THE ECONOMICS OF MONEY, BANKING AND FINANCIAL MARKETS

The Economics of Money, Banking and Financial Markets

European Edition

Frederick S. Mishkin

Kent Matthews

Massimo Giuliodori

PEARSON

Harlow, England • London • New York • Boston • San Francisco • Toronto • Sydney
Auckland • Singapore • Hong Kong • Tokyo • Seoul • Taipei • New Delhi
Cape Town • São Paulo • Mexico City • Madrid • Amsterdam • Munich • Paris • Milan

PEARSON EDUCATION LIMITED
Edinburgh Gate
Harlow CM20 2JE
Tel: +44 (0)1279 623623
Fax: +44 (0)1279 431059
Website: www.pearson.com/uk

First published 2013 (print and electronic)

ISBN: 978-0-273-73180-1 (print)
          978-0-273-79302-1 (ePub)
          978-0-273-8086-1 (eText)

British Library Cataloguing-in-Publication Data
A catalogue record for the print edition is available from the British Library

Library of Congress Cataloging-in-Publication Data
Mishkin, Frederick S.
    The economics of money, banking and financial markets / Frederick S. Mishkin,
Kent Matthews, Massimo Giuliodori. — European ed.
        p. cm.
    ISBN 978-0-273-73180-1
    1. Finance. 2. Money. 3. Banks and banking.   I. Matthews, Kent.   II. Giuliodori, Massimo.   III. Title.
    HG173.M6322 2013
    332—dc23   2012039053

ARP impression 98

Cover image: © Alamy Images

Print edition typeset in 9.5/12.5 pt Charter ITC Std by 73
Print edition printed and bound by Ashford Colour Press Ltd

BRIEF CONTENTS

CONTENTS

CHAPTER 6

The risk and term structure of interest rates   108

CHAPTER 7

The stock market, the theory of rational expectations and the efficient market hypothesis   130

PART 3
FINANCIAL INSTITUTIONS   147

CHAPTER 8

An economic analysis of financial structure   149

CHAPTER 9

Financial crises and the subprime meltdown   176

CHAPTER 10

Banking and the management of financial institutions   205

CHAPTER 22

Aggregate demand and supply analysis

CHAPTER 23

Transmission mechanisms of monetary policy: the evidence

CHAPTER 24

Money and inflation

CHAPTER 25

Rational expectations: implications for policy

Supporting resources

Visit **www.myeconlab.com** to find valuable online resources

- A dynamic eText of the book that you can search, bookmark, annotate and highlight as you please
- Self-assessment questions that identify your strengths before recommending a personalised study plan that points you to the resources which can help you achieve a better grade
- Flashcards to test your understanding of key terms
- links to relevent sites on the web

For more information please contact your local peearson Eduction sales representative or visit **www.myeconlab.com**

PREFACE

Hallmarks

Although this text has undergone a major revision and adaptation for the European context it retains the basic hallmarks of all past Global editions that have made it the best-selling textbook on money and banking over the past editions:

- A unifying, analytic framework that uses a few basic economic principles to organize students' thinking about the structure of financial markets, the foreign exchange markets, financial institution management and the role of monetary policy in the economy
- A careful, step-by-step development of models (an approach found in the best principles of economics textbooks), which makes it easier for students to learn
- The complete integration of an international perspective throughout the text
- A thoroughly up-to-date treatment of the latest developments in monetary theory
- A special feature called 'Following the financial news' to encourage reading of a financial newspaper
- An applications-oriented perspective with numerous applications and special-topic boxes that increase students' interest by showing them how to apply theory to real-world examples

What's new in the European adaptation

The basis of the adaptation was the 9th Global edition. The figures and data have been replaced by or supplemented with UK and other European countries' data. The text in each chapter reflects the Europeanization of the material while retaining the essential features of the original Global editions. There is major new material in every part of the text.

Chapter 1 Why study money, banking and financial markets?

This chapter lays the foundations for the following chapters. It contains new material that refers to the interest rates of the UK and the major economies of the euro area. The broad sweep of the history and volatility of stock markets in the twentieth and twenty-first centuries is discussed by comparing the evolution of the FT30 index and the Dow-Jones from 1935. The foreign exchange market is given greater prominence in the book and is introduced earlier in this chapter.

The structure of the chapter follows closely the 9th Global edition but the examples of money and business cycles and the long-run relationship between inflation and money is taken from the UK. There are two reasons why the UK is used to illustrate the long-run relationships between money, interest rates, the business cycle and inflation. The first is that the euro area has not been in existence for long enough to provide an undisturbed long series of data that will adequately illustrate the economic relationships explored in the chapter. The second reason is that the UK provides an undisturbed example of long-term trends that have relevance for the euro area.

Chapter 2 An overview of the financial system

This chapter stays close to the structure of the 9th Global edition and provides data on the principal money market and capital market instruments in the UK as examples of the types of financial instruments that are traded in an advanced financial market. The principal financial intermediaries in the euro area and the UK are described and the boxes on 'Following the financial news' take examples from the *Financial Times*.

Chapter 3 What is money? A comparative approach to measuring money

The difference between the definition of money and the measurement of money is discussed in a special 'Closer look' box. It uses the evolution of the measures of money in the UK as examples of circumstances when financial innovation blurs the distinction between different means of payment systems, leading to changes in the measures of money while retaining the fundamental definition. The different measures of money in the euro area, the UK and the US are discussed and presented in Table 3.1 and the detailed components of the various measures of the euro area money supply are shown in Table 3.2.

Chapter 4–6 Understanding interest rates, The behaviour of interest rates and The risk and term structure of interest rates

These three chapters have remained largely unchanged as they are theoretical in substance. A notable addition in Chapter 4 is the 'Closer look' box that discusses the observation of real interest rates from the yields on UK index-linked bonds. Additionally Figure 4.1 shows how real interest rates can be backed out by subtracting econometrically generated inflation expectations following the Mishkin (1981) method, from the UK short-term rate of interest. Figure 5.7 uses the UK data on short-term interest to illustrate the relationship between the rate of interest and the business cycle. The 'Following the financial news' box contains a column from the *Financial Times* on UK index-linked bonds which is explained and analysed in the text. Chapter 6 uses the spread between the UK commercial bill rate and the UK risk-free rate of interest to illustrate the risk premium in short-term bonds. It also includes a discussion of the risk premium on interest rates due to sovereign debt default within the euro area. 'Following the financial news' includes a discussion and an analysis on UK yield curves produced by the *Financial Times* for yield curve shapes from 1981 to 2011.

Chapter 8 An economic analysis of financial structure

The context for this chapter is the European sovereign debt crisis that followed the global financial crisis which was itself sparked by the subprime crisis. The banking crisis and the impacts on the financial system in the euro area and the UK are explored in this chapter. The financial structure of the three largest economies in the euro area, the UK and the US are described. The chapter shows data for the sources of external funds for non-financial businesses in the US, the UK, France, Germany and Italy. The euro area and UK financial structure fits in with the eight basic facts about company financial structure. The attempts to remedy conflicts of interest in the US (Sarbanes–Oxley Act of 2002 and the Global Legal Settlement of 2002) are supplemented with a discussion of European Union Directives.

Chapter 9 Financial crises and the subprime meltdown

The 9th Global edition included an extensive analysis of why financial crises like the subprime crisis occur and why they have such devastating effects on the economy. This chapter follows the structure of the original edition and examines why financial crises occur and why they have such devastating effects on the economy. This analysis is used to explain the course of events in a number of past financial crises throughout the world, including the collapse of the European Exchange Rate Mechanism. A particular focus of the chapter is the explanation of the recent subprime crisis and the sovereign debt crisis in the euro area economies. A special section is on the dynamics of the euro area financial crisis and an additional application is the box on the sovereign debt crisis in the EU and the attempts by the ECB, the EU and the IMF to deal with a crisis that keeps on developing. The material in this chapter is very exciting for European students as it is as bang up to date in its information and analysis as the publication of a textbook will allow. As this book goes to print the sovereign debt crisis and the banking crisis have had political upheavals in Europe with changing governments in Italy, France and Greece. Far from coming to any form of resolution, the banking crisis has worsened in Spain.

Chapter 10 Banking and the management of financial institutions

Understanding the workings of banks begins with understanding the balance sheet of the banks. This chapter begins with the consolidated balance sheet of all commercial banks in the euro area. This is then compared with the balance sheet of a single universal bank in Germany as an example with the similarities and differences highlighted in the discussion. The process of maturity transformation is explained and the methods by which banks make profits are described by referring to the income statement of a large German bank.

Chapter 11 Economic analysis of financial regulation

The material in the Global box 'The spread of deposit insurance' has been updated to include information on the spread of deposit insurance as a result of the 2008 financial crisis. The extent of deposit insurance in the European Union is shown in Table 11.1. Examples of direct government help to banks in the European Union and the problem of moral hazard are explained. The notion of 'too important to fail' is explored in a seperate section. This is a case when the government thinks that a bank failure would infect the rest of the financial system, but even though it may not commit public funds to the exercise, the intervention alone could create moral hazard. An explicit exploration of the regulations in the Basle 1 is contained in a 'Closer look' box with an explanation of how the capital-adequacy ratio is calculated. The Global box on International financial regulation has been extended to deal with the Basle 3 regulations that are to be phased in by 2019. An additional section on the advantages and disadvantages of bank regulation is included as well as an EU-wide discussion on where regulation is going in the light of banking crises in Europe and the sovereign debt crisis.

Chapter 12 Banking industry: structure and competition

This chapter begins with the creation and development of the single banking market in the European Union. The result of attempts to promote competition has led to greater consolidation. Deregulation has occured in phases and these phases are discussed in a special section on deregulation and competition. The impact of deregulation and competition on bank structures is discussed in a special section on consolidation and downsizing. A special section on the structure of the banking sector in Europe discusses issues of concentration and competitiveness. A further section discusses the internationalization of banking.

Chapter 13 The goals and structure of central banks

This chapter has been substantially rewritten and contains a wider coverage of the goals and structure of central banks with special emphasis on the Bank of England, the ECB and the Federal Reserve. It includes a box on the benefits of price stability. Also the description of the Federal Reserve System includes a box on the differing styles of Bernanke and Greenspan as Governors. The independence of the ECB contains material that discusses the pressures it faces during the current financial crisis. Additional material in the section on central banks around the world includes a description of the central banks of Sweden and Norway. The chapter also includes an additional section on central banks in transition countries. The discussion on central bank behaviour is expanded and includes two additional boxes on making central banks more accountable and whether independence for central banks leads to lower inflation.

Chapters 14–15 The money supply process and The tools of monetary policy

While retaining the theoretical features of the 9th Global edition, these chapters have been reorganized to reflect the European context. The specific factors that determine the money supply in the context of the money multiplier are elaborated in Chapter 14. The historic trend of the UK M3 money multiplier is described as an example and recent trends are examined with the M3 multiplier of the euro area and the M1 multiplier of the US. A special box describing the operations of the monetary counterparts process explains the link between bank lending, the government budget deficit and funding of the deficit through bond sales. The counterparts process has a stronger resonance with the operations of the monetary process in the UK and the ECB than the simple textbook money supply process. Chapter 15 on the tool of monetary policy has been substantially rewritten to accommodate a more general framework which is useful to analyse the market for reserves in the euro area, the UK and the US, and to understand how the respective central banks can use their tools to affect the interest rates. This chapter also includes a number of boxes describing the unconventional monetary policies implemented by the Bank of England, the ECB and the Fed over the last few years. More specifically, a new box describes the mechanics of quantitative easing by the Bank of England. Further analysis of the European context includes a special box on extraordinary policy responses by the ECB to the current crisis in the form of the enhanced credit support and the securities markets programme. The box on the Fed's response to the crisis has also been updated.

Chapter 16 The conduct of monetary policy: strategy and tactics

The first part of this chapter has a section on the experience of monetary targeting in the UK, the US and Germany. The chapter continues with an extensive discussion of inflation targeting. In order to stress the importance of transparency and regular communication with the public, a special box that describes the working of the inflation fan chart used by the Bank of England is included. This chapter also features an extended coverage of the two-pillar monetary policy strategy of the ECB. After a discussion of the monetary strategy of the Fed, the chapter discusses the main tactics in choosing the policy instruments. Within this context, an updated section on the Taylor rule includes figures that show the rate generated by the Taylor rule and the respective policy rate of the UK and the US. The Fed Watchers box in the 9th Global edition is replaced by a Central Bank Watchers box that focuses on the Bank of England and the ECB.

Chapters 17–18 The foreign exchange market and The international financial system

The structure and theoretical content of the working of the foreign exchange market in Chapter 17 remains mostly unchanged with the context focusing on Europe. Additions worth mentioning are a discussion of alternative methods used in expressing the exchange rate and an updated application on the euro and the global financial crisis. Chapter 18 has also been rewritten to reflect a European focus, but the theoretical aspects remain largely unchanged. The section on the balance of payments describes the UK system as an example. The box on why large current account deficits worry economists has been extended to Germany and the UK. Following the recent proposals of policymakers, a new 'Reading the financial news' section on the Tobin tax has been added. The section that covers dollarization, currency boards and monetary unions now includes an extensive coverage of the benefits and costs of a monetary union. On top of a special box on the potential for a monetary union in the Arab Gulf Cooperation Council, this section features two new boxes discussing whether the existing euro area constitutes an optimal currency area and whether the EU countries outside the euro area will join the euro area.

Chapter 19 The demand for money

Chapter 19 is contextualized in the European setting with long-run movements in the velocity of circulation for broad money in the UK examined alongside the US. In particular the changes in the UK velocity are matched against recessions from 1915 onwards. The stability of the demand for money is examined in the context of the experience of M3 velocity in the euro area.

Chapters 20–23 The *ISLM* model, Monetary and fiscal policy, Aggregate demand and supply analysis and Transmission mechanisms of monetary policy

As theoretical chapters, these have had only a light revision to reflect the European context. In Chapter 20 the application of the collapse of investment spending demonstrates the effect for the UK economy in the 1930s. The application in Chapter 21 of the economic stimulus following the 2008 downturn includes stimulus plans by the European economies. A further application examines the effect of the British fiscal austerity programme of 2010 and the reunification of Germany in 1990. The theoretical model is extended to examine the mix of fiscal and monetary policy in unison. In Chapter 22, the effect of negative supply shocks is traced through unemployment and inflation for the UK and the euro area as well as the US in 1973–5. Similarly the effect of negative demand shocks during the 1980–3 period are traced through on inflation and unemployment in the UK and the US. Finally, this chapter includes a section on the effect of the global financial crisis on unemployment and inflation during 2007–8 for the UK, the US, the euro area and Japan. Chapter 23 includes a discussion of UK reform of the monetary mechanism and its effect on structural model evidence. The section on the traditional interest-rate channels includes a special box that summarizes the research on the pass-through of retail bank rates in the euro area. Additionally the credit view is expanded to include data from the euro area, the UK and the US. The application on the subprime crisis has been extended to include the policy of quantitative easing by the Bank of England.

Chapters 24–25 Money and inflation and Rational expectations: implications for policy

Chapter 24 has been rewritten to reflect global, European and UK episodes of inflation and money growth. It starts with an extended section on the empirical relationship between money and inflation in the UK and the euro area. This chapter also includes an application to the UK experience of inflation during the period 1960–2009 and the underlying political economy factors that explain the rise in inflation to 1980. A final application discusses the importance of credibility for the curbing of inflation in the UK. Chapter 25, being largely theoretical, has remained much the same as in the 9th Global edition, with the context focusing on Europe. A relevant application in the European context is the credibility enhancing condition for entry to EMU enshrined in the Maastricht Treaty of 1992. The evidence on inflation in the euro area is examined in the application.

Flexibility

In using previous editions, adopters, reviewers and survey respondents have continually praised this text's flexibility. There are as many ways to teach money, banking and financial markets as there are instructors. To satisfy the diverse needs of instructors, the text achieves flexibility as follows:

■ Core chapters provide the basic analysis used throughout the book, and other chapters or sections of chapters can be used or omitted according to instructor preferences. For example, Chapter 2 introduces the financial system and basic concepts such as transaction costs, adverse selection and moral hazard. After covering Chapter 2, the instructor may decide to give more detailed coverage of financial structure by assigning Chapter 8, or may choose to skip Chapter 8 and take any of a number of different paths through the book.

- The text also allows instructors to cover the most important issues in monetary theory and policy without having to use the *ISLM* model in Chapters 20 and 21, while more complete treatments of monetary theory make use of the *ISLM* chapters.
- The internationalization of the text through marked international sections within chapters, as well as through complete separate chapters on the foreign exchange market and the international monetary system, is comprehensive yet flexible. Although many instructors will teach all the international material, others will not. Instructors who want less emphasis on international topics can easily skip Chapter 17 on the foreign exchange market and Chapter 18 on the international financial system and monetary policy. The international sections within chapters are self-contained and can be omitted with little loss of continuity.

To illustrate how this book can be used for courses with varying emphases, several course outlines are suggested for a semester teaching schedule. More detailed information about how the text can be used flexibly in your course is available in the Instructor's Manual.

- *General money and banking course:* Chapters 1–5, 10–13, 15, 16, 22, 24, with a choice of 6 of the remaining 12 chapters.
- *General money and banking course with an international emphasis:* Chapters 1–5, 10–13, 15–18, 22, 24 with a choice of 4 of the remaining 10 chapters.
- *Financial markets and institutions course:* Chapters 1–12, with a choice of 7 of the remaining 13 chapters.
- *Monetary theory and policy course:* Chapters 1–5, 13–16, 19, 22–25, with a choice of 5 of the remaining 11 chapters.

Pedagogical aids

In teaching theory or its applications, a textbook must be a solid motivational tool. To this end, we have incorporated a wide variety of pedagogical features to make the material easy to learn:

- **Previews** at the beginning of each chapter tell students where the chapter is heading, why specific topics are important, and how they relate to other topics in the book.
- **Applications**, numbering around 50, demonstrate how the analysis in the book can be used to explain many important real-world situations.
- **'Following the financial news'** boxes introduce students to relevant news articles and data that are reported daily in the press and explain how to read them.
- **Global** boxes include interesting material with an international focus.
- **'Closer look'** boxes highlight dramatic historical episodes, interesting ideas and intriguing facts related to the subject matter.
- **Summary tables** provide a useful study aid in reviewing material.
- **Key statements** are important points set in boldface italic type so that students can easily find them for later reference.
- **Graphs** with captions, numbering more than 150, help students clearly understand the interrelationship of the variables plotted and the principles of analysis.
- **Summary** at the end of each chapter lists the main points covered.
- **Key terms** are important words or phrases, boldface when they are defined for the first time and listed by page number at the end of the chapter.

- **End-of-chapter questions and problems**, numbering more than 400, help students learn the subject matter by applying economic concepts, including a special class of problems that students find particularly relevant, under the heading 'Using economic analysis to predict the future'.
- **Web exercises** encourage students to collect information from online sources or use online resources to enhance their learning experience.
- **Web sources** report the Web URL source of the data used to create the many tables and charts.
- **Useful websites** point the student to websites that provide information or data that supplement the text material.
- **Glossary** at the back of the book provides definitions of all the key terms.

Acknowledgements

We have been guided by the thoughtful commentary of outside reviewers and correspondents. Their feedback has made this a better book. In particular, we thank the following: Siert Vos; Yioryos Makedonis, Queen Mary and University of London; Tom van Veen, Maastricht University/Nyenrode Business Universiteit; Ulrike Neyer, Heinrich-Heine-University Düsseldorf; Gert Peersman, Ghent University; Ian Sharpe, Sheffield Business School; Cian Twomey, NUI Galway; Ozge Senay, University of St Andrews; Roy Dahlstedt, Aalto University School of Economics in Helsinki and Swapnil Singh, University of Amsterdam. In addition, we would like to thank Benjamin Bluhm and Krisztina Orbán for their excellent research assistance, and Martin Admiraal and Luca Benati for providing or sharing some of the data used in this book.

Our special thanks go to the following individuals who edited or contributed to creation of the manuscript: Kate Brewin, Michael Fitch, Stuart Hay, Gemma Papageorgiou, Carole Drummond and Colin Reed.

Frederic S. Mishkin, Kent Matthews and Massimo Giuliodori

ABOUT THE AUTHORS

Frederick S. Mishkin is the Alfred Lerner Professor of Banking and Financial Institutions at the Graduate School of Business, Columbia University. He is also a Research Associate at the National Bureau of Economic Research and past president of the Eastern Economics Association. Since receiving his PhD from the Massachusetts Institute of Technology in 1976, he has taught at the University of Chicago, Northwestern University, Princeton University, and Columbia. He has also received an honorary professorship from the People's (Renmin) University of China. From 1994 to 1997, he was Executive Vice President and Director of Research at the Federal Reserve Bank of New York and an associate economist of the Federal Open Market Committee of the Federal Reserve System. From September 2006 to August 2008, he was a member (governor) of the Board of Governors of the Federal Reserve System.

Professor Mishkin's research focuses on monetary policy and its impact on financial markets and the aggregate economy. He is the author of more than 15 books, including *Financial Markets and Institutions*, sixth edition (Addison-Wesley, 2009); *Monetary Policy Strategy*, (MIT Press, 2007) *The Next Great Globalization: How Disadvantaged Nations Can Harness Their Financial Systems to Get Rich* (Princeton University Press, 2006); *Inflation Targeting: Lessons from the International Experience* (Princeton University Press, 1999); *Money, Interest Rates, and Inflation* (Edward Elgar, 1993); and *A Rational Expectations Approach to Macroeconometrics: Testing Policy Ineffectiveness and Efficient Markets Models* (University of Chicago Press, 1983). In addition, he has published more than 150 articles in such journals as *American Economic Review*, *Journal of Political Economy*, *Econometrica*, *Quarterly Journal of Economics*, *Journal of Finance*, and *Journal of Monetary Economics*.

Professor Mishkin has served on the editorial board of *American Economic Review* and has been an associate editor at *Journal of Business and Economic Statistics*, the *Journal of Applied Econometrics*, and *Journal of Money, Credit and Banking*; he also served as the editor of the Federal Reserve Bank of New York's Economic Policy Review. He is currently an associate editor (member of the editorial board) at six academic journals, including *Macroeconomics and Monetary Economics Abstracts*; *Journal of International Money and Finance; International Finance; Finance India; Economic Policy Review; and Emerging Markets, Finance and Trade.* He has been a consultant to the Board of Governors of the Federal Reserve System, the World Bank, and the International Monetary Fund, as well as to many central banks throughout the world. He was also a member of the International Advisory Board to the Financial Supervisory Service of South Korea and an advisor to the Institute for Monetary and Economic Research at the Bank of Korea. Professor Mishkin was a Senior Fellow at the Federal Deposit Insurance Corporation's Center for Banking Research and was an academic consultant to and served on the Economic Advisory Panel of the Federal Reserve Bank of New York.

Kent Matthews is the Sir Julian Hodge Professor of Banking and Finance at the Cardiff Bussiness School. He is graduate of the London School of Economics, Birkbeck (University of London) and the university of Liverpool and has held research posts at the LSE, National Institute of Economic and Social Research and Bank of England.

Massimo Giuliodori is Associate Professor of Monetary and Fiscal Policy at the Amsterdam School of Economics at the University of Amsterdam and Research Fellow in Macroeconomics and International Economics at the Tinbergen Institute in Amsterdam.

After obtaining his PhD from the Scottish Doctoral Programme at the University of Glasgow in 2003, he moved to the University of Amsterdam, where is currently the Director of the Economics and Business BSc International Programme. Giuliodori's research interest is on the effects of monetary and fiscal policies on the economic activity, and he has published several papers in academic journals including the *Journal of Economic Literature, The Economic Journal, Journal of the European Economic Association and Economic Policy.*

GUIDED TOUR

PREVIEW On the evening TV news you see images of people carrying cardboard boxes leaving a glass-plated building in the City of London. The scene cuts to a trading screen on the London Stock Exchange flashing red numbers and the TV commentary says something about the collapse of a major US bank. You have just heard that the Bank of England is to cut the base rate once again and stock markets in Frankfurt and Paris have shown falls in share prices. Why should financial events in New York have any implications for the stock market in London, Frankfurt or Paris? What effect might the cut in the base rate have on mortgage payments? Will the global collapse of stock markets make it easier or harder for you to get a job next year?

Previews at the beginning of each chapter tell you what topics to expect, why they are important, and how they relate to other topics in the book.

Key terms are important words or phrases, emboldened when they are defined for the first time, and listed by page number at the end of the chapter.

Fiscal policy involves decisions about government spending and taxation. A **budget deficit** is the excess of government expenditures over tax revenues for a particular time period, typically a year, while a **budget surplus** arises when tax revenues exceed government expenditures. The government must finance any deficit by borrowing, which leads to a higher government debt burden while a budget surplus leads to a lower government debt burden. Figure 1.8 shows the budget deficit for the euro economies relative to the size of its economy (as calculated by the **gross domestic product**, or GDP,

CLOSER LOOK
The yield curve as a forecasting tool for inflation and the business cycle

Because the yield curve contains information about future expected interest rates, it should also have the capacity to help forecast inflation and real output fluctuations. To see why, recall from Chapter 5 that rising interest rates are associated with economic booms and falling interest rates with recessions. When the yield curve is either flat or downward-sloping, it suggests that future short-term interest rates are expected to fall and, therefore, that the economy is more likely to enter a recession. Indeed, the yield curve is found to be an accurate predictor of the business cycle.*

In Chapter 4, we also learned that a nominal interest rate is composed of a real interest rate and expected inflation, implying that the yield curve contains

The ability of the yield curve to forecast business cycles and inflation is one reason why the slope of the yield curve is part of the toolkit of many economic forecasters and is often viewed as a useful indicator of the stance of monetary policy, with a steep yield curve indicating loose policy and a flat or downward-sloping yield curve indicating tight policy.

* For example, see Arturo Estrella and Frederic S. Mishkin, 'Predicting US recessions: financial variables as leading indicators', *Review of Economics and Statistics*, 80 (February 1998): 45–61.
† Frederic S. Mishkin, 'What does the term structure tell us about future inflation?', *Journal of Monetary Economics*

'Closer look' boxes encourage you to explore the subject further to deepen your understanding.

Applications demonstrate how the analysis can be used to explain many important real-world situations.

APPLICATION Interpreting yield curves, 1981–2011

Figure 6.8 illustrates several yield curves that have appeared for British government securities in recent years. What do these yield curves tell us about the public's expectations of future movements of short-term interest rates?

The steep inverted yield curve that occurred on 30 September 1981, indicated that short-term interest rates were expected to decline sharply in the future. For longer-term interest rates with their positive liquidity premium to be well below the short-term interest rate, short-term interest rates must be expected to decline so sharply that their average is far below the current short-term rate. Indeed, the public's expectations of sharply lower short-term interest rates evident in the yield curve were realized soon after September; by November, three-month Treasury bill rates had declined from 15.1% to 13.8% and by February 1982 they had fallen to 12.5%.

The steep upward-sloping yield curves on 28 February 1993 and 30 April 2011 indicated that short-term interest rates would climb in the future. The long-term interest rate is higher than the short-term interest rate when short-term interest rates are expected to rise because their average plus the liquidity premium will be higher than the current short-term rate. The moderately upward-sloping yield curves on 30 November 1996 indicated that short-term

FOLLOWING THE FINANCIAL NEWS

The 'Lex' column

The Lex column is a daily feature that appears on the back page of the first section of the *Financial Times* (FT). The Lex is the agenda-setting column of the FT and it comprises a wide set of analyses and opinions covering current business, economic and financial topics, usually from a global perspective. The following is an example of a contemporary topic relating to the effect of the global financial crisis on the credit rating of the UK and other indebted countries.

THE LEX COLUMN

Sterling

Well, it was nice while it lasted. The pound has had a good run this year. Since December's trough, sterling's trade-weighted exchange rate has risen 9 per cent – a big move and one due a correction, or at least a pause. A review of Britain's credit rating provided the excuse yesterday. Sterling tumbled and gilts fell after Standard & Poor's cut the UK's debt outlook to negative, warning the country's ratio of debt

almost quintupled to £8.5bn in April compared with the same month the year before while tax receipts fell almost 10 per cent. But a high debt\GDP ratio need not be disastrous, as economic historians often point out. After all, British national debt was that high after the second world war, even if it was a period of austerity for those who lived through it. Sugar rationing was lifted only in 1953 and, to save

big European economy. But at some point markets will demand compensation for the growing credit risk. The government to be formed after elections that are due at the latest in the middle of next year, therefore, needs to slow growth in the national debt and then reverse it. This will be a painful and unpopular task, as squabbling over the public purse always is. It is probably no accident

'**Following the financial news' boxes** introduce relevant news articles and data that are reported daily in the press and explain how to read them.

INSIDE THE FEDERAL RESERVE
How Bernanke's style differs from Greenspan's

Every Federal Reserve chairman has a different style that affects how policy decisions are made at the Fed. There has been much discussion of how the current chairman of the Fed, Ben Bernanke, differs from Alan Greenspan, who was the chairman of the Federal Reserve Board for nineteen years from 1987 until 2006.

Alan Greenspan dominated the Fed like no other prior Federal Reserve chairman. His background was very different from that of Bernanke, who spent most of his professional life in academia at Princeton University. Greenspan, a disciple of Ayn Rand, is a strong advocate for laissez-faire capitalism and headed a very successful economic consulting firm, Townsend-Greenspan.* Greenspan has never been an economic theorist, but is rather famous for immersing himself in the data – literally so, because he is known to have done this in his bath tub at the beginning of the day – and often focused on rather obscure data series to come up with his forecasts. As a result, Greenspan did not rely exclusively on the Federal Reserve Board staff's forecast in making his policy decisions. A prominent example occurred during

In contrast to Greenspan, Bernanke's background as a top academic economist has meant that he focuses on analytics in making his decisions. The result is a much greater use of model simulations in guiding policy discussions.

The FOMC decision-making process under Greenspan was one where the chairman for the most part made the decision about policy, while Bernanke's procedure is more democratic and enables participants to have greater influence over the chairman's vote.

Another big difference in style is in terms of transparency. Greenspan was famous for being obscure. Bernanke is known for being a particularly clear speaker. Finally, while Greenspan adopted more transparent communication with reluctance, Bernanke has been a much stronger supporter of transparency, having advocated that the Fed announce its inflation objective. Bernanke launched a major initiative in 2006 to study Federal Reserve communications that resulted in substantial increases in Fed transparency in November 2007. A very significant further step towards greater

'**Inside the Federal Reserve' boxes** provide an insight into what is important in the operation and structure of the Federal Reserve system.

GLOBAL
Why a large current account deficit worries economists

Over the recent years, with the exception of Germany which has enjoyed large current account surpluses, many industrialized countries like the UK and in particular the US experienced substantial current account deficits (see Figure 18.2). Massive current account deficits worry economists for several reasons. First, a current account deficit indicates that at current exchange rate values, foreigners' demand for domestic exports is far less than domestic demand for imports. As we saw in the previous chapter, low demand for exports and high demand for imports may lead to a future decline in the value of the domestic currency. Second, the current account deficit means that foreigners' claims on domestic assets are

growing, and these claims will have to be paid back at some point. Domestic citizens are mortgaging their future to foreigners; when the bill comes due, domestic citizens will be poorer. Furthermore, if domestic citizens have a greater preference for domestic assets than foreigners do, the movement of domestic wealth to foreigners could decrease the demand for domestic assets over time, also causing the domestic currency to depreciate. The hope is that the eventual decline in the domestic currency resulting from the large current account deficits will be a gradual one, occurring over a period of several years. If the decline is precipitous, however, it could potentially disrupt financial markets and hurt the domestic economy.

'**Global' boxes** offer an international focus.

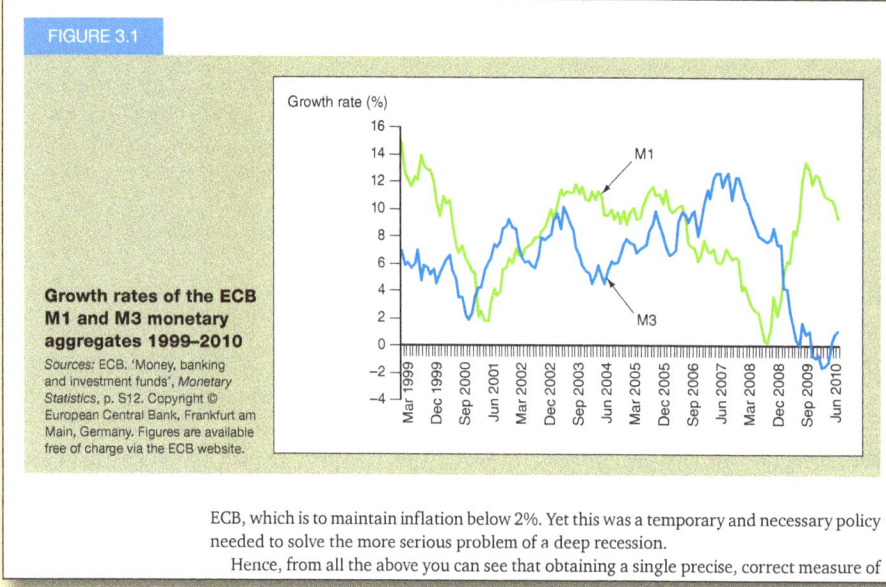

FIGURE 3.1

Growth rates of the ECB M1 and M3 monetary aggregates 1999–2010

Sources: ECB. 'Money, banking and investment funds', *Monetary Statistics*, p. S12. Copyright © European Central Bank, Frankfurt am Main, Germany. Figures are available free of charge via the ECB website.

ECB, which is to maintain inflation below 2%. Yet this was a temporary and necessary policy needed to solve the more serious problem of a deep recession.

Hence, from all the above you can see that obtaining a single precise, correct measure of

Figures and graphs help you clearly understand the principles of the analysis.

Summary tables provide a useful study aid to review material.

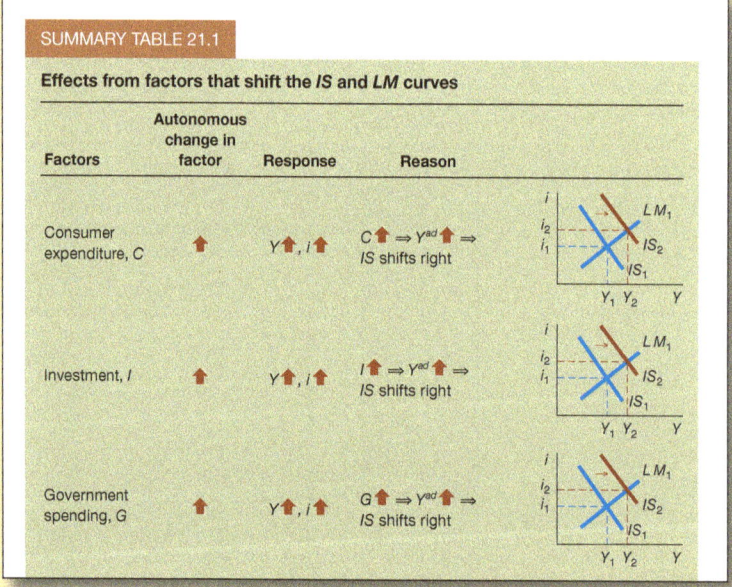

SUMMARY TABLE 21.1

Effects from factors that shift the *IS* and *LM* curves

Factors	Autonomous change in factor	Response	Reason	
Consumer expenditure, C	▲	Y▲, i▲	C▲ ⇒ Y^ad▲ ⇒ IS shifts right	
Investment, I	▲	Y▲, i▲	I▲ ⇒ Y^ad▲ ⇒ IS shifts right	
Government spending, G	▲	Y▲, i▲	G▲ ⇒ Y^ad▲ ⇒ IS shifts right	

Summary

1 To economists, the word *money* has a different meaning from *income* or *wealth*. Money is anything that is generally accepted as payment for goods or services or in the repayment of debts.

2 Money serves three primary functions: as a medium of exchange, as a unit of account and as a store of value. Money as a medium of exchange avoids the problem of double coincidence of wants that arises in a barter economy, and thus lowers transaction costs and encourages specialization and the division of labour. Money as a unit of account reduces the number of prices needed in the economy, which also reduces transaction costs. Money also functions as a store of value, but performs this role poorly if it is rapidly losing value due to inflation.

3 The payments system has evolved over time. Until

still further. We are currently moving toward an electronic payments system in which paper is eliminated and all transactions are handled by computers. Despite the potential efficiency of such a system, obstacles are slowing the movement to the cashless society and the development of new forms of electronic money.

4 There is no uniform definition of monetary aggregates, but in general monetary aggregates range from narrow to broad definitions. Since monetary aggregates do not usually move together, they cannot be used interchangeably by policymakers. It is imperative to measure different monetary aggregates so that the central bank can intervene if any of the components change.

5 Another problem in the measurement of money is that

'Summary' at the end of each chapter lists the main points covered.

'Questions and problems' sections enable you to test your understanding and practise your knowledge by applying economic concepts.

QUESTIONS AND PROBLEMS

All questions and problems are available in MyEconLab at **www.myeconlab.com/mishkin**.

1 Explain why you would be more or less willing to buy a share of Microsoft stock in the following situations:

(a) Your wealth falls.
(b) You expect the stock to appreciate in value.
(c) The bond market becomes more liquid.
(d) You expect gold to appreciate in value.
(e) Prices in the bond market become more volatile.

2 Explain why you would be more or less willing to buy a house under the following circumstances:

(a) You just inherited €100,000.
(b) Real estate commissions fall from 6% of the sales price to 5% of the sales price.
(c) You expect Microsoft stock to double in value next year.
(d) Prices in the stock market become more volatile.
(e) You expect housing prices to fall.

3 Explain why you would be more or less willing to buy gold under the following circumstances:

7 Using both the liquidity preference framework and the supply and demand for bonds framework, show why interest rates are procyclical (rising when the economy is expanding and falling during recessions).

8 Why should a rise in the price level (but not in expected inflation) cause interest rates to rise when the nominal money supply is fixed?

9 Go to **www.ft.com** and click on 'Capital Markets' in markets. Examine the statements made on the online articles, and draw the appropriate supply and demand diagrams that support these statements.

10 What effect will a sudden increase in the volatility of gold prices have on interest rates?

11 How might a sudden increase in people's expectations of future real estate prices affect interest rates?

12 Explain what effect a large government deficit might have on interest rates.

'Web exercises' prompt you to use online resources to enhance your learning.

WEB EXERCISES

1 This chapter discusses how an understanding of adverse selection and moral hazard can help us better understand financial crises. The greatest financial crisis faced by the United States was the Great Depression of 1929–33. Go to www.amatecon.com/greatdepression.html. This site contains a brief discussion of the factors that led to the Great Depression. Write a one-page summary explaining how adverse selection and moral hazard contributed to the Great Depression.

2 Go to the International Monetary Fund's Financial Crisis page at www.imf.org/external/np/exr/key/finstab.htm.

Report on the most recent three countries that the IMF has given emergency loans to in response to a financial crisis. According to the IMF, what caused the crisis in each country?

3 One of the countries hardest hit by the global financial crisis of 2008 was Iceland. Go to assets.opencrs.com/rpts/RS22988_20081120.pdf and summarize the causes and events that led to the crisis in Iceland.

'Useful websites' point you to websites that provide information or data that support the text material.

Useful websites

www.amatecon.com/gd/gdtimeline.html A time line of the Great Depression.

www.imf.org The International Monetary Fund is an organization of 185 countries that works on global policy coordination (both monetary and trade),stable and sustainable economic prosperity, and the reduction of poverty.

www.publicpolicy.umd.edu/news/Reinhart%20paper.pdf Paper by Carmen Reinhart and Kenneth Rogoff comparing the 2007 subprime crisis to other international crises.

www.earth.columbia.edu/sitefiles/File/about/director/pubs/paper27.pdf Non-technical paper by Steven Radelet and Jeffrey Sachs on the causes of the East Asian financial crisis.

assets.opencrs.com/rpts/RS22988_20081120.pdf The Congressional Research Service (CRS) report to congress about Iceland's financial crisis of 2008.

GUIDED TOUR TO MyEconLab®

MyEconLab is an online assessment and revision tool that puts you in control of your learning through a suite of study and practice tools tied to the online eText.

How do I use MyEconLab?

The **Course Home page** is where you can view announcements from your instructor and see an overview of your personal progress.

View the **Calendar** to see the dates for online homework, quizzes and tests that your instructor has set for you.

Your lecturer may have chosen **MyEconLab** to provide online homework, quizzes and texts. Check here to access the homework that has been set for you.

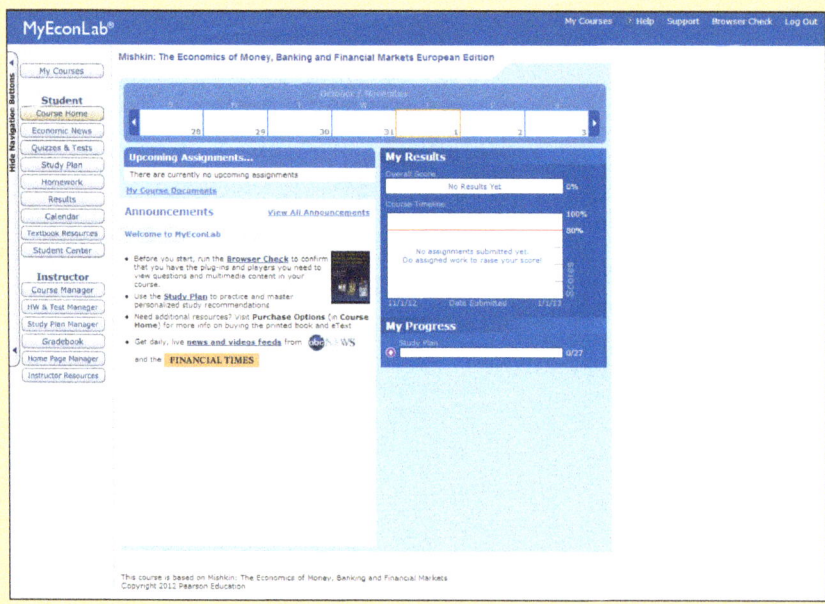

Practice tests for each chapter of the textbook enable you to check your understanding and identify the areas in which you need to do further work. Lecturers can customise and assign the practice tests or students can complete the tests on their own.

Keep track of your results in your own gradebook.

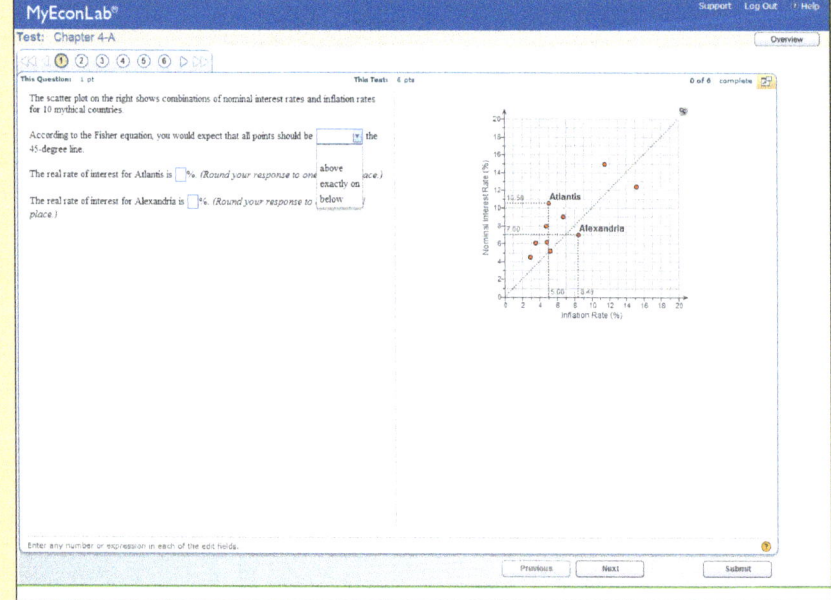

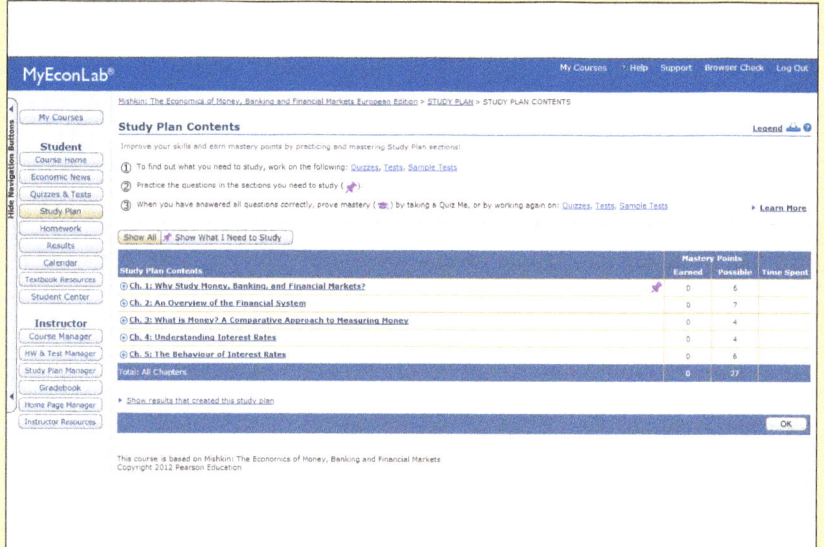

Work through the questions in your personalised **Study Plan** at your own pace. Because the Study Plan is tailored to each student, you will be able to study more efficiently by only reviewing areas where you still need practice. The Study Plan also saves your results, helping you see at a glance exactly which topics you need to review.

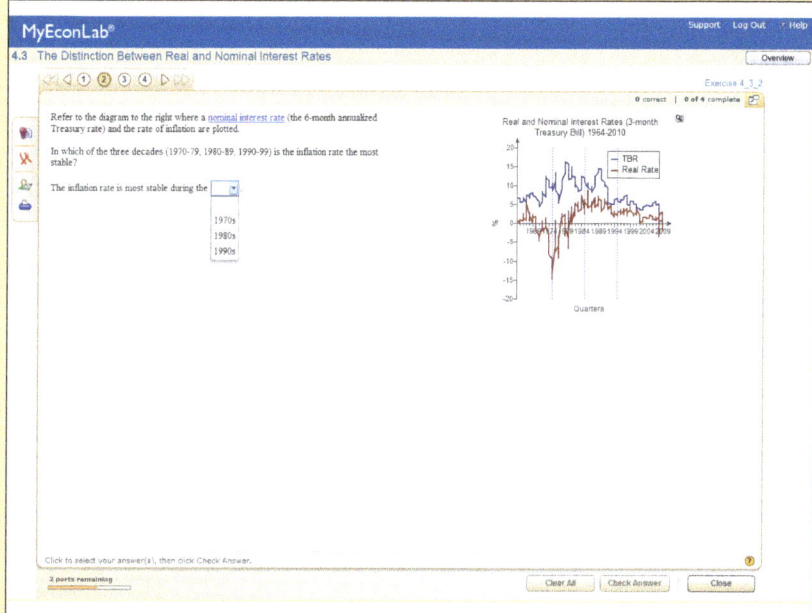

Additional instruction is provided in the form of detailed, step-by-step solutions to worked exercises. The figures in many of the exercises in **MyEconLab** are generated algorithmically, containing different values each time they are used. This means that you can practise individual concepts as often as you like.

There is also a link to the **eText** from every question in the Study Plan, so you can easily review and master the content.

View supporting multimedia resources such as links to the eText and **Glossary Flashcards**.

Lecturer training and support

Our dedicated team of Technology Specialists offer personalised training and support for **MyEconLab**, ensuring that you can maximise the benefits of **MyEconLab**. To make contact with your Technology Specialist, please email **feedback-cw@pearson.com**.

For a visual walkthrough of how to make the most of **MyEconLab**, visit **www.MyEconLab.com**.

To find details of your local sales representatives, go to **www.pearsoned.co.uk/replocator**.

PUBLISHER'S ACKNOWLEDGEMENTS

Matthews Kent - Economics of Money, Banking & Financial Markets European adaptation - 1st Ed.

We are grateful to the following for permission to reproduce copyright material:

Figures

Figure 3.1 from 'Money, Banking and Investment Funds', *Monetary Statistics*, March, p. S12 (ECB 2009), European Central Bank; Figures 6.1a, 6.1b adapted from Statistical Interactive Database, http://www.bankofengland.co.uk (Bank of England Revisions Policy, http://www.bankofengland.co.uk/mfsd/iadb/notesiadb.Revisions.htm); Figure 6.3 from OECD (2012), OECD.Stat (database), http://dx.doi.org/10.1787/data-00285-en, with permission from the OECD; Figure on page 117 from UK Yield Curve, http://markets.ft.com/research/Markets/Bonds, © The Financial Times Limited. All Rights Reserved; Figure 6.4 from ONS website, data from Office for National Statistics licensed under the Open Government Licence v.1.0; Figure 6.7 adapted from http://www.bankofengland.co.uk/statistics/Pages/yieldcurve/default.aspx, with permission from the Bank of England (Bank of England Revisions Policy, http://www.bankofengland.co.uk/mfsd/iadb/notesiadb.Revisions.htm); Figure 8.1 reprinted from 'Financing patterns around the world: Are small firms different?', *Journal of Financial Economics*, 89(3), pp. 467–87 (Beck, T., Demirgüç-Kunt, A. and Maksimovic, V. 2008), Copyright © 2008, with permission from Elsevier; Figure 8.2 from Beck, T.; Demirgüç-Kunt, A. (2009) 'Financial Institutions and Markets across Countries and over Time: Data and Analysis', *World Bank Policy Research Working Paper* no. 4943, May (revised November 2010) © World Bank. http://creativecommons.org/licenses/by/3.0, Creative Commons Attribution CC BY 3.0; Figure 9.9 from http://sdw.ecb.europa.eu/browseSelection.do?DATASET=0&sfl2=4&REF_AREA=308&sfl3=4&INSTRUMENT_FM=BG&sfl4=3&node=2018817&SERIES_KEY=145.IFI.M.U2.BG.2D.G000.CI.Z5.EUR, European Central Bank; Figure 11.1 from Caprio, G.; Klingebiel, D. (1999) *Episodes of Systematic and Borderline Financial Crises, mimeo* © World Bank. http://creativecommons.org/licenses/by/3.0, Creative Commons Attribution 3.0 Unported licence (CC BY); Figures 13.2a, 13.2b from *Facts Presentation. ECB, August 2011, Slides 1&2*, Copyright © European Central Bank, Frankfurt am Main, Germany; Figure 13.3 from 'Central Bank Independence and Macroeconomic Performance: Some Comparative Evidence', *Journal of Money, Credit and Banking*, vol. 25, no. 2, May, pp. 151–62 (Alesina, A. and Summers, L.H., 1993). Copyright 1993. The Ohio State University Press. Reproduced with permission; Figure 14.5 from Friedman, Milton; *A Monetary History of the United States, 1867–1960.* © 1963 NBER, 1991 renewed. Reprinted by permission of Princeton University Press; Figure 15.9 from European Central Bank; Figure 16.2 from *Inflation Report*, February (Bank of England 2012), with permission from the Bank of England (Bank of England Revisions Policy, http://www.bankofengland.co.uk/mfsd/iadb/notesiadb.Revisions.htm); Figure 16.3 from http://www.ecb.int/mopo/strategy/html/index.en.html, European Central Bank; Figure 17.1 adapted from http://www.bankofengland.co.uk/statistics/index.htm, with permission from the Bank of England (Bank of England Revisions Policy, http://www.bankofengland.co.uk/mfsd/iadb/notesiadb.Revisions.htm); Figure 17.9 from http://sdw.ecb.europa.eu/browse.do?node=2018794, European Central Bank; Figures 18.2, 24.12,

24.13 from OECD (2011), *OECD Economic Outlook No. 90*, OECD Economic Outlook: Statistics and Projections (database). http://dx.doi.org/10.1787/data-00588-en; Figure 24.1 from 'Some Monetary Facts', *Federal Reserve Bank of Minneapolis Quarterly Review*, 19, 3, pp.1–11 (McCandless, G. and Weber, W., 1995), with permission from Federal Reserve Bank of Minneapolis; Figures 24.2, 24.11 from 'Long Run Evidence on Money Growth and Inflation', *ECB Working Paper Series* no. 1027 (Benati, L. 2009), copyright European Central Bank, http://www.ecb.europa.eu/home/html/disclaimer.en.html.

Screenshots

Screenshot on page 16 from http://www.bankofengland.co.uk/statistics/Pages/, with permission from the Bank of England; Screenshot on page 16 from Treasury 3 month data from, http://www.bankofengland.co.uk, with permission from the Bank of England; Screenshots on pages 16, 30, 34 Microsoft screenshot frame reprinted with permission from Microsoft Corporation; Screenshots on page 30 from http://markets.ft.com, 4 April 2012, © The Financial Times Limited 2012. All Rights Reserved; Screenshot on page 34 from http://markets.ft.com, 6 August 2009, © The Financial Times Limited. All Rights Reserved.

Tables

Tables 2.2, 2.4a from ONS website, data from Office for National Statistics licensed under the Open Government Licence v.1.0; Table 2.4b from *ECB Monthly Bulletin*, January (ECB 2012), European Central Bank; Table on page 117 from FT.com, Saturday 25 June 2011, http://www.ft.com, © The Financial Times Limited 2011. All Rights Reserved; Table 10.1 from *Monthly Bulletin*, August, Table 2.1 (ECB 2011), European Central Bank; Table 11.2 from 'The World Bank', *Banking Crises Database* (Caprio, G., Klingebiel, D., Laeven, L. and Noguera, G.), http://www1.worldbank.org/finance/html/database_sfd.html. © World Bank. http://creativecommons.org/licenses/by/3.0, Creative Commons Attribution 3.0 Unported licence (CC BY); Tables 12.1, 12.2, 12.4 based on data from OECD (2010), 'Classification of bank assets and liabilities', OECD Banking Statistics (database). http://dx.doi.org/10.1787/data-00269-en; Tables 12.5, 12.7 from Bankscope, published by Bureau Van Dijk; Table 12.6 from 'The Banking Sector and Recovery in the EU Economy', *NIESR*, December (Barrell, R., Fic, T., Fitzgerald, J., Orazgani, A. and Whitworth, R., 2010), National Institute of Economic and Social Research; Table on page 383 from Markets Data: Currencies, *Financial Times*, 9 March 2012, http://markets.ft.com/ft/markets/currencies.asp, © The Financial Times Limited 2012. All Rights Reserved; Table 25.2 from OECD (2011), *OECD Economic Outlook No. 90*, OECD Economic Outlook: Statistics and Projections (database). http://dx.doi.org/10.1787/data-00588-en.

Text

Box on page 95 from Oakley, D. (2011) 'Appeal of gilts is untarnished by their poor performance', FT.com, 4 February, © The Financial Times Limited 2011. All Rights Reserved; Box on page 239 adapted from *Banking Supervision Fact Sheet* (Bank of England 1990) August, with permission from the Bank of England (Bank of England Revisions Policy, http://www.bankofengland.co.uk/mfsd/iadb/notesiadb.Revisions.htm); Box on page 400 from Sterling, Lex column, *Financial Times*, 21 May 2008, © The Financial Times Limited 2008. All Rights Reserved; Box on pages 421–422 from Carnegy, H. and Peel, Q. (2012) 'Financiers attack Sarkozy "Tobin tax" plan', *Financial Times*, 8 January, © The Financial Times Limited 2012. All Rights Reserved.

In some instances we have been unable to trace the owners of copyright material, and we would appreciate any information that would enable us to do so.

PART 1
INTRODUCTION

CHAPTER 1

Why study money, banking and financial markets?

PREVIEW

On the evening TV news you see images of people carrying cardboard boxes leaving a glass-plated building in the City of London. The scene cuts to a trading screen on the London Stock Exchange flashing red numbers and the TV commentary says something about the collapse of a major US bank. You have just heard that the Bank of England is to cut the base rate once again and stock markets in Frankfurt and Paris have shown falls in share prices. Why should financial events in New York have any implications for the stock market in London, Frankfurt or Paris? What effect might the cut in the base rate have on mortgage payments? Will the global collapse of stock markets make it easier or harder for you to get a job next year?

This book provides answers to these and other questions by examining how financial markets (such as those for bonds, stocks and foreign exchange) and financial institutions (banks, insurance companies, mutual funds and other institutions) work and by exploring the role of money in the economy. Financial markets and institutions not only affect your everyday life but also involve flows of billions of pounds and euros throughout the economy, which in turn affect business profits, the production of goods and services in Europe, and even the economic well-being of countries in the Far East. What happens to financial markets, financial institutions and money is of great concern to politicians and can even have a major impact on elections. The study of money, banking and financial markets will reward you with an understanding of many exciting issues. In this chapter, we provide a road map of the book by outlining these issues and exploring why they are worth studying.

Why study financial markets?

Part 2 of this book focuses on **financial markets**, markets in which funds are transferred from people who have an excess of available funds to people who have a shortage. Financial markets such as bond and stock markets are crucial to promoting greater economic efficiency by channelling funds from people who do not have a productive use for them to those who do. Indeed, well-functioning financial markets are a key factor in producing high economic growth, and poorly performing financial markets are one reason that many countries in the world remain desperately poor. Activities in financial markets also have direct effects on personal wealth, the behaviour of businesses and consumers, and the cyclical performance of the economy.

The bond market and interest rates

A **security** (also called a *financial instrument*) is a claim on the issuer's future income or **assets** (any financial claim or piece of property that is subject to ownership). A **bond** is a debt security that promises to make payments periodically for a specified period of time.[1] The bond market is especially important to economic activity because it enables corporations and governments to borrow to finance their activities and because it is where interest rates are determined. An **interest rate** is the cost of borrowing or the price paid for the rental of funds (usually expressed as a percentage of the rental of €100 per year). There are many interest rates in the economy – mortgage interest rates, car loan rates, and interest rates on many different types of bonds.

Interest rates are important on a number of levels. On a personal level, high interest rates could deter you from buying a house or a car because the cost of financing it would be high. Conversely, high interest rates could encourage you to save because you can earn more interest income by putting aside some of your earnings as savings. On a more general level, interest rates have an impact on the overall health of the economy because they affect not only consumers' willingness to spend or save but also businesses' investment decisions. High interest rates, for example, might cause a company to postpone building a new plant that would provide more jobs.

Because changes in interest rates have important effects on individuals, financial institutions, businesses and the overall economy, it is important to explain fluctuations in interest rates that have been substantial over the past thirty years. Take a look at Figure 1.1a which shows the movements of three different interest rates in the UK. Notice how the three-month Treasury bill rate moves close together.

Because different interest rates have a tendency to move in unison, economists frequently lump interest rates together and refer to 'the' interest rate. As Figure 1.1a shows, however, interest rates on several types of financial instruments can differ substantially. The interest rate on three-month Treasury bills, for example, fluctuates more than the other interest rates and is lower, on average. Figure 1.1a shows the interest rate on two types. The interest on 10-year bonds is the interest rate on UK government bonds that have a maturity of 10 years. The interest rate on 10-year bonds follows the same pattern as long-term government bonds that have no maturity date. These types of bonds are referred to as consols. Both 10-year bond rates and consol rates fluctuate less than the Treasury bill rate (TBR) but are higher,

FIGURE 1.1a

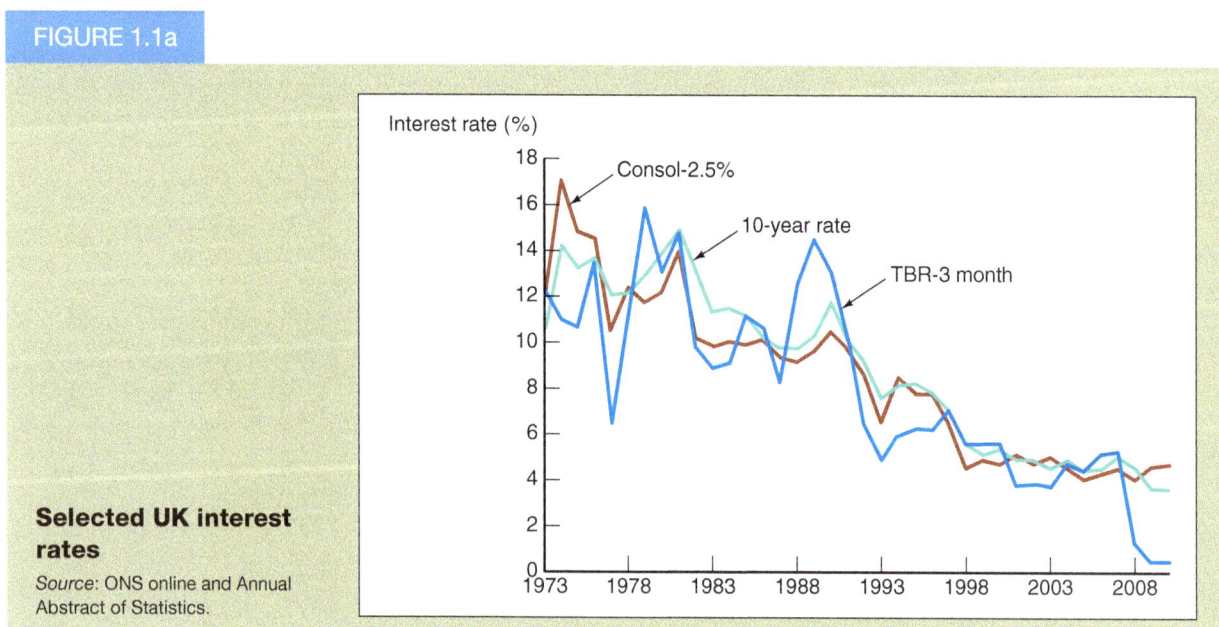

Selected UK interest rates

Source: ONS online and Annual Abstract of Statistics.

FIGURE 1.1b

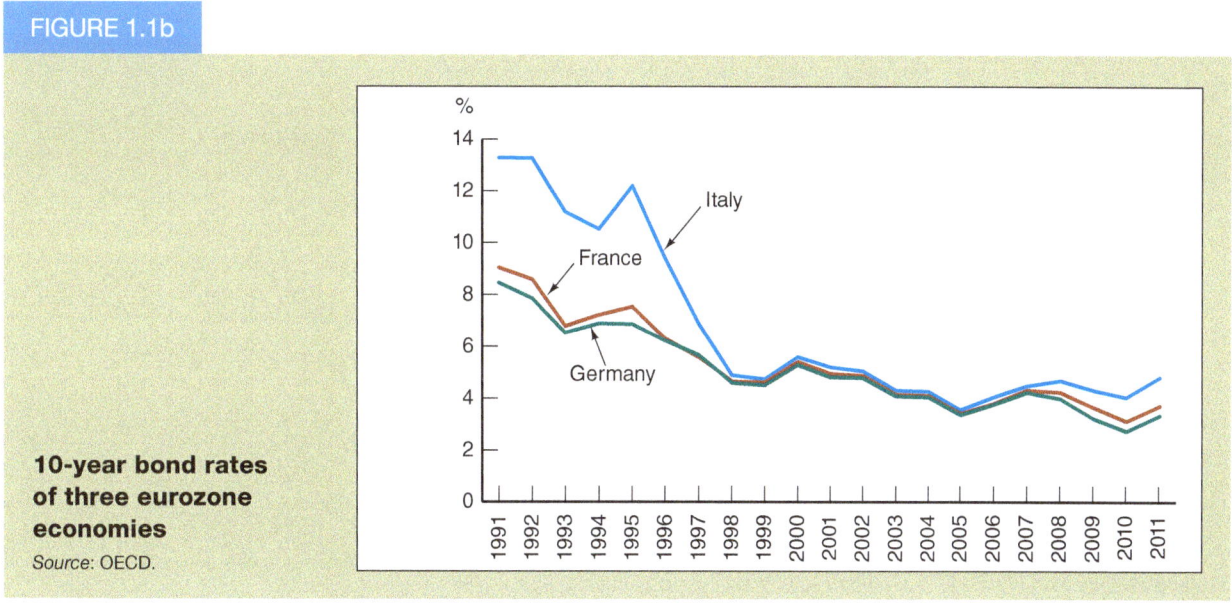

**10-year bond rates
of three eurozone
economies**
Source: OECD.

on average, than the Treasury bill rate. The spread between the consol rate and the Treasury bill rate was greatest during the late 1970s, the late 1980s and in recent years. The interest rate on three-month Treasury bills peaked at over 16% in 1979, fell to 8% in 1987, rose to 15% in 1989, fell to 5% in 1993 and after some wobbles fell to $\frac{1}{2}$% in 2009.

Now look at Figure 1.1b which shows the interest rate on 10-year maturity government bonds for Germany, France and Italy. These interest rates will differ from each other because of differences between the countries relating to inflation risk, political risk and default risk. Notice how the interest rate of Italy differed markedly from that of Germany in the 1990s. This is because Italy had traditionally higher inflation in the past than Germany and Italian bonds had to pay a higher rate of interest to compensate for this risk. Notice how the interest rates converge just prior to the creation of the single currency in Europe. This was because in a single currency the inflation differences between countries should theoretically be like the inflation differences between New England and California in the US. However, this is not the case in reality. California and the New England states are part of a single political union. Not so for Germany, France and Italy. Notice how the interest rates begin to differ after 2007, reflecting the impact of the global banking crisis on the eurozone sovereign debt crisis.

In Chapter 2 we study the role of bond markets in the economy, and in Chapters 4 to 6 we examine what an interest rate is, how the common movements in interest rates come about, and why the interest rates on different bonds vary.

The stock market

A **common stock** (typically just called a **stock**) represents a share of ownership in a corporation. It is a security that is a claim on the earnings and assets of the corporation. Issuing stock and selling it to the public is a way for corporations to raise funds to finance their activities. The stock market, in which claims on the earnings of corporations (shares of stock) are traded, is the most widely followed financial market in almost every country that has one; that's why it is often called simply 'the market'. A big swing in the prices of shares in the stock market is always a major story on the evening news. People often speculate on where the market is heading and get very excited when they can brag about their latest 'big killing', but they become depressed when they suffer a big loss. The attention the market receives can probably be best explained by one simple fact: it is a place where people can get rich – or poor – quickly.

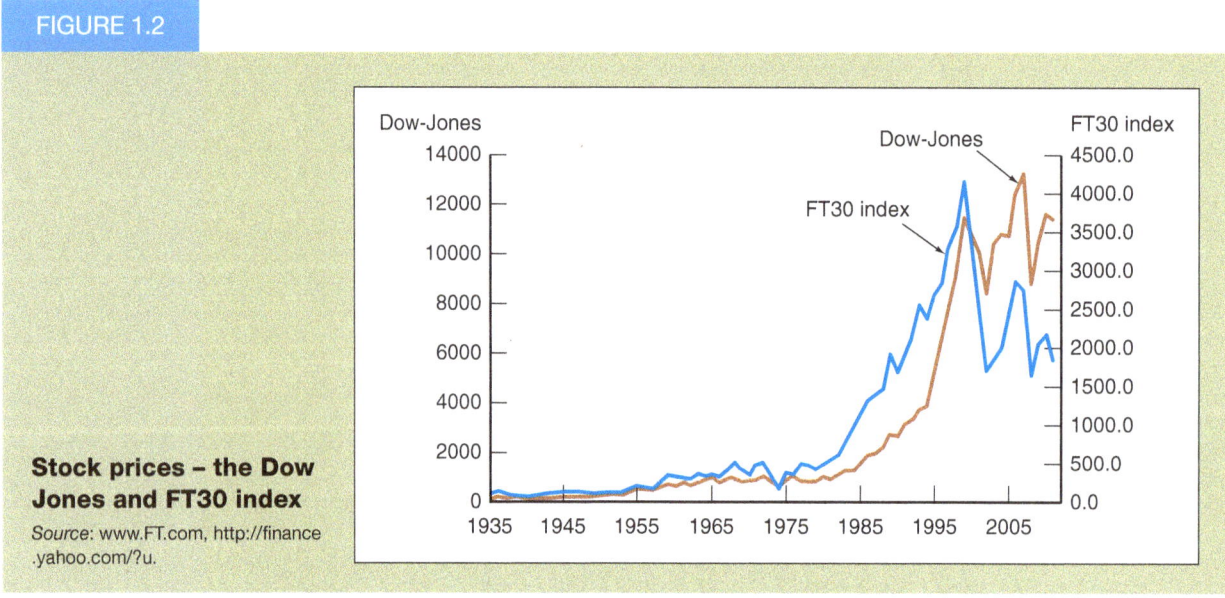

Stock prices – the Dow Jones and FT30 index

Source: www.FT.com, http://finance.yahoo.com/?u.

As Figure 1.2, which shows the FT30 for the UK (right-side axis) and the Dow Jones Industrial Average for the US (left-side axis), indicates, stock prices are extremely volatile. After the market rose in the 1980s, on 'Black Monday', 19 October 1987, markets all over the world experienced sharp falls in share prices following a panic sell-off of shares on Wall Street on the Friday previously. In the USA the market experienced the worst one-day drop in its entire history, with the Dow Jones Industrial Average (DJIA) falling by 22%. In London the FT30 index fell by 10%, wiping out £50 billion of shares. However, as Figure 1.2 shows, from then until 1999, the stock market experienced one of the greatest bull markets in its history. With the collapse of the high-tech bubble in 2000, the stock market fell sharply again, dropping by over 50% by late 2002. It then recovered again and reached a new peak by the end of 2006, only to fall by 43% by the end of 2008 in the wake of the global financial crisis. These considerable fluctuations in stock prices affect the size of people's wealth and as a result may affect their willingness to spend.

The stock market is also an important factor in business investment decisions, because the price of shares affects the amount of funds that can be raised by selling newly issued stock to finance investment spending. A higher price for a firm's shares means that it can raise a larger amount of funds, which it can use to buy production facilities and equipment.

In Chapter 2 we examine the role that the stock market plays in the financial system, and we return to the issue of how stock prices behave and respond to information in the marketplace in Chapter 7.

The foreign exchange market

When funds are transferred from one country to another, they have to be converted from the currency of the country of origin (say sterling or euros) into the currency of the country they are going to (say US dollars). This conversion takes place in the **foreign exchange market**. This is the market where one currency is bought and sold using another currency. The price at which one currency is exchanged for another is known as the **foreign exchange rate**.

Figure 1.3 shows the exchange rate of the pound sterling from 1980 to 2011 measured as the number of US dollars per pound and the same for the number of US dollars per euro. This way of expressing the exchange rate is known as the indirect quote (foreign currency per unit of domestic). The advantage of using this way of expressing the exchange rate is

FIGURE 1.3

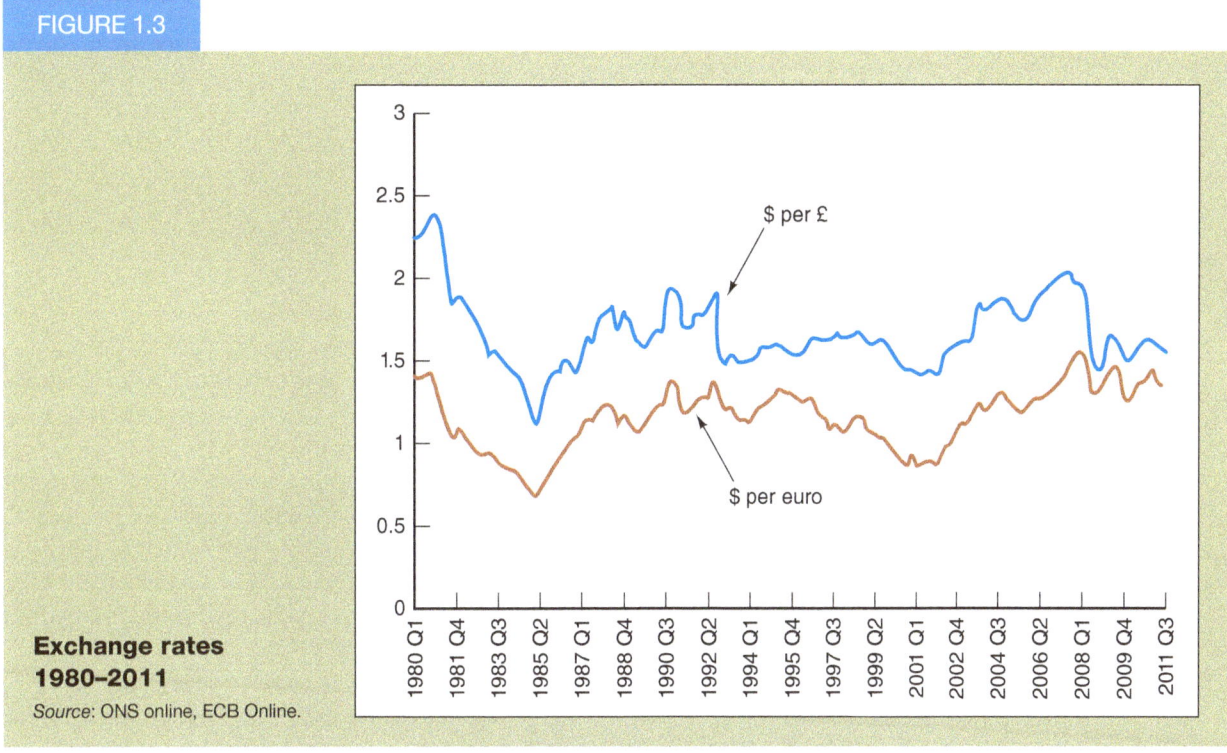

**Exchange rates
1980–2011**

Source: ONS online, ECB Online.

that a rise represents an appreciation and a fall is depreciation. There have been considerable fluctuations in the exchange rate over this period. You can see from Figure 1.3 that the pound sterling against the dollar fell from a peak in late 1980 of $2.39 to a low of $1.12 in early 1985. It then fluctuated between $1.80 and $1.40 and then reached a peak of around $2.00 by 2007. The €/$ exchange rate mirrors the fluctuations in the £/$ exchange rate which means that there was greater stability between the pound and the euro. However, both the euro and the pound sterling fell in 2008, reflecting the fall in demand for sterling and the euro during the global financial crisis.

In Chapter 17 we study how the exchange rate is determined in the foreign exchange market, where pounds sterling or euros are bought and sold for non-EU currencies.

Why study financial institutions and banking?

Part 3 of this book focuses on financial institutions and the business of banking. Banks and other financial institutions are what make financial markets work. Without them, financial markets would not be able to move funds from people who save to people who have productive investment opportunities. Thus they play a crucial role in the economy.

Structure of the financial system

The financial system is complex, comprising many different types of private sector financial institutions, including banks, insurance companies, mutual funds, finance companies and investment banks, all of which are heavily regulated by the government. If an individual wanted to make a loan to BP or BT, for example, he or she would not go directly to the president of the company and offer a loan. Instead, he or she would lend to such companies indirectly through **financial intermediaries**, institutions that borrow funds from people who have saved and in turn make loans to others.

Why are financial intermediaries so crucial to well-functioning financial markets? Why do they extend credit to one party but not to another? Why do they usually write complicated legal documents when they extend loans? Why are they the most heavily regulated businesses in the economy?

We answer these questions in Chapter 8 by developing a coherent framework for analysing financial structure in the eurozone economies and the United Kingdom.

Financial crises

At times, the financial system seizes up and produces **financial crises**, major disruptions in financial markets that are characterized by sharp declines in asset prices and the failures of many financial and non-financial firms. Financial crises have been a feature of capitalist economies for hundreds of years and are typically followed by the worst business cycle downturns. Starting in August of 2007, the United States economy was hit by the worst financial crisis since the Great Depression. Defaults in subprime residential mortgages led to major losses in financial institutions, producing not only numerous bank failures but also the demise of Bear Stearns and Lehman Brothers, two of the largest investment banks in the United States. The interconnectedness of the international financial system meant that the financial crisis that began in the United States was rapidly passed on to the rest of the world, resulting in the global financial crisis and the onset of the 'great recession'.

The sovereign debt crisis of the eurozone arrived hot on the heels of the global financial crisis. The need to protect the banking sector of countries in the eurozone exposed the parlous state of the fiscal deficits of many countries – the debts they owed to investors in their own country and overseas were increased by having to guarantee the debts of the banking system.

Why these crises occur and do so much damage to the economy is discussed in Chapter 9.

Banks and other financial institutions

Banks are financial institutions that accept deposits and make loans. Included under the term *banks* are firms such as commercial banks, building societies (in the UK), mutual savings banks and credit unions. Banks are the financial intermediaries that the average person interacts with most frequently. A person who needs a loan to buy a house or a car usually obtains it from a local bank. Most individuals keep a large proportion of their financial wealth in banks in the form of cheque accounts, savings accounts, or other types of bank deposits. Because banks are the largest financial intermediaries in the economy and are involved in the payments mechanism (which means people use bank cheques, debit cards or other electronic transfers to make payments), they deserve the most careful study. However, banks are not the only important financial institutions. Indeed, in recent years, other financial institutions such as insurance companies, finance companies, pension funds, mutual funds and investment banks have been growing at the expense of banks, so we need to study them as well.

In Chapter 10, we examine how banks and other financial institutions manage their assets and liabilities to make profits. In Chapter 11, we extend the economic analysis in Chapter 8 to understand why financial regulation takes the form it does and what can go wrong in the regulatory process. In Chapter 12, we look at the banking industry; we examine how the competitive environment has changed in this industry and learn why some financial institutions have been growing at the expense of others.

Financial innovation

In the good old days, when you took cash out of the bank or wanted to check your account balance, you got to say hello to a friendly human teller. Nowadays you are more likely to interact with an automatic teller machine (ATM) when withdrawing cash, and you can get your account balance from your home computer. To see why these options have developed, in Chapter 12 we study why and how financial innovation takes place, with particular emphasis on how the dramatic improvements in information technology have led to new means of delivering financial services electronically, in what has become known as **e-finance**. We also study financial innovation because it shows us how creative thinking on the part of financial institutions can lead to higher profits. By seeing how and why financial institutions have been creative in the past, we obtain a better grasp of how they may be creative in the future. This knowledge provides us with useful clues about how the financial system may change over time and will help keep our knowledge about banks and other financial institutions from becoming obsolete.

Why study money and monetary policy?

Money, also referred to as the **money supply**, is defined as anything that is generally accepted in payment for goods or services or in the repayment of debts. Money is linked to changes in economic variables that affect all of us and are important to the health of the economy. The final two parts of the book examine the role of money in the economy.

Money and business cycles

In 1980–1, total production of goods and services (called **aggregate output**) in the UK economy fell and the **unemployment rate** (the percentage of the available labour force unemployed) rose to 10%. After 1982, the economy began to expand rapidly, and by 1990 the unemployment rate had declined to 7%. In 1990, the 8-year expansion came to an end, with the unemployment rate rising above 7%. The economy bottomed out in late 1991, and the subsequent recovery was one of the longest in the UK's history, with the unemployment rate falling to around 5%. Starting in 2008 second quarter, the economy went into recession and by the first quarter of 2010 the unemployment rate rose to 8%.

Why did the economy expand from 1982 to 1990, contract in 1990 to 1991, boom again from 1991 and contract again in 2008? Evidence suggests that money plays an important role in generating **business cycles**, the upward and downward movement of aggregate output produced in the economy. Business cycles affect all of us in immediate and important ways. When output is rising, for example, it is easier to find a good job; when output is falling, finding a good job might be difficult. Figure 1.4 shows the movements of the quarterly rate of money growth for the UK over the 1964–2010 period, with the shaded areas representing **recessions**, periods of declining aggregate output. What we see is that the rate of money growth has declined before every recession, indicating that changes in money might be a driving force behind business cycle fluctuations. However, not every decline in the rate of money growth is followed by a recession.

We explore how money might affect aggregate output in Chapters 19 to 25 in Part 6 of this book, where we study **monetary theory**, the theory that relates changes in the quantity of money to changes in aggregate economic activity and the price level.

Money and inflation

Thirty years ago, the movie you might have paid £8 to see last week would have set you back only 50p for two. In fact, for £8 you could probably have had dinner, seen the movie and bought yourself a tub of ice cream. As shown in Figure 1.5, which illustrates the movement of average prices in the UK from 1950 to 2009, the prices of most items are quite a bit higher now than they were then. The average price of goods and services in an economy is called the **aggregate price level**, or, more simply, the *price level* (a more precise definition is found

FIGURE 1.4

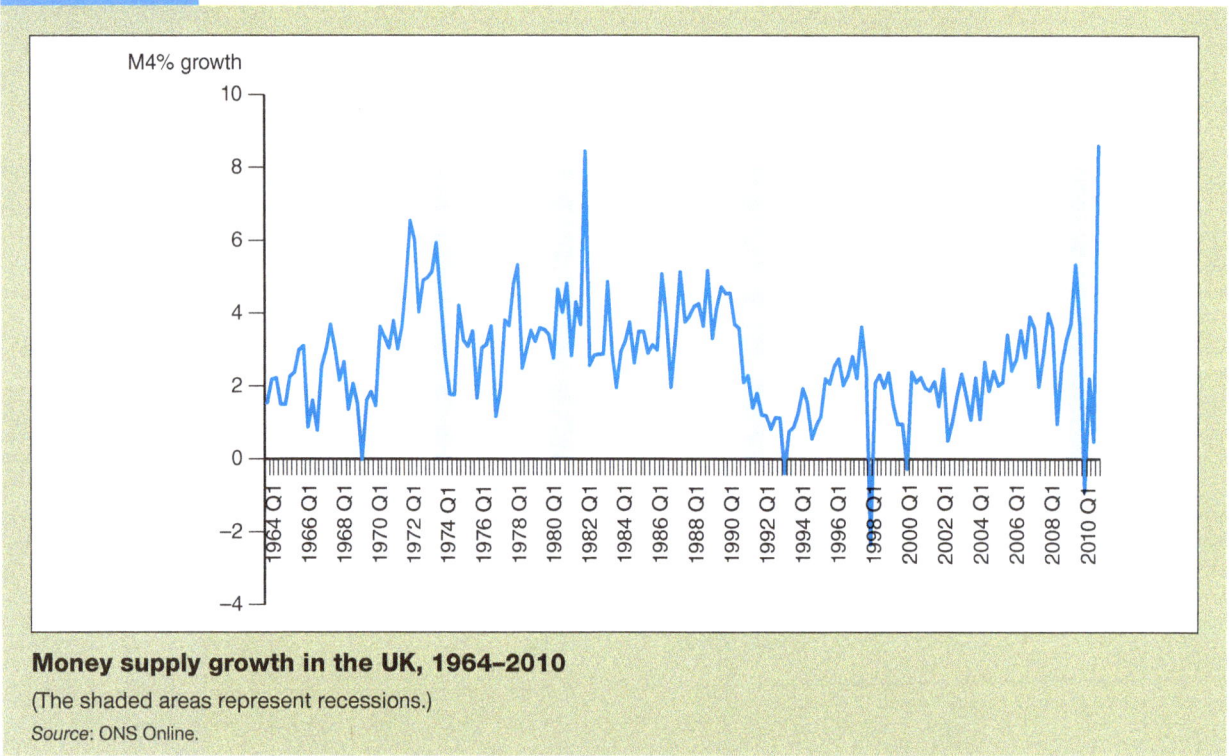

Money supply growth in the UK, 1964–2010

(The shaded areas represent recessions.)

Source: ONS Online.

in the appendix to this chapter). From 1950 to 2009, the price level increased 25-fold. **Inflation**, a continual increase in the price level, affects individuals, businesses and the government. It is generally regarded as an important problem to be solved and is often at the top of the political and policymaking agendas. To solve the inflation problem, we need to know something about its causes.

What explains inflation? One clue to answering this question is found in Figure 1.5, which plots the money supply and the price level. As we can see, the price level and the money supply generally rise together. These data seem to indicate that a continuing increase in the

FIGURE 1.5

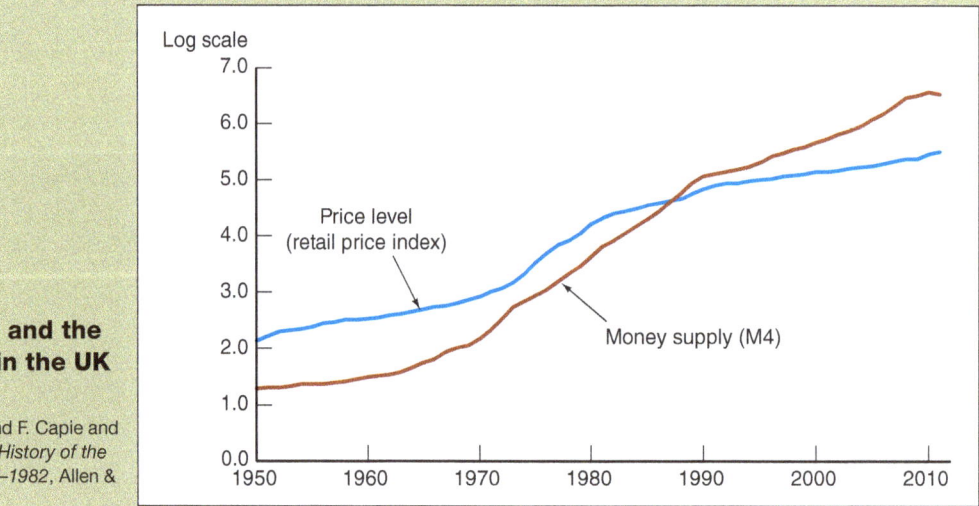

The price level and the money supply in the UK before 1950

Source: ONS online and F. Capie and A. Weber, *A Monetary History of the United Kingdom, 1870–1982*, Allen & Unwin, London, 1985.

FIGURE 1.6

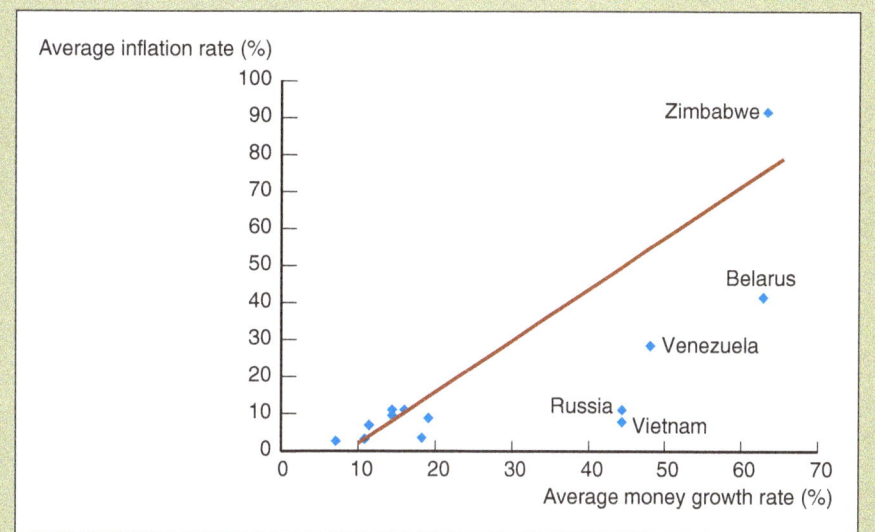

Average inflation rate versus average rate of money growth for selected countries, 1999–2009

Source: Internatonal Monetary Fund.

money supply might be an important factor in causing the continuing increase in the price level that we call inflation.

Further evidence that inflation may be tied to continuing increases in the money supply is found in Figure 1.6. For a number of countries, it plots the average **inflation rate** (the rate of change of the price level, usually measured as a percentage change per year) over the ten-year period 1999–2009 against the average rate of money growth over the same period. As you can see, there is a positive association between inflation and the growth rate of the money supply. The countries with the highest inflation rates are also the ones with the highest money growth rates. Belarus, Brazil, Romania, Russia and Zimbabwe, for example, experienced high inflation during this period, and their rates of money growth were high. By contrast, the United Kingdom and the United States had low inflation rates over the same period, and their rates of money growth have been low. Such evidence led Milton Friedman, a Nobel laureate in economics, to make the famous statement, 'Inflation is always and everywhere a monetary phenomenon'.[2] We look at money's role in creating inflation in Chapter 24.

Money and interest rates

In addition to other factors, money plays an important role in interest-rate fluctuations, which are of great concern to businesses and consumers. Figure 1.7 shows the changes in the interest rate on long-term Treasury bonds in the UK and the rate of money growth. As the money growth rate rose in the 1960s and 1970s, the long-term bond rate rose with it. However, the relationship between money growth and interest rates has been less clear-cut since the late 1980s. We analyse the relationship between money and interest rates when we examine the behaviour of interest rates in Chapter 5.

Conduct of monetary policy

Because money can affect many economic variables that are important to the well-being of the economy, politicians and policymakers throughout the world care about the conduct of **monetary policy**, the management of money and interest rates. The organization

FIGURE 1.7

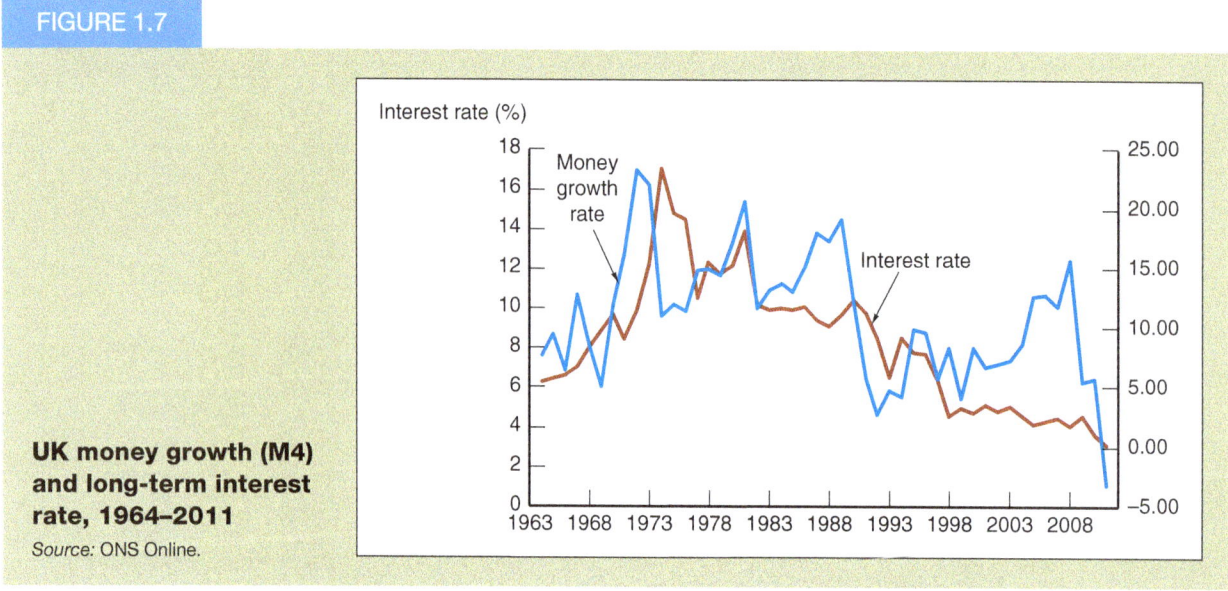

UK money growth (M4) and long-term interest rate, 1964–2011

Source: ONS Online.

responsible for the conduct of a nation's monetary policy is the **central bank**. The central bank of the eurozone countries is the European Central Bank (ECB) in Frankfurt and the central bank for the UK is the Bank of England. In Chapters 13–16 (Part 4), we study how central banks around the world can affect the quantity of money and interest rates in the economy and then we look at how monetary policy is actually conducted in the eurozone, the UK and elsewhere.

Fiscal policy and monetary policy

Fiscal policy involves decisions about government spending and taxation. A **budget deficit** is the excess of government expenditures over tax revenues for a particular time period, typically a year, while a **budget surplus** arises when tax revenues exceed government expenditures. The government must finance any deficit by borrowing, which leads to a higher government debt burden while a budget surplus leads to a lower government debt burden. Figure 1.8 shows the budget deficit for the euro economies relative to the size of its economy (as calculated by the **gross domestic product**, or GDP, a measure of aggregate output described in the appendix to this chapter) and the budget deficit of the UK relative to GDP. As Figure 1.8 shows, the budget deficit, relative to the size of the UK economy, reached its highest in 2009 at 10% of national output. The UK has had more years of budget deficit than surplus since 1970. The budget reached a surplus in 2000 but swung into deficit by 2002 and was strongly in deficit long before the global financial crisis and the great recession hit the UK. Meanwhile, the total budget of the euro economies as a whole was always in deficit over this period. The coordinated fiscal stimulus packages run by governments all over the world in response to the global downturn only pushed the budget deficit higher. What to do about the budget deficit in the euro countries and the UK is a topic that has exercised international investors, the ECB, political parties and the International Monetary Fund.

You may have heard statements in newspapers or on TV that budget surpluses are a good thing while deficits are undesirable. We explore the accuracy of such claims in Chapters 9 and 18 by seeing how budget deficits might lead to a financial crisis as they did in Argentina in 2001 or in Greece in recent years. In Chapter 24, we examine why

FIGURE 1.8

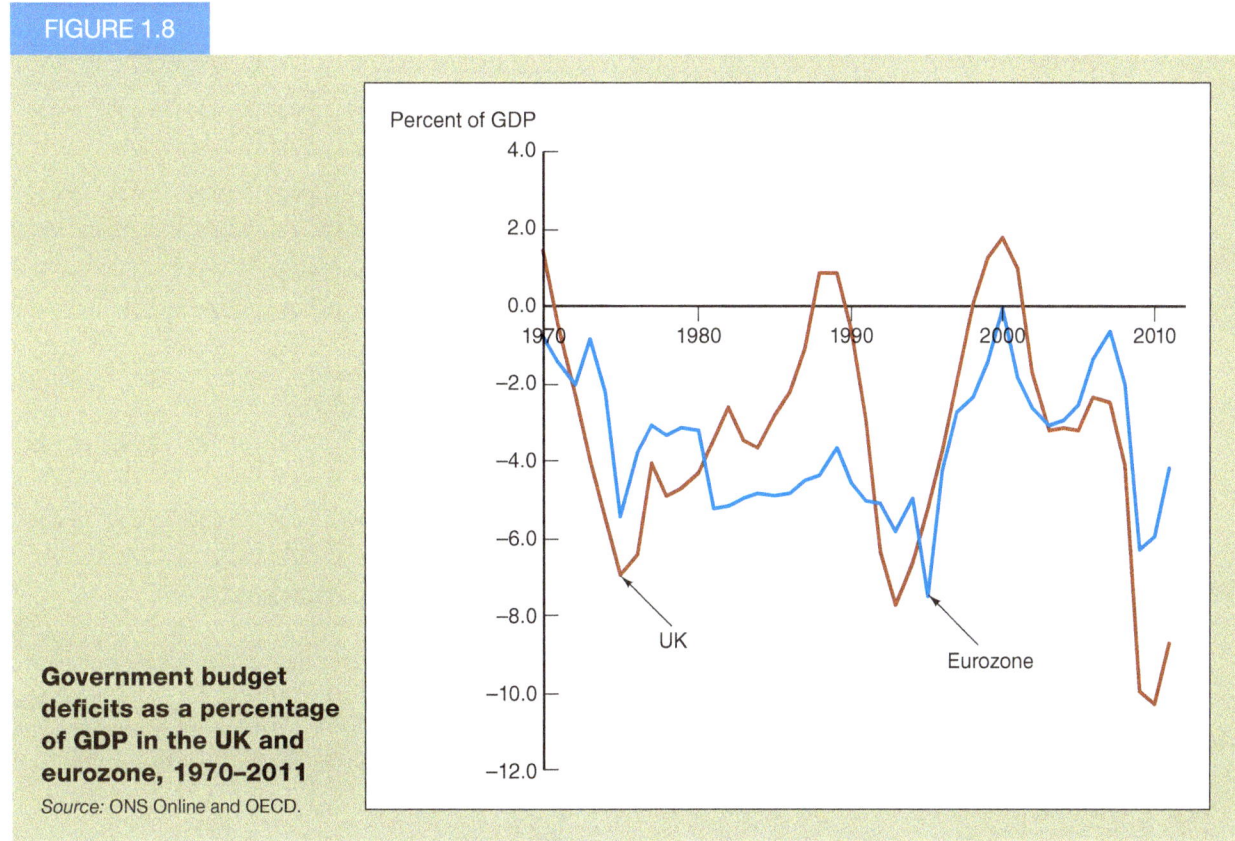

Government budget deficits as a percentage of GDP in the UK and eurozone, 1970–2011
Source: ONS Online and OECD.

deficits might result in a higher rate of money growth, a higher rate of inflation and higher interest rates.

Why study international finance?

The globalization of financial markets has accelerated at a rapid pace in recent years. Financial markets have become increasingly integrated throughout the world. European companies often borrow in foreign financial markets and foreign companies borrow in European financial markets. Banks and other financial institutions, such as JPMorgan Chase, Citigroup, HSBC and Deutsche Bank, have become increasingly international, with operations in many countries throughout the world. Part 5 of this book explores the foreign exchange market and the international financial system.

In Figure 1.3 we looked at the euro and sterling exchange rates for the US dollar. The fluctuations in prices in this market have also been substantial. But what have these fluctuations in the exchange rate meant to households and businesses? A change in the exchange rate has a direct effect on consumers because it affects the cost of imports. In 2007 the pound was worth $2.00 and British consumers could purchase US goods cheaply. Indeed, it was said that British shoppers went to New York to do their Christmas shopping. When the pound subsequently weakened in 2009, US goods became more expensive. Thus a weaker pound leads to more expensive foreign goods, makes holidaying in the US more expensive, and raises the cost of indulging your desire for imported delicacies. Fluctuations in the foreign exchange markets have major consequences for the economy.

In Chapter 17 we study how exchange rates are determined in the foreign exchange market in which dollars are bought and sold for foreign currencies.

The international financial system

The tremendous increase in capital flows among countries heightens the international financial system's impact on domestic economies. Issues we will explore in Chapter 18 include:

- How does a country's decision to fix its exchange rate to that of another nation shape the conduct of monetary policy?
- What is the impact of capital controls that restrict mobility of capital across national borders on domestic financial systems and the performance of the economy?
- What role should international financial institutions such as the International Monetary Fund play in the international financial system?

How we will study money, banking and financial markets

This textbook stresses the economic way of thinking by developing a unifying framework to study money, banking and financial markets. This analytic framework uses a few basic economic concepts to organize your thinking about the determination of asset prices, the structure of financial markets, bank management, and the role of money in the economy. It encompasses the following basic concepts:

- A simplified approach to the demand for assets
- The concept of equilibrium
- Basic supply and demand to explain behaviour in financial markets
- The search for profits
- An approach to financial structure based on transaction costs and asymmetric information
- Aggregate supply and demand analysis

The unifying framework used in this book will keep your knowledge from becoming obsolete and make the material more interesting. It will enable you to learn what *really* matters without having to memorize a mass of dull facts that you will forget soon after the final exam. This framework will also provide you with the tools you need to understand trends in the financial marketplace and in variables such as interest rates, exchange rates, inflation and aggregate output.

To help you understand and apply the unifying analytic framework, simple models are constructed in which the variables held constant are carefully delineated, each step in the derivation of the model is clearly and carefully laid out, and the models are then used to explain various phenomena by focusing on changes in one variable at a time, holding all other variables constant.

To reinforce the models' usefulness, this text uses case studies, applications and special-interest boxes to present evidence that supports or casts doubts on the theories being discussed. This exposure to real-life events and empirical data should dissuade you from thinking that all economists make abstract assumptions and develop theories that have little to do with actual behaviour.

To function better in the real world outside the classroom, you must have the tools to follow the financial news that appears in leading financial publications such as the *Financial Times*. To help and encourage you to read the financial section of your newspaper, this book contains a set of special boxed inserts titled 'Following the financial news' that contain actual columns and data from the *Financial Times*, which typically appear daily or periodically. These applications show you how you can use the analytic framework in the book directly to make sense of the daily columns in an international financial newspaper. In addition to these applications, this book also contains nearly 400 end-of-chapter problems that ask you to apply the analytic concepts you have learned to other real-world issues. Particularly relevant is a special class of problems headed 'Using economic analysis to predict the future'. These give you an opportunity to review and apply many of the important financial concepts and tools presented throughout the book.

Exploring the Web

The World Wide Web has become an extremely valuable and convenient resource for financial research. We emphasize the importance of this tool in several ways. First, wherever we utilize the Web to find information to build the charts and tables that appear throughout the text, we include the source site's URL. These sites often contain additional information and are updated frequently. Second, we have Web exercises towards the end of each chapter. These exercises prompt you to visit sites related to the chapter and to work with real-time data and information. We also have Web references at the end of each chapter that list the URLs of sites related to the material being discussed. Visit these sites to further explore a topic you find of particular interest. Website URLs are subject to frequent change. We have tried to select stable sites, but we realize that even government URLs change. The publisher's website (**www.myeconlab.com/mishkin**) will maintain an updated list of current URLs for your reference.

Collecting and graphing data

The following Web exercise is especially important because it demonstrates how to export data from a website into Microsoft® Excel for further analysis. We suggest you work through this problem on your own so that you will be able to perform this activity when prompted in subsequent Web exercises.

Concluding remarks

The topic of money, banking and financial markets is an exciting field that directly affects your life – interest rates influence earnings on your savings and the payments on loans you may seek on a car or a house, and monetary policy may affect your job prospects and the prices of goods in the future. Your study of money, banking and financial markets will introduce you to many of the controversies about the conduct of economic policy that are hotly debated in the political arena and will help you gain a clearer understanding of economic phenomena you hear about in the news media. The knowledge you gain will stay with you and benefit you long after the course is done.

WEB EXERCISE

You have been hired by Risky Ventures, Inc., as a consultant to help the company analyse interest-rate trends. Your employers are initially interested in determining the historical relationship between long- and short-term interest rates. The biggest task you must immediately undertake is collecting market interest-rate data. You know the best source of this information is the Web.

1 You decide that your best indicator of long-term interest rates is the twenty-year UK Government bonds. Your first task is to gather historical data. Go to **www.bankofengland. co.uk/**

2 Click on Statistics. Now scroll down to 'Statistical Interactive Database – interest & exchange rates data' and click. A list will pop up. Then click on 'Nominal par yields' and go to 20 year and choose end month by ticking the box. There are many different frequencies to choose from.

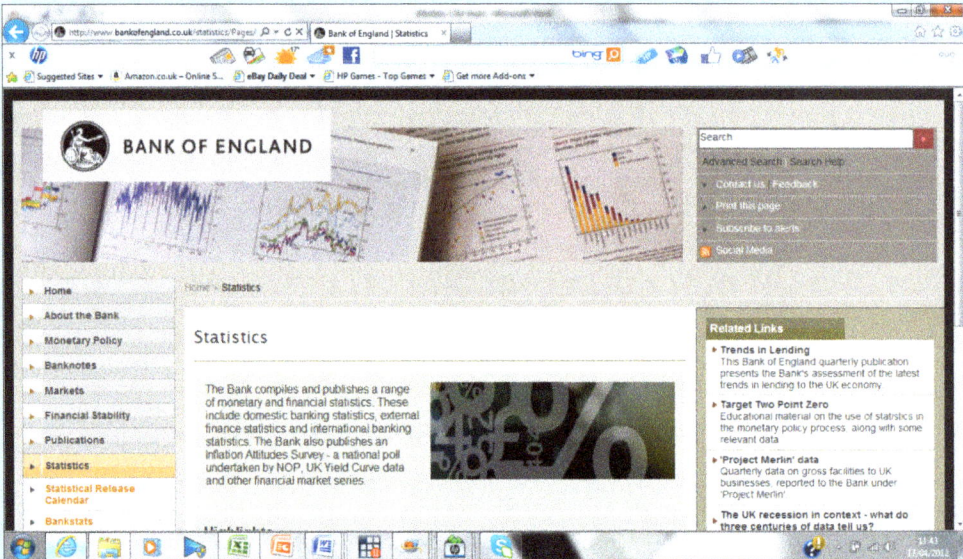

3 Now go back up and click on 'Wholesale interest and discount rates'. Scroll down to Treasury Bills 3 month and tick Sterling end month.

Now you have located an accurate source of historical interest rate data, the next step is getting it onto a spreadsheet. You click 'show data' and a menu will pop up for how you want the data downloaded. Click on the Excel button and the data will be downloaded and appear before you. Save this to a disk or hard drive.

4 You now want to analyse the interest rates by graphing them. Again highlight the two columns of data you just created in Excel. Click on the charts icon on the toolbar (or INSERT/CHART). Select scatter diagram and choose any type of scatter diagram that connects the dots. Let the Excel wizard take you through the steps of completing the graph.

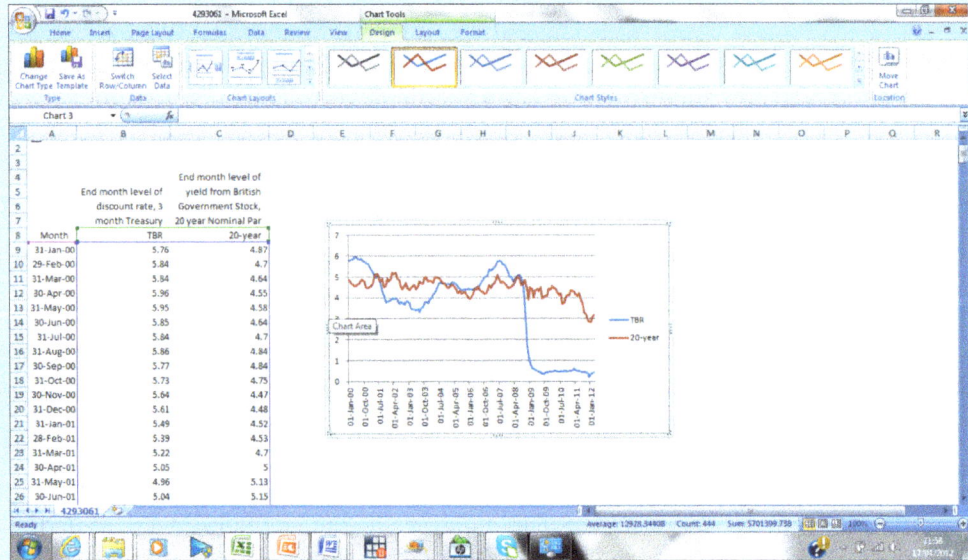

Summary

1 Activities in financial markets have direct effects on individuals' wealth, the behaviour of businesses and the efficiency of our economy. Three financial markets deserve particular attention: the bond market (where interest rates are determined), the stock market (which has a major effect on people's wealth and on firms' investment decisions), and the foreign exchange market (because fluctuations in the foreign exchange rates have major consequences for the eurozone economies and the UK economy).

2 Banks and other financial institutions channel funds from people who might not put them to productive use to people who can do so and thus play a crucial role in improving the efficiency of the economy.

3 Money appears to be a major influence on inflation, business cycles and interest rates. Because these economic variables are so important to the health of the economy, we need to understand how monetary policy is and should be conducted. We also need to study government fiscal policy because it can be an influential factor in the conduct of monetary policy.

4 This textbook stresses the economic way of thinking by developing a unifying analytic framework for the study of money, banking and financial markets using a few basic economic principles. This textbook also emphasizes the interaction of theoretical analysis and empirical data.

Key terms

aggregate income p. 20

aggregate output p. 9

aggregate price level p. 9

asset p. 4

banks p. 8

bond p. 4

budget deficit p. 12

budget surplus p. 12

business cycles p. 9

central bank p. 12

common stock p. 5

e-finance p. 9

financial crises p. 8

financial intermediaries p. 7

financial markets p. 3

fiscal policy p. 12

foreign exchange market p. 6

foreign exchange rate p. 6

gross domestic product p. 12, 20

inflation p. 10

inflation rate p. 11

interest rate p. 4

monetary policy p. 11

monetary theory p. 9

money (money supply) p. 9

recession p. 9

security p. 4

stock p. 5

unemployment rate p. 9

QUESTIONS AND PROBLEMS

All questions and problems are available in MyEconLab at **www.myeconlab.com/mishkin.**

1 Has the inflation rate in the euro area increased or decreased in the past few years? What about interest rates?

2 If history repeats itself and we see a decline in the rate of money growth, what might you expect to happen to

(a) real output?
(b) the inflation rate?
(c) interest rates?

3 When was the most recent recession in the euro area?

4 When interest rates fall, how might you change your economic behaviour?

5 Can you think of any financial innovation in the past ten years that has affected you personally? Has it made you better off or worse off? Why?

6 Is everybody worse off when interest rates rise?

7 What is the basic activity of banks?

8 Why are financial markets important to the health of the economy?

9 What is the typical relationship between interest rates on three-month Treasury bills and long-term government bonds in the euro area?

10 What effect might a fall in stock prices have on business investment?

11 What effect might a rise in stock prices have on consumers' decisions to spend?

12 How does a fall in the value of the pound sterling affect British consumers?

13 How does an increase in the value of the pound sterling affect American businesses?

14 Looking at Figure 1.3, in which years would an American have chosen to visit the Grand Canyon in Arizona rather than the Leaning Tower of Pisa?

15 When the dollar is worth more in relation to currencies of other countries, would an American be more likely to buy American-made or foreign-made jeans? Are US companies that manufacture jeans happier when the dollar is strong or when it is weak? What about an American company that is in the business of importing jeans into the United States?

WEB EXERCISES

1 In this exercise we will practise collecting data from the Web and graphing it using Excel. Use the example on page 16 as a guide. Go to **http://finance.yahoo.com/**, click on FTSE100 at the top of the page, then choose the 'Historical Prices' option. Set the data range to cover the past five years and choose 'weekly' data. Click the 'Get Prices' button.

(a) Using the 'Download to Spreadsheet' link at the bottom of the page, move the data into an Excel spreadsheet.
(b) Using the data from part a, prepare a graph. Use the graphing wizard to properly label your axes.

2 In Web Exercise 1 you collected and graphed the FTSE100. Yahoo! Finance also has data on other stock market indices. Repeat the process for either the German DAX stock market index.

(a) Using the data in Excel, compare the DAX versus the FTSE100 over the past five years.
(b) Yahoo! Finance allows you to compare the performance between several stock markets directly under 'Charts'. Using either the Interactive or Basic Chart, graph the FTSE100 versus the DAX. What differences do you observe between the Yahoo! Finance chart and your own Excel graph? How can they be reconciled?

Notes

1 The definition of *bond* used throughout this book is the broad one in common use by academics, which covers both short- and long-term debt instruments. However, some practitioners in financial markets use the word *bond* to describe only specific long-term debt instruments such as UK government gilt-edged securities.

2 Milton Friedman, *Dollars and Deficits* (Upper Saddle River, NJ: Prentice Hall, 1968), p. 39.

Useful websites

www.ecb.int/home/html/index.en.html Provides euro area data on yields, interest rates, foreign exchange rates and money supply aggrgegates.

www.bankofengland.co.uk Daily, weekly, monthly, quarterly and annual releases and historical data for selected interest rates, foreign exchange rates.

http://www.ons.gov.uk/ons/datasets-and-tables/index.html Provides all data collected by the UK Office for National Statistics.

http://www.reuters.com/financen Reuters Finance is one of the most comprehensive finance sites on the web.

http://www.ft.com/home/uk The *Financial Times* has market data, breaking news and insightful commentary.

http://stockcharts.com/charts/historical Historical charts of various stock indexes over differing time periods.

www.federalreserve.gov General information, monetary policy, banking system, research and economic data of the Federal Reserve.

http://finance.yahoo.com/ Yahoo! Finance allows you to download data, track current news and get corporate data.

MyEconLab Can help you get a better grade

MyEconLab®

If your exam were tomorrow, would you be ready? For each chapter, MyEconLab Practice Tests and Study Plans pinpoint which sections you have mastered and which ones you need to study. That way, you are more efficient with your study time, and you are better prepared for your exams.

Here's how it works:

1 Register and log in at: **www.myeconlab.com/mishkin**

2 Click on 'Take a Test' and select Sample Test A for this chapter.

3 Take the diagnostic test. MyEconLab will grade it automatically and create a personalized Study Plan so you see which sections of the chapter you should study further.

4 The Study Plan will serve up additional practice problems and tutorials to help you master the specific areas on which you need to focus. By practising online, you can track your progress in the Study Plan.

5 After you have mastered the sections, go to 'Take a Test' and select Sample Test B for this chapter. Take the test and see how you do!

MyEconLab®

Defining aggregate output, income, the price level and the inflation rate

Because these terms are used so frequently throughout the text, we need to have a clear understanding of the definitions of *aggregate output*, *income*, the *price level* and the *inflation rate*.

Aggregate output and income

The most commonly reported measure of aggregate output, the **gross domestic product (GDP)**, is the market value of all final goods and services produced in a country during the course of the year. This measure excludes two sets of items that at first glance you might think it would include. Purchases of goods that have been produced in the past, whether a Rembrandt painting or a house built twenty years ago, are not counted as part of GDP, nor are purchases of stocks or bonds. None of these enter into GDP because they are not goods and services produced during the course of the year. Intermediate goods, which are used up in producing final goods and services, such as the sugar in a candy bar or the energy used to produce steel, are also not counted separately as part of GDP. Because the value of the final goods already includes the value of the intermediate goods, to count them separately would be to count them twice.

Aggregate income, the total income of *factors of production* (land, labour and capital) from producing goods and services in the economy during the course of the year, is best thought of as being equal to aggregate output. Because the payments for final goods and services must eventually flow back to the owners of the factors of production as income, income payments must equal payments for final goods and services. For example, if the economy has an aggregate output of €1 trillion, total income payments in the economy (aggregate income) are also €1 trillion.

Real versus nominal magnitudes

When the total value of final goods and services is calculated using current prices, the resulting GDP measure is referred to as *nominal GDP*. The word *nominal* indicates that values are measured using current prices. If all prices doubled but actual production of goods and services remained the same, nominal GDP would double even though people would not enjoy the benefits of twice as many goods and services. As a result, nominal variables can be misleading measures of economic well-being.

A more reliable measure of economic production expresses values in terms of prices for an arbitrary base year. GDP measured with constant prices is referred to as *real GDP*, the word *real* indicating that values are measured in terms of fixed prices. Real variables thus measure the quantities of goods and services and do not change because prices have changed, but rather only if actual quantities have changed.

A brief example will make the distinction clearer. Suppose that you have a nominal income of €30,000 in 2010 and that your nominal income was €15,000 in 2000. If all prices doubled between 2000 and 2010, are you better off? The answer is no: although your income has doubled, your €30,000 buys you only the same amount of goods because prices have also doubled. A real income measure indicates that your income in terms of the goods it can buy is the same. Measured in 2000 prices, the €30,000 of nominal income in 2010 turns out to be only €15,000 of real income. Because your real income is actually the same in the two years, you are no better or worse off in 2010 than you were in 2000.

Because real variables measure quantities in terms of real goods and services, they are typically of more interest than nominal variables. In this text, discussion of aggregate output or aggregate income always refers to real measures (such as real GDP).

Aggregate price level

In this chapter, we defined the aggregate price level as a measure of average prices in the economy. Three measures of the aggregate price level are commonly encountered in economic data. The first is the *GDP deflator*, which is defined as nominal GDP divided by real GDP. Thus, if 2010 nominal GDP is €10 trillion but 2010 real GDP in 2000 prices is €9 trillion,

$$GDP\ deflator = \frac{€10\ trillion}{€9\ trillion} = 1.11$$

The GDP deflator equation indicates that, on average, prices have risen 11% since 2000. Typically, measures of the price level are presented in the form of a price index, which expresses the price level for the base year (in our example, 2000) as 100. Thus the GDP deflator for 2010 would be 111.

Another popular measure of the aggregate price level is the *PCE deflator*, which is similar to the GDP deflator and is defined as nominal personal consumption expenditures (PCE) divided by real PCE.

The measure of the aggregate price level that is most frequently reported in the press is the *consumer price index (CPI)*. The CPI is measured by pricing a 'basket' of goods and services bought by a typical urban household. If, over the course of the year, the cost of this basket of goods and services rises from €500 to €600, the CPI has risen by 20%. The CPI is also expressed as a price index with the base year equal to 100.

The CPI, the PCE deflator and the GDP deflator measures of the price level can be used to convert or deflate a nominal magnitude into a real magnitude. This is accomplished by dividing the nominal magnitude by the price index. In our example, in which the GDP deflator for 2010 is 1.11 (expressed as an index value of 111), real GDP for 2010 equals

$$\frac{€10\ trillion}{1.11} = €9\ trillion\ in\ 2000\ prices$$

which corresponds to the real GDP figure for 2010 assumed earlier.

Growth rates and the inflation rate

The media often talk about the economy's growth rate, and particularly the growth rate of real GDP. A growth rate is defined as the percentage change in a variable, i.e.

$$growth\ rate = \frac{x_t - x_{t-1}}{x_{t-1}} \times 100$$

where t indicates today and $t - 1$ a year earlier.

For example, if real GDP grew from \$9 trillion in 2010 to \$9.5 trillion in 2011, then the GDP growth rate for 2011 would be 5.6%:

$$\text{GDP growth rate} = \frac{\text{€9.5 trillion} = \text{€9 trillion}}{\text{€9 trillion}} \times 100 = 5.6\%$$

The inflation rate is defined as the growth rate of the aggregate price level. Thus, if the GDP deflator rose from 111 in 2010 to 113 in 2011, the inflation rate using the GDP deflator would be 1.8%:

$$\text{inflation rate} = \frac{113 - 111}{111} \times 100 = 1.8\%$$

If the growth rate is for a period less than one year, it is usually reported on an annualized basis; that is, it is converted to the growth rate over a year's time, assuming that the growth rate remains constant. For GDP, which is reported quarterly, the annualized growth rate would be approximately four times the percentage change in GDP from the previous quarter. For example, if GDP rose $\frac{1}{2}$% from the first quarter of 2010 to the second quarter of 2010, then the annualized GDP growth rate for the second quarter of 2010 would be reported as 2% $\left(= 4 \times \frac{1}{2}\% \right)$. (A more accurate calculation would be 2.02%, because a precise quarterly growth rate should be compounded on a quarterly basis.)

CHAPTER 2

An overview of the financial system

PREVIEW

Andrew Gordon was dismissed from *Dragons' Den*, the BBC reality show, for inventing a device that props up wobbly table legs. After his rejection, he took a bank loan to launch his product 'Wobbly wizard' and has since clocked up £1 million of orders. Percy the Pensioner has plenty of savings, which he and his wife accumulated over the years. If Andrew and Percy could have got together so that Percy could provide funds to Andrew to launch his 'Wobbly wizard' Andrew would not have had to take a bank loan. But Percy has partly funded Andrew because he holds his savings in bank deposits, and some bonds and stocks. It was the bank using its deposits that advanced Andrew the funds to start up his business.

Financial markets (bond and stock markets) and financial intermediaries (such as banks, insurance companies, pension funds) have the basic function of getting people like Andrew and Percy together by moving funds from those who have a surplus of funds (Percy) to those who have a shortage of funds (Andrew). More realistically, when Apple invents a better iPad, it may need funds to bring its new product to market. Similarly, when a local government needs to build a road or a school, it may need more funds than local property taxes provide. Well-functioning financial markets and financial intermediaries are crucial to economic health.

To study the effects of financial markets and financial intermediaries on the economy, we need to acquire an understanding of their general structure and operation. In this chapter, we learn about the major financial intermediaries and the instruments that are traded in financial markets as well as how these markets are regulated.

This chapter presents an overview of the fascinating study of financial markets and institutions. We return to a more detailed treatment of the regulation, structure and evolution of the financial system in Chapters 8 to 12.

Function of financial markets

Financial markets perform the essential economic function of channelling funds from households, firms and governments that have saved surplus funds by spending less than their income to those that have a shortage of funds because they wish to spend more than their income. This function is shown schematically in Figure 2.1. Those who have saved and are lending funds, the lender–savers, are at the left, and those who must borrow funds to finance their spending, the borrower–spenders, are at the right. The principal lender–savers are households, but business enterprises and the government (particularly central and local government), as well as foreigners and their governments, sometimes also find themselves with excess funds and so lend them out. The most important borrower–spenders are businesses and the government (particularly the central government), but households

FIGURE 2.1

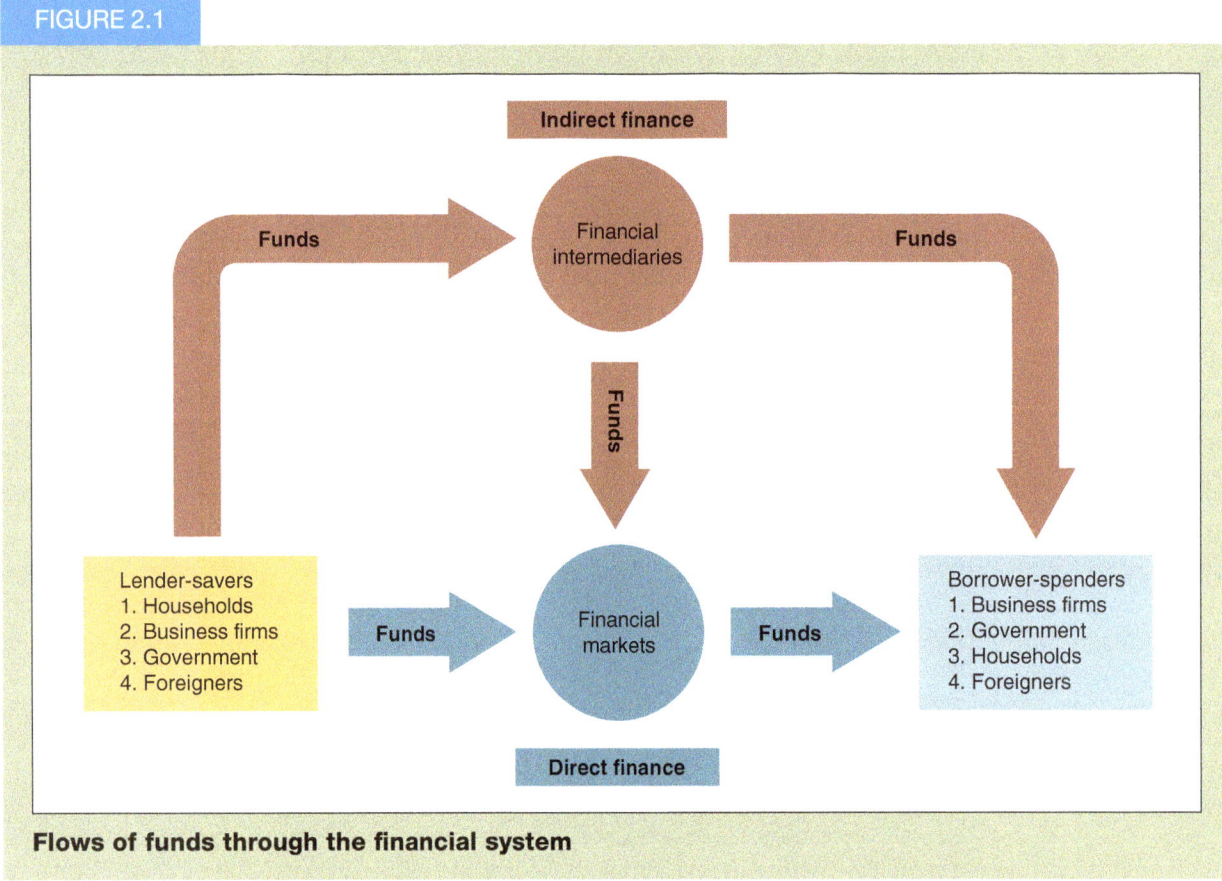

Flows of funds through the financial system

and foreigners also borrow to finance their purchases of cars, furniture and houses. The arrows show that funds flow from lender–savers to borrower–spenders via two routes.

In *direct finance* (the route at the bottom of Figure 2.1), borrowers borrow funds directly from lenders in financial markets by selling them *securities* (also called *financial instruments*), which are claims on the borrower's future income or assets. Securities are assets for the person who buys them but **liabilities** (IOUs or debts) for the individual or firm that sells (issues) them. For example, if Renault needs to borrow funds to pay for a new factory to manufacture electric cars, it might borrow the funds from savers by selling them a *bond*, a debt security, that promises to make payments periodically for a specified period of time, or a *stock*, a security that entitles the owner to a share of the company's profits and assets.

Why is this channelling of funds from savers to spenders so important to the economy? The answer is that the people who save are frequently not the same people who have profitable investment opportunities available to them, the entrepreneurs. Let's first think about this on a personal level. Suppose that you have saved €1,000 this year, but no borrowing or lending is possible because there are no financial markets. If you do not have an investment opportunity that will permit you to earn income with your savings, you will just hold on to the €1,000 and will earn no interest. However, Carl the carpenter has a productive use for your €1,000: he can use it to purchase a new tool that will shorten the time it takes him to build a house, thereby earning an extra €200 per year. If you could get in touch with Carl, you could lend him the €1,000 at a rental fee (interest) of €100 per year, and both of you would be better off. You would earn €100 per year on your €1,000, instead of the zero amount that you would earn otherwise, while Carl would earn €100 more income per year (the €200 extra earnings per year minus the €100 rental fee for the use of the funds).

In the absence of financial markets, you and Carl the carpenter might never get together. You would both be stuck with the status quo, and both of you would be worse off. Without financial markets, it is hard to transfer funds from a person who has no investment opportunities to one who has them. Financial markets are thus essential to promoting economic efficiency.

The existence of financial markets is beneficial even if someone borrows for a purpose other than increasing production in a business. Say that you are recently married, have a good job, and want to buy a house. You earn a good salary, but because you have just started to work, you have not saved much. Over time, you would have no problem saving enough to buy the house of your dreams, but by then you would be too old to get full enjoyment from it. Without financial markets, you are stuck; you cannot buy the house and must continue to live in your tiny apartment.

If a financial market were set up so that people who had built up savings could lend you the funds to buy the house, you would be more than happy to pay them some interest so that you could own a home while you are still young enough to enjoy it. Then, over time, you would pay back your loan. If this loan could occur, you would be better off, as would the persons who made you the loan. They would now earn some interest, whereas they would not if the financial market did not exist.

Now we can see why financial markets have such an important function in the economy. They allow funds to move from people who lack productive investment opportunities to people who have such opportunities. Financial markets are critical for producing an efficient allocation of **capital** (wealth, either financial or physical, that is employed to produce more wealth), which contributes to higher production and efficiency for the overall economy. Indeed, as we will explore in Chapter 9, when financial markets break down during financial crises, as they have in Mexico, East Asia and Argentina in recent years, but most recently the global financial crisis that followed the subprime loans crisis in the USA, severe economic hardship results.

Well-functioning financial markets also directly improve the well-being of consumers by allowing them to time their purchases better. They provide funds to young people to buy what they need and can eventually afford without forcing them to wait until they have saved up the entire purchase price. Financial markets that are operating efficiently improve the economic welfare of everyone in the society.

Structure of financial markets

Now that we understand the basic function of financial markets, let's look at their structure. The following descriptions of several categorizations of financial markets illustrate essential features of these markets.

Debt and equity markets

A firm or an individual can obtain funds in a financial market in two ways. The most common method is to issue a debt instrument, such as a bond or a mortgage, which is a contractual agreement by the borrower to pay the holder of the instrument fixed amounts of euros at regular intervals (interest and principal payments) until a specified date (the maturity date), when a final payment is made. The **maturity** of a debt instrument is the number of years (term) until that instrument's expiration date. A debt instrument is **short-term** if its maturity is less than a year and **long-term** if its maturity is longer than one year.

The second method of raising funds is by issuing **equities**, such as common stock, which are claims to share in the net income (income after expenses and taxes) and the assets of a business. If you own one share of common stock in a company that has issued one million shares, you are entitled to one millionth of the firm's net income and one millionth of the firm's assets. Equities often make periodic payments (**dividends**) to their holders and are considered long-term securities because they have no maturity date. In addition, owning stock means that you own a portion of the firm and thus have the right to vote on issues important to the firm and to elect its directors.

The main disadvantage of owning a corporation's equities rather than its debt is that an equity holder is a *residual claimant*; that is, the corporation must pay all its debt holders before it pays its equity holders. The advantage of holding equities is that equity holders benefit directly from any increases in the corporation's profitability or asset value because equities confer ownership rights on the equity holders. Debt holders do not share in this benefit, because their payments in euros are fixed. We examine the pros and cons of debt versus equity instruments in more detail in Chapter 8, which provides an economic analysis of financial structure.

The total value of equities in the UK has typically fluctuated between £0.9 and £3.8 trillion since 1990, depending on the prices of shares. Although the average person is more aware of the stock market than any other financial market, the size of the debt market is often substantially larger than the size of the equities market: the total value of debt instruments was approximately £7 trillion at the end of 2009.

Primary and secondary markets

A **primary market** is a financial market in which new issues of a security, such as a bond or a stock, are sold to initial buyers by the corporation or government agency borrowing the funds. A **secondary market** is a financial market in which securities that have been previously issued can be resold.

The primary markets for securities are not well known to the public because the selling of securities to initial buyers often takes place behind closed doors. An important financial institution that assists in the initial sale of securities in the primary market is the **investment bank**. It does this by **underwriting** securities: it guarantees a price for a corporation's securities and then sells them to the public.

The New York Stock Exchange, London Stock Exchange and Frankfurt Stock Exchange are the best-known examples of secondary markets, although the bond markets, in which previously issued bonds of major corporations and the UK and other European governments are bought and sold, actually have a larger trading volume. Other examples of secondary markets are foreign exchange markets, futures markets and options markets. Securities brokers and dealers are crucial to a well-functioning secondary market. **Brokers** are agents of investors who match buyers with sellers of securities; **dealers** link buyers and sellers by buying and selling securities at stated prices.

When an individual buys a security in the secondary market, the person who has sold the security receives money in exchange for the security, but the corporation that issued the security acquires no new funds. A corporation acquires new funds only when its securities are first sold in the primary market. Nonetheless, secondary markets serve two important functions. First, they make it easier and quicker to sell these financial instruments to raise cash; that is, they make the financial instruments more **liquid**. The increased liquidity of these instruments then makes them more desirable and thus easier for the issuing firm to sell in the primary market. Second, they determine the price of the security that the issuing firm sells in the primary market. The investors who buy securities in the primary market will pay the issuing corporation no more than the price they think the secondary market will set for this security. The higher the security's price in the secondary market, the higher the price that the issuing firm will receive for a new security in the primary market, and hence the greater the amount of financial capital it can raise. Conditions in the secondary market are therefore the most relevant to corporations issuing securities. It is for this reason that books like this one, which deal with financial markets, focus on the behaviour of secondary markets rather than primary markets.

Exchanges and over-the-counter markets

Secondary markets can be organized in two ways. One method is to organize **exchanges**, where buyers and sellers of securities (or their agents or brokers) meet in one central location to conduct trades. The London Stock Exchange for stocks and the London Metal Exchange for commodities (aluminium, copper, tin, plastics etc.) are examples of organized exchanges.

The other method of organizing a secondary market is to have an **over-the-counter (OTC) market**, in which dealers at different locations who have an inventory of securities stand ready to buy and sell securities 'over the counter' to anyone who comes to them and is willing to accept their prices. Because over-the-counter dealers are in computer contact and know the prices set by one another, the OTC market is very competitive and not very different from a market with an organized exchange.

Many common stocks are traded over-the-counter, although a majority of the largest corporations have their shares traded at organized stock exchanges. The US government bond market, with a larger trading volume than the New York Stock Exchange, by contrast, is set up as an over-the-counter market. Forty or so dealers establish a 'market' in these securities by standing ready to buy and sell US government bonds. Other over-the-counter markets include those that trade other types of financial instruments such as negotiable certificates of deposit, commercial paper and foreign exchange.

Money and capital markets

Another way of distinguishing between markets is on the basis of the maturity of the securities traded in each market. The **money market** is a financial market in which only short-term debt instruments (generally those with original maturity of less than one year) are traded; the **capital market** is the market in which longer-term debt instruments (generally those with original maturity of one year or greater) and equity instruments are traded. Money market securities are usually more widely traded than longer-term securities and so tend to be more liquid. In addition, as we will see in Chapter 4, short-term securities have smaller fluctuations in prices than long-term securities, making them safer investments. As a result, corporations and banks actively use the money market to earn interest on surplus funds that they expect to have only temporarily. Capital market securities, such as stocks and long-term bonds, are often held by financial intermediaries such as insurance companies and pension funds, which have little uncertainty about the amount of funds they will have available in the future.

Financial market instruments

To complete our understanding of how financial markets perform the important role of channelling funds from lender–savers to borrower–spenders, we need to examine the securities (instruments) traded in financial markets. We first focus on the instruments traded in the money market and then turn to those traded in the capital market.

Money market instruments (MMIs)

Because of their short terms to maturity, the debt instruments traded in the money market undergo the least price fluctuations and so are the least risky investments. The money market has undergone great changes in the past three decades, with the amount of some financial instruments growing at a far more rapid rate than others.

The London money market is one of the most liquid in the world. The principal money market instruments are listed in Table 2.1 along with the amount outstanding at the end of 2000 and 2009. The 'Following the financial news' box illustrates how the interest rates on many of the instruments are reported.

<table>
<tr><td colspan="4">TABLE 2.1</td></tr>
</table>

Principal money market instruments (London money market)			
	Amount outstanding (£ billions, end of year)		
Type of instrument	1990	2000	2009
Treasury bills	9.0	3.3	47.6
Bank bills	23.0	11.0	1.4
Sterling certificates of deposit	53.0	151.2	208.9
Commercial paper	5.0	18.0	15.0
Interbank deposits	89.0	151.0	335.4
Gilt repos	–	128.4	373.1

Source: www.bankofengland.co.uk/statistics/bankstats and ONS online.

Treasury bills

These are short-term debt instruments of the UK government and issued in one-, three- and six-month maturities to finance government spending. They pay a set amount at maturity and have no interest payments, but they effectively pay interest by initially selling at a discount, that is, at a price lower than the set amount paid at maturity. For instance, on 6 August 2010 you might buy a three-month Treasury bill for £1,498 that can be redeemed on 5 November 2010 for £1,500.

Treasury bills are highly liquid because they are the easiest to trade. They are also the safest of all money market instruments because there is almost no possibility of default, a situation in which the party issuing the debt instrument (HM government in this case) is unable to make interest payments or pay off the amount owed when the instrument matures. HM government is always able to meet its debt obligations because it can raise taxes or issue currency (paper money or coins) to pay off its debts. Treasury bills are held mainly by banks, although small amounts are held by households, corporations and other financial intermediaries. However, sterling Treasury bills are the smallest in volume of trades compared with other instruments. In 2000 they were less than 1% of the total money market instruments.

Bank bills

Bank bills are like Treasury bills and are issued by the banks and bought mostly by other banks. They have the same maturity as Treasury bills but they differ by being sold at a greater discount (higher implied yield). You can see from the table that in 1990 bank bills were a significant part of the sterling MMIs but by the end of 2009 had fallen to £1.4 billion.

Certificates of deposit

A certificate of deposit (CD) is a debt instrument sold by a bank to depositors that pays annual interest of a given amount and at maturity pays back the original purchase price. Negotiable CDs are CDs that are sold in secondary markets, with the amount outstanding. Negotiable CDs are an extremely important source of funds for commercial banks, from corporations, mutual funds, charitable institutions and government agencies. Certificates of deposits issued by the euro area banks reached €733 billion in 2009, having reached a peak of €822 billion in 2008.

Commercial paper

Commercial paper is a short-term debt instrument issued by large banks and well-known corporations, such as British Telecom and BAT. Growth of the commercial paper market has been substantial: the amount of commercial paper outstanding has increased by over

300% (from £5 billion to £15 billion) in the period 1990–2009. Commercial paper issued by companies in the euro area was €71 billion in 2009 after reaching a peak of €116 billion in 2008. We will discuss why the commercial paper market has had such tremendous growth in Chapter 12.

Interbank deposits

The interbank market is one where surplus banks can lend to cash-short banks sometimes substantial amounts. Interbank deposits are of varying maturities and go from overnight, seven days, one-month, three-, six- and twelve-month maturities. The growth of the interbank market shows the increased dependency of the UK commercial banks on interbank sources of funds. This dependence created a strain on the banks that expected the interbank market to source short-term funds when funds were not forthcoming during the credit crunch period of 2007–8.

Gilt repurchase agreements

Repurchase agreements (repos) are effectively short-term loans (usually with a maturity of less than two weeks) for which UK government gilt-edged securities (bonds, Treasury bills) but also high-grade commercial paper and certificate of deposits act as collateral. The gilt repo market is relatively new in the UK and began in 1996. It is a market where a borrowing institution will sell a gilt-edged security to a lending institution with a promise to buy it back at some predetermined maturity. It is also the market in which the Bank of England makes funds available to the banking system. A repo works as follows: the Bank of England buys a security from a commercial bank, which agrees to repurchase it at a specified period at a slightly higher price. The effect of this agreement is that the Bank of England has made a loan to the commercial bank and holds an equivalent value of gilts until the bank repurchases them to pay off the loan.

Capital market instruments

Capital market instruments are debt and equity instruments with maturities of greater than one year. They have far wider price fluctuations than money market instruments and are considered to be fairly risky investments. The principal capital market instruments are listed in Table 2.2, which shows the amount outstanding at the end of 1990, 2000 and 2009 for the UK. 'The following the financial news' box illustrates how the interest rates on many of these instruments are reported.

Stocks

Stocks are equity claims on the net income and assets of a corporation. Their value of £1.6 trillion at the end of 2009 exceeds that of any other type of security in the capital market. However, the fall in the value of stocks following the global financial crisis has meant that the market value of all quoted shares was lower at the end of 2009 than in 2000. Stocks are held mainly by individuals, pension funds, mutual funds and insurance companies. The total value of shares and equity which includes unquoted shares and private equity investment is typically twice the value of quoted shares shown in Table 2.2. The total value of quoted shares in the euro area was €998 billion in 1990, €5,555 billion in 2000 and €4,410 billion in 2009.

Mortgages

Mortgages are loans to households or firms to purchase housing, land, or other real structures, where the structure or land itself serves as collateral for the loans. The mortgage market is one of the largest debt markets in the UK, with most mortgages being taken by individuals. The building societies' primary asset is residential mortgages. Commercial banks also make residential mortgage loans but have a wider portfolio of lending to firms, individuals and other financial institutions.

Money market rates

The *Financial Times* publishes daily a listing of interest rates on many different financial instruments in its 'Market Interest Rates' column and 'Official interest rates' in the Companies and Markets section. You can access these by logging on to **www.ft.com**

Click on 'markets data' and 'bonds and rates'. Under 'Data Archive' select 'Market Interest Rate Summary' and 'Official Interest Rates'.

The four interest rates in the 'Money rates' and 'Official rates' columns that are monitored by the financial press are these:

- *UK Repo rate:* The interest rate at which the Bank of England makes secured loans to commercial banks
- *£ Libor rate:* The daily reference interest rate at which banks can borrow unsecured funds from other banks in the London wholesale market and is a sensitive indicator of the stance of monetary policy. The rates are set by the British Bankers Association and have maturities ranging from overnight to one year.
- *Euro Repo rate:* The interest rate at which the European Central Bank through the eurozone national central banks make funds available to the banking market (for maturities of usually 2 weeks). The funds are made available through repurchase agreements with a wide range of marketed and non-marketed debt instruments used as collateral **www.ecb .int/mopo/implement/intro/html/index.en.html**.
- *Euro Euribor rate:* A reference rate of interest at which banks in the eurozone offer to make unsecured loans to other banks in the eurozone through the euro wholesale money market.

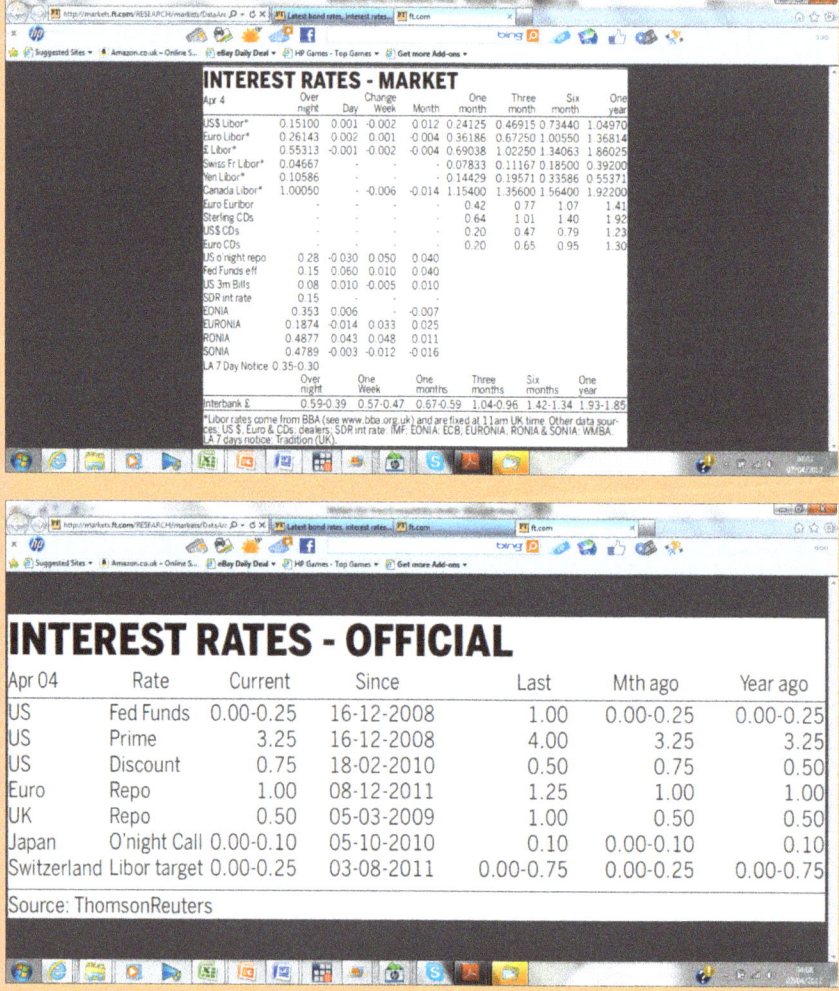

TABLE 2.2

Principal capital market instruments in the UK

Type of instrument	Amount outstanding (£ billions, end of year)		
	1990	2000	2009
Corporate stocks (quoted shares)	452	1754	1600
Mortgages	293	535	1235
Corporate bonds	80	410	1457
UK government securities (marketable long-term bonds)	108	329	798
UK local authority bonds	0.2	0.8	1
Long-term bonds issued by banks and other financial institutions	11	75	389
Bank loans (other than mortgages)	372	697	1601

Source: ONS online.

Corporate bonds

These long-term bonds are issued by corporations with very strong credit ratings. The typical **corporate bond** sends the holder an interest payment twice a year and pays off the face value when the bond matures. Some corporate bonds, called **convertible bonds**, have the additional feature of allowing the holder to convert them into a specified number of shares of stock at any time up to the maturity date. This feature makes these convertible bonds more desirable to prospective purchasers than bonds without it and allows the corporation to reduce its interest payments because these bonds can increase in value if the price of the stock appreciates sufficiently. Because the outstanding amount of both convertible and non-convertible bonds for any given corporation is small, they are not nearly as liquid as other securities such as UK government bonds.

The corporate bond market has been traditionally smaller than the stock market; however, the recent monetary policy of the Bank of England of asset purchases as a means of injecting liquidity into the markets and stimulating the economy following the great recession has encouraged the growth of the corporate bond market. Thus the behaviour of the corporate bond market is probably far more important to a firm's financing decisions than the behaviour of the stock market. The principal buyers of corporate bonds are life insurance companies; pension funds and households are other large holders.

UK government bonds

These long-term debt instruments are issued by the UK government Debt Management Office to finance the deficit of the government. Because UK government bonds have the highest rating (AAA) they are a highly liquid security traded in the capital market. They are held by the Bank of England, commercial banks, pension funds, life insurance companies, households and foreigners.

Local authority bonds

These long-term bonds are issued by various local authorities in the UK and were very popular in the 1980s as a means of financing capital projects in individual cities. At one time it was a standing joke that the bankers of Switzerland had claim to all the public buildings in Liverpool because of the outstanding long-term bonds they held issued by the Liverpool Corporation. Many of these bonds are implicitly guaranteed by the Treasury but the size of the market is small compared to other instruments in the bond market.

Bank and building society bonds

Banks and building societies issue long-term bonds of typically fixed rates of 1 to 5 years maturity. However, some banks issue bonds based on investments in selected stocks and provide a guaranteed minimum rate of return and therefore have some of the properties of equity rather than debt.

Bank and building society loans (excluding mortgages)

These loans are made principally to businesses. Unsecured lending to individuals (consumer credit and credit cards) amount to 10% of total bank loans excluding mortgages.

Internationalization of financial markets

The growing internationalization of financial markets has become an important trend. Before the 1980s, financial markets in the US were much larger than financial markets elsewhere, but in recent years the dominance of US markets has been disappearing. (See the Global box 'Are US capital markets losing their edge?'.) The extraordinary growth of foreign financial markets has been the result of both large increases in the pool of savings in foreign countries such as Japan and the deregulation of foreign financial markets, which has enabled foreign markets to expand their activities. American corporations and banks are

GLOBAL
Are US capital markets losing their edge?

Over the past few decades the United States lost its international dominance in a number of manufacturing industries, including automobiles and consumer electronics, as other countries became more competitive in global markets. Recent evidence suggests that financial markets now are undergoing a similar trend: just as Ford and General Motors have lost global market share to Toyota and Honda, US stock and bond markets recently have seen their share of sales of newly issued corporate securities slip. In 2008 the London and Hong Kong stock exchanges each handled a larger share of initial public offerings (IPO) of stock than did the New York Stock Exchange, which had been by far the dominant exchange in terms of IPO value just five years before. Likewise, the portion of new corporate bonds issued worldwide that are initially sold in US capital markets has fallen below the share sold in European debt markets in each of the past two years.*

Why do corporations that issue new securities to raise capital now conduct more of this business in financial markets in Europe and Asia? Among the factors contributing to this trend are quicker adoption of technological innovation by foreign financial markets, tighter immigration controls in the United States following the terrorist attacks in 2001, and perceptions that listing on American exchanges will expose foreign securities issuers to greater risks of lawsuits. Many people see

burdensome financial regulation as the main cause, however, and point specifically to the Sarbanes–Oxley Act of 2002. Congress passed this act after a number of accounting scandals involving US corporations and the accounting firms that audited them came to light. Sarbanes–Oxley aims to strengthen the integrity of the auditing process and the quality of information provided in corporate financial statements. The costs to corporations of complying with the new rules and procedures are high, especially for smaller firms, but largely avoidable if firms choose to issue their securities in financial markets outside the United States. For this reason, there is much support for revising Sarbanes–Oxley to lessen its alleged harmful effects and induce more securities issuers back to United States financial markets. However, there is not conclusive evidence to support the view that Sarbanes–Oxley is the main cause of the relative decline of US financial markets and therefore in need of reform.

Discussion of the relative decline of US financial markets and debate about the factors that are contributing to it likely will continue. Chapter 8 provides more detail on the Sarbanes–Oxley Act and its effects on the US financial system.

*'Down in the Street', *The Economist*, 25 November 2006, pp. 69–71.

now more likely to tap international capital markets to raise needed funds, and American investors often seek investment opportunities abroad. Similarly, foreign corporations and banks raise funds from Americans, and foreigners have become important investors in the United States. A look at international bond markets and world stock markets will give us a picture of how this globalization of financial markets is taking place.

International bond market, Eurobonds and Eurocurrencies

The traditional instruments in the international bond market are known as **foreign bonds**. Foreign bonds are sold in a foreign country and are denominated in that country's currency. For example, if the German car maker Porsche sells a bond in the United States denominated in US dollars, it is classified as a foreign bond. Foreign bonds have been an important instrument in the international capital market for centuries. In fact, a large percentage of US railroads built in the nineteenth century were financed by sales of foreign bonds in Britain.

A more recent innovation in the international bond market is the **Eurobond**, a bond denominated in a currency other than that of the country in which it is sold – for example, a bond denominated in US dollars sold in London. Currently, over 80% of the new issues in the international bond market are Eurobonds, and the market for these securities has grown very rapidly. As a result, the Eurobond market is now larger than the US corporate bond market.

A variant of the Eurobond is **Eurocurrencies**, which are foreign currencies deposited in banks outside the home country. The most important of the Eurocurrencies are **eurodollars**, which are US dollars deposited in foreign banks outside the United States or in foreign branches of US banks. Because these short-term deposits earn interest, they are similar to short-term Eurobonds. American banks borrow eurodollar deposits from other banks or from their own foreign branches, and eurodollars are now an important source of funds for American banks.

Note that the new currency, the euro, can create some confusion about the terms Eurobond, Eurocurrencies and eurodollars. A bond denominated in euros is called a Eurobond only *if it is sold outside the countries that have adopted the euro.* In fact, most Eurobonds are not denominated in euros but are instead denominated in US dollars. Similarly, eurodollars have nothing to do with euros, but are instead US dollars deposited in banks outside the United States.

World stock markets

Until recently, the US stock market was by far the largest in the world, but other stock markets have been growing in importance, with the United States not always being number one. The increased interest in foreign stocks has prompted the development in the United States of mutual funds that specialize in trading in foreign stock markets. Investors in the USA pay attention not only to the Dow Jones Industrial Average but also to stock price indexes for foreign stock markets such as the Nikkei 300 Average (Tokyo) and the Financial Times Stock Exchange (FTSE) 100-Share Index (London).

The internationalization of financial markets is having profound effects on the United States. Foreigners, particularly Japanese investors, are not only providing funds to corporations in the United States, but are also helping finance the federal government. One of the largest holders of US Treasury bills is the People's Republic of China. Without these foreign funds, the US economy would have grown far less rapidly in the last twenty years. Similarly, in the UK it was the international money market that made funds available to British banks through the interbank market to increase their lending in excess of their own funds prior to the credit crunch. The internationalization of financial markets is also leading the way to a more integrated world economy in which flows of goods and technology

FOLLOWING THE FINANCIAL NEWS

Foreign stock market indexes

Foreign stock market indexes are published daily in the *Financial Times* which reports developments in foreign stock markets. The first column identifies the country of the foreign stock exchange, and the second column gives the market index; for example, the circled entry for the M-DAX in Germany. The third column, gives the closing value of the index on the date at the top of the column which was 10515.43 for the M-DAX Average on 4 April 2012. The next column is the closing value of the index in the previous day which in the case of the M-DAX was 10853.01. You should be able to calculate the percentage change in the index, which is −3.1%.

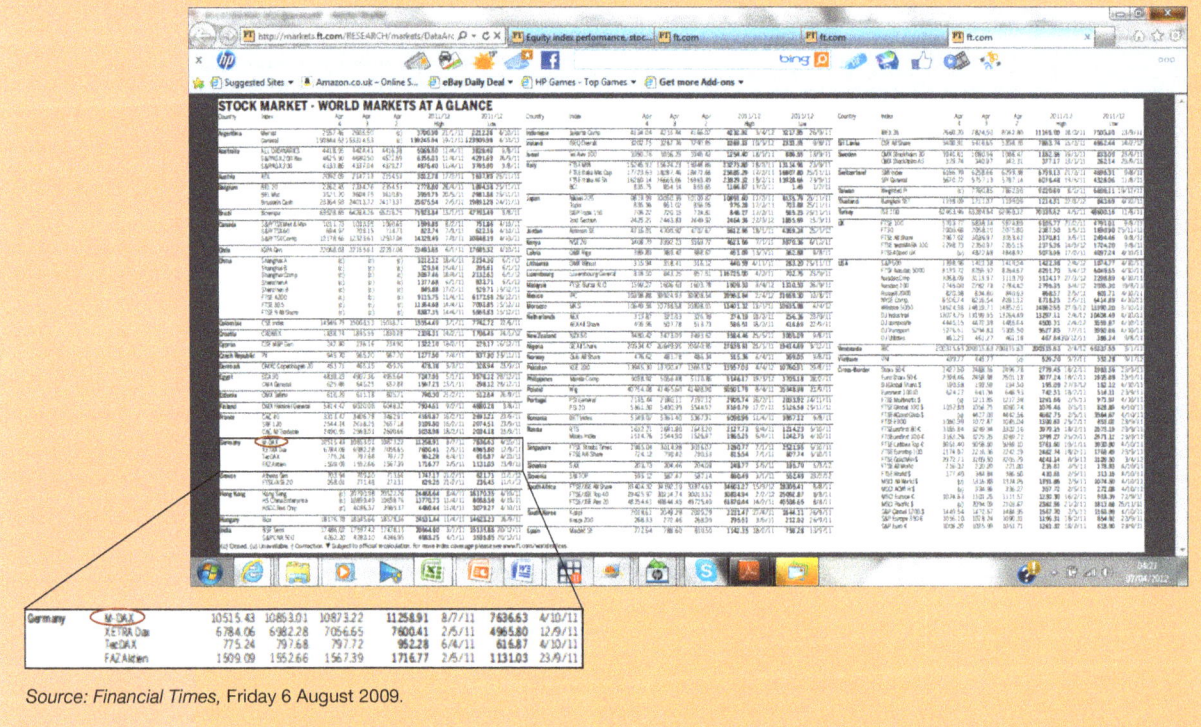

Source: *Financial Times,* Friday 6 August 2009.

between countries are more commonplace. In later chapters, we will encounter many examples of the important roles that international factors play in the US economy (see the 'Following the financial news' box).

Function of financial intermediaries: indirect finance

As shown in Figure 2.1, funds can move from lenders to borrowers by a second route, called *indirect finance* because it involves a financial intermediary that stands between the lender–savers and the borrower–spenders and helps transfer funds from one to the other. A financial intermediary does this by borrowing funds from the lender–savers and then using these funds to make loans to borrower–spenders. For example, a bank might acquire funds by issuing a liability to the public (an asset for the public) in the form of savings deposits. It might then use the funds to acquire an asset by making a loan to British Telecom or by buying a government bond in the financial market. The ultimate result is that funds have been transferred from the public (the lender–savers) to BT or HM Treasury (the borrower–spender) with the help of the financial intermediary (the bank).

The process of indirect finance using financial intermediaries, called **financial intermediation**, has traditionally been the primary route for moving funds from lenders to borrowers. Although the media focus much of their attention on securities markets, particularly the stock market, financial intermediaries are also an important source of financing for corporations. This is also true for other industrialized countries, particularly the eurozone economies (see the Global box overleaf). Why are financial intermediaries and indirect finance so important in financial markets? To answer this question, we need to understand the role of transaction costs, risk sharing and information costs in financial markets.

Transaction costs

Transaction costs, the time and money spent in carrying out financial transactions, are a major problem for people who have excess funds to lend. As we have seen, Carl the carpenter needs €1,000 for his new tool, and you know that it is an excellent investment opportunity. You have the cash and would like to lend him the money, but to protect your investment you have to hire a lawyer to write up the loan contract that specifies how much interest Carl will pay you, when he will make these interest payments, and when he will repay you the €1,000. Obtaining the contract will cost you €500. When you figure in this transaction cost for making the loan, you realize that you can't earn enough from the deal (you spend €500 to make perhaps €100) and reluctantly tell Carl that he will have to look elsewhere.

This example illustrates that small savers like you or potential borrowers like Carl might be frozen out of financial markets and thus be unable to benefit from them. Can anyone come to the rescue? Financial intermediaries can.

Financial intermediaries can substantially reduce transaction costs because they have developed expertise in lowering them; and because their large size allows them to take advantage of **economies of scale**, the reduction in transaction costs per euro of transactions as the size (scale) of transactions increases. For example, a bank knows how to find a good lawyer to produce an airtight loan contract, and this contract can be used over and over again in its loan transactions, thus lowering the legal cost per transaction. Instead of a loan contract (which may not be all that well written) costing €500, a bank can hire a top-flight lawyer for €5,000 to draw up an airtight loan contract that can be used for 2,000 loans at a cost of €2.50 per loan. At a cost of €2.50 per loan, it now becomes profitable for the financial intermediary to lend Carl the €1,000.

Because financial intermediaries are able to reduce transaction costs substantially, they make it possible for you to provide funds indirectly to people like Carl with productive investment opportunities. In addition, a financial intermediary's low transaction costs mean that it can provide its customers with **liquidity services**, services that make it easier for customers to conduct transactions. For example, banks provide depositors with current accounts that enable them to pay their bills easily. In addition, depositors can earn interest on current and savings accounts and yet still convert them into goods and services whenever necessary.

Risk sharing

Another benefit made possible by the low transaction costs of financial institutions is that they can help reduce the exposure of investors to **risk** – that is, uncertainty about the returns investors will earn on assets. Financial intermediaries do this through the process known as **risk sharing**: they create and sell assets with risk characteristics that people are comfortable with, and the intermediaries then use the funds they acquire by selling these assets to purchase other assets that may have far more risk. Low transaction costs allow financial intermediaries to share risk at low cost, enabling them to earn a profit on the

GLOBAL
The importance of financial intermediaries relative to securities markets: an international comparison

Patterns of financing corporations differ across countries, but studies of the major developed countries, including the United States, the United Kingdom, Japan and the eurozone countries show that financing businesses through financial intermediaries has always been greater than the debt securities (bond market).* Even in the United States and the UK, which have the most developed securities markets in the world, loans from financial intermediaries are far more important for corporate finance than securities markets are. The countries that have made the least use of securities markets are the eurozone economies and Japan. In the eurozone, financing from financial intermediaries has been almost ten times greater than that from securities markets. However, after the deregulation of Japanese securities markets in recent years, the share of corporate financing by financial intermediaries has been declining relative to the use of securities markets.

Although the dominance of financial intermediaries over securities markets is clear in all countries, the relative importance of bond versus stock markets differs widely across countries. In the United States, the bond market is far more important as a source of corporate finance than in the UK. In the US 40% of company debt is obtained from the securities market whereas for the UK it is 25-6%. In contrast the euro countries such as France and Italy make more use of equities markets than of the bond market to raise capital.

*See, Task Force of the Monetary Policy Committee of the European System of Central Banks, 'Corporate finance in the euro area', *ECB Occasional Paper*, 63, 2007.

spread between the returns they earn on risky assets and the payments they make on the assets they have sold. This process of risk sharing is also sometimes referred to as **asset transformation**, because in a sense, risky assets are turned into safer assets for investors.

Financial intermediaries also promote risk sharing by helping individuals to diversify and thereby lower the amount of risk to which they are exposed. **Diversification** entails investing in a collection (**portfolio**) of assets whose returns do not always move together, with the result that overall risk is lower than for individual assets. (Diversification is just another name for the old adage, 'You shouldn't put all your eggs in one basket'.) Low transaction costs allow financial intermediaries to do this by pooling a collection of assets into a new asset and then selling it to individuals.

Asymmetric information: adverse selection and moral hazard

The presence of transaction costs in financial markets explains, in part, why financial intermediaries and indirect finance play such an important role in financial markets. An additional reason is that in financial markets, one party often does not know enough about the other party to make accurate decisions. This inequality is called **asymmetric information**. For example, a borrower who takes out a loan usually has better information about the potential returns and risk associated with the investment projects for which the funds are earmarked than the lender does. Lack of information creates problems in the financial system on two fronts: before the transaction is entered into and after.[1]

Adverse selection is the problem created by asymmetric information *before* the transaction occurs. Adverse selection in financial markets occurs when the potential borrowers who are the most likely to produce an undesirable (*adverse*) outcome – the bad credit risks – are the ones who most actively seek out a loan and are thus most likely to be selected. Because adverse selection makes it more likely that loans might be made to bad credit risks, lenders may decide not to make any loans even though there are good credit risks in the marketplace.

To understand why adverse selection occurs, suppose that you have two aunts to whom you might make a loan – Aunt Louise and Aunt Sheila. Aunt Louise is a conservative type who borrows only when she has an investment she is quite sure will pay off. Aunt Sheila, by contrast, is an inveterate gambler who has just come across a get-rich-quick scheme that will make her a millionaire if she can just borrow €1,000 to invest in it. Unfortunately, as with most get-rich-quick schemes, there is a high probability that the investment won't pay off and that Aunt Sheila will lose the €1,000.

Which of your aunts is more likely to call you to ask for a loan? Aunt Sheila, of course, because she has so much to gain if the investment pays off. You, however, would not want to make a loan to her because there is a high probability that her investment will turn sour and she will be unable to pay you back.

If you knew both your aunts very well – that is, if your information were not asymmetric – you wouldn't have a problem, because you would know that Aunt Sheila is a bad risk and so you would not lend to her. Suppose, though, that you don't know your aunts well. You are more likely to lend to Aunt Sheila than to Aunt Louise because Aunt Sheila would be hounding you for the loan. Because of the possibility of adverse selection, you might decide not to lend to either of your aunts, even though there are times when Aunt Louise, who is an excellent credit risk, might need a loan for a worthwhile investment.

Moral hazard is the problem created by asymmetric information *after* the transaction occurs. Moral hazard in financial markets is the risk (*hazard*) that the borrower might engage in activities that are undesirable (*immoral*) from the lender's point of view, because they make it less likely that the loan will be paid back. Because moral hazard lowers the probability that the loan will be repaid, lenders may decide that they would rather not make a loan.

As an example of moral hazard, suppose that you made a €1,000 loan to another relative, Uncle Melvin, who needs the money to purchase a computer so he can set up a business typing students' essays. Once you have made the loan, however, Uncle Melvin is more likely to slip off to the racetrack and play the horses. If he bets on a 20-to-1 long shot and wins with your money, he is able to pay you back your €1,000 and live high off the hog with the remaining €19,000. But if he loses, as is likely, you don't get paid back, and all he has lost is his reputation as a reliable, upstanding uncle. Uncle Melvin therefore has an incentive to go to the track because his gains (€19,000) if he bets correctly are much greater than the cost to him (his reputation) if he bets incorrectly. If you knew what Uncle Melvin was up to, you would prevent him from going to the track, and he would not be able to increase the moral hazard. However, because it is hard for you to keep informed about his whereabouts – that is, because information is asymmetric – there is a good chance that Uncle Melvin will go to the track and you will not get paid back. The risk of moral hazard might therefore discourage you from making the €1,000 loan to Uncle Melvin, even if you were sure that you would be paid back if he used it to set up his business.

The problems created by adverse selection and moral hazard are an important impediment to well-functioning financial markets. Again, financial intermediaries can alleviate these problems.

With financial intermediaries in the economy, small savers can provide their funds to the financial markets by lending these funds to a trustworthy intermediary – say, the Honest John Bank – which in turn lends the funds out either by making loans or by buying securities such as stocks or bonds. Successful financial intermediaries have higher earnings on their investments than small savers, because they are better equipped than individuals to screen out bad credit risks from good ones, thereby reducing losses due to adverse selection. In addition, financial intermediaries have high earnings because they develop expertise in monitoring the parties they lend to, thus reducing losses due to moral hazard. The result is that financial intermediaries can afford to pay lender–savers interest or provide substantial services and still earn a profit.

As we have seen, financial intermediaries play an important role in the economy because they provide liquidity services, promote risk sharing and solve information problems, thereby allowing small savers and borrowers to benefit from the existence of financial markets. The success of financial intermediaries in performing this role is evidenced by the fact that most Americans invest their savings with them and obtain loans from them. Financial intermediaries play a key role in improving economic efficiency because they help financial markets channel funds from lender–savers to people with productive investment opportunities. Without a well-functioning set of financial intermediaries, it is very hard for an economy to reach its full potential. We will explore further the role of financial intermediaries in the economy in Part 3.

Types of financial intermediaries

We have seen why financial intermediaries play such an important role in the economy. Now we look at the principal financial intermediaries themselves and how they perform the intermediation function. They fall into three categories: depository institutions (banks), contractual savings institutions and investment intermediaries. Table 2.3 provides a guide to the discussion of the financial intermediaries that fit into these three categories by describing their primary liabilities (sources of funds) and assets (uses of funds). The relative size of these intermediaries in the UK is indicated in Table 2.4a, which lists the amount of their assets at the end of 1990, 2000 and 2009. Table 2.4b provides a similar breakdown for the financial intermediaries in the euro area.

Depository institutions

Depository institutions (for simplicity, we refer to these as *banks* throughout this text) are financial intermediaries that accept deposits from individuals and institutions and make loans. The study of money and banking focuses special attention on this group of financial institutions, because they are involved in the creation of deposits, an important component of the money supply. These institutions include commercial banks and the building societies and credit unions.

TABLE 2.3

Primary assets and liabilities of financial intermediaries

Type of intermediary	Primary liabilities (sources of funds)	Primary assets (uses of funds)
Depository institutions (banks)		
Commercial banks	Deposits	Business and consumer loans, mortgages, government securities, commercial paper
Building societies	Deposits	Mortgages
Contractual savings institutions		
Life and general insurance companies	Premiums from policies	Government bonds, corporate bonds and stocks
Pension funds	Employer and employee contributions	Government bonds, corporate bonds and stocks
Investment intermediaries		
Finance companies	Commercial paper, stocks, bonds	Consumer and business loans
Mutual funds	Shares	Stocks, bonds

TABLE 2.4a

Principal financial intermediaries and value of their assets in the UK

Type of intermediary	Value of assets (£ billion year end)		
	1990	2000	2009
Depository institutions			
Commercial banks, building societies and credit unions	1,467	3,256	11,952
Contractual savings institutions			
Insurance corporations and pension funds	502	1,657	2,415
Investment intermediaries			
Other financial intermediaries and financial auxiliaries (finance companies, mutual funds, money market mutuals, investment banks)	242	1,034	4,070

Source: ONS online.

TABLE 2.4b

Financial intermediaries and value of their assets in the euro area

Type of intermediary	Value of assets (€ billion year end)		
	1999	2008	2010
Depository institutions			
Commercial banks, and other credit institutions	16,527	34,807	35,380
Contractual savings institutions			
Insurance corporations and pension funds	2,925	4,630	5,321
Investment intermediaries			
Other financial intermediaries and financial auxiliaries (finance companies, mutual funds, money market mutuals, investment banks)	6,621	12,002	15,216

Source: ECB *Monthly Bulletin*, January 2012. Information may be obtained free of charge through the ECB's website.

Commercial banks

These financial intermediaries raise funds primarily by issuing sight deposits (deposits on which cheques can be written), savings deposits (deposits that are payable on demand but do not allow their owner to write cheques), and time deposits (deposits with fixed terms to maturity). They then use these funds to make commercial, consumer and mortgage loans and to buy government securities and commercial paper. There are 203 commercial banks including subsidiaries that belong to the British Banking Association.

Building societies

Building societies are depository institutions in the UK that have the status of mutuals. They are owned by the members (depositors) and numbered 50 in 2010. They obtain funds primarily through savings deposits (often called *shares*) and time and sight deposits. In the past, these institutions were constrained in their activities and mostly made mortgage loans for residential housing. Over time, these restrictions have been loosened so that the distinction between these depository institutions and commercial banks has blurred. These intermediaries have become more alike and are now more competitive with each other. The total assets of building societies amounted to £335 billion at the end of 2009.

Credit unions

These financial institutions, numbering about 500 in the UK, are typically very small cooperative lending institutions organized around a particular group: union members, employees of a particular firm, and so forth. They acquire funds from deposits called *shares* and primarily make consumer loans. They accounted for around £455 million of loans at the end of 2008.

Contractual savings institutions

Contractual savings institutions, such as insurance companies and pension funds, are financial intermediaries that acquire funds at periodic intervals on a contractual basis. Because they can predict with reasonable accuracy how much they will have to pay out in benefits in the coming years, they do not have to worry as much as depository institutions about losing funds quickly. As a result, the liquidity of assets is not as important a consideration for them as it is for depository institutions, and they tend to invest their funds primarily in long-term securities such as corporate bonds, stocks and mortgages.

Life and general insurance companies

Life insurance companies insure people against financial hazards following a death and sell annuities (annual income payments upon retirement). They acquire funds from the premiums that people pay to keep their policies in force and use them mainly to buy government bonds, corporate bonds and stocks. Except for the UK and the Netherlands there are limits on the proportion of assets life insurance companies can hold in the form of stocks. In France the limit is 65% whereas in Italy it is 20%.

Pension funds

Private pension funds and government and government agency retirement funds provide retirement income in the form of annuities to employees who are covered by a pension plan. Funds are acquired by contributions from employers and from employees, who either have a contribution automatically deducted from their pay or contribute voluntarily. The largest asset holdings of pension funds are corporate bonds and stocks.

Investment intermediaries

This category of financial intermediaries includes finance companies, mutual funds and money market mutual funds.

Finance companies

Finance companies raise funds by selling commercial paper (a short-term debt instrument) and by issuing stocks and bonds. They lend these funds to consumers, who make purchases of such items as furniture, automobiles and home improvements, and to small businesses. Some finance companies are organized by a parent corporation to help sell its product. For example, Ford Credit Company makes loans to consumers who purchase Ford automobiles.

Mutual funds

These financial intermediaries acquire funds by selling shares to many individuals and use the proceeds to purchase diversified portfolios of stocks and bonds. Mutual funds allow shareholders to pool their resources so that they can take advantage of lower transaction costs when buying large blocks of stocks or bonds. In addition, mutual funds allow shareholders to hold more diversified portfolios than they otherwise would. Shareholders can sell (redeem) shares at any time, but the value of these shares will be determined by the value of the mutual fund's holdings of securities. Because these fluctuate greatly, the value of mutual fund shares will, too; therefore, investments in mutual funds can be risky.

Money market mutual funds

These financial institutions have the characteristics of a mutual fund but also function to some extent as a depository institution because they offer deposit-type accounts. Like most mutual funds, they sell shares to acquire funds that are then used to buy money market instruments that are both safe and very liquid. The interest on these assets is paid out to the shareholders.

Investment banks

Despite its name, an investment bank is not a bank or a financial intermediary in the ordinary sense; that is, it does not take in deposits and then lend them out. Instead, an investment bank is a different type of intermediary that helps a corporation issue securities. First it advises the corporation on which type of securities to issue (stocks or bonds); then it helps sell (**underwrite**) the securities by purchasing them from the corporation at a predetermined price and reselling them in the market. Investment banks also act as deal makers and earn enormous fees by helping corporations acquire other companies through mergers or acquisitions.

Regulation of the financial system

Financial markets are regulated for two main reasons; first, to increase the information available to investors and, second, to ensure the soundness of the financial system. We will examine how these two reasons have led to the present regulatory environment. As a study aid, the principal regulatory agencies of the European financial system are listed in Table 2.5.

Increasing information available to investors

Asymmetric information in financial markets means that investors may be subject to adverse selection and moral hazard problems that may hinder the efficient operation of financial markets. Risky firms or outright crooks may be the most eager to sell securities to unwary investors, and the resulting adverse selection problem may keep investors out of financial markets. Furthermore, once an investor has bought a security, thereby lending money to a firm, the borrower may have incentives to engage in risky activities or to commit outright fraud. The presence of this moral hazard problem may also keep investors away from financial markets. Government regulation can reduce adverse selection and moral hazard problems in financial markets and increase their efficiency by increasing the amount of information available to investors.

Ensuring the soundness of financial intermediaries

Asymmetric information can lead to the widespread collapse of financial intermediaries, referred to as a **financial panic**. Because providers of funds to financial intermediaries may not be able to assess whether the institutions holding their funds are sound, if they have doubts about the overall health of financial intermediaries, they may want to pull their

TABLE 2.5

Selected regulatory agencies of the European financial system

Regulatory agency	Subject of regulation	Nature of regulations
Autorité des Marchés Financiers (AMP – France)	Organized exchanges, financial markets, company disclosure and financial services provision	Conduct, regulation, authorization, supervision and enforcement. The remit is to safeguard investments and maintain orderly financial markets
Bundesanstalt für Finanzdienstleistungsaufsicht (BaFin – Germany)	Banks and financial services providers, insurance undertakings and securities trading	Remit to ensure the proper functioning, stability and integrity of the German financial system. Regulation covers banking, insurance and securities markets
Financial Services Authority (FSA – UK)	Financial service markets, exchanges and financial intermediaries	Supervision and regulation of financial services. Remit is protection for consumers and to fight financial crime
Banque de France (France)	Financial intermediaries	Supervision of financial intermediaries and provision of services to banks, businesses and public authorities. Remit to maintain financial stability
Deutsche Bundesbank (Germany)	Financial intermediaries	Supervision of financial intermediaries and operation of the payments mechanism
Bank of England (UK)	Monetary policy	Remit to maintain financial stability
European Central Bank (eurozone)	Monetary policy for the euro area	Sets reserve requirements for all banks in the euro area

funds out of both sound and unsound institutions. The possible outcome is a financial panic that produces large losses for the public and causes serious damage to the economy. To protect the public and the economy from financial panics, government has implemented six types of regulations.

Restrictions on entry

Individual regulatory agencies of Europe set regulations governing who is allowed to set up a financial intermediary. Individuals or groups that want to establish a financial intermediary, such as a bank or an insurance company, must obtain an authorization of 'fit and proper'.

Disclosure

There are stringent reporting requirements for financial intermediaries. Their bookkeeping must follow certain strict principles, their books are subject to periodic inspection, and they must make certain information available to the public.

Restrictions on assets and activities

There are restrictions on what financial intermediaries are allowed to do and what assets they can hold. Before you put your funds into a bank or some other such institution, you would want to know that your funds are safe and that the bank or other financial intermediary will be able to meet its obligations to you. One way of doing this is to restrict the financial intermediary from engaging in certain risky activities. One way to limit a financial intermediary's risky behaviour is to restrict it from holding certain risky assets, or at least from holding a greater quantity of these risky assets than is prudent. For example, commercial banks and other depository institutions in the UK are not allowed to hold common stock because stock prices experience substantial fluctuations. However, this is not the case for Germany where banks hold significant stakes in firms through their stock holdings.

Deposit insurance

The government can insure people's deposits so that they do not suffer great financial loss if the financial intermediary that holds these deposits should fail. The extent of deposit insurance varies across the European economies.

Limits on competition

Politicians have often declared that unbridled competition among financial intermediaries promotes failures that will harm the public. Although the evidence that competition has this effect is extremely weak, individual European governments at times have imposed restrictions on the opening of additional locations and placed restrictions on the takeover of banks by other banks within Europe on grounds of national interest.

In later chapters, we will look more closely at government regulation of financial markets and will see whether it has improved their functioning.

Summary

1 The basic function of financial markets is to channel funds from savers who have an excess of funds to spenders who have a shortage of funds. Financial markets can do this either through direct finance, in which borrowers borrow funds directly from lenders by selling them securities, or through indirect finance, which involves a financial intermediary that stands between the lender–savers and the borrower–spenders and helps transfer funds from one to the other. This channelling of funds improves the economic welfare of everyone in the society. Because they allow funds to move from people who have no productive investment opportunities to those who have such opportunities, financial markets contribute to economic efficiency. In addition, channelling of funds directly benefits consumers by allowing them to make purchases when they need them most.

2 Financial markets can be classified as debt and equity markets, primary and secondary markets, exchanges and over-the-counter markets, and money and capital markets.

3 The principal money market instruments (debt instruments with maturities of less than one year) are Treasury bills, bank certificates of deposit, bank bills, interbank deposits, commercial paper, and repurchase agreements. The principal capital market instruments (debt and equity instruments with maturities greater than one year) are stocks, mortgages, corporate bonds, bank bonds, government securities, local government bonds, and consumer and bank commercial loans.

4 An important trend in recent years is the growing internationalization of financial markets. Eurobonds, which are denominated in a currency other than that of the country in which they are sold, are now the dominant security in the international bond market and have surpassed US corporate bonds as a source of new funds. Eurodollars, which are US dollars deposited in foreign banks, are an important source of funds for American banks.

5 Financial intermediaries are financial institutions that acquire funds by issuing liabilities and, in turn, use those funds to acquire assets by purchasing securities or making loans. Financial intermediaries play an important role in the financial system because they reduce transaction costs, allow risk sharing, and solve problems created by adverse selection and moral hazard. As a result, financial intermediaries allow small savers and borrowers to benefit from the existence of financial markets, thereby increasing the efficiency of the economy.

6 The principal financial intermediaries fall into three categories: (a) banks – commercial banks, building societies, mutual savings banks and credit unions; (b) contractual savings institutions – life

and general insurance companies and pension funds; and (c) investment intermediaries – finance companies, mutual funds and money market mutual funds.

7 Government regulates financial markets and financial intermediaries for two main reasons: to increase the information available to investors and to ensure the soundness of the financial system. Regulations include requiring disclosure of information to the public, restrictions on who can set up a financial intermediary, restrictions on what assets financial intermediaries can hold, the provision of deposit insurance, limits on competition, and restrictions on interest rates.

Key terms

adverse selection p. 36

asset transformation p. 36

asymmetric information p. 36

brokers p. 26

capital p. 25

capital market p. 27

capital market instruments p. 29

certificate of deposit p. 28

commercial paper p. 28

convertible bonds p. 31

corporate bonds p. 31

currency p. 28

dealers p. 26

default p. 28

diversification p. 36

dividends p. 26

economies of scale p. 35

equities p. 25

Eurobond p. 33

Eurocurrencies p. 33

eurodollars p. 33

exchanges p. 27

financial intermediation p. 35

financial panic p. 41

foreign bonds p. 33

investment bank p. 26

liabilities p. 24

liquid p. 26

liquidity services p. 35

long-term p. 25

maturity p. 25

money market p. 27

moral hazard p. 37

mortgages p. 29

over-the-counter (OTC) market p. 27

portfolio p. 36

primary market p. 26

repurchase agreements (repos) p. 29

risk p. 35

risk sharing p. 35

secondary market p. 26

short-term p. 25

stocks p. 29

transaction costs p. 35

Treasury bill p. 28

underwrite p. 41

underwriting p. 26

QUESTIONS AND PROBLEMS

All questions and problems are available in MyEconLab at **www.myeconlab.com/mishkin**.

1 Why is a share of Tesco ordinary shares common stock an asset for its owner and a liability for Tesco?

2 If I can buy a car today for €5,000 and it is worth €10,000 in extra income next year to me because it enables me to get a job as a travelling anvil seller, should I take out a loan from Larry the Loan Shark at a 90% interest rate if no one else will give me a loan? Will I be better or worse off as a result of taking out this loan? Can you make a case for legalizing loan-sharking?

3 Some economists suspect that one of the reasons that economies in developing countries grow so slowly is that they do not have well-developed financial markets. Does this argument make sense?

4 The US economy borrowed heavily from the British in the nineteenth century to build a railroad system. What was the principal debt instrument used? Why did this make both countries better off?

5 'Because companies do not actually raise any funds in secondary markets, they are less important to the economy than primary markets.' Comment.

6 If you suspect that a company will go bankrupt next year, which would you rather hold, bonds issued by the company or equities issued by the company? Why?

7 How can the adverse selection problem explain why you are more likely to make a loan to a family member than to a stranger?

8 Think of one example in which you have had to deal with the adverse selection problem.

9 Why do loan sharks worry less about moral hazard in connection with their borrowers than some other lenders do?

10 If you are an employer, what kinds of moral hazard problems might you worry about with your employees?

11 If there were no asymmetry in the information that a borrower and a lender had, could there still be a moral hazard problem?

12 'In a world without information and transaction costs, financial intermediaries would not exist.' Is this statement true, false or uncertain? Explain your answer.

13 Why might you be willing to make a loan to your neighbour by putting funds in a savings account earning a 5% interest rate at the bank and having the bank lend her the funds at a 10% interest rate rather than lend her the funds yourself?

14 How does risk sharing benefit both financial intermediaries and private investors?

15 Discuss some of the manifestations of the globalization of world capital markets.

WEB EXERCISES

1 One of the single best sources of information about US financial institutions is the US Flow of Funds report produced by the Federal Reserve. This document contains data on most financial intermediaries. Go to **www. federalreserve.gov/releases/Z1/**. Go to the most current release. You may have to load Acrobat Reader if your computer does not already have it; the site has a link for a free patch. Go to the Level Tables and answer the following.

(a) What percentage of assets do commercial banks hold in loans? What percentage of assets are held in mortgage loans?

(b) What percentage of assets do savings and loans hold in mortgage loans?

(c) What percentage of assets do credit unions hold in mortgage loans and in consumer loans?

2 The London Stock Exchange (LSE) is one of the world's most important financial markets. Go to **http://www. londonstockexchange.com/home/homepage.htm**.

(a) Under 'Prices and Markets', find out what range of financial instruments are available on the LSE.

(b) What are the key differences for companies listed on the Official List versus the AIM?

Note

1 Asymmetric information and the adverse selection and moral hazard concepts are also crucial problems for the insurance industry.

Useful websites

http://stockcharts.com/charts/historical This page contains historical stock index charts for the Dow Jones Industrial Average, S&P 500, NASDAQ, 30-year Treasury Bond and gold prices.

www.londonstockexchange.com/home/homepage.htm London Stock Exchange's home page.

http://www.reuters.com/finance/markets/europe Reuters has a page dedicated to all the main European stock market indices.

http://www.fese.be/en/ Federation of European Securities Exchanges.

https://europeanequities.nyx.com/ The home page of Euronext, now part of the NYSE Euronext group of stock exchanges. Find listed companies, quotes, company historical data, real-time market indexes, and more.

www.nasdaq.com Detailed market and security information for the Nasdaq OTC stock exchange.

http://finance.yahoo.com/intlindices?e=americas Major world stock indexes, with charts, news and components.

www.ft.com The ft.com page contains information on global stock markets, bond yields and interest rates. It is possible to get financial news subject to registration.

CHAPTER 3

What is money?

A comparative approach to measuring money

PREVIEW   The florin was a gold coin issued by the bankers of Florence which was in wide circulation in early medieval Europe. Paper money arrived much later in Europe and evolved from promissory notes that were redeemed at banks in Europe for gold and silver during the sixteenth and seventeenth centuries. Your parents may remember with nostalgia the Deutschmark, the guilder or the franc. Today, you use coins such as euros or pounds sterling as money, but also cheques written on accounts held at banks. Money has been different things at different times, but it has *always* been important to people and to the economy.

To understand the effects of money on the economy, we must understand exactly what money is. In this chapter, we develop precise definitions by exploring the functions of money, looking at why and how it promotes economic efficiency, tracing how its forms have evolved over time, and examining how money is currently measured.

Meaning of money

As the word *money* is used in everyday conversation, it can mean many things, but to economists, it has a very specific meaning. To avoid confusion, we must clarify how economists' use of the word *money* differs from conventional usage.

Economists define *money* (also referred to as the *money supply*) as anything that is generally accepted in payment for goods or services or in the repayment of debts. Currency, consisting of euros and cents (or pounds and pence), clearly fits this definition and is one type of money. When most people talk about money, they're talking about currency (paper money and coins). If, for example, a mugger held a knife to you and said 'give me your money' you are not likely to say 'What exactly do you mean by "money"?' You should immediately hand over your notes and coins, in other words all the currency you have on you.

But to define money simply as currency is much too narrow for economists. Because cheques and debit cards are also accepted as payment for purchases, bank deposits are considered money as well. An even broader definition of money is often needed, because other items such as time deposits can in effect function as money if they can be quickly and easily converted into currency or into cheque account deposits. As you can see, there is no single, precise definition of money or the money supply, even for economists.

To complicate matters further, the word *money* is frequently used synonymously with *wealth*. When people say, 'Joe is rich – he has an awful lot of money', they may well mean that Joe not only has a lot of currency and a high balance in his current account but also has stocks, bonds, four cars, three houses and a yacht. Thus, while 'currency' is too narrow a definition of money, this other popular usage is much too broad. Economists make a distinction between money in the form of currency, demand deposits and other items that are used to make purchases and **wealth**, the total collection of pieces of property that serve to store value. Wealth includes not only money but also other assets such as bonds, common stock, art, land, furniture, cars and houses.

People also use the word *money* to describe what economists call *income*, as in the sentence 'Sheila would be a wonderful catch; she has a good job and earns a lot of money'. **Income** is a *flow* of earnings per unit of time. Money, by contrast, is a *stock*: it is a certain amount at a given point in time. If someone tells you that he has an income of €1,000, you cannot tell whether he earned a lot or a little without knowing whether this €1,000 is earned per year, per month, or even per day. But if someone tells you that she has €1,000 in her pocket, you know exactly how much this is.

Keep in mind that the money discussed in this book refers to anything that is generally accepted in payment for goods and services or in the repayment of debts and is distinct from income and wealth.

Functions of money

Whether money is shells or rocks or gold or paper, it has three primary functions in any economy: as a medium of exchange, as a unit of account and as a store of value. Of the three functions, its function as a medium of exchange is what distinguishes money from other assets such as stocks, bonds and houses.

Medium of exchange

In almost all market transactions in our economy, money in the form of currency or cheques is a **medium of exchange**; it is used to pay for goods and services. The use of money as a medium

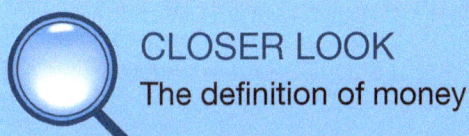

CLOSER LOOK
The definition of money

The definition of money is something many people would regard as an unproductive exercise similar to counting the number of angels that can dance on a pin. After all most people think they know what money is and if asked they would probably show you their wallet or purse and the number of notes and coins they carry. For economists the definition of money is an important exercise. The reason is that once we have a good definition of money it means that if financial innovation leads to a financial product that acts as money, we can immediately recognize this and include it in the measure of money. So how would we come to a definition of money? The definition of anything can follow one of two procedures, namely applying abstraction or realism. The first method provides an abstract description that satisfies certain properties. The second method uses real-world entities and labels them as the object we wish to define. In the case of money, we can point to cash and notes and say this is money and this would be the second method. Using the first method we may say money has to satisfy certain functional properties, namely it is a medium of exchange, unit of account and store of value. Economists have tended to accept the first method. The advantage is that if financial innovation or deregulation leads to a financial instrument that satisfies the three functional properties then it becomes money.

This actually happened in the UK when building society deposits began to be used as cheque accounts but the conventional measure of money M3 was notes and coin + sight deposits + time deposits of banks (but not building societies). But M3 understated the total money supply because it failed to include building society deposits in the measure. The current UK measure of the money supply, M4, includes building society deposits.

of exchange promotes economic efficiency by minimizing the time spent in exchanging goods and services. To see why, let's look at a *barter economy*, one without money, in which goods and services are exchanged directly for other goods and services.

Take the case of Ellen the Economics Professor, who can do just one thing well: give brilliant economics lectures. In a barter economy, if Ellen wants to eat, she must find a farmer who not only produces the food she likes but also wants to learn economics. As you might expect, this search will be difficult and time-consuming, and Ellen might spend more time looking for such an economics-hungry farmer than she will teaching. It is even possible that she will have to quit lecturing and go into farming herself. Even so, she may still starve to death.

The time spent trying to exchange goods or services is called a *transaction cost*. In a barter economy, transaction costs are high because people have to satisfy a 'double coincidence of wants' – they have to find someone who has a good or service they want and who also wants the good or service they have to offer.

Let's see what happens if we introduce money into Ellen the Economics Professor's world. Ellen can teach anyone who is willing to pay money to hear her lecture. She can then go to any farmer (or his representative at the supermarket) and buy the food she needs with the money she has been paid. The problem of the double coincidence of wants is avoided, and Ellen saves a lot of time, which she may spend doing what she does best: teaching.

As this example shows, money promotes economic efficiency by eliminating much of the time spent exchanging goods and services. It also promotes efficiency by allowing people to specialize in what they do best. Money is therefore essential in an economy: it is a lubricant that allows the economy to run more smoothly by lowering transaction costs, thereby encouraging specialization and the division of labour.

The need for money is so strong that almost every society beyond the most primitive invents it. For a commodity to function effectively as money, it has to meet several criteria: (1) it must be easily standardized, making it simple to ascertain its value; (2) it must be widely accepted; (3) it must be divisible, so that it is easy to 'make change'; (4) it must be easy to carry; and (5) it must not deteriorate quickly. Forms of money that have satisfied these criteria have taken many unusual forms throughout human history, ranging from wampum (strings of beads) used by Native Americans, to tobacco and whisky, used by the early American colonists, to cigarettes, used in prisoner-of-war camps during World War II.[1] The diversity of forms of money that have been developed over the years is as much a testament to the inventiveness of the human race as the development of tools and language.

Unit of account

The second role of money is to provide a **unit of account**; that is, it is used to measure value in the economy. We measure the value of goods and services in terms of money, just as we measure weight in terms of grams or distance in terms of kilometres. To see why this function is important, let's look again at a barter economy where money does not perform this function. If the economy has only three goods – say, peaches, economics lectures and movies – then we need to know only three prices to tell us how to exchange one for another: the price of peaches in terms of economics lectures (that is, how many economics lectures you have to pay for a peach), the price of peaches in terms of movies, and the price of economics lectures in terms of movies. If there were 10 goods, we would need to know 45 prices to exchange one good for another; with 100 goods, we would need 4,950 prices; and with 1,000 goods, 499,500 prices.[2]

Imagine how hard it would be in a barter economy to shop at a supermarket with 1,000 different items on its shelves, having to decide whether chicken or fish is a better buy if the price of a pound of chicken were quoted as 4 pounds of butter and the price of a pound of fish as 8 pounds of tomatoes. To make it possible to compare prices, the tag on each item would have to list up to 999 different prices, and the time spent reading them would result in very high transaction costs.

The solution to the problem is to introduce money into the economy and have all prices quoted in terms of units of that money, enabling us to quote the price of economics lectures, peaches and movies in terms of, say, euros or pounds. If there were only three goods in the economy, this would not be a great advantage over the barter system, because we would still need three prices to conduct transactions. But for ten goods we now need only ten prices; for 100 goods, 100 prices; and so on. At the 1,000-goods supermarket, there are now only 1,000 prices to look at, not 499,500!

We can see that using money as a unit of account reduces transaction costs in an economy by reducing the number of prices that need to be considered. The benefits of this function of money grow as the economy becomes more complex.

Store of value

Money also functions as a **store of value**; it is a repository of purchasing power over time. A store of value is used to save purchasing power from the time income is received until the time it is spent. This function of money is useful, because most of us do not want to spend our income immediately upon receiving it, but rather prefer to wait until we have the time or the desire to shop.

Money is not unique as a store of value; any asset – whether money, stocks, bonds, land, houses, art or jewellery – can be used to store wealth. Many such assets have advantages over money as a store of value: they often pay the owner a higher interest rate than money, experience price appreciation, and deliver services such as providing a roof over one's head. If these assets are a more desirable store of value than money, why do people hold money at all?

The answer to this question relates to the important economic concept of **liquidity**, the relative ease and speed with which an asset can be converted into a medium of exchange. Liquidity is highly desirable. Money is the most liquid asset of all because it *is* the medium of exchange; it does not have to be converted into anything else to make purchases. Other assets involve transaction costs when they are converted into money. For example, when you sell your house, you may have to pay a brokerage commission, and if you need cash immediately to pay some pressing bills, you might have to settle for a lower price if you want to sell the house quickly. Because money is the most liquid asset, people are willing to hold it even if it is not the most attractive store of value.

How good a store of value money is depends on the price level. A doubling of all prices, for example, means that the value of money has dropped by half; conversely, a halving of all prices means that the value of money has doubled. During inflation, when the price level is increasing rapidly, money loses value rapidly, and people will be more reluctant to hold their wealth in this form. This is especially true during periods of extreme inflation, known as **hyperinflation**, in which the inflation rate exceeds 50% per month.

Hyperinflation occurred in Germany after World War I, with inflation rates sometimes exceeding 1,000% per month. By the end of the hyperinflation in 1923, the price level had risen to more than 30 billion times what it had been just two years before. The quantity of money needed to purchase even the most basic items became excessive. There are stories, for example, that near the end of the hyperinflation, a wheelbarrow of cash would be required to pay for a loaf of bread. Money was losing its value so rapidly that workers were paid and given time off several times during the day to spend their wages before the money became worthless. No one wanted to hold on to money, so the use of money to carry out transactions declined and barter became more and more dominant. Transaction costs skyrocketed and, as we would expect, output in the economy fell sharply.

Evolution of the payments system

We can obtain a better picture of the functions of money and the forms it has taken over time by looking at the evolution of the **payments system**, the method of conducting transactions in the economy. The payments system has been evolving over centuries and with it the form of money. At one point, precious metals such as gold were used as the principal means of payment and were the main form of money. Later, paper assets such as cheques and currency began to be used in the payments system and viewed as money. Where the payments system is heading has an important bearing on how money will be defined in the future.

Commodity money

To obtain perspective on where the payments system is heading, it is worth exploring how it has evolved. For any object to function as money it must be universally acceptable; everyone must be willing to take it in payment for goods and services. An object that clearly has value to everyone is a likely candidate to serve as money, and a natural choice is a precious metal such as gold or silver. Money made up of precious metals or another valuable commodity is called **commodity money**, and from ancient times until several hundred years ago, commodity money functioned as the medium of exchange in all but the most primitive societies. The problem with a payments system based exclusively on precious metals is that such a form of money is very heavy and is hard to transport from one place to another. Imagine the holes you'd wear in your pockets if you had to buy things only with coins! Indeed, for large purchases such as a house, you'd have to rent a truck to transport the money payment.

Fiat money

The next development in the payments system was *paper currency* (pieces of paper that function as a medium of exchange). Initially, paper currency carried a guarantee that it was convertible into coins or into a fixed quantity of precious metal. However, currency has evolved into **fiat money**, paper currency decreed by governments as legal tender (meaning that legally it must be accepted as payment for debts) but not convertible into coins or precious metal. Paper currency has the advantage of being much lighter than coins or precious metal, but it can be accepted as a medium of exchange only if there is some trust in the authorities who issue it and if printing has reached a sufficiently advanced stage that counterfeiting is extremely difficult. Because paper currency has evolved into a legal arrangement, countries can change the currency that they use at will. Indeed, this is what happened when the eurozone was created in 2002.

Major drawbacks of paper currency and coins are that they are easily stolen and can be expensive to transport in large amounts because of their bulk. To combat this problem, another step in the evolution of the payments system occurred with the development of modern banking: the invention of *cheques*.

Cheques

A **cheque** is an instruction from you to your bank to transfer money from your account to someone else's account when she deposits the cheque. Cheques allow transactions to take place without the need to carry around large amounts of currency. The introduction of cheques was a major innovation that improved the efficiency of the payments system. Frequently, payments made back and forth cancel each other; without cheques, this would involve the movement of a lot of currency. With cheques, payments that cancel each other can be settled by cancelling the cheques, and no currency need be moved. The use of cheques thus reduces the transportation costs associated with the payments system and improves economic efficiency. Another advantage of cheques is that they can be written for any amount up to the balance in the account, making transactions for large amounts much easier. Cheques are also advantageous in that loss from theft is greatly reduced, and because they provide convenient receipts for purchases.

There are, however, two problems with a payments system based on cheques. First, it takes time to get cheques from one place to another, a particularly serious problem if you are paying someone in a different location who needs to be paid quickly. In addition, if you have a cheque account, you know that it usually takes several business days before a bank will allow you to make use of the funds from a cheque you have deposited. If your need for cash is urgent, this feature of paying by cheque can be frustrating. Second, all the paper shuffling required to process cheques is costly; it is estimated that it currently costs £1 to process one cheque whereas it costs 66 pence per electronic transaction. In 2009 the estimated total costs to maintaining a cheque system in the UK was £1.4 billion.

Electronic payment

The development of inexpensive computers and the spread of the Internet now make it cheap to pay bills electronically. In the past, you had to pay your bills by mailing a cheque, but now banks provide websites at which you just log on, make a few clicks, and thereby transmit your payment electronically. Not only do you save the cost of the stamp, but paying bills becomes (almost) a pleasure, requiring little effort. Electronic payment systems provided by banks now even spare you the step of logging on to pay the bill. Instead, recurring bills can be automatically deducted from your bank account. Estimated cost savings when a bill is paid electronically rather than by a cheque are 34 pence per transaction. Electronic payment is thus becoming far more common.

E-money

Electronic payments technology can substitute not only for cheques, but also for cash, in the form of **electronic money** (or **e-money**) – money that exists only in electronic form. The first form of e-money was the *debit card*. Debit cards, which look like credit cards, enable consumers to purchase goods and services by electronically transferring funds directly from their bank accounts to a merchant's account. Debit cards are used in many of the same places that accept credit cards and are now often becoming faster to use than cash. At most supermarkets, for example, you can swipe your debit card through the card reader at the checkout station, press a button, and the amount of your purchases is deducted from your bank account. Most banks and companies such as Visa and MasterCard issue debit cards, and your ATM card typically can function as a debit card.

A more advanced form of e-money is the *stored-value card*. The simplest form of stored-value card is purchased for a preset amount that the consumer pays up front, like a prepaid phonecard. The more sophisticated stored-value card is known as a **smart card**. It contains a computer chip that allows it to be loaded with digital cash from the owner's bank account whenever needed. In Asian countries, such as Japan and Korea, mobile phones now have a smart card feature that raises the expression 'pay by phone' to a new level. Smart cards can be loaded from ATM machines, personal computers with a smart card reader, or specially equipped telephones.

A third form of electronic money is often referred to as **e-cash**, which is used on the Internet to purchase goods or services. A consumer gets e-cash by setting up an account with a bank that has links to the Internet and then has the e-cash transferred to her PC. When she wants to buy something with e-cash, she surfs to a store on the Web and clicks the 'buy' option for a particular item, whereupon the e-cash is automatically transferred

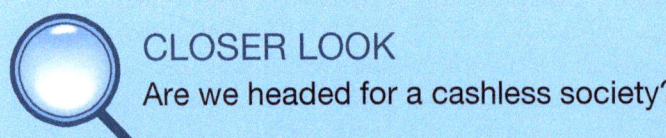

CLOSER LOOK
Are we headed for a cashless society?

Predictions of a cashless society have been around for decades, but they have not come to fruition. For example, *Business Week* predicted in 1975 that electronic means of payment 'would soon revolutionize the very concept of money itself', only to reverse itself several years later. Pilot projects in recent years with smart cards to convert consumers to the use of e-money have not been a success. Mondex, one of the widely touted, early stored-value cards that was launched in the UK in 1995, is only used on a few British university campuses. In Germany and Belgium, millions of people carry bank cards with computer chips embedded in them that enable them to make use of e-money, but very few use them. Why has the movement to a cashless society been so slow in coming?

Although e-money might be more convenient and may be more efficient than a payments system based on paper, several factors work against the disappearance of the paper system. First, it is very expensive to set up the computer, card reader and telecommunications networks necessary to make electronic money the dominant form of payment. Second, electronic means of payment raise security and privacy concerns. We often hear media reports that an unauthorized hacker has been able to access a computer database and to alter information stored there. Because this is not an uncommon occurrence, unscrupulous persons might be able to access bank accounts in electronic payments systems and steal funds by moving them from someone else's accounts into their own. The prevention of this type of fraud is no easy task, and a whole new field of computer science has developed to cope with security issues. A further concern is that the use of electronic means of payment leaves an electronic trail that contains a large amount of personal data on buying habits. There are worries that government, employers and marketers might be able to access these data, thereby encroaching on our privacy.

Finally, cash remains the preferred means of payment for transactions that are either illegal (e.g. drugs and tax evasion) or to be hidden for proprietary reasons (e.g. prostitution). The average size of the shadow economy in the Western developed economies is estimated to be around 16% of GDP (see F. Schneider, Andreas Buehn and Claudio Montenegro (2010), 'Shadow economies all over the world: new estimates for 162 countries from 1999 to 2007', World Bank Policy Research Working Paper 5356).

So the conclusion from this discussion is that although the use of e-money will surely increase in the future, to paraphrase Mark Twain, 'the reports of cash's death are greatly exaggerated'.

from her computer to the merchant's computer. The merchant can then have the funds transferred from the consumer's bank account to his before the goods are shipped.

Given the convenience of e-money, you might think that we would move quickly to a cashless society in which all payments are made electronically. However, this hasn't happened, as discussed in the 'Closer look' box 'Are we headed for a cashless society?'.

Measuring money

The definition of money as anything that is generally accepted in payment for goods and services tells us that money is defined by people's behaviour. People consider an asset as money if they believe it will be accepted by others when making payment. As we have seen, many different assets have performed this role over the centuries, ranging from gold to paper currency to cheque accounts. For that reason, this behavioural definition does not tell us which assets in an economy should be considered as money. To measure money, we need a precise definition that tells us exactly which assets should be included.

Measurement of monetary aggregates

The method by which central banks measure money differs from one economy to another. Variations among measures of money supply, also referred to as **monetary aggregates**, arise from differences in the norms of money holders, the innovation of financial instruments and the variety of issuers of money. Let us see how each of these factors affects the measurement of monetary aggregates.

First, the dissimilarity in measurements of money partly stems from the differences in what members of each society accept as a means of exchange. For example, the Bank of Mexico includes all deposits in both pesos and US dollars in its monetary aggregates. This is because Mexicans are known for holding substantial amounts of their savings in US dollars. Conversely, the People's Bank of China does not include foreign currency deposits in its monetary aggregates, since the Chinese are precluded from legally holding foreign currency deposits.

Moreover, in view of the immense financial innovations mentioned earlier, some assets are accepted as money in some societies but not others. In those countries where banks and depository institutions are not sufficiently widespread to attract household savings, most of the money supply would be in the form of cash. Besides, as people's norms change, the definition of monetary aggregates also changes. Hence, every few years, central banks tend to change their measurement of the money supply whenever they sense a change in the behavioural patterns and conceptions of members of the society.

One last factor that affects the money in the economy is the institutions responsible for issuing monetary aggregates, normally the central bank and depository institutions. Let us compare the European Union, the United Kingdom and United States to show how money issuers differ immensely in these three areas. In the euro area, monetary financial institutions (**MFI**s) are responsible for issuing money. MFIs include: the European Central Bank (**ECB**); the national central banks (**NCB**s) of the euro area countries that have adopted the euro; credit institutions and money market funds located in the euro area (refer to Chapter 13 for a detailed explanation of how the NCBs work under the umbrella of the ECB). In the UK coins are issued by the Royal Mint and notes are issued by the Bank of England as well as banks in Scotland and Northern Ireland. The commercial banks and the building societies issue the deposits and other instruments that make up the UK measure of money. In the US, issuers of money are: the Federal Reserve Banks, which issue currency; the US Treasury, which mints coins; and depository institutions, which hold all other components of monetary aggregates.

For this reason, you would never find a central bank copying the definition of money adopted by another central bank, but generally most central banks range monetary aggregates from narrow to broad. Table 3.1 compares how the Bank of England, the ECB and the Federal Reserve System each defines its monetary aggregates.

Generally the narrowest measure of money that central banks report is **M1** and it is more or less the same for most countries.[3] M1 consists of currency in circulation as well as demand deposits and other chequeable deposits held in depository institutions. Canada is a noteworthy exception, since it adds chequeable deposits at credit unions and other non-bank depository institutions in M1. Currency in the vaults of banks and ATMs are not included in M1. Typically, demand deposits include all deposits in depository institutions that can be withdrawn without prior notice; most of these are non-interest-bearing (except for the UK). Chequeable deposits may be either interest-bearing, or non-interest-bearing.

On the other hand, monetary aggregates broader than M1 considerably differ from one country to another. Even so, we generally find that savings deposits and most time deposits are usually included in **M2**. Savings deposits are interest-bearing non-transaction accounts that can be drawn upon demand at no costs. Time deposits are also interest-bearing deposits or certificates of deposits (CDs) held for a given period of time and can be withdrawn with prior written notice, usually at very low costs. Only the US includes *money market mutual fund shares* (MMMF) in M2. MMMF shares are retail accounts issued by banks, on which households can issue cheques.

M3 is the broadest definition of money and is calculated by many central banks such as the ECB. Table 3.2 shows how the ECB measures its monetary aggregates. Some other

TABLE 3.1

Comparison of compositions of monetary aggregates in the eurozone, UK and US

	Euro area	UK	US
M1	Currency + Overnight and similar deposits	Currency + Non-interest-bearing demand deposits with banks + Interest-bearing demand deposits with banks	Currency + Traveller's cheques + Demand deposits + Other chequeable deposits
M2	M1 + Deposits (2 year maturity) + Deposits redeemable in 3 months	M1 + Interest-bearing retail deposits with building societies + National Savings ordinary accounts	M1 + Small denomination time deposits + Savings deposits and MMDA + Retail MMMF shares
M3	M2 + Repurchase agreements + MMF shares/units + Debt securities up to 2 years	M2 + Time deposits with banks + Certificates of deposits (CD)	
M4		M3 + Time deposits, shares and CDs with building societies − Building society holdings of bank deposits and bank CDs	

TABLE 3.2

Components of monetary aggregates in the euro area

	Value as of June 2010 (€ billions)
M1 = Currency	785
+ Overnight and similar deposits	3,877
Total M1	4,663
M2 = M1	
+ Deposits with agreed maturity within 2 years	1,791
+ Deposits redeemable in 3 months	1,840
Total M2	8,294
M3 = M2	
+ Repurchase agreements	399
+ MMF shares/units	606
+ Debt securities up to 2 years	125
Total M3	9,423

Source: 'Monetary developments in the euro area', June 2010, Press Release, 27 July 2010.

CLOSER LOOK
Where are all the US dollar bills and the euro coins?

The fact that each person in the United States holds more than $2,000 in cash and each person in the euro area holds more than €2,200 in cash is surprising. These currencies are bulky, can be easily stolen, and pay no interest, so it doesn't make sense to keep a lot of it. Do you know anyone who carries these sums in his or her pockets? We have a puzzle: where are all these dollars and euros and who is holding them and why?

Criminals are one group who hold a lot of cash. If you were engaged in illegal activity, you would not conduct your transactions with cheques because they are traceable and, therefore, a potentially powerful piece of evidence against you. That explains why Tony Soprano has so much cash in his backyard. Some businesses also like to retain a lot of cash because if they operate as a cash business that makes their transactions less traceable; thus, they can avoid declaring income on which they would have to pay taxes.

People outside the United States and the eurozone also routinely hold US dollars and euros. In many countries, people do not trust their own currency because they often experience high inflation, which erodes the value of that currency. The currencies of the two largest economic entities in the globe, the European Union and the United States, have become the two major and widely sought-after currencies. Foreigners hold US dollars and euros as a hedge against this inflation risk. Lack of trust in the rouble, for example, has led Russians to hoard enormous amounts of US dollars. More than 80% of US dollars is held abroad.

countries that calculate M3 are Japan, Canada, Switzerland, Australia, New Zealand, Iceland, Thailand, the Philippines, Mexico and Turkey. The definitions of M3 vastly differ from one country to another. A number of central banks no longer calculate M3; for example, the Fed (Federal Reserve Bank) discontinued measuring M3 in March 2006.

Which is the most accurate monetary aggregate?

By influencing the money supply, the central bank can control inflation. If there is too much money in the economy, the result will be more money chasing fewer products, hence leading to inflation. Central banks resort to an expansion of money supply in order to boost GDP growth, albeit with the understanding that this is apt to result in inflation.

But the question that we should ask ourselves is which measurement should central banks consider when they try to affect variables in the economy, such as GDP growth and inflation? Because we cannot be sure which of the monetary aggregates is the true measure of money, it is logical to question if their movements closely parallel one another. If they do, then using one monetary aggregate to predict future economic performance and to conduct policy will produce the same results as using another, and it does not matter much that we are not sure of the appropriate definition of money for a given policy decision. However, if the monetary aggregates do not move together, then what one monetary aggregate tells us is happening to the money supply might be quite different from what another monetary aggregate would tell us.

Figure 3.1 plots the growth rates of M1 and M3 in the euro area from 1999 to 2010. These two measures have more or less moved together till 2006, after which they appear to have taken opposite directions up until mid-2007 after which they moved in the same direction. However, since the second half of 2008, when the crisis hit the financial sector hard, the ECB has consistently expanded the currency in circulation, in order to try to make up for the decrease in customer deposits. The volume of deposits maturing within two years has declined substantially as a result of low interest rates. To compensate for this drop in money supply, the ECB decided to increase currency notes and accordingly M1. This led to inflation levels reaching 4% during 2008, a major deviation from the primary goal of the

FIGURE 3.1

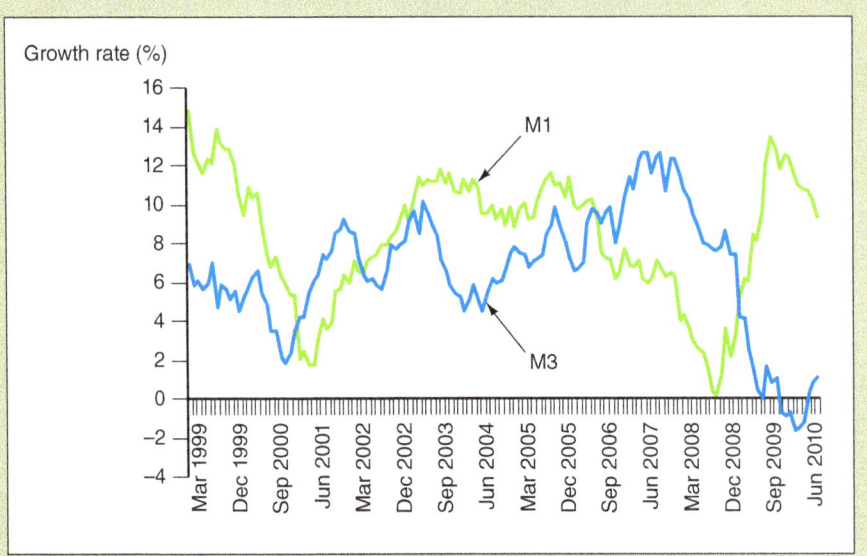

Growth rates of the ECB M1 and M3 monetary aggregates 1999–2010

Sources: ECB. 'Money, banking and investment funds', *Monetary Statistics*, p. S12. Copyright © European Central Bank, Frankfurt am Main, Germany. Figures are available free of charge via the ECB website.

ECB, which is to maintain inflation below 2%. Yet this was a temporary and necessary policy needed to solve the more serious problem of a deep recession.

Hence, from all the above you can see that obtaining a single precise, correct measure of money does seem to matter and that it does make a difference which monetary aggregate policymakers and economists choose as the true measure of money. However, many central banks prefer to keep a close watch on various monetary aggregates, to intervene and make up for any change in any of the components of money supply.

Summary

1 To economists, the word *money* has a different meaning from *income* or *wealth*. Money is anything that is generally accepted as payment for goods or services or in the repayment of debts.

2 Money serves three primary functions: as a medium of exchange, as a unit of account and as a store of value. Money as a medium of exchange avoids the problem of double coincidence of wants that arises in a barter economy, and thus lowers transaction costs and encourages specialization and the division of labour. Money as a unit of account reduces the number of prices needed in the economy, which also reduces transaction costs. Money also functions as a store of value, but performs this role poorly if it is rapidly losing value due to inflation.

3 The payments system has evolved over time. Until several hundred years ago, the payments system in all but the most primitive societies was based primarily on precious metals. The introduction of paper currency lowered the cost of transporting money. The next major advance was the introduction of cheques, which lowered transaction costs still further. We are currently moving toward an electronic payments system in which paper is eliminated and all transactions are handled by computers. Despite the potential efficiency of such a system, obstacles are slowing the movement to the cashless society and the development of new forms of electronic money.

4 There is no uniform definition of monetary aggregates, but in general monetary aggregates range from narrow to broad definitions. Since monetary aggregates do not usually move together, they cannot be used interchangeably by policymakers. It is imperative to measure different monetary aggregates so that the central bank can intervene if any of the components change.

5 Another problem in the measurement of money is that the data are not always as accurate as we would like. Substantial revisions in the data do occur; they indicate that initially released money data are not a reliable guide to short-run (say, month-to-month) movements in the money supply, although they are more reliable over longer periods of time, such as a year.

Key terms

cheques p. 50	income p. 47	NCB p. 53
commodity money p. 50	liquidity p. 49	payments system p. 50
currency p. 46	M1 p. 53	smart card p. 51
e-cash p. 51	M2 p. 53	store of value p. 49
ECB p. 53	M3 p. 53	unit of account p. 48
electronic money (e-money) p. 51	MFI p. 53	wealth p. 47
fiat money p. 50	medium of exchange p. 47	
hyperinflation p. 49	monetary aggregates p. 52	

QUESTIONS AND PROBLEMS

All questions and problems are available in MyEconLab at **www.myeconlab.com/mishkin**.

1 Which of the following three expressions uses the economists' definition of money?

(a) 'How much money did you earn last week?'

(b) 'When I go to the store, I always make sure that I have enough money.'

(c) 'The love of money is the root of all evil.'

2 There are three goods produced in an economy by three individuals:

Good	Producer
Apples	Orchard owner
Bananas	Banana grower
Chocolate	Chocolatier

If the orchard owner likes only bananas, the banana grower likes only chocolate and the chocolatier likes only apples, will any trade between these three persons take place in a barter economy? How will introducing money into the economy benefit these three producers?

3 Why did cavemen not need money?

4 Why were people in the United States in the nineteenth century sometimes willing to be paid by cheques rather than with gold, even though they knew that there was a possibility that the cheques might bounce?

5 In Ancient Greece, why was gold a more likely candidate for use as money than wine was?

6 Was money a better store of value in the United Kingdom in the 1950s than it was in the 1970s? Why or why not? In which period would you have been more willing to hold money?

7 Would you be willing to give up your cheque book and instead use an electronic means of payment if it were made available? Why or why not?

8 Rank the following assets from most liquid to least liquid:

(a) Cheque account deposits

(b) Houses

(c) Currency

(d) Washing machines

(e) Savings deposits

(f) Common stock

9 Why have some economists described money during a hyperinflation as a 'hot potato' that is quickly passed from one person to another?

10 In Brazil, a country that underwent a rapid inflation before 1994, many transactions were conducted in dollars rather than in reals, the domestic currency. Why?

11 Suppose that a researcher discovers that a measure of the total amount of debt in the eurozone economies over the past ten years was a better predictor of the business cycle than M3. Does this discovery mean that we should define money as equal to the total amount of debt in the economy?

12 Look up the numbers of the M1, M2 and M3 monetary aggregates in the European Central Bank *Euro Area Statistics* for the most recent last-year period since the outburst of the global financial crisis. Have their growth rates been similar? What implications does this have for the conduct of monetary policy?

13 Which of the ECB's measures of the monetary aggregates – M1 or M3 – is composed of the most liquid assets? Which is the largest measure?

14 For each of the following assets, indicate which of the monetary aggregates (M1 and M2) includes them:

(a) Currency
(b) Money market mutual funds
(c) Small-denomination time deposits
(d) Chequeable deposits

15 Why are revisions of monetary aggregates less of a problem for measuring long-run movements of the money supply than they are for measuring short-run movements?

WEB EXERCISES

1 Go to the ECB's Monetary Developments in the euro area statistical releases **http://www.ecb.int/press/pr/stats/md/html/index.en.html.**

   (a) What has been the growth rate in M1 and M3 over the last twelve months?
   (b) From what you know about the state of the economy, does this seem expansionary or restrictive?

2 Go to **www.federalreserve.gov/paymentsys.htm** and select one topic on which the Federal Reserve has a written policy. Write a one-paragraph summary of this policy.

3 Hyperinflations can be extremely damaging for a country's economic activity. CNBC has a useful slideshow on the worst hyperinflations of all time (**http://www.cnbc.com/id/41532451**). A paper by Hanke and Krus, "World Hyperinflations" also examines historical cases (**www.cato.org/publications/working-paper/world-hyperinflations**). Which countries have experienced the highest inflation rates? What common characteristics can you identify from these cases?

Notes

1 An extremely entertaining article on the development of money in a prisoner-of-war camp during World War II is R.A. Radford, 'The economic organization of a POW camp', *Economica* 12 (November 1945): 189–201.

2 The formula for telling us the number of prices we need when we have N goods is the same formula that tells us the number of pairs when there are N items. It is $\frac{N(N-1)}{2}$. In the case of 10 goods, for example, we would need $\frac{10(10-1)}{2} = \frac{90}{2} = 45$

3 The Bank of England used to report M0 which is sometimes known as base money. This constitutes currency in circulation with the non-bank public, plus currency reserves held by the banks, plus the reserves of the commercial banks held at the Bank of England.

Useful websites

http://www.ecb.int/stats/services/html/index.en.html ECB's Statistics Data Services gives you access to the euro area statistics including, in some cases, national breakdowns.

http://www.britishmuseum.org/explore/galleries/themes/room_68_money.aspx The British Museum in London has a new Citi Money Gallery devoted to the history of money.

http://www.minneapolisfed.org/community_education/teacher/history.cfm A brief history of money from the Minneapolis Fed.

www.federalreserve.gov/paymentsystems/default.htm This site reports on the Federal Reserve's policies regarding payments systems.

www.federalreserve.gov/releases/h6/Current/ The Federal Reserve reports the current levels of M1 and M2 on its website.

https://stats.ecb.europa.eu/stats/download/bsi_easch02_update/bsi_easch02_update/easch02_update.pdf The European Central Bank reports the details of its monetary aggregates on its website.

PART 2
FINANCIAL MARKETS

Crisis and response: Credit market turmoil and the stock market crash in October 2008

The subprime financial crisis began snowballing as the value of mortgage-backed securities on financial institutions' balance sheets plummeted. When the House of Representatives, fearing the wrath of constituents who were angry about bailing out Wall Street, voted down a $700 billion bailout package proposed by the Bush administration on Monday, 29 September 2008, the subprime financial crisis took an even more virulent turn, despite the bailout package that was passed four days later.

A 'flight to quality' drove three-month Treasury bill rates down to almost zero, which had last happened during the Great Depression of the 1930s. Credit spreads – an indicator of risk – shot through the roof, with the Treasury bill to eurodollar rate (TED) spread going from around 40 basis points (0.40 percentage points) before the subprime crisis started to over 450 basis points in mid-October, the highest value in its history. After earlier sharp declines, the stock market crashed further, with the week beginning on 6 October 2008 showing the worst weekly decline in US history.

The subprime crisis illustrates how volatile financial markets can be. This volatility hit financial consumers directly with difficulty getting loans, falling home values, declining retirement account values, and jobs in jeopardy. How can policy respond to disruptions in financial markets? We begin addressing this question by examining the inner workings of financial markets, particularly interest rate dynamics. Chapter 4 explains what an interest rate is, and the relationship between interest rates, bond prices and returns. Chapter 5 examines how the overall level of interest rates is determined. In Chapter 6, we extend the analysis of the bond market to explain changes in credit spreads and the relationship of long-term to short-term interest rates. Chapter 7 looks at the role of expectations in the stock market and what drives stock prices.

CHAPTER 4

Understanding interest rates

PREVIEW

Interest rates are among the most closely watched variables in the economy. Their movements are reported almost daily by the news media, because they directly affect our everyday lives and have important consequences for the health of the economy. They affect personal decisions such as whether to consume or save, whether to buy a house, and whether to purchase bonds or put funds into a savings account. Interest rates also affect the economic decisions of businesses and households, such as whether to use their funds to invest in new equipment for factories or to save their money in a bank.

Before we can go on with the study of money, banking and financial markets, we must understand exactly what the phrase *interest rates* means. In this chapter, we see that a concept known as the *yield to maturity* is the most accurate measure of interest rates; the yield to maturity is what economists mean when they use the term *interest rate*. We discuss how the yield to maturity is measured. We'll also see that a bond's interest rate does not necessarily indicate how good an investment the bond is because what it earns (its rate of return) does not necessarily equal its interest rate. Finally, we explore the distinction between real interest rates, which are adjusted for inflation, and nominal interest rates, which are not.

Although learning definitions is not always the most exciting of pursuits, it is important to read carefully and understand the concepts presented in this chapter. Not only are they continually used throughout the remainder of this text, but a firm grasp of these terms will give you a clearer understanding of the role that interest rates play in your life as well as in the general economy.

Measuring interest rates

Different debt instruments have very different streams of cash payments to the holder (known as **cash flows**) with very different timing. Thus we first need to understand how we can compare the value of one kind of debt instrument with another before we see how interest rates are measured. To do this, we make use of the concept of *present value*.

Present value

The concept of **present value** (or **present discounted value**) is based on the common-sense notion that a euro paid to you one year from now is less valuable to you than a euro paid to you today: this notion is true because you can deposit a euro today in a savings account that earns interest and have more than a euro in one year. Economists use a more formal definition, as explained in this section.

Let's look at the simplest kind of debt instrument, which we will call a **simple loan**. In this loan, the lender provides the borrower with an amount of funds (called the *principal*) that must be repaid to the lender at the *maturity date,* along with an additional payment for the interest. For example, if you made your friend, Jane, a simple loan of €100 for one year, you would require her to repay the principal of €100 in one year's time along with an additional payment for interest – say, €10. In the case of a simple loan like this one, the interest payment divided by the amount of the loan is a natural and sensible way to measure the interest rate. This measure of the so-called *simple interest rate,i*, is

$$i = \frac{€10}{€100} = 0.10 = 10\%$$

If you make this €100 loan, at the end of the year you would have €110, which can be rewritten as

$$€100 \times (1 + 0.1) = €110$$

If you then lent out the €110, at the end of the second year you would have

$$€110 \times (1 + 0.10) = €121$$

or, equivalently,

$$€100 \times (1 + 0.10) \times (1 + 0.10) = €100 \times (1 + 0.10)^2 = €121$$

Continuing with the loan again, you would have at the end of the third year

$$€121 \times (1 + 0.10) = €100 \times (1 + 0.10)^3 = €133$$

Generalizing, we can see that at the end of n years, your €100 would turn into

$$€100 \times (1 + i)^n$$

The amounts you would have at the end of each year by making the €100 loan today can be seen in the following timeline:

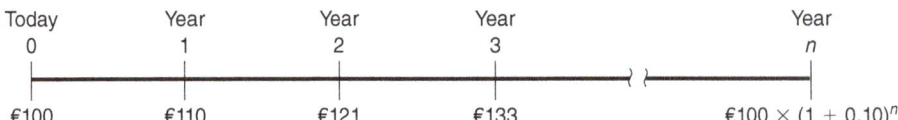

This timeline immediately tells you that you are just as happy having €100 today as having €110 a year from now (of course, as long as you are sure that Jane will pay you back). You are also just as happy having €100 today as having €121 two years from now, or €133 three years from now or €100 × $(1 + 0.10)^n$ n years from now. The timeline tells us that we can also work backward from future amounts to the present. For example, €133 = €100 × $(1 + 0.10)^3$ three years from now is worth €100 today, so that

$$€100 = \frac{€133}{(1 + 0.10)^3}$$

The process of calculating today's value of euros received in the future, as we have done above, is called *discounting the future.* We can generalize this process by writing today's (present) value of €100 as *PV*, the future cash flow (payment) of €133 as *CF*, and replacing 0.10 (the 10% interest rate) by i. This leads to the following formula:

$$PV = \frac{CF}{(1 + i)^n} \tag{4.1}$$

Intuitively, Equation 4.1 tells us that if you are promised €1 of cash flow for certain ten years from now, this euro would not be as valuable to you as €1 is today because if you had the €1 today, you could invest it and end up with more than €1 in ten years.

The concept of present value is extremely useful, because it allows us to figure out today's value (price) of a credit (debt) market instrument at a given simple interest rate i by just adding up the individual present values of all the future payments received. This information allows us to compare the values of two or more instruments with very different timing of their payments.

APPLICATION

Simple present value

What is the present value of €250 to be paid in two years if the interest rate is 15%?

Solution

The present value would be €189.04. Using (4.1),

$$PV = \frac{CF}{(1 + i)^n}$$

where CF = cash flow in two years = €250
i = annual interest rate   = 0.15
n = number of years   = 2

Thus

$$PV = \frac{€250}{(1 + 0.15)^2} = \frac{€250}{1.3225} = €189.04$$

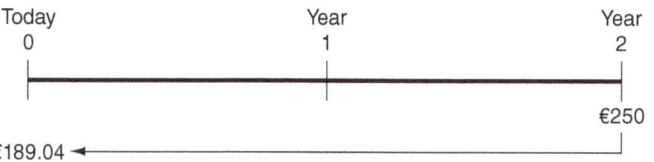

APPLICATION

How much is that jackpot worth?

Assume that you just hit the €20 million jackpot in the Europa State Lottery, which promises you a payment of €1 million for the next twenty years. You are clearly excited, but have you really won €20 million?

Solution

No, not in the present value sense. In today's money, that €20 million is worth a lot less. If we assume an interest rate of 10%, the first payment of €1 million is clearly worth €1 million today, but the next payment next year is only worth €1 million/(1 + 0.10) = €909,090 a lot less than €1 million. The following year the payment is worth €1 million/(1 + 0.10)^2 = €826,446 in today's euros, and so on. When you add all these up, they come to €9.4 million. You are still pretty excited (who wouldn't be?), but because you understand the concept of present value, you recognize that you are the victim of false advertising. In present value terms, you didn't really win €20 million, but instead won less than half as much. ■

Four types of credit market instruments

In terms of the timing of their cash flow payments, there are four basic types of credit market instruments.

1 A simple loan, which we have already discussed, in which the lender provides the borrower with an amount of funds, which must be repaid to the lender at the maturity date along with an additional payment for the interest. Many money market instruments are of this type – for example, commercial loans to businesses.

2 A **fixed-payment loan** (which is also called a **fully amortized loan**) in which the lender provides the borrower with an amount of funds, which must be repaid by making the same payment every period (such as a month), consisting of part of the principal and interest for a set number of years. For example, if you borrowed €1,000, a fixed-payment loan might require you to pay €126 every year for 25 years. Instalment loans (such as car loans) and mortgages are frequently of the fixed-payment type.

3 A **coupon bond** pays the owner of the bond a fixed-interest payment (coupon payment) every year until the maturity date, when a specified final amount (**face value** or **par value**) is repaid. (The coupon payment is so named because the bondholder used to obtain payment by clipping a coupon off the bond and sending it to the bond issuer, who then sent the payment to the holder. Nowadays, it is no longer necessary to send in coupons to receive these payments.) A coupon bond with €1,000 face value, for example, might pay you a coupon payment of €100 per year for ten years, and at the maturity date, repay you the face value amount of €1,000. (The face value of a bond is usually in €1,000 increments.)

A coupon bond is identified by three pieces of information. First is the corporation or government agency that issues the bond. Second is the maturity date of the bond. Third is the bond's **coupon rate**, the money amount of the yearly coupon payment expressed as a percentage of the face value of the bond. In our example, the coupon bond has a yearly coupon payment of €100 and a face value of €1,000. The coupon rate is then €100/€1,000 = 0.10, or 10%. Capital market instruments such as UK government bonds (known as consols) and corporate bonds are examples of coupon bonds.

4 A **discount bond** (also called a **zero-coupon bond**) is bought at a price below its face value (at a discount), and the face value is repaid at the maturity date. Unlike a coupon bond, a discount bond does not make any interest payments; it just pays off the face value. For example, a one-year discount bond with a face value of €1,000 might be bought for €900; in a year's time the owner would be repaid the face value of €1,000. UK Treasury bills, US savings bonds and long-term zero-coupon bonds are examples of discount bonds.

These four types of instruments require payments at different times: simple loans and discount bonds make payment only at their maturity dates, whereas fixed-payment loans and coupon bonds have payments periodically until maturity. How would you decide which of these instruments provides you with more income? They all seem so different because they make payments at different times. To solve this problem, we use the concept of present value, explained earlier, to provide us with a procedure for measuring interest rates on these different types of instruments.

Yield to maturity

Of the several common ways of calculating interest rates, the most important is the **yield to maturity**, the interest rate that equates the present value of cash flow payments received from a debt instrument with its value today.[1] Because the concept behind the calculation of the yield to maturity makes good economic sense, economists consider it the most accurate measure of interest rates.

To understand the yield to maturity better, we now look at how it is calculated for the four types of credit market instruments. In all these examples, the key to understanding the calculation of the yield to maturity is equating today's value of the debt instrument with the present value of all of its future cash flow payments.

Simple loan

Using the concept of present value, the yield to maturity on a simple loan is easy to calculate. For the one-year loan we discussed, today's value is €100, and the payments in one year's time would be €110 (the repayment of €100 plus the interest payment of €10). We can use this information to solve for the yield to maturity i by recognizing that the present value of the future payments must equal today's value of a loan.

Yield to maturity on a simple loan

If Pete borrows €100 from his sister and next year she wants €110 back from him, what is the yield to maturity on this loan?

Solution

The yield to maturity on the loan is 10%.

$$PV = \frac{CF}{(1 + i)^n}$$

where PV = amount borrowed   = €100
         CF = cash flow in one year = €110
          n = number of years   = 1

Thus

$$€100 = \frac{€110}{(1 + i)}$$

$$(1 + i)\,€100 = €110$$

$$(1 + i) = \frac{€110}{€100}$$

$$i = 1.10 - 1 = 0.10 = 10\%$$

Today   Year
  0   1

€100   €110

$i = 10\%$

This calculation of the yield to maturity should look familiar, because it equals the interest payment of €10 divided by the loan amount of €100; that is, it equals the simple interest rate on the loan. An important point to recognize is that **for simple loans, the simple interest rate equals the yield to maturity**. Hence the same term i is used to denote both the yield to maturity and the simple interest rate. ∎

Fixed-payment loan

Recall that this type of loan has the same cash flow payment every period throughout the life of the loan. On a fixed-rate mortgage, for example, the borrower makes the same payment to the bank every month until the maturity date, when the loan will be completely paid off. To calculate the yield to maturity for a fixed-payment loan, we follow the same strategy we used for the simple loan – we equate today's value of the loan with its present value. Because the fixed-payment loan involves more than one cash flow payment, the present value of the fixed-payment loan is calculated as the sum of the present values of all cash flow payments (using Equation 4.1).

In the case of our earlier example, the loan is €1,000 and the yearly payment is €126 for the next 25 years. The present value is calculated as follows: at the end of one year, there is a €126 payment with a PV of €126$/(1 + i)$; at the end of two years, there is another €126 payment with a PV of €126$/(1 + i)^2$; and so on until at the end of the twenty-fifth year, the last payment of €126 with a PV of €126$/(1 + i)^{25}$ is made. Making today's value of the loan (€1,000) equal to the sum of the present values of all the yearly payments gives us

$$€1{,}000 = \frac{€126}{1 + i} + \frac{€126}{(1 + i)^2} + \frac{€126}{(1 + i)^3} + \cdots + \frac{€126}{(1 + i)^{25}}$$

More generally, for any fixed-payment loan,

$$LV = \frac{FP}{1+i} + \frac{FP}{(1+i)^2} + \frac{FP}{(1+i)^3} + \cdots + \frac{FP}{(1+i)^n} \qquad (4.2)$$

where LV = loan value

FP = fixed yearly payment

n = number of years until maturity

For a fixed-payment loan amount, the fixed yearly payment and the number of years until maturity are known quantities, and only the yield to maturity is not. So we can solve this equation for the yield to maturity i. Because this calculation is not easy, many pocket calculators have programs that allow you to find i given the loan's numbers for LV, FP and n. For example, in the case of a 25-year loan with yearly payments of €85.81, the yield to maturity that solves Equation 4.2 is 7%. Real estate brokers always have a pocket calculator that can solve such equations so that they can immediately tell the prospective house buyer exactly what the yearly (or monthly) payments will be if the house purchase is financed by taking out a mortgage.

APPLICATION Yield to maturity and the yearly payment on a fixed-payment loan

You decide to purchase a new home and need a €100,000 mortgage. You take out a loan from the bank that has an interest rate of 7%. What is the yearly payment to the bank to pay off the loan in 20 years?

Solution

The yearly payment to the bank is €9,439.29.

$$LV = \frac{FP}{1+i} + \frac{FP}{(1+i)^2} + \frac{FP}{(1+i)^3} + \cdots + \frac{FP}{(1+i)^n}$$

where LV = loan value amount   = €100,000

i = annual interest rate = 0.07

n = number of years   = 20

Thus

$$€100,000 = \frac{FP}{1+0.07} + \frac{FP}{(1+0.07)^2} + \frac{FP}{(1+0.07)^3} + \cdots + \frac{FP}{(1+0.07)^{20}}$$

To find the monthly payment for the loan using a financial calculator:

n = number of years   = 20

PV = amount of the loan (LV)   = −100,000

FV = amount of the loan after 20 years = 0

i = annual interest rate   = 0.7

Then push the PMT button to give fixed yearly payment (FP) = €9,439.29. ■

Coupon bond

To calculate the yield to maturity for a coupon bond, follow the same strategy used for the fixed-payment loan: equate today's value of the bond with its present value. Because coupon bonds also have more than one cash flow payment, the present value of the bond is calculated as the sum of the present values of all the coupon payments plus the present value of the final payment of the face value of the bond.

The present value of a €1,000-face-value bond with ten years to maturity and yearly coupon payments of €100 (a 10% coupon rate) can be calculated as follows. At the end of one year, there is a €100 coupon payment with a *PV* of €100/(1 + *i*); at the end of the second year, there is another €100 coupon payment with a *PV* of €100/(1 + *i*)^2; and so on until, at maturity, there is a €100 coupon payment with a *PV* of €100/(1 + *i*)^{10} plus the repayment of the €1,000 face value with a *PV* of €1,000/(1 + *i*)^{10}. Setting today's value of the bond (its current price, denoted by *P*) equal to the sum of the present values of all the cash flow payments for this bond gives

$$P = \frac{€100}{1 + i} + \frac{€100}{(1 + i)^2} + \frac{€100}{(1 + i)^3} + \cdots + \frac{€100}{(1 + i)^{10}} + \frac{€1,000}{(1 + i)^{10}}$$

More generally, for any coupon bond,[2]

$$P = \frac{C}{1 + I} + \frac{C}{(1 + i)^2} + \frac{C}{(1 + i)^3} + \cdots + \frac{C}{(1 + i)^n} + \frac{F}{(1 + i)^n} \qquad (4.3)$$

where *P* = price of coupon bond
  C = yearly coupon payment
  F = face value of the bond
  n = years to maturity date

In Equation 4.3, the coupon payment, the face value, the years to maturity and the price of the bond are known quantities, and only the yield to maturity is not. Hence we can solve this equation for the yield to maturity *i*. Just as in the case of the fixed-payment loan, this calculation is not easy, so business-oriented software and pocket calculators have built-in programs that solve this equation for you.

APPLICATION   ### Yield to maturity and the bond price for a coupon bond

Find the price of a 10% coupon bond with a face value of €1,000, a 12.25% yield to maturity and eight years to maturity.

Solution

The price of the bond is €889.20. To solve using a financial calculator:

$$n = \text{years to maturity} \qquad\qquad = 8$$
$$FV = \text{face value of the bond } (F) \quad = 1,000$$
$$i = \text{annual interest rate} \qquad\qquad = 12.25\%$$
$$PMT = \text{yearly coupon payments } (C) = 100$$

Then push the *PV* button to give price of the bond = €889.20.
  Alternatively, you could solve for the yield to maturity given the bond price by putting in €889.20 for *PV* and pushing the *i* button to get a yield to maturity of 12.25%. ■

Table 4.1 shows the yields to maturity calculated for several bond prices. Three interesting facts emerge:

1 When the coupon bond is priced at its face value, the yield to maturity equals the coupon rate.
2 The price of a coupon bond and the yield to maturity are negatively related; that is, as the yield to maturity rises, the price of the bond falls. As the yield to maturity falls, the price of the bond rises.
3 The yield to maturity is greater than the coupon rate when the bond price is below its face value.

These three facts are true for any coupon bond and are really not surprising if you think about the reasoning behind the calculation of the yield to maturity. When you put €1,000 in

Yields to maturity on a 10%-coupon-rate bond maturing in ten years (face value = €1,000)

Price of bond (€)	Yield to maturity (%)
1,200	7.13
1,100	8.48
1,000	10.00
900	11.75
800	13.81

a bank account with an interest rate of 10%, you can take out €100 every year and you will be left with the €1,000 at the end of ten years. This is similar to buying the €1,000 bond with a 10% coupon rate analysed in Table 4.1, which pays a €100 coupon payment every year and then repays €1,000 at the end of ten years. If the bond is purchased at the par value of €1,000, its yield to maturity must equal 10%, which is also equal to the coupon rate of 10%. The same reasoning applied to any coupon bond demonstrates that if the coupon bond is purchased at its par value, the yield to maturity and the coupon rate must be equal.

It is straightforward to show that the bond price and the yield to maturity are negatively related. As i, the yield to maturity, increases, all denominators in the bond price formula (4.3) must necessarily increase. Hence a rise in the interest rate as measured by the yield to maturity means that the price of the bond must fall. Another way to explain why the bond price falls when the interest rate rises is that a higher interest rate implies that the future coupon payments and final payment are worth less when discounted back to the present; hence the price of the bond must be lower.

The third fact, that the yield to maturity is greater than the coupon rate when the bond price is below its par value, follows directly from facts 1 and 2. When the yield to maturity equals the coupon rate, then the bond price is at the face value; when the yield to maturity rises above the coupon rate, the bond price necessarily falls and so must be below the face value of the bond.

There is one special case of a coupon bond that is worth discussing because its yield to maturity is particularly easy to calculate. This bond is called a **consol** or a **perpetuity**; it is a perpetual bond with no maturity date and no repayment of principal that makes fixed coupon payments of €C for ever. Consols were first sold by the British Treasury during the Napoleonic Wars and are still traded today; they are quite rare, however, in non-UK capital markets. The formula in Equation 4.3 for the price of the consol P_c simplifies to the following:[3]

$$P_c = \frac{C}{i_c} \tag{4.4}$$

where P_c = price of the perpetuity (consol)
$\quad C$ = yearly payment
$\quad i_c$ = yield to maturity of the perpetuity (consol)

One nice feature of perpetuities is that you can immediately see that as i_c increases, the price of the bond falls. For example, if a perpetuity pays €100 per year for ever and the interest rate is 10%, its price will be €1,000 = €100/0.10. If the interest rate rises to 20%, its price will fall to €500 = €100/0.20. We can also rewrite this formula as

$$i_c = \frac{C}{P_c} \tag{4.5}$$

| APPLICATION | Perpetuity |

What is the yield to maturity on a bond that has a price of €2,000 and pays €100 of interest annually for ever?

Solution

The yield to maturity would be 5%.

$$i_c = \frac{C}{P_c}$$

where C = yearly payment = €100
 P_c = price of perpetuity (consol) = €2,000

Thus

$$i_c = \frac{€100}{€2,000}$$

$$i_c = 0.05 = 5\%$$

The formula in Equation 4.5, which describes the calculation of the yield to maturity for a perpetuity, also provides a useful approximation for the yield to maturity on coupon bonds. When a coupon bond has a long term to maturity (say, twenty years or more), it is very much like a perpetuity, which pays coupon payments for ever. This is because the cash flows more than twenty years in the future have such small present discounted values that the value of a long-term coupon bond is very close to the value of a perpetuity with the same coupon rate. Thus i_c in Equation 4.5 will be very close to the yield to maturity for any long-term bond. For this reason, i_c, the yearly coupon payment divided by the price of the security, has been given the name **current yield** and is frequently used as an approximation to describe interest rates on long-term bonds.

Discount bond

The yield-to-maturity calculation for a discount bond is similar to that for the simple loan. Let us consider a discount bond such as a one-year Treasury bill, which pays a face value of €1,000 in one year's time. If the current purchase price of this bill is €900, then equating this price to the present value of the €1,000 received in one year, using Equation 4.1, gives

$$€900 = \frac{€1,000}{1 + i}$$

Solving for i,

$$(1 + i) \times €900 = €1,000$$

$$€900 + €900i = €1,000$$

$$€900i = €1,000 - €900$$

$$i = \frac{€1,000 - €900}{€900} = 0.111 = 11.1\%$$

More generally, for any one-year discount bond, the yield to maturity can be written as

$$i = \frac{F - P}{P} \tag{4.6}$$

where F = face value of the discount bond
 P = current price of the discount bond

In other words, the yield to maturity equals the increase in price over the year $(F - P)$ divided by the initial price (P). In normal circumstances, investors earn positive returns

GLOBAL
Negative Treasury bill rates? It can happen

We normally assume that interest rates must always be positive. Negative interest rates would imply that you are willing to pay more for a bond today than you will receive for it in the future (as our formula for yield to maturity on a discount bond demonstrates). Negative interest rates therefore seem like an impossibility because you would do better by holding cash that has the same value in the future as it does today.

Events in Japan in the late 1990s and in the United States during the subprime financial crisis of 2008 have demonstrated that this reasoning is not quite correct. In November 1998, interest rates on Japanese six-month Treasury bills became negative, yielding an interest rate of –0.004%. In September 2008, interest rates on three-month Treasury bills fell very slightly below zero for a

very brief period. Negative interest rates are an extremely unusual event. How could this happen?

As we will see in Chapter 5, the weakness of the economy and a flight to quality during a financial crisis can drive interest rates to low levels, but these two factors can't explain the negative rates. The answer is that large investors found it more convenient to hold these Treasury bills as a store of value rather than holding cash because the bills are denominated in larger amounts and can be stored electronically. For that reason, some investors were willing to hold them, despite their negative rates, even though in monetary terms the investors would be better off holding cash. Clearly, the convenience of Treasury bills goes only so far, and thus their interest rates can go only a little bit below zero.

from holding these securities and so they sell at a discount, meaning that the current price of the bond is below the face value. Therefore, $F - P$ should be positive, and the yield to maturity should be positive as well. However, this is not always the case, as recent extraordinary events in Japan indicate (see the Global box).

An important feature of this equation is that it indicates that for a discount bond, the yield to maturity is negatively related to the current bond price. This is the same conclusion that we reached for a coupon bond. For example, Equation 4.6 shows that a rise in the bond price, say from €900 to €950, means that the bond will have a smaller increase in its price at maturity, and the yield to maturity falls, from 11.1% to 5.3%. Similarly, a fall in the yield to maturity means that the price of the discount bond has risen.

Summary

The concept of present value tells you that a euro in the future is not as valuable to you as a euro today because you can earn interest on this euro. Specifically, a euro received n years from now is worth only $€1/(1 + i)^n$ today. The present value of a set of future cash flow payments on a debt instrument equals the sum of the present values of each of the future payments. The yield to maturity for an instrument is the interest rate that equates the present value of the future payments on that instrument to its value today. Because the procedure for calculating the yield to maturity is based on sound economic principles, this is the measure that economists think most accurately describes the interest rate.

Our calculations of the yield to maturity for a variety of bonds reveal the important fact that current bond prices and interest rates are negatively related: when the interest rate rises (or falls), the price of the bond falls (or rises).

The distinction between interest rates and returns

Many people think that the interest rate on a bond tells them all they need to know about how well off they are as a result of owning it. If Irving the Investor thinks he is better off when he owns a long-term bond yielding a 10% interest rate and the interest rate rises to 20%, he will have a rude awakening: as we will shortly see, if he has to sell the bond, Irving has lost his shirt! How well a person does by holding a bond or any other security over a particular time period is accurately measured by the **return**, or, in more precise terminology, the **rate of return**. We will use the concept of *return* continually throughout this book: understanding it will make the material presented later in the book easier to follow.

For any security, the rate of return is defined as the payments to the owner plus the change in its value, expressed as a fraction of its purchase price. To make this definition clearer, let us see what the return would look like for a €1,000-face-value coupon bond with a coupon rate of 10% that is bought for €1,000, held for one year, and then sold for €1,200. The payments to the owner are the yearly coupon payments of €100, and the change in its value is €1,200 − €1,000 = €200. Adding these together and expressing them as a fraction of the purchase price of €1,000 gives us the one-year holding-period return for this bond:

$$\frac{€100 + €200}{€1,000} = \frac{€300}{€1,000} = 0.3 = 30\%$$

You may have noticed something quite surprising about the return that we have just calculated: it equals 30%, yet as Table 4.1 indicates, initially the yield to maturity was only 10%. This demonstrates that *the return on a bond will not necessarily equal the yield to maturity on that bond*. We now see that the distinction between interest rate and return can be important, although for many securities the two may be closely related.

More generally, the return on a bond held from time t to time $t + 1$ can be written as

$$R = \frac{C + P_{t+1} - P_t}{P_t} \tag{4.7}$$

where R = return from holding the bond from time t to time $t + 1$
    P_t = price of the bond at time t
    P_{t+1} = price of the bond at time $t + 1$
    C = coupon payment

A convenient way to rewrite the return formula in Equation 4.7 is to recognize that it can be split into two separate terms:

$$R = \frac{C}{P_t} + \frac{P_{t+1} - P_t}{P_t}$$

The first term is the current yield i_c (the coupon payment over the purchase price):

$$\frac{C}{P_t} = i_c$$

The second term is the **rate of capital gain**, or the change in the bond's price relative to the initial purchase price:

$$\frac{P_{t+1} - P_t}{P_t} = g$$

where g is the rate of capital gain. Equation 4.7 can then be rewritten as

$$R = i_c + g \tag{4.8}$$

which shows that the return on a bond is the current yield i_c plus the rate of capital gain g. This rewritten formula illustrates the point we just discovered: even for a bond for which the current yield i_c is an accurate measure of the yield to maturity, the return can differ substantially from the interest rate. Returns will differ from the interest rate, especially if there are sizeable fluctuations in the price of the bond that produce substantial capital gains or losses.

One-year returns on different-maturity 10%-coupon-rate bonds when interest rates rise from 10% to 20%

(1) Years to maturity when bond is purchased	(2) Initial current yield (%)	(3) Initial price (€)	(4) Price next year* (€)	(5) Rate of capital gain (%)	(6) Rate of return (2 + 5) (%)
30	10	1,000	503	−49.7	−39.7
20	10	1,000	516	−48.4	−38.4
10	10	1,000	597	−40.3	−30.3
5	10	1,000	741	−25.9	−15.9
2	10	1,000	917	−8.3	+1.7
1	10	1,000	1,000	0.0	+10.0

*Calculated with a financial calculator using Equation 4.3.

To explore this point even further, let's look at what happens to the returns on bonds of different maturities when interest rates rise. Table 4.2 calculates the one-year return using Equation 4.8 above on several 10%-coupon-rate bonds all purchased at par when interest rates on all these bonds rise from 10% to 20%. Several key findings in this table are generally true of all bonds:

- The only bond whose return equals the initial yield to maturity is one whose time to maturity is the same as the holding period (see the last bond in Table 4.2).
- A rise in interest rates is associated with a fall in bond prices, resulting in capital losses on bonds whose terms to maturity are longer than the holding period.
- The more distant a bond's maturity, the greater the size of the percentage price change associated with an interest-rate change.
- The more distant a bond's maturity, the lower the rate of return that occurs as a result of the increase in the interest rate.
- Even though a bond has a substantial initial interest rate, its return can turn out to be negative if interest rates rise.

At first it frequently puzzles students (as it puzzles poor Irving the Investor) that a rise in interest rates can mean that a bond has been a poor investment. The trick to understanding this is to recognize that a rise in the interest rate means that the price of a bond has fallen. A rise in interest rates therefore means that a capital loss has occurred. If this loss is large enough, the bond can be a poor investment indeed. For example, we see in Table 4.2 that the bond that has 30 years to maturity when purchased has a capital loss of 49.7% when the interest rate rises from 10% to 20%. This loss is so large that it exceeds the current yield of 10%, resulting in a negative return (loss) of −39.7%. If Irving does not sell the bond, his capital loss is often referred to as a 'paper loss'. This is a loss nonetheless because if he had not bought this bond and had instead put his money in the bank, he would now be able to buy more bonds at their lower price than he presently owns.

Maturity and the volatility of bond returns: interest-rate risk

The finding that the prices of longer-maturity bonds respond more dramatically to changes in interest rates helps explain an important fact about the behaviour of bond markets: *prices and returns for long-term bonds are more volatile than those for shorter-term bonds*.

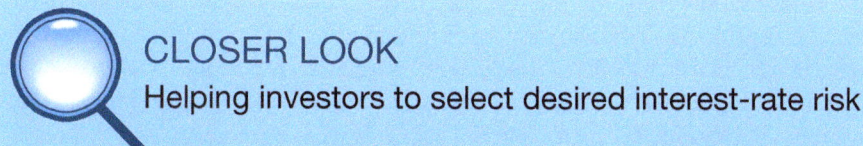

CLOSER LOOK
Helping investors to select desired interest-rate risk

Because many investors want to know how much interest-rate risk they are exposed to, some mutual fund companies try to educate investors about the perils of interest-rate risk, as well as to offer investment alternatives that match their investors' preferences.

Vanguard Group, for example, offers eight separate high-grade bond mutual funds. In its prospectus, Vanguard separates the funds by the average maturity of the bonds they hold and demonstrates the effect of interest-rate changes by computing the percentage change in bond value resulting from a 1% increase and

decrease in interest rates. Three of the bond funds invest in bonds with average maturities of one to three years, which Vanguard rates as having the lowest interest-rate risk. Three other funds hold bonds with average maturities of five to ten years, which Vanguard rates as having medium interest-rate risk. Two funds hold long-term bonds with maturities of 15 to 30 years, which Vanguard rates as having high interest-rate risk.

By providing this information, Vanguard hopes to increase its market share in the sales of bond funds. Not surprisingly, Vanguard is one of the most successful mutual fund companies in the business.

Price changes of and within a year, with corresponding variations in returns, are common for bonds more than twenty years away from maturity.

We now see that changes in interest rates make investments in long-term bonds quite risky. Indeed, the riskiness of an asset's return that results from interest-rate changes is so important that it has been given a special name, **interest-rate risk**.[4] Dealing with interest-rate risk is a major concern of managers of financial institutions and investors, as we will see in later chapters (see also the 'Closer look' box).

Although long-term debt instruments have substantial interest-rate risk, short-term debt instruments do not. Indeed, bonds with a maturity that is as short as the holding period have no interest-rate risk.[5] We see this for the coupon bond at the bottom of Table 4.2, which has no uncertainty about the rate of return because it equals the yield to maturity, which is known at the time the bond is purchased. The key to understanding why there is no interest-rate risk for *any* bond whose time to maturity matches the holding period is to recognize that (in this case) the price at the end of the holding period is already fixed at the face value. The change in interest rates can then have no effect on the price at the end of the holding period for these bonds, and the return will therefore be equal to the yield to maturity known at the time the bond is purchased.[6]

Summary

The return on a bond, which tells you how good an investment it has been over the holding period, is equal to the yield to maturity in only one special case: when the holding period and the maturity of the bond are identical. Bonds whose term to maturity is longer than the holding period are subject to interest-rate risk: changes in interest rates lead to capital gains and losses that produce substantial differences between the return and the yield to maturity known at the time the bond is purchased. Interest-rate risk is especially important for long-term bonds, where the capital gains and losses can be substantial. This is why long-term bonds are not considered to be safe assets with a sure return over short holding periods.

The distinction between real and nominal interest rates

So far in our discussion of interest rates, we have ignored the effects of inflation on the cost of borrowing. What we have up to now been calling the interest rate makes no allowance for inflation, and it is more precisely referred to as the **nominal interest rate**. We distinguish it from the **real interest rate**, the interest rate that is adjusted by subtracting expected changes in the price level (inflation) so that it more accurately reflects the true cost of borrowing. This interest rate is more precisely referred to as the *ex ante real interest rate* because it is adjusted for *expected* changes in the price level. The ex ante real interest rate is most important to economic decisions, and typically it is what economists mean when they make reference to the 'real' interest rate. The interest rate that is adjusted for *actual* changes in the price level is called the *ex post real interest rate*. It describes how well a lender has done in real terms *after the fact*.

The real interest rate is more accurately defined from the *Fisher equation*, named for Irving Fisher, one of the great monetary economists of the twentieth century. The Fisher equation states that the nominal interest rate i equals the real interest rate i_r plus the expected rate of inflation:[7]

$$i = i_r + \pi^e \tag{4.9}$$

Rearranging terms, we find that the real interest rate equals the nominal interest rate minus the expected inflation rate:

$$i_r = i - \pi^e \tag{4.10}$$

To see why this definition makes sense, let us first consider a situation in which you have made a one-year simple loan with a 5% interest rate and you expect the price level to rise by 3% over the course of the year ($\pi^e = 3\%$). As a result of making the loan, at the end of the year you expect to have 2% more in **real terms** – that is, in terms of real goods and services you can buy. In this case, the interest rate you expect to earn in terms of real goods and services is 2%:

$$i_r = 5\% - 3\% = 2\%$$

as indicated by the definition in Equation 4.10.

APPLICATION   ## Calculating real interest rates

What is the real interest rate if the nominal interest rate is 8% and the expected inflation rate is 10% over the course of a year?

Solution

The real interest rate is −2%. Although you will be receiving 8% more pounds at the end of the year, you will be paying 10% more for goods. The result is that you will be able to buy 2% fewer goods at the end of the year, and you will be 2% worse off in real terms.

$$i_r = i - \pi^e$$

where i = nominal interest rate   = 0.08
        π^e = expected inflation rate = 0.10
Thus

$$i_r = 0.08 - 0.10 = -0.02 = -2\%$$

As a lender, you are clearly less eager to make a loan in this case, because in terms of real goods and services you have actually earned a negative interest rate of 2%. By contrast, as the borrower, you fare quite well because at the end of the year, the amounts you will have to pay back will be worth 2% less in terms of goods and services – you as the borrower will be ahead by 2% in real terms. ***When the real interest rate is low, there are greater incentives to borrow and fewer incentives to lend***. ■

FIGURE 4.1

Real and nominal interest rates (3-month Treasury bill), 1964–2010

Sources: Nominal rates from ONS online. The real rate is constructed using the procedure outlined in Frederic S. Mishkin, 'The real interest rate: an empirical investigation', *Carnegie-Rochester Conference Series on Public Policy* 15 (1981): 151–200. This procedure involves estimating expected inflation as a function of past interest rates, inflation and time trends and then subtracting the expected inflation measure from the nominal interest rate.

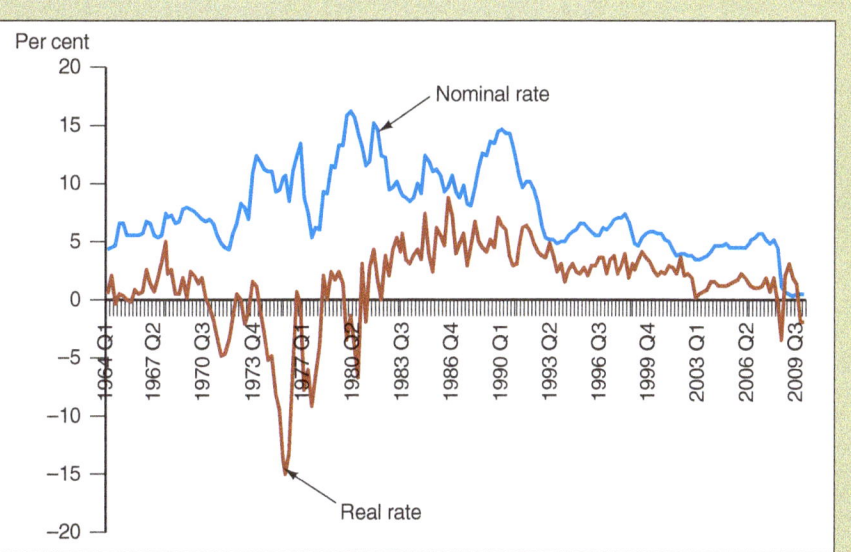

A similar distinction can be made between nominal returns and real returns. Nominal returns, which do not allow for inflation, are what we have been referring to as simply 'returns'. When inflation is subtracted from a nominal return, we have the real return, which indicates the amount of extra goods and services that we can purchase as a result of holding the security.

The distinction between real and nominal interest rates is important because the real interest rate, which reflects the real cost of borrowing, is likely to be a better indicator of the incentives to borrow and lend. It appears to be a better guide to how people will be affected by what is happening in credit markets. Figure 4.1, which presents estimates from 1964 to 2010 of the real and nominal interest rates on three-month UK Government Treasury

CLOSER LOOK
With index-linked gilts, real interest rates have become observable in the UK

Index-linked bonds came into being in March 1981. The sale of index-linked bonds was initially restricted to pension funds but since March 1982 all restrictions of ownership have been removed and a general market for index-linked bonds has been created. The indexation was to the general retail price index.

These indexed securities have successfully carved out a niche in the bond market, enabling governments to raise more funds. In addition, because their interest and principal payments are adjusted for changes in the price level, the interest rate on these bonds provides a direct measure of a real interest rate. These indexed bonds are very useful to policymakers, especially monetary

policymakers, because by subtracting their interest rate from a nominal interest rate on a non-indexed bond, they generate more insight into expected inflation, a valuable piece of information. For example, on 23 September 2005, the UK Treasury issued an index-linked Gilt maturing in 2055. In September 2005 the yield on conventional Treasury stock maturing in 2055 was 4.14% while the yield on index-linked Gilt was 1.08%. By subtracting the real rate from the nominal rate we have the expected average rate of inflation for the next 50 years as 3.06%. In July 2010 the nominal yield was 4.24% and the real yield had fallen to 0.67. The average expected inflation for the next 45 years has therefore risen to 3.57%.

bills, shows us that nominal and real rates often do not move together. (This is also true for nominal and real interest rates in the rest of the world.) In particular, when nominal rates in the UK were high in the mid-1970s and early 1980s, real rates were actually extremely low – often negative. By the standard of nominal interest rates, you would have thought that credit market conditions were tight in this period, because it was expensive to borrow. However, the estimates of the real rates indicate that you would have been mistaken. In real terms, the cost of borrowing was actually quite low.[8]

Real interest rates have been observed in the UK since March 1981 when the first **index-linked bonds** were issued. Index-linked bonds have the coupon and principal adjusted for the general **retail price index**.

Summary

1 The yield to maturity, which is the measure that most accurately reflects the interest rate, is the interest rate that equates the present value of future payments of a debt instrument with its value today. Application of this principle reveals that bond prices and interest rates are negatively related: when the interest rate rises (or falls), the price of the bond must fall (or rise).

2 The return on a security, which tells you how well you have done by holding this security over a stated period of time, can differ substantially from the interest rate as measured by the yield to maturity. Long-term bond prices have substantial fluctuations when interest rates change and thus bear interest-rate risk. The resulting capital gains and losses can be large, which is why long-term bonds are not considered to be safe assets with a sure return.

3 The real interest rate is defined as the nominal interest rate minus the expected rate of inflation. It is a better measure of the incentives to borrow and lend than the nominal interest rate, and it is a more accurate indicator of the tightness of credit market conditions than the nominal interest rate.

Key terms

cash flows p. 61

consol or perpetuity p.68

coupon bond p. 64

coupon rate p. 64

current yield p. 69

discount bond (zero-coupon bond) p. 64

face value (par value) p. 64

fixed-payment loan (fully amortized loan) p. 64

index-linked bond p. 76

interest-rate risk p. 73

nominal interest rate p. 73

present discounted value p. 61

present value p. 61

rate of capital gain p. 71

real interest rate p. 74

real terms p. 74

retail price index p. 76

return (rate of return) p. 71

simple loan p. 62

yield to maturity p. 64

QUESTIONS AND PROBLEMS

All questions and problems are available in MyEconLab at **www.myeconlab.com/mishkin.**

1 Would a euro tomorrow be worth more to you today when the interest rate is 20% or when it is 10%?

2 You have just won €10 million in the lottery, which promises to pay you €1 million (tax free) every year for the next ten years. Have you really won €10 million?

3 If the interest rate is 10%, what is the present value of a security that pays you €1,100 next year, €1,210 the year after and €1,331 the year after that?

4 If the security in problem 3 sold for €3,500, is the yield to maturity greater or less than 10%? Why?

5 Write down the formula that is used to calculate the yield to maturity on a twenty-year 10% coupon bond with €1,000 face value that sells for €2,000.

6 What is the yield to maturity on a €1,000-face-value discount bond maturing in one year that sells for €800?

7 What is the yield to maturity on a simple loan for €1 million that requires a repayment of €2 million in five years' time?

8 To pay for university, you have just taken out a €1,000 government loan that makes you pay €126 per year for 25 years. However, you don't have to start making these payments until you graduate from university two years from now. Why is the yield to maturity necessarily less than 12%, the yield to maturity on a normal €1,000 fixed-payment loan in which you pay €126 per year for 25 years?

9 Which €1,000 bond has the higher yield to maturity, a twenty-year bond selling for €800 with a current yield of 15% or a one-year bond selling for €800 with a current yield of 5%?

10 Pick five Treasury bonds from the bond page of the *Financial Times*, and calculate the current yield. Note when the current yield is a good approximation of the yield to maturity.

11 You are offered two bonds, a one-year Treasury bond with a yield to maturity of 9% and a one-year Treasury bill with a yield on a discount basis of 8.9%. Which would you rather own?

12 If there is a decline in interest rates, which would you rather be holding, long-term bonds or short-term bonds? Why? Which type of bond has the greater interest-rate risk?

13 Francine the Financial Adviser has just given you the following advice: 'Long-term bonds are a great investment because their interest rate is over 20%.' Is Francine necessarily right?

14 If mortgage rates rise from 5% to 10% but the expected rate of increase in housing prices rises from 2% to 9%, are people more or less likely to buy houses?

15 Interest rates were lower in the mid-1980s than they were in the late 1970s, yet many economists have commented that real interest rates were actually much higher in the mid-1980s than in the late 1970s. Does this make sense? Do you think that these economists are right?

WEB EXERCISES

1 In the euro area, the 10-year government bond spread versus the German bund (government bond) is a key indicator of sovereign risk. Go to **http://markets.ft.com/RESEARCH/Markets/Government-Bond-Spreads.**

(a) Which euro area country's bond currently has the highest spread versus bunds?
(b) Which euro area country's bond currently has the lowest spread versus bunds?

2 Yields on key government bonds are available on **www.bloomberg.com/markets/rates-bonds.**

(a) Which of the countries listed currently has the highest 10-year government bond yield?
(b) Which has the lowest 10-year bond yield?
(c) Using the 'Bond Spread Calculator', determine the spread between Italian 10-year government bonds and German 10-year government bonds.
(d) Graph the German 10-year government bond yield (**www.bloomberg.com/quote/GDBR10:IND**) over the past 12 months. How has it changed?
(e) Now choose any other euro area 10-year government bond yield chart over a one year horizon. Is the pattern similar to that for Germany?

3 Investigate the data on UK yields on the Bank of England website (**http://www.bankofengland.co.uk/statistics/Pages/iadb/notesiadb/Yields.aspx**) Read the material and answer the following questions:

(a) What is the flat yield?.
(b) What is the zero coupon yield?.

4 Figure 4.1 in the text shows the estimated real and nominal rates for three-month Treasury bills. Go to **www.martincapital.com/main/charts.htm** and click on 'Nominal vs. Real Rates', then on 'Nominal vs. Real Market Rates'.

(a) Compare the three-month real rate to the long-term real rate. Which is greater?
(b) Compare the short-term nominal rate to the long-term nominal rate. Which appears more volatile?

5 In this chapter we discussed long-term bonds as if there were only one type, coupon bonds. In fact, there are also long-term discount bonds. A discount bond is sold at a low price and the whole return comes in the form of a price appreciation. You can easily compute the current price of a discount bond using the financial calculator at **www.treasurydirect.gov/indiv/tools/tools_savingsbondcalc.htm.**

To compute the values for savings bonds, read the instructions on the page and click 'Get Started'. Fill in the information (you do not need to fill in the 'Bond Serial Number' field) and click on 'calculate'.

Notes

1 In other contexts, it is also called the *internal rate of return*.

2 Most coupon bonds actually make coupon payments on a semiannual basis rather than once a year as assumed here. The effect on the calculations is only very slight and will be ignored here.

3 The bond price formula for a consol is

$$P = \frac{C}{1 + i} + \frac{C}{(1 + i)^2} + \frac{C}{(1 + i)^3} + \cdots$$

which can be written as $P = C(x + x^2 + x^3 + \cdots)$ in which $x = 1/(1 + i)$. The formula for an infinite sum is

$$1 + x + x^2 + x^3 + \cdots = \frac{1}{1 - x}$$

for $x < 1$ and so

$$P = C\left(\frac{1}{1 - x} - 1\right) = C\left[\frac{1}{1 - 1/(1 + i)} - 1\right]$$

which by suitable algebraic manipulation becomes

$$P = C\left(\frac{1 + i}{i} - \frac{i}{i}\right) = \frac{C}{i}$$

4 Interest-rate risk can be quantitatively measured using the concept of *duration*. This concept and its calculation are discussed in an appendix to this chapter, which can be found on this book's website at **www.myeconlab.com/mishkin**.

5 The statement that there is no interest-rate risk for any bond whose time to maturity matches the holding period is literally true only for discount bonds and zero-coupon bonds that make no intermediate cash payments before the holding period is over. A coupon bond that makes an intermediate cash payment before the holding period is over requires that this payment be reinvested. Because the interest rate at which this payment can be reinvested is uncertain, there is some uncertainty about the return on this coupon bond even when the time to maturity equals the holding period. However, the riskiness of the return on a coupon bond from reinvesting the coupon payments is typically quite small, so the basic point that a coupon bond with a time to maturity equalling the holding period has very little risk still holds true.

6 In the text, we are assuming that all holding periods are short and equal to the maturity on short-term bonds and are thus not subject to interest-rate risk. However, if an investor's holding period is longer than the term to maturity of the bond, the investor is exposed to a type of interest-rate risk called *reinvestment risk*. Reinvestment risk occurs because the proceeds from the short-term bond need to be reinvested at a future interest rate that is uncertain. To understand reinvestment risk, suppose that Irving the Investor has a holding period of two years and decides to purchase a €1,000 one-year bond at face value and will then purchase another one at the end of the first year. If the initial interest rate is 10%, Irving will have €1,100 at the end of the year. If the interest rate rises to 20%, as in Table 4.2, Irving will find that buying €1,100 worth of another one-year bond will leave him at the end of the second year

with €1,100 × (1 + 0.2) = €1,320. Thus Irving's two-year return will be (€1,320 − €1,000)/€1,000 = 0.32 = 32%, which equals 14.9% at an annual rate. In this case, Irving has earned more by buying the one-year bonds than if he had initially purchased the two-year bond with an interest rate of 10%. Thus, when Irving has a holding period that is longer than the term to maturity of the bonds he purchases, he benefits from a rise in interest rates. Conversely, if interest rates fall to 5%, Irving will have only €1,155 at the end of two years: €1,100 × (1 + 0.05). His two-year return will be (€1,155 − €1,000)/1,000 = 0.115 = 15.5%, which is 7.2% at an annual rate. With a holding period greater than the term to maturity of the bond, Irving now loses from a decline in interest rates. We have thus seen that when the holding period is longer than the term to maturity of a bond, the return is uncertain because the future interest rate when reinvestment occurs is also uncertain – in short, there is reinvestment risk. We also see that if the holding period is longer than the term to maturity of the bond, the investor benefits from a rise in interest rates and is hurt by a fall in interest rates.

7 A more precise formulation of the Fisher equation is $i = i_r + \pi^e + (i_i \times \pi^e)$ because $1 + i = (1 + i_r)(1 + \pi^e) = 1 + i_r + \pi^e + (i_r \times \pi^e)$ and subtracting 1 from both sides gives us the first equation. For small values of i_r and π^e the term $i_r \times \pi^e$ is so small that we ignore it, as in the text.

8 Because interest income in the UK and other EU countries is subject to income taxes, the true earnings in real terms from holding a debt instrument are not reflected by the real interest rate defined by the Fisher equation but rather by the *after-tax real interest rate*, which equals the nominal interest rate *after income tax payments have been subtracted*, minus the expected inflation rate. For example for a person facing a 30% tax rate, the after-tax interest rate earned on a bond yielding 10% is only 7% because 30% of the interest income must be paid to the Government Revenue Service. Thus the after-tax real interest rate on this bond when expected inflation is 5% equals 2% (= 7% − 5%). More generally, the after-tax real interest rate can be expressed as $i = r(1 - \tau) - \pi^e$ where τ = the income tax rate. This formula for the after-tax real interest rate also provides a better measure of the effective cost of borrowing for many corporations and homeowners in the United States because in calculating income taxes, they can deduct interest payments on loans from their income. Thus, if you face a 30% tax rate and take out a mortgage loan with a 10% interest rate, you are able to deduct the 10% interest payment and lower your taxes by 30% of this amount. Your after-tax nominal cost of borrowing is then 7% (10% minus 30% of the 10% interest payment), and when the expected inflation rate is 5%, the effective cost of borrowing in real terms is again 2% (=7% − 5%). As the example (and the formula) indicates, after-tax real interest rates are always below the real interest rate defined by the Fisher equation. For a further discussion of measures of after-tax real interest rates, see Frederic S. Mishkin, 'The real interest rate: an empirical investigation', *Carnegie-Rochester Conference Series on Public Policy* 15 (1981): 151–200.

Useful websites

www.bloomberg.com/markets/ Under 'Rates & Bonds', you can access information on key interest rates, international government bonds and other fixed income securities.

http://www.calculatedriskblog.com/p/european-bond-yields.html Useful link to the Bloomberg data on several government bond yields within the euro area.

http://www.investinginbonds.com/ Investing in Bonds is a very comprehensive site on bond markets, news and commentary, and some useful educational features.

http://finance.yahoo.com/bonds A useful free resource on primarily US bond data. The bond screener is a useful tool.

http://markets.ft.com/research/Markets/Bonds The *Financial Times* page on bonds includes a 'Data Archive' facility to download recent interest rates and bond yields for several types of fixed income securities.

www.teachmefinance.com A review of the key financial concepts: time value of money, annuities, perpetuities, and so on.

www.martincapital.com/main/charts.htm Go to charts of real versus nominal rates for the US to view 30 years of nominal interest rates compared to real rates for the 30-year T-bond and 90-day T-bill.

MyEconLab can help you get a better grade

MyEconLab®

If your exam were tomorrow, would you be ready? For each chapter, MyEconLab Practice Tests and Study Plans pinpoint which sections you have mastered and which ones you need to study. That way, you are more efficient with your study time, and you are better prepared for your exams.

To see how it works, turn to page 19 and then go to: **www.myeconlab.com/mishkin**

CHAPTER 5

The behaviour of interest rates

PREVIEW

In the early 1950s, nominal interest rates in the UK on three-month Treasury bills were about $1\frac{1}{2}\%$ at an annual rate; by 1981, they had reached just under 15%; in 2003 they reached a low of under 4%, rose to over 5% in 2007 and then fell to $\frac{1}{2}\%$ in 2008. What explains these substantial fluctuations in interest rates? One reason why we study money, banking and financial markets is to provide some answers to this question.

In this chapter, we examine how the overall level of *nominal* interest rates (which we refer to as simply 'interest rates') is determined and which factors influence their behaviour. We learned in Chapter 4 that interest rates are negatively related to the price of bonds, so if we can explain why bond prices change, we can also explain why interest rates fluctuate. We make use of supply and demand analysis for bond markets and money markets to examine how interest rates change.

To derive a demand curve for assets such as money or bonds, the first step in our analysis, we must first understand what determines the demand for these assets. We do this by examining the *theory of asset demand*, an economic theory that outlines criteria that are important when deciding how much of an asset to buy. Armed with this theory, we can then go on to derive the demand curve for bonds or money. After deriving supply curves for these assets, we develop the concept of *market equilibrium*, the point at which the quantity supplied equals the quantity demanded. Then we use this model to explain changes in equilibrium interest rates.

Because interest rates on different securities tend to move together, in this chapter we will proceed as if there were only one type of security and one interest rate in the entire economy. In the following chapter, we expand our analysis to look at why interest rates on different types of securities differ.

Determinants of asset demand

Before going on to our supply and demand analysis of the bond market and the market for money, we must first understand what determines the quantity demanded of an asset. Recall that an asset is a piece of property that is a store of value. Items such as money, bonds, stocks, art, land, houses, farm equipment and manufacturing machinery are all assets. Facing the question of whether to buy and hold an asset or whether to buy one asset rather than another, an individual must consider the following factors:

1 **Wealth**, the total resources owned by the individual, including all assets
2 **Expected return** (the return expected over the next period) on one asset relative to alternative assets

3   **Risk** (the degree of uncertainty associated with the return) on one asset relative to alternative assets

4   **Liquidity** (the ease and speed with which an asset can be turned into cash) relative to alternative assets

Wealth

When we find that our wealth has increased, we have more resources available with which to purchase assets, and so, not surprisingly, the quantity of assets we demand increases. Therefore, the effect of changes in wealth on the quantity demanded of an asset can be summarized as follows: *holding everything else constant, an increase in wealth raises the quantity demanded of an asset.*

Expected returns

In Chapter 4, we saw that the return on an asset (such as a bond) measures how much we gain from holding that asset. When we make a decision to buy an asset, we are influenced by what we expect the return on that asset to be. If a British Telecom (BT) corporate bond, for example, has a return of 15% half the time and 5% the other half of the time, its expected return (which you can think of as the average return) is 10% (= 0.5 × 15% + 0.5 × 5%).[1] If the **expected return** on the BT bond rises relative to expected returns on alternative assets, holding everything else constant, then it becomes more desirable to purchase it, and the quantity demanded increases. This can occur in either of two ways: (1) when the expected return on the BT bond rises while the return on an alternative asset – say, stock in Google – remains unchanged or (2) when the return on the alternative asset, the Google stock, falls while the return on the BT bond remains unchanged. To summarize, *an increase in an asset's expected return relative to that of an alternative asset, holding everything else unchanged, raises the quantity demanded of the asset*.

Risk

The degree of **risk** or uncertainty of an asset's returns also affects the demand for the asset. Consider two assets, stock in Fly-by-Night Airlines and stock in the Feet-on-the-Ground Bus Company. Suppose that Fly-by-Night stock has a return of 15% half the time and 5% the other half of the time, making its expected return 10%, while stock in Feet-on-the-Ground has a fixed return of 10%. Fly-by-Night stock has uncertainty associated with its returns and so has greater risk than stock in Feet-on-the-Ground, whose return is a sure thing.

A *risk-averse* person prefers stock in Feet-on-the-Ground (the sure thing) to Fly-by-Night stock (the riskier asset), even though the stocks have the same expected return, 10%. By contrast, a person who prefers risk is a *risk preferrer* or *risk lover*. Most people are risk-averse, especially in their financial decisions: everything else being equal, they prefer to hold the less risky asset. Hence, *holding everything else constant, if an asset's risk rises relative to that of alternative assets, its quantity demanded will fall.*

Liquidity

Another factor that affects the demand for an asset is how quickly it can be converted into cash at low costs – its **liquidity**. An asset is liquid if the market in which it is traded has depth and breadth; that is, if the market has many buyers and sellers. A house is not a very liquid asset, because it may be hard to find a buyer quickly; if a house must be sold to pay off bills, it might have to be sold for a much lower price. And the transaction costs in selling a house (broker's commissions, lawyer's fees, and so on) are substantial. A government Treasury bill and a highly rated commercial bill, by contrast, is a highly liquid asset. It can be sold in a well-organized market where there are many buyers, so it can be sold quickly at low cost. *The more liquid an asset is relative to alternative assets, holding everything else unchanged, the more desirable it is, and the greater will be the quantity demanded.*

Theory of asset demand

All the determining factors we have just discussed can be assembled into the **theory of asset demand**, which states that, holding all of the other factors constant:

■ The quantity demanded of an asset is positively related to wealth.
■ The quantity demanded of an asset is positively related to its expected return relative to alternative assets.
■ The quantity demanded of an asset is negatively related to the risk of its returns relative to alternative assets.
■ The quantity demanded of an asset is positively related to its liquidity relative to alternative assets.

These results are summarized in Table 5.1.

SUMMARY TABLE 5.1

Response of the quantity of an asset demanded to changes in wealth, expected returns, risk and liquidity

Variable	Change in variable	Change in quantity demanded
Wealth	↑	↑
Expected return relative to other assets	↑	↑
Risk relative to other assets	↑	↓
Liquidity relative to other assets	↑	↑

Note: Only increases in the variables are shown. The effect of decreases in the variables on the change in quantity demanded would be the opposite of those indicated in the rightmost column.

Supply and demand in the bond market

Our first approach to the analysis of interest-rate determination looks at supply and demand in the bond market to see how the price of bonds is determined. Thanks to our understanding of how interest rates are measured from Chapter 4, we know that each bond price is associated with a particular level of the interest rate. Specifically, the negative relationship between bond prices and interest rates means that when a bond price rises (or falls), its interest rate falls (or rises).

The first step in the analysis is to obtain a bond **demand curve**, which shows the relationship between the quantity demanded and the price when all other economic variables are held constant (that is, values of other variables are taken as given). You may recall from previous economics courses that the assumption that all other economic variables are held constant is called *ceteris paribus*, which means 'other things being equal' in Latin.

Demand curve

To clarify our analysis, let us consider the demand for one-year discount bonds, which make no coupon payments but pay the owner the €1,000 face value in a year. If the holding period is one year then, as we have seen in Chapter 4, the return on the bonds is known absolutely and is equal to the interest rate as measured by the yield to maturity. This means that the expected return on this bond is equal to the interest rate i, which, using Equation 4.6, is

$$i = R^e = \frac{F - P}{P}$$

where i = interest rate = yield to maturity
R^e = expected return
F = face value of the discount bond
P = initial purchase price of the discount bond

This formula shows that a particular value of the interest rate corresponds to each bond price. If the bond sells for €950, the interest rate and expected return are

$$\frac{€1,000 - €950}{€950} = 0.053 = 5.3\%$$

At this 5.3% interest rate and expected return corresponding to a bond price of €950, let us assume that the quantity of bonds demanded is €100 billion, which is plotted as point A in Figure 5.1.

At a price of €900, the interest rate and expected return are

$$\frac{€1000 - €900}{€900} = 0.111 = 11.1\%$$

Because the expected return on these bonds is higher, with all other economic variables (such as income, expected returns on other assets, risk and liquidity) held constant, the quantity demanded of bonds will be higher as predicted by the theory of asset demand. Point B in Figure 5.1 shows that the quantity of bonds demanded at the price of €900 has

FIGURE 5.1

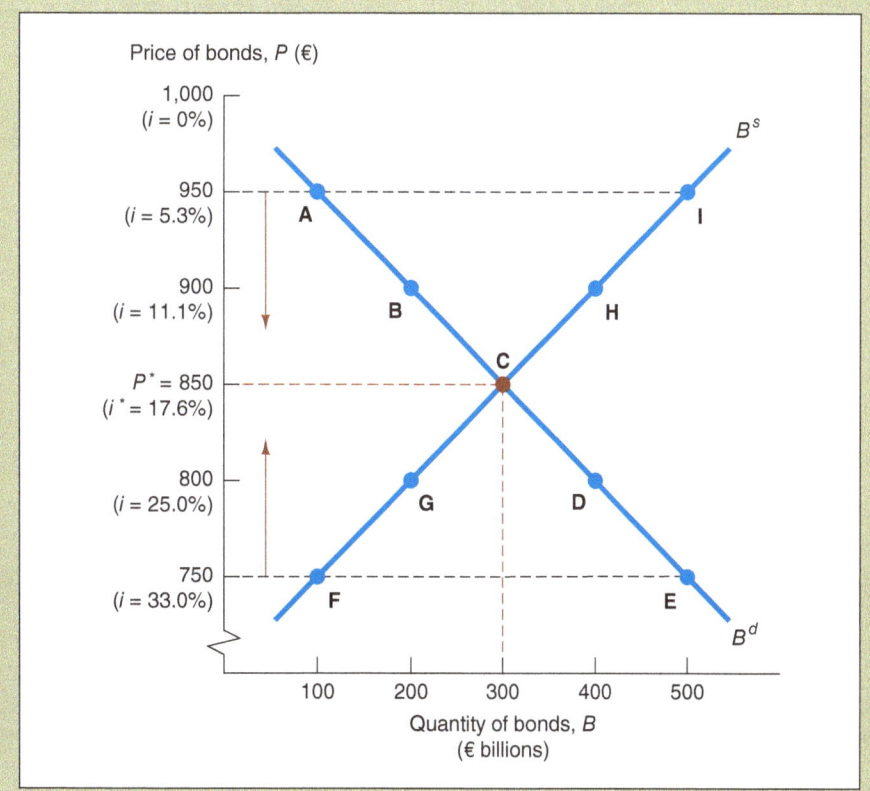

Supply and demand for bonds

Equilibrium in the bond market occurs at point C, the intersection of the demand curve B^d and the bond supply curve B^s. The equilibrium price is $P^* = $ €850, and the equilibrium interest rate is $i^* = 17.6\%$.

risen to €200 billion. Continuing with this reasoning, if the bond price is €850 (interest rate and expected return = 17.6%), the quantity of bonds demanded (point C) will be greater than at point B. Similarly, at the lower prices of €800 (interest rate = 25%) and €750 (interest rate = 33.3%), the quantity of bonds demanded will be even higher (points D and E). The curve B^d, which connects these points, is the demand curve for bonds. It has the usual downward slope, indicating that at lower prices of the bond (everything else being equal), the quantity demanded is higher.[2]

Supply curve

An important assumption behind the demand curve for bonds in Figure 5.1 is that all other economic variables besides the bond's price and interest rate are held constant. We use the same assumption in deriving a **supply curve**, which shows the relationship between the quantity supplied and the price when all other economic variables are held constant.

When the price of the bonds is €750 (interest rate = 33.3%), point F shows that the quantity of bonds supplied is €100 billion for the example we are considering. If the price is €800, the interest rate is the lower rate of 25%. Because at this interest rate it is now less costly to borrow by issuing bonds, firms will be willing to borrow more through bond issues, and the quantity of bonds supplied is at the higher level of €200 billion (point G). An even higher price of €850, corresponding to a lower interest rate of 17.6%, results in a larger quantity of bonds supplied of €300 billion (point C). Higher prices of €900 and €950 result in even greater quantities of bonds supplied (points H and I). The B^s curve, which connects these points, is the supply curve for bonds. It has the usual upward slope found in supply curves, indicating that as the price increases (everything else being equal), the quantity supplied increases.

Market equilibrium

In economics, **market equilibrium** occurs when the amount that people are willing to buy (*demand*) equals the amount that people are willing to sell (*supply*) at a given price. In the bond market, this is achieved when the quantity of bonds demanded equals the quantity of bonds supplied:

$$B^d = B^s \qquad (5.1)$$

In Figure 5.1, equilibrium occurs at point C, where the demand and supply curves intersect at a bond price of €850 (interest rate of 17.6%) and a quantity of bonds of €300 billion. The price of P = €850, where the quantity demanded equals the quantity supplied, is called the *equilibrium* or *market-clearing* price. Similarly, the interest rate of i = 17.6% that corresponds to this price is called the equilibrium or market-clearing interest rate.

The concepts of market equilibrium and equilibrium price or interest rate are useful, because there is a tendency for the market to head toward them. We can see that it does in Figure 5.1 by first looking at what happens when we have a bond price that is above the equilibrium price. When the price of bonds is set too high, at, say, €950, the quantity of bonds supplied at point I is greater than the quantity of bonds demanded at point A. A situation like this, in which the quantity of bonds supplied exceeds the quantity of bonds demanded, is called a condition of **excess supply**. Because people want to sell more bonds than others want to buy, the price of the bonds will fall, which is why the downward arrow is drawn in the figure at the bond price of €950. As long as the bond price remains above the equilibrium price, there will continue to be an excess supply of bonds, and the price will continue to fall. This decline will stop only when the price has reached the equilibrium price of €850, where the excess supply of bonds has been eliminated.

Now let's look at what happens when the price of bonds is below the equilibrium price. If the price of the bonds is set too low, at, say, €750, the quantity demanded at point E is greater than the quantity supplied at point F. This is called a condition of **excess demand**. People now want to buy more bonds than others are willing to sell, so the price of bonds will be driven up. This is illustrated by the upward arrow drawn in the figure at the bond price of €750. Only when the excess demand for bonds is eliminated by the price rising to the equilibrium level of €850 is there no further tendency for the price to rise.

We can see that the concept of equilibrium price is a useful one because it indicates where the market will settle. Because each price on the vertical axis of Figure 5.1 corresponds to a particular value of the interest rate, the same diagram also shows that the interest rate will head toward the equilibrium interest rate of 17.6%. When the interest rate is below the equilibrium interest rate, as it is when it is at 5.3%, the price of the bond is above the equilibrium price, and there will be an excess supply of bonds. The price of the bond then falls, leading to a rise in the interest rate toward the equilibrium level. Similarly, when the interest rate is above the equilibrium level, as it is when it is at 33.3%, there is excess demand for bonds, and the bond price will rise, driving the interest rate back down to the equilibrium level of 17.6%.

Supply and demand analysis

Our Figure 5.1 is a conventional supply and demand diagram with price on the vertical axis and quantity on the horizontal axis. Because the interest rate that corresponds to each bond price is also marked on the vertical axis, this diagram allows us to read the equilibrium interest rate, giving us a model that describes the determination of interest rates. It is important to recognize that a supply and demand diagram like Figure 5.1 can be drawn for *any* type of bond because the interest rate and price of a bond are *always* negatively related for any type of bond, whether a discount bond or a coupon bond.

An important feature of the analysis here is that supply and demand are always in terms of *stocks* (amounts at a given point in time) of assets, not in terms of *flows*. The **asset market approach** for understanding behaviour in financial markets – which emphasizes stocks of assets rather than flows in determining asset prices – is the dominant methodology used by economists, because correctly conducting analyses in terms of flows is very tricky, especially when we encounter inflation.[3]

Changes in equilibrium interest rates

We will now use the supply and demand framework for bonds to analyse why interest rates change. To avoid confusion, it is important to make the distinction between *movements along* a demand (or supply) curve and *shifts in* a demand (or supply) curve. When quantity demanded (or supplied) changes as a result of a change in the price of the bond (or, equivalently, a change in the interest rate), we have a *movement along* the demand (or supply) curve. The change in the quantity demanded when we move from point A to B to C in Figure 5.1, for example, is a movement along a demand curve. A *shift in* the demand (or supply) curve, by contrast, occurs when the quantity demanded (or supplied) changes *at each given price (or interest rate)* of the bond in response to a change in some other factor besides the bond's price or interest rate. When one of these factors changes, causing a shift in the demand or supply curve, there will be a new equilibrium value for the interest rate.

In the following pages, we will look at how the supply and demand curves shift in response to changes in variables, such as expected inflation and wealth, and what effects these changes have on the equilibrium value of interest rates.

Shifts in the demand for bonds

The theory of asset demand demonstrated at the beginning of the chapter provides a framework for deciding which factors cause the demand curve for bonds to shift. These factors include changes in four parameters:

1 Wealth
2 Expected returns on bonds relative to alternative assets

SUMMARY TABLE 5.2

Factors that shift the demand curve for bonds

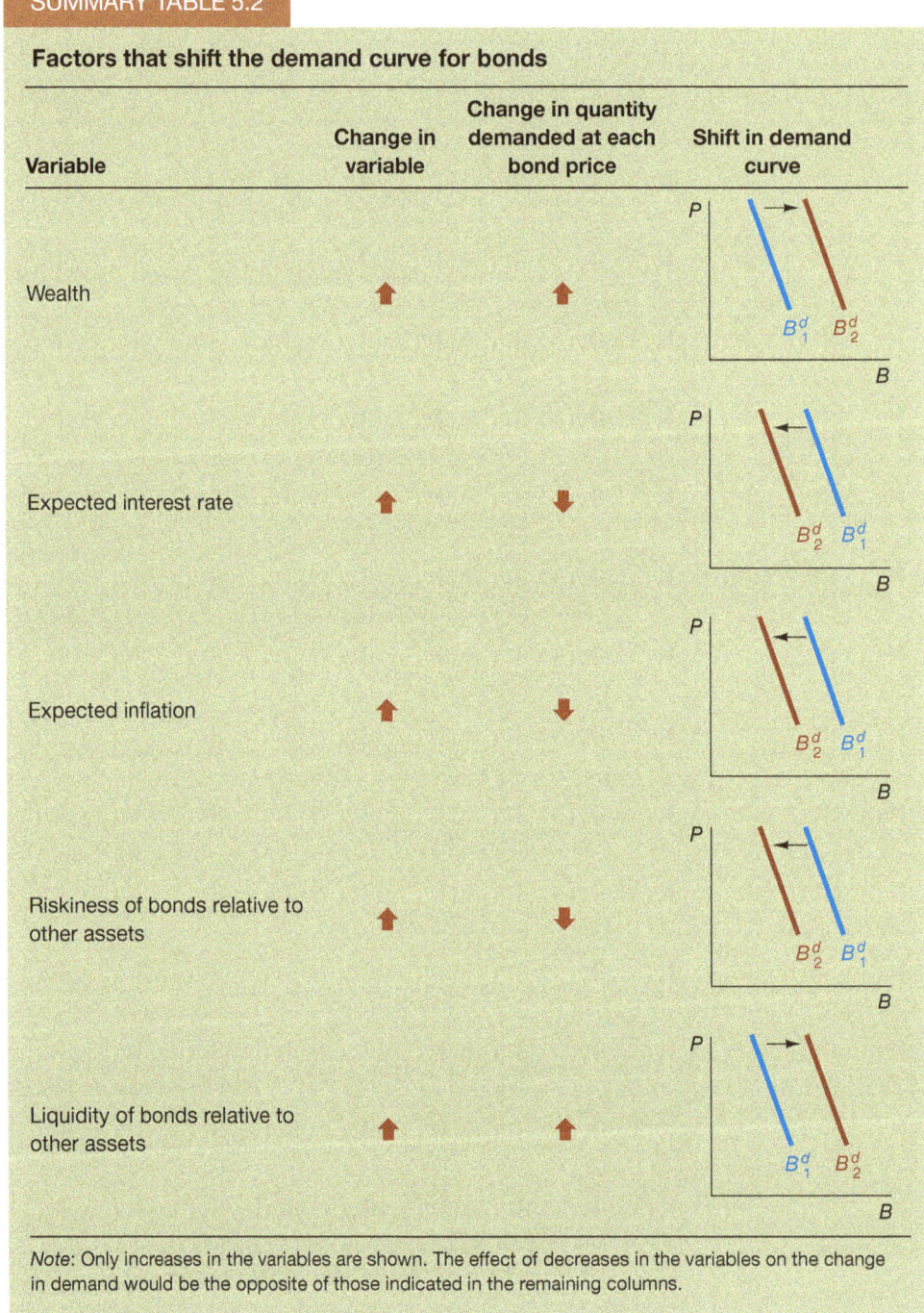

Variable	Change in variable	Change in quantity demanded at each bond price	Shift in demand curve
Wealth	⬆	⬆	
Expected interest rate	⬆	⬇	
Expected inflation	⬆	⬇	
Riskiness of bonds relative to other assets	⬆	⬇	
Liquidity of bonds relative to other assets	⬆	⬆	

Note: Only increases in the variables are shown. The effect of decreases in the variables on the change in demand would be the opposite of those indicated in the remaining columns.

3 Risk of bonds relative to alternative assets
4 Liquidity of bonds relative to alternative assets

To see how a change in each of these factors (holding all other factors constant) can shift the demand curve, let us look at some examples. (As a study aid, Table 5.2 summarizes the effects of changes in these factors on the bond demand curve.)

Wealth

When the economy is growing rapidly in a business cycle expansion and wealth is increasing, the quantity of bonds demanded at each bond price (or interest rate) increases as shown in Figure 5.2. To see how this works, consider point B on the initial demand curve for bonds B_1^d.

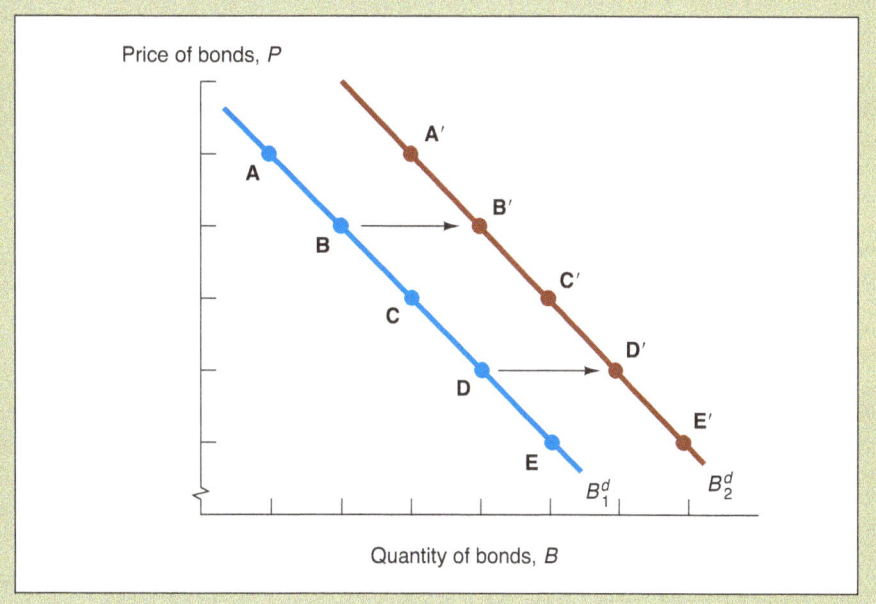

FIGURE 5.2

**Shift in the demand
curve for bonds**
When the demand for bonds
increases, the demand curve
shifts to the right as shown.

With higher wealth, the quantity of bonds demanded at the same price must rise, to point B'. Similarly, for point D the higher wealth causes the quantity demanded at the same bond price to rise to point D'. Continuing with this reasoning for every point on the initial demand curve B_1^d, we can see that the demand curve shifts to the right from B_1^d to B_2^d as is indicated by the arrows.

The conclusion we have reached is that in a business cycle expansion with growing wealth, the demand for bonds rises and the demand curve for bonds shifts to the right. Using the same reasoning, in a recession, when income and wealth are falling, the demand for bonds falls, and the demand curve shifts to the left.

Another factor that affects wealth is the public's propensity to save. If households save more, wealth increases and, as we have seen, the demand for bonds rises and the demand curve for bonds shifts to the right. Conversely, if people save less, wealth and the demand for bonds will fall and the demand curve shifts to the left.

Expected returns

For a one-year discount bond and a one-year holding period, the expected return and the interest rate are identical, so nothing besides today's interest rate affects the expected return.

For bonds with maturities of greater than one year, the expected return may differ from the interest rate. For example, we saw in Table 5.2 that a rise in the interest rate on a long-term bond from 10% to 20% would lead to a sharp decline in price and a very large negative return. Hence, if people began to think that interest rates would be higher next year than they had originally anticipated, the expected return today on long-term bonds would fall, and the quantity demanded would fall at each interest rate. *Higher expected interest rates in the future lower the expected return for long-term bonds, decrease the demand, and shift the demand curve to the left.*

By contrast, a revision downward of expectations of future interest rates would mean that long-term bond prices would be expected to rise more than originally anticipated, and the resulting higher expected return today would raise the quantity demanded at each bond price and interest rate. *Lower expected interest rates in the future increase the demand for long-term bonds and shift the demand curve to the right* (as in Figure 5.2).

Changes in expected returns on other assets can also shift the demand curve for bonds. If people suddenly became more optimistic about the stock market and began to expect higher stock prices in the future, both expected capital gains and expected returns on stocks would rise. With the expected return on bonds held constant, the expected return on bonds today relative to stocks would fall, lowering the demand for bonds and shifting the demand curve to the left.

A change in expected inflation is likely to alter expected returns on physical assets (also called *real assets*) such as automobiles and houses, which affect the demand for bonds. An increase in expected inflation, say, from 5% to 10%, will lead to higher prices on cars and houses in the future and hence higher nominal capital gains. The resulting rise in the expected returns today on these real assets will lead to a fall in the expected return on bonds relative to the expected return on real assets today and thus cause the demand for bonds to fall. Alternatively, we can think of the rise in expected inflation as lowering the real interest rate on bonds, and the resulting decline in the relative expected return on bonds will cause the demand for bonds to fall. *An increase in the expected rate of inflation lowers the expected return for bonds, causing their demand to decline and the demand curve to shift to the left.*

Risk

If prices in the bond market become more volatile, the risk associated with bonds increases, and bonds become a less attractive asset. *An increase in the riskiness of bonds causes the demand for bonds to fall and the demand curve to shift to the left.*

Conversely, an increase in the volatility of prices in another asset market, such as the stock market, would make bonds more attractive. *An increase in the riskiness of alternative assets causes the demand for bonds to rise and the demand curve to shift to the right* (as in Figure 5.2).

Liquidity

If more people started trading in the bond market, and as a result it became easier to sell bonds quickly, the increase in their liquidity would cause the quantity of bonds demanded at each interest rate to rise. *Increased liquidity of bonds results in an increased demand for bonds, and the demand curve shifts to the right* (see Figure 5.2). *Similarly, increased liquidity of alternative assets lowers the demand for bonds and shifts the demand curve to the left.* The reduction of brokerage commissions for trading common stocks that occurred when the fixed-rate commission structure was abolished in 1986 with the Big Bang reforms of the London Stock Market, for example, increased the liquidity of stocks relative to bonds, and the resulting lower demand for bonds shifted the demand curve to the left.

Shifts in the supply of bonds

Certain factors can cause the supply curve for bonds to shift, among them are:

- Expected profitability of investment opportunities
- Expected inflation
- Government budget

We will look at how the supply curve shifts when each of these factors changes (all others remaining constant). (As a study aid, Table 5.3 summarizes the effects of changes in these factors on the bond supply curve.)

Expected profitability of investment opportunities

The more profitable plant and equipment investments that a firm expects it can make, the more willing it will be to borrow to finance these investments. When the economy is growing

SUMMARY TABLE 5.3

Factors that shift the supply of bonds

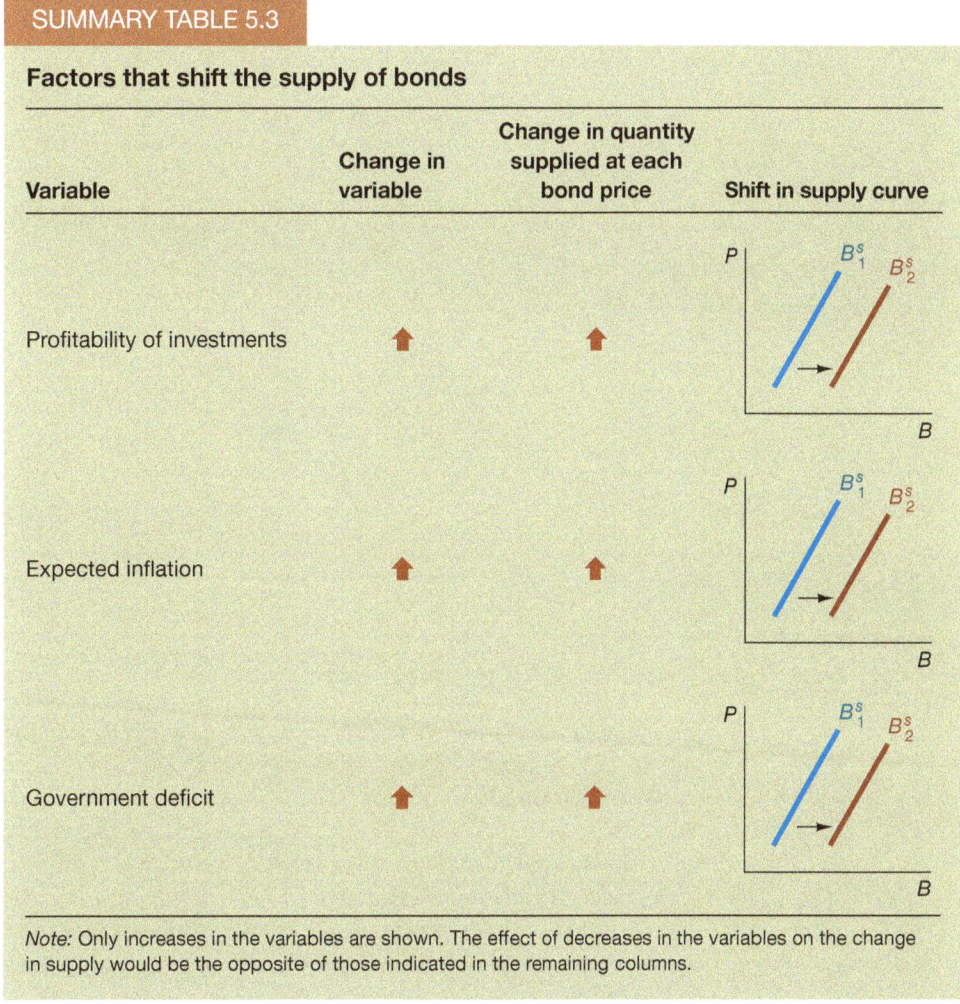

Variable	Change in variable	Change in quantity supplied at each bond price	Shift in supply curve
Profitability of investments	⬆	⬆	
Expected inflation	⬆	⬆	
Government deficit	⬆	⬆	

Note: Only increases in the variables are shown. The effect of decreases in the variables on the change in supply would be the opposite of those indicated in the remaining columns.

rapidly, as in a business cycle expansion, investment opportunities that are expected to be profitable abound, and the quantity of bonds supplied at any given bond price will increase (see Figure 5.3). *Therefore, in a business cycle expansion, the supply of bonds increases, and the supply curve shifts to the right. Likewise, in a recession, when there are far fewer expected profitable investment opportunities, the supply of bonds falls and the supply curve shifts to the left.*

Expected inflation

As we saw in Chapter 4, the real cost of borrowing is more accurately measured by the real interest rate, which equals the (nominal) interest rate minus the expected inflation rate. For a given interest rate (and bond price), when expected inflation increases, the real cost of borrowing falls; hence the quantity of bonds supplied increases at any given bond price. *An increase in expected inflation causes the supply of bonds to increase and the supply curve to shift to the right* (see Figure 5.3).

Government budget

The activities of the government can influence the supply of bonds in several ways. The UK Treasury and the finance departments of other EU governments issue bonds to finance government deficits, the gap between the government's expenditures and its revenues. When these deficits are large, the Treasury sells more bonds, and the quantity of bonds supplied at each bond price increases. *Higher government deficits increase the supply of bonds and shift the supply curve to the right* (see Figure 5.3). *On the other hand,*

FIGURE 5.3

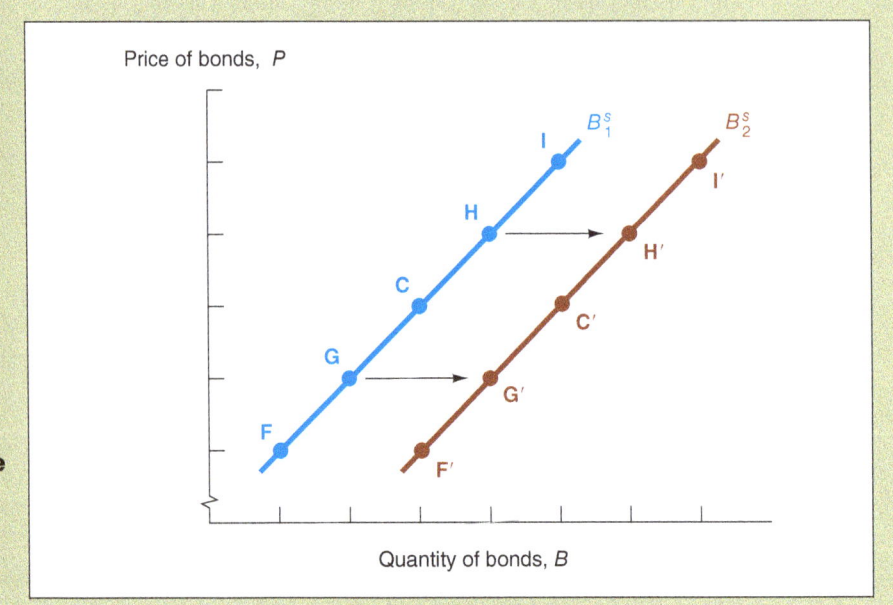

Shift in the supply curve for bonds

When the supply of bonds increases, the supply curve shifts to the right.

government surpluses, as occurred in the late 1990s and early 2000s, decrease the supply of bonds and shift the supply curve to the left.

National and local government authorities also issue bonds to finance their expenditures, and this can also affect the supply of bonds. We will see in later chapters that the conduct of monetary policy involves the purchase and sale of bonds, which in turn influences the supply of bonds.[4]

We now can use our knowledge of how supply and demand curves shift to analyse how the equilibrium interest rate can change. The best way to do this is to pursue several applications that are particularly relevant to our understanding of how monetary policy affects interest rates. In going through these applications, keep two things in mind:

1 When you examine the effect of a variable change, remember that we are assuming that all other variables are unchanged; that is, we are making use of the *ceteris paribus* assumption.

2 Remember that the interest rate is negatively related to the bond price, so when the equilibrium bond price rises, the equilibrium interest rate falls. Conversely, if the equilibrium bond price moves downward, the equilibrium interest rate rises.

APPLICATION

Changes in the interest rate due to expected inflation: the Fisher effect

We have already done most of the work to evaluate how a change in expected inflation affects the nominal interest rate, in that we have already analysed how a change in expected inflation shifts the supply and demand curves. Figure 5.4 shows the effect on the equilibrium interest rate of an increase in expected inflation.

Suppose that expected inflation is initially 5% and the initial supply and demand curves B_1^s and B_1^d intersect at point 1, where the equilibrium bond price is P_1. If expected inflation rises to 10%, the expected return on bonds relative to real assets falls for any given bond price and interest rate. As a result, the demand for bonds falls, and the demand curve shifts to the left from B_1^d to B_2^d. The rise in expected inflation also shifts the supply curve. At any given bond price and interest rate, the real cost of borrowing has declined, causing the quantity of bonds supplied to increase, and the supply curve shifts to the right, from B_1^s to B_2^s.

When the demand and supply curves shift in response to the change in expected inflation, the equilibrium moves from point 1 to point 2, the intersection of B_2^d and B_2^s. The equilibrium bond price has fallen from P_1 to P_2, and because the bond price is negatively related to

FIGURE 5.4

Response to a change in expected inflation

When expected inflation rises, the supply curve shifts from B_1^s to B_2^s, and the demand curve shifts from B_1^d to B_2^d. The equilibrium moves from point 1 to point 2, with the result that the equilibrium bond price falls from P_1 to P_2 and the equilibrium interest rate rises.

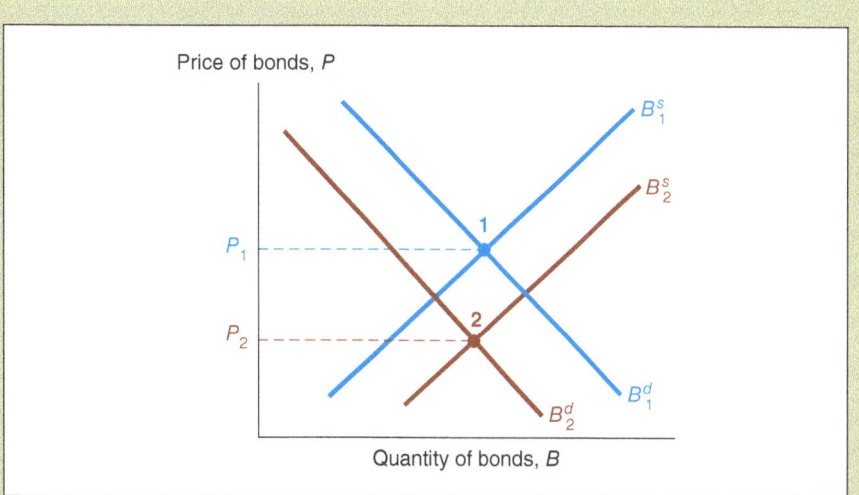

the interest rate, this means that the interest rate has risen. Note that Figure 5.4 has been drawn so that the equilibrium quantity of bonds remains the same for both point 1 and point 2. However, depending on the size of the shifts in the supply and demand curves, the equilibrium quantity of bonds could either rise or fall when expected inflation rises.

Our supply and demand analysis has led us to an important observation: *when expected inflation rises, interest rates will rise*. This result has been named the **Fisher effect**, after

FIGURE 5.5

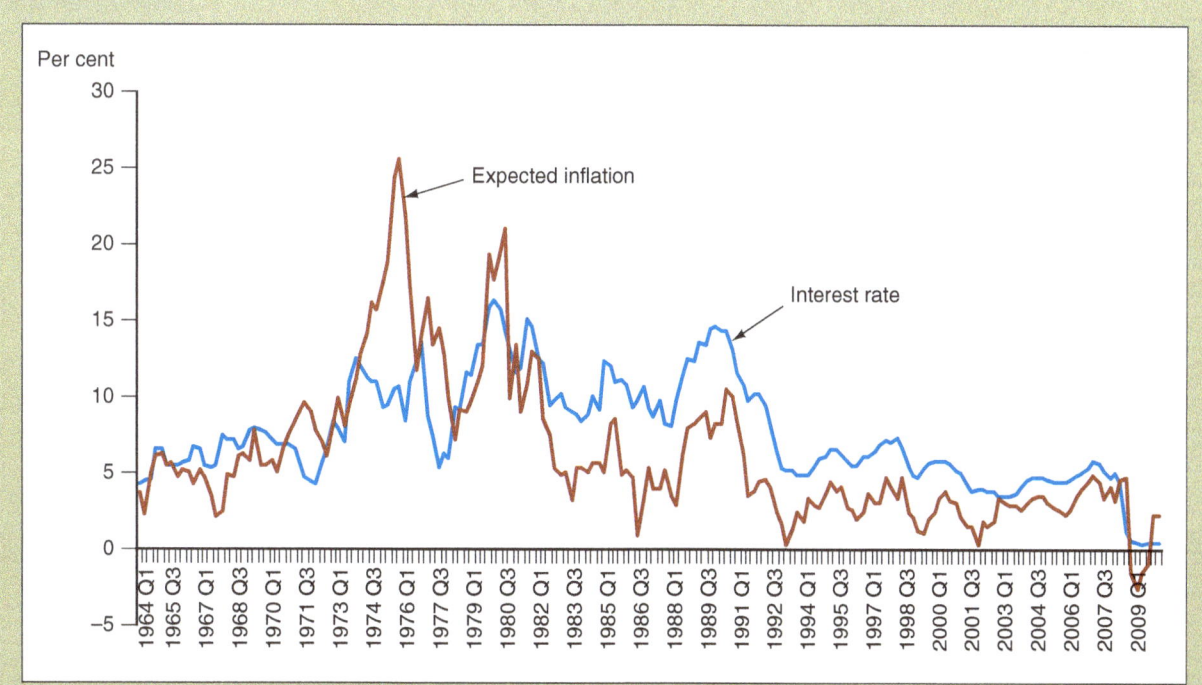

Expected inflation and interest rates (three-month UK treasury bills), 1964–2009

Source: Expected inflation calculated using procedures outlined in Frederic S. Mishkin, 'The Real Interest Rate: An Empirical Investigation', *Carnegie-Rochester Conference Series on Public Policy* 15 (1981): 151–200. These procedures involve estimating expected inflation as a function of past interest rates, inflation and time trends.

Irving Fisher, the economist who first pointed out the relationship of expected inflation to interest rates. The accuracy of this prediction is shown in Figure 5.5. Except during times when monetary policy has actively been used to lower the rate of interest, as in the period during and after the great recession of 2008–9, most of the time the interest rate on three-month Treasury bills has moved along with the expected inflation rate. Consequently, it is understandable that many economists recommend that inflation must be kept low if we want to keep nominal interest rates low. ■

APPLICATION ## Changes in the interest rate due to a business cycle expansion

Figure 5.6 analyses the effects of a business cycle expansion on interest rates. In a business cycle expansion, the amounts of goods and services being produced in the economy increase, so national income increases. When this occurs, businesses will be more willing to borrow, because they are likely to have many profitable investment opportunities for which they need financing. Hence at a given bond price, the quantity of bonds that firms want to sell (that is, the supply of bonds) will increase. This means that in a business cycle expansion, the supply curve for bonds shifts to the right (see Figure 5.6) from B_1^s to B_2^s.

Expansion in the economy will also affect the demand for bonds. As the business cycle expands, wealth is likely to increase, and the theory of asset demand tells us that the demand for bonds will rise as well. We see this in Figure 5.6, where the demand curve has shifted to the right, from B_1^d to B_2^d.

Given that both the supply and demand curves have shifted to the right, we know that the new equilibrium reached at the intersection of B_2^d and B_2^s must also move to the right. However, depending on whether the supply curve shifts more than the demand curve, or vice versa, the new equilibrium interest rate can either rise or fall.

FIGURE 5.6

Response to a business cycle expansion

In a business cycle expansion, when income and wealth are rising, the demand curve shifts rightward from B_1^d to B_2^d, and the supply curve shifts rightward from B_1^s to B_2^s. If the supply curve shifts to the right more than the demand curve, as in this figure, the equilibrium bond price moves down from P_1 to P_2, and the equilibrium interest rate rises.

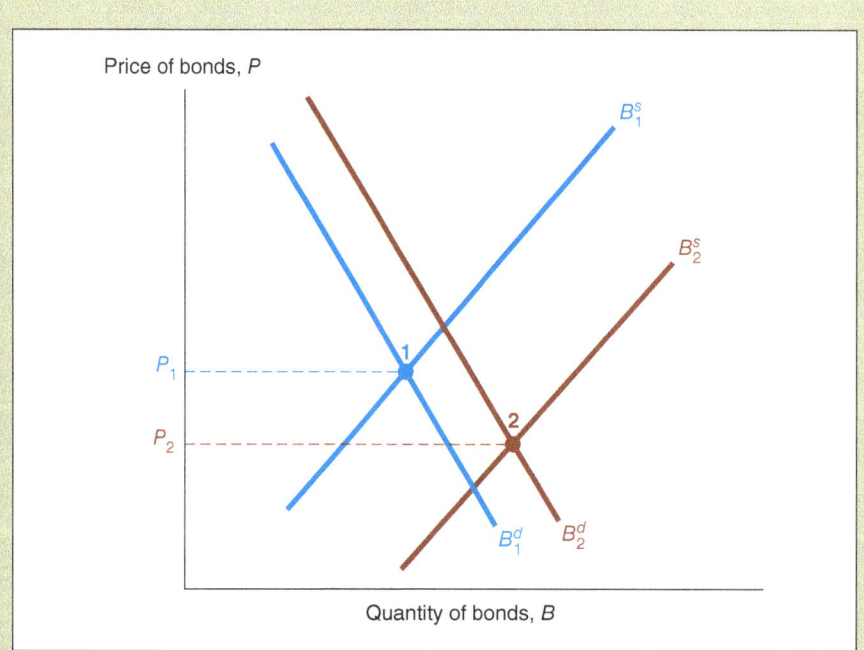

FIGURE 5.7

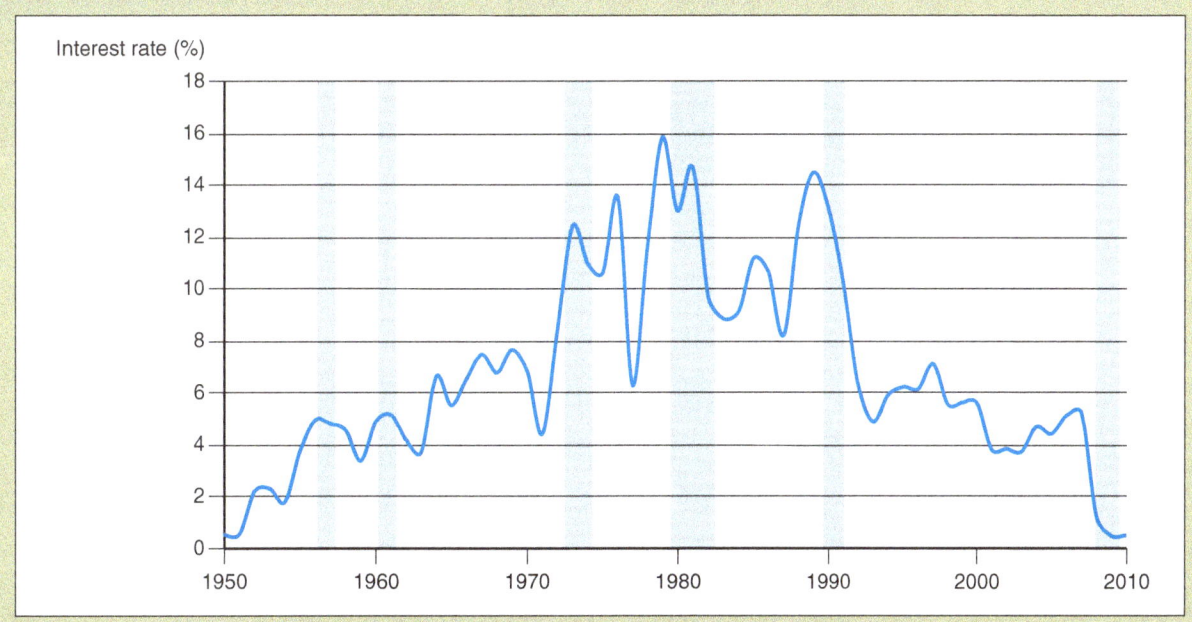

Business cycle and interest rates (three-month Treasury bills), 1950–2010

Shaded areas indicate periods of recession. The figure shows that interest rates rise during business cycle expansions and fall during contractions, which is what Figure 5.6 suggests would happen.

Source: ONS and London & Cambridge Economic Service.

The supply and demand analysis used here gives us an ambiguous answer to the question of what will happen to interest rates in a business cycle expansion. Figure 5.6 has been drawn so that the shift in the supply curve is greater than the shift in the demand curve, causing the equilibrium bond price to fall to P_2, leading to a rise in the equilibrium interest rate. The reason the figure has been drawn so that a business cycle expansion and a rise in income lead to a higher interest rate is that this is the outcome we actually see in the data. Figure 5.7 plots the movement of the interest rate on UK Treasury bills from 1950 to 2010 and indicates when the business cycle is undergoing recessions (shaded areas). As you can see, the interest rate tends to rise during business cycle expansions and fall during recessions, which is what the supply and demand diagram indicates. ■

APPLICATION   Explaining low Japanese interest rates

In the 1990s and early 2000s, Japanese interest rates became the lowest in the world. Indeed, in November 1998, an extraordinary event occurred: interest rates on Japanese six-month Treasury bills turned slightly negative (see Chapter 4). Why did Japanese interest rates drop to such low levels?

In the late 1990s and early 2000s, Japan experienced a prolonged recession, which was accompanied by deflation, a negative inflation rate. Using these facts, analysis similar to that used in the preceding application explains the low Japanese interest rates.

Negative inflation caused the demand for bonds to rise because the expected return on real assets fell, thereby raising the relative expected return on bonds and in turn causing the demand curve to shift to the right. The negative inflation also raised the real interest rate and therefore the real cost of borrowing for any given nominal rate, thereby causing the supply of bonds to contract and the supply curve to shift to the left. The outcome was then exactly the opposite of that graphed in Figure 5.4: the rightward shift of the demand curve and leftward shift of the supply curve led to a rise in the bond price and a fall in interest rates.

The business cycle contraction and the resulting lack of profitable investment opportunities in Japan also led to lower interest rates, by decreasing the supply of bonds and shifting the supply curve to the left. Although the demand curve also would shift to the left because wealth decreased during the business cycle contraction, we have seen in the preceding application that the demand curve would shift less than the supply curve. Thus, the bond price rose and interest rates fell (the opposite outcome to that in Figure 5.6).

Usually, we think that low interest rates are a good thing, because they make it cheap to borrow. But the Japanese example shows that just as there is a fallacy in the adage 'You can never be too rich or too thin' (maybe you can't be too rich, but you can certainly be too thin and do damage to your health), there is a fallacy in always thinking that lower interest rates are better. In Japan, the low and even negative interest rates were a sign that the Japanese economy was in real trouble, with falling prices and a contracting economy. Only when the Japanese economy returns to health will interest rates rise back to more normal levels. ■

APPLICATION   ## Reading the financial news

Now that we have an understanding of how supply and demand determine prices and interest rates in the bond market, we can use our analysis to understand discussions about bond prices and interest rates appearing in the financial press. The *Financial Times* reports regularly on the UK and European government bond market, an example of which is found in the 'Following the financial news' box. Let's see how the news piece can be explained using our supply and demand framework.

The column describes the potential demand for UK government bonds in the near future and discusses the possible movements in the price of bonds and, by implication, the yield for investors. Let's see how our supply and demand framework can be used to understand the news piece.

The column expresses the concern that UK gilts (bonds) may not be such a good investment because of the expectation that bond prices will fall in the coming months. Specifically, it mentions that inflationary pressure will lead to a rise in inflation expectations which will depress the demand for bonds and increase the supply as in Figure 5.4. The expected fall in the price of bonds will result in an expected rise in yields. Other factors that would see an increase in the supply of bonds is that the Bank of England is holding nearly £200 billion of bonds on its balance sheet as a result of extraordinary monetary policy measures associated with quantitative easing. These holdings will have to be unwound by the bank which will also lead to an expected increase in supply and a further depression in prices.

However, the column suggests that in terms of relative performance, UK bonds may be better than eurozone bonds where interest rates are expected to rise higher because of the sovereign debt crisis bedevilling the weaker economies. The demand for UK bonds remains strong and the latest data show that foreign investors took up £80 billion of bonds in 2010 and the demand from financial institutions and banks will remain strong. The bottom line is that while higher inflation expectations and increasing supply of bonds will depress prices and raise yields there is a strong demand for UK bonds for foreign investors and domestic financial institutions that will raise demand and offset some of the negative factors lowering demand. ■

Appeal of gilts is untarnished by their poor performance

It has been a bad week for gilts. So far this year, they are the worst performing government bond market in Western Europe.

Two-year yields this week hit a 20-month high, 10-year yields hit a nine-month high and 30-year yields hit a 10-month high.

Markets have brought forward expectations of interest rate rises, which is bad news for gilts as it suggests inflationary pressures are building up. The first quarter-point rise in rates is now expected in May, brought forward from July after strong manufacturing numbers on Tuesday. Yet Robert Stheeman, head of the UK Debt Management Office and the main person in charge of selling gilts to domestic and international investors, remains sanguine.

This week was the busiest for gilts sales since October and figures published on Tuesday by the Bank of England showed international investors were buying record amounts.

As Mr Stheeman says, the gilt market is in robust health. Gilt investors should therefore be wary about offloading their UK government bonds too soon as there is a natural demand for them at home and abroad that may restrain a sharp lurch higher in yields, even in the most bond unfriendly conditions.

There are, of course, risks.

Inflation is stubbornly high at 3.7 per cent, nearly double the Bank of England's target.

Rising commodity prices may import more inflation to the UK economy, particularly with tensions in Egypt putting pressure on the oil price. Interest rates will almost certainly rise this year, and, let's not forget, the Bank of England holds nearly £200bn in gilts, which some strategists warn it could start selling this year, propelling yields higher. These are all factors that give weight to the dire predictions that gilts could end the year as they stated – one of the worst performing government bond markets.

On a relative value basis, gilts could outperform other eurozone bond markets, where interest rates are expected to rise too.

Rallies in Greek, Irish and Portuguese bonds, dating back to early January, are based on hopes that policymakers will beef up the eurozone's bail-out fund. Many investors think the markets have travelled too far. European policymakers appear to be edging towards some kind of resolution to tackle the eurozone's woes, but question marks remain over whether they will deliver in the way markets hope.

The latest data, published by the Bank of England on Tuesday, showed international investors bought a record £80bn of gilts last year.

At the longer end of the yield curve, pension funds and life insurance companies, which need to match liabilities, will remain buyers, while commercial banks still have to purchase gilts for regulatory reasons.

Supply and demand in the market for money: the liquidity preference framework

Instead of determining the equilibrium interest rate using the supply of and demand for bonds, an alternative model developed by John Maynard Keynes, known as the **liquidity preference framework**, determines the equilibrium interest rate in terms of the supply of and demand for money. Although the two frameworks look different, the liquidity preference analysis of the market for money is closely related to the supply and demand framework of the bond market.[5]

The starting point of Keynes's analysis is his assumption that there are two main categories of assets that people use to store their wealth: money and bonds. Therefore, total wealth in the economy must equal the total quantity of bonds plus money in the economy, which equals the quantity of bonds supplied (B^s) plus the quantity of money supplied (M^s). The quantity of bonds (B^d) and money (M^d) that people want to hold and thus demand must also equal the total amount of wealth, because people cannot purchase more assets than their available resources allow. The conclusion is that the quantity of bonds and money supplied must equal the quantity of bonds and money demanded:

$$B^s + M^s = B^d + M^d \tag{5.2}$$

Collecting the bond terms on one side of the equation and the money terms on the other, this equation can be rewritten as

$$B^s - B^d = M^d - M^s \tag{5.3}$$

The rewritten equation tells us that if the market for money is in equilibrium ($M^s = M^d$), the right-hand side of Equation 5.3 equals zero, implying that $B^s = B^d$, meaning that the bond market is also in equilibrium.

Thus it is the same to think about determining the equilibrium interest rate by equating the supply and demand for bonds or by equating the supply and demand for money. In this sense, the liquidity preference framework, which analyses the market for money, is equivalent to a framework analysing supply and demand in the bond market. In practice, the approaches differ, because by assuming that there are only two kinds of assets, money and bonds, the liquidity preference approach implicitly ignores any effects on interest rates that arise from changes in the expected returns on real assets such as automobiles and houses. In most instances, however, both frameworks yield the same predictions.

The reason that we approach the determination of interest rates with both frameworks is that the bond supply and demand framework is easier to use when analysing the effects from changes in expected inflation, whereas the liquidity preference framework provides a simpler analysis of the effects from changes in income, the price level and the supply of money.

Because the definition of money that Keynes used includes currency (which earns no interest) and cheque account deposits (which in his time typically earned little or no interest), he assumed that money has a zero rate of return. Bonds, the only alternative asset to money in Keynes's framework, have an expected return equal to the interest rate i.[6] As this interest rate rises (holding everything else unchanged), the expected return on money falls relative to the expected return on bonds, and as the theory of asset demand tells us, this causes the quantity of money demanded to fall.

We can also see that the quantity of money demanded and the interest rate should be negatively related by using the concept of **opportunity cost**, the amount of interest (expected return) sacrificed by not holding the alternative asset – in this case, a bond. As the interest rate on bonds, i, rises, the opportunity cost of holding money rises; thus money is less desirable and the quantity of money demanded must fall.

Figure 5.8 shows the quantity of money demanded at a number of interest rates, with all other economic variables, such as income and the price level, held constant. At an interest rate of 25%, point A shows that the quantity of money demanded is €100 billion. If the interest rate is at the lower rate of 20%, the opportunity cost of holding money is lower, and the quantity of money demanded rises to €200 billion, as indicated by the move from point A to point B. If the interest rate is even lower, the quantity of money demanded is even higher, as is indicated by points C, D and E. The curve M^d connecting these points is the demand curve for money, and it slopes downward.

At this point in our analysis, we will assume that a central bank controls the amount of money supplied at a fixed quantity of €300 billion, so the supply curve for money M^s in the figure is a vertical line at €300 billion. The equilibrium where the quantity of money demanded equals the quantity of money supplied occurs at the intersection of the supply and demand curves at point C, where

$$M^d = M^s \tag{5.4}$$

The resulting equilibrium interest rate is at $i^* = 15\%$.

FIGURE 5.8

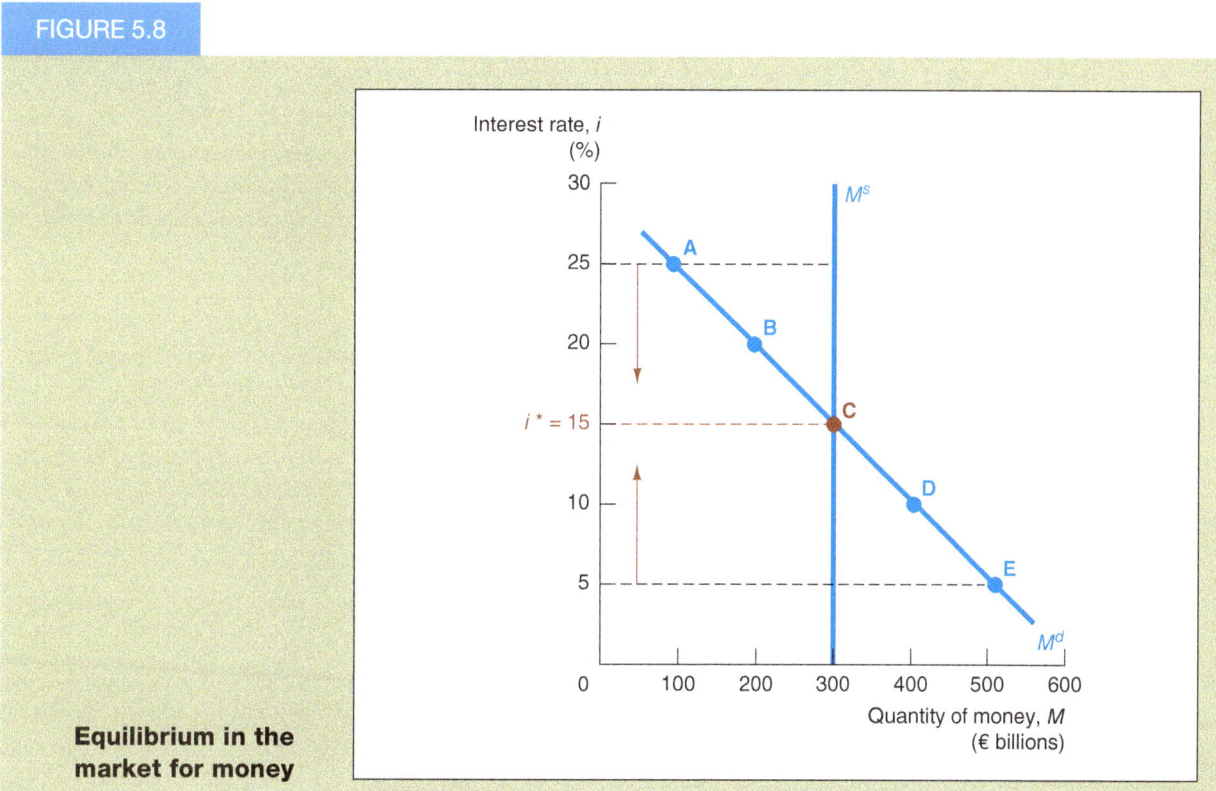

Equilibrium in the market for money

We can again see that there is a tendency to approach this equilibrium by first looking at the relationship of money demand and supply when the interest rate is above the equilibrium interest rate. When the interest rate is 25%, the quantity of money demanded at point A is €100 billion, yet the quantity of money supplied is €300 billion. The excess supply of money means that people are holding more money than they desire, so they will try to get rid of their excess money balances by trying to buy bonds. Accordingly, they will bid up the price of bonds. As the bond price rises, the interest rate will fall toward the equilibrium interest rate of 15%. This tendency is shown by the downward arrow drawn at the interest rate of 25%.

Likewise, if the interest rate is 5%, the quantity of money demanded at point E is €500 billion, but the quantity of money supplied is only €300 billion. There is now an excess demand for money because people want to hold more money than they currently have. To try to obtain more money, they will sell their only other asset – bonds – and the price will fall. As the price of bonds falls, the interest rate will rise toward the equilibrium rate of 15%. Only when the interest rate is at its equilibrium value will there be no tendency for it to move further, and the interest rate will settle to its equilibrium value.

Changes in equilibrium interest rates in the liquidity preference framework

Analysing how the equilibrium interest rate changes using the liquidity preference framework requires that we understand what causes the demand and supply curves for money to shift.

Shifts in the demand for money

In Keynes's liquidity preference analysis, two factors cause the demand curve for money to shift: income and the price level.

Income effect

In Keynes's view, there were two reasons why income would affect the demand for money. First, as an economy expands and income rises, wealth increases and people will want to hold more money as a store of value. Second, as the economy expands and income rises, people will want to carry out more transactions using money as a medium of exchange, with the result that they will also want to hold more money. The conclusion is that *a higher level of income causes the demand for money at each interest rate to increase and the demand curve to shift to the right*.

Price-level effect

Keynes took the view that people care about the amount of money they hold in real terms – that is, in terms of the goods and services that it can buy. When the price level rises, the same nominal quantity of money is no longer as valuable; it cannot be used to purchase as many real goods or services. To restore their holdings of money in real terms to its former level, people will want to hold a greater nominal quantity of money, so *a rise in the price level causes the demand for money at each interest rate to increase and the demand curve to shift to the right*.

Shifts in the supply of money

We will assume that the supply of money is completely controlled by the central bank, which in the euro area is the European Central Bank and in the UK is the Bank of England. (Actually, the process that determines the money supply is substantially more complicated, involving banks, depositors and borrowers from banks. We will study it in more detail later in the book.) For now, all we need to know is that *an increase in the money supply engineered by the central bank will shift the supply curve for money to the right*.

APPLICATION	Changes in the equilibrium interest rate due to changes in income, the price level or the money supply

To see how we can use the liquidity preference framework to analyse the movement of interest rates, we will again look at several applications that will be useful in evaluating the effect of monetary policy on interest rates. In going through these applications, remember to use the *ceteris paribus* assumption: when examining the effect of a change in one variable, hold all other variables constant. (As a study aid, Table 5.4. summarizes the shifts in the demand and supply curves for money.)

Changes in income

When income is rising during a business cycle expansion, we have seen that the demand for money will rise, shown in Figure 5.9 by the shift rightward in the demand curve from M_1^d to M_2^d. The new equilibrium is reached at point 2 at the intersection of the M_1^d curve with the money supply curve M^s. As you can see, the equilibrium interest rate rises from i_1 to i_2. The liquidity preference framework thus generates the conclusion that *when income is rising during a business cycle expansion (holding other economic variables constant), interest rates will rise*. This conclusion is unambiguous when contrasted to the conclusion reached about the effects of a business cycle expansion on interest rates using the bond supply and demand framework.

Changes in the price level

When the price level rises, the value of money in terms of what it can purchase is lower. To restore their purchasing power in real terms to its former level, people will want to hold a

SUMMARY TABLE 5.4

Factors that shift the demand for and supply of money

Variable	Change in variable	Change in money demand (M^d) or supply (M^s) at each interest rate	Change in interest rate	
Income	↑	M^d ↑	↑	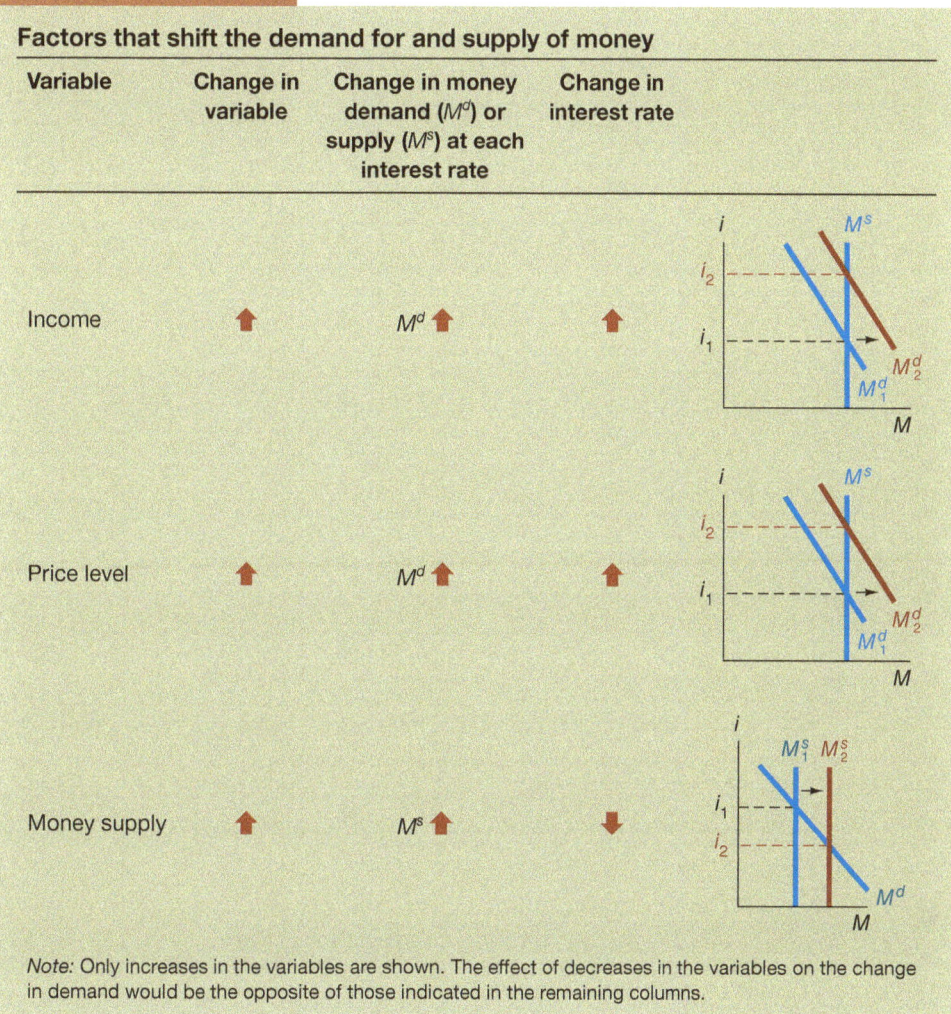
Price level	↑	M^d ↑	↑	
Money supply	↑	M^s ↑	↓	

Note: Only increases in the variables are shown. The effect of decreases in the variables on the change in demand would be the opposite of those indicated in the remaining columns.

FIGURE 5.9

Response to a change in income or the price level

In a business cycle expansion, when income is rising, or when the price level rises, the demand curve shifts from M_1^d to M_2^d. The supply curve is fixed at $M^s = \overline{M}$. The equilibrium interest rate rises from i_1 to i_2.

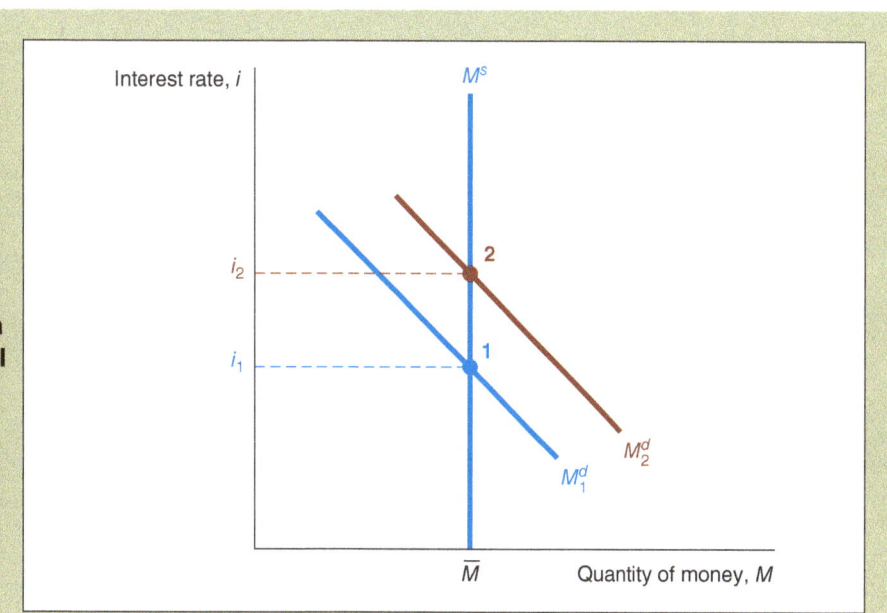

FIGURE 5.10

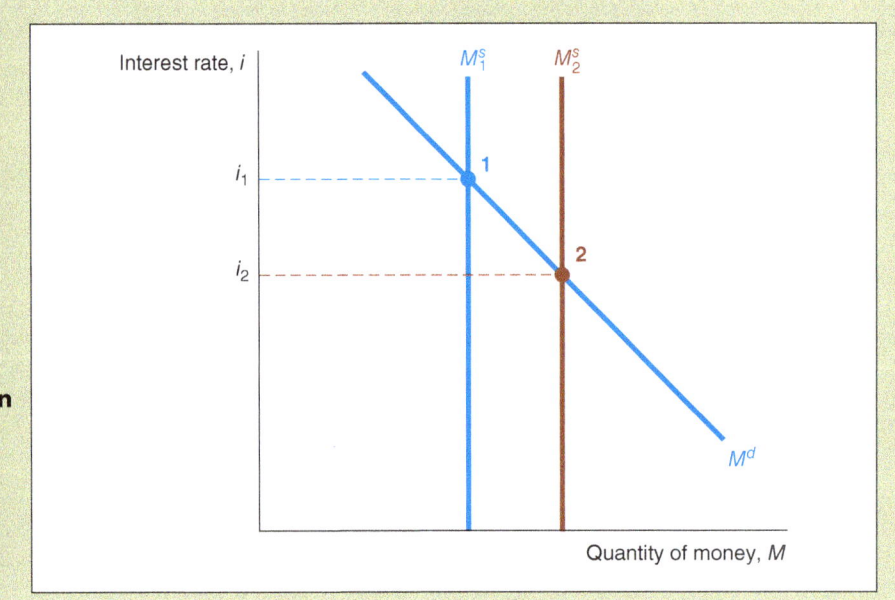

Response to a change in the money supply

When the money supply increases, the supply curve shifts from M_1^s to M_2^s and the equilibrium interest rate falls from i_1 to i_2.

greater nominal quantity of money. A higher price level shifts the demand curve for money to the right from M_1^d to M_2^d (see Figure 5.9). The equilibrium moves from point 1 to point 2, where the equilibrium interest rate has risen from i_1 to i_2, illustrating that **when the price level increases, with the supply of money and other economic variables held constant, interest rates will rise**.

Changes in the money supply

An increase in the money supply due to expansionary monetary policy by the ECB or Bank of England implies that the supply curve for money shifts to the right. As is shown in Figure 5.10 by the movement of the supply curve from M_1^s to M_2^s, the equilibrium moves from point 1 down to point 2, where the M_2^s supply curve intersects with the demand curve M^d and the equilibrium interest rate has fallen from i_1 to i_2. **When the money supply increases (everything else remaining equal), interest rates will decline**.[7] ■

Money and interest rates

The liquidity preference analysis in Figure 5.10 seems to lead to the conclusion that an increase in the money supply will lower interest rates.

But is this conclusion that money and interest rates should be negatively related correct? Might there be other important factors left out of the liquidity preference analysis in Figure 5.10 that would reverse this conclusion? We will provide answers to these questions by applying the supply and demand analysis we have used in this chapter to obtain a deeper understanding of the relationship between money and interest rates.

An important criticism of the conclusion that an increase in the money supply lowers interest rates was raised by Milton Friedman, a Nobel laureate in economics. He acknowledged that the liquidity preference analysis was correct and called the result – that an increase in the money supply (*everything else remaining equal*) lowers interest rates – the *liquidity effect*. However, he viewed the liquidity effect as merely part of the story: an increase in the money supply might not leave 'everything else equal' and will have other effects on the economy that may make interest rates rise. If these effects are substantial, it is entirely possible that when the money supply increases, interest rates may also increase.

We have already laid the groundwork to discuss these other effects because we have shown how changes in income, the price level, and expected inflation affect the equilibrium interest rate.

1 *Income effect*. Because an increasing money supply is an expansionary influence on the economy, it should raise national income and wealth. Both the liquidity preference and bond supply and demand frameworks indicate that interest rates will then rise (see Figures 5.6 and 5.9). Thus *the income effect of an increase in the money supply is a rise in interest rates in response to the higher level of income*.

2 *Price-level effect*. An increase in the money supply can also cause the overall price level in the economy to rise. The liquidity preference framework predicts that this will lead to a rise in interest rates. Thus *the price-level effect from an increase in the money supply is a rise in interest rates in response to the rise in the price level*.

3 *Expected-inflation effect*. The higher inflation rate that results from an increase in the money supply also affects interest rates by affecting the expected inflation rate. Specifically, an increase in the money supply may lead people to expect a higher price level in the future – and hence the expected inflation rate will be higher. The bond supply and demand framework has shown us that this increase in expected inflation will lead to a higher level of interest rates. Therefore, *the expected-inflation effect of an increase in the money supply is a rise in interest rates in response to the rise in the expected inflation rate*.

At first glance it might appear that the price-level effect and the expected-inflation effect are the same thing. They both indicate that increases in the price level induced by an increase in the money supply will raise interest rates. However, there is a subtle difference between the two, and this is why they are discussed as two separate effects.

Suppose that there is a one-time increase in the money supply today that leads to a rise in prices to a permanently higher level by next year. As the price level rises over the course of this year, the interest rate will rise via the price-level effect. Only at the end of the year, when the price level has risen to its peak, will the price-level effect be at a maximum.

The rising price level will also raise interest rates via the expected-inflation effect, because people will expect that inflation will be higher over the course of the year. However, when the price level stops rising next year, inflation and the expected inflation rate will return to zero. Any rise in interest rates as a result of the earlier rise in expected inflation will then be reversed. We thus see that in contrast to the price-level effect, which reaches its greatest impact next year, the expected-inflation effect will have its smallest impact (zero impact) next year. The basic difference between the two effects, then, is that the price-level effect remains even after prices have stopped rising, whereas the expected-inflation effect disappears.

An important point is that the expected-inflation effect will persist only as long as the price level continues to rise. As we will see in our discussion of monetary theory in subsequent chapters, a one-time increase in the money supply will not produce a continually rising price level; only a higher rate of money supply growth will. Thus a higher rate of money supply growth is needed if the expected-inflation effect is to persist.

Does a higher rate of growth of the money supply lower interest rates?

We can now put together all the effects we have discussed to help us decide whether the facts can be explained by the theory. Of all the effects, only the liquidity effect indicates that a higher rate of money growth will cause a decline in interest rates. In contrast, the income, price-level and expected-inflation effects indicate that interest rates will rise when money growth is higher. Which of these effects is largest, and how quickly does it take effect? The answers are critical in determining whether interest rates will rise or fall when money supply growth is increased.

Generally, the liquidity effect from the greater money growth takes effect immediately, because the rising money supply leads to an immediate decline in the equilibrium interest rate. The income and price-level effects take time to work, because it takes time for the increasing money supply to raise the price level and income, which in turn raise interest rates. The expected-inflation effect, which also raises interest rates, can be slow or fast, depending on whether people adjust their expectations of inflation slowly or quickly when the money growth rate is increased.

Three possibilities are outlined in Figure 5.11; each shows how interest rates respond over time to an increased rate of money supply growth starting at time T. Panel (a) shows a case in which the liquidity effect dominates the other effects so that the interest rate falls from i_1 at time T to a final level of i_2. The liquidity effect operates quickly to lower the interest rate, but as time goes by, the other effects start to reverse some of the decline. Because the liquidity effect is larger than the others, however, the interest rate never rises back to its initial level.

Panel (b) has a smaller liquidity effect than the other effects, with the expected-inflation effect operating slowly because expectations of inflation are slow to adjust upward. Initially, the liquidity effect drives down the interest rate. Then the income, price-level and expected-inflation effects begin to raise it. Because these effects are dominant, the interest rate eventually rises above its initial level to i_2. In the short run, lower interest rates result from increased money growth, but eventually they end up climbing above the initial level.

Panel (c) has the expected-inflation effect dominating as well as operating rapidly because people quickly raise their expectations of inflation when the rate of money growth increases. The expected-inflation effect begins immediately to overpower the liquidity effect, and the interest rate immediately starts to climb. Over time, as the income and price-level effects start to take hold, the interest rate rises even higher, and the eventual outcome is an interest rate that is substantially higher than the initial interest rate. The result shows clearly that increasing money supply growth is not the answer to reducing interest rates; rather, money growth should be reduced to lower interest rates!

An important issue for economic policymakers is which of these three scenarios is closest to reality. If a decline in interest rates is desired, then an increase in money supply growth is called for when the liquidity effect dominates the other effects, as in panel (a). A decrease in money growth is appropriate when the other effects dominate the liquidity effect and expectations of inflation adjust rapidly, as in panel (c). If the other effects dominate the liquidity effect but expectations of inflation adjust only slowly, as in panel (b), then whether you want to increase or decrease money growth depends on whether you care more about what happens in the short run or the long run.

Which scenario is supported by the evidence? The relationship of interest rates and money growth from 1964 to 2010 in the UK is plotted in Figure 5.12. You can see that in the period 1969–72 interest rates fell and the rate of growth of money soared to over 20% a year in 1973. When interest rates rose between 1972 and 1974 the rate of growth of money fell back soon after. During this period the liquidity effect dominated the price level, income and expected-inflation effects. Once again, when the rate of interest fell to a low in 1977, the rate of money growth increased rapidly in 1978. Higher interest rates in 1980 led to a fall in money growth in 1981 and 1982. In all these instances the liquidity effect dominated.

Interest rates fell in 1985–6 and money growth rose in the same period but so did inflation, and interest rates were on the way up from 1987 but this time money growth did not fall. Not until interest rates reached a peak in 1989 did money growth begun to fall. From 1989 to 1992 both interest rates and money growth fell, as did inflation. In this instance the expected-inflation effect dominated as the fall in money growth led to a fall in inflation expectations.

Figure 5.12 does not really tell us which one of the three scenarios, panel (a), (b) or (c) of Figure 5.11, is most accurate. It depends critically on how fast people's expectations about inflation adjust. However, recent research using more sophisticated methods than just looking at a graph like Figure 5.12 does indicate that increased money growth temporarily lowers short-term interest rates.[8]

FIGURE 5.11

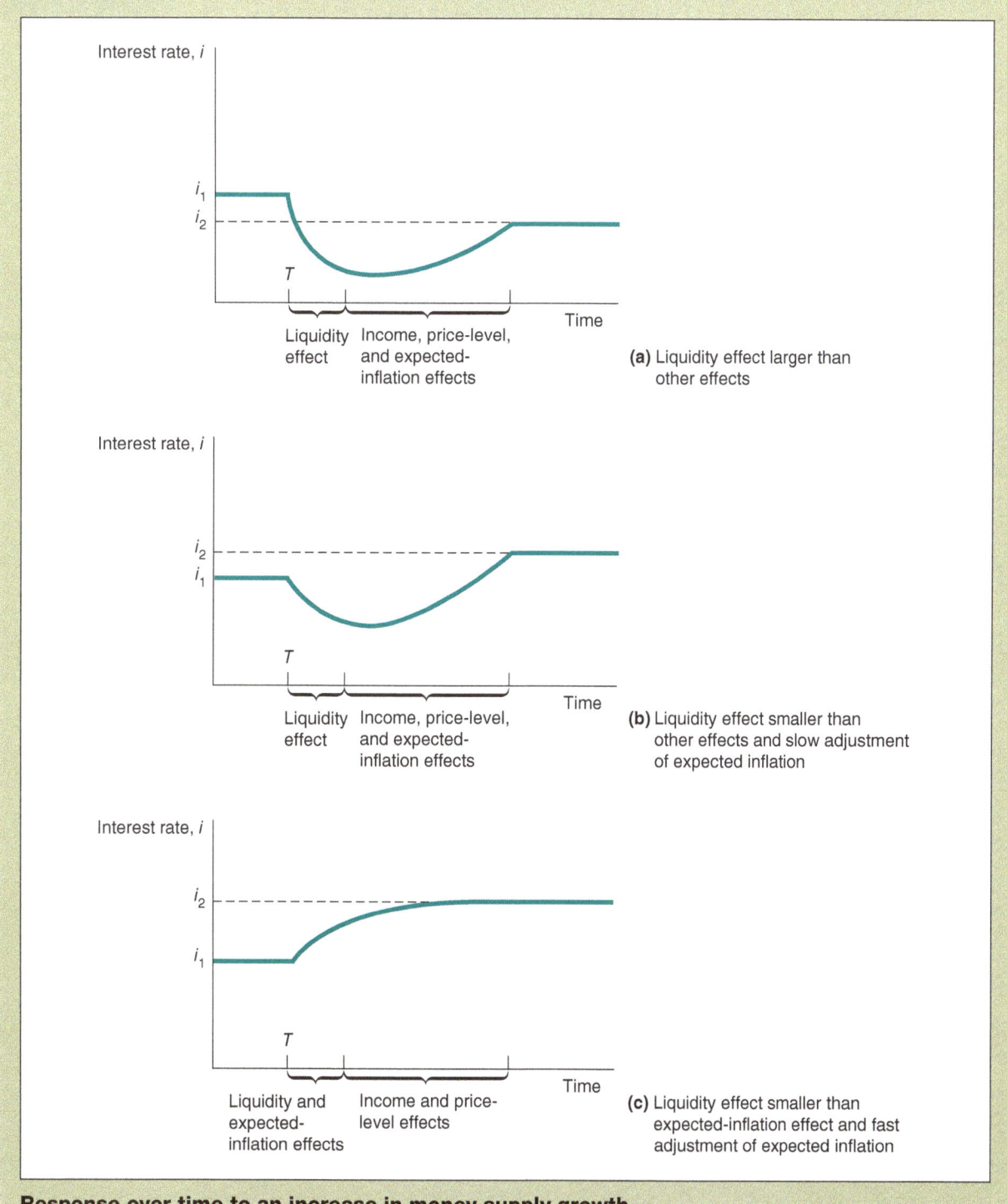

Response over time to an increase in money supply growth

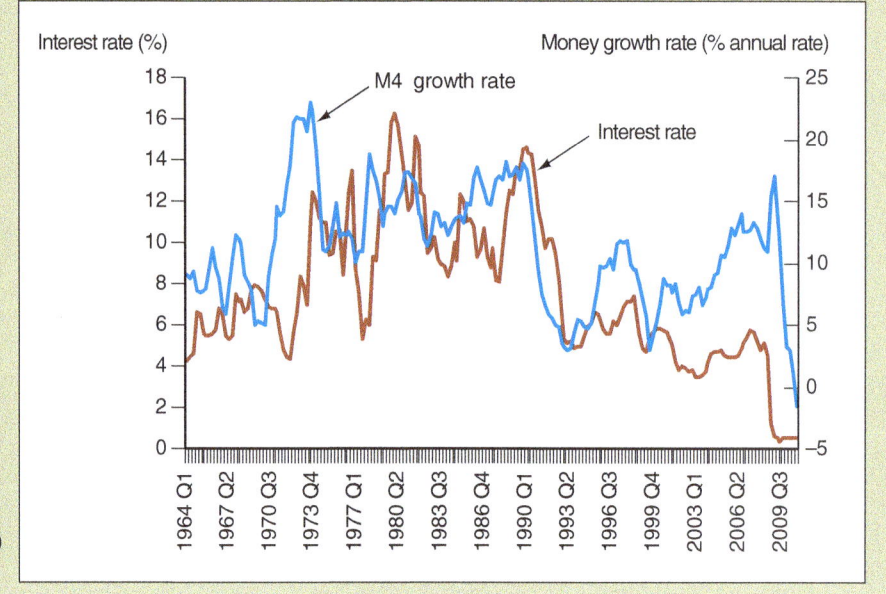

FIGURE 5.12

Money growth (M4, annual rate) and interest rates (three-month Treasury bills), 1964–2010

Sources: ONS online.

Summary

1 The theory of asset demand tells us that the quantity demanded of an asset is (a) positively related to wealth, (b) positively related to the expected return on the asset relative to alternative assets, (c) negatively related to the riskiness of the asset relative to alternative assets, and (d) positively related to the liquidity of the asset relative to alternative assets.

2 The supply and demand analysis for bonds provides one theory of how interest rates are determined. It predicts that interest rates will change when there is a change in demand because of changes in income (or wealth), expected returns, risk or liquidity, or when there is a change in supply because of changes in the attractiveness of investment opportunities, the real cost of borrowing or the government budget.

3 An alternative theory of how interest rates are determined is provided by the liquidity preference framework, which analyses the supply of and demand for money. It shows that interest rates will change when there is a change in the demand for money because of changes in income or the price level or when there is a change in the supply of money.

4 There are four possible effects of an increase in the money supply on interest rates: the liquidity effect, the income effect, the price-level effect and the expected-inflation effect. The liquidity effect indicates that a rise in money supply growth will lead to a decline in interest rates; the other effects work in the opposite direction. The evidence seems to indicate that the income, price-level and expected-inflation effects dominate the liquidity effect such that an increase in money supply growth leads to higher – rather than lower – interest rates.

Key Terms

asset market approach p. 85	Fisher effect p. 91	risk p. 81
demand curve p. 82	liquidity p. 81	supply curve p. 84
excess demand p. 84	liquidity preference framework p. 95	theory of asset demand p. 82
excess supply p. 84	market equilibrium p. 84	
expected return p. 81	opportunity cost p. 96	

QUESTIONS AND PROBLEMS

All questions and problems are available in MyEconLab at **www.myeconlab.com/mishkin**.

1 Explain why you would be more or less willing to buy a share of in Tesco plc in the following situations:

(a) Your wealth falls.
(b) You expect the stock to appreciate in value.
(c) The bond market becomes more liquid.
(d) You expect gold to appreciate in value.
(e) Prices in the bond market become more volatile.

2 Explain why you would be more or less willing to buy a house under the following circumstances:

(a) You just inherited €100,000.
(b) Real estate commissions fall from 6% of the sales price to 5% of the sales price.
(c) You expect Aviva shares to double in value next year.
(d) Prices in the stock market become more volatile.
(e) You expect housing prices to fall.

3 Explain why you would be more or less willing to buy gold under the following circumstances:

(a) Gold again becomes acceptable as a medium of exchange.
(b) Prices in the gold market become more volatile.
(c) You expect inflation to rise, and gold prices tend to move with the aggregate price level.
(d) You expect interest rates to rise.

4 Explain why you would be more or less willing to buy long-term Axa bonds under the following circumstances:

(a) Trading in these bonds increases, making them easier to sell.
(b) You expect a bear market in stocks (stock prices are expected to decline).
(c) Brokerage commissions on stocks fall.
(d) You expect interest rates to rise.
(e) Brokerage commissions on bonds fall.

5 What would happen to the demand for Rembrandt paintings if the stock market undergoes a boom? Why?

Answer each question by drawing the appropriate supply and demand diagrams.

6 An important way in which the relevant monetary authority (ECB or Bank of England) decreases the money supply is by selling bonds to the public. Using a supply and demand analysis for bonds, show what effect this action has on interest rates. Is your answer consistent with what you would expect to find with the liquidity preference framework?

7 Using both the liquidity preference framework and the supply and demand for bonds framework, show why

interest rates are procyclical (rising when the economy is expanding and falling during recessions).

8 Why should a rise in the price level (but not in expected inflation) cause interest rates to rise when the nominal money supply is fixed?

9 Go to the *Financial Times* website **www.ft.com** and click on 'Capital Markets' in markets. Examine the statements made on the online articles, and draw the appropriate supply and demand diagrams that support these statements.

10 What effect will a sudden increase in the volatility of property prices have on interest rates?

11 How might a sudden increase in people's expectations of future real estate prices affect interest rates?

12 Explain what effect a large government deficit might have on interest rates.

13 Using both the supply and demand for bonds and liquidity preference frameworks, show what the effect is on interest rates when the riskiness of bonds rises. Are the results the same in the two frameworks?

14 If the price level falls next year, remaining fixed thereafter, and the money supply is fixed, what is likely to happen to interest rates over the next two years? (*Hint:* Take account of both the price-level effect and the expected-inflation effect.)

15 Will there be an effect on interest rates if brokerage commissions on stocks fall? Explain your answer.

Using economic analysis to predict the future

16 Suppose the Governor of the ECB (currently Mario Draghi), announces that interest rates will rise sharply next year, and the market believes him. What will happen to today's interest rate on government bonds in the euro economies?

17 Predict what will happen to interest rates if the public suddenly expects a large increase in stock prices.

18 Predict what will happen to interest rates if prices in the bond market become more volatile.

19 If the next governor of the ECB has a reputation for advocating an even slower rate of money growth than the current governor, what will happen to interest rates? Discuss the possible resulting situations.

WEB EXERCISES

1 One of the largest single influences on the level of interest rates is inflation. There are a number of sites that report inflation over time. Go to **ftp://ftp.bls.gov /pub/special.requests/cpi/cpiai.txt** and review the data available. Note that the last columns report various averages. Move these data into a spreadsheet using the method discussed in the Web exploration at the end of Chapter 1. What has the average rate of inflation been in the US since 1950, 1960, 1970, 1980 and 1990? Which year had the lowest level of inflation? Which year had the highest level of inflation?

2 Increasing prices erode the purchasing power of the currency. It is interesting to compute what goods would have cost at some point in the past after adjusting for inflation. Go to **http://sdw.ecb.europa.eu /browseSelection.do?DATASET=0&sfl1=3&sfl2=4&REF _AREA=160&sfl3=4&ICP_ITEM=&sfl4=4&node=2120778**. What would a car that cost €22,000 today have cost ten years ago?

3 One of the points made in this chapter is that inflation erodes investment returns. Go to **www.moneychimp.com /articles/econ/inflation_calculator.htm** and review how changes in inflation alter your real return. What happens to the difference between the adjusted value of an investment compared to its inflation-adjusted value as

(a) Inflation increases?
(b) The investment horizon lengthens?
(c) Expected returns increase?

Notes

1 If you are interested in finding out more information on how to calculate expected returns, as well as standard deviations of returns that measure risk, you can look at an appendix to this chapter describing models of asset pricing that is on this book's website at **www.myeconlab.com/mishkin**. This appendix also describes how diversification lowers the overall risk of a portfolio and has a discussion of systematic risk and basic asset pricing models such as the capital asset pricing model and arbitrage pricing theory.

2 Although our analysis indicates that the demand curve is downward-sloping, it does not imply that the curve is a straight line. For ease of exposition, however, we will draw demand curves and supply curves as straight lines.

3 The asset market approach developed in the text is useful in understanding not only how interest rates behave but also how any asset price is determined. A second appendix to this chapter, which is on this book's website at **www .myeconlab.com/mishkin**, shows how the asset market approach can be applied to understanding the behaviour of commodity markets; in particular, the gold market. The analysis of the bond market that we have developed here has another interpretation using a different terminology and framework involving the supply and demand for loanable funds. This loanable funds framework is discussed in a third appendix to this chapter, which is also on the book's website.

4 In the euro area, buying bonds is an unconventional monetary policy measure that is highly controversial.

5 Note that the term *market for money* refers to the market for the medium of exchange, money. This market differs from the *money market* referred to by finance practitioners, which, as discussed in Chapter 2, is the financial market in which short-term debt instruments are traded.

6 Keynes did not actually assume that the expected returns on bonds equalled the interest rate but rather argued that they were closely related. This distinction makes no appreciable difference in our analysis.

7 This same result can be generated using the bond supply and demand framework. As we will see in Chapter 14, the primary way that a central bank produces an increase in the money supply is by buying bonds and thereby decreasing the supply of bonds to the public. The resulting shift to the left of the supply curve for bonds will lead to an increase in the equilibrium price of bonds and a decline in the equilibrium interest rate.

8 See Lawrence J. Christiano and Martin Eichenbaum, 'Identification and the liquidity effect of a monetary policy shock', in *Business Cycles, Growth, and Political Economy*, ed. Alex Cukierman, Zvi Hercowitz and Leonardo Leiderman (Cambridge, MA: MIT Press, 1992), pp. 335–70; Eric M. Leeper and David B. Gordon, 'In search of the liquidity effect', *Journal of Monetary Economics* 29 (1992): 341–70; Steven Strongin, 'The identification of monetary policy disturbances: explaining the liquidity puzzle', *Journal of Monetary Economics* 35 (1995): 463–97; Adrian Pagan and John C. Robertson, 'Resolving the liquidity effect', *Federal Reserve Bank of St. Louis Review* 77 (May–June 1995): 33–54; and Ben S. Bernanke and Ilian Mihov, 'Measuring monetary policy', *Quarterly Journal of Economics* 113, 3 (August 1998): 869–902.

Useful websites

http://www.ecb.int/home/html/index.en.html Contains inflation data for all EU economies and money supply data for the eurozone.

www.bankofengland.co.uk/Pages/home.aspx Contains money and credit market data, interest rates and inflation for the UK

http://sdw.ecb.europa.eu/browse.do?node=2120778 ECB's Statistical Data Warehouse: Consumer Prices data.

ftp://ftp.bls.gov/pub/special.requests/cpi/cpiai.txt Contains historical information about inflation in the US.

www.federalreserve.gov/releases/H6/Current The Federal Reserve reports money supply data for the US.

MyEconLab can help you get a better grade

MyEconLab®

If your exam were tomorrow, would you be ready? For each chapter, MyEconLab Practice Test and Study Plans pinpoint which sections you have mastered and which ones you need to study. That way, you are more efficient with your study time, and you are better prepared for your exams.

To see how it works, turn to page 19 and here go to: **www.myeconlab.com/mishkin**

CHAPTER 6

The risk and term structure of interest rates

PREVIEW

In our supply and demand analysis of interest-rate behaviour in Chapter 5, we examined the determination of just one interest rate. Yet we saw earlier that there are enormous numbers of bonds on which the interest rates can and do differ. In this chapter, we complete the interest-rate picture by examining the relationship of the various interest rates to one another. Understanding why they differ from bond to bond can help businesses, banks, insurance companies and private investors decide which bonds to purchase as investments and which ones to sell.

We first look at why bonds with the same term to maturity have different interest rates. The relationship among these interest rates is called the **risk structure of interest rates**, although risk, liquidity and income tax rules all play a role in determining the risk structure. A bond's term to maturity also affects its interest rate, and the relationship among interest rates on bonds with different terms to maturity is called the **term structure of interest rates**. In this chapter, we examine the sources and causes of fluctuations in interest rates relative to one another and look at a number of theories that explain these fluctuations.

Risk structure of interest rates

Figure 6.1a shows the yields to maturity for two categories of short-term bonds from 1975 to 2011. The short-term bond rates are the rate of interest on UK Treasury bills and the average rate of interest on commercial bills (corporate bonds) of the same maturity as Treasury bills and also of high investment grade. The first thing to notice is how closely the rates of interest move together. This is because they are the interest rates on similar maturities, in this case three months and in the same currency. But there are differences, even if small. A better feel for these differences can be seen by examining the spread (or difference) between the commercial bill yield and the Treasury bill yield. These differences are plotted in Figure 6.1b. What we can see from the spreads is that most of the time they are only a few basis points difference but on some occasions they have been quite large. Huge differences opened up in 1980 and again in 2008. These two years were periods of deep recession in the UK.

Figure 6.1a shows us two important features of interest-rate behaviour for bonds. First, interest rates on different categories of bonds differ from one another in any given year, and second, the spread (or difference) between the interest rates varies over time. The interest rates on corporate bonds, for example, are usually higher than those on UK government (Treasury) bonds. Which factors can explain these phenomena?

FIGURE 6.1a

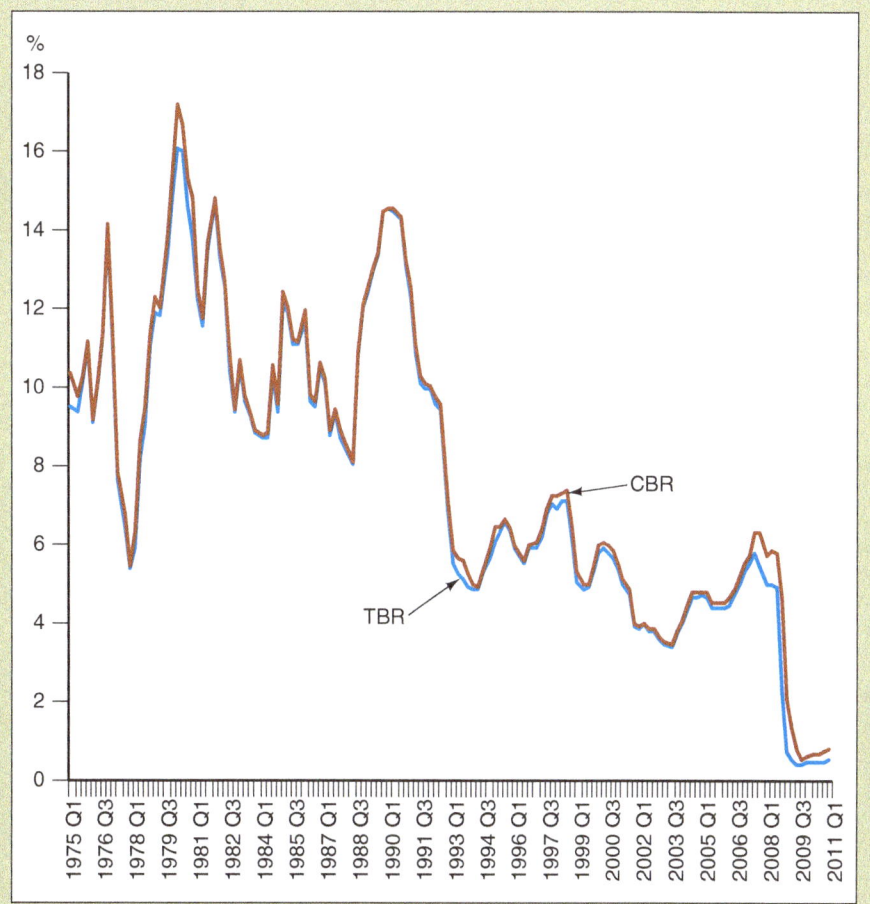

Treasury bill rate (TBR) and commercial bill rate (CBR), 1975–2011

FIGURE 6.1b

Spread between short–term commercial bill rate and UK Treasury bill rate, 1975–2011

Source: www.bankofengland.co.uk/boeapps/iadb/Index.asp?

The data represented are sourced from http://www.bankofengland.co.uk/. Please be advised that data pre-2005 in Tables 6.1a and 6.1b are sourced from series IUQAAJNB of the Interactive Database. Data post 2005 are sourced from series IUQAAJND of the Interactive Database and also uses the Quarterly average of commercial paper rates: 3 month sterling as a representative rate and are sourced from series IUQAL3ESE of the Interactive Database.

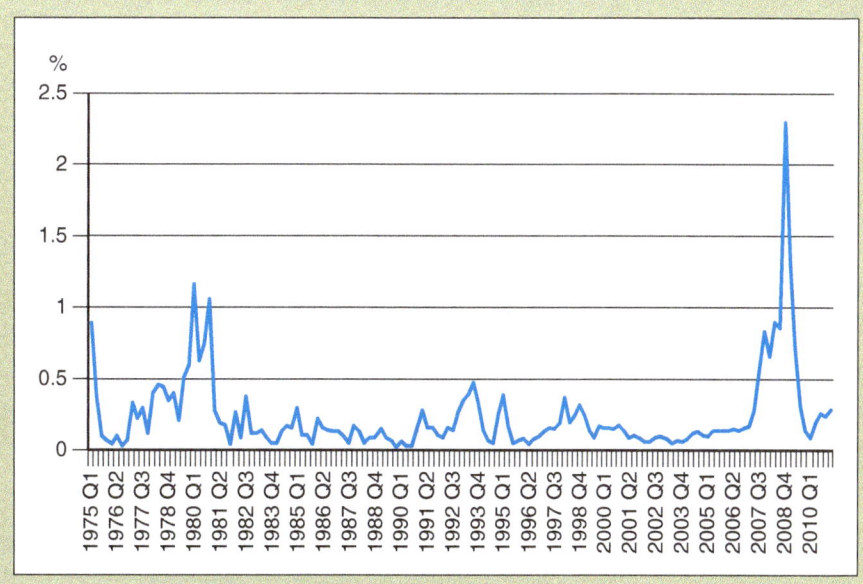

Default risk

One attribute of a bond that influences its interest rate is its risk of **default**, which occurs when the issuer of the bond is unable or unwilling to make interest payments when promised or pay off the face value when the bond matures. A corporation suffering big losses, such as the oil and gas exploration company BP, might be more likely to suspend interest payments on its bonds. Following the Gulf of Mexico oil disaster in 2010, even BP bonds that would have been considered almost equivalent to UK government bonds were downgraded. The default risk on its bonds would therefore be quite high. By contrast, UK Treasury bonds have usually been considered to have no default risk because the UK government can always increase taxes to pay off its obligations. Bonds like these with no default risk are called **default-free bonds**. The spread between the interest rates on bonds with default risk and default-free bonds, both of the same maturity, called the **risk premium**, indicates how much additional interest people must earn to be willing to hold that risky bond. This spread is shown as the difference between the short-term corporate bond rate and the short-term Treasury bill rate in Figure 6.1b. It can be seen from Figure 6.1b that throughout most of this period the spread had been small (roughly 24 basis points – or 0.24%). But there are periods when the gap has been sizeable and these periods coincide with major recessions.

Our supply and demand analysis of the bond market in Chapter 5 can be used to explain why a bond with default risk always has a positive risk premium and why the higher the default risk is, the larger the risk premium will be.

To examine the effect of default risk on interest rates, let us look at the supply and demand diagrams for the default-free bond and corporate bond markets in Figure 6.2. To make the diagrams somewhat easier to read, let's assume that initially corporate bonds have the same default risk as UK Treasury bonds. In this case, these two bonds have the same attributes (identical risk and maturity); their equilibrium prices and interest rates will initially be equal ($P_1^c = P_1^T$ and $i_1^c = i_1^T$), and the risk premium on corporate bonds ($i_1^c - i_1^T$) will be zero.

If the possibility of a default increases because a corporation begins to suffer large losses, the default risk on corporate bonds will increase, and the expected return on these bonds will decrease. In addition, the corporate bond's return will be more uncertain. The theory of asset demand predicts that because the expected return on the corporate bond falls relative to the expected return on the default-free Treasury bond while its relative riskiness rises, the corporate bond is less desirable (holding everything else equal), and demand for it will fall. Another way of thinking about this is that if you were an investor, you would want to hold (demand) a smaller amount of corporate bonds. The demand curve for corporate bonds in panel (a) of Figure 6.2 then shifts to the left, from to D_1^c to D_2^c.

At the same time, the expected return on default-free Treasury bonds increases relative to the expected return on corporate bonds, while their relative riskiness declines. The Treasury bonds thus become more desirable, and demand rises, as shown in panel (b) by the rightward shift in the demand curve for these bonds from D_1^T to D_2^T.

As we can see in Figure 6.2, the equilibrium price for corporate bonds falls from P_1^c to P_2^c, and since the bond price is negatively related to the interest rate, the equilibrium interest rate on corporate bonds rises to i_2^c. At the same time, however, the equilibrium price for the Treasury bonds rises from P_1^t to P_2^T and the equilibrium interest rate falls to i_2^T. The spread between the interest rates on corporate and default-free bonds – that is, the risk premium on corporate bonds – has risen from zero to $i_2^c - i_2^T$. We can now conclude that *a bond with default risk will always have a positive risk premium, and an increase in its default risk will raise the risk premium*.

Because default risk is so important to the size of the risk premium, purchasers of bonds need to know whether a corporation is likely to default on its bonds. This information is

FIGURE 6.2

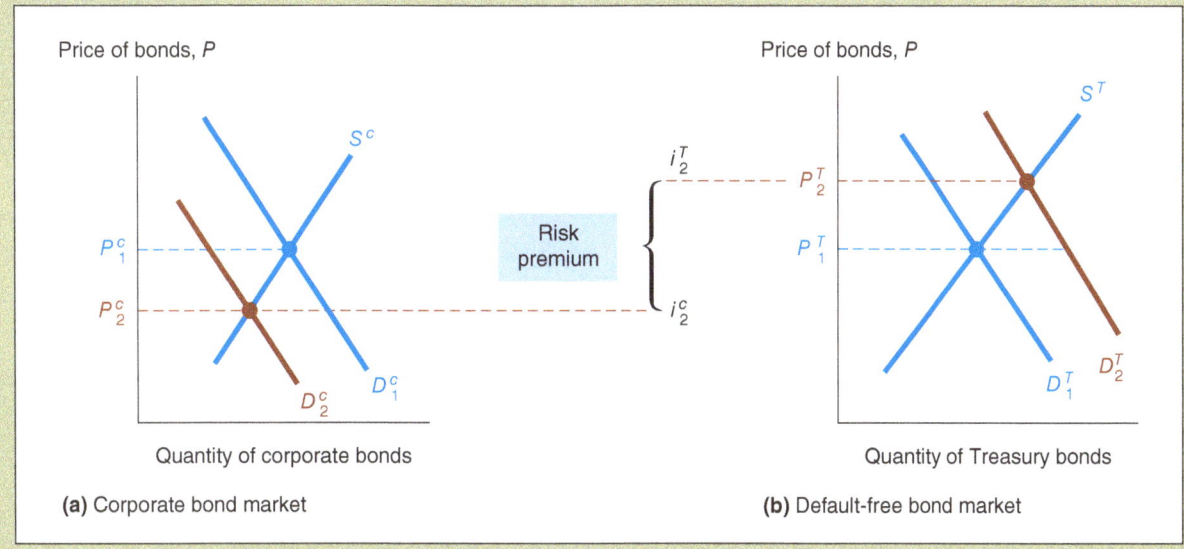

(a) Corporate bond market

(b) Default-free bond market

Response to an Increase in default risk on corporate bonds

Initially P_1^c-P_1^T and the risk premium is zero. An increase in default risk on corporate bonds shifts the demand curve from D_1^c to D_2^c. Simultaneously, it shifts the demand curve for Treasury bonds from to D_1^T to D_2^T. The equilibrium price for corporate bonds falls from P_1^c to P_2^c, and the equilibrium interest rate on corporate bonds rises to i_2^c. In the Treasury market, the equilibrium bond price rises from P_1^T to P_2^T, and the equilibrium interest rate falls to i_2^T. The brace indicates the difference between i_2^c and i_2^T, the risk premium on corporate bonds. (Note that because P_2^c is lower than P_2^T, i_2^c is greater than i_2^T.)

provided by **credit-rating agencies**, investment advisory firms that rate the quality of corporate and municipal bonds in terms of the probability of default. Table 6.1 provides the ratings and their description for the three largest credit-rating agencies, Moody's Investor Service, Standard & Poor's Corporation and Fitch Ratings. Bonds with relatively low risk of default are called *investment-grade* securities and have a rating of Baa (or BBB) and above. Bonds with ratings below Baa (or BBB) have higher default risk and have been aptly dubbed speculative-grade or **junk bonds**. Because these bonds always have higher interest rates than investment-grade securities, they are also referred to as high-yield bonds.

Next let's look at Figure 6.1b at the beginning of the chapter and see if we can explain the relationship between interest rates on corporate and UK Treasury bonds. Corporate bonds always have higher interest rates than UK Treasury bonds because they always have some risk of default, whereas UK Treasury bonds do not. Even AA-rated corporate bonds have a greater default risk than the higher-rated AAA bonds, their risk premium is greater. Similarly the BBB+ rate rated bonds always exceeds the AAA rate. We can use the same analysis to explain the huge jump in the risk premium on corporate bond rates during the years 2008–9. The steep recession in the UK following the global financial crisis led to the expectation of a high rate of business failures and defaults. As we would expect, these factors led to a substantial increase in the default risk for corporate bonds issued by vulnerable corporations, and the risk premium reached unprecedentedly high levels.

TABLE 6.1

Bond ratings by Moody's, Standard & Poor's and Fitch

Rating			
Moody's	S&P	Fitch	Definitions
Aaa	AAA	AAA	Prime maximum safety
Aa1	AA+	AA+	High grade high quality
Aa2	AA	AA	
Aa3	AA−	AA−	
A1	A+	A+	Upper medium grade
A2	A	A	
A3	A−	A−	
Baa1	BBB+	BBB+	Lower medium grade
Baa2	BBB	BBB	
Baa3	BBB−	BBB−	
Ba1	BB+	BB+	Non-investment grade
Ba2	BB	BB	Speculative
Ba3	BB−	BB−	
B1	B+	B+	Highly speculative
B2	B	B	
B3	B−	B−	
Caa1	CCC+	CCC	Substantial risk
Caa2	CCC	—	In poor standing
Caa3	CCC−	—	
Ca	—	—	Extremely speculative
C	—	—	May be in default
—	—	DDD	Default
—	—	DD	—
—	D	D	

APPLICATION   The subprime collapse and the Baa–Treasury spread

Starting in August 2007, the collapse of the subprime mortgage market led to large losses in financial institutions (which we will discuss more extensively in Chapter 9). As a consequence of the subprime collapse, many investors began to doubt the financial health of corporations and even the reliability of the ratings themselves. The perceived increase in default risk for corporate bonds made them less desirable at any given interest rate, decreased the quantity demanded, and shifted the demand curve for corporate bonds to the left. As shown in panel (a) of Figure 6.2, the interest rate on short-term corporate bonds should have risen, which is indeed what happened. The spread between interest rates on eurosterling commercial paper of three-month duration (which is the average rate on short-term sterling borrowing) and UK Treasury bills widened by 231 basis points (2.31 percentage points). The usual spread in normal times was 10–15 basis points (0.1–0.15% difference) but in fact eurosterling commercial paper rates had been rising from quarter 2 of 2007. They rose from an average of 5.74% in quarter 1 2007 to 6.33% in the last quarter of 2007. But the increase in perceived default risk for corporate bonds after the subprime collapse made default-free UK Treasury bonds relatively more attractive and shifted the demand curve for these securities to the right – an outcome described by some analysts as a 'flight to quality'. Just as our analysis predicts in Figure 6.2, interest rates on Treasury bonds fell. The spread between interest rates on corporate bonds and Treasury bonds rose by from 0.19% before the crisis to 2.31% at its peak and only reverted to normal spreads at the end of 2009. ■

APPLICATION | ## Sovereign default risk and the crisis in the euro area

Default risk is not confined to the corporate bond market alone. Tensions in the European Monetary Union that emerged after the onset of the global financial crisis have shown that default risk can occur in the government bond market. The global economic downturn in 2008–10 has worsened the government budget deficits of a number of countries (known as the GIIPS – Greece, Ireland, Italy, Portugal and Spain) in the eurozone. Since the onset of the financial crisis in August 2007, bond markets have shifted attention to the macroeconomic fundamentals of the GIIPS. The macroeconomic fundamentals concern the debt levels of the government and fiscal deficits. The risks are related to whether the governments of the GIIPS are able to repay bondholders the par value of bonds in terms of euros. Default risk rises with the debt levels and the budget deficits of a country. For example, the projected (by the OECD) budget deficit and government debt as a percentage of GDP for Greece is 7.5% and 157% respectively. For Ireland it is 10% and 120% respectively, Portugal is 6% and 110% respectively, Spain is 6% and 74% and Italy is 4% and 129%. However, these figures do not include the potential costs of bailing out insolvent banks by underwriting the deposit liabilities of the banking system. The banking crisis has worsened the financial situation of the GIIPS as the liabilities of insolvent banks are ultimately guaranteed by the government and could end up on the balance sheets of the government sending debt levels to even greater heights.

The spread between 10-year maturity bond rates of the GIIPS economies and 10-year German government bond rates is an indicator of default risk. German government bond rates are viewed by the market as risk-free. Figure 6.3 shows that the spread has widened markedly during 2010 and 2011, with Greek bond rates showing the widest spreads. ■

FIGURE 6.3

Interest rate spreads between selected 10-year government bonds of GIIPS countries and 10-year German government bonds for January 1999 to May 2011 (Greece, January 2001 to May 2011)

Source: Data extracted on 04 July 2011 11:54 UTC (GMT) from OECD (2012), OECD.Stat.

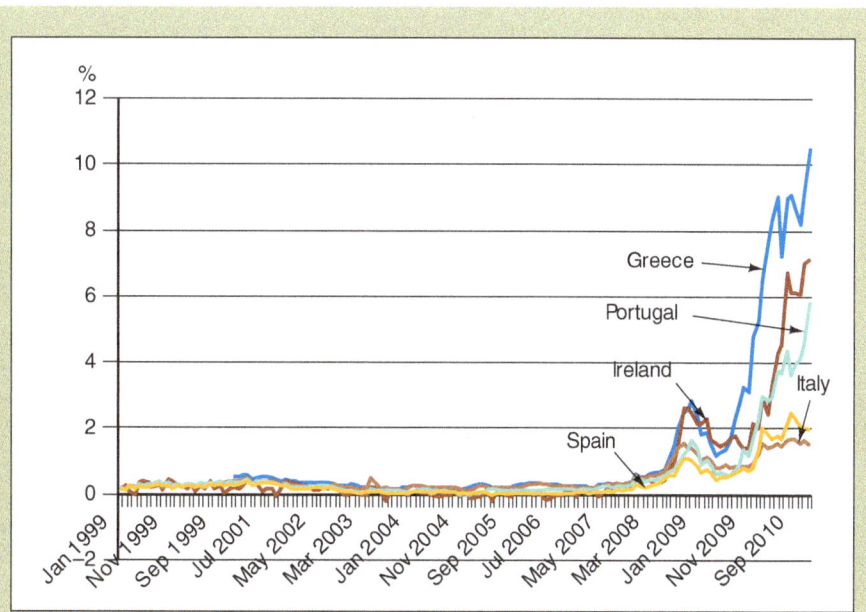

Liquidity

Another attribute of a bond that influences its interest rate is its liquidity. As we learned in Chapter 5, a liquid asset is one that can be quickly and cheaply converted into cash if the need arises. The more liquid an asset is, the more desirable it is (holding everything else constant). UK and US Treasury bonds are the most liquid of all long-term bonds, because they are so widely traded that they are the easiest to sell quickly and the cost of selling them is low. Corporate bonds are not as liquid, because fewer bonds for any one corporation are traded; thus it can be costly to sell these bonds in an emergency, because it might be hard to find buyers quickly.

How does the reduced liquidity of the corporate bonds affect their interest rates relative to the interest rate on Treasury bonds? We can use supply and demand analysis with the same figure that was used to analyse the effect of default risk, Figure 6.2, to show that the lower liquidity of corporate bonds relative to Treasury bonds increases the spread between the interest rates on these two bonds. Let us start the analysis by assuming that initially corporate and Treasury bonds are equally liquid and all their other attributes are the same. As shown in Figure 6.2, their equilibrium prices and interest rates will initially be equal: $P_1^c = P_1^T$ and $i_1^c = i_1^T$. If the corporate bond becomes less liquid than the Treasury bond because it is less widely traded, then (as the theory of asset demand indicates) demand for it will fall, shifting its demand curve from D_1^c to D_2^c as in panel (a). The Treasury bond now becomes relatively more liquid in comparison with the corporate bond, so its demand curve shifts rightward from D_1^T to D_2^T as in panel (b). The shifts in the curves in Figure 6.2 show that the price of the less liquid corporate bond falls and its interest rate rises, while the price of the more liquid Treasury bond rises and its interest rate falls.

The result is that the spread between the interest rates on the two bond types has risen. Therefore, the differences between interest rates on corporate bonds and Treasury bonds (that is, the risk premiums) reflect not only the corporate bond's default risk but also its liquidity. This is why a risk premium is more accurately a 'risk and liquidity premium', but convention dictates that it is called a *risk premium*.

Income tax considerations

Some bonds have tax exemptions that make them particularly attractive to investors. In the US, municipal bonds have tax exemptions. Such bonds no longer exist in the UK or the eurozone but they existed in the UK in a limited form up until the early 1980s. In the US, municipal bonds constitute nearly 10% of the total stock of bonds. However, municipal bonds are certainly not default-free: US state and local governments have defaulted on the municipal bonds they have issued in the past, for example in the case of Orange County, California, in 1994. Also, municipal bonds are not as liquid as Federal government Treasury bonds.

However, the rates on these municipal bonds have had lower interest rates than US Treasury bonds for long periods. How can this be explained? The explanation lies in the fact that interest payments on municipal bonds are exempt from federal income taxes, a factor that has the same effect on the demand for municipal bonds as an increase in their expected return.

Let us imagine that you have a high enough income to put you in the 35% income tax bracket, where for every extra dollar of income you have to pay 35 cents to the federal government. If you own a $1,000-face-value US Treasury bond that sells for $1,000 and has a coupon payment of $100, you get to keep only $65 of the payment after taxes. Although the bond has a 10% interest rate, you actually earn only 6.5% after taxes.

Suppose, however, that you put your savings into a $1,000-face-value municipal bond that sells for $1,000 and pays only $80 in coupon payments. Its interest rate is only 8%, but because it is a tax-exempt security, you pay no federal income taxes on the $80 coupon payment, so you earn 8% after taxes. Clearly, you earn more on the municipal bond after taxes, so you are willing to hold the riskier and less liquid municipal bond even though it has a lower interest rate than the US Treasury bond. (This was not true before World War II, when the tax-exempt status of municipal bonds did not convey much of an advantage because federal income tax rates were extremely low.)

Another way of understanding why municipal bonds have lower interest rates than Treasury bonds is to use the supply and demand analysis depicted in Figure 6.4. We initially assume that municipal and Treasury bonds have identical attributes and so have the same bond prices as drawn in the figure: $P_1^m = P_1^T$, and the same interest rates. Once the municipal bonds are given a tax advantage that raises their after-tax expected return relative to Treasury bonds and makes them more desirable, demand for them rises, and their demand curve shifts to the right, from D_1^m to D_2^m. The result is that their equilibrium bond price rises from P_1^m to P_2^m, and their equilibrium interest rate falls. By contrast, Treasury bonds have now become less desirable relative to municipal bonds; demand for Treasury bonds decreases, and D_1^T shifts to D_2^T. The Treasury bond price falls from P_1^T to P_2^T, and the interest rate rises. The resulting lower interest rates for municipal bonds and higher interest rates for Treasury bonds explain why municipal bonds can have interest rates below those of Treasury bonds.[1]

The risk structure of interest rates (the relationship among interest rates on bonds with the same maturity) is explained by three factors: default risk, liquidity and the income tax treatment of a bond's interest payments. As a bond's default risk increases, the risk premium on that bond (the spread between its interest rate and the interest rate on a default-free Treasury bond) rises. The greater liquidity of Treasury bonds also explains why their interest rates are lower than interest rates on less liquid bonds. If a bond has a favourable tax treatment, as do US municipal bonds, whose interest payments are exempt from federal income taxes, its interest rate will be lower.

Interest rates on municipal and treasury bonds

When the municipal bond is given tax-free status, demand for the municipal bond shifts rightward from D_1^m to D_2^m and demand for the Treasury bond shifts leftward from D_1^T to D_2^T. The equilibrium price of the municipal bond rises from P_1^m to P_2^m, so its interest rate falls, while the equilibrium price of the Treasury bond falls from P_1^T to P_2^T and its interest rate rises. The result is that municipal bonds end up with lower interest rates than those on Treasury bonds.

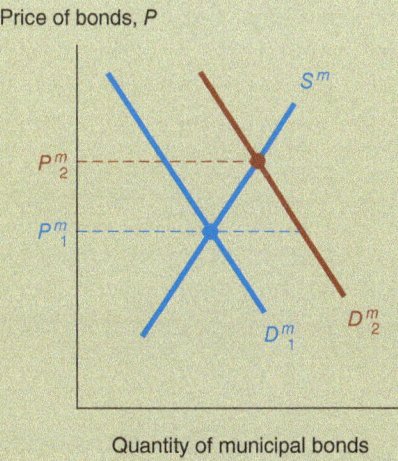
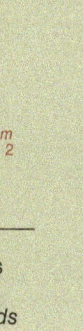
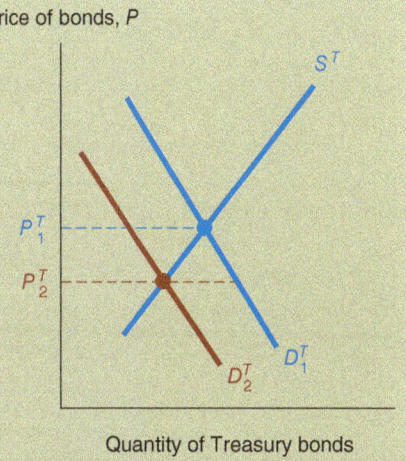

(a) Market for municipal bonds

(b) Market for Treasury bonds

Effects of former President Bush's tax cut on municipal bond
interest rates

The Bush tax cut passed in 2001 scheduled a reduction of the top income tax bracket from
39% to 35% over a ten-year period. What is the effect of this income tax decrease on interest
rates in the municipal bond market relative to those in the Treasury bond market?

Our supply and demand analysis provides the answer. A decreased income tax rate for
wealthy people means that the after-tax expected return on tax-free municipal bonds relative
to that on Treasury bonds is lower, because the interest on Treasury bonds is now taxed at a
lower rate. Because municipal bonds now become less desirable, their demand decreases,
shifting the demand curve to the left, which lowers their price and raises their interest rate.
Conversely, the lower income tax rate makes Treasury bonds more desirable; this change
shifts their demand curve to the right, raises their price and lowers their interest rates.

Our analysis thus shows that the Bush tax cut raised the interest rates on municipal bonds
relative to the interest rate on Treasury bonds.

With the possible repeal of the Bush tax cuts for wealthy people that may occur under
President Obama, the analysis would be reversed. Higher tax rates would raise the after-
tax expected return on tax-free municipal bonds relative to Treasury bonds. Demand for
municipal bonds would increase, shifting the demand curve to the right, which raises their
price and lowers their interest rate. Conversely, the higher tax rate would make Treasury
bonds less desirable, shifting their demand curve to the left, lowering their price and raising
their interest rate. Higher tax rates would thus result in lower interest rates on municipal
bonds relative to the interest rate on Treasury bonds.

Term structure of interest rates

We have seen how risk, liquidity and tax considerations (collectively embedded in the risk
structure) can influence interest rates. Another factor that influences the interest rate on
a bond is its term to maturity: bonds with identical risk, liquidity and tax characteristics
may have different interest rates because their time remaining to maturity is different. A
plot of the yields on bonds with differing terms to maturity but the same risk, liquidity
and tax considerations is called a **yield curve**, and it describes the term structure of
interest rates for particular types of bonds, such as government bonds. The 'Following
the financial news' box shows three yield curves for Treasury bonds that were obtained
from the *Financial Times* online service **http://markets.ft.com/research/Markets/Bonds**.
Yield curves can be classified as upward-sloping, flat, and downward-sloping (the last
sort is often referred to as an **inverted yield curve**). When yield curves slope upward, the
most usual case, the long-term interest rates are above the short-term interest rates; when
yield curves are flat, short-and long-term interest rates are the same; and when yield
curves are inverted, long-term interest rates are below short-term interest rates. Yield
curves can also have more complicated shapes in which they first slope up and then down,
or vice versa. Why do we usually see upward slopes of the yield curve but sometimes
other shapes? Besides explaining why yield curves take on different shapes at different
times, a good theory of the term structure of interest rates must explain the following three
important empirical facts:

1 As we see in Figure 6.5, interest rates on bonds of different maturities move together
over time.
2 When short-term interest rates are low, yield curves are more likely to have an upward
slope; when short-term interest rates are high, yield curves are more likely to slope
downward and be inverted.
3 Yield curves almost always slope upward, as in the 'Following the financial news' box.

Yield curves

The Capital Markets section of the *Financial Times* online **www.ft.com** publishes daily yield curve data of British government bond yields, an example of which is presented here. The same section provides similar information for bond yields in the eurozone, US and Japan. The numbers on the vertical axis indicate the interest rate for the Treasury security, with the maturity given by the numbers on the horizontal axis. It is found in **http://markets.ft.com/research/Markets /Bonds**. The numbers on the vertical axis indicate the interest rate for the government security, with the maturity given by the numbers on the horizontal axis.

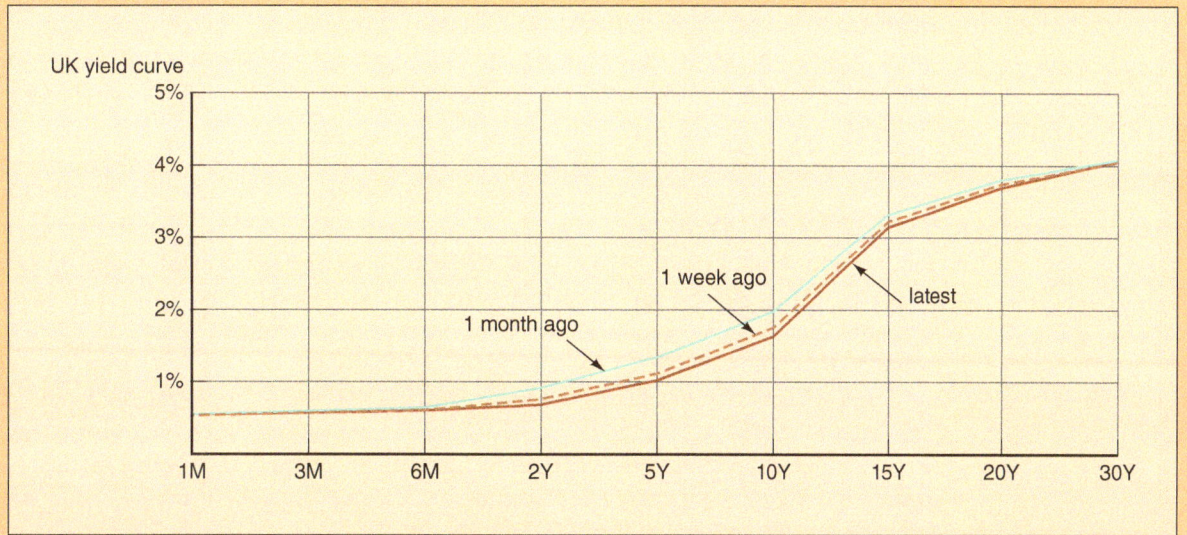

Source: www.ft.com.

UK benchmark yields

Maturity	Yield	Today's change	1 week ago	1 month ago
1 Month	0.55%	0.00	0.55%	0.56%
3 Month	0.58%	0.00	0.58%	0.60%
6 Month	0.60%	0.00	0.61%	0.65%
1 Year	0.54%	0.00	0.58%	0.62%
2 Year	0.70%	−0.02	0.77%	0.92%
3 Year	1.02%	<0.01	1.13%	1.35%
4 Year	1.46%	>−0.01	1.56%	1.79%
5 Year	1.64%	0.00	1.74%	1.97%
7 Year	2.44%	>−0.01	2.53%	2.71%
8 Year	2.77%	<0.01	2.84%	3.00%
9 Year	3.00%	<0.01	3.07%	3.20%
10 Year	3.14%	<0.01	3.21%	3.31%
15 Year	3.69%	+0.01	3.73%	3.79%
20 Year	4.05%	+0.01	4.06%	4.07%
30 Year	4.15%	<0.01	4.16%	4.13%

Source: FT.Com Saturday, 25 June, 2011.

Three theories have been put forward to explain the term structure of interest rates – that is, the relationship among interest rates on bonds of different maturities reflected in yield curve patterns: (1) the expectations theory, (2) the segmented markets theory, and (3) the liquidity premium theory, each of which is described in the following sections. The expectations theory does a good job of explaining the first two facts on our list, but not the third. The segmented markets theory can explain fact 3 but not the other two facts, which are well explained by the expectations theory. Because each theory explains facts that the other cannot, a natural way to seek a better understanding of the term structure is to combine features of both theories, which leads us to the liquidity premium theory, which can explain all three facts.

If the liquidity premium theory does a better job of explaining the facts and is hence the most widely accepted theory, why do we spend time discussing the other two theories? There are two reasons. First, the ideas in these two theories lay the groundwork for the liquidity premium theory. Second, it is important to see how economists modify theories to improve them when they find that the predicted results are inconsistent with the empirical evidence.

Expectations theory

The **expectations theory** of the term structure states the following common-sense proposition: the interest rate on a long-term bond will equal an average of the short-term interest rates that people expect to occur over the life of the long-term bond. For example, if people expect that short-term interest rates will be 10% on average over the coming five years, the expectations theory predicts that the interest rate on bonds with five years to maturity will be 10%, too. If short-term interest rates were expected to rise even higher after this five-year period, so that the average short-term interest rate over the coming 20 years is 11%, then the interest rate on 20-year bonds would equal 11% and would be higher than the interest rate on five-year bonds. We can see that the explanation provided by the expectations theory for why interest rates on bonds of different maturities differ is that short-term interest rates are expected to have different values at future dates.

The key assumption behind this theory is that buyers of bonds do not prefer bonds of one maturity over another, so they will not hold any quantity of a bond if its expected return is less than that of another bond with a different maturity. Bonds that have this characteristic are said to be *perfect substitutes*. What this means in practice is that if bonds with different maturities are perfect substitutes, the expected return on these bonds must be equal.

To see how the assumption that bonds with different maturities are perfect substitutes leads to the expectations theory, let us consider the following two investment strategies:

1 Purchase a one-year bond, and when it matures in one year, purchase another one-year bond.
2 Purchase a two-year bond and hold it until maturity.

Because both strategies must have the same expected return if people are holding both one- and two-year bonds, the interest rate on the two-year bond must equal the average of the two one-year interest rates. For example, let's say that the current interest rate on the one-year bond is 9% and you expect the interest rate on the one-year bond next year to be 11%. If you pursue the first strategy of buying the two one-year bonds, the expected return over the two years will average out to be (9% + 11%)/2 = 10% per year. You will be willing to hold both the one- and two-year bonds only if the expected return per year of the two-year bond equals this return. Therefore, the interest rate on the two-year bond must equal 10%, the average interest rate on the two one-year bonds.

We can make this argument more general. For an investment of €1, consider the choice of holding, for two periods, a two-period bond or two one-period bonds. Using the definitions

i_t = today's (time t) interest rate on a one-period bond

$i_t^e + 1$ = interest rate on a one-period bond expected for next period (time $t + 1$)

i_{2t} = today's (time t) interest rate on the two-period bond

the expected return over the two periods from investing €1 in the two-period bond and holding it for the two periods can be calculated as

$$(1 + i_{2t})(1 + i_{2t}) - 1 = 1 + 2i_{2t} + (i_{2t})^2 - 1 = 2i_{2t} + (i_{2t})^2$$

After the second period, the €1 investment is worth $(1 + i_{2t})(1 + i_{2t})$. Subtracting the €1 initial investment from this amount and dividing by the initial €1 investment gives the rate of return calculated in the previous equation. Because $(i_{2t})^2$ is extremely small – if $i_{2t} = 10\% = 0.10$, then $(i_{2t})^2 = 0.01$ – we can simplify the expected return for holding the two-period bond for the two periods to

$$2i_{2t}$$

With the other strategy, in which one-period bonds are bought, the expected return on the €1 investment over the two periods is

$$(1 + i_t)(1 + i_{t+1}^e) - 1 = 1 + i_t + i_{t+1}^e + i_t(i_{t+1}^e) - 1 = i_t + i_{t+1}^e + i_t(i_{t+1}^e)$$

This calculation is derived by recognizing that after the first period, the €1 investment becomes $1 + i_t$, and this is reinvested in the one-period bond for the next period, yielding an amount $(1 + i_t)(1 + i_{t+1}^e)$. Then subtracting the €1 initial investment from this amount and dividing by the initial investment of €1 gives the expected return for the strategy of holding one-period bonds for the two periods. Because $i_t(i_{t+1}^e)$ is also extremely small – if $i_t = i_{t+1}^e = 0.10$, then $i_t(i_{t+1}^e) = 0.01$ – we can simplify this to

$$i_t + i_{t+1}^e$$

Both bonds will be held only if these expected returns are equal – that is, when

$$2i_{2t} = i_t + i_{t+1}^e$$

Solving for i_{2t} in terms of the one-period rates, we have

$$i_{2t} = \frac{i_t + i_{t+1}^e}{2} \tag{6.1}$$

which tells us that the two-period rate must equal the average of the two one-period rates. Graphically, this can be shown as

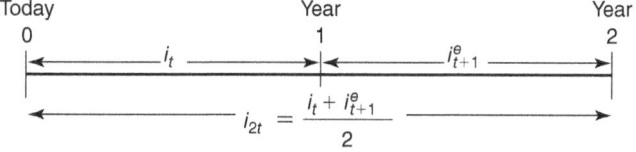

We can conduct the same steps for bonds with a longer maturity so that we can examine the whole term structure of interest rates. Doing so, we will find that the interest rate of i_{nt} on an n-period bond must be

$$i_{nt} = \frac{i_t + i_{t+1}^e + i_{t+2}^e + \cdots + i_{t+(n-1)}^e}{n} \tag{6.2}$$

Equation 6.2 states that the n-period interest rate equals the average of the one-period interest rates expected to occur over the n-period life of the bond. This is a restatement of the expectations theory in more precise terms.[2]

A simple numerical example might clarify what the expectations theory in Equation 6.2 is saying. If the one-year interest rate over the next five years is expected to be 5%, 6%, 7%, 8%, and 9%, Equation 6.2 indicates that the interest rate on the two-year bond would be

$$\frac{5\% + 6\%}{2} = 5.5\%$$

For the five-year bond it would be

$$\frac{5\% + 6\% + 7\% + 8\% + 9\%}{5} = 7\%$$

Doing a similar calculation for the one-, three- and four-year interest rates, you should be able to verify that the one- to five-year interest rates are 5.0%, 5.5%, 6.0%, 6.5% and 7.0%, respectively. Thus we see that the rising trend in expected short-term interest rates produces an upward-sloping yield curve along which interest rates rise as maturity lengthens.

The expectations theory is an elegant theory that explains why the term structure of interest rates (as represented by yield curves) changes at different times. When the yield curve is upward-sloping, the expectations theory suggests that short-term interest rates are expected to rise in the future, as we have seen in our numerical example. In this situation, in which the long-term rate is currently higher than the short-term rate, the average of future short-term rates is expected to be higher than the current short-term rate, which can occur only if short-term interest rates are expected to rise. This is what we see in our numerical example. When the yield curve is inverted (slopes downward), the average of future short-term interest rates is expected to be lower than the current short-term rate, implying that short-term interest rates are expected to fall, on average, in the future. Only when the yield curve is flat does the expectations theory suggest that short-term interest rates are not expected to change, on average, in the future.

The expectations theory also explains fact 1, which states that interest rates on bonds with different maturities move together over time. Historically, short-term interest rates have had the characteristic that if they increase today, they will tend to be higher in the future. Hence a rise in short-term rates will raise people's expectations of future short-term rates. Because long-term rates are the average of expected future short-term rates, a rise in short-term rates will also raise long-term rates, causing short- and long-term rates to move together.

The expectations theory also explains fact 2, which states that yield curves tend to have an upward slope when short-term interest rates are low and are inverted when short-term rates are high. When short-term rates are low, people generally expect them to rise to some normal level in the future, and the average of future expected short-term rates is high relative to the current short-term rate. Therefore, long-term interest rates will be substantially higher than current short-term rates, and the yield curve would then have an upward slope. Conversely, if short-term rates are high, people usually expect them to come back down. Long-term rates would then drop below short-term rates because the average of expected future short-term rates would be lower than current short-term rates and the yield curve would slope downward and become inverted.[3]

The expectations theory is an attractive theory because it provides a simple explanation of the behaviour of the term structure, but unfortunately it has a major shortcoming: it cannot explain fact 3, which says that yield curves usually slope upward. The typical upward slope of yield curves implies that short-term interest rates are usually expected to rise in the future. In practice, short-term interest rates are just as likely to fall as they are to rise, and so the expectations theory suggests that the typical yield curve should be flat rather than upward-sloping.

FIGURE 6.5

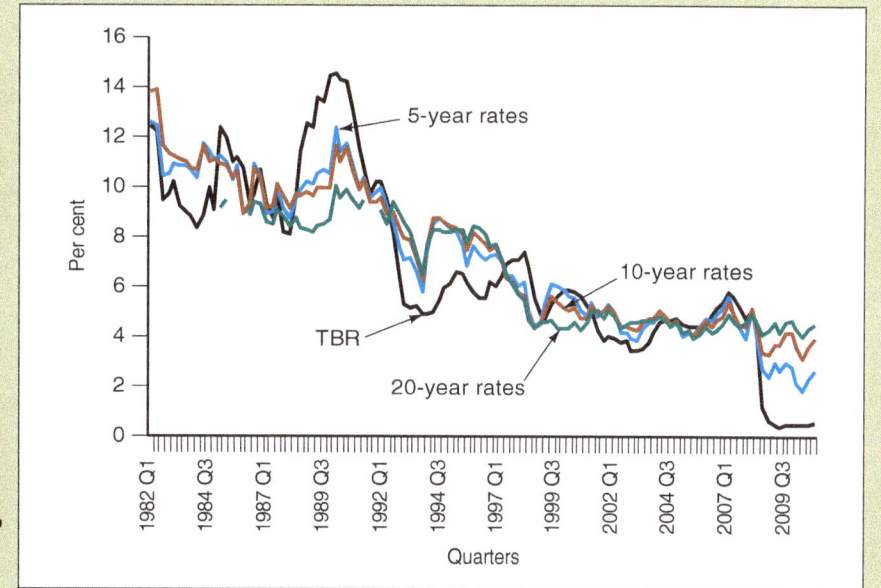

Movements over time of interest rates on British government securities with different maturities, 1982–2011

Source: Data from ONS online

Segmented markets theory

As the name suggests, the **segmented markets theory** of the term structure sees markets for different-maturity bonds as completely separate and segmented. The interest rate for each bond with a different maturity is then determined by the supply of and demand for that bond, with no effects from expected returns on other bonds with other maturities.

The key assumption in the segmented markets theory is that bonds of different maturities are not substitutes at all, so the expected return from holding a bond of one maturity has no effect on the demand for a bond of another maturity. This theory of the term structure is at the opposite extreme to the expectations theory, which assumes that bonds of different maturities are perfect substitutes.

The argument for why bonds of different maturities are not substitutes is that investors have very strong preferences for bonds of one maturity but not for another, so they will be concerned with the expected returns only for bonds of the maturity they prefer. This might occur because they have a particular holding period in mind, and if they match the maturity of the bond to the desired holding period, they can obtain a certain return with no risk at all.[4] (We have seen in Chapter 4 that if the term to maturity equals the holding period, the return is known for certain because it equals the yield exactly, and there is no interest-rate risk.) For example, people who have a short holding period would prefer to hold short-term bonds. Conversely, if you were putting funds away for your young child to go to college, your desired holding period might be much longer, and you would want to hold longer-term bonds.

In the segmented markets theory, differing yield curve patterns are accounted for by supply and demand differences associated with bonds of different maturities. If, as seems sensible, investors have short desired holding periods and generally prefer bonds with shorter maturities that have less interest-rate risk, the segmented markets theory can explain fact 3, which states that yield curves typically slope upward. Because in the typical situation the demand for long-term bonds is relatively lower than that for short-term bonds, long-term bonds will have lower prices and higher interest rates, and hence the yield curve will typically slope upward.

Although the segmented markets theory can explain why yield curves usually tend to slope upward, it has a major flaw in that it cannot explain facts 1 and 2. First, because it views the market for bonds of different maturities as completely segmented, there is no reason for a rise in interest rates on a bond of one maturity to affect the interest rate on a bond of another maturity. Therefore, it cannot explain why interest rates on bonds of different maturities tend to move together (fact 1). Second, because it is not clear how demand and supply for short- versus long-term bonds change with the level of short-term interest rates, the theory cannot explain why yield curves tend to slope upward when short-term interest rates are low and to be inverted when short-term interest rates are high (fact 2).

Because each of our two theories explains empirical facts that the other cannot, a logical step is to combine the theories, which leads us to the liquidity premium theory.

Liquidity premium and preferred habitat theories

The **liquidity premium theory** of the term structure states that the interest rate on a long-term bond will equal an average of short-term interest rates expected to occur over the life of the long-term bond plus a liquidity premium (also referred to as a term premium) that responds to supply and demand conditions for that bond.

The liquidity premium theory's key assumption is that bonds of different maturities are substitutes, which means that the expected return on one bond *does* influence the expected return on a bond of a different maturity, but it allows investors to prefer one bond maturity over another. In other words, bonds of different maturities are assumed to be substitutes but not perfect substitutes. Investors tend to prefer shorter-term bonds because these bonds bear less interest-rate risk. For these reasons, investors must be offered a positive liquidity premium to induce them to hold longer-term bonds. Such an outcome would modify the expectations theory by adding a positive liquidity premium to the equation that describes the relationship between long- and short-term interest rates. The liquidity premium theory is thus written as

$$i_{nt} = \frac{i_t + i_{t+1}^e + i_{t+2}^e + \cdots + i_{t+(n-1)}^e}{n} + l_{nt} \tag{6.3}$$

where l_{nt} is the liquidity (term) premium for the n-period bond at time t, which is always positive and rises with the term to maturity of the bond, n.

Closely related to the liquidity premium theory is the **preferred habitat theory**, which takes a somewhat less direct approach to modifying the expectations hypothesis but comes to a similar conclusion. It assumes that investors have a preference for bonds of one maturity over another, a particular bond maturity (preferred habitat) in which they prefer to invest. Because they prefer bonds of one maturity over another, they will be willing to buy bonds that do not have the preferred maturity (habitat) only if they earn a somewhat higher expected return. Because investors are likely to prefer the habitat of short-term bonds over that of longer-term bonds, they are willing to hold long-term bonds only if they have higher expected returns. This reasoning leads to the same Equation 6.3 implied by the liquidity premium theory with a term premium that typically rises with maturity.

The relationship between the expectations theory and the liquidity premium and preferred habitat theories is shown in Figure 6.6. There we see that because the liquidity premium is always positive and typically grows as the term to maturity increases, the yield curve implied by the liquidity premium theory is always above the yield curve implied by the expectations theory and generally has a steeper slope. (Note that for simplicity we are assuming that the expectations theory yield curve is flat.)

A simple numerical example similar to the one we used for the expectations hypothesis further clarifies what the liquidity premium and preferred habitat theories in Equation 6.3 are saying. Again suppose that the one-year interest rate over the next five years is expected to be 5%, 6%, 7%, 8% and 9%, while investors' preferences for holding short-term bonds means that the liquidity premiums for one- to five-year bonds are 0%, 0.25%, 0.5%, 0.75%

FIGURE 6.6

The relationship between the liquidity premium (preferred habitat) and expectation theory

Because the liquidity premium is always positive and grows as the term to maturity increases, the yield curve implied by the liquidity premium and preferred habitat theories is always above the yield curve implied by the expectations theory and has a steeper slope. For simplicity the yield curve implied by the expectations theory is drawn under the scenario of unchanging future one-year interest rates.

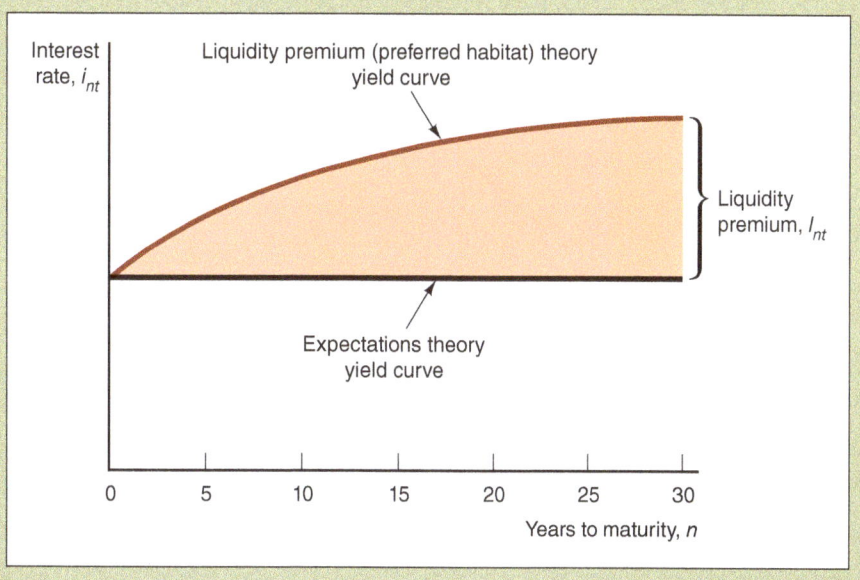

and 1.0%, respectively. Equation 6.3 then indicates that the interest rate on the two-year bond would be

$$\frac{5\% + 6\%}{2} + 0.25\% = 5.75\%$$

For the five-year bond it would be

$$\frac{5\% + 6\% + 7\% + 8\% + 9\%}{5} + 1\% = 8\%$$

Doing a similar calculation for the one-, three- and four-year interest rates, you should be able to verify that the one- to five-year interest rates are 5.0%, 5.75%, 6.5%, 7.25% and 8.0%, respectively. Comparing these findings with those for the expectations theory, we see that the liquidity premium and preferred habitat theories produce yield curves that slope more steeply upward because of investors' preferences for short-term bonds.

Let's see if the liquidity premium and preferred habitat theories are consistent with all three empirical facts we have discussed. They explain fact 1, which states that interest rates on different-maturity bonds move together over time: a rise in short-term interest rates indicates that short-term interest rates will, on average, be higher in the future, and the first term in Equation 6.3 then implies that long-term interest rates will rise along with them.

They also explain why yield curves tend to have an especially steep upward slope when short-term interest rates are low and to be inverted when short-term rates are high (fact 2). Because investors generally expect short-term interest rates to rise to some normal level when they are low, the average of future expected short-term rates will be high relative to the current short-term rate. With the additional boost of a positive liquidity premium, long-term interest rates will be substantially higher than current short-term rates, and the yield curve will then have a steep upward slope. Conversely, if short-term rates are high, people usually expect them to come back down. Long-term rates will then drop below short-term rates because the average of expected future short-term rates will be so far below current short-term rates that despite positive liquidity premiums, the yield curve will slope downward.

FIGURE 6.7

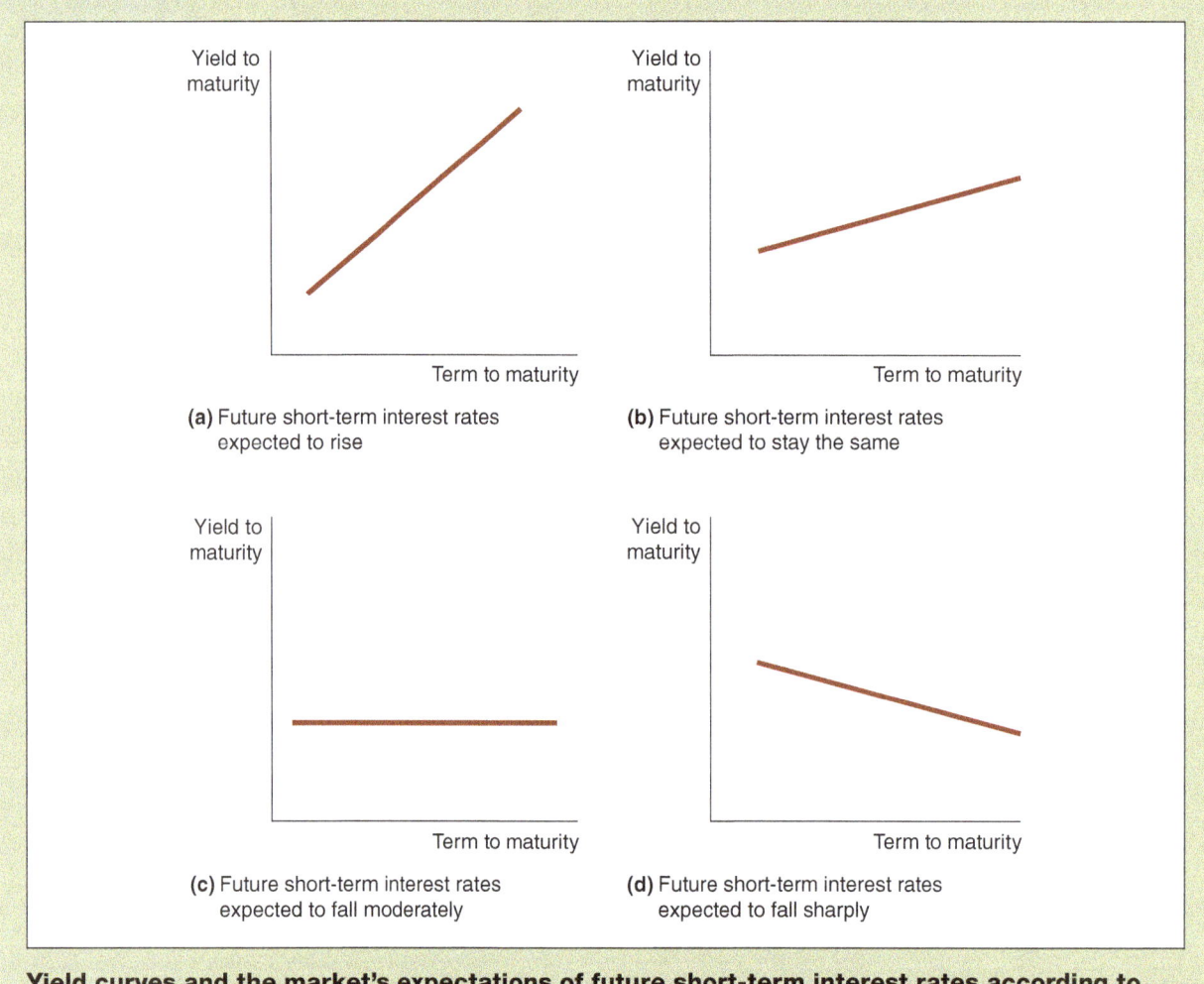

(a) Future short-term interest rates expected to rise

(b) Future short-term interest rates expected to stay the same

(c) Future short-term interest rates expected to fall moderately

(d) Future short-term interest rates expected to fall sharply

Yield curves and the market's expectations of future short-term interest rates according to the liquidity premium (preferred habitat) theory

The liquidity premium and preferred habitat theories explain fact 3, which states that yield curves typically slope upward, by recognizing that the liquidity premium rises with a bond's maturity because of investors' preferences for short-term bonds. Even if short-term interest rates are expected to stay the same on average in the future, long-term interest rates will be above short-term interest rates, and yield curves will typically slope upward.

How can the liquidity premium and preferred habitat theories explain the occasional appearance of inverted yield curves if the liquidity premium is positive? It must be that at times short-term interest rates are expected to fall so much in the future that the average of the expected short-term rates is well below the current short-term rate. Even when the positive liquidity premium is added to this average, the resulting long-term rate will still be lower than the current short-term interest rate.

As our discussion indicates, a particularly attractive feature of the liquidity premium and preferred habitat theories is that they tell you what the market is predicting about future short-term interest rates just from the slope of the yield curve. A steeply rising yield curve, as in panel (a) of Figure 6.7, indicates that short-term interest rates are expected to rise in the future. A moderately steep yield curve, as in panel (b), indicates that short-term interest rates are not expected to rise or fall much in the future. A flat yield curve, as in panel (c), indicates that short-term rates are expected to fall moderately in the future. Finally, an

CLOSER LOOK
The yield curve as a forecasting tool for inflation and the business cycle

Because the yield curve contains information about future expected interest rates, it should also have the capacity to help forecast inflation and real output fluctuations. To see why, recall from Chapter 5 that rising interest rates are associated with economic booms and falling interest rates with recessions. When the yield curve is either flat or downward-sloping, it suggests that future short-term interest rates are expected to fall and, therefore, that the economy is more likely to enter a recession. Indeed, the yield curve is found to be an accurate predictor of the business cycle.*

In Chapter 4, we also learned that a nominal interest rate is composed of a real interest rate and expected inflation, implying that the yield curve contains information about both the future path of nominal interest rates and future inflation. A steep yield curve predicts a future increase in inflation, while a flat or downward-sloping yield curve forecasts a future decline in inflation.†

The ability of the yield curve to forecast business cycles and inflation is one reason why the slope of the yield curve is part of the toolkit of many economic forecasters and is often viewed as a useful indicator of the stance of monetary policy, with a steep yield curve indicating loose policy and a flat or downward-sloping yield curve indicating tight policy.

* For example, see Arturo Estrella and Frederic S. Mishkin, 'Predicting US recessions: financial variables as leading indicators', *Review of Economics and Statistics*, 80 (February 1998): 45–61.
† Frederic S. Mishkin, 'What does the term structure tell us about future inflation?', *Journal of Monetary Economics* 25 (January 1990): 77–95; and Frederic S. Mishkin, 'The information in the longer-maturity term structure about future inflation', *Quarterly Journal of Economics* 55 (August 1990): 815–28.

inverted yield curve, as in panel (d), indicates that short-term interest rates are expected to fall sharply in the future.

Evidence on the term structure

In the 1980s, researchers examining the term structure of interest rates questioned whether the slope of the yield curve provides information about movements of future short-term interest rates.[5] They found that the spread between long- and short-term interest rates does not always help predict future short-term interest rates, a finding that may stem from substantial fluctuations in the liquidity (term) premium for long-term bonds. More recent research using more discriminating tests now favours a different view. It shows that the term structure contains quite a bit of information for the very short run (over the next several months) and the long run (over several years) but is unreliable at predicting movements in interest rates over the intermediate term (the time in between).[6] Research also finds that the yield curve helps forecast future inflation and business cycles (see the 'Closer look' box).

Summary

The liquidity premium and preferred habitat theories are the most widely accepted theories of the term structure of interest rates because they explain the major empirical facts about the term structure so well. They combine the features of both the expectations theory and the segmented markets theory by asserting that a long-term interest rate will be the sum of a liquidity (term) premium and the average of the short-term interest rates that are expected to occur over the life of the bond.

The liquidity premium and preferred habitat theories explain the following facts: (1) Interest rates on bonds of different maturities tend to move together over time, (2) yield curves usually slope upward, and (3) when short-term interest rates are low, yield curves are more likely to have a steep upward slope, whereas when short-term interest rates are high, yield curves are more likely to be inverted.

FIGURE 6.8

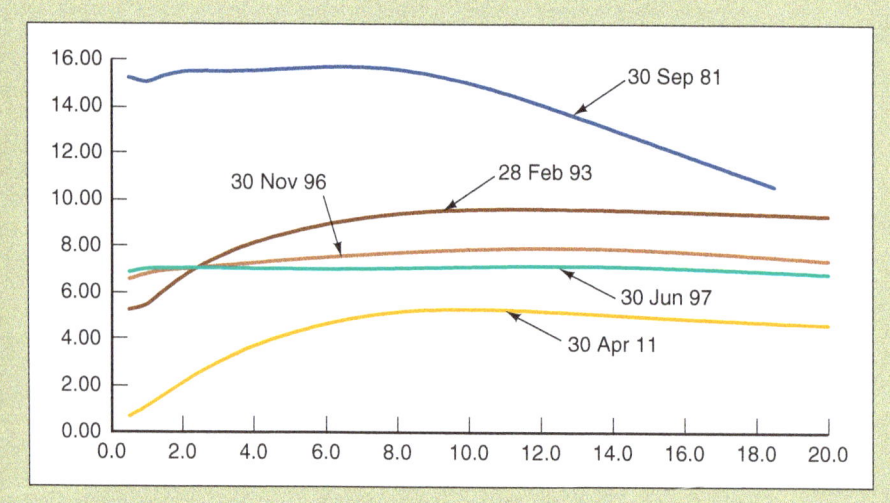

Yield curves for British government securities

Source: www.bankofengland.co.uk
/statistics/Pages/yieldcurve/default
.aspx.

The theories also help us predict the movement of short-term interest rates in the future. A steep upward slope of the yield curve means that short-term rates are expected to rise, a mild upward slope means that short-term rates are expected to remain the same, a flat slope means that short-term rates are expected to fall moderately, and an inverted yield curve means that short-term rates are expected to fall sharply.

APPLICATION   Interpreting yield curves, 1981–2011

Figure 6.8 illustrates several yield curves that have appeared for British government securities in recent years. What do these yield curves tell us about the public's expectations of future movements of short-term interest rates?

The steep inverted yield curve that occurred on 30 September 1981, indicated that short-term interest rates were expected to decline sharply in the future. For longer-term interest rates with their positive liquidity premium to be well below the short-term interest rate, short-term interest rates must be expected to decline so sharply that their average is far below the current short-term rate. Indeed, the public's expectations of sharply lower short-term interest rates evident in the yield curve were realized soon after September; by November, three-month Treasury bill rates had declined from 15.1% to 13.8% and by February 1982 they had fallen to 12.5%.

The steep upward-sloping yield curves on 28 February 1993 and 30 April 2011 indicated that short-term interest rates would climb in the future. The long-term interest rate is higher than the short-term interest rate when short-term interest rates are expected to rise because their average plus the liquidity premium will be higher than the current short-term rate. The moderately upward-sloping yield curves on 30 November 1996 indicated that short-term interest rates were expected neither to rise nor to fall in the near future. In this case, their average remains the same as the current short-term rate, and the positive liquidity premium for longer-term bonds explains the moderate upward slope of the yield curve. The flat yield curve of 30 June 1997 indicated that short-term interest rates were expected to fall slightly. ■

SUMMARY

1 Bonds with the same maturity will have different interest rates because of three factors: default risk, liquidity and tax considerations. The greater a bond's

default risk, the higher its interest rate relative to other bonds; the greater a bond's liquidity, the lower its interest rate; and bonds with tax-exempt status as in the case of US municipal bonds, will have lower interest rates than they otherwise would. The relationship among interest rates on bonds with the same maturity that arises because of these three factors is known as the *risk structure of interest rates*.

2 Four theories of the term structure provide explanations of how interest rates on bonds with different terms to maturity are related. The expectations theory views long-term interest rates as equalling the average of future short-term interest rates expected to occur over the life of the bond. By contrast, the segmented markets theory treats the determination of interest rates for each bond's maturity as the outcome of supply and demand in that market only. Neither of these theories by itself can explain the fact that interest rates on bonds of different maturities move together over time and that yield curves usually slope upward.

3 The liquidity premium (preferred habitat) theory combines the features of the other two theories, and by so doing are able to explain the facts just mentioned. It views long-term interest rates as equalling the average of future short-term interest rates expected to occur over the life of the bond plus a liquidity premium. This theory allows us to infer the market's expectations about the movement of future short-term interest rates from the yield curve. A steeply upward-sloping curve indicates that future short-term rates are expected to rise, a mildly upward-sloping curve indicates that short-term rates are expected to stay the same, a flat curve indicates that short-term rates are expected to decline slightly, and an inverted yield curve indicates that a substantial decline in short-term rates is expected in the future.

KEY TERMS

credit-rating agencies p. 111

default p. 110

default-free bonds p. 110

expectations theory p. 118

inverted yield curve p. 116

junk bonds p. 111

liquidity premium theory p. 122

preferred habitat theory p. 122

risk premium p. 110

risk structure of interest rates p. 108

segmented markets theory p. 121

term structure of interest rates p. 108

yield curve p. 116

QUESTIONS AND PROBLEMS

All questions and problems are available in MyEconLab at **www.myeconlab.com/mishkin**.

1 Which should have the higher risk premium on its interest rates, a corporate bond with a Moody's Baa rating or a corporate bond with a C rating? Why?

2 Why do UK Treasury bills have lower interest rates than large-denomination negotiable bank CDs?

3 Risk premiums on corporate bonds are usually *anticyclical*; that is, they decrease during business cycle expansions and increase during recessions. Why is this so?

4 'If bonds of different maturities are close substitutes, their interest rates are more likely to move together.' Is this statement true, false, or uncertain? Explain your answer.

5 If yield curves, on average, were flat, what would this say about the liquidity (term) premiums in the term structure? Would you be more or less willing to accept the expectations theory?

6 Assuming that the expectations theory is the correct theory of the term structure, calculate the interest rates in the term structure for maturities of one to five years, and plot the resulting yield curves for the following series of one-year interest rates over the next five years:

(a) 5%, 7%, 7%, 7%, 7%

(b) 5%, 4%, 4%, 4%, 4%

How would your yield curves change if people preferred shorter-term bonds over longer-term bonds?

7 Assuming that the expectations theory is the correct theory of the term structure, calculate the interest rates in the term structure for maturities of one to five years, and plot the resulting yield curves for the following paths of one-year interest rates over the next five years:

(a) 5%, 6%, 7%, 6%, 5%

(b) 5%, 4%, 3%, 4%, 5%

How would your yield curves change if people preferred shorter-term bonds over longer-term bonds?

8 If a yield curve looks like the one shown in Figure (a) below, what is the market predicting about the movement of future short-term interest rates? What might the yield curve indicate about the market's predictions for the inflation rate in the future?

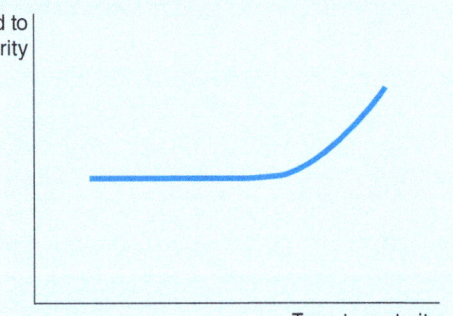

9 If a yield curve looks like the one shown in Figure (b) below, what is the market predicting about the movement of future short-term interest rates? What might the yield curve indicate about the market's predictions for the inflation rate in the future?

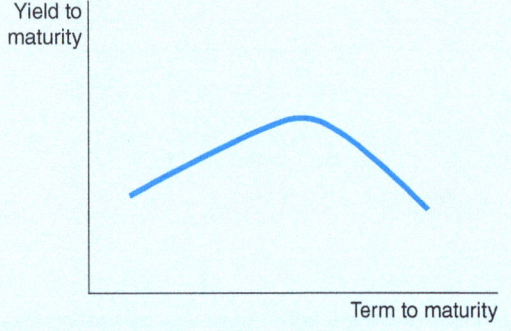

Using economic analysis to predict the future

10 Predict what will happen to interest rates on a given corporate bond if the British government guarantees today that it will pay creditors if the company goes bankrupt in the future. What will happen to the interest rates on UK Treasury bonds?

11 If the US federal income tax exemption on municipal bonds were abolished, what would happen to the interest rates on these bonds? What effect would the change have on interest rates on US Treasury securities?

12 If, for example, the UK yield curve suddenly becomes steeper, how would you revise your predictions of interest rates in the future?

13 If expectations of future short-term interest rates suddenly fall, what would happen to the slope of the yield curve?

WEB EXERCISES

1 The amount of additional interest investors receive due to the various risk premiums changes over time. Sometimes the risk premiums are much larger than at other times. For example, the US default risk premium was very small in the late 1990s when the US economy was so healthy that business failures were rare. This risk premium increases during recessions. Go to **www.federalreserve.gov/releases/ h15** (historical data) and find the interest rate listings for AAA- and Baa-rated bonds at three points in time: the most recent; 1 June 2005; and 1 June 2002. Prepare a graph that shows these three time periods. Are the risk premiums stable or do they change over time?

2 Figure 6.8 shows a number of yield curves at various points in time. Go to **www.bankofengland.co.uk /statistics/Pages/yieldcurve/default.aspx** and click on

the nominal government liability chart. Does the current yield curve fall above or below the most recent one listed in Figure 6.8? Is the current yield curve flatter or steeper than the most recent one reported in Figure 6.8?

3 Within the euro area, there are different yield curves for different sovereign entities. The ECB estimates zero-coupon spot yield curves for AAA-rated government bonds in the euro area and derives forward and par yield curves. Go to **http://www.ecb.int/stats/money/yc/html/ index.en.html** and under 'Data Services' download the latest yield curve data. You can then compare this to a range of historical euro-area government bond yield data. What patterns are noticeable since 2009? You can find explanatory notes on the ECB's yield curve here: **http:// www.ecb.int/stats/money/yc/html/technical_notes.pdf.**

4 Investment companies attempt to explain to investors the nature of the risk the investor incurs when buying shares in their mutual funds. For example, Vanguard carefully explains interest-rate risk and offers alternative funds with different interest rate risks. Go to **https://personal.vanguard.com/us/funds**.

(a) Select the bond fund you would recommend to an investor who has a very low tolerance for risk and a short investment horizon. Justify your answer.

(b) Select the bond fund you would recommend to an investor who has a very high tolerance for risk and a long investment horizon. Justify your answer.

Notes

1 In contrast to corporate bonds, Treasury bonds are exempt from US state and local income taxes. Using the analysis in the text, you should be able to show that this feature of Treasury bonds provides an additional reason why interest rates on corporate bonds are higher than those on Treasury bonds.

2 The analysis here has been conducted for discount bonds. Formulas for interest rates on coupon bonds would differ slightly from those used here, but would convey the same principle.

3 The expectations theory explains another important fact about the relationship between short-term and long-term interest rates. As you can see in Figure 6.5, short-term interest rates are more volatile than long-term rates. If interest rates are *mean-reverting* – that is, if they tend to head back down after they are at unusually high levels or go back up when they are at unusually low levels – then an average of these short-term rates must necessarily have less volatility than the short-term rates themselves. Because the expectations theory suggests that the long-term rate will be an average of future short-term rates, it implies that the long-term rate will have less volatility than short-term rates.

4 The statement that there is no uncertainty about the return if the term to maturity equals the holding period is literally true only for a discount bond. For a coupon bond with a long holding period, there is some risk because coupon payments must be reinvested before the bond matures. Our analysis here is thus being conducted for discount bonds. However, the gist of the analysis remains the same for coupon bonds because the amount of this risk from reinvestment is small when coupon bonds have the same term to maturity as the holding period.

5 Robert J. Shiller, John Y. Campbell and Kermit L. Schoenholtz, 'Forward rates and future policy: interpreting the term structure of interest rates', *Brookings Papers on Economic Activity* 1 (1983): 173–217; N. Gregory Mankiw and Lawrence H. Summers, 'Do long-term interest rates overreact to short-term interest rates?', *Brookings Papers on Economic Activity* 1 (1984): 223–42.

6 Eugene Fama, 'The information in the term structure', *Journal of Financial Economics* 13 (1984): 509–28; Eugene Fama and Robert Bliss, 'The information in long-maturity forward rates', *American Economic Review* 77 (1987): 680–92; John Y. Campbell and Robert J. Shiller, 'Cointegration and tests of the present value models', *Journal of Political Economy* 95 (1987): 1062–88; John Y. Campbell and Robert J. Shiller, 'Yield spreads and interest rate movements: a bird's eye view', *Review of Economic Studies* 58 (1991): 495–514.

Useful websites

http://www.bankofengland.co.uk/statistics/Pages/yieldcurve/default.aspx The Bank of England reports the yield on British government bonds of different maturities and charts them.

http://www.ecb.int/stats/money/yc/html/index.en.html Euro-area government bond yield curve page with current and historical data, as well as technical notes.

www.federalreserve.gov/Releases/h15/update/ The Federal Reserve reports the yields on different quality bonds. Look at the bottom of the listing of interest rates for AAA- and BBB- rated bonds.

http://stockcharts.com/charts/YieldCurve.html This site lets you look at the dynamic yield curve at any point in time since 1995.

CHAPTER 7

The stock market, the theory of rational expectations and the efficient market hypothesis

PREVIEW

Rarely does a day go by that the stock market isn't a major news item. We have witnessed huge swings in the stock market in recent years. The 1990s were an extraordinary decade for stocks all over the world: the Dow Jones and S&P 500 indexes in the USA increased more than 400%, while the tech-laden NASDAQ index rose more than 1,000%. In the UK the FTSE100 rose by 220% and in Germany the DAX rose by 380%. By early 2000, all five indexes had reached record highs. Unfortunately, the good times did not last, and many investors lost their shirts. Starting in early 2000, the stock market began to decline: the NASDAQ crashed, falling by more than 50%, while the Dow Jones and S&P 500 indexes fell by 30% to January 2003. The FTSE100 fell by around 50% to mid-2002 and the DAX fell by 45% to late 2001. After subsequently recovering globally, the stock market crashed again during the subprime financial crisis, falling by over 50% from its peak in late 2007 to late 2008 and through to 2009.

Because so many people invest in the stock market or the pension fund companies invest on their behalf, the price of stocks affects the ability of people to retire comfortably; therefore the market for stocks is undoubtedly the financial market that receives the most attention and scrutiny. In this chapter, we look first at how this important market works.

We begin by discussing the fundamental theories that underlie the valuation of stocks. These theories are critical to understanding the forces that cause the value of stocks to rise and fall minute by minute and day by day. Once we have learned the methods for stock valuation, we need to explore how expectations about the market affect its behaviour. We do so by examining the *theory of rational expectations*. When this theory is applied to financial markets, the outcome is the *efficient market hypothesis*, which has some general implications for how markets in other securities besides stocks operate. The theory of rational expectations is also central to debates about the conduct of monetary policy, to be discussed in Chapter 25.

Computing the price of common stock

Common stock is the principal way that corporations raise equity capital. Holders of common stock own an interest in the corporation consistent with the percentage of outstanding shares owned. This ownership interest gives **stockholders** – those who hold stock in a corporation – a bundle of rights. The most important are the right to vote and to be the **residual claimant** of all funds flowing into the firm (known as **cash flows**), meaning that the stockholder receives whatever remains after all other claims against the firm's assets have been satisfied. Stockholders are paid dividends from the net earnings of the corporation. **Dividends** are payments made periodically, usually every quarter, to stockholders. The board of directors of the firm sets the level of the dividend, usually based on the recommendation of management. In addition, the stockholder has the right to sell the stock.

One basic principle of finance is that the value of any investment is found by computing the present value of all cash flows the investment will generate over its life. For example, a commercial building will sell for a price that reflects the net cash flows (rents − expenses) it is projected to have over its useful life. Similarly, we value common stock as the value in today's dollars of all future cash flows. The cash flows a stockholder might earn from stock are dividends, the sales price, or both.

To develop the theory of stock valuation, we begin with the simplest possible scenario: you buy the stock, hold it for one period to get a dividend, then sell the stock. We call this the *one-period valuation model*.

The one-period valuation model

Suppose that you have some extra money to invest for one year. After a year, you will need to sell your investment to pay tuition. After listening to *The Money Programme* on the BBC, you decide that you want to buy VW stock. You call your broker and find that VW is currently selling for €50 per share and pays €0.16 per year in dividends. The analyst on the radio predicts that the stock will be selling for €60 in one year. Should you buy this stock?

To answer this question, you need to determine whether the current price accurately reflects the analyst's forecast. To value the stock today, you need to find the present discounted value of the expected cash flows (future payments) using the formula in Equation 4.1. In this equation, the discount factor used to discount the cash flows is the required return on investments in equity rather than the interest rate. The cash flows consist of one dividend payment plus a final sales price. When these cash flows are discounted back to the present, the following equation computes the current price of the stock:

$$P_0 = \frac{Div_1}{(1 + k_e)} + \frac{P_1}{(1 + k_e)} \tag{7.1}$$

where P_0 = the current price of the stock. The zero subscript refers to time period zero, or the present

Div_1 = the dividend paid at the end of year 1

k_e = the required return on investments in equity

P_1 = the price at the end of the first period, the assumed sales price of the stock

To see how Equation 7.1 works, let's compute the price of the VW stock if, after careful consideration, you decide that you would be satisfied to earn a 12% return on the investment. If you have decided that $k_e = 0.12$, are told that VW pays €0.16 per year in dividends ($Div_1 = 0.16$), and forecast the share price of €60 for next year ($P_1 = €60$), you get the following from Equation 7.1:

$$P_0 = \frac{0.16}{1 + 0.12} + \frac{€60}{1 + 0.12} = €0.14 + €53.27 = €53.71$$

Based on your analysis, you find that the present value of all cash flows from the stock is €53.71. Because the stock is currently priced at €50 per share, you would choose to buy it. However, you should be aware that the stock may be selling for less than €53.71, because other investors place a different risk on the cash flows or estimate the cash flows to be less than you do.

The generalized dividend valuation model

Using the present value concept, the one-period dividend valuation model can be extended to any number of periods: the value of a stock today is the present value of all future cash flows. The only cash flows that an investor will receive are dividends and a final sales price when the stock is ultimately sold in period n. The generalized multi-period formula for stock valuation can be written as

$$P_0 = \frac{D_1}{(1 + k_e)^1} + \frac{D_2}{(1 + k_e)^2} + \cdots + \frac{D_n}{(1 + k_e)^n} + \frac{P_n}{(1 + k_e)^n} \qquad (7.2)$$

If you tried to use Equation 7.2 to find the value of a share of stock, you would soon realize that you must first estimate the value the stock will have at some point in the future before you can estimate its value today. In other words, you must find P_n before you can find P_0. However, if P_n is far in the future, it will not affect P_0. For example, the present value of a share of stock that sells for €50 seventy-five years from now using a 12% discount rate is just one cent [€50/(1.12^{75}) = €0.01]. This reasoning implies that the current value of a share of stock can be calculated as simply the present value of the future dividend stream. The **generalized dividend model** is rewritten in Equation 7.3 without the final sales price:

$$P_0 = \sum_{t=1}^{\infty} \frac{D_t}{(1 + k_e)^t} \qquad (7.3)$$

Consider the implications of Equation 7.3 for a moment. The generalized dividend model says that the price of stock is determined only by the present value of the dividends and that nothing else matters. Many stocks do not pay dividends, so how is it that these stocks have value? *Buyers of the stock expect that the firm will pay dividends someday*. Most of the time a firm institutes dividends as soon as it has completed the rapid growth phase of its life cycle.

The generalized dividend valuation model requires that we compute the present value of an infinite stream of dividends, a process that could be difficult, to say the least. Therefore, simplified models have been developed to make the calculations easier. One such model is the **Gordon growth model**, which assumes constant dividend growth.

The Gordon growth model

Many firms strive to increase their dividends at a constant rate each year. Equation 7.4 rewrites Equation 7.3 to reflect this constant growth in dividends:

$$P_0 = \frac{D_0 \times (1 + g)^1}{(1 + k_e)^1} + \frac{D_0 \times (1 + g)^2}{(1 + k_e)^2} + \cdots + \frac{D_0 \times (1 + g)^{\infty}}{(1 + k_e)^{\infty}} \qquad (7.4)$$

where D_0 = the most recent dividend paid
g = the expected constant growth rate in dividends
k_e = the required return on an investment in equity

Equation 7.4 has been simplified to obtain Equation 7.5:[1]

$$P_0 = \frac{D_0 \times (1 + g)}{(k_e - g)} = \frac{D_1}{(k_e - g)} \qquad (7.5)$$

This model is useful for finding the value of stock, given a few assumptions:

1 *Dividends are assumed to continue growing at a constant rate for ever.* Actually, as long as they are expected to grow at a constant rate for an extended period of time, the model should yield reasonable results. This is because errors about distant cash flows become small when discounted to the present.
2 *The growth rate is assumed to be less than the required return on equity, k_e.* Myron Gordon, in his development of the model, demonstrated that this is a reasonable assumption. In theory, if the growth rate were faster than the rate demanded by holders of the firm's equity, in the long run the firm would grow impossibly large.

How the market sets stock prices

Suppose you go to an auto auction. The cars are available for inspection before the auction begins, and you find a little Mazda Miata that you like. You test-drive it in the parking lot and notice that it makes a few strange noises, but you decide that you would still like the car. You decide €5,000 would be a fair price that would allow you to pay some repair bills should the noises turn out to be serious. You see that the auction is ready to begin, so you go in and wait for the Miata to enter.

Suppose another buyer also spots the Miata. He test-drives the car and recognizes that the noises are simply the result of worn brake pads that he can fix himself at a nominal cost. He decides that the car is worth €7,000. He also goes in and waits for the Miata to come up for auction.

Who will buy the car and for how much? Suppose only the two of you are interested in the Miata. You begin the bidding at €4,000. Your competitor ups your bid to €4,500. You bid your top price of €5,000. He counters with €5,100. The price is now higher than you are willing to pay, so you stop bidding. The car is sold to the more informed buyer for €5,100.

This simple example raises a number of points. First, the price is set by the buyer willing to pay the highest price. The price is not necessarily the highest price the asset could fetch, but it is incrementally greater than what any other buyer is willing to pay.

Second, the market price will be set by the buyer who can take best advantage of the asset. The buyer who purchased the car knew that he could fix the noise easily and cheaply. As a consequence, he was willing to pay more for the car than you were. The same concept holds for other assets. For example, a piece of property or a building will sell to the buyer who can put the asset to the most productive use.

Finally, the example shows the role played by information in asset pricing. Superior information about an asset can increase its value by reducing its risk. When you consider buying a stock, there are many unknowns about the future cash flows. The buyer who has the best information about these cash flows will discount them at a lower interest rate than will a buyer who is very uncertain.

Now let us apply these ideas to stock valuation. Suppose that you are considering the purchase of stock expected to pay a €2 dividend next year. Market analysts expect the firm to grow at 3% indefinitely. You are *uncertain* about both the constancy of the dividend stream and the accuracy of the estimated growth rate. To compensate yourself for this uncertainty (risk), you require a return of 15%.

Now suppose Jennifer, another investor, has spoken with industry insiders and feels more confident about the projected cash flows. Jennifer requires only a 12% return because her perceived risk is lower than yours. Bud, on the other hand, is dating the CEO of the company. He knows with more certainty what the future of the firm actually is, and thus requires only a 10% return.

What are the values each investor will give to the stock? Applying the Gordon growth model yields the following stock prices:

Investor	Discount rate	Stock price
You	15%	€16.67
Jennifer	12%	€22.22
Bud	10%	€28.57

You are willing to pay €16.67 for the stock. Jennifer would pay up to €22.22, and Bud would pay €28.57. The investor with the lowest perceived risk is willing to pay the most for the stock. If there were no other traders but these three, the market price would be between €22.22 and €28.57. If you already held the stock, you would sell it to Bud.

We thus see that the players in the market, bidding against one another, establish the market price. When new information is released about a firm, expectations change and with them, prices change. New information can cause changes in expectations about the level of future dividends or the risk of those dividends. Because market participants are constantly receiving new information and revising their expectations, it is reasonable that stock prices are constantly changing as well.

APPLICATION | ## Monetary policy and stock prices

Stock market analysts tend to hang on the pronouncements of the ECB governing council or the Monetary Policy Committee of the Bank of England because they know that an important determinant of stock prices is monetary policy. But how does monetary policy affect stock prices?

The Gordon growth model in Equation 7.5 explains this relationship. Monetary policy can affect stock prices in two ways. First, when the Fed lowers interest rates, the return on bonds (an alternative asset to stocks) declines, and investors are likely to accept a lower required rate of return on an investment in equity (k_e). The resulting decline in k_e would lower the denominator in the Gordon growth model (Equation 7.5), lead to a higher value of P_0, and raise stock prices. Furthermore, a lowering of interest rates is likely to stimulate the economy, so that the growth rate in dividends, g, is likely to be somewhat higher. This rise in g also causes the denominator in Equation 7.5 to decrease, which also leads to a higher P_0 and a rise in stock prices.

As we will see in Chapter 24, the impact of monetary policy on stock prices is one of the key ways in which monetary policy affects the economy. ■

APPLICATION | ## The subprime financial crisis and the stock market

The subprime financial crisis that started in August 2007 led to one of the worst bear markets in the last 50 years. Our analysis of stock price valuation, again using the Gordon growth model, can help us understand how this event affected stock prices.

The subprime financial crisis had a major negative impact on the economy, leading to a downward revision of the growth prospects for US companies, thus lowering the dividend growth rate (g) in the Gordon model. The resulting increase in the denominator in Equation 7.5 would lead to a decline in P_0 and hence a decline in stock prices.

Increased uncertainty for the US economy and the widening credit spreads resulting from the subprime crisis would also raise the required return on investment in equity. A higher k_e also leads to an increase in the denominator in Equation 7.5, a decline in P_0, and a general fall in stock prices.

In the early stages of the financial crisis, the decline in growth prospects and credit spreads were moderate and so, as the Gordon model predicts, the stock market decline was also moderate. However, when the crisis entered a particularly virulent stage in October of 2008, credit spreads shot through the roof, the economy nosedived, and as the Gordon model predicts, the stock market crashed, falling by over 40% from its peak value a year earlier. ■

The theory of rational expectations

The analysis of stock price evaluation we outlined in the previous section depends on people's expectations – especially of cash flows. Indeed, it is difficult to think of any sector in the economy in which expectations are not crucial; this is why it is important to examine how expectations are formed. We do so by outlining the *theory of rational expectations*, currently the most widely used theory to describe the formation of business and consumer expectations.

In the 1950s and 1960s, economists regularly viewed expectations as formed from past experience only. Expectations of inflation, for example, were typically viewed as being an average of past inflation rates. This view of expectation formation, called **adaptive expectations**, suggests that changes in expectations will occur slowly over time as past data change.[2] So if inflation had formerly been steady at a 5% rate, expectations of future inflation would be 5%, too. If inflation rose to a steady rate of 10%, expectations of future inflation would rise toward 10%, but slowly: in the first year, expected inflation might rise only to 6%; in the second year, to 7%; and so on.

Adaptive expectations have been faulted on the grounds that people use more information than just past data on a single variable to form their expectations of that variable. Their expectations of inflation will almost surely be affected by their predictions of future monetary policy as well as by current and past monetary policy. In addition, people often change their expectations quickly in the light of new information. To meet these objections to adaptive expectations, John Muth developed an alternative theory of expectations, called **rational expectations**, which can be stated as follows: *expectations will be identical to optimal forecasts (the best guess of the future) using all available information.*[3]

What exactly does this mean? To explain it more clearly, let's use the theory of rational expectations to examine how expectations are formed in a situation that most of us encounter at some point in our lifetime: our drive to work. Suppose that if Joe Commuter travels when it is not rush hour, it takes an average of 30 minutes for his trip. Sometimes it takes him 35 minutes, other times 25 minutes, but the average non-rush-hour driving time is 30 minutes. If, however, Joe leaves for work during the rush hour, it takes him, on average, an additional 10 minutes to get to work. Given that he leaves for work during the rush hour, the best guess of the driving time – the **optimal forecast** – is 40 minutes.

If the only information available to Joe before he leaves for work that would have a potential effect on his driving time is that he is leaving during the rush hour, what does rational expectations theory allow you to predict about Joe's expectations of his driving time? Since the best guess of his driving time using all available information is 40 minutes, Joe's expectation should also be the same. Clearly, an expectation of 35 minutes would not be rational, because it is not equal to the optimal forecast, the best guess of the driving time.

Suppose that the next day, given the same conditions and the same expectations, it takes Joe 45 minutes to drive because he hits an abnormally large number of red lights, and the day after that he hits all the lights right and it takes him only 35 minutes. Do these variations mean that Joe's 40-minute expectation is irrational? No, an expectation of 40 minutes' driving time is still a rational expectation. In both cases, the forecast is off by five minutes, so the expectation has not been perfectly accurate. However, the forecast does not have to be perfectly accurate to be rational – it need only be the *best possible* given the available information; that is, it has to be correct *on average,* and the 40-minute expectation meets this requirement. As there is bound to be some randomness in Joe's driving time regardless of driving conditions, an optimal forecast will never be completely accurate.

The example makes the following important point about rational expectations: *even though a rational expectation equals the optimal forecast using all available information, a prediction based on it may not always be perfectly accurate.*

What if an item of information relevant to predicting driving time is unavailable or ignored? Suppose that on Joe's usual route to work there is an accident that causes a two-hour traffic jam. If Joe has no way of ascertaining this information, his rush-hour expectation of 40 minutes' driving time is still rational, because the accident information is not available to him for incorporation into his optimal forecast. However, if there was a radio or TV traffic report about the accident that Joe did not bother to listen to or heard but ignored, his 40-minute expectation is no longer rational. In light of the availability of this information, Joe's optimal forecast should have been 2 hours and 40 minutes.

Accordingly, there are two reasons why an expectation may fail to be rational:

1 People might be aware of all available information but find it takes too much effort to make their expectation the best guess possible.
2 People might be unaware of some available relevant information, so their best guess of the future will not be accurate.

Nonetheless, it is important to recognize that if an additional factor is important but information about it is not available, an expectation that does not take account of it can still be rational.

Formal statement of the theory

We can state the theory of rational expectations somewhat more formally. If X stands for the variable that is being forecast (in our example, Joe Commuter's driving time), X^e for the expectation of this variable (Joe's expectation of his driving time), and X^{of} for the optimal forecast of X using all available information (the best guess possible of his driving time), the theory of rational expectations then simply says

$$X^e = X^{of} \tag{7.6}$$

That is, the expectation of X equals the optimal forecast using all available information.

Rationale behind the theory

Why do people try to make their expectations match their best possible guess of the future using all available information? The simplest explanation is that it is costly for people not to do so. Joe Commuter has a strong incentive to make his expectation of the time it takes him to drive to work as accurate as possible. If he underpredicts his driving time, he will often be late to work and risk being fired. If he overpredicts, he will, on average, get to work too early and will have given up sleep or leisure time unnecessarily. Accurate expectations are desirable, and there are strong incentives for people to try to make them equal to optimal forecasts by using all available information.

The same principle applies to businesses. Suppose that an appliance manufacturer – say, General Electric – knows that interest-rate movements are important to the sales of appliances. If GE makes poor forecasts of interest rates, it will earn less profit, because it might produce either too many appliances or too few. There are strong incentives for GE to acquire all available information to help it forecast interest rates and use the information to make the best possible guess of future interest-rate movements.

The incentives for equating expectations with optimal forecasts are especially strong in financial markets. In these markets, people with better forecasts of the future get rich. The application of the theory of rational expectations to financial markets (where it is called the **efficient market hypothesis** or the **theory of efficient capital markets**) is thus particularly useful.

Implications of the theory

Rational expectations theory leads to two common-sense implications for the forming of expectations that are important in the analysis of both the stock market and the aggregate economy:

1 *If there is a change in the way a variable moves, the way in which expectations of this variable are formed will change as well.* This tenet of rational expectations theory can be most easily understood through a concrete example. Suppose that interest rates move in such a way that they tend to return to a 'normal' level in the future. If today's interest rate is high relative to the normal level, an optimal forecast of the interest rate in the

future is that it will decline to the normal level. Rational expectations theory would imply that when today's interest rate is high, the expectation is that it will fall in the future.

Suppose now that the way in which the interest rate moves changes so that when the interest rate is high, it stays high. In this case, when today's interest rate is high, the optimal forecast of the future interest rate, and hence the rational expectation, is that it will stay high. Expectations of the future interest rate will no longer indicate that the interest rate will fall. The change in the way the interest-rate variable moves has therefore led to a change in the way that expectations of future interest rates are formed. The rational expectations analysis here is generalizable to expectations of any variable. Hence, when there is a change in the way any variable moves, the way in which expectations of this variable are formed will change, too.

2 **The forecast errors of expectations will, on average, be zero and cannot be predicted ahead of time.** The forecast error of an expectation is $X - X^e$, the difference between the realization of a variable X and the expectation of the variable. That is, if Joe Commuter's driving time on a particular day is 45 minutes and his expectation of the driving time is 40 minutes, the forecast error is 5 minutes.

Suppose that in violation of the rational expectations tenet, Joe's forecast error is not, on average, equal to zero; instead, it equals five minutes. The forecast error is now predictable ahead of time because Joe will soon notice that he is, on average, five minutes late for work and can improve his forecast by increasing it by five minutes. Rational expectations theory implies that this is exactly what Joe will do because he will want his forecast to be the best guess possible. When Joe has revised his forecast upward by five minutes, on average, the forecast error will equal zero so that it cannot be predicted ahead of time. Rational expectations theory implies that forecast errors of expectations cannot be predicted.

The efficient market hypothesis: rational expectations in financial markets

While monetary economists were developing the theory of rational expectations, financial economists were developing a parallel theory of expectations formation in financial markets. It led them to the same conclusion as that of the rational expectations theorists: expectations in financial markets are equal to optimal forecasts using all available information.[4] Although financial economists gave their theory another name, calling it *the efficient market hypothesis,* in fact their theory is just an application of rational expectations to the pricing of stocks and also other securities.

The efficient market hypothesis is based on the assumption that prices of securities in financial markets fully reflect all available information. You may recall from Chapter 4 that the rate of return from holding a security equals the sum of the capital gain on the security (the change in the price), plus any cash payments, divided by the initial purchase price of the security:

$$R = \frac{P_{t+1} - P_t + C}{P_t} \tag{7.7}$$

where R = rate of return on the security held from time t to $t + 1$
      (say, the end 2010 to the end of 2011)
  P_{t+1} = price of the security at time $t + 1$, the end of the holding period
    P_t = price of the security at time t, the beginning of the holding period
     C = cash payment (coupon or dividend payments) made in the period t to $t + 1$

Let's look at the expectation of this return at time t, the beginning of the holding period. Because the current price P_t and the cash payment C are known at the beginning, the only variable in the definition of the return that is uncertain is the price next period, P_{t+1}.[5] Denoting the expectation of the security's price at the end of the holding period as, the expected return R^e is

$$R^e = \frac{P^e_{t+1} - P_t + C}{P_t}$$

The efficient market hypothesis views expectations of future prices as equal to optimal forecasts using all currently available information. In other words, the market's expectations of future securities prices are rational, so that

$$P^e_{t+1} = P^{of}_{t+1}$$

which in turn implies that the expected return on the security will equal the optimal forecast of the return:

$$R^e = R^{of} \tag{7.8}$$

Unfortunately, we cannot observe either R^e or, p^e_{t+1}, so the rational expectations equations by themselves do not tell us much about how the financial market behaves. However, if we can devise some way to measure the value of R^e, these equations will have important implications for how prices of securities change in financial markets.

The supply and demand analysis of the bond market developed in Chapter 5 shows us that the expected return on a security (the interest rate, in the case of the bond examined) will have a tendency to head toward the equilibrium return that equates the quantity demanded to the quantity supplied. Supply and demand analysis enables us to determine the expected return on a security with the following equilibrium condition: the expected return on a security R^e equals the equilibrium return R^*, which equates the quantity of the security demanded to the quantity supplied; that is,

$$R^e = R^* \tag{7.9}$$

The academic field of finance explores the factors (risk and liquidity, for example) that influence the equilibrium returns on securities. For our purposes, it is sufficient to know that we can determine the equilibrium return and thus determine the expected return with the equilibrium condition.

We can derive an equation to describe pricing behaviour in an efficient market by using the equilibrium condition to replace R^e with R^* in the rational expectations equation (Equation 7.8). In this way, we obtain

$$R^{of} = R^* \tag{7.10}$$

This equation tells us that *current prices in a financial market will be set so that the optimal forecast of a security's return using all available information equals the security's equilibrium return.* Financial economists state it more simply: in an efficient market, a security's price fully reflects all available information.

Rationale behind the hypothesis

To see why the efficient market efficient hypothesis makes sense, we make use of the concept of **arbitrage**, in which market participants (*arbitrageurs*) eliminate **unexploited profit opportunities**, i.e. returns on a security that are larger than what is justified by the characteristics of that security. There are two types of arbitrage, *pure arbitrage*, in which the elimination of unexploited profit opportunities involves no risk, and the type of arbitrage we discuss here in which the arbitrageur takes on some risk when eliminating the unexploited profit opportunities. To see how arbitrage leads to the efficient market hypothesis, suppose that, given its risk characteristics, the normal return on a security, say, ExxonMobil common stock, is 10% at an annual rate, and its current price P_t is lower than the optimal forecast of tomorrow's price P_{t+1}^{of} so that the optimal forecast of the return at an annual rate is 50%, which is greater than the equilibrium return of 10%. We are now able to predict that, on average, ExxonMobil's return would be abnormally high so that there is an unexploited profit opportunity. Knowing that, on average, you can earn such an abnormally high rate of return on ExxonMobil because $R^{of} > R^*$, you would buy more, which would in turn drive up its current price P_t relative to the expected future price P_{t+1}^{of}, thereby lowering R^{of}. When the current price had risen sufficiently so that R^{of} equalled R^* and the efficient market condition (Equation 7.10) was satisfied, the buying of ExxonMobil would stop, and the unexploited profit opportunity would disappear.

Similarly, a security for which the optimal forecast of the return is -5% and the equilibrium return is 10% ($R^{of} < R^*$) would be a poor investment, because, on average, it earns less than the equilibrium return. In such a case, you would sell the security and drive down its current price relative to the expected future price until R^{of} rose to the level of R^* and the efficient market condition was again satisfied. What we have shown can be summarized as follows:

$$R^{of} > R^* \rightarrow P_t \uparrow \rightarrow R^{of} \downarrow$$
$$R^{of} < R^* \rightarrow P_t \downarrow \rightarrow R^{of} \uparrow$$
$$\text{until}$$
$$R^{of} = R^*$$

Another way to state the efficient market condition is this: *in an efficient market, all unexploited profit opportunities will be eliminated*.

An extremely important factor in this reasoning is that *not everyone in a financial market must be well informed about a security or have rational expectations for its price to be driven to the point at which the efficient market condition holds*. Financial markets are structured so that many participants can play. As long as a few keep their eyes open for unexploited profit opportunities (often referred to as 'smart money'), they will eliminate the profit opportunities that appear, because in so doing, they make a profit. The efficient market hypothesis makes sense, because it does not require everyone in a market to be cognizant of what is happening to every security.

Stronger version of the efficient market hypothesis

Many financial economists take the efficient market hypothesis one step further in their analysis of financial markets. Not only do they define efficient markets as those in which expectations are rational – that is, equal to optimal forecasts using all available information – but they also add the condition that an efficient market is one in which prices reflect the true fundamental (intrinsic) value of the securities. Thus, in an efficient market, all prices are always correct and reflect market fundamentals (items that have a direct impact on future income streams of the securities). This stronger view of market efficiency has several important implications in the academic field of finance. First, it implies that in an efficient capital market, one investment is as good as any other because the securities' prices are correct. Second, it implies that a security's price reflects all available information about the intrinsic value of the security. Third, it implies that security prices can be used by managers of both financial and non-financial firms to assess their cost of capital (cost of financing their investments) accurately and hence that security prices can be used to help them make the correct decisions about whether a specific investment is worth making. The stronger version of market efficiency is a basic tenet of much analysis in the finance field.

APPLICATION Practical guide to investing in the stock market

The efficient market hypothesis has numerous applications to the real world.[6] It is especially valuable because it can be applied directly to an issue that concerns many of us: how to get rich (or at least not get poor) in the stock market. (The 'Following the financial news' box shows how stock prices are reported daily.) A practical guide to investing in the stock market, which we develop here, provides a better understanding of the use and implications of the efficient market hypothesis.

How valuable are published reports by investment advisers?

Suppose you have just read in the 'Lex' column of the *Financial Times* that investment advisers are predicting a boom in oil stocks because an oil shortage is developing. Should you proceed to withdraw all your hard-earned savings from the bank and invest it in oil stocks?

The efficient market hypothesis tells us that when purchasing a security, we cannot expect to earn an abnormally high return, a return greater than the equilibrium return. Information in newspapers and in the published reports of investment advisers is readily available to many market participants and is already reflected in market prices. So acting on this information will not yield abnormally high returns, on average. The empirical evidence for the most part confirms that recommendations from investment advisers cannot help us outperform the general market. Indeed, as the 'Closer look' box suggests, human investment advisers in San Francisco do not, on average, even outperform an orang utan!

Probably no other conclusion is met with more scepticism by students than this one when they first hear it. We all know or have heard of someone who has been successful in the stock market for a period of many years. We wonder, 'How could someone be so consistently successful if he or she did not really know how to predict when returns would be abnormally high?' The following story, reported in the press, illustrates why such anecdotal evidence is not reliable.

A get-rich-quick artist invented a clever scam. Every week, he wrote two letters. In letter A, he would pick team A to win a particular football game; in letter B, he would pick the opponent, team B. He would then separate a mailing list into two groups, and he would send letter A to the people in one group and letter B to the people in the other. The following week he would do the same thing but would send these letters only to the group who had received the first letter with the correct prediction. After doing this for ten games, he had a small cluster of people who had received letters predicting the correct winning team for every game. He then mailed a final letter to them, declaring that since he was obviously an expert predictor of the outcome of football games (he had picked winners ten weeks in a row) and since his predictions were profitable for the recipients who bet on the games, he would continue to send his predictions only if he were paid a substantial amount of money. When one of his clients figured out what he was up to, the con man was prosecuted and thrown in jail!

What is the lesson of the story? Even if no forecaster is an accurate predictor of the market, there will always be a group of consistent winners. A person who has done well regularly in the past cannot guarantee that he or she will do well in the future. Note that there will also be a group of persistent losers, but you rarely hear about them because no one brags about a poor forecasting record.

Should you be sceptical of hot tips?

Suppose your broker phones you with a hot tip to buy stock in the Happy Feet Corporation (HFC) because it has just developed a product that is completely effective in curing athlete's foot. The stock price is sure to go up. Should you follow this advice and buy HFC stock?

The efficient market hypothesis indicates that you should be sceptical of such news. If the stock market is efficient, it has already priced HFC stock so that its expected return will

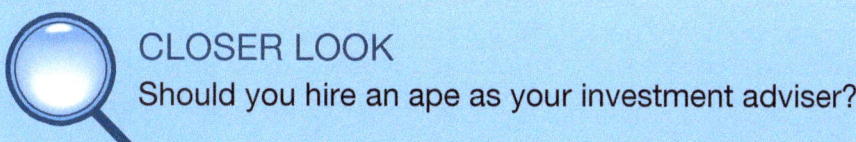

CLOSER LOOK
Should you hire an ape as your investment adviser?

The *San Francisco Chronicle* came up with an amusing way of evaluating how successful investment advisers are at picking stocks. They asked eight analysts to pick five stocks at the beginning of the year and then compared the performance of their stock picks to those chosen by Jolyn, an orang utan living at Marine

World/Africa USA in Vallejo, California. Consistent with the results found in the 'Investment Dartboard' feature of the *Wall Street Journal*, Jolyn beat the investment advisers as often as they beat her. Given this result, you might be just as well off hiring an orang utan as your investment adviser as you would hiring a human being!

equal the equilibrium return. The hot tip is not particularly valuable and will not enable you to earn an abnormally high return.

You might wonder, though, if the hot tip is based on new information and would give you an edge on the rest of the market. If other market participants have got this information before you, the answer is no. As soon as the information hits the street, the unexploited profit opportunity it creates will be quickly eliminated. The stock's price will already reflect the information, and you should expect to realize only the equilibrium return. But if you are one of the first to gain the new information, it can do you some good. Only then can you be one of the lucky ones who, on average, will earn an abnormally high return by helping eliminate the profit opportunity by buying HFC stock.

Do stock prices always rise when there is good news?

If you follow the stock market, you might have noticed a puzzling phenomenon: when good news about a stock, such as a particularly favourable earnings report, is announced, the price of the stock frequently does not rise. The efficient market hypothesis explains this phenomenon.

Because changes in stock prices are unpredictable, when information is announced that has already been expected by the market, the stock price will remain unchanged. The announcement does not contain any new information that should lead to a change in stock prices. If this was not the case and the announcement led to a change in stock prices, it would mean that the change was predictable. Because that is ruled out in an efficient market, **stock prices will respond to announcements only when the information being announced is new and unexpected**. If the news is expected, there will be no stock price response. This is exactly what the evidence shows: stock prices do reflect publicly available information.

Sometimes an individual stock price declines when good news is announced. Although this seems somewhat peculiar, it is completely consistent with the workings of an efficient market. Suppose that although the announced news is good, it is not as good as expected. HFC's earnings may have risen 15%, but if the market expected earnings to rise by 20%, the new information is actually unfavourable, and the stock price declines.

Efficient market prescription for the investor

What does the efficient market hypothesis recommend for investing in the stock market? It tells us that hot tips and investment advisers' published recommendations – all of which make use of publicly available information – cannot help an investor outperform the market. Indeed, it indicates that anyone without better information than other market participants cannot expect to beat the market. So what is an investor to do?

The efficient market hypothesis leads to the conclusion that such an investor (and almost all of us fit into this category) should not try to outguess the market by constantly buying and selling securities. This process does nothing but boost the income of brokers, who earn commissions on each trade.[7] Instead, the investor should pursue a 'buy and hold' strategy – purchase stocks and hold them for long periods of time. This will lead to the same returns, on average, but the investor's net profits will be higher, because fewer brokerage commissions will have to be paid.

It is frequently a sensible strategy for a small investor, whose costs of managing a portfolio may be high relative to its size, to buy into a mutual fund rather than to buy individual stocks. Because the efficient market hypothesis indicates that no mutual fund can consistently outperform the market, an investor should not buy into one that has high management fees or that pays sales commissions to brokers, but rather should purchase a no-load (commission-free) mutual fund that has low management fees.

The evidence indicates that it will not be easy to beat the prescription suggested here, although some anomalies to the efficient market hypothesis suggest that an extremely clever investor (which rules out most of us) may be able to outperform a buy-and-hold strategy. ▪

APPLICATION ## What do the Black Monday crash of 1987 and the tech crash of 2000 tell us about rational expectations and efficient markets?

On 19 October 1987, dubbed 'Black Monday', the Dow Jones Industrial Average declined more than 20%, the largest one-day decline in US history. The collapse of the high-tech companies' share prices from their peaks in March 2000 caused the heavily tech-laden NASDAQ index to fall from around 5,000 in March 2000 to around 1,500 in 2001 and 2002, a decline of well over 60%. These two crashes have caused many economists to question the validity of the efficient market hypothesis and rational expectations. They do not believe that a rational marketplace could have produced such a massive swing in share prices. To what degree should these stock market crashes make us doubt the validity of rational expectations and the efficient market hypothesis?

Nothing in rational expectations theory rules out large changes in stock prices. A large change in stock prices can result from new information that produces a dramatic decline in optimal forecasts of the future valuation of firms. However, economists are hard pressed to come up with fundamental changes in the economy that can explain the Black Monday and tech crashes. One lesson from these crashes is that factors other than market fundamentals probably have an effect on stock prices. Hence these crashes have convinced many economists that the stronger version of the efficient market hypothesis, which states that asset prices reflect the true fundamental (intrinsic) value of securities, is incorrect. They attribute a large role in determination of stock prices to market psychology and to the institutional structure of the marketplace. However, nothing in this view contradicts the basic reasoning behind rational expectations or the efficient market hypothesis – that market participants eliminate unexploited profit opportunities. Even though stock market prices may not always solely reflect market fundamentals, this does not mean that rational expectations do not hold. As long as stock market crashes are unpredictable, the basic lessons of the theory of rational expectations hold.

Some economists have come up with theories of what they call *rational bubbles* to explain stock market crashes. A **bubble** is a situation in which the price of an asset differs from its fundamental market value. In a rational bubble, investors can have rational expectations that a bubble is occurring because the asset price is higher than its fundamental value but continue to hold the asset anyway. They might do so because they believe that someone else will buy the asset for a higher price in the future. In a rational bubble, asset prices can therefore deviate from their fundamental value for a long time because the bursting of the bubble cannot be predicted and so there are no unexploited profit opportunities.

However, other economists believe that the Black Monday crash of 1987 and the tech crash of 2000 suggest that there may be unexploited profit opportunities and that the theory of rational expectations and the efficient market hypothesis might be fundamentally flawed. The controversy over whether capital markets are efficient or expectations are rational continues. ∎

Behavioural finance

Doubts about the efficient market hypothesis, particularly after the stock market crash of 1987, have led to the emergence of a new field of study, **behavioural finance**. It applies concepts from other social sciences such as anthropology, sociology and, particularly, psychology to understand the behaviour of securities prices.[8]

As we have seen, the efficient market hypothesis assumes that unexploited profit opportunities are eliminated by 'smart money' market participants. But can smart money dominate ordinary investors so that financial markets are efficient? Specifically, the efficient market hypothesis suggests that smart money participants will sell when a stock price goes up irrationally, with the result that the stock price falls back down to a level that is justified by fundamentals. For this to occur, smart money investors must be able to engage in **short sales**; that is, they must borrow stock from brokers and then sell it in the market, with the aim that they earn a profit by buying the stock back again ('covering the short') after it has fallen in price. Work by psychologists, however, suggests that people are subject to loss aversion: they are more unhappy when they suffer losses than they are happy when they achieve gains. Short sales can result in losses far in excess of an investor's initial investment if the stock price climbs sharply higher than the price at which the short sale is made (and losses have the possibility of being unlimited if the stock price climbs to astronomical heights).

Loss aversion can thus explain an important phenomenon: very little short selling actually takes place. Short selling may also be constrained by rules restricting it because it seems unsavoury for someone to make money from another person's misfortune. The existence of so little short selling can explain why stock prices are sometimes overvalued. That is, the lack of enough short selling means that smart money does not drive stock prices back down to their fundamental value.

Psychologists have also found that people tend to be overconfident in their own judgements. As a result, investors tend to believe that they are smarter than other investors. Because investors are willing to assume that the market typically doesn't get it right, they trade on their beliefs, rather than on pure facts. This theory may explain why securities markets have such a large trading volume – something that the efficient market hypothesis does not predict.

Overconfidence and social contagion (fads) provide an explanation for stock market bubbles. When stock prices go up, investors attribute their profits to their intelligence and talk up the stock market. This word-of-mouth enthusiasm and glowing media reports then can produce an environment in which even more investors think stock prices will rise in the future. The result is a positive feedback loop in which prices continue to rise, producing a speculative bubble, which finally crashes when prices get too far out of line with fundamentals.[9]

The field of behavioural finance is a young one, but it holds out hope that we might be able to explain some features of securities markets' behaviour that are not well explained by the efficient market hypothesis.

Summary

1 Stocks are valued as the present value of future dividends. Unfortunately, we do not know very precisely what these dividends will be. This uncertainty introduces a great deal of error into the valuation process. The Gordon growth model is a simplified method of computing stock value

that depends on the assumption that the dividends are growing at a constant rate for ever. Given our uncertainty regarding future dividends, this assumption is often the best we can do.

2 The interaction among traders in the market is what actually sets prices on a day-to-day basis. The trader who values the security the most (either because of less uncertainty about the cash flows or because of greater estimated cash flows) will be willing to pay the most. As new information is released, investors will revise their estimates of the true value of the security and will either buy or sell it depending on how the market price compares to their estimated valuation. Because small changes in estimated growth rates or required return result in large changes in price, it is not surprising that the markets are often volatile.

3 The efficient market hypothesis states that current security prices will fully reflect all available information, because in an efficient market, all unexploited profit opportunities are eliminated. The elimination of unexploited profit opportunities necessary for a financial market to be efficient does not require that all market participants be well informed.

4 The efficient market hypothesis indicates that hot tips, investment advisers' published recommendations, cannot help an investor outperform the market. The prescription for investors is to pursue a buy-and-hold strategy – purchase stocks and hold them for long periods of time. Empirical evidence generally supports these implications of the efficient market hypothesis in the stock market.

5 The stock market crash of 1987 and the tech crash of 2000 convinced many financial economists that the stronger version of the efficient market hypothesis, which states that asset prices reflect the true fundamental (intrinsic) value of securities, is not correct. It is less clear that these crashes show that the weaker version of the efficient market hypothesis is wrong. Even if the stock market was driven by factors other than fundamentals, these crashes do not clearly demonstrate that many of the basic lessons of the efficient market hypothesis are no longer valid, as long as these crashes could not have been predicted.

6 The new field of behavioural finance applies concepts from other social sciences such as anthropology, sociology and psychology to understand the behaviour of securities prices. Loss aversion, overconfidence and social contagion can explain why trading volume is so high, stock prices become overvalued and speculative bubbles occur.

Key terms

adaptive expectations p. 135

arbitrage p. 138

behavioural finance p. 143

bubble p. 142

cash flows p. 131

dividends p. 131

efficient market hypothesis p. 136

generalized dividend model p. 132

Gordon growth model p. 132

market fundamentals p. 139

optimal forecast p. 135

rational expectations p. 135

residual claimant p. 131

short sales p. 143

stockholders p. 130

theory of efficient capital markets p. 136

unexploited profit opportunity p. 138

QUESTIONS AND PROBLEMS

All questions and problems are available in MyEconLab at **www.myeconlab.com/mishkin**.

1 What basic principle of finance can be applied to the valuation of any investment asset?

2 Identify the cash flows available to an equity investor. How reliably can these cash flows be estimated? Compare the problem of estimating stock cash flows to estimating bond cash flows. Which security would you predict to be more volatile?

3 Compute the price of a share of stock that pays a €1 per year dividend and that you expect to be able to sell in one year for €20, assuming you require a 15% return.

4 After careful analysis, you have determined that a firm's dividends should grow at 7% on average in the foreseeable future. The firm's last dividend was €3. Compute the current price of this stock, assuming the required return is 18%.

5 Some economists think that the central banks should try to prick bubbles in the stock market before they get out of hand and cause later damage when they burst. How can monetary policy be used to prick a bubble? Explain how it can do this using the Gordon growth model.

6 'Forecasters' predictions of inflation are notoriously inaccurate, so their expectations of inflation cannot be rational'. Is this statement true, false, or uncertain? Explain your answer.

7 'Whenever it is snowing when Joe Commuter gets up in the morning, he misjudges how long it will take him to drive to work. Otherwise, his expectations of the driving time are perfectly accurate. Considering that it snows only once every ten years where Joe lives, Joe's expectations are almost always perfectly accurate.' Are Joe's expectations rational? Why or why not?

8 If a forecaster spends hours every day studying data to forecast interest rates but his expectations are not as accurate as predicting that tomorrow's interest rates will be identical to today's interest rate, are his expectations rational?

9 'If stock prices did not follow a random walk, there would be unexploited profit opportunities in the market.' Is this statement true, false, or uncertain? Explain your answer.

10 Suppose that increases in the money supply lead to a rise in stock prices. Does this mean that when you see that the money supply has had a sharp increase in the past week, you should go out and buy stocks? Why or why not?

11 If the public expects a company to lose €5 per share this quarter and it actually loses €4, which is still the largest loss in the history of the company, what does the efficient market hypothesis say will happen to the price of the stock when the €4 loss is announced?

12 If you read in the *Financial Times* that the 'stock pickers' on Lombard Street expect stock prices to fall, should you follow that lead and sell all your stocks?

13 If your broker has been right in her five previous buy and sell recommendations, should you continue listening to her advice?

14 Can a person with rational expectations expect the price of a share of Google to rise by 10% in the next month?

15 'If most participants in the stock market do not follow what is happening to the monetary aggregates, prices of common stocks will not fully reflect information about them.' Is this statement true, false, or uncertain? Explain your answer.

16 'An efficient market is one in which no one ever profits from having better information than the rest.' Is this statement true, false, or uncertain? Explain your answer.

17 If higher money growth is associated with higher future inflation, and if announced money growth turns out to be extremely high but is still less than the market expected, what do you think would happen to long-term bond prices?

18 'Foreign exchange rates, like stock prices, should follow a random walk.' Is this statement true, false, or uncertain? Explain your answer.

19 Can we expect the value of the euro to rise by 2% next week against the US dollar if our expectations are rational?

20 'Human fear is the source of stock market crashes, so these crashes indicate that expectations in the stock market cannot be rational.' Is this statement true, false, or uncertain? Explain your answer.

WEB EXERCISES

1 Visit **www.forecasts.org/data/index.htm**. Click on 'Stock Index' at the very top of the page. Now choose 'US Stock Indices – monthly.' Review the indexes for the DJIA, the S&P 500 and the NASDAQ composite. Which index appears most volatile? In which index would you have rather invested in 1985 if the investment had been allowed to compound until now?

2 The Internet is a great source of information on stock prices and stock price movements. Yahoo! Finance UK & Ireland is one useful (and free) source for current and historical stock market data. Go to **http://uk.finance. yahoo.com/** and click on the DAX (under the 'Europe' tab) or FTSE100 (under the 'UK' tab) at the top of the page to view current data on the DAX or FTSE100. Click on the 'Charts' section to get historical charts for the different indices. Change the time range and observe the stock trend over various intervals. Have stock prices been going up or down over the last day, week, three months, and year? Using 'Interactive Charts', compare the relative performance of the FTSE100, DAX and S&P500 over different time horizons.

3 Information on the FTSE100 index can also be found on the London Stock Exchange website. Locate the current value of the FTSE100 (**http://www. londonstockexchange.com/exchange/prices-and-markets/stocks/indices/summary/summary-indices. html?index=UKX**) and constituents here (**http://www. londonstockexchange.com/exchange/prices-and-markets/stocks/indices/summary/summary-indices-constituents.html?index=UKX**). Choose any one of the 100 companies and examine its profile, fundamentals, and news events.

Notes

1 To generate Equation 7.5 from Equation 7.4, first multiply both sides of Equation 7.4 by $(1 + k_e)/(1 + g)$ and subtract Equation 7.4 from the result. This yields $\frac{P_0 \times (1 + k_e)}{(1 + g)} - P_0 = D_0 \frac{D_0 \times (1 + g)^\infty}{(1 + k_e)^\infty}$ Assuming that k_e is greater than g, the term on the far right will approach zero and can be dropped. Thus, after factoring P_0 out of the left-hand side, $P_0 \times \left[\frac{1 + k_e}{1 + g} - 1 \right] = D_0$ Next, simplify by combining terms: $P_0 \times \frac{(1 + k_e) - (1 + g)}{1 + g} = D_0$

$$P_0 = \frac{D_0 \times (1 + g)}{k_e - g} = \frac{D_1}{k_e - g}$$

2 More specifically, adaptive expectations – say, of inflation – are written as a weighted average of past inflation rates:

$$\pi_t^e = (1 + \lambda) \sum_{j=0}^{\infty} \lambda^j \pi_{t-j}$$

where π_t^e = adaptive expectation of inflation at time t
π_{t-j} = inflation at time $t - j$
λ = a constant between the values of 0 and 1

3 John Muth, 'Rational expectations and the theory of price movements', *Econometrica* 29 (1961): 315–35.

4 The development of the efficient market hypothesis was not wholly independent of the development of rational expectations theory, in that financial economists were aware of Muth's work.

5 There are cases where C might not be known at the beginning of the period, but that does not make a substantial difference to the analysis. We would in that case assume that not only price expectations but also the expectations of C are optimal forecasts using all available information.

6 The empirical evidence on the efficient markets hypothesis is discussed in an appendix to this chapter, which can be found on this book's website at **www.myeconlab.com/mishkin**.

7 The investor may also have to pay the government capital gains taxes on any profits that are realized when a security is sold – an additional reason why continual buying and selling does not make sense.

8 Surveys of this field can be found in Hersh Shefrin, *Beyond Greed and Fear: Understanding of Behavioral Finance and the Psychology of Investing* (Boston: Harvard Business School Press, 2000); Andrei Shleifer, *Inefficient Markets* (Oxford, UK: Oxford University Press, 2000); and Robert J. Shiller, 'From efficient market theory to behavioral finance', Cowles Foundation Discussion Paper No. 1385 (October 2002).

9 See Robert J. Shiller, *Irrational Exuberance* (New York: Broadway Books, 2001).

Useful websites

http://www.stoxx.com/indices/index_information.html?symbol=sx5E Detailed information on the EURO STOXX 50 Index, Europe's leading blue-chip index for the euro zone.

http://www.londonstockexchange.com/home/homepage.htm The London Stock Exchange official website is a fantastic resource for prices, news, and other stock market information (**http://www.londonstockexchange.com/exchange/prices-and-markets/stocks/indices/summary/summary-indices-constituents.html?index=UKX**).

http://stocks.tradingcharts.com Access detailed stock quotes, charts, and historical stock data.

There are several websites on where you can learn more about the efficient market hypothesis:

http://www.e-m-h.org/

www.investorhome.com/emh.htm

http://v2.moneyscience.com/Information_Base/The_Efficient_Markets_Hypothesis_(EMH).html

PART 3
FINANCIAL INSTITUTIONS

Crisis upon crisis: The euro crisis hot on the heels of the global financial crisis

Beginning in mid-2007, the global financial system experienced a financial crisis of unprecedented magnitude. The crisis began with the drying up of liquidity in the interbank market, resulting in sharp increases in interest rates at which banks lend to each other. Both the ECB and the Bank of England provided liquidity to the market. But in September 2008 the collapse of Lehman Brothers signalled a seismic elevation of the crisis to global proportions. Immediately governments and central banks around the developed world swung into action with extraordinary monetary policy measures. In October 2008 the US House of Representatives passed the Emergency Economic Stabilization Act which paved the way for a $700 billion bailout package of the banks. The act authorized the US Treasury to purchase troubled mortgage assets from struggling financial institutions or to inject capital into banking institutions. In March 2009, the Bank of England instituted its policy of quantitative easing (QE) to purchase mainly government bonds to the amount of £200 billion, and in May 2009 the ECB announced a policy of purchasing €60 billion denominated covered bonds, with the aim of easing credit conditions. As the European sovereign debt crisis gathered pace, the ECB launched the Securities Markets Programme in May 2010 to purchase private and public debt securities with the objective of stabilizing bond markets and arresting the rise in bond yields in specific sovereign bonds.

The aim of these policies was to inject liquidity into the market and avoid a systemic crisis with the ultimate objective of buttressing the downturn in the economy from being worse than it could have been. As it happened, the downturn in the UK and other European economies was even deeper than expected. Real GDP fell by more than 5% by mid-2009 in the UK and the eurozone countries. Unemployment in Europe tipped 10%. How could injecting liquidity into the financial system help those fearful of losing their job or, worse yet, suddenly without work?

Following close on the heels of the global financial crisis was the euro economies' sovereign debt crisis emanating principally from Greece but also Portugal, Spain, Ireland and Italy (see Chapter 24). In May 2010 a bailout fund for Greece of €110 billion by the EU and the IMF was agreed upon and soon after bailout funds were agreed for Ireland and Portugal. The bailout policy was instituted to forestall a default by countries like Greece, Portugal and Spain. The problem is not just that the government debt of these countries will be worth less than its face value because of default but because the holders of this debt are the banks in the European Union. A default would mean deterioration in bank assets, and would signal a further round of bank crises.

The central role of financial institutions in the working of the economy – the focus of Part 3 – was overlooked. Banks and other financial institutions make financial markets work by moving funds from people who save to people who have productive investment opportunities. That bank branch on the high street was not going to be able to lend freely to a small business owner or recent college graduate looking to fund a new car purchase until capital once again flowed.

The subprime crisis and the eurozone debt crisis highlight how the financial system changes over time, be it from financial innovations or hard lessons from crises such as the one at hand. Chapter 8 analyses financial structure in Europe and the US. In Chapter 9, we develop a framework to understand the dynamics of financial crises – and focus in particular on the subprime crisis of 2007–8 and the continuing eurozone debt crisis. In Chapter 10, we look at the business and process of banking. In Chapter 11, we extend the economic analysis developed in Chapter 8 to understand the motivations for bank regulation and we examine the pitfalls in the regulatory process. Chapter 12 examines the development of the banking system over time and the growing internationalization of banking.

CHAPTER 8

An economic analysis of financial structure

PREVIEW

A healthy and vibrant economy requires a financial system that moves funds from people who save to people who have productive investment opportunities. But how does the financial system make sure that your hard-earned savings get channelled to Paula the Productive Investor rather than to Benny the Bum?

This chapter answers that question by providing an economic analysis of how our financial structure is designed to promote economic efficiency. The analysis focuses on a few simple but powerful economic concepts that enable us to explain features of our financial system, such as why financial contracts are written as they are and why financial intermediaries are more important than securities markets for getting funds to borrowers. The analysis also demonstrates the important link between the financial system and the performance of the aggregate economy, which is the subject of Part 5 of the book.

Basic facts about financial structure throughout the world

The financial system is complex in structure and function throughout the world. It includes many different types of institutions: banks, pension funds, insurance companies, stock and bond markets, and so on – all of which are regulated by a government-sanctioned authority. The financial system channels trillions of pounds and euros per year from savers to people with productive investment opportunities. If we take a close look at financial structure all over the world, we find eight basic facts, some of which are quite surprising, that we need to explain to understand how the financial system works.

The bar chart in Figure 8.1 shows how businesses financed their activities using external funds (those obtained from outside the business itself) in the period 1995–9 for the four largest economies in the European Union and the United States. The *bank credit* category is made up primarily of loans from depository institutions but includes lease finance from other financial institutions and loans from development banks; *trade credit* is composed of credit extended by one company to another in the process of transactions between each other; *equity* consists of new issues of equity (stock market shares); and *other* includes informal sources (e.g. venture capital). This chart shows the external sources of financing of company investment during the period 1995–9 and includes the financing of small and medium-sized enterprises (SMEs).

It is important to understand that Figure 8.1 relates to flows of external investment finance and the data relates to the 1990s. An important item that is missing from Figure 8.1 is the use of the private bond market to finance investment. Figure 8.2 shows the composition

FIGURE 8.1

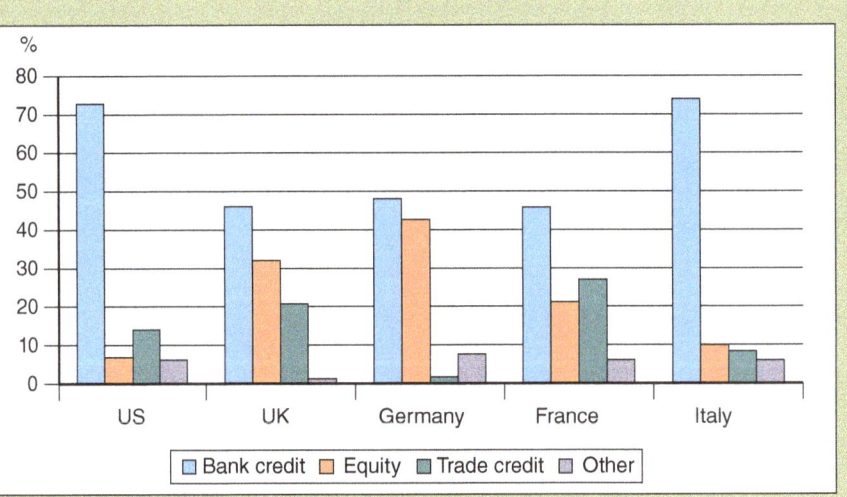

Sources of external funds for non-financial companies, 1995–9

Source: Thorsten Beck, Asli Demirgüç-Kunt and Vokislav Maksimovic, 'Financing patterns around the world: are small firms different?', *Journal of Financial Economics*, 89 (2008): 467–87.

of the total amount of liabilities of the non-financial company sector as a percentage of GDP during the 2000s. They are the stock of bank credit advanced to the non-financial company sector, the stock of bonds issued by the non-financial company sector and the stock market capitalization (market value of stocks) of the non-financial company sector. These figures are averages for the period 2000–9.

Now let us explore the eight facts.

1 *Stocks are not the most important source of external financing for businesses.* Because so much attention in the media is focused on the stock market, many people have the impression that stocks are the most important sources of financing for companies. However, as we can see from the bar chart in Figure 8.1, the stock market accounted for only a fraction of the external financing of businesses in the US, the UK, France and Italy in 1995–9 and only Germany shows a significant share of external financing from stocks.[1] Similarly small

FIGURE 8.2

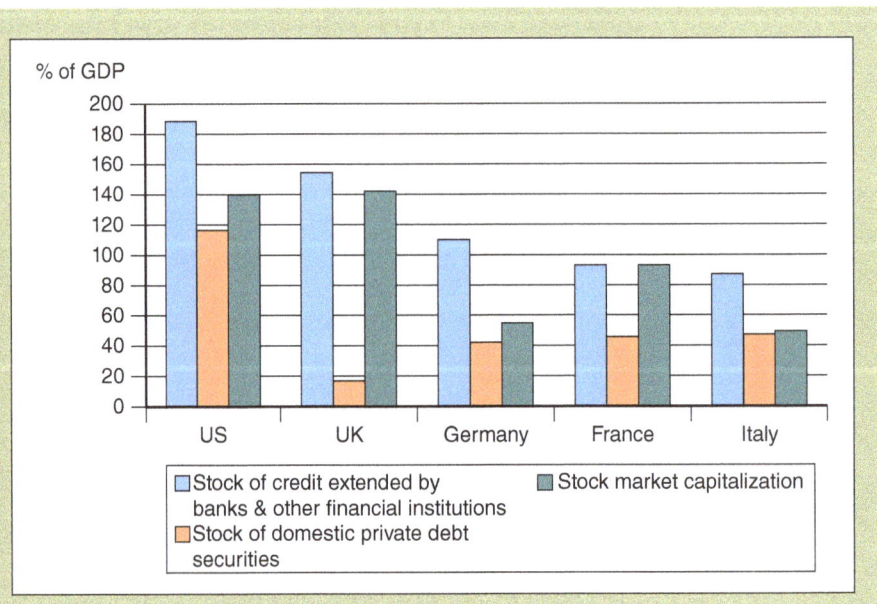

Financial structure of non-financial company sector, 2000–9

Source: Thortsen Beck and Asli Demirgüç-Kunt, 'Financial institutions and markets across countries and over time: data and analysis', *World Bank Policy Research Working Paper* No. 4943, May 2009 (Revised November 2010).

figures apply in the other countries presented in Figure 8.1 as well. Why is the stock market less important than other sources of financing in most countries?

2 *Issuing equities is not the only type of marketable security by which businesses finance their operations*. Figure 8.2 shows that bonds are also a significant source of external finance. In Germany, France and Italy the domestic private stock of bond liabilities of the company sector was 40–45% of GDP whereas in the United States it was 116% of GDP. You can see from Figure 8.2 that the outstanding value of stocks and shares as a percentage of GDP is very large for Germany, France and Italy and above 100 for the UK and the US. How does this square with Figure 8.1 which shows that financing from the stock markets is quite small relative to bank credit? In reality the amount of finance raised by the issue of new shares each year is smaller than the amount of bank credit advanced. The reason why the value of stocks as a percentage of GDP is so high is because the market price of the existing stock of shares has risen. You were shown how the market sets stock prices in Chapter 7. Other research[2] shows that stocks and bonds combined, which make up the total share of marketable securities, supply less than one-half of the external funds corporations need to finance their activities in the US and Germany. Why don't businesses use marketable securities more extensively to finance their activities?

3 *Indirect finance, which involves the activities of financial intermediaries, is many times more important than direct finance, in which businesses raise funds directly from lenders in financial markets*. Direct finance involves the sale to households of marketable securities such as stocks and bonds. The share of stocks and bonds as a source of external financing for businesses actually greatly overstates the importance of direct finance. In general households buy only a fraction of newly issued corporate bonds and commercial paper and stocks. The majority of securities have been bought primarily by financial intermediaries such as insurance companies, pension funds and mutual funds. In most countries marketable securities are a less important source of finance and direct finance is also less important than indirect finance. Why are financial intermediaries and indirect finance so important in financial markets? In recent years, indirect finance has been declining in importance. Why is this happening?

4 *Financial intermediaries, particularly banks, are the most important source of external funds used to finance businesses*. As we can see in Figure 8.1, the primary source of external funds for businesses throughout the world comprises loans made by banks and other non-bank financial intermediaries such as insurance companies, pension funds and finance companies (45–50% in the United Kingdom, Germany and France, but more than 70% in the US and Italy). Thus the data suggest that banks in these countries have the most important role in financing business activities. In developing countries, banks play an even more important role in the financial system than they do in the industrialized countries. What makes banks so important to the workings of the financial system? Although banks remain important, their share of external funds for businesses has been declining in recent years. What is driving this decline?

5 *The financial system is among the most heavily regulated sectors of the economy*. The financial system is one of the most heavily regulated in the European economies and the United States. Governments regulate financial markets primarily to promote the provision of information, and to ensure the soundness (stability) of the financial system. Why are financial markets so extensively regulated throughout the world?

6 *Only large, well-established corporations have easy access to securities markets to finance their activities*. Individuals and smaller businesses that are not well established are less likely to raise funds by issuing marketable securities. Instead, they most often obtain their financing from banks. Why do only large, well-known corporations find it easier to raise funds in securities markets?

7 *Collateral is a prevalent feature of debt contracts for both households and businesses*. **Collateral** is property that is pledged to a lender to guarantee payment in the event that the

borrower is unable to make debt payments. Collateralized debt (also known as **secured debt** to contrast it with **unsecured debt**, such as credit card debt, which is not collateralized) is the predominant form of household debt and is widely used in business borrowing as well. The majority of household debt in the United Kingdom and other EU economies consists of collateralized loans: your car is collateral for your car loan, and your house is collateral for your mortgage. Corporate bonds and other bank loans also often involve pledges of collateral. Why is collateral such an important feature of debt contracts?

8 *Debt contracts typically are extremely complicated legal documents that place substantial restrictions on the behaviour of the borrower.* Many students think of a debt contract as a simple IOU that can be written on a single piece of paper. The reality of debt contracts is far different, however. In all countries, bond or loan contracts typically are long legal documents with provisions (called **restrictive covenants**) that restrict and specify certain activities that the borrower can engage in. Restrictive covenants are not just a feature of debt contracts for businesses; for example, personal automobile loan and home mortgage contracts have covenants that require the borrower to maintain sufficient insurance on the automobile or house purchased with the loan. Why are debt contracts so complex and restrictive?

As you may recall from Chapter 2, an important feature of financial markets is that they have substantial transaction and information costs. An economic analysis of how these costs affect financial markets provides us with explanations of the eight facts, which in turn provide us with a much deeper understanding of how our financial system works. In the next section, we examine the impact of transaction costs on the structure of our financial system. Then we turn to the effect of information costs on financial structure.

Transaction costs

Transaction costs are a major problem in financial markets. An example will make this clear.

How transaction costs influence financial structure

Say you have €5,000 you would like to invest, and you think about investing in the stock market. Because you have only €5,000, you can buy only a small number of shares. Even if you use online trading, your purchase is so small that the brokerage commission for buying the stock you picked will be a large percentage of the purchase price of the shares. If instead you decide to buy a bond, the problem is even worse, because the smallest denomination for some bonds you might want to buy is as much as €10,000, and you do not have that much to invest. You are disappointed and realize that you will not be able to use financial markets to earn a return on your hard-earned savings. You can take some consolation, however, in the fact that you are not alone in being stymied by high transaction costs. This is a fact of life for many of us: Only around one in five of UK households own any securities.[3]

You also face another problem because of transaction costs. Because you have only a small amount of funds available, you can make only a restricted number of investments because a large number of small transactions would result in very high transaction costs. That is, you have to put all your eggs in one basket, and your inability to diversify will subject you to a lot of risk.

How financial intermediaries reduce transaction costs

This example of the problems posed by transaction costs and the example outlined in Chapter 2 when legal costs kept you from making a loan to Carl the Carpenter illustrate that small savers like you are frozen out of financial markets and are unable to benefit from them. Fortunately, financial intermediaries, an important part of the financial structure, have evolved to reduce transaction costs and allow small savers and borrowers to benefit from the existence of financial markets.

Economies of scale

One solution to the problem of high transaction costs is to bundle the funds of many investors together so that they can take advantage of *economies of scale*, the reduction in transaction costs per euro of investment as the size (scale) of transactions increases. Bundling investors' funds together reduces transaction costs for each individual investor. Economies of scale exist because the total cost of carrying out a transaction in financial markets increases only a little as the size of the transaction grows. For example, the cost of arranging a purchase of 10,000 shares of stock is not much greater than the cost of arranging a purchase of 50 shares of stock.

The presence of economies of scale in financial markets helps explain why financial intermediaries developed and have become such an important part of our financial structure. The clearest example of a financial intermediary that arose because of economies of scale is a mutual fund. A *mutual fund* is a financial intermediary that sells shares to individuals and then invests the proceeds in bonds or stocks. Because it buys large blocks of stocks or bonds, a mutual fund can take advantage of lower transaction costs. These cost savings are then passed on to individual investors after the mutual fund has taken its cut in the form of management fees for administering their accounts. An additional benefit for individual investors is that a mutual fund is large enough to purchase a widely diversified portfolio of securities. The increased diversification for individual investors reduces their risk, making them better off.

Economies of scale are also important in lowering the costs of things such as computer technology that financial institutions need to accomplish their tasks. Once a large mutual fund has invested a lot of money in setting up a telecommunications system, for example, the system can be used for a huge number of transactions at a low cost per transaction.

Expertise

Financial intermediaries are also better able to develop expertise to lower transaction costs. Their expertise in computer technology enables them to offer customers convenient services like being able to log on to Internet services that show how well their investments are doing, to transfer funds between accounts and to pay bills electronically.

An important outcome of a financial intermediary's low transaction costs is the ability to provide its customers with *liquidity services*, services that make it easier for customers to conduct transactions. Banks can pay interest on the average amount of funds kept in an account and enable customers to pay bills electronically. Some money market mutual funds in the US also, not only pay shareholders high interest rates, but also allow them to write cheques for convenient bill-paying.

Asymmetric information: adverse selection and moral hazard

The presence of transaction costs in financial markets explains in part why financial intermediaries and indirect finance play such an important role in financial markets (fact 3). To understand financial structure more fully, however, we turn to the role of information in financial markets.[4]

Asymmetric information – a situation that arises when one party's insufficient knowledge about the other party involved in a transaction makes it impossible to make accurate decisions when conducting the transaction – is an important aspect of financial markets. For example, managers of a corporation know whether they are honest or have better information about how well their business is doing than the stockholders do. The presence of asymmetric information leads to adverse selection and moral hazard problems, which were introduced in Chapter 2.

Adverse selection is an asymmetric information problem that occurs *before* the transaction: potential bad credit risks are the ones that most actively seek out loans. Thus the parties who are the most likely to produce an undesirable outcome are the ones most likely to want to engage in the transaction. For example, big risk takers or outright crooks might be the most eager to take out a loan because they know that they are unlikely to pay it back. Because adverse selection increases the chances that a loan might be made to a bad credit risk, lenders might decide not to make any loans, even though there are good credit risks in the marketplace.

Moral hazard arises *after* the transaction occurs: the lender runs the risk that the borrower will engage in activities that are undesirable from the lender's point of view because they make it less likely that the loan will be paid back. For example, once borrowers have obtained a loan, they may take on big risks (which have possible high returns but also run a greater risk of default) because they are playing with someone else's money. Because moral hazard lowers the probability that the loan will be repaid, lenders may decide that they would rather not make a loan.

The analysis of how asymmetric information problems affect economic behaviour is called **agency theory**. We will apply this theory here to explain why financial structure takes the form it does, thereby explaining the facts outlined at the beginning of the chapter.

The lemons problem: how adverse selection influences financial structure

A particular aspect of the way the adverse selection problem interferes with the efficient functioning of a market was outlined in a famous article by Nobel Prize winner George Akerlof. It is called the 'lemons problem', because it resembles the problem created by 'lemons' in the used-car market.[5] Potential buyers of used cars are frequently unable to assess the quality of the car; that is, they can't tell whether a particular used car is a car that will run well or a lemon that will continually give them grief. The price that a buyer pays must therefore reflect the *average* quality of the cars in the market, somewhere between the low value of a lemon and the high value of a good car.

The owner of a used car, by contrast, is more likely to know whether the car is a peach or a lemon. If the car is a lemon, the owner is more than happy to sell it at the price the buyer is willing to pay, which, being somewhere between the value of a lemon and that of a good car, is greater than the lemon's value. However, if the car is a peach, the owner knows that the car is undervalued at the price the buyer is willing to pay, and so the owner may not want to sell it. As a result of this adverse selection, few good used cars will come to the market. Because the average quality of a used car available in the market will be low and because few people want to buy a lemon, there will be few sales. The used-car market will function poorly, if at all.

Lemons in the stock and bond markets

A similar lemons problem arises in securities markets – that is, the debt (bond) and equity (stock) markets. Suppose that our friend Irving the Investor, a potential buyer of securities such as common stock, can't distinguish between good firms with high expected profits and low risk and bad firms with low expected profits and high risk. In this situation, Irving will be willing to pay only a price that reflects the *average* quality of firms issuing securities – a price that lies between the value of securities from bad firms and the value of those from good firms. If the owners or managers of a good firm have better information than Irving and *know* that they are a good firm, they know that their securities are undervalued and will not want to sell them to Irving at the price he is willing to pay. The only firms willing to sell Irving securities will be bad firms (because his price is higher than the securities are worth). Our friend Irving is not stupid; he does not want to hold securities in bad firms, and hence he will decide not to purchase securities in the market. In an outcome similar to that in the used-car market, this securities market will not work very well because few firms will sell securities in it to raise capital.

The analysis is similar if Irving considers purchasing a corporate debt instrument in the bond market rather than an equity share. Irving will buy a bond only if its interest rate is high enough to compensate him for the average default risk of the good and bad firms trying to sell the debt. The knowledgeable owners of a good firm realize that they will be paying a higher interest rate than they should, so they are unlikely to want to borrow in this market. Only the bad firms will be willing to borrow, and because investors like Irving are not eager to buy bonds issued by bad firms, they will probably not buy any bonds at all. Few bonds are likely to sell in this market, so it will not be a good source of financing.

The analysis we have just conducted explains fact 2 – why marketable securities are not the primary source of financing for businesses in any country in the world. It also partly explains fact 1 – why stocks are not the most important source of financing for American businesses. The presence of the lemons problem keeps securities markets such as the stock and bond markets from being effective in channelling funds from savers to borrowers.

Tools to help solve adverse selection problems

In the absence of asymmetric information, the lemons problem goes away. If buyers know as much about the quality of used cars as sellers, so that all involved can tell a good car from a bad one, buyers will be willing to pay full value for good used cars. Because the owners of good used cars can now get a fair price, they will be willing to sell them in the market. The market will have many transactions and will do its intended job of channelling good cars to people who want them.

Similarly, if purchasers of securities can distinguish good firms from bad, they will pay the full value of securities issued by good firms, and good firms will sell their securities in the market. The securities market will then be able to move funds to the good firms that have the most productive investment opportunities.

Private production and sale of information

The solution to the adverse selection problem in financial markets is to eliminate asymmetric information by furnishing the people supplying funds with full details about the individuals or firms seeking to finance their investment activities. One way to get this material to saver–lenders is to have private companies collect and produce information that distinguishes good from bad firms and then sell it. In the United States, companies such as Standard & Poor's, Moody's and Value Line gather information on firms' balance sheet positions and investment activities, publish these data, and sell them to subscribers (individuals, libraries and financial intermediaries involved in purchasing securities).

The system of private production and sale of information does not completely solve the adverse selection problem in securities markets, however, because of the **free-rider problem**. The free-rider problem occurs when people who do not pay for information take advantage of the information that other people have paid for. The free-rider problem suggests that the private sale of information will be only a partial solution to the lemons problem. To see why, suppose that you have just purchased information that tells you which firms are good and which are bad. You believe that this purchase is worthwhile because you can make up the cost of acquiring this information, and then some, by purchasing the securities of good firms that are undervalued. However, when our savvy (free-riding) investor Irving sees you buying certain securities, he buys right along with you, even though he has not paid for any information. If many other investors act as Irving does, the increased demand for the undervalued good securities will cause their low price to be bid up immediately to reflect the securities' true value. Because of all these free riders, you can no longer buy the securities for less than their true value. Now because you will not gain any profits from purchasing the information, you realize that you never should have paid for this information in the first place. If other investors come to the same realization, private firms and individuals may not be able to sell enough of this information to make it worth their while to gather and produce it. The weakened ability of private firms to profit from selling information will mean that less information is produced in the marketplace, so adverse selection (the lemons problem) will still interfere with the efficient functioning of securities markets.

Government regulation to increase information

The free-rider problem prevents the private market from producing enough information to eliminate all the asymmetric information that leads to adverse selection. Could financial markets benefit from government intervention? The government could, for instance, produce information to help investors distinguish good firms from bad firms and provide it to the public free of charge. This solution, however, would involve the government in releasing negative information about firms, a practice that might be politically difficult. A second possibility (and one followed by the governments of the developed economies) is for the government to regulate securities markets in a way that encourages firms to reveal honest information about them so that investors can determine how good or bad the firms are. In the United Kingdom the Financial Services Authority (FSA) is the listing authority (UK Listing Authority – UKLA) that ensures that companies have undertaken proper disclosure of information and auditing prior to listing on the stock exchange. Similar regulations are found in other countries. However, disclosure requirements do not always work well, as the collapse of Enron and accounting scandals at other corporations, such as WorldCom (in the US) and Parmalat (in Italy) suggest (see the 'Closer look' box, 'The Enron implosion').

The asymmetric information problem of adverse selection in financial markets helps explain why financial markets are among the most heavily regulated sectors in the economy (fact 5). Government regulation to increase information for investors is needed to reduce the adverse selection problem, which interferes with the efficient functioning of securities (stock and bond) markets.

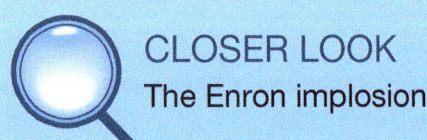

CLOSER LOOK
The Enron implosion

Until 2001, Enron Corporation, a firm that specialized in trading in the energy market, appeared to be spectacularly successful. It had a quarter of the energy-trading market and was valued as high as $77 billion in August 2000 (just a little over a year before its collapse), making it the seventh-largest corporation in the United States at that time. However, toward the end of 2001, Enron came crashing down. In October 2001, Enron announced a third-quarter loss of $618 million and disclosed accounting 'mistakes'. The Securities and Exchange Commission in the US then engaged in a formal investigation of Enron's financial dealings with partnerships led by its former finance chief. It became clear that Enron was engaged in a complex set of transactions by which it was keeping substantial amounts of debt and financial contracts off its balance sheet. These transactions enabled Enron to hide its financial difficulties. Despite securing as much

as $1.5 billion of new financing from JPMorgan Chase and Citigroup, the company was forced to declare bankruptcy in December 2001, up to then the largest bankruptcy in US history.

The Enron collapse illustrates that government regulation can lessen asymmetric information problems, but cannot eliminate them. Managers have tremendous incentives to hide their companies' problems, making it hard for investors to know the true value of the firm.

The Enron bankruptcy not only increased concerns in financial markets about the quality of accounting information supplied by corporations, but also led to hardship for many of the firm's former employees, who found that their pensions had become worthless. Outrage against the duplicity of executives at Enron has been high, and several have been indicted, with some being already convicted and sent to jail.

Although government regulation lessens the adverse selection problem, it does not eliminate it. Even when firms provide information to the public about their sales, assets or earnings, they still have more information than investors: there is a lot more to knowing the quality of a firm than statistics can provide. Furthermore, bad firms have an incentive to make themselves look like good firms, because this would enable them to fetch a higher price for their securities. Bad firms will slant the information they are required to transmit to the public, thus making it harder for investors to sort out the good firms from the bad.

Financial intermediation

So far we have seen that private production of information and government regulation to encourage provision of information lessen, but do not eliminate, the adverse selection problem in financial markets. How, then, can the financial structure help promote the flow of funds to people with productive investment opportunities when there is asymmetric information? A clue is provided by the structure of the used-car market.

An important feature of the used-car market is that most used cars are not sold directly by one individual to another. An individual considering buying a used car might pay for privately produced information by subscribing to a magazine like *Which?* to find out if a particular make of car has a good repair record. Nevertheless, reading a *Which?* report does not solve the adverse selection problem, because even if a particular make of car has a good reputation, the specific car someone is trying to sell could be a lemon. The prospective buyer might also bring the used car to a mechanic for a once-over. But what if the prospective buyer doesn't know a mechanic who can be trusted or if the mechanic would charge a high fee to evaluate the car?

Because these problems make it hard for individuals to acquire enough information about used cars, most used cars are not sold directly by one individual to another. Instead, they are sold by an intermediary, a used-car dealer who purchases used cars from individuals and resells them to other individuals. Used-car dealers produce information in the market by becoming experts in determining whether a car is a peach or a lemon. Once they know that a car is good, they can sell it with some form of a guarantee: either a guarantee that is explicit, such as a warranty, or an implicit guarantee, in which they stand by their reputation for honesty. People are more likely to purchase a used car because of a dealer's guarantee, and the dealer is able to make a profit on the production of information about automobile quality by being able to sell the used car at a higher price than the dealer paid for it. If dealers purchase and then resell cars on which they have produced information, they avoid the problem of other people free-riding on the information they produced.

Just as used-car dealers help solve adverse selection problems in the automobile market, financial intermediaries play a similar role in financial markets. A financial intermediary, such as a bank, becomes an expert in producing information about firms, so that it can sort out good credit risks from bad ones. Then it can acquire funds from depositors and lend them to the good firms. Because the bank is able to lend mostly to good firms, it is able to earn a higher return on its loans than the interest it has to pay to its depositors. The resulting profit that the bank earns gives it the incentive to engage in this information production activity.

An important element in the bank's ability to profit from the information it produces is that it avoids the free-rider problem by primarily making private loans rather than by purchasing securities that are traded in the open market. Because a private loan is not traded, other investors cannot watch what the bank is doing and bid up the loan's price to the point that the bank receives no compensation for the information it has produced. The bank's role as an intermediary that holds mostly non-traded loans is the key to its success in reducing asymmetric information in financial markets.

Our analysis of adverse selection indicates that financial intermediaries in general – and banks in particular, because they hold a large fraction of non-traded loans – should play a greater role in moving funds to corporations than securities markets do. Our analysis thus explains facts 3 and 4: why indirect finance is so much more important than direct finance and why banks are the most important source of external funds for financing businesses.

Another important fact that is explained by the analysis here is the greater importance of banks in the financial systems of developing countries. As we have seen, when the quality of information about firms is better, asymmetric information problems will be less severe, and it will be easier for firms to issue securities. Information about private firms is harder to collect in developing countries than in industrialized countries; therefore, the smaller role played by securities markets leaves a greater role for financial intermediaries such as banks. A corollary of this analysis is that as information about firms becomes easier to acquire, the role of banks should decline. A major development in the past twenty years in the United States has been huge improvements in information technology. Thus the analysis here suggests that the lending role of financial institutions such as banks in the US and UK should have declined, and this is exactly what has occurred (see Chapter 12).

Our analysis of adverse selection also explains fact 6, which questions why large firms are more likely to obtain funds from securities markets, a direct route, rather than from banks and financial intermediaries, an indirect route. The better known a corporation is, the more information about its activities is available in the marketplace. Thus it is easier for investors to evaluate the quality of the corporation and determine whether it is a good firm or a bad one. Because investors have fewer worries about adverse selection with well-known corporations, they will be willing to invest directly in their securities. Our adverse selection analysis thus suggests that there should be a pecking order for firms that can issue securities. Hence we have an explanation for fact 6: the larger and more established a corporation is, the more likely it will be to issue securities to raise funds.

Collateral and net worth

Adverse selection interferes with the functioning of financial markets only if a lender suffers a loss when a borrower is unable to make loan payments and thereby defaults. *Collateral*, property promised to the lender if the borrower defaults, reduces the consequences of adverse selection because it reduces the lender's losses in the event of a default. If a borrower defaults on a loan, the lender can sell the collateral and use the proceeds to make up for the losses on the loan. For example, if you fail to make your mortgage payments, the lender can take title to your house, auction it off, and use the receipts to pay off the loan. Lenders are thus more willing to make loans secured by collateral, and borrowers are willing to supply collateral because the reduced risk for the lender makes it more likely they will get the loan in the first place and perhaps at a better loan rate. The presence of adverse selection in credit markets thus provides an explanation for why collateral is an important feature of debt contracts (fact 7).

Net worth (also called **equity capital**), the difference between a firm's assets (what it owns or is owed) and its liabilities (what it owes), can perform a similar role to collateral. If a firm has a high net worth, then even if it engages in investments that cause it to have negative profits and so defaults on its debt payments, the lender can take title to the firm's net worth, sell it off, and use the proceeds to recoup some of the losses from the loan. In addition, the more net worth a firm has in the first place, the less likely it is to default, because the firm has a cushion of assets that it can use to pay off its loans. Hence, when firms seeking credit have high net worth, the consequences of adverse selection are less important and lenders are more willing to make loans. This analysis lies behind the often-heard lament, 'Only the people who don't need money can borrow it!'

Summary

So far we have used the concept of adverse selection to explain seven of the eight facts about financial structure introduced earlier: the first four emphasize the importance of financial intermediaries and the relative unimportance of securities markets for the financing of corporations; the fifth, that financial markets are among the most heavily regulated sectors of the economy; the sixth, that only large, well-established corporations have access to securities markets; and the seventh, that collateral is an important feature of debt contracts. In the next section, we will see that the other asymmetric information concept of moral hazard provides additional reasons for the importance of financial intermediaries and the relative unimportance of securities markets for the financing of corporations, the prevalence of government regulation, and the importance of collateral in debt contracts. In addition, the concept of moral hazard can be used to explain our final fact (fact 8): why debt contracts are complicated legal documents that place substantial restrictions on the behaviour of the borrower.

How moral hazard affects the choice between debt and equity contracts

Moral hazard is the asymmetric information problem that occurs after the financial transaction takes place, when the seller of a security may have incentives to hide information and engage in activities that are undesirable for the purchaser of the security. Moral hazard has important consequences for whether a firm finds it easier to raise funds with debt than with equity contracts.

Moral hazard in equity contracts: the principal–agent problem

Equity contracts, such as common stock, are claims to a share in the profits and assets of a business. Equity contracts are subject to a particular type of moral hazard called the **principal–agent problem**. When managers own only a small fraction of the firm they work for, the stockholders who own most of the firm's equity (called the *principals*) are not the same people as the managers of the firm, who are the *agents* of the owners. This separation of ownership and control involves moral hazard, in that the managers in control (the agents) may act in their own interest rather than in the interest of the stockholder–owners (the principals) because the managers have less incentive to maximize profits than the stockholder–owners do.

To understand the principal–agent problem more fully, suppose that your friend Steve asks you to become a silent partner in his ice-cream store. The store requires an investment of €10,000 to set up and Steve has only €1,000. So you purchase an equity stake (stock shares) for €9,000, which entitles you to 90% of the ownership of the firm, while Steve owns only 10%. If Steve works hard to make tasty ice cream, keeps the store clean, smiles at all the customers and hustles to wait on tables quickly, after all expenses (including Steve's salary), the store will have €50,000 in profits per year, of which Steve receives 10% (€5,000) and you receive 90% (€45,000).

But if Steve doesn't provide quick and friendly service to his customers, uses the €50,000 in income to buy artwork for his office, and even sneaks off to the beach while he should be at the store, the store will not earn any profit. Steve can earn the additional €5,000 (his 10% share of the profits) over his salary only if he works hard and forgoes unproductive investments (such as art for his office). Steve might decide that the extra €5,000 just isn't enough to make him expend the effort to be a good manager; he might decide that it would be worth his while only if he earned an extra €10,000. If Steve feels this way, he does not have enough incentive to be a good manager and will end up with a beautiful office, a good tan and a store that doesn't show any profits. Because the store won't show any profits, Steve's decision not to act in your interest will cost you €45,000 (your 90% of the profits if he had chosen to be a good manager instead).

The moral hazard arising from the principal–agent problem might be even worse if Steve were not totally honest. Because his ice-cream store is a cash business, Steve has the incentive to pocket €50,000 in cash and tell you that the profits were zero. He now gets a return of €50,000, and you get nothing.

Further indications that the principal–agent problem created by equity contracts can be severe are provided by recent scandals in corporations such as Enron and Tyco International, in which managers have been accused of diverting funds for their own personal use. Besides pursuing personal benefits, managers might also pursue corporate strategies (such as the acquisition of other firms) that enhance their personal power but do not increase the corporation's profitability.

The principal–agent problem would not arise if the owners of a firm had complete information about what the managers were up to and could prevent wasteful expenditures or fraud. The principal–agent problem, which is an example of moral hazard, arises only because a manager, such as Steve, has more information about his activities than the stockholder does – that is, there is asymmetric information. The principal–agent problem would also not arise if Steve alone owned the store and there were no separation of ownership and control. If this were the case, Steve's hard work and avoidance of unproductive investments would yield him a profit (and extra income) of €50,000, an amount that would make it worth his while to be a good manager.

Tools to help solve the principal–agent problem

Production of information: monitoring

You have seen that the principal–agent problem arises because managers have more information about their activities and actual profits than stockholders do. One way for stockholders to reduce this moral hazard problem is for them to engage in a particular type of information production, the monitoring of the firm's activities: auditing the firm frequently and checking on what the management is doing. The problem is that the monitoring process can be expensive in terms of time and money, as reflected in the name economists give it, **costly state verification**. Costly state verification makes the equity contract less desirable, and it explains, in part, why equity is not a more important element in our financial structure.

As with adverse selection, the free-rider problem decreases the amount of information production that would reduce the moral hazard (principal–agent) problem. In this example, the free-rider problem decreases monitoring. If you know that other stockholders are paying to monitor the activities of the company you hold shares in, you can take a free ride on their activities. Then you can use the money you save by not engaging in monitoring to vacation on a Caribbean island. If you can do this, though, so can other stockholders. Perhaps all the stockholders will go to the islands, and no one will spend any resources on monitoring the firm. The moral hazard problem for shares of common stock will then be severe, making it hard for firms to issue them to raise capital (providing an additional explanation for fact 1).

Government regulation to increase information

As with adverse selection, the government has an incentive to try to reduce the moral hazard problem created by asymmetric information, which provides another reason why the financial system is so heavily regulated (fact 5). Governments everywhere have laws to force firms to adhere to standard accounting principles that make profit verification easier. They also pass laws to impose stiff criminal penalties on people who commit the fraud of hiding and stealing profits. However, these measures can be only partly effective. Catching this kind of fraud is not easy; fraudulent managers have the incentive to make it very hard for government agencies to find or prove fraud.

Financial intermediation

Financial intermediaries have the ability to avoid the free-rider problem in the face of moral hazard, and this is another reason why indirect finance is so important (fact 3). One financial intermediary that helps reduce the moral hazard arising from the principal–agent problem is the **venture capital firm**. Venture capital firms pool the resources of their partners and use the funds to help budding entrepreneurs start new businesses. In exchange for the use of the venture capital, the firm receives an equity share in the new business. Because verification of earnings and profits is so important in eliminating moral hazard, venture capital firms usually insist on having several of their own people participate as members of the managing body of the firm, the board of directors, so that they can keep a close watch on the firm's activities. When a venture capital firm supplies start-up funds, the equity in the firm is not marketable to anyone *except* the venture capital firm. Thus other investors are unable to take a free ride on the venture capital firm's verification activities. As a result of this arrangement, the venture capital firm is able to garner the full benefits of its verification activities and is given the appropriate incentives to reduce the moral hazard problem. Venture capital firms have been important in the development of the technology sector in the UK, which has resulted in job creation, economic growth and increased international competitiveness.

Debt contracts

Moral hazard arises with an equity contract, which is a claim on profits in all situations, whether the firm is making or losing money. If a contract could be structured so that moral hazard would exist only in certain situations, there would be a reduced need to monitor managers, and the contract would be more attractive than the equity contract. The debt contract has exactly these attributes because it is a contractual agreement by the borrower to pay the lender *fixed* monetary amounts at periodic intervals. When the firm has high profits, the lender receives the contractual payments and does not need to know the exact profits of the firm. If the managers are hiding profits or are pursuing activities that are personally beneficial but don't increase profitability, the lender doesn't care as long as these activities do not interfere with the ability of the firm to make its debt payments on time. Only when the firm cannot meet its debt payments, thereby being in a state of default, is there a need for the lender to verify the state of the firm's profits. Only in this situation do lenders involved in debt contracts need to act more like equity holders; now they need to know how much income the firm has to get their fair share.

The less frequent need to monitor the firm, and thus the lower cost of state verification, helps explain why debt contracts are used more frequently than equity contracts to raise capital. The concept of moral hazard thus helps explain fact 1, why stocks are not the most important source of financing for businesses.[6]

How moral hazard influences financial structure in debt markets

Even with the advantages just described, debt contracts are still subject to moral hazard. Because a debt contract requires the borrowers to pay out a fixed amount and lets them keep any profits above this amount, the borrowers have an incentive to take on investment projects that are riskier than the lenders would like.

For example, suppose that because you are concerned about the problem of verifying the profits of Steve's ice-cream store, you decide not to become an equity partner. Instead, you lend Steve the €9,000 he needs to set up his business and have a debt contract that pays you an interest rate of 10%. As far as you are concerned, this is a surefire investment because there is a strong and steady demand for ice cream in your neighbourhood. However, once you give Steve the funds, he might use them for purposes other than you intended. Instead of opening up the ice-cream store, Steve might use your €9,000 loan to invest in chemical research equipment because he thinks he has a 1-in-10 chance of inventing a diet ice cream that tastes every bit as good as the premium brands but has no fat or calories.

Obviously, this is a very risky investment, but if Steve is successful, he will become a multimillionaire. He has a strong incentive to undertake the riskier investment with your money, because the gains to him would be so large if he succeeded. You would clearly be very unhappy if Steve used your loan for the riskier investment, because if he were unsuccessful, which is highly likely, you would lose most, if not all, of the money you gave him. And if he were successful, you wouldn't share in his success – you would still get only a 10% return on the loan because the principal and interest payments are fixed. Because of the potential moral hazard (that Steve might use your money to finance a very risky venture), you would probably not make the loan to Steve, even though an ice-cream store in the neighbourhood is a good investment that would provide benefits for everyone.

Tools to help solve moral hazard in debt contracts

Net worth and collateral

When borrowers have more at stake because their net worth (the difference between their assets and their liabilities) is high or the collateral they have pledged to the lender is valuable, the risk of moral hazard – the temptation to act in a manner that lenders find objectionable – will be greatly reduced because the borrowers themselves have a lot to lose. Another way to say this is that if borrowers have more 'skin in the game' because they have higher net worth or pledge collateral, they are likely to take less risk at the lender's expense. Let's return to Steve and his ice-cream business. Suppose that the cost of setting up either the ice-cream store or the research equipment is €100,000 instead of €10,000. So Steve needs to put €91,000 of his own money into the business (instead of €1,000) in addition to the €9,000 supplied by your loan. Now if Steve is unsuccessful in inventing the no-calorie non-fat ice cream, he has a lot to lose – the €91,000 of net worth (€100,000 in assets minus the €9,000 loan from you). He will think twice about undertaking the riskier investment and is more likely to invest in the ice-cream store, which is more of a sure thing. Thus, when Steve has more of his own money (net worth) in the business, and hence more skin in the game, you are more likely to make him the loan. Similarly, if you have pledged your house as collateral, you are less likely to go to Monaco and gamble away your earnings that month because you might not be able to make your mortgage payments and might lose your house.

One way of describing the solution that high net worth and collateral provides to the moral hazard problem is to say that it makes the debt contract **incentive-compatible**; that is, it aligns the incentives of the borrower with those of the lender. The greater the borrower's net worth and collateral pledged, then the greater the borrower's incentive to behave in the way that the lender expects and desires, the smaller the moral hazard problem in the debt contract, and the easier it is for the firm or household to borrow. Conversely, when the borrower's net worth and collateral are lower, the moral hazard problem is greater, and it is harder to borrow.

Monitoring and enforcement of restrictive covenants

As the example of Steve and his ice-cream store shows, if you could make sure that Steve doesn't invest in anything riskier than the ice-cream store, it would be worth your while to make him the loan. You can ensure that Steve uses your money for the purpose *you* want it to be used for by writing provisions (restrictive covenants) into the debt contract that restrict his firm's activities. By monitoring Steve's activities to see whether he is complying with the restrictive covenants and enforcing the covenants if he is not, you can make sure that he will not take on risks at your expense. Restrictive covenants are directed at reducing moral hazard either by ruling out undesirable behaviour or by encouraging desirable behaviour. There are four types of restrictive covenants that achieve this objective:

1 *Covenants to discourage undesirable behaviour.* Covenants can be designed to lower moral hazard by keeping the borrower from engaging in the undesirable behaviour of undertaking risky investment projects. Some covenants mandate that a loan can be used only to finance specific activities, such as the purchase of particular equipment or inventories. Others restrict the borrowing firm from engaging in certain risky business activities, such as purchasing other businesses.

2 *Covenants to encourage desirable behaviour.* Restrictive covenants can encourage the borrower to engage in desirable activities that make it more likely that the loan will be paid off. One restrictive covenant of this type requires the breadwinner in a household to carry life insurance that pays off the mortgage upon that person's death. Restrictive covenants of this type for businesses focus on encouraging the borrowing firm to keep its net worth high because higher borrower net worth reduces moral hazard and makes it less likely that the lender will suffer losses. These restrictive covenants typically specify that the firm must maintain minimum holdings of certain assets relative to the firm's size.

3 *Covenants to keep collateral valuable.* Because collateral is an important protection for the lender, restrictive covenants can encourage the borrower to keep the collateral in good condition and make sure that it stays in the possession of the borrower. This is the type of covenant ordinary people encounter most often. Automobile loan contracts, for example, require the car owner to maintain a minimum amount of collision and theft insurance and prevent the sale of the car unless the loan is paid off. Similarly, the recipient of a home mortgage must have adequate insurance on the home and must pay off the mortgage when the property is sold.

4 *Covenants to provide information.* Restrictive covenants also require a borrowing firm to provide information about its activities periodically in the form of quarterly accounting and income reports, thereby making it easier for the lender to monitor the firm and reduce moral hazard. This type of covenant may also stipulate that the lender has the right to audit and inspect the firm's books at any time.

We now see why debt contracts are often complicated legal documents with numerous restrictions on the borrower's behaviour (fact 8): debt contracts require complicated restrictive covenants to lower moral hazard.

Financial intermediation

Although restrictive covenants help reduce the moral hazard problem, they do not eliminate it completely. It is almost impossible to write covenants that rule out *every* risky activity. Furthermore, borrowers may be clever enough to find loopholes in restrictive covenants that make them ineffective.

Another problem with restrictive covenants is that they must be monitored and enforced. A restrictive covenant is meaningless if the borrower can violate it knowing that the lender won't check up or is unwilling to pay for legal recourse. Because monitoring and enforcement of restrictive covenants are costly, the free-rider problem arises in the debt securities (bond) market just as it does in the stock market. If you know that other bondholders are monitoring and enforcing the restrictive covenants, you can free-ride on their monitoring and enforcement. But other bondholders can do the same thing, so the likely outcome is that not enough resources are devoted to monitoring and enforcing the restrictive covenants. Moral hazard therefore continues to be a severe problem for marketable debt.

As we have seen before, financial intermediaries – particularly banks – have the ability to avoid the free-rider problem as long as they make primarily private loans. Private loans are not traded, so no one else can free-ride on the intermediary's monitoring and enforcement of the restrictive covenants. The intermediary making private loans thus receives the benefits of monitoring and enforcement and will work to shrink the moral hazard problem inherent in debt contracts. The concept of moral hazard has provided us with additional reasons why financial intermediaries play a more important role in channelling funds from savers to borrowers than marketable securities do, as described in facts 3 and 4.

Summary

The presence of asymmetric information in financial markets leads to adverse selection and moral hazard problems that interfere with the efficient functioning of those markets. Tools to help solve these problems involve the private production and sale of information, government regulation to increase information in financial markets, the importance of collateral and net worth to debt contracts, and the use of monitoring and restrictive covenants. A key finding from our analysis is that the existence of the free-rider problem for traded securities such as stocks and bonds indicates that financial intermediaries – particularly banks – should play a greater role than securities markets in financing the activities of businesses. Economic analysis of the consequences of adverse selection and moral hazard has helped explain the basic features of our financial system and has provided solutions to the eight facts about our financial structure outlined at the beginning of this chapter.

To help you keep track of all the tools that help solve asymmetric information problems, Table 8.1 summarizes the asymmetric information problems and tools that help solve them. In addition, it notes how these tools and asymmetric information problems explain the eight facts of financial structure described at the beginning of the chapter.

SUMMARY TABLE 8.1

Asymmetric information problems and tools to solve them

Asymmetric information problem	Tools to solve it	Explains fact number
Adverse selection	Private production and sale of information	1, 2
	Government regulation to increase information	5
	Financial intermediation	3, 4, 6
	Collateral and net worth	7
Moral hazard in equity contracts (principal–agent problem)	Production of information: monitoring	1
	Government regulation to increase information	5
	Financial intermediation	3
	Debt contracts	1
Moral hazard in debt contracts	Collateral and net worth	6, 7
	Monitoring and enforcement of restrictive covenants	8
	Financial intermediation	3, 4

Note: List of facts:
[1] Stocks are not the most important source of external financing.
[2] Stocks are not the only form of marketable security available as a source of finance.
[3] Indirect finance is more important than direct finance.
[4] Banks are the most important source of external funds.
[5] The financial system is heavily regulated.
[6] Only large, well-established firms have access to securities markets.
[7] Collateral is prevalent in debt contracts.
[8] Debt contracts have numerous restrictive covenants.

Financial development and economic growth

Recent research has found that an important reason why many developing countries or ex-communist countries like Russia (which are referred to as *transition countries*) experience very low rates of growth is that their financial systems are underdeveloped (a situation referred to as *financial repression*).[7] The economic analysis of financial structure helps explain how an underdeveloped financial system leads to a low state of economic development and economic growth.

The financial systems in developing and transition countries face several difficulties that keep them from operating efficiently. As we have seen, two important tools used to help solve adverse selection and moral hazard problems in credit markets are collateral and restrictive covenants. In many developing countries, the system of property rights (the rule of law, constraints on government expropriation, absence of corruption) functions poorly, making it hard to use these two tools effectively. In these countries, bankruptcy procedures are often extremely slow and cumbersome. For example, in many countries, creditors (holders of debt) must first sue the defaulting debtor for payment, which can take several years; then, once a favourable judgement has been obtained, the creditor has to sue again to obtain title to the collateral. The process can take in excess of five years, and by the time the lender acquires the collateral, it may well have been neglected and thus have little value. In addition, governments often block lenders from foreclosing on borrowers in politically powerful sectors such as agriculture. Where the market is unable to use collateral effectively, the adverse selection problem will be worse, because the lender will need even more information about the quality of the borrower so that it can screen out a good loan from a bad one. The result is that it will be harder for lenders to channel funds to borrowers with the most productive investment opportunities. There will be less productive investment, and hence a slower-growing economy. Similarly, a poorly developed or corrupt legal system may make it extremely difficult for lenders to enforce restrictive covenants. Thus they may have a much more limited ability to reduce moral hazard on the part of borrowers and so will be less willing to lend. Again the outcome will be less productive investment and a lower growth rate for the economy. The importance of an effective legal system in promoting economic growth suggests that lawyers play a more positive role in the economy than we give them credit for (see the 'Closer look' box, 'Should we kill *all* the lawyers?')

Governments in developing and transition countries often use their financial systems to direct credit to themselves or to favoured sectors of the economy by setting interest rates at artificially low levels for certain types of loans, by creating development finance institutions to make specific types of loans, or by directing existing institutions to lend to certain entities. As we have seen, private institutions have an incentive to solve adverse selection and moral hazard problems and lend to borrowers with the most productive investment opportunities. Governments have less incentive to do so because they are not driven by the profit motive and thus their directed credit programmes may not channel funds to sectors that will produce high growth for the economy. The outcome is again likely to result in less efficient investment and slower growth.

In addition, banks in many developing and transition countries are owned by their governments. Again, because of the absence of the profit motive, these **state-owned banks** have little incentive to allocate their capital to the most productive uses. Not surprisingly, the primary loan customer of these state-owned banks is often the government or state-owned enterprises, which do not always use the funds wisely.

We have seen that government regulation can increase the amount of information in financial markets to make them work more efficiently. Many developing and transition countries have an underdeveloped regulatory apparatus that retards the provision of adequate information to the marketplace. For example, these countries often have weak accounting standards, making it very hard to ascertain the quality of a borrower's balance sheet. As a result, asymmetric information problems are more severe, and the financial system is severely hampered in channelling funds to the most productive uses.

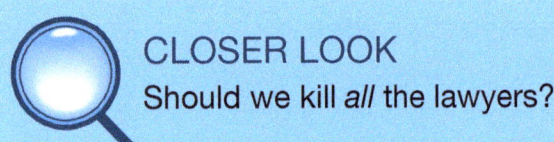

CLOSER LOOK
Should we kill *all* the lawyers?

Lawyers are often an easy target for would-be comedians. Countless jokes centre on ambulance chasing and shifty filers of frivolous lawsuits. Hostility to lawyers is not just a recent phenomenon: in Shakespeare's *Henry VI*, written in the late sixteenth century, Dick the Butcher recommends, 'The first thing we do, let's kill all the lawyers'. Is Shakespeare's Dick the Butcher right?

Most legal work is actually not about ambulance chasing, criminal law and frivolous lawsuits. Instead, it involves the writing and enforcement of contracts, which is how property rights are established. Property rights are essential to protect investments. A good system of laws, by itself, does not provide incentives to invest, because property rights without enforcement are meaningless. This is where lawyers come in. When someone encroaches on your land or makes use of your property without your permission, a lawyer can stop him or her. Without lawyers,

you would be unwilling to invest. With zero or limited investment, there would be little economic growth.

The United States has more lawyers per capita than any other country in the world. It is also among the richest countries in the world with a financial system that is superb at getting capital to new productive uses such as the technology sector. Is this just a coincidence? Or could the US legal system actually be beneficial to its economy? Recent research suggests the American legal system, which is based on the Anglo-Saxon legal system, is an advantage of the US economy.*

*See Rafael La Porta, Florencio Lopez-de-Silanes, Andrei Shleifer and Robert W. Vishny, 'Legal determinants of external finance', *The Journal of Finance* 52, 3 (July 1997): 1131–50; and Rafael La Porta, Florencio Lopez-de-Silanes, Andrei Shleifer and Robert W. Vishny, 'Law and finance', *Journal of Political Economy* 106, 6 (December 1998): 1113–55.

The institutional environment of a poor legal system, weak accounting standards, inadequate government regulation, and government intervention through directed credit programmes and state ownership of banks all help explain why many countries stay poor while others grow richer. ■

APPLICATION   ## Is China a counter-example to the importance of financial development?

Although China appears to be on its way to becoming an economic powerhouse, its financial development remains in the early stages. The country's legal system is weak so that financial contracts are difficult to enforce, while accounting standards are lax so that high-quality information about creditors is hard to find. Regulation of the banking system is still in its formative stages, and the banking sector is dominated by large state-owned banks. Yet the Chinese economy has enjoyed one of the highest growth rates in the world over the last twenty years. How has China been able to grow so rapidly given its low level of financial development?

As noted above, China is in an early stage of development, with a per capita income that is still less than $7,500, one-fifth of the per capita income in Germany. With an extremely high savings rate, averaging around 40% over the last two decades, the country has been able to rapidly build up its capital stock and shift a massive pool of underutilized labour from the subsistence-agriculture sector into higher-productivity activities that use capital. Even though available savings have not been allocated to their most productive uses, the huge increase in capital combined with the gains in productivity from moving labour out of low-productivity, subsistence agriculture have been enough to produce high growth.

As China gets richer, however, this strategy is unlikely to continue to work. The Soviet Union provides a graphic example. In the 1950s and 1960s, the Soviet Union shared many characteristics with modern-day China: high growth fuelled by a high savings rate, a massive buildup of capital, and shifts of a large pool of underutilized labour from subsistence agriculture to manufacturing. During this high-growth phase, however, the Soviet Union was unable to develop the institutions needed to allocate capital efficiently. As a result, once the pool of subsistence labourers was used up, the Soviet Union's growth slowed dramatically and it was unable to keep up with the Western economies. Today no one considers the Soviet Union to have been an economic success story, and its inability to develop the institutions necessary to sustain financial development and growth was an important reason for the demise of this superpower.

To move into the next stage of development, China will need to allocate its capital more efficiently, which requires that it must improve its financial system. The Chinese leadership is well aware of this challenge: the government has announced that state-owned banks are being put on the path to privatization. In addition, the government is engaged in legal reform to make financial contracts more enforceable. New bankruptcy law is being developed so that lenders have the ability to take over the assets of firms that default on their loan contracts. Whether the Chinese government will succeed in developing a first-rate financial system, thereby enabling China to join the ranks of developed countries, is a big question mark. ■

Conflicts of interest

Earlier in this chapter, we saw how financial institutions play an important role in the financial system. Specifically, their expertise in interpreting signals and collecting information from their customers gives them a cost advantage in the production of information. Furthermore, because they are collecting, producing and distributing this information, financial institutions can use the information over and over again in as many ways as they would like, thereby realizing economies of scale. By providing multiple financial services to their customers, such as offering them bank loans or selling their bonds for them, they can also achieve **economies of scope**; that is, they can lower the cost of information production for each service by applying one information resource to many different services. A bank, for example, can evaluate how good a credit risk a corporation is when making a loan to the firm, which then helps the bank decide whether it would be easy to sell the bonds of this corporation to the public. Additionally, by providing multiple financial services to their customers, financial institutions develop broader and longer-term relationships with firms. These relationships both reduce the cost of producing information and increase economies of scope.

What are conflicts of interest and why do we care?

Although the presence of economies of scope may substantially benefit financial institutions, it also creates potential costs in terms of **conflicts of interest**. Conflicts of interest are a type of moral hazard problem that arise when a person or institution has multiple objectives (interests) and, as a result, has conflicts between those objectives. Conflicts of interest are especially likely to occur when a financial institution provides multiple services. The potentially competing interests of those services may lead an individual or firm to conceal information or disseminate misleading information. Here we use the analysis of asymmetric information problems to understand why conflicts of interest are important, why they arise, and what can be done about them.

We care about conflicts of interest because a substantial reduction in the quality of information in financial markets increases asymmetric information problems and prevents financial markets from channelling funds into the most productive investment opportunities. Consequently, the financial markets and the economy become less efficient.

Why do conflicts of interest arise?

Three types of financial service activities have led to prominent conflicts-of-interest problems in financial markets in recent years:[8] underwriting and research in investment banks, auditing and consulting in accounting firms, and credit assessment and consulting in credit-rating agencies. Why do combinations of these activities so often produce conflicts of interest?

Underwriting and research in investment Banking

Investment banks perform two tasks: they *research* companies issuing securities, and they *underwrite* these securities by selling them to the public on behalf of the issuing corporations. Investment banks often combine these distinct financial services because information synergies are possible: that is, information produced for one task may also be useful in the other task. A conflict of interest arises between the brokerage and underwriting services because the banks are attempting to simultaneously serve two client groups – the security-issuing firms and the security-buying investors. These client groups have different information needs. Issuers benefit from optimistic research, whereas investors desire unbiased research. However, the same information will be produced for both groups to take advantages of economies of scope. When the potential revenues from underwriting greatly exceed the brokerage commissions from selling, the bank will have a strong incentive to alter the information provided to investors to favour the issuing firm's needs or else risk losing the firm's business to competing investment banks. For example, an internal Morgan Stanley memo excerpted in the *Wall Street Journal* on 14 July 1992, stated, 'Our objective . . . is to adopt a policy, fully understood by the entire firm, including the Research Department, that we do not make negative or controversial comments about our clients as a matter of sound business practice.'

Because of directives like this one, analysts in investment banks might distort their research to please issuers, and indeed this seems to have happened during the stock market tech boom of the 1990s. Such actions undermine the reliability of the information that investors use to make their financial decisions and, as a result, diminish the efficiency of securities markets.

Another common practice that exploits conflicts of interest is **spinning**. Spinning occurs when an investment bank allocates hot, but underpriced, **initial public offerings (IPOs)** – that is, shares of newly issued stock – to executives of other companies in return for their companies' future business with the investment banks. Because hot IPOs typically immediately rise in price after they are first purchased, spinning is a form of kickback meant to persuade executives to use that investment bank. When the executive's company plans to issue its own shares, he or she will be more likely to go to the investment bank that distributed the hot IPO shares, which is not necessarily the investment bank that would get the highest price for the company's securities. This practice may raise the cost of capital for the firm, thereby diminishing the efficiency of the capital market.

Auditing and consulting in accounting firms

Traditionally, an auditor checks the books of companies and monitors the quality of the information produced by firms to reduce the inevitable information asymmetry between the firm's managers and its shareholders. In auditing, threats to truthful reporting arise from several potential conflicts of interest. The conflict of interest that has received the most attention in the media occurs when an accounting firm provides its client with both auditing services and non-audit consulting services such as advice on taxes, accounting, management information systems and business strategy. Supplying clients with multiple services allows for economies of scale and scope, but creates two potential sources of conflicts of interest. First, auditors may be willing to skew their judgements and opinions to win consulting business from these same clients. Second, auditors may be auditing information systems or tax and financial plans put in place by their non-audit counterparts within the firm, and therefore may be reluctant to criticize the systems or advice. Both types of conflicts may lead to biased audits, with the result that less reliable information is available in financial markets and investors find it difficult to allocate capital efficiently.

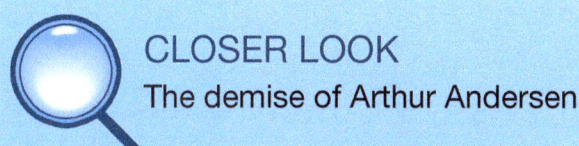

CLOSER LOOK
The demise of Arthur Andersen

In 1913, Arthur Andersen, a young accountant who had denounced the slipshod and deceptive practices that enabled companies to fool the investing public, founded his own firm. Up until the early 1980s, auditing was the most important source of profits within this firm. However, by the late 1980s, the consulting part of the business experienced high revenue growth with high profit margins, while audit profits slumped in a more competitive market. Consulting partners began to assert more power within the firm, and the resulting internal conflicts split the firm in two. Arthur Andersen (the auditing service) and Andersen Consulting were established as separate companies in 2000.

During the period of increasing conflict before the split, Andersen's audit partners had been under increasing pressure to focus on boosting revenue and profits from audit services. Many of Arthur Andersen's clients that later went bust – Enron, WorldCom, Qwest and Global

Crossing – were also the largest clients in Arthur Andersen's regional offices. The combination of intense pressure to generate revenue and profits from auditing and the fact that some clients dominated regional offices translated into tremendous incentives for regional office managers to provide favourable audit stances for these large clients. The loss of a client like Enron or WorldCom would have been devastating for a regional office and its partners, even if that client contributed only a small fraction of the overall revenue and profits of Arthur Andersen.

The Houston office of Arthur Andersen, for example, ignored problems in Enron's reporting. Arthur Andersen was indicted in March 2002 and then convicted in June 2002 for obstruction of justice for impeding the SEC's investigation of the Enron collapse. Its conviction – the first ever against a major accounting firm – barred Arthur Andersen from conducting audits of publicly traded firms. This development contributed to the firm's demise.

Another conflict of interest arises when an auditor provides an overly favourable audit to solicit or retain audit business. The unfortunate collapse of Arthur Andersen – one of the largest global accounting firms at that time – suggests that this may be the most dangerous conflict of interest (see the 'Closer look' box above).

Credit assessment and consulting in credit-rating agencies

Investors use credit ratings (e.g. Aaa or Baa) that reflect the probability of default to determine the creditworthiness of particular debt securities. As a consequence, debt ratings play a major role in the pricing of debt securities and in the regulatory process. Conflicts of interest can arise when multiple users with divergent interests (at least in the short term) depend on the credit ratings. Investors and regulators are seeking a well-researched, impartial assessment of credit quality; the issuer needs a favourable rating. In the credit-rating industry, the issuers of securities pay a rating firm such as Standard & Poor's or Moody's to have their securities rated. Because the issuers are the parties paying the credit-rating agency, investors and regulators worry that the agency may bias its ratings upward to attract more business from the issuer.

Another kind of conflict of interest may arise when credit-rating agencies also provide ancillary consulting services. Debt issuers often ask rating agencies to advise them on how to structure their debt issues, usually with the goal of securing a favourable rating. In this situation, the credit-rating agencies would be auditing their own work and would experience a conflict of interest similar to the one found in accounting firms that provide both auditing and consulting services. Furthermore, credit-rating agencies may deliver favourable ratings to garner new clients for the ancillary consulting business. The possible decline in the quality of credit assessments issued by rating agencies could increase asymmetric information in financial markets, thereby diminishing their ability to allocate credit. Such conflicts of interest came to the forefront because of the damaged reputations of the credit-rating agencies during the subprime financial crisis starting in 2007 (see the 'Closer look' box, 'Credit-rating agencies and the subprime financial crisis').

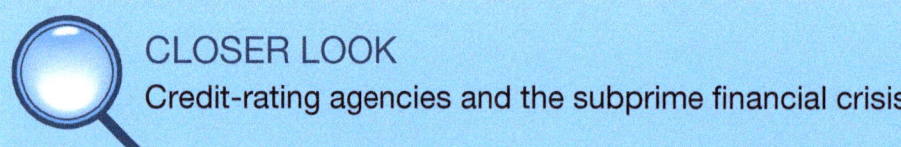

CLOSER LOOK
Credit-rating agencies and the subprime financial crisis

The credit-rating agencies have come under severe criticism for the role they played during the subprime financial crisis. Credit-rating agencies advised clients on how to structure complex financial instruments that paid out cash flows from subprime mortgages. At the same time, they were rating these identical products, leading to the potential for severe conflicts of interest. Specifically, the large fees they earned from advising clients on how to structure products that they were rating meant they did not have sufficient incentives to make sure their ratings were accurate.

When housing prices began to fall and subprime mortgages began to default, it became crystal clear that the ratings agencies had done a terrible job of assessing the risk in the subprime products they had helped to structure. Many AAA-rated products had to be downgraded over and over again until they reached junk status. The resulting massive losses on these assets were one reason why so many financial institutions that were holding them got into trouble, with absolutely disastrous consequences for the economy, as discussed in the next chapter.

Criticisms of the credit-rating agencies led the SEC to propose comprehensive reforms in 2008. The SEC concluded that the credit-rating agencies' models for rating subprime products were not fully developed and that conflicts of interest may have played a role in producing inaccurate ratings. To address conflicts of interest, the SEC prohibited credit-rating agencies from structuring the same products they rate, prohibited anyone who participates in determining a credit rating from negotiating the fee that the issuer pays for it, and prohibited gifts from bond-issuers to those who rate them in any amount over $25. In order to make credit-rating agencies more accountable, the SEC's new rules also required more disclosure of how the credit-rating agencies determine ratings. For example, credit-rating agencies were required to disclose historical ratings performance, including the dates of downgrades and upgrades, information on the underlying assets of a product that were used by the credit-rating agencies to rate a product, and the kind of research they used to determine the rating. In addition, the SEC required the rating agencies to differentiate the ratings on structured products from those issued on bonds. The expectation is that these reforms will bring increased transparency to the ratings process and reduce conflicts of interest that played such a large role in the subprime debacle.

What has been done to remedy conflicts of interest?

In the US two major policy measures were implemented to deal with conflicts of interest: the Sarbanes–Oxley Act and the Global Legal Settlement. In the European Union proposed directives to reform the credit rating agencies were made in November 2011 with the overall objective of *'reducing the risks to financial stability and restoring investor and other market participants' confidence in financial markets and ratings quality'*.[9]

Sarbanes–Oxley Act of 2002

The public outcry in the USA over the corporate and accounting scandals led in 2002 to the passage of the Public Accounting Return and Investor Protection Act, more commonly referred to as the Sarbanes–Oxley Act, after its two principal authors in Congress. This act increased supervisory oversight to monitor and prevent conflicts of interest:

- It established a Public Company Accounting Oversight Board (PCAOB), overseen by the SEC, to supervise accounting firms and ensure that audits are independent and controlled for quality.
- It increased the SEC's budget to supervise securities markets.

Sarbanes–Oxley also directly reduced conflicts of interest:

- It made it illegal for a registered public accounting firm to provide any non-audit service to a client contemporaneously with an impermissible audit (as determined by the PCAOB).

Sarbanes–Oxley provided incentives for investment banks not to exploit conflicts of interest:

■ It beefed up criminal charges for white-collar crime and obstruction of official investigations.

Sarbanes–Oxley also had measures to improve the quality of information in the financial markets:

■ It required a corporation's chief executive officer (CEO) and chief financial officer (CFO), as well as its auditors, to certify that periodic financial statements and disclosures of the firm (especially regarding off-balance-sheet transactions) are accurate (Section 404).
■ It required members of the audit committee (the subcommittee of the board of directors that oversees the company's audit) to be 'independent'; that is, they cannot be managers in the company or receive any consulting or advisory fee from the company.

Global legal settlement of 2002

The second major policy measure in the US arose out of a lawsuit brought by New York Attorney General Eliot Spitzer against the ten largest investment banks (Bear Stearns, Credit Suisse First Boston, Deutsche Bank, Goldman Sachs, JPMorgan, Lehman Brothers, Merrill Lynch, Morgan Stanley, Salomon Smith Barney, and UBS Warburg). A global settlement was reached on 20 December 2002 with these investment banks by the SEC, the New York Attorney General, NASD, NASAA, NYSE and New York state regulators. Like Sarbanes–Oxley, this settlement directly reduced conflicts of interest:

■ It required investment banks to sever the links between research and securities underwriting.
■ It banned spinning.

The global legal settlement also provided incentives for investment banks not to exploit conflicts of interest:

■ It imposed $1.4 billion of fines on the accused investment banks.

The global settlement had measures to improve the quality of information in financial markets:

■ It required investment banks to make their analysts' recommendations public.
■ Over a five-year period, investment banks were required to contract with at least three independent research firms that would provide research to their brokerage customers.
■ It is too early to evaluate the impact of the Sarbanes–Oxley Act and the global legal settlement, but the most controversial elements were the separation of functions (research from underwriting and auditing from non-audit consulting). Although such a separation of functions may reduce conflicts of interest, it might also diminish economies of scope and thus potentially lead to a reduction of information in financial markets. In addition, there is a serious concern that implementation of these measures, particularly Sarbanes–Oxley, is too costly and is leading to a decline in US capital markets (see the 'Closer look' box 'Has Sarbanes–Oxley led to a decline in US capital markets?').

European Union directives

Outside the US, the attempt to mitigate conflicts of interest has been slow in getting off the ground. Regulations setting out the rules of conduct of credit-rating agencies (CRAs) came into force in December 2010. However aspects of conflict of interest and the overreliance of financial markets on rating agencies particularly the rating of sovereign debt remained unaddressed. Other issues of concern were the degree of concentration in the credit-rating market (Fitch, Moody's and S&P) and also the way the agencies are remunerated.

The European Union proposed reforms in 2011 that impact on the credit-rating agencies as well as the rated institutions. The problem, as the EU Commission sees it, was the overreliance

CLOSER LOOK
Has Sarbanes–Oxley led to a decline in US capital markets?

There has been much debate in the United States in recent years regarding the impact of Sarbanes–Oxley, especially Section 404, on US capital markets. Section 404 requires both management and company auditors to certify the accuracy of their financial statements. There is no question that Sarbanes–Oxley has led to increased costs for corporations, and this is especially true for smaller firms with revenues of less than $100 million, where the compliance costs have been estimated to exceed 1% of sales. These higher costs could result in smaller firms listing abroad and discourage IPOs (initial public offerings) in the United States, thereby shrinking US capital markets relative to those abroad. However, improved accounting standards could work to encourage stock market listings and IPOs because better information could raise the valuation of common stocks.

Critics of Sarbanes–Oxley have cited it, as well as higher litigation and weaker shareholder rights, as the cause of declining US stock listings and IPOs, but other factors are likely to be at work. The European financial system experienced a major liberalization in the 1990s, along with the introduction of the euro which helped make its financial markets more integrated and efficient. As a result, it became easier for European firms to list in their home countries. The fraction of European firms that list in their home countries has risen to over 90% currently from around 60% in 1995. As the importance of the United States in the world economy has diminished because of the growing importance of other economies, the US capital markets have become less dominant over time. This process is even more evident in the corporate bond market. In 1995, corporate bond issues were double those of Europe, while issues of corporate bonds in Europe now exceed those in the United States.

of the market on three agencies that controlled 95% of the market, which leads to precipitous effects on the market when ratings are altered, particularly ratings of sovereign debt. The other issue for the Commission is independence of CRAs due to conflicts of interest arising from the 'issuer-pays' model.

The proposals are that financial institutions use more than one credit agency and also improve disclosure of structured financial products. Small and medium-sized credit agencies are encouraged to be set up. Further recommendations include the publication of the methodology used to arrive at ratings and to extend power to competent authorities to oversee the rating agencies through legal compliance. Other proposals are aimed at improving the independence of the credit-rating agencies and ensuring that agencies are transparent in the pricing of their services.

A looser version of the Sarbanes–Oxley Act exists in the EU in the form of the 8th Company Law Directive (2006). However in the US Sarbanes–Oxley requires that material weakness be disclosed to the market and not just to the auditors, where the EU does not, enabling European firms to fix the weakness. The Directive is also a framework and does not have the same force in law as it leaves member countries to interpret, add or subtract to it according to 'national requirements'.

Summary

1 There are eight basic facts about company financial structure. The first four emphasize the importance of financial intermediaries and the relative unimportance of securities markets for the financing of corporations; the fifth recognizes that financial markets are among the most heavily regulated sectors of the economy; the sixth states that only large, well-established corporations have access to securities markets; the seventh indicates that collateral is an important feature of debt contracts; and the eighth presents debt contracts as complicated legal documents that place substantial restrictions on the behaviour of the borrower.

2 Transaction costs freeze many small savers and borrowers out of direct involvement with financial markets. Financial intermediaries can take advantage

of economies of scale and are better able to develop expertise to lower transaction costs, thus enabling their savers and borrowers to benefit from the existence of financial markets.

3 Asymmetric information results in two problems: adverse selection, which occurs before the transaction, and moral hazard, which occurs after the transaction. Adverse selection refers to the fact that bad credit risks are the ones most likely to seek loans, and moral hazard refers to the risk of the borrower's engaging in activities that are undesirable from the lender's point of view.

4 Adverse selection interferes with the efficient functioning of financial markets. Tools to help reduce the adverse selection problem include private production and sale of information, government regulation to increase information, financial intermediation, and collateral and net worth. The free-rider problem occurs when people who do not pay for information take advantage of information that other people have paid for. This problem explains why financial intermediaries, particularly banks, play a more important role in financing the activities of businesses than securities markets do.

5 Moral hazard in equity contracts is known as the principal–agent problem, because managers (the agents) have less incentive to maximize profits than stockholders (the principals). The principal–agent

problem explains why debt contracts are so much more prevalent in financial markets than equity contracts. Tools to help reduce the principal–agent problem include monitoring, government regulation to increase information, and financial intermediation.

6 Tools to reduce the moral hazard problem in debt contracts include net worth, monitoring and enforcement of restrictive covenants, and financial intermediaries.

7 Conflicts of interest arise when financial service providers or their employees are serving multiple interests and have incentives to misuse or conceal information needed for the effective functioning of financial markets. We care about conflicts of interest because they can substantially reduce the amount of reliable information in financial markets, thereby preventing them from channelling funds to parties with the most productive investment opportunities. Three types of financial service activities have had the greatest potential for conflicts of interest: underwriting and research in investment banking, and auditing and consulting in accounting firms. In the US a major policy measure has been implemented to deal with conflicts of interest: the Sarbanes–Oxley Act of 2002. In the EU, directives dealing with conflicts of interest and transparency have been proposed but not uniformly implemented.

Key terms

agency theory p. 154

collateral p. 151

conflicts of interest p. 167

costly state verification p. 160

economies of scope p. 167

free-rider problem p. 155

incentive-compatible p. 162

initial public offering (IPO) p. 168

net worth (equity capital) p. 158

principal–agent problem p. 159

restrictive covenants p. 152

secured debt p. 152

spinning p. 168

state-owned banks p. 165

unsecured debt p. 152

venture capital firm p. 161

QUESTIONS AND PROBLEMS

All questions and problems are available in MyEconLab at **www.myeconlab.com/mishkin**.

1 How can economies of scale help explain the existence of financial intermediaries?

2 Describe two ways in which financial intermediaries help lower transaction costs in the economy.

3 Would moral hazard and adverse selection still arise in financial markets if information were not asymmetric? Explain.

4 How do standard accounting principles help financial markets work more efficiently?

5 Do you think the lemons problem would be more severe for stocks traded on the New York Stock Exchange or those traded over the counter? Explain.

6 Which firms are most likely to use bank financing rather than to issue bonds or stocks to finance their activities? Why?

7 How can the existence of asymmetric information provide a rationale for government regulation of financial markets?

8 Would you be more willing to lend to a friend if she put all of her life savings into her business than you would if she had not done so? Why?

9 Wealthy people often worry that others will seek to marry them only for their money. Is this a problem of adverse selection?

10 The more collateral there is backing a loan, the less the lender has to worry about adverse selection. Is this statement true, false, or uncertain? Explain your answer.

11 How does the free-rider problem aggravate adverse selection and moral hazard problems in financial markets?

12 Explain how the separation of ownership and control in companies might lead to poor management.

13 Why can the provision of several types of financial services by one firm lead to a lower cost of information production?

14 How does the provision of several types of financial services by one firm lead to conflicts of interest?

15 How can conflicts of interest make financial service firms less efficient?

16 Describe two conflicts of interest that occur when underwriting and research are provided by a single investment firm.

17 How does spinning lead to a less efficient financial system?

18 Describe two conflicts of interest that occur in accounting firms.

19 Which provisions of Sarbanes–Oxley do you think are beneficial, and which are not?

20 Which provisions of the global legal settlement do you think are beneficial, and which are not?

WEB EXERCISE

In this chapter we discuss the lemons problem and its effect on the efficient functioning of a market. This theory was initially developed by George Akerlof in his 1970 paper 'The Market for Lemons: Quality Uncertainty and the Market Mechanism'. Akerlof (alongside Michael Spence and Joseph Stiglitz) was awarded the Sveriges Riksbank Prize in Economic Sciences in Memory of Alfred Nobel in 2001. George Akerlof's lecture can be found on this page: **http://www.nobelprize.org/nobel_prizes/ economics/laureates/2001/akerlof-lecture.html.**Read the lecture and the accompanying profile of George Akerlof. Summarize his research ideas in one page.

Notes

1 The figure for the percentage of external financing provided by stocks is based on the flows of external funds to corporations. Figure 8.1 does not include the flow figure for bond financing. However, the stocks flow figure is somewhat misleading, because when a share of stock is issued, it raises funds permanently; whereas when a bond is issued, it raises funds only temporarily until they are paid back at maturity. To see this, suppose that a firm raises €1,000 by selling a share of stock and another €1,000 by selling a €1,000 one-year bond. In the case of the stock issue, the firm can hold on to the €1,000 it raised this way, but to hold on to the €1,000 it raised through debt, it has to issue a new €1,000 bond every year. If we look at the flow of funds to corporations over a 5-year period, as in Figure 8.1, the firm will have raised €1,000 with a stock issue only once in the 5-year period, while it will have raised €1,000 with debt five times, once in each of the 5 years. Thus it will look as though debt is five times more important than stocks in raising funds, even though our example indicates that they are actually equally important for the firm.

2 Andreas Hackenthal and Reinhardt H. Schmidt, 'Financing patterns: measurement concepts and empirical results',

Johan Wolfgang Goethe-Universitat Working Paper No 125, January 2004.

3 James Banks and Sarah Tanner, 'Household saving in the UK', Institute of Fiscal Studies, October 1999.

4 An excellent survey of the literature on information and financial structure that expands on the topics discussed in the rest of this chapter is contained in Mark Gertler, 'Financial structure and aggregate economic activity: an overview', *Journal of Money, Credit and Banking* 20 (1988): 559–88.

5 George Akerlof, 'The market for "lemons": quality, uncertainty and the market mechanism', *Quarterly Journal of Economics* 84 (1970): 488–500. Two important papers that have applied the lemons problem analysis to financial markets are Stewart Myers and N. S. Majluf, 'Corporate financing and investment decisions when firms have information that investors do not have', *Journal of Financial Economics* 13 (1984): 187–221; and Bruce Greenwald, Joseph E. Stiglitz and Andrew Weiss, 'Information imperfections in the capital market and macroeconomic fluctuations', *American Economic Review* 74 (1984): 194–9.

6 An important factor that encourages the use of debt contracts in the UK rather than equity contracts is that debt interest payments are a deductible expense, whereas dividend payments to equity shareholders are not.

7 See World Bank, *Finance for Growth: Policy Choices in a Volatile World* (World Bank and Oxford University Press, 2001) and Frederic S. Mishkin, *The Next Great Globalization: How Disadvantaged Nations Can Harness, Their Financial Systems to Get Rich* (Princeton University Press, 2006) for a survey of the literature linking economic growth with financial development and a list of additional references.

8 Another important type of conflict of interest arises in universal banking, in which banks engage in multiple financial service activities, including commercial banking, investment banking and insurance. For further analysis of these conflicts of interest, see Andrew Crockett, Trevor Harris, Frederic S. Mishkin and Eugene N. White, *Conflicts of Interest in the Financial Services Industry: What Should We Do about Them?*, Geneva Reports on the World Economy 4 (Geneva and London: International Centre for Monetary and Banking Studies and Center for Economic Policy Research, 2003).

9 EU – 'Proposal for a Regulation amending Regulation (EC) No 1060/2009 on credit rating agencies and a Proposal for a Directive amending Directive 2009/65/EC on coordination on laws, regulations and administrative provisions relating to undertakings for collective investment in transferable securities (UCITS) and Directive 2011/61/EU on Alternative Investment Fund Managers', Brussels, XXX SEC(2011), 1355/2.

Useful website

http://nobelprize.org/nobel_prizes/economics/laureates/2001/public.html A complete discussion of the lemons problem on a site dedicated to Nobel Prize winners.

CHAPTER 9

Financial crises and the subprime meltdown

PREVIEW

Financial crises are major disruptions in financial markets characterized by sharp declines in asset prices and firm failures. Beginning in August 2007, defaults in the subprime mortgage market (for borrowers with weak credit records) sent a shudder through the world financial markets, leading to the worst global financial crisis since the Great Depression. Alan Greenspan, former Chairman of the US Federal Reserve, described the subprime financial crisis as a 'once-in-a-century credit tsunami'. Wall Street firms and commercial banks suffered hundreds of billions of dollars of losses. All over the world, stock markets crashed. Many financial firms, including commercial banks, investment banks and insurance companies, went belly up. Economic growth in the developed economies slumped during 2008–9 but in 2010 there appeared the signs of recovery in the world economy, then in the summer of 2011 a fresh gale of financial crisis hit the global economy. The European sovereign debt crisis which had been bubbling under the surface during 2009–10 finally broke through in August 2011 with stock markets all over the world wiping out hundreds of billions of euros worth of shares, with bank shares being the worst affected.

Why did these financial crises occur? Why have financial crises been so prevalent throughout the history of the developed economies, and what insights do they provide on the current crisis? Why are financial crises almost always followed by severe contractions in economic activity? We will examine these questions in this chapter by developing a framework to understand the dynamics of financial crises. Building on Chapter 8, we make use of agency theory, the economic analysis of the effects of asymmetric information (adverse selection and moral hazard) on financial markets and the economy, to see why financial crises occur and why they have such devastating effects on the economy. We will then apply the analysis to explain the course of events in a number of past financial crises throughout the world, including the recent subprime crisis.

Factors causing financial crises

In the previous chapter we saw that a well-functioning financial system solves asymmetric information problems so that capital is allocated to its most productive uses. A **financial crisis** occurs when an increase in asymmetric information from a disruption in the financial system causes severe adverse selection and moral hazard problems that render financial markets incapable of channelling funds efficiently from savers to households and firms with productive investment opportunities. When financial markets fail to function efficiently, economic activity contracts sharply.

To understand why financial crises occur and, more specifically, how they lead to contractions in economic activity, we need to examine the factors that cause them. Six categories of factors play an important role in financial crises: asset market effects on balance sheets, deterioration in financial institutions' balance sheets, banking crisis, increases in uncertainty, increases in interest rates and government fiscal imbalances. We will examine each of these factors and their impact on lending, investment and economic activity.

Asset market effects on balance sheets

The state of borrowers' balance sheets has important implications for the severity of asymmetric information problems in the financial system.

Stock market decline

A sharp decline in the stock market is one factor that can cause a serious deterioration in borrowing firms' balance sheets. In turn, this deterioration can increase adverse selection and moral hazard problems in financial markets and provoke a financial crisis. A decline in the stock market means that the net worth of corporations has fallen, because share prices are the valuation of a corporation's net worth. The decline in net worth makes lenders less willing to lend because, as we have seen, the net worth of a firm plays a role similar to that of collateral. When the value of collateral declines, it provides less protection to lenders, meaning that losses on loans are likely to be more severe. Because lenders are now less protected against the consequences of adverse selection, they decrease their lending, which in turn causes investment and aggregate output to decline. In addition, the decline in corporate net worth as a result of a stock market decline increases moral hazard by providing incentives for borrowing firms to make risky investments, as they now have less to lose if their investments go sour. The resulting increase in moral hazard makes lending less attractive – another reason why a stock market decline and the resultant decline in net worth leads to decreased lending and economic activity.

Unanticipated decline in the price level

In economies with moderate inflation, which characterizes most industrialized countries, many debt contracts with fixed interest rates are typically of fairly long maturity, ten years or more. In this institutional environment, unanticipated declines in the aggregate price level also decrease the net worth of firms. Because debt payments are contractually fixed in nominal terms, an unanticipated decline in the price level raises the value of borrowing firms' liabilities in real terms (increases the burden of the debt) but does not raise the real value of firms' assets. The result is that net worth in real terms (the difference between assets and liabilities in real terms) declines. A sharp drop in the price level therefore causes a substantial decline in real net worth for borrowing firms and an increase in adverse selection and moral hazard problems facing lenders. An unanticipated decline in the aggregate price level thus leads to a drop in lending and economic activity.

Unanticipated decline in the value of the domestic currency

Because of uncertainty about the future value of the domestic currency in developing countries (and in some industrialized countries), many non-financial firms, banks and governments in developing countries find it easier to issue debt denominated in foreign currencies rather than in their own currency. This can lead to a financial crisis in a similar fashion to an unanticipated decline in the price level. With debt contracts denominated in foreign currency, when there is an unanticipated decline in the value of the domestic currency, the debt burden of domestic firms increases. Since assets are typically denominated in domestic currency, there is a resulting deterioration in firms' balance sheets and a decline in net worth, which then increases adverse selection and moral hazard problems along the lines just described. The increase in asymmetric information problems leads to a decline in investment and economic activity.

Asset write-downs

Asset price declines also lead to a write-down of the value of the assets side of the balance sheets of financial institutions. This deterioration in their balance sheets can also lead to a contraction of lending, as the next factor indicates.

Deterioration in financial institutions' balance sheets

Financial institutions, particularly banks, play a major role in financial markets because they are well positioned to engage in information-producing activities that facilitate productive investment for the economy. The state of banks' and other financial intermediaries' balance sheets has an important effect on lending. Suppose financial institutions suffer a deterioration in their balance sheets and so have a substantial contraction in their capital. They will have fewer resources to lend, and lending will decline. The contraction in lending then leads to a decline in investment spending, which slows economic activity.

Banking crisis

If the deterioration in financial institutions' balance sheets is severe enough, they will start to fail. Fear can spread from one institution to another, causing even healthy ones to go under. Because banks have deposits that can be pulled out very quickly, they are particularly prone to contagion of this type. A **bank panic** occurs when multiple banks fail simultaneously. The source of the contagion is asymmetric information. In a panic, depositors, fearing for the safety of their deposits (in the absence of or with limited amounts of deposit insurance) and not knowing the quality of banks' loan portfolios, withdraw their deposits to the point that the banks fail. When a large number of banks fail in a short period of time, there is a loss of information production in financial markets and a direct loss of banks' financial intermediation.

The decrease in bank lending during a banking crisis decreases the supply of funds available to borrowers, which leads to higher interest rates. Bank panics result in an increase in adverse selection and moral hazard problems in credit markets: these problems produce an even sharper decline in lending to facilitate productive investments and lead to an even more severe contraction in economic activity.

Increases in uncertainty

A dramatic increase in uncertainty in financial markets, due perhaps to the failure of a prominent financial or non-financial institution, a recession or a stock market crash, makes it hard for lenders to screen good from bad credit risks. The resulting inability of lenders to solve the adverse selection problem makes them less willing to lend, which leads to a decline in lending, investment and aggregate economic activity.

Increases in interest rates

As we saw in Chapter 8, individuals and firms with the riskiest investment projects are those that are willing to pay the highest interest rates. If increased demand for credit or a decline in the money supply market drives up interest rates sufficiently, good credit risks are less likely to want to borrow while bad credit risks are still willing to borrow. Because of the resulting increase in adverse selection, lenders will no longer want to make loans. The substantial decline in lending will lead to a substantial decline in investment and aggregate economic activity.

Increases in interest rates also play a role in promoting a financial crisis through their effect on cash flow, the difference between cash receipts and expenditures. A firm with sufficient cash flow can finance its projects internally, and there is no asymmetric information because it knows how good its own projects are. (Indeed, American businesses fund around two-thirds of their investments with internal funds.) An increase in interest rates and therefore in household and firm interest payments decreases their cash flow. With less cash flow, the firm has fewer internal funds and must raise funds from an external source, say, a bank, which does not know the firm as well as its owners or managers. How can the bank be sure if the firm will invest in safe projects or instead take on big risks and then be unlikely to pay back the loan? Because of this increased adverse selection and moral hazard, the bank may choose not to lend firms, even those with good risks, the money to undertake potentially profitable investments. Thus when cash flow drops as a result of an increase in interest rates, adverse selection and moral hazard problems become more severe, again curtailing lending, investment and economic activity.

Government fiscal imbalances

Government fiscal imbalances may create fears of default on government debt. A recent example is the eurozone sovereign debt crisis that is particularly affecting the GIIPS countries (Greece, Ireland, Italy, Portugal and Spain). As a result, demand from individual investors for government bonds may fall, causing the government to force financial institutions to purchase them. If the debt then declines in price – which, as we have seen in Chapter 6, will occur if a government default is likely – financial institutions' balance sheets will weaken and their lending will contract for the reasons described earlier. Fears of default on the government debt can also spark a foreign exchange crisis in which the value of the domestic currency falls sharply because investors pull their money out of the country. The decline in the domestic currency's value will then lead to the destruction of the balance sheets of firms with large amounts of debt denominated in foreign currency. These balance sheet problems lead to an increase in adverse selection and moral hazard problems, a decline in lending and a contraction of economic activity.

Dynamics of past financial crises in developed countries

The subprime crisis has dominated recent news headlines, but it is only one of a number of financial crises in the history of the developed world. We will now examine trends in past crises – and uncover insights on present-day challenges along the way.

Financial crises have typically progressed in two and sometimes three stages. To help you understand how these crises have unfolded, refer to Figure 9.1, a diagram that identifies the stages and sequence of events in developed countries' financial crises.

Stage 1: Initiation of financial crisis

There are several possible ways that financial crises start – mismanagement of financial liberalization or innovation, asset price booms and busts, spikes in interest rates, or a general increase in uncertainty when there are failures of major financial institutions.

Mismanagement of financial liberalization/innovation

The seeds of a financial crisis are often sown when countries engage in **financial liberalization**, the elimination of restrictions on financial markets and institutions, or when major financial innovations are introduced to the marketplace, as occurred recently with subprime residential mortgages. Financial innovation or liberalization is highly beneficial in the long run because it facilitates the process of financial development discussed in

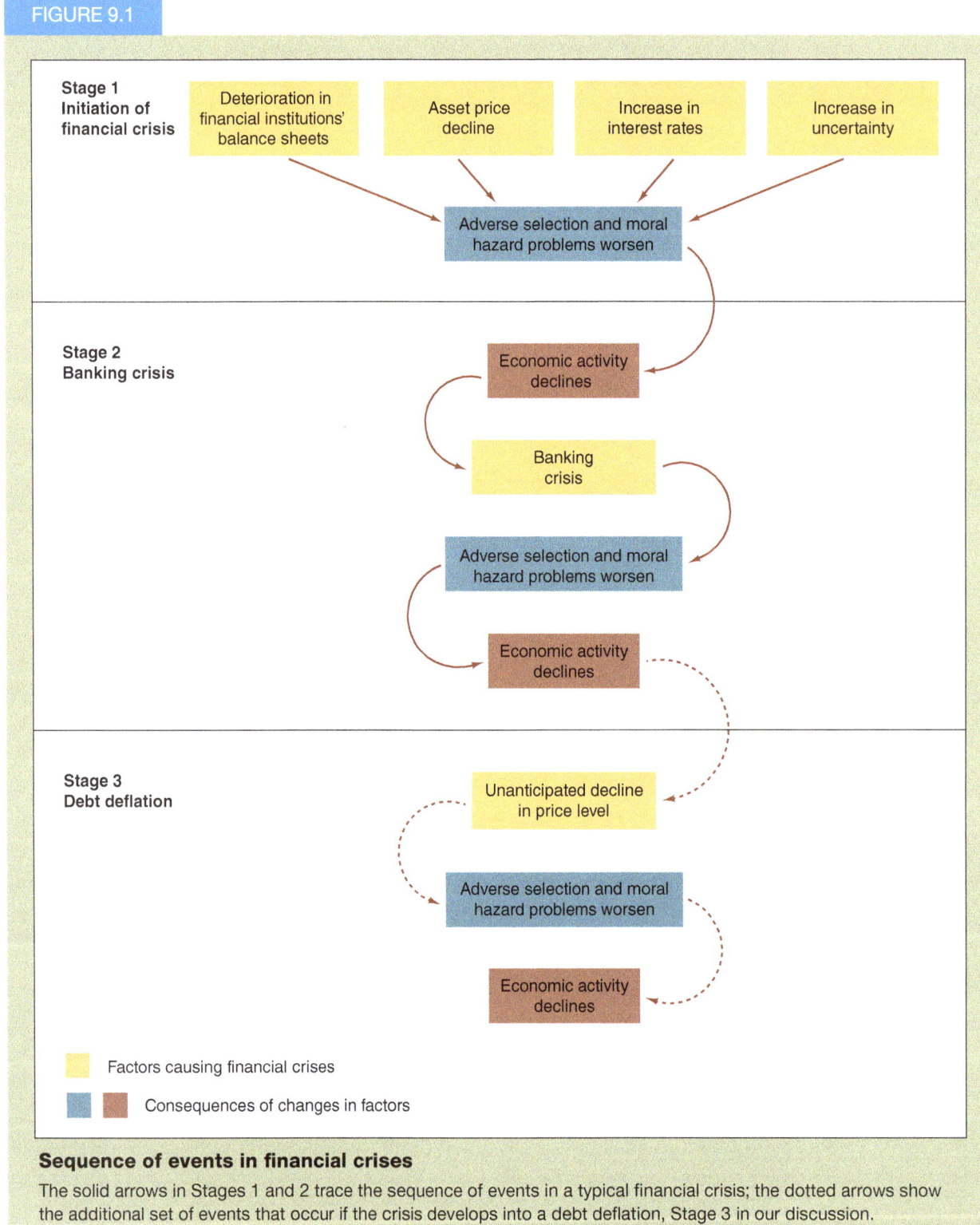

Sequence of events in financial crises

The solid arrows in Stages 1 and 2 trace the sequence of events in a typical financial crisis; the dotted arrows show the additional set of events that occur if the crisis develops into a debt deflation, Stage 3 in our discussion.

the previous chapter, which leads to a more efficient financial system that can allocate capital better. However, financial liberalization or innovation has a dark side: if managed improperly, it can lead financial institutions to take on excessive risk. With restrictions lifted or new financial products introduced, financial institutions frequently go on a lending spree, often called a **credit boom**, and expand their lending at a rapid pace. Unfortunately, the managers of these financial institutions may not have the expertise to manage risk appropriately in these new lines of business. Even if the required managerial expertise is initially present, the rapid growth of credit will likely outstrip the information resources available to these institutions, leading to overly risky lending.

As we will discuss in Chapter 11, most governments try to prevent bank panics and encourage banks to keep on lending during bad times by providing a government safety net. If depositors and other providers of funds to banks are protected from losses, they will keep on supplying banks with funds so banks can continue to lend and will not fail. However, there is a catch: the government safety net weakens market discipline for the bank. With a safety net, depositors know that they will not lose anything if a bank fails. Thus the bank can still acquire funds even if it takes on excessive risk. The government safety net therefore increases the moral hazard incentive for banks to take on greater risk than they otherwise would, because if their risky, high-interest loans pay off, the banks make a lot of money; if they don't and the bank fails, taxpayers pay most of the bill for the safety net that protects the banks' depositors. In other words, banks can play the game of 'heads, I win: tails, the taxpayer loses'.

The presence of a government safety net requires regulation and government supervision of the financial system to prevent excessive risk taking. However, new lines of business and rapid credit growth stretch the resources of the government's supervisory agencies. Financial supervisors find themselves without the expertise or the additional resources needed to appropriately monitor the new lending activities. Without this monitoring, risk taking can explode.

Eventually, this risk taking comes home to roost. Losses on loans begin to mount and the drop in the value of the loans (on the asset side of the balance sheet) falls relative to liabilities, thereby driving down the net worth (capital) of banks and other financial institutions. With less capital, these financial institutions cut back on their lending, a process that is called **deleveraging**. Furthermore, with less capital, banks and other financial institutions become riskier, causing depositors and other potential lenders to these institutions to pull out their funds. Fewer funds mean fewer loans and a credit freeze. The lending boom turns into a lending crash.

As we have seen, banks and other financial intermediaries play a crucial role in financial markets because they are well suited to collect information about businesses and industries. This ability in turn enables these institutions to distinguish good loan prospects from bad ones. When financial intermediaries deleverage and cut back on their lending, no one else can step in to collect this information and make these loans. The ability of the financial system to cope with the asymmetric information problems of adverse selection and moral hazard is therefore severely hampered (as shown in the arrow pointing from the first factor in the top row of Figure 9.1). As loans become scarcer, firms are no longer able to fund their attractive investment opportunities; they decrease their spending and economic activity contracts.

Asset price boom and bust

Asset prices, in the stock market and real estate, can be driven well above their fundamental economic values by investor psychology (dubbed 'irrational exuberance' by Alan Greenspan when he was Chairman of the Federal Reserve). The result is an **asset-price bubble**, such as the tech stock market bubble of the late 1990s or the housing price bubble of the 2000s that we will discuss later in this chapter.

Asset-price bubbles are often also driven by credit booms, in which the large increase in credit is used to fund purchases of assets, thereby driving up their price. When the bubble bursts and asset prices realign with fundamental economic values, the resulting decline in net worth increases asymmetric information (as shown by the arrow pointing from the second factor in the top row of Figure 9.1), making borrowers less creditworthy and causing a contraction in lending and spending along the lines we discussed in the previous section.

The asset price bust can also, as we have seen, lead to a deterioration in financial institutions' balance sheets (as shown by the arrow pointing from the second factor in the top row of Figure 9.1), which causes them to deleverage, further contributing to the decline in economic activity.

Spikes in interest rates

Many financial crises in the nineteenth century were precipitated by increases in interest rates, either when interest rates shot up in London, which at the time was the world's financial centre, or when bank panics led to a scramble for liquidity in the United States that produced sharp upward spikes in interest rates (sometimes rising by 100 percentage points in a couple of days).

The higher interest rates led to a decline in cash flow for households and firms and a reduction in the number of good credit risks who are willing to borrow, both of which increase adverse selection and moral hazard (as shown by the arrow pointing from the third factor in the top row of Figure 9.1), causing a decline in economic activity. An example of this was the financial crisis of 1825 that resulted from capital flows from London to finance infrastructure spending in South America following the overthrow of the Spanish empire. To halt the outflow of gold from London the Bank of England raised interest rates which resulted in banking panics in the US and currency collapses in South America.

Increase in uncertainty

Financial crises in the developed economies almost always have started when uncertainty is high, either after a recession has begun or the stock market has crashed. The failure of a major financial institution is a particularly important source of heightened uncertainty that features prominently in financial crises. Examples in US history abound: the Ohio Life Insurance and Trust Company in 1857; Jay Cooke and Company in 1873; Grant and Ward in 1884; the Knickerbocker Trust Company in 1907; the Bank of the United States in 1930; and Bear Stearns, Lehman Brothers and AIG in 2008. In Europe, the collapse of the Austrian bank Credit-Anstalt in 1931 signalled the start of the global banking collapse that led to the Great Depression. With information harder to come by in a period of high uncertainty, adverse selection and moral hazard problems increase, leading to a decline in lending and economic activity (as shown by the arrow pointing from the last factor in the top row of Figure 9.1).

Stage 2: Banking crisis

Because of the worsening business conditions and uncertainty about their banks' health, depositors begin to withdraw their funds from banks and a banking crisis or bank panic often ensues. The resulting decline in the number of banks results in a loss of their information capital, worsening adverse selection and moral hazard problems in the credit markets, leading to a further spiralling down of the economy. Figure 9.1 represents this progression in the Stage 2 portion. Bank panics were a feature of all financial crises in the US during the nineteenth and twentieth centuries until World War II, occurring every twenty years or so – 1819, 1837, 1857, 1873, 1884, 1893, 1907 and 1930–3. The collapse of Credit-Anstalt in May 1931 brought down banks in Amsterdam and Warsaw, and the crisis spread to Germany, Latvia, Turkey and Egypt by June 1931. A few months later the panic spread leading to bank failures in Australia, Belgium, Greece, Italy, Portugal, Spain, Scandinavia and the US.

Typically, in a financial crisis, there is then a sorting out of firms that are insolvent (had a negative net worth) from healthy firms by bankruptcy proceedings. The same process occurs for banks, often with the help of public and private authorities. Once this sorting out is complete, uncertainty in financial markets declines, the stock market recovers, and interest rates fall. The overall result is that adverse selection and moral hazard problems diminish and the financial crisis subsides. With the financial markets able to operate well again, the stage is set for the recovery of the economy, bringing us to the next possible stage.

Stage 3: Debt deflation

If, however, the economic downturn leads to a sharp decline in prices, the recovery process can be short-circuited. In this situation, shown as Stage 3 in Figure 9.1, a process called **debt deflation** occurs, in which a substantial unanticipated decline in the price level sets in, leading to a further deterioration in firms' net worth because of the increased burden of indebtedness. With debt deflation, the adverse selection and moral hazard problems become more severe so that lending, investment spending and aggregate economic activity remain depressed for a long time. The most significant financial crisis that included debt deflation was the Great Depression, the worst economic contraction in US history.

APPLICATION   ### The mother of all financial crises: the Great Depression

In 1928 and 1929, prices doubled in the US stock market. Federal Reserve officials viewed the stock market boom as excessive speculation. To curb it, they pursued a tight monetary policy to raise interest rates; the Fed got more than it bargained for when the stock market crashed in October 1929, falling by 20%.

Although the 1929 crash had a great impact on the minds of a whole generation, most people forget that by the middle of 1930, more than half of the stock market decline had been reversed. Indeed, credit market conditions remained quite stable and there was little evidence that a major financial crisis was under way.

What might have been a normal recession turned into something far different, however, when adverse shocks to the agricultural sector led to bank failures in agricultural regions that then spread to the major banking centres. A sequence of bank panics followed from October 1930 until March 1933. More than one-third of US banks went out of business (events described in more detail in Chapter 14).

The continuing decline in stock prices after mid-1930 (by mid-1932 stocks had declined to 10% of their value at the 1929 peak) and the increase in uncertainty from the unsettled business conditions created by the economic contraction worsened adverse selection and moral hazard problems in the credit markets. The loss of one-third of the banks reduced the amount of financial intermediation. Intensified adverse selection and moral hazard problems decreased the ability of financial markets to channel funds to firms with productive investment opportunities. As our analysis predicts, the amount of outstanding commercial loans fell by half from 1929 to 1933, and investment spending collapsed, declining by 90% from its 1929 level.

The short-circuiting of the process that kept the economy from recovering quickly, which it does in most recessions, occurred because of a fall in the price level by 25% in the 1930–3 period. This huge decline in prices triggered a debt deflation in which net worth fell because of the increased burden of indebtedness borne by firms. The decline in net worth and the resulting increase in adverse selection and moral hazard problems in the credit markets led to a prolonged economic contraction in which unemployment rose to 25% of the labour force. The financial crisis in the Great Depression was the worst ever experienced in the United States, and it explains why this economic contraction was also the most severe ever experienced by that nation.[1] ■

The subprime financial crisis of 2007–8

Now that our framework for analysing financial crises is in place, we are prepared to tackle the most recent financial crisis that came out of the US. Mismanagement of financial innovation in the subprime residential mortgage market and a bursting of a bubble in housing prices were the underlying forces behind the financial crisis of 2007–8.

Financial innovations emerge in the mortgage markets

Before 2000, only the most creditworthy (prime) borrowers were able to obtain residential mortgages. Advances in computer technology and new statistical techniques, known as data mining, however, led to enhanced, quantitative evaluation of the credit risk for a new class of riskier residential mortgages. **Subprime mortgages** are mortgages for borrowers with less-than-stellar credit records. **Alt-A mortgages** are mortgages for borrowers with higher expected default rates than prime (A-paper), but with better credit records than subprime borrowers. Households with credit records could now be assigned a numerical credit score, known as a FICO score (named after the Fair Isaac Corporation that developed it), that would predict how likely they would be to default on their loan payments. In addition, by lowering transaction costs, computer technology enabled the bundling together of smaller loans (like mortgages) into standard debt securities, a process known as **securitization**.

   The ability to cheaply bundle and quantify the default risk of the underlying high-risk mortgages in a standardized debt security called **mortgage-backed securities** provided a new source of financing for these mortgages. The financial innovation of subprime and alt-A mortgages was born. Financial innovation didn't stop there. **Financial engineering**, the development of new, sophisticated financial instruments products, led to **structured credit products** that are derived from cash flows of underlying assets and can be tailored to have particular risk characteristics that appeal to investors with differing preferences. Particularly notorious were **collateralized debt obligations (CDOs)**, which paid out the cash flows from subprime mortgage-backed securities in different tranches, with the highest-rated tranche paying out first, while lower ones paid out less if there were losses on the mortgage-backed securities. There were even CDO2s and CDO3s that sliced and diced risk even further, paying out the cash flows from CDOs and CDO2s.

Housing price bubble forms

Aided by liquidity from cash flows surging into the United States from countries like China and India, the subprime mortgage market took off after the recession was over in 2001, becoming an over a trillion dollar market by 2007. The development of the subprime mortgage market was lauded by economists and politicians alike because it led to a 'democratization of credit' and helped raise US homeownership rates to the highest levels in history. The asset price boom in housing, which took off after the 2000–1 recession was over, also helped stimulate the growth of the subprime market. Higher housing prices meant that subprime borrowers could refinance their houses with even larger loans when their homes appreciated in value. Subprime borrowers were also unlikely to default because they could always sell their house to pay off the loan, making investors happy because the securities backed by cash flows from subprime mortgages had high returns. The growth of the subprime mortgage market, in turn, increased the demand for houses and so fuelled the boom in housing prices.

Agency problems arise

But all was not well in the subprime mortgage market. All the agency problems described in the previous chapter were coming to the fore. The subprime mortgage market was based on a so-called **originate-to-distribute** business model, in which the mortgage was originated by a separate party, typically a mortgage broker, and then distributed to an investor as an underlying asset in a security. Unfortunately, the originate-to-distribute model is subject to the principal–agent problem because the agent for the investor, the mortgage originator, has little incentive to make sure that the mortgage is a good credit risk. Once the mortgage broker earns her fee, why should she care if the borrower makes good on his payment? The more volume the broker originates, the more she makes.

Not surprisingly, given these incentives, mortgage brokers often did not make a strong effort to evaluate whether the borrower could pay off the loan. Adverse selection then became especially severe: risk-loving investors were able to obtain loans to acquire houses that would be very profitable if housing prices went up, but they could just 'walk away' from houses if housing prices went down. The principal–agent problem also created incentives for mortgage brokers to encourage households to take on mortgages they could not afford, or to commit fraud by falsifying information on borrowers' mortgage applications in order to qualify them for their mortgages. Compounding this problem was lax regulation of originators, who were not required to disclose information to borrowers that would have helped them assess whether they could afford the loans.

The agency problems went even deeper. Commercial and investment banks, which were earning large fees by underwriting mortgage-backed securities and structured credit products like CDOs, also had weak incentives to make sure that the ultimate holders of the securities would be paid off. The credit-rating agencies that were evaluating these securities also were subject to conflicts of interest: they were earning fees from rating them and also from advising clients on how to structure these securities to get the highest ratings. The integrity of these ratings was thus more likely to be compromised.

Information problems surface

Although financial engineering has the potential benefit to create products and services that better match investors' risk appetites, it, too, has a dark side. The structured products like CDOs, CDO2s and CDO3s can get so complicated that it can be hard to value the cash flows of the underlying assets for a security or to determine who actually owns these assets. Indeed, in a speech in October 2007, Ben Bernanke, the chairman of the Federal Reserve, joked that he 'would like to know what those damn things are worth'. In other words, the increased complexity of structured products can actually destroy information, thereby making asymmetric information worse in the financial system and increasing the severity of adverse selection and moral hazard problems.

Housing price bubble bursts

As housing prices rose and profitability for mortgage originators and lenders was high, the underwriting standards for subprime mortgages fell to lower and lower standards. Riskier borrowers were able to obtain mortgages, and the amount of the mortgage relative to the value of the house, the loan-to-value ratio (LTV), rose. Borrowers were often able to get piggyback second and third mortgages on top of their original 80% LTV mortgage, so that they had to put almost no money down. When asset prices rise too far out of line with fundamentals, however, they must come down, and eventually the housing price bubble burst. With housing prices falling after their peak in 2006, the rot in the financial system began to be revealed. The decline in housing prices led to many subprime borrowers finding that their mortgages were 'under water', that is, the value of the house fell below the amount of the mortgage. When this happened, struggling homeowners had tremendous incentives to walk away from their homes and just send the keys back to the lender. Defaults on mortgages shot up sharply, eventually leading to over 1 million mortgages in foreclosure.

Crisis spreads globally

Although the problem originated in the United States, the wake-up call came from Europe, a sign of how extensive the globalization of financial markets had become. After Fitch and Standard & Poor's announced ratings downgrades on mortgage-backed securities and CDOs totalling more than $10 billion, the asset-based commercial paper market seized up and a French investment house, BNP Paribas, suspended redemption of shares held in some of its money market funds on 7 August 2007. Despite huge injections of liquidity into the financial system by the European Central Bank and the Federal Reserve, which will be discussed later in Chapter 15, banks began to hoard cash and were unwilling to lend to each other. As can be seen in Figure 9.2, the **Treasury Bill-to-Eurodollar rate (TED)** spread, a good measure of liquidity in the interbank market, shot up from an average of 40 basis points (0.40 percentage points) during the first half of 2007 to a peak of 240 by 20 August 2007. The drying up of credit led to the first major bank failure in the United Kingdom in over 100 years when Northern Rock, which had relied on wholesale short-term borrowing rather than deposits for its funding, collapsed in September 2008.

Banks' balance sheets deteriorate

The decline in US housing prices, which now accelerated, led to rising defaults on mortgages. As a result, the value of mortgage-backed securities and CDOs collapsed, leading to ever-larger write-downs at banks and other financial institutions. The balance sheets of these institutions deteriorated because of the losses from their holdings of these securities and because many of these institutions had to take back onto their balance sheets some of the *structured investment vehicles (SIVs)* they had sponsored. **Structured investment vehicles** are similar to CDOs in that they pay off cash flows from pools of assets such as mortgages; instead of issuing long-term debt as in CDOs, they issued asset-backed commercial paper. With weaker balance sheets, these banks and other financial institutions began to deleverage, selling off assets and restricting the availability of credit to both

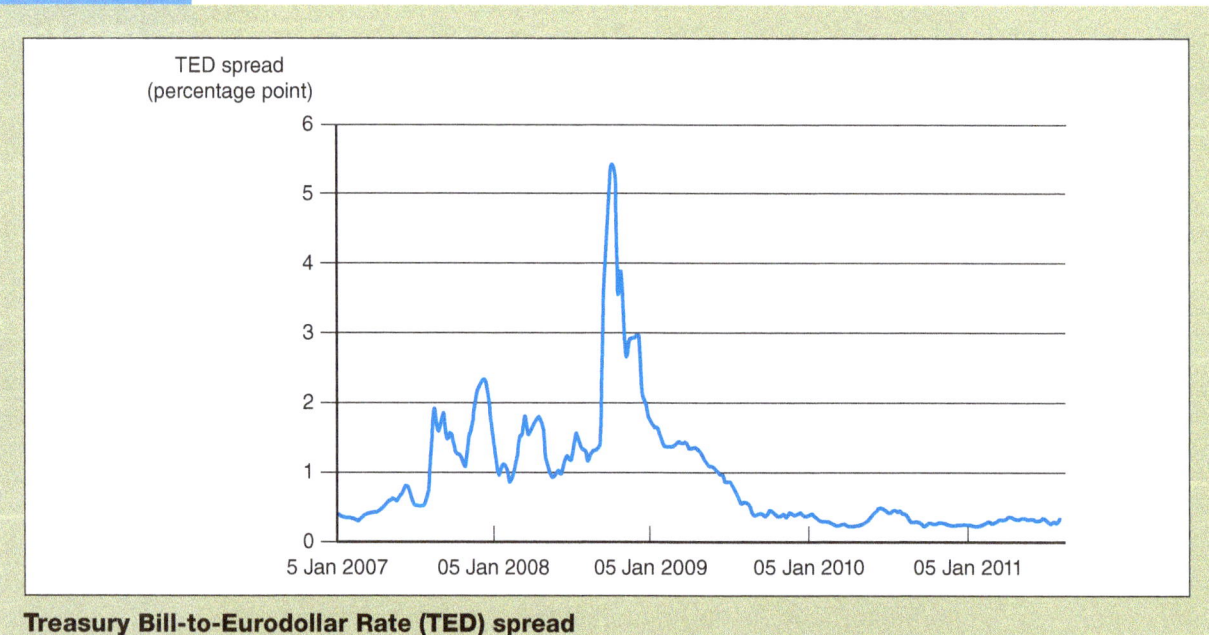

FIGURE 9.2

Treasury Bill-to-Eurodollar Rate (TED) spread

Source: www.federalreserve.gov/releases/h15/data.htm.

households and businesses. With no one else able to step in to collect information and make loans, adverse selection and moral hazard problems increased in the credit markets, leading to a slowing of the US economy and rising unemployment levels.

High-profile firms fail

In March 2008, Bear Stearns, the fifth-largest investment bank, which had invested heavily in subprime-related securities, had a run on its funding and was forced to sell itself to JPMorgan for less than 5% of what it was worth just a year earlier. In order to broker the deal, the Federal Reserve had to take over $30 billion of Bear Stearns's hard-to-value assets. In July, Fannie Mae and Freddie Mac, the two privately owned government-sponsored enterprises that together insured over $5 trillion of mortgages or mortgage-backed assets, had to be propped up by the US Treasury and the Federal Reserve after suffering substantial losses from their holdings of subprime securities. In early September 2008, they were then put into conservatorship (in effect run by the government).

Worse was yet to come. On Monday, 15 September 2008, after suffering losses in the subprime market, Lehman Brothers, the fourth-largest investment bank by asset size with over $600 billion in assets and 25,000 employees, filed for bankruptcy, making it the largest bankruptcy filing in US history. The day before, Merrill Lynch, the third-largest investment bank, which also suffered large losses on its holding of subprime securities, announced its sale to Bank of America for a price 60% below its price a year earlier. On Tuesday, 16 September, AIG, an insurance giant with assets of over $1 trillion, suffered an extreme liquidity crisis when its credit rating was downgraded. It had written over $400 billion of insurance contracts called credit default swaps which had to make payouts on possible losses from subprime mortgage securities. The Federal Reserve then stepped in with an $85 billion loan to keep AIG afloat (with total loans from the Fed and the government later increased to $173 billion).

Also on 16 September, as a result of its losses from exposure to Lehman Brothers' debt, one large money market mutual fund, the Reserve Primary Fund, with over $60 billion of assets, 'broke the buck' – that is, it could no longer redeem its shares at the par value of $1. A run on money market funds then ensued, with the Treasury putting in place a temporary guarantee for all money market mutual fund redemptions in order to stem withdrawals. On 25 September 2008, Washington Mutual (WAMU), the sixth-largest bank in the United States with over $300 billion in assets, was put into receivership by the Federal Deposit Insurance Corporation (FDIC) and sold to JPMorgan, making it the largest bank failure in US history.

Bailout package debated

The financial crisis then took an even more virulent turn after the House of Representatives, fearing the wrath of constituents who were angry about bailing out Wall Street, voted down a $700 billion dollar bailout package proposed by the Bush administration on Monday, 29 September 2008. The Emergency Economic Stabilization Act was finally passed on Friday, 3 October. The stock market crash accelerated, with the week beginning on 6 October showing the worst weekly decline in US history. Credit spreads went through the roof over the next three weeks, with the Treasury Bill-to-Eurodollar rate (TED) spread going to over 500 basis points (5.00 percentage points), the highest value in its history (see Figure 9.2). The crisis then spread to Europe with a string of failures of financial institutions.

Recovery in sight?

The increase in uncertainty from the failures of so many financial institutions, the deterioration in financial institutions' balance sheets and the decline in the stock market of over 40% from its peak all increased the severity of adverse selection and moral

GLOBAL
The Treasury Asset Relief Plan and government bailouts

The Economic Recovery Act of 2008 had several provisions to promote recovery from the subprime financial crisis. The most important was the Treasury Asset Relief Plan (TARP), which authorized the Treasury to spend $700 billion purchasing subprime mortgage assets from troubled financial institutions or to inject capital into banking institutions. The hope was that by buying subprime assets, their price would rise above fire-sale levels, thus creating a market for them, while at the same time increasing capital in financial institutions. Along with injections of capital, this would enable these institutions to start lending again. In addition, the act raised the federal deposit insurance limit temporarily from $100,000 to $250,000 in order to limit withdrawals from banks and required the Treasury, as the owner of these assets, to encourage the servicers of the underlying mortgages to restructure them to minimize foreclosures. Shortly thereafter, the FDIC put in place a guarantee for certain debt newly issued by banks, and the Treasury guaranteed for a year money market mutual fund shares at par value.

The spreading bank failures in Europe in autumn 2008 led to bailouts of financial institutions: the Netherlands, Belgium and Luxembourg injected

€11 billion to prop up Fortis, a major European bank; the Netherlands injected €10 billion into ING, a banking and insurance giant; Germany provided a €52 billion rescue package for Hypo Real Estate Holdings; and Iceland took over its three largest banks after its banking system collapsed. Ireland's government guaranteed all the deposits of its commercial banks as well as interbank lending, as did Greece. Spain implemented a bailout package similar to the United States' to buy up to €50 billion of assets in its banks in order to encourage them to lend. The UK Treasury set up a bailout plan with a similar price tag to that of the US Treasury's plan of £400 billion. It guaranteed £250 billion of bank liabilities, added £100 billion to a facility that swaps these assets for government bonds, and allowed the UK government to buy up to £50 billion of equity stakes in British banks. Bailout plans to the tune of over $100 billion in South Korea, $200 billion in Sweden, $400 billion in France and $500 billion in Germany, all of which guaranteed the debt of their banks as well as injecting capital into them, then followed. Both the scale of these bailout packages and the degree of international coordination was unprecedented.

hazard problems in the credit markets. The resulting decline in lending has led to the US unemployment rate rising to 8.2% in March 2012 with worse likely to come. Growth in the US picked up in the end of 2009, fell back at the end of 2010 and showed a robust growth of 3.0% in the final quarter of 2011. By March 2012, individual sectors in the US were showing signs of recovery but not all sectors were showing the same pace of growth. The financial crisis led to a slowing of economic growth worldwide and massive government bailouts of financial institutions (see the Global box, 'The Treasury Asset Relief Plan and government bailouts'). Whether TARP has resulted in a permanent improvement in the US economy is arguable and we can only wait and see.

Dynamics of financial crises in emerging market economies

Hot on the heels of the subprime crisis was the European sovereign debt crisis. As a result of the economic downturn following the global financial crisis sparked by the subprime loans crisis, investors around the world became nervous that some countries in the eurozone will be unable to pay the debts their respective governments have amassed. The result of this nervousness has been volatility in bond and stock markets and a series of European intergovernmental efforts to bail out the affected economies. Financial crises associated with sovereign debt crises are not new. There are many examples of financial crises brought on by governments amassing more debt than they are able to service or repay. For other examples of financial crises, economists have looked at the non-developed economies.

Emerging market economies, economies in an earlier stage of market development that have recently opened up to the flow of goods, services and capital from the rest of the world, are particularly vulnerable. With the opening up of their economies to markets, emerging market countries have been no stranger to devastating financial crises in recent years. The dynamics of financial crises in emerging market economies have many of the same elements as those found in the developed economies, but with some important differences. Figure 9.3 outlines the key stages and common sequence of events in financial crises in developed and emergent economies that we will address in this section.

Stage 1: Initiation of financial crisis

Typically there are two paths to financial crises. One involving the mismanagement of financial liberalization and globalization is typically associated with emerging economies and the other which is common to even developed economies involving severe fiscal

FIGURE 9.3

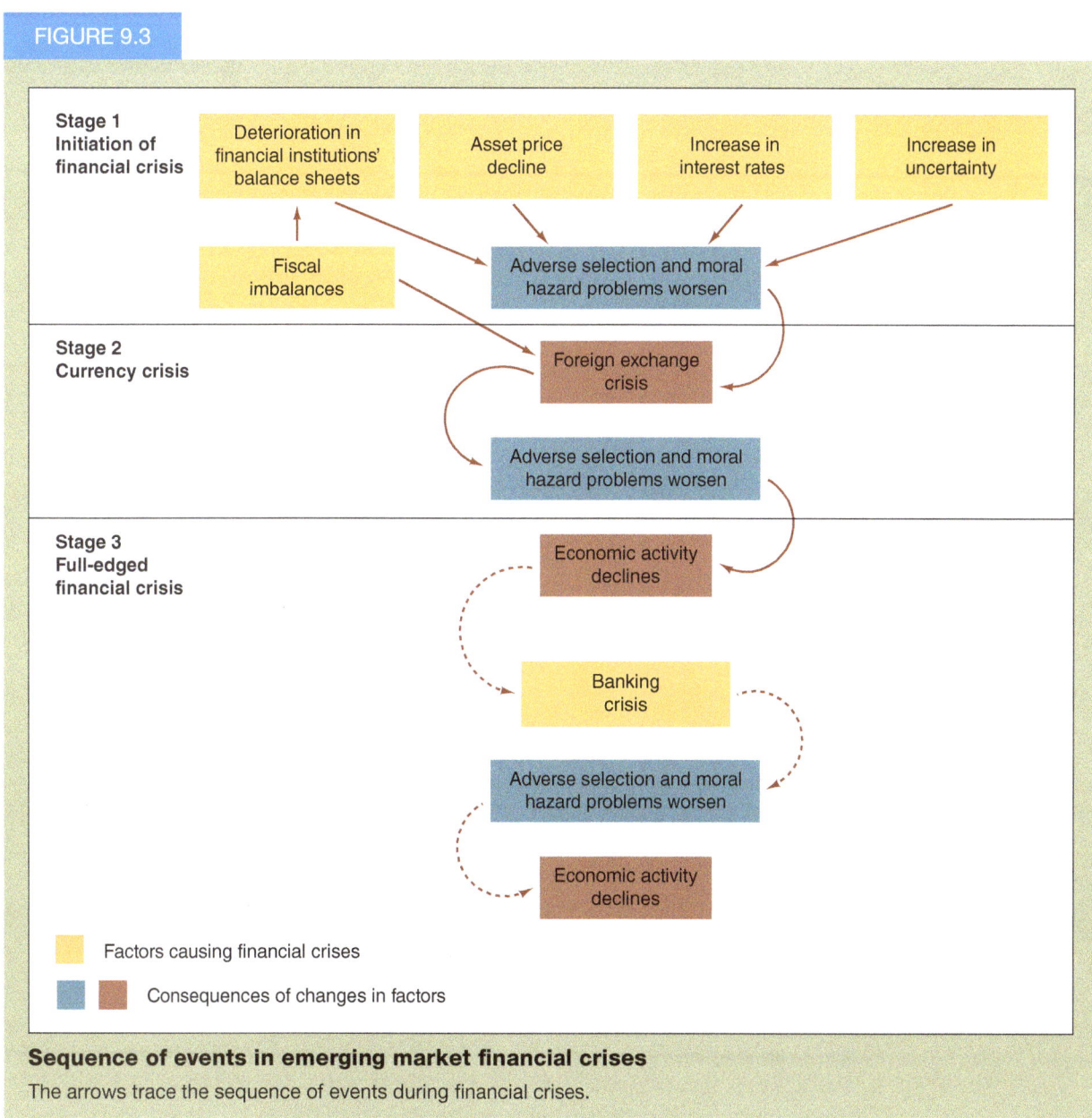

Sequence of events in emerging market financial crises
The arrows trace the sequence of events during financial crises.

imbalances. We will see that a common factor in past financial crises of emerging markets and that of the current financial crisis of the eurozone starts with severe fiscal imbalances.

Path 1: Mismanagement of financial liberalization/globalization

As has occurred in the developed economies, the seeds of a financial crisis in emerging market countries are often sown when countries liberalize their financial systems. Liberalization occurs by eliminating restrictions on financial institutions and markets domestically and opening up their economies to flows of capital and financial firms from other nations, a process called **financial globalization**.

Emerging market countries typically have very weak supervision by bank regulators and a lack of expertise in the screening and monitoring of borrowers by banking institutions. Consequently, the lending boom that is a result after a financial liberalization often leads to even riskier lending than is typical in advanced countries, and enormous loan losses result. The financial globalization process adds fuel to the fire because it allows domestic banks to borrow abroad. The banks pay high interest rates to attract foreign capital and so can rapidly increase their lending. The capital inflow is further stimulated by government policies that keep exchange rates fixed to the dollar, which gives foreign investors a sense of lower risk.

At some point, all of the highly risky lending starts producing high loan losses, which then lead to a deterioration in bank balance sheets and banks cut back on their lending. Just as in advanced countries like the United States, the lending boom ends in a lending crash. In emerging market countries, banks play an even more important role in the financial system than in advanced countries because securities markets and other financial institutions are not as well developed. The decline in bank lending thus means that there are really no other players to solve adverse selection and moral hazard problems (as shown by the arrow pointing from the first factor in the top row of Figure 9.3). The deterioration in their balance sheets therefore has even more negative impacts on lending and economic activity than in advanced countries.

The story told so far suggests that a lending boom and crash are inevitable outcomes of financial liberalization and globalization in emerging market countries, but this is not the case. They only occur when there is an institutional weakness that prevents the nation from successfully handling the liberalization/globalization process. More specifically, if prudential regulation and supervision to limit excessive risk-taking were strong, the lending boom and bust would not happen. Why do regulation and supervision instead end up being weak? The answer is the principal–agent problem discussed in the previous chapter which encourages powerful domestic business interests to pervert the financial liberalization process. Politicians and prudential supervisors are ultimately agents for voter–taxpayers (principals); that is, the goal of politicians and prudential supervisors is, or should be, to protect the taxpayers' interest. Taxpayers almost always bear the cost of bailing out the banking sector if losses occur.

Once financial markets have been liberalized, powerful business interests that own banks will want to prevent the supervisors from doing their job properly. Powerful business interests that contribute heavily to politicians' campaigns are often able to persuade politicians to weaken regulations that restrict their banks from engaging in high-risk/high-payoff strategies. After all, if bank owners achieve growth and expand bank lending rapidly, they stand to make a fortune. But, if the bank gets in trouble, the government is likely to bail it out and the taxpayer foots the bill. In addition, these business interests can also make sure that the supervisory agencies, even in the presence of tough regulations, lack the resources to effectively monitor banking institutions or to close them down.

As we will see in Chapter 11, powerful business interests also have acted to prevent supervisors from doing their job properly in advanced countries. The weaker institutional environment in emerging market countries makes this perversion of the financial liberalization process even worse. In emerging market economies, business interests are far more powerful than they are in advanced economies where a better-educated public and a free press monitor (and punish) politicians and bureaucrats who are not acting in the public interest. Not surprisingly, then, the cost to the society of the principal–agent problem we have been describing here is particularly high in emerging market economies.

Path 2: Severe fiscal imbalances

The second path through which emerging market countries experience a financial crisis is government fiscal imbalances that entail substantial budget deficits that need to be financed. The financial crisis in Argentina in 2001–2 is of this type. Other recent crises are, for example, Russia in 1998, Ecuador in 1999 and Turkey in 2001; which also have some elements of deficit-driven fiscal imbalances.

When Willie Sutton, a famous bank robber, was asked why he robbed banks, he answered, 'Because that's where the money is'. Governments in emerging market countries have the same attitude. When they face large fiscal imbalances and cannot finance their debt, they often cajole or force banks to purchase government debt. Investors who lose confidence in the ability of the government to repay this debt unload the bonds, which causes their prices to plummet. Now the banks that are holding this debt have a big hole on the asset side of their balance sheets, with a huge decline in their net worth. The deterioration in bank balance sheets then causes a decline in bank lending and can even lead to a bank panic. Severe fiscal imbalances spill over into and weaken the banking system (as shown by the arrow from the factor in the second row of Figure 9.3), which leads to a worsening of adverse selection and moral hazard problems.

Additional factors

Other factors also play a role in the first stage in some crises. For example, another precipitating factor in some crises is a rise in interest rates that comes from events abroad, such as a tightening of monetary policy. When interest rates rise, riskier firms are most willing to pay the higher interest rates, so the adverse selection problem is more severe. In addition, the higher interest rates reduce firms' cash flows, forcing them to seek funds in external capital markets in which asymmetric problems are greater. Increases in interest rates abroad that raise domestic interest rates can then increase adverse selection and moral hazard problems (as shown by the arrow from the second factor in the top row of Figure 9.3).

Because asset markets are not as large in emerging market countries as they are in advanced countries, they play a less prominent role in financial crises. Asset-price declines in the stock market do, nevertheless, decrease the net worth of firms and so increase adverse selection problems. There is less collateral for lenders to grab on to, which increases moral hazard problems because with lower net worth the owners of the firm have less to lose if they engage in riskier activities. Asset-price declines can therefore have some role in worsening adverse selection and moral hazard problems directly (as shown by the arrow pointing from the third factor in the first row of Figure 9.3) as well as indirectly by causing a deterioration in banks' balance sheets from asset write-downs.

As in developed economies, when an emerging market economy is in a recession or a prominent firm fails, people become more uncertain about the returns on investment projects. But in emerging market countries, another source of uncertainty can come from their political systems, which are often notoriously unstable. When uncertainty increases, it becomes harder for lenders to screen out good credit risks from bad and to monitor the activities of firms to whom they have loaned money, so that adverse selection and moral hazard problems worsen (as shown by the arrow pointing from the last factor in the first row of Figure 9.3).

Stage 2: Currency crisis

As the effects of any or all of the factors in Stage 1 in Figure 9.3 build on each other, participants in the foreign exchange market sense an opportunity: they can make huge profits if they bet on a depreciation of the currency. As the currency sales flood the market, supply far outstrips demand, the value of the currency collapses, and a currency crisis ensues (see the Stage 2 section of Figure 9.3). High interest rates abroad, increases in uncertainty and falling asset prices all play a role. The deterioration in bank balance sheets and severe fiscal imbalances, however, are the two key factors that trigger the **speculative attacks** and plunge the economies into a full-scale, vicious downward spiral of currency crisis, financial crisis and meltdown.

How deterioration of bank balance sheets triggers currency crises

When banks and other financial institutions are in trouble, governments have a limited number of options. Defending their currencies by raising interest rates should encourage capital inflows. If the government raises interest rates, banks must pay more to obtain funds. This increase in costs decreases bank profitability, which may lead them to insolvency. Thus when the banking system is in trouble, the government and central bank are now between a rock and a hard place: if they raise interest rates too much they will destroy their already weakened banks, and if they don't, they can't maintain the value of their currency.

Speculators in the market for foreign currency are able to recognize the troubles in a country's financial sector and realize when the government's ability to defend the currency is limited. They will seize an almost sure-thing bet because the currency has only one way to go, downward in value. Speculators engage in a feeding frenzy and sell the currency in anticipation of its decline, which will provide them with huge profits. These sales rapidly use up the country's holdings of reserves of foreign currency because the country has to sell its reserves to buy the domestic currency and keep it from falling in value. Once the country's central bank has exhausted its holdings of foreign currency reserves, the cycle ends. It no longer has the resources to intervene in the foreign exchange market and must let the value of the domestic currency fall; that is, the government must allow a devaluation.

While the above scenario is typical for a currency crisis in the emerging economies it could be argued that this is exactly what happened during the collapse of the **Exchange Rate Mechanism (ERM)** of the **European Monetary System (EMS)** in 1992–3. On 16 September 1992, the UK suspended its membership of the ERM which was a fixed-exchange-rate system pegged against the German Deutschmark. The UK joined the ERM in October 1990 at an exchange rate of 2.95 Deutschmarks to the pound. Germany had begun a policy of raising interest rates to offset the inflationary costs of reunification. Raising interest rates caused considerable stress within the ERM but particularly for the UK and also Italy as both countries also had rising fiscal deficits. After spending billions of pounds defending the currency against speculative attack, raising interest rates from 10% to 12% and then to 15% in one day, the pound devalued against the Deutschmark.

How severe fiscal imbalances trigger currency crises

We have seen that severe fiscal imbalances can lead to a deterioration of bank balance sheets, and so can help produce a currency crisis along the lines just described. Fiscal imbalances can also directly trigger a currency crisis. When government budget deficits spin out of control, foreign and domestic investors begin to suspect that the country may not be able to pay back its government debt and so will start pulling money out of the country and selling the domestic currency. Recognition that the fiscal situation is out of control thus results in a speculative attack against the currency, which eventually results in its collapse.

Stage 3: Full-fledged financial crisis

In the case of emerging economies, debt contracts are often denominated in foreign currency, and there is an unanticipated depreciation or devaluation of the domestic currency, the debt burden of domestic firms increases in terms of domestic currency. That is, it takes more domestic currency to pay back the debt denominated in foreign currency. Since the goods and services produced by most firms are priced in the domestic currency, the firms' assets do not rise in value in terms of the domestic currency, while the debt does. The depreciation of the domestic currency increases the value of debt relative to assets, and the firm's net worth declines. The decline in net worth then increases adverse selection and moral hazard problems described earlier. A decline in investment and economic activity then follows (as shown by the Stage 3 section of Figure 9.3).

We now see how the institutional structure of debt markets in emerging market countries interacts with the currency devaluations to propel the economies into full-fledged financial crises. Economists often call a concurrent currency and financial crisis the 'twin crises'. Many firms in these emerging market countries have debt denominated in foreign currencies like the dollar and the yen. Depreciation of their currencies thus results in increases in their indebtedness in domestic currency terms, even though the value of their assets remains unchanged.

The collapse of a currency also can lead to higher inflation. The central banks in most emerging market countries have little credibility as inflation fighters. Thus a sharp depreciation of the currency after a currency crisis leads to immediate upward pressure on import prices. A dramatic rise in both actual and expected inflation will likely follow. The resulting increase in interest payments causes reductions in firms' cash flow, which lead to increased asymmetric information problems since firms are now more dependent on external funds to finance their investment. As the asymmetric information analysis suggests, the resulting increase in adverse selection and moral hazard problems leads to a reduction in investment and economic activity.

As shown in Figure 9.3, further deterioration in the economy occurs. The collapse in economic activity and the deterioration of cash flow and balance sheets of firms and households means that many of them are no longer able to pay off their debts, resulting in substantial losses for banks. Sharp rises in interest rates also have a negative effect on banks' profitability and balance sheets. Even more problematic for the banks is the sharp increase in the value of their foreign-currency-denominated liabilities after the devaluation. Thus bank balance sheets are squeezed from both sides – the value of their assets falls as the value of their liabilities rises.

Under these circumstances, the banking system will often suffer a banking crisis in which many banks are likely to fail (as happened in the 1930s in the USA). The banking crisis and the contributing factors in the credit markets explain a further worsening of adverse selection and moral hazard problems and a further collapse of lending and economic activity in the aftermath of the crisis.

APPLICATION   ## Financial crisis in East Asia, 1997–8

When emerging market countries opened up their markets to the outside world in the 1990s, they had high hopes that globalization would stimulate economic growth and eventually make them rich. Instead of leading to high economic growth and reduced poverty, however, many of them experienced financial crises that were every bit as devastating as the Great Depression of the 1930s.

The most dramatic of these crises was the East Asian crisis, which started in July 1997. We now apply the asymmetric information analysis of the dynamics of financial crises to explain why a developing country can shift dramatically from a path of high growth before a financial crisis – as was true in the East Asian countries of Thailand, Malaysia, Indonesia, the Philippines and South Korea – to a sharp decline in economic activity.

Before the crisis, the East Asian countries had achieved a sound fiscal policy. The East Asian countries ran budget surpluses. The key precipitating factor driving these crises was the deterioration in banks' balance sheets because of increasing loan losses. When financial markets in these countries were liberalized and opened to foreign capital markets in the early 1990s, a lending boom ensued. Bank credit to the private non-financial business sector accelerated sharply, with lending expanding at 15% to 30% per year. Because of weak supervision by bank regulators, aided and abetted by powerful business interests (see the Global box 'The perversion of the financial liberalization/globalization process: chaebols and the South Korean crisis') and a lack of expertise in screening and monitoring borrowers at banking institutions, losses on loans began to mount, causing an erosion of banks' net worth (capital). As a result of this erosion, banks had fewer resources to lend. This lack of lending led to a contraction of economic activity along the lines outlined in the previous section.

Consistent with the experience of developed economies, stock market declines and increases in uncertainty initiated and contributed to full-blown financial crises in Thailand and South Korea. (The stock market declines in Malaysia, Indonesia and the Philippines, on the other hand, occurred simultaneously with the onset of these crises.) Right before their crises, Thailand and South Korea experienced major failures of financial and non-financial firms that increased general uncertainty in financial markets. ■

GLOBAL
The perversion of the financial liberalization/globalization process: chaebols and the South Korean crisis

Although there are similarities with the perversion of the financial liberalization and globalization process that occurred in many emerging market economies, South Korea exhibited some particularly extraordinary elements because of the unique role of the chaebols, large family-owned conglomerates. Because of their massive size – sales of the top five chaebols were nearly 50% of GDP right before the crisis – the chaebols were politically very powerful. The chaebols' influence extended the government safety net far beyond the financial system because the government had a long-standing policy of viewing the chaebols as being 'too big to fail'. With this policy in place, the chaebols would receive direct government assistance or directed credit if they got into trouble. Not surprisingly, given this guarantee, chaebols borrowed like crazy and were highly leveraged.

In the 1990s, the chaebols were in trouble: they weren't making any money. From 1993 to 1996, the return on assets for the top thirty chaebols was never much more than 3% (a comparable figure for US corporations is 15–20%). In 1996, right before the crisis hit, the rate of return on assets had fallen to 0.2%. Furthermore, only the top five chaebols had any profits: the sixth to thirtieth chaebols never had a rate of return on assets much above 1% and in many years had negative rates of returns. With this poor profitability and the already high leverage, any banker would pull back on lending to these conglomerates if there were no government safety net. Because the banks knew the government would make good on the chaebols' loans if they were in default, the opposite occurred: banks continued to lend to the chaebols and, in effect, threw good money after bad.

Even though the chaebols were getting substantial financing from commercial banks, it was not enough to feed their insatiable appetite for more credit. The chaebols decided that the way out of their troubles was to pursue growth, and they needed massive amounts of funds to do it. Even with the vaunted Korean national savings rate of over 30%, there just were not enough loanable funds to finance the chaebols' planned expansion. Where could they get it? The answer was in the international capital markets.

The chaebols encouraged the Korean government to accelerate the process of opening up Korean financial markets to foreign capital as part of the liberalization process. In 1993, the government expanded the ability of domestic banks to make loans denominated in foreign currency by expanding the types of loans for which this was possible. At the same time, the Korean government effectively allowed unlimited short-term foreign borrowing by financial institutions, but maintained quantity restrictions on long-term borrowing as a means of managing capital flows into the country. Opening up short-term but not long-term to foreign capital flows made no economic sense. It is short-term capital flows that make an emerging market economy financially fragile: *short-term* capital can fly out of the country extremely rapidly if there is any whiff of a crisis.

Opening up primarily to short-term capital, however, made complete political sense: the chaebols needed the money and it is much easier to borrow short-term funds at lower interest rates in the international market because long-term lending is much riskier for foreign creditors. Keeping restrictions on long-term international borrowing, however, allowed the government to say that it was still restricting foreign capital inflows and to claim that it was opening up to foreign capital in a prudent manner. In the aftermath of these changes, Korean banks opened 28 branches in foreign countries that gave them access to foreign funds.

The perversion of the financial liberalization and globalization process (*continued*)

Although Korean financial institutions now had access to foreign capital, the chaebols still had a problem. They were not allowed to own commercial banks and so the chaebols might not get all of the bank loans that they needed. What was the answer? The chaebols needed to get their hands on financial institutions that they could own, that were allowed to borrow abroad and that were subject to very little regulation. The financial institution could then engage in connected lending by borrowing foreign funds and then lending them to the chaebols which owned the institution.

An existing type of financial institution specific to South Korea perfectly met the chaebols' requirements: the merchant bank. Merchant banking corporations were wholesale financial institutions that engaged in underwriting securities, leasing and short-term lending to the corporate sector. They obtained funds for these loans by issuing bonds and commercial paper and by borrowing from interbank and foreign markets.

At the time of the Korean crisis, merchant banks were allowed to borrow abroad and were virtually unregulated. The chaebols saw their opportunity. Government officials, often lured with bribery and kickbacks, allowed many finance companies (some already owned by the chaebols) that were not allowed to borrow abroad to be converted into merchant banks, which could. In 1990 there were only six merchant banks and all of them were foreign-affiliated. By 1997, after the chaebols had exercised their political influence, there were thirty merchant banks, sixteen of which were owned by chaebols, two of which were foreign-owned but in which chaebols were major stockholders, and twelve of which were independent of the chaebols, but Korean-owned. The chaebols were now able to exploit connected lending with a vengeance: the merchant banks channelled massive amounts of funds to their chaebol owners, where they flowed into unproductive investments in steel, automobile production and chemicals. When the loans went sour, the stage was set for a disastrous financial crisis.

As we have seen, an increase in uncertainty and a decrease in net worth as a result of a stock market decline increase asymmetric information problems. It becomes harder to screen out good from bad borrowers. The decline in net worth decreases the value of firms' collateral and increases their incentives to make risky investments because there is less equity to lose if the investments are unsuccessful. The increase in uncertainty and stock market declines that occurred before the crises, along with the deterioration in banks' balance sheets, worsened adverse selection and moral hazard problems and made the economies ripe for a serious financial emergency.

In the case of Thailand, concerns about the large current account deficit and weakness in the Thai financial system, culminating with the failure of a major finance company, Finance One, led to a successful speculative attack. The Thai central bank was forced to allow the baht to depreciate in July 1997. Soon thereafter, speculative attacks developed against the other countries in the region, leading to the collapse of the Philippine peso, the Indonesian rupiah, the Malaysian ringgit and the South Korean won.

The institutional structure of debt markets in East Asia now interacted with the currency devaluations to propel the economies into full-fledged financial crises. Because so many firms in these countries had debt denominated in foreign currencies like the dollar and the yen, depreciation of their currencies resulted in increases in their indebtedness in domestic currency terms, even though the value of their assets remained unchanged. When the Thai, Philippine, Malaysian and South Korean currencies lost between one-third and one-half of their value by the beginning of 1998, firms' balance sheets took a big negative hit, causing a dramatic increase in adverse selection and moral hazard problems. This negative shock was especially severe for Indonesia which saw the value of its currency fall by more than 70%, resulting in insolvency for firms with substantial amounts of debt denominated in foreign currencies.

The collapse of currencies also led to a rise in actual and expected inflation in these countries. Market interest rates rose sky-high. The resulting increase in interest payments caused reductions in household and firm cash flows. A feature of debt markets in emerging market countries, like those in East Asia, is that debt contracts have very short durations, typically less than one month. Thus the rise in short-term interest rates in these countries made the effect on cash flow and hence on balance sheets substantial. As our asymmetric information analysis suggests, this deterioration in households' and firms' balance sheets increased adverse selection and moral hazard problems in the credit markets, making domestic and foreign lenders even less willing to lend.

The banking crisis, along with other factors that increased adverse selection and moral hazard problems in the credit markets of Mexico, East Asia and Argentina, explains the collapse of lending and hence economic activity in the aftermath of the crisis.

Dynamics of the eurozone financial crisis

The dynamics of the eurozone financial crisis can be described in the same way as past financial crises in developed economies and emerging economies.

Cheap credit, fiscal imbalances and mismanagement of financial innovation

The seeds of the eurozone financial crisis were sown when countries with a history of fiscal indiscipline joined the single currency. Joining the euro for some countries, in particular the **GIIPS** (Greece, Ireland, Italy, Portugal and Spain), meant access to lower interest rates and cheaper financing of government borrowing and bank credit. Figure 9.4 shows the interest rate on 10-year government bonds for countries in the eurozone before the creation of the single currency, and the evolution of interest rates after joining the single currency.

FIGURE 9.4

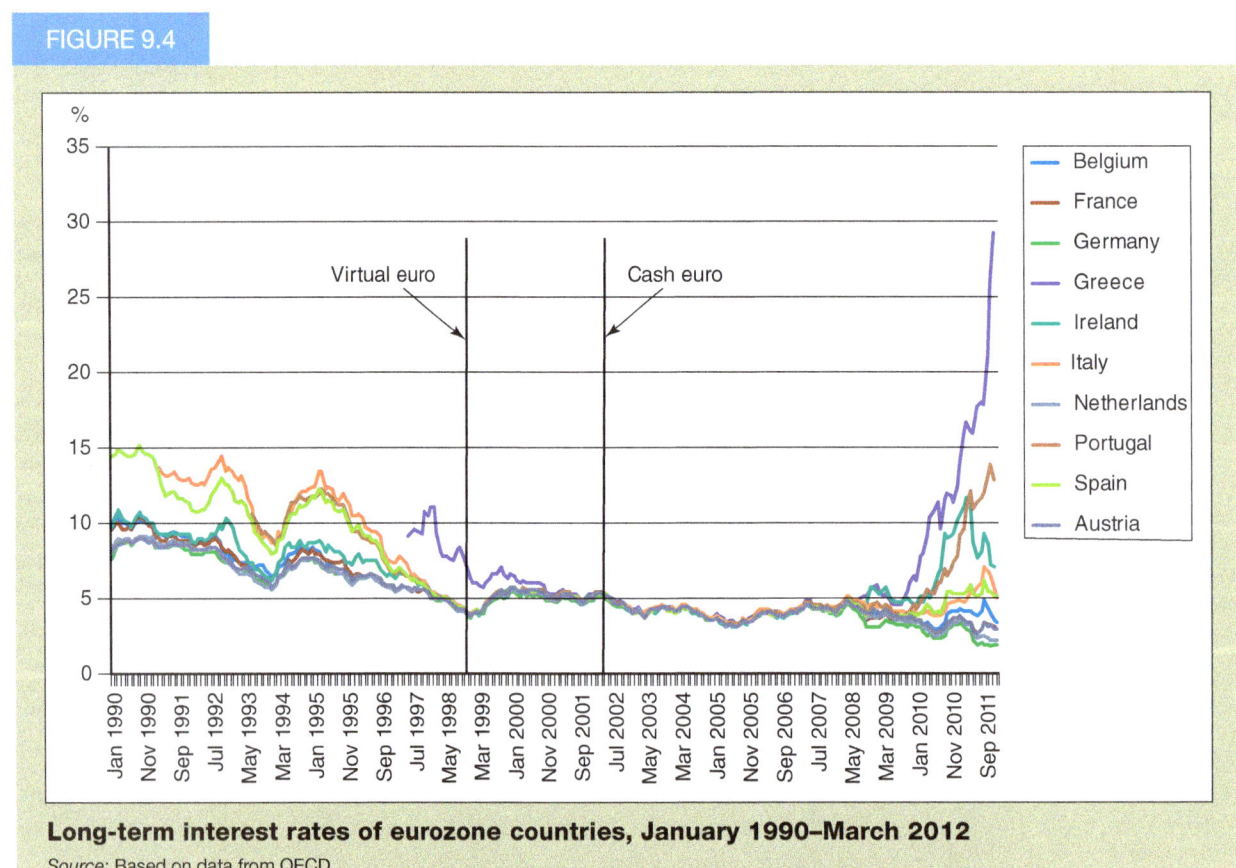

Long-term interest rates of eurozone countries, January 1990–March 2012
Source: Based on data from OECD.

You can see that for some countries, notably Greece, Portugal and Italy, joining the euro led to interest rates falling close to the levels of Germany. Governments in these countries found that their debt service burden had declined rapidly and they were able to borrow cheaply. Households borrowed from banks recognizing that low interest rates meant that the costs of servicing the debt were low relative to disposable income. Mortgage lending soared and house prices began to rise rapidly in the countries of the southern part of Europe and in Ireland. Companies borrowed to engage in merger and acquisition activity and investment and banks borrowed in the wholesale markets to finance domestic borrowing as well as market new financial products. As in the dynamics of past financial crises of Figure 9.1 the financial institutions went on a lending spree that culminated in a credit boom. Similar to the scenario drawn in Figure 9.1, risk management took a back seat in dealing with new financial products.

Regulators failed to spot the telltale signs of a credit boom that weakened bank balance sheets. In part this was because inflation remained under control and therefore the bank credit growth, the expansion in household spending and the rapid rise in house prices were viewed as benign.

As with the dynamics of financial crises of the developed economies the risk taking of the banks comes home to roost. The trigger for the banks in the eurozone countries came with the subprime loans crisis and the collapse of Lehman Brothers in the US. House prices began to decline and losses on loans begin to mount. The decline in the value of the loans relative to banks' liabilities drives down the net worth (capital) of banks and other financial institutions. As with the dynamics of financial crises for developed economies, with less capital, financial institutions cut back on their lending not just to the private sector but also to each other. Figure 9.5 shows the spread between the Euribor and the OIS rates (the difference between the three-month euro interbank offered rate and overnight index swaps rate). This spread is an indicator of banks' reluctance to lend to each other in Europe. It conveys the same signal as the TED spread in Figure 9.2.

The stages of the financial crisis in the eurozone can be followed in Figure 9.6. Stage 1 is the same as that of Figure 9.1 except that fiscal imbalances were already uncomfortably high for some countries in the eurozone although financial markets expected these to dicline in the future. Stage 2 develops into the banking crisis but governments initiate bailouts which burden the already heavily indebted economies like the GIIPS. Stage 3 sees the banks' balance sheets being underwritten by their respective governments. At stage 3

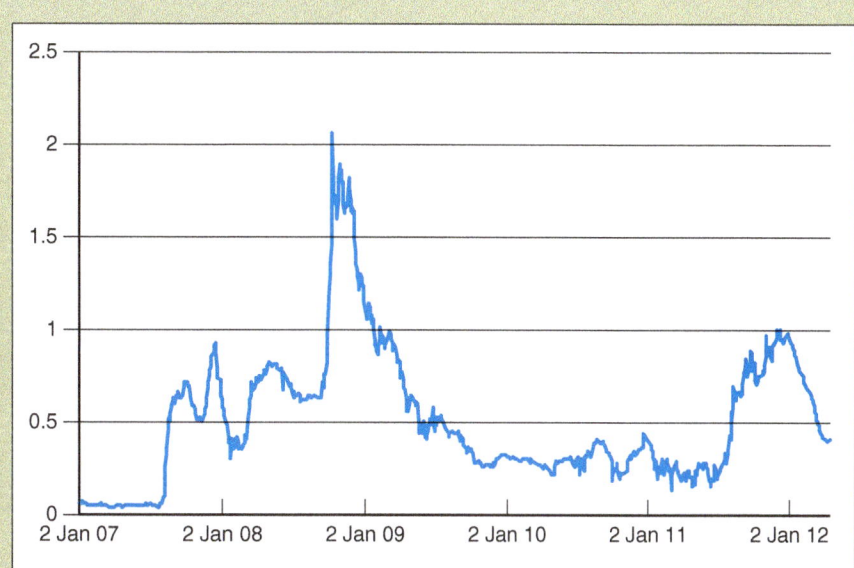

FIGURE 9.5

Spread between 3-month Euribor and OIS rates, January 2007–March 2012
Source: Based on Bloomberg.

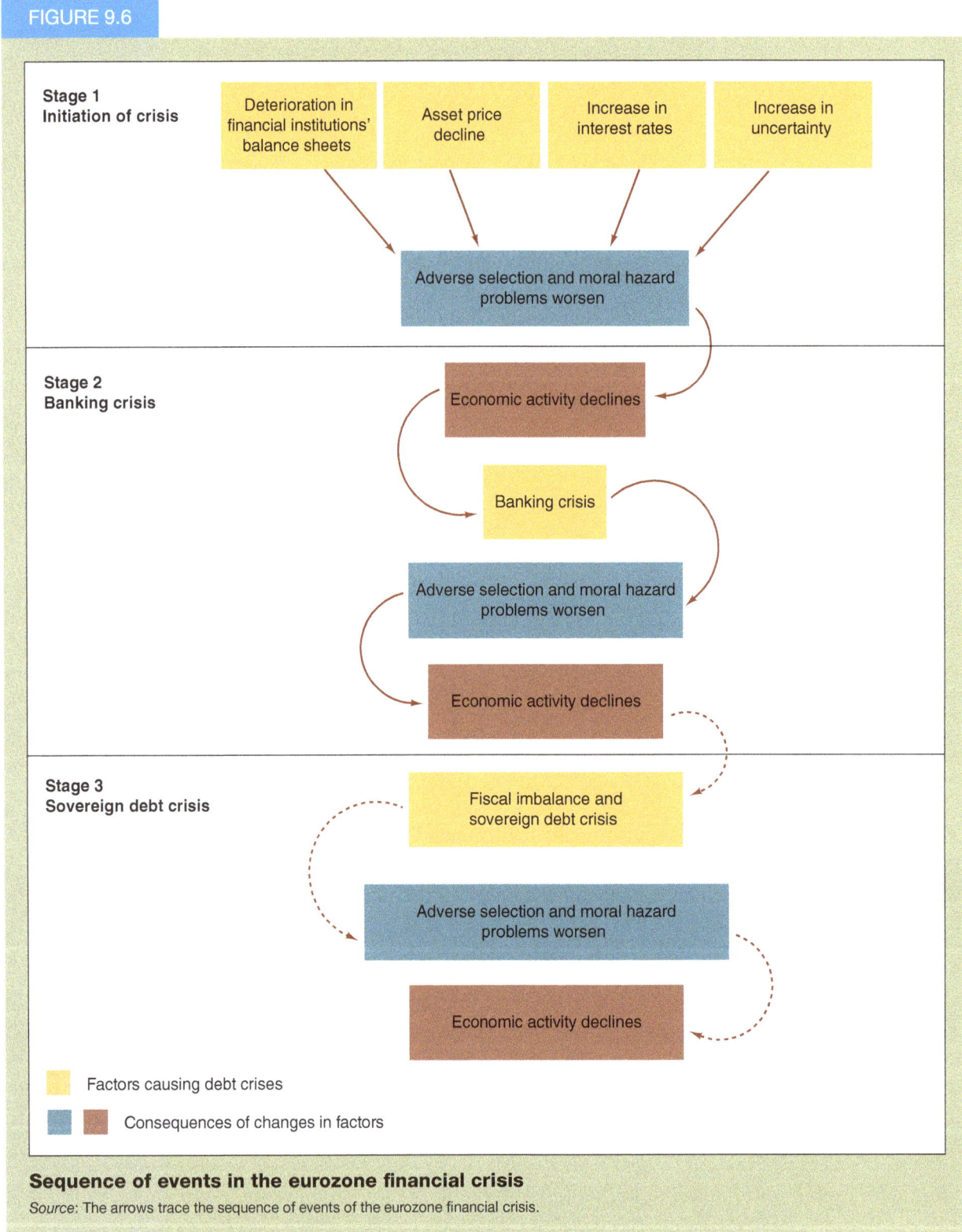

FIGURE 9.6

Stage 1
Initiation of crisis

Deterioration in financial institutions' balance sheets

Asset price decline

Increase in interest rates

Increase in uncertainty

Adverse selection and moral hazard problems worsen

Stage 2
Banking crisis

Economic activity declines

Banking crisis

Adverse selection and moral hazard problems worsen

Economic activity declines

Stage 3
Sovereign debt crisis

Fiscal imbalance and sovereign debt crisis

Adverse selection and moral hazard problems worsen

Economic activity declines

Factors causing debt crises

Consequences of changes in factors

Sequence of events in the eurozone financial crisis

Source: The arrows trace the sequence of events of the eurozone financial crisis.

financial markets are made aware that some countries' budget deficits and the debt they have absorbed from the banks have increased the risk of sovereign debt default. Interest rates on government bonds begin to reflect the risk of default and we have a full-blown sovereign debt crisis. If these countries had their own currencies, stage 2 would be a

FIGURE 9.7

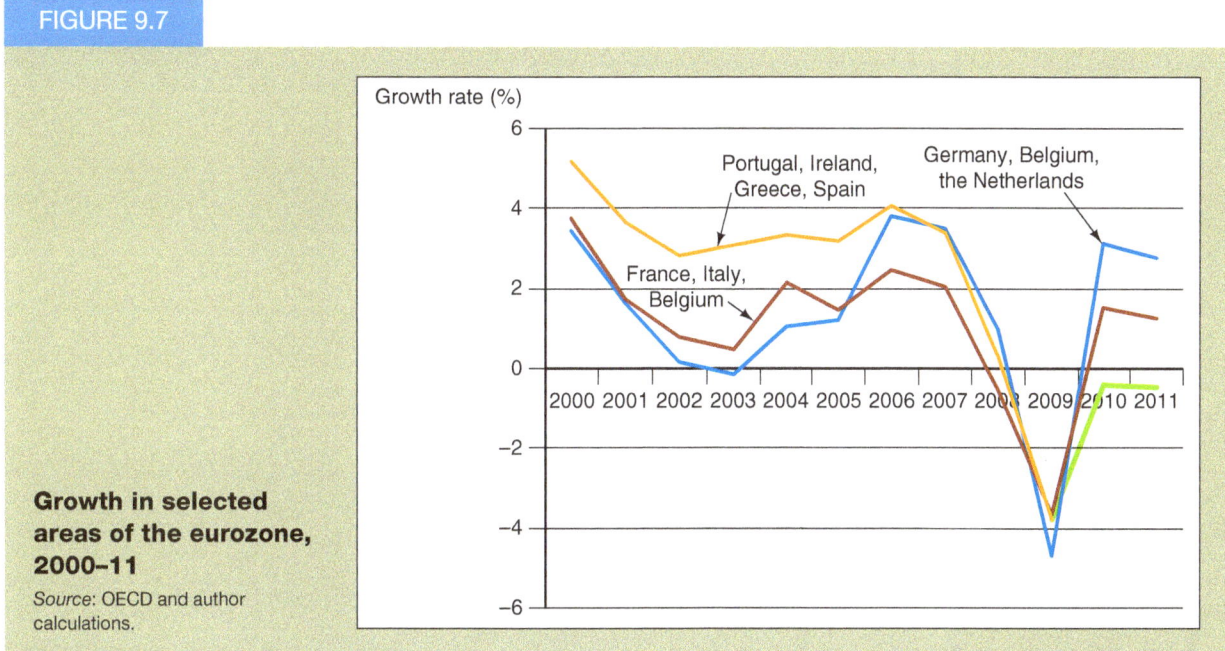

Growth in selected areas of the eurozone, 2000–11

Source: OECD and author calculations.

currency crisis similar to the ERM crisis of 1991–2. However, being in a single currency the option of devaluation is ruled out. The only available option is to restore fiscal discipline through a policy of austerity, which involves cuts in government expenditure and raising tax revenue.

Too rapid a cut in government spending can worsen the downturn in the economy. Figure 9.7 shows the rate of growth of GDP in selected economies of the eurozone. You can see that countries like Germany, Austria and the Netherlands have bounced back strongly from the recession of 2008–9, while Greece, Portugal and Ireland have remained in negative growth for longer.

Part of the reason for the continued recession in some countries in the eurozone is the high interest rates they have to pay for borrowing and the speed of government cuts in expenditure. But a more fundamental problem is the loss of competitiveness in those economies. Figure 9.8 shows the evolution of the price level for selected regions of the eurozone. You can see from this chart that the price level of Greece, Ireland, Portugal and Spain combined has risen by over 40% in the decade from 1999 whereas the combined price level for Germany, the Netherlands and Austria has risen by about 24%. The consequence for the low-growth countries in the eurozone is the loss of competitiveness against Germany and other countries and a balance of trade deficit with those same countries.

These issues are fundamental ones for countries like Greece, Portugal and Ireland. Some economists argue that the crisis cannot be resolved until financial austerity in countries like Greece and Portugal leads to a reduction in overall government debt and a decline in the fiscal deficit. Others argue that countries like Greece and Portugal need to devalue, and to do that they need to exit from the euro. Yet other economists argue that the fundamental problems of competitiveness cannot be solved by devaluation alone, and exit from the eurozone will have repercussions on the remaining member countries, therefore countries like Greece should remain in the euro and the governments of the member countries should engage in greater fiscal coordination and transfers to counterbalance the single monetary policy.

The sovereign debt crisis in Europe is as much a political crisis as an economic one. Bailout packages and lending by the ECB to member countries' commercial banks are but temporary measures. At the time of writing, there is no resolution to the crisis on the horizon. The application below gives a timeline analysis of the euro sovereign debt crisis.

FIGURE 9.8

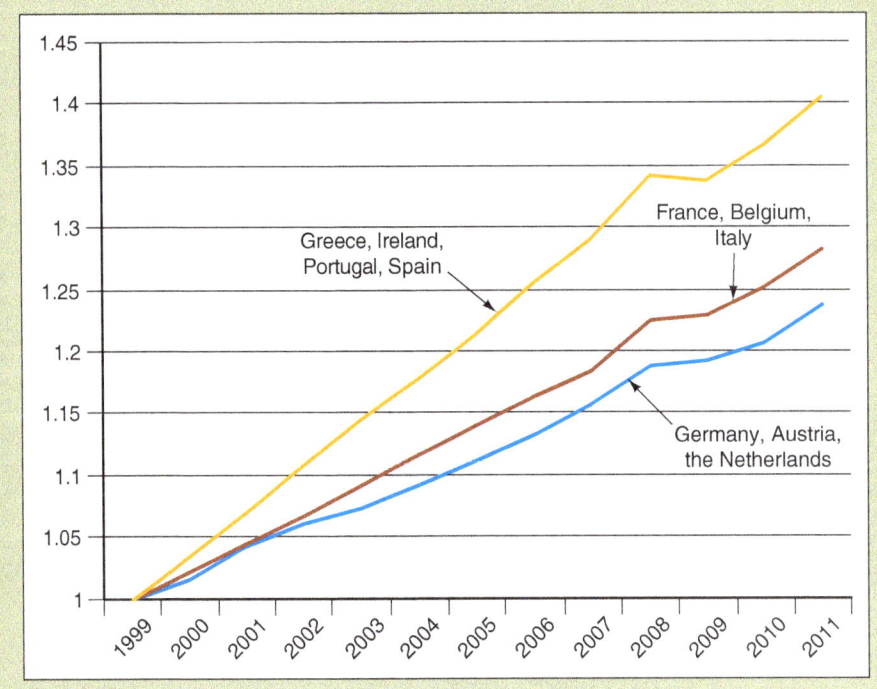

Price developments in selected areas of the eurozone, 1999–2011 (Index: 1999-1)

Source: OECD and author calculations.

APPLICATION ## Euro sovereign debt crisis

The global financial crisis that was sparked by the subprime loans crisis revealed some of the weaknesses in the banks of the EU economies and ultimately in the economies themselves. The banking crisis that soon followed led to EU governments providing bailout funds for their respective banks. In 2009 the collective cost was approximately €1,107 billion with €827 billion on underwriting bank liabilities, €141 billion in capital injections, €110 billion in relief for impaired bank assets and €29 billion for providing liquidity to the banks. For a number of countries that already had high fiscal deficits taking on the burden of bank liabilities pushed the overall debts of the government and the deficits to unsustainable levels. In Figure 9.6, the link between the banking crisis in stage 2 and the sovereign debt crisis in stage 3 needs to be clarified as not all countries had serious fiscal imbalances at the onset of the financial crisis. Ireland is a case in point where the Irish government guaranteed the deposits of the Irish banks that had lent to finance a property bubble that collapsed. The assets of the Irish banks deteriorated sharply and they were unable to raise funds. The government guarantees that were put in place in 2008 were renewed in September 2010. In November 2010 a joint EU/IMF bailout package of €85 billion for Ireland was agreed.

In countries like Greece (and latterly Portugal, Spain and Italy) that already had high fiscal deficits and hidden public-sector debts, the global financial crisis focused attention on their ability to repay debts, raising the risk of sovereign debt default. The consequence was a sharp rise in the rate of interest at which the government could borrow. Figure 9.9 shows the spread between the rate of interest on 10-year government bonds of Greece, Portugal, Ireland, Spain and Italy against Germany (which is considered to be default-free). The spread is an indicator of default risk.

If Greece (and Portugal, Ireland, Spain and Italy) had its own currency, we would be witnessing stage 2 of Figure 9.6 – a full-blown currency crisis. However, as these countries are in the eurozone they are unable to go through devaluation. The high interest rates that governments such as Greece have to pay for borrowing also has an effect on the borrowing

FIGURE 9.9

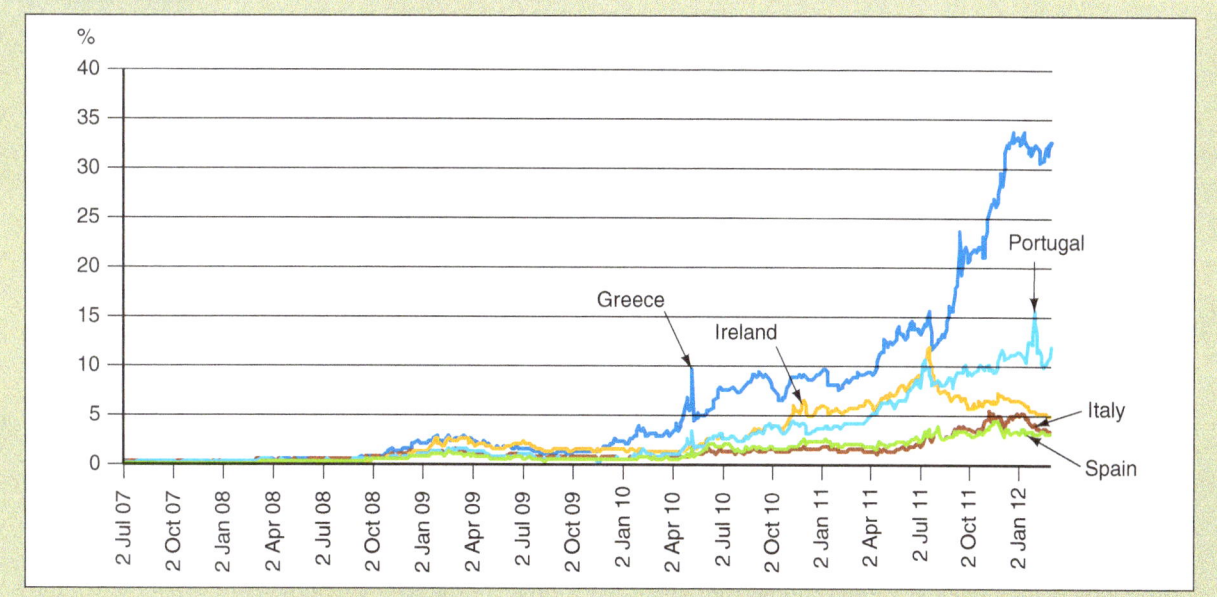

Spread of 10-year government bond yields and equivalent German government bond yields, July 2007–March 2012

Source: http://sdw.ecb.europa.eu/browseSelection.do?DATASET=0&sfl2=4&REF_AREA=308&sfl3=4&INSTRUMENT_FM=BG&sfl4=3&node=201 8817&SERIES_KEY=145.IFI.M.U2.BG.2D.G000.CI.Z5.EUR. Information may be obtained free of charge through the ECB's website.

costs of the corporate sector which has an effect on economic activity and the spectre of recession raises its head once again. Stock markets react to the uncertainty caused by the economy going into recession.

Following a first rescue package of €110 billion in May 2010, the leaders of the eurozone economies agreed to a further bailout package in July 2011 of €100 billion to be provided by the newly created *European Financial Stability Facility* (EFSF). In October 2011 the leaders of the eurozone economies agreed to increase the funds to the EFSF to €440 billion, €200 billion for bailouts to Greece, Portugal and Ireland and hold €240 billion as a contingency reserve. In a marathon meeting in February 2012 the euro countries agreed on a second bailout fund of €130 billion for Greece. It was also agreed that banks should increase their capital adequacy to 9% as well as accepting that the 'haircut' on Greek bonds will be nearly 50%.

The problem for the eurozone banks is that they collectively held the debt of the high deficit countries. The high rates of interest increase the borrowing costs for corporations which have an adverse effect on the economy. Fears that Greece would be unable to grow its way out of debt raised the possibility of a sovereign default. The prospect of a default by Greece has two effects on the eurozone economy. The fear of default can spread to other high deficit countries as indeed Figure 9.9 shows. A possible default leads to further deterioration of the balance sheets of the banks that hold Greek and other high deficit country debt and a second bank crisis may result. Banks face higher funding costs at a time when balance sheets are shrinking, and this in turn can lead to a credit crunch and a further downturn in the EU economy. Stock markets react nervously as sellers overwhelm buyers and share prices plummet. Household and firms' wealth is destroyed with consequences for aggregate demand.

What's in store for the eurozone? Holders of Greek and other country debt might have to take even a larger 'haircut' (a term that means a lower value for the debt than its face value). The EU bailout fund can be increased by the core countries such as Germany and France. The ECB can buy government bonds issued by the member states that belong in the eurozone, creating a eurozone type of quantitative easing (see Chapter 15 for quantitative easing).

While all the respective governments of the eurozone economies accept that some or all of these policies may be necessary, none of these options is politically acceptable to all of the countries – particularly German taxpayers who feel that they are paying for the largesse of governments on the periphery of the EU. German as well as Greek taxpayers will have to pay for fiscal deficits and bank bailouts or there has to be an orderly exit from the euro for some countries. A third and fearsome option is the creation of inflation to reduce the real value of debt created by fiscal profligacy. ■

Summary

1 A financial crisis occurs when a disruption in the financial system causes an increase in asymmetric information that makes adverse selection and moral hazard problems far more severe, thereby rendering financial markets incapable of channelling funds to households and firms with productive investment opportunities, and causing a sharp contraction in economic activity. Six categories of factors play an important role in financial crises: asset market effects on balance sheets, deterioration in financial institutions' balance sheets, banking crisis, increases in uncertainty, increases in interest rates, and government fiscal imbalances.

2 There are several possible ways that financial crises can start in advanced countries: mismanagement of financial liberalization or innovation, asset price booms and busts, spikes in interest rates, or a general increase in uncertainty when there are failures of major financial institutions. The result is a substantial increase in adverse selection and moral hazard problems that lead to a contraction of lending and a decline in economic activity. The worsening business conditions and deterioration in bank balance sheets then triggers the second stage of the crisis, the simultaneous failure of many banking institutions, that is, a banking crisis. The resulting decline in the number of banks causes a loss of their information capital, leading to a further decline of lending and a spiralling down of the economy. In some instances, the resulting economic downturn leads to a sharp decline of prices, which increases the real liabilities of firms and therefore lowers their net worth, leading to a debt deflation. The decline in firms' net worth worsens adverse selection and moral hazard problems, so that lending, investment spending and aggregate economic activity remain depressed for a long time. The most significant financial crisis in US history, which led to the Great Depression, displayed the debt deflation phenomenon.

3 The global financial crisis starting in 2007 was triggered by mismanagement of financial innovations involving subprime residential mortgages and the bursting of a housing price bubble.

4 Financial crises in emerging market countries develop along two basic paths: one involving the mismanagement of financial liberalization and globalization that weakens bank balance sheets and the other involving severe fiscal imbalances. Both lead to a speculative attack on the domestic currency, and eventually to a currency crisis in which there is a sharp decline in the currency's value. The decline in the value of the domestic currency causes a sharp rise in the debt burden of domestic firms, which leads to a decline in firms' net worth, as well as increases in inflation and interest rates. Adverse selection and moral hazard problems then worsen, leading to a collapse of lending and economic activity. The worsening economic conditions and increases in interest rates result in substantial losses for banks, leading to a banking crisis, which further depresses lending and aggregate economic activity.

5 The financial crises in East Asia in 1997–8, led to great economic hardship and weakened the social fabric of these countries.

6 The sovereign debt crisis in Europe has the potential to create serious hardship in Europe. The geopolitical effects of a disorderly exit from the euro by some countries could have serious social and political repercussions in the rest of Europe. Financial institutions in Europe are strongly interconnected. German, Dutch and French financial institutions are the holders of Greek and Spanish debt through intricate swap arrangements that could endanger the stability of their banks if a disorderly exit occurred. The sovereign debt crisis in Europe has the potential to plunge Europe into a serious debt deflationary spiral that would destabilise the rest of the world.

Key terms

alt-A mortgages p. 184

asset-price bubble p. 181

bank panic p. 178

collateralized debt obligations (CDOs) p. 184

credit boom p. 181

debt deflation p. 183

deleveraging p. 181

emerging market economies p. 189

European Monetary System (EMS) p. 192

eurozone p. 179

Exchange Rate Mechanism p. 192

financial crisis p. 176

financial engineering p. 184

financial globalization p. 190

financial liberalization p. 179

GIIPS p. 196

mortgage-backed securities p. 184

originate-to-distribute model p. 185

securitization p. 184

speculative attack p. 192

structured credit products p. 184

structured investment vehicles (SIVs) p. 186

subprime mortgages p. 184

Treasury Bill-to-Eurodollar rate (TED) p. 186

QUESTIONS AND PROBLEMS

All questions and problems are available in MyEconLab at **www.myeconlab.com/mishkin**.

1 How can a bursting of an asset-price bubble in the stock market help trigger a financial crisis?

2 How does an unanticipated decline in the price level cause a drop in lending?

3 When can a decline in the value of a country's currency exacerbate adverse selection and moral hazard problems? Why?

4 How can a decline in house prices cause deleveraging and a decline in lending?

5 How does a deterioration in balance sheets of financial institutions and the simultaneous failures of these institutions cause a decline in economic activity?

6 How does a general increase in uncertainty as a result of a failure of a major financial institution lead to an increase in adverse selection and moral hazard problems?

7 What are the two ways that spikes in interest rates lead to an increase in adverse selection and moral hazard problems?

8 How can government fiscal imbalances lead to a financial crisis?

9 How can financial liberalizations lead to financial crises?

10 What role does weak financial regulation and supervision play in causing financial crises?

11 Why do debt deflations occur in advanced countries, but not in emerging market countries?

12 What technological innovations led to the development of the subprime mortgage market?

13 Why is the originate-to-distribute business model subject to the principal–agent problem?

14 True, false, or uncertain: financial engineering always leads to a more efficient financial system.

15 How did a decline in housing prices help trigger the subprime financial crisis starting in 2007?

16 How can opening up to capital flows from abroad lead to a financial crisis?

17 Why are more resources not devoted to adequate prudential supervision of the financial system to limit excessive risk taking, when it is clear that this supervision is needed to prevent financial crises?

18 Why does the 'twin crises' phenomenon of currency and banking crises occur in emerging market countries?

19 How can a currency crisis lead to higher interest rates?

20 How has the European sovereign debt crisis led to higher borrowing costs for governments?

21 How can deterioration in bank balance sheets lead to a currency crisis?

22 How can the deterioration in bank balance sheets lead to a sovereign debt crisis?

WEB EXERCISES

1 This chapter discusses how an understanding of adverse selection and moral hazard can help us better understand financial crises. The greatest financial crisis faced by the United States was the Great Depression of 1929–33. Go to **www.amatecon.com/greatdepression.html**. This site contains a brief discussion of the factors that led to the Great Depression. Write a one-page summary explaining how adverse selection and moral hazard contributed to the Great Depression.

2 Go to the International Monetary Fund's Financial Crisis page at **www.imf.org/external/np/exr/key/finstab.htm**.

Report on the most recent three countries that the IMF has given emergency loans to in response to a financial crisis. According to the IMF, what caused the crisis in each country?

3 One of the countries hardest hit by the global financial crisis of 2008 was Iceland. Go to **assets.opencrs.com /rpts/RS22988_20081120.pdf** and summarize the causes and events that led to the crisis in Iceland.

Note

1 For a discussion of the role of asymmetric information problems in the Great Depression period, see Ben Bernanke, 'Nonmonetary effects of the financial crisis in the propagation of the Great Depression', *American Economic Review* 73 (1983): 257–76, and Charles Calomiris, 'Financial factors and the Great Depression', *Journal of Economic Perspectives* (Spring 1993): 61–85.

Useful websites

http://epp.eurostat.ec.europa.eu/portal/page/portal/financial_crisis/introduction Eurostat – the Statistical Office of the European Union – has a dedicated section on measuring aspects of the recent financial crisis.

http://www.ecb.int/ecb/html/crisis.en.html ECB's timeline of the recent financial crisis.

www.amatecon.com/gd/gdtimeline.html A time line of the Great Depression.

www.imf.org The International Monetary Fund is an organization of 185 countries that works on global policy coordination (both monetary and trade), stable and sustainable economic prosperity, and the reduction of poverty.

http://www.imf.org/external/country/index.htm IMF Country Level reports and analysis.

http://www.economics.harvard.edu/files/faculty/51_This_Time_Is_Different.pdf 'This Time is Different: A Panoramic View of Eight Centuries of Financial Crises' – a seminal paper by Carmen Reinhart and Kenneth Rogoff comparing the 2007 subprime crisis to other international crises over the past eight centuries.

http://www.cid.harvard.edu/archive/hiid/papers/bpeasia.pdf *The East Asian Financial Crisis: Diagnosis, Remedies, Prospects*: a non-technical survey paper by Steven Radelet and Jeffrey Sachs on the causes of the East Asian financial crisis.

http://www.cepr.org/pubs/PolicyInsights/CEPR_Policy_Insight_026.asp *The Icelandic banking crisis and what to do about it* – Willem Buiter and Anne Sibert's CEPR paper analysing the causes of the Icelandic banking crisis.

CHAPTER 10

Banking and the management of financial institutions

PREVIEW   Because banking plays such a major role in channelling funds to borrowers with productive investment opportunities, this financial activity is important in ensuring that the financial system and the economy run smoothly and efficiently. In 2010 banks (depository institutions) in the euro area supplied more than €95 billion in credit. They provide loans to businesses, help us finance our college educations or the purchase of a new car or home, and provide us with services such as cheque and savings accounts.

In this chapter, we examine how banking is conducted to earn the highest profits possible: how and why banks make loans, how they acquire funds and manage their assets and liabilities (debts), and how they earn income. Although we focus on commercial banking, because this is the most important financial intermediary activity, many of the same principles are applicable to other types of financial intermediation.

The bank balance sheet

To understand how banking works, we start by looking at the bank **balance sheet**, a list of the bank's assets and liabilities. As the name implies, this list balances; that is, it has the characteristic that

$$\text{total assets} = \text{total liabilities} + \text{capital}$$

A bank's balance sheet is also a list of its *sources* of bank funds (liabilities) and *uses* to which the funds are put (assets). Banks obtain funds by borrowing and by issuing other liabilities such as deposits. They then use these funds to acquire assets such as securities and loans. Banks make profits by charging an interest rate on their asset holdings of securities and loans that is higher than the interest and other expenses on their liabilities. The balance sheet of all commercial banks in the eurozone as of June 2011 appears in Table 10.1.

Liabilities

A bank acquires funds by issuing (selling) liabilities, such as deposits, which are the *sources of funds* the bank uses. The funds obtained from issuing liabilities are used to purchase income-earning assets.

Table 10.1 shows the balance sheet for all banks in the eurozone but this is the aggregation of all the banks in the eurozone. Not all banks have exactly the same structure. Compare Table 10.1 with the balance sheet of the largest bank in the eurozone. Table 10.2

TABLE 10.1

Balance sheet of all commercial banks in the eurozone (items as a percentage of the total, June 2011)

Assets (uses of funds)		Liabilities (sources of funds)	
Reserves and cash items	10%	Customer sight deposits	32%
Bonds and other securities	19%	Customer time deposits	12%
		Bank's deposits and borrowing	18%
		Foreign currency deposits	13%
Loans		Debt and other securities	17%
Non-financial corporations	12%	Bank capital	8%
Mortgages	10%		
Consumer	14%		
Banks	17%		
Foreign currency loans	14%		
Other assets (for example, physical capital)	4%		
Total (€31,712.4 billion)	100	Total	100

Source: ECB *Monthly Bulletin* August 2011. Table 2.1. Information may be obtained free of charge through the ECB's website.

shows the balance sheet of Deutsche Bank in 2010. The total amount of assets in Table 10.1 is €31.7 trillion, whereas Deutsche Bank reported a total assets position of €1.6 trillion (or 5% of the total level of bank assets in the eurozone).

There are some similarities and also some big differences. We will discuss each item of the balance sheet in turn.

TABLE 10.2

Balance sheet of Deutsche Bank (items as a percentage of the total, 31 December 2010)

Assets (uses of funds)		Liabilities (sources of funds)	
Reserves and cash items	7%	Customer sight deposits	21%
Bonds and other securities	3%	Customer time deposits	12%
		Bank's deposits	38%
		Foreign currency deposits	3%
Loans		Debt and other securities	21%
Mortgages	2%	Bank capital	5%
Consumers and firms	29%		
Banks	26%		
Foreign currency loans	4%		
Net trading assets	20%		
Other assets (for example, physical capital)	9%		
Total €1,620.2 billion	100%	Total	100%

Source: Annual Financial Statement and Management Report Deutsche Bank AG 2010.

Sight deposits

Sight deposits are bank accounts that allow the owner of the account to write cheques to third parties or to draw cash out of ATMs without loss of interest. Sight deposits include all accounts on which cheques can be drawn: non-interest-bearing accounts (demand deposits) and interest-bearing cheque accounts. Table 10.1 shows that the category of sight deposits is an important source of bank funds, making up 32% of bank liabilities for all banks in the eurozone. Notice that in the case of Deutsche Bank, at 21% this source accounts for much less than for other banks.

Sight deposits are payable on demand, hence they are sometimes known as demand deposits; that is, if a depositor shows up at the bank and requests payment by making a withdrawal, the bank must pay the depositor immediately. Similarly, if a person who receives a cheque written on an account from a bank presents that cheque at the bank, it must pay the funds out immediately (or credit them to that person's account).

A sight deposit is an asset for the depositor because it is part of his or her wealth. Because the depositor can withdraw funds and the bank is obliged to pay, sight deposits are a liability for the bank. They are usually the lowest-cost source of bank funds because banks pay no interest or a very small amount of interest on these deposits and depositors are willing to forgo some interest to have access to a liquid asset that they can use to make purchases. The bank's costs of maintaining cheque deposits include interest payments and the costs incurred in servicing these accounts – processing, preparing and sending out monthly statements, providing efficient tellers (human or otherwise), maintaining an impressive head office and conveniently located branches, and advertising and marketing to entice customers to deposit their funds with a given bank.

Time deposits

Time deposits cannot be withdrawn on demand like sight deposits. They have a fixed term to maturity which means that the funds have to be kept in the account for a minimum period to earn interest. Depositors cannot write cheques on time deposits, but the interest rates paid on these deposits are usually higher than those on sight deposits. Time deposits also include savings accounts.

Time deposits have a fixed maturity length, ranging from several months to over five years, and assess substantial penalties for early withdrawal (the forfeiture of several months' interest). Notice that Deutsche Bank sources 12% of its funds from time deposits, as do the rest of the banks in the eurozone.

Banks' deposits and other funding

Banks borrow and lend to each other through the interbank market. These interbank deposits can be the same as demand deposits or they can have fixed maturities of one month, three months or even several years. The function of the interbank market is to distribute funds between banks that have surplus funds and banks that have shortages of funds. So a loan from one bank to another is not like a loan from a bank to a customer. Banks deposit funds (lend) in the interbank market and other banks bid (borrow) funds. The process of bid and offer produces a market rate of interest at which banks are willing to lend to each other or borrow from each other. A bank can also borrow from the central bank at times.

Banks' deposits in Table 10.1 are 18% of total assets but Deutsche Bank borrows proportionately more from the interbank market than the banks in the eurozone do as a whole.

Debt and other securities

Banks also obtain funds by borrowing from the financial market. They do this by issuing bonds and certificates of deposits (CDs). CDs are negotiable; like bonds, they can be resold in a secondary market before they mature. For this reason, negotiable CDs are held by corporations, money market mutual funds, and other financial institutions as alternative assets to Treasury bills and other short-term bonds. You can see that this avenue of sourcing funds is important to the banks in the eurozone and to Deutsche Bank.

Foreign currency deposits

An international bank also borrows and lends in foreign currency. Certain foreign currency deposits like US dollars can be held by domestic residents and foreigners can also deposit funds in their own currency. Holding foreign currency deposits exposes the banks to foreign currency risk. If a bank holds US dollar deposits of $100 and the exchange rate is $1.40 to the € it has liabilities of €71.43. If the exchange rate were to depreciate to $1.25, the bank now faces a liability of €80. The bank would have to hedge against currency fluctuations. The most common way is to maturity match by holding an equivalent amount of $ assets. So if the exchange rate were to change the banks' net foreign currency exposure (foreign currency assets less foreign currency liabilities) is small.

Bank capital

The final category on the liabilities side of the balance sheet is bank capital, the bank's net worth, which equals the difference between total assets and liabilities (8% of total bank assets in Table 10.1 and 5% in Table 10.2). Bank capital is raised by selling new equity (stock) or from retained earnings. Bank capital is a cushion against a drop in the value of its assets, which could force the bank into insolvency (having liabilities in excess of assets, meaning that the bank can be forced into liquidation).

Assets

A bank uses the funds that it has acquired by issuing liabilities to purchase income-earning assets. Bank assets are thus naturally referred to as *uses of funds*, and the interest payments earned on them are what enable banks to make profits.

Reserves

All banks hold some of the funds they acquire as deposits in an account at the central bank. **Reserves** are these deposits plus currency that is physically held by banks (called **vault cash** because it is stored in bank vaults overnight). Although reserves earn a low interest rate, banks hold them for two reasons. First, some reserves, called **required reserves**, are held because of **reserve requirements**, the regulation that for every euro of sight deposits at a bank, a certain fraction must be kept as reserves. This fraction is called the **required reserve ratio**. Banks hold additional reserves, called **excess reserves**, because they are the most liquid of all bank assets and a bank can use them to meet its obligations when funds are withdrawn, either directly by a depositor or indirectly when a cheque is written on an account.

Securities

A bank's holdings of securities are an important income-earning asset: Securities (made up entirely of debt instruments for commercial banks) account for 19% of bank assets in Table 10.1. These securities can be classified into three categories: government and agency securities such as Treasury bills and short-term government bonds, commercial paper and private-sector bonds, and other securities. Treasury bills and other short-term government debt are the most liquid because they can be easily traded and converted into cash with low transaction costs. Because of their high liquidity, short-term government securities are called **secondary reserves**.

Banks also hold commercial paper and other short-term securities of the non-financial company sector for two reasons. First, companies are more likely to do business with banks that hold their securities. And second, short-term company securities are liquid, but less liquid and riskier than equivalent maturity government securities, primarily because of default risk: there is some possibility that the issuer of the securities may not be able to make its interest payments or pay back the face value of the securities when they mature. Therefore the interest rate on commercial paper is normally higher than that on Treasury bills. Notice that in Table 10.2 Deutsche Bank holds only 3% of its assets in bonds and securities compared with 19% for banks in the eurozone as a whole.

Loans

Banks make their profits primarily by issuing loans. In Table 10.1, some 67% of bank assets are in the form of loans (61% in the case of Deutsche Bank). A loan is a liability for the individual or corporation receiving it, but an asset for a bank, because it provides income to the bank. Loans are typically less liquid than other assets, because they cannot be turned into cash until the loan matures. If the bank makes a one-year loan, for example, it cannot get its funds back until the loan comes due in one year. Loans also have a higher probability of default than other assets. Because of the lack of liquidity and higher default risk, the bank earns its highest return on loans.

As you saw in Table 10.1, the largest categories of loans for commercial banks are commercial and industrial loans made to businesses, consumers and mortgage loans (total 36% and 31% in Table 10.2). Commercial banks also make consumer loans and lend to each other. The bulk of these interbank loans are short-term loans lent in the interbank market. You may notice that from Table 10.1, the banks within the eurozone borrow and lend to each other roughly the same amount (the differences are items in transit, items from outside the eurozone and rounding and measurement error), but individual banks will borrow or lend more than the average bank according to the needs of their operations. For instance you can see that in Table 10.2 Deutsche Bank borrows 38% of its liabilities from the interbank market but lends 26% of its assets in the same. Notice also that net foreign currency loans (foreign currency loans minus foreign currency deposits) is 1% in both Tables 10.1 and 10.2 which means that eurozone banks in general and Deutsche Bank in particular lend more in foreign currency than they borrow by a small margin.

The major difference in the balance sheets of the various depository institutions is primarily in the type of loan in which they specialize. Savings banks and UK-type building societies, for example, specialize in mortgages, while credit banks tend to make consumer loans.

Net trading assets

Trading assets are government securities, asset-backed securities or commercial securities such as derivatives that the bank holds for the purpose of selling them for a profit. They are valued at the existing market price (known as mark-to-market) and are bought at a low price and sold at a high price. These assets are held for a short period so as to gain from a profit in trade. The bank also holds trading liabilities where they might guarantee or sell asset-backed securities and derivatives. The subtraction of these from its assets gives its net trading assets. You can see from Table 10.2 that only some banks have a major exposure to this area of activity. Deutsche Bank reports 20% of its assets as net trading assets.

Other assets

The physical capital (bank buildings, computers and other equipment) owned by the banks is included in this category.

Basic banking

Before proceeding to a more detailed study of how a bank manages its assets and liabilities to make the highest profit, you should understand the basic operation of a bank. In other words, how a bank makes money.

In general terms, banks make profits by selling liabilities with one set of characteristics (a particular combination of liquidity, risk, size and return) and using the proceeds to buy assets with a different set of characteristics. This process is often referred to as *asset transformation*. For example, a savings deposit held by one person can provide the funds that enable the bank to make a mortgage loan to another person. The bank has, in effect, transformed the savings deposit (an asset held by the depositor) into a mortgage loan (an asset held by the bank). Another way this process of asset transformation is described is to say that the bank 'borrows short and lends long' because it makes long-term loans and funds them by issuing short-dated deposits.

How does a bank get away with lending out 'long' its deposits that can be withdrawn on demand on 'short' notice? It does this by applying the 'law of large numbers' to liability management. Normally, depositors do not withdraw their deposits at the same time as other customers. Recognizing that depositors withdraw their funds at different times means that banks only need to hold a certain amount as reserves to meet day-to-day withdrawals and lend the rest in long-term loans. This process is known as **maturity transformation**. This is the process by which banks accept short maturity deposits and convert them into long maturity loans.

The process of transforming assets and providing a set of services (cheque clearing, record keeping, credit analysis and so forth) is like any other production process in a firm. If the bank produces desirable services at low cost and earns substantial income on its assets, it earns profits; if not, the bank suffers losses.

To better understand how a bank makes profit and the sources of its revenues and costs let us examine the profit and loss account of the Deutsche Bank in 2010. Table 10.3 shows the income statement of Deutsche Bank on 31 December 2010.

TABLE 10.3

Income statement for the period 1 January 2010 to 31 December 2010

Item	€ million
Interest Income	18,524
Loans	10,414
Securities	3,884
Other	4,226
Interest expenses	11,164
Net interest income	7,360
Other operating income	2,344
Commission income	7,143
Commission expenses	1,439
Net commission income	5,704
Net income from trading	2,619
Administrative expenses	11,617
Other expenses	4,504
Loan loss provisions	305
Write downs	956
Taxes	157
Net income	488

Source: Annual Financial Statement and Management Report Deutsche Bank AG 2010.

Interest income comes from interest received on loans to households and firms, interest from fixed-income securities such as government bills and commercial paper, and receivables from equity-related securities and variable-income securities. Interest expenses are interest paid to depositors and to loans taken from other banks through the interbank market. Net interest income accounts for 43% of revenues to Deutsche Bank.

Commission income is the fees the bank charges for its various financial services and investment activities and net commission is the net income after subtracting the costs associated with these services. Net commission income accounted for 31% of revenues in 2010.

Other operating income is income derived from leasing activity or sale of assets that are not on the trading account and net trading income is net revenue obtained from the buying and selling of financial securities.

Administrative expenses are largely costs of labour and other expenses related to all other variable costs such as running premises, computers, security etc. Loan loss provisions are special reserves held on anticipation of defaults of loans and write-downs are loans that have gone bad and are unrecoverable. After deducting all costs from earnings streams and subtracting tax Deutsche Bank made €488 million profit on its domestic bank operations. Now let's turn to an analysis of the banks' operation.

To make our analysis of the operation of a bank more concrete, we use a tool called a **T-account**. A T-account is a simplified balance sheet, with lines in the form of a T, that lists only the changes that occur in balance sheet items starting from some initial balance sheet position. Let's say that Ingrid Schmidt has heard that the First Euro Bank provides excellent service, so she opens an account with a €100 note. She now has a €100 sight deposit at the bank, which shows up as a €100 liability on the bank's balance sheet. The bank now puts her €100 into its vault so that the bank's assets rise by the €100 increase in vault cash. The T-account for the bank looks like this:

First Euro Bank			
Assets		**Liabilities**	
Vault cash	+€100	Sight deposits	+€100

Because vault cash is also part of the bank's reserves, we can rewrite the T-account as follows:

Assets		**Liabilities**	
Reserves	+€100	Sight deposits	+€100

Note that Ingrid Schmidt's opening of an account leads to an increase in the bank's reserves equal to the increase in sight deposits.

If Ingrid had opened her account with a €100 cheque written on an account at another bank, say, the Second Euro Bank, we would get the same result. The initial effect on the T-account of the First Euro Bank is as follows:

Assets		**Liabilities**	
Cash items in process of collection	+€100	Sight deposits	+€100

Sight deposits increase by €100 as before, but now the First Euro Bank is owed €100 by the Second Euro Bank. This asset for the First Euro Bank is entered in the T-account as €100 of cash items in process of collection because the First Euro Bank will now try to collect the funds that it is owed. It could go directly to the Second Euro Bank and ask for payment of the funds, but if the two banks are in separate areas, that would be a time-consuming and costly process. Instead, the First Euro Bank presents the cheque at a clearing house, and the clearing house collects the funds from the Second Euro Bank. The result is that the clearing house transfers €100 of reserves from the Second Euro Bank to the First Euro Bank, and the final balance sheet positions of the two banks are as follows:

First Euro Bank				Second Euro Bank			
Assets		**Liabilities**		**Assets**		**Liabilities**	
Reserves	+€100	Sight deposits	+€100	Reserves	−€100	Sight deposits	−€100

The process initiated by Ingrid Schmidt can be summarized as follows: when a cheque written on an account at one bank is deposited in another, the bank receiving the deposit gains reserves equal to the amount of the cheque, while the bank on which the cheque is written sees its reserves fall by the same amount. Therefore, *when a bank receives additional deposits, it gains an equal amount of reserves; when it loses deposits, it loses an equal amount of reserves*.

A clearing house is a process by which cheques are netted out between banks and only the net amount is debited or credited from a bank's balance sheet. In most countries in Europe the netting process is done electronically through the use of debit cards and the process of 'pinning' (the use of your PIN number for electronic transactions).

Now that you understand how banks gain and lose reserves, we can examine how a bank rearranges its balance sheet to make a profit when it experiences a change in its deposits. Let's return to the situation when the First Euro Bank has just received the extra €100 of sight deposits. As you know, the bank is obliged to keep a certain fraction of its sight deposits as required reserves. If the fraction (the required reserve ratio) is 10%, the First Euro Bank's required reserves have increased by €10, and we can rewrite its T-account as follows:

First Euro Bank			
Assets		**Liabilities**	
Required reserves	+€10	Sight deposits	+€100
Excess reserves	+€90		

Let's see how well the bank is doing as a result of the additional sight deposits. Servicing the extra €100 of sight deposits is costly, because the bank must keep records, pay tellers, pay for cheque clearing, and so forth. Since reserves earn little interest the bank is taking a loss! The situation is even worse if the bank makes interest payments on the deposits. If it is to make a profit, the bank must put to productive use all or part of the €90 of excess reserves it has available. One way to do this is to invest in securities. The other is to make loans; loans account for approximately 56% of the total value of Deutsche Bank's assets (uses of funds). Because lenders are subject to the asymmetric information problems of adverse selection and moral hazard (discussed in Chapter 8), banks take steps to reduce the incidence and severity of these problems. Bank loan officers evaluate potential borrowers using what are called the 'five Cs': character, capacity (ability to repay), collateral, conditions (in the local and euro economies) and capital (net worth) before they agree to lend. (Later in this chapter is a more detailed discussion of the methods banks use to reduce the risk involved in lending.)

Let us assume that the bank chooses not to hold any excess reserves but to make loans instead. The T-account then looks like this:

Assets		Liabilities	
Required reserves	+€10	Sight deposits	+€100
Loans	+€90		

The bank is now making a profit because it holds short-term liabilities such as sight deposits and uses the proceeds to fund longer-term assets such as loans with higher interest rates. As mentioned earlier, this process of asset transformation is frequently described by saying that banks are in the business of 'borrowing short and lending long'. For example, if the loans have an interest rate of 10% per year, the bank earns €9 in income from its loans over the year. If the €100 of sight deposits is in an account with a 5% interest rate and it costs another €3 per year to service the account, the cost per year of these deposits is €8. The bank's profit on the new deposits is then €1 per year, plus any interest that is paid on required reserves.

General principles of bank management

Now that you have some idea of how a bank operates, let's look at how a bank manages its assets and liabilities to earn the highest possible profit. The bank manager has four primary concerns. The first is to make sure that the bank has enough ready cash to pay its depositors when there are **deposit outflows** – that is, when deposits are lost because depositors make withdrawals and demand payment. To keep enough cash on hand, the bank must engage in **liquidity management**, the acquisition of sufficiently liquid assets to meet the bank's obligations to depositors. Second, the bank manager must pursue an acceptably low level of risk by acquiring assets that have a low rate of default and by diversifying asset holdings (**asset management**). The third concern is to acquire funds at low cost (**liability management**). Finally, the manager must decide the amount of capital the bank should maintain and then acquire the needed capital (**capital adequacy management**).

To understand bank and other financial institution management fully, we must go beyond the general principles of bank asset and liability management described next and look in more detail at how a financial institution manages its assets. The two sections following this one provide an in-depth discussion of how a financial institution manages **credit risk**, the risk arising because borrowers may default, and how it manages **interest-rate risk**, the riskiness of earnings and returns on bank assets that result from interest-rate changes.

Liquidity management and the role of reserves

Let us see how a typical bank, the First Euro Bank, can deal with deposit outflows that occur when its depositors withdraw cash from demand or time accounts, write cheques or electronically transfer funds that are deposited in other banks. In the example that follows, we assume that the bank has ample excess reserves and that all deposits have the same required reserve ratio of 10% (the bank is required to keep 10% of deposits as reserves). Suppose that the First Euro Bank's initial balance sheet is as follows:

Assets		Liabilities	
Reserves	€20 million	Deposits	€100 million
Loans	€80 million	Bank capital	€10 million
Securities	€10 million		

The bank's required reserves are 10% of €100 million, or €10 million. Given that it holds €20 million of reserves, the First Euro Bank has excess reserves of €10 million.

If a deposit outflow of €10 million occurs, the bank's balance sheet becomes

Assets		Liabilities	
Reserves	€10 million	Deposits	€90 million
Loans	€80 million	Bank capital	€10 million
Securities	€10 million		

The bank loses €10 million of deposits *and* €10 million of reserves, but because its required reserves are now 10% of only €90 million (€9 million), its reserves still exceed this amount by €1 million. In short, *if a bank has ample excess reserves, a deposit outflow does not necessitate changes in other parts of its balance sheet.*

The situation is quite different when a bank holds insufficient excess reserves. Let's assume that instead of initially holding €10 million in excess reserves, the First Euro Bank makes additional loans of €10 million, so that it holds no excess reserves. Its initial balance sheet would then be

Assets		Liabilities	
Reserves	€10 million	Deposits	€100 million
Loans	€90 million	Bank capital	€10 million
Securities	€10 million		

When it suffers the €10 million deposit outflow, its balance sheet becomes

Assets		Liabilities	
Reserves	€0	Deposits	€90 million
Loans	€90 million	Bank capital	€10 million
Securities	€10 million		

After €10 million has been withdrawn from deposits and hence reserves, the bank has a problem: it has a reserve requirement of 10% of €90 million, or €9 million, but it has no reserves! To eliminate this shortfall, the bank has four basic options. One is to acquire reserves to meet a deposit outflow by borrowing them from other banks in the central bank funds market or by borrowing from corporations.[1] If the First Euro Bank acquires the €9 million shortfall in reserves by borrowing it from other banks or corporations, its balance sheet becomes

Assets		Liabilities	
Reserves	€9 million	Deposits	€90 million
Loans	€90 million	Borrowings from other banks or corporations	€9 million
Securities	€10 million	Bank capital	€10 million

The cost of this activity is the interest rate on these borrowings, such as the central bank's funds rate.

A second alternative is for the bank to sell some of its securities to help cover the deposit outflow. For example, it might sell €9 million of its securities and deposit the proceeds with the central bank, resulting in the following balance sheet:

Assets		Liabilities	
Reserves	€9 million	Deposits	€90 million
Loans	€90 million	Bank capital	€10 million
Securities	€1 million		

The bank incurs some brokerage and other transaction costs when it sells these securities. The government securities that are classified as secondary reserves are very liquid, so the transaction costs of selling them are quite modest. However, the other securities the bank holds are less liquid, and the transaction cost can be appreciably higher.

A third way that the bank can meet a deposit outflow is to acquire reserves by borrowing from the central bank. In our example, the First Euro Bank could leave its security and loan holdings the same and borrow €9 million in discount loans from the central bank (CB). Its balance sheet would then be

Assets		Liabilities	
Reserves	€9 million	Deposits	€90 million
Loans	€90 million	Borrowing from the central bank	€9 million
Securities	€10 million	Bank capital	€10 million

The cost associated with (CB borrowing) discount loans is the interest rate that must be paid to the central bank (in the euro area this is the main refinancing operations rate, in the UK this is the bank rate and in the US it is the discount rate).

Finally, a bank can acquire the €9 million of reserves to meet the deposit outflow by reducing its loans by this amount and depositing the €9 million it then receives with the central bank, thereby increasing its reserves by €9 million. This transaction changes the balance sheet as follows:

Assets		Liabilities	
Reserves	€9 million	Deposits	€90 million
Loans	€81 million	Bank capital	€10 million
Securities	€10 million		

The First Euro Bank is once again in good shape because its €9 million of reserves satisfies the reserve requirement.

However, this process of reducing its loans is the bank's costliest way of acquiring reserves when there is a deposit outflow. If the First Euro Bank has numerous short-term loans renewed at fairly short intervals, it can reduce its total amount of loans outstanding fairly quickly by *calling in* loans – that is, by not renewing some loans when they come due. Unfortunately for the bank, this is likely to antagonize the customers whose loans are not being renewed because they have not done anything to deserve such treatment. Indeed, they are likely to take their business elsewhere in the future, a very costly consequence for the bank.

A second method for reducing its loans is for the bank to sell them off to other banks. Again, this is very costly because other banks do not personally know the customers who have taken out the loans and so may not be willing to buy the loans at their full value. (This is just the lemons adverse selection problem described in Chapter 8.)

The foregoing discussion explains why banks hold excess reserves even though loans or securities earn a higher return. When a deposit outflow occurs, holding excess reserves allows the bank to escape the costs of (1) borrowing from other banks or corporations, (2) selling securities, (3) borrowing from the central bank, or (4) calling in or selling off loans. *Excess reserves are insurance against the costs associated with deposit outflows. The higher the costs associated with deposit outflows, the more excess reserves banks will want to hold.*

Just as you and I would be willing to pay an insurance company to insure us against a casualty loss such as the theft of a car, a bank is willing to pay the cost of holding excess reserves (the opportunity cost, the earnings forgone by not holding income-earning assets such as loans or securities) to insure against losses due to deposit outflows. Because excess reserves, like insurance, have a cost, banks also take other steps to protect themselves; for example, they might shift their holdings of assets to more liquid securities (secondary reserves).

Asset management

Now that you understand why a bank has a need for liquidity, we can examine the basic strategy a bank pursues in managing its assets. To maximize its profits, a bank must simultaneously seek the highest returns possible on loans and securities, reduce risk, and make adequate provisions for liquidity by holding liquid assets. Banks try to accomplish these three goals in four basic ways.

First, banks try to find borrowers who will pay high interest rates and are unlikely to default on their loans. They seek out loan business by advertising their borrowing rates and by approaching corporations directly to solicit loans. It is up to the bank's loan officer to decide if potential borrowers are good credit risks who will make interest and principal payments on time (i.e. engage in screening to reduce the adverse selection problem). Typically, banks are conservative in their loan policies; the default rate is usually less than 1%. It is important, however, that banks not be so conservative that they miss out on attractive lending opportunities that earn high interest rates.

Second, banks try to purchase securities with high returns and low risk. Third, in managing their assets, banks must attempt to lower risk by diversifying. They accomplish this by purchasing many different types of assets (short- and long-term, government bonds and highly rated commercial bonds) and approving many types of loans to a number of customers. Banks that have not sufficiently sought the benefits of diversification often come to regret it later. For example, in the US, banks that had overspecialized in making loans to energy companies, real estate developers or farmers suffered huge losses in the 1980s with the slump in energy, property and farm prices. Indeed, many of these banks went broke because they had 'put too many eggs in one basket'.

Finally, the bank must manage the liquidity of its assets so that it can satisfy its reserve requirements without bearing huge costs. This means that it will hold liquid securities even if they earn a somewhat lower return than other assets. The bank must decide, for example, how much in excess reserves must be held to avoid costs from a deposit outflow. In addition, it will want to hold Treasury bills or other government securities as secondary reserves so that even if a deposit outflow forces some costs on the bank, these will not be terribly high. Again, it is not wise for a bank to be too conservative. If it avoids all costs associated with deposit outflows by holding only excess reserves, the bank suffers losses because reserves earn low interest, while the bank's liabilities are costly to maintain. The bank must balance its desire for liquidity against the increased earnings that can be obtained from less liquid assets such as loans.

Liability management

Before the 1960s, liability management was a staid affair: for the most part, banks took their liabilities as fixed and spent their time trying to achieve an optimal mix of assets. There were two main reasons for the emphasis on asset management. First, the majority of the sources of bank funds were obtained through sight (demand) deposits that by law could not pay any interest. Thus banks could not actively compete with one another for these deposits by paying interest on them, and so their amount was effectively a given for an individual bank. Second, because the interbank market was not well developed, banks rarely borrowed from other banks to meet their reserve needs.

Starting in the 1960s, however, large banks in London and New York began to explore ways in which the liabilities on their balance sheets could provide them with reserves and liquidity. This led to the development of the interbank market, and the development of new financial instruments such as negotiable certificates of deposits (CDs) which enabled banks with surplus funds to lend to banks in need of funds through the interbank market.

This new flexibility in liability management meant that banks could take a different approach to bank management. They no longer needed to depend on sight deposits as the primary source of bank funds and as a result no longer treated their sources of funds (liabilities) as given. Instead, they aggressively set target goals for their asset growth and tried to acquire funds (by issuing liabilities) as they were needed.

For example, today, when a bank finds an attractive loan opportunity, it can acquire funds by selling a negotiable CD. Or, if it has a reserve shortfall, it can borrow funds from another bank in the interbank market without incurring high transaction costs. The interbank market can also be used to finance loans. Because of the increased importance of liability management, most banks now manage both sides of the balance sheet together in an *asset–liability management (ALM) committee*.

The greater emphasis on liability management explains some of the important changes over the past three decades in the composition of banks' balance sheets. While negotiable CDs and bank borrowings have greatly increased in importance as a source of bank funds in recent years, sight deposits have decreased in importance. New-found flexibility in liability management and the search for higher profits have also stimulated banks to increase the proportion of their assets held in loans, which earn higher income: 53% in Table 10.1.

Capital adequacy management

Banks have to make decisions about the amount of capital they need to hold for three reasons. First, bank capital helps prevent *bank failure*, a situation in which the bank cannot satisfy its obligations to pay its depositors and other creditors and so goes out of business. Second, the amount of capital affects returns for the owners (equity holders) of the bank. Third, a minimum amount of bank capital (bank capital requirements) is required by regulatory authorities.

How bank capital helps prevent bank failure

Let's consider two banks with identical balance sheets, except that the High Capital Bank has a ratio of capital to assets of 10% while the Low Capital Bank has a ratio of 4%.

Suppose that both banks get caught up in the euphoria of the housing market, only to find that €5 million of their housing loans became worthless later. When these bad

High Capital Bank				Low Capital Bank			
Assets		Liabilities		Assets		Liabilities	
Reserves	€10 million	Deposits	€90 million	Reserves	€10 million	Deposits	€96 million
Loans	€90 million	Bank capital	€10 million	Loans	€90 million	Bank capital	€4 million

loans are written off (valued at zero), the total value of assets declines by €5 million. As a consequence, bank capital, which equals total assets minus liabilities, also declines by €5 million. The balance sheets of the two banks now look like this:

High Capital Bank				Low Capital Bank			
Assets		**Liabilities**		**Assets**		**Liabilities**	
Reserves	€10 million	Deposits	€90 million	Reserves	€10 million	Deposits	€96 million
Loans capital	€85 million	Bank capital	€5 million	Loans capital	€85 million	Bank	−€1 million

The High Capital Bank takes the €5 million loss in its stride because its initial cushion of €10 million in capital means that it still has a positive net worth (bank capital) of €5 million after the loss. The Low Capital Bank, however, is in big trouble. Now the value of its assets has fallen below its liabilities, and its net worth is now −€1 million. Because the bank has a negative net worth, it is insolvent: it does not have sufficient assets to pay off all holders of its liabilities. When a bank becomes insolvent, government regulators close the bank, its assets are sold off, and its managers are fired. Because the owners of the Low Capital Bank will find their investment wiped out, they would clearly have preferred the bank to have had a large enough cushion of bank capital to absorb the losses, as was the case for the High Capital Bank. We therefore see an important rationale for a bank to maintain a sufficient level of capital: *a bank maintains bank capital to lessen the chance that it will become insolvent*.

How the amount of bank capital affects returns to equity holders

Because owners of a bank must know whether their bank is being managed well, they need good measures of bank profitability. A basic measure of bank profitability is the **return on assets (ROA)**, the net profit after taxes per euro of assets:

$$\text{ROA} = \frac{\text{net profit after taxes}}{\text{assets}}$$

The return on assets provides information on how efficiently a bank is being run, because it indicates how much profits are generated on average by each euro of assets. For example from Table 10.2 and 10.3 the ROA of Deutsche Bank in 2010 was (488/1620164) = 0.3%.

However, what the bank's owners (equity holders) care about most is how much the bank is earning on their equity investment. This information is provided by the other basic measure of bank profitability, the **return on equity (ROE)**, the net profit after taxes per euro of equity (bank) capital:

$$\text{ROE} = \frac{\text{net profit after taxes}}{\text{equity capital}}$$

There is a direct relationship between the return on assets (which measures how efficiently the bank is run) and the return on equity (which measures how well the owners are doing on their investment). This relationship is determined by the **equity multiplier (EM)**, the amount of assets per euro of equity capital:

$$\text{EM} = \frac{\text{assets}}{\text{equity capital}}$$

To see this, we note that

$$\frac{\text{net profit after taxes}}{\text{equity capital}} = \frac{\text{net profit after taxes}}{\text{assets}} \times \frac{\text{assets}}{\text{equity capital}}$$

which, using our definitions, yields

$$\text{ROE} = \text{ROA} \times \text{EM} \tag{10.1}$$

The formula in Equation 10.1 tells us what happens to the return on equity when a bank holds a smaller amount of capital (equity) for a given amount of assets. As we have seen, the High Capital Bank initially has €100 million of assets and €10 million of equity, which gives it an equity multiplier of (10 = €100 million/€10 million). The Low Capital Bank, by contrast, has only €4 million of equity, so its equity multiplier is higher, equalling (25 = €100 million/€4 million). Suppose that these banks have been equally well run so that they both have the same return on assets, 1%. The return on equity for the High Capital Bank equals 1% × 10 = 10% while the return on equity for the Low Capital Bank equals 1% × 25 = 25%. The equity holders in the Low Capital Bank are clearly a lot happier than the equity holders in the High Capital Bank because they are earning more than twice as high a return. We now see why owners of a bank may not want it to hold too much capital. *Given the return on assets, the lower the bank capital, the higher the return for the owners of the bank.*

Trade-off between safety and returns to equity holders

We now see that bank capital has both benefits and costs. Bank capital benefits the owners of a bank in that it makes their investment safer by reducing the likelihood of bankruptcy. But bank capital is costly because the higher it is, the lower will be the return on equity for a given return on assets. In determining the amount of bank capital, managers must decide how much of the increased safety that comes with higher capital (the benefit) they are willing to trade off against the lower return on equity that comes with higher capital (the cost).

In more uncertain times, when the possibility of large losses on loans increases, bank managers might want to hold more capital to protect the equity holders. Conversely, if they have confidence that loan losses won't occur, they might want to reduce the amount of bank capital, have a high equity multiplier, and thereby increase the return on equity.

Bank capital requirements

Banks also hold capital because they are required to do so by regulatory authorities. Because of the high costs of holding capital for the reasons just described, bank managers often want to hold less bank capital relative to assets than is required by the regulatory authorities. In this case, the amount of bank capital is determined by the bank capital requirements. We discuss the details of bank capital requirements and their important role in bank regulation in Chapter 11.

APPLICATION Strategies for managing bank capital

Suppose that as the manager of the First Euro Bank, you have to make decisions about the appropriate amount of bank capital. Looking at the balance sheet of the bank, which like the High Capital Bank has a ratio of bank capital to assets of 10% (€10 million of capital and €100 million of assets), you are concerned that the large amount of bank capital is causing the return on equity to be too low. You conclude that the bank has a capital surplus and should increase the equity multiplier to increase the return on equity. What should you do?

To lower the amount of capital relative to assets and raise the equity multiplier, you can do any of three things. (1) You can reduce the amount of bank capital by buying back some of the bank's stock. (2) You can reduce the bank's capital by paying out higher dividends to its stockholders, thereby reducing the bank's retained earnings. (3) You can keep bank capital constant but increase the bank's assets by acquiring new funds – say, by issuing CDs – and then seeking out loan business or purchasing more securities with these new funds. Because you think that it would enhance your position with the stockholders, you decide to pursue the second alternative and raise the dividend on the First Euro Bank stock.

Now suppose that the First Euro Bank is in a similar situation to the Low Capital Bank and has a ratio of bank capital to assets of 4%. You now worry that the bank is short on capital relative to assets because it does not have a sufficient cushion to prevent bank failure. To raise the amount of capital relative to assets, you now have the following three choices. (1) You can raise capital for the bank by having it issue equity (common stock). (2) You can raise capital by reducing the bank's dividends to shareholders, thereby increasing retained earnings that it can put into its capital account. (3) You can keep capital at the same level but reduce the bank's assets by making fewer loans or by selling off securities and then using the proceeds to reduce its liabilities. Suppose that raising bank capital is not easy to do at the current time because capital markets are tight or because shareholders will protest if their dividends are cut. Then you might have to choose the third option and decide to shrink the size of the bank.

Our discussion of strategies for managing bank capital for the First Euro Bank leads to the following conclusion that deserves some emphasis: *a shortfall of bank capital is likely to lead to a bank reducing its assets and therefore a contraction in lending*. In past years, many banks experienced capital shortfalls and had to restrict asset and lending growth. The important consequences of this for the credit markets are illustrated by the application that follows.

APPLICATION   How a capital crunch caused a credit crunch in 2008

The dramatic slowdown in the growth of credit in the wake of the financial crisis starting in 2007 triggered a 'credit crunch' in which credit was hard to get. As a result, the performance of the economy in 2008 was very poor. What caused the credit crunch?

Our analysis of how a bank manages its capital indicates that the 2008 credit crunch was caused, at least in part, by the capital crunch, in which shortfalls of bank capital led to slower credit growth.

As we discussed in the previous chapter, there was a major boom and bust in the housing market that led to huge losses for banks from their holdings of securities backed by residential mortgages. In addition, banks had to take back onto their balance sheets many of the structured investment vehicles (SIVs) they had sponsored. The losses that reduced bank capital, along with the need for more capital to support the assets coming back onto their balance sheets, led to capital shortfalls: banks had to either raise new capital or restrict asset growth by cutting back on lending. Banks did raise some capital but with the growing weakness of the economy, raising new capital was extremely difficult, so banks also chose to tighten their lending standards and reduce lending. Both of these helped produce a weak economy in 2008.

Managing credit risk

As seen in the earlier discussion of general principles of asset management, banks and other financial institutions must make successful loans that are paid back in full (and so subject the institution to little credit risk) if they are to earn high profits. The economic concepts of adverse selection and moral hazard (discussed in Chapters 2 and 8) provide a framework for understanding the principles that financial institutions have to follow to reduce credit risk and make successful loans.[2]

Adverse selection in loan markets occurs because bad credit risks (those most likely to default on their loans) are the ones who usually line up for loans; in other words, those who are most likely to produce an *adverse* outcome are the most likely to be *selected*. Borrowers with very risky investment projects have much to gain if their projects are successful, so they are the most eager to obtain loans. Clearly, however, they are the least desirable borrowers because of the greater possibility that they will be unable to pay back their loans.

Moral hazard exists in loan markets because borrowers may have incentives to engage in activities that are undesirable from the lender's point of view. In such situations, it is more likely that the lender will be subjected to the *hazard* of default. Once borrowers have obtained a loan, they are more likely to invest in high-risk investment projects – projects that pay high returns to the borrowers if successful. The high risk, however, makes it less likely that they will be able to pay the loan back.

To be profitable, financial institutions must overcome the adverse selection and moral hazard problems that make loan defaults more likely. The attempts of financial institutions to solve these problems help explain a number of principles for managing credit risk: screening and monitoring, establishment of long-term customer relationships, loan commitments, collateral and compensating balance requirements, and credit rationing.

Screening and monitoring

Asymmetric information is present in loan markets because lenders have less information about the investment opportunities and activities of borrowers than borrowers do. This situation leads to two information-producing activities by banks and other financial institutions – screening and monitoring. Indeed, Walter Wriston, a former head of Citicorp, was often quoted as stating that the business of banking is the production of information.

Screening

Adverse selection in loan markets requires that lenders screen out the bad credit risks from the good ones so that loans are profitable to them. To accomplish effective screening, lenders must collect reliable information from prospective borrowers. Effective screening and information collection together form an important principle of credit risk management.

When you apply for a consumer loan (such as a car loan or a mortgage to purchase a house), the first thing you are asked to do is fill out forms that elicit a great deal of information about your personal finances. You are asked about your salary, your bank accounts and other assets (such as cars, insurance policies and furnishings), and your outstanding loans; your record of loan, credit card and charge account repayments; the number of years you've worked and who your employers have been. You also are asked personal questions such as your age, marital status and number of children. The lender uses this information to evaluate how good a credit risk you are by calculating your credit score, a statistical measure derived from your answers that predicts whether you are likely to have trouble making your loan payments. Deciding on how good a risk you are cannot be entirely scientific, so the lender must also use judgement. The loan officer, whose job is to decide whether you should be given the loan, might call your employer or talk to some of the personal references you supplied. The officer might even make a judgement based on your demeanour or your appearance. (This is why most people dress neatly and conservatively when they go to a bank to apply for a loan.)

The process of screening and collecting information is similar when a financial institution makes a business loan. It collects information about the company's profits and losses (income) and about its assets and liabilities. The lender also has to evaluate the likely future success of the business. So in addition to obtaining information on such items as sales figures, a loan officer might ask questions about the company's future plans, the purpose of the loan, and the competition in the industry. The officer may even visit the company to obtain a first-hand look at its operations. The bottom line is that, whether for personal or business loans, bankers and other financial institutions need to be nosy.

Specialization in lending

One puzzling feature of bank lending is that a bank often specializes in lending to local firms or to firms in particular industries, such as energy. In one sense, this behaviour seems surprising, because it means that the bank is not diversifying its portfolio of loans and thus is exposing itself to more risk. But from another perspective, such specialization makes perfect sense. The adverse selection problem requires that the bank screen out bad credit risks. It is easier for the bank to collect information about local firms and determine their creditworthiness than to collect comparable information on firms that are far away. Similarly, by concentrating its lending on firms in specific industries, the bank becomes more knowledgeable about these industries and is therefore better able to predict which firms will be able to make timely payments on their debt.

Monitoring and enforcement of restrictive covenants

Once a loan has been made, the borrower has an incentive to engage in risky activities that make it less likely that the loan will be paid off. To reduce this moral hazard, financial institutions must adhere to the principle for managing credit risk that a lender should write provisions (restrictive covenants) into loan contracts that restrict borrowers from engaging in risky activities. By monitoring borrowers' activities to see whether they are complying with the restrictive covenants and by enforcing the covenants if they are not, lenders can make sure that borrowers are not taking on risks at their expense. The need for banks and other financial institutions to engage in screening and monitoring explains why they spend so much money on auditing and information-collecting activities.

Long-term customer relationships

An additional way for banks and other financial institutions to obtain information about their borrowers is through long-term customer relationships, another important principle of credit risk management.

If a prospective borrower has had a transactions (cheque) or savings account or other loans with a bank over a long period of time, a loan officer can look at past activity on the accounts and learn quite a bit about the borrower. The balances in the transaction and savings accounts tell the banker how liquid the potential borrower is and at what time of year the borrower has a strong need for cash. A review of the transactions the borrower has written reveals the borrower's suppliers. If the borrower has borrowed previously from the bank, the bank has a record of the loan payments. Thus long-term customer relationships reduce the costs of information collection and make it easier to screen out bad credit risks.

The need for monitoring by lenders adds to the importance of long-term customer relationships. If the borrower has borrowed from the bank before, the bank has already established procedures for monitoring that customer. Therefore, the costs of monitoring long-term customers are lower than those for new customers.

Long-term relationships benefit the customers as well as the bank. A firm with a previous relationship will find it easier to obtain a loan at a low interest rate because the bank has an easier time determining if the prospective borrower is a good credit risk and incurs fewer costs in monitoring the borrower.

A long-term customer relationship has another advantage for the bank. No bank can think of every contingency when it writes a restrictive covenant into a loan contract; there will always be risky borrower activities that are not ruled out. However, what if a borrower wants to preserve a long-term relationship with a bank because it will be easier to get future loans at low interest rates? The borrower then has the incentive to avoid risky activities that would upset the bank, even if restrictions on these risky activities are not specified in the loan contract. Indeed, if a bank doesn't like what a borrower is doing even when the borrower isn't violating any restrictive covenants, it has some power to discourage the borrower from such activity: the bank can threaten not to let the borrower have new loans in the future. Long-term customer relationships therefore enable banks to deal with even unanticipated moral hazard contingencies.

Loan commitments

Banks also create long-term relationships and gather information by issuing **loan commitments** to commercial customers. A loan commitment is a bank's commitment (for a specified future period of time) to provide a firm with loans up to a given amount at an interest rate that is tied to some market interest rate. The majority of commercial and industrial loans are made under the loan commitment arrangement. The advantage for the firm is that it has a source of credit when it needs it. The advantage for the bank is that the loan commitment promotes a long-term relationship, which in turn facilitates information collection. In addition, provisions in the loan commitment agreement require that the firm continually supply the bank with information about the firm's income, asset and liability position, business activities and so on. A loan commitment arrangement is a powerful method for reducing the bank's costs for screening and information collection.

Collateral and compensating balances

Collateral requirements for loans are important credit risk management tools. Collateral, which is property promised to the lender as compensation if the borrower defaults, lessens the consequences of adverse selection because it reduces the lender's losses in the case of a loan default. It also reduces moral hazard because the borrower has more to lose from a default. If a borrower defaults on a loan, the lender can sell the collateral and use the proceeds to make up for its losses on the loan. One particular form of collateral required when a bank makes commercial loans is called **compensating balances**: a firm receiving a loan must keep a required minimum amount of funds in a cheque account at the bank. For example, a business getting a €10 million loan may be required to keep compensating balances of at least €1 million in its cheque account at the bank. This €1 million in compensating balances can then be taken by the bank to make up some of the losses on the loan if the borrower defaults.

Besides serving as collateral, compensating balances help increase the likelihood that a loan will be paid off. They do this by helping the bank monitor the borrower and consequently reduce moral hazard. Specifically, by requiring the borrower to use a cheque account at the bank, the bank can observe the firm's cheque payment practices, which may yield a great deal of information about the borrower's financial condition. For example, a sustained drop in the borrower's cheque account balance may signal that the borrower is having financial trouble, or account activity may suggest that the borrower is engaging in risky activities; perhaps a change in suppliers means that the borrower is pursuing new lines of business. Any significant change in the borrower's payment procedures is a signal to the bank that it should make inquiries. Compensating balances therefore make it easier for banks to monitor borrowers more effectively and are another important credit risk management tool.

Credit rationing

Another way in which financial institutions deal with adverse selection and moral hazard is through **credit rationing**: refusing to make loans even though borrowers are willing to pay the stated interest rate or even a higher rate. Credit rationing takes two forms. The first occurs when a lender refuses to make a loan *of any amount* to a borrower, even if the borrower is willing to pay a higher interest rate. The second occurs when a lender is willing to make a loan but restricts the size of the loan to less than the borrower would like.

At first you might be puzzled by the first type of credit rationing. After all, even if the potential borrower is a credit risk, why doesn't the lender just extend the loan but at a higher interest rate? The answer is that adverse selection prevents this solution. Individuals and firms with the riskiest investment projects are exactly those that are willing to pay the highest interest rates. If a borrower took on a high-risk investment and succeeded, the borrower would become extremely rich. But a lender wouldn't want to make such a loan precisely because the credit risk is high; the likely outcome is that the borrower will *not* succeed and the lender will not be paid back. Charging a higher interest rate just makes adverse selection worse for the lender; that is, it increases the likelihood that the lender is lending to a bad credit risk. The lender would therefore rather not make any loans at a higher interest rate; instead, it would engage in the first type of credit rationing and would turn down loans.

Financial institutions engage in the second type of credit rationing to guard against moral hazard: they grant loans to borrowers, but not loans as large as the borrowers want. Such credit rationing is necessary because the larger the loan, the greater the benefits from moral hazard. If a bank gives you a €1,000 loan, for example, you are likely to take actions that enable you to pay it back because you don't want to hurt your credit rating for the future. However, if the bank lends you €10 million, you are more likely to fly to Rio to celebrate. The larger your loan, the greater your incentives to engage in activities that make it less likely that you will repay the loan. Because more borrowers repay their loans if the loan amounts are small, financial institutions ration credit by providing borrowers with smaller loans than they seek.

Managing interest-rate risk

With the increased volatility of interest rates that occurred in the 1980s, banks and other financial institutions became more concerned about their exposure to interest-rate risk, the riskiness of earnings and returns that is associated with changes in interest rates. To see what interest-rate risk is all about, let's again take a look at the First Euro Bank, which has the following balance sheet:

First Euro Bank			
Assets		**Liabilities**	
Rate-sensitive assets	€20 million	Rate-sensitive liabilities	€50 million
Variable-rate and short-term loans		Variable-rate CDs	
Short-term securities		Money market deposit accounts	
Fixed-rate assets	€80 million	Fixed-rate liabilities	€50 million
Reserves		Sight deposits	
Long-term loans		Savings deposits	
Long-term securities		Long-term CDs	
		Equity capital	

A total of €20 million of its assets are rate-sensitive, with interest rates that change frequently (at least once a year), and €80 million of its assets are fixed-rate, with interest rates that remain unchanged for a long period (over a year). On the liabilities side, the First Euro Bank has €50 million of rate-sensitive liabilities and €50 million of fixed-rate liabilities. Suppose that interest rates rise by 5 percentage points on average, from 10% to 15%. The income on the assets increases by €1 million (= 5% × €20 million of rate-sensitive assets), while the payments on the liabilities increase by €2.5 million (= 5% × €50 million of rate-sensitive liabilities). The First Euro Bank's profits now decline by €1.5 million (= €1 million − €2.5 million). Conversely, if interest rates fall by 5 percentage points, similar reasoning tells us that the First Euro Bank's profits increase by €1.5 million. This example illustrates the following point: *if a bank has more rate-sensitive liabilities than assets, a rise in interest rates will reduce bank profits and a decline in interest rates will raise bank profits*.

Gap and duration analysis

The sensitivity of bank profits to changes in interest rates can be measured more directly using gap analysis, in which the amount of rate-sensitive liabilities is subtracted from the amount of rate-sensitive assets. In our example, this calculation (called the 'gap') is −30 million (= €20 million − €50 million) By multiplying the gap times the change in the interest rate, we can immediately obtain the effect on bank profits. For example, when interest rates rise by 5 percentage points, the change in profits is 5% × −€30 million, which equals −€1.5 million, as we saw.

The analysis we just conducted is known as *basic gap analysis*, and it can be refined in two ways. Clearly, not all assets and liabilities in the fixed-rate category have the same maturity. One refinement, the *maturity bucket approach*, is to measure the gap for several maturity subintervals, called *maturity buckets*, so that effects of interest-rate changes over a multi-year period can be calculated. The second refinement, called *standardized gap analysis*, accounts for the differing degrees of rate sensitivity for different rate-sensitive assets and liabilities.

An alternative method for measuring interest-rate risk, called duration analysis, examines the sensitivity of the market value of the bank's total assets and liabilities to changes in interest rates. Duration analysis is based on what is known as Macaulay's concept of *duration*, which measures the average lifetime of a security's stream of payments.[3] Duration is a useful concept because it provides a good approximation of the sensitivity of a security's market value to a change in its interest rate:

$$\text{percent change in market value of security} \approx$$
$$- \text{ percentage-point change in interest rate} \times \text{duration in years}$$

where ≈ denotes 'approximately equals'.

Duration analysis involves using the average (weighted) duration of a financial institution's assets and of its liabilities to see how its net worth responds to a change in interest rates. Going back to our example of the First Euro Bank, suppose that the average duration of its assets is three years (that is, the average lifetime of the stream of payments is three years), while the average duration of its liabilities is two years. In addition, the First Euro Bank has €100 million of assets and, say, €90 million of liabilities, so its bank capital is 10% of assets. With a 5-percentage-point increase in interest rates, the market value of the bank's assets falls by (= −5% × 3 years), a decline of €15 million on the €100 million of assets. However, the market value of the liabilities falls by (= −5% × 2 years), a decline of €9 million on the €90 million of liabilities. The net result is that the net worth (the market value of the assets minus the liabilities) has declined by €6 million, or 6% of the total original asset value. Similarly, a 5-percentage-point decline in interest rates increases the net worth of the First Euro Bank by 6% of the total asset value.

As our example makes clear, both duration analysis and gap analysis indicate that the First Euro Bank will suffer if interest rates rise but will gain if they fall. Duration analysis and gap analysis are thus useful tools for telling a manager of a financial institution its degree of exposure to interest-rate risk.

APPLICATION   ## Strategies for managing interest-rate risk

Suppose that, as the manager of the First Euro Bank, you have done a duration and gap analysis for the bank as discussed in the text. Now you need to decide which alternative strategies you should pursue to manage the interest-rate risk.

If you firmly believe that interest rates will fall in the future, you may be willing to take no action because you know that the bank has more rate-sensitive liabilities than rate-sensitive assets and so will benefit from the expected interest-rate decline. However, you also realize that the First Euro Bank is subject to substantial interest-rate risk because there is always a possibility that interest rates will rise rather than fall. What should you do to eliminate this interest-rate risk? One thing you could do is to shorten the duration of the bank's assets to increase their rate sensitivity. Alternatively, you could lengthen the duration of the liabilities. By this adjustment of the bank's assets and liabilities, the bank's income will be less affected by interest-rate swings.

One problem with eliminating the First Euro Bank's interest-rate risk by altering the balance sheet is that doing so might be very costly in the short run. The bank may be locked into assets and liabilities of particular durations because of where its expertise lies. Fortunately, recently developed financial instruments known as financial derivatives – financial forwards and futures, options and swaps – can help the bank reduce its interest-rate risk exposure but do not require that the bank rearrange its balance sheet.

Off-balance-sheet activities

Although asset and liability management has traditionally been the major concern of banks, in the more competitive environment of recent years banks have been aggressively seeking out profits by engaging in off-balance-sheet activities.[4] **Off-balance-sheet activities** involve trading financial instruments and generating income from fees and loan sales, activities that affect bank profits but do not appear on bank balance sheets. Indeed, off-balance-sheet activities have been growing in importance for banks: the income from these activities as a percentage of assets has nearly doubled since 1980.

Loan sales

One type of off-balance-sheet activity that has grown in importance in recent years involves income generated by loan sales. A **loan sale**, also called a *secondary loan participation*, involves a contract that sells all or part of the cash stream from a specific loan and thereby removes the loan so that it no longer is an asset on the bank's balance sheet. Banks earn profits by selling loans for an amount slightly greater than the amount of the original loan. Because the high interest rate on these loans makes them attractive, institutions are willing to buy them, even though the higher price means that they earn a slightly lower interest rate than the original interest rate on the loan, usually of the order of 0.15 percentage point.

Generation of fee income

Another type of off-balance-sheet activity involves the generation of income from fees that banks receive for providing specialized services to their customers, such as making foreign exchange trades on a customer's behalf, servicing a mortgage-backed security by collecting interest and principal payments and then paying them out, guaranteeing debt securities such as banker's acceptances (by which the bank promises to make interest and principal payments if the party issuing the security cannot), and providing backup lines of credit. There are several types of backup lines of credit. We have already mentioned the most important, the loan commitment, under which for a fee the bank agrees to provide a loan at the customer's request, up to a given euro amount, over a specified period of time. Credit lines are also now available to bank depositors with 'overdraft privileges' – these bank customers can write cheques or withdraw funds in excess of their deposit balances and, in effect, write themselves a loan. Other lines of credit for which banks get fees include standby letters of credit to back up issues of commercial paper and other securities and credit lines (called *note issuance facilities*, NIFs, and *revolving underwriting facilities*, RUFs) for underwriting Euronotes, which are medium-term Eurobonds.

You can see how important this source of revenue is to banks by examining the generation of net commissions and fees in Table 10.3. Net commission income was 31% of the net revenues of Deutsche Bank in 2010.

Off-balance-sheet activities involving guarantees of securities and backup credit lines increase the risk a bank faces. Even though a guaranteed security does not appear on a bank's balance sheet, it still exposes the bank to default risk: if the issuer of the security defaults, the bank is left holding the bag and must pay off the security's owner. Backup credit lines also expose the bank to risk because the bank may be forced to provide loans when it does not have sufficient liquidity or when the borrower is a very poor credit risk.

Banks also earn fees by creating financial instruments like the structured investment vehicles (SIVs) mentioned earlier and selling them off to investors. However, as became clear during the subprime financial crisis starting in 2008, when they decline in value, many of these financial instruments have to be taken back onto the balance sheet of the bank (like Citigroup) sponsoring them, because to do otherwise would severely damage the reputation of the bank. Even though these financial instruments at first appear to be off-balance-sheet, in reality they are back on the balance sheet if they are subjected to large losses. To their regret, banks such as Citigroup ended up taking large losses on these financial instruments during the subprime financial crisis, indicating that these off-balance-sheet vehicles exposed banks to just as much risk as if they had been part of their balance sheets from the outset.

Trading activities and risk management techniques

We have already mentioned that banks' attempts to manage interest-rate risk led them to trading in financial futures, options for debt instruments and interest-rate swaps. Banks engaged in international banking also conduct transactions in the foreign exchange market. All transactions in these markets are off-balance-sheet activities because they do not have a direct effect on the bank's balance sheet. Although bank trading in these markets is often directed toward reducing risk or facilitating other bank business, banks also try to outguess the markets and engage in speculation. This speculation can be a very risky business and indeed has led to bank insolvencies, the most dramatic being the failure of Barings, a British bank, in 1995. But it is also one of the ways profit is generated from its investment arm. In 2010, Deutsche Bank earned 14% of its net revenues from the profits from trading activity.

Trading activities, although often highly profitable, are dangerous because they make it easy for financial institutions and their employees to make huge bets quickly. A particular problem for management of trading activities is that the principal–agent problem, discussed in Chapter 8, is especially severe. Given the ability to place large bets, a trader (the agent), whether she trades in bond markets, in foreign exchange markets or in financial derivatives, has an incentive to take on excessive risks: if her trading strategy leads to large profits, she is likely to receive a high salary and bonuses, but if she takes large losses, the financial institution (the principal) will have to cover them. As the Barings Bank failure in 1995 so forcefully demonstrated, a trader subject to the principal–agent problem can take an institution that is quite healthy and drive it into insolvency very rapidly (see the Global box).

To reduce the principal–agent problem, managers of financial institutions must set up internal controls to prevent debacles like the one at Barings. Such controls include the complete separation of the people in charge of trading activities from those in charge of the bookkeeping for trades. In addition, managers must set limits on the total amount of traders' transactions and on the institution's risk exposure. Managers must also scrutinize risk assessment procedures using the latest computer technology. One such method involves the value-at-risk approach. In this approach, the institution develops a statistical model with which it can calculate the maximum loss that its portfolio is likely to sustain over a given

GLOBAL

Barings, Daiwa, Sumitomo and Société Générale: rogue traders and the principal–agent problem

The demise of Barings, a venerable British bank more than a century old, is a sad morality tale of how the principal–agent problem operating through a rogue trader can take a financial institution that has a healthy balance sheet one month and turn it into an insolvent tragedy the next.

In July 1992, Nick Leeson, Barings' new head clerk at its Singapore branch, began to speculate on the Nikkei, the Japanese version of the Dow Jones stock index. By late 1992, Leeson had suffered losses of $3 million, which he hid from his superiors by stashing the losses in a secret account. He even fooled his superiors into thinking he was generating large profits, thanks to a failure of internal controls at his firm, which allowed him to execute trades on the Singapore exchange *and* oversee the bookkeeping of those trades. (As anyone who runs a cash business, such as a bar, knows, there is always a lower likelihood of fraud if more than one person handles the cash. Similarly for trading operations, you never mix management of the back room with management of the front room; this principle was grossly violated by Barings management.)

Things didn't get better for Leeson, who by late 1994 had losses exceeding $250 million. In January and February 1995, he bet the net worth of the bank. On 17 January 1995, the day of the earthquake at Kobe in Japan, he lost €75 million, and by the end of the week he had lost more than $150 million. When the stock market declined on 23 February, leaving him with a further loss of $250 million, he called it quits and fled Singapore. Three days later, he turned himself in at Frankfurt airport. By the end of his wild ride, Leeson's losses, $1.3 billion in all, ate up Barings' capital and caused the bank to fail. Leeson was subsequently convicted and sent to jail in Singapore for his activities. He was released in 1999 and apologized for his actions.

Our asymmetric information analysis of the principal–agent problem explains Leeson's behaviour and the danger of Barings' management lapse. By letting Leeson control both his own trades and the back room, it increased asymmetric information, because it reduced the principal's (Barings') knowledge about Leeson's trading activities. This lapse increased the moral hazard incentive for him to take risks at the bank's expense, as he was now less likely to be caught. Furthermore, once he had experienced large losses, he had even greater incentives to take on even higher risk because if his bets worked out, he could reverse his losses and keep in good standing with the company, whereas if his bets soured, he had little to lose because he was out of a job anyway. Indeed, the bigger his losses, the more he had to gain by bigger bets, which explains the escalation of the amount of his trades as his losses mounted. If Barings' managers had understood the principal–agent problem, they would have been more vigilant at finding out what Leeson was up to, and the bank might still be here today.

Unfortunately, Nick Leeson is no longer a rarity in the rogue traders' billionaire club, those who have lost more than $1 billion. Over eleven years, Toshihide Iguchi, an officer in the New York branch of Daiwa Bank, also had control of both the bond trading operation and the back room, and he racked up $1.1 billion in losses over the period. In July 1995, Iguchi disclosed his losses to his superiors, but the management of the bank did not disclose them to its regulators. The result was that Daiwa was slapped with a $340 million fine and the bank was thrown out of the country by US bank regulators.

Yasuo Hamanaka is another member of the billionaire club. In July 1996, he topped Leeson's and Iguchi's record, losing $2.6 billion for his employer, the Sumitomo Corporation, one of Japan's top trading companies. Jerome Kerviel's loss for his bank, Société Générale, in January 2008 set the all-time record for a rogue trader: His unauthorized trades cost the French bank $7.2 billion.

The moral of these stories is that management of firms engaged in trading activities must reduce the principal–agent problem by closely monitoring their traders' activities, or the rogues' gallery will continue to grow.

time interval, dubbed the value at risk, or VaR. For example, a bank might estimate that the maximum loss it would be likely to sustain over one day with a probability of 1 in 100 is €1 million; the €1 million figure is the bank's calculated value at risk. Another approach is called 'stress testing'. In this approach, a manager asks models what would happen if a doomsday scenario occurs; that is, she looks at the losses the institution would sustain if an unusual combination of bad events occurred. With the value-at-risk approach and stress testing, a financial institution can assess its risk exposure and take steps to reduce it.

Bank regulators have become concerned about the increased risk that banks are facing from their off-balance-sheet activities, and, as we will see in Chapter 11, are encouraging banks to pay increased attention to risk management. In addition, the Bank for International Settlements is developing additional bank capital requirements based on value-at-risk calculations for a bank's trading activities.

Summary

1 The balance sheet of commercial banks can be thought of as a list of the sources and uses of bank funds. The bank's liabilities are its sources of funds, which include sight deposits, time deposits, loans from the central bank, borrowings from other banks and corporations, and bank capital. The bank's assets are its uses of funds, which include reserves, cash items in process of collection, deposits at other banks, securities, loans and other assets (mostly physical capital).

2 Banks make profits through the process of asset transformation: they borrow short (accept deposits) and lend long (make loans). When a bank takes in additional deposits, it gains an equal amount of reserves; when it pays out deposits, it loses an equal amount of reserves.

3 Although more-liquid assets tend to earn lower returns, banks still desire to hold them. Specifically, banks hold excess and secondary reserves because they provide insurance against the costs of a deposit outflow. Banks manage their assets to maximize profits by seeking the highest returns possible on loans and securities while at the same time trying to lower risk and making adequate provisions for liquidity. Although liability management was once a staid affair, large banks now actively seek out sources of funds by issuing liabilities such as negotiable CDs or by actively borrowing from other banks and corporations. Banks manage the amount of capital they hold to prevent bank failure and to

meet bank capital requirements set by the regulatory authorities. However, they do not want to hold too much capital because by so doing they will lower the returns to equity holders.

4 The concepts of adverse selection and moral hazard explain many credit risk management principles involving loan activities: screening and monitoring, establishment of long-term customer relationships and loan commitments, collateral and compensating balances, and credit rationing.

5 With the increased volatility of interest rates that occurred in the 1980s, financial institutions became more concerned about their exposure to interest-rate risk. Gap and duration analyses tell a financial institution if it has more rate-sensitive liabilities than assets (in which case a rise in interest rates will reduce profits and a fall in interest rates will raise profits). Financial institutions manage their interest-rate risk by modifying their balance sheets but can also use strategies involving financial derivatives.

6 Off-balance-sheet activities consist of trading financial instruments and generating income from fees and loan sales, all of which affect bank profits but are not visible on bank balance sheets. Because these off-balance-sheet activities expose banks to increased risk, bank management must pay particular attention to risk assessment procedures and internal controls to restrict employees from taking on too much risk.

Key terms

asset management p. 213

balance sheet p. 205

capital adequacy management p. 213

compensating balance p. 223

credit rationing p. 223

credit risk p. 213

deposit outflows p. 213

duration analysis p. 225

equity multiplier (EM) p. 218

excess reserves p. 208

gap analysis p. 225

interest-rate risk p. 213

liability management p. 213

liquidity management p. 213

loan commitment p. 223

loan sale p. 226

maturity transformation p. 210

off-balance-sheet activities p. 226

required reserve ratio p. 208

required reserves p. 208

reserve requirements p. 208

reserves p. 208

return on assets (ROA) p. 218

return on equity (ROE) p. 218

secondary reserves p. 208

sight deposit p. 207

t-account p. 211

time deposit p. 207

vault cash p. 208

QUESTIONS AND PROBLEMS

All questions and problems are available in MyEconLab at **www.myeconlab.com/mishkin**.

1 Why might a bank be willing to borrow funds from other banks at a higher rate than it can borrow from the relevant central bank?

2 Rank the following bank assets from most to least liquid:

(a) Commercial loans
(b) Securities
(c) Reserves
(d) Physical capital

3 Using the T-accounts of the First Euro Bank and the Second Euro Bank, describe what happens when Ingrid Schmidt writes a €50 cheque on her account at the First Euro Bank to pay her friend Joe Green, who in turn deposits the cheque in his account at the Second Euro Bank.

4 What happens to reserves at the First Euro Bank if one person withdraws €1,000 of cash and another person deposits €500 of cash? Use T-accounts to explain your answer.

5 The bank you own has the following balance sheet:

Assets		Liabilities	
Reserves	€75 million	Deposits	€500 million
Loans	€525 million	Bank capital	€100 million

If the bank suffers a deposit outflow of €50 million with a required reserve ratio on deposits of 10%, what actions must you take to keep your bank from failing?

6 If a deposit outflow of €50 million occurs, which balance sheet would a bank rather have initially, the balance sheet in Problem 5 or the following balance sheet? Why?

Assets		Liabilities	
Reserves	€100 million	Deposits	€500 million
Loans	€500 million	Bank capital	€100 million

7 Why has the development of overnight loan markets made it more likely that banks will hold fewer excess reserves?

8 If the bank you own has no excess reserves and a sound customer comes in asking for a loan, should you automatically turn the customer down, explaining that you don't have any excess reserves to lend out? Why or why not? What options are available for you to provide the funds your customer needs?

9 If a bank finds that its Return on Equity (ROE) is too low because it has too much bank capital, what can it do to raise its ROE?

10 If a bank is falling short of meeting its capital requirements by €1 million, what three things can it do to rectify the situation?

11 Why is being nosy a desirable trait for a banker?

12 A bank almost always insists that the firms it lends to keep compensating balances at the bank. Why?

13 'Because diversification is a desirable strategy for avoiding risk, it never makes sense for a bank to specialize in making specific types of loans.' Is this statement true, false, or uncertain? Explain your answer.

14 Suppose that you are the manager of a bank whose €100 billion of assets have an average duration of four years and whose €90 billion of liabilities have an average duration of six years. Conduct a duration analysis for the bank, and show what will happen to the net worth of the bank if interest rates rise by 2 percentage points. What actions could you take to reduce the bank's interest-rate risk?

15 Suppose that you are the manager of a bank that has €15 million of fixed-rate assets, €30 million of rate-sensitive assets, €25 million of fixed-rate liabilities and €20 million of rate-sensitive liabilities. Conduct a gap analysis for the bank, and show what will happen to bank profits if interest rates rise by 5 percentage points. What actions could you take to reduce the bank's interest-rate risk?

WEB EXERCISES

1 Table 10.1 reports the balance sheet of all commercial banks based on aggregate data in the euro area. Compare this table to the most recent balance sheet reported by Deutsche Bank. Go to **www.deutsche–bank.de/ir/en/content/reports.htm** and click on Annual Reports to view the balance sheet. Does Bank of America have more or less of its portfolio in loans than the average bank? Which type of loan is most common?

2 It is relatively easy to find up-to-date information on banks because of their extensive reporting requirements. Go to **www.eba.europa.eu/Supervisory-Disclosure /Statistical-Data.aspx**. This is the site of the newly established European Banking Authority (EBA). You will find summary data on EU financial institutions. Go to the most recent Excel file on national banking statistics.

(a) Which country has the highest equity multiplier in the EU?

(b) Which country has the highest increase in core capital in the two most recent years?

(c) Which country has the largest number of financial institutions reporting to the EBA?

Notes

1 One way that the First Euro Bank can borrow from other banks and corporations is by selling negotiable certificates of deposit. This method for obtaining funds is discussed in the section on liability management.

2 Other financial intermediaries, such as insurance companies, pension funds and finance companies, also make private loans, and the credit risk management principles we outline here apply to them as well.

3 Algebraically, Macaulay's duration, D, is defined as

$$D = \sum_{\tau=1}^{N} \tau \frac{CP_\tau}{(1 + i)} \bigg/ \sum_{\tau=1}^{N} \tau \frac{CP_\tau}{(1 + i)}$$

where

τ = time until cash payment is made
CP_τ = cash payment (interest plus principal) at time τ
i = interest rate
N = time to maturity of the security

For a more detailed discussion of duration gap analysis using the concept of Macaulay's duration, you can look at an appendix to this chapter that is on this book's website at **www.myeconlab.com/mishkin**.

4 Managers of financial institutions also need to know how well their banks are doing at any point in time. A second appendix to this chapter discusses how bank performance is measured; it can be found on the book's website at **www.myeconlab.com/mishkin**.

Useful websites

www.deutsche-bank.de/ir/en/content/reports.htm Click on the year for the Annual Reports to view the balance sheet.

www.eba.europa.eu/Home.aspx Click on supervisory disclosure and then on statistics to obtain EU-wide statistics on bank assets and capital adequacy. Similar data for Germany only can be found on **www.bundesbank.de/sdtf/index4.htm**.

www.federalreserve.gov/boarddocs/SupManual/default.htm#trading The Federal Reserve Bank Trading and Capital Market Activities Manual offers an in-depth discussion of a wide range of risk management issues encountered in trading operations.

MyEconLab can help you get a better grade

MyEconLab®

If your exam were tomorrow, would you be ready? For each chapter, MyEconLab Practice Test and Study Plans pinpoint which sections you have mastered and which ones you need to study. That way, you are more efficient with your study time, and you are better prepared for your exams.

To see how it works, turns to page 19 and then go to **www.myeconlab.com/mishkin**

CHAPTER 11

Economic analysis of financial regulation

PREVIEW

As we have seen in the previous chapters, the financial system is among the most heavily regulated sectors of the economy, and banks are among the most heavily regulated of financial institutions. In this chapter, we develop an economic analysis of why regulation of the financial system takes the form it does.

Unfortunately, the regulatory process may not always work very well, as evidenced by the subprime meltdown and other financial crises, in Europe, the United States and many other countries throughout the world. Here we also use our economic analysis of financial regulation to explain the worldwide crises in banking and to consider how the regulatory system can be reformed to prevent future disasters.

Asymmetric information and financial regulation

In earlier chapters, we have seen how asymmetric information – the fact that different parties in a financial contract do not have the same information – leads to adverse selection and moral hazard problems that have an important impact on the financial system. The concepts of asymmetric information, adverse selection and moral hazard are especially useful in understanding why government has chosen the form of financial regulation we see in Europe and in other countries. There are eight basic categories of financial regulation: the government safety net, restrictions on asset holdings, capital requirements, prompt corrective action, licensing and examination, assessment of risk management, disclosure requirements, and consumer protection.

Government safety net

As we saw in Chapter 8, financial intermediaries, like banks, are particularly well suited to solving adverse selection and moral hazard problems because they make private loans that help avoid the free-rider problem. However, this solution to the free-rider problem creates another asymmetric information problem, because depositors lack information about the quality of these private loans. This asymmetric information problem leads to several reasons why the financial system might not function well.

Bank panics and the need for deposit insurance

Before the existence of deposit insurance, a **bank failure** (in which a bank is unable to meet its obligations to pay its depositors and other creditors and so must go out of business) meant that depositors would have to wait to get their deposit funds until the bank was liquidated (until its assets had been turned into cash); at that time, they would be paid only a fraction of the value of their deposits. Unable to learn if bank managers were taking on too much risk or were outright crooks, depositors would be reluctant to put money in the bank, thus making banking institutions less viable. Second, depositors' lack of information about the quality of bank assets can lead to bank panics, which, as we saw in Chapter 9, can have serious harmful consequences for the economy. To see this, consider the following situation. There is no deposit insurance, and an adverse shock hits the economy. As a result of the shock, 5% of the banks have such large losses on loans that they become insolvent (have a negative net worth and so are bankrupt). Because of asymmetric information, depositors are unable to tell whether their bank is a good bank or one of the 5% that are insolvent. Depositors at bad *and* good banks recognize that they may not get back 100 cents on the euro for their deposits and will want to withdraw them. Indeed, because banks operate on a 'sequential service constraint' (a first-come, first-served basis), depositors have a very strong incentive to show up at the bank first, because if they are last in line, the bank may run out of funds and they will get nothing. Uncertainty about the health of the banking system in general can lead to runs on banks both good and bad, and the failure of one bank can hasten the failure of others (referred to as the *contagion effect*). If nothing is done to restore the public's confidence, a bank panic can ensue.

Bank panics have existed throughout history and were typically associated with bad harvests and speculative bubbles such as the Dutch tulip mania (1634–7) and the British South Sea bubble (1717–19). But bank runs were commonplace in the US in the nineteenth and early twentieth centuries, with major ones occurring every 20 years or so, in 1819, 1837, 1857, 1873, 1884, 1893, 1907 and 1930–3. Bank failures were a serious problem even during the boom years of the 1920s, when the number of bank failures averaged around 600 per year. In September 2007 the British bank Northern Rock faced a bank run that witnessed long lines of depositors patiently waiting to withdraw their deposits. Other types of runs are the quiet ones that do not see lines of depositors withdrawing funds but other banks and financial institutions withdrawing funds from an individual bank. A silent run on the investment bank Bear-Stearns in March 2008 was only halted when the Federal Reserve Bank of New York helped JPMorgan Chase acquire it.

A government safety net for depositors can short-circuit runs on banks and bank panics, and by providing protection for the depositor, it can overcome reluctance to put funds in the banking system. One form of the safety net is deposit insurance, a guarantee such as that provided by the central bank or government-backed deposit insurance institutions such as the Federal Deposit Insurance Corporation (FDIC) in the United States in which depositors are paid off in full on the first $100,000 they have deposited in a bank if the bank fails. (FDIC coverage was temporarily raised to $250,000 during the subprime financial crisis in October 2008.) With fully insured deposits, depositors don't need to run to the bank to make withdrawals – even if they are worried about the bank's health – because in many cases their deposits will be worth 100 cents on the dollar no matter what. From 1930 to 1933, the years immediately preceding the creation of the FDIC, the number of bank failures averaged more than 2,000 per year. After the establishment of the FDIC in 1934, bank failures averaged fewer than 15 per year until 1981.

Deposit insurance is an accepted part of the landscape of government safety net arrangements. Table 11.1 shows the extent and coverage of deposit insurance in the European Union. In recent years, government deposit insurance has grown in popularity and has spread to many countries throughout the world. Whether this trend is desirable is discussed in the Global box, 'The spread of government deposit insurance throughout the world: is this a good thing?'

Other forms of the government safety net

Deposit insurance is not the only form of government safety net. Governments have often stood ready to provide support to domestic banks facing runs even in the absence of explicit deposit insurance. Furthermore, banks are not the only financial intermediaries

> **TABLE 11.1**
>
> **Deposit insurance in the European Union**
>
> In response to the global banking crisis in 2008 the countries of the EU widened the scope and coverage of their individual deposit insurance schemes. Below is a list of the deposit insurance schemes of the countries of the European Union.
>
> | Country | Limit | Coverage | History |
> |---------|-------|----------|---------|
> | Belgium | €100,000 | 100% | €20,000 before 2009 |
> | Bulgaria | €100,000 | 100% | Valid since 31 December 2010. Previously €51,129 |
> | Czech Republic | €100,000 | 100% | Since 2002, 90% of deposits up to €25,000. In 2008 100% up to €50,000. 2011 limit increased to €100,000 |
> | Denmark | Kr750,000 | 100% | Valid 30 September 2010. In period October 2008 – September 2010 the coverage was unlimited |
> | Finland | €100,000 | 100% | Since 1998, increased from €25,000 to €50,000 on October 2008 and €100,000 since 1 January 2011 |
> | France | €100,000 | 100% | |
> | Germany | €100,000 | 100% | |
> | Ireland | Unlimited | 100% | Since September 2008 |
> | Italy | €103,291 | 100% | Since December 1996 |
> | Netherlands | €100,000 | 100% | October 2008. Previously 100% of first €20,000 and 90% of next €20,000 |
> | Poland | €100,000 | 100% | Raised from €50,000 on December 2010 |
> | Portugal | €100,000 | 100% | Raised from €25,000 in November 2008 |
> | Slovakia | Unlimited | 100% | Since July 2010 |
> | Spain | €100,000 | 100% | |
> | Sweden | SKr500,000 | 100% | Since October 2008. Previously SKr250,000 |
> | United Kingdom | £85,000 | 100% | Since January 2011. Previously 100% of first £2,000 and 90% of £2,000 – £35,000 until October 2008 when the ceiling was raised to £50,000 |
>
> *Source:* Based on various web sources.

that can pose a systemic threat to the financial system, as our discussion of financial crises in Chapter 9 has illustrated. When financial institutions are very large or highly interconnected with other financial institutions or markets, their failure has the potential to bring down the entire financial system.

One way governments provide support is through lending from the central bank to troubled institutions, as the Federal Reserve did during the subprime financial crisis. This form of support is often referred to as the 'lender of last resort' role of the central bank. In other cases, funds are provided directly to troubled institutions, as was done by the Bank of England in 2008 during a particularly virulent phase of the financial crisis. Governments can also take over (nationalize) troubled institutions and guarantee that all creditors will be repaid their loans in full. Following the banking crisis the UK government took a 43% stake in the Lloyds Banking Group in 2009. In 2008 the Royal Bank of Scotland Group, one of the largest banks in the world, received a capital injection from the UK government which took a share of 60% of the company. In 2009 a further capital injection took the

GLOBAL
The spread of government deposit insurance throughout the world: is this a good thing?

For the first 30 years after federal deposit insurance was established in the United States, only six countries emulated the United States and adopted deposit insurance. However, this began to change in the late 1960s, with the trend accelerating in the 1990s, when the number of countries adopting deposit insurance topped 70. Government deposit insurance has taken off throughout the world because of growing concern about the health of banking systems, particularly after the increasing number of banking crises in recent years (documented at the end of this chapter). As a result of the 2008 global banking crisis even more countries like New Zealand that never had deposit insurance have introduced it. By June 2008 there were 99 countries with deposit insurance in operation. Has this spread of deposit insurance been a good thing? Has it helped improve the performance of the financial system and prevent banking crises?

The answer seems to be no under many circumstances. Research at the World Bank has found that, on average, the adoption of explicit government deposit insurance is associated with less banking sector stability and a higher incidence of banking crises.* Furthermore, on average, it seems to retard financial development. However, the negative effects of deposit insurance appear only in countries with weak institutional environments: an absence of rule of law, ineffective regulation and supervision of the financial sector, and high corruption. This is exactly what might be expected because, as we will see later in this chapter, a strong institutional environment is needed to limit the moral hazard incentives for banks to engage in the excessively risky behaviour encouraged by deposit insurance.
The problem is that developing a strong institutional environment may be very difficult to achieve in many emerging market countries. This leaves us with the following conclusion: adoption of deposit insurance may be exactly the wrong medicine for promoting stability and efficiency of banking systems in emerging market countries.

* See World Bank, *Finance for Growth: Policy Choices in a Volatile World* (Oxford: World Bank and Oxford University Press, 2001).

government stake in the bank to 84%. The DEXIA Group is a Franco-Belgian banking group that came under pressure during the financial crisis of 2008 and received direct capital injections from the Belgian and French governments totalling €6 billion. Following a €4 billion loss announced in July 2011 after marking down the value of Greek bond holdings, the Belgian government announced the purchase of the Belgian arm of the bank for €4 billion. Similarly, in October 2008 the Dutch government purchased a 49% stake in the Dutch operations of Fortis Bank.

Moral hazard and the government safety net

Although a government safety net can help protect depositors and other creditors and prevent, or ameliorate, financial crises, it is a mixed blessing. The most serious drawback of the government safety net stems from moral hazard, the incentives of one party to a transaction to engage in activities detrimental to the other party. Moral hazard is an important concern in insurance arrangements in general because the existence of insurance provides increased incentives for taking risks that might result in an insurance payoff. For example, some drivers with automobile collision insurance that has a low excess might be more likely to drive recklessly, because if they get into an accident, the insurance company pays most of the costs for damage and repairs.

Moral hazard is a prominent concern in government arrangements to provide a safety net. With a safety net depositors and creditors know that they will not suffer losses if a financial institution fails, so they do not impose the discipline of the marketplace on these institutions by withdrawing funds when they suspect that the financial institution is taking on too much risk. Consequently, financial institutions with a government safety net have an incentive to take on greater risks than they otherwise would, with taxpayers paying the bill if the bank subsequently goes belly up. Financial institutions have been given the following bet: 'Heads I win, tails the taxpayer loses'.

Adverse selection and the government safety net

A further problem with a government safety net like deposit insurance arises because of adverse selection, the fact that the people who are most likely to produce the adverse outcome insured against (bank failure) are those who most want to take advantage of the insurance. For example, bad drivers are more likely than good drivers to take out automobile collision insurance with a low deductible. Because depositors and creditors protected by a government safety net have little reason to impose discipline on financial institutions, risk-loving entrepreneurs might find the financial industry a particularly attractive one to enter – they know that they will be able to engage in highly risky activities. Even worse, because protected depositors and creditors have so little reason to monitor the financial institution's activities, without government intervention outright crooks might also find finance an attractive industry for their activities because it is easy for them to get away with fraud and embezzlement.

'Too big to fail'

The moral hazard created by a government safety net and the desire to prevent financial institution failures have presented financial regulators with a particular quandary. Because the failure of a very large financial institution makes it more likely that a major financial disruption will occur, financial regulators are naturally reluctant to allow a big institution to fail and cause losses to its depositors and creditors.

The term 'too big to fail' was first used in the bailout of Continental Illinois, one of the ten largest banks in the United States when it became insolvent in May 1984. Not only did the FDIC guarantee depositors up to the $100,000 insurance limit, but it also guaranteed accounts exceeding $100,000 and even prevented losses for Continental Illinois bondholders. Shortly thereafter, the Comptroller of the Currency (the regulator of national banks) testified to Congress that eleven of the largest banks would receive a similar treatment to that of Continental Illinois. The term 'too big to fail', which was actually used by US politician Stewart McKinney in those hearings, is now applied to a policy in which the government provides guarantees of repayment of large uninsured creditors of the largest banks, so that no depositor or creditor suffers a loss, even when they are not automatically entitled to this guarantee. The deposit insurance guarantors (typically the central bank) would do this by using the purchase and assumption method, giving the insolvent bank a large infusion of capital and then finding a willing merger partner to take over the bank and its deposits. The too-big-to-fail policy was extended to big banks that were not even among the eleven largest. In fact the term 'too big to fail' is somewhat misleading because when a financial institution is closed or merged into another financial institution, the managers are usually fired and the stockholders in the financial institution lose their investment.

One problem with the too-big-to-fail policy is that it increases the moral hazard incentives for big banks. If the central bank were willing to close a bank using the payoff method, paying depositors only up to the €100,000 limit, large depositors with more than €100,000 would suffer losses if the bank failed. Thus they would have an incentive to monitor the bank by examining the bank's activities closely and pulling their money out if the bank was taking on too much risk. To prevent such a loss of deposits, the bank would be more likely to engage in less risky activities. However, once large depositors know that a bank is too big to fail, they have no incentive to monitor the bank and pull out their deposits when it takes on too much risk: no matter what the bank does, large depositors will not suffer any losses. The result of the too-big-to-fail policy is that big banks might take on even greater risks, thereby making bank failures more likely.[1]

Similarly, the too-big-to-fail policy increases the moral hazard incentives for non-bank financial institutions that are extended a government safety net. Knowing that the financial institution will get bailed out, creditors have little incentive to monitor the institution and pull their money out when the institution is taking on excessive risk. As a result, large or interconnected financial institutions will be more likely to engage in highly risky activities, making it more likely that a financial crisis will occur.

'Too important to fail'

The problem of moral hazard could occur even if the safety net was not provided by the government or a government-sponsored agency. If the central bank organized a bailout of a financial institution that was in trouble because it thought that failure would infect the rest of the financial system, even though it may not commit public funds to the exercise, the intervention alone could create moral hazard. In 1998 a hedge fund called Long Term Capital Management (LTCM) was on the verge of filing for bankruptcy. Many large financial institutions in New York and in the rest of the world were heavily exposed to LTCM. Fearing that a collapse of the hedge fund could lead to the failure of other financial institutions resulting in a run on the banks in New York, the Federal Reserve Bank of New York organized a bailout of $3.62 million with LTCM's main creditors to recapitalize the hedge fund. The criticism of the Fed's action was that the intervention helped the shareholders and managers to get a better deal than they otherwise would have (an alternative deal led by Warren Buffet was rejected by the LTCM board). This is not so much an example of 'too big to fail' as 'too important to fail'.

Financial consolidation and the government safety net

With financial innovation and the globalization of banking, financial consolidation has been proceeding at a rapid pace, leading to both larger and more complex financial organizations. Financial consolidation poses two challenges to financial regulation because of the existence of the government safety net. First, the increased size of financial institutions as a result of financial consolidation increases the too-big-to-fail problem, because there will now be more large institutions whose failure would expose the financial system to systemic (system-wide) risk. Thus more financial institutions are likely to be treated as too big to fail, and the increased moral hazard incentives for these large institutions to take on greater risk can then increase the fragility of the financial system. Second, financial consolidation of banks with other financial services firms means that the government safety net may be extended to new activities such as securities underwriting, insurance or real estate activities, as has occurred in the US with government support for Fannie Mae and Freddie Mac, the two large mortgage providers, and AIG, the global insurance company, during the subprime financial crisis in 2008. This increases incentives for greater risk taking in these activities that can also weaken the fabric of the financial system. Limiting the moral hazard incentives for the larger, more complex financial organizations that have arisen as a result of recent changes in legislation will be one of the key issues facing banking regulators in the aftermath of the subprime financial crisis.

Restrictions on asset holdings

As we have seen, the moral hazard associated with a government safety net encourages too much risk taking on the part of financial institutions. Bank regulations that restrict asset holdings are directed at minimizing this moral hazard, which can cost the taxpayers dearly.

Even in the absence of a government safety net, financial institutions still have the incentive to take on too much risk. Risky assets may provide the financial institution with higher earnings when they pay off; but if they do not pay off and the institution fails, depositors and creditors are left holding the bag. If depositors and creditors were able to monitor the bank easily by acquiring information on its risk-taking activities, they would immediately withdraw their funds if the institution was taking on too much risk. To prevent such a loss of funds, the institution would be more likely to reduce its risk-taking activities. Unfortunately, acquiring information on an institution's activities to learn how much risk it is taking can be a difficult task. Hence most depositors and many creditors are incapable of imposing discipline that might prevent financial institutions from engaging in risky activities. A strong rationale for government regulation to reduce risk taking on the part of financial institutions therefore existed even before the establishment of government safety nets.

Because banks are most prone to panics, they are subjected to strict regulations to restrict their holding of risky assets such as common stocks. Bank regulations also promote diversification, which reduces risk by limiting the euro amount of loans in particular categories or to individual borrowers. For example different countries apply different maximum loan-to-value (mortgage loan relative to the value of the property) regulations to mortgages from 60% in Germany to 80% in Denmark. With the extension of the government safety net during the subprime financial crisis, it is likely that non-bank financial institutions may face greater restrictions on their holdings of risky assets. There is a danger, however, that these restrictions may become so onerous that the efficiency of the financial system will be impaired.

Capital requirements

Government-imposed capital requirements are another way of minimizing moral hazard at financial institutions. When a financial institution is forced to hold a large amount of equity capital, the institution has more to lose if it fails and is thus more likely to pursue less risky activities. In addition, as was illustrated in Chapter 10, capital functions as a cushion when bad shocks occur, making it less likely that the financial institution will fail, thereby directly adding to the safety and soundness of financial institutions.

Bank regulators have also become increasingly worried about banks' holdings of risky assets and about the increase in banks' **off-balance-sheet activities**, activities that involve trading financial instruments and generating income from fees, which do not appear on bank balance sheets but nevertheless expose banks to risk. An agreement among banking officials from industrialized nations set up the **Basel Committee on Banking Supervision** (because it meets under the auspices of the Bank for International Settlements in Basel, Switzerland), which has implemented the **Basel Accord** that deals with a second type of capital requirements, risk-based capital requirements. The Basel Accord, which required that banks hold as capital at least 8% of their risk-weighted assets, has been adopted by all the major economies. Assets and off-balance-sheet activities were allocated into four categories, each with a different weight to reflect the degree of credit risk. The first category carries a zero weight and includes items that have little default risk, such as reserves and government securities issued by the Organisation for Economic Co-operation and Development (OECD – industrialized) countries. The second category has a 20% weight and includes claims on banks in OECD countries. The third category has a weight of 50% and includes municipal bonds and residential mortgages. The fourth category has the maximum weight of 100% and includes loans to consumers and corporations. Off-balance-sheet activities are treated in a similar manner by assigning a credit-equivalent percentage that converts them to on-balance-sheet items to which the appropriate risk weight applies. The 1996 Market Risk Amendment to the Basel Accord set minimum capital requirements for risks in banks' trading accounts.

Over time, limitations of the Basel Accord have become apparent, because the regulatory measure of bank risk as stipulated by the risk weights can differ substantially from the actual risk the bank faces. This has resulted in **regulatory arbitrage**, a practice in which banks keep on their books assets that have the same risk-based capital requirement but are relatively risky, such as a loan to a company with a very low credit rating, while taking off their books low-risk assets, such as a loan to a company with a very high credit rating. The Basel Accord could thus lead to increased risk taking, the opposite of its intent. Another weakness was that the categories of credit risk were too crude and insufficiently differentiated. Also Basel 1 led to biases like lending to the government. To address these limitations, the Basel Committee on Bank Supervision released proposals for a new capital accord, often referred to as Basel 2, but it is not clear if it is workable (see the Global box, 'Basel 2: An obsolete proposal?').

The Basel Committee's work on bank capital requirements is never-ending. Indeed, with the extension of the government safety net to non-bank financial institutions during

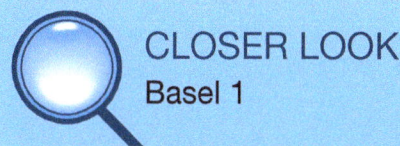

CLOSER LOOK
Basel 1

The Basel Accord of 1988 set out a common minimum risk-weighted capital – asset ratio for international banks amounting to 8% of risk-weighted assets (RWA). It has largely been superseded by Basel 2 and latterly Basel 3. Basel 1 was only viewed as a minimum. Individual regulators imposed further restrictions on banks. In 1996 the Basel Accord was extended to include losses from trading. We describe below an example of how the 8% RWA is made up. Each item in the balance has a weight applied to it which gives the weighted value. The weighted value for each item is summed to produce a total of RWA. In the case of off-balance-sheet items, an appropriate risk weight is applied. Guarantees of commercial loans are contingent claims and could appear on the balance sheet as a loan (with a risk weight of unity). However, it is uncertain if they would appear on the balance sheet at all so the weight is less than one, namely 0.5.

Risk–asset ratio – an illustrative example

Asset	€ million	Weight	Weighted value
Cash	25	0.0	0.0
Treasury Bills	5	0.0	0.0
Government bonds	70	0.0	0.0
Money market loans	100	0.2	20.0
Municipal bonds	50	0.5	25.0
Foreign OECD bonds	25	0.0	0.0
Commercial bonds	25	1.0	25.0
Commercial loans	400	1.0	400.0
Personal loans	200	1.0	200.0
Mortgages	100	0.5	50.0
Total assets	1,000		
Off-balance-sheet risks			
Guarantees of commercial loans	20	0.5	10.0
Letters of credit	50	0.5	25.0
Total risk-weighted assets (RWA)			755.0
Capital ratio 8%			60.4

Source: Adapted from Bank of England 'Banking supervision' Fact Sheet, August 1990.

the subprime financial crisis, capital requirements for these other financial institutions will receive more scrutiny in the future. As the financial industry changes, regulation of capital must change with it to ensure the safety and soundness of financial institutions. It is increasingly likely that the Basel Committee will have an even greater role in exploring capital requirements for a wider range of financial institutions in the future.

Prompt corrective action

If the amount of a financial institution's capital falls to low levels, there are two serious problems. First, the bank is more likely to fail because it has a smaller capital cushion if it suffers loan losses or other asset write-downs. Second, with less capital, a financial institution has less 'skin in the game' and is therefore more likely to take on excessive risks.

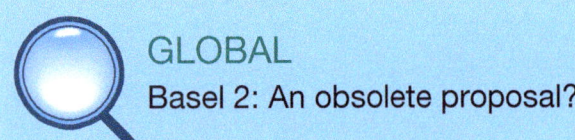

GLOBAL
Basel 2: An obsolete proposal?

Starting in June 1999, the Basel Committee on Banking Supervision released several proposals to reform the original 1988 Basel Accord. These efforts have culminated in what bank supervisors refer to as Basel 2, which is based on three pillars.

1 Pillar 1 links capital requirements for large, internationally active banks more closely to actual risk of three types: market risk, credit risk and operational risk. It does so by specifying many more categories of assets with different risk weights in its standardized approach. Alternatively, it allows sophisticated banks to pursue an internal ratings-based approach that permits banks to use their own models of credit risk.

2 Pillar 2 focuses on strengthening the supervisory process, particularly in assessing the quality of risk management in banking institutions and evaluating whether these institutions have adequate procedures to determine how much capital they need.

3 Pillar 3 focuses on improving market discipline through increased disclosure of details about a bank's credit exposures, its amount of reserves and capital, the officials who control the bank, and the effectiveness of its internal rating system.

Although Basel 2 makes great strides toward limiting excessive risk taking by internationally active banking institutions, it has greatly increased the complexity of the accord. The document describing the original Basel Accord was 26 pages, while the final draft of Basel 2 exceeded 500 pages. The original timetable called for the completion of the final round of consultation by the end of 2001, with the new rules taking effect by 2004. However, criticism from banks, trade associations and national regulators led to several postponements.

The final draft was not published until June 2004 and Basel 2 started to be implemented at the beginning of 2008 by European banks. United States banks submitted plans for compliance with Basel 2 in 2008, but full implementation did not occur until 2009. Only the dozen or so largest US banks are subject to Basel 2: all others will be allowed to use a simplified version of the standards it imposes.

There are several serious criticisms of Basel 2 that cast doubts on how well it will work. First, its complexity could make it unworkable. Second, risk weights in the standardized approach are heavily reliant on credit ratings. Since these credit ratings have proved to be very unreliable on subprime mortgage products during the recent financial crisis, there are serious doubts that the standardized approach using credit ratings will produce reliable risk weights. Third, Basel 2 is very procyclical. That is, it demands that banks hold less capital when times are good, but more when times are bad, thereby exacerbating credit cycles. Because the probability of default and expected losses for different classes of assets rises during bad times, Basel 2 may require more capital at exactly the time when capital is most short. This has been a particularly serious concern in the aftermath of the subprime financial crisis. As a result of this crisis, banks' capital balances eroded, leading to a cutback on lending that was a big drag on the economy. Basel 2 may make this cutback in lending even worse, doing even more harm to the economy.

As a consequence of the shortcomings of Basel 2 that emerged during the global financial crisis following the subprime crisis, the Bank of International Settlements brought a further set of regulatory proposals known as Basel 3 (see below).

In other words, the moral hazard problem becomes more severe, making it more likely that the institution will fail and the taxpayer will be left holding the bag.

Financial supervision: bank licensing and examination

Overseeing who operates financial institutions and how they are operated, referred to as **financial supervision** or **prudential supervision**, is an important method for reducing adverse selection and moral hazard in the financial industry. Because financial institutions can be used by crooks or overambitious entrepreneurs to engage in highly speculative activities, such undesirable people would be eager to run a financial institution. Licensing financial institutions is one method for preventing this adverse selection problem; through chartering, proposals for new institutions are screened to prevent undesirable people from controlling them.

Regular on-site examinations, which allow regulators to monitor whether the institution is complying with capital requirements and restrictions on asset holdings, also function to limit moral hazard. Bank examiners give banks a *CAMELS rating.* The acronym is based on the six areas assessed: capital adequacy, asset quality, management, earnings, liquidity and sensitivity to market risk. With this information about a bank's activities, regulators can enforce regulations by taking such formal actions as *cease and desist orders* to alter the bank's behaviour or even close a bank if its CAMELS rating is sufficiently low. Actions taken to reduce moral hazard by restricting banks from taking on too much risk help reduce the adverse selection problem further, because with less opportunity for risk taking, risk-loving entrepreneurs will be less likely to be attracted to the banking industry. Note that the methods regulators use to cope with adverse selection and moral hazard have their counterparts in private financial markets (see Chapters 8 and 10). Licensing is similar to the screening of potential borrowers, regulations restricting risky asset holdings are similar to restrictive covenants that prevent borrowing firms from engaging in risky investment activities, capital requirements act like restrictive covenants that require minimum amounts of net worth for borrowing firms, and regular examinations are similar to the monitoring of borrowers by lending institutions.

Once a bank has been licensed, it is required to file periodic reports that reveal the bank's assets and liabilities, income and dividends, ownership, foreign exchange operations and other details. The bank is also subject to examination by the bank regulatory agencies to ascertain its financial condition at least once a year. Bank examinations are conducted by bank examiners, who sometimes make unannounced visits to the bank (so that nothing can be 'swept under the rug' in anticipation of their examination). The examiners study a bank's books to see whether it is complying with the rules and regulations that apply to its holdings of assets. If a bank is holding securities or loans that are too risky, the bank examiner can force the bank to get rid of them. If a bank examiner decides that a loan is unlikely to be repaid, the examiner can force the bank to declare the loan worthless (to write off the loan, which reduces the bank's capital). If, after examining the bank, the examiner feels that it does not have sufficient capital or has engaged in dishonest practices, the bank can be declared a 'problem bank' and will be subject to more frequent examinations.

Assessment of risk management

Traditionally, on-site examinations have focused primarily on assessment of the quality of a financial institution's balance sheet at a point in time and whether it complies with capital requirements and restrictions on asset holdings. Although the traditional focus is important for reducing excessive risk taking by financial institutions, it is no longer felt to be adequate in today's world, in which financial innovation has produced new markets and instruments that make it easy for financial institutions and their employees to make huge bets easily and quickly. In this new financial environment, a financial institution that is healthy at a particular point in time can be driven into insolvency extremely rapidly from trading losses. Thus an examination that focuses only on a financial institution's position at a point in time may not be effective in indicating whether it will, in fact, be taking on excessive risk in the near future.

This change in the environment for financial institutions has resulted in a major shift in thinking about the prudential supervisory process throughout the world. Bank examiners, for example, are now placing far greater emphasis on evaluating the soundness of a bank's management processes with regard to controlling risk. Now bank examiners give a separate risk management rating from 1 to 5 that feeds into the overall management rating as part of the CAMELS system. A number of elements of sound risk management are assessed to come up with the risk management rating: (1) the quality of oversight provided by the board of directors and senior management, (2) the adequacy of policies and limits for all activities that present significant risks, (3) the quality of the risk measurement and monitoring systems, (4) the adequacy of internal controls to prevent fraud or unauthorized activities on the part of employees and (5) since 2010 a number of regulatory authorities have published guidelines on bankers' remuneration and bonuses that feed into risk-taking behaviour.

This shift toward focusing on management processes has resulted in the adoption of processes to deal with trading risk and risk based on market movements. These guidelines require the bank's board of directors to establish interest-rate risk limits, appoint officials of the bank to manage this risk, and monitor the bank's risk exposure. The guidelines also require that senior management of a bank develop formal risk management policies and procedures to ensure that the board of directors' risk limits are not violated and to implement internal controls to monitor interest-rate risk and compliance with the board's directives. Particularly important is the implementation of *stress testing*, which calculates losses under dire scenarios, or value-at-risk (VaR) calculations, which measure the size of the loss on a trading portfolio that might happen 1% of the time – say, over a two-week period. In addition to these guidelines, bank examiners will continue to consider interest-rate risk in deciding the bank's capital requirements.

Disclosure requirements

The free-rider problem described in Chapter 8 indicates that individual depositors and creditors will not have enough incentive to produce private information about the quality of a financial institution's assets. To ensure that there is better information in the marketplace, regulators can require that financial institutions adhere to certain standard accounting principles and disclose a wide range of information that helps the market assess the quality of an institution's portfolio and the amount of its exposure to risk. More public information about the risks incurred by financial institutions and the quality of their portfolios can better enable stockholders, creditors and depositors to evaluate and monitor financial institutions and so act as a deterrent to excessive risk taking.

Disclosure requirements are a key element of financial regulation. Basel 2 puts a particular emphasis on disclosure requirements with one of its three pillars focusing on increasing market discipline by mandating increased disclosure by banking institutions of their credit exposure, amount of reserves, and capital. Regulation to increase disclosure is needed to limit incentives to take on excessive risk and to improve the quality of information in the marketplace so that investors can make informed decisions, thereby improving the ability of financial markets to allocate capital to its most productive uses. Particularly controversial in the wake of the subprime financial crisis is the move to so-called **mark-to-market accounting**, also called **fair-value accounting**, in which assets are valued in the balance sheet at what they could sell for in the market (see the 'Closer look' box, 'Mark-to-market accounting and the subprime financial crisis').

Consumer protection

The existence of asymmetric information also suggests that consumers may not have enough information to protect themselves fully. Consumer protection regulation in the EU has been sparse and mainly concerned with harmonization of the regulation to enable consumer credit transactions to occur smoothly across borders. The Consumer Credit Directive of 1987 was the first of this type of regulation that was applied EU-wide. The rapid evolution of financial products led to a further consumer credit directive which was brought into national law in June 2010. The regulation requires all lenders, not just banks, to provide information to consumers about the cost of borrowing, including a standardized interest rate (called the *annual percentage rate*, or *APR*) and the total finance charges on the loan. Other regulations relate to the right of withdrawal by the consumer within fourteen days of the credit contract at no financial penalty and the right to repay a debt contract early and to incur only reasonable costs.

CLOSER LOOK
Mark-to-market accounting and the subprime financial crisis

The controversy over mark-to-market accounting has made accounting a hot topic. Mark-to-market accounting was made standard practice in the accounting industry in 1993. The rationale behind mark-to-market accounting is that market prices provide the best basis for estimating the true value of assets, and hence capital, in the firm. Before mark-to-market accounting, firms relied on the traditional historical-cost (book value) basis in which the value of an asset was set at its initial purchase price. The problem with historical-cost accounting is that fluctuations in the value of assets and liabilities because of changes in interest rates or default are not reflected in the calculation of the firm's equity capital. Yet changes in the market value of assets and liabilities – and hence changes in the market value of equity capital – are what indicate if a firm is in good shape, or alternatively, if it is getting into trouble and may therefore be more susceptible to moral hazard.

Mark-to-market accounting, however, is subject to a major flaw. At times markets stop working, as occurred during the subprime financial crisis. The price of an asset sold at a time of financial distress does not reflect its fundamental value. That is, the fire-sale liquidation value of an asset can at times be well below the present value of its expected future cash flows. Many people, particularly bankers, criticized mark-to-market accounting during the recent subprime financial crisis episode, claiming that it has been an important factor driving the crisis. They claim that the seizing up of financial markets has led to market prices being well below fundamental values. Mark-to-market accounting requires that the financial firms' assets be marked down in value. This markdown creates a shortfall in capital that leads to a cutback in lending, which causes a further deterioration in asset prices, which in turn causes a further cutback in lending. The resulting adverse feedback loop can then make the financial crisis even worse. Although the criticisms of mark-to-market accounting have some validity, some of the criticism by bankers is self-serving. The criticism was made only when asset values were falling, when mark-to-market accounting was painting a bleaker picture of banks' balance sheets, as opposed to when asset prices were booming, when it made banks' balance sheets look very good.

Summary

Asymmetric information analysis explains what types of financial regulations are needed to reduce moral hazard and adverse selection problems in the financial system. However, understanding the theory behind regulation does not mean that regulation and supervision of the financial system are easy in practice. Getting regulators and supervisors to do their job properly is difficult for several reasons. First, as we will see in the discussion of financial innovation in Chapter 12, in their search for profits, financial institutions have strong incentives to avoid existing regulations by loophole mining. Thus regulation applies to a moving target: regulators are continually playing cat-and-mouse with financial institutions – financial institutions think up clever ways to avoid regulations, which then lead regulators to modify their regulation activities. Regulators continually face new challenges in a dynamically changing financial system – and unless they can respond rapidly to change, they may not be able to keep financial institutions from taking on excessive risk. This problem can be exacerbated if regulators and supervisors do not have the resources or expertise to keep up with clever people in financial institutions seeking to circumvent the existing regulations.

Financial regulation and supervision are difficult for two other reasons. In the regulation and supervision game, the devil is in the details. Subtle differences in the details may have unintended consequences; unless regulators get the regulation and supervision just right, they may be unable to prevent excessive risk taking. In addition, regulated firms may lobby politicians to lean on regulators and supervisors to go easy on them. For all these reasons, there is no guarantee that regulators and supervisors will be successful in promoting a healthy financial system. These same problems bedevil financial regulators in all countries, as the Global box 'International financial regulation and Basel 3' indicates. Indeed, as we will see, financial regulation and supervision have not always worked well, leading to banking crises throughout the world.

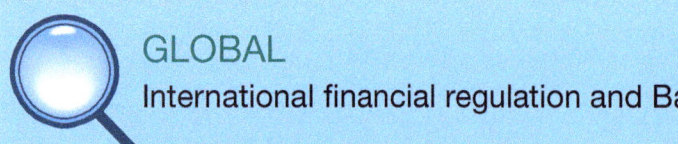

GLOBAL
International financial regulation and Basel 3

Because asymmetric information problems in the banking industry are a fact of life throughout the world, countries have similar financial regulations. Financial institutions are licensed and supervised by government regulators or the central banks. Disclosure requirements for financial institutions and corporations issuing securities are similar in other developed countries. Deposit insurance is also a feature of the regulatory systems in most other countries. We have also seen that capital requirements are standardized across countries with agreements like the Basel Accord.

Particular problems in financial regulation occur when financial institutions operate in many countries and thus can readily shift their business from one country to another. Financial regulators closely examine the domestic operations of financial institutions in their country, but they often do not have the knowledge or ability to keep a close watch on operations in other countries, either by domestic institutions' foreign affiliates or by foreign institutions with domestic branches. In addition, when a financial institution operates in many countries, it is not always clear which national regulatory authority should have primary responsibility for keeping the institution from engaging in overly risky activities.

The difficulties inherent in international financial regulation were highlighted by the collapse of the Bank of Credit and Commerce International (BCCI). BCCI, which was operating in more than 70 countries, including the United States and the United Kingdom, was supervised by Luxembourg, a tiny country unlikely to be up to the task. When massive fraud was discovered, the Bank of England closed BCCI down, but not before depositors and stockholders were exposed to huge losses. Cooperation among regulators in different countries and standardization of regulatory requirements provide potential solutions to the problems of international financial regulation. The world has been moving in this direction through agreements like the Basel Accord and oversight procedures announced by the Basel Committee in July 1992, which require a bank's worldwide operations to be under the scrutiny of a single home-country regulator with enhanced powers to acquire information on the bank's activities. Also, the Basel Committee ruled that regulators in other countries can restrict the operations of a foreign bank if they feel that it lacks effective oversight.

It is generally accepted that one of many factors that contributed to the global banking crisis that began in late 2007 was a failure of bank regulation that allowed banks to take risky positions without sufficient capital backing. At the height of the credit crunch in 2007–8 banks reduced their lending to each other, causing a sharp rise in spreads in the interbank market and a drying up of liquidity. In September 2010 the Basel Committee on Banking Supervision announced a set of regulations that has come to be known as Basel 3. The new set of regulatory arrangements addresses the problem of liquidity shortage that arose during the period of the credit crunch, higher capital requirements and in particular better quality capital, and countercyclical measures aimed at addressing the destabilizing implications of Basel 2 and dampening the procyclical credit cycle that sees bank credit growing and receding with the ups and down of the business cycle.

The Basel 3 recommendation is that banks should hold liquidity sufficient to withstand a stressed case of cash outflow over a period of 30 days. The practical implication is that banks will have to hold higher levels of low-yielding liquid assets which will reduce their lending capacity and interest earnings. Capital requirements are to be strengthened and simplified which will see the total proportion of capital as a proportion of risk-weighted assets rising from the Basel 1 minimum of 8% to 10.5%, which includes an additional conservation buffer of 2.5% made up of common equity to absorb losses during periods of economic stress. Finally, the Committee recommends a countercyclical buffer within the range of 0%–2.5% of common equity to be implemented by national regulatory authorities to support other macro-prudential measures it applies to dampen the excess credit growth that tends to move with the business cycle.

The immediate impact of Basel 3 if adopted universally will be to raise capital requirements at a time when banks are exhorted by their governments to aid the global recovery by lending to businesses. For this reason and others the Basel 3 proposals are to be phased in over a period of time to 2019. In the short term, banks are likely to meet the additional capital requirements by widening spreads, retaining profits and shrinking bank lending. In the medium term, higher capital requirements could mean wider spreads and more expensive credit as banks pass on the additional costs of capital to their customers. A counter-argument is that a better capitalised bank is a safer bank and will be able to command a lower cost of capital. Whether the higher capital requirements will lead to more expensive credit and dampened business cycles in the future is an open question.

Advantages and disadvantages of bank regulation

The case for regulation of the banking system is based on the argument by the famous economist Ronald Coase that unregulated private actions create outcomes whereby social marginal costs are greater than private marginal costs.[2] The experience of the global banking crisis shows that the costs of a bank failure are met by the shareholders but the costs of the wider crisis are borne by the rest of the economy. Regulation has to walk a fine line in that too much regulation can stifle enterprise and risk taking necessary for a market-led economy but too little regulation can lead to periodic bank crises which impose enormous costs on the rest of the economy. Arguably, the global banking crisis has tipped the balance in favour of greater regulation.

Regulation is also necessary to protect the depositor (and the investors in general). Most depositors do not have the capacity or the inclination to monitor the risk-taking activity of the bank managers. Content to leave the business of monitoring the banks to others (the free-rider problem) the depositor is more likely to 'run' on the bank at times of stress rather than monitor. We have seen that bank runs can cause contagion and systemic problems for the banking system that can result in a breakdown of the financial system and the economy (as it did in the Great Depression in the 1930s). Therefore regulation is needed not just to protect the depositor but also to safeguard the stability of the financial system. Deposit insurance has the effect of curbing a bank run but we have seen that it also has the disadvantage of creating moral hazard which might lead to cases of 'too big to fail' or 'too important to fail'.

Other disadvantages of regulation are the direct costs of compliance that regulation places on banks. Compliance costs have been estimated by various agencies as lying between 5% and 10% of banks' operational costs. Regulation also requires well-trained regulators that know what the banks are about. In many cases, regulators are recruited from the ranks of the regulated giving rise to the potential for 'regulatory capture' and too cosy a relationship between the regulator and the regulated. Designing a proper regulatory system is therefore not an easy matter for the regulators. Self-regulation which was the ethos of the UK banking regulatory system has been deemed to have been too lax, whereas excessive regulation can be too costly. By curbing enterprise and risk taking, regulation can also reduce the efficiency of the financial system.

Banking crises throughout the world

Because misery loves company, it may make you feel better to know that the banking crises are universal and not just confined to Europe and the United States. Indeed, as Figure 11.1 and Table 11.2 illustrate, banking crises have struck a large number of countries throughout the world, and many of them have been substantially worse than the one we experienced in the 1980s.

'Déjà vu all over again'

In the banking crises in these different countries, history keeps repeating itself. The parallels between the banking crisis episodes in all these countries are remarkably similar, creating a feeling of déjà vu. They all started with financial liberalization or innovation, with weak bank regulatory systems and a government safety net. Although financial liberalization is generally a good thing because it promotes competition and can make a financial system more efficient, it can lead to an increase in moral hazard, with more risk taking on the part of banks if there is lax regulation and supervision; the result can then be banking crises.[3]

FIGURE 11.1

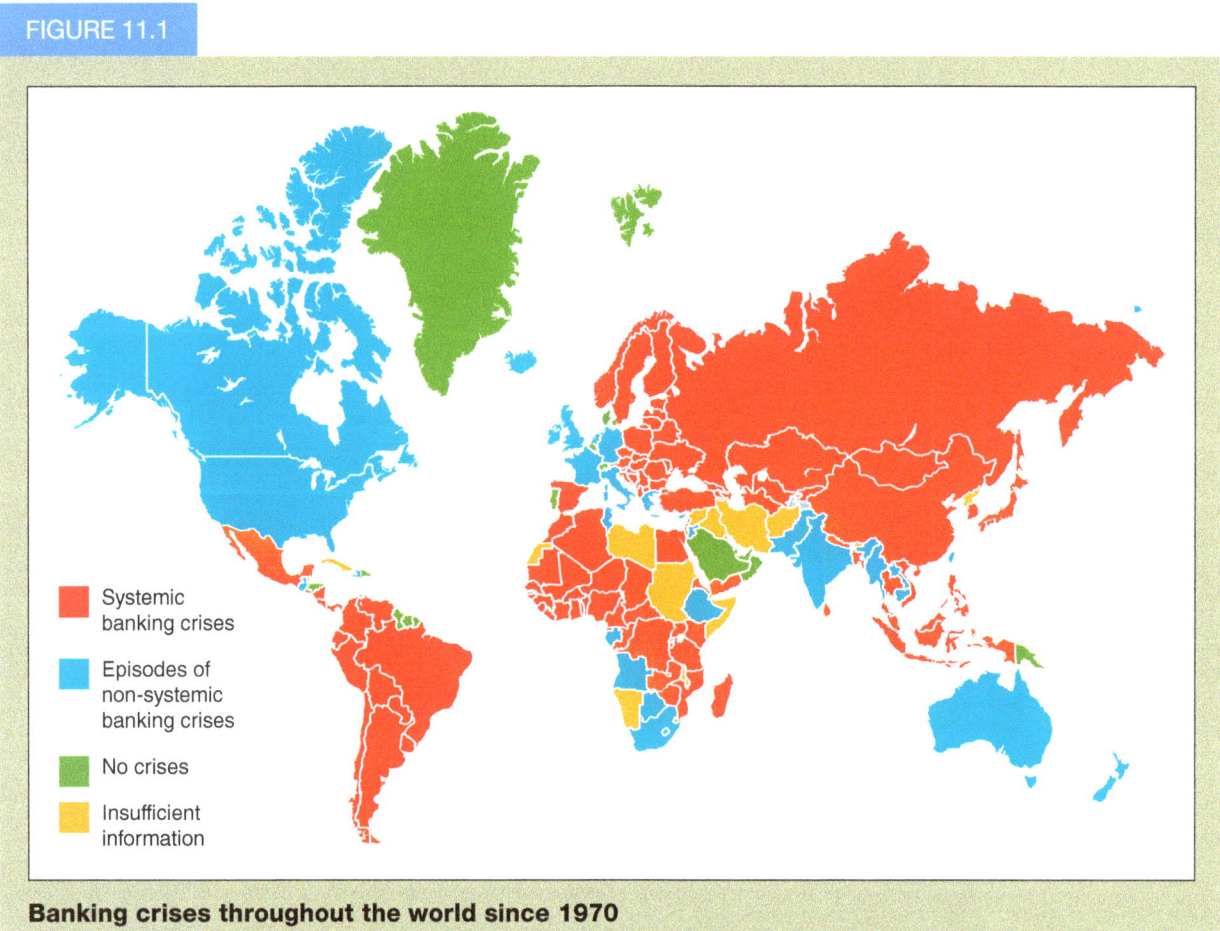

Systemic banking crises

Episodes of non-systemic banking crises

No crises

Insufficient information

Banking crises throughout the world since 1970

Source: Gerard Caprio and Daniela Klingebiel, 'Episodes of systemic and borderline financial crises', mimeo, World Bank, October 1999.

However, the banking crisis episodes listed in Table 11.2 do differ in that deposit insurance has not played an important role in many of the countries experiencing banking crises. For example, the Japanese Deposit Insurance Corporation did not play a prominent role in the banking system and exhausted its resources almost immediately with the first bank failures. This example indicates that deposit insurance is not to blame for some of these banking crises. However, what is common to all the countries discussed here is the existence of a government safety net, in which the government stands ready to bail out banks whether deposit insurance is an important feature of the regulatory environment or not. It is the existence of a government safety net, and not deposit insurance per se, that increases moral hazard incentives for excessive risk taking on the part of banks.

Whither financial regulation after the subprime financial crisis?

The global financial crisis has resulted in popular pressure to regulate banks and curb the remuneration and bonus culture that permeated the banking industry. The result has been the call for banks to hold more capital against losses and better quality of capital. The populist view is that the bonuses of bankers were linked to the performance of the bank which encouraged excessive risk taking. From January 2010 the Financial Services Authority of the UK set out new guidelines for the remuneration practices of the major banks in London. Other regulatory authorities in the EU also set out guidelines for the setting of bankers' remuneration.

TABLE 11.2

The cost of rescuing banks in several countries

Country	Date 1980–2009	Cost as a percentage of GDP
Indonesia	1997–2001	57
Argentina	1980–2	55
Thailand	1997–2000	44
Chile	1981–5	43
Turkey	2000–1	32
South Korea	1997–8	31
Israel	1977	30
Ecuador	1998–2002	22
Mexico	1994–6	19
China	1998	18
Malaysia	1997–9	16
Philippines	1997–2001	13
Brazil	1994–8	13
Finland	1991–5	13
Argentina	2001–3	10
Jordan	1989–91	10
Hungary	1991–5	10
Czech Republic	1996–2000	7
Sweden	1991–5	4
United States	1988	4
Norway	1991–3	3
	2007–9	
Iceland	2007–9	13
Ireland	2007–9	8
Luxembourg	2007–9	8
Netherlands	2007–9	7
Belgium	2007–9	5
United Kingdom	2007–9	5
United States	2007–9	4
Germany	2007–9	1

Sources: Luc Laeven and Fabian Valencia, 'Resolution of Banking Crises: The Good, the Bad and the Ugly', IMF Working Paper No. WP/10/46 (June 2010) and Luc Laeven, Banking Crisis Database at http://www.luclaeven. com/Data.htm.

The Independent Commission on Banking in the UK reported in September 2011 with a proposal to 'ring-fence' retail banking from wholesale banking activity by delineating day-to-day retail activity from risky trading and investment activity. The Commission does not ask for the break-up of the banks between its retail and investment arms but for stronger capital requirements of at least 10% of risk-weighted assets.

In January 2011 the **European Banking Authority (EBA)** was set up to oversee national bank regulators in the European Union and if necessary provide a common framework of regulation that reduces the possibility of 'regulatory arbitrage' (the potential for financial firms to locate in areas of weaker regulation). One of the areas of the EBA's sphere of control is the guideline for setting bankers' remuneration. Another is the setting of minimum capital requirements for banks operating in the EU. Following a 'stress testing' exercise on a sample of 90 European banks in July 2011, the EBA announced the recommendation that national regulatory authorities call on their banks to raise capital ratios (capital to risk-weighted assets) up to 9% by June 2012.

The euro sovereign debt crisis has made European banks vulnerable to the marking down of Greek (and also Portuguese, Spanish, Irish and even Italian) bonds. During 2010–11 bank shares fell faster than stock prices in general signalling the fragility of the banks. Banks were unable to raise capital from their shareholders. The only alternative would be retained profits, converting other forms of liabilities (certain types of debt) into equity, or reducing lending. The estimated amount of capital required is in the order of €235–€245billion for the euro area. The argument made by the banks is that raising this much capital in the fragile economic conditions of 2011 can only be achieved by charging customers higher interest rates, reducing credit (to meet the higher capital ratio), and weakening the economic recovery by starving businesses of funds for growth. In the medium term, the higher capital ratio means paying more dividends that have to be met from the consumer through wider spreads.

The counter-argument made by academic economists and bank regulators is that banks with higher capital ratios are actually safer banks that would pay a lower 'risk premium' for their funding and therefore face a lower cost of capital. More capital is like a tax on the banks. It will be costly for the banks and they will try to pass this cost on to customers but it is also true that a well-capitalized bank is one that will be able to command a lower cost of funds. It is unclear which of these two forces will prevail and what it means for the cost of credit to the customer.

It is too soon to tell how much the global banking crisis will impact on regulation, the customer, the banks and the taxpayer. It is unclear how large the costs of rescuing the banks will be as a result of this episode (which is why they are not listed in Table 11.2). However, given the size of the bailouts and the nationalization of so many financial institutions, it is safe to assume that the system of financial regulation will surely never be the same. Here we can speculate on where financial regulation might be heading as a result of this crisis.

The financial innovations of subprime mortgages and structured credit products like collateralized debt obligations helped trigger the crisis. Although these innovations have the positive potential for promoting the 'democratization of credit', that is, increasing the access of poorer members of society to credit, they went horribly wrong because of the agency problems of the originate-to-distribute business model. Future regulation will surely focus on limiting these agency problems to make the originate-to-distribute model and the financial system overall work better. A number of regulations likely to be seen in the future are described below.

Increased regulation of mortgage brokers

Mortgage brokers, who did not have proper incentives to ensure that mortgages were given on 'ability to pay' principles, are likely to be subjected to grater regulatory scrutiny. Licensing requirements for mortgage originators are likely to be tightened up, and more regulations will require them to disclose mortgage terms more clearly and prevent them from encouraging borrowers to take on more debt than they can afford.

Fewer subprime mortgage products

Some of the complex mortgage products that were offered to subprime borrowers may be banned by regulation. Even with full disclosure of these products' characteristics, they may still be so complicated that subprime borrowers, who are unlikely to be financially sophisticated, cannot understand them and make informed choices. Government ban or regulation of certain mortgage products might help prevent subprime borrowers from 'getting in over their heads' again in the future.

Regulation of bankers' compensation

Compensation schemes for all the parties in the chain from origination of mortgages to the eventual distribution of mortgage-related securities may be constrained by government regulation. The high fees and executive compensation that have so outraged the public created incentives for the financial industry to push out securities that turned out to be much more risky than advertised and have proved to be disastrous.

Higher capital requirements

Regulation and supervision of financial institutions to ensure that they have enough capital to cope with the amount of risk they take are likely to be strengthened. Given the risks they were taking, investment banks did not have enough capital relative to their assets and their risky activities. Capital requirements at banks are likely to be tightened up, particularly for some of their off-balance-sheet activities. Banks' sponsoring of structured investment vehicles (SIVs), which were supposedly off balance sheet but came back on the balance sheet once the SIVs got into trouble, indicate that some off-balance-sheet activities should be treated as though they were on the balance sheet.

Countercyclical capital requirements

Individual regulatory authorities will apply variable capital requirements that will phase in with the business cycle. The aim of this will be to support macro-prudential measures in the central bank's toolkit to dampen the cycle. Higher capital requirements in the upswing of the business cycle is expected to raise the cost of credit to borrowers as banks pass on the increased cost of capital to their borrowers. It is also expected that the central bank will play its part by tightening monetary policy and raising borrowing costs generally.

Heightened regulation to limit financial institutions' risk taking

With the extension of the government safety net to a wider range of financial institutions, regulation will be needed to limit risk taking by financial firms. This will require stricter regulation of investment banks – some of this will automatically occur because the largest ones that have survived are now part of bank holding companies and thus will be regulated and supervised like banks – as well as insurance companies.

Increased regulation of credit-rating agencies

Regulations to restrict conflicts of interest at credit-rating agencies and to give them greater incentives to provide reliable ratings have already been strengthened, but even more is likely to be done. The inaccurate ratings provided by credit-rating agencies helped promote risk taking throughout the financial system and led to investors not having the information they needed to make informed choices about their investments. The reliance on credit ratings in the Basel 2 capital requirements may also have to be rethought, given the poor performance of credit-rating agencies in recent years.

Additional regulation of derivatives

More regulations both on disclosure and how derivatives are traded are likely to be put in place, particularly on derivatives such as credit-default swaps. These derivatives ended up being 'weapons of mass destruction' that helped lead to a financial meltdown when the US insurance company AIG had to be rescued after making overly extensive use of them. Preventing this from happening again will be a high priority.

The danger of overregulation

Many of the suggestions for re-regulation discussed above are in advanced stages of consultation with regulatory agencies in the EU and have appeared as EU Commission Directives. For example it is mooted that systematically important financial institutions be forced to hold more capital. But whatever happens to re-regulation in banking, as a result of the subprime financial crisis, the world of financial regulation will never be the same. Although it is clear that more regulation is needed to prevent such a crisis from ever occurring again, there is a substantial danger that too much or poorly designed regulation could hamper the efficiency of the financial system. If new regulations choke off financial innovation that can benefit both households and businesses, economic growth in the future will suffer.

Summary

1 The concepts of asymmetric information, adverse selection and moral hazard help explain the main types of financial regulation that we see in the developed economies: the government safety net, restrictions on financial institutions' asset holdings, capital requirements, financial institution supervision, assessment of risk management, disclosure requirements, consumer protection and restrictions on competition.

2 Financial innovation and deregulation increased adverse selection and moral hazard problems in the 1980s and 1990s in both developed and developing economies.

3 The parallels between the banking crisis episodes that have occurred in countries throughout the world are striking, indicating that similar forces are at work.

Key terms

bank failure p. 232

Basel Accord p. 238

Basel Committee on Banking Supervision p. 238

European Banking Authority (EBA) p. 247

fair-value accounting p. 242

financial supervision (prudential supervision) p. 240

mark-to-market accounting p. 242

off-balance-sheet activities p. 238

regulatory arbitrage p. 238

QUESTIONS AND PROBLEMS

All questions and problems are available in MyEconLab at **www.myeconlab.com/mishkin**.

1 Give one example each of moral hazard and adverse selection in private insurance arrangements.

2 If casualty insurance companies provided fire insurance without any restrictions, what kind of adverse selection and moral hazard problems might result?

3 Which bank regulation is designed to reduce adverse selection problems for deposit insurance? Will it always work?

4 Which bank regulations are designed to reduce moral hazard problems created by deposit insurance? Will they completely eliminate the moral hazard problem?

5 What are the costs and benefits of a too-big-to-fail policy?

6 Why did the US Savings & Loans crisis not occur until the 1980s?

7 Why is regulatory forbearance a dangerous strategy for a deposit insurance agency?

8 Do you think that eliminating or limiting the amount of deposit insurance would be a good idea? Explain your answer.

9 How could higher deposit insurance premiums for banks with riskier assets benefit the economy?

10 How might limiting the too-big-to-fail policy help reduce the risk of a future banking crisis?

11 What are the key objectives of the European Banking Authority (EBA)?

WEB EXERCISES

1 **http://ec.europa.eu/internal_market/bank/regcapital/ index_en.htm**: This site reports on EU rules on capital requirements for credit institutions and investment firms. These aim to put in place a comprehensive and risk-sensitive framework and to foster enhanced risk management amongst financial institutions .Summarize the most recent bank regulatory initiatives listed on this site related to capital requirements.

2 In the UK, the Financial Services Authority (FSA) is one of the key regulators for the financial services industry.Go to **http://www.fsa.gov.uk/.** Click on 'what we do' **(http://www.fsa.gov.uk/pages/about/what/index.shtml** and summarize its key roles).

3 In the aftermath of the Global Financial Crisis, regulation is being implemented at an international, rather than national, level. Use the international section of the FSA website to summarize the key initiatives that have taken place in recent years at a European level **(http://www.fsa.gov.uk/about/what/international)**.

4 The Basel Committee on Banking Supervision is currently implementing the 'International Regulatory Framework for Banks' or Basel III. Go to **http://www.bis. org/bcbs/basel3.htm** and describe any recent highlights on its implementation around the world.

Notes

1 Evidence reveals, as our analysis predicts, that large banks took on riskier loans than smaller banks and that this led to higher loan losses for big banks; see John Boyd and Mark Gertler, 'US commercial banking: trends, cycles and policy', *NBER Macroeconomics Annual*, 1993, pp. 319–68.

2 R. H. Coase, *The Firm, the Market and the Law* - (Chicago, IL: University of Chicago Press, 1988).

3 An appendix to this chapter on this book's website, **www .myeconlab.com/mishkin**, discusses in detail many of the episodes of banking crises listed in Table 11.2.

Useful websites

www.financialregulationforum.com/ Keep abreast of all regulatory changes at this international site.

www.bankofengland.co.uk/financialstability/Pages/overseeing_fs/default.aspx A summary of the changes to the UK regulatory framework from the Bank of England.

www.ecb.europa.eu/pub/pdf/other/art3_mb201107en_pp85-94en.pdf A report from the ECB on the new framework for financial crisis management.

www.federalreserve.gov/Regulations/default.htm Access regulatory publications of the US Federal Reserve Board.

www.fdic.gov/regulations/laws/important/index.html Describes the most important laws that have affected the banking industry in the United States.

www.bis.org/bcbs/ The official website of the Basel Committee on Banking Supervision.

MyEconLab can help you get a better grade   MyEconLab®

If your exam were tomorrow, would you be ready? For each chapter, MyEconLab Practice Test and Study Plans pinpoint which sections you have mastered and which ones you need to study. That way, you are more efficient with your study time, and you are better prepared for your exams.

To see how it works, turn to page 19 and then go to: **www.myeconlab.com/mishkin**

CHAPTER 12

Banking industry: structure and competition

PREVIEW

The operations of individual banks (how they acquire, use and manage funds to make a profit) are roughly similar throughout the world. In all countries, banks are financial intermediaries in the business of earning profits. Except for the United States, the structure and operation of the banking industry in developed countries as a whole consists of four or five large banks that dominate the banking industry. In the United States there are in the order of 7,000 commercial banks, 1,200 savings and loan associations (mortgage credit companies) and 900 mutual savings banks, making a total of about 9,000 deposit-taking institutions. No single country in the developed world comes close to this level of bank provision and diversity. However, the European Union as a whole, which has a comparable population to the US, has 2,000 commercial banks, nearly 4,000 mortgage credit and specialist institutions, and over 4,000 mutual savings banks – or around 10,000 deposit-taking institutions.

The European Union has been engaged in developing a single banking market for its citizens that transcends national boundaries. However, strong national identities in banking still exist. Has the single market programme in banking been successful in creating a more competitive and therefore more economically efficient and sound banking system? We try to answer these questions by examining the recent trends in the banking industry and its overall structure.

We start by examining the details of the single banking market in the European Union and how the three trends in international banking, namely deregulation, financial innovation and globalization, have increased the competitive environment for the banking industry. We go on to look at the structure of the commercial banking industry in detail. Finally we examine the forces behind the growth in international banking.

The single banking market in Europe

International banking has gone through a process of deregulation and globalization during the last twenty years of the twentieth century, which has resulted in increased competitive pressure in banking markets. The creation of a **single banking market** in the European Union was designed with the aim of accelerating the process of competition created by the opening up of banking markets and deregulation. By offering consumers and firms banking services across national boundaries, the single banking market is supposed to improve welfare by promoting lower interest rates for loans and mortgages and higher interest rates for savings and deposits. The objective of the single banking market is that any banking service provider in the EU can establish an equivalent provision, or acquire another banking service provider across the EU. Any EU customer can bank with any legally constituted banking institution across the EU.

The single banking market is based on several directives that addressed the key issues of barriers to cross-border activity, capital ratios and deposit protection. The process began with two key banking directives. The First Banking Directive (1977) set the framework for the integration of the banking market within the EU. It was designed to establish the rules for banks to establish branches in other member states based on host-country regulations. This created a platform for cross-border EU bank entrants to behave like domestic banks and operate under host-country regulations. A level playing field was created but by doing so an incoming bank could not exploit any competitive advantage it may have had because it had to operate under host-country regulations for its branches operating cross-border and home-country regulations in its home market.

The Second Banking Directive (1988), implemented in 1993, had at its core two elements: first, the principle of home-country control or mutual recognition of regulatory authorities; and second, the concept of the 'single banking passport'. Home-country control means that banks are regulated according to the legislative framework of their home country. If a bank in one EU member state conducts business in another EU state, the regulatory authority in the 'host' country will recognize the primacy of the home country. The 'single passport' means that if a bank is licensed to do business in one EU state, it is similarly entitled to do business in any other EU state. In this way an EU state-based bank can set up a branch or subsidiary in any other EU state or, perhaps more importantly, take over any bank in another state. This passport provision is intended to open up the EU banking market, exposing domestic banks to the threat of foreign acquisition if uncompetitive. States are not allowed to impose barriers to this external threat for example by imposing an obligation upon non-domestic but nevertheless EU-based banks to establish separate capital bases for entities established within their borders, or by requiring the permission from officials prior to the launching of takeover bids.

Other directives such as the Own Funds Directive (1989, 1991) and the Solvency Ratio Directive (1989) were intended to set common capital adequacy standards across the EU market. One of the central objectives was to bring about greater cross-border activity whilst removing the ability of domestic regulators to obstruct ownership of banks passing into foreign control. The Financial Service Action Plan (1999) provided a time frame for the creation of a single market in wholesale financial services, to open retail banking services and to strengthen the rules on prudential supervision. In the case of the latter objective, the European Banking Authority was set up in 2011 to act as a European bank regulatory agency that oversees national regulatory agencies and even overrules national regulatory agencies if it thinks proper regulatory oversight is not being carried out. The stated objective is to have a common set of regulations to avoid 'regulatory arbitrage' and regulatory competition.

The principles of the single banking market have been harmonization, national treatment, mutual recognition and common regulation. The reality has been much more modest. Formidable obstacles remain to a full integration of EU banking markets. These include language and culture, home bias in the case of retail banking, branch network, differences in legal systems, and discriminatory tax treatment. However, the most important obstacle is the acceptance of the 'general good' principle that opens up the possibility of opt-outs from specific directives. Other barriers are informal such as implicit government or official interventions to favour national banks.[1]

Competition and bank consolidation

What has been the result of deregulation, and the drive to a single European banking market? First, it has to be realized that the process of deregulation and the opening up of the banking market was a worldwide phenomenon and not just confined to Europe.

The deregulation and removal of barriers in banking had been growing apace with the trend in globalization throughout the world. The process of globalization of financial markets had been proceeding throughout the 1970s followed by rapid financial innovation and the development of securitization (see below). The 1980s and 1990s saw a progressive relaxation of capital controls and the General Agreement in Trade in Services (GATS) relating to financial services in the mid-1990s encouraged the further opening up of banking and financial markets globally. The European single banking market and the drive to a single currency were but one of the forces relating to the three trends in banking, namely deregulation, financial innovation and globalization.

Deregulation and competition

The impact of deregulation can be separated into three distinct phases. The first phase involved the removals of quantitative barriers to growth in banking (in the UK and continental Europe these were restrictions on bank lending, in the US it was Regulation Q which imposed a ceiling on the rate of interest paid on deposits). The result of phase one was the growth in bank assets and services leading to a rise in prices for its products and an increase in profits.

The second phase saw an increase in competition from new entrants from overseas, competition from non-bank financial institutions (such as building societies in the UK, savings institutions, credit institutions and private equity institutions) and even competition from non-financial institutions (such as Virgin, Tesco, Marks & Spencer etc.), leading to the growth of a significant 'shadow banking' system. This second phase saw the banks reacting by narrowing spreads and cutting the relative cost of loans as competition bit into profits.

The third phase was the growth of non-traditional business as banks fought the competition by increasing their revenue sources from off-balance-sheet activity such as financial market trading, derivatives and securitization.

Table 12.1 shows the improved profit position of banks during the 1990s for the eurozone economies and the UK. The return on assets (ROA) is the ratio of after-tax profits of a year divided by the assets of the bank in the particular year. It is a conventional accounting

TABLE 12.1

Return on average assets (ROA) (%)

Country	1990	2000	2008
Austria	0.33	0.44	−0.14
Belgium	0.22	0.52	−0.26
Finland	0.26	1.02	0.41
France	0.27	0.54	−0.19
Germany	0.22	0.20	−0.30
Greece	0.69	1.46	−0.08
Ireland	0.43	0.30	0.04
Italy	0.58	0.79	0.22
Luxembourg	0.16	0.41	0.02
Netherlands	0.41	0.55	−0.01
Portugal	0.24	0.14	0.13
Spain	0.95	0.81	0.61
UK	0.35	0.85	−0.62

Source: Adapted from OECD (2010) Classification of bank assets and liabilities.

measure used to measure profit performance. Table 12.1 shows that despite the rapid growth in assets in the 1990s, in most economies bank profits increased. Bank assets grew at a rate of 11% a year in the eurozone and 14% a year in the UK between 1990 and 2000. The low or negative values in 2008 indicate the losses the banks made in the global financial crisis.

As in any industry faced with increased competition, prices fall and quantities increase as newcomers into the industry bid for business from the existing suppliers. Banking is no different. In phase two, banks began to offer cheaper loans and higher interest rates on their deposit savings. The spread between the average interest earned on banks' earning assets and the average interest paid on their funds narrowed in response to the increased competition. Banks charge different interest rates to different customers conditioned by risk, maturity, costs and required return on capital. Similarly the interest rate on various types of deposits will vary according to maturity and size. Therefore there is no single spread between a loan rate of interest and a deposit rate of interest. However, an aggregate measure that includes the spread can be obtained from banks' income statements.

A conventional accounting measure of earnings on intermediation is the **net interest margin (NIM)**. This measure is the interest earnings from assets less interest costs of funds, all divided by earnings assets, which contains the average spread.[2] Table 12.2 shows the net interest margin of the banks from 1990 to 2008 for the eurozone and the UK. It can be seen that increased competition in the banking industry led to a narrowing of the net interest margin as competition drove down the average interest rate charged on loans and drove up the average interest rate paid on deposits.

In the third phase of deregulation and competition, banks responded by developing new business lines. The way banks have sought to maintain former profit levels is to pursue new off-balance-sheet activities that are more profitable. Commercial banks in the UK and continental Europe did this during the 1980s, increasing the share of their income coming from off-balance-sheet non-interest-income activities. Non-traditional bank activities can be riskier and, therefore, result in excessive risk taking by banks. Indeed, they led to a substantial weakening of bank balance sheets during the subprime financial crisis. Figure 12.1 shows the development of non-interest earnings in the Big-3 economies of the EU (Germany, France and the UK). The figure shows the percentage contribution of non-interest income to gross income of the banking sector in each country.

TABLE 12.2

Net interest margins (in % of earning assets)

Country	1990	1994	2000	2008
Austria	1.8	1.9	1.2	0.8
Belgium	1.5	1.3	1.0	0.9
Finland	2.2	1.6	1.9	0.8
France	1.7	1.3	1.0	0.5
Germany	2.3	2.2	1.3	1.3
Greece	2.0	1.4	2.8	1.9
Ireland	n/a	3.0	1.6	1.0
Italy	3.4	2.7	2.4	1.4
Luxembourg	0.8	0.8	0.6	0.8
Portugal	4.1	2.6	1.8	1.8
Spain	4.0	3.1	2.2	1.6
UK	3.0	2.4	1.8	0.9

Source: Adapted from OECD (2010) Classification of bank assets and liabilities.

FIGURE 12.1

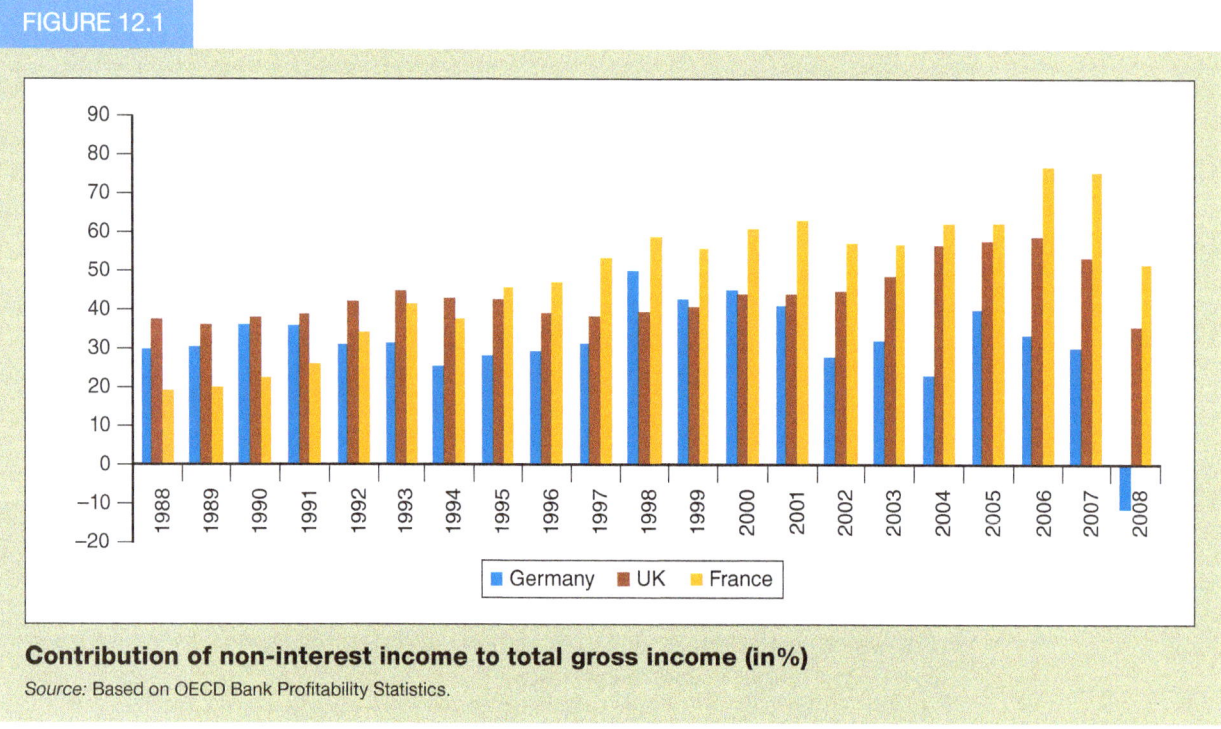

Contribution of non-interest income to total gross income (in%)

Source: Based on OECD Bank Profitability Statistics.

Both France and the UK show a consistent pattern of an increasing contribution to revenues while Germany shows growth till the end of the 1990s and then dips down in the 2000s. The statistics show the trend for all banks in France and the UK but in the case of Germany the figures relate to commercial banks only. The reason is that Germany has a much more disparate banking system than any other country in the EU. In 2008 it had 1,800 local credit and deposit-taking institutions that specialized in traditional banking activity. The commercial banks operate globally and are more susceptible to the pressures and incentives of globalization, deregulation and financial innovation. It should be noted that non-interest income fell dramatically in 2008 following on from the global banking crisis and in the case of Germany made a negative contribution to total revenue because of large losses on financial operations.

To sum up, the decline of banks' traditional business has meant that the banking industry has been driven to seek out new lines of business. This could be beneficial because, by so doing, banks can keep vibrant and healthy. Indeed, bank profitability was sustained up until 2008 by non-traditional and off-balance-sheet activities.

Consolidation and downsizing

How have the banks in Europe and elsewhere responded to the forces of competition unleashed by deregulation, globalization and financial innovation? In much the same way as any industry would respond faced with increased competition – through consolidation. Banks have been merging to create larger entities or have been buying up other banks. Just like firms that reduce costs and increase productivity to survive, banks have been following strategies of consolidation through merger and acquisition and downsizing through branch closure and personnel contraction and increase in productivity by utilizing technology.

Despite the single banking market programme and the single currency in the eurozone, cross-border mergers in the EU (even in the euro area) have been few and far between. Most mergers and acquisitions (M&A) have been within domestic boundaries. The number of mergers between financial institutions in the EU varied between 40 and 110 a year in the 1990s and the 2000s. These included a number of spectacular large-value mergers as shown

---

TABLE 12.3

Major merger or acquisition deals of banking institutions in the EU

Year	Origin of Target bank	Groups involved	Value of deal (€ bn)
1995	UK	TSB Group and Lloyds Bank	12.5
1998	Belgium	Fortis AG and Générale de Banque SA	11.2
1999	France	Banque Nationale de Paris and Paribas	11.2
1999	Italy	Banca Intesa SpA and Banca Commerciale Italiana SpA	10.9
1999	Spain	Banco de Santander and Banco Central Hispanoamericano	9.6
2000	UK	National Westminster Bank and Royal Bank of Scotland	37.3
2001	UK	Halifax and Bank of Scotland to form HBOS	45.0
2004	UK	Banco Santander and Abbey National	12.5
2007	Netherlands	ABN AMRO by RBS	72.0
2007	Italy	Unicredit and Capitalia	20.7

Source: Caterina Figueira, Joseph Nellis and Richard Shoenberg, 'Travel abroad or stay at home? Investigating the patterns of bank industry M&As in the EU', *European Business Review*, 19, 1 (2007): 23–30 and web sources.

---

in Table 12.3 but they include only two cross-border mergers or acquisition within the EU and one acquisition outside.

The number of banking financial institutions in the economies of the eurozone has fallen from a total of 11,877 in 1988 to 6,842 in 2008, a contraction of 5,035 over two decades or 250 institutions a year. A further 483 credit institutions closed in the two years to 2010.[3] The consolidation in the banking industry has not just been about merger and acquisition but also branch closure and de-staffing of the industry. Table 12.4 shows the decline in banking and credit institutions in the Big-4 economies of the EU in the two decades to 2008.

All said and done, has the competitive process driven by the single banking market programme resulted in a convergence in the price of credit across the EU economies and in particular the eurozone? The evidence is inconclusive. Economic theory suggests that a competitive market will result in a convergence in the price of homogeneous products and any differences will be accounted for by transactions costs. It is precisely the eradication of transactions costs that the single banking market is supposed to address. The empirical evidence suggests that differences in borrowing rates remain within the euro area and that

---

TABLE 12.4

Number of monetary financial institutions, 1988–2008

Country	1988	2008	Change
France	2050	338	−1712
Germany	4223	1816	−2407
Italy	1006	768	−238
UK	52	23	−29

Source: Adapted from OECD (2010) Classification of bank assets and liabilities.

markets are still segmented by national boundaries.[4] Bank credit is fairly homogeneous and it should not matter whether a mortgage loan of €250,000 over the same repayment period is issued by a Dutch bank or a German bank, so why should there be any difference in the rate of interest.

Some economists argue differences in the rate of interest rates charged for similar products by different banks do not necessarily indicate a lack of competitiveness. This is because banks differentiate from each other by selling a 'bundled product' of which retail loans, mortgages, credit and other loan products are bundled in with fee-based other financial services. Banks may underprice one product using a 'loss-leader' strategy so as to sell a premium priced product at a later stage. Therefore, it is the prices of the bundled products that should be compared with each other. However, measuring the price of a bundled service is easier said than done.

Is bank consolidation a good thing?

Advocates of 'bigger is better' banking believe that it will produce more efficient banks and a healthier banking system less prone to bank failures. However, critics of bank consolidation fear that it will eliminate small banks, and that this will result in less lending to small businesses. In addition, they worry that a few banks will come to dominate the industry, making the banking business less competitive.

Most economists are sceptical of these criticisms of bank consolidation. As long as the banking industry in the EU does not impose barriers to entry, the threat of entry will behave in a highly competitive manner, more so considering that banks have the single currency and the single banking programme to spur on competition.

Economists see some important benefits from bank consolidation. The elimination of geographic restrictions on banking will increase competition and drive inefficient banks out of business, increasing the efficiency of the banking sector. The move to larger banking organizations also means that there will be some increase in efficiency because they can take advantage of economies of scale and scope.[5] The increased diversification of banks' loan portfolios may lower the probability of a banking crisis in the future. In the 1980s and early 1990s, bank failures were often concentrated in countries with weak economies. Thus EU-wide banking is seen as a major step toward creating a banking system that is less vulnerable to banking crises.

Two concerns remain about the effects of bank consolidation – that it may lead to a reduction in lending to small businesses and that banks rushing to expand into new geographic markets may take increased risks, leading to bank failures. The jury is still out on these concerns, but most economists see the benefits of bank consolidation and EU-wide banking as outweighing the costs.

Financial innovation and the growth of the 'shadow banking system'

Although banking institutions remain the most important financial institutions in European economies, in recent years the traditional banking business of making loans that are funded by deposits has been in decline. Some of this business has been replaced by the **shadow banking system**, in which bank lending has been replaced by lending via the securities market.

To understand how this happened, we must first understand the process of financial innovation, which has transformed the entire financial system. Like other industries, the financial industry is in business to earn profits by selling its products. If a soap company perceives that there is a need in the marketplace for a laundry detergent with fabric softener, it develops a product to fit the need. Similarly, to maximize their profits, financial institutions develop new products to satisfy their own needs as well as those of their customers; in other words, innovation – which can be extremely beneficial to the economy – is driven by the desire to get (or stay) rich. This view of the innovation process leads to the following simple analysis: *a change in the financial environment will stimulate a search by financial institutions for innovations that are likely to be profitable*.

Starting in the 1960s, individuals and financial institutions operating in financial markets were confronted with drastic changes in the economic environment: inflation and interest rates climbed sharply and became harder to predict, a situation that changed demand conditions in financial markets. The rapid advance in computer technology changed supply conditions. In addition, financial regulations became more burdensome. Financial institutions found that many of the old ways of doing business were no longer profitable; the financial services and products they had been offering to the public were not selling. Many financial intermediaries found that they were no longer able to acquire funds with their traditional financial instruments, and without these funds they would soon be out of business. To survive in the new economic environment, financial institutions had to research and develop new products and services that would meet customer needs and prove profitable, a process referred to as **financial engineering**. In their case, necessity was the mother of innovation.

Our discussion of why financial innovation occurs suggests that there are three basic types of financial innovation: responses to changes in demand conditions, responses to changes in supply conditions, and avoidance of existing regulations. These three motivations often interact to produce particular financial innovations. Now that we have a framework for understanding why financial institutions produce innovations, let's look at examples of how financial institutions in their search for profits have produced financial innovations of the three basic types.

Responses to changes in demand conditions: interest-rate volatility

The most significant change in the economic environment that altered the demand for financial products in recent years has been the dramatic increase in the volatility of interest rates. In the 1950s, under the Bretton Woods system of fixed exchange rates where most currencies were fixed against the US dollar, interest rate fluctuations were modest. In the 1970s, after the break-up of the system of fixed exchange rates interest fluctuations were greater. Large fluctuations in interest rates led to substantial capital gains or losses and greater uncertainty about returns on investments. Recall that the risk that is related to the uncertainty about interest-rate movements and returns is called *interest-rate risk*, and high volatility of interest rates, such as we saw in the 1970s and 1980s, leads to a higher level of interest-rate risk.

We would expect the increase in interest-rate risk to increase the demand for financial products and services that could reduce that risk. This change in the economic environment would thus stimulate a search for profitable innovations by financial institutions that meet this new demand and would spur the creation of new financial instruments that help lower interest-rate risk. An example of financial innovations that appeared in the 1970s confirms these prediction, namely financial derivatives.

Financial derivatives

Given the greater demand for the reduction of interest-rate risk, commodity exchanges such as the Chicago Board of Trade recognized that if they could develop a product that would help investors and financial institutions to protect themselves from, or **hedge**, interest-rate risk, then they could make profits by selling this new instrument. **Futures contracts**, in which the seller agrees to provide a certain standardized commodity to the buyer on a specific future date at an agreed-on price, had been around for a long time.

Officials at the Chicago Board of Trade realized that if they created futures contracts in financial instruments, which are called **financial derivatives** because their payoffs are linked to (i.e. derived from) previously issued securities, they could be used to hedge risk. Thus, in 1975, financial derivatives were born and soon came to be traded worldwide.

Responses to changes in supply conditions: information technology

The most important source of the changes in supply conditions that stimulate financial innovation has been the improvement in computer and telecommunications technology. This technology, called *information technology*, has had two effects. First, it has lowered the cost of processing financial transactions, making it profitable for financial institutions to create new financial products and services for the public. Second, it has made it easier for investors to acquire information, thereby making it easier for firms to issue securities. The rapid developments in information technology have resulted in many new financial products and services that we examine here.

Bank credit and debit cards

Credit cards have been around since well before World War II. Many individual stores institutionalized charge accounts by providing customers with cards that allowed them to make purchases at these stores without cash. However, credit cards were not established until after World War II, when Diners Club developed one to be used in restaurants all over the world. Similar credit card programmes were started by American Express and Carte Blanche, but because of the high cost of operating these programmes, cards were issued only to selected persons and businesses that could afford expensive purchases.

A firm issuing credit cards earns income from loans it makes to credit card holders and from payments made by stores on credit card purchases (a percentage of the purchase price, say 5%). A credit card programme's costs arise from loan defaults, stolen cards and the expense involved in processing credit card transactions.

Seeing the success of Diners Club, American Express and Carte Blanche, bankers wanted to share in the profitable credit card business. Several commercial banks attempted to expand the credit card business to a wider market in the 1950s, but the cost per transaction of running these programmes was so high that their early attempts failed.

In the late 1960s, improved computer technology, which lowered the transaction costs for providing credit card services, made it more likely that bank credit card programmes would be profitable. The banks tried to enter this business again, and this time their efforts led to the creation of two successful bank credit card programmes: BankAmericard (originally started by Bank of America but now an independent organization called Visa) and MasterCharge (now MasterCard, run by the Interbank Card Association). These programmes have become phenomenally successful; more than 200 million of their cards are in use. Indeed, bank credit cards have been so profitable that non-financial institutions such as Marks & Spencer, General Motors, Tesco and Virgin have also entered the credit card business. Consumers have benefited because credit cards are more widely accepted than cheques to pay for purchases (particularly abroad), and they allow consumers to take out loans more easily.

The success of bank credit cards has led these institutions to come up with a new financial innovation, *debit cards*. Debit cards often look just like credit cards and can be used to make purchases in an identical fashion. However, in contrast to credit cards, which extend the purchaser a loan that does not have to be paid off immediately, a debit card purchase is immediately deducted from the cardholder's bank account. Debit cards depend even more on low costs of processing transactions, because their profits are generated entirely from the fees paid by merchants on debit card purchases at their stores. Debit cards have grown extremely popular in recent years.

Electronic banking

The wonders of modern computer technology have also enabled banks to lower the cost of bank transactions by having the customer interact with an electronic banking (e-banking) facility rather than with a human being. One important form of an e-banking facility is the **automated teller machine (ATM)**, an electronic machine that allows customers to get cash, make deposits, transfer funds from one account to another, and check balances. The ATM has the advantage that it does not have to be paid overtime and never sleeps, thus being available for use 24 hours a day. Not only does this result in cheaper transactions for the bank, but it also provides more convenience for the customer. Because of their low cost, ATMs can be put at locations other than a bank or its branches, further increasing customer convenience. Furthermore, it is now as easy to get local currency from an ATM when you are travelling abroad as it is to get cash from your local bank.

With the drop in the cost of telecommunications, banks have developed another financial innovation, *home banking.* It is now cost-effective for banks to set up an electronic banking facility in which the bank's customer is linked up with the bank's computer to carry out transactions by using either a telephone or a personal computer. Now a bank's customers can conduct many of their bank transactions without ever leaving the comfort of home. The advantage for the customer is the convenience of home banking, while banks find that the cost of transactions is substantially less than having the customer come to the bank. The success of ATMs and home banking has led to another innovation, the **automated banking machine (ABM)**, which combines in one location an ATM, an Internet connection to the bank's website and a telephone link to customer service.

With the decline in the price of personal computers and their increasing presence in the home, we have seen a further innovation in the home banking area, the appearance of a new type of banking institution, the **virtual bank**, a bank that has no physical location but rather exists only in cyberspace. In 1998, *First Direct*, the telephone banking arm of Midland (later taken over by HSBC), began to offer an array of banking services on the Internet – accepting cheque account and savings deposits, issuing ATM cards, providing bill-paying facilities and so on. The virtual bank thus takes home banking one step further, enabling the customer to have a full set of banking services at home 24 hours a day. Will virtual banking be the predominant form of banking in the future (see the 'Closer look' box, 'Will "clicks" dominate "bricks" in the banking industry')?

Junk bonds

With the improvement in information technology in the 1970s, it became easier for investors to acquire financial information about corporations, making it easier to screen out bad from good credit risks. With easier screening, investors were more willing to buy long-term debt securities from less-well-known corporations with lower credit ratings. With this change in supply conditions, we would expect that some smart individual would pioneer the concept of selling new public issues of junk bonds, not for fallen angels but for companies that had not yet achieved investment-grade status. This is exactly what Michael Milken of Drexel Burnham Lambert, an investment banking firm, started to do in 1977. Junk bonds became an important factor in the corporate bond market. Although there was a sharp slowdown in activity in the junk bond market after Milken was indicted for securities law violations in 1989, it heated up again in the 1990s and 2000s. Junk bonds do not just include bonds that have not reached investment grade status but the term also refers to bonds that have been downgraded by the credit-rating agencies to junk bond status.

Commercial paper market

Commercial paper is a short-term debt security issued by large banks and corporations. The commercial paper market has undergone tremendous growth in the 1980s and reached €250 billion by 2000. Indeed, commercial paper has been one of the fastest-growing money market instruments.

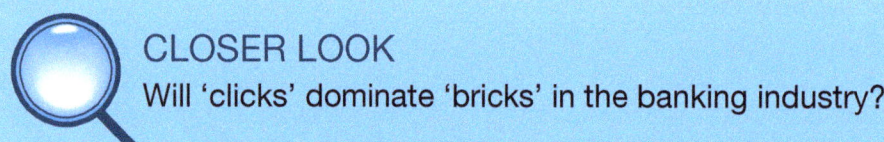

CLOSER LOOK
Will 'clicks' dominate 'bricks' in the banking industry?

With the advent of virtual banks ('clicks') and the convenience they provide, a key question is whether they will become the primary form in which banks do their business, eliminating the need for physical bank branches ('bricks') as the main delivery mechanism for banking services. Indeed, will stand-alone Internet banks be the wave of the future?

The answer seems to be no. Internet-only banks such as Wingspan (owned by Bank One), First-e (Dublin-based) and Egg (a British Internet-only bank owned by Prudential) have had disappointing revenue growth and profits. The result is that pure online banking has not been the success that proponents had hoped for. Why has Internet banking been a disappointment?

There are several strikes against Internet banking. First, bank depositors want to know that their savings are secure, and so are reluctant to put their money into new institutions without a long track record. Second, customers worry about the security of their online transactions

and whether their transactions will truly be kept private. Traditional banks are viewed as being more secure and trustworthy in terms of releasing private information. Third, customers may prefer services provided by physical branches. For example, banking customers seem to prefer to purchase long-term savings products face-to-face. Fourth, Internet banking has run into technical problems – server crashes, slow connections over phone lines, mistakes in conducting transactions – that will probably diminish over time as technology improves.

The wave of the future thus does not appear to be pure Internet banks. Instead it looks like 'clicks and bricks' will be the predominant form of banking, in which online banking is used to complement the services provided by traditional banks. Nonetheless, the delivery of banking services is undergoing massive changes, with more and more banking services delivered over the Internet and the number of physical bank branches likely to decline in the future.

Improvements in information technology also help provide an explanation for the rapid rise of the commercial paper market. We have seen that the improvement in information technology made it easier for investors to screen out bad from good credit risks, thus making it easier for corporations to issue debt securities. Not only did this make it easier for corporations to issue long-term debt securities as in the junk bond market, but it also meant that they could raise funds by issuing short-term debt securities such as commercial paper more easily. Many corporations that used to do their short-term borrowing from banks now frequently raise short-term funds in the commercial paper market instead.

Securitization

An important example of a financial innovation arising from improvements in both transaction and information technology is securitization, one of the most important financial innovations in the past two decades, which played an especially prominent role in the development of the subprime mortgage market in the mid-2000s. **Securitization** is the process of transforming otherwise illiquid financial assets (such as residential mortgages, auto loans and credit card receivables), which have typically been the bread and butter of banking institutions, into marketable capital market securities. As we have seen, improvements in the ability to acquire information have made it easier to sell capital market securities. In addition, with low transaction costs because of improvements in computer technology, financial institutions find that they can cheaply bundle together a portfolio of loans (such as mortgages) with varying small denominations, collect the interest and principal payments on the mortgages in the bundle, and then 'pass them through' (pay them out) to third parties. By dividing the portfolio of loans into standardized amounts, the financial institution can then sell the claims to these interest and principal payments to third parties as securities. The standardized amounts of these securitized loans make them liquid securities, and the fact that they are made up of a bundle of loans helps diversify risk, making them desirable. The financial institution selling the securitized loans makes a profit by servicing the loans (collecting the interest and principal payments and paying them out) and charging a fee to the third party for this service.

Avoidance of existing regulations

The process of financial innovation we have discussed so far is much like innovation in other areas of the economy: it occurs in response to changes in demand and supply conditions. However, because the financial industry is more heavily regulated than other industries, government regulation is a much greater spur to innovation in this industry. Government regulation leads to financial innovation by creating incentives for firms to skirt regulations that restrict their ability to earn profits. Edward Kane, an economist at Boston College, describes this process of avoiding regulations as 'loophole mining'. The economic analysis of innovation suggests that when the economic environment changes such that regulatory constraints are so burdensome that large profits can be made by avoiding them, loophole mining and innovation are more likely to occur.

Because banking is one of the most heavily regulated industries in all countries, loophole mining is especially likely to occur. The rise in inflation and interest rates from the late 1960s to 1980 made the regulatory constraints imposed on this industry even more burdensome, leading to financial innovation.

In countries outside Europe and the US, banks also faced increased competition from the expansion of securities markets and the growth of the shadow banking system. Both financial deregulation and fundamental economic forces in other countries have improved the availability of information in securities markets, making it easier and less costly for firms to finance their activities by issuing securities rather than going to banks. Further, even in countries where securities markets have not grown, banks have still lost loan business because their best corporate customers have had increasing access to foreign and offshore capital markets, such as the Eurobond market. In smaller economies, like Australia, which still do not have as well-developed corporate bond or commercial paper markets, banks have lost loan business to international securities markets. In addition, the same forces that drove the securitization process in the United States have been at work in other countries and have undercut the profitability of traditional banking in these countries as well. The United States has not been unique in seeing its banks face a more difficult competitive environment. Thus, although the decline of traditional banking occurred earlier in the United States than in other countries, the same forces have caused a decline in traditional banking elsewhere.

Technology

Not surprisingly, the advent of the Web and improved computer technology is another factor driving bank consolidation. Economies of scale have increased, because large upfront investments are required to set up many information technology platforms for financial institutions. To take advantage of these economies of scale, banks have needed to get bigger, and this development has led to additional consolidation. Information technology has also been increasing **economies of scope**, the ability to use one resource to provide many different products and services. For example, details about the quality and creditworthiness of firms not only inform decisions about whether to make loans to them, but also can be useful in determining at what price their shares should trade. Similarly, once you have marketed one financial product to an investor, you probably know how to market another. Business people describe economies of scope by saying that there are 'synergies' between different lines of business, and information technology is making these synergies more likely. The result is that consolidation is taking place not only to make financial institutions bigger, but also to increase the combination of products and services they can provide. This consolidation has had two consequences. First, different types of financial intermediaries are encroaching on each other's territory, making them more alike. Second, consolidation has led to the development of what the Federal Reserve in the US has named **large, complex banking organizations (LCBOs)**.

Financial innovation and the decline of traditional banking

The traditional financial intermediation role of banking has been to make long-term loans and to fund them by issuing short-term deposits, a process of asset transformation commonly referred to as 'borrowing short and lending long'. Here we examine how financial innovations have created a more competitive environment for the banking industry, causing the industry to change dramatically, with its traditional banking business going into decline.

To understand why traditional banking business has declined in size we need to look at how the financial innovations described earlier have caused banks to suffer declines in their cost advantages in acquiring funds – that is, on the liabilities side of their balance sheet – while at the same time they have lost income advantages on the assets side of their balance sheet. The simultaneous decline of cost and income advantages has resulted in reduced profitability of traditional banking and an effort by banks to leave this business and engage in new and more profitable activities.

One of the problems banks faced was that the rise in inflation during the 1970s led to higher interest rates which made savers more aware of interest rate differentials between savings instruments. Demand deposits traditionally paid no interest and depositors were finding homes for their funds outside the banking system, leading to what is termed the process of *disintermediation*. During the late 1970s banks began to pay interest on deposits that responded to changes in market rates of interest. Although these changes helped make banks more competitive in their quest for funds, it also meant that their cost of acquiring funds had risen substantially, thereby reducing their earlier cost advantage over other financial institutions.

The loss of cost advantages on the liabilities side of the balance sheet for banks is one reason that they have become less competitive, but they have also been hit by a decline in income advantages on the assets side from the financial innovations we discussed earlier – junk bonds, securitization and the rise of the commercial paper market. The resulting loss of income advantages for banks relative to these innovations has resulted in a loss of market share and has led to the growth of the shadow banking system, which has made use of these innovations to enable borrowers to bypass the traditional banking system.

We have seen also that improvements in information technology have made it easier for firms to issue securities directly to the public. This has meant that instead of going to banks to finance short-term credit needs, many of the banks' best business customers now find it cheaper to go instead to the commercial paper market for funds. In addition, the commercial paper market has allowed finance companies, which depend primarily on commercial paper to acquire funds, to expand their operations at the expense of banks. Finance companies, which lend to many of the same businesses that borrow from banks, have increased their market share relative to banks.

We have also seen that improvements in computer technology have led to securitization, whereby illiquid financial assets such as bank loans and mortgages are transformed into marketable securities. Computers enable other financial institutions to originate loans because they can now accurately evaluate credit risk with statistical methods, while computers have lowered transaction costs, making it possible to bundle these loans and sell them as securities. When default risk can be easily evaluated with computers, banks no longer have an advantage in making loans. Without their former advantages, banks have lost loan business to other financial institutions even though the banks themselves are involved in the process of securitization. Securitization has been a particular problem for mortgage-issuing institutions such as savings and loan companies, because most residential mortgages are now securitized.

Banks' responses

In any industry, a decline in profitability usually results in an exit from the industry (often due to widespread bankruptcies) and shrinkage of market share. We have seen that within the European Union exit through bankruptcy has not been the adopted route. Banks have exited from the industry through consolidation.

In an attempt to survive and maintain adequate profit levels, banks faced two alternatives. First, they could attempt to maintain their traditional lending activity by expanding into new and riskier areas of lending. For example, banks particularly in the UK increased their risk taking by placing a greater percentage of their total funds in commercial real estate loans, traditionally a riskier type of loan. In addition, they increased lending for corporate takeovers and leveraged buyouts, which are highly leveraged transaction loans. The decline in the profitability of banks' traditional business may thus have helped lead to the crisis in banking starting in 2007.

Structure of the European commercial banking industry

There were 6,334 commercial banks in the eurozone economies in 2010, comparable with around 7,000 in the United States. In contrast, in the United Kingdom five or fewer banks dominate the industry. The ten largest commercial banks in the United States together hold just 53% of the assets in their industry. In comparison the ten largest banks in the euro area hold 47% of the assets in the banking industry (see Table 12.5). In terms of size and structure the euro area banking system is not dissimilar to that of the US if viewed from cross-border euro perspective. However, within borders there are large differences in terms of structure. For instance in the Netherlands three to four banks dominated 80 – 90% of the entire Dutch banking sector.

However, like the US, where the restrictions on interstate banking that became policy following the Great Depression years made banking develop for local economy needs, banking in Europe has largely developed within borders. Despite the best intentions of the single banking market programme, we have seen that the competitive pressure exerted by

TABLE 12.5

Ten largest banks in the eurozone, 30 December 2010

Bank	Assets (€ billions)	Share of all commercial bank assets (%)
1 BNP Paribas (France)	1,998.2	7.7
2 Deutsche Bank (Germany)	1,905.6	7.4
3 Credit Agricole (France)	1,730.8	6.7
4 ING Group (Netherlands)	1,247.1	4.8
5 Banco Santander (Spain)	1,217.5	4.7
6 Société Générale (France)	1,132.1	4.4
7 Unicredit Group (Italy)	929.5	3.6
8 Commerzbank (Germany)	754.3	2.9
9 Intesa Sanpaolo (Italy)	658.8	2.6
10 Dexia (Belgium)	566.7	2.1
Total	2,5826.1	47.0

Source: Bankscope.

TABLE 12.6

Ownership of domestic banks by cross-border source (%), December 2010

	France	Germany	Italy	UK
France	93.67	0.45	2.28	0.04
Germany	0.02	90.39	0.70	0.07
Italy	0.01	4.72	95.12	0.01
UK	2.73	0.26	0.04	81.53
Other EU	0.09	3.32	1.63	4.11
Non-EU	3.48	0.86	0.23	14.24

Source: Ray Barrell, Tatiana Fic, John Fitzgerald, Ali Orazgani and Rachel Whitworth, 'The banking sector and recovery in the EU economy', *National Institute of Economic and Social Research*, December 2010.

it, and even with the advantage of the single currency area, the convergence to a common rate of interest for loan products has had only limited success. There is also a strong home bias in the ownership of banks, with few cross-border transactions in the consolidation process. Table 12.6 shows the ownership share of the banks in the Big-4 economies of the EU. The Big-3 of the euro area have little other EU country ownership of their banks. Only the UK has nearly 20% foreign ownership of domestic banks. It is very likely that the latter result is more to do with London being an international centre for banking and finance rather than the pressure caused by the single banking market.

Does the large number of banks in the commercial banking industry and the absence of a few dominant firms suggest that commercial banking is competitive in the euro area? Table 12.6 suggests that despite the advantages that a single currency may produce for the competitive process and the imperatives of the single banking market, banking in the eurozone remains territorial. Within the boundaries of each country in the EU, banking is dominated by a few large banks. So while superficially having similarities between the banking industry in Europe as a whole and the US, the model of banking in continental Europe is strikingly different from the banking tradition of the Anglo-Saxon economies. There are three basic frameworks for the banking and securities industries.

The first framework is *universal banking,* which exists in Germany, the Netherlands and Switzerland. It provides no separation at all between the banking and securities industries. In a universal banking system, commercial banks provide a full range of banking, securities, real estate and insurance services, all within a single legal entity. Banks are allowed to own sizeable equity shares in commercial firms, and often they do.

The *British-style universal banking system,* the second framework, is found in the United Kingdom and countries with close historical ties to it, such as Canada and Australia, and now the United States. The British-style universal bank engages in securities underwriting, but it differs from the German-style universal bank in three ways: separate legal subsidiaries are more common, bank equity holdings of commercial firms are less common, and combinations of banking and insurance firms are less common.

The third framework features some legal separation of the banking and other financial services industries, as in Japan. A major difference between the UK and Japanese banking systems is that Japanese banks are allowed to hold substantial equity stakes in commercial firms, whereas UK and American banks cannot. While the banking and securities industries are legally separated in Japan under Section 65 of the Japanese Securities Act, commercial banks are increasingly being allowed to engage in securities activities and are becoming more like British-style universal banks.

CLOSER LOOK
The subprime financial crisis and the demise of large, free-standing investment banks in the US

Although the move toward bringing financial service activities into larger, complex banking organizations was inevitable after the repeal of the Glass – Steagall Act that separated commercial banking from investment banking, no one expected it to occur as rapidly as it did in 2008. Over a six-month period from March to September 2008, all five of the largest, free-standing investment banks in the US ceased to exist in their old form. When Bear Stearns, the fifth-largest investment bank, revealed its large losses from investments in subprime mortgage securities, it had to be bailed out by the Federal Reserve in March 2008; the price it paid was a forced sale to JPMorgan for less than one-tenth what it had been worth only a year or so before. The Bear Stearns bailout made it clear that the government safety net had been extended to investment banks. The trade-off is that investment banks will be subject to more regulation, along the lines of commercial banks, in the future.

Next to go was Lehman Brothers, the fourth-largest investment bank, which declared bankruptcy on 15 September. Only one day before, Merrill Lynch, the third-largest investment bank, which also suffered large losses on its holdings of subprime securities, announced its sale to Bank of America for less than half of its year-earlier price. Within a week Goldman Sachs and Morgan Stanley, the first- and second-largest investment banks, both of which had smaller exposure to subprime securities, nevertheless saw the writing on the wall. They realized that they would soon become regulated on a similar basis and decided to become bank holding companies so they could access insured deposits, a more stable funding base.

It was the end of an era. Large, free-standing investment banking firms are now a thing of the past.

International banking

The dominance of Britain in global trade in the nineteenth century provided the economic impetus for the expansion of banking overseas. In some ways it can be argued that banking has always been global, either through the creation of overseas branches or through *correspondent banking*, where a bank in one country would have a commercial relationship with a bank in another country. Through overseas branches and correspondent relationships, London banks were able to follow their customers across the British Empire and help in the process of developing global trade relationships.

However, modern international banking as it is understood today really took off after the Second World War with the setting up of US bank branches in London and other financial centres. The US banks imported modern management styles and methods of banking that were soon adopted by banks all over the world. In 1960, only eight US banks operated branches in foreign countries, and their total assets were less than $4 billion. Currently, around 100 American banks have branches abroad, with assets totalling more than $2.5 trillion. The spectacular growth in international banking can be explained by three factors.

First is the rapid growth in international trade and multinational (worldwide) corporations that has occurred since 1960. When American firms operate abroad, they need banking services in foreign countries to help finance international trade. For example, they might need a loan in a foreign currency to operate a factory abroad. And when they sell goods abroad, they need to have a bank exchange the foreign currency they have received for their goods into dollars. Although these firms could use foreign banks to provide them with these international banking services, many of them prefer to do business with the US banks with which they have established long-term relationships and which understand American business customs and practices. As international trade has grown, international banking has grown with it.

Second, American banks have been able to earn substantial profits by being very active in global investment banking, in which they underwrite foreign securities. They also sell insurance abroad, and they derive substantial profits from these investment banking and insurance activities.

Third, American banks have wanted to tap into the large pool of dollar-denominated deposits in foreign countries known as eurodollars. To understand the structure of US banking overseas, let us first look at the eurodollar market, an important source of growth for international banking.

Eurodollar market

Eurodollars are created when deposits in accounts in the United States are transferred to a bank outside the country and are kept in the form of dollars. (For a discussion of the birth of the eurodollar, see the Global box, 'Ironic birth of the eurodollar market'.) For example, if Rolls-Royce PLC deposits a $1 million cheque, written on an account at an American bank, in its bank in London – specifying that the deposit is payable in dollars – $1 million in eurodollars is created.[6] More than 90% of eurodollar deposits are time deposits, more than half of them certificates of deposit with maturities of 30 days or more. The total amount of eurodollars outstanding is of the order of $5.2 trillion, making the eurodollar market one of the most important financial markets in the world economy.

Why would companies such as Rolls-Royce want to hold dollar deposits outside the United States? First, the dollar is the most widely used currency in international trade, so Rolls-Royce might want to hold deposits in dollars to conduct its international transactions. Second, eurodollars are 'offshore' deposits – they are held in countries that will not subject them to regulations such as reserve requirements or restrictions (called *capital controls*) on taking the deposits outside the country.[7]

The main centre of the eurodollar market is London, a major international financial centre for hundreds of years. Eurodollars are also held outside Europe in locations that provide offshore status to these deposits – for example, Singapore, the Bahamas and the Cayman Islands.

The minimum transaction in the eurodollar market is typically $1 million, and approximately 75% of eurodollar deposits are held by banks. Plainly, you and I are unlikely to come into direct contact with eurodollars. The eurodollar market is, however, an important source of funds to US banks. Rather than using an intermediary and borrowing all the deposits from foreign banks, American banks decided that they could earn higher profits by opening their own branches abroad to attract these deposits. Consequently, the eurodollar market has been an important stimulus to US banking overseas.

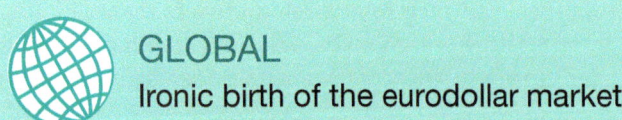

GLOBAL
Ironic birth of the eurodollar market

One of capitalism's great ironies is that the eurodollar market, one of the most important financial markets used by capitalists, was fathered by the Soviet Union. In the early 1950s, at the height of the Cold War, the Soviets had accumulated a substantial amount of dollar balances held by banks in the United States. Because the Russians feared that the US government might freeze these assets in the United States, they wanted to move the deposits to Europe, where they would be safe from expropriation.

(This fear was not unjustified – consider the US freeze on Iranian assets in 1979 and Iraqi assets in 1990.) However, they also wanted to keep the deposits in dollars so that they could be used in their international transactions. The solution to the problem was to transfer the deposits to European banks but to keep the deposits denominated in dollars. When the Soviets did this, the eurodollar was born.

Ten largest banks in the world, 30 December 2010

Bank	Assets (US $ billions)
1 BNP Paribas, France	2,669.9
2 Deutsche Bank AG, Germany	2,546.3
3 HSBC, UK	2,454.7
4 Mitsubishi UFJ Financial Group, Japan	2,384.4
5 Barclays plc, UK	2,331.9
6 Credit Agricole, France	2,312.7
7 Royal Bank of Scotland, UK	2,275.5
8 Bank of America, US	2,264.9
9 JPMorgan Chase, US	2,117.6
10 Industrial and Commercial Bank of China, China	2,032.1

Source: Bankscope.

The internationalization of banking

Another development has been the importance of foreign banks in international banking. The growth in international trade has not only encouraged banks in Europe, the UK and the US to open offices overseas, but has also encouraged non-EU and non-US banks to establish offices in the United States and the EU.

The internationalization of banking, by UK and other European banks going abroad and by foreign banks setting up in London or Frankfurt, has meant that financial markets throughout the world have become more integrated. As a result, there is a growing trend toward international coordination of bank regulation, one example of which is the Basel Regulations to standardize bank capital and liquidity requirements in industrialized countries, as discussed in Chapter 11. Financial market integration has also encouraged bank consolidation abroad, culminating in the creation of the first trillion-dollar bank with the merger of the Industrial Bank of Japan, Dai-Ichi Kangyo Bank and Fuji Bank in 2002. Another development has been the importance of non-US banks in international banking. As is shown in Table 12.7, in 2010, eight of the ten largest banking groups (in terms of assets) in the world were non-US. The implications of this financial market integration for the operation of the economy are examined further in Chapter 18 when we discuss the international financial system in more detail.

Summary

1 The three main trends in banking have been the trend of deregulation, the trend to globalization and the trend in financial innovation. These trends have worked together to improve the competitiveness of banking in Europe.

2 In Europe the Single Banking Market was developed to provide further impetus for improving competition in banking and financial services in the EU. The programme has had some success in improving competition and narrowing spreads but it is unclear if the SBM programme did more than what would have happened as a result of the major trends in world banking.

3 A change in the economic environment will stimulate financial institutions to search for financial innovations. Changes in demand conditions, especially an increase in interest-rate risk; changes in supply conditions, especially improvements in information technology; and the desire to avoid costly regulations have been major driving forces behind financial innovation. Financial innovation has caused banks to suffer declines in cost advantages in

acquiring funds and in income advantages on their assets. The resulting squeeze has hurt profitability in banks' traditional lines of business and has led to a decline in traditional banking.

4 Since the mid-1980s, bank consolidation has been occurring at a rapid pace. Most economists believe that the benefits of bank consolidation will outweigh the costs.

5 With the rapid growth of world trade since 1960, international banking has grown dramatically. Banks engage in international banking activities by opening branches abroad, owning controlling interests in foreign banks and operating international banking facilities.

Key terms

automated banking machine (ABM) p. 261

automated teller machine (ATM) p. 261

economies of scope p. 263

financial derivatives p. 260

financial engineering p. 259

futures contracts p. 259

hedge p. 259

large, complex banking organizations (LCBOs) p. 264

net interest margin (NIM) p. 255

securitization p. 262

shadow banking system p. 258

single banking market p. 252

virtual bank p. 261

QUESTIONS AND PROBLEMS

All questions and problems are available in MyEconLab at **www.myeconlab.com/mishkin**.

1 Why was the United States one of the last of the major industrialized countries to have a central bank?

2 Explain the key objectives of the Single Banking Market in Europe.

3 What were the three phases of bank deregulation within the European Union?

4 Why did new technology make it harder to enforce limitations on bank branching?

5 Why has there been such a dramatic increase in bank holding companies?

6 How have the banks in Europe and elsewhere responded to the forces of competition?

7 Explain any economic benefits from bank consolidation across Europe.

8 What incentives have regulatory agencies created to encourage international banking? Why have they done this?

9 What are the key differences between the structure of commercial banking in the United Kingdom versus the United States?

10 If the bank at which you keep your current account is owned by investors outside Europe (e.g. Saudi Arabians), should you worry that your deposits are less safe than if the bank were owned by Europeans?

11 What are the key advantages to corporate borrowers and/or banks of using Eurodollars?

12 What are the key characteristics of universal banking as found in, for example, Germany?

13 'The invention of the computer is the major factor behind the decline of the banking industry.' Is this statement true, false, or uncertain? Explain your answer.

WEB EXERCISES

1 In response to the eurozone sovereign debt crisis, there have been moves towards a single banking regulator (**http://ec.europa.eu/internal_market/bank/index_en.htm**). As stated, achieving an integrated market for banks and financial conglomerates is a core component of the European financial services policy. From their 'News' feed – **http://ec.europa.eu/internal_market/bank/news/index_en.htm** – discuss any recent developments in European banking policy.

2 In 2011, a High-level Expert Group was formed to examine possible reforms to the structure of the EU's banking sector. Its mandate was to determine whether, in addition to ongoing regulatory reforms, structural reforms of EU banks would strengthen financial stability and improve efficiency and consumer protection. Read their October 2012 report here and summarize their key recommendations: **http://ec.europa.eu/internal_market/bank/docs/high-level_expert_group/report_en.pdf**.

3 Despite the regulations that protect banks from failure, some do fail. The FDIC in the United States maintains a useful database of bank failures (**http://www.fdic.gov/bank/historical/bank/**). How many bank failures occurred in the United States during the most recent complete calendar year? What were the total assets held by the banks that failed? How many banks failed in each of the past 10 years?

4 Northern Rock is a high-profile victim of the recent financial crisis. Several case studies examine its failure. The most comprehensive is 'The Failure of Northern Rock - A Multidimensional Case Study' (**http://www.suerf.org/download/studies/study20091.pdf**). What three issues stand out from this analysis of the failure of Northern Rock?

Notes

1 An example of this is the attempt of the former governor of the Italian Central Bank Antonio Fazio to rig the takeover of Banca Antonveneta by another Italian bank rather than a non-Italian bank in 2005. Antonio Fazio was convicted of attempting to rig the sale of Banca Nazionale del Lavoro (BNL) so that it would not be taken over by BBVA of Spain. It was ultimately taken over by BNP Paribas in 2005.

2 We can see that from the following expression. Let interest earnings (IE) be given by $r_A A$ where r_A is the average interest on earning assets (A) and interest costs (IC) be given by $r_D D$ where r_D is the average interest rate on deposits (D).

$$NIM = \frac{r_A A - r_D D}{A} = r_A - r_D \frac{D}{A} = r_A - r_D + (1 - \frac{D}{A})r_D$$
$$= spread + (1 - \frac{D}{A})r_D$$

3 Table 2.11 European Central Bank, *The Monetary Policy of the ECB*, 2011.

4 Massimiliano Affinito and Fabio Farabullini, 'Does the law of one price hold in the euro-area retail banking? An empirical analysis of interest rate differentials across monetary union', *International Journal of Central Banking*, 5, 1 (2009): 5–37.

5 Economies of scope occur when the production of more than one good or service jointly is cheaper than producing them individually. In the case of banking, a bank can reduce unit costs if it not only dispenses loan products but also cross-sells other financial services.

6 Note that the London bank keeps the $1 million on deposit at the American bank, so the creation of eurodollars has not caused a reduction in the amount of bank deposits in the United States.

7 Although most offshore deposits are denominated in dollars, some are denominated in other currencies. Collectively, these offshore deposits are referred to as Eurocurrencies. A Japanese yen-denominated deposit held in London, for example, is called a euroyen.

Useful websites

www.bankofengland.co.uk/statistics/Pages/bankstats/default.aspx Bank of England's 'Bankstats' (Monetary & Financial Statistics).

www.ecb.int/stats/money/consolidated/html/index.en.html ECB page with information on the aggregate consolidated profitability, balance sheets and solvency of EU banks.

http://sdw.ecb.europa.eu/browse.do?node=2018773 Statistics regarding monetary financial institutions (MFIs), investment funds, financial stability and financial markets, and payments within the euro area.

www.fdic.gov/bank/ The FDIC gathers data about individual US financial institutions and the banking industry.

PART 4
CENTRAL BANKING

Crisis and response: The monetary policy of the ECB, the Bank of England and the Fed

The onset of the subprime financial crisis in August 2007 was a curve ball for Ben Bernanke, the Chairman of the Federal Reserve, and his fellow members of the FOMC (Federal Open Market Committee). The subprime financial crisis, described by former Chairman Alan Greenspan as a 'once-in-a-century credit tsunami', had the potential to devastate the economy.

The Federal Reserve resolved to come to the rescue. Starting in September 2007, the Fed lowered the federal funds rate target, bringing it down to zero by the end of 2008. At the same time, the Fed implemented large liquidity injections into the credit markets to try to get them lending again. In a similar vein, the Bank of England reduced the official bank rate from 5.75% to 0.5% from December 2007 to March 2009. The ECB reacted slightly later, but quite aggressively as well. Its main refinancing rate was dropped from 4.25% in July 2008 to 1% in May 2009. At first, it appeared that the central banks' actions would keep the growth slowdown mild and prevent a recession. However, the economy proved to be weaker than expected and financial markets highly volatile. With official interest rates almost at zero, central banks started implementing unconventional policies. The Bank of England, for instance, implemented a 'quantitative easing' policy by purchasing government and corporate bonds from the private sector. In the euro area, the ECB undertook non-standard measures exploiting the flexibility of its existing conventional tools.

The recent crisis has demonstrated the importance of central banks like the ECB, the Bank of England and the Federal Reserve to the health of the financial system and the economy. Chapter 13 outlines what central banks are trying to achieve, what motivates them, and how they are set up. Chapter 14 describes how the money supply is determined. In Chapter 15, we look at the tools that central banks like the ECB have at their disposal and how they use them. Chapter 16 extends the discussion of how monetary policy is conducted to focus on the broader picture of central banks' strategies and tactics.

CHAPTER 13

The goals and structure
of central banks

PREVIEW

Among the most important players in financial markets throughout the world are central banks, the government authorities in charge of monetary policy. Central banks' actions affect interest rates, the amount of credit and the money supply, all of which have direct impacts not only on financial markets, but also on aggregate output and inflation. To understand the role that central banks play in financial markets and the overall economy, we need to understand how these organizations work. Who controls central banks and determines their actions? What motivates their behaviour? Who holds the reins of power?

In this chapter, we look at the goals and institutional structure of major central banks, with a particular focus on the European Central Bank (ECB), the Bank of England and the Federal Reserve. We start by examining what central banks are trying to do, and then focus on the elements of the institutional structure of these three central banks that determine where the true power lies. By understanding who makes the decisions, we will have a better idea of how they are made. We then shall take a quick tour around the world to look at the organization of several other major central banks, in a number of industrial nations, emerging economies and developing countries. Finally, we examine what explains central bank behaviour and whether it is a good idea to make central banks independent by insulating them from politicians. With this context in place, we will be prepared to comprehend the actual conduct of monetary policy described in the following chapters.

The price stability goal and the nominal anchor

Over the past few decades, policymakers throughout the world have become increasingly aware of the social and economic costs of inflation and more concerned with maintaining a stable price level as a goal of economic policy. Indeed, **price stability**, which central bankers define as low and stable inflation, is increasingly viewed as the most important goal of monetary policy. Price stability is desirable because a rising price level (inflation) creates uncertainty in the economy, and that uncertainty might hamper economic growth (see Closer look box: 'What are the benefits of price stability?'). This view is supported by a growing body of evidence suggesting that inflation leads to lower economic growth.[1] The most extreme example of unstable prices is *hyperinflation*, such as Argentina, Brazil and Russia have experienced in the recent past. Hyperinflation has proved to be very damaging to the workings of the economy. Furthermore, inflation can strain a country's social fabric, resulting in severe conflicts. In the first half of 2008, the higher cost of living spawned violent rioting in countries ranging from Côte d'Ivoire and Egypt to Haiti, Indonesia and

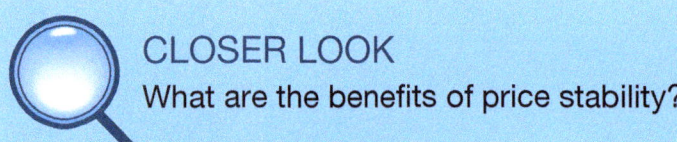

CLOSER LOOK
What are the benefits of price stability?

Inflation may pose a serious threat to a country's economic welfare and social freedom. Beyond these general risks, economic theory provides several reasons for price stability to be a primary policy objective. In the following we will restrict ourselves to the main arguments officially stressed by the European Central Bank in support of price stability as the major goal of monetary policy.*

First, price stability facilitates the efficient allocation of resources in the economy by making it easier for people to disentangle changes in relative prices (that is movements in prices of individual goods and services) from changes of the general price level. For example, let us assume that the price of a certain product rises. If the overall price level remains stable, consumption of the product may fall because consumers know that the relative price of the product has increased. If, however, uncertainty about the overall price level is high, people cannot assess the relative price change of the product. In our example consumers may be unaware of the fact that the price increase of the product simply reflects a rise in the general price level. As a result, consumers may buy less of the product if they mistakenly assume a rise in the relative price of the product. This simple example shows that price stability, by leading to a higher transparency of relative prices, allows the market to allocate resources more efficiently.

Second, price stability reduces the distortionary effects of the tax and social security systems. Fiscal systems do not normally allow for the indexation of tax rates and social security contributions to the inflation rate. As a result, inflation or deflation exacerbates these distortionary effects. To clarify this point, let us take a simple case in which an investor buys a stock today at €100. One year later he sells the stock for €110. The nominal capital gain of €10 will be subject to taxation. Now, assuming an inflation rate of 10% over the one-year period, the real capital gain of the investor will be zero. However, despite not being better off in real terms, the investor will be liable to pay capital gain taxes on the €10 nominal gain.

Third, low and predictable inflation prevents the arbitrary redistribution of wealth. High inflation is associated with high uncertainty about the future inflation rate, implying that actual inflation is likely to deviate from expected inflation. Unexpected inflation is bad since it leads to unintended wealth transfers between creditors and debtors. To understand this, consider two parties agreeing on a loan of €100 with a maturity of one year. Both parties agree on a real interest rate of 2%. Since

expected inflation is 2%, the nominal interest rate is fixed at 4%. Suppose now that actual inflation runs at 6% instead of the expected 2%. If both parties had correctly anticipated the inflation rate, they would have agreed on a nominal interest rate of 8%. Then the creditor would have received a final repayment of €108 instead of the agreed €104. In fact, unexpected inflation has led to an unintended wealth redistribution of €4 from the creditor to the debtor.

Fourth, price stability benefits economic growth via a reduction of inflation-risk premia in interest rates. If investors are uncertain about the general price development, they will ask for an inflation-risk premium to compensate them for the possibility of rising inflation. By reducing these risk premia in the real interest rates, price stability contributes to the efficient allocation of resources operating through the capital markets, increasing the incentives to invest.

Fifth, stable prices contribute to avoiding unnecessary hedging activities. If prices are unstable people and firms tend to protect (i.e. to 'hedge') themselves against inflation or deflation. For example, a high-inflation environment may lead to the stockpiling of real goods since they retain their value better than money and other financial assets. The means being eaten up by hedging activities reduces the amount of available resources that can be channelled into productive capacities. A lack of price stability therefore prevents an efficient allocation of resources in the economy, thereby hindering economic growth.

Finally, stable prices increase the benefits of holding cash. Since higher inflation leads to higher nominal interest rates, the opportunity cost of holding money increases with a rising price level. Consequently, people will reduce their cash holdings. If people decrease their money balances they must make more frequent trips to the bank. For example, they may withdraw €100 from their bank account twice a week instead of €200 once a week. The inconvenience arising from the reduced money holdings is commonly referred to as 'shoe-leather costs' as more frequent trips to the bank cause one's shoes to wear out more quickly. With lower inflation these trips would become redundant and people could be spending their time on other things instead.

---

* This box is based on benefits of price stability listed on pages 56–7 of Chapter 3 of ECB, *The Monetary Policy of the ECB* (2011), which can be found at www.ecb.int/pub/html/index .en.html.

the Philippines. Against these high economic and social costs public opinion surveys, not surprisingly, indicate that the public is hostile to inflation.

The role of a nominal anchor

Because price stability is so crucial to the long-run health of an economy, a central element in successful monetary policy is the use of a nominal anchor, a nominal variable such as the nominal exchange rate, wage and price controls, or the money supply, which ties down the price level to achieve price stability. Adherence to a nominal anchor that keeps the nominal variable within a narrow range promotes price stability by directly promoting low and stable inflation expectations. A more subtle reason for a nominal anchor's importance is that it can limit the time-inconsistency problem, in which monetary policy conducted on a discretionary, day-by-day basis leads to poor long-run outcomes.[2]

The time-inconsistency problem

The time-inconsistency problem is something we deal with continually in everyday life. We often have a plan that we know will produce a good outcome in the long run, but when tomorrow comes, we just can't help ourselves and we renege on our plan because doing so has short-run gains. For example, we make a New Year's resolution to go on a diet, but soon thereafter we can't resist having one more bite of that rocky road ice cream – and then another bite, and then another bite – and the weight begins to pile back on. In other words, we find ourselves unable to *consistently* follow a good plan over *time*; the good plan is said to be *time-inconsistent* and will soon be abandoned.

Monetary policymakers also face the time-inconsistency problem. They are always tempted to pursue a discretionary monetary policy that is more expansionary than firms or people expect because such a policy would boost economic output (or lower unemployment) in the short run. The best policy, however, is *not* to pursue expansionary policy, because decisions about wages and prices reflect workers' and firms' expectations about policy; when they see a central bank pursuing expansionary policy, workers and firms will raise their expectations about inflation, driving wages and prices up. The rise in wages and prices will lead to higher inflation, but will not result in higher output on average. (We examine this issue more formally in Chapter 25.)

A central bank will have better inflation performance in the long run if it does not try to surprise people with an unexpectedly expansionary policy, but instead keeps inflation under control. However, even if a central bank recognizes that discretionary policy will lead to a poor outcome (high inflation with no gains in output), it still may not be able to pursue the better policy of inflation control, because politicians are likely to apply pressure on the central bank to try to boost output with overly expansionary monetary policy.

A clue as to how we should deal with the time-inconsistency problem comes from 'Supernanny' TV programmes on parenting. Parents know that giving in to a child to keep him from acting up will produce a very spoiled child. Nevertheless, when a child throws a tantrum, many parents give him what he wants just to keep him quiet. Because parents don't stick to their 'do not give in' plan, the child expects that he will get what he wants if he behaves badly, so he will throw tantrums over and over again. Parenting programmes suggest a solution to the time-inconsistency problem (although they don't call it that): parents should set behaviour rules for their children and stick to them.

A nominal anchor is like a behaviour rule. Just as rules help to prevent the time-inconsistency problem in parenting by helping the adults to resist pursuing the discretionary policy of giving in, a nominal anchor can help prevent the time-inconsistency problem in monetary policy by providing an expected constraint on discretionary policy.

Other possible goals of monetary policy

While price stability is the primary goal of most central banks, five other goals are continually mentioned by central bank officials when they discuss the objectives of monetary policy: (1) high employment, (2) economic growth, (3) stability of financial markets, (4) interest-rate stability and (5) stability in foreign exchange markets.

High employment

High employment is a worthy goal for two main reasons: (1) the alternative situation – high unemployment – causes much human misery, and (2) when unemployment is high, the economy has both idle workers and idle resources (closed factories and unused equipment), resulting in a loss of output (lower GDP).

Although it is clear that high employment is desirable, how high should it be? At what point can we say that the economy is at full employment? At first, it might seem that full employment is the point at which no worker is out of a job – that is, when unemployment is zero. But this definition ignores the fact that some unemployment, called *frictional unemployment*, which involves searches by workers and firms to find suitable matches, is beneficial to the economy. For example, a worker who decides to look for a better job might be unemployed for a while during the job search. Workers often decide to leave work temporarily to pursue other activities (raising a family, travel, returning to education), and when they decide to re-enter the job market, it may take some time for them to find the right job.

Another reason that unemployment is not zero when the economy is at full employment is *structural unemployment*, a mismatch between job requirements and the skills or availability of local workers. Clearly, this kind of unemployment is undesirable. Nonetheless, it is something that monetary policy can do little about.

This goal for high employment is not an unemployment level of zero but a level above zero, consistent with full employment, at which the demand for labour equals the supply of labour. This level is called the **natural rate of unemployment**.

Although this definition sounds neat and authoritative, it leaves a troublesome question unanswered. What unemployment rate is consistent with full employment? In some cases, it is obvious that the unemployment rate is too high: the US unemployment rate in excess of 20% during the Great Depression, for example, was clearly far too high. In the early 1960s, on the other hand, policymakers thought that a reasonable goal was 4%, a level that was probably too low, because it led to accelerating inflation. Current estimates of the natural rate of unemployment place it between 4% and 6%, but even this estimate is subject to much uncertainty and disagreement. It is possible, for example, that appropriate government policy, such as the provision of better information about job vacancies or job training programmes, could decrease the natural rate of unemployment.

Economic growth

The goal of steady economic growth is closely related to the high-employment goal because businesses are more likely to invest in capital equipment to increase productivity and economic growth when unemployment is low. Conversely, if unemployment is high and factories are idle, it does not pay for a firm to invest in additional plants and equipment. Although the two goals are closely related, policies can be specifically aimed at promoting economic growth by directly encouraging firms to invest or by encouraging people to save, which provides more funds for firms to invest. In fact, this is the stated purpose of *supply-side economics* policies, which are intended to spur economic growth by providing tax incentives for businesses to invest in facilities and equipment and for taxpayers to save more. There is also an active debate about what role monetary policy can play in boosting growth.

Stability of financial markets

As our analysis in Chapter 9 showed, financial crises can interfere with the ability of financial markets to channel funds to people with productive investment opportunities and lead to a sharp contraction in economic activity. The promotion of a more stable financial system in which financial crises are avoided is thus an important goal for a central bank. Indeed, as we will discuss in this chapter, the Federal Reserve System was created in response to the bank panic of 1907 to promote financial stability. As we will discuss in Chapter 15, during the global financial crisis of 2007–9, the stabilization of the financial markets was a prominent goal for central banks.

Interest-rate stability

Interest-rate stability is desirable because fluctuations in interest rates can create uncertainty in the economy and make it harder to plan for the future. Fluctuations in interest rates that affect consumers' willingness to buy houses, for example, make it more difficult for consumers to decide when to purchase a house and for construction firms to plan how many houses to build. A central bank may also want to reduce upward movements in interest rates for the reasons we will discuss in this chapter: upward movements in interest rates generate hostility toward central banks and lead to demands that their power be curtailed.

The stability of financial markets is also fostered by interest-rate stability, because fluctuations in interest rates create great uncertainty for financial institutions. An increase in interest rates produces large capital losses on long-term bonds and mortgages, losses that can cause the failure of the financial institutions holding them.

Stability in foreign exchange markets

With the increasing importance of international trade, the value of the domestic currency of a country relative to foreign currencies has become a major consideration for the central banks. For example, a rise in the value of the national currency makes domestic industries less competitive with those abroad, and declines in the value of the national currency stimulate inflation in the economy. In addition, preventing large changes in the value of the domestic currency makes it easier for firms and individuals purchasing or selling goods abroad to plan ahead. Stabilizing extreme movements in the value of the domestic currency in foreign exchange markets is thus an important goal of monetary policy. In those countries which are very dependent on foreign trade, stability in foreign exchange markets takes on even greater importance.

Should price stability be the primary goal of monetary policy?

In the long run, there is no inconsistency between the price stability goal and the other goals mentioned earlier. The natural rate of unemployment is not lowered by high inflation, so higher inflation cannot produce lower unemployment or more employment in the long run. In other words, there is no long-run trade-off between inflation and employment. In the long run, price stability promotes economic growth as well as financial and interest-rate stability.[3] Although price stability is consistent with the other goals in the long run, in the short run price stability often conflicts with the goals of high employment and interest-rate stability. For example, when the economy is expanding and unemployment is falling, the economy may become overheated, leading to a rise in inflation. To pursue the price stability goal, a central bank would prevent this overheating by raising interest rates, an action that would initially lower employment and increase interest-rate instability. How should a central bank resolve this conflict among goals?

Hierarchical versus dual mandates

Because price stability is crucial to the long-run health of the economy, many countries have decided that price stability should be the primary, long-run goal for central banks. For example, the **Maastricht Treaty**, which created the European Central Bank, states, 'The primary objective of the European System of Central Banks [ESCB] shall be to maintain price stability. Without prejudice to the objective of price stability, the ESCB shall support the general economic policies in the Community', which include objectives such as 'a high level of employment' and 'sustainable and non-inflationary growth'. Also, the Bank [of England] Act of 1998 states, 'In relation to monetary policy, the objectives of the Bank of England shall be to maintain price stability, and, subject to that, to support the economic policy of Her Majesty's Government, including its objectives for growth and employment.' Mandates of this type, which put the goal of price stability first, and then say that as long as it is achieved other goals can be pursued, are known as **hierarchical mandates**. They are the directives governing the behaviour of central banks such as the European Central Bank and the Bank of England.

In contrast, the legislation defining the mission of the Federal Reserve states, 'The Board of Governors of the Federal Reserve System and the Federal Open Market Committee shall maintain long-run growth of the monetary and credit aggregates commensurate with the economy's long-run potential to increase production, so as to promote effectively the goals of maximum employment, stable prices, and moderate long-term interest rates.' Because, as we learned in Chapter 5, long-term interest rates will be very high if there is high inflation, this statement in practice is a **dual mandate** to achieve two co-equal objectives: price stability and maximum employment.

Is it better for an economy to operate under a hierarchical mandate or a dual mandate?

Price stability as the primary, long-run goal of monetary policy

Because there is no inconsistency between achieving price stability in the long run and the natural rate of unemployment, these two types of mandates are not very different *if* maximum employment is defined as the natural rate of employment. In practice, however, there could be a substantial difference between these two mandates, because the public and politicians may believe that a hierarchical mandate puts too much emphasis on inflation control and not enough on reducing business-cycle fluctuations.

Because low and stable inflation rates promote economic growth, central bankers have come to realize that price stability should be the primary, long-run goal of monetary policy. Nevertheless, because output fluctuations should also be a concern of monetary policy, the goal of price stability should be seen as the primary goal only in the long run. It is likely that attempts to keep inflation at the same level in the short run, no matter what, would lead to excessive output fluctuations.

As long as price stability is a long-run goal, but not a short-run goal, central banks can focus on reducing output fluctuations by allowing inflation to deviate from the long-run goal for short periods of time and, therefore, can operate under a dual mandate. However, if a dual mandate leads a central bank to pursue short-run expansionary policies that increase output and employment without worrying about the long-run consequences for inflation, the time-inconsistency problem may recur. Concerns that a dual mandate could lead to an overly expansionary policy is a key reason why central bankers often favour hierarchical mandates, in which the pursuit of price stability takes precedence. Hierarchical mandates can also be a problem if they lead to a central bank behaving as what the Governor of the Bank of England, Mervyn King, has referred to as an 'inflation nutter' – that is, a central bank that focuses solely on inflation control, even in the short run, and so undertakes policies that lead to large output fluctuations. The choice of which type of mandate is better for a central bank ultimately depends on the subtleties of how it will work in practice. Either type of mandate is acceptable as long as it operates to make price stability the primary goal in the long run, but not the short run.

Structure of central banks

As seen above, nowadays most central banks aim at price stability in the long run. The way the central banks are set up, however, differs from country to country. This section describes their structures, starting with one of the oldest central banks in the world, the Bank of England. Then the Federal Reserve System of the United States and the European Central Bank of the euro area will be described.

The Bank of England

Founded in 1694, the **Bank of England** is one of the oldest central banks in the world. The economic, financial and political history of the United Kingdom critically influenced the history of the Bank. The establishment of the Bank of England was driven by two major developments. First, public finances were weak at the end of the seventeenth century. The government's pressing need for money called for a bank designed to provide and arrange loans to the government. Second, there was a sense of being on the brink of an enormous expansion of trade. A national bank was needed to mobilize the country's resources in order to provide finance for trade. During the eighteenth century the Bank of England was entrusted with a few additional tasks. It took deposits and issued notes, managed the government's accounts and acted as the bankers' bank. In the nineteenth century the Bank's sphere was extended to responsibility for monetary and financial stability. Concern for monetary stability emerged from the inflationary excesses at the beginning of the century following a long period of uncontrolled credit growth during the Napoleonic wars. The Bank of England also became responsible for the stability of the financial system by acting as the lender of last resort during several banking crises of the mid-nineteenth century. In the twentieth century, the Bank increasingly took on the role of a central bank and in the meantime distanced itself from commercial business. The Bank Act of 1946 gave the government statutory authority over the Bank of England. Therefore final authority over monetary policy was transferred to the Treasury. Following a global trend towards more independence of monetary policy this transfer of power was reversed in 1997.

The current governance framework of the Bank of England is based on the Bank Act of 1998, whose most important innovation is the establishment of the **Monetary Policy Committee (MPC)**.

The MPC is responsible for the formulation of monetary policy and meets monthly for a two-day meeting, usually on the Wednesday and Thursday after the first Monday of each month. Decisions are made by a vote of the Committee on a one-person one-vote basis. The MPC consists of nine members: the Governor of the Bank of England (who chairs the MPC), two Deputy Governors of the Bank, two members appointed by the Governor after consultation with the Chancellor of the Exchequer (normally central bank officials), plus four outside economic experts appointed by the Chancellor of the Exchequer. According to the Bank Act of 1998, the main policy objectives of the MPC are to maintain price stability, and, subject to that, to support the government's economic policy in terms of growth and employment. The Act also requires that the Chancellor of the Exchequer specify annually in writing what the price stability is to be taken to consist of, and what government's economic policy ought to be.

How independent is the Bank of England?

Stanley Fischer, who was a professor at MIT and is now governor of the Bank of Israel, has defined two different types of independence of central banks: **instrument independence**, the ability of the central bank to set monetary policy instruments, and **goal independence**, the ability of the central bank to set the goals of monetary policy.

Until 1997, the Bank of England was the least independent of the central banks that we will examine in this chapter because the decision to raise or lower interest rates resided not within the Bank of England but with the Chancellor of the Exchequer. All of this changed when the Labour government came to power in May 1997. At that time, the Chancellor of the Exchequer, Gordon Brown, made a surprise announcement that the Bank of England would henceforth have the power to set interest rates. However, the Bank was not granted total instrument independence: the government can overrule the Bank and set rates 'in extreme economic circumstances' and 'for a limited period'. Nonetheless, because overruling the Bank would be so public and is supposed to occur only in highly unusual circumstances and for a limited time, it is likely to be a rare occurrence. In 1997 the Bank of England was stripped of two of its prime functions, namely the national debt management and the supervision of the banking sector. Both these roles were hived off to the Debt Management Office (DMO) and the Financial Services Authority (FSA) respectively. However, the experience of the recent global financial crisis has led policymakers to abolish the tripartite regime. The FSA was criticized for weak enforcement of regulations and for the inability to properly monitor and regulate the financial sector, hence contributing to the current global financial crisis. In favour of a more efficient system of prudential regulation it is planned to return full responsibility over financial supervision to the Bank of England.

Because the United Kingdom is not a member of the euro area, the Bank of England makes its monetary policy decisions independently from the European Central Bank. The decision to set interest rates resides with the MPC. The inflation target for the Bank of England is, however, set by the Chancellor of the Exchequer, so, as we will see below, the Bank of England is also less goal-independent than the Fed and the ECB.

The Federal Reserve System

Of all the central banks in the world, the Federal Reserve System probably has the most unusual structure. To understand why this structure arose, we must go back to before 1913, when the Federal Reserve System was created.

Before the twentieth century, a major characteristic of American politics was the fear of centralized power. Open hostility of the American public to the existence of a central bank resulted in the demise of the first two experiments in central banking, whose function was to police the banking system. In absence of a national supervisory body, in the nineteenth and early twentieth centuries nationwide bank panics became a regular event, culminating in the panic of 1907. The 1907 panic resulted in such widespread bank failures and such substantial losses to depositors that the public was finally convinced that a central bank was needed to prevent future panics.

The hostility of the American public to banks and centralized authority created great opposition to the establishment of a single central bank like the Bank of England. In 1913, a compromise was struck in the Federal Reserve Act, which created the Federal Reserve System. The writers of the Act wanted to diffuse power along regional lines, between the private sector and the government, and among bankers, business people and the public. This initial diffusion of power has resulted in the evolution of the Federal Reserve System to include the following main entities: the twelve **Federal Reserve banks**, the **Board of Governors of the Federal Reserve System** and the **Federal Open Market Committee (FOMC)**.

Federal Reserve banks

Each of the twelve Federal Reserve districts has one main Federal Reserve bank, which may have branches in other cities in the district. The locations of these districts, the Federal Reserve banks, and their branches are shown in Figure 13.1. The three largest Federal

FIGURE 13.1

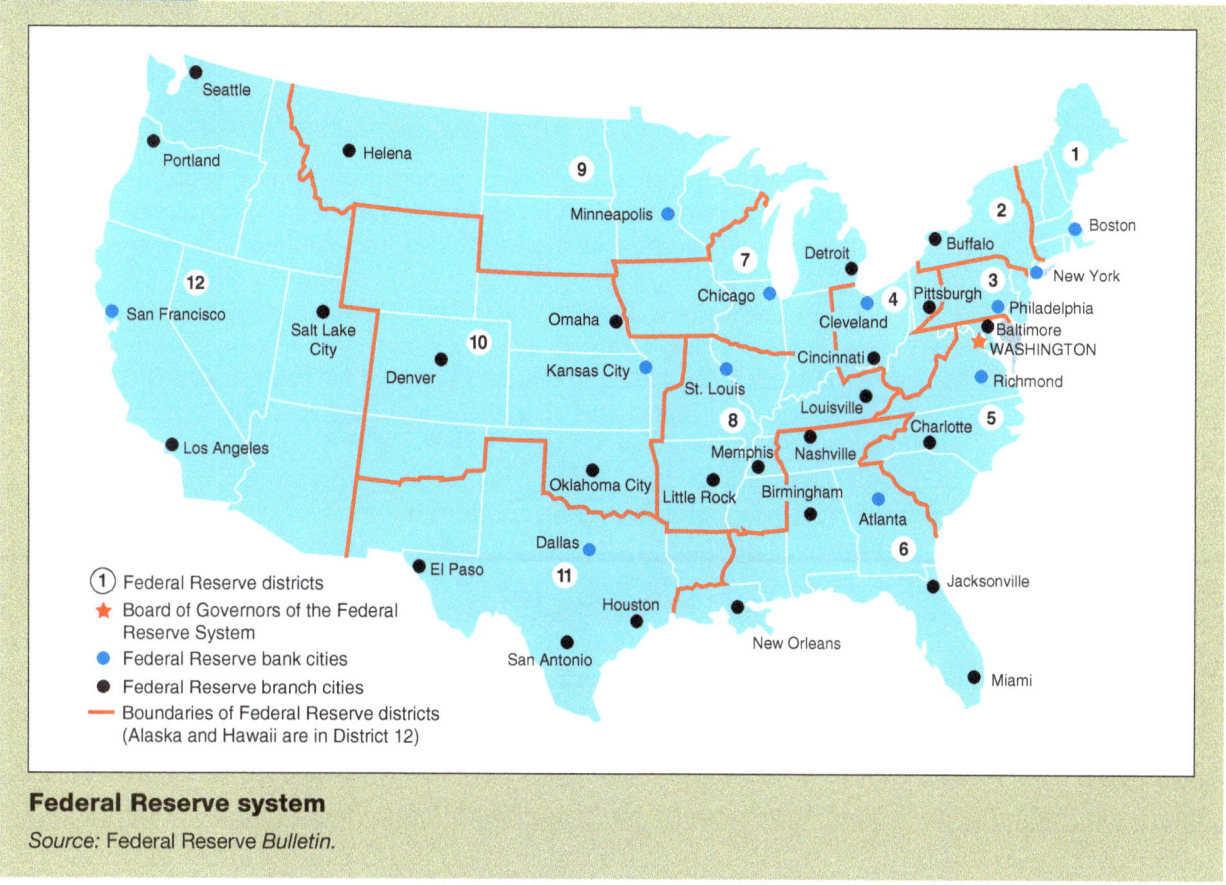

Federal Reserve system

Source: Federal Reserve *Bulletin.*

Reserve banks in terms of assets are those of New York, Chicago and San Francisco. The New York bank, with around one-quarter of the assets, is the most important.

Reserve banks are quasi-public (part private, part government) institutions owned by the private commercial banks in their district that are members of the Federal Reserve System. These member banks have purchased stock in their district Federal Reserve bank (a requirement of membership). The member banks elect six directors for each district bank; three more are appointed by the Board of Governors. Together, these nine directors appoint the president of the bank (subject to the approval of the Board of Governors).

The twelve Federal Reserve banks perform the following main functions:

- Hold deposits for the banks in their district
- Administer and make loans to banks in their district
- Operate and ensure the proper working of the payment system for clearing cheques and transferring of electronic payments
- Supervise and regulate financial institutions in their district, and evaluate proposed mergers and applications for banks to expand their activities
- Issue new currency and withdraw damaged currency from circulation
- Collect and make available data on local business conditions. Moreover, they use their staffs of professional economists to research topics related to the conduct of monetary policy

The twelve Federal Reserve banks are directly involved in formulating monetary policy. In fact, five of the twelve bank presidents each have a vote on the Federal Open Market Committee, which directs **open market operations** (the purchase and sale of government securities that affect both interest rates and the amount of reserves in the banking system). The president of the New York Fed is a permanent member of the FOMC, and therefore always has a vote on the FOMC, making it the most important of the banks; the other four votes allocated to the district banks rotate annually among the remaining eleven presidents.

Board of Governors of the Federal Reserve System

At the head of the Federal Reserve System is the seven-member Board of Governors, headquartered in Washington, DC. Each governor is appointed by the president of the United States and confirmed by the Senate. To limit the president's control over the Fed and insulate the Fed from other political pressures, the governors can serve one full non-renewable fourteen-year term plus part of another term, with one governor's term expiring every other January. The governors (many are professional economists) are required to come from different Federal Reserve districts to prevent the interests of one region of the country from being overrepresented. The chairman of the Board of Governors is chosen from among the seven governors and serves a four-year, renewable term. It is expected that once a new chairman is chosen, the old chairman resigns from the Board of Governors, even if there are many years left to his or her term as a governor.

The Board of Governors is actively involved in decisions concerning the conduct of monetary policy. All seven governors are members of the FOMC and vote on the conduct of open market operations. Because there are only twelve voting members on this committee (seven governors and five presidents of the district banks), the Board has the majority of the votes. The Board also sets reserve requirements (within limits imposed by legislation) and effectively controls the discount rate. The chairman of the Board advises the president of the United States on economic policy, testifies in Congress, and speaks for the Federal Reserve System to the media. The chairman and other governors may also represent the United States in negotiations with foreign governments on economic matters. The Board has a staff of professional economists (larger than those of individual Federal Reserve banks), which provides economic analysis that the board uses in making its decisions.

The Board has substantial bank regulatory functions: it approves bank merger applications, supervises and regulates the Reserve Banks (including their budget), and together with the Federal Banks, supervises and regulates the banking system.

Federal Open Market Committee (FOMC)

The FOMC usually meets eight times a year (about every six weeks) and makes decisions regarding the conduct of open market operations, which influence the money supply and interest rates. Indeed, the FOMC is often referred to as the 'Fed' in the press: for example, when the media say that the Fed is meeting, they actually mean that the FOMC is meeting. The committee consists of the seven members of the Board of Governors, the president of the Federal Reserve Bank of New York, and the presidents of four other Federal Reserve banks. The chairman of the Board of Governors also presides as the chairman of the FOMC. Even though only the presidents of five of the Federal Reserve banks are voting members of the FOMC, the other seven presidents of the district banks attend FOMC meetings and participate in discussions. Hence they have some input into the committee's decisions.

Because open market operations are the most important policy tool that the Fed has, the FOMC is necessarily the focal point for policymaking in the Federal Reserve System. Although reserve requirements and the discount rate are not actually set by the FOMC, decisions in regard to these policy tools are effectively made there. The FOMC does not actually carry out securities purchases or sales. Instead, it issues directives to the trading desk at the Federal Reserve Bank of New York, where the manager for domestic open market operations supervises a roomful of people who execute the purchases and sales of the government or agency securities. The manager communicates daily with the FOMC members and their staffs concerning the activities of the trading desk.

How independent is the Fed?

The Federal Reserve has both instrument and goal independence and is remarkably free of the political pressures that influence other government agencies. Not only are the members of the Board of Governors appointed for a fourteen-year term (and so cannot be ousted from office), but also the term is technically not renewable, eliminating some of the incentive for the governors to seek the approval of president and Congress.

Probably even more important to its independence from the whims of Congress is the Fed's independent and substantial source of revenue from its holdings of securities and, to a lesser extent, from its loans to banks. Because it returns the bulk of these earnings to the Treasury, it does not get rich from its activities, but this income gives the Fed an important advantage over other government agencies: it is not subject to the appropriations process usually controlled by Congress. Indeed, the Government Accountability Office, the auditing agency of the federal government, cannot audit the monetary policy or foreign exchange market functions of the Federal Reserve. Because the power to control the purse strings is usually synonymous with the power of overall control, this feature of the Federal Reserve System contributes to its independence more than any other factor.

Yet the Federal Reserve is still subject to the influence of Congress, because the legislation that structures it is written by Congress and is subject to change at any time. When legislators are upset with the Fed's conduct of monetary policy, they frequently

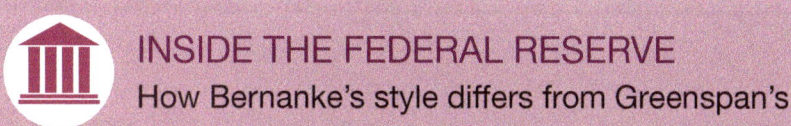

INSIDE THE FEDERAL RESERVE
How Bernanke's style differs from Greenspan's

Every Federal Reserve chairman has a different style that affects how policy decisions are made at the Fed. There has been much discussion of how the current chairman of the Fed, Ben Bernanke, differs from Alan Greenspan, who was the chairman of the Federal Reserve Board for nineteen years from 1987 until 2006.

Alan Greenspan dominated the Fed like no other prior Federal Reserve chairman. His background was very different from that of Bernanke, who spent most of his professional life in academia at Princeton University. Greenspan, a disciple of Ayn Rand, is a strong advocate for laissez-faire capitalism and headed a very successful economic consulting firm, Townsend-Greenspan.* Greenspan has never been an economic theorist, but is rather famous for immersing himself in the data – literally so, because he is known to have done this in his bath tub at the beginning of the day – and often focused on rather obscure data series to come up with his forecasts. As a result, Greenspan did not rely exclusively on the Federal Reserve Board staff's forecast in making his policy decisions. A prominent example occurred during 1997, when the Board staff was forecasting a surge in inflation, which would have required a tightening of monetary policy. Yet Greenspan believed that inflation would not rise and convinced the FOMC not to tighten monetary policy. Greenspan proved to be right and was dubbed the 'maestro' by the media.

In contrast to Greenspan, Bernanke's background as a top academic economist has meant that he focuses on analytics in making his decisions. The result is a much greater use of model simulations in guiding policy discussions.

The FOMC decision-making process under Greenspan was one where the chairman for the most part made the decision about policy, while Bernanke's procedure is more democratic and enables participants to have greater influence over the chairman's vote.

Another big difference in style is in terms of transparency. Greenspan was famous for being obscure. Bernanke is known for being a particularly clear speaker. Finally, while Greenspan adopted more transparent communication with reluctance, Bernanke has been a much stronger supporter of transparency, having advocated that the Fed announce its inflation objective. Bernanke launched a major initiative in 2006 to study Federal Reserve communications that resulted in substantial increases in Fed transparency in November 2007. A very significant further step towards greater transparency was taken in January 2012, when the FOMC released a statement specifying the Committee's long-term goals (see Chapter 16).

* For biographical information on Alan Greenspan, see his autobiography, *The Age of Turbulence: Adventures in a New World* (New York: Penguin Press, 2007).

threaten to take control of the Fed's finances and force it to submit a budget request like other government agencies. A recent example was the call by Senators Dorgan and Reid in 1996 for Congress to have budgetary authority over the non-monetary activities of the Federal Reserve. This is a powerful club to wield, and it certainly has some effect in keeping the Fed from straying too far from congressional wishes.

Congress also passed legislation in 1978, requiring the Federal Reserve to issue a *Monetary Policy Report to the Congress* semiannually, with accompanying testimony by the chairman of the Board of Governors, to explain how the conduct of monetary policy is consistent with the objectives given by the Federal Reserve Act.

The president can also influence the Federal Reserve. Because congressional legislation can affect the Fed directly or affect its ability to conduct monetary policy, the president can be a powerful ally through his influence on Congress. Second, although ostensibly a president might be able to appoint only one or two members to the Board of Governors during each presidential term, in actual practice the president appoints members far more often. One reason is that most governors do not serve out a full fourteen-year term. (Governors' salaries are substantially below what they can earn in the private sector or even at universities, thus providing an incentive for them to return to academia or take private-sector jobs before their term expires.) In addition, the president is able to appoint a new chairman of the Board of Governors every four years, and a chairman who is not reappointed is expected to resign from the board so that a new member can be appointed.

The European Central Bank

Until recently, the Federal Reserve had no rivals in terms of its importance in the central banking world. However, this situation changed in January 1999 with the start-up of the **European Central Bank (ECB)** which now conducts monetary policy for countries that are members of the **Economic and Monetary Union (EMU)**. These countries, taken together, have a population that exceeds that of the United States and a GDP comparable with that of the United States. The agreement to form the EMU was signed in the Maastricht Treaty in 1992. The Treaty was the first step to the creation of the **European System of Central Banks (ESCB)**, which comprises the ECB and the **National Central Banks (NCBs)** of the 27 **European Union (EU)** members whether or not they use the euro as their domestic currency. The ECB and the NCBs of the seventeen (in 2012) countries that have adopted the euro form the **Eurosystem**. As for the euro area, it refers to only the EU countries using the euro as their currency. The ECB is owned by the NCBs of the euro area and it was established as the centre of the ESCB and the Eurosystem. While the ECB has a legal personality under public international law, the ESCB does not. It is intended that the Eurosystem and the ESCB will coexist as long as there are EU member states outside the euro area. Once all 27 members of the ESCB adopt the euro, the two institutions will merge. Figure 13.2 shows the member nations of the ESCB and the Eurosystem.

The organizational structure of the Eurosystem mirrors that of the Federal Reserve System. Namely, the Eurosystem includes the following three main entities: the national central banks, which are similar to the Federal Reserve banks; the **Executive Board**, which is comparable to the Board of Governors; and the **Governing Council**, which is the de facto decision maker, just like the FOMC.[4]

Governing Council and the Executive Board

The Governing Council, the supreme decision-making body of the ECB, comprises the six members of the Executive Board, plus the governors of the national central banks of the euro area countries. The main responsibility of the Governing Council is to formulate the monetary policy for the euro area. The monetary policy decisions of the Governing

FIGURE 13.2

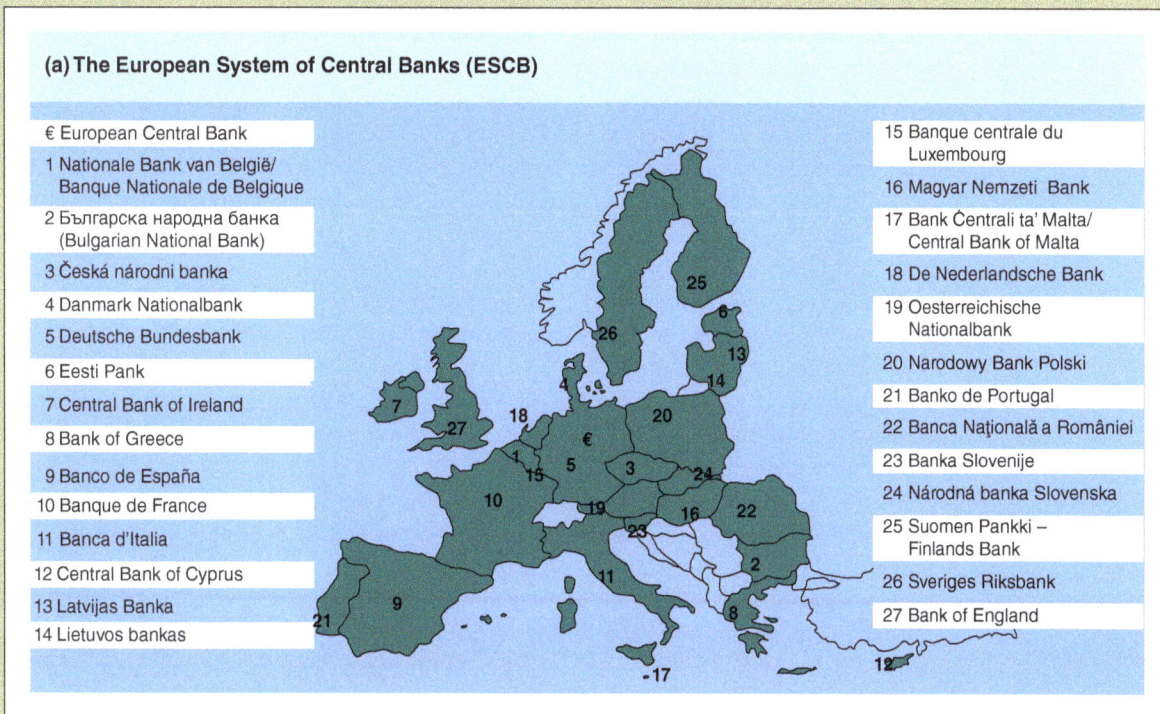

(a) The European System of Central Banks (ESCB)

€ European Central Bank
1 Nationale Bank van België/ Banque Nationale de Belgique
2 Българска народна банка (Bulgarian National Bank)
3 Česká národni banka
4 Danmark Nationalbank
5 Deutsche Bundesbank
6 Eesti Pank
7 Central Bank of Ireland
8 Bank of Greece
9 Banco de España
10 Banque de France
11 Banca d'Italia
12 Central Bank of Cyprus
13 Latvijas Banka
14 Lietuvos bankas

15 Banque centrale du Luxembourg
16 Magyar Nemzeti Bank
17 Bank Ċentrali ta' Malta/ Central Bank of Malta
18 De Nederlandsche Bank
19 Oesterreichische Nationalbank
20 Narodowy Bank Polski
21 Banko de Portugal
22 Banca Naţională a României
23 Banka Slovenije
24 Národná banka Slovenska
25 Suomen Pankki – Finlands Bank
26 Sveriges Riksbank
27 Bank of England

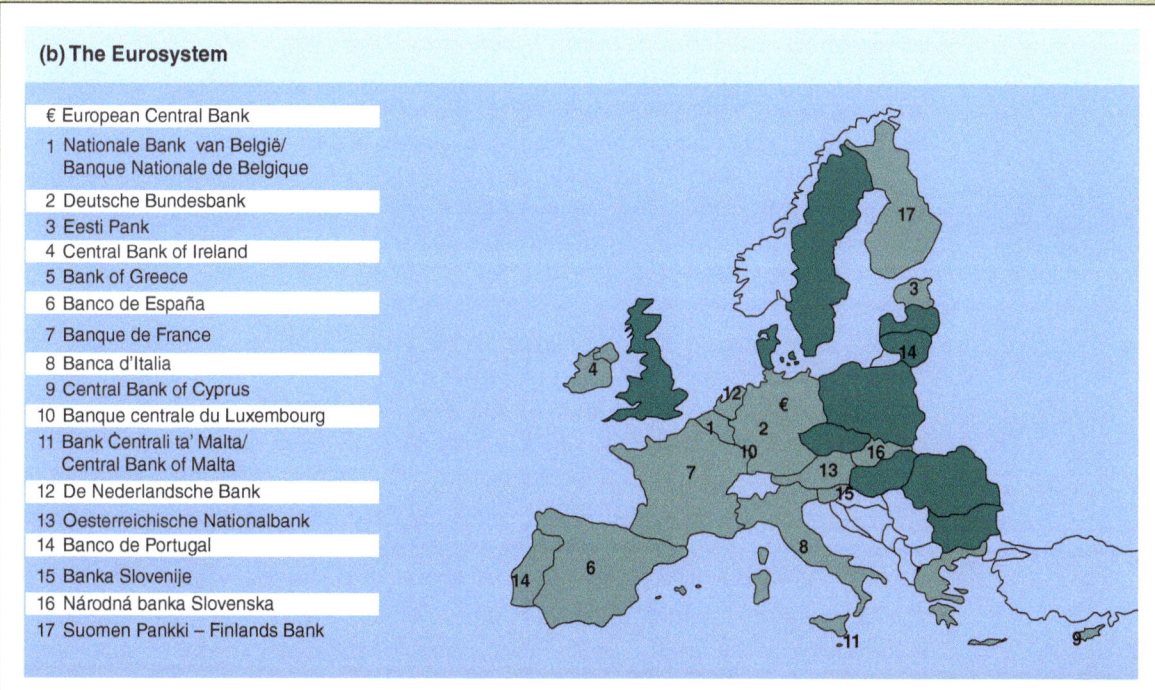

(b) The Eurosystem

€ European Central Bank
1 Nationale Bank van België/ Banque Nationale de Belgique
2 Deutsche Bundesbank
3 Eesti Pank
4 Central Bank of Ireland
5 Bank of Greece
6 Banco de España
7 Banque de France
8 Banca d'Italia
9 Central Bank of Cyprus
10 Banque centrale du Luxembourg
11 Bank Ċentrali ta' Malta/ Central Bank of Malta
12 De Nederlandsche Bank
13 Oesterreichische Nationalbank
14 Banco de Portugal
15 Banka Slovenije
16 Národná banka Slovenska
17 Suomen Pankki – Finlands Bank

The European System of Central Banks vs. the Eurosystem

Source: Facts Presentation. ECB, August 2011, Slides 1 and 2. Copyright © European Central Bank, Frankfurt am Main, Germany. Figures are available free of charge via the ECB website.

Council relate to meeting the general monetary objectives of the eurozone, authorization of the NCBs to issue currency notes, changes in interest rates and supervising the proper management of foreign reserves. It is also responsible for giving guidelines to NCBs for the implementation of those decisions. Therefore, differently from the Federal Reserve System, the decisions in the Eurosystem are implemented via the NCBs in a decentralized way.

The Governing Council convenes on a fortnightly basis at the Eurotower in Frankfurt, Germany. During its first meeting each month, members of the Governing Council assess the economic and monetary conditions and developments in the EMU in order to take decisions regarding its monthly monetary policies. During its second meeting, the council discusses issues pertaining to other responsibilities of the ECB and the detailed implementation process by each of the NCBs.

The Governing Council has decided that although its members have the legal right to vote, no formal vote will actually be taken; instead, the Council operates by consensus. One reason the Governing Council has decided not to take votes is because of worries that the casting of individual votes could lead the heads of NCBs to support a monetary policy that would be appropriate for their individual countries, but not necessarily for the countries in the euro area as a whole.

Just as the Federal Reserve releases the FOMC's decision on the setting of the policy interest rate (the federal funds rate) immediately after the meeting is over, the ECB does the same after the Governing Council meeting concludes (announcing the target for a similar short-term interest rate for interbank loans). However, whereas the Fed simply releases a statement about the setting of the monetary policy instruments, the ECB goes further by having a press conference in which the president and vice-president of the ECB take questions from the news media. Holding such a press conference so soon after the meeting is tricky because it requires the president and vice-president to be quick on their feet in dealing with the press. The first president of the ECB, Willem F. Duisenberg, caused uncomfortable situations at some of these press conferences, and the ECB came under some sharp criticism. His successor, Jean-Claude Trichet, a more successful communicator, encountered fewer problems in this regard. The current president, Mario Draghi, seems to carry on the good communication skills of his predecessor.

The Executive Board consists of the president, vice-president and four other members who are appointed by common agreement of the heads of states of the euro area countries. Its main tasks are to ensure the day-to-day implementation of the monetary policy through giving detailed instructions to all NCBs in accordance with the guidelines of the Governing Council. Moreover, the Executive Board is responsible for managing the daily business of the ECB.

With more countries opting to join the euro area it becomes more difficult to reach a consensus. To deal with this potential problem, the Governing Council has decided on a complex system of rotation, somewhat like that for the FOMC, in which national central banks from the larger countries will vote more often than national central banks from the smaller countries. Moreover, once the member nations of the eurozone reach 18, a two-thirds majority will be followed instead of the current consensus.

How do national central banks operate within the Eurosystem?

The NCBs play an essential role in the Eurosystem and exercise powers delegated to them by the Governing Council. But the question that immediately comes to mind is how do individual national central banks act in accordance with ECB guidelines? In order to have a better understanding of the system, it is helpful to focus on one of the most significant members of the ECB, namely the Deutsche Bundesbank. The reason for selecting the Bundesbank is that it is the largest national central bank within the ECB and also more than half of the short-term interbank borrowing by euro-area banks from the central banks is attributable to the Bundesbank. It also contributes almost 20% of the capital of the ECB. Moreover, the ECB was modelled after the Deutsche Bundesbank in a manner that fully ensures its independence.

Deutsche Bundesbank

In 1948, the Allied forces created the Bank deutscher *Länder* (BdL) to act as the central bank of the Federal Republic of Germany (West Germany). A two-tier central banking system was established comprising the BdL and the *Länder* (or state) central banks whose presidents were appointed by the *Länder* governments. A higher council comprised the governors of the *Länder* central banks, a federal-appointed president and the president of the BdL. In this highly decentralized central banking system, the BdL assumed the main tasks of conducting monetary policy, coordinating the policies and tasks of the *Länder* central banks and managing the foreign exchange system of the country. In the meantime, the *Länder* central banks were greatly autonomous, with each state issuing currency notes, along with the BdL.

In 1957 the Bundesbank replaced the BdL as the new central bank of West Germany and a new structure was adopted. The Bundesbank, nicknamed the 'Buba', became the sole issuer of the Deutsche Mark currency notes and was required to cooperate with other policymaking institutions to ensure harmonious objectives and policies. The Central Bank Council comprised ten central government representatives and eleven *Länder* central bank presidents, selected by the *Länder* governments. This structure served the dual objectives of coordinated policies, while ensuring that the *Länder* central banks still maintained some autonomy.

After the unification of East and West Germany, the Bundesbank was reorganized in 1990 to allow for the incorporation of East Germany into the system. The composition of the council was altered, so that it comprised eight government appointees and nine *Länder* central bank presidents, while key states retained their central banks. This new structure of the Bundesbank strikes a balance between granting the federal or central government relative say in policymaking, while preserving the majority status of the state central bank presidents. This guaranteed the continued independence of the Bundesbank.

Till 2008 the Bundesbank had 9 regional offices and 47 branches throughout Germany. In 2008 it posted a profit of 6.3 billion, which accrued to *Länder* banks, since they are the legal owners of the Bundesbank. Since 2009 the Executive Board of the Bundesbank has consisted of six instead of eight members. Three members are now nominated by the federal government and three by the Bundesrat (or the German Federal Council) and all members are appointed by the President of Germany.

How does the ECB differ from the Bundesbank?

After its introduction in 2001, Germany adopted the euro as its currency to replace the Deutsche Mark. The Bundesbank no longer exists as an independent body, but is part of the European Central Bank. Its objectives are harmonious with those of the ECB, with the primary goal of price stability. The Governing Council of the ECB has the prime goal of maintaining the inflation rate in the euro area below, but close to 2% over the medium term. The inflation rate is a weighted (by the size of the gross domestic product) average of the inflation rates of all EMU members.

The Bundesbank has five core tasks that it jointly performs with the ECB.

■ The core function of the Bundesbank is to implement the Eurosystem monetary policy as laid down in the EC Treaty. It has to ensure stable prices and this is executed through voting in the monthly meeting of the Governing Council of the ECB where monetary policy decisions are made. The president of the Bundesbank is a voting member in the Governing Council of the ECB and consults experts before voting each month. The Bundesbank does not have the right to issue currency notes and coins at its own discretion, but only after authorization from the ECB.

■ It also performs the main function as the clearing house for its member banks and the banks' banker. All central banks within the eurozone are now members of an advanced payment system, known as TARGET 2, that allows banks to make payments in real time and also permits them to use counter-payment as cover. The ECB does not have the task of supervising banks, but this task is delegated to each of the national banks such as the Bundesbank which is responsible for the supervision of the solvency, liquidity and risk management systems of 2,300 credit institutions in Germany. The Bundesbank also ensures that banks hold adequate capital requirements in accordance with the legal requirements.

■ The Bundesbank is the state's banker and the federal government's fiscal agent. Moreover, the Bundesbank advises the government on issues of monetary policy.

■ It also manages the currency reserves of Germany; the ECB has no say as to how much foreign reserves each of the national central banks should hold. But each NCB is required to contribute to the ECB foreign reserves equivalent to its contribution to the capital of the ECB.

■ Finally, the Bundesbank may also cooperate with other international institutions to maintain a stable financial system. For example, during the global financial crisis, it cooperated with the Fed to improve dollar liquidity in the euro area and to help stabilize the money market.

How independent is the ECB?

Although the Federal Reserve is a highly independent central bank, the Maastricht Treaty, which established the Eurosystem, has made the ECB the most independent central bank in the world. Like the Board of Governors, the members of the Executive Board have long terms (eight years), while heads of NCBs are required to have terms at least five years long. Like the Fed, the Eurosystem determines its own budget, and the governments of the member countries are not allowed to issue instructions to the ECB. These elements of the Maastricht Treaty make the ECB highly independent.

Another element that grants the ECB more independence is that it is prohibited from granting loans to national public-sector entities, in order to shield it from any influences by public authorities. Moreover, to ensure the independence of NCBs, the ECB strictly forbids them from taking instructions from European Community institutions, any government of an EU member state or any other international body. This ensures total conformity of the NCBs with monetary policy decisions undertaken by the Governing Council.

Other central banks around the world

Now let us tour the globe to examine the structure and degree of independence of central banks around the world. We shall first start with a selected number of industrial nations, followed by some central banks in transition economies and finally we shall take a look at how central banks operate in a number of developing countries.

Bank of Sweden

Established in 1668, the Bank of Sweden (Riksbank) is the oldest among all central banks in the world. The Executive Board, as the decision-making body of the Bank, comprises six members all of whom are appointed for a period of five or six years. The members of the Executive Board are nominated by the General Council, a group of representatives appointed by the Swedish parliament after each general election. One of the Board members is appointed chairman and serves as the governor of the Bank of Sweden.

Until 1999 political independence of monetary policy in Sweden was low. In 1999 a change in the governance structure of the Bank of Sweden granted formal independence from the government. Since then the Executive Board has full responsibility for monetary policy. The government may not give instructions or advise on issues relating to monetary policy. The Bank has to inform the government, however, prior to the implementation of important monetary policy decisions. The Bank of Sweden also enjoys a high degree of goal independence. It has defined low and stable inflation as the primary objective of monetary policy. In order to achieve this objective the Bank of Sweden has specified an inflation target of 2% laid down in law. Next to goal independence the Bank is also free to choose its monetary policy instruments. Like its neighbour Norway, Sweden abandoned its fixed exchange rate system in 1992 following international currency unrest.

Central Bank of Norway

Norway's central bank (Norges Bank) was founded in 1816. Responsibility for the conduct of monetary policy lies within the Executive Board consisting of seven members appointed by the King in Council. Serving as a chairman and deputy chairman, the central bank governor and deputy central bank governor, respectively, are appointed for a term of six years. The other five members hold office for four-year terms. Working as professional economists and experts in academia or the financial industry they do not form part of the Bank's staff.

According to the Norges Bank Act of 1985 the Ministry of Finance possesses the right to issue instructions to the central bank in matters of special importance. Therefore, by law the Central Bank of Norway must be considered less independent than the Fed or the ECB. Nevertheless the government's right to intervene in the Bank's decisions has never been executed in practice. So as a matter of fact actual control over monetary policy is situated within the Central Bank of Norway. The degree of goal independence is similar to the case of the Bank of England. In fact, the government has specified a target for price stability, the primary objective of monetary policy as defined in the Royal Decree of 2001.

Bank of Japan

The Bank of Japan (Nippon Ginko) was founded in 1882 during the Meiji Restoration. Monetary policy is determined by the Policy Board, which is composed of the governor, two vice-governors and six outside members appointed by the cabinet and approved by the parliament, all of whom serve for five-year terms.

Until recently, the Bank of Japan was not formally independent of the government, with the ultimate power residing with the Ministry of Finance. However, the Bank of Japan Law, which took effect in April 1998 and was the first major change in the powers of the Bank of Japan in 55 years, changed this situation. In addition to stipulating that the objective of monetary policy is to attain price stability, the law granted greater instrument and goal independence to the Bank of Japan. Before this, the government had two voting members on the Policy Board, one from the Ministry of Finance and the other from the Economic Planning Agency. Now the government may send two representatives from these agencies to board meetings, but they no longer have voting rights, although they do have the ability to request delays in monetary policy decisions. In addition, the Ministry of Finance lost its authority to oversee many of the operations of the Bank of Japan, particularly the right to dismiss senior officials. However, the Ministry of Finance continues to have control over the part of the Bank's budget that is unrelated to monetary policy, which might limit its independence to some extent.

Central banks in transition economies

In the early 1990s, socialism collapsed in a number of countries in east and central Europe and the former USSR. As these countries were moving from central planning and public ownership to more liberalization and private property rights, a number of institutions were changed, while totally new ones were created. This transition process was quite painful and cumbersome for many of these nations, as it entailed substantial structural changes and the formation of the previously non-existent markets.

Prior to 1990, most of the transition nations possessed one state-owned bank that assumed the dual roles of a commercial bank and a central bank, while a few others already possessed a separate central bank that supervised the operations of other state-owned banks. By the 1990s, the economies of these nations were in shambles, where the banking sector had a huge non-performing debt portfolio owed by the inefficient public sector firms. Moreover, with the abrupt introduction of markets to these economies they suffered from inflationary pressures due to the liberalization of prices, along with substantial deficits in their balance of payments and massive devaluations of their domestic currencies.

Hence, it was imperative to create new central banks, by breaking up the mono-bank into a central bank and a commercial bank, or to grant some degree of independence to the already existing ones. This required multiple central bank reforms in order to substantially upgrade both the instrument and the goal independence of these newly reformed institutions. Central bank independence in Eastern European nations and the Commonwealth of Independent Nations (the fifteen nations that gained their independence after the collapse of the USSR) was granted, albeit not being fully functional.

With the increase in the levels of law enforcement in transition economies, gradual central bank independence has been granted and implemented, leading to more successful solutions to the problems of inflation and bank supervision. Among the most independent central banks in transition nations are the Czech, Bulgarian and Hungarian central banks, which have proved successful in controlling inflation.

Central banks in developing countries and emerging economies

Developing nations are those economies with a low-to-middle GDP. While such economies make up about 80% of the global population, they produce a little less than 20% of the world's GDP. An emerging economy, on the other hand, is a developing country or transition economy that is embarking on a new economic reform programme in order to achieve higher economic performance and more efficiency in the capital markets and foreign exchange system reforms. Such nations are apt to attract considerable foreign investment through financial markets as well as in their service sector and other productive industries. Even though the term is quite loosely used, emerging economies range from India and China to countries in Latin America, Africa, the Middle East and Asia.

Many of these nations are relative newcomers to the concept of central banking. The degree of independence of their central banks highly relates to the level of development of the financial sector and political institutions. Yet, one main barrier that renders the independence of central banks in some of these nations as futile is the low level of capitalization and their inability to generate sources of revenue. The case of the central bank of Costa Rica is a typical example of a relatively independent central bank, albeit lacking the necessary resources to provide it with de facto effectiveness to implement monetary policy. Another example of an emerging economy facing similar problems of insufficient capital is the Bank of Indonesia, which had insufficient capital at the turn of the century and hence was unable to extend credit assistance to the ailing banks during the 1997 Asian Crisis. For this reason, when central banks suffer from precarious financial conditions that may compromise the conduct of monetary policy, it becomes imperative to recapitalize central banks.

In order to ensure the independence and sovereignty of their central banks, many governments of developing nations and emerging economies have started to periodically increase the capital of their central banks. On the other hand, central banks of the Gulf Cooperation Council nations possess adequate capital but enjoy limited independence. This has urged them to try to form a multinational central bank to ensure independence from national government controls.

Among the most independent central banks that freely implement monetary policy in Africa are the Reserve Bank of Africa and Central Bank of Egypt, which have considerable levels of independence from political pressures. However, this does not mean that these central banks are oblivious to the general macroeconomic goals of the country. On the contrary, in many cases central banks act in coordination with the fiscal agents of the government, especially at times of crisis.

People's Bank of China

The People's Bank of China (PBC), established in December 1948, is an example of a relatively new central bank in an emerging economy. It acted as China's sole mono-bank, undertaking both commercial banking and central banking roles. This was the pattern of banking in most socialist regimes, since private banks were prohibited from operating in these economic systems. Only in 1980 did the State Council of China divide the commercial banking activities into four state-owned banks; in 1985 the People's Bank of China legally started its functions as a full-fledged central bank with its headquarters in Beijing and nine other regional offices. Since that date, gradual reforms have been introduced to grant the PBC control over the banking sector and the authority to implement monetary policy. However, the PBC is required to report its decisions, even before their implementation, to the State Council with regard to monetary policy, the volume of money supply, interest rates and foreign exchange rates. Thus, this high level of involvement of the State Council in its activities gives the PBC limited independence compared to most central banks in industrial nations. The official objective of the monetary policy of the PBC is to maintain the stability of the value of the currency and thereby promote economic growth.

Central bank reforms in Latin America

In various Latin American countries central banks have found themselves in considerable financial distress, leading to recurrent banking crises. In the 1980s, Latin American countries were in an especially serious situation as three- or four-digit rates of inflation were reported. For this reason, governments embarked on central bank reforms; Chile was the pioneer, when in 1989 its central bank was granted more independence in return for enhanced transparency and accountability. In order to reverse inflation, central banks in Brazil, Chile, Colombia, Mexico and Peru adopted a nominal anchor by introducing inflation targeting. Moreover, since the 1990s most South American nations have started to separate central bank appointments from electoral calendars and granted central banks the right to conduct monetary policy without government interference. In exchange, central banks were made accountable for achieving specific inflation targets rather than focusing on economic growth.

Should the central banks be independent?

As our survey of the structure and independence of the major central banks indicates, in recent years we have seen a remarkable trend toward increasing independence. It used to be that the Federal Reserve was substantially more independent than almost all other central banks. Now the newly established European Central Bank is far more independent than the Fed, and greater independence has been granted to central banks such as the Bank of England and the Bank of Japan.

But should the central bank be independent, or would we be better off with a central bank under the control of the president or the parliament? What are the arguments for and against an independent central bank? What is the empirical evidence in favour of the recent trend towards granting greater independence? In the following sections we will try to answer these questions.

The case for independence

The strongest argument for an independent central bank rests on the view that subjecting the central banks to more political pressures would impart an inflationary bias to monetary policy. In the view of many observers, politicians may be short-sighted because they are driven by the need to win their next election. With this as the primary goal, they are unlikely to focus on long-run objectives, such as promoting a stable price level. Instead, they will seek short-run solutions to problems, such as high unemployment and high interest rates, even if the short-run solutions have undesirable long-run consequences. For example, we saw in Chapter 5 that high money growth could lead initially to a drop in interest rates but may cause an increase later as inflation heats up. Would a central bank under the control of the parliament or the president be more likely to pursue a policy of excessive money growth when interest rates are high, even though it would eventually lead to inflation and even higher interest rates in the future? The advocates of an independent central bank say yes. They believe that a politically insulated central bank is more likely to be concerned with long-run objectives and thus be a defender of a sound exchange rate and a stable price level.

A variation on the preceding argument is that the political process in democratic societies could lead to a **political business cycle**, in which just before an election, expansionary policies are pursued to lower unemployment and interest rates. After the election, the bad effects of these policies – high inflation and high interest rates – cause problems, requiring contractionary policies that politicians hope the public will forget before the next election. There is some evidence that such a political business cycle exists in the United States, and a Federal Reserve under the control of Congress or the president may make the cycle even more pronounced.

Putting the central bank under the control of the Treasury or fiscal agent of the government (making it more subject to influence by the leader of the country) is also considered dangerous because the central bank can be used to facilitate financing of large budget deficits by its purchases of government securities.[5] Government pressure on the central bank to 'help out' could lead to more inflation in the economy. An independent central bank is better able to resist this pressure from the government.

Another argument for central bank independence is that control of monetary policy is too important to leave to politicians, a group that has repeatedly demonstrated a lack of expertise at making hard decisions on issues of great economic importance, such as reducing the budget deficit or reforming the banking system. Another way to state this argument is in terms of the principal–agent problem. Both the central bank and politicians are agents of the public (the principals), and as we have seen, both politicians and the central bank have incentives to act in their own interest rather than in the interest of the public. The argument supporting central bank independence is that the principal–agent problem is worse for politicians than for the central bank because politicians have fewer incentives to act in the public interest.

Indeed, some politicians may prefer to have an independent central bank, which can be used as a public 'whipping boy' to take some of the heat off their backs. It is possible that a politician who in private opposes an inflationary monetary policy will be forced to support such a policy in public for fear of not being re-elected. An independent central bank can pursue policies that are politically unpopular, yet in the public interest.

The case against independence

Proponents of a central bank under the control of the president or the parliament argue that it is undemocratic to have monetary policy (which affects almost everyone in the economy) controlled by an elite group that is responsible to no one. If the central bank performs badly, there is no provision for replacing members (as there is with politicians). In view of the danger that an independent central bank will not be accountable, delegation of power

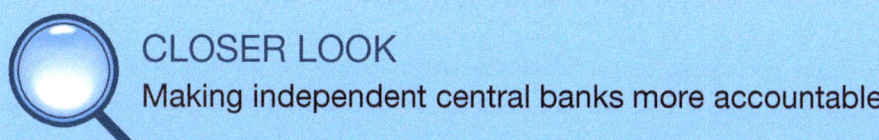

CLOSER LOOK
Making independent central banks more accountable

The movement towards greater central bank independence implies the delegation of power to independent unelected officials. Concerns about the democratic legitimacy as well as the lack of direct political control over monetary policy associated with the high degree of central bank autonomy provide a strong rationale for *accountability* of decision-makers and *transparency* of monetary policy objectives. The introduction of an accountability mechanism requires the central bank to justify and explain its decisions and actions to the public and democratically elected institutions and to respond to concerns about its policy. Higher transparency of monetary policy objectives through more disclosure of information facilitates accountability in a way that it becomes easier for the public to monitor the performance of the central bank in relation to its policy goals. Together, accountability and transparency can increase public support for central bank independence by implementing an effective system of checks and balances to the autonomy awarded to the central bank.

In order to balance the costs associated with greater central bank independence a number of accountability mechanisms have been introduced by the major central banks. In discharge of their obligation to clarify the objectives of monetary policy and to explain the central

bank's performance in achieving these objectives central bank officials periodically have to bear witness before parliament or a committee of a designated public authority. Accountability to the use of resources entrusted to the central bank is achieved through public disclosure of audited financial statements and information on the operating expenses and revenues of the central bank. To prevent conflicts of interest central bank officials and staff have to abide by a set of guidelines and rules defining the principles for the conduct of personal financial affairs.

Steps taken towards higher transparency of monetary policy include the definition of responsibilities and objectives in relevant legislation and regulation, the description and explanation of the framework, instruments and strategy used to pursue the goals of monetary policy to the public and the dissemination of information on monetary policy decisions. Beyond the accountability objective higher transparency also promises to strengthen the effectiveness of monetary policy. If higher transparency through more disclosure of information contributes to a better understanding of monetary policy in the public, reduced uncertainty about monetary policy decisions is likely to facilitate better decision-making of economic agents.

to an independent institution requires guaranteeing its **accountability**. For this reason, in the last decade, several institutional reforms geared towards more accountability of central banks have been implemented in order to limit the costs associated with a higher degree of autonomy (see box 'Making independent central banks more accountable').

The public holds the president, the cabinet and the parliament responsible for the economic well-being of the country, yet they lack control over the government agency that may well be the most important factor in determining the health of the economy. In addition, to achieve a cohesive programme that will promote economic stability, monetary policy must be coordinated with fiscal policy (management of government spending and taxation). Only by placing monetary policy under the control of the politicians who also control fiscal policy can these two policies be prevented from working at cross-purposes.

Another argument against central bank independence is that an independent central bank has not always used its freedom successfully. To cite an example, the Fed failed miserably in its stated role as lender of last resort during the Great Depression, and its independence certainly didn't prevent it from pursuing an overly expansionary monetary policy in the 1960s and 1970s that contributed to rapid inflation in that period.

Some economists also suggest that central banks are not immune from political pressures and that independence may encourage them to pursue a course of narrow self-interest rather than the public interest.[6] In particular, the *theory of bureaucratic behaviour* argues that an important factor affecting central banks' behaviour is their attempt to increase their power and prestige. An implication of this incentive is that central banks will fight vigorously to preserve their autonomy and will try to avoid conflict with political groups that may threaten to curtail their power and reduce their autonomy.

There is yet no consensus on whether central bank independence is a good thing, although public support for independence of the central bank seems to have been growing throughout the world. As you may expect, people who like the central bank policies are more likely to support its independence, while those who dislike its policies advocate a less independent central bank.

Central bank independence and macroeconomic performance

We have seen that advocates of an independent central bank believe that macroeconomic performance will be improved by making the central bank more independent. Early empirical research seems to support this conjecture: when central banks are ranked from least independent to most independent, inflation performance is found to be the best for countries with the most independent central banks.[7] This relationship is illustrated in Figure 13.3 where the average inflation rate is depicted along the vertical axis and an index of central bank independence is depicted along the horizontal axis. This figure shows that in the past the countries with the most independent central banks (e.g. Germany and Switzerland) enjoyed the lowest-level inflation, whereas countries with the least independent central banks like New Zealand, Italy and Spain experienced much higher levels of inflation. Although a more independent central bank appears to lead to a lower inflation rate, it was found that this is not achieved at the expense of poorer real economic performance. Countries with independent central banks are no more likely to have high unemployment or greater output fluctuations than countries with less independent central banks.

Despite the empirical evidence on the relationship between independence and inflation not being free of criticism (see Closer look box: 'Does an independent central bank lead to lower inflation?'), however, over the last few years an increasing number of nations have granted their central banks more independence with the hope of achieving or maintaining low and stable inflation. The greater independence granted to the Bank of England in

FIGURE 13.3

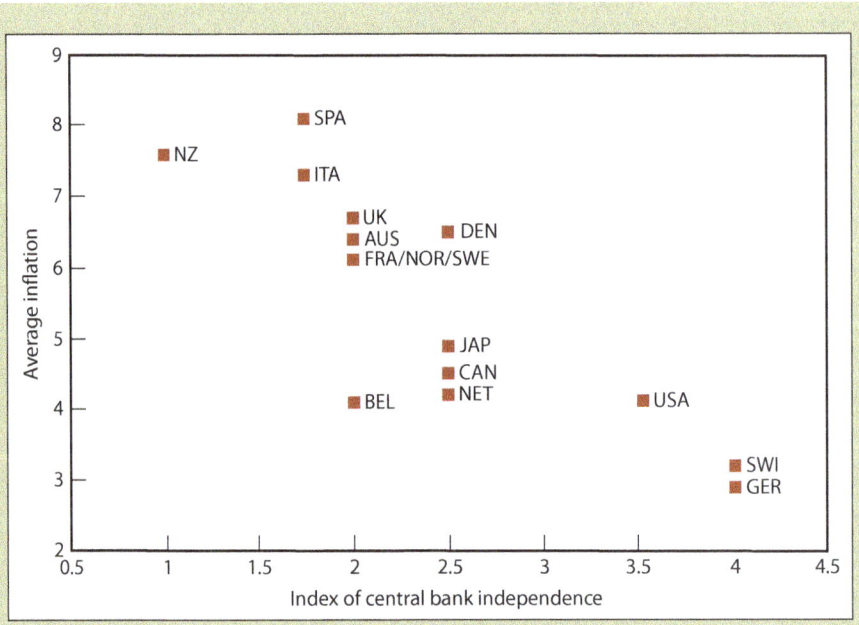

Inflation and central bank independence

Average inflation refers to the period 1973 to 1988.

Source: Alesina, Alberto and Summer, Lowrence H. (1993) 'Central bank independence and macroeconomic performance: some comparative evidence', *Journal of Money, Credit and Banking*, Vol. 25, pp. 151–62. Copyright 1993 The Ohio State University Press. Reproduced with permission.

CLOSER LOOK
Does an independent central bank lead to lower inflation?

The early empirical evidence by Alesina and Summer in 1993 on the relationship between inflation and central bank independence (CBI) seemed to show a clear negative correlation between the level of autonomy awarded to a central bank and the rates of inflation in the country under consideration (see Figure 13.3). However, these conclusions are not free of criticism. First, correlation is not the same as causality. For instance, Adam Posen, 'Central bank independence and disinflationary credibility: a missing link', Federal Reserve Bank of New York Staff Report No. 1, May 1995, has cast some doubt on whether the causality runs from CBI to improved inflation performance. In fact the introduction of an independent central bank may be simply the result of past high inflation. For instance, the historical experience of a hyperinflation in Germany is generally thought to have raised the German public aversion to inflation and its propensity to have an independent central bank committed to price stability.

Second, no consensus exists on the relative importance of the various criteria measuring the level of central bank independence. Different researchers assign different weights to the characteristics typically associated with CBI. As a result, country rankings of central bank independence vary across studies, and alternative weighting schemes may significantly weaken the observed strength of the link between the degree of independence and inflation. In this respect, a recent paper by Jeroen Klomp and Jakob de Haan, 'Central bank independence and inflation revised', *Public Choice*, Vol. 144, pp. 445–57, 2010, casts doubts on the robustness of the negative relationship between inflation and independence. In particular, they proxy CBI by the central bank governor's turnover rate and an indicator based on central bank laws in place, and they re-examine the inflation-independence relationship with a sample of more than 120 countries in the period 1980 to 2005. They conclude that there exists no general significant negative relation, and that central bank independence has only a significant effect in less than 20% of their countries. Even though these results suggest that CBI may be less relevant than originally thought by the early empirical literature, they do conclude that in various countries central bank independence is related to inflation.

1997 and the creation of the European Central Bank (ECB) which is the most independent central bank in the world are clear examples in this respect. However, the recent large-scale purchases of government bonds by the Bank of England (see Chapter 15) as well as the emergency actions of the ECB as part of the EU response to the problems facing Greece and the other euro countries during the recent sovereign debt crisis (discussed in Chapter 9 and 15) have led to a lot being written by many commentators about a weakening of the independence of these central banks.[8]

Summary

1 The six basic goals of monetary policy are price stability (the primary goal), high employment, economic growth, stability of financial markets, interest-rate stability, and stability in foreign exchange markets.

2 Having a strong nominal anchor is a key element in successful monetary policy. It helps promote price stability by tying down inflation expectations and limiting the time-inconsistency problem, in which monetary policymakers conduct monetary policy in a discretionary way that focuses on short-run objectives but produces poor long-run outcomes.

3 The Bank of England was founded in 1694 to act as the government's banker and debt-manager. The Bank of England is one of the oldest central banks in the world. The current governance framework of the Bank of England is based on the Bank Act of 1998, whose most important innovation was the establishment of the Monetary Policy Committee (MPC). The MPC is responsible for the formulation of monetary policy.

4 Because the United Kingdom is not a member of the euro area, the Bank of England makes its monetary policy decisions independently from the European Central Bank. The decision to set interest rates resides with the MPC. However, the inflation target

for the Bank of England is set by the Chancellor of the Exchequer. So in this respect the Bank of England is less goal-independent than the Fed and the ECB.

5 The Federal Reserve System was created in 1913 to lessen the frequency of bank panics. Because of public hostility to central banks and the centralization of power, the Federal Reserve System was created with many checks and balances to diffuse power.

6 The structure of the Federal Reserve System consists of 12 regional Federal Reserve banks, around 2,900 member commercial banks, the Board of Governors of the Federal Reserve System, the Federal Open Market Committee (FOMC) and the Federal Advisory Council. Although on paper the Federal Reserve System appears to be decentralized, in practice it has come to function as a unified central bank controlled by the Board of Governors, especially the board's chairman.

7 The Federal Reserve is more independent than most agencies of the US government, but it is still subject to political pressures because the legislation that structures the Fed is written by Congress and can be changed at any time.

8 The Eurosystem has a fairly similar structure to the Federal Reserve System, with each member country having a national central bank, and an Executive Board of the European Central Bank being located in Frankfurt, Germany. The Governing Council, which is made up of the six members of the Executive Board (which includes the president of the European Central Bank) and the presidents of the national central banks, makes the decisions on monetary policy. The Eurosystem, which was established under the terms of the Maastricht Treaty, is even more independent than the Federal Reserve System because its charter cannot be changed by legislation. Indeed, it is the most independent central bank in the world.

9 Most developing nations and transition economies have reformed their central banks and granted them increasing levels of independence during the last decades of the twentieth century.

10 There has been a remarkable trend toward increasing independence of central banks throughout the world. Greater independence has been granted to central banks such as the Bank of England and the Bank of Japan in recent years, as well as to other central banks in such diverse countries as New Zealand and Sweden. Both theory and experience suggest that more independent central banks produce better monetary policy.

11 The theory of bureaucratic behaviour suggests that one factor driving central banks' behaviour might be an attempt to increase their power and prestige. This view explains many central bank actions, although central banks may also act in the public interest.

12 The case for an independent central bank rests on the view that curtailing its independence and subjecting it to more political pressures would impart an inflationary bias to monetary policy. An independent central bank can afford to take the long view and not respond to short-run problems that will result in expansionary monetary policy and a political business cycle. The case against an independent central bank holds that it is undemocratic to have monetary policy (so important to the public) controlled by an elite that is not accountable to the public. An independent central bank also makes the coordination of monetary and fiscal policy difficult.

Key terms

accountability p. 295

Bank of England p. 286

Board of Governors of the Federal Reserve System p. 282

dual mandate p. 280

Economic and Monetary Union (EMU) p. 286

European Central Bank (ECB) p. 286

European System of Central Banks (ESCB) p. 286

European Union p. 286

Eurosystem p. 286

Executive Board p. 286

Federal Open Market Committee (FOMC) p. 282

Federal Reserve banks p. 282

goal independence p.281

Governing Council p. 286

hierarchical mandates p. 280

instrument independence p. 281

Maastricht Treaty p. 280

Monetary Policy Committee (MPC) p. 281

national central banks (NCBs) p. 286

natural rate of unemployment p. 278

nominal anchor p. 277

open market operations p. 283

political business cycle p. 294

price stability p. 275

time-inconsistency problem p. 277

QUESTIONS AND PROBLEMS

All questions and problems are available in MyEconLab at **www.myeconlab.com/mishkin**.

1 Compare the structure and independence of the European System of Central Banks (ESCB) and the US Federal Reserve System.

2 Which entities in the European Central Bank and the Federal Reserve System control the tools of monetary policy?

3 In what ways can the national central banks (NCBs) of the Eurosystem influence the conduct of monetary policy in the euro area?

4 Why was the Federal Reserve System set up with twelve regional Federal Reserve banks rather than one central bank, as in other countries like the United Kingdom?

5 On the ECB's website, their mission is stated as have as their 'primary objective the maintenance of price stability for the common good'. What reasons lie behind the ECB's adoption of price stability as its key objective?

6 The Fed is the most independent of all US government agencies. What is the main difference between it and other government agencies that explains the Fed's greater independence?

7 What the mechanisms are used to promote greater transparency of the ECB's monetary policy?

8 What are the main difficulties encountered by the newly established central banks in transition economies?

9 What are the reasons that compel some developing nations to adopt currency unions?

10 Why could eliminating the central bank's independence lead to a more pronounced political business cycle?

11 'The independence of the ECB leaves it completely unaccountable for its actions.' Is this statement true, false, or uncertain? Explain your answer.

12 'The independence of the central bank has meant that it takes the long view and not the short view.' Is this statement true, false, or uncertain? Explain your answer.

13 While the ECB holds a press conference after each of its meetings, the Fed promotes secrecy by not releasing the minutes of the FOMC meetings to Congress or the public immediately. Discuss the pros and cons of each of these policies.

WEB EXERCISES

1 Go to the 'Independence' section of the European Central Bank website **http://www.ecb.int/ecb/orga/independence/html/index.en.html**. What are the main provisions that characterize the independence of the ECB?

2 The ECB has put together €CONOMIA as an online monetary policy game and smartphone app. Go to **http://www.ecb.int/ecb/educational/economia/html/index.en.html** Play €CONOMIA with the goal of keeping inflation low and stable at just under 2%. Your tool: the key interest rate.

3 Go to **www.bankofengland.co.uk/Pages/home.aspx** and click on 'About the Bank'. Then click on 'History'. How many governors have served since the foundation of the Bank of England in 1694?

4 Go to **www.federalreserve.gov**/ and click on 'About the Fed'. Then click on 'The Federal Reserve System' and then on 'Structure'. According to the Federal Reserve, what is the most important responsibility of the Board of Governors?

Notes

1 For example, see Stanley Fischer, 'The role of macroeconomic factors in growth', *Journal of Monetary Economics* 32 (1993): 485–512.

2 The time-inconsistency problem was first outlined in papers by Nobel Prize winners Finn Kydland and Edward Prescott, 'Rules rather than discretion: the inconsistency of optimal plans', *Journal of Political Economy* 85 (1977): 473–91; Guillermo Calvo, 'On the time consistency of optimal policy in the monetary economy', *Econometrica* 46 (November 1978): 1411–28; and Robert J. Barro and

David Gordon, 'A positive theory of monetary policy in a natural rate model', *Journal of Political Economy* 91 (August 1983): 589–610.

3 In the paper 'Monetary policy strategy: lesson from the crisis', NBER Working Paper (2011), no. 16755, Frederic Mishkin argues that before the recent financial crisis, the common view, both in academia and in central banks was that achieving price and output stability would promote financial stability. However, he points out that the benign economic environment leading up to 2007 and the low volatility

of both inflation and output fluctuations may have even promoted excessive risk taking and made the financial system more fragile. Although price and output stability are surely beneficial, the recent crisis indicates that a policy focus solely on these objectives may not be enough to produce financial stability.

4 Another decision-making body of the Eurosystem is the General Council of the ECB. The General Council includes the president and the vice-president of the ECB, representatives of the euro area countries and the non-eurozone EU member states. The president of the EU Council and a member of the European Commission may attend the meetings of the General Council, but they have no voting rights. The General Council is a transitional body that will be dissolved once all EU member states introduce the single currency. It performs advisory tasks to the ECB, collects statistical information and standardizes the accounting operations of the NCBs.

5 Most central banks are prohibited from buying government securities directly from the fiscal agent of the government (except to roll over maturing securities); instead, central banks buy these securities on the open market. One possible reason for this prohibition is that the central bank would find it very costly to finance large fiscal budget deficits.

6 For evidence on this issue, see Robert E. Weintraub, 'Congressional supervision of monetary policy', *Journal of*

Monetary Economics 4 (1978): 341–62. Some economists suggest that lessening the independence of the Fed might even reduce the incentive for politically motivated monetary policy; see Milton Friedman, 'Monetary policy: theory and practice', *Journal of Money, Credit and Banking* 14 (1982): 98–118.

7 Alberto Alesina and Lawrence H. Summers, 'Central bank independence and macroeconomic performance: some comparative evidence', *Journal of Money, Credit and Banking* 25 (1993): 151–62. See also Alex Cukierman, 'Central bank independence, political influence and macroeconomic performance: a survey of recent developments', *Cuadernos de Economía* (Santiago) 30 (1993): 271–91.

8 This view is strongly challenged by central bankers. For instance in a speech at the Barclays Capital 14th Annual Global Inflation-Linked Conference (New York) on 14 June 2010, Adam Posen, the external member of the Monetary Policy Committee (MPC) of the Bank of England stated that 'What matters for our independence is our ability to say no and to mean it, and to be responsible about when we choose to say yes'. More specifically, he argued that in the case of the Bank of England's policy of quantitative easing (see Chapter 15 for a full description), it was undertaken on the initiative of the MPC because it was consistent with their mandate to deliver price stability.

Useful websites

www.ecb.int/home/html/index.en.html The website for the European Central Bank.

www.ecb.europa.eu/mopo/intro/html/index.en.html ECB's description of the objective of monetary policy.

http://www.ecb.europa.eu/pub/pdf/other/monetarypolicy2011en.pdf A more detailed analysis of the ECB's monetary policy.

http://www.youtube.com/ecbeuro A dedicated ECB YouTube channel with several educational and media presentations.

www.bankofengland.co.uk/Pages/home.aspx The website for the Bank of England.

http://www.bankofengland.co.uk/monetarypolicy/Pages/default.aspx The Bank of England describes how they conduct monetary policy.

http://www.youtube.com/bankofenglanduk A dedicated Bank of England YouTube channel with several useful presentations.

www.federalreserve.gov/pubs/frseries/frseri.htm Information on the structure of the Federal Reserve System.

www.federalreserve.gov/bios/boardmembership.htm Lists all the members of the Board of Governors of the Federal Reserve since its inception.

www.federalreserve.gov/fomc Find general information on the FOMC; its schedule of meetings, statements, minutes and transcripts; information on its members; and the 'beige book'.

CHAPTER 14

The money supply process

PREVIEW

As we saw in Chapter 5 and will see in later chapters on monetary theory, movements in the money supply affect interest rates and the overall health of the economy and thus affect us all. Because of its far-reaching effects on economic activity, it is important to understand how the money supply is determined. Who controls it? What causes it to change? How might control of it be improved? In this and subsequent chapters, we answer these questions by providing a detailed description of the *money supply process*, the mechanism that determines the level of the money supply.

Because deposits at banks are by far the largest component of the money supply, understanding how these deposits are created is the first step in understanding the money supply process. This chapter provides an overview of how the banking system creates deposits, describes the basic principles of the money supply process, and critically assesses the limitations of the central bank's ability to control the quantity of money. This will help us to understand the evolution in the use of tools and the choice of monetary strategies which will be developed in later chapters.

Three players in the money creation process

The 'cast of characters' in the money supply story is as follows:

1 The *central bank* – the government agency that oversees the banking system and is responsible for the conduct of monetary policy; in the euro area, it is the Eurosystem, in the United Kingdom, the Bank of England, and in the United States, the Federal Reserve System.
2 *Banks* (depository institutions) – the financial intermediaries that accept deposits from individuals and institutions and make loans: commercial banks, building societies, savings banks, mortgage banks, mutual banks, etc.
3 *Depositors* – individuals and institutions that hold deposits in banks.

Of the three players, the central bank is the most important. The central bank's conduct of monetary policy involves actions that affect its balance sheet (holdings of assets and liabilities), to which we turn now.

The central bank's balance sheet

The operation of the central bank and its monetary policy involve actions that affect its balance sheet, its holdings of assets and liabilities. Here we discuss a simplified balance sheet that includes just four items that are essential to our understanding of the money supply process.[1]

Central bank	
Assets	**Liabilities**
Government securities	Currency in circulation
Loans to banks	Reserves

Liabilities

The two liabilities on the balance sheet, currency in circulation and reserves, are often referred to as the *monetary liabilities* of the central bank. They are an important part of the money creation story, because increases in either or both will lead to an increase in the money supply (everything else being constant). The sum of the central bank's monetary liabilities (currency in circulation and bank reserves) makes up the **monetary base**.

1 *Currency in circulation.* The central bank issues currency. Currency in circulation is the amount of currency in the hands of the public. Currency held by depository institutions is also a liability of the central bank, but is counted as part of the reserves.

   Central banks' notes are IOUs from the central bank to the bearer and are also liabilities, but unlike most, they promise to pay back the bearer solely with banknotes; that is, they pay off IOUs with other IOUs. Accordingly, if you bring a €50 note to the European Central Bank and demand payment, you will receive either five €10s, ten €5 notes or fifty €1 coins.

   People are more willing to accept IOUs from the central bank than from you or me because central bank notes are a recognized medium of exchange; that is, they are accepted as a means of payment and so function as money. Unfortunately, neither you nor I can convince people that our IOUs are worth anything more than the paper they are written on.[2]

2 *Reserves.* All banks have an account at the central bank in which they hold deposits. **Reserves** consist of deposits at the central bank plus currency that is physically held by banks (called vault cash because it is stored in bank vaults). Reserves are assets for the banks but liabilities for the central bank, because the banks can demand payment on them at any time and the central bank is required to satisfy its obligation by paying notes. As you will see, an increase in reserves leads to an increase in the level of deposits and hence in the money supply.

   Total reserves can be divided into two categories: reserves that the central bank requires banks to hold (**required reserves**) and any additional reserves the banks choose to hold (**excess reserves**). For example, the ECB might require that for every euro of deposits at a depository institution, a certain fraction (say, 10 cents) must be held as reserves. This fraction (10%) is called the **required reserve ratio**.[3]

Assets

The two assets on the central bank's balance sheet are particularly important because changes in the asset items lead to changes in reserves, the monetary base, and consequently to changes in the money supply.

1 *Government securities.* This category of assets covers the central bank's holdings of securities issued by the government. As you will see, one way the central bank can provide reserves to the banking system is by purchasing bonds, thereby increasing its holdings of these assets. An increase in government bonds (e.g. euro countries' government bonds in the euro area, *gilts* in the UK or Treasury bonds in the US) held by the central bank leads to an increase in the money supply.

2 *Loans to banks.* The second way the central bank can provide reserves to the banking system is by making loans to banks. For these banks, the loans they have taken out are

referred to as *borrowings from the central bank* or, alternatively, as *borrowed reserves*. These loans appear as a liability on banks' balance sheets. An increase in loans can also be the source of an increase in the money supply. Central banks charge an interest rate to banks for these loans.

Control of the monetary base

The *monetary base* (also called **high-powered money**) equals currency in circulation C plus the total reserves in the banking system R.[4] The monetary base MB can be expressed as

$$MB = C + R$$

The central bank exercises control over the monetary base through its purchases or sale of government securities in the open market, called **open market operations**, and through its extension of loans to banks.

Open market operations

The primary way in which the central bank causes changes in the monetary base is through its open market operations. A purchase of bonds by the central bank is called an **open market purchase**, and a sale of bonds by the central bank is called an **open market sale**. The term 'open market' refers to commercial banks and the non-bank public.

Open market purchase from a commercial bank

Suppose that the central bank purchases €100 of bonds from a bank and pays for them with a €100 cheque. To understand what occurs as a result of this transaction, we look at *T-accounts*, which list only the changes that occur in balance sheet items starting from the initial balance sheet position. The bank will either deposit the cheque in its account with the central bank or cash it in for currency, which will be counted as vault cash. Either action means that the bank will find itself with €100 more reserves and a reduction in its holdings of securities of €100. The T-account for the banking system, then, is

Banking system		
Assets		**Liabilities**
Securities	−€100	
Reserves	+€100	

The central bank, meanwhile, finds that its liabilities have increased by the additional €100 of reserves, while its assets have increased by the €100 of additional securities that it now holds. Its T-account is

Central bank		
Assets		**Liabilities**
Securities	+€100	Reserves	+€100

The net result of this open market purchase is that reserves have increased by €100, the amount of the open market purchase. Because there has been no change of currency in circulation, the monetary base has also risen by €100.

Open market purchase from the non-bank public

To understand what happens when there is an open market purchase from the non-bank public, we must look at two cases. First, let's assume that the person or corporation that sells the €100 of bonds to the central bank deposits the central bank's cheque in the local bank. The non-bank public's T-account after this transaction is

Non-bank public			
Assets		**Liabilities**	
Securities	−€100		
Chequable deposits	+€100		

When the bank receives the cheque, it credits the depositor's account with the €100 and then deposits the cheque in its account with the central bank, thereby adding to its reserves. The banking system's T-account becomes

Banking system			
Assets		**Liabilities**	
Reserves	+€100	Chequable deposits	+€100

The effect on the central bank's balance sheet is that it has gained €100 of securities in its assets column, while it has an increase of €100 of reserves in its liabilities column:

Central bank			
Assets		**Liabilities**	
Securities	+€100	Reserves	+€100

As you can see in the above T-account, when the central bank's cheque is deposited in a bank, the net result of the central bank's open market purchase from the non-bank public is identical to the effect of its open market purchase from a bank: reserves increase by the amount of the open market purchase, and the monetary base increases by the same amount.

If, however, the person or corporation selling the bonds to the central bank cashes the cheque at a local bank for currency, the effect on reserves is different.[5] This seller will receive currency of €100 while reducing holdings of securities by €100. The non-bank public's seller's T-account will be

Non-bank public			
Assets		**Liabilities**	
Securities	−€100		
Currency	+€100		

The central bank now finds that it has exchanged €100 of currency for €100 of securities, so its T-account is

Central bank			
Assets		**Liabilities**	
Securities	+€100	Currency in circulation	+€100

The net effect of the open market purchase in this case is that reserves are unchanged, while currency in circulation increases by the €100 of the open market purchase. Thus the monetary base increases by the €100 amount of the open market purchase, while reserves do not. This contrasts with the case in which the seller of the bonds deposits the central bank's cheque in a bank; in that case, reserves increase by €100, and so does the monetary base.

The analysis reveals that *the effect of an open market purchase on reserves depends on whether the seller of the bonds keeps the proceeds from the sale in currency or in deposits*. If the proceeds are kept in currency, the open market purchase has no effect on reserves; if the proceeds are kept as deposits, reserves increase by the amount of the open market purchase.

The effect of an open market purchase on the monetary base, however, is always the same (the monetary base increases by the amount of the purchase) whether the seller of the bonds keeps the proceeds in deposits or in currency. The impact of an open market purchase on reserves is much more uncertain than its impact on the monetary base. Therefore, the central bank can control the monetary base with open market operations more effectively than it can control reserves.[6]

Currency withdrawal

Even if the central bank does not conduct open market operations, a shift from deposits to currency will affect the reserves in the banking system. However, such a shift will have no effect on the monetary base – another reason why the central bank has more control over the monetary base than over reserves.

Let's suppose that Tony Brown (who opened a €100 cheque account at Safe Bank) decides that tellers are so abusive in all banks that she closes her account by withdrawing the €100 balance in cash and vows never to deposit it in a bank again. The effect on the T-account of the non-bank public is

Non-bank public			
Assets		**Liabilities**	
Chequable deposits	−€100		
Currency	+€100		

The banking system loses €100 of deposits and hence €100 of reserves:

Banking system			
Assets		**Liabilities**	
Reserves	−€100	Chequable deposits	−€100

For the central bank, Tony Brown's action means that there is €100 of additional currency circulating in the hands of the public, while reserves in the banking system have fallen by €100. The central bank's T-account is

Central bank		
Assets	**Liabilities**	
	Currency in circulation	+€100
	Reserves	−€100

The net effect on the monetary liabilities of the central bank is zero; the monetary base is unaffected by Tony Brown's disgust at the banking system. But reserves are affected. Random fluctuations of reserves can occur as a result of random shifts into currency and out of deposits, and vice versa. The same is not true for the monetary base, making it a more stable variable.

Loans to banks

In this chapter so far we have seen how changes in the monetary base occur as a result of open market operations. However, the monetary base is also affected when the central bank makes a loan to a bank. When the central bank makes a €100 loan to Safe Bank, the bank is credited with €100 of reserves from the proceeds of the loan. The effects on the balance sheets of the banking system and the central bank are illustrated by the following T-accounts:

Banking system		
Assets	**Liabilities**	
Reserves +€100	Loans (from central bank)	+€100

Central bank		
Assets	**Liabilities**	
Loans (to banking system) +€100	Reserves +€100	

The monetary liabilities of the central bank have now increased by €100, and the monetary base, too, has increased by this amount. However, if a bank pays off a loan from the central bank, thereby reducing its borrowings from the central bank by €100, the T-accounts of the banking system and the central bank are as follows:

Banking system		
Assets	**Liabilities**	
Reserves −€100	Loans (from central bank)	−€100

Central bank		
Assets	**Liabilities**	
Loans (to banking system) −€100	Reserves −€100	

The net effect on the monetary liabilities of the central bank, and hence on the monetary base, is a reduction of €100. We see that the *monetary base changes one-for-one with the change in the borrowings from the central bank*.

Overview of the central bank's ability to control the monetary base

Our discussion above indicates that there are two primary features that determine the monetary base, open market operations and lending to banks. Whereas the amount of open market purchases or sales is completely controlled by the central bank's placing orders with dealers in bond markets, the central bank cannot unilaterally determine, and therefore cannot perfectly predict, the amount of borrowing by banks from the central bank. Central banks set the interest rate on loans to banks, and then banks make decisions about whether to borrow. The amount of loans, though influenced by the central bank's setting of the interest rate, is not completely controlled by the central bank; banks' decisions play a role, too.

Therefore, we might want to split the monetary base into two components: one that the central bank can control completely and another that is less tightly controlled. The less tightly controlled component is the amount of the base that is created by banks' loans from the central bank. The remainder of the base (called the **non-borrowed monetary base**) is under the central bank's control, because it results primarily from open market operations. The non-borrowed monetary base is formally defined as the monetary base minus banks' borrowings from the central bank, which are referred to as **borrowed reserves**:

$$MB_n = MB - BR$$

where MB_n = non-borrowed monetary base
          MB = monetary base
          BR = borrowed reserves from the central bank

This split of the monetary base into components that are fully or partially controlled by the central bank will help us to understand the factors affecting the money supply process. However, changes in the monetary base are only the first half of this process. In what follows we discuss how changes in the monetary base lead to changes in the money supply. As we have seen in Chapter 3, one of the main components of money supply is bank deposits. Therefore, we start investigating how central bank can affect the level of deposits.

Multiple deposit creation: a simple model

With our understanding of how the central bank controls the monetary base and how banks operate (Chapter 10), we now have the tools necessary to explain how deposits are created. When the central bank supplies the banking system with a certain amount of additional reserves, deposits increase by a multiple of this amount – a process called **multiple deposit creation**.

Deposit creation: the single bank

Suppose that the €100 open market purchase described earlier was conducted with Safe Bank. After the central bank has bought the €100 bond from Safe Bank, the bank finds that it has an increase in excess reserves of €100. To analyse what the bank will do with these excess reserves, assume that the bank does not want to hold excess reserves because it earns little interest on them. We begin the analysis with the following T-account:

Safe Bank		
Assets		**Liabilities**
Securities	−€100	
Reserves	+€100	

Because the bank has no increase in its chequable deposits, the bank finds that its additional €100 of reserves means that its excess reserves have increased by €100. Let's say that the bank decides to make a loan equal in amount to the €100 increase in excess reserves. When the bank makes the loan, it sets up a cheque account for the borrower and puts the proceeds of the loan into this account. In this way, the bank alters its balance sheet by increasing its liabilities with €100 of chequable deposits and at the same time increasing its assets with the €100 loan. The resulting T-account looks like this:

Safe Bank				
Assets			**Liabilities**	
Securities	−€100		Chequable deposits	+€100
Reserves	+€100			
Loans	+€100			

The bank has created chequable deposits by its act of lending. Because chequable deposits are part of the money supply, the bank's act of lending has, in fact, created money.

In its current balance sheet position, Safe Bank still has excess reserves and so might want to make additional loans. However, these reserves will not stay at the bank for very long. The borrower took out a loan not to leave €100 idle at Safe Bank but to purchase goods and services from other individuals and corporations. When the borrower makes these purchases by writing cheques, they will be deposited at other banks, and the €100 of reserves will leave Safe Bank. *A bank cannot safely make loans for an amount greater than the excess reserves it has before it makes the loan*.

The final T-account of Safe Bank is

Safe Bank				
Assets			**Liabilities**	
Securities	−€100			
Loans	+€100			

The increase in reserves of €100 has been converted into additional loans of €100 at Safe Bank, plus an additional €100 of deposits that have made their way to other banks. (All the cheques written on accounts at Safe Bank are deposited in banks rather than converted into cash, because we are assuming that the public does not want to hold any additional currency.) Now let's see what happens to these deposits at the other banks.

Deposit creation: the banking system

To simplify the analysis, let us assume that the €100 of deposits created by Safe Bank's loan is deposited at Bank A and that this bank and all other banks hold no excess reserves. Bank A's T-account becomes

Bank A				
Assets			**Liabilities**	
Reserves	+€100		Chequable deposits	+€100

If the required reserve ratio r is 10%, this bank will now find itself with a €10 increase in required reserves, leaving it €90 of excess reserves. Because Bank A (like Safe Bank) does not want to hold on to excess reserves, it will make loans for the entire amount. Its loans and chequable deposits will then increase by €90, but when the borrower spends the €90 of chequable deposits, they and the reserves at Bank A will fall back down by this same amount. The net result is that Bank A's T-account will look like this:

Bank A			
Assets		**Liabilities**	
Reserves	+€10	Chequable deposits	+€100
Loans	+€90		

If the money spent by the borrower to whom Bank A lent the €90 is deposited in another bank, such as Bank B, the T-account for Bank B will be

Bank B			
Assets		**Liabilities**	
Reserves	+€90	Chequable deposits	+€90

The chequable deposits in the banking system have increased by another €90, for a total increase of €190 (€100 at Bank A plus €90 at Bank B). In fact, the distinction between Bank A and Bank B is not necessary to obtain the same result on the overall expansion of deposits. If the borrower from Bank A writes cheques to someone who deposits them at Bank A, the same change in deposits would occur. The T-accounts for Bank B would just apply to Bank A, and its chequable deposits would increase by the total amount of €190.

Bank B will want to modify its balance sheet further. It will keep 10% of €90 (€9) as required reserves and has 90% of €90 (€81) in excess reserves and so can make loans of this amount. Bank B will make an €81 loan to a borrower, who spends the proceeds from the loan. Bank B's T-account will be

Bank B			
Assets		**Liabilities**	
Reserves	+€9	Chequable deposits	+€90
Loans	+€81		

The €81 spent by the borrower from Bank B will be deposited in another bank (Bank C). Consequently, from the initial €100 increase of reserves in the banking system, the total increase of chequable deposits in the system so far is €271 (= €100 + €90 + €81).

Following the same reasoning, if all banks make loans for the full amount of their excess reserves, further increments in chequable deposits will continue (at Banks C, D, E and so on), as depicted in Table 14.1. Therefore, the total increase in deposits from the initial €100 increase in reserves will be €1,000: the increase is tenfold, the reciprocal of the 10% (0.10) required reserve ratio.

If the banks choose to invest their excess reserves in securities, the result is the same. If Bank A had taken its excess reserves and purchased securities instead of making loans, its T-account would have looked like this:

TABLE 14.1

Creation of deposits (assuming 10% required reserve ratio and a €100 increase in reserves)

Bank	Increase in deposits (€)	Increase in loans (€)	Increase in reserves (€)
Safe Bank	0.00	100.00	0.00
A	100.00	90.00	10.00
B	90.00	81.00	9.00
C	81.00	72.90	8.10
D	72.90	65.61	7.29
E	65.61	59.05	6.56
F	59.05	53.14	5.91
.	.	.	.
.	.	.	.
.	.	.	.
Total for all banks	1,000.00	1,000.00	100.00

Bank A

Assets		Liabilities	
Reserves	€ +10	Chequable deposits	€ + 100
Securities	€ + 90		

When the bank buys €90 of securities, it writes a €90 cheque to the seller of the securities, who in turn deposits the €90 at a bank such as Bank B. Bank B's chequable deposits increase by €90, and the deposit expansion process is the same as before. *Whether a bank chooses to use its excess reserves to make loans or to purchase securities, the effect on deposit expansion is the same*.

You can now see the difference in deposit creation for the single bank from that for the banking system as a whole. Because a single bank can create deposits equal only to the amount of its reserves, it cannot by itself generate multiple deposit expansion. A single bank cannot make loans greater in amount than its reserves, because the bank will lose these reserves as the deposits created by the loan find their way to other banks.[7] However, the banking system as a whole can generate a multiple expansion of deposits, because when a bank loses its reserves, these reserves do not leave the banking system even though they are lost to the individual bank. So as each bank makes a loan and creates deposits, the reserves find their way to another bank, which uses them to make additional loans and create additional deposits. As you have seen, this process continues until the initial increase in reserves results in a multiple increase in deposits.

The multiple increase in deposits generated from an increase in the banking system's reserves is called the **simple deposit multiplier**.[8] In our example with a 10% required reserve ratio, the simple deposit multiplier is 10. More generally, the simple reserve multiplier equals the reciprocal of the required reserve ratio *r*, expressed as a fraction (10 = 1/0.10), so the formula for the multiple expansion of deposits can be written as follows:[9]

$$\Delta D = \frac{1}{r} \times \Delta R \qquad (14.1)$$

where ΔD = change in total chequable deposits in the banking system

      r = required reserve ratio (0.10 in the example)

     ΔR = change in reserves for the banking system (€100 in the example)

Deriving the formula for multiple deposit creation

The formula for the multiple creation of deposits can also be derived directly using algebra. We obtain the same answer for the relationship between a change in deposits and a change in reserves, but more quickly.

Our assumption that banks do not hold on to any excess reserves means that the total amount of required reserves for the banking system RR will equal the total reserves in the banking system R:

$$RR = R$$

The total amount of required reserves equals the required reserve ratio r times the total amount of chequable deposits D:

$$RR = r \times D$$

Substituting for $r \times D$ in the first equation

$$r \times D = R$$

and dividing both sides of the preceding equation by r gives

$$D = \frac{1}{r} \times R$$

Taking the change in both sides of this equation and using delta to indicate a change gives

$$\Delta D = \frac{1}{r} \times \Delta R$$

which is the same formula for deposit creation found in Equation 14.1.

This derivation provides us with another way of looking at the multiple creation of deposits, because it forces us to look directly at the banking system as a whole rather than at one bank at a time. For the banking system as a whole, deposit creation (or contraction) will stop only when all excess reserves in the banking system are gone; that is, the banking system will be in equilibrium when the total amount of required reserves equals the total amount of reserves, as seen in the equation $RR=R$. When $r \times D$ is substituted for RR, the resulting equation $R = r \times D$ tells us how high chequable deposits will have to be for required reserves to equal total reserves. Accordingly, a given level of reserves in the banking system determines the level of chequable deposits when the banking system is in equilibrium (when $ER = 0$); put another way, the given level of reserves supports a given level of chequable deposits.

In our example, the required reserve ratio is 10%. If reserves increase by €100, chequable deposits must rise by €1,000 for total required reserves also to increase by €100. If the increase in chequable deposits is less than this, say €900, then the increase in required reserves of €90 remains below the €100 increase in reserves, so there are still excess reserves somewhere in the banking system. The banks with the excess reserves will now make additional loans, creating new deposits, and this process will continue until all reserves in the system are used up. This occurs when chequable deposits rise by €1,000.

We can also see this by looking at the T-account of the banking system as a whole (including Safe Bank) that results from this process:

Banking system			
Assets		**Liabilities**	
Securities	−€100	Chequable deposits	+€1,000
Reserves	+€100		
Loans	+€1,000		

The procedure of eliminating excess reserves by loaning them out means that the banking system (Safe Bank and Banks A, B, C, D and so on) continues to make loans up to the €1,000 amount until deposits have reached the €1,000 level. In this way, €100 of reserves supports €1,000 (ten times the quantity) of deposits.

Critique of the simple model

Our model of multiple deposit creation seems to indicate that the central bank is able to exercise complete control over the level of chequable deposits by setting the required reserve ratio and the level of reserves. The actual creation of deposits is much less mechanical than the simple model indicates. If proceeds from Bank A's €90 loan are not deposited but are kept in currency, nothing is deposited in Bank B and the deposit creation process ceases. The total increase in the money supply is now the €90 increase in currency plus the initial €100 of deposits deposited at Bank A, for a total of only €190 – considerably less than the €1,000 we calculated with the simple model above. Another way of saying this is that currency has no multiple deposit expansion, while deposits do. Thus, if some proceeds from loans are used to raise the holdings of currency, there is less multiple expansion overall, and the money supply will not increase by as much as our simple model of multiple deposit creation tells us.

Another situation ignored in our model is one in which banks do not make loans or buy securities in the full amount of their excess reserves. If Bank A decides to hold on to all €90 of its excess reserves, no deposits would be made in Bank B, and this would also stop the deposit creation process. The total increase in deposits would be only €100 and not the €1,000 increase in our example. Hence, if banks choose to hold all or some of their excess reserves, the full expansion of deposits predicted by the simple model of multiple deposit creation again does not occur.

Our examples indicate that the central bank is not the only player whose behaviour influences the level of deposits and therefore the money supply. Depositors' decisions regarding how much currency to hold and banks' decisions regarding the amount of excess reserves to hold can cause the money supply to change.

The money multiplier

Because the central bank can control the monetary base better than it can control reserves, it makes sense to link the money supply M to the monetary base MB through a relationship such as the following:

$$M = m \times MB \qquad (14.2)$$

where the variable m is the money multiplier, and tells us how much the money supply changes for a given change in the monetary base. Because the money multiplier is larger than 1, the alternative name for the monetary base, *high-powered money*, is logical: a €1 change in the monetary base leads to more than a €1 change in the money supply.

Deriving the money multiplier

Let's assume that the desired holdings of currency C and excess reserves ER grows proportionally with chequable deposits D; moreover, banks hold a fixed proportion of chequable deposits into required reserves RR. In other words, we assume that the ratios of these items to chequable deposits are constants in equilibrium, as the braces in the following expressions indicate:

$$c = \{C/D\} \quad = \text{currency ratio}$$
$$r = \{RR/D\} \quad = \text{required reserves ratio}$$
$$e = \{ER/D\} \quad = \text{excess reserves ratio}$$

We will now derive a formula that describes how the currency ratio desired by depositors, the excess reserves ratio desired by banks, and the required reserve ratio set by the central bank affect the multiplier m. We begin the derivation of the model of the money supply with the following equation:

$$R = RR + ER$$

which states that the total amount of reserves in the banking system R equals the sum of required reserves RR and excess reserves ER.

Because the monetary base MB equals currency C plus reserves R, we can generate an equation that links the amount of the monetary base to the levels of chequable deposits and currency by adding currency to both sides of the equation:

$$MB = R + C = RR + ER + C$$

Another way of thinking about this equation is to recognize that it reveals the amount of the monetary base needed to support the existing amounts of chequable deposits, currency and excess reserves.

To derive the money multiplier formula in terms of the currency ratio $c = \{C/D\}$ and the excess reserves ratio $e = \{ER/D\}$ and the required reserve ratio $r = \{RR/D\}$, we rewrite the last equation, specifying C as $c \times D$, ER as $e \times D$ and RR as $r \times D$

$$MB = (r \times D) + (e \times D) + (c \times D) = (r + e + c) \times D$$

We next divide both sides of the equation by the term inside the parentheses to get an expression linking chequable deposits D to the monetary base MB:

$$D = \frac{1}{r + e + c} \times MB \tag{14.3}$$

Using the M1 definition of the money supply as currency plus chequable deposits ($M = D + C$) and again specifying C as $c \times D$

$$M = D + (c \times D) = (1 + c) \times D$$

Substituting in this equation the expression for D from Equation 14.3, we have

$$M = \frac{1 + c}{r + e + c} \times MB \tag{14.4}$$

We have derived an expression in the form of our earlier Equation 14.2. As you can see, the ratio that multiplies MB is the money multiplier, which tells how much the money supply changes in response to a given change in the monetary base (high-powered money). The money multiplier m is thus

$$m = \frac{1 + c}{r + e + c} \tag{14.5}$$

It is a function of the currency ratio set by depositors c, the excess reserves ratio set by banks e, and the required reserve ratio r set by the central bank.[10]

Intuition behind the money multiplier

To get a feel for what the money multiplier means, let us construct a numerical example with hypothetical numbers for the following variables:

$$r = \text{required reserve ratio} = 0.10$$
$$C = \text{currency in circulation} = €400 \text{ billion}$$
$$D = \text{chequable deposits} = €800 \text{ billion}$$
$$ER = \text{excess reserves} = €0.8 \text{ billion}$$
$$M = \text{money supply (M1)} = C + D = €1,200 \text{ billion}$$

From these numbers we can calculate the values for the currency ratio c and the excess reserves ratio e:

$$c = \frac{€400 \text{ billion}}{€800 \text{ billion}} = 0.5$$

$$e = \frac{€0.8 \text{ billion}}{€800 \text{ billion}} = 0.001$$

The resulting value of the money multiplier is

$$m = \frac{1 + 0.5}{0.1 + 0.001 + 0.5} = \frac{1.5}{0.601} = 2.5$$

The money multiplier of 2.5 tells us that, given the required reserve ratio $r = 10\%$, a currency ratio $c = 0.5$ and an excess reserve ratio $e = 0.001$, a unit increase in the monetary base leads to a 2.5 increase in the money supply (M1).

An important characteristic of the money multiplier is that it is less than the simple deposit multiplier of 10 found earlier in the chapter. The key to understanding this result is to realize that *although there is multiple expansion of deposits, there is no such expansion for currency*. Thus, if some portion of the increase in high-powered money finds its way into currency, this portion does not undergo multiple deposit expansion. In our simple model earlier in the chapter, we did not allow for this possibility, and so the increase in reserves led to the maximum amount of multiple deposit creation. However, in our current model of the money multiplier, the level of currency does increase when the monetary base MB and chequable deposits D increase because c is greater than zero. As previously stated, any increase in MB that goes into an increase in currency is not multiplied, so only part of the increase in MB is available to support chequable deposits that undergo multiple expansion. The overall level of multiple deposit expansion must be lower, meaning that the increase in M, given an increase in MB, is smaller than the simple model earlier in the chapter indicated.[11]

Factors that determine the money supply

By recognizing that the monetary base is $MB = MB_n + BR$, it is useful to rewrite Equation 14.4 as:

$$M = \frac{1 + c}{r + e + c} \times (MB_n + BR) \tag{14.6}$$

Now we are ready to look at how the money supply M changes in response to changes in the variables in our model: MB_n, BR, r, c and e. The 'game' we are playing is a familiar one in economics. We ask what happens when one of these variables changes, leaving all other variables the same (*ceteris paribus*).

Changes in the non-borrowed monetary base, MB_n

As shown earlier in the chapter, the central bank's open market purchases increase the non-borrowed monetary base, and its open market sales decrease it. Holding all other variables constant, an increase in MB_n arising from an open market purchase increases the amount of the monetary base and reserves, so that multiple deposit creation occurs and the money supply increases. Similarly, an open market sale that decreases MB_n shrinks the amount of the monetary base and reserves, thereby causing a multiple contraction of deposits and the money supply decrease. We have the following result: *the money supply is positively related to the non-borrowed monetary base MB_n*.

Changes in borrowed reserves, *BR,* from the central bank

An increase in loans to banks from the central bank provides additional borrowed reserves, and thereby increases the amount of the monetary base and reserves, so that multiple deposit creation occurs and the money supply increases. If banks reduce the level of their borrowing from central banks, all other variables held constant, the monetary base and amount of reserves would fall, and the money supply would decrease. The result is this: *the money supply is positively related to the level of borrowed reserves, BR, from the central bank*. However, because central banks normally keep the interest rate on loans to the banking sector above market rates at which banks can lend from each other, banks have very little incentive to take our loans. Borrowed reserves, *BR*, is thus very small except under exceptional circumstances that will be discussed in the next chapter.

Changes in the required reserve ratio, *r*

If the required reserve ratio on chequable deposits increases while all other variables, such as the monetary base, stay the same, we have seen that there is less multiple deposit expansion (the money multiplier becomes smaller), and hence the money supply falls. If, on the other hand, the required reserve ratio falls, multiple deposit expansion is higher (the money multiplier increases) and the money supply rises. We now have the following result: *the money supply is negatively related to the required reserve ratio r*. In the past, central banks sometimes used reserve requirements to affect the size of the money supply. In recent years, however, reserve requirements have become a less important factor in the determination of the money multiplier and the money supply, as we shall see in the next chapter.

Changes in currency ratio, *c*

As shown before, chequable deposits undergo multiple expansions while currency does not. Hence, when chequable deposits are converted into currency, holding the monetary base and other variables constant, there is a switch from a component of the money supply that undergoes multiple expansion to one that does not. The overall level of multiple expansion declines, and so must the money multiplier, which leads to a fall in the money supply. On the other hand, if currency holdings fall, there would be a switch into chequable deposits that undergo multiple deposit expansion, so the money multiplier would increase causing a rise of the money supply. This analysis suggests the following result: *the money supply is negatively related to the currency ratio c*.

Changes in excess reserves ratio, *e*

When banks increase their holdings of excess reserves relative to the chequable deposits, those reserves are no longer being used to make loans, causing multiple deposit creation to stop dead in its tracks, thus causing a contraction of the money multiplier and the money supply. If, on the other hand, banks chose to hold less excess reserves, loans and multiple deposit creation would go up and the money supply would rise. *The money supply is negatively related to the excess reserves ratio e*.

Recall from Chapter 10 that the primary benefit to a bank of holding excess reserves is that they provide insurance against losses due to deposit outflows; that is, they enable the bank experiencing deposit outflows to escape the costs of calling in loans, selling securities, borrowing from the central bank or other corporations, or bank failure. If banks fear that deposit outflows are likely to increase (that is, if expected deposit outflows increase), they will want more insurance against this possibility and excess reserves will increase.

SUMMARY TABLE 14.2

Money supply response

Player	Variable	Change in variable	Money supply response	Reason
Central bank	Non-borrowed monetary base, MB_n	⬆	⬆	More *MB* for deposit creation
	Borrowed reserves, *BR*	⬆	⬆	More *MB* for deposit creation
	Required reserve ratio, *r*	⬆	⬇	Less multiple deposit expansion
Depositors	Currency ratio, *c*	⬆	⬇	Less multiple deposit expansion
Depositors and banks	Excess reserves ratio, *e*	⬆	⬇	Less loans and deposit creation

Note: Only increases (⬆) in the variables are shown. The effects of decreases on the money supply would be the opposite of those indicated in the 'Money supply response' column.

Overview of the money creation process

We now have a model of the money supply process in which all three of the players – the central bank, banks and depositors – directly influence the money supply. As a study aid, Summary Table 14.2 charts the money supply response to the five factors discussed above and gives a brief synopsis of the reasoning behind them.

The variables are grouped by the players who are the primary influence behind the variable. The ECB, the Bank of England and the Fed, for instance, influence the money supply by controlling the first three variables (called tools of the central bank). Depositors influence the money supply through their decisions about their holdings of currency, while banks influence the money supply with their decisions about excess reserves. However, because depositors' behaviour influences bankers' expectations about deposit outflows, which as we have seen affects banks' decisions to hold excess reserves, depositors are also listed as a player determining excess reserves.

Limits of the central bank's ability to control the money supply

So far we have discussed the main factors affecting the money supply. We are now ready to answer a key question of this chapter. Do central banks have the ability to fully control the money supply? If we assume that the behaviour of banks on reserve holding and of depositors on desired currency holding is stable and predictable, then we can expect a close link between the monetary base and the quantity of money supply. In this case, we should observe a stable money multiplier. As such, the central bank may opt to exploit this relationship for policy purposes. If, on the other hand, the money multiplier is volatile and its changes unpredictable, then such a link is weak and central banks may not be able to fully control the quantity of money.

To see which of these two scenarios belongs to the real world, we start looking at movements of the money multiplier for M3 in the UK using historical data over the

FIGURE 14.1

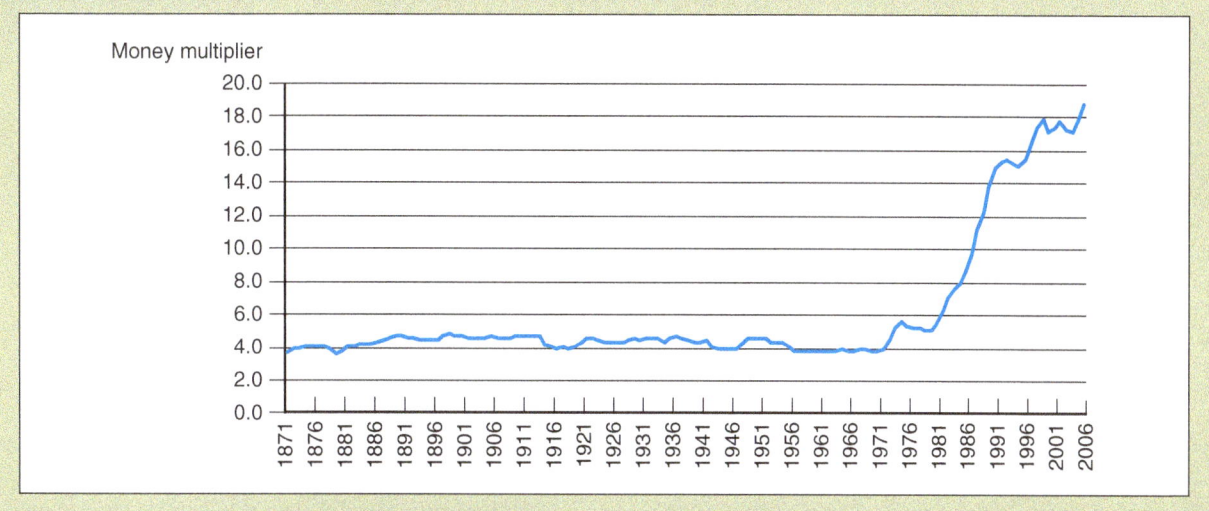

M3 money multiplier in the UK, 1871–2005

Sources: Own calculation from the monetary base and M3 annual series provided by Forrest Cappie and Alan Webber, *A Monetary History of the United Kingdom, 1870–1982* (London: George Allen & Unwin, 1985) up to 1969 and Bank of England afterwards. The Monetary Base series was discontinued in April 2006.

period 1871 to 2005. Figure 14.1 shows that this multiplier fluctuated within a moderate band for almost 100 years. Since the introduction of the Competition and Credit Control in 1971 and the ending of the conventional minimum reserve ratio, however, the M3 multiplier rose sharply from around 4 to more than 18 at the end of 2005. The increase in the multiplier was partly due the drop in the required reserve ratio r implemented by the government, but it was also related to a huge decrease in the currency ratio c. Figure 14.1 clearly indicates that the UK M3 money multiplier went through remarkable changes in the past.

But what is the behaviour of money multipliers during more recent times? Figure 14.2 shows the M3 multiplier for the euro area since 1999. This multiplier rose from around 10 to 13 during the early years of the monetary union, to fall steadily back to its initial value up to the beginning of the recent financial turmoil where the multiplier dropped significantly and became also highly volatile. The instability of the money multiplier and its response to the financial crisis are even more clear-cut from Figure 14.3 which graphs the M1 multiplier for the US since January 1980 up to the beginning of 2012. The US M1 multiplier rose from early 1980 to January 1987, mostly due to a fall in the currency ratio c. In the period from January 1987 to April 1991, the currency ratio underwent a substantial rise, which led to a fall in m. After a moderate decline in c and a subsequent increase of m during the April 1991 to December 1993 period, the currency ratio rose sharply and led the M1 multiplier to fall from 2.8 to 1.6 in 2008. The financial crisis of 2007–9 led to a dramatic change in the US multiplier. In September 2008, following the collapse of Lehman Brothers, banks increased their excess reserves holding due to the increased risk of deposit withdrawals and their reluctance to lend to the private sector. The sharp increase in the excess reserve ratio e led to a dramatic drop in the M1 multiplier from 1.6 to 0.8. The recent financial crisis as well as the experience of the Great Depression (see Application: 'The Great Depression bank panics, 1930–3') show us that the ability of the central bank to fully control the money supply is particularly limited during periods of banking and financial panics.

FIGURE 14.2

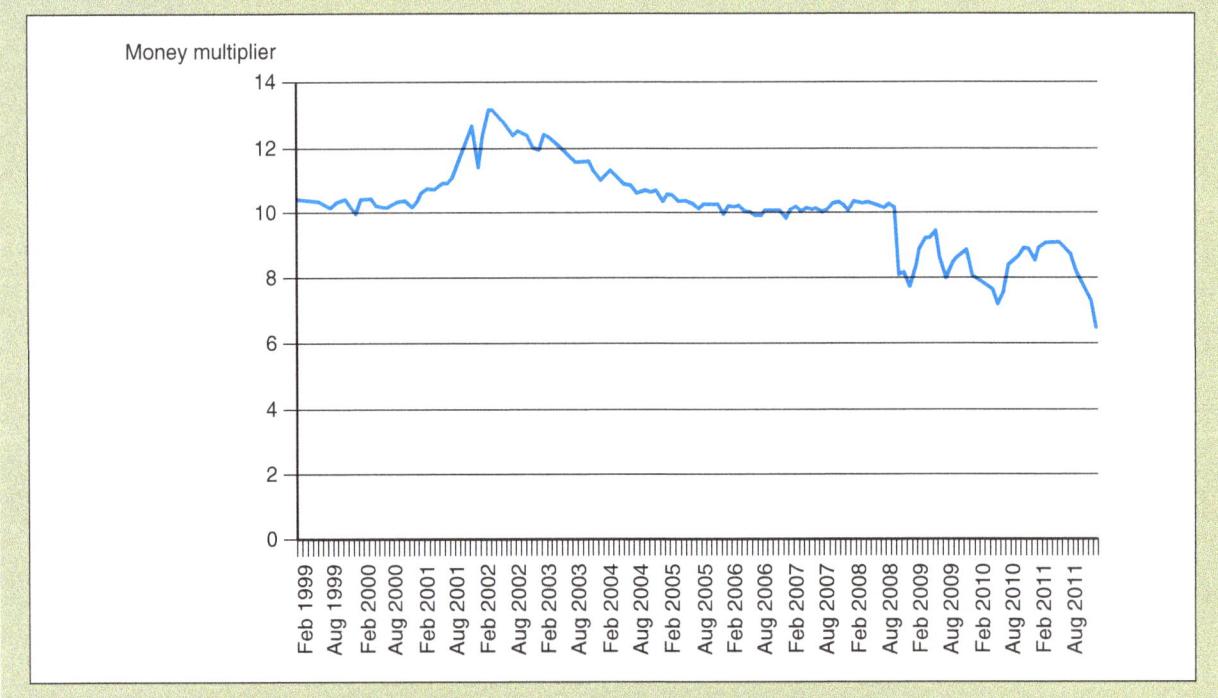

M3 money multiplier in the euro area, February 1999 to January 2012

Sources: Own calculations from monthly outstanding values of monetary base and M3 series provided by the ECB Statistical Data Warehouse http://sdw.ecb.europa.eu/.

FIGURE 14.3

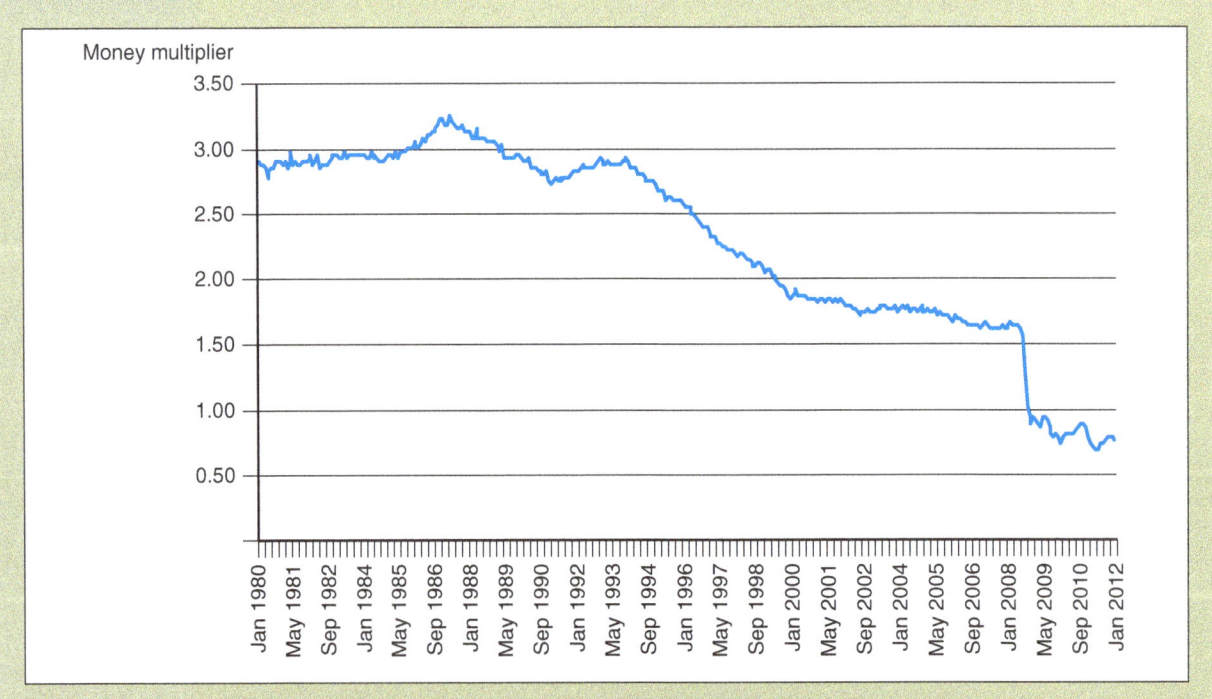

M1 money multiplier in the US, January 1980 to February 2012

Source: Own calculation from the monetary base and M1 monthly series provided by the Federal Reserve www.federalreserve.gov/.

| APPLICATION | The Great Depression bank panics, 1930–3 |

In Chapter 9, we discussed bank panics and saw that they could harm the economy by making asymmetric information problems more severe in credit markets, as they did during the Great Depression. Here we can see that another consequence of bank panics is that they can cause a substantial reduction in the money supply. As we will see in the chapters on monetary theory later in the book, such reductions can also cause severe damage to the economy.

The first bank panic, from October 1930 to January 1931, corresponded with a rise in the amount of deposits at failed banks. Because there was no deposit insurance at the time (the FDIC wasn't established until 1934), when a bank failed, depositors would receive only partial repayment of their deposits. Therefore, when banks were failing during a bank panic, depositors knew that they would be likely to suffer substantial losses on deposits and thus the expected return on deposits would be negative. The theory of asset demand predicts that with the onset of the first bank crisis, depositors would shift their holdings from chequable deposits to currency by withdrawing currency from their bank accounts, and c would rise. Our earlier analysis of the excess reserves ratio suggests that the resulting surge in deposit outflows would cause the banks to protect themselves by substantially increasing their excess reserves ratio e. Both of these predictions are borne out by the data in Figure 14.4. During the first bank panic (October 1930–January 1931) c began to climb. Even more striking is the behaviour of e, which more than doubled from November 1930 to January 1931.

The money supply model predicts that when e and c increase, the money supply will contract. The rise in c results in a decline in the overall level of multiple deposit expansion,

| FIGURE 14.4 |

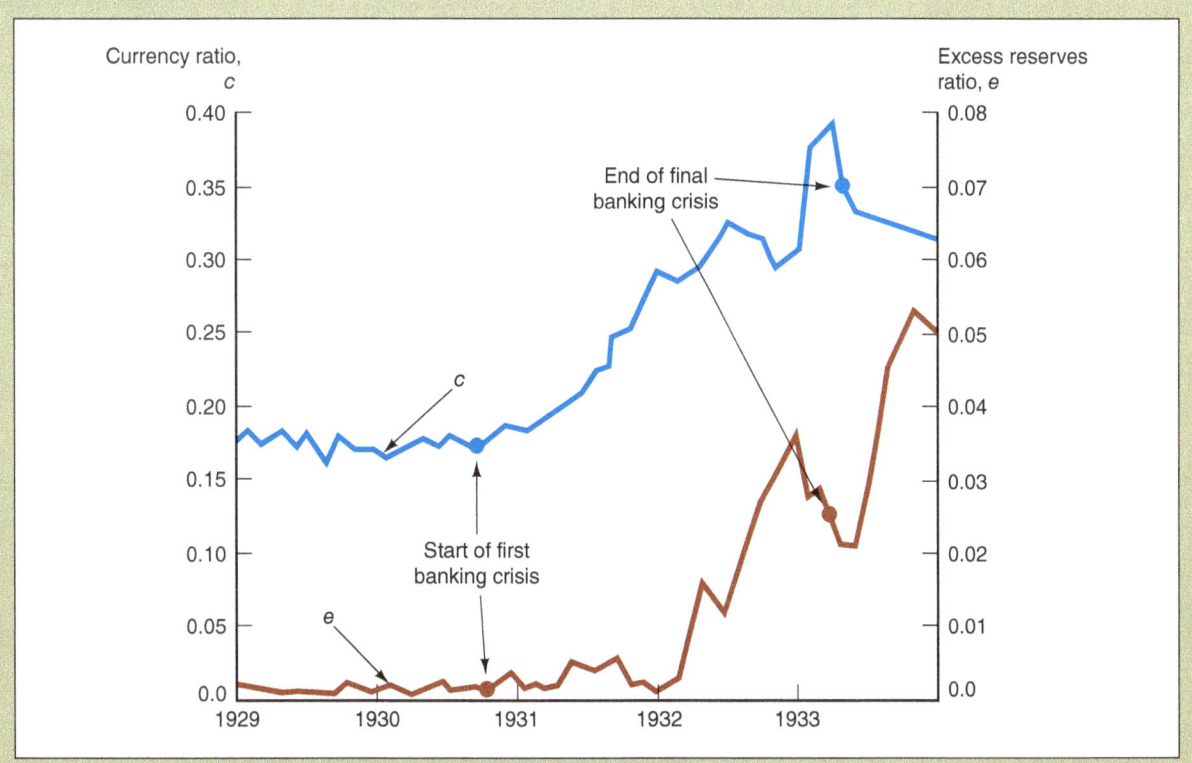

Excess reserves ratio and currency ratio, 1929–33

Sources: Federal Reserve *Bulletin*; Milton Friedman and Anna Jacobson Schwartz, *A Monetary History of the United States, 1867–1960* (Princeton, NJ: Princeton University Press, 1963), p. 333.

FIGURE 14.5

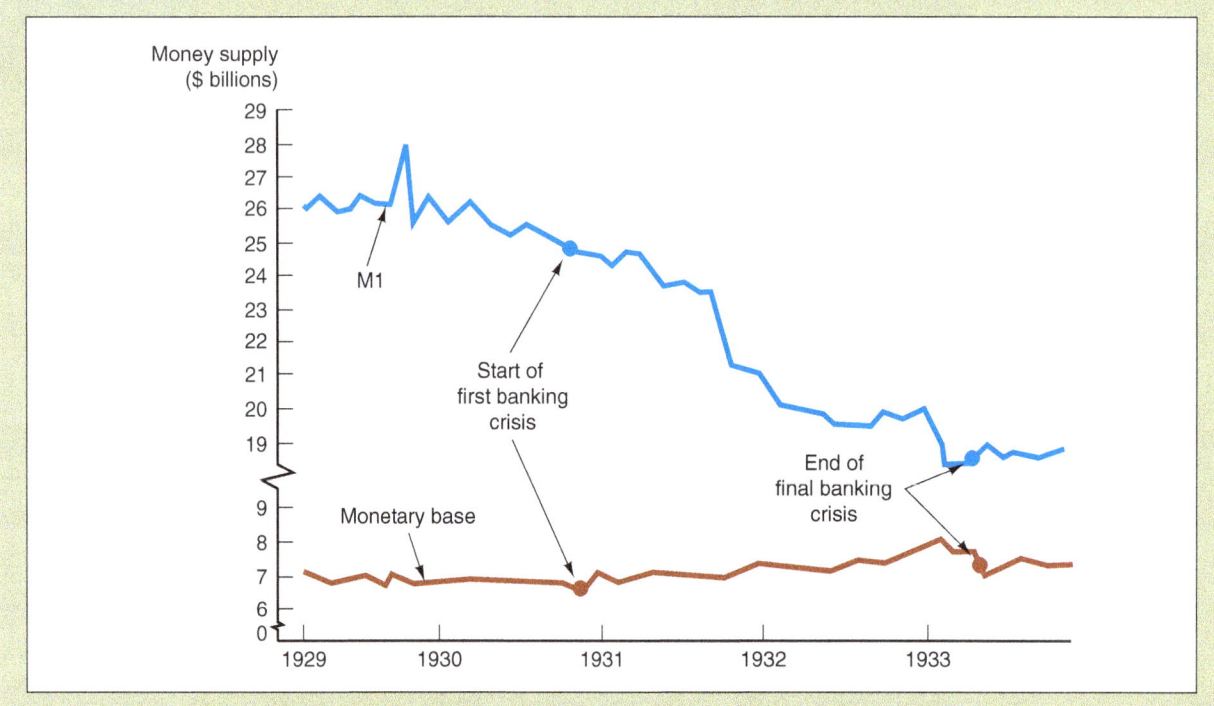

M1 and the monetary base, 1929–33

Source: Milton Friedman. *A Monetary History of the United States, 1867–1960.* © NBER,1991 renewed. Reprinted by permission of Princeton University Press.

leading to a smaller money multiplier and a decline in the money supply, while the rise in *e* reduces the amount of reserves available to support deposits and also causes the money supply to decrease. Thus our model predicts that the rise in *e* and *c* after the onset of the first bank crisis would result in a decline in the money supply – a prediction borne out by the evidence in Figure 14.5.

Banking crises continued to occur from 1931 to 1933, and the pattern predicted by our model persisted: *c* continued to rise, and so did *e*. By the end of the crises in March 1933, the money supply (M1) had declined by over 25% – by far the largest decline in all of American history – and it coincided with the nation's worst economic contraction (see Chapter 9). Even more remarkable is that this decline occurred despite a 20% rise in the level of the monetary base – which illustrates how important the changes in *c* and *e* during bank panics can be in the determination of the money supply. It also illustrates that the central bank's job of conducting monetary policy can be complicated by depositor and bank behaviour.

At the same time, the Fed learned a key lesson from the 1930s which turned out to be useful in responding to the recent financial crisis in 2007–9. Namely, in order to avoid a complete collapse of the money supply due to the sharp increase in the excess reserves demanded by banks and the subsequent drop in the money multiplier (see Figure 14.5), the Fed (as well as central banks across the world) increased the monetary base to record levels, which prevented the collapse of money supply. ■

All in all, the above analysis indicates that money multipliers are not stable and that central banks may find it difficult to exploit systematically the relationship between the monetary base and the quantity of money supply for policy purposes. This explains why in the past a number of industrialized countries (e.g. the UK and the US) failed in pursuing a strategy of monetary targeting (see Chapter 16 for a full discussion). A structural weakness of the money multiplier model is that it is based on the stability of currency and reserve ratios, which, however, in reality fluctuate in response to changes in economic, financial and institutional conditions both in the short and the medium–long run. For instance, the declining role or the ending of reserve requirements in many industrialized countries has made the multiplier approach theoretically less appealing. Another structural weakness of this model is that it is based on the assumption that bank lending is constrained by the amount of reserves supplied by central banks. As we discussed in Chapter 10, with the financial innovation process of the recent decades banks have made increasingly use of wholesale markets for their funds needs, in response to changes in lending demand (liability management). This has made banks less reserve-constrained, and shifted the focus onto lending demand rather than supply of reserves.

It is therefore not surprising that some central banks like the Bank of England have traditionally preferred an alternative model of money supply determination, which focuses on bank lending to the private sector as the main determinant of the quantity of money. This model, which is based on the '**credit counterparts**' approach (see Closer look box: 'The credit counterparts model'), is also theoretically more attractive in those monetary systems in which the central bank targets short-term interest rates. As we shall see in the next chapters, nowadays central banks throughout the world generally use short-term interest rates as the primary instrument of monetary policy. When central banks set the interest rate, the amount of money supply is endogenously determined by the quantity of loans and deposits demanded by their customers, at the prevailing interest rates.

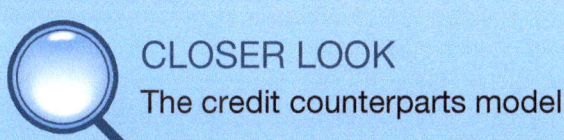

CLOSER LOOK
The credit counterparts model

The central assumption of the money multiplier model is that central banks affect the quantity of money by changing the amount of reserves and monetary base through open market operations. Traditionally, the Bank of England has preferred an alternative model to describe the money supply process which is based on *flow of funds*. This model, also called the credit counterparts model, is obtained by the interaction of the balance sheets of the banking sector, the private sector and the public sector, in which the central bank and the government are aggregated. The starting point to understand this model is to remember that the banking sector's total deposit liabilities are matched by total loans provided by the banking sector (this is of course the case only when banks hold no capital, which is what we assume for simplicity). Bank loans can be provided both to the private sector (e.g. residential mortgages, consumer credit, overdraft facilities, etc.) and to the public sector in the form of direct loans to the government or banks' holding of government bonds. The resulting simplified balance sheet of the banking sector will look like:

$$D = R + LP + LG$$

which implies that total amount of deposits of the private sector (D) should be equal to the sum of total reserves held by the banking sector at the central bank (R), loans to the non-bank private sector (LP), and loans to the public sector (LG).

The public sector (central bank and government) financing constraint is given by:

$$G - T = \Delta MB + \Delta B + \Delta LG$$

which states that government expenditures (G) in excess of tax revenues (T) should be financed either with an increase in monetary base (ΔMB), or with an increase in net sales of government bonds to the non-bank private sector (ΔB), or by borrowing from the banking system (ΔLG), or a combination of the three.[*]

Using the definitions of the monetary base $MB = C + R$ and the money supply $M = C + D$, the banking sectors balance sheet can also be written as:

$$M = MB + LP + LG$$

Taking differences of this last expression and plugging it for the change in monetary base in the public sector financing constraint give $G - T = \Delta M - \Delta LP + \Delta B$. Rearranging this last identity, we can derive the money supply credit counterparts as:

$$\Delta M = [G - T) - \Delta B] + \Delta LP$$

This expression tells us that the change in the money supply equals that part of the budget deficit $(G - T)$ not financed by the net sales of bonds to the non-bank private sector (ΔB) plus the change in loans to the non-bank private sector (ΔLP). This approach emphasizes a direct link from bank lending to the private sector to the money supply.

Now we see why British authorities have historically preferred this model of money supply determination. First, in the UK there has always been a widespread use of overdraft facilities, in which the amount of lending is at the discretion of customers. More generally, the amount of bank lending to the private sector has been a special focus of monetary policy. Second, this approach allows all the credit counterparts to changes in the money supply to be identified. In particular those components

related to the budget deficit and its financing through net sales of bonds (which was common practice before the independence of the Bank of England in 1997) are clearly identifiable. Third, the credit counterparts approach can be directly applied to broader definitions of monetary aggregates (e.g. M3 and M4) which, by embracing the whole banking sector, have been traditionally monitored by British authorities. More recently, also the ECB has increasingly used the credit counterparts approach in its monetary analysis, one of the two pillars of its monetary strategy (see Chapter 16 for a full discussion). Finally, this approach stresses the fact that when a central bank targets short-term interest rates, the resulting change in the demand for private lending will determine the change in money supply.

---

* The public sector can also borrow from abroad by selling foreign exchange for domestic currency, providing an 'external' source of finance. In this section, as in this chapter, we abstract from foreign open market operations, which will be covered in Chapter 18.

Summary

1 There are three players in the money supply process: the central bank, banks (depository institutions) and depositors.

2 Four items in the central bank's balance sheet are essential to our understanding of the money supply process: the two liability items, currency in circulation and reserves, which together make up the monetary base, and the two asset items, government securities and discount loans.

3 The central bank controls the monetary base through open market operations and extension of loans to banks and has better control over the monetary base than over reserves.

4 A single bank can make loans up to the amount of its excess reserves, thereby creating an equal amount of deposits. The banking system can create a multiple expansion of deposits, because as each bank makes a loan and creates deposits, the reserves find their way to another bank, which uses them to make loans and create additional deposits. In the simple model of multiple deposit creation in which banks do not hold on to excess reserves and the public holds no currency, the multiple increase in chequable deposits (simple deposit multiplier) equals the reciprocal of the required reserve ratio.

5 The simple model of multiple deposit creation has serious deficiencies. Decisions by depositors to increase their holdings of currency or of banks to hold excess reserves will result in a smaller expansion of deposits than the simple model predicts. All three players – the central bank, banks and depositors – are important in the determination of the money supply.

6 The money supply is positively related to the non-borrowed monetary base MB_n, which is determined by open market operations, and the level of borrowed reserves (loans to banks) from the central bank, BR. The money supply is negatively related to the required reserve ratio, r, holdings of currency, and excess reserves. The model of the money supply process takes into account the behaviour of all three players in the money supply process: the central bank through open market operations, lending, and setting of the required reserve ratio; depositors through their decisions about their holding of currency and banks through their decisions about excess reserves which are also influenced by depositors' decisions about deposit outflows.

7 The monetary base is linked to the money supply using the concept of the money multiplier, which tells us how much the money supply changes when there is a change in the monetary base.

Key terms

QUESTIONS AND PROBLEMS

All questions and problems are available in MyEconLab at **www.myeconlab.com/mishkin**.

1 If the central bank sells €2 million of bonds to the Safe Bank, what happens to reserves and the monetary base? Use T-accounts to explain your answer.

2 If the central bank sells €2 million of bonds to Irving the Investor, who pays for the bonds with a briefcase filled with currency, what happens to reserves and the monetary base? Use T-accounts to explain your answer.

3 If the central bank lends five banks an additional total of €100 million but depositors withdraw €50 million and hold it as currency, what happens to reserves and the monetary base? Use T-accounts to explain your answer.

4 The Safe Bank receives an extra €100 of reserves but decides not to lend any of these reserves out. How much deposit creation takes place for the entire banking system?

Unless otherwise noted, the following assumptions are made in all the remaining problems: the required reserve ratio on checkable deposits (current accounts) is 10%, banks do not hold any excess reserves and the public's holdings of currency do not change.

5 Using T-accounts, show what happens to checkable deposits in the banking system when the central bank lends an additional €1 million to the Safe Bank.

6 Using T-accounts, show what happens to checkable deposits in the banking system when the central bank sells €2 million of bonds to the Safe Bank.

7 Suppose that the central bank buys €1 million of bonds from the Safe Bank. If the Safe Bank and all other banks use the resulting increase in reserves to purchase securities only and not to make loans, what will happen to checkable deposits?

8 If the central bank buys €1 million of bonds from the Safe Bank, but an additional 10% of any deposit is held as excess reserves, what is the total increase in chequable deposits? (*Hint:* Use T-accounts to show what happens at each step of the multiple expansion process.)

9 If a bank depositor withdraws €1,000 of currency from an account, what happens to reserves and checkable deposits?

10 If reserves in the banking system increase by €1 billion as a result of discount loans of €1 billion and chequable deposits increase by €9 billion, why isn't the banking system in equilibrium? What will continue to happen in the banking system until equilibrium is reached? Show the T-account for the banking system in equilibrium.

11 If the central bank reduces reserves by selling €5 million worth of bonds to the banks, what will the T-account of the banking system look like when the banking system is in equilibrium? What will have happened to the level of chequable deposits?

12 If a bank decides that it wants to hold €1 million of excess reserves, what effect will this have on chequable deposits in the banking system?

13 If a bank sells €10 million of bonds to the central bank to pay back €10 million on the discount loan it owes, what will be the effect on the level of chequable deposits?

14 If you decide to hold €100 less cash than usual and therefore deposit €100 in cash in the bank, what effect will this have on chequable deposits in the banking system if the rest of the public keeps its holdings of currency constant?

15 'The money multiplier is necessarily greater than 1.' Is this statement true, false, or uncertain? Explain your answer.

16 During the Great Depression years, 1930–3, the currency ratio *c* rose dramatically. What do you think happened to the money supply? Why?

17 During the Great Depression, the excess reserves ratio *e* rose dramatically. What do you think happened to the money supply? Why?

18 Did central banks' response to the global financial crisis of 2007–9 prove that they learned from the lessons of the Great Depression?

Using economic analysis to predict the future

19 The central bank buys €100 million of bonds from the public and also lowers *r*. What will happen to the money supply?

20 If the central bank sells €1 million of bonds and banks reduce their borrowings from the central bank by €1 million, predict what will happen to the money supply.

21 Predict what will happen to the money supply if there is a sharp rise in the currency ratio.

WEB EXERCISES

1 Go to **http://sdw.ecb.europa.eu/** and look at the latest dynamics of M3 for the euro area. Has the rate of growth of money increased over the last three years?

2 Go to **http://sdw.ecb.europa.eu/** and click on 'Monetary operations'. Then click on 'Minimum reserves and liquidity' and download the 'Base Money' series for the euro area. Then go to 'Money, banking and financial markets' and find the monetary aggregates for M1, M2 and M3. Calculate the correspondent multipliers and comment on their developments over the last five years.

3 Go to **www.bankofengland.co.uk/boeapps/iadb/ NewIntermed.asp** and search for the monthly average outstanding of total M0 and M4 for the UK. Calculate and plot the M4 multiplier since the early 1980s and compare it to the dynamics of the M3 multiplier displayed in Figure 14.1. How do the two multipliers differ from each other during the overlapping period? Can you provide an explanation for these differences?

4 In May 2006, the Bank of England ceased publication of M0 and instead began publishing series for reserve balances at the Bank of England to accompany notes and coins in circulation. Using the sum of these two series as the measure of monetary base, and the M4 data collected from the previous exercise, calculate the M4 money multiplier since May 2006. How did this multiplier develop during the quantitative easing policy of the Bank of England?

5 Go to **www.federalreserve.gov/boarddocs/hh/** and find the most recent Monetary Policy Report to the Longress (the annual report of the Federal Reserve). Read the first section of the annual report that summarizes monetary policy and the economic outlook. Write a one-page summary of this section of the report.

6 Go to **www.federalreserve.gov/releases/h6/hist/** and find the historical report of M1 and M2. Compute the growth rate in each aggregate over each of the last three years (it will be easier to do if you move the data into Excel as demonstrated in Chapter 1). Does it appear that the Fed has been increasing or decreasing the rate of growth of the money supply? Is this consistent with what you understand the economy needs? Why?

7 An important aspect of the supply of money is reserve balances. Go to **www.federalreserve.gov/Releases/h41/** and locate the most recent release. This site reports changes in factors that affect depository reserve balances.

(a) What is the current reserve balance?
(b) What is the change in reserve balances since a year ago?
(c) Based on parts a and b, does it appear that the money supply should be increasing or decreasing?

Notes

1 This simplified balance sheet does not include other basic items. On the asset side, an important category is given by 'international reserves', which are the central bank's assets denominated in a foreign currency. These are generally held in the form of bonds issued by foreign governments and used in 'foreign exchange interventions' (these will be discussed in Chapter 18). On the liability side, an important component is given by the 'government's account'. Just like commercial banks provide banking services to their customers, the central bank acts as the government's bank by providing the government with a bank account. A discussion of the full composition of the balance sheets of the European Central Bank, the Bank of England and the Fed, and the factors that affect the monetary base can be found in their respective web pages.

2 The currency item on our balance sheet refers only to currency in *circulation* – that is, the amount in the hands of the public. Currency that has been printed is not automatically a liability of the central bank. For example, consider the importance of having €1 million of your own IOUs printed up. You give out €100 worth to other people and keep the other €999,900 in your pocket. The €999,900 of IOUs does not make you richer or poorer and does not affect your indebtedness. You care only about the €100 of liabilities from the €100 of circulated IOUs. The same reasoning applies for the central bank in regard to its notes. For similar reasons, the currency component of the money supply, no matter how it is defined, includes only currency in circulation. It does not include any additional currency that is not yet in the hands of the public. The fact that

currency has been printed but is not circulating means that it is not anyone's asset or liability and thus cannot affect anyone's behaviour. Therefore, it makes sense not to include it in the money supply.

3 In some monetary systems (e.g. in the eurozone, the US and China) banks are required, by regulation, to hold reserves in proportion to their holding of deposits. On the other hand, there are monetary systems (e.g. in the UK, Australia, Canada, New Zealand and Switzerland) with no reserve requirements, relying mostly on banks voluntarily holding reserves for self-imposed prudential reasons and to facilitate the everyday interbank payments and settlement. Chapter 15 will provide a full discussion of the reserve requirements in the euro area, the UK and the US.

4 Here currency in circulation includes both banknotes and coins.

5 If the bond seller cashes the cheque at the local bank, the bank's balance sheet will be unaffected, because the €100 of vault cash that it pays out will be exactly matched by the deposit of the €100 cheque at the central bank. Thus its reserves will remain the same, and there will be no effect on its T-account. That is why a T-account for the banking system does not appear here.

6 Open market operations can also be implemented in other assets besides government bonds and have the same effects on the monetary base we have described here. For instance, as we will see in Chapter 18, the central bank can purchase or sell foreign assets through foreign exchange interventions.

7 The deposit expansion by a single bank is still possible if the money returns to another account holder at the same bank.

8 This multiplier should not be confused with the Keynesian multiplier, which is derived through a similar step-by-step analysis. That multiplier relates an increase in income to an increase in investment, whereas the simple deposit multiplier relates an increase in deposits to an increase in reserves.

9 A formal derivation of this formula follows. Using the reasoning in the text, the change in chequable deposits is €100 ($=\Delta R \times 1$) plus [$=\Delta R \times (1-r)$] plus €81[$=\Delta R \times (1-r)^2$] and so on, which can be rewritten as $\Delta D = \Delta R \times [1 + (1-r) + (1-r)^2 + (1-r)^3 + \cdots]$ Using the formula for the sum of an infinite series found in note 5 in Chapter 4, this can be rewritten as $\Delta D = \Delta R \times \dfrac{1}{1-(1-r)} = \dfrac{1}{r} \times \Delta R$

10 All the above results can be derived more generally from Equation 14.5 as follows. When r or e increases, the denominator of the money multiplier increases, and therefore the money multiplier must decrease. As long as $r + e$ is less than 1 (as is the case using the realistic numbers as above), an increase in c raises the denominator of the money multiplier proportionally by more than it raises the numerator. The increase in c causes the multiplier to fall. For more background on the currency ratio c, consult the Web appendix to this chapter at www.myeconlab.com/mishkin. Recall that the money multiplier in Equation 14.5 is for the M1 definition of money. Another appendix on the website discusses how the multiplier for a broader definition of M is determined.

11 Another reason the money multiplier is smaller is that e is a constant fraction greater than zero, indicating that an increase in MB and D leads to higher excess reserves. The resulting higher amount of excess reserves means that the amount of reserves used to support chequable deposits will not increase as much as it otherwise would. Hence the increase in chequable deposits and the money supply will be lower, and the money multiplier will be smaller. However, because e is often tiny, the impact of this ratio on the money multiplier can be quite small. But there are periods when e is much larger and so has a more important role in lowering the money multiplier. The Application on the Great Depression at the end of this chapter and the recent financial crisis provide clear examples.

Useful websites

http://sdw.ecb.europa.eu/ The ECB Statistical Data Warehouse. This site provides the statistical interactive dataset of the European Central Bank.

www.bankofengland.co.uk/boeapps/iadb/NewIntermed.asp Statistical interactive dataset of the Bank of England.

www.richmondfed.org/about_us/visit_us/tours/money_museum/index.cfm A virtual tour of the Federal Reserve Bank of Richmond's money museum.

www.federalreserve.gov/Releases/h3/ The Federal Reserve website reports data about aggregate reserves and the monetary base. This site also reports on the volume of borrowings from the Fed.

www.federalreserve.gov/Releases/h6/ This site reports current and historical levels of M1 and M2, and other data on the money supply.

CHAPTER 15

The tools of monetary policy

PREVIEW

In the chapters describing the structure of central banks and the money supply process, we mentioned three policy tools that central banks can use to manipulate the money supply and interest rates: open market operations, which affect the quantity of reserves and the monetary base; changes in borrowed reserves, which affect the monetary base; and changes in reserve requirements, which affect the money multiplier. Because the central bank's use of these policy tools has such an important impact on interest rates and economic activity, it is important to understand how the central bank wields them in practice and how relatively useful each tool is.

In recent years, central banks have been signalling the stance of their monetary policy by controlling or targeting the **overnight interbank interest rate** (the interest rate on loans of reserves from one bank to another). Changes in interbank rates have an impact on the interest rates set by banks on loans and deposits, and therefore play a fundamental role in the way central banks can affect the economy and achieve their goals. Typically, the central bank announces an official short-term interest rate at each of its meetings, an announcement that is watched closely by market participants because it affects interest rates throughout the economy. This **official interest rate** is called the Main Refinancing Rate in the euro area, the Bank Rate in the UK and the Federal Funds Rate Target in the US. These policy rates are used by central banks in their open market operations, and are linked to the interest rates applied in their standing (lending and deposit) facilities. Thus, to fully understand how central banks' tools are used in the conduct of monetary policy, we must understand not only their effect on the money supply, but also their direct effects on the interbank interest rate. The chapter therefore begins with a supply and demand analysis of the market for reserves to explain how the central bank's settings for the tools of monetary policy determine the interbank rate in normal times. We then go on to look in more detail at each of the tools to see how they are used in practice by the European Central Bank, the Bank of England and the Federal Reserve and to ask whether the use of these tools could be modified to improve the conduct of monetary policy.

As a result of the financial crisis of 2007–9, many central banks around the world introduced a number of **unconventional monetary policy tools**. These measures were implemented both to stabilize the financial markets and to provide further stimulus to the economy and prevent the risk of deflation. These measures aimed at supplementing the **conventional monetary policy tools**, which seemed to have exhausted their stimulating effects. This chapter will also discuss those unconventional tools used by the ECB, the Bank of England and the Fed in response to the crisis.

The market for reserves and the overnight interest rate

In Chapter 14, we saw how open market operations and loans to banks affect the balance sheet of the central bank and the amount of reserves. The market for reserves is where the overnight interbank rate is determined, and this is why we turn to a supply and demand analysis of this market to analyse how all tools of monetary policy affect this rate.

Demand and supply in the market for reserves

The analysis of the market for reserves proceeds in a similar fashion to the analysis of the bond market we conducted in Chapter 5. We derive a demand and supply curve for reserves. Then the market equilibrium in which the quantity of reserves demanded equals the quantity of reserves supplied determines the overnight rate, the interest rate charged on the loans of these reserves. The overnight interbank rate has a different name according to the country we refer to. In the euro area, it is called the **EONIA (euro overnight index average)**, in the United Kingdom the SONIA (sterling overnight index average) and in the United States the **federal funds rate**.[1]

Demand curve

To derive the demand curve for reserves, we need to ask what happens to the quantity of reserves demanded by banks, holding everything else constant, as the overnight rate changes. Recall from Chapter 14 that the amount of reserves can be split up into two components: (1) required reserves, which equal the required reserve ratio times the amount of deposits on which reserves are required,[2] and (2) excess reserves, the additional reserves banks choose to hold. Therefore, the quantity of reserves demanded by banks equals required reserves plus the quantity of excess reserves demanded. Excess reserves are insurance against deposit outflows, and the cost of holding these excess reserves is their opportunity cost, the interest rate that could have been earned on lending these reserves out, minus the interest rate that is offered by the central bank in its **deposit facility**, that is the **deposit rate**, i_d. Nowadays, most major central banks including the ECB, the Bank of England and the Fed offer deposit facilities, in which banks are allowed to deposit excess reserves at the central bank and receive a fixed interest rate below the respective **official interest rate** (see the Closer look box: 'Why do central banks need to pay interest on excess reserves?'). When the overnight rate is above the deposit rate, i_d, as the overnight rate decreases, the opportunity cost of holding excess reserves falls. Holding everything else constant, including the quantity of required reserves, the quantity of total reserves demanded rises. Consequently, the demand curve for reserves, R^d, slopes downward in Figure 15.1 when the overnight rate i is above i_d. If, however, the overnight rate begins to fall below the deposit rate i_d, banks would not lend in the interbank market at a lower interest rate. Instead, they would just keep on adding to their holdings of deposits indefinitely. The result is that the demand curve for reserves, R^d, becomes flat (infinitely elastic) at i_d in Figure 15.1.

Supply curve

The supply of reserves, R^s, can be broken up into two components: the amount of reserves that are supplied by the central bank's open market operations, called non-borrowed reserves (NBR), and the amount of reserves borrowed from the central bank, called *borrowed reserves* (BR). The primary cost of borrowing from the central bank is the interest rate the central bank charges on these loans in its **lending facility**, the **lending rate** (i_l). This rate is set at a fixed amount above the official rate and thus changes when the latter changes.[3] Because borrowing reserves from other banks is a substitute for borrowing from the central bank, if the overnight rate i is below the lending rate i_l, then banks will not borrow from the central bank and borrowed reserves will be zero because borrowing in the interbank market is cheaper. Thus, as long as i remains below i_l, the supply of reserves will

FIGURE 15.1

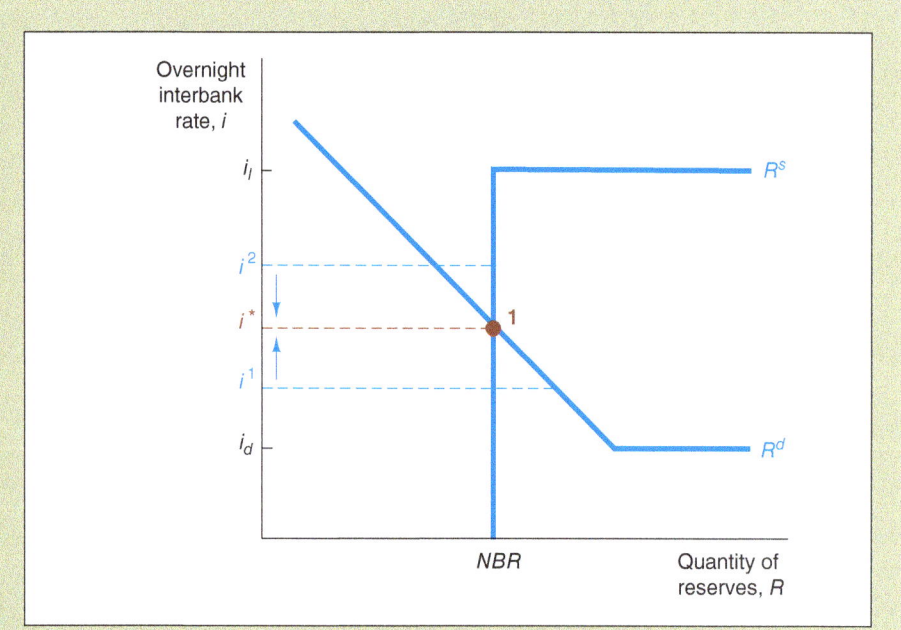

Equilibrium in the market for reserves

Equilibrium occurs at the intersection of the supply curve R^s and the demand curve R^d at point 1 and an interest rate of i^*.

just equal the amount of non-borrowed reserves supplied by the central bank, *NBR*, and so the supply curve will be vertical as shown in Figure 15.1. However, as the overnight rate begins to rise above the lending rate, banks would want to keep borrowing more and more at i_l from the central bank and then lending out the proceeds in the interbank market at the higher rate, i. The result is that the supply curve becomes flat (infinitely elastic) at i_l, as shown in Figure 15.1.

Market equilibrium

Market equilibrium occurs where the quantity of reserves demanded equals the quantity supplied, $R^s = R^d$. Equilibrium therefore occurs at the intersection of the demand curve R^d and the supply curve R^s at point 1, with an equilibrium overnight rate of i^*. When the overnight rate is above the equilibrium rate at i^2, there are more reserves supplied than demanded (excess supply) and so the overnight rate falls to i^* as shown by the downward arrow. When the overnight rate is below the equilibrium rate at i^1, there are more reserves demanded than supplied (excess demand) and so the overnight rate rises as shown by the upward arrow. (Note that Figure 15.1 is drawn so that i_l is above i^* because the central bank normally keeps the lending rate at a fixed level above the target for the overnight rate.)

How changes in the tools of monetary policy affect the overnight rate

Now that we understand how the overnight interbank rate is determined, we can examine how changes in the tools of monetary policy – open market operations, standing (lending and deposit) facilities and reserve requirements – affect the market for reserves and the equilibrium overnight rate.

Open market operations

The effect of an open market operation depends on whether the supply curve initially intersects the demand curve in its downward-sloped section versus its flat section.

CLOSER LOOK
Why do central banks need to pay interest on excess reserves?

Since the beginning of the Economic and Monetary Union (EMU) in January 1999, the ECB has been paying interest rates on required reserves and as well as balances deposited overnight by banks with their respective national central banks. In May 2006, as one of the main reforms to its operational framework, the Bank of England introduced deposit facilities which allowed banks to deposit overnight reserves at the Bank at rates set below the official Bank Rate. For years, the Federal Reserve asked Congress to pass legislation allowing the Fed to pay interest on reserves. In 2006 legislation was passed to go into effect in 2011, but the starting date was moved up to October 2008 during the subprime financial crisis. Why is paying interest on reserves so important to central banks?

One argument for paying interest on reserves is that it helps improve implementation of monetary policy. As we learned in Chapter 14, the amount of excess reserves fluctuates with changes in the opportunity cost of holding reserves. With the interest rate on reserves set at a fixed amount below official policy rate, the opportunity cost of reserves no longer fluctuates as much. As a result, fluctuations in excess reserves are potentially reduced when interest rates change, which, as we saw in Chapter 14, makes for fewer fluctuations and therefore tighter control of the money supply. In addition, as the supply and demand analysis of the market for reserves outlined in this chapter shows, paying interest on reserves sets a floor for the overnight rate, and so limits fluctuations of the overnight rate around the official policy target.

The second argument for paying interest on reserves became especially relevant for the Fed during the subprime financial crisis of 2007–9. As discussed below, during that period the Fed needed to provide liquidity to particular parts of the financial system using its lending facilities in order to limit the damage from the financial crisis. As the discussion of the central bank's balance sheet in Chapter 14 shows, when the Fed provides liquidity through its lending facilities, the monetary base and the amount of reserves will expand, which will raise the money supply and also cause the federal funds rate to decline, as the supply and demand analysis of the market for reserves in this chapter shows. In order to prevent this, the Fed can conduct offsetting, open market

sales of its securities to 'sterilize' the liquidity created by its lending and so keep the money supply and the federal funds rate at their prior levels. This sterilization process leads to a reduction of the holdings of these securities on the Fed's balance sheet. If the Fed were to run out of these securities, it would no longer be able to sterilize the liquidity created by its lending: in other words, it would have used up its balance sheet capacity to channel liquidity to specific sectors of the financial system that needed it, without altering monetary policy. This problem became particularly acute during the subprime financial crisis when the huge lending operations of the Fed caused a precipitous drop in the Fed's holdings of securities, raising fears that the Fed would not be able to engage in further lending operations.

Having the ability to pay interest on reserves helps solve this balance-sheet-capacity problem. With interest paid on reserves, the Fed can expand its lending facilities as much as it wants, and yet as our supply and demand analysis of the market for reserves demonstrates, the federal funds rate will not fall below the interest rate paid on reserves. If the interest rate paid on reserves is set close to the federal funds rate target, the expansion of the Fed's lending will then not drive down the federal funds rate much below its intended target. The Fed can then do all the lending it wants without having much of an effect on its monetary policy instrument, the federal funds rate.*

Given the huge expansion in the Fed's lending facilities during the subprime financial crisis, it is no surprise that Chairman Bernanke requested that Congress move up the date when the Fed could pay interest on reserves. This request was granted in the Emergency Economic Stabilization Act passed in October 2008.

---

* With interest paid on reserves, the expansion of Federal Reserve lending also would not lead to an expansion of the money supply. The supply and demand analysis of the market for reserves shows that once the federal funds rate hits the floor set by the interest rate paid on reserves, increasing the reserves supplied by increasing Fed lending leads to a continuing rise in excess reserves. However, as we saw in Chapter 14, the rise in reserves would not lead to a rise in the money supply: with the increase in reserves going into excess reserves, there would be no multiple deposit expansion and hence no increase in the money supply.

FIGURE 15.2

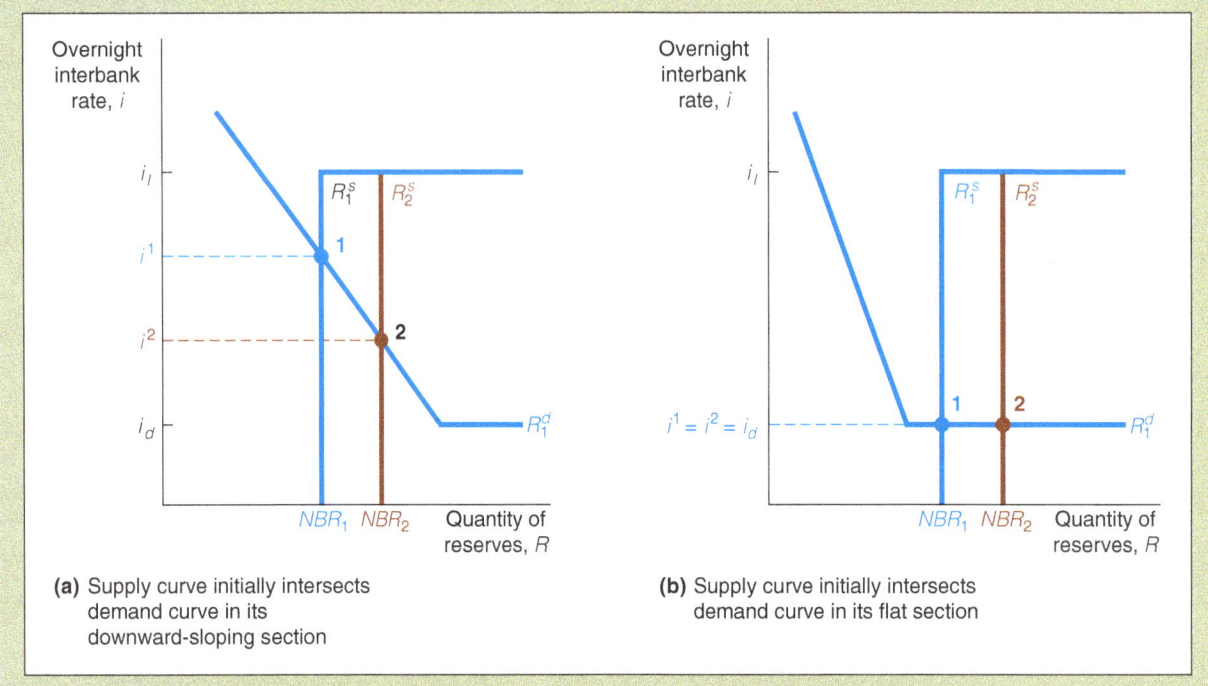

(a) Supply curve initially intersects demand curve in its downward-sloping section

(b) Supply curve initially intersects demand curve in its flat section

Response to an open market operation

An open market purchase increases non-borrowed reserves and hence the reserves supplied, and shifts the supply curve from R_1^s to R_2^s. In panel (a), the equilibrium moves from point 1 to point 2, lowering the overnight rate from i^1 to i^2. In panel (b), the equilibrium moves from point 1 to point 2, but the overnight rate remains unchanged, $i^1 = i^2 = i_d$.

Panel (a) of Figure 15.2 shows what happens if the intersection initially occurs on the downward-sloped section of the demand curve. We have already seen that an open market purchase leads to a greater quantity of reserves supplied; this is true at any given overnight rate because of the higher amount of non-borrowed reserves, which rises from NBR_1 to NBR_2. An open market purchase therefore shifts the supply curve to the right from R_1^s to R_2^s and moves the equilibrium from point 1 to point 2, lowering the overnight rate from i^1 to i^2.[4] The same reasoning implies that an open market sale decreases the quantity of non-borrowed reserves supplied, shifts the supply curve to the left, and causes the overnight rate to rise. Because this is the typical situation – since the central bank usually keeps the overnight rate target above the deposit rate – the conclusion is that **an open market purchase causes the overnight rate to fall, whereas an open market sale causes the overnight rate to rise**.

However, if the supply curve initially intersects the demand curve on its flat section, as in panel (b) of Figure 15.2, open market operations have no effect on the overnight rate. To see this, let's again look at an open market purchase that raises the quantity of reserves supplied, which shifts the demand curve from R_1^s to R_2^s, but now where initially $i^1 = i_d$. The shift in the supply curve moves the equilibrium from point 1 to point 2, but the overnight rate remains unchanged at i_d because **the deposit rate i_d, sets a floor for the overnight rate**.

Standing facilities

As we discussed above, most major central banks offer two main types of standing facilities: lending and deposit facilities. Lending facilities are operated to provide (against eligible collateral) overnight reserves to banks at a lending rate, which is typically set above the official rate. Deposit facilities are offered for absorbing overnight reserves of banks wishing to deposit at the central bank at a deposit rate, which is set below the official rate.

Lending rate

The effect of a lending rate change depends on whether the demand curve intersects the supply curve in its vertical section versus its flat section. Panel (a) of Figure 15.3 shows what happens if the intersection occurs on the vertical section of the supply curve so there is no lending to banks and borrowed reserves, BR, are zero. In this case, when the lending rate is lowered by the central bank from i_l^1 to i_l^2, the horizontal section of the supply curve falls, as in R_2^s, but the intersection of the supply and demand curves remains at point 1. Thus, in this case, there is no change in the equilibrium overnight rate, which remains at i^1. Because this is the typical situation – since central banks usually keep the lending rate above its target – the conclusion is that *most changes in the lending rate have no effect on the overnight rate*.

However, if the demand curve intersects the supply curve on its flat section, so there is some lending (i.e. $BR > 0$), as in panel (b) of Figure 15.3, changes in the lending rate do affect the overnight rate. In this case, initially lending is positive and the equilibrium overnight rate equals the lending rate, $i^1 = i_l^1$. When the lending rate is lowered by the central bank from i_l^1 to i_l^2, the horizontal section of the supply curve R_2^s falls, moving the equilibrium from point 1 to point 2, and the equilibrium overnight rate falls from i^1 to $i^2(= i_l^2)$ in panel (b).

Deposit rate

The effect of a deposit rate change depends on whether the supply curve intersects the demand curve in its downward-sloped section or in its flat section. Panel (a) of Figure 15.4 shows what happens if the intersection occurs on the downward-sloped section of the demand curve, so that there are no deposits of banks. In this case, when the deposit rate is lowered by the central bank from i_d^1 to i_d^2, the horizontal section of the demand curve falls, as

---

FIGURE 15.3

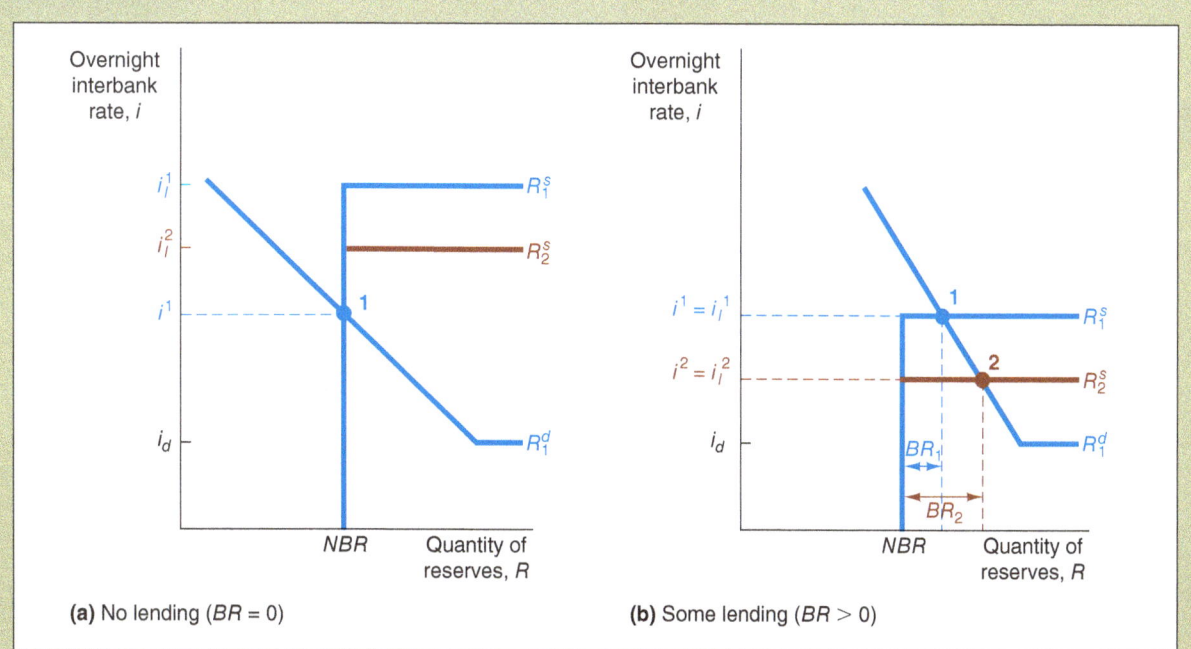

(a) No lending ($BR = 0$)

(b) Some lending ($BR > 0$)

Response to a change in the lending rate

In panel (a) when the lending rate is lowered by the central bank from i_l^1 to i_l^2, the horizontal section of the supply curve falls, as in R_2^s, and the equilibrium overnight rate remains unchanged at i^1. In panel (b) when the lending rate is lowered by the central bank from i_l^1 to i_l^2, the horizontal section of the supply curve R_2^s falls, and the equilibrium overnight rate falls from i^1 to i^2 as borrowed reserves increase.

FIGURE 15.4

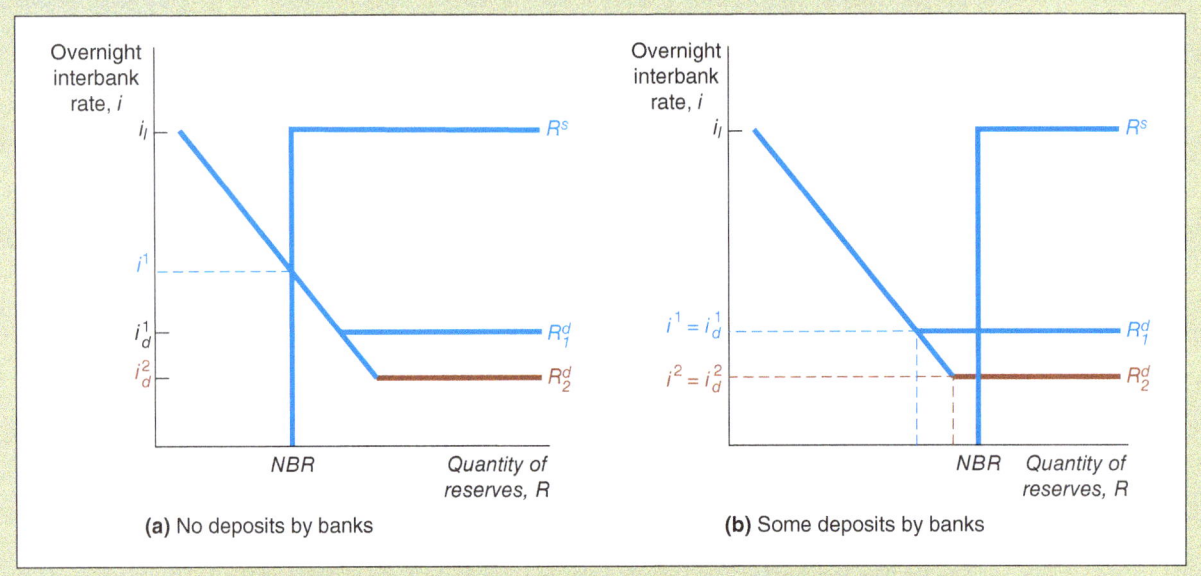

Response to a change in the deposit rate

In panel (a) when the deposit rate is lowered by the central bank from i_d^1 to i_d^2, the horizontal section of the demand curve falls, as in R_2^d, and the equilibrium overnight rate remains unchanged at i^1. In panel (b) when the deposit rate is lowered by the central bank from i_d^1 to i_d^2, the horizontal section of the demand curve R_2^d falls, and the equilibrium overnight rate falls from i^1 to i^2.

in R_2^d, but the intersection of the supply and demand curves remains at point 1. Thus, in this case, there is no change in the equilibrium overnight rate, which remains at i^1. Similarly to the lending facility, this is the typical situation – since central banks usually keep the deposit rate below its target – the conclusion is that **most changes in the deposit rate have no effect on the overnight rate**.

However, if the supply curve intersects the demand curve on its flat section, so that there are some deposits by banks at the central bank (as in panel (b) of Figure 15.4), changes in the deposit rate do affect the overnight rate. In this case, initially the equilibrium overnight rate equals the deposit rate, $i^1 = i_d^1$. When the deposit rate is lowered by the central bank from i_d^1 to i_d^2, the horizontal section of the demand curve R_2^d falls, moving the equilibrium from point 1 to point 2, and the equilibrium overnight rate falls from i^1 to $i^2 (= i_d^2)$ in panel (b).

Reserve requirements

When the required reserve ratio increases, required reserves increase and hence the quantity of reserves demanded increases for any given interest rate. Thus a rise in the required reserve ratio shifts the demand curve to the right from R_1^d to R_2^d in Figure 15.5, moves the equilibrium from point 1 to point 2, and in turn raises the overnight rate from i^1 to i^2. The result is that when the central bank raises reserve requirements, the overnight rate rises.[5]

Similarly, a decline in the required reserve ratio lowers the quantity of reserves demanded, shifts the demand curve to the left, and causes the overnight rate to fall. **When the central bank decreases reserve requirements, the overnight rate falls**.

Now that we understand how the three tools of monetary policy – open market operations, standing facilities and reserve requirements – can be used by the central bank to manipulate the money supply and interest rates, we will look at each of them in turn to see how the Bank of England, the ECB and the Fed wield them in practice and how relatively useful each tool is.

FIGURE 15.5

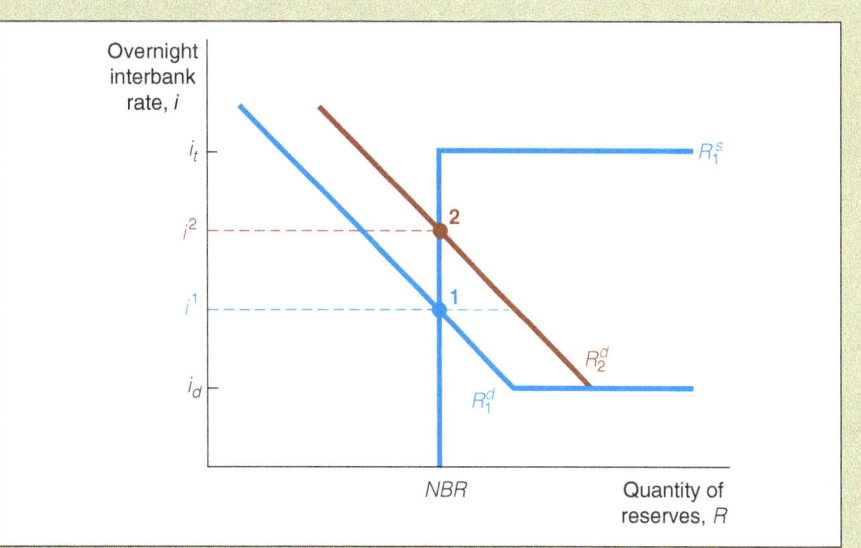

Response to a change in required reserves

When the central bank raises reserve requirements, required reserves increase, which increases the demand for reserves. The demand curve shifts from R_1^d to R_2^d, the equilibrium moves from point 1 to point 2, and the overnight rate rises from i^1 to i^2.

Open market operations

Open market operations (OMOs) are the most important monetary policy tool, because they are the primary determinants of changes in interest rates and the monetary base, the main source of fluctuations in the money supply. Open market purchases expand reserves and the monetary base, thereby increasing the money supply and lowering short-term interest rates. Open market sales shrink reserves and the monetary base, decreasing the money supply and raising short-term interest rates.

In general, central banks use two main categories of open market operations. The first are called *outright* open market operations, in which the central bank conducts an outright purchase or sale of securities in the secondary market, permanently adding or draining reserve balances. The second category refers to *temporary* open market operations. These transactions take two basic forms. In a **repurchase agreement** (often called a **repo**), the central bank purchases securities with an agreement that the seller will repurchase them in a pre-specified period of time, anywhere from one day to one year from the original date of purchase. Because the effects on reserves of a repo are reversed on the day the agreement matures, a repo is actually a temporary open market purchase and is an especially desirable way of conducting an open market purchase that will be reversed. When the central bank wants to conduct a temporary open market sale, it engages in a **reverse repurchase agreement** (sometimes called a **reverse repo**) in which the central bank sells securities and the buyer agrees to sell them back to the central bank in the future.

Now that we understand the main broad categories of open market operations, we can examine the specific details on how the Bank of England, the ECB and the Federal Reserve conduct open market operations with the objective of controlling short-term interest rates and the amount of reserves.

Bank of England: In order to meet its monetary policy objective of maintaining overnight interest rates in line with the official **Bank Rate**, in May 2006 the Bank of England introduced significant changes in its operational framework.[6] As one of the main reforms, the Bank introduced the *reserve average scheme*, according to which for the period running from one scheduled Monetary Policy Committee (MPC) decision date until the day before the next (reserves maintenance period), each participating bank has to define a target for the expected amount of reserves it needs to hold in view of its liquidity needs. In order to supply the right amount of reserves to allow banks in aggregate to hold their target reserves, the Bank of England uses three main types of open market operations: short-term repos, long-term repos and outright purchases of bonds. In normal times the Bank of England predominantly lends through weekly repos at one week maturity.[7] On the final day of each maintenance period the Bank also undertakes 'fine-tuning' overnight operations, lending or borrowing as necessary. Weekly and fine-tuning repos are undertaken at the official Bank Rate. Other sources of liquidity to the banking system are long-term repos (at maturities of 3–12 months) at market rates determined in monthly OMOs, and outright purchases of high-quality bonds. In response to the financial crisis, the Bank first conducted large amounts of three-month repos to satisfy the demand of the reserves beyond the amount needed for banks to meet their pre-arranged reserve targets. As the crisis intensified, the Bank first dropped the Bank Rate to 0.5%, the lowest level in the Bank of England's 300 year history. It then engaged in the unconventional monetary policy of 'quantitative easing' which aimed at increasing the quantity of reserves through purchases of bonds beyond the level needed to maintain its policy rate target (see the box 'Quantitative easing').

European Central Bank: Similarly to the Bank of England, the ECB uses open market operations as its primary tool for conducting monetary policy to steer the overnight rate and affect the supply of reserves. The ECB decentralizes its open market operations by having them be conducted by the individual national central banks of the euro area. **Main refinancing operations (MROs)**, the predominant form of open market operations, normally take place in the form of reverse transactions that are conducted regularly on a weekly basis and with a maturity of one week. In these reverse transactions, the central bank buys assets under repurchase agreements or grants a loan against assets pledged as collateral. In the MROs, credit institutions submit bids, and the central bank decides which bids to accept. The ECB accepts the most attractively priced bids and makes purchases to the point where the desired amount of reserves is supplied. The official policy rate of the ECB is the minimum bid rate which is the minimum rate allowed at these refinancing auctions, and is fixed by the Governing Council in its monetary policy meetings.[8] This rate is commonly known as the **Main Refinancing Rate**.

A second category of open market operations is the **longer-term refinancing operations (LTROs)**, which in normal times are a much smaller source of liquidity for the euro-area banking system. These operations normally are carried out with a monthly frequency and a maturity of three months. They are not used for signalling the monetary policy stance, but instead are aimed at providing euro-area banks access to longer-term funds. During the recent financial crisis, the ECB made extensive use of long-term refinancing operations (see the box 'The Enhanced Credit Support" programme of the ECB'). On top of these regular OMOs, on an *ad hoc* basis, the ECB can also initiate both *fine-tuning operations* and *structural operations*, both of which can take the form of repos or outright operations.[9]

Federal Reserve: The Fed conducts most of its open market operations in US Treasury securities because the market for these securities is the most liquid and has the largest trading volume. As we saw in Chapter 13, the decision-making authority for open market operations is the Federal Open Market Committee (FOMC), which sets a target for the federal funds rate. Differently from the Eurosystem, the actual execution of these operations, however, is daily and centralized by the Trading Desk at the Federal Reserve Bank of New York. Typically, each morning the staff of the Trading Desk estimates the demand for reserves of the banking system. This information will help decide how large a change in the supply of reserves is needed to reach the **Federal Funds Rate Target**. If the amount of reserves in the banking system is too large, many banks will have excess reserves to lend that other banks may have little desire to hold, and the federal funds rate will fall. If the level of reserves is too low, banks seeking to borrow reserves from the few banks that have excess reserves to lend may push the funds rate higher than the desired

GLOBAL
Quantitative easing

The global financial crisis that started in August 2007 and the following meltdown in the global economy has confronted monetary policy in the major industrialized countries with unprecedented challenges. The severe financial turmoil and the associated sharp economic downturn led central banks to respond with unconventional measures of monetary policy.

The precise nature of the unconventional measures implemented by the Bank of England, the ECB and the Fed differed significantly. For example, due to the strong relevance of bank lending in the euro area countries (see Chapter 8), the ECB implemented its programme mostly vis-à-vis the banking sector. By contrast, in order to ensure the flow of credit in the economy, the Bank of England

and the Fed undertook large-scale asset purchases predominantly from non-bank counterparties. Despite these differences, all three central banks witnessed a ballooning expansion in the size of their balance sheets. As shown in Figure 15.6, since the collapse of Lehman Brothers in September 2008, the total size of the balance sheet of the ECB more than doubled, while those of the Bank of England and the Fed almost quadrupled (as of the beginning of March 2012).

Whereas the ECB's non-standard measures mainly focused on an expansion of the existing operational framework, the Bank of England and the Fed engaged in large-scale asset purchases, a process commonly known as **'quantitative easing' (QE)**. The term 'quantitative

FIGURE 15.6

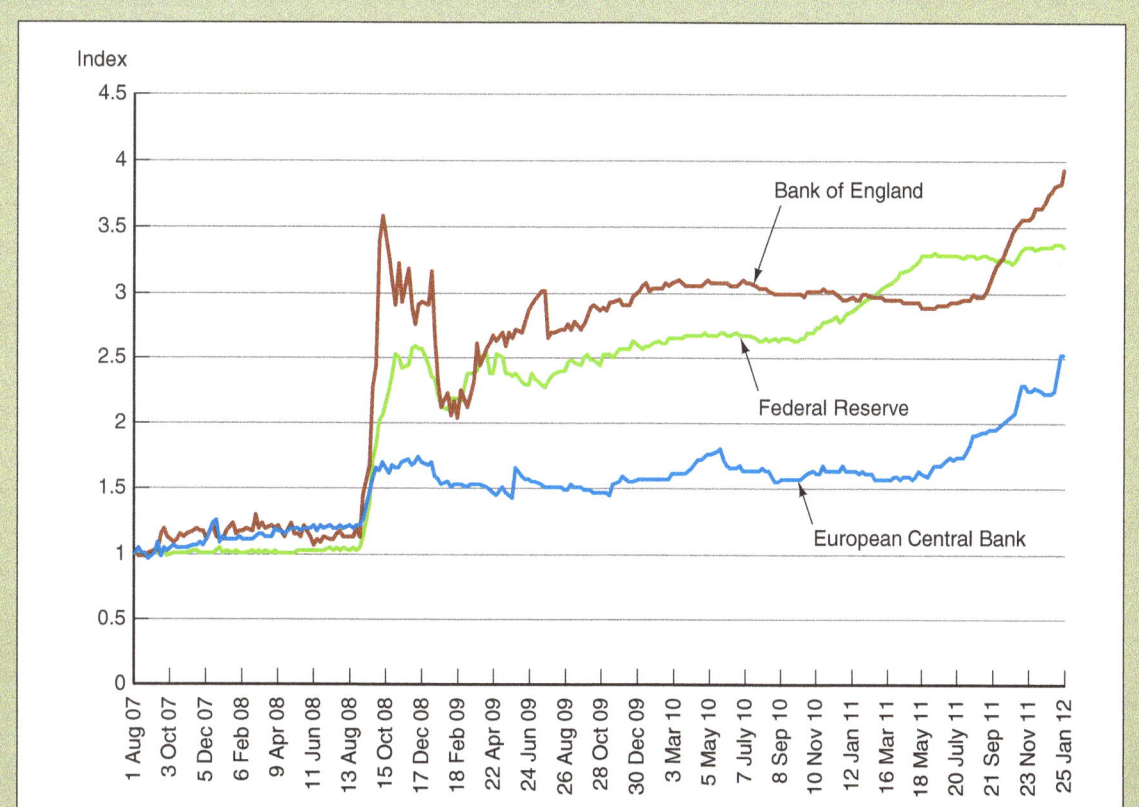

Size of the balance sheet of the ECB, Bank of England and Fed, August 2007 to March 2012

The size of the balance sheet refers to total assets of the respective central banks. August 2007 = 1.
Sources: ECB, Bank of England and Federal Reserve.

Quantitative easing (*continued*)

easing' was first used to describe the monetary policy of Japan during the period from 2001 to 2006, in which the Bank of Japan implemented a programme of outright purchases of government bonds amounting to some 13% of nominal GDP. With QE the central bank expands the supply of reserves beyond the level that would be needed to maintain its policy rate target. This mechanism is clearly displayed in Figure 15.7 from which we can see that once the overnight market rate reaches the lower (in the figure the zero) bound set by the deposit rate (or interest rate paid on excess reserves), the central bank can add limitlessly to the supply of reserves without affecting the overnight market rate. In doing so, the focus of monetary policy shifts from the price (e.g. the overnight rate) to the quantity of reserves.

The central bank that more openly and transparently used the term QE to describe its unconventional response to the financial crisis was the Bank of England. After cutting the Bank Rate to just 0.5% at its March 2009 meeting, the Monetary Policy Committee (MPC) agreed that more stimulus was needed to mitigate the risk of depression and deflation. As a result the Bank launched the Asset Purchase Facility (APF) programme, in which the MPC started buying UK government securities (gilts) in the secondary market as well as smaller quantities of high-quality private-sector assets (including commercial paper and corporate bonds),

financed by the issuance of central bank reserves. The amount allocated to the APF programme was initially set to £75 billion, but was progressively extended till reaching £325 billion in March 2012, an amount equivalent to about a fifth of the annual output of the United Kingdom and around a third of the total stock of UK government debt in issue.

But how can 'quantitative easing' stimulate the economy? Although a full discussion of the monetary transmission mechanisms is developed in Chapter 23, we can already identify some important expansionary channels underlying a QE policy. First, as shown in Chapter 4, an increase in the demand of bonds will push their price up and lower the corresponding yield, effectively reducing the cost of borrowing to firms and households, leading to more consumption and investment. For instance, the Bank of England bought nearly all gilts with medium- and long-term maturities, and estimated that these asset purchases may have lowered interest rates at 5–25-year maturity by around 100 basis points. Second, introducing quantitative easing as an additional element of monetary policy may send a strong signal to market participants to expect policy rates to remain low in the future. As the expectation theory of the term structure of Chapter 5 demonstrates, expectations of low future policy rates will lower today's long-term interest rates, which stimulate economic activity.

FIGURE 15.7

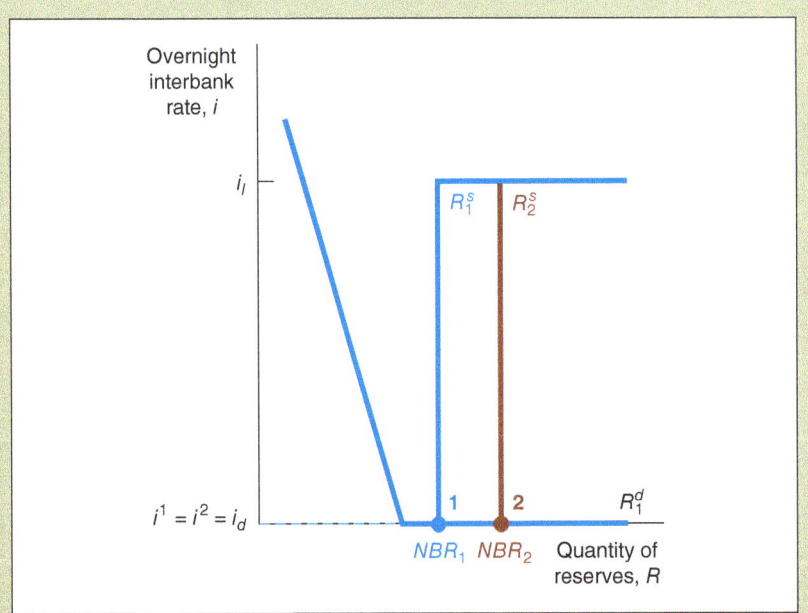

Quantitative easing

With quantitative easing, the central bank shifts the supply of non-borrowed reserves from R_1^s, the level needed to keep the overnight market rate at its policy rate, to R_2^s. The equilibrium moves from point 1 to point 2, with an unchanged level of the overnight rate, $i^1 = i^2 = i_d$, but a higher supply of non-borrowed reserves.

INSIDE THE EUROPEAN CENTRAL BANK
The 'Enhanced Credit Support' programme of the ECB

The global financial crisis that began with financial tensions in August 2007, and the subsequent economic downturn called for unprecedented policy responses by all major central banks.* As we have seen above, the Bank of England implemented a 'quantitative easing' policy by purchasing long-term Treasury bonds predominately from non-banks. On the other hand, reflecting the financial structure of the euro area, the non-standard measures undertaken by the ECB were primarily bank-based. These measures exploited the flexibility of the existing conventional tools of the ECB and are contained in the programme of so-called '**Enhanced Credit Support**' **(ECS)**. The latter is a set of non-standard measures to support financing conditions and the flow of credit beyond what could be achieved through reductions in key ECB interest rates alone. The first set of non-standard measures was adopted in October 2008 and additional ones in May 2009. This included:

Extension of the maturity of liquidity provision: The Eurosystem had already increased the amount of liquidity provided in LTROs after the ECB's decision to introduce supplementary refinancing operations with maturities of three and six months during the period of financial turmoil. After the collapse of Lehman Brothers, the maximum maturity of the LTROs was temporarily extended to twelve months. This increased the Eurosystem's intermediation role aimed at easing refinancing concerns of the euro area banking system, especially for term maturities. Reduced uncertainty and a longer liquidity planning horizon was expected to encourage banks to continue providing credit to the economy. Moreover, the measures were expected to contribute to keeping money market interest rates at low levels.

Fixed-rate full allotment: A fixed-rate full allotment tender procedure was also adopted for all refinancing operations during the financial crisis. Thus, contrary to normal practice, eligible euro area financial institutions had unlimited access to central bank liquidity at the main refinancing rate, subject to adequate collateral.

Currency swap agreements: The Eurosystem also temporarily provided liquidity in foreign currencies during the financial crisis, most notably in US dollars, at various maturities. It used reciprocal currency arrangements with the Federal Reserve System to provide funding in US dollars against Eurosystem eligible collateral at various maturities at fixed interest rates with full allotment. This measure supported banks which otherwise faced a massive shortfall in US dollar funding during the period of financial crisis.

Collateral requirements: The list of eligible collateral accepted in Eurosystem refinancing operations was extended during the financial crisis, and this allowed banks to use a larger range and proportion of their assets to obtain central bank liquidity. The ability to refinance illiquid assets through the central bank provided an effective remedy to liquidity shortages caused by a sudden halt in interbank lending. This included, for instance, asset-backed securities, which became illiquid when the market collapsed after the default of Lehman Brothers.

Covered bond purchase programme (CBPP): Within the scope of this programme, the Eurosystem purchased euro-denominated covered bonds issued in the euro area. The first CBPP of the Eurosystem was launched for a value of €60 billion between May 2009 and June 2010. The covered bonds market had virtually dried up in terms of liquidity, issuance and spreads. The aim of the covered bond purchase programme was to revive the covered bond market, which is a primary source of financing for banks in the euro area.

The above non-standard monetary policy measures contributed to the improvement of market conditions until the outbreak of the euro sovereign debt crisis in May 2010 which corresponded to the first large increases in the spreads between the yields on ten-year bonds of some euro area governments and the German Bund yield (see Figure 6.3). In response to these tensions, the Eurosystem introduced the '**Securities Markets Programme**' **(SMP)**, which entailed the outright purchase of public and private debt instruments. Officially the SMP was launched to ensure the market functioning of specific market segments, and restore the functioning of the monetary transmission mechanism. In line with the Maastricht Treaty, the purchases of government bonds were strictly limited to secondary markets and sterilized. In other words, every liquidity-enhancing operation resulting from these purchases was offset by an equal-size liquidity-absorbing operation, so as to maintain the net injection of central bank reserves unchanged. Therefore, the SMP was fundamentally different from a pure quantitative easing policy, where the main objective is the increase of the supply of reserves.

In second half of July 2011 and the first week of August 2011, tensions that before had broadly been confined to Greece, Portugal and Ireland spread increasingly to Italy and Spain. As a result, ten-year government bond spreads reached record highs in most euro area countries. Fears of contagion and dysfunctional money markets in the euro area led the ECB to take a

The 'Enhanced Credit Support' programme of the ECB (*continued*)

number of additional non-standard actions extending the ECS programme and re-activating the SMP. At its meeting of 4 August 2011, the Governing Council announced that the provision of liquidity to banks by means of full allotment at fixed rates would be extended until at least early 2012. In order to support bank funding enabling banks to continue lending to the private sector, the Council also announced a further longer-term refinancing operation with a maturity of approximately six months as a fixed rate tender procedure with full allotment. On 7 August it was also announced that the ECB would again begin actively implementing the SMP, which, introduced first in May 2010 in practice was stopped after the end of March 2011. On top of these actions, between October and December 2011 the Governing Council implemented additional ECS measures. More specifically, on 6 October 2011 it launched a new covered bond purchase programme for an amount of €40 billion. Then, on 8 December it decided to reduce the minimum reserve ratio from 2% to 1%, to increase availability of collateral,

and most importantly to conduct two longer-term refinancing operations (LTROs) with a maturity of three years. The first operation took place on 21 December 2011 and provided almost €500 billion to more than 500 credit institutions, whereas the second operation was conducted on 29 February 2012 and saw the allotment of €530 billion to 800 credit institutions. As of the first half of 2012, the full impact of these non-standard measures on banks' lending to the private sector was hard to assess, but it was likely to have helped to contain spillovers from the euro sovereign debt crisis to credit and financial markets. For sure, these extraordinary measures showed a strong commitment from the ECB to support bank lending and liquidity in the euro area.

*The first part of this box is based on Box 5.1 'The Eurosystem's non-standard measures since August 2007', in ECB, *The Monetary Policy of the ECB* (2011). The second part is drawn from information provided in several issues of the *Monthly Bulletin* of the ECB.

level. On the basis of these projections, the Trading Desk will formulate and propose a course of action to be taken that day, which may involve plans to add reserves to or drain reserves from the banking system through open market operations. If an operation is contemplated, the type, size and maturity will be discussed. After the plan is approved by the members of the Monetary Affairs Division at the Board of Governors and one of the four voting Reserve Bank presidents outside of New York, the Trading Desk is instructed to execute immediately any temporary open market operations that were planned for that day. These daily transactions take the form of repo (or reverse repo) with maturities which generally go from overnight to two weeks. At times, the desk may see the need to address a persistent reserve shortage or surplus and wish to arrange an operation that will have a more permanent impact on the supply of reserves. Outright transactions, which involve a purchase or sale of securities that is not self-reversing, can also be conducted. These operations are traditionally executed at times of day when temporary operations are not being conducted.

Advantages of open market operations

Open market operations have several advantages over the other tools of monetary policy.

1　Open market operations occur at the initiative of the central bank, which has complete control over their volume. This control is not found, for example, in lending facilities, in which the central bank can encourage or discourage banks to borrow reserves by altering the lending rate but cannot directly control the volume of borrowed reserves.

2　Open market operations are flexible and precise; they can be used to any extent. No matter how small a change in reserves or the monetary base is desired, open market operations can achieve it with a small purchase or sale of securities. Conversely, if the desired change in reserves or the base is very large, the open market operations tool is strong enough to do the job through a very large purchase or sale of securities.

3　Open market operations are easily reversed. If a mistake is made in conducting an open market operation, the central bank can immediately reverse it. If the central bank decides that the overnight rate is too low because it has made too many open market purchases, it can immediately make a correction by conducting open market sales.

4 Open market operations can be implemented quickly; they involve no administrative delays. When the central bank decides that it wants to change the monetary base or reserves, it can just execute them immediately.

Standing facilities

Standing facilities aim to provide and absorb overnight reserves. The facility at which banks can borrow (against eligible collateral) overnight reserves from the central bank is called the lending facility. The facility at which banks can deposit overnight reserves is called the deposit facility. Nowadays, most major central bank systems offer standing facilities. However, the specific terminology and operational details differ slightly from system to system.

Bank of England: With the new operational framework of May 2006, the Bank of England introduced the operational standing facilities (OSFs). These facilities allow eligible UK banks and building societies to borrow and deposit overnight reserves of unlimited size. In normal times, these facilities carry a penalty, relative to the official Bank Rate, of plus or minus 25 basis points on the last day of the reserves maintenance period, and of plus or minus 100 basis points on all other days. The standing lending facility is for overnight repo against eligible collateral, which comprises high-quality securities like gilts, Treasury bills, etc.[10]

European Central Bank: The next most important tool of monetary policy for the ECB after open market operations involves lending to banking institutions, which is carried out in a decentralized manner by the national central banks. This lending takes place through a standing facility called the **marginal lending facility**, which is available to the banks on their own initiative. Here, banks can borrow (against eligible collateral) overnight loans from the national central banks at the **marginal lending rate**, which is normally set at 100 basis points above the minimum bid rate. The marginal lending rate provides a ceiling for the overnight market interest rate in the euro area. Just as in the UK, Canada, Australia, New Zealand, and very recently in the US, the Eurosystem also has a deposit facility, in which banks on their own initiative can deposit overnight reserves and receive a deposit rate which is normally 100 basis points below the minimum bid rate. The deposit rate provides a floor for the overnight market interest rate, while the marginal lending rate sets a ceiling. This creates a corridor system which limits fluctuations in the overnight rate (see the Application 'How standing facilities limit fluctuations in the overnight interest rate').

APPLICATION   How standing facilities limit fluctuations in the overnight interest rate

An important advantage of a central bank's procedure for offering standing facilities is that they limit fluctuations in the overnight market rate. We can use our supply and demand analysis of the market for reserves to see why.

Suppose that initially the equilibrium overnight rate is at the official policy target of $i*$ in Figure 15.8. If the demand for reserves has a large unexpected increase, the demand curve would shift to the right to $R^{d''}$, where it now intersects the supply curve for reserves on the flat portion where the equilibrium overnight rate i'' equals the lending rate i_l. No matter how far the demand curve shifts to the right, the equilibrium overnight rate i'' will just stay at i_l because borrowed reserves will just continue to increase, matching the increase in demand. Similarly, if the demand for reserves has a large unexpected decrease, the demand curve would shift to the left to $R^{d'}$, and the supply curve intersects the demand curve on its flat portion where

FIGURE 15.8

How the standing facilities limit fluctuations in the overnight rate

A rightward shift in the demand curve for reserves to $R^{d''}$ will raise the equilibrium federal funds rate to a maximum of $i'' = i_l$ while a leftward shift of the demand curve to $R^{d'}$ will lower the overnight rate to a minimum of $i' = i_d$.

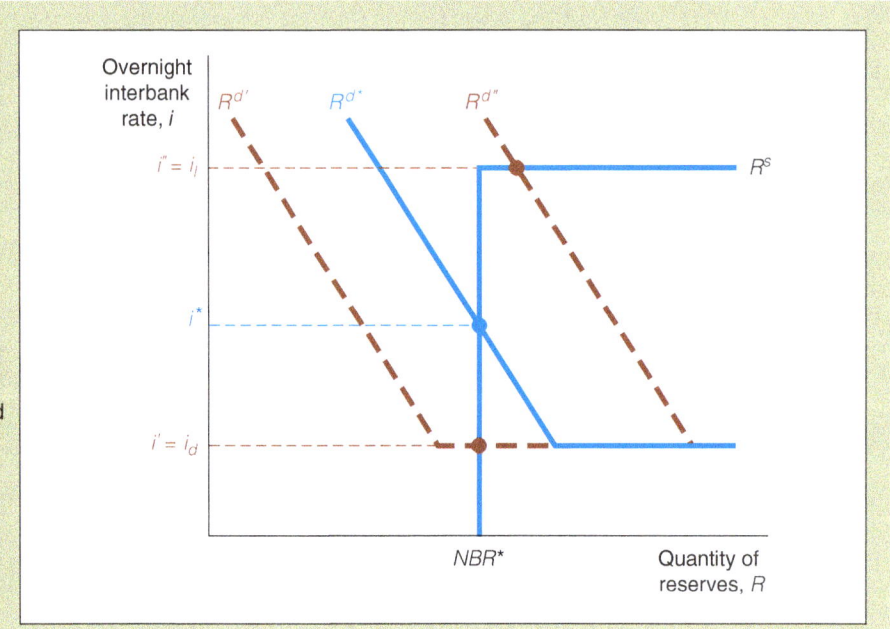

the equilibrium overnight rate i'' equals the interest rate paid on deposit i_d. No matter how far the demand curve shifts to the left, the equilibrium overnight rate i' will stay at i_d because deposits will just keep on increasing so that the quantity demanded of reserves equals the quantity of non-borrowed reserves supplied.

Our analysis therefore shows that the ***central bank's standing facilities limit the fluctuations of the overnight market rate to between*** i_d *and* i_l. If the range between i_d and i_l is kept narrow enough, then the fluctuations around the target rate will be small. But is this conclusion confirmed by the data? Figure 15.9 shows the fluctuations of the EONIA rate (the overnight interbank interest rate in the euro area) since January 1999. As we can see, this rate fluctuated around the official policy rate, but it always remained within the band delimited by the marginal lending rate and the deposit rate. The proven success of the ECB's corridor system in maintaining control over the overnight interest rate has been taken as a model for the reform of the development of the standing facilities of the Bank of England in May 2006 and the introduction of the Fed's deposit rate in October 2008. What is interesting to observe, however, is that since the beginning of the global financial crisis the EONIA rate has often stayed well below the official policy rate and much closer to the deposit rate. This behaviour was due to the large amount of reserves provided by the ECB within its enhanced credit support policy (see the box 'The "Enhance Credit Support" of the ECB'), and the increased use of the ECB's deposit facilities by banks. Yet, even during this exceptional period, the EONIA rate has remained well within the band. ■

Federal Reserve: Under the umbrella of the so-called **discount window** facility, the Federal Reserve makes three types of loans: primary credit secondary credit and seasonal credit.[11] *Primary credit* is the discount lending that plays the most important role in monetary policy. Healthy banks are allowed to borrow all they want at very short maturities (usually overnight) from the primary credit facility, and it is therefore referred to as a standing lending facility, which is the analogue of the ECB's marginal lending facility. The interest rate on these loans is the **discount rate**, and, as we mentioned before, it is set higher than the federal funds rate target, usually by 100 basis points. *Secondary credit* is given to banks that are in financial trouble

FIGURE 15.9

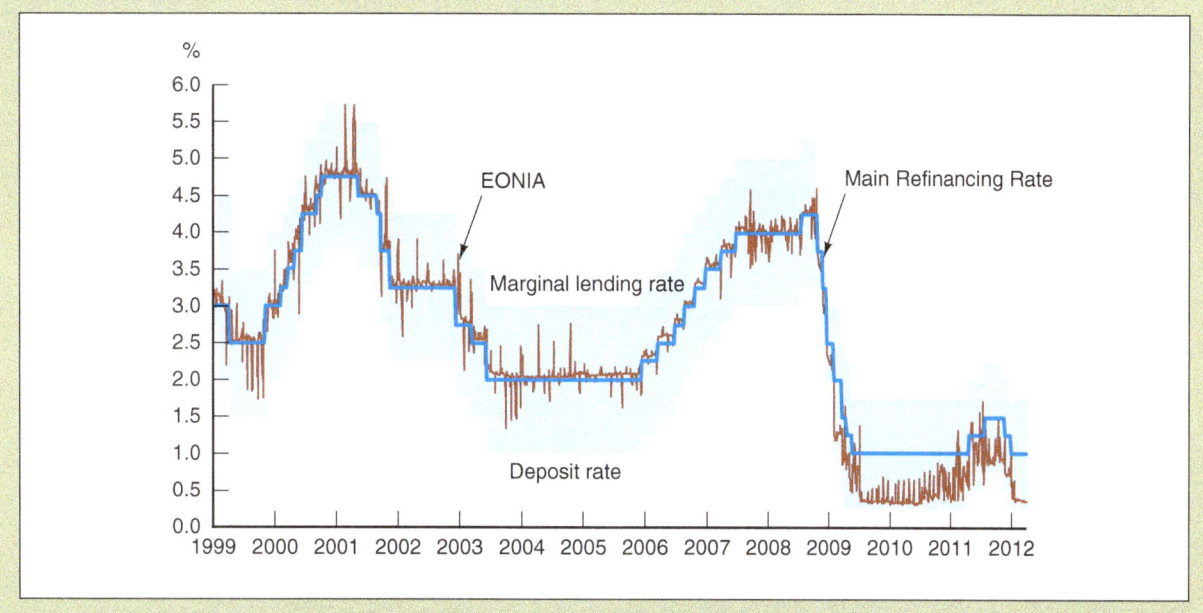

Key ECB interest rates and the EONIA, January 1999 to March 2012

Sources: ECB. The EONIA (euro overnight index average) is an effective overnight rate computed as weighted average of all overnight unsecured lending transactions in the interbank market in the euro area. Between June 2000 and October 2008, the official rate refers to the minimum bid rate. Information may be obtained free of charge through the ECB's website

and are experiencing severe liquidity problems. The interest rate on secondary credit is set at 50 basis points (0.5 percentage point) above the discount rate. The interest rate on these loans is set at a higher, penalty rate to reflect the less-sound condition of these borrowers. *Seasonal credit* is given to meet the needs of a limited number of small banks in vacation and agricultural areas that have a seasonal pattern of deposits. The interest rate charged on seasonal credit is tied to the average of the federal funds rate and certificate of deposit rates. The Federal Reserve has questioned the need for the seasonal credit facility because of improvements in credit markets and is thus contemplating eliminating it in the future. As we discussed above, since October 2008 the Fed has been offering deposit facilities in which banks can deposit overnight excess reserves and receive an interest rate set below the federal funds rate target.[12] While this reform was simply an anticipation of a previously planned extension of the conventional toolkit of the Fed, similarly to other major central banks, the Federal Reserve made use of unconventional tools (see box 'The response of the Fed to the financial crisis').

Advantages and disadvantages of lending facilities

In addition to its use as a tool to control the overnight market rate, the most important advantage of lending facilities is that the central bank can use it to perform its role of **lender of last resort** in preventing and coping with financial and bank panics. As we discussed in Chapter 13, in the nineteenth century the Bank of England became responsible for the stability of the financial system by acting as the lender of last resort during several banking crises of that time. Similarly, when the Federal Reserve System was created, its most important role was intended to be as the lender of last resort; to prevent bank failures from spinning out of control, it was to provide reserves to banks when no one else would, thereby preventing bank and financial panics. Discounting is a particularly effective way to provide reserves to the banking system during a banking crisis because reserves are immediately channelled to the banks that need them most.

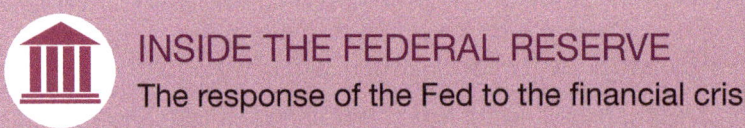

INSIDE THE FEDERAL RESERVE
The response of the Fed to the financial crisis

The onset of the subprime financial crisis in August 2007 led to a massive increase in Federal Reserve lending facilities to contain the crisis. Since mid-August 2007, the Fed lowered the discount rate to just 25 basis points (0.25 percentage point) above the federal funds rate target from the normal 100 basis points. In addition, the Fed expanded the types of securities that would be eligible for use as collateral and extended the term of discount window loans from overnight (or very short-term) to 90 days; and set up several lending facilities to provide liquidity directly to borrowers and investors in key credit markets. These *temporary lending facilities* included:

Term Auction Facility (TAF): Announced on 12 December 2007, the TAF allowed the Fed to make discount loans at a rate determined through competitive auctions. This facility carried less of a stigma for banks than the normal discount window facility. It was more widely used than the discount window facility because it enabled banks to borrow at a rate less than the discount rate and because the rate was determined competitively, rather than being set at a penalty rate. The TAF auctions started at amounts of $20 billion, but as the crisis worsened, the amounts were raised dramatically, with a total outstanding of over $400 billion. The final TAF auction was conducted on 8 March 2010.

Term Securities Lending Facility (TSLF): Created on 11 March 2008, in this facility the Fed lent Treasury securities to primary dealers for terms longer than overnight, with the primary dealers pledging other securities. The TSLF's purpose was to supply more Treasury securities to primary dealers so they had sufficient Treasury securities to act as collateral, thereby helping the orderly functioning of financial markets. The TSLF expired on 1 February 2010.

Primary Dealer Credit Facility (PDCF): Announced on 16 March 2008, under this facility primary dealers, many of them investment banks, could borrow on similar terms to depository institutions using the traditional discount window facility. The PDCF was closed on 1 February 2010.

Asset-backed Commercial Paper Money Market Mutual Fund Liquidity Facility (AMLF): On 19 September 2008, after money market mutual funds were subject to large amounts of redemptions by investors, the Fed announced the AMLF, in which the Fed would lend to primary dealers so that they could purchase asset-backed commercial paper from money market mutual funds. By so doing, money market mutual funds would be able to unload their asset-backed commercial paper

when they needed to sell it to meet the demands for redemptions from their investors. The AMLF expired on 1 February 2010.

Money Market Investor Funding Facility (MMIFF): This facility was set up on 21 October 2008, to lend to special-purpose vehicles that could buy a wider range of money market mutual funds assets. The MMIFF expired on 30 October 2009.

Commercial Paper Funding Facility (CPFF): On 7 October 2008, the Fed announced another liquidity facility to promote the smooth functioning of the commercial paper market that had also begun to seize up. With this facility, the Fed could buy commercial paper directly from issuers at a rate 100 basis points above the expected federal funds rate over the term of the commercial paper. To restrict the facility to rolling over existing commercial paper, the Fed stipulated that each issuer could sell only an amount of commercial paper that was less than or equal to its average amount outstanding in August 2008. The CPFF was closed on 1 February 2010.

Term Asset-Backed Securities Loan Facility (TALF): Created on 25 November 2008, in this facility the Federal Reserve Bank of New York (FRBNY) committed to lend up to $200 billion (later raised to $1 trillion) to holders of high-rated newly issued asset-backed securities (ABS), backed by the ABS as collateral.

Support for Specific Institutions: In the aftermath of the Lehman Brothers failure, the Fed also extended large amounts of credit directly to financial institutions that needed to be bailed out. In late September, the Fed agreed to lend over $100 billion to prop up AIG and also authorized the Federal Reserve Bank of New York to purchase mortgage-backed and other risky securities from AIG to pump more liquidity into the company. In November, the Fed committed over $200 billion to absorb 90% of losses resulting from the federal government's guarantee of Citigroup's risky assets, while in January, it did the same thing for Bank of America, committing over $80 billion.

The second phase of the response of the Fed to the crisis began in March 2009. As the performance of financial markets started improving, which led to the closure of most of the lending facilities outlined above, in order to stimulate the economy and prevent the risk of deflation, the Fed began implementing *large-scale asset purchases* programmes. During 2009–11, within its Government Sponsored Entities Purchase Program, the Fed purchased more than $1 trillion of agency mortgage-backed securities (MBSs) and up to $170 billion of agency debt issued by Fannie Mae and Freddie Mac and other government-sponsored enterprises (GSEs). Moreover, similarly to the QE policy of the Bank of England, the Fed bought also up to $1.6 trillion of US Treasury securities. Collectively, as shown in Figure 15.10, the outright holding of securities by March 2012 was more than $2.6 trillion, a threefold increase of the Fed securities holdings relative to the pre-crisis period.* Early research on the effect of the Fed's large-scale asset purchases during the global financial crisis shows that these programmes lowered long-term bond rates relative to short rates on the order of 50 basis points, and lowered interest rates on mortgage-backed securities even further.

The temporary lending facilities, together with the large-scale asset purchases undertaken by the Fed, have been given by the president of the Federal Reserve, Ben Bernanke, the name '**credit easing**' **(CE)**. This is conceptually distinct from pure 'quantitative easing' (QE). In QE, the focus of policy is the quantity of bank reserves, which are liabilities of the central bank, and the composition of lending and securities on the asset side of the central bank's balance sheet is incidental. In contrast, with CE, the central bank aims at shifting the composition of the balance sheet from risk-free assets (like Treasury bills) towards risky assets (like mortgage-backed securities). Whereas the unconventional policies

implemented by the Fed are consistent with both CE and QE, there is no doubt that the size of the balance sheet of the Fed expanded to unprecedented levels.

On top of the temporary lending facilities and the large-scale asset purchase programmes, the Fed also adopted a third unconventional tool of monetary policy based on the **management of expectations**. In particular, in March 2009, the Federal Open Market Committee stated that it would maintain 'exceptionally low' interest rates 'for an extended period'. This policy was also adopted in January 2012, when the Fed extended its promise of exceptionally low interest rate from mid-2013 until late 2014. This commitment to keep short-term rates aimed at lowering long-term interest rates and also raising inflation expectations, thereby reducing the real interest rates. Although the overall effects of these unconventional policies on the economy will be a major topic of research for years to come, there is no doubt that the Fed demonstrated a strong commitment to get the financial markets working again and to support to the economy.

*In September 2011, the Fed announced the Maturity Extension Program and Reinvestment Policy (also known as 'Operation Twist') in which the Fed intended to 'twist' and flatten the yield curve by selling short-term Treasury bonds and buying an equivalent amount of long-term Treasury bonds.

FIGURE 15.10

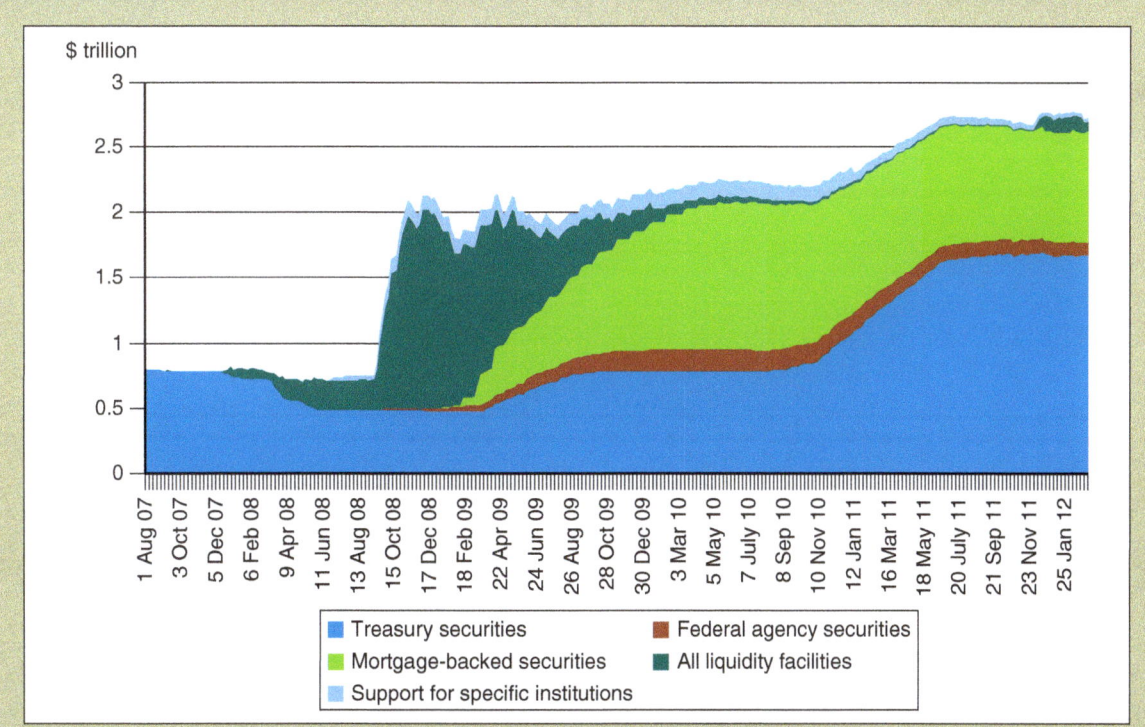

Selected assets of the Federal Reserve in $ trillions, August 2007 to March 2012

Sources: Federal Reserve http://www.federalreserve.gov/monetarypolicy/bst_recenttrends.htm.

Unfortunately, the discount tool has not always been used by the Fed to prevent financial panics, as the massive failures during the Great Depression attest. The Fed learned from its mistakes of that period and has performed admirably in its role of lender of last resort in the post-World War II period. The Fed has used its discount lending weapon several times to avoid bank panics by extending loans to troubled banking institutions, thereby preventing further bank failures.

Not only can the Fed be a lender of last resort to banks, but it can also play the same role for the financial system as a whole. The existence of the Fed's discount window can help prevent and cope with financial panics that are not triggered by bank failures. This was the case during the recent financial crisis, but also in the past. The Black Monday stock market crash of 1987, and the terrorist destruction of the World Trade Center in September 2001 are clear examples (see box 'Using the discount window to prevent a financial panic').

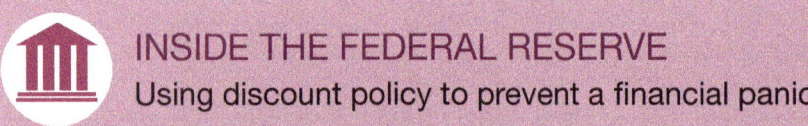

INSIDE THE FEDERAL RESERVE
Using discount policy to prevent a financial panic

The Black Monday stock market crash of 1987 and the terrorist destruction of the World Trade Center in September 2001

Although 19 October 1987, dubbed 'Black Monday', will go down in the history books as the largest one-day percentage decline in stock prices to date (the Dow Jones Industrial Average declined by more than 20%), it was on Tuesday, 20 October 1987 that financial markets almost stopped functioning. Felix Rohatyn, one of the most prominent men on Wall Street, stated flatly: 'Tuesday was the most dangerous day we had in 50 years'.* Much of the credit for prevention of a market meltdown after Black Monday must be given to the Federal Reserve System and then-chairman of the Board of Governors, Alan Greenspan.

The stress of keeping markets functioning during the sharp decline in stock prices on Monday 19 October meant that many brokerage houses and specialists (dealer–brokers who maintain orderly trading on the stock exchanges) were severely in need of additional funds to finance their activities. However, understandably enough, New York banks, as well as foreign and regional US banks, growing very nervous about the financial health of securities firms, began to cut back credit to the securities industry at the very time when it was most needed. Panic was in the air. One chairman of a large specialist firm commented that on Monday, 'from 2 p.m. on, there was total despair. The entire investment community fled the market. We were left alone on the field.' It was time for the Fed, like the cavalry, to come to the rescue.

Upon learning of the plight of the securities industry, Alan Greenspan and E. Gerald Corrigan, then president of the Federal Reserve Bank of New York and the Fed

official most closely in touch with Wall Street, became fearful of a spreading collapse of securities firms. To prevent this from occurring, Greenspan announced before the market opened on Tuesday 20 October the Federal Reserve System's 'readiness to serve as a source of liquidity to support the economic and financial system'. In addition to this extraordinary announcement, the Fed made it clear that it would provide discount loans to any bank that would make loans to the securities industry, although this did not prove to be necessary. As one New York banker said, the Fed's message was, 'We're here. Whatever you need, we'll give you.'

The outcome of the Fed's timely action was that a financial panic was averted. The markets kept functioning on Tuesday, and a market rally ensued that day, with the Dow Jones Industrial Average climbing over 100 points.

A similar lender-of-last-resort operation was carried out in the aftermath of the destruction of the World Trade Center in New York City on Tuesday 11 September 2001 – the worst terrorist incident in US history. Because of the disruption to the most important financial centre in the world, the liquidity needs of the financial system skyrocketed. To satisfy these needs and to keep the financial system from seizing up, within a few hours of the incident, the Fed made an announcement similar to that made after the crash of 1987: 'The Federal Reserve System is open and operating. The discount window is available to meet liquidity needs'.[†]

The Fed then proceeded to provide $45 billion to banks through the discount window, a 200-fold increase over the previous week. As a result of this action, along with the injection of as much as $80 billion of reserves into the banking system through open market operations, the financial system kept functioning. When the stock market reopened on Monday 17 September, trading was orderly, although the Dow Jones average did decline 7%.

The terrorists were able to bring down the twin towers of the World Trade Center, with nearly 3,000 dead. However, they were unable to bring down the US financial system because of the timely actions of the Federal Reserve.

* 'Terrible Tuesday: how the stock market almost disintegrated a day after the crash', *Wall Street Journal*, 20 November, 1987, p. 1. This article provides a fascinating and more detailed view of the events described here and is the source of all the quotations cited.

† 'Economic front: how policy makers regrouped to defend the financial system', *Wall Street Journal*, 18 September 2001, p. A1, provides more detail on this episode.

Although the central bank's role as the lender of last resort has the benefit of preventing bank and financial panics, it does have a cost. If a bank expects that the central bank will provide it with lending when it gets into trouble, it will be willing to take on more risk knowing that the central bank will come to the rescue. The central bank's lender-of-last-resort role has thus created a **moral hazard** problem similar to the one created by deposit insurance (discussed in Chapter 11). Banks take on more risk, thus exposing the deposit insurance agency, and hence taxpayers, to greater losses. The moral hazard problem is most severe for large banks, which may believe that the central bank views them as 'too big to fail'; that is, they will always receive central bank loans when they are in trouble because their failure would be likely to precipitate a bank panic. When the central bank considers using the lending weapon to prevent panics, it therefore needs to consider the trade-off between the moral hazard cost of its role as lender of last resort and the benefit of preventing financial panics. This trade-off explains why central banks must be careful not to perform their role as lender of last resort too frequently.

Reserve requirements

As we saw in Chapter 14, changes in reserve requirements affect the money supply by causing the money supply multiplier to change. A rise in reserve requirements reduces the amount of deposits that can be supported by a given level of the monetary base and will lead to a contraction of the money supply. A rise in reserve requirements also increases the demand for reserves and raises the overnight market rate. Conversely, a decline in reserve requirements leads to an expansion of the money supply and a fall in the overnight market rate. Central banks have the authority to vary reserve requirements. However, whereas in the past this was a powerful way of affecting the money supply and interest rates, nowadays this tool is less important.

One of the disadvantages of using reserve requirements to control the money supply and interest rates is that raising the requirements can cause immediate liquidity problems for banks where reserve requirements are binding. Moreover, continually fluctuating reserve requirements would also create more uncertainty for banks and make their liquidity management more difficult. Since the policy tool of changing reserve requirements does not have much to recommend it, it is not used actively by central banks. If anything, over recent years, central banks in many countries in the world have been reducing or even eliminating entirely their reserve requirements. This downward trend is explained by the fact that, if not remunerated, reserve requirements act as a tax on banks and, as a result, reduce bank competitiveness. These costs have been recognized by those central banks still requiring reserves, and explain why required reserves are nowadays remunerated.

But are there any advantages of maintaining reserve requirements at all in the current operational frameworks? The answer is yes. Besides the macro-prudential function of ensuring that credit institutions hold a minimum level of liquidity (see Chapter 10 for a discussion), today the main function of reserve requirements is to stabilize the demand for reserves by creating a structural liquidity shortage of the banking sector. This makes it easier for the central bank to control the interest rates.

Bank of England: As anticipated in Chapter 14, the Bank of England does not impose reserve requirements. However, with the reform of the its operational framework in May 2006, the Bank introduced the reserves-averaging scheme, according to which for the period running from one scheduled MPC decision date until the day before the next (the maintenance period), each participating bank has to define a target for the expected amount of reserves it needs to hold in view of its liquidity needs. But why would a bank not subject to legal reserve requirements choose to voluntarily hold a certain amount of reserve at all? The answer is twofold. First, banks need to meet everyday cash withdrawals by customers. This can be done by using vault cash or deposits at the central bank which can be immediately converted into cash. In this respect, it is prudent for banks to hold positive reserves at the central bank. Secondly, banks hold reserves at the central bank to settle payments among themselves and on behalf of their customers. Therefore, having positive levels of reserves at the central bank facilitates the payment system amongst banks.

Reserves are remunerated at the official Bank Rate as long as average reserve holdings during the maintenance period are within a certain range around the target each scheme member chooses, otherwise interest penalties are applied. As a result, the reserves-average scheme creates a stable demand for reserves, which helps the Bank of England to steer the overnight market rate in line with the Bank Rate.[13]

European Central Bank: The ECB imposes minimum reserve requirements such that all deposit-taking institutions are required to hold a certain fraction of the total amount of chequing deposits and other short-term deposits in reserve accounts with their respective national central banks. The minimum reserve ratio was set to 2% from the beginning of the monetary union in 1999 to the end of 2011. However, as a result of the intensification of the euro sovereign debt crisis and the resulting increasing stress on the banking sector, in December the ECB reduced it to 1%. The minimum reserve system enables credit institutions to make use of averaging provisions. This implies that compliance with the reserve requirement is determined on the basis of the institutions' average daily reserve holdings over a maintenance period of about one month. The reserve maintenance periods start on the settlement day of the main refinancing operation (MRO) following the Governing Council meeting, and ends on the day before the corresponding settlement day in the following month. All institutions that are subject to minimum reserve requirements have access to the ECB's standing lending facilities and participate in open market operations. The ECB pays interest rates on required reserves, corresponding to the average interest rate over the maintenance period of the main refinancing operations. Consequently, the banks' cost of complying with reserve requirements is low.

Federal Reserve: All depository institutions, including commercial banks, savings and loan associations, mutual savings banks and credit unions, are subject to the same reserve requirements. As of the end of 2011, required reserves on all chequable deposits – including non-interest-bearing chequing accounts, NOW (negotiable order of withdrawal) accounts super-NOW accounts, and ATS (automatic transfer savings) accounts – were equal to 0% between 0 and $11.5 million of the bank's chequable deposits, 3% between $11.5 and $71 million and 10% of the chequable deposits over $71 million.[14] At the beginning of October 2008, in order to eliminate effectively the implicit tax that reserve requirements used to impose on depository institutions, the Fed started paying interest rates on required reserves. This rate is the average targeted federal funds rate established by the Fed over each two-week maintenance period less 10 basis points.[15]

Summary

1 A supply and demand analysis of the market for reserves yields the following results: when the central bank makes an open market purchase or lowers reserve requirements, the overnight interbank interest rate declines. When the central bank makes an open market sale or raises reserve requirements, the overnight rate rises. Changes in the lending and deposit rates may also affect the overnight rate.

2 The amount of open market operations conducted by the central banks is determined by the expected demand for reserves. Open market operations are the primary tool used by the central bank to control the money supply because they occur at the initiative of the central bank, are flexible, are easily reversed and can be implemented quickly.

3 The volume of loans to banks (borrowed reserves) is affected by the lending rate. Besides its effect on the monetary base and the money supply, lending allows the central bank to perform its role as the lender of last resort. However, because the decisions by banks to take out loans (borrow reserves) are not controlled by the central bank, the use of lending policy to conduct monetary policy has little to recommend it.

4 Changing reserve requirements is too blunt a tool to use for controlling the money supply, and is no longer used as a policy tool.

5 The monetary policy tools used by the major central banks in the world like the European Central Bank, the Bank of England and the Federal Reserve are similar to each other and involve open market operations, standing (lending and deposit) facilities and reserve requirements. Temporary open market operations are the primary tool to set the overnight rate at the target financing rate. The central banks also operate standing lending and deposit facilities that operate to ensure that the overnight rate remains within the corridor set by the lending and deposit rates.

6 As a result of the financial crisis of 2007–9, many central banks around the world introduced a number of unconventional measures to stimulate the economy and prevent the risk of deflation. The precise nature of the unconventional tools implemented by the Bank of England, the ECB and the Fed differed from country to country. The Bank of England and the Fed overtook 'quantitative easing' policies by purchasing large amounts of assets, whereas the ECB implemented 'enhanced credit support' measures. These actions led to a ballooning of the size of the balance sheets of these central banks.

Key terms

Bank Rate p. 333

conventional monetary policy tools p. 326

credit easing (CE) p. 343

deposit facility p. 327

deposit rate p. 339

discount rate p. 340

discount window p. 340

enhanced credit support (ECS) p. 337

euro overnight index average (EONIA) p. 327

federal funds rate p. 327

Federal Funds Rate Target p. 334

lender of last resort p. 341

lending facility p. 327

lending rate p. 327

longer-term refinancing operations (LTROs) p. 334

Main Refinancing Operations (MROs) p. 334

Main Refinancing Rate p. 334

management of expectations p. 343

marginal lending facility p. 339

marginal lending rate p. 339

moral hazard p. 345

official interest rate p. 327

operational standing facilities (OSFs) p. 339

overnight interbank interest rate p. 326

quantitative easing (QE) p. 335

repurchase agreement (repo) p. 333

reverse repurchase agreement (reverse repo) p. 333

Securities Markets Programme (SMP) p. 337

unconventional monetary policy tools p. 326

QUESTIONS AND PROBLEMS

All questions and problems are available in MyEconLab at **www.myeconlab.com/mishkin.**

1 During Christmas-time, when the public's holdings of currency increase, what kind of open market operations are typically implemented by central banks? Why?

2 'The only way that the central bank can affect the level of borrowed reserves is by adjusting the lending rate.' Is this statement true, false, or uncertain? Explain your answer.

3 Using the supply and demand analysis of the market for reserves, show what happens to the overnight interest rate, holding everything else constant, if the economy is surprisingly strong, leading to an increase in the amount of chequable deposits.

4 If there is a switch from deposits into currency, what happens to the overnight interest rate? Use the supply and demand analysis of the market for reserves to explain your answer.

5 During the recent financial crisis, the ECB narrowed the corridor of its standing facilities. Can you think of the main reason behind this action?

6 The benefits of using marginal lending facilities (or discount operations) to prevent bank panics are straightforward. What are the costs?

7 'If reserve requirements were eliminated, it would be harder to control interest rates.' True, false, or uncertain?

8 'Considering that raising reserve requirements to 100% makes complete control of the money supply possible, the ECB should be authorized to raise reserve requirements to this level.' Discuss.

9 Compare the use of open market operations, lending facilities and changes in reserve requirements to control the money supply on the following criteria: flexibility, reversibility, effectiveness and speed of implementation.

10 Many commentators argue that the large increase in the amount of reserves which accompanied quantitative easing will have large inflationary effects. Can the central bank reduce this risk by changing the deposit rate? Explain how.

WEB EXERCISES

1 Go to **www.ecb.int/stats/monetary/rates/html/index.en.html**. This site reports the key interest rates of the ECB. Identify the dates in which the corridor system was smaller than 200 basis points. What is the difference between main refinancing operations (MROs) carried out through fixed-rate and variable-rate tender procedures?

2 Go to **www.ecb.int/mopo/decisions/html/index.en.html** and look for the latest non-standard measures of monetary policy. Did the ECB implement additional measures after the beginning of 2012?

3 Go to **www.bankofengland.co.uk/monetarypolicy/mpcvoting.xls**. This worksheet reports the voting outcomes by each individual MPC member on monetary policy decisions from May 1997 until the present date. Look for the most recent MPC meeting. How many

members voted to increase the Bank Rate? How many voted to maintain the same amount of Asset Purchases?

4 Go to **www.federalreserve.gov/fomc/**. This site reports activity by the FOMC. Go to the 'Meeting calendars, statements and minutes' section and click on the statement released after the last meeting. Summarize this statement in one paragraph. Be sure to note whether the committee has decided to increase or decrease the federal funds rate target. Now review the statements of the last two meetings. Has the stance of the committee changed?

5 Go to **www.federalreserve.gov/releases/h15/update/**. What is the current federal funds rate? What is the current Federal Reserve discount rate (define this rate as well)? Have short-term rates increased or declined since the end of 2008?

Notes

1 It is important to clarify from the outset that while the Federal Reserve officially targets the federal funds rate, the ECB and the Bank of England do not set policy in terms of a target for a specific money market interest rate. However, the EONIA and the SONIA are the key market interest rates that these central banks aim at steering with their tools.

2 As discussed in Chapter 14, minimum reserve requirements do not apply to UK banks. However, since May 2006, the Bank of England has introduced a voluntary reserve target, according to which banks contractually commit themselves to hold a pre-specified level of reserves at the Bank of England over the maintenance period (that is, from the date of the scheduled monthly MPC policy decision and announcement, to the day before the next scheduled MPC announcement). Deviations from the pre-specified target imply financial penalties for banks. Therefore, although this level of reserves is self-imposed, in the UK the behaviour of banks in terms of daily liquidity management during the maintenance period is similar to those banks operating in require reserve systems like the euro area and the US. A more detailed discussion of the reserve requirements is provided in a later section of this chapter.

3 The distinction between non-borrowed and borrowed reserves may seem misleading in the institutional environment of the euro area. In fact, as we will see below, the open market operations undertaken by the ECB with respect to the banking sector take also the form of credit operations against assets pledged as collateral. A crucial difference between these refinancing operations and the lending provided through the marginal lending facility is that the former is conducted on the initiative of the ECB, whereas the latter is on the initiative of banks. So in this contest, non-borrowed reserves can be interpreted as reserves supplied on the initiative of the central bank, whereas borrowed reserves are reserves supplied on the initiative of banks.

4 We come to the same conclusion using the money supply framework in Chapter 14, along with the liquidity preference framework in Chapter 5. An open market purchase raises reserves and the money supply, and then the liquidity preference framework shows that interest rates fall as a result.

5 Because an increase in the required reserve ratio means that the same amount of reserves is able to support a smaller amount of deposits, a rise in the required reserve ratio leads to a decline in the money supply. Using the liquidity preference framework, the fall in the money supply results in a rise in interest rates, yielding the same conclusion as in the text – that raising reserve requirements leads to higher interest rates.

6 The framework governing the Bank's operations in the money markets is known as the 'Sterling Monetary Framework' and is set out in the Bank's Red Book, which can be found on the Bank's website at **www.bankofengland .co.uk/markets/sterlingoperations/redbook.htm**. The Red Book is periodically updated to reflect changes to the Bank's operations.

7 Repos are sold at prices determined in an auction where bids with the highest interest rates are accepted first. Subsequently funds are allocated to bids with successively lower rates until the desired amount of reserves supplied is exhausted.

8 The MROs described above are known as 'variable-rate' tender operations. In these transactions, credit institutions bid both the amount of reserves they wish to transact and the interest rate at which they wish to enter into the transaction. However, MROs can also be conducted in the form of 'fixed-rate' tenders, in which the credit institutions bid the amount of reserves they wish to transact at a fixed interest rate specified in advance by the Governing Council of the ECB (e.g. the Main Refinancing Rate). Due to dysfunctional money markets which followed the financial market tension in 2007, from October 2008 all MROs were conducted as fixed-rate tenders with full allotment, meaning that the ECB supplied all the reserves demanded by the credit institutions (see box 'The "Enhanced Credit Support" programme of the ECB'). As of the beginning of 2012, the full allotment procedure was still in place.

9 A full and detailed description of the operational framework of the ECB can be found in the book *The Monetary Policy of the ECB* (2011), which can be downloaded from the ECB's website.

10 As a result of the intensification of the financial crisis, in 2008 the Bank of England launched the Discount Window Facility (DWF) designed to provide insurance against short-term system-wide liquidity shocks. In particular, the DWF allows banks to borrow against a wider range of collateral compared to the operational standing facility.

11 The procedures for administering the discount window were changed in January 2003. The primary credit facility replaced an adjustment credit facility whose discount rate was typically set below market interest rates, so banks were restricted in their access to this credit. In contrast, now healthy banks can borrow all they want from the primary credit facility. The secondary credit facility replaced the extended credit facility, which focused somewhat more on longer-term credit extensions. The seasonal credit facility remains basically unchanged.

12 As a result of the recent financial crisis, the Fed has created the Term Deposit Facility (TDF), in which Federal Reserve Banks offer term deposits, and all institutions that are eligible to receive earnings on their balances at Reserve Banks may participate in the term deposit programme. With this facility, the Fed can manage the aggregate quantity of reserve balances held by depository institutions. Funds placed in term deposits are removed from the accounts of participating institutions for the life of the term deposit and thereby drain reserve balances from the banking system.

13 The policy of 'quantitative easing' undertaken by the Bank of England created the risk of large misalignments of supply and demand for reserves. Under the usual reserves-average scheme this supply–demand mismatch was likely to cause large fluctuations in short-term interest rates. To prevent this, in August 2009 the Bank of England suspended the reserves average scheme and banks were remunerated at Bank Rate on any level of reserves. This implies that there is no incentive for banks to lend in the interbank market at less than Bank Rate.

14 The percentage set initially at 10% can be varied between 8% and 14%, at the Fed's discretion. In extraordinary circumstances, the percentage can be raised as high as 18%. The $71 million figure refers to the end of 2011. Each year, this figure is adjusted upward by 80% of the percentage increase in chequable deposits in the US.

15 One argument for paying interest on required reserves is that it reduces the effective tax on deposits, thereby increasing economic efficiency. As pointed out above, the opportunity cost for a bank of holding reserves is the interest the bank could earn by lending out the reserves minus the interest payment that it receives from the central bank. When there was no interest paid on reserves, this opportunity cost of holding them was quite high, and banks went to extraordinary lengths to reduce them (for example, US banks were sweeping out deposits every night into repurchase agreements in order to reduce their required reserve balances). With the interest rate on reserves set close to the federal funds rate target, this opportunity cost is lowered dramatically, sharply reducing the need for banks to engage in unnecessary transactions to avoid this opportunity cost.

Useful websites

www.ecb.europa.eu/pub/pdf/other/gendoc2011en.pdf Full description of the Eurosystem monetary policy instruments and procedures.

www.ecb.int/mopo/decisions/html/index.en.html Information on the monetary policy decisions of the ECB.

http://www.ecb.int/ecb/html/crisis.en.html An ECB timeline of the financial crisis.

www.bankofengland.co.uk/statistics/rates/baserate.xls Document providing the official Bank Rate set by the Bank of England from 1694 till now.

www.bankofengland.co.uk/monetarypolicy/Pages/qe/default.aspx A comprehensive explanation of 'Quantitative Easing' provided by the Bank of England, including links to speeches and videos.

http://www.hm-treasury.gov.uk/ukecon_mon_index.htm An overview of monetary policy issues in the UK as outlined by HM Treasury.

www.federalreserve.gov/pubs/bulletin/1997/199711lead.pdf Article providing information on open market operations of the Federal Reserve.

www.frbdiscountwindow.org/ Information on the operation of the discount window and data on current and historical interest rates.

www.federalreserve.gov/monetarypolicy/bst.htm A description of the credit and liquidity programmes undertaken by the Federal Reserve.

http://www.newyorkfed.org/markets/omo/dmm/fedfundsdata.cfm Historical data on the Federal Funds and Discount Rates.

http://www.europarl.europa.eu/document/activities/cont/201207/20120702ATT48168/20120702ATT48168EN.pdf *Central Banks in Time of Crisis: The Fed versus the ECB*: a paper published by the European Parliament compares the ECB unfavorably versus the Federal Reserve in its management of the crisis.

CHAPTER 16

The conduct of monetary policy: strategy and tactics

PREVIEW

Getting monetary policy right is crucial to the health of the economy. Overly expansionary monetary policy leads to high inflation, which decreases the efficiency of the economy and hampers economic growth. Monetary policy that is too tight can produce serious recessions in which output falls and unemployment rises. It can also lead to deflation, a fall in the price level, such as occurred in the United Kingdom in 1921–33, in the United States during the Great Depression and in Japan more recently. As we saw in Chapter 9, deflation can be especially damaging to an economy, because it promotes financial instability and can worsen financial crises.

Now that we understand the tools that central banks use to conduct monetary policy, we can consider how central banks *should* conduct monetary policy. To explore this subject, in this chapter we first examine three monetary policy strategies, all of which focus on price stability as the primary, long-run goal of monetary policy. We then look at tactics, that is, the choice and setting of the monetary policy instrument.

Monetary targeting

In pursuing a strategy of **monetary targeting**, the central bank announces that it will achieve a certain value (the target) of the annual growth rate of a monetary aggregate, such as a 5% growth rate of M1 or a 6% growth rate of M2. The central bank then is accountable for hitting the target.

Monetary targeting in the United States, the United Kingdom and Germany

In the 1970s, monetary targeting was adopted by several countries – most notably, Germany, Switzerland, Canada, the United Kingdom, Japan and the United States. Monetary targeting in practice was quite different from Milton Friedman's suggestion that the chosen monetary aggregate be targeted to grow at a constant rate. Indeed, in all of these countries, the central banks never adhered to strict, ironclad rules for monetary growth. In some of these countries, monetary targeting was not pursued very seriously.

United States

In 1970, Arthur Burns was appointed chairman of the Board of Governors of the Federal Reserve, and soon thereafter the Fed stated that it was committing itself to the use of monetary targets to guide monetary policy. In 1975, in response to a congressional resolution, the Fed began to announce publicly its targets for money supply growth, though it often missed them. In October 1979, two months after Paul Volcker became chairman of the Board of Governors, the Fed switched to an operating procedure that focused more on non-borrowed reserves and control of the monetary aggregates and less on the federal funds rate. Despite the change in focus, the performance in hitting monetary targets was even worse: in all three years of the 1979–82 period, the Fed missed its M1 growth target ranges. What went wrong?

There are several possible answers to this question. The first is that the US economy was exposed to several shocks during this period that made monetary control more difficult: the acceleration of financial innovation and deregulation, which added new categories of deposits such as NOW accounts to the measures of monetary aggregates; the imposition by the Fed of credit controls from March to July 1980, which restricted the growth of consumer and business loans; and the back-to-back recessions of 1980 and 1981–2.[1]

A more persuasive explanation for poor monetary control, however, is that controlling the money supply was never really the intent of Volcker's policy shift. Despite Volcker's statements about the need to target monetary aggregates, he was not committed to these targets. Rather, he was far more concerned with using interest-rate movements to wring inflation out of the economy. Volcker's primary reason for changing the Fed's operating procedure was to free his hand to manipulate interest rates and thereby fight inflation. It was necessary to abandon interest-rate targets if Volcker were to be able to raise interest rates sharply when a slowdown in the economy was required to dampen inflation. This view of Volcker's strategy suggests that the Fed's announced attachment to monetary aggregate targets may have been a smokescreen to keep the Fed from being blamed for the high interest rates that would result from the new interest-rate policy.

In 1982, with inflation in check, the Fed decreased its emphasis on monetary targets. In July 1993, Board of Governors chairman Alan Greenspan testified in Congress that the Fed would no longer use any monetary aggregates as a guide for conducting monetary policy.

United Kingdom

The Bank of England made commitments to monetary targets around the same time as the Federal Reserve. After internal monetary targeting for M3 had already started in 1973, in response to rising inflation concerns and the exchange rate crisis, the Bank of England officially introduced a binding numerical target for broad money supply (£M3) in July 1976.

Similarly to the experiences of the Federal Reserve, the Bank of England had great difficulties in meeting its £M3 target. Not only were targets consistently overshot in the 1976–79 period, but the Bank of England also frequently revised its target. Following a peak in inflation of nearly 20% in 1980, the UK government pressed for a policy change in order to bring down inflation back to normal levels. In March 1980 the Bank of England launched the so-called Medium-Term Financial Strategy (MTFS), on the basis of which a gradual reduction in the growth of broad money was set. Moreover, to restore public confidence in the government's commitment to monetary targeting all other macroeconomic objectives were subordinated to the achievement of this target. The policy shift did, however, not yield the desired progress. As the Bank of England still found itself unable to control the money supply, in October 1985 £M3 was officially abandoned as a money target. Subsequently a target for narrow money (the monetary base) was introduced and remained in place until 1992, the beginning of the inflation targeting framework. However, the demise of the monetary targeting regime is generally thought to have taken place in 1985 as for the remainder of the decade the Bank of England turned towards exchange-rate targeting, attempting to stop the appreciation of the pound.

The Bank of Canada adopted a monetary targeting regime around the same time as the Bank of England and the Federal Reserve and had similar experiences to that in the United Kingdom and the United States. By the 1980s, it became clear that monetary aggregates were not a reliable guide to monetary policy and, as with the Bank of England and the Federal Reserve, monetary targeting was abandoned. Gerald Bouey, the governor of the Bank of Canada, described his bank's experience colourfully by saying, 'We didn't abandon monetary aggregates; they abandoned us'.

There are two main interpretations for the failure of monetary targeting in these countries. One is that the rise of financial innovation did not allow for proper controllability of the targeted monetary aggregates. The other is that monetary targeting was not pursued seriously and as a result monetary control never had a chance to be successful.

Germany

Starting in the mid-1970s and continuing through the next two decades, both Germany and Switzerland engaged in monetary targeting. The success of monetary targeting in controlling inflation in these two countries explains why monetary targeting still has strong advocates and is an element of the official policy regime for the European Central Bank (see the box 'The two-pillar monetary strategy of the ECB'). Because the success of the German monetary targeting regime in producing low inflation has received the most attention, we'll concentrate on Germany's experience.

Germany's central bank, the Bundesbank, chose to focus on a narrow monetary aggregate called *central bank money*, the sum of currency in circulation and bank deposits weighted by the 1974 required reserve ratios. In 1988, the Bundesbank switched targets from central bank money to M3.

The key fact about the monetary targeting regime in Germany is that it was not a Friedman-type monetary targeting rule in which a monetary aggregate is kept on a constant-growth-rate path and is the primary focus of monetary policy. The Bundesbank allowed growth outside of its target ranges for periods of two to three years, and overshoots of its targets were subsequently reversed. Monetary targeting in Germany was instead primarily a method of communicating the strategy of monetary policy focused on long-run considerations and the control of inflation.

The calculation of monetary target ranges put great stress on making policy transparent (clear, simple and understandable) and on regular communication with the public. First and foremost, a numerical inflation goal was prominently featured in the setting of target ranges. Second, monetary targeting, far from being a rigid policy rule, was flexible in practice. The target ranges for money growth were missed about 50% of the time in Germany, often because of the Bundesbank's concern about other objectives, including output and exchange rates. Furthermore, the Bundesbank demonstrated its flexibility by allowing its inflation goal to vary over time and to converge gradually to the long-run inflation goal.

The monetary targeting regime in Germany demonstrated a strong commitment to clear communication of the strategy to the general public. The money growth targets were continually used as a framework to explain the monetary policy strategy, and the Bundesbank expended tremendous effort in its publications and in frequent speeches by central bank officials to communicate to the public what the central bank was trying to achieve. Given that the Bundesbank frequently missed its money growth targets by significant amounts, its monetary targeting framework is best viewed as a mechanism for transparently communicating how monetary policy is being directed to achieve inflation goals and as a means for increasing the accountability of the central bank.

There are two key lessons to be learned from our discussion of German monetary targeting. First, a monetary targeting regime can restrain inflation in the longer run, even when the regime permits substantial target misses. Thus adherence to a rigid policy rule is not necessary to obtain good inflation outcomes. Second, the key reason why monetary targeting was reasonably successful, despite frequent target misses, is that the objectives of monetary policy were clearly stated and the central bank actively engaged in communicating the strategy of monetary policy to the public, thereby enhancing the transparency of monetary policy and the accountability of the central bank.

As we will see in the next section, these key elements of a successful monetary-targeting regime – flexibility, transparency and accountability – are also important elements in inflation-targeting regimes. German monetary policy was actually closer in practice to inflation targeting than it was to Friedman-like monetary targeting, and thus might best be thought of as 'hybrid' inflation targeting.

Advantages of monetary targeting

One advantage of monetary targeting is that information on whether the central bank is achieving its target is known almost immediately – figures for monetary aggregates are typically reported within a couple of weeks. Thus monetary targets can send almost immediate signals to the public and markets about the stance of monetary policy and the intentions of the policymakers to keep inflation in check. In turn, these signals help fix inflation expectations and produce less inflation. Monetary targets also allow almost immediate accountability for monetary policy to keep inflation low, thus helping to constrain the monetary policymaker from falling into the time-inconsistency trap.

Disadvantages of monetary targeting

All of the above advantages of monetary aggregate targeting depend on a big *if*: there must be a strong and reliable relationship between the goal variable (inflation or nominal income) and the targeted monetary aggregate. If the relationship between the monetary aggregate and the goal variable is weak, monetary aggregate targeting will not work; this seems to have been a serious problem in those countries that pursued monetary targets. The weak relationship implies that hitting the target will not produce the desired outcome on the goal variable and thus the monetary aggregate will no longer provide an adequate signal about the stance of monetary policy. As a result, monetary targeting will not help fix inflation expectations and will not be a good guide for assessing central bank accountability. In addition, an unreliable relationship between monetary aggregates and goal variables makes it difficult for monetary targeting to serve as a communications device that increases the transparency of monetary policy and makes the central bank accountable to the public.

Inflation targeting

Given the breakdown of the relationship between monetary aggregates and goal variables such as inflation, many countries have recently adopted inflation targeting as their monetary policy strategy to achieve price stability. New Zealand was the first country to formally adopt inflation targeting in 1990, followed by Canada in 1991, the United Kingdom in 1992, Sweden and Finland in 1993, and Australia and Spain in 1994. Israel, Chile and Brazil, among others, have also adopted a form of inflation targeting.

Inflation targeting involves several elements: (1) public announcement of medium-term numerical objectives (targets) for inflation; (2) an institutional commitment to price stability as the primary, long-run goal of monetary policy and a commitment to achieve the inflation goal; (3) an information-inclusive approach in which many variables (not just monetary aggregates) are used in making decisions about monetary policy; (4) increased transparency of the monetary policy strategy through communication with the public and the markets about the plans and objectives of monetary policymakers; and (5) increased accountability of the central bank for attaining its inflation objectives.

Inflation targeting in New Zealand, Canada and the United Kingdom

We begin our look at inflation targeting with New Zealand, because it was the first country to adopt it. We then go on to look at the experiences in Canada and the United Kingdom, which were next to adopt this strategy.[2]

New Zealand

As part of a general reform of the government's role in the economy, the New Zealand parliament passed a new Reserve Bank of New Zealand Act in 1989, which became effective on 1 February 1990. Besides increasing the independence of the central bank, moving it from being one of the least independent to one of the most independent among the developed countries, the act committed the Reserve Bank to a sole objective of price stability. The Act stipulated that the minister of finance and the governor of the Reserve Bank should negotiate and make public a Policy Targets Agreement, a statement that sets out the targets by which monetary policy performance will be evaluated, specifying numerical target ranges for inflation and the dates by which they are to be reached. An unusual feature of the New Zealand legislation is that the governor of the Reserve Bank is held highly accountable for the success of monetary policy. If the goals set forth in the Policy Targets Agreement are not satisfied, the governor is subject to dismissal.

The first Policy Targets Agreement, signed by the minister of finance and the governor of the Reserve Bank on 2 March 1990, directed the Reserve Bank to achieve an annual inflation rate within a 3–5% range. Subsequent agreements lowered the range to 0–2% until the end of 1996, when the range was changed to 0–3% and later to 1–3% in 2002. As a result of tight monetary policy, the inflation rate was brought down from above 5% to below 2% by the end of 1992 (see Figure 16.1, panel a), but at the cost of a deep recession and a sharp rise in unemployment. Since then, inflation has typically remained within the targeted range, with the exception of brief periods in 1995, 2000 and 2008 when it exceeded the range by a small amount. (Under the Reserve Bank Act, the governor could have been dismissed, but after parliamentary debates he retained his job.) Since 1992, New Zealand's growth rate has generally been high, with some years exceeding 5%, and unemployment has come down significantly.

Canada

On 26 February 1991, a joint announcement by the minister of finance and the governor of the Bank of Canada established formal inflation targets. The target ranges were 2–4% by the end of 1992, 1.5–3.5% by June 1994 and 1–3% by December 1996. After the new government took office in late 1993, the target range was set at 1–3% from December 1995 until December 1998 and has been kept at this level. Canadian inflation has also fallen dramatically since the adoption of inflation targets, from above 5% in 1991, to a 0% rate in 1995 and to around 2% subsequently (see Figure 16.1, panel b). As was the case in New Zealand, however, this decline was not without cost: unemployment soared to above 10% from 1991 until 1994, but then declined substantially.

United Kingdom

In October 1992, the United Kingdom adopted an inflation target as its nominal anchor, and the Bank of England began to produce an *Inflation Report*, a quarterly report on the progress being made in achieving that target. The inflation target range was initially set at 1–4% until the next election (spring 1997 at the latest), with the intent that the inflation rate should settle down to the lower half of the range (below 2.5%). In May 1997, the inflation target was set at 2.5% and the Bank of England was given the power to set interest rates henceforth, granting it a more independent role in monetary policy.

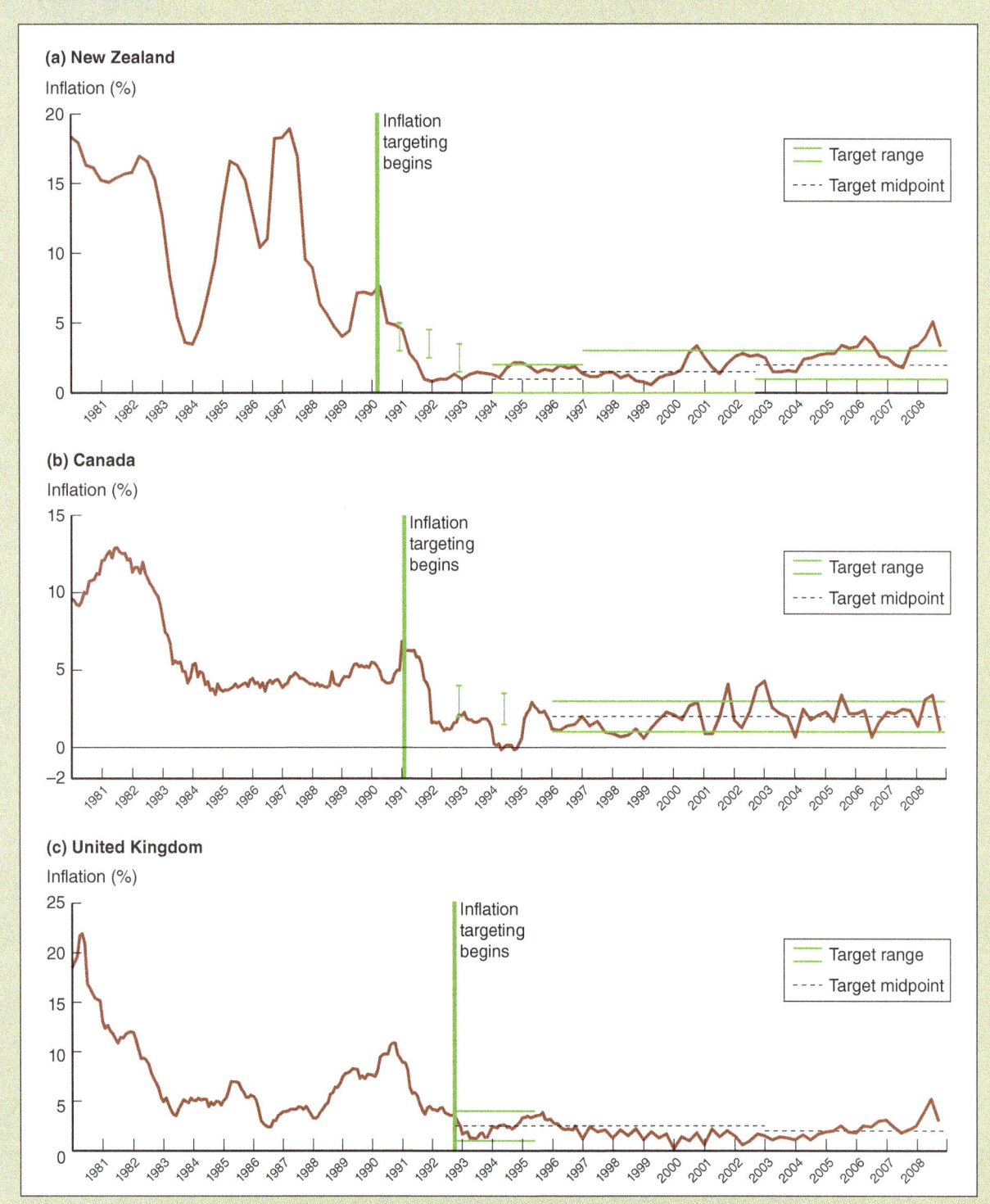

FIGURE 16.1

Inflation rates and inflation targets for New Zealand, Canada and the United Kingdom, 1980–2008 (a) New Zealand; (b) Canada; (c) United Kingdom

Source: Ben S. Bernanke, Thomas Laubach, Frederic S. Mishkin and Adam S. Posen, *Inflation Targeting: Lessons from the International Experience* (Princeton, NJ: Princeton University Press, 1999), updates from the same sources and www.rbnz.govt.nz/statistics/econind/a3/ha3.xls.

Before the adoption of inflation targets, inflation had already been falling in the United Kingdom, with a peak of 9% at the beginning of 1991 and a rate of 4% at the time of adoption (see Figure 16.1, panel c). By the third quarter of 1994, it was at 2.2%, within the intended range. Subsequently inflation rose, climbing slightly above the 2.5% level by the end of 1995, but then fell and has remained close to the target since then except for 2008. In December 2003, the target was changed to 2.0% for a slightly different measure of inflation. Meanwhile, growth of the UK economy was strong until 2008, causing a substantial reduction in the unemployment rate.

Advantages of inflation targeting

Inflation targeting has several advantages over monetary targeting as a strategy for the conduct of monetary policy. With inflation targeting, stability in the relationship between money and inflation is not critical to its success, because it does not rely on this relationship. An inflation target allows the monetary authorities to use all available information, not just one variable, to determine the best settings for monetary policy.

Inflation targeting also has the key advantage that it is readily understood by the public and is thus highly transparent. Monetary targets, in contrast, are less likely to be easily understood by the public, and if the relationship between the growth rates of monetary aggregates and the inflation goal variable is subject to unpredictable shifts, as has occurred in many countries, monetary targets lose their transparency because they are no longer able to accurately signal the stance of monetary policy.

Because an explicit numerical inflation target increases the accountability of the central bank, inflation targeting has the potential to reduce the likelihood that the central bank will fall into the time-inconsistency trap of trying to expand output and employment in the short run by pursuing overly expansionary monetary policy. A key advantage of inflation targeting is that it can help focus the political debate on what a central bank can do in the long run – that is, control inflation – rather than what it cannot do – permanently increase economic growth and the number of jobs through expansionary monetary policy. Thus inflation targeting has the potential to reduce political pressures on the central bank to pursue inflationary monetary policy and thereby to reduce the likelihood of the time-inconsistency problem.

Inflation-targeting regimes also put great stress on making policy transparent and on regular communication with the public. Inflation-targeting central banks have frequent communications with the government, some mandated by law and some in response to informal inquiries, and their officials take every opportunity to make public speeches on their monetary policy strategy. While these techniques are also commonly used in countries that have not adopted inflation targeting, inflation-targeting central banks have taken public outreach a step further: not only do they engage in extended public information campaigns, including the distribution of glossy brochures, but they also publish documents like the Bank of England's *Inflation Report*. The publication of these documents is particularly noteworthy, because they depart from the usual dull-looking, formal reports of central banks and use fancy graphics (see the box 'The inflation "fan chart" of the Bank of England'), boxes, and other eye-catching design elements to engage the public's interest.

The above channels of communication are used by central banks in inflation-targeting countries to explain the following concepts to the general public, financial market participants and politicians: (1) the goals and limitations of monetary policy, including the rationale for inflation targets; (2) the numerical values of the inflation targets and how they were determined; (3) how the inflation targets are to be achieved, given current economic conditions; and (4) reasons for any deviations from targets. These communications have improved private-sector planning by reducing uncertainty about monetary policy, interest rates and inflation; they have promoted public debate of monetary policy, in part by educating

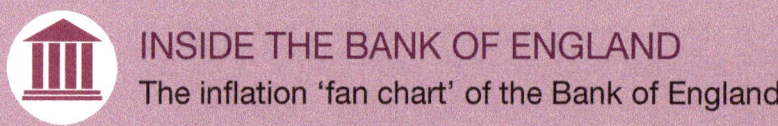

INSIDE THE BANK OF ENGLAND
The inflation 'fan chart' of the Bank of England

Since February 1996, the Bank of England's inflation forecast has been published in what is now known as the 'fan chart'. The fan chart is an easy-to-understand way of communicating the best collective judgement of the Bank of England regarding the degree of uncertainty about future inflation in the medium-term horizon. Figure 16.2 displays the fan chart for CPI inflation for the UK published in the February 2012 *Inflation Report*. The solid red line reports the realized inflation, whereas the red fan depicts the probability of various outcomes for inflation throughout the forecast period (up to three years). More specifically, if the same economic circumstances are expected to prevail on 100 occasions, the darkest red central band represents the best collective judgement by the Monetary Policy Committee (MPC) for future inflation on only 10 of these occasions. The fan chart is constructed so that out-turns of inflation are expected to lie within each pair of the lightest red areas on 10 occasions. Therefore, in any forecasting quarter, inflation is expected to lie within the fan on 90 out of 100 occasions. So, according to this fan chart in

Figure 16.2 there is a 90% probability that at the end of the two-year forecasting horizon (the dashed vertical line), inflation will roughly lie between 0% and 5%. Someone may argue that this is a rather broad range to be of any significant use, but it represents an honest reflection of the high degree of uncertainty about inflation forecasts faced by the MPC, and more in general by central banks.

Fan charts are a typical example of an increasing trend towards greater transparency by central banks around the world. In order to help the public and the market participants understand central banks' actions, the central banks of Norway and New Zealand have even been announcing projections of the path of future policy interest rates. But how far should central bank transparency go? This a difficult question to answer, but it can be argued that transparency can go too far if it complicates communication with the public. In the future, central banks are likely to experiment further with different approaches to providing more information to the public.

FIGURE 16.2

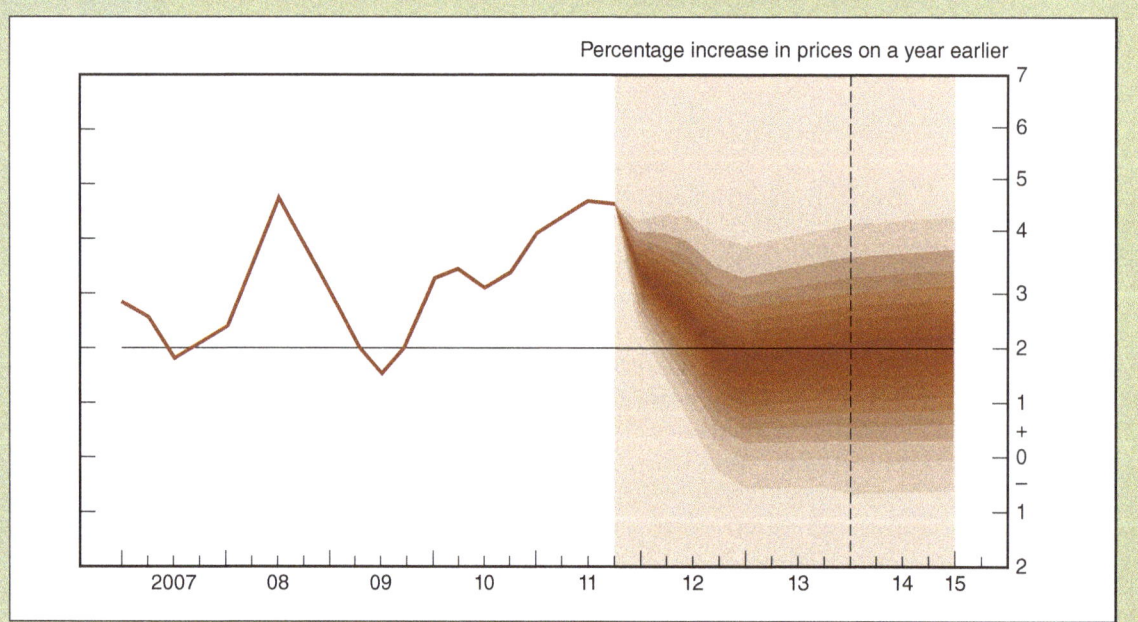

Fan chart for CPI inflation in the United Kingdom (February 2012)

Source: Bank of England's *Inflation Report* of February 2012. The dashed line is drawn at the two-year point. See the box on pages 48–9 of the May 2002 *Inflation Report* for a full description of the fan chart.

the public about what a central bank can and cannot achieve; and they have helped clarify the responsibilities of the central bank and of politicians in the conduct of monetary policy.

Another key feature of inflation-targeting regimes is the tendency toward increased accountability of the central bank. Indeed, transparency and communication go hand in hand with increased accountability. In the United Kingdom, if inflation moves away from the target by more than 1 percentage point in either direction, the Governor is required to send an open letter to the Chancellor. In it, the Governor explains why inflation has moved away from the target, the policy action that the Committee is taking to deal with it, the period within which the Committee expects inflation to return to the target, and how this approach meets the government's monetary policy objectives (see Chapter 13). The strongest case of accountability of a central bank in an inflation-targeting regime is in New Zealand, where the government has the right to dismiss the Reserve Bank's governor if the inflation targets are breached, even for one quarter. In other inflation-targeting countries, the central bank's accountability is less formalized. Nevertheless, the transparency of policy associated with inflation targeting has tended to make the central bank highly accountable to the public and the government. Sustained success in the conduct of monetary policy as measured against a pre-announced and well-defined inflation target can be instrumental in building public support for a central bank's independence and for its policies. This building of public support and accountability occurs even in the absence of a rigidly defined and legalistic standard of performance evaluation and punishment.

The performance of inflation-targeting regimes has been quite good. Inflation-targeting countries seem to have significantly reduced both the rate of inflation and inflation expectations beyond what would be likely to have occurred in the absence of inflation targets. Furthermore, once down, inflation in these countries has stayed down; following disinflations, the inflation rate in targeting countries has not bounced back up during subsequent cyclical expansions of the economy.

Disadvantages of inflation targeting

Critics of inflation targeting cite four disadvantages of this monetary policy strategy: delayed signalling, too much rigidity, the potential for increased output fluctuations, and low economic growth. We look at each in turn and examine the validity of these criticisms.

Delayed signalling

In contrast to monetary aggregates, inflation is not easily controlled by the monetary authorities. Furthermore, because of the long lags in the effects of monetary policy, inflation outcomes are revealed only after a substantial lag. Thus an inflation target is unable to send immediate signals to both the public and markets about the stance of monetary policy. However, we have seen that the signals provided by monetary aggregates may not be very strong. Hence it is not at all clear that monetary targeting is superior to inflation targeting on these grounds.

Too much rigidity

Some economists have criticized inflation targeting because they believe it imposes a rigid rule on monetary policymakers and limits their ability to respond to unforeseen circumstances. However, useful policy strategies exist that are 'rule-like' in that they involve forward-looking behaviour that limits policymakers from systematically engaging in policies with undesirable long-run consequences. Such policies avoid the time-inconsistency problem and would best be described as 'constrained discretion'.

Indeed, inflation targeting can be described exactly in this way. Inflation targeting, as actually practised, is far from rigid and is better described as 'flexible inflation targeting'. First, inflation targeting does not prescribe simple and mechanical instructions on how the central bank should conduct monetary policy. Rather, it requires the central bank to use all available information to determine which policy actions are appropriate to achieve the inflation target.

INSIDE THE EUROPEAN CENTRAL BANK
The two-pillar monetary policy strategy of the ECB

The European Central Bank (ECB) pursues a hybrid monetary policy strategy that has elements in common with the monetary-targeting strategy previously used by the Bundesbank but also includes some elements of inflation targeting.* Like inflation targeting, the ECB has announced its definition of price stability 'as a year-on-year increase in the Harmonized Index of Consumer Prices (HICP) for the euro area of below, but close to, 2% to be maintained over the medium term'. Moreover, the ECB's monetary decisions are based on a comprehensive analysis of the risks to price stability founded on a two-pillar strategy: the 'economic' analysis and the 'monetary' analysis (see Figure 16.3).

The objective of the 'economic analysis' pillar is to assess short- to medium-term risks to price stability. Here the focus is mostly on current real activity and financial conditions in the euro area, on the information content of asset prices and financial yields, and on a thorough analysis of the nature and magnitude of the economic shocks hitting the euro area economy. A key element in the economic analysis is the conduct of short- to medium-term exercises projecting the main macroeconomic variables in the euro area such as real GDP growth and inflation.

The second pillar of the ECB's strategy is the 'monetary analysis', which focuses on a longer-term

horizon than the economic analysis. The basic assumption behind this pillar is the close link between money and prices over the long run. Not only is this relationship well founded in economic theory, but also has empirical evidence provided significant support in favour of inflation being a monetary phenomenon (see Chapter 24 for a more elaborated discussion). In order to provide a benchmark for the assessment of monetary developments, initially the ECB announced a 'reference value' (to be reviewed annually) of 4.5% for the annual growth rate of the broad monetary aggregate M3. However, also in response to heavy criticisms by many commentators and economists which, in the words of the ECB, led to 'occasional misconceptions' that the former practice implied a monetary targeting, since May 2003, the ECB decided to no longer review this reference value on an annual basis, and the 'numerical' emphasis has been progressively downgraded. Since January 2011, the ECB has defined the reference value as 'the annual growth of M3 that is deemed to be compatible with price stability over the medium term'. As the growth of broad money is subject to various influences, some of which are likely to exert a sustained impact on prices whereas others are not, short- to medium-term deviations from the reference may not be very informative about the risks to price stability.

FIGURE 16.3

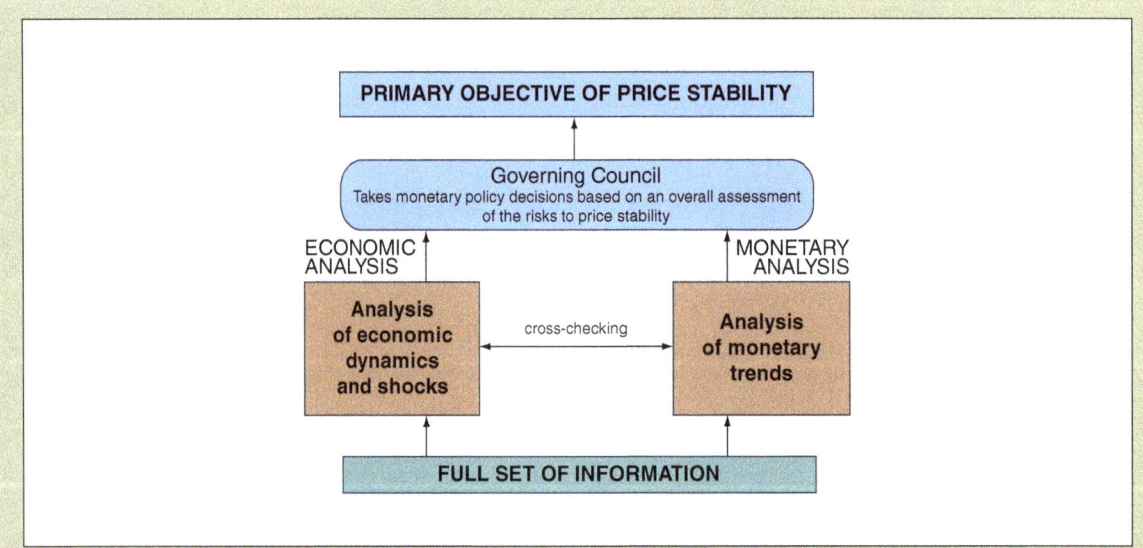

The ECB's two-pillar monetary policy strategy

Source: www.ecb.int/mopo/strategy/html/index.en.html. Information may be obtained free of charge through the EGB's website.

Therefore, the ECB does not react mechanically to deviations of M3 growth from the reference value. As part of the monetary analysis, ECB experts monitor not only M3, but also other indicators such as M1 and M2, and their components and credit counterparts (e.g. loans to non-financial corporations and loans to households).

The idea behind the two-pillar strategy is to ensure the use of all relevant information regarding decisions on the appropriate stance of monetary policy. Against this background this strategy provides a cross-check of inflation signals arising from the short- to medium-term economic analysis with those from the long-term monetary analysis.

The ECB's strategy is somewhat confusing and has been subject to criticism for this reason. Although the 'below, but close to, 2%' goal for inflation sounds like an inflation target, the ECB has repeatedly stated that it does not have an inflation target. The ECB seems to have decided to try to 'have its cake and eat it' by not committing too strongly to either a monetary-targeting strategy or an inflation-targeting strategy. The resulting difficulty of assessing the ECB's strategy has the potential to reduce the accountability of the institution. However, the legal framework of the ECB includes a number of mechanisms designed to hold central bank officials accountable for their decisions on monetary policy. Those

mechanisms relate to various reporting obligations and transparency guidelines. As a central reporting requirement, the president of the ECB has to bear witness to the governing bodies of the European Union, explaining and justifying the performance of monetary policy in relation to its mandate. A strong commitment to transparency is achieved through regular public announcement of the ECB's monetary policy strategy and assessment of economic developments. The efforts to enhance transparency facilitate public scrutiny of monetary policy actions and therefore raise the incentives for decision makers to fulfil their mandate in an appropriate manner.

All in all, the performance of the ECB in terms of price stability has been mostly successful. The success of monetary policy in the euro area can be inferred from Figure 16.4 which shows the annual HICP inflation rate and two different measures of medium- to long-term inflation forecasts from surveys (Consensus Economic Forecasts and the ECB Survey of Professional Forecasters) since the introduction of the euro. The figure yields two messages. First, since the establishment of the ECB, the average inflation rate in the euro area has been broadly in line with the ECB's definition of price stability, although inflation volatility increased significantly during the recent turbulent period. Second, the close alignment of inflation forecasts with the price stability

FIGURE 16.4

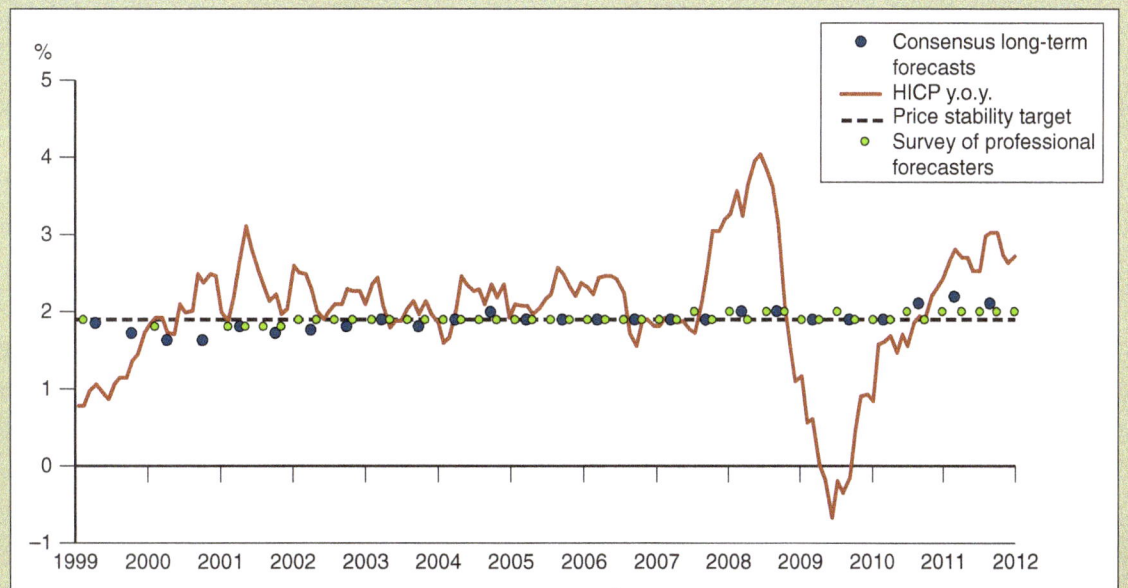

Expected and realized inflation in the euro area 1999–2012

Sources: Consensus forecasts are calculated on the basis of prominent financial and economic forecasters and refer to annual rate of inflation expected to prevail between six and ten years ahead. Survey of Professional Forecasters (conducted by the ECB) refers to five years ahead. Own calculations from ECB data.

The two-pillar monetary policy strategy of the ECB (*continued*)

objective points towards well-anchored inflation expectations. In particular, the indicators of long-term inflation expectations in the euro area have remained close to the 2%, even around the financial crisis period which was characterized by more a volatile inflation rate. The strong conformity of inflation forecasts with the ECB's definition of price stability indicates that

the ECB has been successful in anchoring long-term inflation expectations and enjoyed a high degree of credibility, which is crucial for the conduct of monetary policy.

*For a full description of the ECB's monetary policy strategy, go to the ECB's website at **www.ecb.int**.

Unlike simple policy rules, inflation targeting never requires the central bank to focus solely on one key variable. Second, inflation targeting as practised contains a substantial degree of policy discretion. Inflation targets have been modified depending on economic circumstances, as we have seen. Moreover, central banks under inflation-targeting regimes have left themselves considerable scope to respond to output growth and fluctuations through several devices.

Potential for increased output fluctuations

An important criticism of inflation targeting is that a sole focus on inflation may lead to monetary policy that is too tight when inflation is above target and thus may lead to larger output fluctuations. Inflation targeting does not, however, require a sole focus on inflation – in fact, experience has shown that inflation targeters display substantial concern about output fluctuations. All the inflation targeters have set their inflation targets above zero.[3] For example, currently, New Zealand, the United Kingdom, Canada and Sweden set the midpoint of their inflation target at 2%, while Australia has its midpoint at 2.5%.

There are two main reasons for inflation targeters to choose inflation targets above zero. First, monetary policymakers are concerned that particularly low inflation can have substantial negative effects on real economic activity. Deflation (negative inflation in which the price level actually falls) is especially to be feared because of the possibility that it may promote financial instability and precipitate a severe economic contraction (Chapter 9). The deflation in Japan in recent years has been an important factor in the weakening of the Japanese financial system and economy. Targeting inflation rates of above zero makes periods of deflation less likely. This is one reason why some economists both within and outside of Japan have been calling on the Bank of Japan to adopt an inflation target at levels of 2% or higher.[4] The second reason for choosing inflation targets above zero reflects the importance of real wage flexibility as an adjustment mechanism. If nominal wages suffer from downward rigidities, cuts in real wages will only be possible with positive levels of inflation. Therefore, an inflation rate of zero may prevent necessary adjustment processes in labour markets, thereby hampering the efficient allocation of resources in the economy.

Inflation targeting also does not ignore traditional stabilization goals. Central bankers in inflation-targeting countries continue to express their concern about fluctuations in output and employment, and the ability to accommodate short-run stabilization goals to some degree is built into all inflation-targeting regimes. All inflation-targeting countries have been willing to minimize output declines by gradually lowering medium-term inflation targets toward the long-run goal.

Low economic growth

Another common concern about inflation targeting is that it will lead to low growth in output and employment. Although inflation reduction has been associated with below-normal output during disinflationary phases in inflation-targeting regimes, once low inflation levels were achieved, output and employment returned to levels at least as high as they were before. A conservative conclusion is that once low inflation is achieved, inflation targeting is not harmful to the real economy. Given the strong economic growth after disinflation in many countries (such as New Zealand) that have adopted inflation targets, a case can be made that inflation targeting promotes real economic growth, in addition to controlling inflation.

Monetary policy with an implicit nominal anchor

Until the subprime financial crisis occurred, the United States achieved excellent macroeconomic performance (including low and stable inflation), without using an explicit nominal anchor such as a monetary aggregate or an inflation target. Although the Federal Reserve had not articulated an explicit strategy, a coherent strategy for the conduct of monetary policy existed nonetheless. This strategy involved an implicit but not an explicit nominal anchor in the form of an overriding concern by the Federal Reserve to control inflation in the long run. In addition, it involved forward-looking behaviour in which there is careful monitoring for signs of future inflation using a wide range of information, coupled with periodic 'pre-emptive strikes' by monetary policy against the threat of inflation.

As emphasized by Milton Friedman, monetary policy effects have long lags. In industrialized countries with a history of low inflation, the inflation process seems to have tremendous inertia: estimates from large macroeconometric models of the US economy, for example, suggest that monetary policy takes over a year to affect output and over two years to have a significant impact on inflation. For countries that have experienced highly variable inflation, and therefore have more flexible prices, the lags may be shorter.

The presence of long lags means that monetary policy cannot wait to respond until inflation has begun. If the central bank waits until overt signs of inflation appear, it will already be too late to maintain stable prices, at least not without a severe tightening of policy: inflation expectations will already be embedded in the wage- and price-setting process, creating an inflation momentum that will be hard to halt. Inflation becomes much harder to control once it has been allowed to gather momentum, because higher inflation expectations become ingrained in various types of long-term contracts and pricing agreements.

To prevent inflation from getting started, therefore, monetary policy needs to be forward-looking and pre-emptive. That is, depending on the lags from monetary policy to inflation, monetary policy needs to act long before inflationary pressures appear in the economy. For example, suppose it takes roughly two years for monetary policy to have a significant impact on inflation. In this case, even if inflation is currently low but policymakers believe inflation will rise over the next two years with an unchanged stance of monetary policy, they must tighten monetary policy *now* to prevent the inflationary surge.

Under Alan Greenspan, the Federal Reserve was successful in pursuing a pre-emptive monetary policy. For example, the Fed raised interest rates from 1994 to 1995 before a rise in inflation got a toehold. As a result, inflation not only did not rise, but fell slightly. This pre-emptive, forward-looking monetary policy strategy is clearly also a feature of inflation-targeting regimes, because monetary policy instruments are adjusted to take account of the long lags in their effects in an effort to hit future inflation targets. However, before the recent move towards a more explicit nominal anchor (see box 'Chairman Bernanke and inflation targeting'), the policy regime of the Federal Reserve was described as a 'just do it' policy, and differed from inflation targeting in that it did not officially have a nominal anchor and was much less transparent in its monetary policy strategy.

Advantages of the 'just do it' approach

The 'just do it' approach, which has some of the key elements of inflation targeting, has many of the same advantages. It also does not rely on a stable money–inflation relationship. As with inflation targeting, the central bank uses many sources of information to determine the best settings for monetary policy. The Fed's forward-looking behaviour and stress on price stability also helped to discourage overly expansionary monetary policy, thereby ameliorating the time-inconsistency problem.

Another key argument for the 'just do it' strategy is its demonstrated success. The Federal Reserve reduced inflation in the United States from double-digit levels in 1980 to an average rate close to 3% over the last 30 years, which is arguably consistent with the price stability goal. At the same time, economic growth has been high, averaging around 3% over the same period, with relatively steady growth up until the subprime financial crisis hit the economy hard. Indeed, up until recently, the performance of the US economy was the envy of the industrialized world.

Disadvantages of the 'just do it' approach

Given the success of the 'just do it' strategy in the United States, why did the United States move to a more explicit monetary policy strategy? The answer is that the 'just do it' strategy has some disadvantages.

One disadvantage of the strategy is its lack of transparency. The Fed's close-mouthed approach about its intentions gave rise to a constant guessing game about what it was going to do. This high level of uncertainty led to unnecessary volatility in financial markets and created doubt among producers and the general public about the future course of inflation and output. Furthermore, the opacity of its policymaking made it hard to hold the Federal Reserve accountable to Congress and the general public: the Fed could not be held accountable if there were no predetermined criteria for judging its performance. Low accountability may make the central bank more susceptible to the time-inconsistency problem, whereby it may pursue short-term objectives at the expense of long-term ones.

Probably the most serious problem with the 'just do it' approach is its strong dependence on the preferences, skills and trustworthiness of the individuals in charge of the central bank. In recent years in the United States, Federal Reserve chairmen Alan Greenspan and Ben Bernanke and other Federal Reserve officials have emphasized forward-looking policies and inflation control, with great success. The Fed's prestige and credibility with the American public have risen accordingly. But as the Fed's leadership was periodically changing, there was no guarantee that it would have been committed to the same approach. Nor was there any guarantee that the relatively good working relationship that had existed between the Fed and the executive branch would have continued. In a different economic or political environment, the Fed might have faced strong pressure to engage in over-expansionary policies, raising the possibility that time inconsistency may have become a more serious problem. In the past, after a successful period of low inflation, the Federal Reserve had reverted to inflationary monetary policy – the 1970s are one example – and without an explicit nominal anchor, this could have certainly happened again.

Another disadvantage of the 'just do it' approach is that it had some inconsistencies with democratic principles. As described in Chapter 13, there are good reasons – notably, insulation from short-term political pressures – for the central bank to have some degree of independence, and the evidence does generally support central bank independence. Yet the practical economic arguments for central bank independence coexist uneasily with the presumption that government policies should be made democratically, rather than by an elite group.

In contrast, inflation targeting can make the institutional framework for the conduct of monetary policy more consistent with democratic principles and avoid some of the above problems. The inflation-targeting framework promotes the accountability of the central bank to elected officials, who are given some responsibility for setting the goals for monetary policy and then monitoring the economic outcomes. However, under inflation targeting as it has generally been practised, the central bank has complete control over operational decisions, so that it can be held accountable for achieving its assigned objectives.

Because of these disadvantages, since the appointment of chairman Ben Bernanke, the Fed's monetary policy strategy has progressively moved towards inflation targeting. To many commentators, this has not been a huge surprise, because Bernanke, a former professor at Princeton University, has been an advocate of inflation targeting (see box 'Chairman Bernanke and inflation targeting').

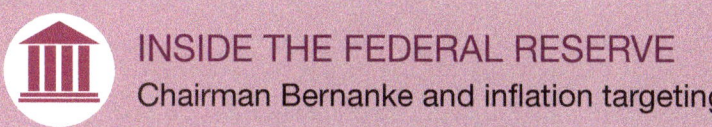

INSIDE THE FEDERAL RESERVE
Chairman Bernanke and inflation targeting

Ben Bernanke, a former professor at Princeton University, became the Federal Reserve chairman in February 2006, after serving as a member of the Board of Governors from 2002 to 2005 and then as chairman of the Council of Economic Advisors. Bernanke is a world-renowned expert on monetary policy and while an academic wrote extensively on inflation targeting, including articles and a book written with one of the authors of this text.*

Bernanke's writings suggest that he is a strong proponent of inflation targeting and increased transparency in central banks. In an important speech given at a conference at the Federal Reserve Bank of St. Louis in 2004 he described how the Federal Reserve might approach a movement toward inflation targeting: the Fed should announce a numerical value for its long-run inflation goal.[†] Bernanke emphasized that announcing a numerical objective for inflation would have been completely consistent with the Fed's dual mandate of achieving price stability and maximum employment, and therefore might have been called a *mandate-consistent inflation objective*, because it would have been set above zero to avoid deflations, which have harmful effects on employment. In addition, it would have not been intended to be a short-run target that might lead to excessively tight control of inflation at the expense of overly high employment fluctuations.

After becoming Fed chairman, Bernanke made it clear that any movement toward inflation targeting must have resulted from a consensus within the FOMC. After Chairman Bernanke set up a subcommittee to discuss Federal Reserve communication, which included discussions about announcing a specific numerical inflation objective, the FOMC made a partial step in the direction of inflation targeting in November 2007 when it announced a new communication strategy that lengthened the horizon for FOMC participants' inflation projections to three years. In many cases, the three-year horizon was sufficiently long that the projection for inflation under 'appropriate policy' was reflecting each participant's inflation objective because at that horizon

inflation should converge to the long-run objective. But a very significant step towards inflation targeting was made on 25 January 2012, when following its meeting the FOMC released a statement intended to provide greater clarity about the Committee's longer-term goals and monetary policy strategy.[‡] More specifically, the FOMC announced that 'The Committee judges that inflation at the rate of 2 percent, as measured by the annual change in the price index for personal consumption expenditures, is most consistent over the longer run with the Federal Reserve's statutory mandate.' In stressing the Fed's commitment to pursue its dual mandate to achieve stable prices and maximum employment, the FOMC also indicated that 'In the most recent projections, FOMC participants' estimates of the longer-run normal rate of unemployment had a central tendency of 5.2 percent to 6.0 percent.' In the same statement it was noted that these statutory objectives are generally complementary, but when they are not, the Committee will take a balanced approach in its efforts to return both inflation and employment to their desired levels. This announcement was seen by many commentators as a significant move towards a flexible inflation targeting. Time will tell if these steps in the direction of greater transparency and predictability of the Fed's monetary policy strategy will be successful.

* Ben S. Bernanke and Frederic S. Mishkin, 'Inflation targeting: a new framework for monetary policy', *Journal of Economic Perspectives* 11, 2 (1997); Ben S. Bernanke, Frederic S. Mishkin and Adam S. Posen, 'Inflation targeting: fed policy after greenspan', *Milken Institute Review* (Fourth Quarter, 1999): 48–56; Ben S. Bernanke, Frederic S. Mishkin and Adam S. Posen, 'What happens when Greenspan is gone', *Wall Street Journal*, 5 January 2000: A22; and Ben S. Bernanke, Thomas Laubach, Frederic S. Mishkin and Adam S. Posen, *Inflation Targeting: Lessons from the International Experience* (Princeton, NJ: Princeton University Press 1999).

† Ben S. Bernanke, 'Inflation targeting', Federal Reserve Bank of St. Louis, Review 86, 4 (July/August 2004); 165–8.

‡ See the press release of the Board of Governors of the Federal Reserve System, 25 January 2012, www.federalreserve.gov /newsevents/press/monetary/20120125c.htm.

Advantages and disadvantages of different monetary policy strategies

	Monetary targeting	Inflation targeting	Implicit nominal anchor
Advantages	Immediate signal on achievement of target	Simplicity and clarity of target	Does not rely on stable money–inflation relationship
		Does not rely on stable money–inflation relationship Increased accountability of central bank	Demonstrated success in United States
		Reduced effects of inflationary shocks	
Disadvantages	Relies on stable money–inflation relationship	Delayed signal about achievement of target	Lack of transparency
		Could impose rigid rule (though has not in practice)	Success depends on individuals in charge
		Larger output fluctuations if sole focus on inflation (though not in practice)	Low accountability

As a study aid, the advantages and disadvantages of monetary targeting as well as the other monetary policy strategies are listed in Summary Table 16.1.

Tactics: choosing the policy instrument

Now that we are familiar with the alternative strategies for monetary policy, let's look at how monetary policy is conducted on a day-to-day basis. Central banks directly control the tools of monetary policy – open market operations, interest rates on standing (lending and deposit) facilities, and reserve requirements – but knowing the tools and the strategies for implementing a monetary policy does not tell us whether policy is easy or tight. The **policy instrument** (also called an **operating instrument**) is a variable that responds to the central bank's tools and indicates the stance (easy or tight) of monetary policy. Central banks have at their disposal two basic types of policy instruments: reserve aggregates (total reserves, non-borrowed reserves, the monetary base and the non-borrowed base) and interest rates (the short-term interest rates). (Central banks in small countries can choose another policy instrument, the exchange rate, but we leave this topic to Chapter 18.) The policy instrument might be linked to an **intermediate target**, such as a monetary aggregate like M3 or a long-term interest rate. Intermediate targets stand between the policy instrument and the goals of monetary policy (e.g. price stability, output growth); they are not as directly affected by the tools of monetary policy, but might be more closely linked to the goals of monetary policy. As a study aid, Figure 16.5 shows a schematic of the linkages between the tools of monetary policy, policy instruments, intermediate targets, and the goals of monetary policy.

As an example, suppose the central bank's employment and inflation goals are consistent with a nominal GDP growth rate of 5%. The central bank might believe that the 5% nominal

FIGURE 16.5

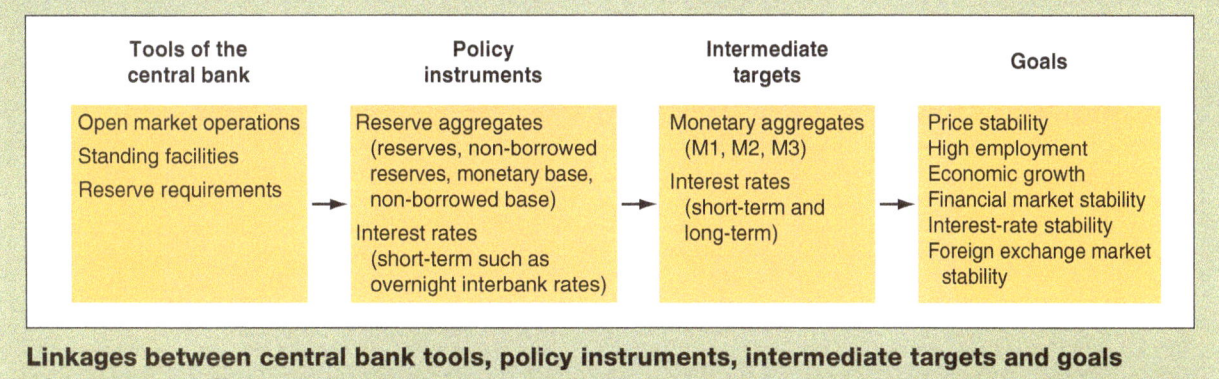

Tools of the central bank	Policy instruments	Intermediate targets	Goals
Open market operations Standing facilities Reserve requirements	Reserve aggregates (reserves, non-borrowed reserves, monetary base, non-borrowed base) Interest rates (short-term such as overnight interbank rates)	Monetary aggregates (M1, M2, M3) Interest rates (short-term and long-term)	Price stability High employment Economic growth Financial market stability Interest-rate stability Foreign exchange market stability

Linkages between central bank tools, policy instruments, intermediate targets and goals of monetary policy

GDP growth rate will be achieved by a 4% growth rate for M2 (an intermediate target), which will in turn be achieved by a growth rate of 3% for non-borrowed reserves (the policy instrument). Alternatively, the central bank might believe that the best way to achieve its objectives would be to set the short-term interest rate (a policy instrument) at, say, 4%. Can the central bank choose to target both the non-borrowed reserves and the short-term interest rate policy instruments at the same time? The answer is no. The application of supply and demand analysis to the market for reserves we developed in Chapter 15 explains why a central bank must choose one or the other.

Let's first see why choosing an aggregate target involves losing control of the interest rate. Figure 16.6 contains a supply and demand diagram for the market for reserves. Although the central bank expects the demand curve for reserves to be at R^{d*}, it fluctuates between $R^{d'}$ and $R^{d''}$ because of unexpected fluctuations in deposits (and hence required reserves) and changes in banks' desire to hold excess reserves. If the central bank has a non-borrowed reserves target of NBR^* (say, because it has a target growth rate of the money

FIGURE 16.6

Result of targeting on non-borrowed reserves

Targeting on non-borrowed reserves of NBR^* will lead to fluctuations in the interest rate between i' and i'' because of fluctuations in the demand for reserves between $R^{d'}$ and $R^{d''}$.

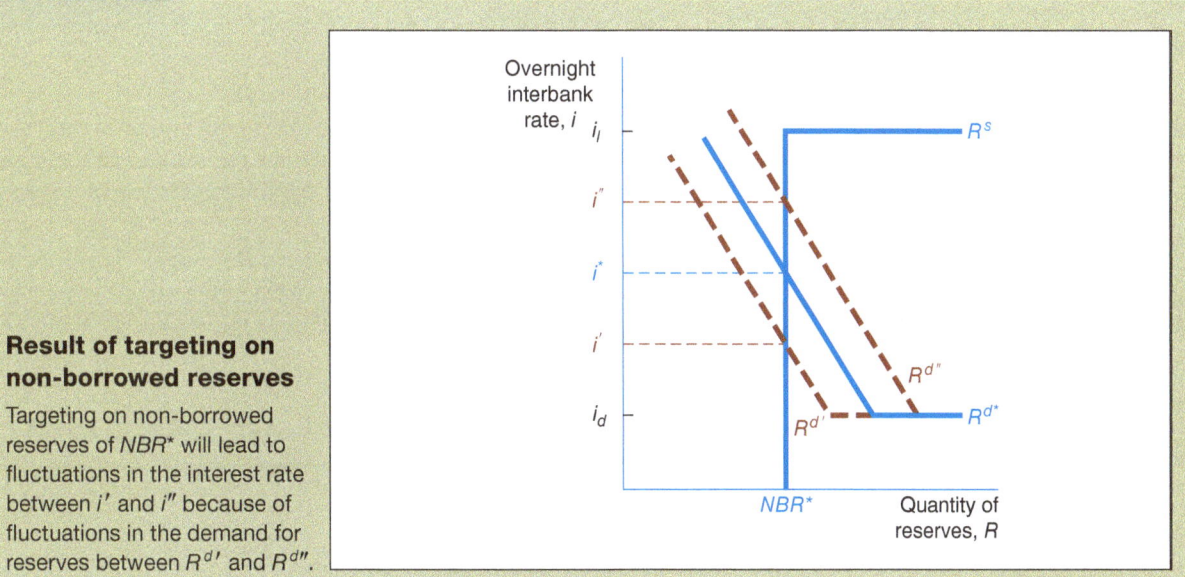

FIGURE 16.7

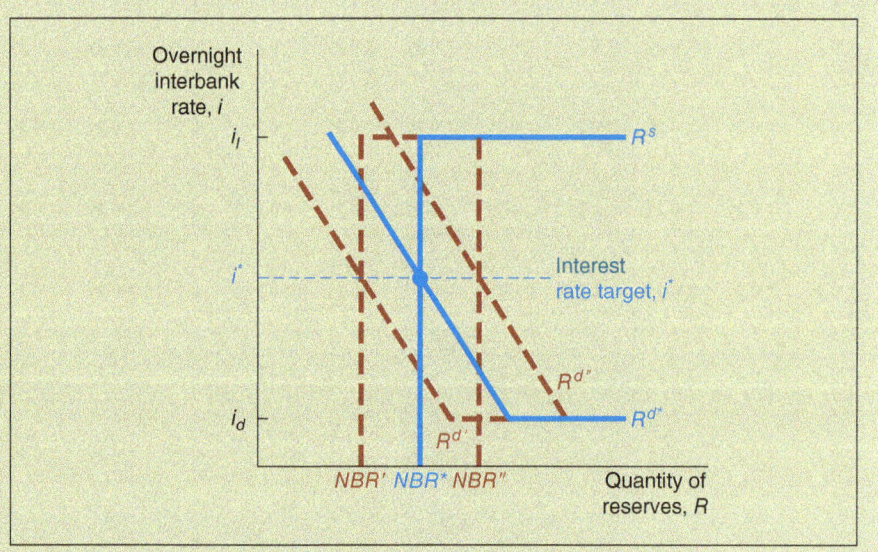

Result of targeting on the short-term interest rate

Targeting on the interest rate i^* will lead to fluctuation in non-borrowed reserves because of fluctuations in the demand for reserves between $R^{d'}$ and $R^{d''}$.

supply of 4%), it expects that the short-term interest rate will be i^*. However, as the figure indicates, the fluctuations in the reserves demand curve between $R^{d'}$ and $R^{d''}$ will result in a fluctuation in the short-term interest rate between i' and i''. Pursuing an aggregate target implies that interest rates will fluctuate.

The supply and demand diagram in Figure 16.7 shows the consequences of an interest-rate target set at i^*. Again the central bank expects the reserves demand curve to be at R^{d^*} but it fluctuates between $R^{d'}$ and $R^{d''}$ due to unexpected changes in deposits or banks' desire to hold excess reserves. If the demand curve rises to $R^{d''}$, the overnight interest rate will begin to rise above i^* and the central bank will engage in open market purchases of bonds until it raises the supply of non-borrowed reserves to NBR'', at which point the equilibrium short-term interest rate is again at i^*. Conversely, if the demand curve falls to $R^{d'}$ and lowers the overnight rate, the central bank would keep making open market sales until non-borrowed reserves fall to NBR' and the interest rate returns to i^*. The central bank's adherence to the interest-rate target thus leads to a fluctuating quantity of non-borrowed reserves and the money supply.

The conclusion from the supply and demand analysis is that interest-rate and reserve (monetary) aggregate targets are incompatible. A central bank can hit one or the other, but not both. Because a choice between them has to be made, we need to examine what criteria should be used to select a policy instrument. It is, however, true that in the corridor systems currently operated by the major central banks in the world (see Chapter 15), the quantity of non-borrowed reserves can be expanded beyond the level that would be needed to maintain the interest-rate target. More specifically, if the interest-rate target corresponds to the lower floor set by the deposit rate (or interest rate paid on excess reserves), as the central bank can actively target both the interest rate and the quantity of non-borrowed reserves.

Criteria for choosing the policy instrument

Three criteria apply when choosing a policy instrument: the instrument must be observable and measurable, it must be controllable by the central bank and it must have a predictable effect on the goals.

Observability and measurability

Quick observability and accurate measurement of a policy instrument is necessary, because it will be useful only if it signals the policy stance rapidly. Reserve aggregates like non-borrowed reserves are straightforward to measure, but there is still some lag in reporting of reserve aggregates (a delay of two weeks). Short-term interest rates like the short-term interbank rate, by contrast, not only are easy to measure, but also are observable immediately. Thus, it seems that interest rates are more observable and measurable than are reserves and, therefore, are a better policy instrument.

However, as we learned in Chapter 4, the interest rate that is easiest to measure and observe is the nominal interest rate. It is typically a poor measure of the real cost of borrowing, which indicates with more certainty what will happen to the real GDP. This real cost of borrowing is more accurately measured by the real interest rate – that is, the nominal interest rate adjusted for expected inflation ($i_r = i - \pi^e$). Unfortunately, real interest rates are extremely difficult to measure, because we do not have a direct way to measure expected inflation. Given that both interest rates and aggregates have observability and measurability problems, it is not clear whether one should be preferred to the other as a policy instrument.

Controllability

A central bank must be able to exercise effective control over a variable if it is to function as a useful policy instrument. If the central bank cannot control the policy instrument, knowing that it is off track does little good, because the central bank has no way of getting it back on track.

Because of shifts in and out of currency, even reserve aggregates such as non-borrowed reserves are not completely controllable. Conversely, central banks can control short-term interest rates very tightly. It might appear, therefore, that short-term interest rates would dominate reserve aggregates on the controllability criterion. However, a central bank cannot set short-term real interest rates because it does not have control over expectations of inflation. Once again, a clear-cut case cannot be made that short-term interest rates are preferable to reserve aggregates as a policy instrument, or vice versa.

Predictable effect on goals

The most important characteristic of a policy instrument is that it must have a predictable effect on a goal. If a central bank can accurately and quickly measure the price of tea in China and can completely control its price, what good will that do? The central bank cannot use the price of tea in China to affect unemployment or the price level in its country. Because the ability to affect goals is so critical to the usefulness of any policy instrument, the tightness of the link from reserve or monetary aggregates to goals (output, employment and inflation) or, alternatively, from interest rates to these goals, is a matter of much debate. In recent years, most central banks have concluded that the link between interest rates and goals such as inflation is tighter than the link between monetary aggregates and inflation. For this reason, central banks throughout the world now generally use short-term interest rates as their policy instrument.

Tactics: the Taylor rule

As we have seen in Chapter 15, most central banks currently conduct monetary policy by setting a target for short-term interest rates. But how should this target be chosen?

John Taylor of Stanford University has come up with an answer, called the **Taylor rule**. The Taylor rule indicates that the policy interest rate should be set equal to the inflation rate plus an 'equilibrium' real policy interest rate (the real interest rate that is consistent with full employment in the long run) plus a weighted average of two gaps: (1) an inflation gap, current inflation minus a target rate, and (2) an output gap, the percentage deviation of real GDP from an estimate of its potential full employment level.[5] This rule can be written as follows:

$$\text{interest rate target} = \text{inflation rate} + \text{equilibrium real interest rate}$$
$$+ \tfrac{1}{2}(\text{inflation gap}) + \tfrac{1}{2}(\text{output gap})$$

In his seminal paper, Taylor assumes that the equilibrium real interest rate is 2% and that an appropriate target for inflation would also be 2%, with equal weights of $\tfrac{1}{2}$ on the inflation and output gaps. For an example of the Taylor rule in practice, suppose that the inflation rate were at 3%, leading to a positive inflation gap of $1\%(= 3\% - 2\%)$, and real GDP was 1% above its potential, resulting in a positive output gap of 1%. Then the Taylor rule suggests that the interest rate should be set at $6\%[= 3\% \text{ inflation} + 2\% \text{ equilibrium real interest rate} + \tfrac{1}{2} (1\% \text{ inflation gap}) + \tfrac{1}{2} (1\% \text{ output gap})]$.

An important feature of the Taylor rule is that the coefficient on the inflation gap is positive and equal to $\tfrac{1}{2}$. If the inflation rate rises by 1 percentage point, then the interest rate target is raised by 1.5 percentage points, and so by more than one-to-one. In other words, a rise in inflation by 1 percentage point leads to a real interest rate increase of $\tfrac{1}{2}$ percentage point. The principle that the monetary authorities should raise nominal interest rates by more than the increase in the inflation rate has been named the **Taylor principle**, and it is critical to the success of monetary policy. Suppose the Taylor principle is not followed and nominal rates rise by *less* than the rise in the inflation rate so that real interest rates *fall* when inflation rises. There will then be serious instability because a rise in inflation leads to an effective easing of monetary policy, which then leads to even higher inflation in the future. Indeed, this was a feature of monetary policy in the 1970s that led to a loss of the nominal anchor and the era of the so-called 'Great Inflation', when inflation rates climbed to double-digit levels. Fortunately, since 1979, the Taylor principle has become a feature of monetary policy, with much happier outcomes on both the inflation and aggregate output fronts.

The presence of an output gap in the Taylor rule might indicate that the central bank should care not only about keeping inflation under control, but also about minimizing business-cycle fluctuations of output around its potential. Caring about both inflation and output fluctuations is consistent with many statements by Federal Reserve officials that controlling inflation and stabilizing real output are important concerns of the Fed. However, this is more difficult to reconcile with the ECB's and the Bank of England's hierarchical mandates towards price stability (see Chapter 13). So how can we justify the presence of the output gap in the Taylor rule for central banks whose main goal is to achieve price stability?

An answer to this question is that the output gap is an indicator of future inflation as stipulated in **Phillips curve theory**. Phillips curve theory indicates that changes in inflation are influenced by the state of the economy relative to its productive capacity, as well as by other factors. This productive capacity can be measured by potential GDP, which is a function of the natural rate of unemployment, the rate of unemployment consistent with full employment. A related concept is the **NAIRU**, the **non-accelerating inflation rate of unemployment**, the rate of unemployment at which there is no tendency for inflation to change.[6] Simply put, the theory states that when the unemployment rate is above NAIRU with output below potential, inflation will come down, but if it is below NAIRU with output above potential, inflation will rise. For example, from the mid-1990s to the mid-2000s, the NAIRU in the UK was thought to reside persistently above the unemployment rate. However, with no significant increase in inflation, some critics have questioned the value of Phillips curve theory. Either they claim that it just doesn't work any more or, alternatively, they believe that there is great uncertainty about the value of NAIRU, which may have fallen to levels similar to the actual unemployment rate for reasons that are not absolutely clear. Phillips curve theory is now highly controversial, and many economists believe that it should not be used as a guide for the conduct of monetary policy.

But how do interest rate decisions by central banks compare with the Taylor rule?

As Figure 16.8 shows, the Taylor rule does a pretty good job of describing the setting of interest rates by the Bank of England and the Federal Reserve. (It did not work very well in the 1970s, which reflects that the Taylor principle was not being followed, which explains why monetary policy outcomes were so poor.) Does this mean that the central bank should fire all its economists and put a computer in charge that just has to compute the Taylor rule setting for the policy rate? This would certainly save the taxpayers a lot of money.

There are several reasons why the answer is no. First, monetary policy has long lags, that is, it takes a long time for policy actions to affect the economy. Therefore, monetary policy

FIGURE 16.8

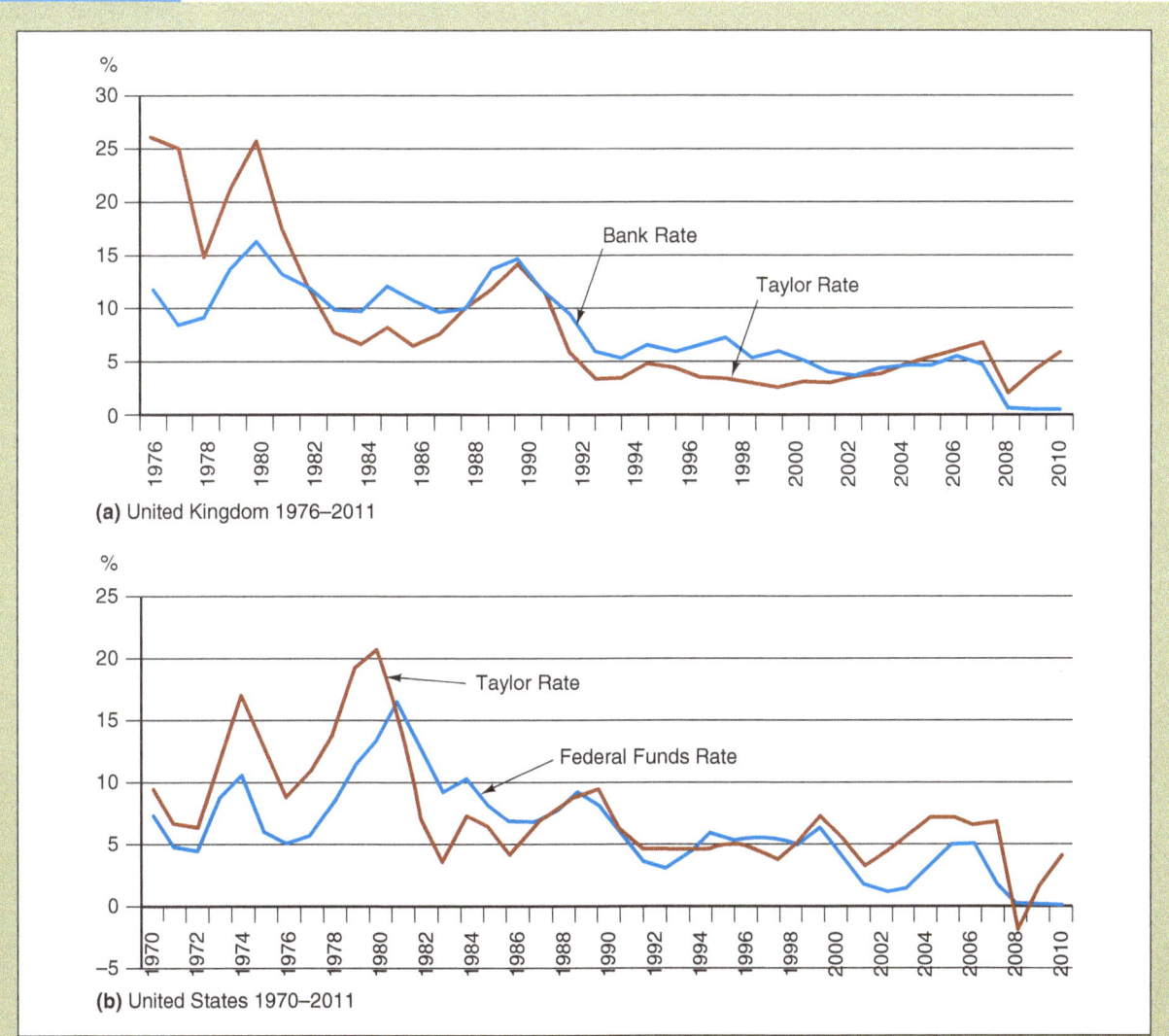

(a) United Kingdom 1976–2011

(b) United States 1970–2011

The Taylor rule for the United Kingdom and the United States

Source: The output gap and inflation rate are collected from the OECD Economic Outlook, December 2011. The 'Bank Rate' is the annual average of the official Bank Rate of the Bank of England. The 'Federal Funds Rate' is the federal funds effective rate available from the Federal Reserve. The inflation rate is based on the CPI index, with the exception of the UK where the retail price index (excluding mortgage payments) is used for the pre-1991 period. The 'Taylor Rate' is constructed assuming an equilibrium real interest rate equal to 2% and a target for inflation of 2%.

necessarily needs to be forward-looking. Good monetary policy requires that the central bank forecast where inflation and economic activity are going to be in the future, and then adjust the policy instrument accordingly. Central banks will therefore look at a much wider range of information than just the current inflation rate and output gap in setting policy, as is done in the Taylor rule. Second, no one really knows what the true model of the economy is. Monetary policymakers therefore need to apply a lot of judgement in deciding the appropriate stance of monetary policy. In other words, the conduct of monetary policy is as much an art as it is a science. The Taylor rule leaves out all the art, and so is unlikely to produce the best monetary policy outcomes. Third, the economy is changing all the time, so the Taylor rule coefficients would be unlikely to stay constant. Fourth, financial crises such as the recent subprime meltdown may require very different monetary policy because changes in credit spreads may alter the relationship between the policy interest rate and other interest rates more relevant to investment decisions, and therefore to economic activity. The bottom line is that putting monetary policy on autopilot using the Taylor rule with fixed coefficients would be a bad idea.

Given the above reasons, it is no surprise that the Taylor rule does not explain all the movements in the policy rates. The Taylor rule is, however, useful as a guide to monetary policy. If the setting of the policy instrument is very different from what the Taylor rule suggests, then policymakers should ask whether they have a good reason for deviating from this rule. If they don't, then they might be making a mistake.

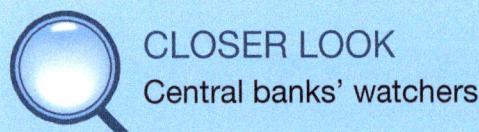

CLOSER LOOK
Central banks' watchers

As we have seen, the most important player in the determination of the money supply and interest rates is the central bank. When the central bank wants to inject reserves into the system, it conducts open market purchases of bonds, which cause bond prices to increase and their interest rates to fall, at least in the short term. If the central bank withdraws reserves from the system, it sells bonds, thereby depressing their price and raising their interest rates. From a longer-run perspective, if the central bank pursues an expansionary monetary policy with high money growth, inflation will rise and, as we saw in Chapter 5, interest rates will rise as well. Contractionary monetary policy is likely to lower inflation in the long run and lead to lower interest rates.

Knowing what actions the central bank might be taking can thus help investors and financial institutions to predict the future course of interest rates with greater accuracy. Because, as we have seen, changes in interest rates have a major impact on investors and financial institutions' profits, they are particularly interested in scrutinizing the central bank's behaviour. To assist in this task, financial institutions hire experts on central bank behaviour who may have worked in the central bank

and so have an insider's view of its operations. Besides personal experience, a key input for the prediction of future interest rates are the minutes of the central bank's meetings. For instance, since October 1998, the MPC of the Bank of England publishes the minutes of its monthly meetings on the Wednesday of the second week after the meetings take place. In these minutes analysts are able to look at the voting outcome on the monetary policy decision and judge whether a certain monetary stance is expected to change in the near future.

Also the Federal Reserve publishes the minutes of the FOMC meetings, but three weeks after the day of the policy decision. The ECB does not publish the minutes, but shortly after the Governing Council meeting the president of the ECB comments on the considerations underlying the policy decisions at a (very busy) press conference. Not surprisingly, the vast majority of the questions by financial journalists aim at pushing the president to provide clues on the future policy actions of the ECB. A central bank watcher who can accurately predict the course of monetary policy is a very valuable commodity, and successful watchers therefore often earn very high salaries, well into the six-figure range and sometimes even higher.

Central banks' response to asset-price bubbles: lessons from the subprime crisis

Over the centuries, economies have been periodically subject to **asset-price bubbles**, pronounced increases in asset prices that depart from fundamental values, which eventually burst resoundingly. The story of the subprime financial crisis, discussed in Chapter 9, indicates how costly these bubbles can be. The bursting of the asset-price bubble in the housing market brought down the financial system, leading to an economic downturn, a rise in unemployment, disrupted communities and direct hardship for families forced to leave their homes after foreclosures.

The high cost of asset-price bubbles raises the question: what should central banks do about them? Should they use monetary policy to try to pop bubbles? Are there regulatory measures they can take to rein in asset-price bubbles? To answer these questions, we need to ask whether there are different kinds of bubbles that require different types of response.

Two types of asset-price bubbles

There are two types of asset-price bubbles: one that is driven by credit and a second that is driven purely by overly optimistic expectations (which former chairman of the Fed, Alan Greenspan, referred to as 'irrational exuberance').

Credit-driven bubbles

When a credit boom begins, it can spill over into an asset-price bubble: easier credit can be used to purchase particular assets and thereby raise their prices. The rise in asset values, in turn, encourages further lending for these assets, either because it increases the value of collateral, making it easier to borrow, or because it raises the value of capital at financial institutions, which gives them more capacity to lend. The lending for these assets can then increase demand for them further and hence raise their prices even more. This feedback loop – in which a credit boom drives up asset prices, which in turn fuels the credit boom, which drives asset prices even higher, and so on – can generate a bubble in which asset prices rise well above their fundamental values.

Credit-driven bubbles are particularly dangerous, as the recent subprime financial crisis has demonstrated. When asset prices come back down to earth and the bubble bursts, the collapse in asset prices then leads to a reversal of the feedback loop in which loans go sour, lenders cut back on credit supply, the demand for assets declines further, and prices drop even more. These were exactly the dynamics in housing markets during the subprime financial crisis. Driven by a credit boom in subprime lending, housing prices rose way above fundamental values; but when housing prices crashed, credit shrivelled up and housing prices plummeted.

The resulting losses on subprime loans and securities eroded the balance sheets of financial institutions, causing a decline in credit (deleveraging) and a sharp fall in business and household spending, and therefore in economic activity. As we saw during the subprime financial crisis, the interaction between housing prices and the health of financial institutions following the collapse of the housing price bubble endangered the operation of the financial system as a whole and had direct consequences for the economy.

Bubbles driven solely by irrational exuberance

Bubbles that are driven solely by overly optimistic expectations, but which are not associated with a credit boom, pose much less risk to the financial system. For example, the bubble in technology stocks in the late 1990s described in Chapter 7 was not fuelled by credit, and the bursting of the tech-stock bubble was not followed by a marked deterioration in financial institutions' balance sheets. The bursting of the tech-stock bubble thus did not have a very severe impact on the economy and the recession that followed was quite mild. Bubbles driven solely by irrational exuberance are therefore far less dangerous than those driven by credit booms.

Should central banks respond to bubbles?

The general consensus is that the central bank should not respond to bubbles, mostly because bubbles are nearly impossible to identify. If central banks or government officials knew that a bubble was in progress, why wouldn't market participants know as well? If so, then a bubble would be unlikely to develop, because market participants would know that prices were getting out of line with fundamentals. This argument applies very strongly to asset-price bubbles that are driven by irrational exuberance, as is often the case for bubbles in the stock market. Unless central bank or government officials are smarter than market participants, which is unlikely given the especially high wages that savvy market participants garner, they will be unlikely to identify when bubbles of this type are occurring. There is then a strong argument for not responding to these kinds of bubbles.

On the other hand, when asset-price bubbles are rising rapidly at the same time that credit is booming, there is a greater likelihood that asset prices are deviating from fundamentals, because laxer credit standards are driving asset prices upward. In this case, central bank or government officials have a greater likelihood of identifying that a bubble is in progress; this was indeed the case during the housing market bubble in the United States because these officials did have information that lenders had weakened lending standards and that credit extension in the mortgage markets was rising at abnormally high rates.

Should monetary policy try to prick asset-price bubbles?

Not only are credit-driven bubbles possible to identify but, as we saw above, they are the ones that are capable of doing serious damage to the economy. There is thus a much stronger case that central banks should respond to possible credit-driven bubbles. But what is the appropriate response? Should monetary policy be used to try to prick a possible asset-price bubble that is associated with a credit boom by raising interest rates above what is desirable for keeping the economy on an even keel? Or are there other measures that are more suited to dealing with credit-driven bubbles?

There are three strong arguments against using monetary policy to prick bubbles by raising interest rates more than is necessary for achieving price stability and minimizing economic fluctuations. First, even if an asset-price bubble is of the credit-driven variety and so can be identified, the effect of raising interest rates on asset prices is highly uncertain. Although some economic analysis suggests that raising interest rates can diminish rises in asset prices, raising interest rates may be very ineffective in restraining the bubble, because market participants expect such high rates of return from buying bubble-driven assets. Furthermore, raising interest rates has often been found to cause a bubble to burst more severely, thereby increasing the damage to the economy. Another way of saying this is that bubbles are departures from normal behaviour, and it is unrealistic to expect that the usual tools of monetary policy will be effective in abnormal conditions.

Second, there are many different asset prices, and at any one time a bubble may be present in only a fraction of assets. Monetary policy actions are a very blunt instrument in such a case, as such actions would be likely to affect asset prices in general, rather than the specific assets that are experiencing a bubble.

Third, monetary policy actions to prick bubbles can have harmful effects on the aggregate economy. If interest rates are raised significantly to curtail a bubble, the economy will slow, people will lose jobs and inflation can fall below its desirable level. Indeed, as the first two arguments suggest, the rise in interest rates necessary to prick a bubble may be so high that it can only be done at great cost to workers and the economy. This is not to say that monetary policy should not respond to asset prices per se. As we will see in Chapter 23, the level of asset prices does affect aggregate demand and thus the evolution of the economy. Monetary policy should react to fluctuations in asset prices to the extent that they affect inflation and economic activity.

Although it is controversial, the basic conclusion from the above reasoning is that monetary policy should not be used to prick bubbles.

Are other types of policy responses appropriate?

As argued above, there is a case for responding to credit-driven bubbles because they are more identifiable and can do great damage to the economy, but monetary policy does not seem to be the way to do it. Regulatory policy to affect what is happening in credit markets in the aggregate, referred to as **macro-prudential regulation**, on the other hand, does seem to be the right tool for the job of reining in credit-driven bubbles.

Financial regulation and supervision, by either central banks or other government entities, with the usual elements of a well-functioning prudential regulatory and supervisory system described in Chapter 11 can prevent excessive risk taking that can trigger a credit boom, which in turn leads to an asset-price bubble. These elements include adequate disclosure and capital requirements, prompt corrective action, close monitoring of financial institutions' risk-management procedures and close supervision to enforce compliance with regulations. More generally, regulation should focus on preventing future feedback loops from credit booms to asset prices, asset prices to credit booms, credit booms to asset prices, and so on. As the subprime financial crisis demonstrated, the rise in asset prices that accompanied the credit boom resulted in higher capital buffers at financial institutions, supporting further lending in the context of unchanging capital requirements; in the bust, the value of the capital dropped precipitously, leading to a cut in lending. Capital requirements that are countercyclical, that is, adjusted upward during a boom and downward during a bust, might help eliminate the pernicious feedback loops that promote credit-driven bubbles.

A rapid rise in asset prices accompanied by a credit boom provides a signal that market failures or poor financial regulation and supervision might be causing a bubble to form. Central banks and other government regulators could then consider implementing policies to rein in credit growth directly or implement measures to make sure credit standards are sufficiently high.

An important lesson from the subprime financial crisis is that central banks and other regulators should not have a laissez-faire attitude and let credit-driven bubbles proceed without any reaction. Appropriate macro-prudential regulation can help limit credit-driven bubbles and improve the performance of both the financial system and the economy.

Summary

1 Monetary targeting has the advantage that information on whether the central bank is achieving its target is known almost immediately. Monetary targeting suffers from the disadvantage that it works well only if there is a reliable relationship between the monetary aggregate and the goal variable, inflation – a relationship that has often not held in different countries.

2 The Bank of England is currently adopting inflation targeting. Inflation targeting has several advantages: (1) it enables monetary policy to focus on domestic considerations; (2) stability in the relationship between money and inflation is not critical to its success; (3) it is readily understood by the public and is highly transparent; (4) it increases accountability of the central bank; and (5) it appears to ameliorate the effects of inflationary shocks. It does have some disadvantages, however: (1) inflation is not easily controlled by the monetary authorities, so that an inflation target is unable to send immediate signals to both the public and markets; (2) it might impose a rigid rule on policymakers, although this has not been the case in practice; and (3) a sole focus on inflation may lead

to larger output fluctuations, although this has also not been the case in practice.

3 The European Central Bank pursues a hybrid monetary policy strategy that has elements in common with the monetary-targeting strategy previously used by the Bundesbank, but also includes some elements of inflation targeting.

4 Until recently, the Federal Reserve followed a strategy of having an implicit, not an explicit, nominal anchor. This strategy has the following advantages: (1) it enables monetary policy to focus on domestic considerations; (2) it does not rely on a stable money–inflation relationship; and (3) it had a demonstrated success, producing low inflation with the longest business-cycle expansion in US history. However, it does have some disadvantages: (1) it has a lack of transparency; (2) it is strongly dependent on the preferences, skills and trustworthiness of individuals in the central bank and the government; and (3) it has some inconsistencies with democratic principles, because the central bank is not highly accountable. Because of these disadvantages the Fed has recently moved to a more explicit nominal anchor.

5 Because interest-rate and aggregate policy instruments are incompatible, a central bank must choose between them on the basis of three criteria:

measurability, controllability and the ability to affect goal variables predictably. Central banks now typically use short-term interest rates as their policy instrument.

6 The Taylor rule indicates that the interest rate should be set equal to the inflation rate plus an 'equilibrium' real interest rate plus a weighted average of two gaps: (1) an inflation gap, current inflation minus a target rate, and (2) an output gap, the percentage deviation of real GDP from an estimate of its potential full employment level. The output gap in the Taylor rule could represent an indicator of future inflation as stipulated in Phillips curve theory. However, this theory is controversial, because high output relative to potential as measured by low unemployment has not seemed to produce higher inflation in recent years.

7 There are two types of bubbles, credit-driven bubbles that are highly dangerous and so deserve a response from central banks, and bubbles driven solely by irrational exuberance, which do not. Although there are strong arguments against using monetary policy to prick bubbles, appropriate macro-prudential regulation to rein in credit-driven bubbles can improve the performance of both the financial system and the economy.

Key terms

accountability p. 354
asset-price bubble p. 373
inflation targeting p. 354
intermediate target p. 366
macro-prudential regulation p. 375

monetary targeting p. 351
non-accelerating inflation rate of unemployment (NAIRU) p. 370
operating instrument p. 366
Phillips curve theory p. 370

policy instrument p. 366
Taylor principle p. 370
Taylor rule p. 369
Transparency p. 354

QUESTIONS AND PROBLEMS

All questions and problems are available in MyEconLab at **www.myeconlab.com/mishkin**.

1 'Unemployment is a bad thing, and the government should make every effort to eliminate it.' Do you agree or disagree? Explain your answer.

2 Classify each of the following as either a policy instrument or an intermediate target, and explain why.

(a) The ten-year Treasury bond rate
(b) The monetary base
(c) M2

3 'If the demand for reserves did not fluctuate, the central bank could pursue both an aggregate target and an

interest-rate target at the same time.' Is this statement true, false, or uncertain? Explain your answer.

4 If the central bank has an interest-rate target, why will an increase in the demand for reserves lead to a rise in the money supply?

5 What procedures can the central bank use to control the short-term interest rate? Why does control of this interest rate imply that the central bank will lose control of non-borrowed reserves?

6 Compare the monetary base to M2 on the grounds of controllability and measurability. Which do you prefer as an intermediate target? Why?

7 'Interest rates can be measured more accurately and more quickly than reserve aggregates. Hence an interest rate is preferred over the reserve aggregates as a policy instrument.' Do you agree or disagree? Explain your answer.

8 What are the benefits of using a nominal anchor for the conduct of monetary policy?

9 Give an example of the time-inconsistency problem that you experience in your everyday life.

10 What incentives arise for a central bank to fall into the time-inconsistency trap of pursuing overly expansionary monetary policy?

11 What are the advantages of monetary targeting as a strategy for the conduct of monetary policy?

12 What is the big *if* necessary for the success of monetary targeting? Does the experience with monetary targeting suggest that the big *if* is a problem?

13 What methods have inflation-targeting central banks used to increase communication with the public and increase the transparency of monetary policymaking?

14 Why might inflation targeting increase support for the independence of the central bank to conduct monetary policy?

15 'Because the public can see whether a central bank hits its monetary targets almost immediately, whereas it takes time before the public can see whether an inflation target is achieved, monetary targeting makes central banks more accountable than inflation targeting does.' Is this statement true, false, or uncertain? Explain your answer.

16 'Because inflation targeting focuses on achieving the inflation target, it will lead to excessive output fluctuations.' Is this statement true, false, or uncertain? Explain your answer.

17 'A central bank with a dual mandate will achieve lower unemployment in the long run than a central bank with a hierarchical mandate in which price stability takes precedence.' Is this statement true, false, or uncertain?

18 What is the advantage that monetary targeting, inflation targeting, and a monetary strategy with an implicit, but not an explicit, nominal anchor have in common?

19 Explain why, according to the Taylor principle, the monetary authorities should raise nominal interest rates by more than the increase in the inflation rate.

WEB EXERCISES

1 Go to the ECB web site **www.ecb.int/press/pr/activities/ecb/html/index.en.html** and download the latest press release of the monetary policy decision. Try to answer the following questions:

(a) What did the Governing Council decide to do about short-term interest rates? What indicators were mostly monitored in the economic analysis?

(b) How does the ECB justify its policy decision on the basis of its monetary analysis?

2 The Monetary Policy Committee (MPC) of the Bank of England meets about every month to assess the state of the economy and to decide what actions the central bank should take. The minutes of this meeting are released on the Wednesday of the second week after the meetings take place; however, a brief news release is made available immediately after the meeting. Go to **www.bankofengland.co.uk/Pages/home.aspx**, click on 'Publications' and then on 'Minutes'. Find the MPC minutes and try to answer the following questions:

(a) When was the last scheduled meeting of the MPC? When is the next meeting?

(b) Review the news release from the last meeting. What did the committee decide to do about short-term interest rates?

(c) Review the most recently published meeting minutes. What areas of the economy seemed to be of most concern to the committee members?

3 Go to **www.bankofengland.co.uk/publications/Pages/inflationreport/default.aspx** and find the latest *Inflation Report* of the Bank of England.

(a) What does the latest 'fan chart' for CPI inflation look like?

(b) What is the Committee's best collective judgement on the chances of inflation being either above or below the 2% inflation target in the medium term?

4 New Zealand was the first country to use inflation targeting. Use the Reserve Bank of New Zealand site **(http://www.rbnz.govt.nz/)** to write a short report about how New Zealand has implemented inflation targeting and discuss whether it has been a successful strategy.

5 Many countries have central banks that are responsible for their nation's monetary policy. Go to **www.bis.org/cbanks.htm** and select one of the central banks (for example, Norway's). Review that bank's website to determine its policies regarding application of monetary policy. How does this bank's policies compare to those of the ECB?

Notes

1 Another explanation focuses on the technical difficulties of monetary control when using a non-borrowed reserves operating target under a system of lagged reserve requirements, in which required reserves for a given week are calculated on the basis of the level of deposits two weeks earlier. See David Lindsey, 'Non-borrowed reserve targeting and monetary control', in *Improving Money Stock Control*, ed. Laurence Meyer (Boston: Kluwer-Nijhoff, 1983), pp. 3–41.

2 For further discussion of experiences with inflation targeting, particularly in other countries, see Leonardo Leiderman and Lars E. O. Svensson, *Inflation Targeting* (London: Centre for Economic Policy Research, 1995); Frederic S. Mishkin and Adam Posen, 'Inflation targeting: lessons from four countries', Federal Reserve Bank of New York, *Economic Policy Review* 3 (August 1997), 9–110; Ben S. Bernanke, Thomas Laubach, Frederic S. Mishkin and Adam S. Posen, *Inflation Targeting: Lessons from the International Experience* (Princeton, NJ: Princeton University Press, 1999); and Frederick S. Mishkin and Klaus Schmidt-Hebbel, 'Does inflation targeting matter?', in Frederic S. Mishkin and Klaus Schmidt-Hebbel, eds., *Monetary Policy under Inflation Targeting* (Santiago: Central Bank of Chile, 2007), pp. 19–372.

3 Consumer price indexes have been found to have an upward bias in the measurement of true inflation, so it is not surprising that inflation targets would be chosen to exceed zero. However, the actual targets have been set to exceed the estimates of this measurement bias, indicating that inflation targeters have decided to have targets for inflation that exceed zero even after measurement bias is accounted for.

4 A zero inflation target increases the risk of deflation also due to the existence of inflation differentials across different regions. With the existence of heterogeneous inflation levels, an average inflation rate of zero forces some regions to operate at negative inflation rates, i.e. deflation. This risk is particularly evident in the euro area where structural inflation differences continue to persist.

5 John B. Taylor, 'Discretion versus policy rules in practice', *Carnegie-Rochester Conference Series on Public Policy* 39 (1993): 195–214. A more intuitive discussion with a historical perspective can be found in John B. Taylor, 'A historical analysis of monetary policy rules', in *Monetary Policy Rules*, ed. John B. Taylor (Chicago: University of Chicago Press, 1999), pp. 319–41.

6 There are, however, subtle differences between the two concepts, as is discussed in Arturo Estrella and Frederic S. Mishkin, 'The role of NAIRU in monetary policy: implications of uncertainty and model selection', in *Monetary Policy Rules*, ed. John Taylor (Chicago: University of Chicago Press, 1999), pp. 405–30.

Useful websites

www.ecb.int/pub/pdf/other/monetarypolicy2011en.pdf?3af2040fd5d35974777cc1ef5b066be7 Detailed description of the ECB's monetary policy and its economic and institutional background.

www.ecb.int/pub/pdf/other/art1_mb201011en_pp71-83en.pdf?d9b2ed2532f8e617426a2ce2cfa617bb Article from the ECB *Monthly Bulletin* (November 2010) describing the role of asset prices in the conduct of monetary policy.

www.ecb.int/ecb/educational/economia/html/index.en.html Link to the monetary policy game from the ECB webpage.

www.bankofengland.co.uk/publications/inflationreport/index.htm Complete series of the *Inflation Reports* of the Bank of England.

www.federalreserve.gov/pf/pf.htm Review of the primary purposes and functions of the Federal Reserve.

MyEconLab can help you get a better grade

MyEconLab®

If your exam were tomorrow, would you be ready? For each chapter, MyEconLab Practice Test and Study Plans pinpoint which sections you have mastered and which ones you need to study. That way, you are more efficient with your study time, and you are better prepared for your exams.

To see how it works, turn to page 19 and then go to: **www.myeconlab.com/mishkin**

PART 5

INTERNATIONAL FINANCE AND MONETARY POLICY

Crisis and response: Foreign exchange market turmoil

From 2002 until 2008, the euro steadily increased in value relative to other currencies. Indeed, a major concern of policymakers was that the strong euro might have adverse effects on economic activity in the euro area. The euro's higher value made imported goods – ranging from computers to books – cheaper to purchase and travelling abroad more affordable. But at the same time, goods produced in the euro area become more expensive for foreigners. With the credit markets seizing up in September and November of 2008, an amazing thing happened. Instead of continuing its rise, the euro depreciated sharply. Investors wanted to put their money in the safest assets possible: US Treasury securities, and this resulted in an increase in the demand for dollar assets and a sharp appreciation of the dollar against the euro and other currencies. In this environment, many countries in Latin America and Eastern Europe found their currencies in free fall. The International Monetary Fund (IMF) stepped in and set up a new lending facility to make loans to distressed countries with fewer strings attached than was true for the IMF's previous lending programmes. The IMF started making loans to the tune of billions of dollars. The IMF, which had looked like it was on the sidelines as the subprime financial crisis spread worldwide, now was moving to front and centre.

The subprime crisis has demonstrated that events in the United States have worldwide ramifications and that international financial institutions like the IMF have an important role in responding to make sure that the international financial system continues to work well. Chapter 17 outlines how the foreign exchange market functions and how exchange rates between different countries' currencies are determined. In Chapter 18, we examine how the international financial system operates and how it affects monetary policy.

The foreign exchange market: exchange rates and applications

During the second half of the 1980s, British businesses became less competitive with their foreign counterparts; subsequently, in the 1990s, their competitiveness increased. Did this swing in competitiveness occur primarily because British management fell down on the job in the 1980s and then got its act together afterwards? Not really. British business became less competitive in the 1980s because British pounds became worth more in terms of foreign currencies, making British goods more expensive relative to foreign goods. By the 1990s, the value of the pound had fallen appreciably from its temporary high at the end of the 1980s, making British goods cheaper and British businesses more competitive.

The price of one currency in terms of another is called the **exchange rate**. As you can see in Figure 17.1, exchange rates are highly volatile. The exchange rate affects the economy and our daily lives, because when the domestic currency becomes more valuable relative to foreign currencies, foreign goods become cheaper in the domestic market and domestic goods become more expensive for foreigners. When the domestic currency falls in value, foreign goods become more expensive in the domestic market and domestic goods become cheaper for foreigners.

Fluctuations in the exchange rate also affect both inflation and output, and are an important concern to monetary policymakers. When the domestic currency falls in value, the higher prices of imported goods feed directly into a higher price level and inflation. At the same time, a declining domestic currency, which makes domestic (exported) goods cheaper for foreigners, increases the demand for domestic goods and leads to higher production and output.

We begin our study of international finance by examining the **foreign exchange market**, the financial market where exchange rates are determined.

Foreign exchange market

Most countries of the world have their own currencies: the euro area has the euro, the United Kingdom the pound sterling, the United States the dollar, Sweden the krona and China the yuan. Trade between countries involves the mutual exchange of different currencies (or, more usually, bank deposits denominated in different currencies). When a German firm buys foreign goods, services or financial assets, for example, euros (typically, bank deposits denominated in euros) must be exchanged for foreign currency (bank deposits denominated in the foreign currency).

FIGURE 17.1

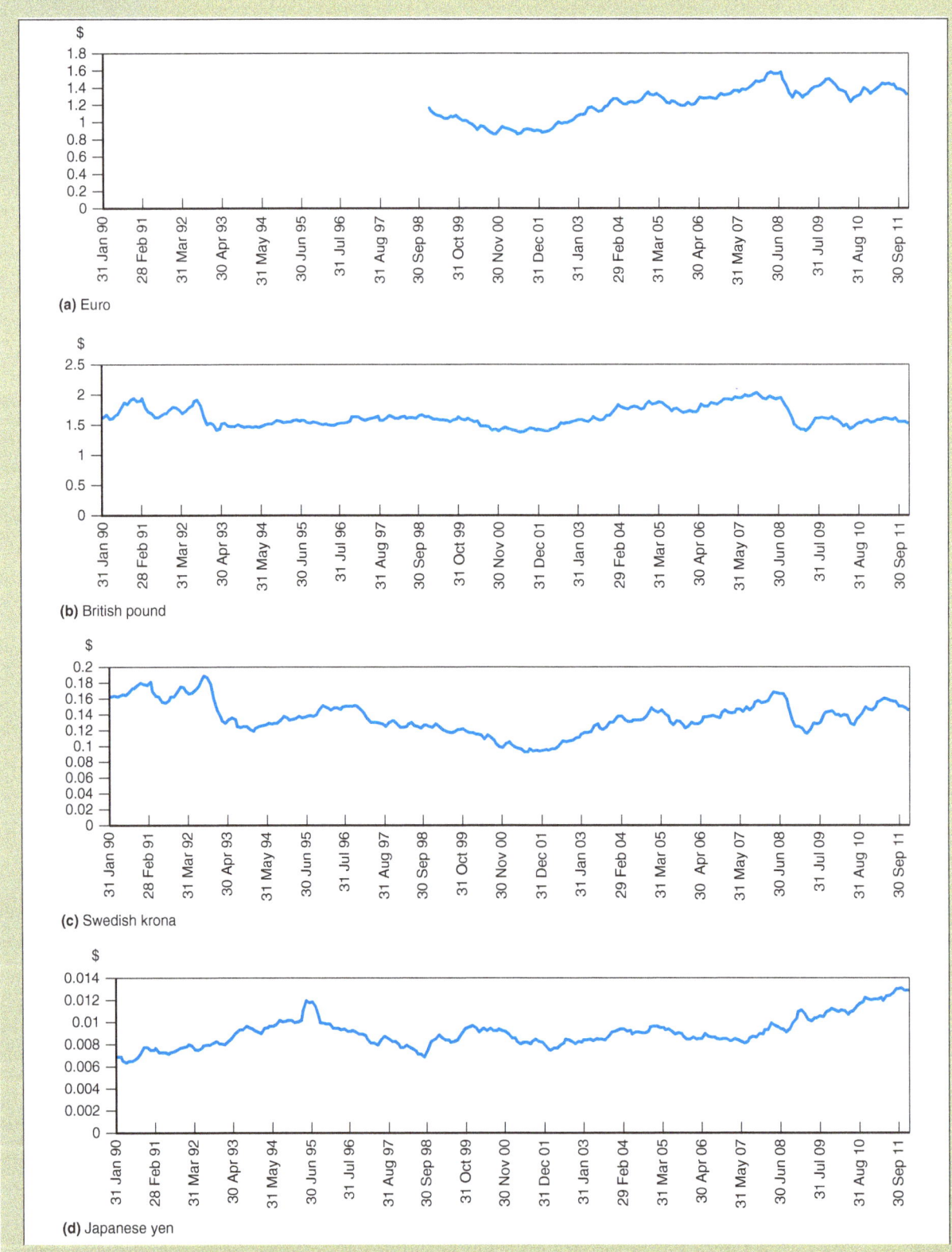

(a) Euro

(b) British pound

(c) Swedish krona

(d) Japanese yen

Exchange rates, 1990–2011

US dollar prices of selected currencies. Note that a rise in these plots indicates a strengthening of the domestic currency.

Source: Bank of England: www.bankofengland.co.uk/statistics/index.htm.

The trading of currencies and bank deposits denominated in particular currencies takes place in the foreign exchange market. Transactions conducted in the foreign exchange market determine the rates at which currencies are exchanged, which in turn determine the cost of purchasing foreign goods and financial assets.

What are foreign exchange rates?

The currency of a country has to be valued in terms of another currency. In most cases, global currencies are widely quoted against the two major currencies in the world: the euro and the US dollar. However, most countries also quote their national currencies against currencies other than the euro and the dollar; these are known as currency cross rates. The 'Following the financial news' box 'Foreign exchange rates' shows how cross rates are quoted for the four major currencies in the world.

There are two kinds of exchange rate transactions. The predominant ones, called **spot transactions**, involve the immediate (two-day) exchange of bank deposits. The **spot exchange rate** is the exchange rate for the spot transaction, and the **forward exchange rate** is the exchange rate for the **forward transaction**. Forward transactions involve the exchange of bank deposits at some specified future date, usually one, three, six or twelve months. While the rate is decided upon today, the actual transfer of funds occurs in the future, thereby protecting

FOLLOWING THE FINANCIAL NEWS

Foreign exchange rates

Log on to the website of the *Financial Times* and select the cross rates for as many currencies as you wish. The following quotations are for spot transactions for only eight currencies, where payment takes place two working days from the day the transaction was made. As you can see, each currency is quoted against the four major global currencies: the euro, the pound sterling, the US dollar and the Japanese yen.

Currencies cross rates

	GBP £	EUR €	USD $	JPY ¥
Australia 1.00 AUD	0.67460	0.8055	1.0573	87.13
Canada 1.00 CAD	0.644	0.7689	1.0093	83.18
European Union 1.00 EUR	0.8372	N/A	1.3121	108.13
Hong Kong 1.00 HKD	0.08224	0.0982	0.1289	10.6223
Japan 1.00 JPY	0.00774	0.00924	0.01212	N/A
Switzerland 1.00 CHF	0.6942	0.8289	1.088	89.66
United Kingdom 1.00 GBP	N/A	1.1937	1.5668	129.12
United States 1.00 USD	0.638	0.7618	N/A	82.41

Source: *Financial Times*, 9 March 2012, http://markets.ft.com/ft/markets/currencies.asp.

against foreign exchange rate fluctuations. Most importers and exporters engage in forward transactions in order to hedge against foreign exchange risks.

The exchange rate is the price of one currency in terms of another. In this respect, there are two methods of expressing it. In the **direct method**, the exchange rate is quoted as units of domestic currency per unit of foreign currency. When the exchange rate *increases*, you need more units of domestic currency to buy a unit of foreign currency, and the domestic currency undergoes **depreciation**; when the exchange rate *falls*, the domestic currency experiences **appreciation**. This convention is used in professional writing by economists and in most countries including the euro area. For example, assuming the domestic currency is the euro, in March 2011, the US dollar was valued at €0.713; on 9 March 2012, the US dollar was traded for €0.762. The euro *depreciated* by 6.9% against the US dollar: $((0.762 - 0.713)/0.713) = 0.069 = 6.9\%$.

In the **indirect method**, the exchange rate is expressed as units of foreign currency for unit of domestic currency. When the exchange rate *increases*, more units of foreign currency are needed to buy a unit of domestic currency, implying an appreciation of the domestic currency; when the exchange rate *falls*, the domestic currency experiences depreciation. This is the definition most commonly used in the UK. For example, assuming now that the domestic currency is the pound, in March 2001, the pound was valued at $1.457, whereas on 9 March 2012 it was $1.567. The rise in the exchange rate now indicates that the pound *appreciated* by 7.5% against the dollar: $(1.567 - 1.457)/1.457 = 0.075 = 7.5\%$. The reader will notice that the indirect method is simply the reciprocal of the direct method. For the purpose of this chapter and this book, we define the exchange rate on the basis of the indirect method, because it is more intuitive to think of an appreciation of the domestic currency as a rise in the exchange rate.

Why are exchange rates important?

Exchange rates are important because they affect the relative price of domestic and foreign goods. The price of German goods to an American is determined by the interaction of two factors: the price of German goods in euros and the dollar/euro exchange rate.

Suppose that Wanda, an American, decides to buy a brand new BMW. If the price of the car in Germany is €50,000 and the exchange rate is $1.50 to the euro, the car will cost Wanda $75,000 (= €50,000 * $1.50/€). Now suppose that Wanda delays her purchase by two months, at which time the euro has appreciated to $2 per euro. If the domestic price of the BMW remains €50,000, its dollar cost will have risen from $75,000 to $100,000.

The same currency appreciation, however, makes the price of foreign goods in that country less expensive. At an exchange rate of $1.50 per euro, a Dell computer priced at $3,000 costs Mark the Programmer €2,000; if the exchange rate increases to $2 per euro, the computer will cost only €1,500.

A depreciation of the euro lowers the cost of German goods in America but raises the cost of American goods in Germany. If the euro drops in value to $1.00 per euro, Wanda's BMW will cost her only $50,000 instead of $75,000, whereas the Dell computer will cost Mark €3,000 instead of €2,000.

Such reasoning leads to the following conclusion: *when a country's currency appreciates the country's goods abroad become more expensive and foreign goods in that country become cheaper (holding domestic prices constant in the two countries). Conversely, when a country's currency depreciates, its goods abroad become cheaper and foreign goods in that country become more expensive.*

Depreciation of a currency makes it easier for domestic manufacturers to sell their goods abroad and makes foreign goods less competitive in domestic markets. From 1999 to 2001, for instance, the depreciated euro helped German industries sell more goods, but it hurt German consumers because foreign goods were more expensive. The prices of American computers and the cost of holidays in the US all rose as a result of the weak euro.

How is foreign exchange traded?

You cannot go to a centralized location to watch exchange rates being determined; currencies are not traded on exchanges such as the London Stock Exchange and the New York Stock Exchange. Instead, the foreign exchange market is organized as an over-the-counter market in which several hundred dealers (mostly banks) stand ready to buy and sell deposits denominated in foreign currencies. Because these dealers are in constant telephone and computer contact, the market is very competitive; in effect, it functions no differently from a centralized market.

An important point to note is that while banks, companies and governments talk about buying and selling currencies in foreign exchange markets, they do not take a fistful of dollar bills and sell them for euro notes. Rather, most trades involve the buying and selling of bank deposits denominated in different currencies. So when we say that a bank is buying dollars in the foreign exchange market, what we actually mean is that the bank is buying *deposits denominated in dollars*. According to the Bank for International Settlements (BIS), the total average daily volume in foreign exchange markets is colossal, exceeding $3.98 trillion per day, as of April 2010. The main centre for foreign exchange trading is London with a share of 36.7% of the total, followed by New York 17.9% and Tokyo with 6.2%.

Trades in the foreign exchange market consist of transactions in excess of $1 million. The market that determines the exchange rates in the 'Following the financial news' box is not where one would buy foreign currency for a trip abroad. Instead, we buy foreign currency in the retail market from dealers such as commercial banks. Because retail prices are higher than wholesale, when we buy foreign exchange, we obtain fewer units of foreign currency per sterling, that is, we pay a higher price for foreign currency than exchange rates in the box indicate.

Exchange rates in the long run

Like the price of any good or asset in a free market, exchange rates are determined by the interaction of supply and demand. To simplify our analysis of exchange rates in a free market, we divide it into two parts. First, we examine how exchange rates are determined in the long run; then we use our knowledge of the long-run determinants of the exchange rates to help us understand how they are determined in the short run.

Law of one price

The starting point for understanding how exchange rates are determined is a simple idea called the **law of one price**: if two countries produce an identical good, and transportation costs and trade barriers are very low, the price of the good should be the same throughout the world no matter which country produces it. Suppose that German steel costs €100 per ton and identical US steel costs $200 per ton. For the law of one price to hold, the exchange rate between the dollar and the euro must be 2 dollars per euro so that one ton of German steel sells for $200 in the US (the price of American steel) and one ton of American steel sells for €100 in Germany (the price of German steel). If the exchange rate were 4 dollars to the euro, American steel would sell for €50 per ton in Germany or half the price of German steel, and German steel would sell for $400 per ton in the US, twice the price of American steel. Because German steel would be more expensive than American steel in both countries and is identical to American steel, the demand for German steel would go to zero. Given a fixed euro price for German steel, the resulting excess supply of German steel will be eliminated only if the exchange rate falls to 2 dollars per euro, making the price of German steel and American steel the same in both countries.

Theory of purchasing power parity

One of the most prominent theories of how exchange rates are determined is the **theory of purchasing power parity (PPP)**. It states that exchange rates between any two currencies will adjust to reflect changes in the price levels of the two countries. The theory of PPP is simply an application of the law of one price to national price levels rather than to individual prices. Suppose that the dollar price of American steel rises 10% (to $220) relative to the euro price of German steel (unchanged at €100). For the law of one price to hold, the exchange rate must rise to 2.2 dollars to the euro, a 10% appreciation of the euro. Applying the law of one price to the price levels in the two countries produces the theory of purchasing power parity, which maintains that if the US price level rises 10% relative to the German price level, the euro will appreciate by 10%.

Another way of thinking about purchasing power parity is through a concept called the **real exchange rate**, the rate at which domestic goods can be exchanged for foreign goods. In effect, it is the price of domestic goods relative to the price of foreign goods denominated in the domestic currency. For example, if a basket of goods in Berlin costs €50, while the cost of the same basket of goods in New York is €75 because it costs $150 while the exchange rate is at 2 dollars per euro, then the real exchange rate is 0.66 (= €50/€75). The real exchange rate is below 1.0, indicating that it is cheaper to buy the basket of goods in Germany than in the United States. The real exchange rate for the euro is currently low against many other currencies, and this is why we are seeing a huge demand for German goods by so many foreign countries. It is the real exchange rate that indicates whether a currency is relatively cheap or not. Another way of describing the theory of PPP is to say that it predicts the real exchange rate is always equal to 1.0, so that the purchasing power of the euro is the same as the purchasing power of other currencies such as the US dollar and the yen.

As our German/US example demonstrates, the theory of PPP suggests that if one country's price level rises relative to another's, its currency should depreciate (the other country's currency should appreciate). As you can see in Figure 17.2, this prediction is borne out in the long run. From 1973 to the end of 2011, the US price level fell by 35.1%

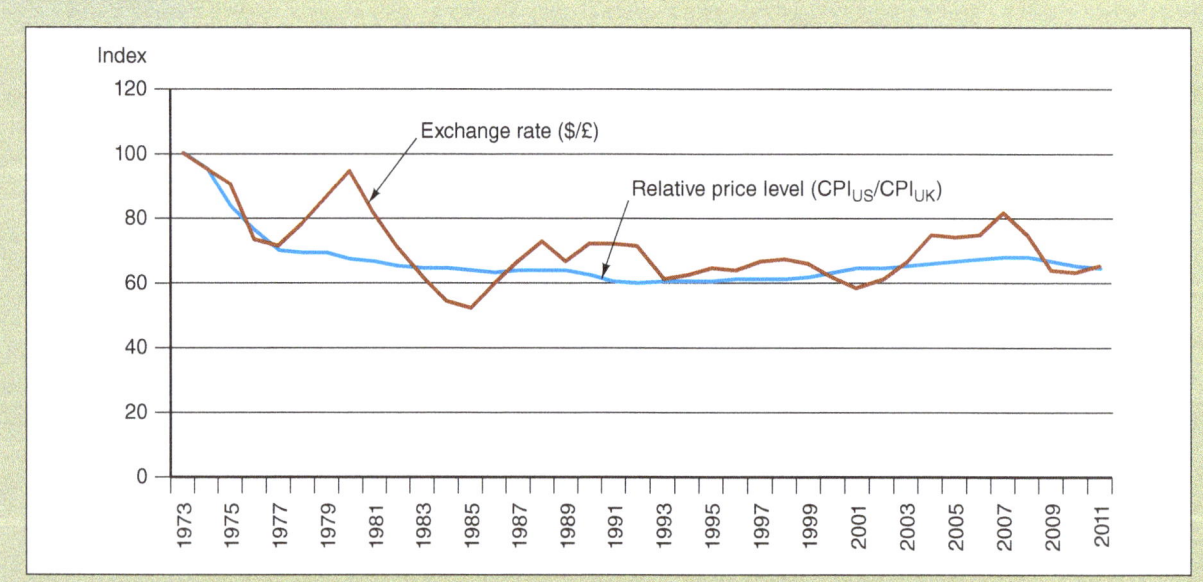

FIGURE 17.2

Purchasing power parity, United States/United Kingdom, 1973–2011 (index: 1973 = 100)

Source: The US CPI price level is from ftp://ftp.bls.gov/pub/special.requests/cpi/cpiai.txt. The average annual bilateral US$/pound exchange rate is from the OECD Economic Outlook. The British price level is from www.bankofengland.co.uk.

relative to the British price level, and as the theory of PPP predicts, the pound depreciated against the US dollar by 34.6%, an amount almost identical to that predicted by PPP.

Yet, as the same figure indicates, PPP theory often has little predictive power in the short run. From early 1985 to the end of 1990, for example, the British price level rose relative to that of the United States. Instead of depreciating, as PPP theory predicts, the British pound actually appreciated by 38.4% against the dollar. So even though PPP theory provides some guidance to the long-run movement of exchange rates, it is not perfect and in the short run is a particularly poor predictor. What explains PPP theory's failure to predict well?

Why the theory of purchasing power parity cannot fully explain exchange rates

The PPP conclusion that exchange rates are determined solely by changes in relative price levels rests on the assumption that all goods are identical in both countries and that transportation costs and trade barriers are very low. When this assumption is true, the law of one price states that the relative prices of all these goods (that is, the relative price level between the two countries) will determine the exchange rate. The assumption that goods are identical may not be too unreasonable for German and American steel, but is it a reasonable assumption for German and American cars? Is a Chevrolet the equivalent of a BMW?

Because Chevrolets and BMWs are obviously not identical, their prices do not have to be equal. Chevrolets can be more expensive relative to BMWs and both Germans and Americans will still purchase Chevrolets. Because the law of one price does not hold for all goods, a rise in the price of Chevrolets relative to BMWs will not necessarily mean that the dollar must depreciate against the euro by the amount of the relative price increase of Chevrolets over BMWs.

PPP theory furthermore does not take into account that many goods and services (whose prices are included in a measure of a country's price level) are not traded across borders. Housing, land and services such as restaurant meals, haircuts and golf lessons are not traded goods. So even though the prices of these items might rise and lead to a higher price level relative to another country's, there would be little direct effect on the exchange rate.

Factors that affect exchange rates in the long run

In the long run, four major factors affect the exchange rate: relative price levels, trade barriers, preferences for domestic versus foreign goods, and productivity. We examine how each of these factors affects the exchange rate while holding the others constant.

The basic reasoning proceeds along the following lines: anything that increases the demand for domestically produced goods that are traded relative to foreign traded goods tends to appreciate the domestic currency because domestic goods will continue to sell well even when the value of the domestic currency is higher. Similarly, anything that increases the demand for foreign goods relative to domestic goods tends to depreciate the domestic currency because domestic goods will continue to sell well only if the value of the domestic currency is lower. In other words, *if a factor increases the demand for domestic goods relative to foreign goods, the domestic currency will appreciate; if a factor decreases the relative demand for domestic goods, the domestic currency will depreciate.*

Relative price levels

In line with PPP theory, when prices of German goods rise (holding prices of foreign goods constant), the demand for German goods falls and the euro tends to depreciate so that German goods can still sell well. By contrast, if prices of American goods rise so that the relative prices of German goods fall, the demand for German goods increases, and the euro tends to appreciate, because German goods will continue to sell well even with a higher value of the domestic currency. *In the long run, a rise in a country's price level (relative to the foreign price level) causes its currency to depreciate, and a fall in the country's relative price level causes its currency to appreciate*.

Trade barriers

Barriers to free trade such as **tariffs** (taxes on imported goods) and **quotas** (restrictions on the quantity of foreign goods that can be imported) can affect the exchange rate. Suppose that Germany increases its tariff or puts a lower quota on American steel. These increases in trade barriers increase the demand for German steel, and the euro tends to appreciate because German steel will still sell well even with a higher value of the euro. *Increasing trade barriers causes a country's currency to appreciate in the long run.*

Preferences for domestic versus foreign goods

If the Americans develop an appetite for German goods – say, for German cars – the increased demand for German goods (exports) tends to appreciate the euro, because the German goods will continue to sell well even at a higher value for the euro. Likewise, if Germans decide that they prefer American cars to German cars, the increased demand for American goods (imports) tends to depreciate the euro. *Increased demand for a country's exports causes its currency to appreciate in the long run; conversely, increased demand for imports causes the domestic currency to depreciate.*

Productivity

When productivity in a country rises, it tends to rise in domestic sectors that produce traded goods rather than non-traded goods. Higher productivity, therefore, is associated with a decline in the price of domestically produced traded goods relative to foreign traded goods. As a result, the demand for domestic traded goods rises, and the domestic currency tends to appreciate. If, however, a country's productivity lags behind that of other countries, its traded goods become relatively more expensive, and the currency tends to depreciate. *In the long run, as a country becomes more productive relative to other countries, its currency appreciates*.[1]

Our long-run theory of exchange rate behaviour is summarized in Table 17.1. As discussed above, we use the convention that the exchange rate E is quoted so that an appreciation of the domestic currency corresponds to a rise in the exchange rate. In the case of Germany, this means that we are quoting the exchange rate as units of foreign currency per euro (say, dollar per euro, yen per euro).

SUMMARY TABLE 17.1

Factors that affect exchange rates in the long run

Factor	Change in factor	Response of the exchange rate*, E
Domestic price level[†]	⬆	⬇
Trade barriers[†]	⬆	⬆
Import demand	⬆	⬇
Export demand	⬆	⬆
Productivity[†]	⬆	⬆

*Units of foreign currency per unit of domestic currency: ⬆ indicates domestic currency appreciation; ⬇, depreciation.

[†]Relative to other countries.

Exchange rates in the short run: a supply and demand analysis

We have developed a theory of the long-run behaviour of exchange rates. However, because factors driving long-run changes in exchange rates move slowly over time, if we are to understand why exchange rates exhibit such large changes (sometimes several percentage points) from day to day, we must develop a supply and demand analysis of how current exchange rates (spot exchange rates) are determined in the short run.

The key to understanding the short-run behaviour of exchange rates is to recognize that an exchange rate is the price of domestic assets (bank deposits, bonds, equities, etc., denominated in the domestic currency) in terms of foreign assets (similar assets denominated in the foreign currency). Because the exchange rate is the price of one asset in terms of another, the natural way to investigate the short-run determination of exchange rates is with a supply and demand analysis that uses an asset market approach, which relies heavily on the theory of asset demand developed in Chapter 5. As you will see, however, the long-run determinants of the exchange rate we have just outlined also play an important role in the short-run asset market approach.[2]

In the past, supply and demand approaches to exchange rate determination emphasized the role of import and export demand. The more modern asset market approach used here emphasizes stocks of assets rather than the flows of exports and imports over short periods, because export and import transactions are small relative to the amount of domestic and foreign assets at any given time. Thus, over short periods, decisions to hold domestic or foreign assets play a much greater role in exchange rate determination than the demand for exports and imports does.

Supply curve for domestic assets

We start by discussing the supply curve. In this analysis, we treat Germany as the home country, so domestic assets are denominated in euros. For simplicity, we use dollars to stand for any foreign country's currency, so foreign assets are denominated in dollars.

The quantity of domestic assets supplied is primarily the quantity of bank deposits, bonds and equities in the home country, and for all practical purposes we can take this amount as fixed with respect to the exchange rate. The quantity supplied at any exchange rate does not change, so the supply curve, S, is vertical, as shown in Figure 17.3.

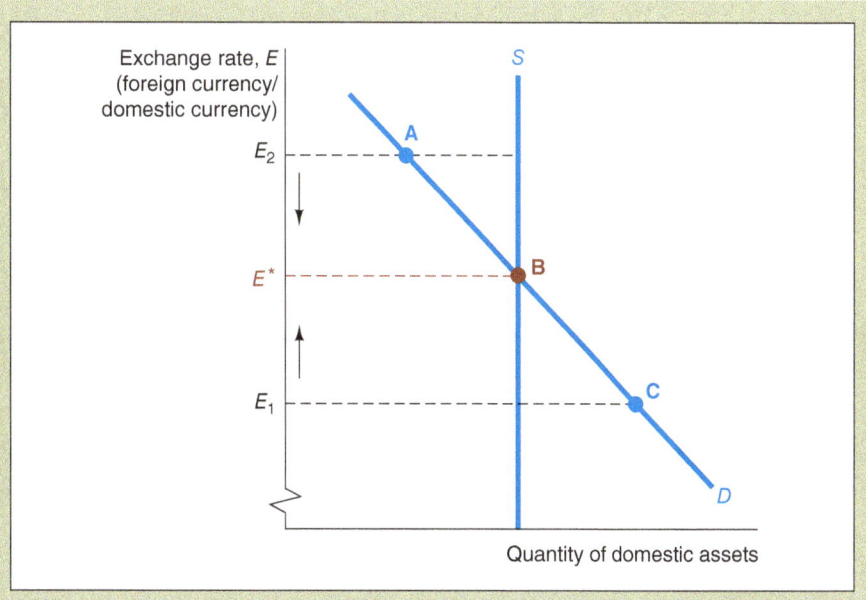

Equilibrium in the foreign exchange market

Equilibrium in the foreign exchange market occurs at point B, the intersection of the demand curve D and the supply curve S at an exchange rate of E^*.

Demand curve for domestic assets

The demand curve traces out the quantity demanded at each current exchange rate by holding everything else constant. Suppose we start at point A in Figure 17.3 where the current exchange rate (the spot exchange rate) is at E_2. A lower value of the exchange rate, say at E^*, implies that the domestic currency depreciates, making domestic assets relatively more attractive to foreigners. The greater the decrease (depreciation) of the domestic currency, the cheaper are domestic assets and the higher their quantity demanded. If the current exchange rate falls even further to E_1, there is an even higher depreciation of the domestic currency, and therefore an even greater quantity of domestic assets demanded. This is shown in point C in Figure 17.3. The resulting demand curve, D, which connects these points, is downward sloping, indicating that at lower current values of the domestic currency (everything else equal), the quantity demanded of domestic assets is higher.

Equilibrium in the foreign exchange market

As in the usual supply and demand analysis, the market is in equilibrium when the quantity of foreign assets demanded equals the quantity supplied. In Figure 17.3, equilibrium occurs at point B, the intersection of the demand and supply curves. At point B, the exchange rate is E^*.

Suppose that the exchange rate is at E_2, which is higher than the equilibrium exchange rate of E^*. As we can see in Figure 17.3, the quantity of domestic assets supplied is then greater than the quantity demanded, a condition of excess supply. Given that more people want to sell domestic assets than want to buy them, the value of the domestic currency will fall. As long as the exchange rate remains above the equilibrium exchange rate, there will continue to be an excess supply of domestic assets, and the domestic currency will fall in value until it reaches the equilibrium exchange rate of E^*.

Similarly, if the exchange rate is less than the equilibrium exchange rate at E_1, the quantity of domestic assets demanded will exceed the quantity supplied, a condition of excess demand. Given that more people want to buy domestic assets than want to sell them, the value of the domestic currency will rise until the excess demand disappears and the value of the domestic currency is again at the equilibrium exchange rate of E^*.

Explaining changes in exchange rates

The supply and demand analysis of the foreign exchange market illustrates how and why exchange rates change. We can simplify this analysis by assuming the amount of domestic assets is fixed: the supply curve is vertical at a given quantity and does not shift. Under this assumption, we need to look at only those factors that shift the demand curve for domestic assets to explain how exchange rates change over time.

Shifts in the demand for domestic assets

As we have seen in the theory of asset demand in Chapter 5, the quantity of domestic assets demanded depends on four main factors: wealth, the relative risk, the relative liquidity and the relative expected return of domestic assets. To see how the demand curve shifts, we need to determine how the quantity demanded changes, holding the current exchange rate, E_t, constant, when other factors change.

Changes in foreign wealth

Suppose that, as a result of an increase in wealth, foreigners have more resources available with which to purchase domestic assets. At every value of the exchange rate, the quantity of domestic assets demanded will increase, as shown by the rightward shift of the demand

FIGURE 17.4

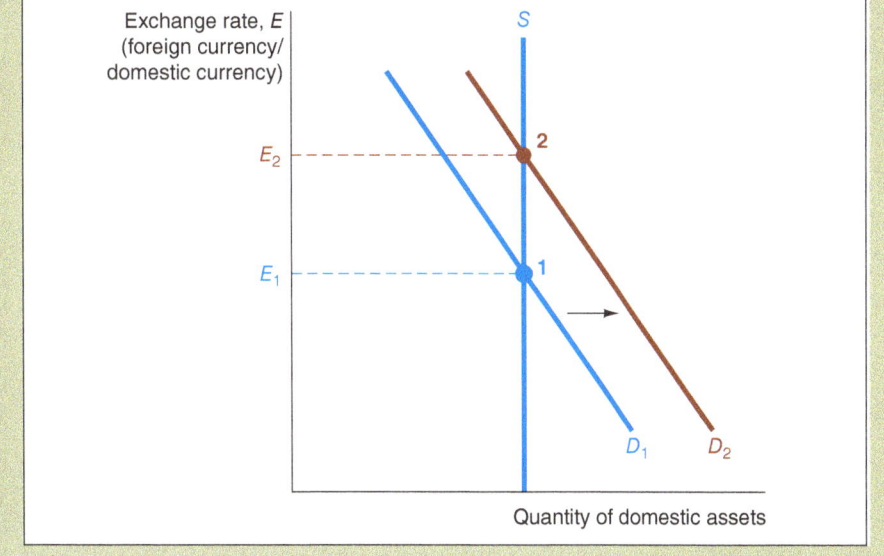

Response to an increase in the demand for domestic assets

When the demand curve for domestic assets shifts to the right, the equilibrium exchange rate rises from E_1 to E_2.

curve in Figure 17.4 from D_1 to D_2. The new equilibrium is reached at point 2, the intersection of D_2 and S, and the equilibrium exchange rate rises from E_1 to E_2. *An increase in the foreign wealth shifts the demand curve for domestic assets, D, to the right and causes the domestic currency to appreciate* ($E\uparrow$).

Changes in relative risk of domestic assets

The degree of risk or uncertainty of an asset's return also affects the demand for the asset at a certain value of the current exchange rate. If the risk associated with domestic assets increases relative to the risk of foreign assets, holding the current exchange rate and everything else constant, people want to hold fewer domestic assets, and the quantity demanded decreases at every value of the exchange rate. This scenario is shown by the leftward shift of the demand curve in Figure 17.5 from D_1 to D_2. The new equilibrium is reached at point 2, when the value of the domestic currency has fallen. Conversely, a decrease in the risk of domestic assets relative to foreign assets, shifts the demand curve to the right, and raises the exchange rate. To summarize, *an increase in the relative risk of domestic assets shifts the demand curve D to the left and causes the domestic currency to depreciate; a fall in the relative risk of domestic assets shifts the demand curve D to the right and causes the domestic currency to appreciate.*

Changes in relative liquidity of domestic assets

The degree of liquidity of domestic assets relative to foreign assets also affects the demand for the asset at a certain value of the current exchange rate. If the liquidity associated with domestic assets increases relative to the liquidity of foreign assets, holding the current exchange rate and everything else constant, people want to hold more domestic assets, and the quantity demanded increases at every value of the exchange rate. This scenario is shown by the rightward shift of the demand curve in Figure 17.4 from D_1 to D_2. The new equilibrium is reached at point 2, when the value of the domestic currency has increased. Conversely, a decrease in the liquidity of domestic assets relative to foreign assets shifts the demand curve to the left and raises the exchange rate. To summarize, *an increase in the relative liquidity of domestic assets shifts the demand curve D to the right and causes the*

FIGURE 17.5

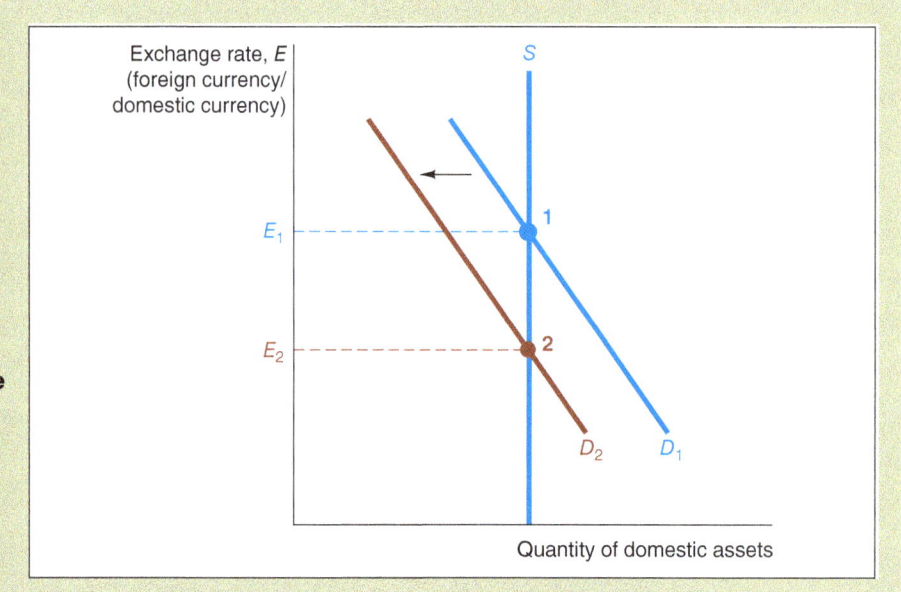

Response to a decrease in the demand for domestic assets

When the demand curve for domestic assets shifts to the left, the equilibrium exchange rate falls from E_1 to E_2.

domestic currency to appreciate; a fall in the relative liquidity of domestic assets shifts the demand curve D to the left and causes the domestic currency to depreciate.

Changes in relative expected return of domestic assets

Domestic interest rate, i^D

Suppose that domestic assets pay an interest rate of i^D. When the domestic interest rate on domestic assets i^D rises, holding the current exchange rate E_t and everything else constant, the return on domestic assets increases relative to foreign assets, so people will want to hold more domestic assets. The quantity of domestic assets demanded increases at every value of the exchange rate, as shown by the rightward shift of the demand curve in Figure 17.4 from D_1 to D_2. The new equilibrium is reached at point 2, the intersection of D_2 and S, and the equilibrium exchange rate rises from E_1 to E_2. *An increase in the domestic interest rate i^D shifts the demand curve for domestic assets, D, to the right and causes the domestic currency to appreciate (E ↑).*

Conversely, if i^D falls, the relative expected return on domestic assets falls, the demand curve shifts to the left, and the exchange rate falls. *A decrease in the domestic interest rate i^D shifts the demand curve for domestic assets, D, to the left and causes the domestic currency to depreciate (E ↓).*

Foreign interest rate, i^F

Suppose that the foreign asset pays an interest rate of i^F. When the foreign interest rate i^F rises, holding the current exchange rate and everything else constant, the return on foreign assets rises relative to domestic assets. Thus the relative expected return on domestic assets falls. Now people want to hold fewer domestic assets, and the quantity demanded decreases at every value of the exchange rate. This scenario is shown by the leftward shift of the demand curve in Figure 17.5 from D_1 to D_2. The new equilibrium is reached at point 2, when the value of the domestic currency has fallen. Conversely, a decrease in i^F raises the relative expected return on domestic assets, shifts the demand curve to the right, and raises the exchange rate. To summarize, *an increase in the foreign interest rate i^F shifts the demand curve D to the left and causes the domestic currency to depreciate; a fall in the foreign interest rate i^F shifts the demand curve D to the right and causes the domestic currency to appreciate.*

Changes in the expected future exchange rate, E_{t+1}^e

Expectations about the future value of the exchange rate play an important role in shifting the current demand curve, because the demand for domestic assets, like the demand for any durable good, depends on the future resale price. Any factor that causes the expected future exchange rate, E_{t+1}^e, to rise increases the expected appreciation of the domestic currency. The result is a higher relative expected return on domestic assets, which increases the demand for domestic assets at every exchange rate, thereby shifting the demand curve to the right in Figure 17.6 from D_1 to D_2. The equilibrium exchange rate rises to point 2 at the intersection of the D_2 and S curves. *A rise in the expected future exchange rate, E_{t+1}^e, shifts the demand curve to the right and causes an appreciation of the domestic currency.* Using the same reasoning, *a fall in the expected future exchange rate, E_{t+1}^e, shifts the demand curve to the left and causes a depreciation of the currency*.

Earlier in the chapter we discussed the determinants of the exchange rate in the long run: the relative price level, relative trade barriers, import and export demand, and relative productivity (refer to Summary Table 17.1). These four factors influence the expected future exchange rate. The theory of purchasing power parity suggests that if a higher domestic price level relative to the foreign price level is expected to persist, the domestic currency will depreciate in the long run. A higher expected relative domestic price level should thus have a tendency to lower E_{t+1}^e, lower the relative expected return on domestic assets, shift the demand curve to the left, and lower the current exchange rate.

Similarly, the other long-run determinants of the exchange rate can influence the relative expected return on domestic assets and the current exchange rate. Briefly, the following changes, all of which increase the demand for domestic goods relative to foreign goods, will raise E_{t+1}^e: (1) expectations of a fall in the domestic price level relative to the foreign price level; (2) expectations of higher domestic trade barriers relative to foreign trade barriers; (3) expectations of lower domestic import demand; (4) expectations of higher foreign demand for domestic exports; and (5) expectations of higher domestic productivity relative to foreign productivity. By increasing E_{t+1}^e, all of these changes increase the relative expected return on domestic assets, shift the demand curve to the right, and cause an appreciation of the domestic currency.

FIGURE 17.6

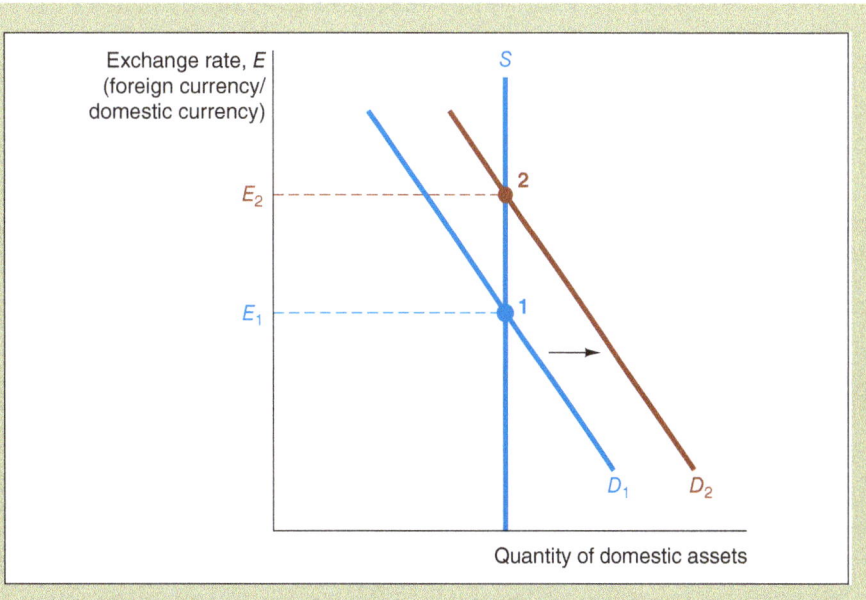

Response to an increase in the expected future exchange rate, E_{t+1}^e

When the expected future exchange rate increases, the relative expected return on domestic assets rises and the demand curve shifts to the right. The equilibrium exchange rate rises from E_1 to E_2.

Recap: factors that change the exchange rate

Summary Table 17.2 outlines all the factors that shift the demand curve for domestic assets and thereby cause the exchange rate to change. Shifts in the demand curve occur when one factor changes, holding everything else constant, including the current exchange rate. Again, the theory of asset demand tells us that changes in wealth, relative risk, relative liquidity, relative expected return on domestic assets are the source of shifts in the demand curve.

Let's review what happens when each of the ten factors in Table 17.2 changes. Remember that to understand which direction the demand curve shifts, consider what happens to the relative expected return on domestic assets when the factor changes. If the relative expected return rises, holding the current exchange rate constant, the demand curve shifts to the right. If the relative expected return falls, the demand curve shifts to the left.

1 When the foreign wealth rises, foreign investors will demand more domestic assets at each exchange rate and so the quantity demanded increases. The demand curve therefore shifts to the right, and the equilibrium exchange rate rises, as is shown in the first row of Table 17.2.

2 When the risk of domestic assets increases relative to the risk of foreign assets, the quantity demanded of domestic assets falls, the demand curve shifts to the left, and the exchange rate declines, as in the second row of Table 17.2.

3 When the liquidity of domestic assets increases relative to the liquidity of foreign assets, the demand curve for domestic assets shifts to the right, and the equilibrium exchange rate rises, as is shown in the third row of Table 17.2.

4 When the interest rates on domestic assets i^D rise, the expected return on domestic assets rises at each exchange rate and so the quantity demanded increases. The demand curve therefore shifts to the right, and the equilibrium exchange rate rises, as is shown in the fourth row of Table 17.2.

5 When the foreign interest rate i^F rises, the return on foreign assets rises, so the relative expected return on domestic assets falls. The quantity demanded of domestic assets then falls, the demand curve shifts to the left, and the exchange rate declines, as in the fifth row of Table 17.2.

6 When the expected price level is higher, our analysis of the long-run determinants of the exchange rate indicates that the value of the dollar will fall in the future. The expected return on domestic assets thus falls, the quantity demanded declines, the demand curve shifts to the left, and the exchange rate falls, as in the sixth row of Table 17.2.

7 With higher expected trade barriers, the value of the domestic currency is higher in the long run and the expected return on domestic assets is higher. The quantity demanded of domestic assets thus rises, the demand curve shifts to the right, and the exchange rate rises, as in the seventh row of Table 17.2.

8 When expected import demand rises, we expect the exchange rate to depreciate in the long run, so the expected return on domestic assets falls. The quantity demanded of domestic assets at each value of the current exchange rate therefore falls, the demand curve shifts to the left, and the exchange rate declines, as in the eighth row of Table 17.2.

9 When expected export demand rises, the opposite occurs because the exchange rate is expected to appreciate in the long run. The expected return on domestic assets rises, the demand curve shifts to the right, and the exchange rate rises, as in the ninth row of Table 17.2.

10 With higher expected domestic productivity, the exchange rate is expected to appreciate in the long run, so the expected return on domestic assets rises. The quantity demanded at each exchange rate therefore rises, the demand curve shifts to the right, and the exchange rate rises, as in the tenth row of Table 17.2.

SUMMARY TABLE 17.2

Factors that shift the demand curve for domestic assets and affect the exchange rate

Factor	Change in factor	Change in quantity demanded of domestic assets at each exchange rate	Response of exchange rate*, E	
Foreign wealth	↑	↑	↑	
Risk[†]	↑	↓	↓	
Liquidity[†]	↑	↑	↑	
Domestic interest rate, i^D	↑	↑	↑	
Foreign interest rate, i^F	↑	↓	↓	
Expected domestic price level[†]	↑	↓	↓	
Expected trade barriers[†]	↑	↑	↑	
Expected import demand	↑	↓	↓	
Expected export demand	↑	↑	↑	
Expected productivity[†]	↑	↑	↑	

*Units of foreign currency per unit of domestic currency: ↑ indicates domestic currency appreciation; ↓, depreciation.

[†]Relative to other countries.

Note: Only increases (↑) in the factors are shown; the effects of decreases in the variables on the exchange rate are the opposite of those indicated in the 'Response' column.

APPLICATION | Changes in the equilibrium exchange rate: two examples

Our analysis has revealed the factors that affect the value of the equilibrium exchange rate. Now we use this analysis to take a closer look at the response of the exchange rate to changes in interest rates and money growth.

Changes in interest rates

Changes in domestic interest rates i^D are often cited as a major factor affecting exchange rates. But is the view always correct?

Not necessarily, because to analyse the effects of interest rate changes, we must carefully distinguish the sources of the changes. The Fisher equation (Chapter 4) states that a nominal interest rate such as i^D equals the *real* interest rate plus expected inflation: $i = i_r + \pi^e$. The Fisher equation thus indicates that the interest rate i^D can change for two reasons: either the real interest rate i_r changes or the expected inflation rate π^e changes. The effect on the exchange rate is quite different, depending on which of these two factors is the source of the change in the nominal interest rate.

Suppose that the domestic real interest rate increases so that the nominal interest rate i^D rises while expected inflation remains unchanged. In this case, it is reasonable to assume that the expected appreciation of the domestic currency will be unchanged because expected inflation is unchanged. In this case, the increase in i^D increases the relative expected return on domestic assets, increases the quantity of domestic assets demanded at each level of the exchange rate, and shifts the demand curve to the right. We end up with the situation depicted in Figure 17.4, which analyses an increase in i^D, holding everything else constant. Our model of the foreign exchange market produces the following result: **when domestic real interest rates rise, the domestic currency appreciates**.

When the nominal interest rate rises because of an increase in expected inflation, we get a different result from the one shown in Figure 17.4. The rise in expected domestic inflation leads to a decline in the expected appreciation of the domestic currency, which is typically thought to be larger than the increase in the domestic interest rate i^D.[3] As a result, at any given exchange rate, the relative expected return on domestic assets falls, the demand curve shifts to the left, and the exchange rate falls from E_1 to E_2 as shown in Figure 17.7. Our analysis leads to this conclusion: **when domestic interest rates rise due to an expected increase in inflation, the domestic currency depreciates.**

FIGURE 17.7

Effect of a rise in the domestic interest rate as a result of an increase in expected inflation

Because a rise in domestic expected inflation leads to a decline in expected appreciation of the domestic currency that is larger than the increase in the domestic interest rate, the relative expected return on domestic assets falls. The demand curve shifts to the left, and the equilibrium exchange rate falls from E_1 to E_2.

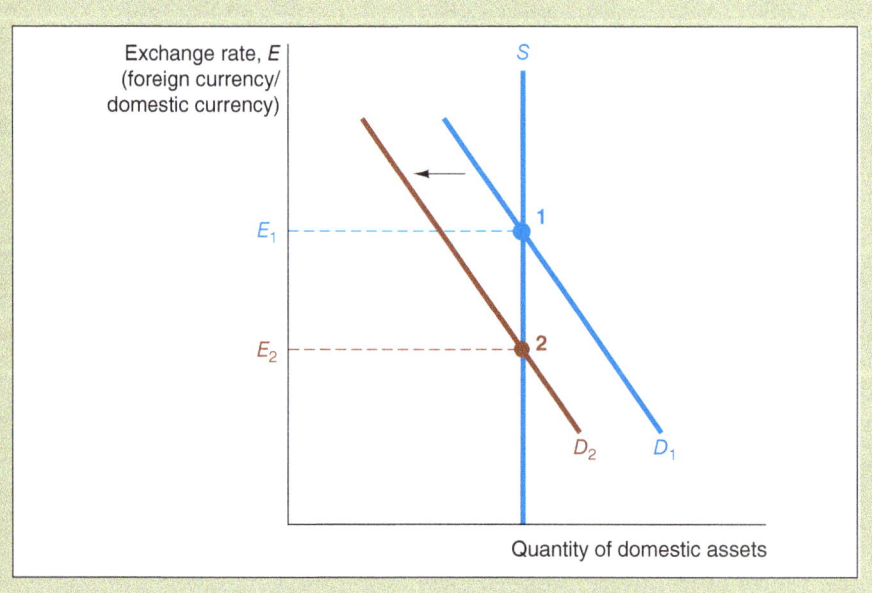

Because this conclusion is completely different from the one reached when the rise in the domestic interest rate is associated with a higher real interest rate, we must always distinguish between *real* and *nominal* measures when analysing the effects of interest rates on exchange rates.

Changes in the money supply

Suppose that the central bank decides to increase the level of the money supply in an attempt to reduce unemployment, which it believes to be excessive. The higher money supply will lead to a higher domestic price level in the long run (as we will see in Chapter 22) and hence to a lower expected future exchange rate. The resulting decline in the expected appreciation of the domestic currency lowers the quantity of domestic assets demanded at each level of the exchange rate and shifts the demand curve to the left. In addition, the higher money supply will lead to a higher real money supply M/P, because the price level does not immediately increase in the short run. As suggested in Chapter 5, the resulting rise in the real money supply causes the domestic interest rate to fall, which also lowers the relative expected return on domestic assets, providing a further reason why the demand curve shifts to the left. As we can see in Figure 17.8, the demand curve shifts to D_2, and the exchange rate declines from E_1 to E_2. The conclusion: **a higher domestic money supply causes the domestic currency to depreciate**.

Exchange rate overshooting

Our analysis of the effect of an increase in the money supply on the exchange rate is not yet over – we still need to look at what happens to the exchange rate in the long run. A basic proposition in monetary theory, called **monetary neutrality**, states that in the long run, a one-time percentage rise in the money supply is matched by the same one-time percentage rise in the price level, leaving unchanged the real money supply and all other economic variables such as interest rates. An intuitive way to understand this proposition is to think of what would happen if the ECB announced overnight that an old euro would now be worth 100 new euros. The money supply in new euros would be 100 times its old value and the price level would also be 100 times higher, but nothing in the economy would really have changed: real and nominal interest rates and the real money supply would remain the same. Monetary neutrality tells us that

---

Effect of a rise in the money supply

A rise in the money supply leads to a higher domestic price level, which in turn leads to a lower expected future exchange rate. In addition, the higher money supply leads to a decline in domestic interest rates. The decline in both the expected appreciation of the domestic currency and the domestic interest rate lowers the relative expected return on domestic assets, shifting the demand curve leftward from D_1 to D_2. In the short run, the equilibrium exchange rate falls from E_1 to E_2. In the long run, however, the interest rate rises back up again to its initial level and the demand curve shifts rightward to D_3. The exchange rate rises from E_2 to E_3 in the long run.

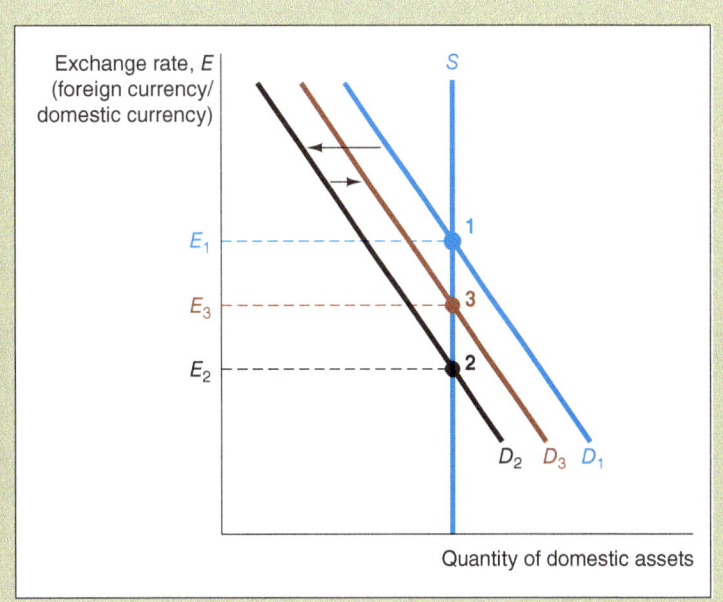

in the long run, the rise in the money supply would not lead to a change in the domestic interest rate so it would rise back to its old level. The demand curve would shift to the right to D_3, but not all the way back to D_1, because the price level will still be higher in the long run. As we can see in Figure 17.8, this means that the exchange rate would rise from E_2 to E_3 in the long run.

The phenomenon we have described here in which the exchange rate falls by more in the short run than it does in the long run when the money supply increases is called **exchange rate overshooting**. It is important because, as we will see in the following application, it can help explain why exchange rates exhibit so much volatility.

Another way of thinking about why exchange rate overshooting occurs is to recognize that when the domestic interest rate falls in the short run, equilibrium in the foreign exchange market means that the expected return on foreign deposits must be lower. With the foreign interest rate given, this lower expected return on foreign deposits means that there must be an expected appreciation of the domestic currency for the expected return on foreign deposits to decline when the domestic interest rate falls. This can occur only if the current exchange rate falls below its long-run value. ■

APPLICATION | Why do some nations peg their currencies?

So far, we have been discussing the exchange rates for currencies that are freely floating and tradable on foreign exchange markets. Till 1971, all currencies in the world were pegged against the US dollar, which was valued at US $35 per ounce of gold. Since the dollar was unable to maintain this price towards gold, all major economies followed a floating rate regime.

Yet, a number of central banks in developing nations still peg their currencies against either the US dollar, or a basket of major currencies including the euro, the Japanese yen, the pound sterling and the Swiss franc to create a stable environment for foreign investment. With a pegged or fixed currency, investors will not have to worry about daily fluctuations and foreign direct investment will pour into the economy, owing to greater confidence in the stability of the pegged currency.

However, since a peg is difficult to maintain in the long run, these fixed systems have resulted in financial panics in the past, since the central banks generally maintain an overvalued currency. Fearing that the central banks may no longer be able to meet the demands to convert the local currency into the foreign currency at the pegged rate, savers and investors may panic and rush to convert their local currency into foreign currency. A scenario such as this resulted in the financial crisis of Mexico in 1994, where the Bank of Mexico was forced to devalue the peso by 30%. Similarly, the 1997 Thai financial crisis resulted in the local currency, the bhat, losing 50% of its value as the Thai central bank floated its currency.

In order to avoid these negative effects, some central banks may choose to have a 'floating', or 'crawling' peg, whereby they re-evaluate and adjust the value of the peg periodically. Among the countries that use this method are the Arab oil-rich nations, whose GDP is highly dependent on oil. This is to reduce shocks to the economy, especially given the immense volatility of oil prices. ■

APPLICATION | The global financial crisis and the euro

As the subprime financial crisis erupted in the US in August 2007, the euro began an accelerated rise in value, increasing by almost 16% against the dollar to reach its highest level in July 2008. How can a subprime problem born in the US have such substantial effects on the exchange rate of the euro? In order to answer this question, we have to examine the effect of interest rates on the foreign exchange market, first in 2007 and again in 2008.

During 2007, the negative effects of the subprime crisis on US economic activity had started to become visible and were mostly confined to the United States. From September 2007 to December 2008, the Fed responded by substantially lowering the discount rate, as well as the target range for the federal funds rate, between 0% and 0.25%. Yet, the ECB did not lower interest rates. Following a policy of inflation targeting, the main concern of the ECB before the spread of the crisis was to neutralize the effect of the high oil prices that reached a peak of US $147 per barrel in July 2008. With this interest rate differential between the US dollar and the euro, the relative expected return on euro assets thus increased, shifting the demand curve for euro assets to the right, as shown in Figure 17.4, leading to a rise in the equilibrium exchange rate. Our analysis of the foreign exchange market thus explains why the early phase of the subprime crisis led to a rise in the value of the euro against the dollar in 2007 (see Figure 17.9).

Let us now turn to the fall in the value of the euro and the corresponding rise in the value of the dollar and the subsequent large fluctuations starting in August 2008 and ending in December 2008. By then the spillover effects of the subprime crisis in the US began to spread violently throughout the world, hitting European banks most harshly. In reaction, the ECB had no option but to gradually cut its interest rates by 325 basis points from October 2008 to reach the lowest ever rate of 1% in May 2009. Most other central banks round the world followed similar policies as measures against economic contractionary pressures. With interest rates for the euro and the dollar converging, the former being 1% and the latter around 0.25%, what do you expect to happen to the relative expected returns for both the euro and the dollar? Your answer may be that for most people, interest rates at 0.25% are no different from zero interest rates. But there is another factor at force. When the global financial crisis reached a particularly virulent stage in September and November 2008, both Americans and Europeans then wanted to put their money in the safest assets possible: US Treasury securities. The resulting increase in the demand for dollar assets provided a strong reason for the demand curve for euro assets to shift to the left, thereby helping to produce a sharp depreciation of the euro against the dollar. This 'fight to quality' factor has also strongly contributed to the weakening of the euro during different phases of the euro debt crisis that erupted in May 2010. This was especially the case when the markets were particularly nervous about the possibility of Greece going into default or even exiting the euro. ■

| APPLICATION | Reading the *Financial Times*: the 'Lex' column |

Now after accumulating enough theoretical knowledge about how foreign exchange markets operate, let us turn to other factors that may have an influence on foreign exchange rates. It is best that we test our knowledge by following some releases in the financial press. Let us take the example of the Lex column, which appears on a daily basis in the *Financial Times*

FIGURE 17.9

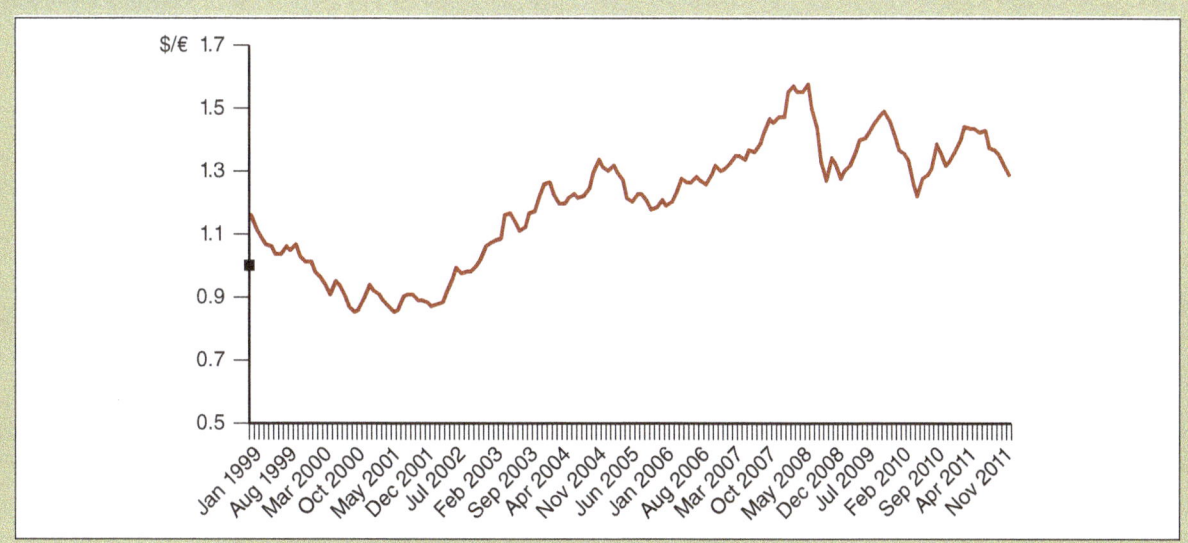

Euro nominal exchange rate, January 1999 to January 2012

Source: http://sdw.ecb.europa.eu/browse.do?node=2018794. Information may be obtained free of charge through the EGB's website.

and discusses global developments relating to a vast range of foreign exchange, financial and business issues.

The column entitled 'Sterling', in the 'Following the financial news' box , discusses yet another factor that may affect the foreign exchange rates relating to the current financial crisis. In order to emerge out of the current crisis, many nations including the US and the UK increased their foreign borrowings, in order to finance their expansionary fiscal expenditure programme needed for economic recovery. In response, the credit rating firm, Standard & Poor's, downgraded the debt outlook of the UK on 22 May 2009, due to its mounting debt/ GDP ratio. The immediate effect was a slide in the value of the pound, soon to be followed by its rebound by the end of the same trading day. Normally, you would expect the demand for assets denominated in sterling to decline and the demand for other currencies (including the US dollar) to rise. This would have resulted in a leftward shift in the demand curve for the pound. But this did not happen, since the US, France, Germany, Italy and a number of

FOLLOWING THE FINANCIAL NEWS

The 'Lex' column

The Lex column is a daily feature that appears on the back page of the first section of the *Financial Times* (FT). The Lex is the agenda-setting column of the FT and it comprises a wide set of analyses and opinions covering current business, economic and financial topics, usually from a global perspective. The following is an example of a contemporary topic relating to the effect of the global financial crisis on the credit rating of the UK and other indebted countries.

THE LEX COLUMN

Sterling

Well, it was nice while it lasted. The pound has had a good run this year. Since December's trough, sterling's trade-weighted exchange rate has risen 9 per cent – a big move and one due a correction, or at least a pause. A review of Britain's credit rating provided the excuse yesterday. Sterling tumbled and gilts fell after Standard & Poor's cut the UK's debt outlook to negative, warning the country's ratio of debt to gross domestic product could soon double to 100 per cent and then stay there.

There is, though, little new about such calculations. Sure, new data showed that government borrowing almost quintupled to £8.5bn in April compared with the same month the year before while tax receipts fell almost 10 per cent. But a high debt\GDP ratio need not be disastrous, as economic historians often point out. After all, British national debt was that high after the second world war, even if it was a period of austerity for those who lived through it. Sugar rationing was lifted only in 1953 and, to save foreign exchange, bananas were a rarity.

What does matter is how long UK debt continues to rise. For now, gilt spreads over German Bunds remain tighter than for any other big European economy. But at some point markets will demand compensation for the growing credit risk. The government to be formed after elections that are due at the latest in the middle of next year, therefore, needs to slow growth in the national debt and then reverse it. This will be a painful and unpopular task, as squabbling over the public purse always is. It is probably no accident that the governments of other European countries that have debt to GDP ratios of about 100 per cent, such as Italy, Greece and Belgium, are characterised by fractious, fragile and fleeting coalitions.

Reprinted by permission of the Financial Times FT Lex column, 21 May 2009.

other nations equally suffered from high debt/GDP ratios. If anything, this downgrading of the creditworthiness of the UK rang an alarm bell for the dire need for the UK to reduce its public deficit more rapidly once the economy embarks on its recovery path. Otherwise, the value of sterling will take a downward slide, especially if other nations prove more successful in settling their foreign debt. ■

Summary

1 Foreign exchange rates (the price of one country's currency in terms of another's) are important because they affect the price of domestically produced goods sold abroad and the cost of foreign goods bought domestically.

2 The theory of purchasing power parity suggests that long-run changes in the exchange rate between two countries' currencies are determined by changes in the relative price levels in the two countries. Other factors that affect exchange rates in the long run are tariffs and quotas, import demand, export demand and productivity.

3 In the short run, exchange rates are determined by changes in the relative expected return on domestic assets, which cause the demand curve to shift. Any

factor that changes the relative expected return on domestic assets will lead to changes in the exchange rate. Such factors include changes in the interest rates on domestic and foreign assets as well as changes in any of the factors that affect the long-run exchange rate and hence the expected future exchange rate. Changes in the money supply lead to exchange rate overshooting, causing the exchange rate to change by more in the short run than in the long run.

4 The asset market approach to exchange rate determination can explain both the volatility of exchange rates and the dynamics of the euro against the dollar since 1999.

Key Terms

QUESTIONS AND PROBLEMS

All questions and problems are available in MyEconLab at **www.myeconlab.com/mishkin**.

1 When the euro appreciates, is an American more likely to drink Californian or French wine?

2 'A country is always worse off when its currency is weak (falls in value).' Is this statement true, false, or uncertain? Explain your answer.

3 In a newspaper, check the exchange rates for the foreign currencies listed in the 'Following the financial

news box' on page 383. Which of these currencies have appreciated and which have depreciated since 9 March 2012?

4 If the US price level rises by 5% relative to the price level in Germany, what does the theory of purchasing power parity predict will happen to the value of the US dollar in terms of the euro?

5 If the demand for a country's exports falls at the same time that tariffs on imports are raised, will the country's currency tend to appreciate or depreciate in the long run?

6 In the mid-to-late 1970s, the yen appreciated relative to the dollar even though Japan's inflation rate was higher than America's. How can this be explained by an improvement in the productivity of Japanese industry relative to American industry?

Using economic analysis to predict the future

Answer the remaining questions by drawing the appropriate exchange market diagrams.

7 The president of the European Central Bank announces that he will reduce inflation with a new anti-inflation programme. If the public believes him, predict what will happen to the trade-weighted Euro exchange rate for the euro.

8 If the Bank of England prints money to reduce unemployment, what will happen to the value of the pound versus other countries in the short run and the long run?

9 If the Indian government unexpectedly announces that it will be imposing higher tariffs on foreign goods one year from now, what will happen to the value of the Indian rupee today?

10 If nominal interest rates in America rise but real interest rates fall, predict what will happen to the US exchange rate.

11 If American car companies make a breakthrough in automotive technology and are able to produce a car that gets 60 miles to the gallon, what will happen to the US exchange rate?

12 If Mexicans go on a spending spree and buy twice as much French perfume, Japanese TVs, British sweaters, Swiss watches and Italian wine, what will happen to the value of the Mexican peso?

13 If expected inflation drops in Europe, leading to a fall in interest rates, predict what will happen to the exchange rate for the US dollar.

14 If the European Central Bank decides to contract the money supply to fight inflation, what will happen to the value of the euro versus the US dollar?

15 If there is a strike in France, making it harder to buy French goods, what will happen to the value of the euro?

WEB EXERCISES

1 Go to **http://markets.ft.com/ft/markets/currencies .asp** and look at the most recent currency cross rates. How do they compare with the ones shown in Figure 17.1?

2 Go to **www.ecb.int/stats/exchange/eurofxref/html /index.en.htm**l and look at the latest developments of the dollar/euro exchange rate. Do you see any trend that can be associated to the factors we discussed in this chapter? Can you explain the recent dynamics of the dollar/euro exchange rate on the basis of the non-standard measures adopted by the ECB and the Fed? See Chapter 15 for a discussion of the unconventional tools used by the ECB and the Fed.

3 The Federal Reserve maintains a website that lists the exchange rates between the US dollar and many other currencies. Go to the historical data from 1999 and later and find the euro **www.newyorkfed.org/markets/fxrates/ historical/home.cfm.**

(a) What has the percentage change in the euro/dollar exchange rate been between introduction and now?

(b) What has been the annual percentage change in the euro/dollar exchange rate for each year since the euro's introduction?

4 International travellers and business people frequently need to accurately convert from one currency to another. It is often easy to find the rate needed to convert the US dollar into another currency. It can be more difficult to find exchange rates between two non-US currencies. Go to **www.xe.com/ucc/full/.** This site lets you convert from any currency into any other currency. How many Lithuanian litas can you currently buy with one Chilean peso?

Notes

1 A country might be so small that a change in productivity or the preferences for domestic or foreign goods would have no effect on prices of these goods relative to foreign goods. In this case, changes in productivity or changes in preferences for domestic or foreign goods affect the country's income but will not necessarily affect the value of the currency. In our analysis, we are assuming that these factors can affect relative prices and consequently the exchange rate.

2 For a further description of the modern asset market approach to exchange rate determination that we use here,

see Paul Krugman and Maurice Obstfeld, *International Economics*, 8th ed. (Boston: Pearson Addison Wesley, 2009).

3 This conclusion is standard in asset market models of exchange rate determination; see Rudiger Dornbusch, 'Expectations and exchange rate dynamics', *Journal of Political Economy* 84 (1976): 1061–76. It is also consistent with empirical evidence that suggests that nominal interest rates do not rise one-for-one with increases in expected inflation. See Frederic S. Mishkin, 'The real interest rate: an empirical investigation', *Carnegie-Rochester Conference Series on Public Policy* 15 (1981): 151–200; and Lawrence Summers, 'The nonadjustment of nominal interest rates: a study of the Fisher effect', in *Macroeconomics, Prices and Quantities,* ed. James Tobin (Washington, DC: Brookings Institution, 1983), pp. 201–40.

Useful websites

http://markets.ft.com/ft/markets/currencies.asp Link to the website of the *Financial Times* where the latest currency cross rates are shown.

www.ecb.int/stats/exchange/eurofxref/html/index.en.html Go to this website to get the charts of the bilateral exchange rate between the euro and a number of foreign currencies since 1999.

http://www.fxstreet.com/ FX Street is a comprehensive site for Forex data, news. It includes live currency rates.

http://www.bankofengland.co.uk/statistics/index.htm Link to the Bank of England with bilateral and effective exchange rate since 1975.

www.newyorkfed.org/markets/foreignex.html Get detailed information about the foreign exchange market in the United States.

http://quotes.ino.com/chart/ Go to this website and click on 'Foreign Exchange' to get market rates and time charts for the exchange rate of the US dollar to major world currencies.

www.oecd.org/department/0,3355,en_2649_34357_1_1_1_1_1,00.html The purchasing power parities home page includes the PPP programme overview, statistics, research, publications and OECD meetings on PPP.

www.federalreserve.gov/releases/ The Federal Reserve reports current and historical exchange rates for many countries.

http://fx.sauder.ubc.ca The Pacific Exchange Rate Service at the University of British Columbia's Sauder School of Business provides information on how market conditions are affecting exchange rates and allows easy plotting of exchange rate data.

www.bis.org/publ/rpfxf10t.htm Link to the Triennial Central Bank Survey of Foreign Exchange and Derivatives Market Activity in 2010 from the Bank for International Settlements.

http://www.forexrate.co.uk/ Forex Rate has live charts, rates and a number of useful Forex trading tools.

The interest parity condition

All the results in the text can be derived with a concept that is widely used in international finance. The *interest parity condition* shows the relationship between domestic interest rates, foreign interest rates and the expected appreciation of the domestic currency. To derive this condition, we examine how expected returns on domestic and foreign assets are compared.

Comparing expected returns on domestic and foreign assets

As in the chapter we treat Germany as the domestic country, so domestic assets are denominated in euros. For simplicity, we use dollars to stand for any foreign country's currency, so foreign assets are denominated in dollars. To illustrate further, suppose that domestic assets pay an interest rate of i^D and do not have any possible capital gains, so that they have an expected return payable in euros of i^D. Similarly, foreign assets have an interest rate of i^F and an expected return payable in the foreign currency, dollars, of i^F. To compare the expected returns on domestic assets and foreign assets, investors must convert the returns into the currency unit they use.

First let us examine how Bill the Foreigner compares the returns on euro assets and foreign assets denominated in his currency, the dollar. When he considers the expected return on euro assets in terms of dollars, he recognizes that it does not equal i^D; instead, the expected return must be adjusted for any expected appreciation or depreciation of the euro. If Bill expects the euro to appreciate by 3%, for example, the expected return on euro assets in terms of dollars would be 3% higher than i^D because the euro is expected to become worth 3% more in terms of dollars. Thus, if the interest rate on euro assets is 4%, with an expected 3% appreciation of the euro, the expected return on euro assets in terms of dollars is 7%: the 4% interest rate plus the 3% expected appreciation of the euro. Conversely, if the euro were expected to depreciate by 3% over the year, the expected return on euro assets in terms of dollars would be only 1%: the 4% interest rate minus the 3% expected depreciation of the euro.

Writing the current exchange rate (the spot exchange rate) as E_t and the expected exchange rate for the next period as E^e_{t+1}, the expected rate of appreciation of the domestic currency is $(E^e_{t+1} - E_t)/E_t$. Our reasoning indicates that the expected return on domestic (euro) assets R^D in terms of foreign (dollar) currency can be written as the sum of the interest rate on domestic assets plus the expected appreciation of the domestic currency.[4]

$$R^D \text{ in terms of dollars } = i^D + \frac{E^e_{t+1} - E_t}{E_t}$$

However, Bill's expected return on foreign assets R^F in terms of dollars is just i^F. Thus, in terms of dollars, the relative expected return on euro assets (that is, the difference between the expected return on euro assets and dollar assets) is calculated by subtracting i^F from the expression above to yield

$$\text{relative } R^D = i^D - i^F + \frac{E^e_{t+1} - E_t}{E_t} \tag{17.1}$$

As the relative expected return on domestic assets increases, foreigners will want to hold more domestic assets and fewer foreign assets.

Next let us look at the decision to hold euro assets versus dollar assets from the point of view of Mark the German. Following the same reasoning we used to evaluate the decision for Bill, we know that the expected return on foreign assets R^F in terms of euros is the interest rate on foreign assets i^F plus the expected appreciation of the foreign currency, equal to minus the expected appreciation of the euro, $(E^e_{t+1} - E_t)/E_t$:

$$R^F \text{ in terms of euros } = i^F - \frac{E^e_{t+1} - E_t}{E_t}$$

If the interest rate on dollar assets is 5%, for example, and the euro is expected to appreciate by 3%, then the expected return on dollar assets in terms of euros is 2%. Mark earns the 5% interest rate, but he expects to lose 3% because he expects the dollar to be worth 3% less in terms of euros as a result of the euro's appreciation.

Mark's expected return on the euro assets R^D in terms of euros is just i^D. Hence, in terms of euros, the relative expected return on euro assets is calculated by subtracting the expression just given from i^D to obtain

$$\text{relative } R^D = i^D - \left(i^F - \frac{E^e_{t+1} - E_t}{E_t} \right) = i^D - i^F + \frac{E^e_{t+1} - E_t}{E_t}$$

This equation is the same as Equation 17.1 describing Bill's relative expected return on euro assets (calculated in terms of dollars). The key point here is that the relative expected return on euro assets is the same – whether it is calculated by Bill in terms of dollars or by Mark in terms of euros. Thus, as the relative expected return on euro assets increases, both foreigners and domestic residents respond in exactly the same way – both will want to hold more domestic assets and fewer foreign assets.

Interest parity condition

We currently live in a world in which there is **capital mobility**: foreigners can easily purchase domestic assets, and domestic residents can easily purchase foreign assets. If there are few impediments to capital mobility and we are looking at assets that have similar risk and liquidity – say, foreign and domestic bank deposits – then it is reasonable to assume that the assets are perfect substitutes (that is, equally desirable). When capital is mobile and when assets are perfect substitutes, if the expected return on domestic assets is above that on foreign assets, both foreign and domestic residents will want to hold only domestic assets and will be unwilling to hold foreign assets. Conversely, if the expected return on foreign assets is higher than on domestic assets, both foreign and domestic residents will not want to hold any domestic assets and will want to hold only foreign assets. For existing supplies of both domestic assets and foreign assets to be held, it must therefore be true that there is no difference in their expected returns; that is, the relative expected return in Equation 17.1 must equal zero. This condition can be rewritten as

$$i^D = i^F - \frac{E^e_{t+1} - E_t}{E_t} \tag{17.2}$$

This equation, which is called the **interest parity condition**, states that the domestic interest rate equals the foreign interest rate minus the expected appreciation of the domestic currency. Equivalently, this condition can be stated in a more intuitive way: the domestic interest rate equals the foreign interest rate plus the expected appreciation of the foreign currency. If the domestic interest rate is higher than the foreign interest rate, there is a positive expected appreciation of the foreign currency, which compensates for the lower foreign interest rate. A domestic interest rate of 5% versus a foreign interest rate of 3% means that the expected appreciation of the foreign currency must be 2% (or, equivalently, that the expected depreciation of the domestic currency must be 2%).

There are several ways to look at the interest parity condition. First, recognize that interest parity means simply that the expected returns are the same on both domestic assets and foreign assets. To see this, note that the left side of the interest parity condition (Equation 17.2) is the expected return on domestic assets, while the right side is the expected return on foreign assets, both calculated in terms of domestic currency. Given our assumption that domestic and foreign assets are perfect substitutes (equally desirable), the interest parity condition is an equilibrium condition for the foreign exchange market. Only when the exchange rate is such that expected returns on domestic and foreign assets are equal – that is, when interest parity holds – will investors be willing to hold both domestic and foreign assets.

With some algebraic manipulation, we can rewrite the interest parity condition in Equation 17.2 as

$$E_t = \frac{E_{t+1}^e}{i^F - i^D + 1}$$

This equation produces exactly the same results that we find in the supply and demand analysis in the text. If i^D rises, the denominator falls and so E_t rises. If i^F rises, the denominator rises and so E_t falls. If E_{t+1}^e rises, the numerator rises and so E_t rises.

Notes

4 This expression is actually an approximation of the expected return in terms of foreign currency, which can be more precisely calculated by thinking how a foreigner invests in domestic assets. Suppose that Bill decides to put one dollar into euro assets. First he buys $1/E_t$ of euros assets (recall that E_t, the exchange rate between euro and dollar assets, is quoted in dollars per euro), and at the end of the period he is paid $(1 + i^D)(1/E_t)$ in euros. To convert this amount into the number of dollars he expects to receive at the end of the period, he multiplies this quantity by E_{t+1}^e. Bill's expected return on his initial investment of one dollar can thus be written as $(1 + i^D)(E_{t+1}^e/E_t)$ minus his initial investment of one dollar: $(1 + i^D)\left(\frac{E_{t+1}^e}{E_t}\right) - 1$ This expression can be

rewritten as $i^D\left(\frac{E_{t+1}^e}{E_t}\right) + \frac{E_{t+1}^e - E_t}{E_t}$ which is approximately equal to the expression in the text because, E_{t+1}^e/E_t is typically close to 1. To see this, consider the example in the text in which $i^D = 0.04$; $(E_{t+1}^e - E_t)/E_t = 0.03$, so $E_{t+1}^e/E_t = 1.03$. Then Bill's expected return on euro assets is $(0.04 \times 1.03) + 0.03 = 0.0712 = 7.12\%$, rather than the 7% reported in the text.

CHAPTER 18

The international financial system

PREVIEW   As the economies of the world grow more interdependent, a country's monetary policy can no longer be conducted without taking international considerations into account. In this chapter, we examine how international financial transactions and the structure of the international financial system affect monetary policy. We also examine the evolution of the international financial system during the past half-century and consider where it may be heading in the future.

Intervention in the foreign exchange market

In Chapter 17, we analysed the foreign exchange market as if it were a completely free market that responds to all market pressures. Like many other markets, however, the foreign exchange market is not free of government intervention; central banks regularly engage in international financial transactions called **foreign exchange interventions** to influence exchange rates. In our current international environment, exchange rates fluctuate from day to day, but central banks attempt to influence their countries' exchange rates by buying and selling currencies. We can use the exchange rate analysis we developed in Chapter 17 to explain the impact of central bank intervention on the foreign exchange market.

Foreign exchange intervention and the money supply

The first step in understanding how central bank intervention in the foreign exchange market affects exchange rates is to see the impact on the monetary base from a central bank sale in the foreign exchange market of some of its holdings of assets denominated in a foreign currency (called **international reserves**). Suppose that the central bank decides to sell €1 million of its foreign assets in exchange for €1 million of domestic currency. The central bank's purchase of foreign assets has two effects. First, it reduces the central bank's holding of international reserves by €1 million. Second, because the central bank's purchase of currency removes it from the hands of the public, currency in circulation falls by €1 million. We can see this in the following T-account for the central bank:

Central bank			
Assets		**Liabilities**	
Foreign assets (international reserves)	−€1 million	Currency in circulation	−€1 million

Because the monetary base is made up of currency in circulation plus reserves, this decline in currency implies that the monetary base has fallen by €1 million.

If instead of paying for the foreign assets sold by the central bank with currency, the persons buying the foreign assets pay for them by cheques written on accounts at domestic banks, then the central bank deducts the €1 million from the reserve deposits it holds for these banks. The result is that deposits with the central bank (reserves) decline by €1 million, as shown in the following T-account:

Central bank			
Assets		**Liabilities**	
Foreign assets (international reserves)	− €1 million	Deposits with the central bank (reserves)	− €1 million

In this case, the outcome of the central bank's sale of foreign assets and the purchase of domestic deposits is a €1 million decline in reserves and, as before, a €1 million decline in the monetary base because reserves are also a component of the monetary base.

We now see that the outcome for the monetary base is exactly the same when a central bank sells foreign assets to purchase domestic bank deposits or domestic currency. This is why when we say that a central bank has purchased its domestic currency, we do not have to distinguish whether it actually purchased currency or bank deposits denominated in the domestic currency. We have thus reached an important conclusion: *a central bank's purchase of domestic currency and corresponding sale of foreign assets in the foreign exchange market leads to an equal decline in its international reserves and the monetary base*.

We could have reached the same conclusion by a more direct route. A central bank sale of a foreign asset is no different from an open market sale of a government bond. We learned in our exploration of the money supply process that an open market sale leads to an equal decline in the monetary base; therefore, a sale of foreign assets also leads to an equal decline in the monetary base. By similar reasoning, a central bank purchase of foreign assets paid for by selling domestic currency, like an open market purchase, leads to an equal rise in the monetary base. Thus we reach the following conclusion: *a central bank's sale of domestic currency to purchase foreign assets in the foreign exchange market results in an equal rise in its international reserves and the monetary base*.

The intervention we have just described, in which a central bank allows the purchase or sale of domestic currency to have an effect on the monetary base, is called an **unsterilized foreign exchange intervention**. But what if the central bank does not want the purchase or sale of domestic currency to affect the monetary base? All it has to do is to counter the effect of the foreign exchange intervention by conducting an offsetting open market operation in the government bond market. For example, in the case of a €1 million purchase of foreign currency by the central bank and a corresponding €1 million sale of foreign assets, which, as we have seen, would decrease the monetary base by €1 million, the central bank can conduct an open market purchase of €1 million of government bonds, which would increase the monetary base by €1 million. The resulting T-account for the foreign exchange intervention and the offsetting open market operation leaves the monetary base unchanged:

Central bank			
Assets		**Liabilities**	
Foreign assets (international reserves)	− €1 million	Monetary base	0
Government bonds	+ €1 million		

A foreign exchange intervention with an offsetting open market operation that leaves the monetary base unchanged is called a **sterilized foreign exchange intervention**.

Now that we understand that there are two types of foreign exchange interventions – unsterilized and sterilized – let's look at how each affects the exchange rate.

Unsterilized intervention

Your intuition might lead you to suspect that if a central bank wants to lower the value of the domestic currency, it should sell its currency in the foreign exchange market and purchase foreign assets. Indeed, this intuition is correct for the case of an unsterilized intervention.

Recall that in an unsterilized intervention, if the central bank decides to sell domestic currency so that it can buy foreign assets in the foreign exchange market, this works just like an open market purchase of bonds to increase the monetary base. Hence the sale of domestic currency leads to an increase in the money supply, and we find ourselves analysing a similar situation to that described in Figure 17.8 which is reproduced here as Figure 18.1.[1] The higher money supply leads to a higher domestic price level in the long run and so to a lower expected future exchange rate. The resulting decline in the expected appreciation of the domestic currency lowers the relative expected return on domestic assets and shifts the demand curve to the left. In addition, the increase in the money supply will lead to a higher real money supply in the short run, which causes the interest rate on domestic assets to fall, also lowering the relative expected return on domestic assets, and providing another reason for the demand curve to shift to the left. The demand curve shifts from D_1 to D_2, and the exchange rate falls to E_2. Because the domestic interest rate will rise back to its initial level in the long run, the relative expected return of domestic assets will increase somewhat, sending the demand curve to D_3, but not all the way back to D_1 because the price level will still be higher in the long run. The exchange rate thus rises from E_2 to E_3, which is still below the initial value of E_1. The result is the same one we found in the previous chapter, in which there is exchange rate overshooting – that is, the exchange rate falls by more in the short run than in the long run.

Our analysis leads us to the following conclusion about unsterilized interventions in the foreign exchange market: an unsterilized intervention in which domestic currency is sold to purchase foreign assets leads to a gain in international reserves, an increase in the money supply and a depreciation of the domestic currency.

The reverse result is found for an unsterilized intervention in which domestic currency is purchased by selling foreign assets. The purchase of domestic currency by selling foreign assets (reducing international reserves) works like an open market sale to reduce the monetary base and the money supply. The decrease in the money supply raises the interest rate on domestic assets and lowers the long-run price level, thereby increasing the future expected exchange rate. The resulting increase in the relative expected return on domestic assets means that people will buy more domestic assets, so the demand curve shifts to the right and the exchange rate rises. *An unsterilized intervention in which domestic currency is purchased by selling foreign assets leads to a drop in international reserves, a decrease in the money supply and an appreciation of the domestic currency.*

Sterilized intervention

The key point to remember about a sterilized intervention is that the central bank engages in offsetting open market operations, so that there is no impact on the monetary base and the money supply. In the context of the model of exchange rate determination we have developed here, it is straightforward to show that a sterilized intervention has almost *no effect* on the exchange rate. A sterilized intervention leaves the money supply unchanged and so has no direct way of affecting interest rates or the expected future exchange rate.[2] Because the relative expected return on domestic assets is unaffected, the demand curve would remain at D_1 in Figure 18.1, and the exchange rate would remain unchanged at E_1.

Effect of a sale of domestic currency and a purchase of foreign assets

A sale of domestic currency and the consequent open market purchase of foreign assets increase the monetary base. The resulting rise in the money supply leads to a decline in domestic interest rates and a higher domestic price level in the long run, which produces a lower expected future exchange rate. The decline in both the expected appreciation of the domestic currency and the domestic interest rate lowers the relative expected return on domestic assets, shifting the demand curve leftward from D_1 to D_2. In the short run, the equilibrium exchange rate falls from E_1 to E_2. In the long run, the interest rate rises back to its initial level and the demand curve shifts rightward to D_3. The exchange rate rises from E_2 to E_3 in the long run.

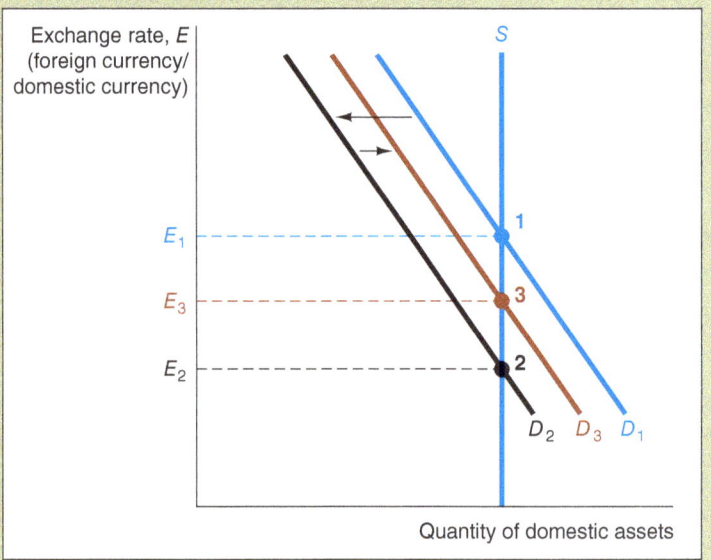

At first it might seem puzzling that a central bank purchase or sale of domestic currency that is sterilized does not lead to a change in the exchange rate. A central bank's sterilized purchase of domestic currency cannot raise the exchange rate, because with no effect on the domestic money supply or interest rates, any resulting rise in the exchange rate would mean that there would be an excess supply of domestic assets. With more people willing to sell domestic assets than to buy them, the exchange rate would have to fall back to its initial equilibrium level, where the demand and supply curves intersect.

Balance of payments

Because international financial transactions such as foreign exchange interventions have considerable effects on monetary policy, it is worth knowing how these transactions are measured. The **balance of payments** is a bookkeeping system for recording all receipts and payments that have a direct bearing on the movement of funds between a nation (private sector and government) and foreign countries. Here we examine the key items in the balance of payments that you often hear about in the media.

The **current account** records international transactions that involve currently produced goods and services. The difference between merchandise exports and imports, the net receipts from trade, is called the **trade balance**. When merchandise imports are greater than exports, we have a trade deficit; if exports are greater than imports, we have a trade surplus. For instance, in 2010, the UK net trade in goods was a deficit of £98.5 billion, whereas the UK net trade in services was a surplus of £58.8 billion. As a result the UK trade balance was a deficit of £39.7 billion.

Additional items included in the current account are the net receipts (cash flows received from abroad minus cash flows sent abroad) from two categories: income and other transfers. Net income is the earnings from foreign financial assets such as bonds and stocks (e.g. investment income) and net earnings of home workers abroad and foreign workers in the home country (e.g. compensation of employees). Net transfers include foreign aid payments and gifts to and from foreigners. For example, in 2010 the UK net income was a surplus of £23.1 billion, because the British received more investment income and compensation of employees from abroad than they paid out. Moreover, because the UK made more unilateral transfers to foreign countries than foreigners made to the UK, net transfers were a deficit of £20.1 billion. The sum of net income and net transfers balances plus the trade balance is the current account balance, which in 2010 showed a deficit of £36.7 billion ($-£39.7 + £23.1 - £20.1 = -£36.7$). The current account can obviously also be in surplus. For instance, in the same year 2010, Germany had a current account surplus of €141.4 billion.

Another important item of the balance of payments is the **capital account**, which records all the net receipts from capital transactions (e.g. purchases and sale of shares, bonds and real estate, bank loans, etc.). In other words, the capital account measures the amount that a country lends to the rest of the world minus the amount that it borrows from it. In 2010 the UK capital account was £30.6 billion, indicating that less capital flowed out of the UK than came in. Another way of saying this is that the UK had a net capital inflow of £30.6 billion.[3] The sum of the current account and the capital account equals the **official reserve transactions balance** (net change in government international reserves), which shows the net change in a country's holding of foreign reserve assets.[4] In 2010, the official reserve balance amounted to $-£6.1$ billion ($-£36.7 + £30.6 = -£6.1$ billion), which means that the UK authorities decreased their foreign official reserves. When economists refer to a surplus or deficit of the balance of payments, they actually mean a surplus or deficit in the official reserve account.

Because the balance of payments must balance, the official reserve transactions balance, which equals the current account plus the capital account, tells us the net amount of international reserves that must move between governments (as represented by their central banks) to finance international transactions: i.e.

$$\text{current account } + \text{ capital account } = \text{ net change in government international reserves}$$

This equation shows us why the current account receives so much attention from economists and the media. The current account balance tells us whether a country (private sector and government combined) is increasing or decreasing its claims on foreign wealth. A surplus indicates that the country is increasing its claims on foreign wealth and thus is increasing its holdings of foreign assets (both good things for domestic residents); a deficit indicates that the country is reducing its holdings of foreign assets and foreign countries are increasing their claims on the domestic country.[5] The large current account deficits of many industrialized countries (in particular the US) in recent years have raised serious concerns that these deficits may have negative consequences for the economy (see box 'Why a large current account deficit worries economists').

Exchange rate regimes in the international financial system

Exchange rate regimes in the international financial system are classified into two basic types: fixed and floating. In a **fixed exchange rate regime**, the value of a currency is pegged relative to the value of one other currency (called the **anchor currency**) so that the exchange rate is fixed in terms of the anchor currency. In a **floating exchange rate regime**, the value of a currency is allowed to fluctuate against all other currencies. When countries intervene in foreign exchange markets in an attempt to influence their exchange rates by buying and selling foreign assets, the regime is referred to as a **managed float regime** (or a **dirty float**).

In examining past exchange rate regimes, we start with the gold standard of the late nineteenth and early twentieth centuries.

Gold standard

Before World War I, the world economy operated under the **gold standard**, a fixed exchange rate regime in which the currency of most countries was convertible directly into gold at fixed rates, so exchange rates between currencies were also fixed. American dollar

GLOBAL
Why a large current account deficit worries economists

Over the recent years, with the exception of Germany which has enjoyed large current account surpluses, many industrialized countries like the UK and in particular the US experienced substantial current account deficits (see Figure 18.2). Massive current account deficits worry economists for several reasons. First, a current account deficit indicates that at current exchange rate values, foreigners' demand for domestic exports is far less than domestic demand for imports. As we saw in the previous chapter, low demand for exports and high demand for imports may lead to a future decline in the value of the domestic currency. Second, the current account deficit means that foreigners' claims on domestic assets are

growing, and these claims will have to be paid back at some point. Domestic citizens are mortgaging their future to foreigners; when the bill comes due, domestic citizens will be poorer. Furthermore, if domestic citizens have a greater preference for domestic assets than foreigners do, the movement of domestic wealth to foreigners could decrease the demand for domestic assets over time, also causing the domestic currency to depreciate. The hope is that the eventual decline in the domestic currency resulting from the large current account deficits will be a gradual one, occurring over a period of several years. If the decline is precipitous, however, it could potentially disrupt financial markets and hurt the domestic economy.

FIGURE 18.2

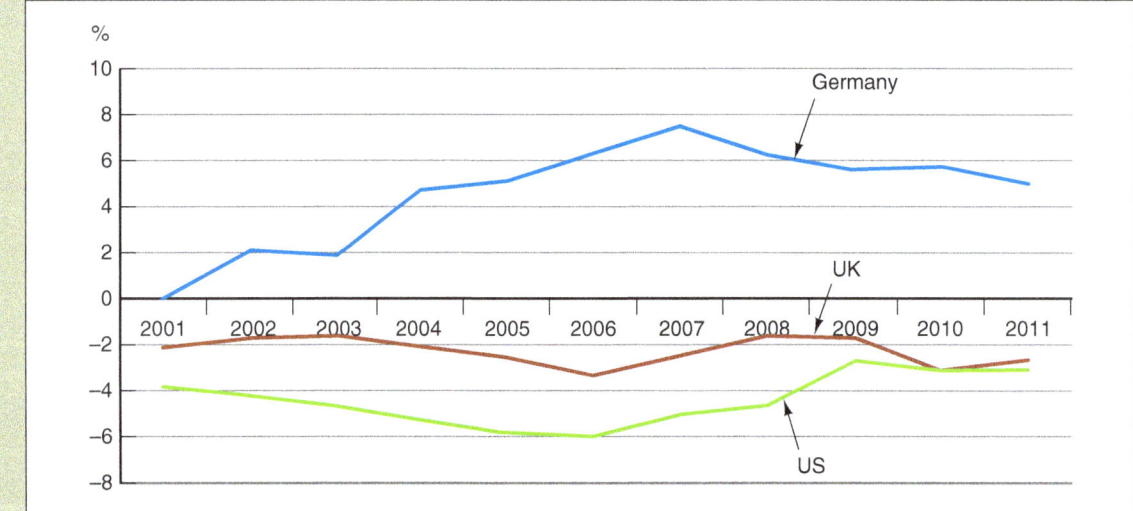

Current account over GDP in Germany, the UK and the US, 2001–11

Source: OECD Economic Outlook, December 2011.

bills, for example, could be turned in to the US Treasury and exchanged for approximately $\frac{1}{20}$ ounce of gold. Likewise, the British Treasury would exchange $\frac{1}{4}$ ounce of gold for £1 sterling. Because an American could convert $20 into 1 ounce of gold, which could be used to buy £4, the exchange rate between the pound and the dollar was effectively fixed at $5 to the pound. The fixed exchange rates under the gold standard had the important advantage of encouraging world trade by eliminating the uncertainty that occurs when exchange rates fluctuate.

As long as countries abided by the rules under the gold standard and kept their currencies backed by and convertible into gold, exchange rates remained fixed. However, adherence to the gold standard meant that a country had no control over its monetary policy, because its money supply was determined by gold flows between countries. Furthermore, monetary policy throughout the world was greatly influenced by the production of gold and gold discoveries. When gold production was low in the 1870s and 1880s, the money supply throughout the world grew slowly and did not keep pace with the growth of the world economy. The result was deflation (falling price levels). Gold discoveries in Alaska and South Africa in the 1890s greatly expanded gold production, causing money supplies to increase rapidly and price levels to rise (inflation) until World War I.

The Bretton Woods system

After World War II, the victors set up a fixed exchange rate system that became known as the **Bretton Woods system**, after the New Hampshire town in which the agreement was negotiated in 1944. The Bretton Woods system remained in effect until 1971.

The Bretton Woods agreement created the **International Monetary Fund (IMF)**, headquartered in Washington, DC, which had 30 original member countries in 1945 and currently has over 180. The IMF was given the task of promoting the growth of world trade by setting rules for the maintenance of fixed exchange rates and by making loans to countries that were experiencing balance-of-payments difficulties. As part of its role of monitoring the compliance of member countries with its rules, the IMF also took on the job of collecting and standardizing international economic data.

The Bretton Woods agreement also set up the International Bank for Reconstruction and Development, commonly referred to as the **World Bank**. Headquartered in Washington, DC, it provides long-term loans to help developing countries build dams, roads and other physical capital that would contribute to their economic development. The funds for these loans are obtained primarily by issuing World Bank bonds, which are sold in the capital markets of the developed countries. In addition, the General Agreement on Tariffs and Trade (GATT), headquartered in Geneva, Switzerland, was set up to monitor rules for the conduct of trade between countries (tariffs and quotas). The GATT has since evolved into the **World Trade Organization (WTO)**.

Because the United States emerged from World War II as the world's largest economic power, with over half of the world's manufacturing capacity and the greater part of the world's gold, the Bretton Woods system of fixed exchange rates was based on the convertibility of US dollars into gold (for foreign governments and central banks only) at $35 per ounce. The fixed exchange rates were to be maintained by intervention in the foreign exchange market by central banks in countries besides the United States that bought and sold dollar assets, which they held as international reserves. The US dollar, which was used by other countries to denominate the assets that they held as international reserves, was called the **reserve currency**. Thus an important feature of the Bretton Woods system was the establishment of the United States as the reserve currency country.

The Bretton Woods system was abandoned in 1971. From 1979 to 1990, however, the European Union instituted among its members its own fixed exchange rate system, the European Monetary System (EMS). In the *exchange rate mechanism (ERM)* in this system, the exchange rate between any pair of currencies of the participating countries was not supposed to fluctuate outside narrow limits, called the 'snake'. In practice, all of the countries in the EMS pegged their currencies to the German mark.

How a fixed exchange rate regime works

Figure 18.3 shows how a fixed exchange rate regime works in practice by using the supply and demand analysis of the foreign exchange market we learned about in the previous chapter. Panel (a) describes a situation in which the domestic currency is fixed relative to an anchor currency at E_{par}, while the demand curve has shifted left to D_1, perhaps because foreign interest rates have risen, thereby lowering the relative expected return of domestic assets. At E_{par}, the exchange rate is now *overvalued*: the demand curve D_1 intersects the supply curve at an exchange rate E_1, which is lower than the fixed (par) value of the

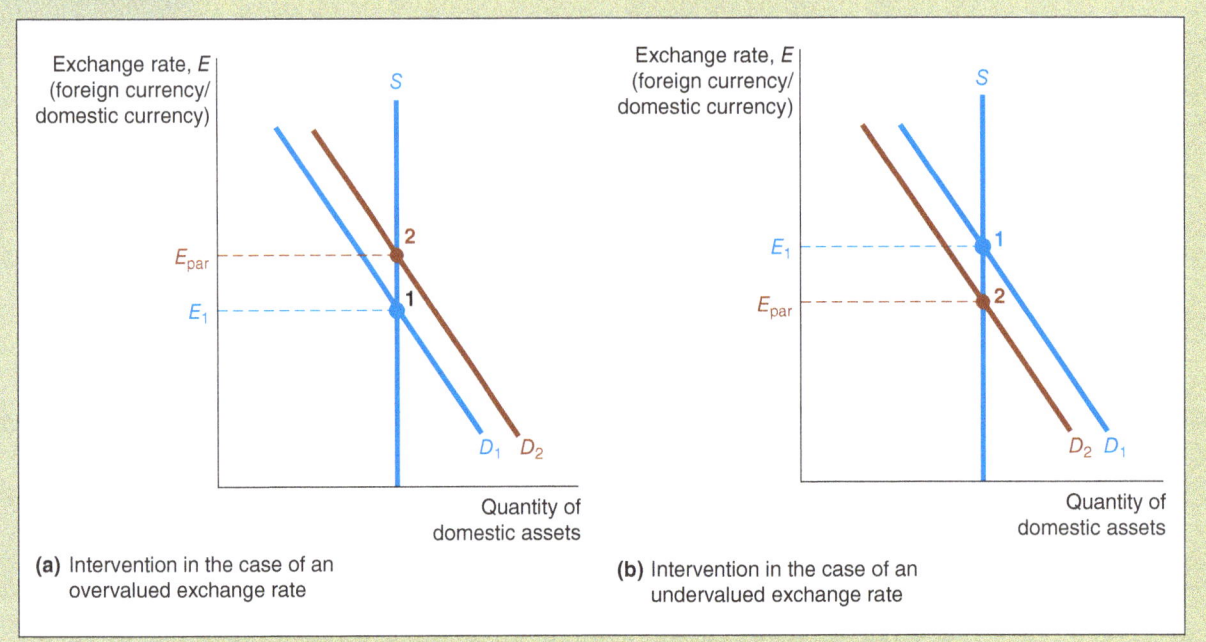

FIGURE 18.3

Intervention in the foreign exchange market under a fixed exchange rate regime

In panel (a), the exchange rate at E_{par} is overvalued. To keep the exchange rate at E_{par} (point 2), the central bank must purchase domestic currency to shift the demand curve to D_2. In panel (b), the exchange rate at E_{par} is undervalued, so the central bank must sell domestic currency to shift the demand curve to D_2 and keep the exchange rate at E_{par} (point 2).

exchange rate E_{par}. To keep the exchange rate at E_{par}, the central bank must intervene in the foreign exchange market to purchase domestic currency by selling foreign assets. This action, like an open market sale, means that both the monetary base and the money supply decline, driving up the interest rate on domestic assets, i^D.[6] This increase in the domestic interest rate raises the relative expected return on domestic assets, shifting the demand curve to the right. The central bank will continue purchasing domestic currency until the demand curve reaches D_2 and the equilibrium exchange rate is at E_{par} at point 2 in panel (a).

We have thus come to the conclusion that when the domestic currency is overvalued, the central bank must purchase domestic currency to keep the exchange rate fixed, but as a result it loses international reserves.

Panel (b) in Figure 18.3 describes the situation in which the demand curve has shifted to the right to D_1 because the relative expected return on domestic assets has risen and hence the exchange rate is undervalued: the initial demand curve D_1 intersects the supply curve at exchange rate E_1, which is above E_{par}. In this situation, the central bank must sell domestic currency and purchase foreign assets. This action works like an open market purchase to increase the money supply and lower the interest rate on domestic assets i^D. The central bank keeps selling domestic currency and lowering i^D until the demand curve shifts all the way to D_2, where the equilibrium exchange rate is at E_{par} – point 2 in panel (b). Our analysis thus leads us to the following result: *when the domestic currency is undervalued, the central bank must sell domestic currency to keep the exchange rate fixed, but as a result, it gains international reserves.*

As we have seen, if a country's currency is overvalued, its central bank's attempts to keep the currency from depreciating will result in a loss of international reserves. If the country's central bank eventually runs out of international reserves, it cannot keep its currency from depreciating, and a **devaluation** must occur, in which the par exchange rate is reset at a lower level.

If, by contrast, a country's currency is undervalued, its central bank's intervention to keep the currency from appreciating leads to a gain of international reserves. As we will see shortly, the central bank might not want to acquire these international reserves, and so it might want to reset the par value of its exchange rate at a higher level (a **revaluation**).

If there is perfect capital mobility – that is, if there are no barriers to domestic residents purchasing foreign assets or foreigners purchasing domestic assets – then a sterilized exchange rate intervention cannot keep the exchange rate at E_{par} because, as we saw earlier in the chapter, the relative expected return of domestic assets is unaffected. For example, if the exchange rate is overvalued, a sterilized purchase of domestic currency will leave the relative expected return and the demand curve unchanged – so pressure for a depreciation of the domestic currency is not removed. If the central bank keeps purchasing its domestic currency but continues to sterilize, it will just keep losing international reserves until it finally runs out of them and is forced to let the value of the currency seek a lower level.

One important implication of the foregoing analysis is that a country that ties its exchange rate to an anchor currency of a larger country loses control of its monetary policy. If the larger country pursues a more contractionary monetary policy and decreases its money supply, this would lead to lower expected inflation in the larger country, thus causing an appreciation of the larger country's currency and a depreciation of the smaller country's currency. The smaller country, having locked in its exchange rate to the anchor currency, will now find its currency overvalued and will therefore have to sell the anchor currency and buy its own to keep its currency from depreciating. The result of this foreign exchange intervention will then be a decline in the smaller country's international reserves, a contraction of its monetary base, and thus a decline in its money supply. Sterilization of this foreign exchange intervention is not an option because this would just lead to a continuing loss of international reserves until the smaller country was forced to devalue its currency. The smaller country no longer controls its monetary policy, because movements in its money supply are completely determined by movements in the larger country's money supply.

Another way to see that when a country fixes its exchange rate to a larger country's currency it loses control of its monetary policy is through the interest parity condition discussed in the appendix to the previous chapter. There we saw that when there is capital mobility, the domestic interest rate equals the foreign interest rate minus the expected appreciation of the domestic currency. With a fixed exchange rate, expected appreciation of the domestic currency is zero, so that the domestic interest rate equals the foreign interest rate. Therefore changes in the monetary policy in the large anchor country that affect its interest rate are directly transmitted to interest rates in the small country. Furthermore, because the monetary authorities in the small country cannot make their interest rate deviate from that of the larger country, they have no way to use monetary policy to affect their economy.

APPLICATION   How did China accumulate over $3 trillion of international reserves?

By 2011, China had accumulated over $3 trillion of international reserves. How did the Chinese get their hands on this vast amount of foreign assets? After all, China is not yet a rich country.

The answer is that China pegged its exchange rate to the US dollar at a fixed rate of 12 cents to the yuan (also called the renminbi) in 1994. Because of China's rapidly growing productivity and an inflation rate that is lower than in the United States, the long-run value of the yuan has increased, leading to a higher relative expected return for yuan assets and a rightward shift of the demand for yuan assets. As a result, the Chinese have found themselves in the situation depicted in panel (b) of Figure 18.3, in which the yuan is undervalued. To keep the yuan from appreciating above E_{par} to E_1 in the figure, the Chinese central bank has been engaging in massive purchases of US dollar assets. According to the US Treasury, today China owns $1.2 trillion of the Treasury debt, and is one of the largest holders of US government bonds in the world.

The pegging of the yuan to the US dollar has created several problems for Chinese authorities. First, the Chinese now own a lot of US assets, particularly US Treasury securities, which have very low returns. Second, the undervaluation of the yuan has meant that Chinese goods are so cheap abroad that many countries have threatened to erect trade barriers against these goods if the Chinese government does not allow an upward revaluation of the yuan. Third, as we learned earlier in the chapter, the Chinese purchase of dollar assets has resulted in a substantial increase in the Chinese monetary base and money supply, which has the potential to produce high inflation in the future. Because the Chinese authorities have created substantial blocks to capital mobility, they have been able to sterilize most of their exchange rate interventions while maintaining the exchange rate peg. Nevertheless, they still worry about inflationary pressures. In July 2005, China finally made its peg somewhat more flexible by letting the value of the yuan rise 2.1% and subsequently allowed it to appreciate at a gradual pace. The central bank also indicated that it would no longer fix the yuan to the US dollar, but would instead maintain its value relative to a basket of currencies.

Why did the Chinese authorities maintain this exchange rate peg for so long despite the problems? One answer is that they wanted to keep their export sector humming by keeping the prices of their export goods low. A second answer might be that they wanted to accumulate a large amount of international reserves as a 'war chest' that could be sold to buy yuan in the event of a speculative attack against the yuan at some future date. Given the pressure on the Chinese government to further revalue its currency from government officials in the United States and Europe, there are likely to be further adjustments in China's exchange rate policy in the future.

How the Bretton Woods system worked

Under the Bretton Woods system, exchange rates were supposed to change only when a country was experiencing a 'fundamental disequilibrium' – that is, large persistent deficits or surpluses in its balance of payments. To maintain fixed exchange rates when countries had balance-of-payments deficits and were losing international reserves, the IMF would loan deficit countries international reserves contributed by other members. As a result of its power to dictate loan terms to borrowing countries, the IMF could encourage deficit countries to pursue contractionary monetary policies that would strengthen their currency or eliminate their balance-of-payments deficits. If the IMF loans were not sufficient to prevent depreciation of a currency, the country was allowed to devalue its currency by setting a new, lower exchange rate.

A notable weakness of the Bretton Woods system was that although deficit countries losing international reserves could be pressured into devaluing their currencies or pursuing contractionary policies, the IMF had no way to force surplus countries to revise their exchange rates upward or pursue more expansionary policies. Particularly troublesome in this regard was the fact that the reserve currency country, the United States, could not devalue its currency under the Bretton Woods system even if the dollar was overvalued. When the United States attempted to reduce domestic unemployment in the 1960s by pursuing an inflationary monetary policy, a fundamental disequilibrium of an overvalued dollar developed. Because surplus countries were not willing to revise their exchange rates upward, adjustment in the Bretton Woods system did not take place, and the system collapsed in 1971. Attempts to patch up the Bretton Woods system with the Smithsonian Agreement in December 1971 proved unsuccessful, and by 1973 America and its trading partners had agreed to allow exchange rates to float.

Managed float

Although most exchange rates are currently allowed to change daily in response to market forces, central banks have not been willing to give up their option of intervening in the foreign exchange market. Preventing large changes in exchange rates makes it easier for firms and individuals purchasing or selling goods abroad to plan into the future. Furthermore, countries with surpluses in their balance of payments frequently do not want to see their currencies appreciate, because it makes their goods more expensive abroad and foreign goods cheaper in their country. Because an appreciation might hurt sales for domestic businesses and increase unemployment, surplus countries have often sold their currency in the foreign exchange market and acquired international reserves.

Countries with balance-of-payments deficits do not want to see their currency lose value, because it makes foreign goods more expensive for domestic consumers and can stimulate inflation. To keep the value of the domestic currency high, deficit countries have often bought their own currency in the foreign exchange market and given up international reserves.

The current international financial system is a hybrid of a fixed and a flexible exchange rate system. Rates fluctuate in response to market forces but are not determined solely by them. Furthermore, many countries continue to keep the value of their currency fixed against other currencies, as was the case in the European Monetary System before the introduction of the euro (to be described shortly).

Another important feature of the current system is the continuing de-emphasis of gold in international financial transactions. Not only has the United States suspended convertibility of dollars into gold for foreign central banks, but since 1970 the IMF has been issuing a paper substitute for gold, called **special drawing rights (SDRs)**. Like gold in the Bretton Woods system, SDRs function as international reserves. Unlike gold, whose quantity is determined by gold discoveries and the rate of production, SDRs can be created by the IMF whenever it decides that there is a need for additional international reserves to promote world trade and economic growth.

The use of gold in international transactions was further de-emphasized by the IMF's elimination of the official gold price in 1975 and by the sale of gold by the US Treasury and the IMF to private investors in an effort to demonetize it. Currently, the price of gold is determined in a free market. Investors who want to speculate in it are able to purchase and sell gold at will, as are jewellers and dentists who use gold in their businesses.

European Monetary System (EMS)

In March 1979, eight members of the European Economic Community (Germany, France, Italy, the Netherlands, Belgium, Luxembourg, Denmark and Ireland) set up the European Monetary System (EMS), in which they agreed to fix their exchange rates vis-à-vis one another and to float jointly against the US dollar. Spain joined the EMS in June 1989, the United Kingdom in October 1990 and Portugal in April 1992. The EMS created a new monetary unit, the *European currency unit* (ECU), whose value was tied to a basket of specified amounts of European currencies.

The exchange rate mechanism (ERM) of the European Monetary System worked as follows. The exchange rate between every pair of currencies of the participating countries was not allowed to fluctuate outside narrow limits around a fixed exchange rate. (The limits were typically ±2.25% but were raised to ±15% in August 1993.) When the exchange rate between two countries' currencies moved outside these limits, the central banks of both countries were supposed to intervene in the foreign exchange market. If, for example, the French franc depreciated below its lower limit against the German mark, the Bank of France was required to buy francs and sell marks, thereby giving up international reserves. Similarly, the German central bank was required to intervene to sell marks and buy francs and consequently increase its international reserves. The EMS thus required that intervention be symmetric when a currency fell outside the limits, with the central bank with the weak currency giving up international reserves and the one with the strong currency gaining them. Central bank intervention was also very common even when the exchange rate was within the limits, but in this case, if one central bank intervened, no others were required to intervene as well.

A serious shortcoming of fixed exchange rate systems such as the Bretton Woods system or the European Monetary System is that they can lead to foreign exchange crises involving a 'speculative attack' on a currency – massive sales of a weak currency or purchases of a strong currency that cause a sharp change in the exchange rate. In the following application, we use our model of exchange rate determination to understand how the September 1992 exchange rate crisis that rocked the European Monetary System came about.

| APPLICATION | ### The foreign exchange crisis of September 1992 |

In the aftermath of German reunification in October 1990, the German central bank, the Bundesbank, faced rising inflationary pressures, with inflation having accelerated from below 3% in 1990 to near 5% by 1992. To get monetary growth under control and to dampen inflation, the Bundesbank raised German interest rates to near double-digit levels. Figure 18.4 shows the consequences of these actions by the Bundesbank in the foreign exchange market for British pounds. Note that in the diagram, the pound is the domestic currency and the German mark (Deutschmark, DM, Germany's currency before the advent of the euro in 1999) is the foreign currency.

The increase in German interest rates i^F lowered the relative expected return of British pound assets and shifted the demand curve to D_2 in Figure 18.4. The intersection of the supply and demand curves at point 2 was now below the lower exchange rate limit at that time (2.778 marks per pound, denoted E_{par}). To increase the value of the pound relative to the mark and to restore the mark/pound exchange rate to within the exchange rate mechanism limits, one of two things had to happen. The Bank of England would have to pursue a contractionary monetary policy, thereby raising British interest rates sufficiently to shift the demand curve back to D_1 so that the equilibrium would remain at point 1, where the exchange rate would remain at E_{par}. Alternatively, the Bundesbank would have to pursue an expansionary monetary policy, thereby lowering German interest rates. Lower German interest rates would raise the relative expected return on British assets and shift the demand curve back to D_1 so the exchange rate would be at E_{par}.

| FIGURE 18.4 |

Foreign exchange market for British pounds in 1992

The realization by speculators that the United Kingdom would soon devalue the pound decreased the relative expected return on British pound assets, resulting in a leftward shift of the demand curve from D_2 to D_3. The result was the need for a much greater purchase of pounds by the British central bank to raise the interest rate so that the demand curve would shift back to D_1 and keep the exchange rate E_{par} at 2.778 German marks per pound.

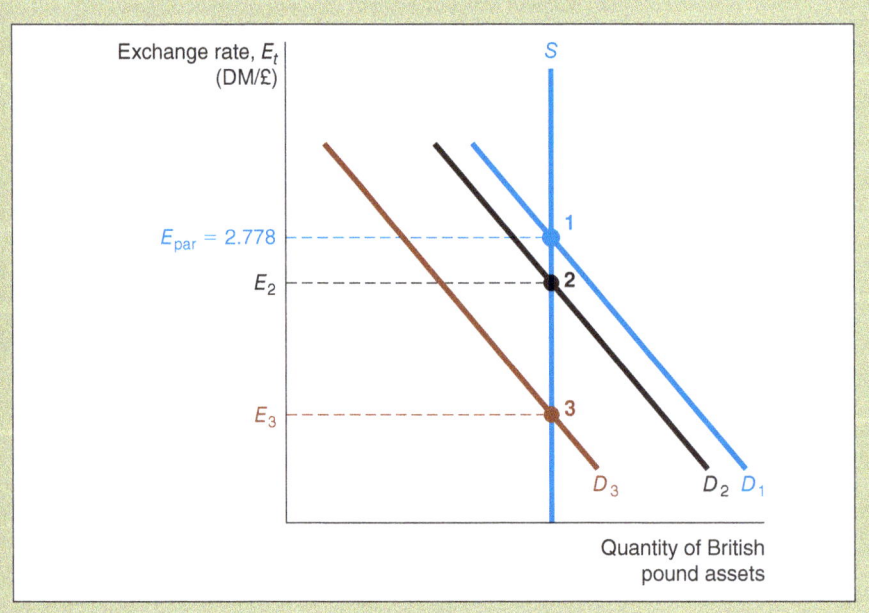

The catch was that the Bundesbank, whose primary goal was fighting inflation, was unwilling to pursue an expansionary monetary policy, and the British, who were facing their worst recession in the post-war period, were unwilling to pursue a contractionary monetary policy to prop up the pound. This impasse became clear when in response to great pressure from other members of the EMS, the Bundesbank was willing to lower its lending rates by only a token amount on 14 September after a speculative attack was mounted on the currencies of the Scandinavian countries. So at some point in the near future, the value of the pound would have to decline to point 2. Speculators now knew that the depreciation of the pound was imminent. As a result, the relative expected return of the pound fell sharply, shifting the demand curve left to D_3 in Figure 18.3.

As a result of the large leftward shift of the demand curve, there was now a huge excess supply of pound assets at the par exchange rate E_{par}, which caused a massive sell-off of pounds (and purchases of marks) by speculators. The need for the British central bank to intervene to raise the value of the pound now became much greater and required a huge rise in British interest rates. After a major intervention effort on the part of the Bank of England, which included a rise in its lending rate from 10% to 15%, which still wasn't enough, the British were finally forced to give up on 16 September: they pulled out of the ERM indefinitely and allowed the pound to depreciate by 10% against the mark.

Speculative attacks on other currencies forced devaluation of the Spanish peseta by 5% and the Italian lira by 15%. To defend its currency, the Swedish central bank was forced to raise its daily lending rate to the astronomical level of 500%! By the time the crisis was over, the British, French, Italian, Spanish and Swedish central banks had intervened to the tune of $100 billion; the Bundesbank alone had laid out $50 billion for foreign exchange intervention. Because foreign exchange crises lead to large changes in central banks' holdings of international reserves and thus significantly affect the official reserve asset items in the balance of payments, these crises are also referred to as **balance-of-payments crises**.

The attempt to prop up the European Monetary System was not cheap for these central banks. It is estimated that they lost $4 to $6 billion as a result of exchange rate intervention during the crisis. What the central banks lost, the speculators gained. A speculative fund run by George Soros ran up $1 billion of profits during the crisis, and Citibank traders reportedly made $200 million. When an exchange rate crisis comes, life can certainly be sweet for exchange rate speculators.

APPLICATION   ## Recent foreign exchange crises in emerging market countries: Mexico 1994, East Asia 1997, Brazil 1999 and Argentina 2002

Major currency crises in emerging market countries have been a common occurrence in recent years. We can use Figure 18.3 to understand the sequence of events during the currency crises in Mexico in 1994, East Asia in 1997, Brazil in 1999 and Argentina in 2002. To do so, we just need to recognize that dollars are the foreign currency, while the domestic currency was pesos, baht or reals. (Note that the exchange rate label on the vertical axis would be in terms of dollars/domestic currency and that the label on the horizontal axis would be the quantity of domestic currency (say, pesos) assets.)

In Mexico in March 1994, political instability (the assassination of the ruling party's presidential candidate) sparked investors' concerns that the peso might be devalued. The result was that the relative expected return on domestic assets fell, thus moving the demand curve from D_1 to D_2 in Figure 18.3. In the case of Thailand in May 1997, the large current account deficit and the weakness of the Thai financial system raised similar concerns about the devaluation of the domestic currency, with the same effect on the demand curve. In Brazil in late 1998 and Argentina in 2001, concerns about fiscal situations that could lead to the printing of money to finance the deficit, and thereby raise inflation, also meant that a devaluation was more likely to occur. The concerns thus lowered the relative expected return on domestic assets and shifted the demand curve from D_1 to D_2. In all of these cases, the result was that the intersection of the supply and demand curves was below the pegged value of the domestic currency at E_{par}.

To keep their domestic currencies from falling below E_{par}, these countries' central banks needed to buy the domestic currency and sell dollars to raise interest rates and shift the demand curve to the right, in the process losing international reserves. At first, the central banks were successful in containing the speculative attacks. However, when more bad news broke, speculators became even more confident that these countries could not defend their currencies. (The bad news was everywhere: In Mexico, there was an uprising in Chiapas and revelations about problems in the banking system; in Thailand, there was a failure of a major financial institution; Brazil had a worsening fiscal situation, along with a threat by a governor to default on his state's debt; and in Argentina, a full-scale bank panic and an actual default on the government debt occurred.) As a result, the relative expected returns on domestic assets fell further, and the demand curve moved much farther to the left to D_3, and the central banks lost even more international reserves. Given the stress on the economy from rising interest rates and the loss of reserves, eventually the monetary authorities could no longer continue to defend the currency and were forced to give up and let their currencies depreciate. This scenario happened in Mexico in December 1994, in Thailand in July 1997, in Brazil in January 1999 and in Argentina in January 2002.

Concerns about similar problems in other countries then triggered speculative attacks against them as well. This contagion occurred in the aftermath of the Mexican crisis (jauntily referred to as the 'tequila effect') with speculative attacks on other Latin American currencies, but there were no further currency collapses. In the East Asian crisis, however, fears of devaluation spread throughout the region, leading to a scenario akin to that depicted in Figure 18.3. Consequently, one by one, Indonesia, Malaysia, South Korea and the Philippines were forced to devalue sharply. Even Hong Kong, Singapore and Taiwan were subjected to speculative attacks, but because these countries had healthy financial systems, the attacks were successfully averted.

As we saw in Chapter 9, the sharp depreciations in Mexico, East Asia and Argentina led to full-scale financial crises that severely damaged these countries' economies. The foreign exchange crisis that shocked the European Monetary System in September 1992 cost central banks a lot of money, but the public in European countries were not seriously affected. By contrast, the public in Mexico, Argentina and the crisis countries of East Asia were not so lucky: the collapse of these currencies triggered by speculative attacks led to the financial crises described in Chapter 9, producing severe depressions that caused hardship and political unrest. ◼

Capital controls

Because capital flows were an important element in the currency crises in Mexico and East Asia, politicians and some economists have advocated that emerging market countries avoid financial instability by restricting capital mobility. Are capital controls a good idea?

Controls on capital outflows

Capital outflows can promote financial instability in emerging market countries, because when domestic residents and foreigners pull their capital out of a country, the resulting capital outflow forces the country to devalue its currency. This is why some politicians in emerging market countries have recently found capital controls particularly attractive. For example, Prime Minister Mahathir of Malaysia instituted capital controls in 1998 to restrict outflows in the aftermath of the East Asian crisis.

Although these controls sound like a good idea, they suffer from several disadvantages. First, empirical evidence indicates that controls on capital outflows are seldom effective during a crisis because the private sector finds ingenious ways to evade them and has little difficulty moving funds out of the country.[7] Second, the evidence suggests that capital flight may even increase after controls are put into place, because confidence in the government is weakened. Third, controls on capital outflows often lead to corruption, as government officials get paid off to look the other way when domestic residents are trying to move funds abroad. Fourth, controls on capital outflows may lull governments into thinking they do not have to take the steps to reform their financial systems to deal with the crisis, with the result that opportunities are lost to improve the functioning of the economy.

Controls on capital inflows

Although most economists find the arguments against controls on capital outflows persuasive, controls on capital inflows receive more support. Supporters reason that if speculative capital cannot come in, then it cannot go out suddenly and create a crisis. Our analysis of the financial crises in East Asia in Chapter 9 provides support for this view by suggesting that capital inflows can lead to a lending boom and excessive risk taking on the part of banks, which then helps trigger a financial crisis.

FOLLOWING THE FINANCIAL NEWS

Time for a Tobin tax?

The 2007–9 global financial crisis was associated with large swings in asset prices. High volatility across various types of financial assets is generally thought to have substantially amplified the economic downturn. To reduce the future risk of destabilizing booms and bursts in asset prices, in the aftermath of the crisis some political leaders have argued in favour of introducing a financial transactions tax, also known as a 'Tobin tax'.[8] The main idea of a Tobin tax is to discourage short-term speculation through invoking a cost on financial transactions, thereby contributing to greater stability in financial markets. The article below, taken from the *Financial Times*, discusses a recent proposal by former French President Nicolas Sarkozy to introduce a Tobin tax. The column highlights an enduring debate relating to the usefulness of the Tobin tax in achieving a higher degree of financial stability.

The main objection often raised against the Tobin tax relates to its unilateral implementation which may provoke a flight of capital to countries with more favourable tax legislation. As a result, financing conditions of households and firms may worsen, leading to a lower level of private spending and investment growth in the economy. In order to avoid the destabilizing effects from capital flight to other jurisdictions, a multilateral tax agreement is widely believed to be essential to the success of the Tobin tax. Other challenges associated with the Tobin tax relate to its particular design. For example, a tax on all types of financial transactions may penalize speculation but also discourage long-term investors. Moreover, job creation in the financial sector and other industries may be sensible to the specific level of the tax rate.

Financiers attack Sarkozy 'Tobin tax' plan

By Hugh Carnegy in Paris and Quentin Peel in Berlin

France's financial and business establishment has attacked President Nicolas Sarkozy's threat to introduce unilaterally a tax on financial transactions, saying it would hit the economy and damage the role of Paris as a financial centre.

'Introducing a financial transaction tax which was not at least European, would weaken the French economy . . . and Paris's place in the European and world economy,' said Paris Europlace, a financial markets association, which said it was speaking for industrial

Financiers attack Sarkozy 'Tobin tax' plan (*continued*)

companies, insurers and institutional investors, as well as the banks.

Mr. Sarkozy confirmed on Friday that his centre-right government would seek to enact a so-called Tobin tax before the presidential election in April, if necessary in advance of other countries. Further delay was 'unacceptable', he said.

He is expected to explain his position to Angela Merkel, German chancellor, at a meeting in Berlin on Monday. Germany is keen to forge a common position with France over the coming weeks, but Mr. Sarkozy is frustrated by the difficulty of reaching wider European agreement on a tax, which is adamantly opposed by Britain and other countries.

Paris Europlace made clear that unilateral introduction of the tax faced strong opposition from the French financial and broader business sector. Arnaud de Bresson, managing director, said Europlace had consulted with industry and other financial organizations before issuing its statement.

'It is important that we are taking such a strong position, not just in the name of financial institutions,' he told the Financial Times. 'At a time when this tax could be added to new financial regulations (on banks and insurers) it could have consequences on the way the financial sector finances the economy.'

Europlace also warned that unilateral application of an FTT would drive banking, insurance and asset management business out of Paris, to the advantage of other large financial centres.

Steffen Seibert, Ms Merkel's chief spokesman, said last week that Germany's preference was for a European Union-wide FTT – although Britain has ruled that out. David Cameron, UK prime minister, said on Sunday that France was free to go ahead with a tax on its own, but London would not agree to any such tax unless it had full international backing.

Wolfgang Schäuble, German finace minister, has said he would be prepared to accept a eurozone-wide tax as an alternative.

'Mr Sarkozy will have to spell out his position,' a senior official said on Sunday, saying that Berlin wanted to agree on a 'common postion' with Paris before the next Franco-German ministerial council meeting in early February.

Source: Carnegy, H. and Peel, Q. (2012) 'Financiers attack Sarkozy "Tobin tax plan"', *Financial Times, 8 January.*

However, controls on capital inflows have the undesirable feature that they may block from entering a country funds that would be used for productive investment opportunities. Although such controls may limit the fuel supplied to lending booms through capital flows, over time they produce substantial distortions and misallocation of resources as households and businesses try to get around them. Indeed, just as with controls on capital outflows, controls on capital inflows can lead to corruption. There are serious doubts whether capital controls can be effective in today's environment, in which trade is open and where there are many financial instruments that make it easier to get around these controls.

On the other hand, there is a strong case for improving bank regulation and supervision so that capital inflows are less likely to produce a lending boom and encourage excessive risk taking by banking institutions. For example, restricting banks in how fast their borrowing can grow might substantially limit capital inflows. Supervisory controls that focus on the sources of financial fragility, rather than the symptoms, can enhance the efficiency of the financial system, rather than hampering it.

The role of the IMF

The International Monetary Fund was originally set up under the Bretton Woods system to help countries deal with balance-of-payments problems and stay with the fixed exchange rates by lending to deficit countries. When the Bretton Woods system of fixed exchange rates collapsed in 1971, the IMF took on new roles.

The IMF continues to function as a data collector and provide technical assistance to its member countries. Although the IMF no longer attempts to encourage fixed exchange rates, its role as an international lender has become more important recently. This role first came to the fore in the 1980s during the Third World debt crisis, in which the IMF assisted developing countries in repaying their loans. The financial crises in Mexico in 1994–5 and in East Asia in 1997–8 led to huge loans by the IMF to these and other affected countries to help them recover from their financial crises and to prevent the spread of these crises to other countries. This role, in which the IMF acts like an international lender of last resort to cope with financial instability, is indeed highly controversial.

Should the IMF be an international lender of last resort?

As we saw in Chapter 15, in industrialized countries when a financial crisis occurs and the financial system threatens to seize up, domestic central banks can address matters with a lender-of-last-resort operation to limit the degree of instability in the banking system. In emerging market countries, however, where the credibility of the central bank as an inflation-fighter may be in doubt and debt contracts are typically short-term and denominated in foreign currencies, a lender-of-last-resort operation becomes a double-edged sword – as likely to exacerbate the financial crisis as to alleviate it. For example, when the US Federal Reserve engaged in a lender-of-last-resort operation during the 1987 stock market crash and after the 2001 terrorist destruction of the World Trade Center (Chapter 15), there was almost no sentiment in the markets that there would be substantially higher inflation. However, for a central bank with less inflation-fighting credibility than the Fed, central bank lending to the financial system in the wake of a financial crisis – even under the lender-of-last-resort rhetoric – may well arouse fears of inflation spiralling out of control, causing an even greater currency depreciation and still greater deterioration of balance sheets. The resulting increase in moral hazard and adverse selection problems in financial markets, along the lines discussed in Chapter 9, would only worsen the financial crisis.

Central banks in emerging market countries therefore have only a very limited ability to successfully engage in a lender-of-last-resort operation. However, liquidity provided by an international lender of last resort does not have these undesirable consequences, and in helping to stabilize the value of the domestic currency, it strengthens domestic balance sheets. Moreover, an international lender of last resort may be able to prevent contagion, the situation in which a successful speculative attack on one emerging market currency leads to attacks on other emerging market currencies, spreading financial and economic disruption as it goes. Because a lender of last resort for emerging market countries is needed at times, and because it cannot be provided domestically, there is a strong rationale for an international institution to fill this role. Indeed, since Mexico's financial crisis in 1994, the International Monetary Fund and other international agencies have stepped into the lender-of-last-resort role and provided emergency lending to countries threatened by financial instability.

However, support from an international lender of last resort brings risks of its own, especially the risk that the perception it is standing ready to bail out irresponsible financial institutions may lead to excessive risk taking of the sort that makes financial crises more likely. In the Mexican and East Asian crises, governments in the crisis countries used IMF support to protect depositors and other creditors of banking institutions from losses. This safety net creates a well-known moral hazard problem because the depositors and other creditors have less incentive to monitor these banking institutions and withdraw their deposits if the institutions are taking on too much risk. The result is that these institutions are encouraged to take on excessive risks. Indeed, critics of the IMF – most prominently, the Congressional Commission headed by Professor Alan Meltzer of Carnegie-Mellon University – contend that IMF lending in the Mexican crisis, which was used to bail out foreign lenders, set the stage for the East Asian crisis, because these lenders expected to be bailed out if things went wrong, and thus provided funds that were used to fuel excessive risk taking.[9]

An international lender of last resort must find ways to limit this moral hazard problem, or it can actually make the situation worse. The international lender of last resort can make it clear that it will extend liquidity only to governments that put the proper measures in place to prevent excessive risk taking. In addition, it can reduce the incentives for risk taking by restricting the ability of governments to bail out stockholders and large uninsured creditors of domestic financial institutions. Some critics of the IMF believe that the IMF has not put enough pressure on the governments to which it lends to contain the moral hazard problem.

One problem that arises for international organizations like the IMF engaged in lender-of-last-resort operations is that they know that if they don't come to the rescue, the emerging market country will suffer extreme hardship and possible political instability. Politicians in the crisis country may exploit these concerns and engage in a game of chicken with the international lender of last resort: they resist necessary reforms, hoping that the IMF will cave in. Elements of this game were present in the Mexican crisis of 1994 and were also a particularly important feature of the negotiations between the IMF and Indonesia during the East Asian crisis.

How should the IMF operate?

The IMF would produce better outcomes if it made clear that it will not play this game. Just as giving in to ill-behaved children may be the easy way out in the short run, but supports a pattern of poor behaviour in the long run, some critics worry that the IMF may not be tough enough when confronted by short-run humanitarian concerns. For example, these critics have been particularly critical of the IMF's lending to the Russian government, which resisted adopting appropriate reforms to stabilize its financial system.

The IMF has also been criticized for imposing on the East Asian countries so-called austerity programmes that focus on tight macroeconomic policies rather than on microeconomic policies to fix the crisis-causing problems in the financial sector. Such programmes are likely to increase resistance to IMF recommendations, particularly in emerging market countries. Austerity programmes allow politicians in these countries to label institutions such as the IMF as being anti-growth, rhetoric that helps the politicians mobilize the public against the IMF and avoid doing what they really need to do to reform the financial system in their country. IMF programmes focused instead on reforms of the financial sector would increase the likelihood that the IMF will be seen as a helping hand in the creation of a more efficient financial system.

An important historical feature of successful lender-of-last-resort operations is that the faster the lending is done, the lower the amount that actually has to be lent. An excellent example involving the Federal Reserve occurred in the aftermath of the stock market crash on 19 October 1987 (Chapter 15). At the end of that day, to service their customers' accounts, securities firms needed to borrow several billion dollars to maintain orderly trading. However, given the unprecedented developments, banks were nervous about extending further loans to these firms. Upon learning this, the Federal Reserve engaged in an immediate lender-of-last-resort operation, making it clear that it would provide liquidity to banks making loans to the securities industry. What is striking about this episode is that the extremely quick intervention of the Fed not only resulted in a negligible impact of the stock market crash on the economy, but also meant that the amount of liquidity that the Fed needed to supply to the economy was not very large.

The ability of the Fed to engage in a lender-of-last-resort operation within a day of a substantial shock to the financial system stands in sharp contrast to the amount of time it has taken the IMF to supply liquidity during the recent crises in emerging market countries. Because IMF lending facilities were originally designed to provide funds after a country was experiencing a balance-of-payments crisis and because the conditions for the loan had to be negotiated, it took several months before the IMF made funds available. By this time, the crisis had got much worse – and much larger sums of funds were needed to cope with the crisis, often stretching the resources of the IMF. One reason central banks can lend so much more quickly than the IMF is that they have set up procedures in advance to provide loans, with the terms and conditions for this lending agreed upon beforehand. The need for quick provision of liquidity, to keep the loan amount manageable, argues for similar credit facilities at the international lender of last resort, so that funds can be provided quickly, as long as the borrower meets conditions such as properly supervising its banks or keeping budget deficits low.

The flaws in IMF lending programmes discussed above led to countries avoiding borrowing from the IMF in recent years. Countries did not want to be subjected to harsh austerity programmes and also were unhappy with IMF delays in disbursing funds during a crisis. As an alternative to the IMF, countries built up substantial cushions of international reserves to deal with balance-of-payments problems on their own. IMF lending therefore shrunk to very low levels, even creating a shortfall of revenue for its operations because it was no longer earning income by making loans. The IMF was at risk of becoming irrelevant – until the subprime financial crisis. With the subprime financial crisis, the IMF's role as an international lender of last resort returned, as can be seen in the box, 'The subprime financial crisis and the IMF'.

The debate on whether the world will be better off with the IMF operating as an international lender of last resort is currently a hot one. Much attention is being focused on making the IMF more effective in performing this role, and redesign of the IMF is at the centre of proposals for a new international financial architecture to help reduce international financial instability.

GLOBAL
The subprime financial crisis and the IMF

Because financial institutions in emerging market countries had limited exposure to subprime mortgages, the early stages of the subprime financial crisis had little impact on their economies. However, when the subprime crisis became more virulent in October 2008, a number of emerging market countries, including former communist countries, as well as Iceland, found that foreigners were pulling funds out of their financial systems, putting not only domestic banks under stress, but also causing a sharp depreciation of their currencies.

The role of the IMF as an international lender of last resort now came to the fore. Toward the end of October, the IMF extended $25 billion in loans to Hungary, $16.5 billion to Ukraine and $2 billion to Iceland. These loans stipulated that the countries would have to undergo belt-tightening in order to get their fiscal houses in order.

The IMF recognized, however, that, as the former Managing Director of the IMF, Dominique Strauss-Kahn put it, 'exceptional times call for an exceptional response', and that a new type of lending programme was needed to overcome the reluctance of countries to borrow from it during the crisis at hand. The IMF created a new lending programme at the end of October 2008, called the Short-Term Liquidity Facility, with $100 billion of funds. It provides three-month loans to countries whose economies are judged by the IMF to be basically sound, but under stress. These condition-free loans could be disbursed very quickly. In addition, these loans would not have austerity programmes attached to them, making them far more attractive to potential borrowing countries.

In 1999, the IMF tried to implement a similar facility called the Contingent Credit Line, but it was unsuccessful because it required prior approval from the IMF, and countries were reluctant to apply for it because doing so might suggest that they were likely to get into trouble. The new Short-term Liquidity Facility does not require countries to apply for it. The IMF can just determine that a country has access and give it a loan if it needs it. It is too soon to determine whether this new lending facility will overcome some of the criticisms levelled against previous IMF lending programmes, but it does appear to be a step in the right direction.

International considerations and monetary policy

Our analysis in this chapter so far has suggested several ways in which monetary policy can be affected by international matters. Awareness of these effects can have significant implications for the way monetary policy is conducted.

Direct effects of the foreign exchange market on the money supply

When central banks intervene in the foreign exchange market, they acquire or sell off international reserves, and their monetary base is affected. When a central bank intervenes in the foreign exchange market, it gives up some control of its money supply. For example, in the early 1970s, the German central bank faced a dilemma. In attempting to keep the German mark from appreciating too much against the US dollar, the Germans acquired huge quantities of international reserves, leading to a rate of money growth that the German central bank considered inflationary.

The Bundesbank could have tried to halt the growth of the money supply by stopping its intervention in the foreign exchange market and reasserting control over its own money supply. Such a strategy has a major drawback when the central bank is under pressure not to allow its currency to appreciate: the lower price of imports and higher price of exports as a result of an appreciation in its currency will hurt domestic producers and increase unemployment.

Because the US dollar has been a reserve currency, the US monetary base and money supply have been less affected by developments in the foreign exchange market. As long as foreign central banks, rather than the Fed, intervene to keep the value of the dollar from changing, American holdings of international reserves are unaffected. The ability to conduct monetary policy is typically easier when a country's currency is a reserve currency.[10]

Balance-of-payments considerations

Under the Bretton Woods system, balance-of-payments considerations were more important than they are under the current managed float regime. When a non-reserve currency country is running balance-of-payments deficits, it necessarily gives up international reserves. To keep from running out of these reserves, under the Bretton Woods system it had to implement contractionary monetary policy to strengthen its currency – exactly what occurred in the United Kingdom before its devaluation of the pound in 1967. When policy became expansionary, the balance of payments deteriorated, and the British were forced to 'slam on the brakes' by implementing a contractionary policy. Once the balance of payments improved, policy became more expansionary until the deteriorating balance of payments again forced the British to pursue a contractionary policy. Such on-again, off-again actions became known as a 'stop-go' policy, and the domestic instability it created was criticized severely.

Because the United States is a major reserve currency country, it can run large balance-of-payments deficits without losing huge amounts of international reserves. This does not mean, however, that the Federal Reserve is never influenced by developments in the US balance of payments. Current account deficits in the United States suggest that American businesses may be losing some of their ability to compete because the value of the dollar is too high. In addition, large US balance-of-payments deficits lead to balance-of-payments surpluses in other countries, which can in turn lead to large increases in their holdings of international reserves (this was especially true under the Bretton Woods system). Because such increases put a strain on the international financial system and may stimulate world inflation, the Fed worries about US balance-of-payments and current account deficits. To help shrink these deficits, the Fed might pursue a more contractionary monetary policy.

Exchange rate considerations

Unlike balance-of-payments considerations, which have become less important under the current managed float system, exchange rate considerations now play a greater role in the conduct of monetary policy. If a central bank does not want to see its currency fall in value, it may pursue a more contractionary monetary policy of reducing the money supply to raise the domestic interest rate, thereby strengthening its currency. Similarly, if a country experiences an appreciation in its currency, its domestic industry may suffer from increased foreign competition and may pressure the central bank to pursue a higher rate of money growth so as to lower the exchange rate.

The pressure to manipulate exchange rates seems to be greater for central banks in countries other than the United States, but even the Federal Reserve is not completely immune. The growing tide of protectionism stemming from the inability of American firms to compete with foreign firms because of the strengthening dollar from 1980 to early 1985 stimulated congressional critics of the Fed to call for a more expansionary monetary policy to lower the value of the dollar. As we saw in Chapter 16, the Fed let money growth surge. A policy to bring the dollar down was confirmed in the Plaza Agreement of September 1985, in which the finance ministers from the five most important industrial nations in the free world (the United Kingdom, the United States, Japan, West Germany and France) agreed to intervene in foreign exchange markets to achieve a decline in the dollar. The dollar continued to fall rapidly after the Plaza Agreement, and the Fed played an important role in this decline by continuing to expand the money supply at a rapid rate.

To peg or not to peg: exchange-rate targeting as an alternative monetary policy strategy

In Chapter 16, we discussed several monetary policy strategies that could be followed to promote price stability: monetary targeting, inflation targeting and monetary policy with an implicit (not explicit) nominal anchor. One other strategy also uses a strong nominal anchor to promote price stability: **exchange-rate targeting** (sometimes referred to as an **exchange-rate peg**).

Targeting the exchange rate is a monetary policy strategy with a long history. It can take the form of fixing the value of the domestic currency to a commodity such as gold, the key feature of the gold standard described earlier in the chapter. More recently, fixed exchange rate regimes have involved fixing the value of the domestic currency to that of a large, low-inflation country like Germany (or the euro area since 1999) or the United States (the *anchor country*). Another alternative is to adopt a *crawling target* or *peg*, in which a currency is allowed to depreciate at a steady rate so that the inflation rate in the pegging country can be higher than that of the anchor country.

Advantages of exchange-rate targeting

Exchange-rate targeting has several advantages. First, the nominal anchor of an exchange-rate target directly contributes to keeping inflation under control by tying the inflation rate for internationally traded goods to that found in the anchor country. It does this because the foreign price of internationally traded goods is set by the world market, while the domestic price of these goods is fixed by the exchange-rate target. For example, until 2002 in Argentina the exchange rate for the Argentine peso was exactly one to the dollar, so that a bushel of wheat traded internationally at five dollars had its price set at five pesos. If the exchange-rate target is credible (i.e. expected to be adhered to), the exchange-rate target has the added benefit of anchoring inflation expectations to the inflation rate in the anchor country.

Second, an exchange-rate target provides an automatic rule for the conduct of monetary policy that helps mitigate the time-inconsistency problem described in Chapter 13. As we saw earlier in the chapter, an exchange-rate target forces a tightening of monetary policy when there is a tendency for the domestic currency to depreciate or a loosening of policy when there is a tendency for the domestic currency to appreciate, so that discretionary monetary policy is less of an option. The central bank will therefore be constrained from falling into the time-inconsistency trap of trying to expand output and employment in the short run by pursuing an overly expansionary monetary policy.

Third, an exchange-rate target has the advantage of simplicity and clarity, which makes it easily understood by the public. A 'sound currency' is an easy-to-understand rallying cry for monetary policy. In the past, for example, this aspect was important in France, where an appeal to the '*franc fort*' (strong franc) was often used to justify tight monetary policy.

Given its advantages, it is not surprising that exchange-rate targeting has been used successfully to control inflation in industrialized countries. Both France and the United Kingdom, for example, successfully used exchange-rate targeting to lower inflation by tying the values of their currencies to the German mark. In 1987, when France first pegged its exchange rate to the mark, its inflation rate was 3%, two percentage points above the German inflation rate. By 1992, its inflation rate had fallen to 2%, a level that can be argued is consistent with price stability, and was even below that in Germany. By 1996, the French and German inflation rates had converged, to a number slightly below 2%. Similarly, after pegging to the German mark in 1990, the United Kingdom was able to lower its inflation rate from 10% to 3% by 1992, when it was forced to abandon the exchange rate mechanism (ERM).

Exchange-rate targeting has also been an effective means of reducing inflation quickly in emerging market countries. For example, before the devaluation in Mexico in 1994, its exchange-rate target enabled it to bring inflation down from levels above 100% in 1988 to below 10% in 1994.

Disadvantages of exchange-rate targeting

Despite the inherent advantages of exchange-rate targeting, there are several serious criticisms of this strategy. The problem (as we saw earlier in the chapter) is that with capital mobility the targeting country can no longer pursue its own independent monetary policy and use it to respond to domestic shocks that are independent of those hitting the anchor country. Furthermore, an exchange-rate target means that shocks to the anchor country are directly transmitted to the targeting country, because changes in interest rates in the anchor country lead to a corresponding change in interest rates in the targeting country.

A striking example of these problems occurred when Germany was reunified in 1990. In response to concerns about inflationary pressures arising from reunification and the massive fiscal expansion required to rebuild East Germany, long-term German interest rates rose until February 1991 and short-term rates rose until December 1991. This shock to the anchor country in the exchange rate mechanism (ERM) was transmitted directly to the other countries in the ERM whose currencies were pegged to the mark, and their interest rates rose in tandem with those in Germany. Continuing adherence to the exchange-rate target slowed economic growth and increased unemployment in countries such as France that remained in the ERM and adhered to the exchange-rate peg.

A second problem with exchange-rate targets is that they leave countries open to speculative attacks on their currencies. Indeed, one aftermath of German reunification was the foreign exchange crisis of September 1992. As we saw earlier, the tight monetary policy in Germany following reunification meant that the countries in the ERM were subjected to a negative demand shock that led to a decline in economic growth and a rise in unemployment. It was certainly feasible for the governments of these countries to keep their exchange rates fixed relative to the mark in these circumstances, but speculators began to question whether these countries' commitment to the exchange-rate peg would weaken. Speculators reasoned that these countries would not tolerate the rise in unemployment resulting from keeping interest rates high enough to fend off attacks on their currencies.

At this stage, speculators were, in effect, presented with a one-way bet, because the currencies of countries like France, Spain, Sweden, Italy and the United Kingdom could go in only one direction and depreciate against the mark. Selling these currencies before the likely depreciation occurred gave speculators an attractive profit opportunity with potentially high expected returns. The result was the speculative attack in September 1992. Only in France was the commitment to the fixed exchange rate strong enough so that France did not devalue. The governments in the other countries were unwilling to defend their currencies at all costs and eventually allowed their currencies to fall in value.

The different responses of France and the United Kingdom after the September 1992 exchange-rate crisis illustrate the potential cost of an exchange-rate target. France, which continued to peg its currency to the mark and was thus unable to use monetary policy to respond to domestic conditions, found that economic growth remained slow after 1992 and unemployment increased. The United Kingdom, on the other hand, which dropped out of the ERM exchange-rate peg and adopted inflation targeting, had much better economic performance: economic growth was higher, the unemployment rate fell and yet its inflation was not much worse than France's.

In contrast to industrialized countries, emerging market countries (including the transition countries of Eastern Europe) may not lose much by giving up an independent monetary policy when they target exchange rates. Because many emerging market countries have not developed the political or monetary institutions that allow the successful use of discretionary monetary policy, they may have little to gain from an independent monetary policy, but a lot to lose. Thus they would be better off by, in effect, adopting the monetary policy of a country like the United States through targeting exchange rates than by pursuing their own independent policy. This is one of the reasons that so many emerging market countries have adopted exchange-rate targeting.

Nonetheless, exchange-rate targeting is highly dangerous for these countries, because it leaves them open to speculative attacks that can have far more serious consequences for their economies than for the economies of industrialized countries. Indeed, the successful speculative attacks in Mexico in 1994, East Asia in 1997 and Argentina in 2002 plunged their economies into full-scale financial crises that devastated their economies.

An additional disadvantage of an exchange-rate target is that it can weaken the accountability of policymakers, particularly in emerging market countries. Because exchange-rate targeting fixes the exchange rate, it eliminates an important signal that can help constrain monetary policy from becoming too expansionary and thereby limit the time-inconsistency problem. In industrialized countries, particularly in the United States, the bond market provides an important signal about the stance of monetary policy. Overly expansionary monetary policy or strong political pressure to engage in overly expansionary monetary policy produces an inflation scare in which inflation expectations surge, interest rates rise because of the Fisher effect (described in Chapter 5), and there is a sharp decline in long-term bond prices. Because both central banks and the politicians want to avoid this kind of scenario, overly expansionary monetary policy will be less likely.

In many countries, particularly emerging market countries, the long-term bond market is essentially non-existent. Under a floating exchange rate regime, however, if monetary policy is too expansionary, the exchange rate will depreciate. In these countries the daily fluctuations of the exchange rate can, like the bond market in the United States, provide an early warning signal that monetary policy is too expansionary. Just as the fear of a visible inflation scare in the bond market constrains central bankers from pursuing overly expansionary monetary policy and constrains politicians from putting pressure on the central bank to engage in overly expansionary monetary policy, fear of exchange-rate depreciations can make overly expansionary monetary policy and the time-inconsistency problem less likely.

The need for signals from the foreign exchange market may be even more acute for emerging market countries, because the balance sheets and actions of their central banks are not as transparent as they are in industrialized countries. Targeting the exchange rate can make it even harder to ascertain the central bank's policy actions. The public is less able to keep a watch on the central bank and the politicians pressuring it, which makes it easier for monetary policy to become too expansionary.

When is exchange-rate targeting desirable for industrialized countries?

Given the above disadvantages with exchange-rate targeting, when might it make sense? In industrialized countries, the biggest cost to exchange-rate targeting is the loss of an independent monetary policy to deal with domestic considerations. If an independent, domestic monetary policy can be conducted responsibly, this can be a serious cost indeed, as the comparison between the post-1992 experiences of France and the United Kingdom indicates. However, not all industrialized countries have found that they are capable of conducting their own monetary policy successfully, either because the central bank is not independent or because political pressures on the central bank lead to an inflationary bias in monetary policy. In these cases, giving up independent control of domestic monetary policy may not be a great loss, while the gain of having monetary policy determined by a better-performing central bank in the anchor country can be substantial.

Italy provides an example: it was not a coincidence that the Italian public had the most favourable attitude of all those in Europe toward the EMU. The past record of Italian monetary policy was not good, and the Italian public recognized that having monetary policy controlled by more responsible outsiders had benefits that far outweighed the costs of losing the ability to focus monetary policy on domestic considerations.

A second reason why industrialized countries might find targeting exchange rates useful is that it encourages integration of the domestic economy with its neighbours. Clearly this was the rationale for long-standing pegging of the exchange rate to the Deutschmark by countries such as Austria and the Netherlands, and the more recent exchange-rate pegs that preceded the creation of the euro area.

To sum up, exchange-rate targeting for industrialized countries is probably not the best monetary policy strategy to control the overall economy unless (1) domestic monetary and political institutions are not conducive to good monetary policymaking or (2) there are other important benefits of an exchange-rate target that have nothing to do with monetary policy.

When is exchange-rate targeting desirable for emerging market countries?

In countries whose political and monetary institutions are particularly weak and which therefore have been experiencing continued bouts of hyperinflation, a characterization that applies to many emerging market (including transition) countries, exchange-rate targeting may be the only way to break inflationary psychology and stabilize the economy. In this situation, exchange-rate targeting is the stabilization policy of last resort. However, if the exchange-rate targeting regimes in emerging market countries are not always transparent, they are more likely to break down, often resulting in disastrous financial crises.

Currency boards, dollarization and monetary unions

Are there exchange-rate strategies that make it less likely that the exchange-rate regime will break down? Two such strategies that have received increasing attention in recent years are currency boards and dollarization. These so-called 'hard-peg' exchange-rate regimes-are characterized by more transparency and a stronger commitment to the fixed exchange rate. An even more extreme form of exchange rate targeting is the creation of a monetary union, in which the exchange rate is fixed irrevocably and irreversibly. In what follows we provide a description of the main features of these systems, with their specific advantages and disadvantages.

Currency boards

One solution to the problem of lack of transparency and commitment to the exchange-rate target is the adoption of a **currency board**, in which the domestic currency is backed 100% by a foreign currency (say, dollars or the euro) and in which the note-issuing authority, whether the central bank or the government, establishes a fixed exchange rate to this foreign currency and stands ready to exchange domestic currency for the foreign currency at this rate whenever the public requests it. A currency board is just a variant of a fixed exchange-rate target in which the commitment to the fixed exchange rate is especially strong because the conduct of monetary policy is in effect put on autopilot, and taken completely out of the hands of the central bank and the government. In contrast, the typical fixed or pegged exchange-rate regime does allow the monetary authorities some discretion in their conduct of monetary policy because they can still adjust interest rates or print money.

A currency board arrangement thus has important advantages over a monetary policy strategy that just uses an exchange-rate target. First, the money supply can expand only when foreign currency is exchanged for domestic currency at the central bank. Thus the increased amount of domestic currency is matched by an equal increase in foreign exchange reserves. The central bank no longer has the ability to print money and thereby cause inflation. Second, the currency board involves a stronger commitment by the central bank to the fixed exchange rate and may therefore be effective in bringing down inflation quickly and in decreasing the likelihood of a successful speculative attack against the currency.

Although they solve the transparency and commitment problems inherent in an exchange-rate target regime, currency boards suffer from some of the same shortcomings: the loss of an independent monetary policy and increased exposure of the economy to shocks from the anchor country, and the loss of the central bank's ability to create money and act as a lender of last resort. Other means must therefore be used to cope with potential banking crises. Also, if there is a speculative attack on a currency board, the exchange of the domestic currency for foreign currency leads to a sharp contraction of the money supply, which can be highly damaging to the economy.

Currency boards have been established in the territory of Hong Kong (1983) and countries such as Argentina (1991), Estonia (1992), Lithuania (1994), Bulgaria (1997) and Bosnia (1998). Argentina's currency board, which operated from 1991 to 2002 and required the central bank to exchange US dollars for new pesos at a fixed exchange rate of 1 to 1, is one of the most interesting. For more on this subject, see the box 'Argentina's currency board'.

Dollarization

Another solution to the problems created by a lack of transparency and commitment to the exchange-rate target is **dollarization**, the adoption of a sound currency, like the US dollar, as a country's money. Indeed, dollarization is just another variant of a fixed exchange-rate target with an even stronger commitment mechanism than a currency board provides. As we have seen in Argentina, a currency board can be abandoned, allowing a change in the value of the currency, but a change of value is impossible with dollarization. A dollar bill is always worth one dollar, whether it is held in the United States or outside of it.

Dollarization has been advocated as a monetary policy strategy for emerging market countries. Panama has been dollarized since its independence in 1904. Dollarization was discussed actively by Argentine officials in the aftermath of the devaluation of the Brazilian real in January 1999 and was adopted by Ecuador in 2000 and El Salvador in 2001. Dollarization's key advantage is that it completely avoids the possibility of a speculative attack on the domestic currency (because there is none). (Such an attack is still a danger even under a currency board arrangement.)

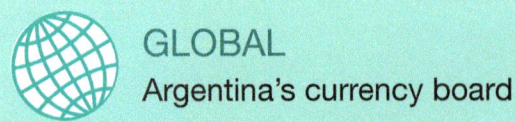

GLOBAL
Argentina's currency board

Argentina has had a long history of monetary instability, with inflation rates fluctuating dramatically and sometimes surging to beyond 1,000% per year. To end this cycle of inflationary surges, Argentina decided to adopt a currency board in April 1991. The Argentine currency board worked as follows. Under Argentina's convertibility law, the peso/dollar exchange rate was fixed at one to one, and a member of the public could go to the Argentine central bank and exchange a peso for a dollar, or vice versa, at any time.

The early years of Argentina's currency board looked stunningly successful. Inflation, which had been running at an 800% annual rate in 1990, fell to less than 5% by the end of 1994, and economic growth was rapid, averaging almost 8% per year from 1991 to 1994. In the aftermath of the Mexican peso crisis, however, concern about the health of the Argentine economy resulted in the public pulling money out of the banks (deposits fell by 18%) and exchanging pesos for dollars, thus causing a contraction of the Argentine money supply. The result was a sharp drop in Argentine economic activity, with real GDP shrinking by more than 5% in 1995 and the unemployment rate jumping above 15%. Only in 1996 did the economy begin to recover.

Because the central bank of Argentina had no control over monetary policy under the currency board system, it was relatively helpless to counteract the contractionary monetary policy stemming from the public's behaviour. Furthermore, because the currency board did not allow

the central bank to create pesos and lend them to the banks, it had very little capability to act as a lender of last resort. With help from international agencies, such as the IMF, the World Bank and the Inter-American Development Bank, which lent Argentina more than $5 billion in 1995 to help shore up its banking system, the currency board survived.

However, in 1998 Argentina entered another recession, which was both severe and very long-lasting. By the end of 2001, unemployment reached nearly 20%, a level comparable to that experienced in the United States during the Great Depression of the 1930s. The result has been civil unrest and the fall of the elected government, as well as a major banking crisis and a default on nearly $150 billion of government debt. Because the central bank of Argentina had no control over monetary policy under the currency board system, it was unable to use monetary policy to expand the economy and get out of its recession. Furthermore, because the currency board did not allow the central bank to create pesos and lend them to banks, it had very little capability to act as a lender of last resort. In January 2002, the currency board finally collapsed and the peso depreciated by more than 70%. The result was the full-scale financial crisis described in Chapter 9, with inflation shooting up and an extremely severe depression. Clearly, the Argentine public is not as enamoured of its currency board as it once was.

Dollarization is subject to the usual disadvantages of an exchange-rate target (the loss of an independent monetary policy, increased exposure of the economy to shocks from the anchor country, and the inability of the central bank to create money and act as a lender of last resort). Dollarization has one additional disadvantage not characteristic of currency boards or other exchange-rate target regimes. Because a country adopting dollarization no longer has its own currency, it loses the revenue that a government receives by issuing money, which is called **seignorage**. Because governments (or their central banks) do not have to pay interest on their currency, they earn revenue (seignorage) by using this currency to purchase income-earning assets such as bonds. If an emerging market country dollarizes and gives up its currency, it needs to make up this loss of revenue somewhere, which is not always easy for a poor country.

Monetary unions

A **monetary union** is formed when two or more countries abandon their own national currencies for a common currency managed by a common central bank. These countries fix their exchange rates *irrevocably* and *irreversibly* towards the common currency. Because of its irrevocability and irreversibility, a monetary union is often viewed as the most extreme variant of exchange-rate targeting. A monetary union differs from dollarization in that dollarized countries like Ecuador and Panama, for example, do not have any influence on the

Fed's monetary policy decisions. On the other hand, countries participating in a monetary union take part in monetary decision processes and share governance. Moreover, union members also share the revenues that come from printing money.

There are several existing monetary unions around the world. Probably, the most well known is the **Economic and Monetary Union (EMU)**. Formed on 1 January 1999, the EMU currently (as of 2012) comprises 17 European countries which irrevocably and irreversibly fixed the values of their national currency against the euro, and, as we describe in Chapter 13, created the European Central Bank (ECB) which conducts monetary policy for the entire euro area. Other examples of monetary unions include the West African Economic and Monetary Union (WAEMU), which engulfs eight West African nations that use the West African CFA franc as their common currency, and the Economic and Monetary Community of Central Africa, which comprises six Central African nations and uses the Central African CFA franc as their legal tender. There are monetary unions yet to be formed: the Gulf Cooperation Council (established in May 1981) aims at full economic and monetary union (see box below).

But why would a certain group of independent countries decide to give up their currencies? More specifically, what are the benefits and the costs of a monetary union?[11]

Benefits of monetary union

The benefits of a monetary union are mostly microeconomic in nature. They include: increased price transparency, reduced transaction costs and reduced exchange rate uncertainty. First, sharing one currency increases **price transparency**. If consumers see prices in the same unit of account, they are better able to compare them. This increases competition among sellers and thus leads to efficiency gains. To see an example, suppose you live in Austria and want to buy a mountain bike for your next adventure in the Scottish Highlands. You start searching the Internet for possible bikes to buy, and find your preferred model both from an Austrian bike shop for €600 and from a German portal in Munich, but for €400. Because a bicycle can be transported relatively easily and cheaply, you will probably buy the bike in Munich. A monetary union, by easing price comparison, reduces price differentials through higher competition.

GLOBAL
Will the monetary union of the six-nation Arab Gulf Cooperation Council be achieved?

The Gulf Cooperation Council (GCC) is a trade bloc comprising six of the fastest-growing Arab nations lying on the Persian Gulf, namely Bahrain, Kuwait, Oman, Qatar, Saudi Arabia and the United Arab Emirates. The GCC was established in May 1981 but the GCC common market was founded only on 1 January 2008. The GCC common market removes all trade barriers between the member nations, and grants national treatment to GCC businesses and citizens. Its nominal GDP grew from $823 billion in 2007 to $1,223 billion in 2008. Moreover, the GCC nations control nearly half the oil reserves in the world.

The heads of five of the central banks of these nations decided at the dawn of 2009 to establish a new central bank that is expected to be named the Gulf Central Bank (GCB). Oman withdrew in 2006 in order to maintain independent monetary policy. The prime goal of the GCB would be to establish the long-awaited currency union in the six Arab Gulf nations by the end of 2010. The new common GCC currency is supposed to be named the 'khaliji' or 'gulf' and would be pegged to a basket of currencies including the US dollar, the euro, the Japanese yen and the British pound. The prime goal of the common currency, aside from facilitating trade, is to price oil in the new khaliji currency rather than in the volatile US dollar. This should enable these six nations to have a better grip on the price of oil. Yet, on 20 May 2009 the United Arab Emirates, the second largest Arab economy after Saudi Arabia, abruptly withdrew from the currency union in protest at the decision to locate the GCB in Saudi Arabia's capital, Riyadh. This means that only four nations remain highly committed to the currency union. However, the United Arab Emirates has vowed to consider joining the currency union in the event it proves to be successful.

Second, a monetary union reduces foreign transaction costs, related to commission charges or margins between the buy and the sell exchange rates charged by banks and currency exchanges. For instance, the European Commission has estimated that the gains of eliminating foreign transaction costs may arrive at 0.3-0.5% of EU GDP each year. Third, with a common currency, the uncertainty associated with future exchange rate movements is eliminated. Of course, exchange rate uncertainty can be reduced through hedging (protecting oneself against future exchange rate movements). But hedging costs money. Both the elimination of the exchange rate risk and the reduction of transaction costs stimulate trade among the members of a monetary union. For instance, recent empirical studies estimate that EMU boosted eurozone trade by something between 5% and 20%.[12]

Besides these traditional microeconomic benefits, a single currency has also the main macroeconomic advantage of anchoring inflation expectations and reducing inflation uncertainty. If the newly created common central bank is credibly committed to the goal of price stability, the monetary union will help anchor inflationary expectations to low levels also in those countries of the union which in the past had a weak anti-inflationary reputation. Therefore these countries may benefit to a great extent from joining a monetary union. A clear example in this respect is given by Italy, which since joining the EMU has been able to bring down inflation to a considerable extent.

Finally, the creation of a common central bank with a strong anti-inflation reputation may have the additional benefit of making the new common currency increasingly used as reserve currency in international financial transactions. This will stimulate activity for domestic financial markets, creating enhanced investment opportunities for bank and non-bank businesses in the monetary union. In this respect, with the creation of the euro in 1999, many commentators have argued that the supremacy of the US dollar as reserve currency may be subject to a serious challenge (see the Closer look box: 'The euro's challenge to the dollar').

Let us now move to the costs of a monetary union.

Costs of monetary union

The costs of a monetary union, as in the other forms of exchange-rate targeting, derive from the loss of an independent monetary policy to deal with domestic considerations. In particular, union members are no longer able to influence the exchange rate of their currency, and are unable to set their own short-term interest rates or determine the amount of money supply in their country. But how costly is it to lose the monetary instruments to deal with domestic considerations in a monetary union? The answer to this question is at the heart of

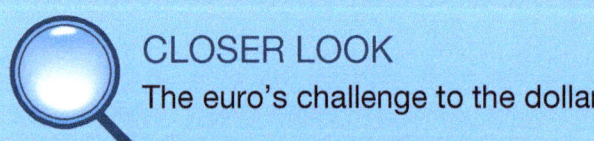

CLOSER LOOK
The euro's challenge to the dollar

With the creation of the Economic and Monetary Union and the euro in 1999, the US dollar is facing a challenge to its position as the key reserve currency in international financial transactions. Adoption of the euro increases integration of Europe's financial markets, which could rival those in the United States. The resulting increase in the use of euros in financial markets will make it more likely that international transactions are carried out in the euro. The economic clout of the euro area rivals that of the United States: both have a similar share of world GDP (around 20%) and world exports (around 15%). If the European Central Bank can make sure that inflation remains low so that the euro becomes a sound currency, this should bode well for the euro.

However, for the euro to eat into the dollar's position as a reserve currency, the euro area must function as a cohesive political entity that can exert its influence on the world stage. There are serious doubts on this score, however, with the 'no' votes on the European constitution by France and the Netherlands in 2005 and particularly with the lack of political consensus shown by European leaders to deal with euro debt crisis. Most analysts think it will be a long time before the euro drives out the dollar in international financial transactions.

the theory of **Optimal Currency Area (OCA)**, pioneered by Robert Mundell, the 1999 Nobel Prize winner and economics professor at Columbia University in New York. On the basis of this theory, a geographical region constitutes an optimal currency area when the use of a common currency leads to no loss of welfare related to the loss of the monetary policy instruments. In particular, two main criteria can be identified. First, the optimality of a currency area depends on how important **asymmetric shocks** in the monetary union really are. Second, if asymmetric shocks are present, the question is whether or not there are **adjustment mechanisms** that help the economy return to equilibrium. Let us address these two aspects in turn.

An asymmetric shock is a shock that hits only one of the countries in the monetary union. Because a country-specific shock may have a small impact on the economic conditions of the union as a whole, it cannot be addressed by the common central bank. Therefore, the effects of an asymmetric shock have to be dealt with by the country itself. Because of the absence of exchange rate adjustments, dealing with such shocks can be costly. If asymmetric shocks are large and frequent, the cost of losing monetary policy as a tool to manage the economy may be high.

To see an example, let us consider the case in which two countries A, and B, form a monetary union. Therefore, countries A and B share the same currency, which is managed by the new common central bank. Now, let us suppose that countries A and B are hit by an asymmetric demand shock, because for instance there has been a shift of demand from the products of country A to the products of country B. As a result, in country A output declines and unemployment rises, whereas in country B output grows and unemployment falls. Both countries are now in disequilibrium, and need adjustment.

If the two countries had not been in a monetary union and had chosen a flexible exchange rate regime, the adjustment mechanism would have been the following. The central bank of country A would have lowered its interest rate to stimulate aggregate demand, whereas country B would have followed the opposite policy. The resulting depreciation of the currency of country A relative to the currency of country B would have further stimulated the aggregate demand of country A, and reduced that of country B, leading to a return to equilibrium in both countries. On the other hand, if both countries are part of a monetary union, the interest rate and exchange rate instruments cannot be used to address domestic conditions. This simple example shows that *one condition for a currency area to be optimal is the absence of asymmetric shocks*.[13] But are there other adjustment mechanisms that would help the two countries in a monetary union to return to equilibrium?

Alternative adjustment mechanisms helping to restore equilibrium is through **wage flexibility** and **labour mobility**. If wages in the two countries are flexible, due to high unemployment in country B workers will reduce their wage claims, making the products of country B cheaper and more competitive. In country A, on the other hand, the excess demand for labour will lead to increased wages and production prices, making products in country A more expensive and less competitive. As a consequence, equilibrium will be restored. Another mechanism that can help restore equilibrium requires labour mobility. If people from country A (where there is excess supply of labour) are ready to move to country B (where there is excess demand for labour), then equilibrium is restored without changes in the wage and price level in the two countries. Wage flexibility and labour mobility are the two key adjustment mechanisms of the original OCA theory. *Therefore, the second condition for a currency area to be optimal is the presence of sufficient flexibility of the labour market*.

Another adjustment mechanism which may help restore equilibrium works through **fiscal policy**. Suppose that in the monetary union there exists a centralized fiscal authority that can levy taxes and make transfers (e.g. pensions and unemployment benefits) to residents of countries A and B. Under these circumstances, a potential adjustment mechanism may work through **automatic transfers** from country B to country A. The higher tax revenues deriving from the rise in output of country B, can be for instance automatically transferred to country A in the form of higher unemployment benefits. With such a system of redistribution in place, the problems of the adjustment mechanisms are reduced. If the centralization of the budget is non-existent, national fiscal authorities of countries A and B can still deal with the effects of asymmetric shocks individually. An example of centralized fiscal authority in a monetary union is given by the US, whereas the model of decentralized fiscal authorities is in place in the euro area.

Now that we know the main criteria to judge how optimal a monetary union is, we are ready to tackle two important questions which have kept many economists, policymakers and commentators rather busy over the last few years. That is, is the euro area an optimal currency area? Will the euro area expand in the future? In the next two boxes we will address these two questions in turn.

CLOSER LOOK
Is the euro area an optimal currency area?

When evaluating how optimal a currency area is, the presence of adjustment mechanisms to absorb asymmetric shocks hitting the countries in the monetary union is of crucial importance. First, however, we need to see how often such shocks occur. Some early evidence in the 1990s showed that in the pre-EMU period economic shocks hitting the European countries were uncorrelated, and the business cycles not fully synchronized. The general conclusion from this empirical literature was that a monetary union of all EU members was not optimal. But is it correct to judge the optimality of a currency area before the adoption of the common currency? By joining a monetary union, countries intensify their trade relationships which leads to more business cycle synchronization. Work carried out by two American economists, Jeffrey Frankel and Andy Rose, seems to support this view. They find that the more countries trade with each other, the more correlated their business cycles are. Similar results are also found in more recent empirical studies. This tells us that a currency area may not be optimal *ex ante*, but it may become so *ex post*.

The enhanced trade integration and increased business cycle convergence do not imply the absence of asymmetric shocks in EMU. Therefore the question whether adjustment mechanisms are available remains relevant. In terms of flexibility of labour markets, European countries show a relatively poor record. First, European wages are very inflexible, mainly due to labour unions that are relatively much stronger in European countries than in other industrialized countries. Second, the degree of labour mobility across European countries is much lower than within US regions. But why are Europeans so immobile? When considering moving to another country, people consider not only economic incentives (availability of jobs, higher wages, career opportunities in general, social benefits, etc.), but also weigh factors such as cultural differences, language barriers, traditions, and family and friends left behind. Apparently for Europeans the prospect of better labour market conditions does not weigh enough against the disadvantages of leaving their country of residence. This will probably change in the future as a result of economic

and political integration, but this process is working rather slowly.

If the labour market is not flexible enough, is the adjustment mechanism working through fiscal policy operative in Europe? Currently, the EU centralized budget accounts for a mere 1% of the EU GDP. Thus no significant centralized redistribution system is in place in Europe. This is in clear contrast with the US, where it is estimated that between 20% and 30% of the effects of asymmetric shocks are compensated by transfers of the federal government. Moreover, euro members cannot make full use of national fiscal policy. In fact, in order to ensure fiscal discipline of member states, in 1997 European leaders introduced the **Stability and Growth Pact (SGP)**, which imposes constraints on the national fiscal policies of EU countries. More specifically, according to the SGP the budget deficit/GDP ratio should not exceed 3% and government debt/GDP ratio should stay below 60%. As such, the SGP limits the ability to use fiscal policy as a stabilizing tool.

To sum up, we have seen that as for the occurrence of asymmetric shocks and business cycle convergence, the EMU countries are showing gradual improvement. However, on the basis of the labour and fiscal adjustment mechanisms, the EMU is far from being an OCA. So, why did European leaders introduce the euro? Commentators such as Barry Eichengreen and Martin Feldstein argue that the euro was introduced for political reasons, and view the EMU as the outcome of a bargain between Germany striving for more political integration and France trying to acquire a say in monetary policy. Other economists, like Charles Wyplosz, give more credit to the economic arguments behind EMU and point to the 'impossible trilogy', the simultaneous existence of free capital mobility, monetary independence and a fixed exchange rate. With full capital mobility, the European countries had no other choice than to move to a union. The alternatives would have been continued German monetary hegemony or a float with long and disruptive swings in the nominal exchange rates.

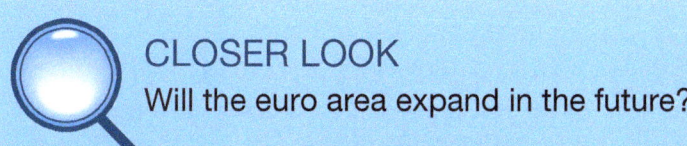

CLOSER LOOK
Will the euro area expand in the future?

As of 2012, 17 of the 27 European Union (EU) member countries were part of the EMU, whereas 10 EU countries had not adopted the euro. The latter are three of the old EU countries (Denmark, Sweden and the UK) and seven of the new EU member states (Bulgaria, the Czech Republic, Hungary, Latvia, Lithuania, Poland and Romania). Will these countries join the euro area in the future? Before answering this question, we need to discuss the **convergence criteria** of the Maastricht Treaty, which was signed in December 1991 and is the foundation stone of the process towards monetary unification in Europe.

According to the Maastricht Treaty, in order for an EU member to join the eurozone it has to fulfil four main convergence criteria, all of which stress macroeconomic convergence between countries before accession to the eurozone. The first criterion determines that the inflation rate in the acceding country should not exceed the average of the three lowest inflation rates in the EU plus 1.5%. The second criterion states that the long-term interest rate should not be more than 2% higher than the average observed in these three low-inflation countries. According to the budgetary criterion, the budget deficit/GDP ratio should not exceed 3% (if it does, it should be declining continuously and substantially to approach the desired level) and government debt/GDP ratio should stay below 60% (if it is not currently under this threshold it should have a declining trend and approach the threshold level at a swift enough rate). Finally, the fourth criterion ensures exchange rate stability. In particular, would-be members of the eurozone should join the ERM system and spend at least two years without devaluation prior to joining. The rationale behind the convergence criteria is ensuring macroeconomic convergence with the eurozone members. All the convergence criteria (through different mechanisms) have the goal of avoiding inflation differentials in the eurozone. This is necessary because traditionally low-inflation countries (e.g. Germany) agreed to the adoption of the euro if they received some guarantee that with the new currency, the euro, they will be able to keep low inflation in their economies.

Whereas the seven countries that entered the EU in or after 2004 will have to introduce the euro once they have fulfilled the convergence criteria, the three old EU members (Denmark, Sweden and the UK) decided not to join the EMU. Despite satisfying the convergence criteria, Denmark was given the right

to condition its entry on the result of a referendum. Sweden, by refusing to enter ERM, did not join as the exchange-rate criterion was not fulfilled. Finally, the UK obtained an 'opt-out' clause, which gives it the right to decide whether to join or not at its discretion. But will the UK join the euro at some point in the future?

In 1997 the Blair government expressed its will to enter the eurozone conditional on five economic tests being passed. The five economic tests, some of which closely resemble the criteria of an OCA, are as follows. (1) Are business cycles and economic structures compatible so that we and others could live with euro interest rates on a permanent basis? (2) If problems emerge, is there sufficient flexibility to deal with them? (3) Would joining EMU create better conditions for firms making long-term decisions to invest in Britain? (4) What impact would entry into EMU have on the financial services industry? (5) In summary, will joining EMU promote higher growth, stability and a lasting increase in jobs? The outcome of the evaluation in 1997 was that the UK had not yet passed the first test. In 2003 the Treasury repeated the analysis and reached the same conclusion. In particular, it was concluded that the timing of the UK business cycle was significantly different from that of the rest of the EU. By 2003 significant progress on convergence had been made and business cycles were more convergent with those of the euro area. But the presence of significant structural differences, in particular between the housing market in the UK and in the rest of Europe, led to the conclusion that the UK was not fit to join the euro. Although the establishment of the five economic tests shows that economic arguments are important, as we have seen in the previous Application, adopting the euro is also (if not mostly) a political decision. Many British leaders have regarded the adoption of the euro as a certain loss of political sovereignty. This seems to be the view of the new Liberal–Conservative government, which ruled out entry to the euro at least till the next election.

Over the last few years, due to the dramatic developments of the euro sovereign debt crisis (see Chapter 9) public and political support towards entry has weakened. In fact, as of early 2012, the question is not whether and when the euro area will expand, but it is rather if the EMU will contract or even break up. For instance, the quick deterioration of the Greek fiscal position opened the possibility of Greece exiting the eurozone.

Summary

1 An unsterilized central bank intervention in which the domestic currency is sold to purchase foreign assets leads to a gain in international reserves, an increase in the money supply and a depreciation of the domestic currency. Available evidence suggests, however, that sterilized central bank interventions have little long-term effect on the exchange rate.

2 The balance of payments is a bookkeeping system for recording all payments between a country and foreign countries that have a direct bearing on the movement of funds between them. The official reserve transactions balance is the sum of the current account balance and the items in the capital account. It indicates the amount of international reserves that must be moved between countries to finance international transactions.

3 Before World War I, the gold standard was predominant. Currencies were convertible into gold, thus fixing exchange rates between countries. After World War II, the Bretton Woods system and the IMF were established to promote a fixed exchange rate system in which the US dollar, the reserve currency, was convertible into gold. The Bretton Woods system collapsed in 1971. We now have an international financial system that has elements of a managed float and a fixed exchange rate system. Some exchange rates fluctuate from day to day, although central banks intervene in the foreign exchange market, while other exchange rates are fixed.

4 Controls on capital outflows receive support because they may prevent domestic residents and foreigners from pulling capital out of a country during a crisis and make devaluation less likely. Controls on capital inflows make sense under the theory that if speculative capital cannot flow in, then it cannot go out suddenly and create a crisis. However, capital controls suffer from several disadvantages: they are seldom effective, they lead to corruption and they may allow governments to avoid taking the steps needed to reform their financial systems to deal with the crisis.

5 The IMF has recently taken on the role of an international lender of last resort. Because central banks in emerging market countries are unlikely to be able to perform a lender-of-last-resort operation successfully, an international lender of last resort like the IMF is needed to prevent financial instability. However, the IMF's role as an international lender of last resort creates a serious moral hazard problem that can encourage excessive risk taking and make a financial crisis more likely, but refusing to lend may be politically hard to do. In addition, it needs to be able to provide liquidity quickly during a crisis to keep manageable the amount of funds lent.

6 Three international considerations affect the conduct of monetary policy: direct effects of the foreign exchange market on the money supply, balance-of-payments considerations, and exchange rate considerations. Inasmuch as the United States has been a reserve currency country in the post-World War II period, US monetary policy has been less affected by developments in the foreign exchange market and its balance of payments than is true for other countries. However, in recent years, exchange rate considerations have been playing a more prominent role in influencing US monetary policy.

Exchange-rate targeting has the following advantages as a monetary policy strategy: (1) it directly keeps inflation under control by tying the inflation rate for internationally traded goods to that found in the anchor country to which its currency is pegged; (2) it provides an automatic rule for the conduct of monetary policy that helps mitigate the time-inconsistency problem; and (3) it is simple and clear. Exchange-rate targeting also has serious disadvantages: (1) it results in a loss of independent monetary policy; (2) it leaves the country open to speculative attacks; and (3) it can weaken the accountability of policymakers because the exchange-rate signal is lost. Two strategies that make it less likely that the exchange-rate regime will break down are currency boards, in which the central bank stands ready to automatically exchange domestic for foreign currency at a fixed rate, and dollarization, in which a sound currency like the US dollar is adopted as the country's money.

7 A monetary union is formed when two or more countries abandon their own national currencies for a common currency managed by a common central bank. These countries fix their exchange rates irrevocably and irreversibly towards the common currency. A monetary union has several benefits which are in common with the other exchange-rate regimes, but it does not leave the country open to speculative attacks. The costs of a monetary union, as in the other forms of exchange-rate targeting, derive from the loss of an independent monetary policy to deal with domestic considerations. According to the Optimal Currency Area (OCA) literature these costs depend on the importance of asymmetric shocks and the presence of adjustment mechanisms helping economies return to equilibrium. The main adjustment mechanisms are working through wage flexibility and labour mobility.

Key terms

QUESTIONS AND PROBLEMS

All questions and problems are available in MyEconLab at **www.myeconlab.com/mishkin**.

1 If the ECB buys euros in the foreign exchange market but conducts an offsetting open market operation to sterilize the intervention, what will be the impact on international reserves, the money supply and the exchange rate?

2 If the ECB buys euros in the foreign exchange market but does not sterilize the intervention, what will be the impact on international reserves, the money supply and the exchange rate?

3 For each of the following, identify in which part of the UK Balance of Payments account it appears (current account, capital account or net change in international reserves) and whether it is a receipt or a payment.

(a) An American subject's purchase of a share of Vodafone shares

(b) A British subject's purchase of an airline ticket from British Airways

(c) The Swiss government's purchase of UK government bonds

(d) A Japanese's purchase of British pies

(e) £50 million of foreign aid to Honduras

(f) A loan by a British bank to Mexico

(g) A British bank's borrowing of Eurodollars

4 Why does a balance-of-payments deficit for the United States have a different effect on its international reserves than a balance-of-payments deficit for the Netherlands?

5 Under the gold standard, if the UK became more productive relative to the United States, what would happen to the money supply in the two countries? Why would the changes in the money supply help preserve a fixed exchange rate between the United States and the UK?

6 If a country's par exchange rate was undervalued during the Bretton Woods fixed exchange rate regime, what kind of intervention would that country's central bank be forced to undertake, and what effect would it have on its international reserves and the money supply?

7 How can a large balance-of-payments surplus contribute to the country's inflation rate?

8 'If a country wants to keep its exchange rate from changing, it must give up some control over its money supply.' Is this statement true, false, or uncertain? Explain your answer.

9 Why can balance-of-payments deficits force some countries to implement a contractionary monetary policy?

10 'Balance-of-payments deficits always cause a country to lose international reserves.' Is this statement true, false, or uncertain? Explain your answer.

11 How can persistent US balance-of-payments deficits stimulate world inflation?

12 'Inflation is not possible under the gold standard.' Is this statement true, false, or uncertain? Explain your answer.

13 Why is it that in a pure flexible exchange rate system, the foreign exchange market has no direct effects on the money supply? Does this mean that the foreign exchange market has no effect on monetary policy?

14 'The abandonment of fixed exchange rates after 1973 has meant that countries have pursued more independent monetary policies.' Is this statement true, false, or uncertain? Explain your answer.

15 What are the key advantages of exchange-rate targeting as a monetary policy strategy?

16 Why did the exchange-rate peg lead to difficulties for the countries in the ERM when German reunification occurred?

17 How can exchange-rate targets lead to a speculative attack on a currency?

18 Why may the disadvantage of exchange-rate targeting of not having an independent monetary policy be less of an issue for emerging market countries than for industrialized countries?

19 How can the long-term bond market help reduce the time-inconsistency problem for monetary policy? Can the foreign exchange market also perform this role?

20 When is exchange-rate targeting likely to be a sensible strategy for industrialized countries? When is exchange-rate targeting likely to be a sensible strategy for emerging market countries?

21 What are the advantages and disadvantages of a currency board over a monetary policy that just uses an exchange-rate target?

22 What are the key advantages and disadvantages of dollarization over other forms of exchange-rate targeting?

23 What are the main benefits and costs of a monetary union? What are the main criteria for the optimality of a currency area?

24 What are the main convergence criteria of the Maastricht Treaty?

WEB EXERCISES

1 Go to **www.oecd.org/std/bop** and search for the latest figures of the current account balances (in national currency) of Germany, Italy and France. Compare these figures and comment on the possible economic implications for the euro exchange rate.

2 Go to **www.ons.gov.uk/ons/index.html** and find the latest edition of the 'Pink Book' containing estimates of the Balance of Payments of the United Kingdom. Go to the table 'Summary of balance of payments' and plot and discuss the evolution of the current account as percentage of GDP since 1947.

3 There are many exchange rate arrangements and monetary frameworks across the worlds. From the International Monetary Fund **(http://www.imf.org/ external/NP/mfd/er/index.aspx)** find two countries for each of the regimes identified by the IMF.

4 The International Monetary Fund stands ready to help nations facing monetary crises. Go to **www.imf.org**. Click on the tab labelled 'About IMF'. What is the stated purpose of the IMF? How many nations participate and when was it established?

Notes

1 An unsterilized intervention in which the central bank sells domestic currency increases the amount of foreign assets slightly because it leads to an increase in the monetary base while leaving the amount of government bonds in the hands of the public unchanged. The curve depicting the supply of domestic assets would thus shift to the right slightly, which also works toward lowering the exchange rate, yielding the same conclusion derived from Figure 18.1. Because the resulting increase in the monetary base would be only a minuscule fraction of the total amount of domestic assets outstanding, the supply curve would shift by an imperceptible amount. This is why Figure 18.1 is drawn with the supply curve unchanged.

2 A sterilized intervention changes the amount of foreign securities relative to domestic securities in the hands of the public, called a *portfolio balance effect*. Through this effect, the central bank might be able to affect the interest differential between domestic and foreign assets, which in turn affects the relative expected return of domestic assets. Empirical evidence has not revealed this portfolio balance effect to be significant. However, a sterilized intervention *could* indicate what central banks want to happen to the future exchange rate and so might provide a signal about the course of future monetary policy. In this way a sterilized intervention could lead to shifts in the demand curve for domestic assets and ultimately affect the exchange rate. However, the future change in monetary policy – not the sterilized intervention – is the source of the exchange rate effect. For a further discussion of the signalling and portfolio balance effects and the possible differential effects of sterilized versus unsterilized intervention, see Paul Krugman and Maurice Obstfeld, *International Economics*, 8th ed. (Boston: Addison-Wesley, 2008).

3 The capital account balance number reported here includes a statistical discrepancy item, called 'net errors and omissions' that represents errors due to unrecorded transactions involving smuggling and other capital flows. Many experts believe that the statistical discrepancy item, which keeps the balance of payments in balance, is primarily the result of large hidden capital flows, and this is why it is included in the capital account balance. In 2010, the 'net errors and omissions' of the UK balance of payments amounted to –£8.5 billion.

4 In practice, the official reserves are an item of the capital account. However, here they are identified separately in order to understand that the change in official reserves acts as a gap between the current account and the capital account balances.

5 The current account balance can also be viewed as showing the amount by which total saving exceeds private-sector

and government investment in the domestic country. Total domestic saving equals the increase in total wealth held by the domestic private sector and government. Total investment equals the increase in the domestic capital stock (wealth physically in the domestic country). The difference between them is the increase in domestic claims on foreign wealth.

6 Because the exchange rate will continue to be fixed at E_{par}, the expected future exchange rate remains unchanged and so does not need to be addressed in the analysis.

7 See Sebastian Edwards, 'How effective are capital controls?', *Journal of Economic Perspectives* 13 (Winter 2000): 65-84.

8 The original proposal by James Tobin was to introduce a tax on all foreign exchange transactions in order to curb excessive exchange-rate fluctuations. Nowadays the term 'Tobin tax' is commonly applied to the idea of a broader financial transaction tax.

9 See international Financial Institution Advisory Commission, *Report* (IFIAC: Washington, DC, 2000).

10 However, the central bank of a reserve currency country must worry about a shift away from the use of its currency for international reserves.

11 For a more detailed discussion of the economics of monetary unions, see Paul de Grauwe, *Economics of Monetary Union*, 8th ed. (Boston: Oxford University Press, 2009).

12 The empirical evidence on the effects of a monetary union on trade is quite mixed. Early studies find that the effects of exchange rate variability on bilateral trade flows are rather weak and insignificant. Other authors, as for instance Andy Rose from the University of California (Berkeley), even claim that countries that are part of a monetary union have bilateral trade flows that are on average 200% higher than those of countries that do not form a monetary union.

13 According to Ronald McKinnon, another contributor of the original OCA theory, the higher is the *degree of openness* of a country, the lower will be the cost of the loss of the exchange rate tool. The argument works as follows. In small open economies, the same exchange rate depreciation will lead to higher increase in domestic prices (because of the higher share of imports) than in relatively more closed economies. As a result, the systematic use of the exchange rate tool in open economies will lead to systematically higher price variability, which is costly. Thus, the loss of an independent monetary policy is likely to be costly in relatively more open economies. Another criterion of the original OCA theory is provided by Peter Kenen, who argues that the more *diversified* a country is, the less vulnerable it is to sector-specific shocks and the smaller is the stabilization cost joining a monetary union.

Useful websites

www.oecd.org/std/bop Link to the OECD balance of payments statistics providing a systematic summary of economic transactions between an economy and the rest of the world, for a specific time period.

www.ons.gov.uk/ons/taxonomy/index.html?nscl=Balance+of+Payments Link from the Office for National Statistics (ONS) of the United Kingdom explaining the balance of payments and providing the latest data.

www.treasury.gov/resource-centre/data-chart-centre/tic/Documents/mfh.txt Link of the US Department of the Treasury showing the major foreign holders of Treasury securities.

https://www.cia.gov/library/publications/the-world-factbook/rankorder/2188rank.html Webpage updated by the Central Intelligence Agency (CIA) ranking countries according to their holding of foreign reserves and gold.

http://ec.europa.eu/economy_finance/economic_governance/sgp/index_en.htm Link of the European Commission providing a description of the Stability and Growth Pact.

http://research.stlouisfed.org/fred2 This website contains exchange rates, balance of payments, and trade data.

http://faculty.washington.edu/danby/bls324/macro/categories.html A nice explanation of the balance of payments.

www.imf.org/external/np/exr/facts/sdr.htm Find information about special drawing rights, allocation, valuation, and SDR users' guide.

MyEconLab can help you get A better grade   MyEconLab®

If your exam were tomorrow, would you be ready? For each chapter, MyEconLab Practice Test and Study Plans pinpoint which sections you have mastered and which ones you need to study. That way, you are more efficient with your study time, and you are better prepared for your exams.

To see how it works, turn to page 19 and then go to: **www.myeconlab.com/mishkin**

PART 6

MONETARY THEORY

Crisis and response: The perfect storm of 2007–9

In 2007 and 2008, the euro area, the UK and the US were hit by a perfect storm of formidable shocks. Higher demand for oil from rapidly growing developing countries like China and India and slowing of production in places like Mexico, Russia and Nigeria drove up oil prices sharply from around the $60 per barrel level at the beginning of 2007. By the end of the year, oil prices had risen to $100 per barrel and reached a peak of over $140 in July 2008. The oil price shock was both contractionary and inflationary, and as a result led to both higher inflation and unemployment – and many unhappy drivers at the pumps.

If this supply shock were not bad enough, the subprime financial crisis hit the industrialized economies starting in August 2007 and caused a contraction in both household and business spending. This shock led to a further rise in unemployment, with some weakening of inflationary pressure further down the road.

The result of this perfect storm of adverse shocks was a rise in unemployment in most European economies and the US between 2006 and 2009. During the same period, inflation also accelerated, but with the increase in the unemployment rate and the decline of oil and other commodity prices by the autumn of 2008, inflation rapidly came back down again.

Although the aggressive monetary policies of the ECB, the Bank of England and the Fed aimed to address the contractionary forces in their economies, policymakers wanted additional action. In February 2008 and then again in February 2009, the US Congress passed stimulus packages, first of $150 billion and then of $787 billion. During this period, also European leaders announced a Recovery Plan to drive Europe's recovery from the economic crisis. The Plan included a coordinated fiscal stimulus of around €200 billion, mostly implemented within national budgets of the individual European countries. However, although the expansionary monetary and the fiscal policies helped boost the GDP, the European economies and the US were overwhelmed by the continuing worsening of the financial crisis, and their economy went into a tailspin.

The impact of the perfect storm of adverse shocks highlights that we need to understand how monetary and other government policies affect the price level and economic activity. Chapter 19 discusses how theories of the demand for money have evolved. Chapters 20 and 21 outline the *ISLM* model, which explains how interest rates and total output in the economy are determined. In Chapter 22, we develop a basic tool, aggregate supply and demand analysis, that will enable us to study the effect of monetary policy on output and prices. Chapter 23 outlines how monetary policy affects the aggregate economy. In Chapter 24, we expand on aggregate supply and demand analysis in order to understand the inflation process. Chapter 25 examines the rational expectations revolution in monetary theory and what it implies for analysing the impact of monetary policy on inflation and economic activity.

CHAPTER 19

The demand for money

In earlier chapters, we spent a lot of time and effort learning what the money supply is, how it is determined, and what role central banks play in it. Now we are ready to explore the role of the money supply in determining the price level and total production of goods and services (aggregate output) in the economy. The study of the effect of money on the economy is called **monetary theory**, and we examine this branch of economics in the chapters of Part 6.

When economists mention *supply,* the word *demand* is sure to follow, and the discussion of money is no exception. The supply of money is an essential building block in understanding how monetary policy affects the economy, because it suggests the factors that influence the quantity of money in the economy. Not surprisingly, another essential part of monetary theory is the demand for money.

This chapter describes how the theories of the demand for money have evolved. We begin with the classical theories refined at the start of the twentieth century by economists such as Irving Fisher, Alfred Marshall and A.C. Pigou; then we move on to the Keynesian theories of the demand for money. We end with Milton Friedman's modern quantity theory.

A central question in monetary theory is whether or to what extent the quantity of money demanded is affected by changes in interest rates. Because this issue is crucial to how we view money's effects on aggregate economic activity, we focus on the role of interest rates in the demand for money.[1]

Quantity theory of money

Developed by the classical economists in the nineteenth and early twentieth centuries, the quantity theory of money is a theory of how the nominal value of aggregate income is determined. Because it also tells us how much money is held for a given amount of aggregate income, it is a theory of the demand for money. The most important feature of this theory is that it suggests that interest rates have no effect on the demand for money.

Velocity of money and equation of exchange

The clearest exposition of the classical quantity theory approach is found in the work of the American economist Irving Fisher, in his influential book *The Purchasing Power of Money,* published in 1911. Fisher wanted to examine the link between the total quantity of money M (the money supply) and the total amount of spending on final goods and services produced in the economy $P \times Y$, where P is the price level and Y is aggregate output (income). (Total spending $P \times Y$ is also thought of as aggregate nominal income for the economy or as nominal GDP.) The concept that provides the link between M and $P \times Y$

is called the **velocity of money** (often reduced to *velocity*), the average number of times per year (turnover) that a euro is spent in buying the total amount of goods and services produced in the economy. Velocity V is defined more precisely as total spending $P \times Y$ divided by the quantity of money M:

$$V = \frac{P \times Y}{M} \tag{19.1}$$

If, for example, nominal GDP ($P \times Y$) in a year is €5 trillion and the quantity of money is €1 trillion, velocity is 5, meaning that the average euro coin is spent five times in purchasing final goods and services in the economy.

By multiplying both sides of this definition by M, we obtain the **equation of exchange**, which relates nominal income to the quantity of money and velocity:

$$M \times V = P \times Y \tag{19.2}$$

The equation of exchange thus states that the quantity of money multiplied by the number of times that this money is spent in a given year must equal nominal income (the total nominal amount spent on goods and services in that year).[2]

As it stands, Equation 19.2 is nothing more than an identity – a relationship that is true by definition. It does not tell us, for instance, that when the money supply M changes, nominal income ($P \times Y$) changes in the same direction; a rise in M, for example, could be offset by a fall in V that leaves $M \times V$ (and therefore $P \times Y$) unchanged. To convert the equation of exchange (an *identity*) into a *theory* of how nominal income is determined requires an understanding of the factors that determine velocity.

Irving Fisher reasoned that velocity is determined by the institutions in an economy that affect the way individuals conduct transactions. If people use charge accounts and credit cards to conduct their transactions, as they can today, and consequently use money less often when making purchases, less money is required to conduct the transactions generated by nominal income (M falls relative to $P \times Y$), and velocity ($P \times Y$)/M will increase. Conversely, if it is more convenient for purchases to be paid for with cash or cheque (both of which are money), more money is used to conduct the transactions generated by the same level of nominal income, and velocity will fall. Fisher took the view that the institutional and technological features of the economy would affect velocity only slowly over time, so velocity would normally be reasonably constant in the short run.

Quantity theory

Fisher's view that velocity is fairly constant in the short run transforms the equation of exchange into the **quantity theory of money**, which states that nominal income is determined solely by movements in the quantity of money: when the quantity of money M doubles, $M \times V$ doubles and so must $P \times Y$ the value of nominal income. To see how this works, let's assume that velocity is 5, nominal income (GDP) is initially €5 trillion, and the money supply is €1 trillion. If the money supply doubles to €2 trillion, the quantity theory of money tells us that nominal income will double to €10 trillion (= 5 × €2 trillion).

Because the classical economists (including Fisher) thought that wages and prices were completely flexible, they believed that the level of aggregate output Y produced in the economy during normal times would remain at the full-employment level, so Y in the equation of exchange could also be treated as reasonably constant in the short run. The quantity theory of money then implies that if M doubles, P must also double in the short run, because V and Y are constant. In our example, if aggregate output is €5 trillion, the velocity of 5 and a money supply of €1 trillion indicate that the price level equals 1 because 1 times €5 trillion equals the nominal income of €5 trillion. When the money supply doubles to €2 trillion, the price level must also double to 2 because 2 times €5 trillion equals the nominal income of €10 trillion.

For the classical economists, the quantity theory of money provided an explanation of movements in the price level: *movements in the price level result solely from changes in the quantity of money*.

Quantity theory of money demand

Because the quantity theory of money tells us how much money is held for a given amount of aggregate income, it is, in fact, a theory of the demand for money. We can see this by dividing both sides of the equation of exchange by V, thus rewriting it as

$$M = \frac{1}{V} \times PY$$

where nominal income $P \times Y$ is written as PY. When the money market is in equilibrium, the quantity of money M that people hold equals the quantity of money demanded M^d, so we can replace M in the equation by M^d. Using k to represent the quantity $1/V$ (a constant, because V is a constant), we can rewrite the equation as

$$M^d = k \times PY \tag{19.3}$$

Equation 19.3 tells us that because k is a constant, the level of transactions generated by a fixed level of nominal income PY determines the quantity of money M^d that people demand. Therefore, Fisher's quantity theory of money suggests that the demand for money is purely a function of income, and interest rates have no effect on the demand for money.[3]

Fisher came to this conclusion because he believed that people hold money only to conduct transactions and have no freedom of action in terms of the amount they want to hold. The demand for money is determined (1) by the level of transactions generated by the level of nominal income PY and (2) by the institutions in the economy that affect the way people conduct transactions and thus determine velocity and hence k.

Is velocity a constant?

The classical economists' conclusion that nominal income is determined by movements in the money supply rested on their belief that velocity PY/M could be treated as reasonably constant.[4] Is it reasonable to assume that velocity is constant? To answer this, let's look at Figures 19.1 and 19.2, which show the year-to-year changes in velocity over a long period of time in the US and the UK (nominal income is represented by nominal GDP and the money supply by M1 and M2 in the US and M3 in the UK).

What we see in Figure 19.1 is that even in the short run, velocity fluctuates too much to be viewed as a constant. Prior to 1950, the US velocity exhibited large swings up and down. This may reflect the substantial instability of the economy in this period, which included two world wars and the Great Depression. (Velocity actually falls, or at least its rate of growth declines, in years when recessions are taking place.) After 1950, velocity appears to have more moderate fluctuations, yet there are large differences in the growth rate of velocity from year to year. The percentage change in M1 velocity (GDP/M1) from 1981 to 1982, for example, was –2.5%, whereas from 1980 to 1981 velocity grew at a rate of 4.2%. This difference of 6.7% means that nominal GDP was 6.7% lower than it would have been if velocity had kept growing at the same rate as in 1980–1.[5] The drop is enough to account for the severe recession that took place in 1981–2. After 1982, M1 velocity appears to have become even more volatile, a fact that has puzzled researchers when they examine the empirical evidence on the demand for money (discussed later in this chapter). M2 velocity remained more stable than M1 velocity after 1982, with the result that the Federal Reserve dropped its M1 targets in 1987 and began to focus more on M2 targets. However, instability of M2 velocity in the early 1990s resulted in the Fed's announcement in July 1993 that it

FIGURE 19.1

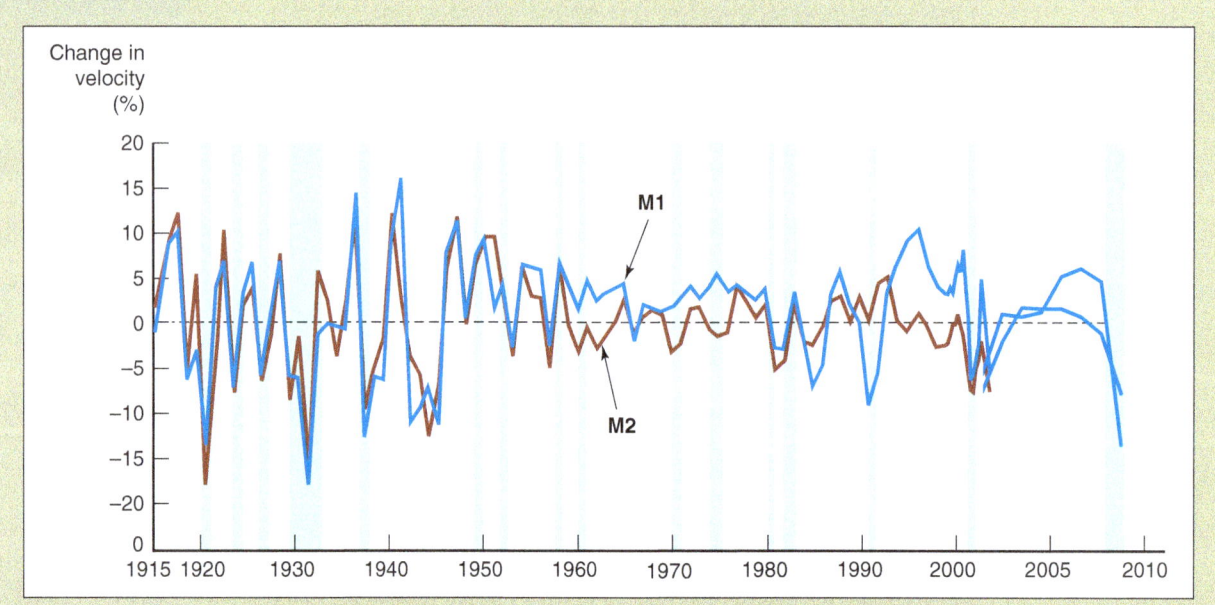

Change in the velocity of M1 and M2 from year to year in the US, 1915–2008
Shaded areas indicate recessions. Velocities are calculated using nominal GNP before 1959 and nominal GDP thereafter.
Sources: Economic Report of the President; Banking and Monetary Statistics; www.federalreserve.gov/releases/h6/hist/h6hist1.txt.

no longer felt that any of the monetary aggregates, including M2, was a reliable guide for monetary policy.

Figure 19.2 shows the UK velocity for the broad monetary aggregate M3.[6] Also in this case, the growth rate of velocity appears to have large fluctuations with a tendency to decline during recessions. Moreover, it is interesting to see that in the 1980s, the velocity showed persistent negative growth rates, reflecting the fact that nominal GDP grew more quickly than M3 throughout this period. Incidentally, as discussed in Chapter 16, this period corresponded to the time in which the Bank of England adopted monetary targeting. Despite upwards revisions of their annual target ranges, the British authorities saw themselves continuously missing their targets and were forced to gradually reduce their emphasis on monetary aggregates.[7] Similarly to the United States, this unstable relationship between the rate of money growth and the rate of growth of nominal GDP has been associated to financial deregulation and liberalization, which in the case of the UK resulted in banks' balance sheets expanding more rapidly than nominal income.

Until the Great Depression, economists did not recognize that velocity declines sharply during severe economic contractions. Why did the classical economists not recognize this fact when it is easy to see in the pre-Depression period in Figures 19.1 and 19.2? Unfortunately, accurate data on GDP and the money supply did not exist before World War II. (Only after the war did governments start to collect these data.) Economists had no way of knowing that their view of velocity as a constant was demonstrably false. The decline in velocity during the Great Depression years was so great, however, that even the crude data available to economists at that time suggested that velocity was not constant. This explains why, after the Great Depression, economists began to search for other factors influencing the demand for money that might help explain the large fluctuations in velocity.

Let us now examine the theories of money demand that arose from this search for a better explanation of the behaviour of velocity.

FIGURE 19.2

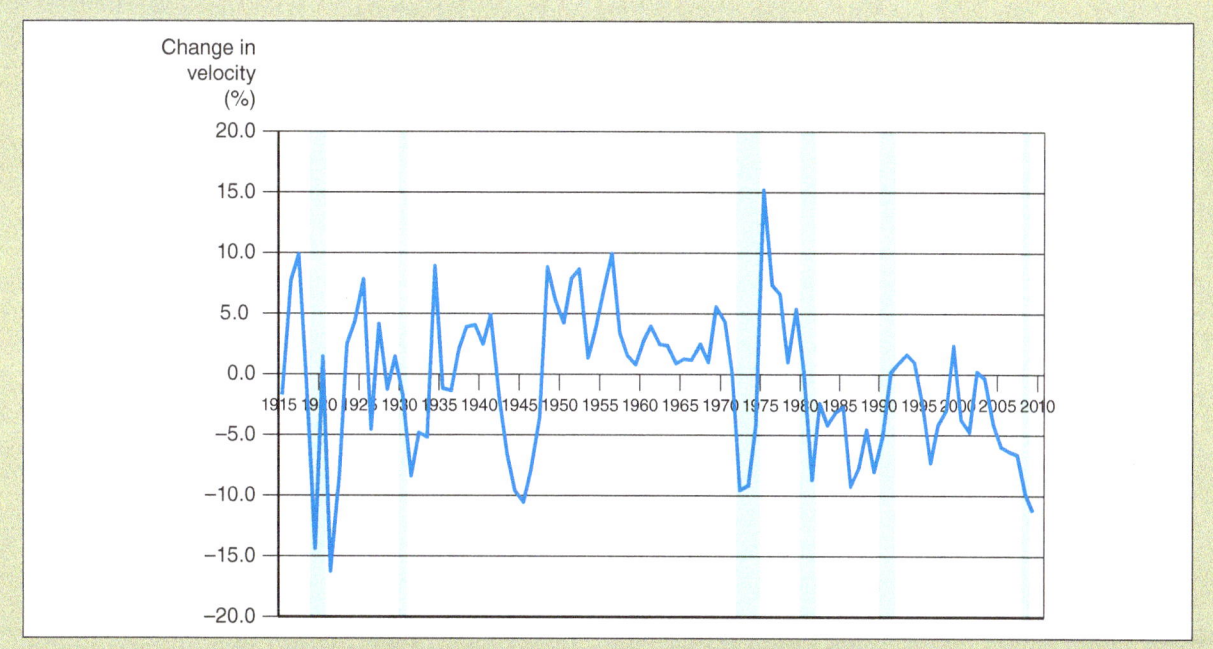

Change in the velocity of M3 from year to year in the UK, 1915–2009

Shaded areas indicate recessions. Velocity is calculated using nominal GNP before 1969 and nominal GDP thereafter.

Sources: Forrest Cappie and Alan Webber, *A Monetary History of the United Kingdom, 1870–1982* (London: George Allen & Unwin, 1985) up to 1969, and ONS and Bank of England datasets afterwards.

Keynes's liquidity preference theory

In his famous 1936 book *The General Theory of Employment, Interest, and Money*, John Maynard Keynes abandoned the classical view that velocity was a constant and developed a theory of money demand that emphasized the importance of interest rates. His theory of the demand for money, which he called the **liquidity preference theory**, asked the question: why do individuals hold money? He postulated that there are three motives behind the demand for money: the transactions motive, the precautionary motive and the speculative motive.

Transactions motive

In the classical approach, individuals are assumed to hold money because it is a medium of exchange that can be used to carry out everyday transactions. Following the classical tradition, Keynes emphasized that this component of the demand for money is determined primarily by the level of people's transactions. Because he believed that these transactions were proportional to income, like the classical economists, he took the transactions component of the demand for money to be proportional to income.

Precautionary motive

Keynes went beyond the classical analysis by recognizing that in addition to holding money to carry out current transactions, people hold money as a cushion against an unexpected need. Suppose that you've been thinking about buying a fancy sound system; you walk by a store that is having a 50%-off sale on the one you want. If you are holding money as a precaution for just such an occurrence, you can purchase the stereo right away; if you are not holding precautionary money balances, you cannot take advantage of the sale.

Precautionary money balances also come in handy if you are hit with an unexpected bill – say, for car repair or private health care.

Keynes believed that the precautionary money balances people want to hold are determined primarily by the level of transactions that they expect to make in the future and that these transactions are proportional to income. Therefore, he postulated, the demand for precautionary money balances is proportional to income.

Speculative motive

If Keynes had ended his theory with the transactions and precautionary motives, income would be the only important determinant of the demand for money, and he would not have added much to the classical approach. However, Keynes took the view that people also hold money as a store of wealth. He called this reason for holding money the *speculative motive*. Because he believed that wealth is tied closely to income, the speculative component of money demand would be related to income. However, Keynes looked more carefully at other factors that influence the decisions regarding how much money to hold as a store of wealth, especially interest rates.

Keynes divided the assets that can be used to store wealth into two categories: money and bonds. He then asked the following question. Why would individuals decide to hold their wealth in the form of money rather than bonds?

Thinking back to the discussion of the theory of asset demand (Chapter 5), you would want to hold money if its expected return was greater than the expected return from holding bonds. Keynes assumed that the expected return on money was zero because in his time, unlike today, most chequable deposits did not earn interest. For bonds, there are two components of the expected return: the interest payment and the *expected* rate of capital gains.

You learned in Chapter 4 that when interest rates rise, the price of a bond falls. If you expect interest rates to rise, you expect the price of the bond to fall and therefore expect to suffer a negative capital gain – that is, a capital loss. If you expect the rise in interest rates to be substantial enough, the capital loss might outweigh the interest payment, and your *expected* return on the bond would be negative. In this case, you would want to store your wealth as money because its expected return is higher; its zero return exceeds the negative return on the bond.

Keynes assumed that individuals believe that interest rates gravitate to some normal value (an assumption less plausible in today's world). If interest rates are below this normal value, individuals expect the interest rate on bonds to rise in the future and so expect to suffer capital losses on them. As a result, individuals will be more likely to hold their wealth as money rather than bonds, and the demand for money will be high.

What would you expect to happen to the demand for money when interest rates are above the normal value? In general, people will expect interest rates to fall, bond prices to rise and capital gains to be realized. At higher interest rates, they are more likely to expect the return from holding a bond to be positive, thus exceeding the expected return from holding money. They will be more likely to hold bonds than money, and the demand for money will be quite low. From Keynes's reasoning, we can conclude that as interest rates rise, the demand for money falls, and therefore **money demand is negatively related to the level of interest rates**.

Putting the three motives together

In putting the three motives for holding money balances together into a demand for money equation, Keynes was careful to distinguish between nominal quantities and real quantities. Money is valued in terms of what it can buy. If, for example, all prices in the economy double (the price level doubles), the same nominal quantity of money will be able to buy only half as many goods. Keynes thus reasoned that people want to hold a certain amount of **real money balances** (the quantity of money in real terms) – an amount that his three motives indicated would be related to real income Y and to interest rates i. Keynes wrote down the following demand for money equation, known as the *liquidity preference function*, which says that the demand for real money balances M^d/P is a function of (related to) i and Y:[8]

$$\frac{M^d}{P} = f(\underset{-}{i}, \underset{+}{Y}) \qquad (19.4)$$

The minus sign below i in the liquidity preference function means that the demand for real money balances is negatively related to the interest rate i, and the plus sign below Y means that the demand for real money balances and real income Y are positively related. Keynes's conclusion that the demand for money is related not only to income but also to interest rates is a major departure from Fisher's view of money demand, in which interest rates have no effect on the demand for money.

The money demand function in Equation 19.4 is the same one used in our analysis of money demand in Chapter 5 and in Chapter 20 that describes the *ISLM* model. Because money demand is negatively related to the interest rate, a fall in i leads to a rise in the quantity of money demanded M^d, and so the money demand curve is downward sloping as in Figure 5.8. By deriving the liquidity preference function for velocity PY/M, we can see that Keynes's theory of the demand for money implies that velocity is not constant, but instead fluctuates with movements in interest rates. The liquidity preference equation can be rewritten as

$$\frac{P}{M^d} = \frac{1}{f(i,Y)}$$

Multiplying both sides of this equation by Y and recognizing that M^d can be replaced by M because they must be equal in money market equilibrium, we solve for velocity:

$$V = \frac{PY}{M} = \frac{Y}{f(i,Y)} \qquad (19.5)$$

We know that the demand for money is negatively related to interest rates; when i goes up, $f(i,Y)$ declines, and therefore velocity rises. In other words, a rise in interest rates encourages people to hold lower real money balances for a given level of income; therefore, the rate at which money turns over (velocity) must be higher. This reasoning implies that because interest rates have substantial fluctuations, the liquidity preference theory of the demand for money indicates that velocity has substantial fluctuations as well.

An interesting feature of Equation 19.5 is that it explains some of the velocity movements in Figures 19.1 and 19.2, in which we noted that when recessions occur, velocity falls or its rate of growth declines. What fact regarding the cyclical behaviour of interest rates (discussed in Chapter 5) might help us explain this phenomenon? You might recall that interest rates are procyclical, rising in expansions and falling in recessions. The liquidity preference theory indicates that a rise in interest rates will cause velocity to rise also. The procyclical movements of interest rates should induce procyclical movements in velocity, and that is exactly what we see in Figures 19.1 and 19.2.

Keynes's model of the speculative demand for money provides another reason why velocity might show substantial fluctuations. What would happen to the demand for money if the view of the normal level to which interest rates gravitate changes? For example, what if people expect the future normal interest rate to be higher than the current normal interest rate? Because interest rates are then expected to be higher in the future, more people will expect the prices of bonds to fall and will anticipate capital losses. The expected returns from holding bonds will decline, and money will become more attractive relative to bonds. As a result, the demand for money will increase. This means that $f(i, Y)$ will increase and so velocity will fall. Velocity will change as expectations about future normal levels of interest rates change, and unstable expectations about future movements in normal interest rates can lead to instability of velocity. This is one more reason why Keynes rejected the view that velocity could be treated as a constant.

FIGURE 19.3

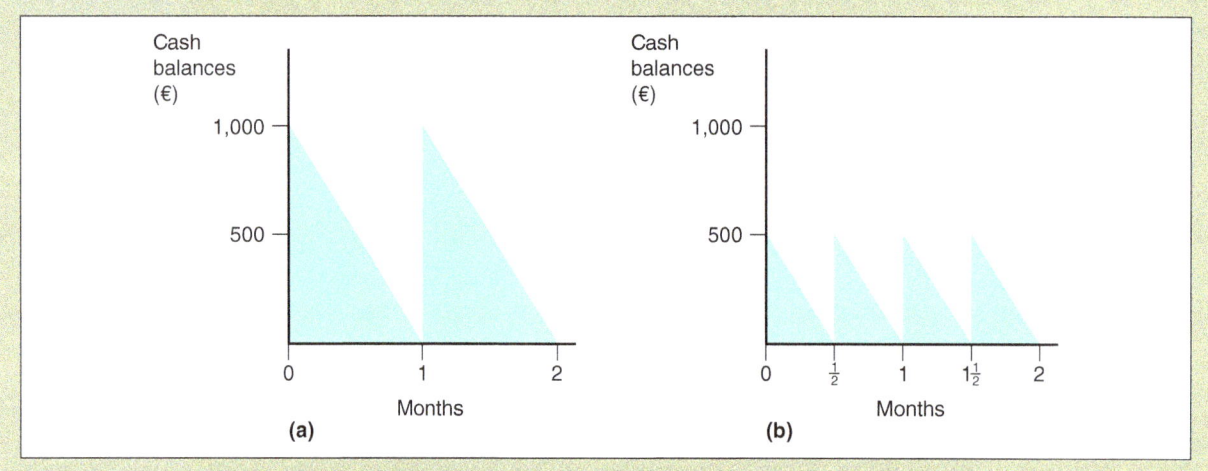

Cash balances in the Baumol–Tobin model

In panel (a), the €1,000 payment at the beginning of the month is held entirely in cash and is spent at a constant rate until it is exhausted by the end of the month. In panel (b), half of the monthly payment is put into cash and the other half into bonds. At the middle of the month, cash balances reach zero and bonds must be sold to bring balances up to €500. By the end of the month, cash balances again dwindle to zero.

In summary, Keynes's liquidity preference theory postulated three motives for holding money: the transactions motive, the precautionary motive and the speculative motive. Although Keynes took the transactions and precautionary components of the demand for money to be proportional to income, he reasoned that the speculative motive would be negatively related to the level of interest rates.

Keynes's model of the demand for money has the important implication that velocity is not constant, but instead is positively related to interest rates, which fluctuate substantially. His theory also rejected the constancy of velocity, because changes in people's expectations about the normal level of interest rates would cause shifts in the demand for money that would cause velocity to shift as well. Thus Keynes's liquidity preference theory casts doubt on the classical quantity theory that nominal income is determined primarily by movements in the quantity of money.

Further developments in the Keynesian approach

After World War II, economists began to take the Keynesian approach to the demand for money even further by developing more precise theories to explain the three Keynesian motives for holding money. Because interest rates were viewed as a crucial element in monetary theory, a key focus of this research was to understand better the role of interest rates in the demand for money.

Transactions demand

William Baumol and James Tobin independently developed similar demand for money models, which demonstrated that even money balances held for transactions purposes are sensitive to the level of interest rates.[9] In developing their models, they considered a hypothetical individual who receives a payment once a period and spends it over the course of this period. In their model, money, which earns zero interest, is held only because it can be used to carry out transactions.

To refine this analysis, let's say that Grant Smith receives €1,000 at the beginning of the month and spends it on transactions that occur at a constant rate during the course of the month. If Grant keeps the €1,000 in cash to carry out his transactions, his money balances follow the sawtooth pattern displayed in panel (a) of Figure 19.3. At the beginning of the month he has €1,000, and by the end of the month he has no cash left because he has spent it all. Over the course of the month, his holdings of money will on average be €500 (his holdings at the beginning of the month, €1,000, plus his holdings at the end of the month, €0, divided by 2).

At the beginning of the next month, Grant receives another €1,000 payment, which he holds as cash, and the same decline in money balances begins again. This process repeats monthly, and his average money balance during the course of the year is €500. Since his yearly nominal income is €12,000 and his holdings of money average €500, the velocity of money ($V = PY/M$) is €12,000/€500 = 24.

Suppose that as a result of taking a money and banking course, Grant realizes that he can improve his situation by not always holding cash. In January, then, he decides to hold part of his €1,000 in cash and puts part of it into an income-earning security such as bonds. At the beginning of each month, Grant keeps €500 in cash and uses the other €500 to buy a Treasury bond. As you can see in panel (b), he starts out each month with €500 of cash, and by the middle of the month, his cash balance has run down to zero. Because bonds cannot be used directly to carry out transactions, Grant must sell them and turn them into cash so that he can carry out the rest of the month's transactions. In the middle of the month, then, Grant's cash balance rises back up to €500. By the end of the month, the cash is gone. When he again receives his next €1,000 monthly payment, he again divides it into €500 of cash and €500 of bonds, and the process continues. The net result of this process is that the average cash balance held during the month is €500/2 = €250 – just half of what it was before. Velocity has doubled to €12,000/€250 = 48.

What has Grant Smith gained from his new strategy? He has earned interest on €500 of bonds that he held for half the month. If the interest rate is 1% per month, he has earned an additional €2.50 ($= \frac{1}{2} \times$ €500 $\times$ 1%) per month.

Sounds like a pretty good deal, doesn't it? In fact, if he had kept €333.33 in cash at the beginning of the month, he would have been able to hold €666.67 in bonds for the first third of the month. Then he could have sold €333.33 of bonds and held on to €333.34 of bonds for the next third of the month. Finally, two-thirds of the way through the month, he would have had to sell the remaining bonds to raise cash. The net result of this is that Grant would have earned €3.33 per month $\left[= (\frac{1}{3} \times €666.67 \times 1\%) \times (\frac{1}{3} \times €333.34 \times 1\%)\right]$. This is an even better deal. His average cash holdings in this case would be €333.33/2 = €166.67. Clearly, the lower his average cash balance, the more interest he will earn.

As you might expect, there is a catch to all this. In buying bonds, Grant incurs transaction costs of two types. First, he must pay a straight brokerage fee for the buying and selling of the bonds. These fees increase when average cash balances are lower because Grant will be buying and selling bonds more often. Second, by holding less cash, he will have to take time to sell the bonds to get the cash. Because time is money, this must also be counted as part of the transaction costs.

Grant faces a trade-off. If he holds very little cash, he can earn a lot of interest on bonds, but he will incur greater transaction costs. If the interest rate is high, the benefits of holding bonds will be high relative to the transaction costs, and he will hold more bonds and less cash. Conversely, if interest rates are low, the transaction costs involved in holding a lot of bonds may outweigh the interest payments, and Grant would then be better off holding more cash and fewer bonds.

The conclusion of the Baumol–Tobin analysis may be stated as follows: as interest rates increase, the amount of cash held for transactions purposes will decline, which in turn means that velocity will increase as interest rates increase.[10] Put another way, the *transactions component of the demand for money is negatively related to the level of interest rates*.

The basic idea in the Baumol–Tobin analysis is that there is an opportunity cost of holding money – the interest that can be earned on other assets. There is also a benefit to holding money – the avoidance of transaction costs. When interest rates increase, people will try to economize on their holdings of money for transactions purposes, because the opportunity cost of holding money has increased. By using simple models, Baumol and Tobin revealed something that we might not otherwise have seen: that the transactions demand for money, and not just the speculative demand, will be sensitive to interest rates. The Baumol–Tobin analysis presents a nice demonstration of the value of economic modelling.[11]

The idea that as interest rates increase, the opportunity cost of holding money increases so that the demand for money falls, can be stated equivalently with the terminology of expected returns used in Chapter 5. As interest rates increase, the expected return on the other asset, bonds, increases, causing the relative expected return on money to fall, thereby lowering the demand for money. These two explanations are in fact identical, because as we saw in Chapter 5, changes in the opportunity cost of an asset are just a description of what is happening to the relative expected return. Baumol and Tobin used opportunity cost terminology in their work on the transactions demand for money, and that is why we use this terminology here.

Precautionary demand

Models that explore the precautionary motive of the demand for money have been developed along lines similar to the Baumol–Tobin framework, so we will not go into great detail about them here. We have already discussed the benefits of holding precautionary money balances, but weighed against these benefits must be the opportunity cost of the interest forgone by holding money. We therefore have a trade-off similar to the one for transactions balances. As interest rates rise, the opportunity cost of holding precautionary balances rises, so the holdings of these money balances fall. We then have a result similar to the one found for the Baumol–Tobin analysis.[12] *The precautionary demand for money is negatively related to interest rates*.

Speculative demand

Keynes's analysis of the speculative demand for money was open to several serious criticisms. It indicated that an individual holds only money as a store of wealth when the expected return on bonds is less than the expected return on money and holds only bonds when the expected return on bonds is greater than the expected return on money. Only when people have expected returns on bonds and money that are exactly equal (a rare instance) would they hold both. Keynes's analysis therefore implies that practically no one holds a diversified portfolio of bonds and money simultaneously as a store of wealth. Because diversification is apparently a sensible strategy for choosing which assets to hold, the fact that it rarely occurs in Keynes's analysis is a serious shortcoming of his theory of the speculative demand for money.

Tobin developed a model of the speculative demand for money that attempted to avoid this criticism of Keynes's analysis.[13] His basic idea was that not only do people care about the expected return on one asset versus another when they decide what to hold in their portfolio, but they also care about the riskiness of the returns from each asset. Specifically, Tobin assumed that most people are risk-averse – that they would be willing to hold an asset with a lower expected return if it is less risky. An important characteristic of money is that its return is certain; Tobin assumed it to be zero. Bonds, by contrast, can have substantial fluctuations in price, and their returns can be quite risky and sometimes negative. So even if the expected returns on bonds exceed the expected return on money, people might still want to hold money as a store of wealth because it has less risk associated with its return than bonds do.

The Tobin analysis also shows that people can reduce the total amount of risk in a portfolio by diversifying – that is, by holding both bonds and money. The model suggests that individuals will hold bonds and money simultaneously as stores of wealth. Because this is probably a more realistic description of people's behaviour than Keynes's, Tobin's rationale for the speculative demand for money seems to rest on more solid ground.

Tobin's attempt to improve on Keynes's rationale for the speculative demand for money was only partly successful, however. It is still not clear that the speculative demand even exists. What if there are assets that have no risk – like money – but earn a higher return? Will there be any speculative demand for money? No, because an individual will always be better off holding such an asset rather than money. The resulting portfolio will enjoy a higher expected return yet has no higher risk. Do such assets exist in the economy? The answer is yes. Treasury bills and other assets that have no default risk provide certain returns that are greater than those available on money. Therefore, why would anyone want to hold money balances as a store of wealth (ignoring for the moment transactions and precautionary reasons)?

Although Tobin's analysis did not explain why money is held as a store of wealth, it was an important development in our understanding of how people should choose among assets. Indeed, his analysis was an important step in the development of the academic field of finance, which examines asset pricing and portfolio choice (the decision to buy one asset over another).

To sum up, further developments of the Keynesian approach have attempted to give a more precise explanation for the transactions, precautionary and speculative demand for money. The attempt to improve Keynes's rationale for the speculative demand for money has been only partly successful; it is still not clear that this demand even exists. However, the models of the transactions and precautionary demand for money indicate that these components of money demand are negatively related to interest rates. Hence Keynes's proposition that the demand for money is sensitive to interest rates – suggesting that velocity is not constant and that nominal income might be affected by factors other than the quantity of money – is still supported.

Friedman's modern quantity theory of money

In 1956, Milton Friedman developed a theory of the demand for money in a famous article, 'The quantity theory of money: a restatement'.[14] Although Friedman frequently referred to Irving Fisher and the quantity theory, his analysis of the demand for money was actually closer to that of Keynes.

Like his predecessors, Friedman pursued the question of why people choose to hold money. Instead of analysing the specific motives for holding money, as Keynes did, Friedman simply stated that the demand for money must be influenced by the same factors that influence the demand for any asset. Friedman then applied the theory of asset demand to money.

The theory of asset demand (Chapter 5) indicates that the demand for money should be a function of the resources available to individuals (their wealth) and the expected returns on other assets relative to the expected return on money. Like Keynes, Friedman recognized that people want to hold a certain amount of real money balances (the quantity of money in real terms). From this reasoning, Friedman expressed his formulation of the demand for money as follows:

$$\frac{M^d}{P} = f(\underset{+}{Y_p}, \underset{-}{r_b - r_m}, \underset{-}{r_e - r_m}, \underset{-}{\pi^e - r_m}) \tag{19.6}$$

where M^d/P = demand for real money balances

Y_p = Friedman's measure of wealth, known as *permanent income* (technically, the present discounted value of all expected future income, but more easily described as expected average long-run income)

r_m = expected return on money

r_b = expected return on bonds

r_e = expected return on equity (common stocks)

π^e = expected inflation rate

The signs underneath the equation indicate whether the demand for money is positively (+) related or negatively (−) related to the terms that are immediately above them.[15]

Let us look in more detail at the variables in Friedman's money demand function and what they imply for the demand for money.

Because the demand for an asset is positively related to wealth, money demand is positively related to Friedman's wealth concept, permanent income (indicated by the plus sign beneath it). Unlike our usual concept of income, permanent income (which can be thought of as expected average long-run income) has much smaller short-run fluctuations, because many movements of income are transitory (short-lived). For example, in a business cycle expansion, income increases rapidly, but because some of this increase is temporary, average long-run income does not change very much. Hence in a boom, permanent income rises much less than income. During a recession, much of the income decline is transitory, and average long-run income (hence permanent income) falls less than income. One implication of Friedman's use of the concept of permanent income as a determinant of the demand for money is that the demand for money will not fluctuate much with business cycle movements.

An individual can hold wealth in several forms besides money. Friedman categorized them into three types of assets: bonds, equity (common stocks) and goods. The incentives for holding these assets rather than money are represented by the expected return on each of these assets relative to the expected return on money, the last three terms in the money demand function. The minus sign beneath each indicates that as each term rises, the demand for money will fall.

The expected return on money r_m, which appears in all three terms, is influenced by two factors:

1 The services provided by banks on deposits included in the money supply, such as provision of receipts in the form of cancelled cheques or the automatic paying of bills. When these services are increased, the expected return from holding money rises.
2 The interest payments on money balances. NOW accounts and other deposits that are included in the money supply currently pay interest. As these interest payments rise, the expected return on money rises.

The terms $r_b - r_m$ and $r_e - r_m$ represent the expected return on bonds and equity relative to money; as they rise, the relative expected return on money falls, and the demand for money falls. The final term, $\pi^e - r_m$, represents the expected return on goods relative to money. The expected return from holding goods is the expected rate of capital gains that occurs when their prices rise and hence is equal to the expected inflation rate π^e. If the expected inflation rate is 10%, for example, then goods' prices are expected to rise at a 10% rate, and their expected return is 10%. When $\pi^e - r_m$ rises, the expected return on goods relative to money rises and the demand for money falls.

Distinguishing between the Friedman and Keynesian theories

There are several differences between Friedman's theory of the demand for money and the Keynesian theories. One is that by including many assets as alternatives to money, Friedman recognized that more than one interest rate is important to the operation of the aggregate economy. Keynes, for his part, lumped financial assets other than money into one big category – bonds – because he felt that their returns generally move together. If this is so, the expected return on bonds will be a good indicator of the expected return on other financial assets, and there will be no need to include them separately in the money demand function.

Also in contrast to Keynes, Friedman viewed money and goods as substitutes; that is, people choose between them when deciding how much money to hold. That is why Friedman included the expected return on goods relative to money as a term in his money demand function. The assumption that money and goods are substitutes indicates that changes in the quantity of money may have a direct effect on aggregate spending.

In addition, Friedman stressed two issues in discussing his demand for money function that distinguish it from Keynes's liquidity preference theory. First, Friedman did not take the expected return on money to be a constant, as Keynes did. When interest rates rise in the economy, banks make more profits on their loans, and they want to attract more deposits to increase the volume of their now more profitable loans. If there are no restrictions on interest payments on deposits, banks attract deposits by paying higher interest rates on them. Because the industry is competitive, the expected return on money held as bank deposits then rises with the higher interest rates on bonds and loans. The banks compete to get deposits until there are no excess profits, and in doing so they close the gap between interest earned on loans and interest paid on deposits. The net result of this competition in the banking industry is that $r_b - r_m$ stays relatively constant when the interest rate i rises.[16]

What if there are restrictions on the amount of interest that banks can pay on their deposits? Will the expected return on money be a constant? As interest rates rise, will $r_b - r_m$ rise as well? Friedman thought not. He argued that although banks might be restricted from making pecuniary payments on their deposits, they can still compete on the quality dimension. For example, they can provide more services to depositors by hiring more tellers, paying bills automatically or making more cash machines available at more accessible locations. The result of these improvements in money services is that the expected return from holding deposits will rise. So despite the restrictions on pecuniary interest payments, we might still find that a rise in market interest rates will raise the expected return on money sufficiently so that $r_b - r_m$ will remain relatively constant. ***Unlike Keynes's theory, which indicates that interest rates are an important determinant of the demand for money, Friedman's theory suggests that changes in interest rates should have little effect on the demand for money***.

Therefore, Friedman's money demand function was essentially one in which permanent income is the primary determinant of money demand, and his money demand equation can be approximated by

$$\frac{M^d}{P} = f(Y_p) \tag{19.7}$$

In Friedman's view, the demand for money was insensitive to interest rates – not because he viewed the demand for money as insensitive to changes in the incentives for holding other assets relative to money, but rather because changes in interest rates should have little effect on these incentive terms in the money demand function. The incentive terms remain relatively constant, because any rise in the expected returns on other assets as a result of the rise in interest rates would be matched by a rise in the expected return on money.

The second issue Friedman stressed was the stability of the demand for money function. In contrast to Keynes, Friedman suggested that random fluctuations in the demand for money are small and that the demand for money can be predicted accurately by the money demand function. When combined with his view that the demand for money is insensitive to changes in interest rates, this means that velocity is highly predictable. We can see this by writing down the velocity that is implied by the money demand equation (Equation 19.7):

$$V = \frac{Y}{f(Y_p)} \tag{19.8}$$

Because the relationship between Y and Y_p is usually quite predictable, a stable money demand function (one that does not undergo pronounced shifts, so that it predicts the demand for money accurately) implies that velocity is predictable as well. If we can predict what velocity will be in the next period, a change in the quantity of money will produce a predictable change in aggregate spending. Even though velocity is no longer assumed to be constant, the money supply continues to be the primary determinant of nominal income as in the quantity theory of money. Therefore, Friedman's theory of money demand is indeed a restatement of the quantity theory, because it leads to the same conclusion about the importance of money to aggregate spending.

You may recall that we said that the Keynesian liquidity preference function (in which interest rates are an important determinant of the demand for money) is able to explain the procyclical movements of velocity that we find in the data. Can Friedman's money demand formulation explain this procyclical velocity phenomenon as well?

The key clue to answering this question is the presence of permanent income rather than measured income in the money demand function. What happens to permanent income in a business cycle expansion? Because much of the increase in income will be transitory, permanent income rises much less than measured income. Friedman's money demand function then indicates that the demand for money rises only a small amount relative to the rise in measured income and, as Equation 19.8 indicates, velocity rises. Similarly, in a recession, the demand for money falls less than measured income, because the decline in permanent income is small relative to measured income, and velocity falls. In this way, we have the procyclical movement in velocity.

To summarize, Friedman's theory of the demand for money used a similar approach to that of Keynes but did not go into detail about the motives for holding money. Instead, Friedman made use of the theory of asset demand to indicate that the demand for money will be a function of permanent income and the expected returns on alternative assets relative to the expected return on money. There are two major differences between Friedman's theory and Keynes's. Friedman believed that changes in interest rates have little effect on the expected returns on other assets relative to money. Thus, in contrast to Keynes, he viewed the demand for money as insensitive to interest rates. In addition, he differed from Keynes in stressing that the money demand function does not undergo substantial shifts and is therefore stable. These two differences also indicate that velocity is predictable, yielding a quantity theory conclusion that money is the primary determinant of aggregate spending. The conclusion that money is the primary determinant of aggregate spending was the basis of **monetarism**, the view that the money supply is the primary source of movements in the price level and aggregate output.

Empirical evidence on the demand for money

As we have seen, the alternative theories of the demand for money can have very different implications for our view of the role of money in the economy. Which of these theories is an accurate description of the real world is an important question, and it is the reason why evidence on the demand for money has been at the centre of many debates on the effects of monetary policy on aggregate economic activity. Here we examine the empirical evidence on the two primary issues that distinguish the different theories of money demand and affect their conclusions about whether the quantity of money is the primary determinant of aggregate spending: is the demand for money sensitive to changes in interest rates, and is the demand for money function stable over time?[17]

Interest rates and money demand

Earlier in the chapter, we saw that if interest rates do not affect the demand for money, velocity is more likely to be a constant – or at least predictable – so that the quantity theory view that aggregate spending is determined by the quantity of money is more likely to be true. However, the more sensitive the demand for money is to interest rates, the more unpredictable velocity will be, and the less clear the link between the money supply and aggregate spending will be. Indeed, there is an extreme case of ultrasensitivity of the demand for money to interest rates, called the *liquidity trap*, in which monetary policy has no direct effect on aggregate spending, because a change in the money supply has no effect on interest rates. (If the demand for money is ultrasensitive to interest rates, a tiny change in interest rates produces a very large change in the quantity of money demanded. Hence, in this case, the demand for money is completely flat in the supply and demand diagrams of Chapter 5. Therefore, a change in the money supply that shifts the money supply curve to the right or left results in it intersecting the flat money demand curve at the same unchanged interest rate.)

The evidence on the interest sensitivity of the demand for money found by different researchers is remarkably consistent. Neither extreme case is supported by the data: in situations in which nominal interest rates have not hit a floor of zero, the demand for money is sensitive to interest rates, and there is little evidence that a liquidity trap has ever existed. However, as we saw in Chapter 4, when interest rates fall to zero, they can go no lower. In this situation, a liquidity trap has occurred because the demand for money is now completely flat. Indeed, Japan has been experiencing a liquidity trap of this type in recent years, which is one reason why it has been difficult for Japanese monetary authorities to stimulate the economy.

Stability of money demand

If the money demand function, like Equation 19.4 or 19.6, is unstable and undergoes substantial unpredictable shifts, as Keynes thought, then velocity is unpredictable, and the quantity of money may not be tightly linked to aggregate spending, as it is in the modern quantity theory. The stability of the money demand function is also crucial to whether the central bank should target interest rates or the money supply (see Chapter 16). Thus it is important to look at the question of whether the money demand function is stable, because it has important implications for how monetary policy should be conducted.

By the early 1970s, evidence strongly supported the stability of the money demand function. However, after 1973, the rapid pace of financial innovation, which changed which items could be used as money, led to substantial instability in estimated money demand functions. The recent instability of the money demand function calls into question whether our theories and empirical analyses are adequate. It also has important implications for the way monetary policy should be conducted, because it casts doubt on the usefulness of the money demand function as a tool to provide guidance to policymakers. In particular, because the money demand function has become unstable, velocity is now harder to predict and, as discussed in Chapter 16, setting rigid money supply targets to control aggregate spending in the economy may not be an effective way to conduct monetary policy.

This view is currently shared by the main central banks across the world, and in particular by the Bank of England and the Federal Reserve. On the other hand, as discussed in Chapter 16, monetary aggregates, although not strictly targeted, play a more prominent role in the monetary policy strategy of the ECB. Why does the ECB see things so differently from the Bank of England and the Fed? There are two main reasons.[18] First, their institutional histories are different. The ECB carries forward the tradition of the German Bundesbank which successfully followed monetary targeting in the past (see Chapter 16). Second, the empirical support on the stability of money demand is stronger in the euro area than in the US and the UK. One way to assess the stability of the money demand is to look at Figure 19.4 which shows the velocity of M3 money in the euro area since the early 1970s. Here we see that the velocity has been relatively stable and predictable up the 2000s. The conventional explanation for this stable relationship between money and nominal GDP in the euro area is that financial innovation and other institutional and regulatory changes (e.g. introduction of new instruments, changes to the regime of remuneration on deposits, increased banking competition, etc.) may not have affected money demand for continental European countries as strongly as in other economies.[19] However, Figure 19.4 also shows that since the early 2000s M3 velocity has started to decline at a higher rate. This unpredicted change has been repeatedly stressed by a number of economists and commentators as clear evidence for the fact that the ECB should de-emphasize the role of money in its monetary strategy, and move closer to the approach of monetary policy of the Bank of England and the Federal Reserve.

FIGURE 19.4

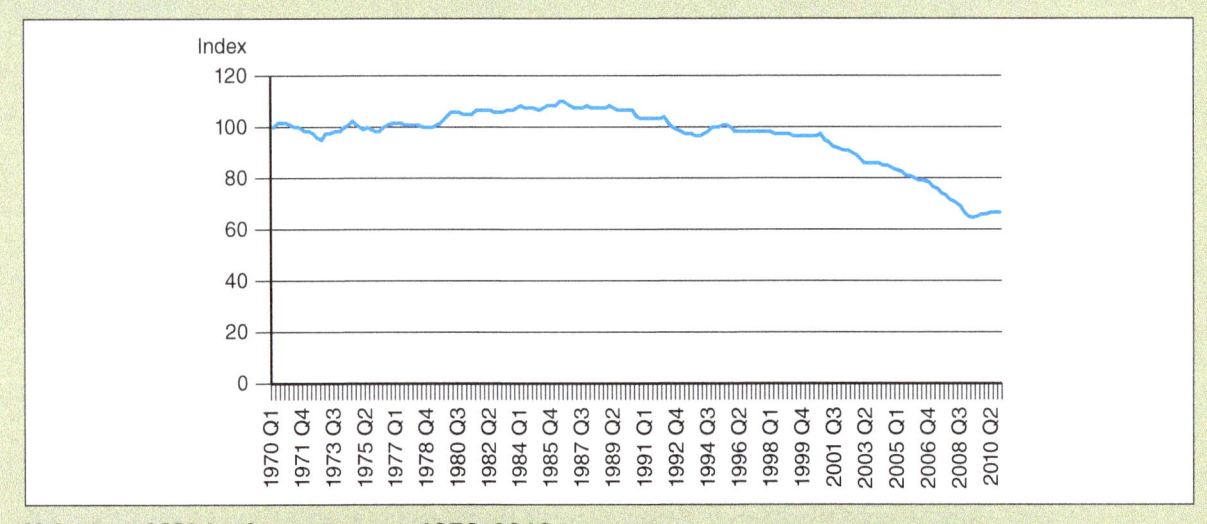

Velocity of M3 in the euro area, 1970–2010

Sources: Nominal GDP and M3 for the euro area are taken from the Area Wide Model (AWM) and the Real Time Database (RTDB) which are available in www.eabcn.org/index.shtml. The velocity of M3 is defined as the ratio of nominal GDP to the M3 monetary aggregate of the euro area. Index 1970Q1=100.

Summary

1 Irving Fisher developed a transactions-based theory of the demand for money in which the demand for real balances is proportional to real income and is insensitive to interest-rate movements. An implication of his theory is that velocity, the rate at which money turns over, is constant. This generates the quantity theory of money, which implies that aggregate spending is determined solely by movements in the quantity of money.

2 The classical view that velocity can be effectively treated as a constant is not supported by the data. The non-constancy of velocity became especially clear to the economics profession after the sharp drop in velocity during the years of the Great Depression.

3 John Maynard Keynes suggested three motives for holding money: the transactions motive, the precautionary motive and the speculative motive. His resulting liquidity preference theory views the transactions and precautionary components of money demand as proportional to income. However, the speculative component of money demand is viewed as sensitive to interest rates as well as to expectations about the future movements of interest rates. This theory, then, implies that velocity is unstable and cannot be treated as a constant.

4 Further developments in the Keynesian approach provided a better rationale for the three Keynesian motives for holding money. Interest rates were found to be important to the transactions and precautionary components of money demand as well as to the speculative component.

5 Milton Friedman's theory of money demand used a similar approach to that of Keynes. Treating money like any other asset, Friedman used the theory of asset demand to derive a demand for money that is a function of the expected returns on other assets relative to the expected return on money and permanent income. In contrast to Keynes, Friedman believed that the demand for money is stable and insensitive to interest-rate movements. His belief that velocity is predictable (though not constant) in turn leads to the quantity theory conclusion that money is the primary determinant of aggregate spending.

6 There are two main conclusions from the research on the demand for money: the demand for money is sensitive to interest rates, but there is little evidence that it is or has been ultrasensitive (liquidity trap). Since the early 1970s, money demand functions in the UK and the US have been found to be unstable, with the most likely source of the instability being the rapid pace of financial innovation. At the same time, the latter seems to have had a more subdued effect in the euro area, where there is a stronger empirical support for a stable money demand.

Key terms

QUESTIONS AND PROBLEMS

All questions and problems are available in MyEconLab at **www.myeconlab.com/mishkin**.

1 Suppose the money supply *M* has been growing at 10% per year, and nominal GDP *PY* has been growing at 20% per year. The data are as follows (in billions of euros):

	2010	2011	2012
M	100	110	121
PY	1,000	1,200	1,440

Calculate the velocity in each year. At what rate is velocity growing?

2 Calculate what happens to nominal GDP if velocity remains constant at 5 and the money supply increases from €200 billion to €300 billion.

3 What happens to nominal GDP if the money supply grows by 20% but velocity declines by 30%?

4 If credit cards were made illegal by legislation, what would happen to velocity? Explain your answer.

5 If velocity and aggregate output are reasonably constant (as the classical economists believed), what happens to the price level when the money supply increases from €1 trillion to €4 trillion?

6 If velocity and aggregate output remain constant at 5 and 1,000, respectively, what happens to the price level if the money supply declines from €400 billion to €300 billion?

7 Looking at Figure 19.1, when were the two largest falls in velocity? What do declines like this suggest about how velocity moves with the business cycle? Given the data in Figure 19.1, is it reasonable to assume, as the classical

economists did, that declines in aggregate spending are caused by declines in the quantity of money?

8 In Keynes's analysis of the speculative demand for money, what will happen to money demand if people suddenly decide that the normal level of the interest rate has declined? Why?

9 Why is Keynes's analysis of the speculative demand for money important to his view that velocity will undergo substantial fluctuations and thus cannot be treated as constant?

10 If interest rates on bonds go to zero, what does the Baumol–Tobin analysis suggest Grant Smith's average holdings of money balances should be?

11 If brokerage fees go to zero, what does the Baumol–Tobin analysis suggest Grant Smith's average holdings of money should be?

12 'In Tobin's analysis of the speculative demand for money, people will hold both money and bonds, even if bonds are expected to earn a positive return.' Is this statement true, false, or uncertain? Explain your answer.

13 Both Keynes's and Friedman's theories of the demand for money suggest that as the relative expected return on money falls, demand for it will fall. Why does Friedman think that money demand is unaffected by changes in interest rates? Why did Keynes think that money demand is affected by changes in interest rates?

14 Why does Friedman's view of the demand for money suggest that velocity is predictable, whereas Keynes's view suggests the opposite?

WEB EXERCISES

1 Go to **http://sdw.ecb.europa.eu** and download the latest series for the nominal GDP and M3 of the euro area. Calculate the change in velocity of M3 from the first quarter of 2007 and suggest reasons for its dynamics since that time.

2 Refer to Figure 19.2. The formula for computing the velocity of money is GDP/M. Go to the Office of National Statistics (ONS) dataset (**http://www.ons.gov.uk/ons/ datasets-and-tables/index.html**) and look up the quarterly nominal GDP series. Next go to the Bank of England (**http://www.bankofengland.co.uk/statistics/Pages/iadb/notesiadb/m4.aspx**) to collect the time series of M4. Compute the velocity of money and compare it to the M3 velocity of the euro area shown in Figure 19.4. Has the velocity of money in the UK been more or less stable than in the euro area during the financial crisis? Suggest reasons for its change since that time.

3 Data on money velocity for the US is available on the St Louis Fed 'FRED Economic Data' (**http://research.stlouisfed.org/fred2/categories/32242**). Use the 'Add to New Graph' tool to compare the velocity of M1 and M2 over the past 5 and 10 years. What patterns are most noticeable?

Notes

1 In Chapter 21, we will see that the responsiveness of the quantity of money demanded to changes in interest rates has important implications for the relative effectiveness of monetary policy and fiscal policy in influencing aggregate economic activity.

2 Fisher actually first formulated the equation of exchange in terms of the nominal value of transactions in the economy PT: $MV_T = PT$ where P = average price per transaction, T = number of transactions conducted in a year, $V_T = PT/M$ = transactions velocity of money. Because the nominal value of transactions T is difficult to measure, the quantity theory has been formulated in terms of aggregate output Y as follows: T is assumed to be proportional to Y so that $T = vY$, where v is a constant of proportionality. Substituting vY for T in Fisher's equation of exchange yields $MV_T = vPY$, which can be written as Equation 19.2 in the text, in which $V = V_T/v$.

3 While Fisher was developing his quantity theory approach to the demand for money, a group of classical economists in Cambridge, England led by Alfred Marshall and A. C. Pigou, came to similar conclusions, although with slightly different reasoning. They derived Equation 19.3 by recognizing that two properties of money motivate people to hold it: its utility as a medium of exchange and as a store of wealth.

4 Actually, the classical conclusion still holds if velocity grows at some uniform rate over time that reflects changes in transaction technology. Hence the concept of a constant velocity should more accurately be thought of here as a lack of upward and downward fluctuations in velocity.

5 We reach a similar conclusion if we use M2 velocity. The percentage change in M2 velocity (GDP/M2) from 1981 to 1982 was −5.0%, whereas from 1980 to 1981 it was +2.3%. This difference of 7.3% means that nominal GDP was 7.3% lower than it would have been if M2 velocity had kept growing at the same rate as in 1980–1.

6 As discussed in a 'Closer look' in Chapter 3, M3 has been superseded by the money aggregate M4 which consists of M3 plus building societies' deposits. In Figure 19.2 we use M3 to have a consistent series over a longer period of time.

7 At the Loughborough University Banking Centre annual lecture in finance given on 22 October 1986 the Governor of the Bank of England remarked that the 'Intermediate objective was chosen in the belief that there was a reasonably stable relationship between the rate of monetary growth and the rate of growth of nominal incomes. But in practice our ability to use an estimate of that relationship for target setting, and to meet those targets, has, quite frankly, been less than impressive.'

8 The classical economists' money demand equation can also be written in terms of real money balances by dividing both sides of Equation 19.3 by the price level P to obtain:
$$\frac{M^d}{P} = k \times Y$$

9 William J. Baumol, 'The transactions demand for cash: an inventory theoretic approach', *Quarterly Journal of Economics* 66 (1952): 545–56; and James Tobin, 'The interest elasticity of the transactions demand for cash', *Review of Economics and Statistics* 38 (1956): 241–7.

10 Similar reasoning leads to the conclusion that as brokerage fees increase, the demand for transactions money balances increases as well. When these fees rise, the benefits from holding transactions money balances increase because by holding these balances, an individual will not have to sell bonds as often, thereby avoiding these higher brokerage costs. The greater benefits to holding money balances relative to the opportunity cost of interest forgone, then, lead to a higher demand for transactions balances.

11 The mathematics behind the Baumol–Tobin model can be found in an appendix to this chapter on this book's website at **www.myeconlab.com/mishkin**.

12 These models of the precautionary demand for money also reveal that as uncertainty about the level of future transactions grows, the precautionary demand for money increases. This is so because greater uncertainty means that individuals are more likely to incur transaction costs if they are not holding precautionary balances. The benefit of holding such balances then increases relative to the opportunity cost of forgone interest, and so the demand for them rises.

13 James Tobin, 'Liquidity preference as behavior towards risk', *Review of Economic Studies* 25 (1958): 65–86.

14 Milton Friedman, 'The quantity theory of money: a restatement', in *Studies in the Quantity Theory of Money*, ed. Milton Friedman (Chicago: University of Chicago Press, 1956), pp. 3–21.

15 Friedman also added to his formulation a term h that represented the ratio of human to non-human wealth. He reasoned that if people had more permanent income coming from labour income and thus from their human capital, they would be less liquid than if they were receiving income from financial assets. In this case, they might want to hold more money because it is a more

liquid asset than the alternatives. The term h plays no essential role in Friedman's theory and has no important implications for monetary theory. That is why we ignore it in the money demand function.

16 Friedman suggested that there is some increase in $r_{ib} - r_{am}$ when I rises because part of the money supply (especially currency) is held in forms that cannot pay interest in a pecuniary or non-pecuniary form. See, for example, Milton Friedman, 'Why a surge of inflation is likely next year', *Wall Street Journal*, 1 September 1983, p. 24.

17 If you are interested in a more detailed discussion of the empirical research on the demand for money, you can find it in an appendix to this chapter on this book's website at **www.myeconlab.com/mishkin**.

18 For a comprehensive overview of the main factors underlying the different approaches to monetary aggregates in the euro area and the United States, see George A. Kahn and Scott Benolkin, 'The role of money in monetary policy: why do the Fed and ECB see it so differently', *Economic Review*, Federal Reserve Bank of Kansas City (2007): 5–36. For an overall assessment of the role of money in the monetary policy strategy of the

ECB, refer to the book edited by Lucas D. Papademos and Jurgen Stark, *Enhancing Monetary Analysis*, Frankfurt am Main: European Central Bank (2010).

19 This seems to be the case for Germany, the largest economy in the euro area. According to Otmar Issing, former member of the Board of the Bundesbank and the Executive Board of the ECB, the weaker and more predictable impact of financial innovation on German broad money was related to the fact that banks were able to satisfy the needs of the private sector with the traditional range of products and to a more conservative attitude of money holders. For an early literature review on the stability of the money demand in the euro area, see Alessandro Calza and Joao Sousa, 'Why has broad money demand been more stable in the euro area than in other countries? A literature review', *ECB Working Paper Series*, no. 261 (2003). For a recent summary of the studies on the stability of money demand in the euro area see Annex I of Chapter 3 of Lucas D. Papademos and Jurgen Stark, *Enhancing Monetary Analysis*, Frankfurt am Main: European Central Bank (2010), pp. 156–63.

Useful websites

http://sdw.ecb.europa.eu The Statistical Data Warehouse (SDW) of the ECB providing statistics for the euro area.

www.eabcn.org/index.shtml It provides a number of variable for the euro area and the individual countries.

www.statistics.gov.uk/default.asp Office for National Statistics (ONS) dataset for the United Kingdom.

www.bankofengland.co.uk/mfsd/iadb/NewIntermed.asp Bank of England's statistical interactive dataset.

www.ecb.int/pub/pdf/other/enhancingmonetaryanalysis2010en.pdf Link to the book edited by Lucas D. Papademos and Jurgen Stark, *Enhancing Monetary Analysis*, Frankfurt am Main: European Central Bank (2010).

http://www.hsbcukeconomyexplained.co.uk/Pages/Contents/09_Money_Banking_Regulation/9-3_Velocity_of_Circulation.aspx Short overview by HSBC on the velocity of money.

www.usagold.com/gildedopinion/puplava/20020614.html A summary of how various factors affect the velocity of money.

CHAPTER 20

The *ISLM* model

PREVIEW   In the media, you often see forecasts of GDP and interest rates by economists and government agencies. At times, these forecasts seem to come from a crystal ball, but economists actually make their predictions using a variety of economic models. One model widely used by economic forecasters is the *ISLM* model, which was developed by Sir John Hicks in 1937 and is based on the analysis in John Maynard Keynes's influential book *The General Theory of Employment, Interest and Money*, published in 1936.[1] The *ISLM* model explains how interest rates and total output produced in the economy (aggregate output or, equivalently, aggregate income) are determined, given a fixed price level (a reasonable assumption in the short run).

The *ISLM* model is valuable not only because it can be used in economic forecasting, but also because it provides a deeper understanding of how government policy can affect aggregate economic activity. In Chapter 21 we use it to evaluate the effects of monetary and fiscal policy on the economy and to learn some lessons about how monetary policy might best be conducted.

In this chapter, we begin by developing the simplest framework for determining aggregate output, in which all economic actors (consumers, firms and others) except the government play a role. Government fiscal policy (spending and taxes) is then added to the framework to see how it can affect the determination of aggregate output. Finally, we achieve a complete picture of the *ISLM* model by adding monetary policy variables: the money supply and the interest rate.

Determination of aggregate output

Keynes was especially interested in understanding movements of aggregate output because he wanted to explain why the Great Depression had occurred and how government policy could be used to increase employment in a similar economic situation. Keynes's analysis started with the recognition that the total quantity demanded of an economy's output was the sum of four types of spending: (1) **consumer expenditure** (C), the total demand for consumer goods and services (hamburgers, electronics, rock concerts, visits to the doctor and so on); (2) **planned investment spending** (I), the total planned spending by businesses on new physical capital (machines, computers, factories, raw materials and the like) plus planned spending on new homes; (3) **government spending** (G), the spending by all levels of government on goods and services (aircraft carriers, government workers, red tape and so forth); and (4) **net exports** (NX), the net foreign spending on domestic goods and services, equal to exports minus imports.[2] The total quantity demanded of an economy's output, called **aggregate demand** (Y^{ad}), can be written as

$$Y^{ad} = C + I + G + NX \tag{20.1}$$

Using the common-sense concept from supply and demand analysis, Keynes recognized that equilibrium would occur in the economy when total quantity of output supplied (aggregate output produced) Y equals quantity of output demanded Y^{ad}:

$$Y = Y^{ad} \qquad (20.2)$$

When this equilibrium condition is satisfied, producers are able to sell all of their output and have no reason to change their production. Keynes's analysis explains two things: (1) why aggregate output is at a certain level (which involves understanding which factors affect each component of aggregate demand) and (2) how the sum of these components can add up to an output smaller than the economy is capable of producing, resulting in less than full employment of resources.

Keynes was especially concerned with explaining the low level of output and employment during the Great Depression. Because inflation was not a serious problem during this period, he assumed that output could change without causing a change in prices. ***Keynes's analysis assumes that the price level is fixed***; that is, monetary amounts for variables such as consumer expenditure, investment and aggregate output do not have to be adjusted for changes in the price level to tell us how much the real quantities of these variables change. Because the price level is assumed to be fixed, when we talk in this chapter about changes in nominal quantities, we are talking about changes in real quantities as well.

Our discussion of Keynes's analysis begins with a simple framework of aggregate output determination in which the role of government, net exports and the possible effects of money and interest rates are ignored. Because we are assuming that government spending and net exports are zero ($G = 0$ and $NX = 0$), we need examine only consumer expenditure and investment spending to explain how aggregate output is determined. This simple framework is unrealistic, because both government and monetary policy are left out of the picture, and because it makes other simplifying assumptions, such as a fixed price level. Still, the model is worth studying, because its simplified view helps us understand the key factors that explain how the economy works. It also clearly illustrates the Keynesian idea that the economy can come to rest at a level of aggregate output below the full-employment level. Once you understand this simple framework, we can proceed to more complex and more realistic models.

Consumer expenditure and the consumption function

Ask yourself what determines how much you spend on consumer goods and services. Your likely response is that your income is the most important factor, because if your income rises, you will be willing to spend more. Keynes reasoned similarly that consumer expenditure is related to **disposable income**, the total income available for spending, equal to aggregate income (which is equivalent to aggregate output) minus taxes ($Y-T$). He called this relationship between disposable income Y_D and consumer expenditure C the **consumption function** and expressed it as follows:

$$C = a + (mpc \times Y_D) \qquad (20.3)$$

The term a stands for **autonomous consumer expenditure**, the amount of consumer expenditure that is independent of disposable income and is the intercept of the consumption function line. It tells us how much consumers will spend when disposable income is 0 (they still must have food, clothing and shelter). If a is €200 billion when disposable income is 0, consumer expenditure will equal €200 billion.[3]

The term mpc, the **marginal propensity to consume**, is the slope of the consumption function line ($\Delta C/\Delta Y_D$) and reflects the change in consumer expenditure that results from an additional euro of disposable income. Keynes assumed that mpc was a constant between the values of 0 and 1. If, for example, a €1.00 increase in disposable income leads to an increase in consumer expenditure of €0.50, then $mpc = 0.5$.

TABLE 20.1

Consumption function: schedule of consumer expenditure C when *mpc* = 0.5 and *a* = 200 (€ billions)

Point in Figure 20.1	Disposable income Y_D (1)	Change in disposable income ΔY_D (2)	Change in consumer expenditure ΔC $(0.5 \times \Delta Y_D)$ (3)	Consumer expenditure C (4)
E	0	–	–	200 (= *a*)
F	400	400	200	400
G	800	400	200	600
H	1,200	400	200	800

A numerical example of a consumption function using the values of $a = 200$ and $mpc = 0.5$ will clarify the preceding concepts. The €200 billion of consumer expenditure at a disposable income of 0 is listed in the first row of Table 20.1 and is plotted as point E in Figure 20.1. (Remember that throughout this chapter, euro amounts for all variables in the figures correspond to real quantities, because Keynes assumed that the price level is fixed.) Because $mpc = 0.5$, when disposable income increases by €400 billion, the change in consumer expenditure – ΔC in column 3 of Table 20.1 – is €200 billion (0.5×400 billion). Thus, when disposable income is €400 billion, consumer expenditure is €400 billion (initial value of €200 billion when income is 0 plus the €200 billion change in consumer expenditure). This combination of consumer expenditure and disposable income is listed in the second row of Table 20.1 and is plotted as point F in Figure 20.1. Similarly, at point G, where disposable income has increased by another €400 billion to €800 billion, consumer expenditure will rise by another €200 billion to €600 billion. By the same reasoning, at point H, at which disposable income is €1,200 billion, consumer expenditure will be €800 billion. The line connecting these points in Figure 20.1 graphs the consumption function.

FIGURE 20.1

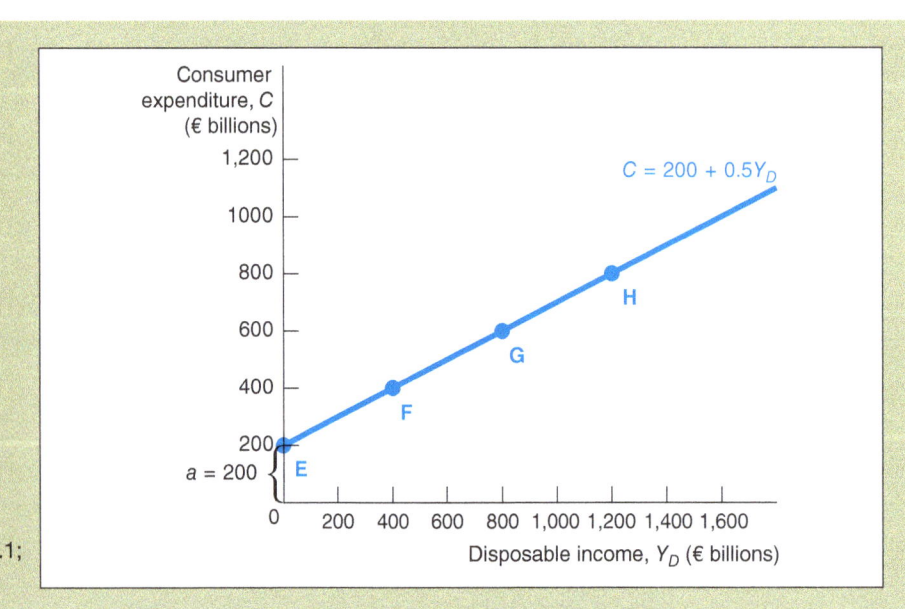

Consumption function

The consumption function plotted here is from Table 20.1; $a = 200$ and $mpc = 0.5$.

Investment spending

It is important to understand that there are two types of investment. The first type, **fixed investment**, is the spending by firms on equipment (machines, computers, aeroplanes) and structures (factories, office buildings, shopping centres) and planned spending on residential housing. The second type, **inventory investment**, is spending by firms on additional holdings of raw materials, parts and finished goods, calculated as the change in holdings of these items in a given time period – say a year. (The 'Closer look' box explains how economists' use of the word *investment* differs from everyday use of the term.)

Suppose that BMW, a company that produces cars, has 10,000 cars sitting in its warehouses on 31 December 2011, ready to be shipped to car dealers. If each car has a wholesale price of €30,000, BMW has an inventory worth €300 million. If by 31 December 2012, its inventory of cars has risen to €450 million, its inventory investment in 2012 is €150 million, the *change* in the level of its inventory over the course of the year (€450 million minus €300 million). Now suppose that there is a drop in the level of inventories; inventory investment will then be negative.

BMW may also have additional inventory investment if the level of raw materials and parts that it is holding to produce these cars increases over the course of the year. If on 31 December 2011, it holds €20 million of gear boxes used to produce its cars and on 31 December 2012, it holds €30 million, it has an additional €10 million of inventory investment in 2012.

An important feature of inventory investment is that – in contrast to fixed investment, which is always planned – some inventory investment can be unplanned. Suppose that the reason BMW finds itself with an additional €150 million of cars on 31 December 2012, is that €150 million less of its cars were sold in 2012 than expected. This €150 million of inventory investment in 2012 was unplanned. In this situation, BMW is producing more cars than it can sell and will cut production.

Planned investment spending, a component of aggregate demand Y^{ad}, is equal to planned fixed investment plus the amount of inventory investment *planned* by firms. Keynes mentioned two factors that influence planned investment spending: interest rates and businesses' expectations about the future. How these factors affect investment spending is discussed later in this chapter. For now, planned investment spending will be treated as a known value. At this stage, we want to explain how aggregate output is determined for a given level of planned investment spending; we can then examine how interest rates and business expectations influence aggregate output by affecting planned investment spending.

Equilibrium and the Keynesian cross diagram

We have now assembled the building blocks (consumer expenditure and planned investment spending) that will enable us to see how aggregate output is determined when we ignore

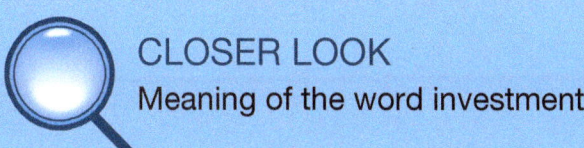

CLOSER LOOK
Meaning of the word investment

Economists use the word *investment* somewhat differently than other people do. When non-economists say that they are making an investment, they are normally referring to the purchase of common stocks or bonds, purchases that do not necessarily involve newly produced goods and services. But when economists speak of investment spending, they are referring to the purchase of *new* physical assets such as new machines or new houses – purchases that add to aggregate demand.

the government and net exports. Although unrealistic, this stripped-down analysis clarifies the basic principles of output determination. In the following sections, government and net exports enter the picture and makes our model more realistic.

The diagram in Figure 20.2, known as the *Keynesian cross diagram*, shows how aggregate output is determined. The vertical axis measures aggregate demand and the horizontal axis measures the level of aggregate output. The 45° line shows all the points at which aggregate output Y equals aggregate demand Y^{ad}; that is, it shows all the points at which the equilibrium condition $Y = Y^{ad}$ is satisfied. Because government spending and net exports are zero ($G = 0$ and $NX = 0$), aggregate demand is

$$Y^{ad} = C + I$$

Because there is no government sector to collect taxes, there are none in our simplified economy; disposable income Y_D then equals aggregate output Y (remember that aggregate income and aggregate output are equivalent; see the appendix to Chapter 1). Thus the consumption function with $a = 200$ and $mpc = 0.5$ plotted in Figure 20.1 can be written as $C = 200 + 0.5Y$ and is plotted in Figure 20.2. Given that planned investment spending is €300 billion, aggregate demand can then be expressed as follows:

$$Y^{ad} = C + I = 200 + 0.5Y + 300 = 500 + 0.5Y$$

This equation, plotted in Figure 20.2, represents the quantity of aggregate demand at any given level of aggregate output and is called the **aggregate demand function**.

The aggregate demand function $Y^{ad} = C + I$ is the vertical sum of the consumption function line ($C = 200 + 0.5Y$) and planned investment spending ($I = 300$). The point at which the aggregate demand function crosses the 45° line $Y = Y^{ad}$ indicates the equilibrium level of aggregate demand and aggregate output. In Figure 20.2, equilibrium occurs at point J, with both aggregate output Y^* and aggregate demand Y^{ad*} at €1,000 billion.

As you learned in Chapter 5, the concept of equilibrium is useful only if there is a tendency for the economy to settle there. To see whether the economy heads toward the equilibrium output level of €1,000 billion, let's first look at what happens if the amount of output produced in the economy is above the equilibrium level at €1,200 billion. At this level of output, aggregate demand is €1,100 billion (point K), €100 billion less than the €1,200 billion of output (point L on the 45° line). Because output exceeds aggregate demand by €100 billion, firms are saddled with €100 billion of unsold inventory. To

---

FIGURE 20.2

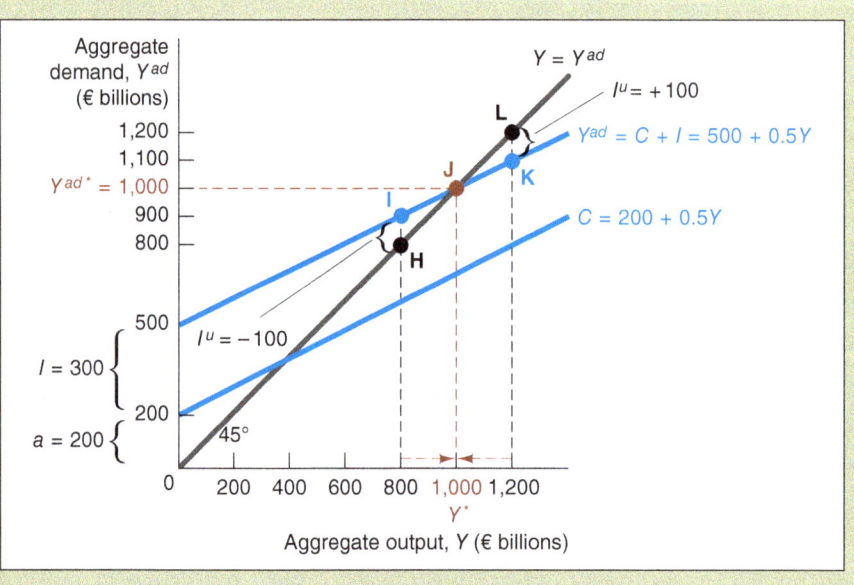

Keynesian cross diagram

When $I = 300$ and $C = 200 + 0.5Y$, equilibrium output occurs at $Y^* = 1,000$, where the aggregate demand function $Y^{ad} = C + I$ intersects with the 45° line $Y = Y^{ad}$.

keep from accumulating unsold goods, firms will cut production. As long as it is above the equilibrium level, output will exceed aggregate demand and firms will cut production, sending aggregate output toward the equilibrium level.

Another way to observe a tendency of the economy to head toward equilibrium at point J is from the viewpoint of inventory investment. When firms do not sell all output produced, they add unsold output to their holdings of inventory, and inventory investment increases. At an output level of €1,200 billion, for instance, the €100 billion of unsold goods leads to €100 billion of unplanned inventory investment, which firms do not want. Companies will decrease production to reduce inventory to the desired level, and aggregate output will fall (indicated by the arrow near the horizontal axis). This viewpoint means that unplanned inventory investment for the entire economy I^u equals the excess of output over aggregate demand. In our example, at an output level of €1,200 billion, I^u = €100 billion. If I^u is positive, firms will cut production and output will fall. Output will stop falling only when it has returned to its equilibrium level at point J, where I^u = 0.

What happens if aggregate output is below the equilibrium level of output? Let's say output is €800 billion. At this level of output, aggregate demand at point I is €900 billion, €100 billion higher than output (point H on the 45° line). At this level, firms are selling €100 billion more goods than they are producing, so inventory falls below the desired level. The negative unplanned inventory investment (I^u = −€100 billion) will induce firms to increase their production so that they can raise inventory to the desired levels. As a result, output rises toward the equilibrium level, shown by the arrow in Figure 20.2. As long as output is below the equilibrium level, unplanned inventory investment will remain negative, firms will continue to raise production and output will continue to rise. We again see the tendency for the economy to settle at point J, where aggregate demand Y equals output Y^{ad} and unplanned inventory investment is zero (I^u = 0).

Expenditure multiplier

Now that we understand that equilibrium aggregate output is determined by the position of the aggregate demand function, we can examine how different factors shift the function and consequently change aggregate output. We will find that either a rise in planned investment spending or a rise in autonomous consumer expenditure shifts the aggregate demand function upward and leads to an increase in aggregate output.

Output response to a change in planned investment spending

Suppose that a new electric motor is invented that makes all factory machines three times more efficient. Because firms are suddenly more optimistic about the profitability of investing in new machines that use this new motor, planned investment spending increases by €100 billion from an initial level of I_1 = €300 billion to I_2 = €400 billion. What effect does this have on output?

The effects of this increase in planned investment spending are analysed in Figure 20.3 using a Keynesian cross diagram. Initially, when planned investment spending I_1 is €300 billion, the aggregate demand function is Y_1^{ad}, and equilibrium occurs at point 1, where output is €1,000 billion. The €100 billion increase in planned investment spending adds directly to aggregate demand and shifts the aggregate demand function upward to Y_2^{ad}. Aggregate demand now equals output at the intersection of Y_2^{ad} with the 45° line Y = Y^{ad} (point 2). As a result of the €100 billion increase in planned investment spending, equilibrium output rises by €200 billion to €1,200 billion (Y_2). For every euro increase in planned investment spending, aggregate output has increased twofold.

The ratio of the change in aggregate output to a change in planned investment spending, $\Delta Y / \Delta I$, is called the **expenditure multiplier**. (This multiplier should not be confused with the money supply multiplier developed in Chapter 14, which measures the ratio of the change in the money supply to the change in the monetary base.) In Figure 20.3, the expenditure multiplier is 2.

FIGURE 20.3

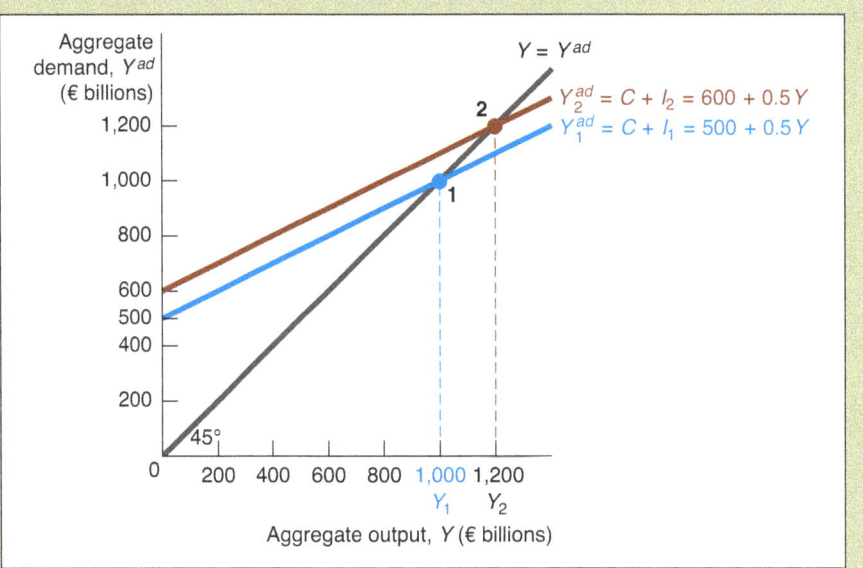

Response of aggregate output to a change in planned investment

A €100 billion increase in planned investment spending from $I_1 = 300$ to $I_2 = 400$ shifts the aggregate demand function upward from Y_1^{ad} to Y_2^{ad}. The equilibrium moves from point 1 to point 2, and equilibrium output rises from $Y_1 = 1,000$ to $Y_2 = 1,200$.

Why does a change in planned investment spending lead to an even larger change in aggregate output so that the expenditure multiplier is greater than 1? The expenditure multiplier is greater than 1 because an increase in planned investment spending, which raises output, leads to an additional increase in consumer expenditure ($mpc \times \Delta Y$). The increase in consumer expenditure, in turn, raises aggregate demand and output further, resulting in a multiple change of output from a given change in planned investment spending. This conclusion can be derived algebraically by solving for the unknown value of Y in terms of a, mpc and I, resulting in the following equation:[4]

$$Y = (a + I) \times \frac{1}{1 - mpc} \tag{20.4}$$

Because I is multiplied by the term $1/(1 - mpc)$, this equation tells us that a €1 change in I leads to a €$1/(1 - mpc)$ change in aggregate output; thus $1/(1 - mpc)$ is the expenditure multiplier. When $mpc = 0.5$, the change in output for a €1 change in I is €$2[=1/(1 - 0.5)]$; if $mpc = 0.8$, the change in output for a €1 change in I is €5. The larger the marginal propensity to consume, the higher the expenditure multiplier.

Response to changes in autonomous spending

Because a is also multiplied by the term $1/(1 - mpc)$ in Equation 20.4, a €1 change in autonomous consumer expenditure a also changes aggregate output by $1/(1 - mpc)$, the amount of the expenditure multiplier. Therefore, we see that the expenditure multiplier applies equally well to changes in autonomous consumer expenditure. In fact, Equation 20.4 can be rewritten as

$$Y = A \times \frac{1}{1 - mpc} \tag{20.5}$$

in which A = autonomous spending = $a + I$.

This rewritten equation tells us that any change in autonomous spending, whether from a change in a, in I, or in both, will lead to a multiplied change in Y. If both a and I decrease by €100 billion each, so that A decreases by €200 billion, and $mpc = 0.5$, the expenditure multiplier is $2[=1/(1 - 0.5)]$, and aggregate output Y will fall by $2 \times$ €200 billion = €400 billion.

Conversely, a rise in *I* by €100 billion that is offset by a €100 billion decline in *a* will leave autonomous spending *A*, and hence *Y*, unchanged. The expenditure multiplier $1/(1 - mpc)$ can therefore be defined more generally as the ratio of the change in aggregate output to the change in autonomous spending $(\Delta Y/\Delta A)$.

Another way to reach this conclusion – that any change in autonomous spending will lead to a multiplied change in aggregate output – is to recognize that the shift in the aggregate demand function in Figure 20.3 did not have to come from an increase in *I*; it could also have come from an increase in *a*, which directly raises consumer expenditure and therefore aggregate demand. Alternatively, it could have come from an increase in both *a* and *I*. Changes in the attitudes of consumers and firms about the future, which cause changes in their spending, will result in multiple changes in aggregate output.

Keynes believed that changes in autonomous spending are dominated by unstable fluctuations in planned investment spending, which is influenced by emotional waves of optimism and pessimism – factors he labelled '**animal spirits**'. His view was coloured by the collapse in investment spending during the Great Depression, which he saw as the primary reason for the economic contraction. We will examine the consequences of this fall in investment spending in the following application.

APPLICATION

The collapse of investment spending and the Great Depression

Along with the world economy, the UK suffered from the fallout of the Great Depression in the US following the great crash of 1929 and the banking crisis. From 1929 to 1933, the UK economy experienced the largest percentage decline in investment spending ever recorded. One explanation for the investment collapse was the ongoing set of financial crises that followed the stock market collapse of 1929 which had a serious effect on the US economy and global trade. In 2010 pounds, investment spending fell from £31 billion to £19 billion – a decline of about 40%. What does the Keynesian analysis developed so far suggest should have happened to aggregate output in this period?

Figure 20.4 demonstrates how the £12 billion drop in planned investment spending would shift the aggregate demand function downward from Y_1^{ad} to Y_2^{ad}, moving the economy from point 1 to point 2. Aggregate output would then fall sharply; real GDP actually fell by £15 billion (a multiple of the £12 billion drop in investment spending), from £251 billion to £236 billion (in 2010 prices). The fall in output resulted in unemployment rising from 1.2 million in 1929 to 2.8 million in 1932.

Government's role

After witnessing the events in the Great Depression, Keynes took the view that an economy would continually suffer major output fluctuations because of the volatility of autonomous spending, particularly planned investment spending. He was especially worried about sharp declines in autonomous spending, which would inevitably lead to large declines in output and an equilibrium with high unemployment. If autonomous spending fell sharply, as it did during the Great Depression, how could an economy be restored to higher levels of output and more reasonable levels of unemployment? Not by an increase in autonomous investment and consumer spending, because the business outlook was so grim. Keynes's answer to this question involved looking at the role of government in determining aggregate output.

Keynes realized that government spending and taxation could also affect the position of the aggregate demand function and hence be manipulated to restore the economy to full employment. As shown in the aggregate demand equation $Y^{ad} = C + I + G + NX$, government spending *G* adds directly to aggregate demand. Taxes, however, do not affect aggregate demand directly, as government spending does. Instead, taxes lower the amount of income that consumers have available for spending and affect aggregate demand by influencing consumer expenditure. When there are taxes, disposable income Y_D does not

FIGURE 20.4

Response of aggregate output to the collapse of investment spending, 1929–33

The decline of £12 billion (in 2010 prices) in planned investment spending from 1929 to 1933 shifted the aggregate demand function down from Y_1^{ad} to Y_2^{ad} and caused the economy to move from point 1 to point 2, where output fell by £15 billion.

Source: 'The British economy: key statistics, 1900–1970', London and Cambridge Economic Service (1973).

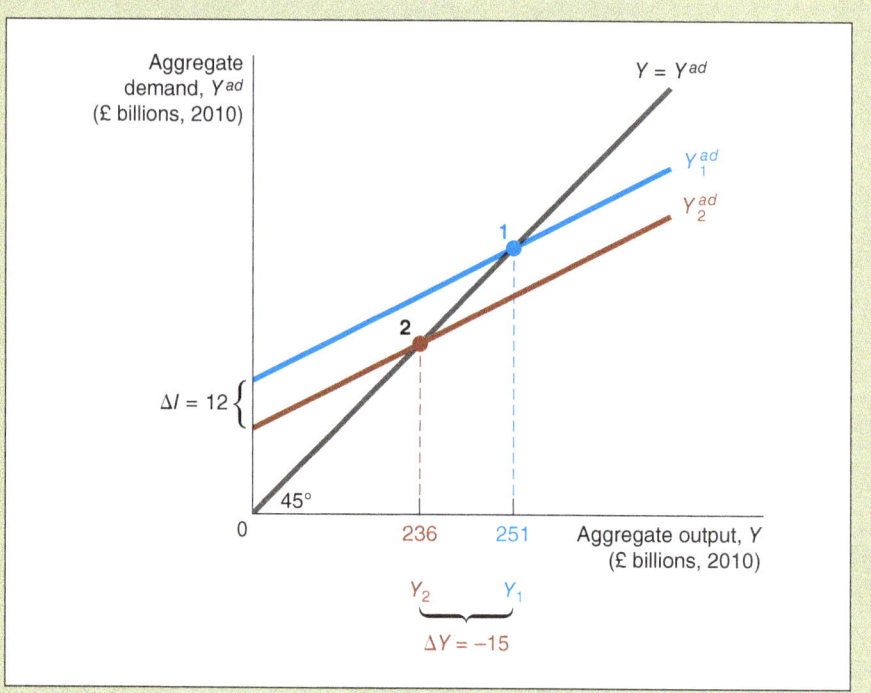

equal aggregate output; it equals aggregate output Y minus taxes T: $Y_D = Y - T$. The consumption function $C = a + (mpc \times Y_D)$ can be rewritten as follows:

$$C = a + \big[mpc \times (Y - T)\big] = a + (mpc \times Y) - (mpc \times T) \qquad (20.6)$$

This consumption function looks similar to the one used in the absence of taxes, but it has the additional term $-(mpc \times T)$ on the right side. This term indicates that if taxes increase by €100, consumer expenditure declines by mpc multiplied by this amount; if $mpc = 0.5$, consumer expenditure declines by €50. This occurs because consumers view €100 of taxes as equivalent to a €100 reduction in income and reduce their expenditure by the marginal propensity to consume times this amount.

To see how the inclusion of government spending and taxes modifies our analysis, first we will observe the effect of a positive level of government spending on aggregate output in the Keynesian cross diagram of Figure 20.5. Let's say that in the absence of government spending or taxes, the economy is at point 1, where the aggregate demand function $Y_1^{qd} = C + I = 500 + 0.5Y$ crosses the 45° line $Y = Y^{ad}$. Here equilibrium output is at €1,000 billion. Suppose, however, that the economy reaches full employment at an aggregate output level of €1,800 billion. How can government spending be used to restore the economy to full employment at €1,800 billion of aggregate output?

If government spending is set at €400 billion, the aggregate demand function shifts upward to $Y_2^{qd} = C + I + G = 900 + 0.5Y$. The economy moves to point 2, and aggregate output rises by €800 billion to €1,800 billion. Figure 20.5 indicates that aggregate output is positively related to government spending and that a change in government spending leads to a multiplied change in aggregate output, equal to the expenditure multiplier, $1/(1 - mpc) = 1/(1 - 0.5) = 2$. Therefore, declines in planned investment spending that produce high unemployment (as occurred during the Great Depression) can be offset by raising government spending.

What happens if the government decides that it must collect taxes of €400 billion to balance the budget? Before taxes are raised, the economy is in equilibrium at the same point

FIGURE 20.5

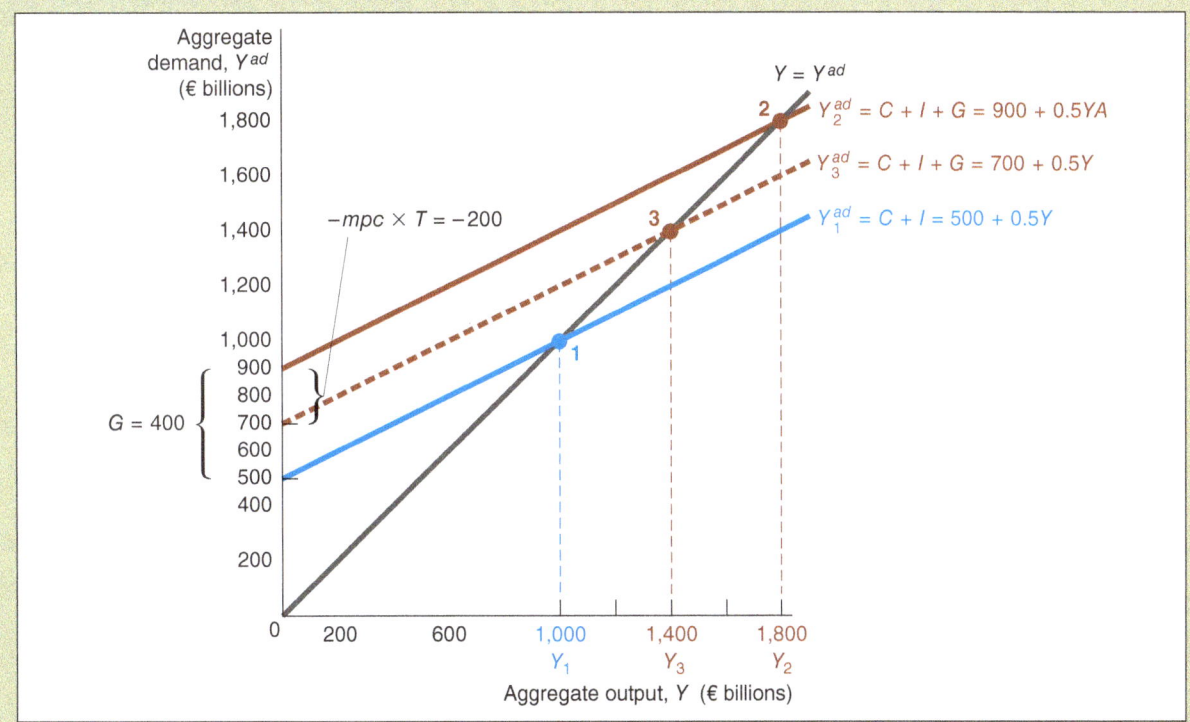

Response of aggregate output to government spending and taxes

With no government spending or taxes, the aggregate demand function is Y_1^{ad} and equilibrium output is $Y_1 = 1,000$. With government spending of €400 billion, the aggregate demand function shifts upward to Y_2^{ad} and aggregate output rises by €800 billion to $Y_2 = $ €1,800 billion. Taxes of €400 billion lower consumer expenditure and the aggregate demand function by €200 billion from Y_2^{ad} to Y_6^{ad} and aggregate output falls by €400 billion to $Y_3 = $ €1,400 billion.

2 found in Figure 20.5. Our discussion of the consumption function (which allows for taxes) indicates that taxes T reduce consumer expenditure by $mpc \times T$ because there is T less income now available for spending. In our example, $mpc = 0.5$, so consumer expenditure and the aggregate demand function shift downward by €200 billion (= 0.5×400); at the new equilibrium, point 3, the level of output has declined by twice this amount (the expenditure multiplier) to €1,400 billion.

Although you can see that aggregate output is negatively related to the level of taxes, it is important to recognize that the change in aggregate output from the €400 billion increase in taxes ($\Delta Y = -$€400 billion) is smaller than the change in aggregate output from the €400 billion increase in government spending ($\Delta Y = $€800 billion). If both taxes and government spending are raised equally – by €400 billion, as occurs in going from point 1 to point 3 in Figure 20.5 – aggregate output will rise.[5]

The Keynesian framework indicates that the government can play an important role in determining aggregate output by changing the level of government spending or taxes. If the economy enters a deep recession, in which output drops severely and unemployment climbs, the analysis we have just developed provides a prescription for restoring the economy to health. The government might raise aggregate output by increasing government spending, or it could lower taxes and reverse the process described in Figure 20.5 (that is, a tax cut makes more income available for spending at any level of output, shifting the aggregate demand function upward and causing the equilibrium level of output to rise).

Role of international trade

International trade also plays a role in determining aggregate output because net exports (exports minus imports) are a component of aggregate demand. To analyse the effect of net exports in the Keynesian cross diagram of Figure 20.6, suppose that initially net exports are equal to zero ($NX_1 = 0$) so that the economy is at point 1, where the aggregate demand function $Y_1^{ad} = C + I + G + NX_1 = 500 + 0.5Y$ crosses the 45° line $Y = Y_1^{ad}$. Equilibrium output is again at €1,000 billion. Now foreigners suddenly get an urge to buy more European products so that net exports rise to €100 billion ($NX_2 = 100$). The €100 billion increase in net exports adds directly to aggregate demand and shifts the aggregate demand function upward to $Y_2^{ad} = C + I + G + NX_2 = 600 + 0.5Y$. The economy moves to point 2, and aggregate output rises by €200 billion to €1,200 billion (Y_2). Figure 20.6 indicates that, just as we found for planned investment spending and government spending, a rise in net exports leads to a multiplied rise in aggregate output, equal to the expenditure multiplier, $1/(1 - mpc) = 1/(1 - 0.5) = 2$. Therefore, changes in net exports can be another important factor affecting fluctuations in aggregate output.

Summary of the determinants of aggregate output

Our analysis of the Keynesian framework so far has identified five autonomous factors (factors independent of income) that shift the aggregate demand function and hence the level of aggregate output:

1 Changes in autonomous consumer expenditure (a)
2 Changes in planned investment spending (I)
3 Changes in government spending (G)
4 Changes in taxes (T)
5 Changes in net exports (NX)

The effects of changes in each of these variables on aggregate output are summarized in Table 20.2 and discussed next in the text.

FIGURE 20.6

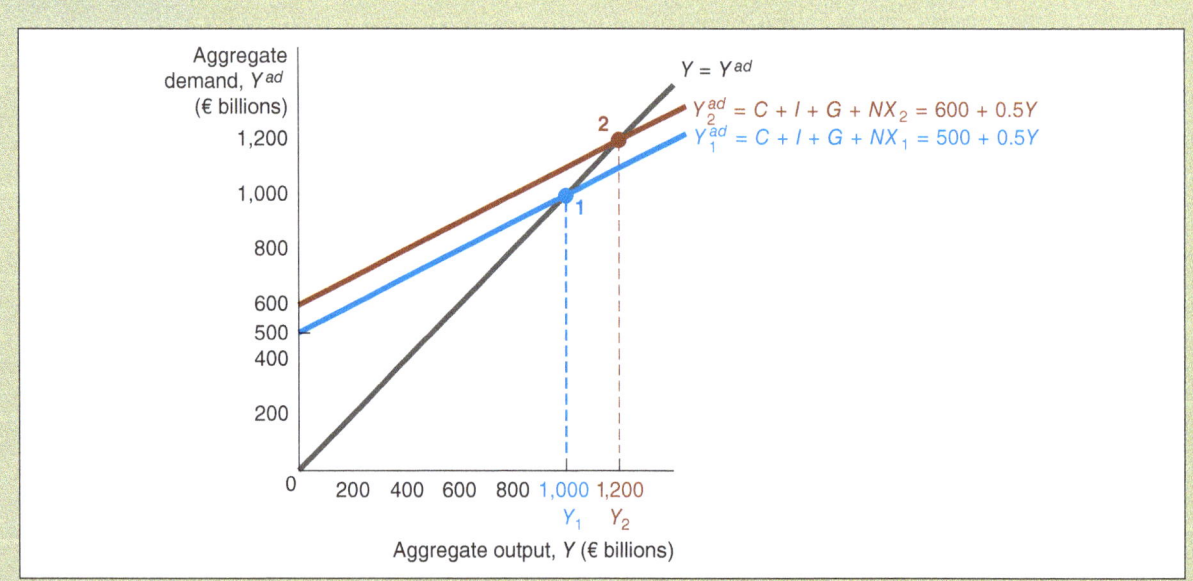

Response of aggregate output to a change in net exports

A €100 billion increase in net exports from $NX_1 = 0$ to $NX_2 = 100$ shifts the aggregate demand function upward from Y_1^{ad} to Y_2^{ad}. The equilibrium moves from point 1 to point 2 and equilibrium output rises from $Y_1 = $ €1,000 billion to $Y_2 = $ €1,200 billion.

SUMMARY TABLE 20.2

Response of aggregate output *Y* to autonomous changes in *a*, *I*, *G*, *T* and *NX*

Variable	Change in variable	Response of aggregate output, *Y*	
Autonomous consumer expenditure, *a*	↑	↑	
Investment, *I*	↑	↑	
Government spending, *G*	↑	↑	
Taxes, *T*	↑	↓	
Net exports, *NX*	↑	↑	

Note: Only increases (↑) in the variables are shown; the effects of the decreases in the variables on aggregate output would be the opposite of the those increased in the 'Response' column.

Changes in autonomous consumer spending (*a*)

A rise in autonomous consumer expenditure a (say, because consumers become more optimistic about the economy when the stock market booms) directly raises consumer expenditure and shifts the aggregate demand function upward, resulting in an increase in aggregate output. A decrease in a causes consumer expenditure to fall, leading ultimately to a decline in aggregate output. Therefore, *aggregate output is positively related to autonomous consumer expenditure a*.

Changes in planned investment spending (*I*)

A rise in planned investment spending adds directly to aggregate demand, raising the aggregate demand function and aggregate output. A fall in planned investment spending lowers aggregate demand and causes aggregate output to fall. Therefore, *aggregate output is positively related to planned investment spending I*.

Changes in government spending (G)

A rise in government spending also adds directly to aggregate demand and raises the aggregate demand function, increasing aggregate output. A fall directly reduces aggregate demand, lowers the aggregate demand function and causes aggregate output to fall. Therefore, *aggregate output is positively related to government spending G*.

Changes in taxes (T)

A rise in taxes does not affect aggregate demand directly, but does lower the amount of income available for spending, reducing consumer expenditure. The decline in consumer expenditure then leads to a fall in the aggregate demand function, resulting in a decline in aggregate output. A lowering of taxes makes more income available for spending, raises consumer expenditure and leads to higher aggregate output. Therefore, *aggregate output is negatively related to the level of taxes T*.

Changes in net exports (NX)

A rise in net exports adds directly to aggregate demand and raises the aggregate demand function, increasing aggregate output. A fall directly reduces aggregate demand, lowers the aggregate demand function and causes aggregate output to fall. Therefore, *aggregate output is positively related to net exports NX*.

Size of the effects from the five factors

The aggregate demand function in the Keynesian cross diagrams shifts vertically by the full amount of the change in a, I, G or NX, resulting in a multiple effect on aggregate output through the effects of the expenditure multiplier, $1/(1 - mpc)$. A change in taxes has a smaller effect on aggregate output, because consumer expenditure changes only by mpc times the change in taxes ($- mpc \times \Delta T$), which in the case of $mpc = 0.5$ means that aggregate demand shifts vertically by only half of the change in taxes.

If there is a change in one of these autonomous factors that is offset by a change in another (say, I rises by €100 billion, but a, G or NX falls by €100 billion or T rises by €200 billion when $mpc = 0.5$), the aggregate demand function will remain in the same position and aggregate output will remain unchanged.[6]

The *ISLM* model

So far, our analysis has excluded monetary policy. We now include money and interest rates in the Keynesian framework to develop the more intricate *ISLM* model of how aggregate output is determined, in which monetary policy plays an important role. Why another complex model? The *ISLM* model is versatile and allows us to understand economic phenomena that cannot be analysed with the simpler Keynesian cross framework used earlier. The *ISLM* model will help us understand how monetary policy affects economic activity and interacts with fiscal policy (changes in government spending and taxes) to produce a certain level of aggregate output; how the level of interest rates is affected by changes in investment spending as well as by changes in monetary and fiscal policy; how monetary policy is best conducted; and how the *ISLM* model generates the aggregate demand curve, an essential building block for the aggregate supply and demand analysis used in Chapter 22 and thereafter.

Like our simplified Keynesian model, the full *ISLM* model examines an equilibrium in which aggregate output produced equals aggregate demand, and, because it assumes a fixed price level, in which real and nominal quantities are the same. The first step in constructing the *ISLM* model is to examine the effect of interest rates on planned investment spending and hence on aggregate demand. Next we use a Keynesian cross diagram to see how the interest rate affects the equilibrium level of aggregate output. The resulting relationship between equilibrium aggregate output and the interest rate is known as the **IS curve**.

Just as a demand curve alone cannot tell us the quantity of goods sold in a market, the *IS* curve by itself cannot tell us what the level of aggregate output will be because the interest rate is still unknown. We need another relationship, called the **LM curve**, to describe the combinations of interest rates and aggregate output for which the quantity of money demanded equals the quantity of money supplied. When the *IS* and *LM* curves are combined in the same diagram, the intersection of the two determines the equilibrium level of aggregate output as well as the interest rate. Finally, we will have obtained a more complete analysis of the determination of aggregate output in which monetary policy plays an important role.

Equilibrium in the goods market: the *IS* curve

In Keynesian analysis, the primary way that interest rates affect the level of aggregate output is through their effects on planned investment spending and net exports. After explaining why interest rates affect planned investment spending and net exports, we will use Keynesian cross diagrams to learn how interest rates affect equilibrium aggregate output.[7]

Interest rates and planned investment spending

Businesses make investments in physical capital (machines, factories and raw materials) as long as they expect to earn more from the physical capital than the interest cost of a loan to finance the investment. When the interest rate is high, few investments in physical capital will earn more than the cost of borrowed funds, so planned investment spending is low. When the interest rate is low, many investments in physical capital will earn more than the interest cost of borrowed funds. Therefore, when interest rates are lower, business firms are more likely to undertake an investment in physical capital and planned investment spending will be higher.

Even if a company has surplus funds and does not need to borrow to undertake an investment in physical capital, its planned investment spending will be affected by the interest rate. Instead of investing in physical capital, it could purchase a security, such as a bond. If the interest rate on this security is high, the opportunity cost (forgone interest earnings) of an investment is high, and planned investment spending will be low, because the firm would probably prefer to purchase the security than to invest in physical capital. As the interest rate and the opportunity cost of investing fall, planned investment spending will increase because investments in physical capital are more likely than the security to earn greater income for the firm.

The relationship between the amount of planned investment spending and any given level of the interest rate is illustrated by the investment schedule in panel (a) of Figure 20.7. The downward slope of the schedule reflects the negative relationship between planned investment spending and the interest rate. At a low interest rate i_1, the level of planned investment spending I_1 is high; for a high interest rate i_3, planned investment spending I_3 is low.

Interest rates and net exports

As discussed in more detail in Chapter 17, when interest rates rise (with the price level fixed), assets denominated in domestic currency become more attractive relative to assets denominated in foreign currencies, thereby causing an increased demand for domestic assets and thus a rise in the exchange rate. The higher value of the domestic currency resulting from the rise in interest rates makes domestic goods more expensive than foreign goods, thereby causing a fall in net exports. The resulting negative relationship between interest rates and net exports is shown in panel (b) of Figure 20.7. At a low interest rate i_1, the exchange rate is low and net exports NX_1 are high; at a high interest rate i_3, the exchange rate is high and net exports NX_3 are low.

Deriving the *IS* curve

We can now use what we have learned about the relationship of interest rates to planned investment spending and net exports in panels (a) and (b) to examine the relationship between interest rates and the equilibrium level of aggregate output (holding government spending and autonomous consumer expenditure constant). The three levels of planned investment spending and net exports in panels (a) and (b) are represented in the three

FIGURE 20.7

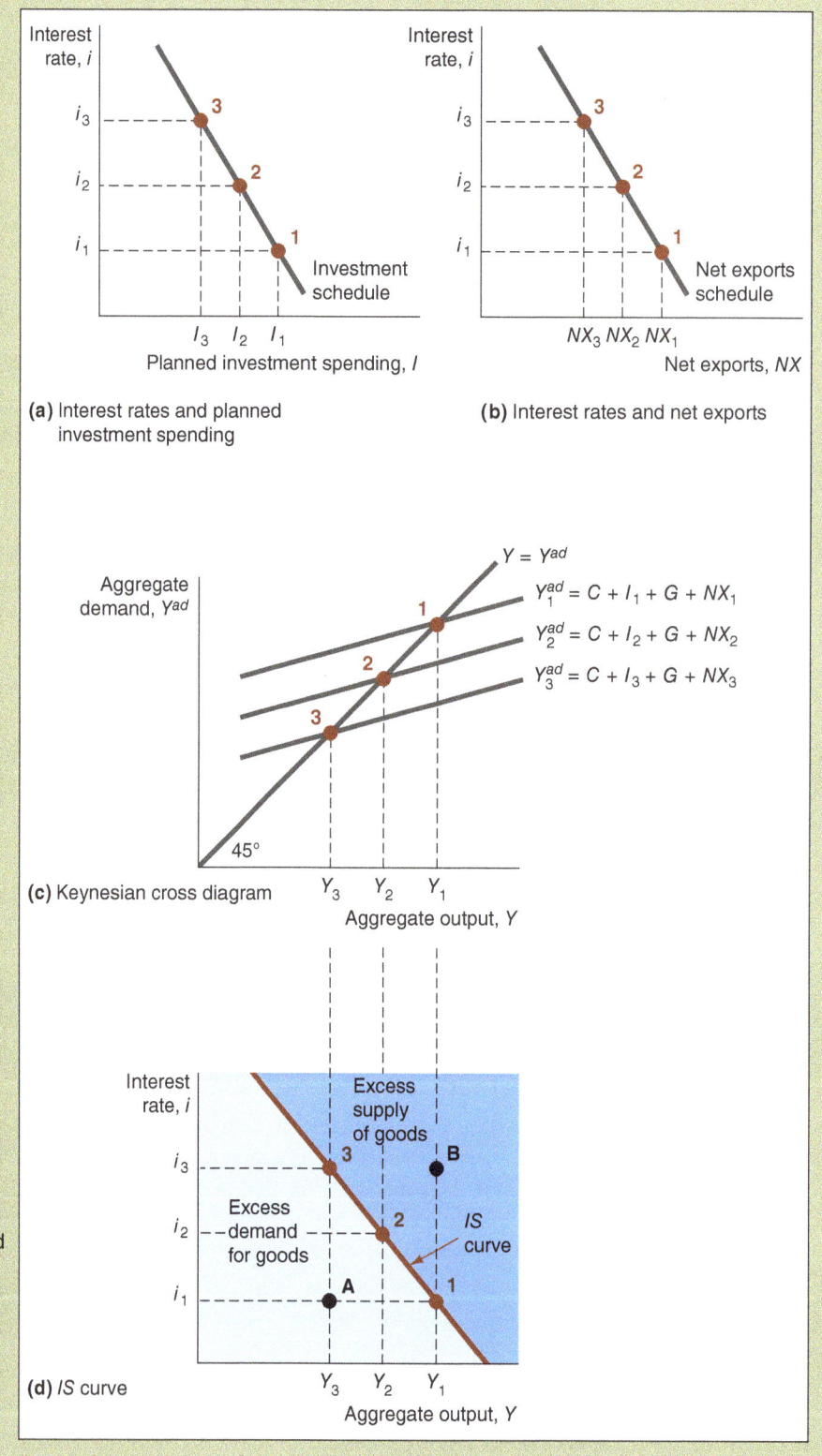

Deriving the *IS* curve

The investment schedule in panel (a) shows that as the interest rate rises from i_1 to i_2 to i_3, planned investment spending falls from I_1 to I_2 to I_3. Panel (b) shows that net exports also fall from NX_1 to NX_2 to NX_3 as the interest rate rises. Panel (c) then indicates the levels of equilibrium output Y_1, Y_2 and Y_3 that correspond to those three levels of planned investment and net exports. Finally, panel (d) plots the level of equilibrium output corresponding to each of the three interest rates; the line that connects these points is the *IS* curve.

(a) Interest rates and planned investment spending

(b) Interest rates and net exports

(c) Keynesian cross diagram

(d) *IS* curve

aggregate demand functions in the Keynesian cross diagram of panel (c). The lowest interest rate i_1 has the highest level of both planned investment spending I_1 and net exports NX_1, and hence the highest aggregate demand function Y_1^{ad}. Point 1 in panel (d) shows the resulting equilibrium level of output Y_1, which corresponds to interest rate i_1. As the interest rate rises to i_2, both planned investment spending and net exports fall, to I_2 and NX_2, respectively, so equilibrium output falls to Y_2. Point 2 in panel (d) shows the lower level of output Y_2, which corresponds to interest rate i_2. Finally, the highest interest rate i_3 leads to the lowest level of planned investment spending and net exports, and hence the lowest level of equilibrium output, which is plotted as point 3.

The line connecting the three points in panel (d), the *IS* curve, shows the combinations of interest rates and equilibrium aggregate output for which aggregate output produced equals aggregate demand. The negative slope indicates that higher interest rates result in lower planned investment spending and net exports, and hence lower equilibrium output.

What the *IS* curve tells us

The *IS* curve traces out the points at which the total quantity of goods produced equals the total quantity of goods demanded. It describes points at which the goods market is in equilibrium. For each given level of the interest rate, the *IS* curve tells us what aggregate output must be for the goods market to be in equilibrium. As the interest rate rises, planned investment spending and net exports fall, which in turn lowers aggregate demand; aggregate output must be lower for it to equal aggregate demand and satisfy goods market equilibrium.

The *IS* curve is a useful concept because output tends to move toward points on the curve that satisfy goods market equilibrium. If the economy is located in the area to the right of the *IS* curve, it has an excess supply of goods. At point B, for example, aggregate output Y_1 is greater than the equilibrium level of output Y_3 on the *IS* curve. This excess supply of goods results in unplanned inventory accumulation, which causes output to fall toward the *IS* curve. The decline stops only when output is again at its equilibrium level on the *IS* curve.

If the economy is located in the area to the left of the *IS* curve, it has an excess demand for goods. At point A, aggregate output Y_3 is below the equilibrium level of output Y_1 on the *IS* curve. The excess demand for goods results in an unplanned decrease in inventory, which causes output to rise toward the *IS* curve, stopping only when aggregate output is again at its equilibrium level on the *IS* curve.

Significantly, equilibrium in the goods market does not produce a unique equilibrium level of aggregate output. Although we now know where aggregate output will head for a given level of the interest rate, we cannot determine aggregate output because we do not know what the interest rate is. To complete our analysis of aggregate output determination, we need to introduce another market that produces an additional relationship that links aggregate output and interest rates. The market for money fulfils this function with the *LM* curve. When the *LM* curve is combined with the *IS* curve, a unique equilibrium that determines both aggregate output and the interest rate is obtained.

Equilibrium in the market for money: the *LM* curve

Just as the *IS* curve is derived from the equilibrium condition in the goods market (aggregate output equals aggregate demand), the *LM* curve is derived from the equilibrium condition in the market for money, which requires that the quantity of money demanded equal the quantity of money supplied. The main building block in Keynes's analysis of the market for money is the demand for money he called *liquidity preference*. Let us briefly review his theory of the demand for money (discussed at length in Chapters 5 and 19).

Keynes's liquidity preference theory states that the demand for money in real terms M^d/P depends on income Y (aggregate output) and interest rates i. The demand for money is positively related to income for two reasons. First, a rise in income raises the level of transactions in the economy, which in turn raises the demand for money because it is used to carry out these transactions. Second, a rise in income increases the demand for money because it increases the wealth of individuals who want to hold more assets, one of which is money. The opportunity cost of holding money is the interest sacrificed by not holding other assets (such as bonds) instead. As interest rates rise, the opportunity cost of holding money rises and the demand for money falls. According to the liquidity preference theory, the demand for money is positively related to aggregate output and negatively related to interest rates.

Deriving the *LM* curve

In Keynes's analysis, the level of interest rates is determined by equilibrium in the market for money (when the quantity of money demanded equals the quantity of money supplied). Figure 20.8 depicts what happens to equilibrium in the market for money as the level of output changes. Because the *LM* curve is derived holding the real money supply at a fixed level, it is fixed at the level of $\overline{M}/P$ in panel (a).[8] Each level of aggregate output has its own money demand curve because as aggregate output changes, the level of transactions in the economy changes, which in turn changes the demand for money.

When aggregate output is Y_1, the money demand curve is $M^d(Y_1)$: it slopes downward because a lower interest rate means that the opportunity cost of holding money is lower, so the quantity of money demanded is higher. Equilibrium in the market for money occurs at point 1, at which the interest rate is i_1. When aggregate output is at the higher level Y_2, the money demand curve shifts rightward to $M^d(Y_2)$ because the higher level of output means that at any given interest rate the quantity of money demanded is higher. Equilibrium in the market for money now occurs at point 2, at which the interest rate is at the higher level of i_2. Similarly, a still higher level of aggregate output Y_3 results in an even higher level of the equilibrium interest rate i_3.

Panel (b) plots the equilibrium interest rates that correspond to the different output levels, with points 1, 2 and 3 corresponding to the equilibrium points 1, 2 and 3 in panel (a). The line connecting these points is the *LM* curve, which shows the combinations of interest rates and output for which the market for money is in equilibrium. The positive slope arises because higher output raises the demand for money and thus raises the equilibrium interest rate.

What the *LM* curve tells us

The *LM* curve traces out the points that satisfy the equilibrium condition that the quantity of money demanded equals the quantity of money supplied. For each given level of aggregate output, the *LM* curve tells us what the interest rate must be for there to be equilibrium in the market for money. As aggregate output rises, the demand for money increases and the

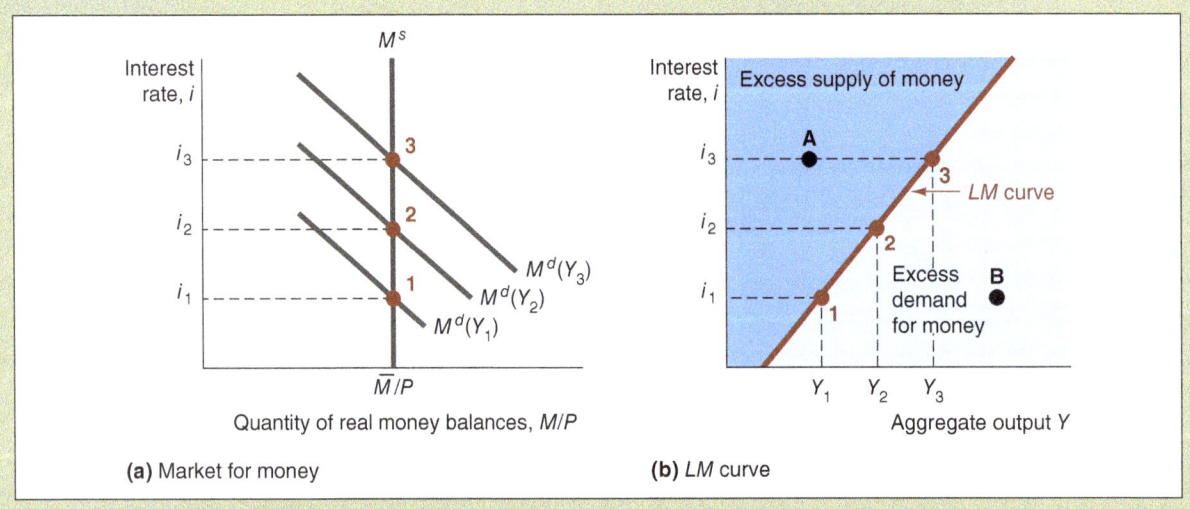

FIGURE 20.8

(a) Market for money

(b) *LM* curve

Deriving the *LM* curve

Panel (a) shows the equilibrium levels of the interest rate in the market for money that arise when aggregate output is at Y_1, Y_2 and Y_3. Panel (b) plots the three levels of the equilibrium interest rate i_1, i_2 and i_3 corresponding to these three levels of output; the line that connects these points is the *LM* curve.

interest rate rises, so that money demanded equals money supplied and the market for money is in equilibrium.

Just as the economy tends to move toward the equilibrium points represented by the *IS* curve, it also moves toward the equilibrium points on the *LM* curve. If the economy is located in the area to the left of the *LM* curve, there is an excess supply of money. At point A, for example, the interest rate is i_3 and aggregate output is Y_1. The interest rate is above the equilibrium level and people are holding more money than they want to. To eliminate their excess money balances, they will purchase bonds, which causes the price of the bonds to rise and their interest rate to fall. (The inverse relationship between the price of a bond and its interest rate is discussed in Chapter 4.) As long as an excess supply of money exists, the interest rate will fall until it comes to rest on the *LM* curve.

If the economy is located in the area to the right of the *LM* curve, there is an excess demand for money. At point B, for example, the interest rate i_1 is below the equilibrium level, and people want to hold more money than they currently do. To acquire this money, they will sell bonds and drive down bond prices, and the interest rate will rise. This process will stop only when the interest rate rises to an equilibrium point on the *LM* curve.

ISLM approach to aggregate output and interest rates

Now that we have derived the *IS* and *LM* curves, we can put them into the same diagram (Figure 20.9) to produce a model that enables us to determine both aggregate output and the interest rate. The only point at which the goods market and the market for money are in simultaneous equilibrium is at the intersection of the *IS* and *LM* curves, point E. At this point, aggregate output equals aggregate demand (*IS*) and the quantity of money demanded equals the quantity of money supplied (*LM*). At any other point in the diagram, at least one of these equilibrium conditions is not satisfied, and market forces move the economy toward the general equilibrium, point E.

To learn how this works, let's consider what happens if the economy is at point A, which is on the *IS* curve but not the *LM* curve. Even though at point A the goods market is in equilibrium, so that aggregate output equals aggregate demand, the interest rate is above its equilibrium level, so the demand for money is less than the supply. Because people have more money than they want to hold, they will try to get rid of it by buying bonds. The

FIGURE 20.9

ISLM diagram: simultaneous determination of output and the interest rate

Only at point E, when the interest rate is *i** and output is *Y**, is there equilibrium simultaneously in both the goods market (as measured by the *IS* curve) and the market for money (as measured by the *LM* curve). At other points, such as A, B, C or D, one of the two markets is not in equilibrium, and there will be a tendency to head toward the equilibrium, point E.

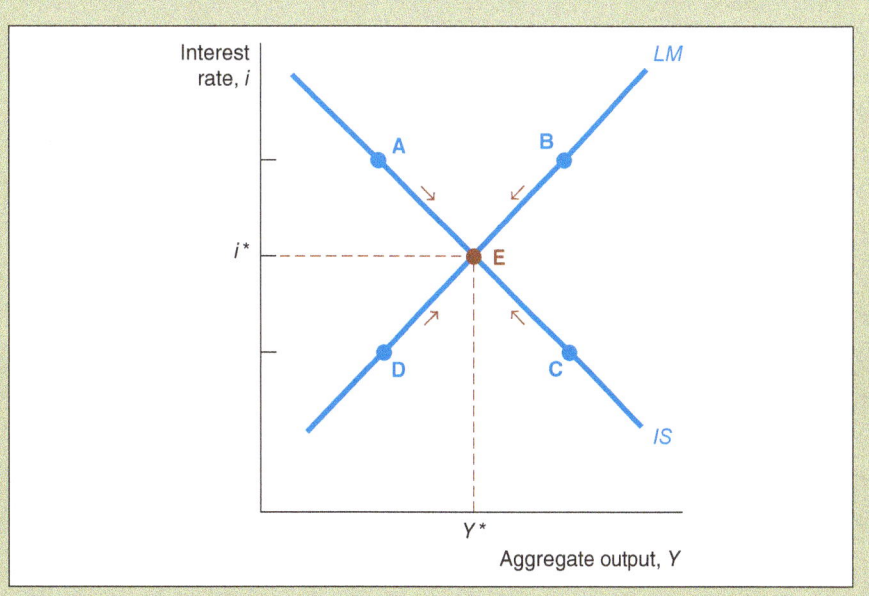

resulting rise in bond prices causes a fall in interest rates, which in turn causes both planned investment spending and net exports to rise, and thus aggregate output rises. The economy then moves down along the *IS* curve, and the process continues until the interest rate falls to i^* and aggregate output rises to Y^* – that is, until the economy is at equilibrium point E.

If the economy is on the *LM* curve but off the *IS* curve at point B, it will also head toward the equilibrium at point E. At point B, even though money demand equals money supply, output is higher than the equilibrium level and exceeds aggregate demand. Firms are unable to sell all their output, and unplanned inventory accumulates, prompting firms to cut production and lower output. The decline in output means that the demand for money will fall, lowering interest rates. The economy then moves down along the *LM* curve until it reaches equilibrium point E.

We have finally developed a model, the *ISLM* model, that tells us how both interest rates and aggregate output are determined when the price level is fixed. Although we have demonstrated that the economy will head toward an aggregate output level of Y^*, there is no reason to assume that at this level of aggregate output the economy is at full employment. If the unemployment rate is too high, government policymakers might want to increase aggregate output to reduce it. The *ISLM* apparatus indicates that they can do this by manipulating monetary and fiscal policy. We will conduct an *ISLM* analysis of how monetary and fiscal policy can affect economic activity in the next chapter.

Summary

1 In the simple Keynesian framework in which the price level is fixed, output is determined by the equilibrium condition in the goods market that aggregate output equals aggregate demand. Aggregate demand equals the sum of consumer expenditure, planned investment spending, government spending and net exports. Consumer expenditure is described by the consumption function, which indicates that consumer expenditure will rise as disposable income increases. Keynes's analysis shows that aggregate output is positively related to autonomous consumer expenditure, planned investment spending, government spending and net exports, and negatively related to the level of taxes. A change in any of these factors leads, through the expenditure multiplier, to a multiple change in aggregate output.

2 The *ISLM* model determines aggregate output and the interest rate for a fixed price level using the *IS* and *LM* curves. The *IS* curve traces out the combinations of the interest rate and aggregate output for which the goods market is in equilibrium, and the *LM* curve traces out the combinations for which the market for money is in equilibrium. The *IS* curve slopes downward, because higher interest rates lower planned investment spending and net exports and so lower equilibrium output. The *LM* curve slopes upward, because higher aggregate output raises the demand for money and so raises the equilibrium interest rate.

3 The simultaneous determination of output and interest rates occurs at the intersection of the *IS* and *LM* curves, where both the goods market and the market for money are in equilibrium. At any other level of interest rates and output, at least one of the markets will be out of equilibrium, and forces will move the economy toward the general equilibrium point at the intersection of the *IS* and *LM* curves.

Key terms

aggregate demand p. 464

aggregate demand function p. 468

'animal spirits' p. 471

autonomous consumer expenditure p. 465

consumer expenditure p. 464

consumption function p. 465

disposable income p. 465

expenditure multiplier p. 469

fixed investment p. 467

government spending p. 464

inventory investment p. 467

IS curve p. 476

LM curve p. 477

marginal propensity to consume p. 465

net exports p. 464

planned investment spending p. 464

QUESTIONS AND PROBLEMS

All questions and problems are available in MyEconlab at **www.myeconlab.com/mishkin**.

1 Calculate the value of the consumption function at each level of disposable income in Table 20.1 if $a = 100$ and $mpc = 0.9$.

2 Why do companies cut production when they find that their unplanned inventory investment is greater than zero? If they didn't cut production, what effect would this have on their profits? Why?

3 Plot the consumption function $C = 100 + 0.75Y$ on graph paper.

(a) Assuming no government sector or net exports, if planned investment spending is 200, what is the equilibrium level of aggregate output? Show this equilibrium level on the graph you have drawn.

(b) If businesses become more pessimistic about the profitability of investment and planned investment spending falls by 100, what happens to the equilibrium level of output?

4 If the consumption function is $C = 100 + 0.8Y$ and planned investment spending is 200, what is the equilibrium level of output? If planned investment falls by 100, how much does the equilibrium level of output fall?

5 Why are the multipliers in Problems 3 and 4 different? Explain intuitively why one is higher than the other.

6 If firms suddenly become more optimistic about the profitability of investment and planned investment spending rises by €100 billion, while consumers become more pessimistic and autonomous consumer spending falls by €100 billion, what happens to aggregate output?

7 'A rise in planned investment spending by €100 billion at the same time that autonomous consumer expenditure falls by €50 billion has the same effect on aggregate output as a rise in autonomous consumer expenditure alone by €50 billion.' Is this statement true, false, or uncertain? Explain your answer.

8 If the consumption function is $C = 100 + 0.75Y$, $I = 200$, and government spending is 200, what will be the equilibrium level of output? Demonstrate your answer with a Keynesian cross diagram. What happens to aggregate output if government spending rises by 100?

9 If the marginal propensity to consume is 0.5, how much would government spending have to rise to increase output by €1,000 billion?

10 Suppose that government policymakers decide that they will change taxes to raise aggregate output by €400 billion, and $mpc = 0.5$. By how much will taxes have to be changed?

11 What happens to aggregate output if both taxes and government spending are lowered by €300 billion and $mpc = 0.5$? Explain your answer.

12 Will aggregate output rise or fall if an increase in autonomous consumer expenditure is matched by an equal increase in taxes?

13 If a change in the interest rate has no effect on planned investment spending or net exports, trace out what happens to the equilibrium level of aggregate output as interest rates fall. What does this imply about the slope of the *IS* curve?

14 Using a supply and demand diagram for the market for money, show what happens to the equilibrium level of the interest rate as aggregate output falls. What does this imply about the slope of the *LM* curve?

15 'If the point describing the combination of the interest rate and aggregate output is not on either the *IS* curve or the *LM* curve, the economy will have no tendency to head toward the intersection of the two curves.' Is this statement true, false, or uncertain? Explain your answer.

WEB EXERCISES

1 Go to **www.fgn.unisg.ch/eurmacro/Tutor /keynesiancross.html**. Make sure the following settings are used: $t = 0$, $G = 200$, $c = 0.8$ and $m = 0.0$. Click on the 'memorize' button. Note the value of equilibrium output. Now, decrease G by 50. What is the value of equilibrium output? What is the implied multiplier?

2 Go to **www.fgn.unisg.ch/eurmacro/Tutor /keynesiancross.html**. Make sure the following settings are used: $t = 0.25$, $G = 400$, $c = 0.8$ and $m = 0.0$. Click the 'memorize' button. Note the value of equilibrium output. Now, decrease G by 50. What is the value of equilibrium output? What is the implied multiplier? Compare your answer with the answer to Question 1.

Notes

1 John Hicks, 'Mr Keynes and the classics: a suggested interpretation', *Econometrica* (1937): 147–59.

2 Imports are subtracted from exports in arriving at the net exports component of the total quantity demanded of an economy's output because imports are already counted in C, I and G but do not add to the demand for the economy's output.

3 Consumer expenditure can exceed income if people have accumulated savings to tide them over during bad times. An alternative is to have parents who will give you money for food (or to pay for school) when you have no income. The situation in which consumer expenditure is greater than disposable income is called *dissaving*.

4 Substituting the consumption function $C = a + (mpc \times Y)$ into the aggregate demand function $Y^{ad} = C + I$ yields $Y^{ad} = a + (mpc \times Y) + I$. In equilibrium, where aggregate output equals aggregate demand, $Y = Y^{ad} = a + (mpc \times Y) + I$. Subtracting the term $mpc \times Y$ from both sides of this equation to collect the terms involving Y on the left side, we have $Y - (mpc \times Y) = Y(1 - mpc) = a + 1$. Dividing both sides by $1 - mpc$ to solve for Y leads to Equation 20.4 in the text.

5 This is also called the 'Haavelmo effect', in honour of Trygve Haavelmo, the economist who first demonstrated this result. See Trygve Haavelmo, 'Multiplier effects of a balanced budget', *Econometrica* 13, 4 (Oct. 1945): 311–18.

6 These results can be derived algebraically as follows. Substituting the consumption function allowing for taxes (Equation 20.6) into the aggregate demand function (Equation 20.1), we have $Y^{ad} = a - (mpc \times T) + (mpc \times Y) + I + G + NX$. If we assume that taxes T are unrelated to income, we can define autonomous spending in the aggregate demand function to be $A = a - (mpc \times T) + I + G + NX$. The expenditure equation can be rewritten as $Y^{ad} = A + (mpc \times Y)$. In equilibrium, aggregate demand equals aggregate output: $Y = A + (mpc \times Y)$ which can be solved for Y. The resulting equation $Y = A \times \dfrac{1}{1 - mpc}$ is the same equation that links autonomous spending and aggregate output in the text (Equation 20.5), but it now allows for additional components of autonomous spending in A. We see that any increase in autonomous expenditure leads to a multiple increase in output. Thus any component of autonomous spending that enters A with a positive sign (a, I, G, and NX) will have a positive relationship with output, and any component with a negative sign ($-mpc \times T$) will have a negative relationship with output. This algebraic analysis also shows us that any rise in a component of A that is offset by a movement in another component of A, leaving A unchanged, will leave output unchanged.

7 More modern Keynesian approaches suggest that consumer expenditure, particularly for consumer durables (cars, furniture, appliances), is influenced by the interest rate. This interest sensitivity of consumer expenditure can be allowed for in the model here by defining planned investment spending more generally to include the interest-sensitive component of consumer expenditure.

8 As pointed out in earlier chapters on the money supply process, the money supply is positively related to interest rates, so the M^s-curve in panel (a) should actually have a positive slope. The M^s-curve is assumed to be vertical in panel (a) to simplify the graph, but allowing for a positive slope leads to identical results.

Useful websites

http://demonstrations.wolfram.com/TheKeynesianISLMModel/ An interactive tool from Wolfram that replicates the IS-LM model.

http://sdw.ecb.europa.eu. The Statistical Data Warehouse (SDW) of the ECB providing statistics for the euro area.

http://www.statistics.gov.uk/default.asp Office for National Statistics (ONS) dataset for the United Kingdom.

http://research.stlouisfed.org/fred2 Information about the US macroeconomic variables.

MyEconLab can help you get a better grade　　　　**MyEconLab®**

If your exam were tomorrow, would you be ready? For each chapter, MyEconLab Practice Test and Study Plans pinpoint which sections you have mastered and which ones you need to study. That way, you are more efficient with your study time, and you are better prepared for your exams.

To see how it works, turn to page 19 and then go to: **www.myeconlab.com/mishkin**

CHAPTER 21

Monetary and fiscal policy in the *ISLM* model

PREVIEW

Since World War II, government policymakers have tried to promote high employment without causing inflation. If the economy experiences a recession such as the one that began with the recent financial crisis, policymakers have two principal sets of tools that they can use to affect aggregate economic activity: *monetary policy*, the control of interest rates or the money supply, and *fiscal policy,* the control of government spending and taxes.

The *ISLM* model can help policymakers predict what will happen to aggregate output and interest rates if they decide to increase the money supply or increase government spending. In this way, *ISLM* analysis enables us to answer some important questions about the usefulness and effectiveness of monetary and fiscal policy in influencing economic activity.

But which is better? When is monetary policy more effective than fiscal policy at controlling the level of aggregate output, and when is it less effective? Will fiscal policy be more effective if it is conducted by changing government spending rather than changing taxes? Should the monetary authorities conduct monetary policy by manipulating the money supply or interest rates?

In this chapter, we use the *ISLM* model to help answer these questions and to learn how the model generates the aggregate demand curve featured prominently in the aggregate demand and supply framework (examined in Chapter 22), which is used to understand changes not only in aggregate output but also in the price level. Our analysis will show why economists focus so much attention on topics such as the stability of the demand for money function and whether the demand for money is strongly influenced by interest rates.

First, however, let's examine the *ISLM* model in more detail to see how the *IS* and *LM* curves developed in Chapter 20 shift and the implications of these shifts. (We continue to assume that the price level is fixed so that real and nominal quantities are the same.)

Factors that cause the *IS* curve to shift

You have already learned that the *IS* curve describes equilibrium points in the goods market – the combinations of aggregate output and interest rate for which aggregate output produced equals aggregate demand. The *IS* curve shifts whenever a change in autonomous factors (factors independent of aggregate output) occurs that is unrelated to the interest rate. (A change in the interest rate that affects equilibrium aggregate output causes only a movement along the *IS* curve.) We have already identified five candidates as autonomous factors that can shift aggregate demand and hence affect the level of equilibrium output. We can now ask how changes in each of these factors affect the IS curve.

1 *Changes in autonomous consumer expenditure.* A rise in autonomous consumer expenditure shifts the aggregate demand function upward and shifts the IS curve to the right (see Figure 21.1). To see how this shift occurs, suppose that the IS curve is initially at IS_1 in panel (a) and that, because of a huge increase in confidence level, consumers now become more optimistic about the future health of the economy, and autonomous consumer expenditure rises. What happens to the equilibrium level of aggregate output as a result of this rise in autonomous consumer expenditure when the interest rate is held constant at i_A?

   The IS_1 curve tells us that equilibrium aggregate output is at Y_A when the interest rate is at i_A (point A). Panel (b) shows that this point is an equilibrium in the goods market because the aggregate demand function Y_1^{ad} at an interest rate i_A crosses the 45° line $Y = Y^{ad}$ at an aggregate output level of Y_A. When autonomous consumer expenditure rises because of confidence boost, the aggregate demand function shifts upward to Y_2^{ad} and equilibrium output rises to $Y_{A'}$. This rise in equilibrium output from Y_A to $Y_{A'}$ when the interest rate is i_A is plotted in panel (a) as a movement from point A to point A'. The same analysis can be applied to every point on the initial IS_1 curve; therefore, the rise in autonomous consumer expenditure shifts the IS curve to the right from IS_1 to IS_2 in panel (a).

   A decline in autonomous consumer expenditure reverses the direction of the analysis. For any given interest rate, the aggregate demand function shifts downward, the equilibrium level of aggregate output falls, and the IS curve shifts to the left.

2 *Changes in investment spending unrelated to the interest rate.* In Chapter 20, we learned that changes in the interest rate affect planned investment spending and hence the equilibrium level of output. This change in investment spending merely causes a movement along the IS curve and not a shift. A rise in planned investment spending unrelated to the interest rate (say, because companies become more confident too) shifts the aggregate demand function upward, as in panel (b) of Figure 21.1. For any given interest rate, the equilibrium level of aggregate output rises, and the IS curve will shift to the right, as in panel (a).

   A decrease in investment spending because companies become more pessimistic about investment profitability shifts the aggregate demand function downward for any given interest rate; the equilibrium level of aggregate output falls, shifting the IS curve to the left.

3 *Changes in government spending.* An increase in government spending will also cause the aggregate demand function at any given interest rate to shift upward, as in panel (b). The equilibrium level of aggregate output rises at any given interest rate, and the IS curve shifts to the right. Conversely, a decline in government spending shifts the aggregate demand function downward, and the equilibrium level of output falls, shifting the IS curve to the left.

4 *Changes in taxes.* Unlike changes in other factors that directly affect the aggregate demand function, a decline in taxes shifts the aggregate demand function by raising consumer expenditure and shifting the aggregate demand function upward at any given interest rate. A decline in taxes raises the equilibrium level of aggregate output at any given interest rate and shifts the IS curve to the right (as in Figure 21.1). Recall, however, that a change in taxes has a smaller effect on aggregate demand than an equivalent change in government spending. So for a given change in taxes, the IS curve will shift less than for an equal change in government spending.

   A rise in taxes lowers the aggregate demand function and reduces the equilibrium level of aggregate output at each interest rate. Therefore, a rise in taxes shifts the IS curve to the left.

5 *Changes in net exports unrelated to the interest rate.* As with planned investment spending, changes in net exports arising from a change in interest rates merely cause a movement along the IS curve and not a shift. An autonomous rise in net exports unrelated to the interest rate – say, because European-made cloths become more chic than American-made cloths – shifts the aggregate demand function upward and causes the IS curve to shift to the right, as in Figure 21.1. Conversely, an autonomous fall in net exports shifts the aggregate demand function downward, and the equilibrium level of output falls, shifting the IS curve to the left.

FIGURE 21.1

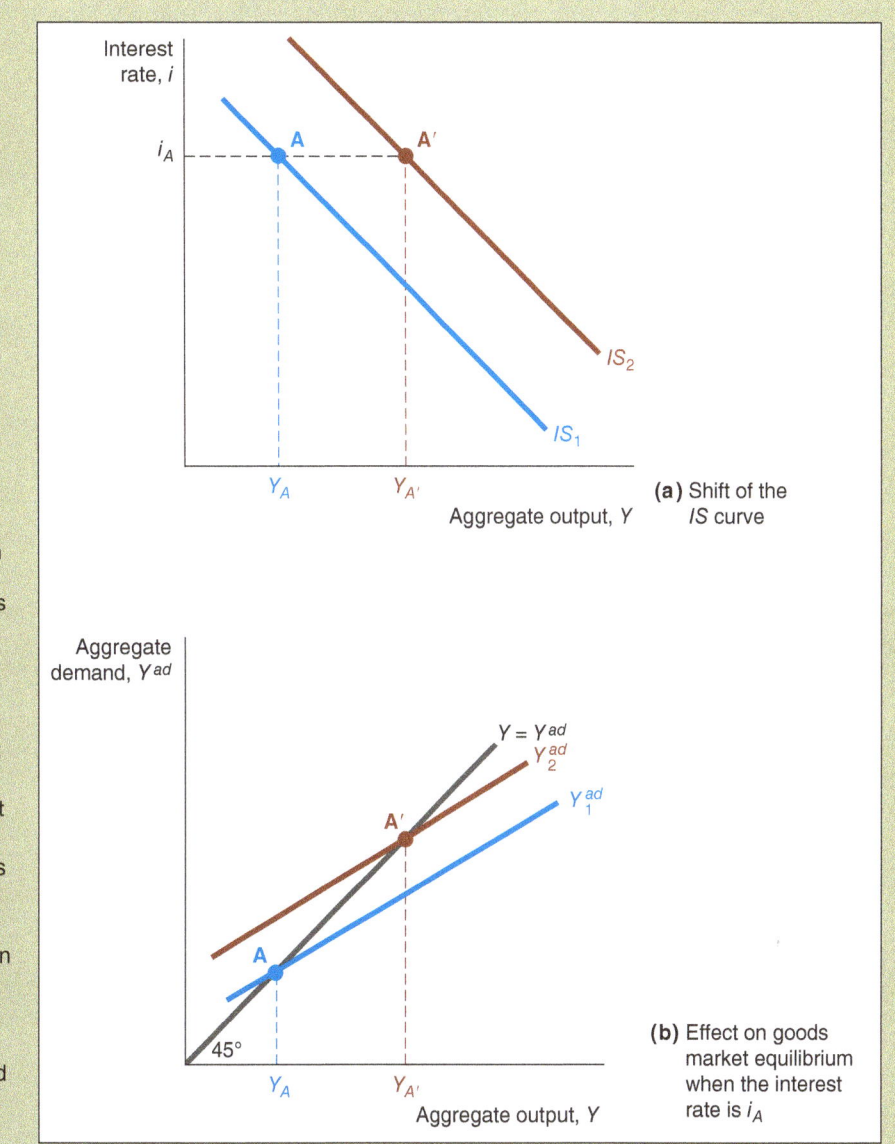

Shift in the *IS* curve

The *IS* curve will shift from IS_1 to IS_2 as a result of (1) an increase in autonomous consumer spending, (2) an increase in planned investment spending due to business optimism, (3) an increase in government spending, (4) a decrease in taxes, or (5) an increase in net exports that is unrelated to interest rates. Panel (b) shows how changes in these factors lead to the rightward shift in the *IS* curve using a Keynesian cross diagram. For any given interest rate (here i_A), these changes shift the aggregate demand function upward and raise equilibrium output from Y_A to $Y_{A'}$.

(a) Shift of the *IS* curve

(b) Effect on goods market equilibrium when the interest rate is i_A

Factors that cause the *LM* curve to shift

The *LM* curve describes the equilibrium points in the market for money – the combinations of aggregate output and interest rate for which the quantity of money demanded equals the quantity of money supplied. Whereas five factors can cause the *IS* curve to shift (changes in autonomous consumer expenditure, planned investment spending unrelated to the interest rate, government spending, taxes and net exports unrelated to the interest rate), only two factors can cause the *LM* curve to shift: autonomous changes in money demand and changes in the money supply. How do changes in these two factors affect the *LM* curve?

1 *Changes in the money supply.* A rise in the money supply shifts the *LM* curve to the right, as shown in Figure 21.2. To see how this shift occurs, suppose that the *LM* curve is initially at LM_1 in panel (a) and the central bank conducts open market purchases that increase the

FIGURE 21.2

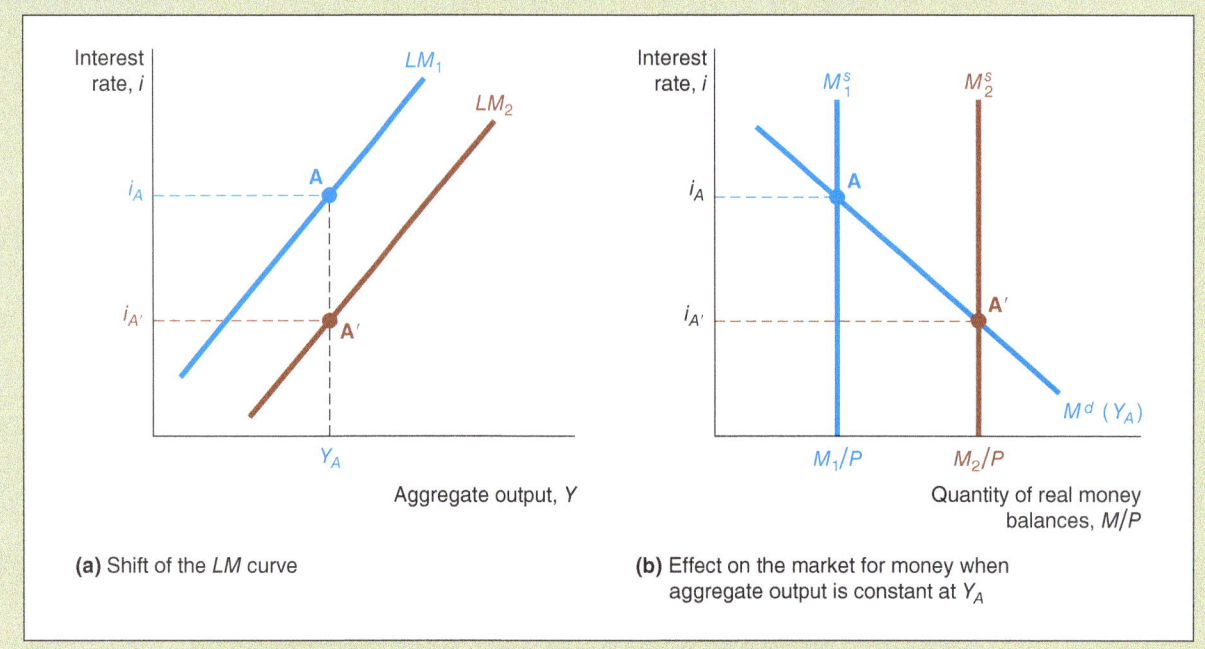

(a) Shift of the *LM* curve

(b) Effect on the market for money when aggregate output is constant at Y_A

Shift in the *LM* curve from an increase in the money supply

The *LM* curve shifts to the right from LM_1 to LM_2 when the money supply increases because, as indicated in panel (b), at any given level of aggregate output (say, Y_A), the equilibrium interest rate falls (point A to A').

money supply. If we consider point A, which is on the initial LM_1 curve, we can examine what happens to the equilibrium level of the interest rate, holding output constant at Y_A.

Panel (b), which contains a supply and demand diagram for the market for money, depicts the equilibrium interest rate initially as i_A at the intersection of the supply curve for money M_1^s and the demand curve for money M^d. The rise in the quantity of money supplied shifts the supply curve to M_2^s and, holding output constant at Y_A, the equilibrium interest rate falls to $i_{A'}$. In panel (a), this decline in the equilibrium interest rate from i_A to $i_{A'}$ is shown as a movement from point A to point A'. The same analysis can be applied to every point on the initial LM_1 curve, leading to the conclusion that at any given level of aggregate output, the equilibrium interest rate falls when the money supply increases. Thus LM_2 is below and to the right of LM_1.

Reversing this reasoning, a decline in the money supply shifts the LM curve to the left. A decline in the money supply results in a shortage of money at points on the initial *LM* curve. This condition of excess demand for money can be eliminated by a rise in the interest rate, which reduces the quantity of money demanded until it again equals the quantity of money supplied.

2 *Autonomous changes in money demand.* The theory of asset demand outlined in Chapter 5 indicates that there can be an autonomous rise in money demand (that is, a change not caused by a change in the price level, aggregate output or the interest rate). For example, an increase in the volatility of bond returns would make bonds riskier relative to money and would increase the quantity of money demanded at any given interest rate, price level or amount of aggregate output. The resulting autonomous increase in the demand for money shifts the *LM* curve to the left, as shown in Figure 21.3. Consider point A on the initial LM_1 curve. Suppose that a massive financial panic occurs, sending many companies into bankruptcy. Because bonds have become a riskier asset, people

FIGURE 21.3

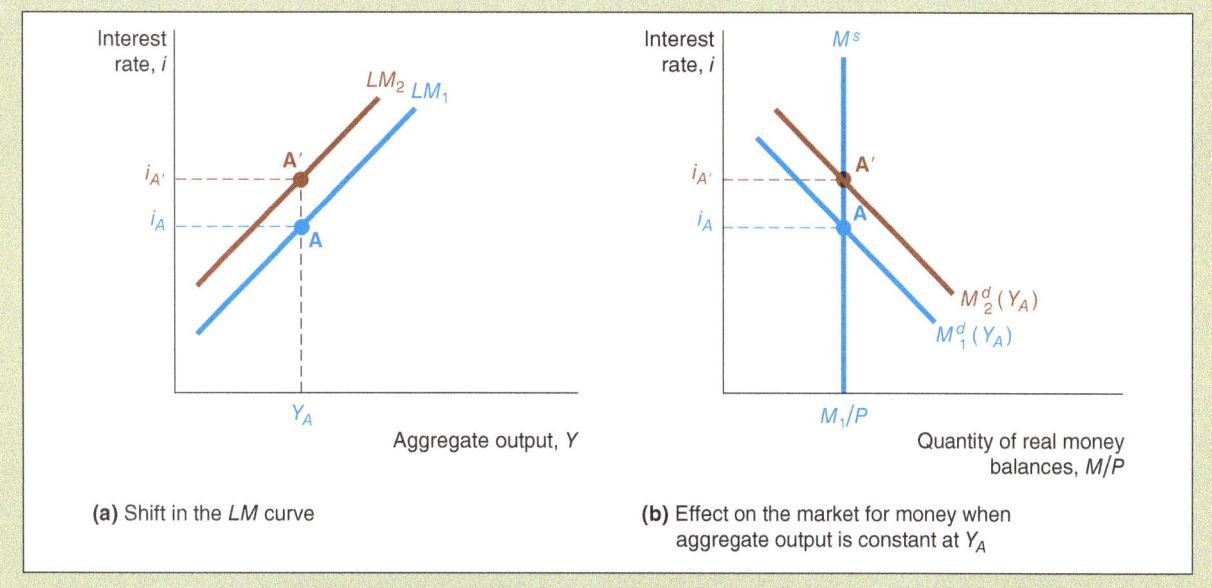

(a) Shift in the *LM* curve

(b) Effect on the market for money when aggregate output is constant at Y_A

Shift in the *LM* curve when money demand increases

The *LM* curve shifts to the left from LM_1 to LM_2 when money demand increases because, as indicated in panel (b), at any given level of aggregate output (say, Y_A), the equilibrium interest rate rises (point A to A').

want to shift from holding bonds to holding money; they will hold more money at all interest rates and output levels. The resulting increase in money demand at an output level of Y_A is shown by the shift of the money demand curve from M_1^d to M_2^d in panel (b). The new equilibrium in the market for money now indicates that if aggregate output is constant at $Y_{A'}$, the equilibrium interest rate will rise to i_A, and the point of equilibrium moves from A to A'.

Conversely, an autonomous decline in money demand would lead to a rightward shift in the *LM* curve. The fall in money demand would create an excess supply of money, which is eliminated by a rise in the quantity of money demanded that results from a decline in the interest rate.

Changes in equilibrium level of the interest rate and aggregate output

You can now use your knowledge of factors that cause the *IS* and *LM* curves to shift for the purpose of analysing how the equilibrium levels of the interest rate and aggregate output change in response to changes in monetary and fiscal policies.

Response to a change in monetary policy

Figure 21.4 illustrates the response of output and interest rate to an increase in the money supply. Initially, the economy is in equilibrium for both the goods market and the market for money at point 1, the intersection of IS_1 and LM_1. Suppose that at the resulting level of aggregate output Y_1, the economy is suffering from an unemployment rate of 10%, and the central bank decides it should try to raise output and reduce unemployment by raising the money supply. Will the central bank's change in monetary policy have the intended effect?

FIGURE 21.4

Response of aggregate output and the interest rate to an increase in the money supply.

The increase in the money supply shifts the *LM* curve to the right from *LM₁* to *LM₂*; the economy moves to point 2, where output has increased to *Y₂* and the interest rate has declined to *i₂*.

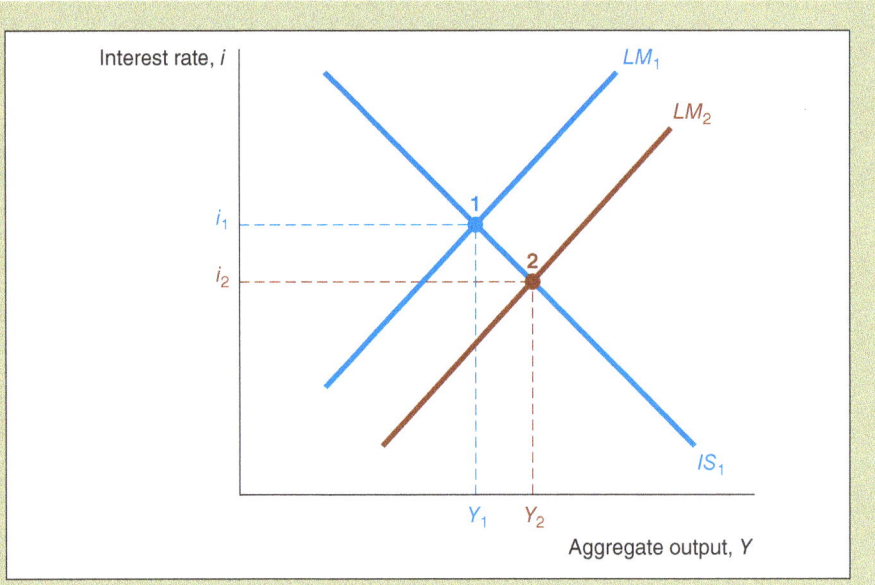

The rise in the money supply causes the *LM* curve to shift rightward to *LM₂*, and the equilibrium point for both the goods market and the market for money moves to point 2 (intersection of *IS₁* and *LM₂*). As a result of an increase in the money supply, the interest rate declines to i_2, as we found in Figure 21.2, and aggregate output rises to Y_2; the central bank's policy has been successful in improving the health of the economy.

For a clear understanding of why aggregate output rises and the interest rate declines, think about exactly what has happened in moving from point 1 to point 2. When the economy is at point 1, the increase in the money supply (rightward shift of the *LM* curve) creates an excess supply of money, resulting in a decline in the interest rate. The decline causes investment spending and net exports to rise, which in turn raises aggregate demand and causes aggregate output to rise. The excess supply of money is eliminated when the economy reaches point 2 because both the rise in output and the fall in the interest rate have raised the quantity of money demanded until it equals the new higher level of the money supply.

A decline in the money supply reverses the process; it shifts the *LM* curve to the left, causing the interest rate to rise and output to fall. Accordingly, ***aggregate output is positively related to the money supply***; aggregate output expands when the money supply increases and falls when it decreases.

Response to a change in fiscal policy

Suppose that the central bank is not willing to increase the money supply when the economy is suffering from a 10% unemployment rate at point 1. Can the government come to the rescue and manipulate government spending and taxes to raise aggregate output and reduce the massive unemployment?

The *ISLM* model demonstrates that it can. Figure 21.5 depicts the response of output and the interest rate to an expansionary fiscal policy (increase in government spending or decrease in taxes). An increase in government spending or a decrease in taxes causes the *IS* curve to shift to *IS₂*, and the equilibrium point for both the goods market and the market for money moves to point 2 (intersection of *IS₂* with *LM₁*). The result of the

SUMMARY TABLE 21.1

Effects from factors that shift the *IS* and *LM* curves

Factors	Autonomous change in factor	Response	Reason	
Consumer expenditure, C	⬆	Y⬆, i⬆	C⬆ ⟹ Y^{ad}⬆ ⟹ IS shifts right	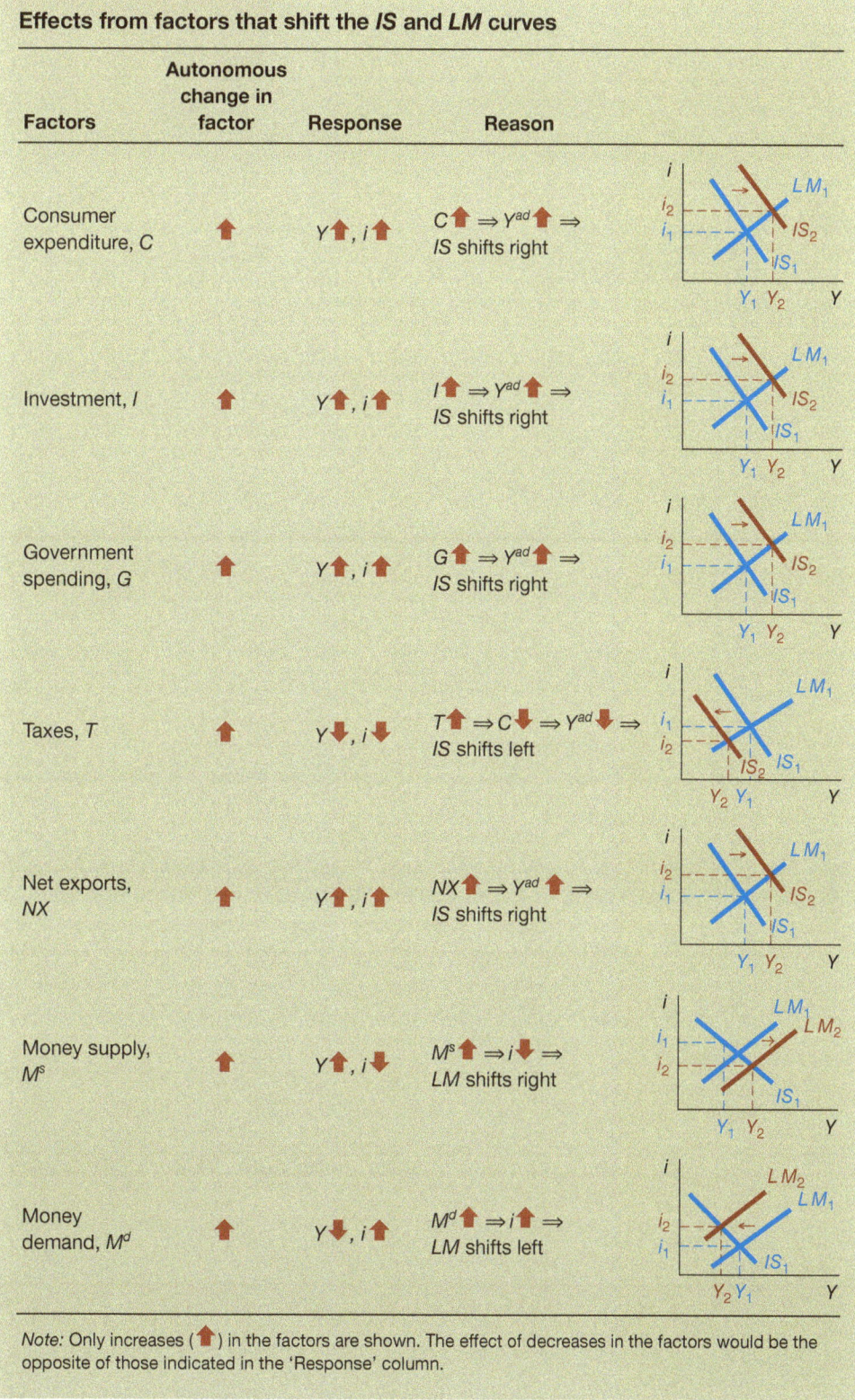
Investment, I	⬆	Y⬆, i⬆	I⬆ ⟹ Y^{ad}⬆ ⟹ IS shifts right	
Government spending, G	⬆	Y⬆, i⬆	G⬆ ⟹ Y^{ad}⬆ ⟹ IS shifts right	
Taxes, T	⬆	Y⬇, i⬇	T⬆ ⟹ C⬇ ⟹ Y^{ad}⬇ ⟹ IS shifts left	
Net exports, NX	⬆	Y⬆, i⬆	NX⬆ ⟹ Y^{ad}⬆ ⟹ IS shifts right	
Money supply, M^s	⬆	Y⬆, i⬇	M^s⬆ ⟹ i⬇ ⟹ LM shifts right	
Money demand, M^d	⬆	Y⬇, i⬆	M^d⬆ ⟹ i⬆ ⟹ LM shifts left	

Note: Only increases (⬆) in the factors are shown. The effect of decreases in the factors would be the opposite of those indicated in the 'Response' column.

FIGURE 21.5

Response of aggregate output and the interest rate to an expansionary fiscal policy.

Expansionary fiscal policy (a rise in government spending or a decrease in taxes) shifts the *IS* curve to the right from *IS₁* to *IS₂*; the economy moves to point 2, aggregate output increases to *Y₂*, and the interest rate rises to *i₂*.

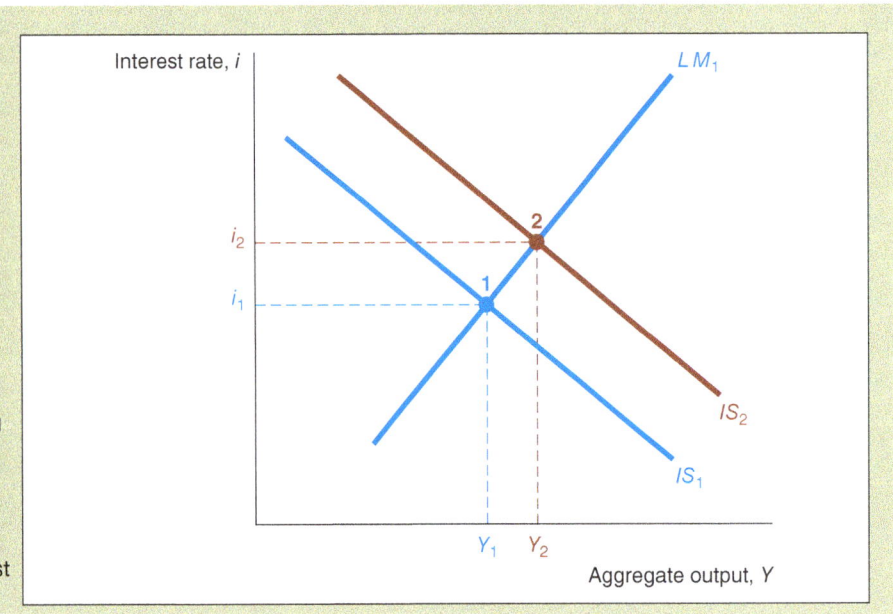

change in fiscal policy is a rise in aggregate output to Y_2 and a rise in the interest rate to i_2. Note the difference in the effect on the interest rate between an expansionary fiscal policy and an expansionary monetary policy. In the case of an expansionary fiscal policy, the interest rate rises, whereas in the case of an expansionary monetary policy, the interest rate falls.

Why does an increase in government spending or a decrease in taxes move the economy from point 1 to point 2, causing a rise in both aggregate output and the interest rate? An increase in government spending raises aggregate demand directly; a decrease in taxes makes more income available for spending and raises aggregate demand by raising consumer expenditure. The resulting increase in aggregate demand causes aggregate output to rise. The higher level of aggregate output raises the quantity of money demanded, creating an excess demand for money, which in turn causes the interest rate to rise. At point 2, the excess demand for money created by a rise in aggregate output has been eliminated by a rise in the interest rate, which lowers the quantity of money demanded.

A contractionary fiscal policy (decrease in government spending or increase in taxes) reverses the process described in Figure 21.5; it causes aggregate demand to fall, which shifts the *IS* curve to the left and causes both aggregate output and the interest rate to fall. *Aggregate output and the interest rate are positively related to government spending and negatively related to taxes*.

As a study aid, Summary Table 21.1 indicates the effect on aggregate output and interest rates of a change in the seven factors that shift the *IS* and *LM* curves.

APPLICATION ### The economic stimulus packages of 2008 and 2009

In February 2008, the US Congress passed the Economic Stimulus Act of 2008 in order to counter the contractionary effects on the economy from the subprime financial crisis. The most important feature of the legislation was the issuance of over $100 billion of rebate payments to low- and middle-income taxpayers, although the bill also included tax incentives for businesses to invest and help for homeowners who were facing foreclosure. During the same period also European leaders implemented expansionary fiscal policies. In November 2008, EU policymakers announced a European Economic Recovery Plan (EERP) to drive Europe's recovery from the economic crisis. The Plan included a coordinated fiscal stimulus of around €200 billion or 1.5% of European Union GDP, within both national budgets of the EU member states (around €170 billion, 1.2% of GDP) and EU and European Investment Bank budgets (around €30 billion, 0.3% of GDP).

Our ISLM analysis can indicate the likely impact of these measures. Similar to the situation depicted in Figure 21.5, an expansionary fiscal policy (increase in government spending or decrease in taxes) shifts the IS curve to the right, raising both interest rates and aggregate output. Although economists have estimated that the stimulus packages did increase spending a little bit and so had some of the effects described in Figure 21.5, the continuing deterioration in credit market conditions overwhelmed the expansionary effect of the stimulus packages. As a result, aggregate spending actually fell rather than rose. Consequently, instead of the *IS* curve shifting to the right, as depicted in Figure 21.5, the *IS* curve shifted to the left and aggregate output and interest rates ended up declining rather than rising during this period.

With the subsequent deterioration in the economy, in February 2009 the Obama administration quickly passed an additional $787 billion stimulus package, the so-called American Recovery and Reinvestment Act (ARRA) of 2009. This economic stimulus package was to provide temporary relief programmes for those most affected by the recession and included direct spending in infrastructure, education, health and energy, federal tax incentives and expansion of unemployment benefits. On the other hand, due to fiscal sustainability concerns, many European countries started implementing restrictive fiscal policies (mainly through government spending cuts and increase in taxes), which for many economists further delayed the economic recovery. How effective these actions have been in practice is still an open question and will be a debated topic of economic research for years to come. ■

Effectiveness of monetary versus fiscal policy

Our discussion of the effects of fiscal and monetary policy suggests that a government can easily lift an economy out of a recession by implementing any of a number of policies (changing the money supply, government spending or taxes). But how can policymakers decide which of these policies to use if faced with too much unemployment? Should they decrease taxes, increase government spending, raise the money supply, or do all three? And if they decide to increase the money supply, by how much? Economists do not pretend to have all the answers, and although the *ISLM* model will not clear the path to aggregate economic bliss, it can help policymakers decide which policies may be most effective under certain circumstances.

Monetary policy versus fiscal policy: the case of complete crowding out

The *ISLM* model developed so far in this chapter shows that both monetary and fiscal policy affect the level of aggregate output. To understand when monetary policy is more effective than fiscal policy, we will examine a special case of the *ISLM* model in which money demand is unaffected by the interest rate (money demand is said to be interest-inelastic) so that monetary policy affects output but fiscal policy does not.

Consider the slope of the *LM* curve if the demand for money is unaffected by changes in the interest rate. If point 1 in panel (a) of Figure 21.6 is such that the quantity of money demanded equals the quantity of money supplied, then it is on the *LM* curve. If the interest rate rises to, say, i_2, the quantity of money demanded is unaffected, and it will continue to equal the *unchanged* quantity of money supplied only if aggregate output remains *unchanged* at Y_1 (point 2). Equilibrium in the market for money will occur at the same level of aggregate output regardless of the interest rate, and the *LM* curve will be vertical, as shown in both panels of Figure 21.6.

Suppose that the economy is suffering from a high rate of unemployment, which policymakers try to eliminate with either expansionary fiscal or monetary policy. Panel (a) depicts what happens when an expansionary fiscal policy (increase in government spending or cut in taxes) is implemented, shifting the *IS* curve to the right from IS_1 to IS_2. As you can see in panel (a), the fiscal expansion has no effect on output; aggregate output remains at Y_1 when the economy moves from point 1 to point 2.

In our earlier analysis, expansionary fiscal policy always increased aggregate demand and raised the level of output. Why doesn't that happen in panel (a)? The answer is that because the *LM* curve is vertical, the rightward shift of the *IS* curve raises the interest rate to i_2, which causes investment spending and net exports to fall enough to offset completely the increased spending of the expansionary fiscal policy. Put another way, increased spending that results from expansionary fiscal policy has *crowded out* investment spending and net

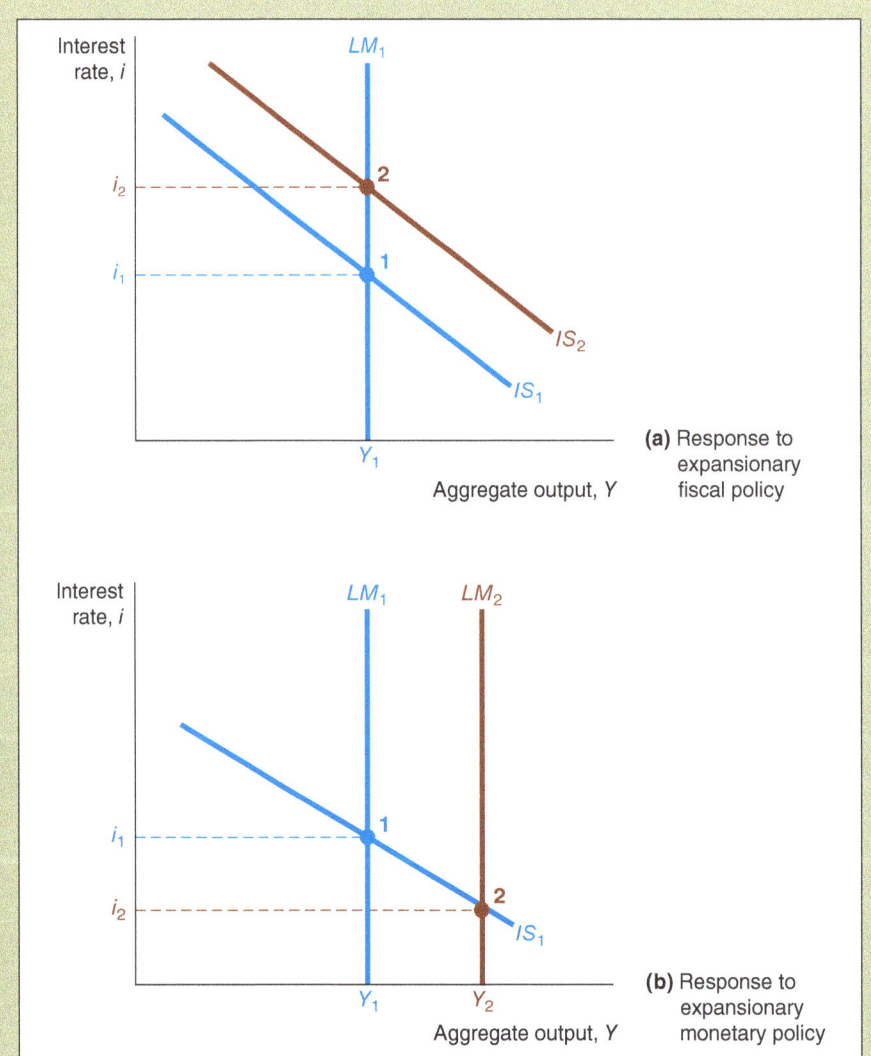

FIGURE 21.6

Effectiveness of monetary and fiscal policy when money demand is unaffected by the interest rate

When the demand for money is unaffected by the interest rate, the *LM* curve is vertical. In panel (a), an expansionary fiscal policy (increase in government spending or a cut in taxes) shifts the *IS* curve from IS_1 to IS_2 and leaves aggregate output unchanged at Y_1. In panel (b), an increase in the money supply shifts the *LM* curve from LM_1 to LM_2 and raises aggregate output from Y_1 to Y_2. Therefore, monetary policy is effective, but fiscal policy is not.

(a) Response to expansionary fiscal policy

(b) Response to expansionary monetary policy

exports, which decrease because of the rise in the interest rate. This situation in which expansionary fiscal policy does not lead to a rise in output is frequently referred to as a case of **complete crowding out**.[1]

Panel (b) shows what happens when the central bank tries to eliminate high unemployment through an expansionary monetary policy (increase in the real money supply, M/P). Here the *LM* curve shifts to the right from LM_1 to LM_2, because at each interest rate, output must rise so that the quantity of money demanded rises to match the increase in the money supply. Aggregate output rises from Y_1 to Y_2 (the economy moves from point 1 to point 2), and expansionary monetary policy does affect aggregate output in this case.

We conclude from the analysis in Figure 21.6 that if the demand for money is unaffected by changes in the interest rate (money demand is interest-inelastic), monetary policy is effective but fiscal policy is not. An even more general conclusion can be reached: *the less interest-sensitive money demand is, the more effective monetary policy is relative to fiscal policy*.[2]

Because the interest sensitivity of money demand is important to policymakers' decisions regarding the use of onetary or fiscal policy to influence economic activity, the subject has been studied extensively by economists and has been the focus of many debates. Findings on the interest sensitivity of money demand are discussed in Chapter 19.

APPLICATION   ## The policy mix: the British fiscal austerity programme of 2010 and the German reunification in 1990

So far we have looked at monetary and fiscal policy in isolation. This is useful to understand the theoretical effects of each policy on the aggregate demand and interest rates. In practice, however, the two are often used together. The combination of monetary and fiscal policy is known as the monetary–fiscal policy mix or simply the **policy mix**. Two interesting examples of policy mix which resulted in different outcomes are the British fiscal austerity programme in 2010 and the German reunification in 1990.

In opposition to the fiscal stimulus implemented by the Labour government during the early years of global financial crisis 2007–9, as soon as they came to power in 2010, the Conservatives announced that in order to restore financial confidence and remove the threat of fiscal collapse, the government would have followed an austerity programme of deficit reduction. During the same period, the Bank of England supported the economy with the aggressive expansionary monetary policy of quantitative easing, in which the central bank buys securities to increase the money supply (see Chapter 15 for a full discussion). Can our *ISLM* analysis help us to predict the effects of this monetary–fiscal policy mix? As shown in panel (a) of Figure 21.7, a decrease in spending and an increase in taxes shift the *IS* curve to the left, whereas a monetary expansion moves the *LM* curve the right. The overall effect of these policies is an unchanged level of aggregate output and a reduction of the interest rate. This seems to be precisely what happened in the UK, where output was flat for most of 2011–12 and interest rates were at historically low levels.

A different scenario can be illustrated in the case of the German reunification and its aftermath. In order to smooth the transition to the unification of the large and rich economy of West Germany with the smaller and much poorer East Germany, Germany implemented an expansionary fiscal policy, aiming at stimulating consumption and aggregate demand of East Germans. However, this policy resulted in rising inflationary pressures, with inflation accelerating from below 3% in 1990 to near 5% by 1992. To dampen inflation, the German Bundesbank started to drastically reduce money growth. The end result of this lack of coordination can be observed in panel (b) of Figure 21.7, which shows that the combination of expansionary fiscal and restrictive monetary policy may lead to no effect on aggregate output and an increase of the interest rate. This is precisely what happened in reality. During

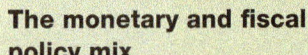

FIGURE 21.7

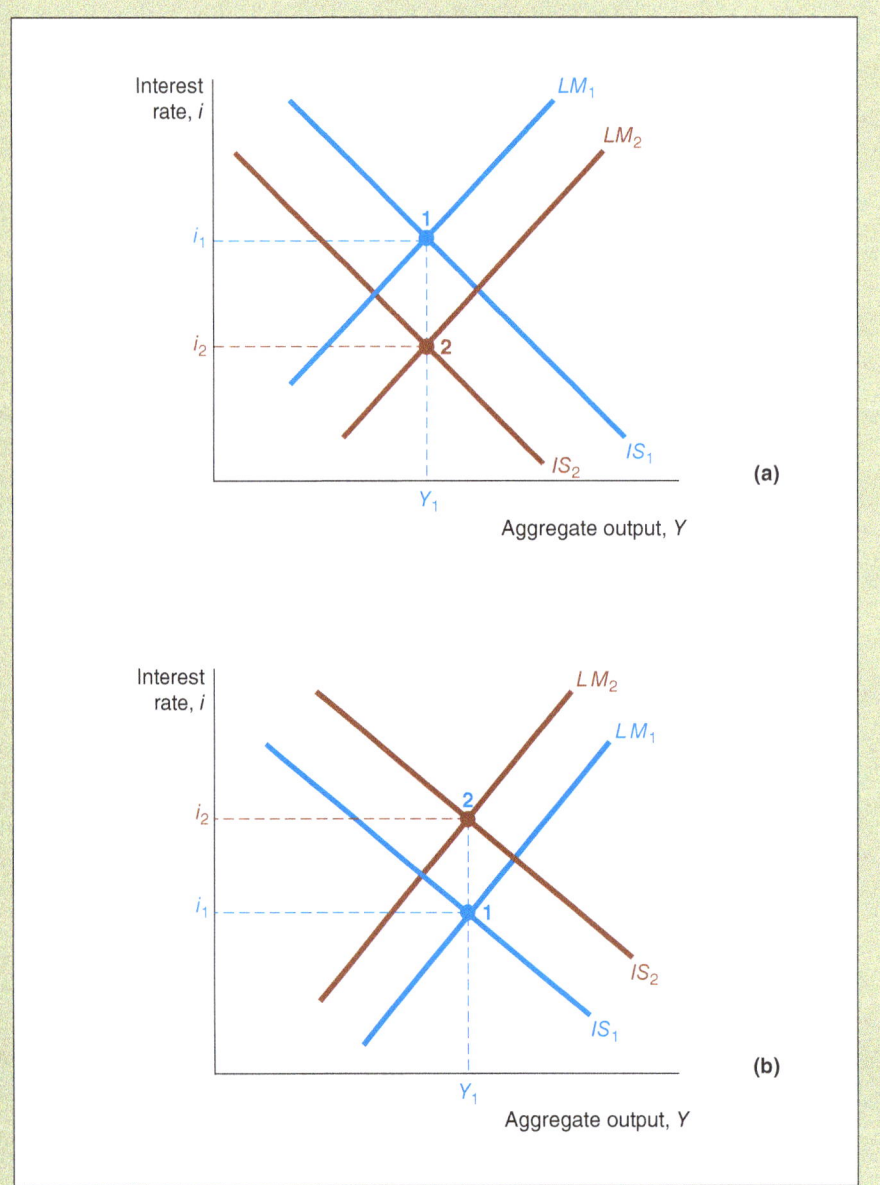

The monetary and fiscal policy mix

In panel (a) a restrictive fiscal policy (decrease in government spending or an increase in taxes) shifts the *IS* curve from IS_1 to IS_2, and an expansionary monetary policy shifts the *LM* curve from LM_1 to LM_2. This policy mix decreases the interest rate from i_1 to i_2 and leaves aggregate output unchanged at Y_1. In panel (b), an expansionary fiscal policy (increase in government spending or a cut in taxes) shifts the *IS* curve from IS_1 to IS_2 and a restrictive monetary policy shifts the *LM* curve from LM_1 to LM_2. This policy mix increases the interest rate from i_1 to i_2 and leaves aggregate output unchanged at Y_1.

this period German interest rates rose to near double-digit levels, initiating a series of speculative attacks in 1992 (see the Application 'The foreign exchange crisis of September 1992' in Chapter 18). ■

Targeting money supply versus interest rates

In the 1970s and early 1980s, central banks in many countries pursued a strategy of *monetary targeting* – that is, they used their policy tools to make the money supply equal a target value. However, as we saw in Chapter 16, many of these central banks abandoned monetary targeting in the 1980s to pursue interest-rate targeting instead because of the breakdown of the stable relationship between the money supply and economic activity. The *ISLM* model has important implications for which variable a central bank should target and we can apply it to explain why central banks have abandoned monetary targeting for interest-rate targeting.[3]

As we saw in Chapter 16, when the central bank attempts to hit a reserve aggregate or a money supply target, it cannot at the same time pursue an interest-rate target; it can hit one target or the other but not both. Consequently, it needs to know which of these two targets will produce more accurate control of aggregate output.

In contrast to the textbook world you have been inhabiting, in which the *IS* and *LM* curves are assumed to be fixed, the real world is one of great uncertainty in which *IS* and *LM* curves shift because of unanticipated changes in autonomous spending and money demand. To understand whether the central bank should use a money supply target or an interest-rate target, we need to look at two cases: one in which uncertainty about the *IS* curve is far greater than uncertainty about the *LM* curve, and another in which uncertainty about the *LM* curve is far greater than uncertainty about the *IS* curve.

The *ISLM* diagram in Figure 21.8 illustrates the outcome of the two targeting strategies for the case in which the *IS* curve is unstable and uncertain, so it fluctuates around its expected value of *IS** from *IS'* to *IS''*, while the *LM* curve is stable and certain, so it stays at *LM**. Because the central bank knows that the expected position of the *IS* curve is at *IS** and desires aggregate output of *Y**, it will set its interest-rate target at *i** so that the expected level of output is *Y**. This policy of targeting the interest rate at *i** is labelled 'Interest-Rate Target'.

How would the central bank keep the interest rate at its target level of *i**? Recall from Chapter 16 that the central bank can hit its interest-rate target by buying and selling bonds when the interest rate differs from *i**. When the *IS* curve shifts out to *IS''*, the interest rate would rise above *i** with the money supply unchanged. To counter this rise in interest rates, however, the central bank would need to buy bonds just until their price is driven back up so that the interest rate comes back down to *i**. (The result of these open market purchases, as we have seen in Chapter 13 and 14, is that the monetary base and the money supply rise until the *LM* curve shifts to the right to intersect the *IS''* curve at *i** – not shown in the diagram for simplicity.) When the interest rate is below *i**, the central bank needs to sell bonds to lower their price and raise the interest rate back up to *i**. (These open market sales reduce the monetary base and the money supply until the *LM* curve shifts to the left to intersect the *IS*

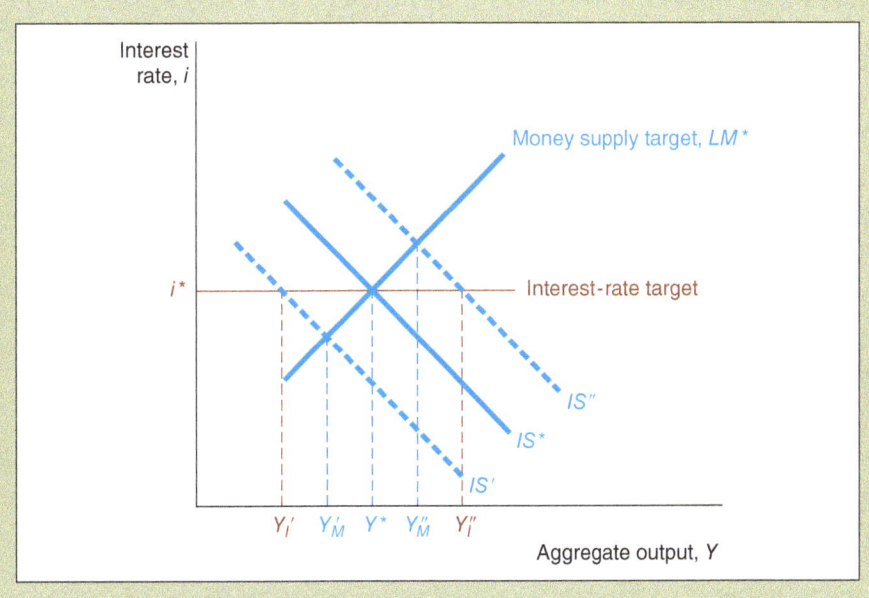

FIGURE 21.8

Money supply and interest-rate targets when the *IS* curve Is unstable and the *LM* curve is stable

The unstable *IS* curve fluctuates between *IS'* and *IS''*. The money supply target produces smaller fluctuations in output (Y_M' to Y_M'') than the interest-rate target (Y_I' to Y_I''). Therefore, the money supply target is preferred.

curve at i^* – again not shown in the diagram.) The result of pursuing the interest-rate target is that aggregate output fluctuates between Y_1' and Y_1'' in Figure 21.8.

If, instead, the central bank pursues a money supply target, it will set the money supply so that the resulting LM curve LM^* intersects the IS^* curve at the desired output level of Y^*. This policy of targeting the money supply is labelled 'Money Supply Target'. Because it is not changing the money supply and so keeps the LM curve at LM^*, aggregate output will fluctuate between Y_M' and Y_M'' under the money supply target policy.

As you can see in the figure, the money supply target leads to smaller output fluctuations around the desired level than the interest-rate target. A rightward shift of the IS curve to IS'', for example, causes the interest rate to rise, given a money supply target, and this rise in the interest rate leads to a lower level of investment spending and net exports and hence to a smaller increase in aggregate output than occurs under an interest-rate target. Because smaller output fluctuations are desirable, the conclusion is that *if the IS curve is more unstable than the LM curve, a money supply target is preferred.*

The outcome of the two targeting strategies for the case of a stable IS curve and an unstable LM curve caused by unanticipated changes in money demand is illustrated in Figure 21.9. Again, the interest-rate and money supply targets are set so that the expected level of aggregate output equals the desired level Y^*. Because the LM curve is now unstable, it fluctuates between LM' and LM'' even when the money supply is fixed, causing aggregate output to fluctuate between Y_M' and Y_M''.

The interest-rate target, by contrast, is not affected by uncertainty about the LM curve, because it is set by the central bank's adjustment of the money supply whenever the interest rate tries to depart from i^*. When the interest rate begins to rise above i^* because of an increase in money demand, the central bank again just buys bonds, driving up their price and bringing the interest rate back down to i^*. The result of these open market purchases is a rise in the monetary base and the money supply. Similarly, if the interest rate falls below i^*, the central bank sells bonds to lower their price and raise the interest rate back to i^*, thereby causing a decline in the monetary base and the money supply. The only effect of the fluctuating LM curve, then, is that the money supply fluctuates more as a result of the interest-rate target policy. The outcome of the interest-rate target is that output will be exactly at the desired level with no fluctuations.

FIGURE 21.9

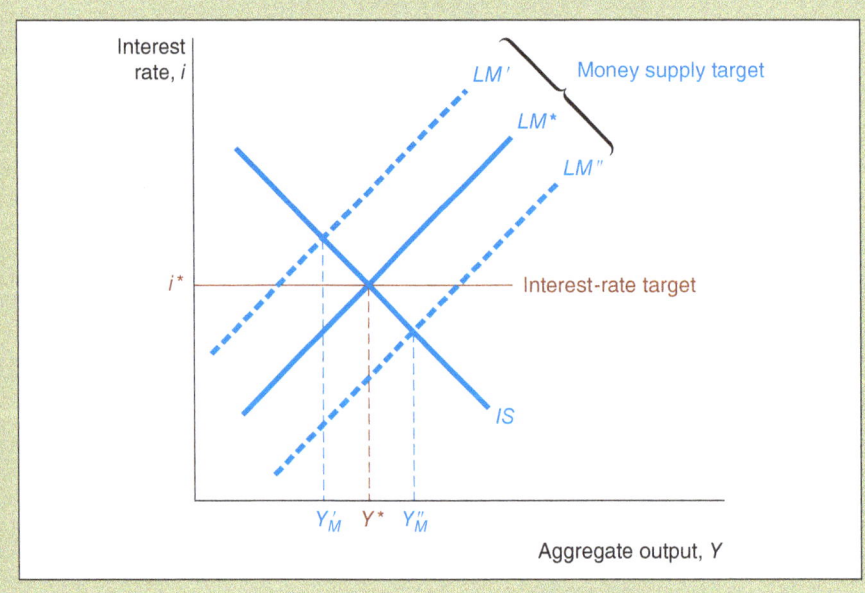

Money supply and interest-rate targets when the *LM* curve is unstable and the *IS* curve is stable

The unstable LM curve fluctuates between LM' and LM''. The money supply target then produces bigger fluctuations in output (Y_M' to Y_M'') than the interest-rate target (which leaves output fixed at Y^*). Therefore, the interest-rate target is preferred.

Because smaller output fluctuations are desirable, the conclusion from Figure 21.9 is that *if the LM curve is more unstable than the IS curve, an interest-rate target is preferred.*

We can now see why central banks like the Bank of England and the Federal Reserve decided to abandon monetary targeting for interest-rate targeting in the 1980s and 1990s. With the rapid proliferation of new financial instruments whose presence can affect the demand for money (see Chapter 19), money demand (which is embodied in the *LM* curve) became highly unstable. Thus central banks in these countries recognized that they were more likely to be in the situation depicted in Figure 21.9 and decided that they would be better off with an interest-rate target than a money supply target.[4] At the same time, this simple model also shows why the ECB gives more importance to money supply in its monetary strategy. This is justified by the empirical evidence that, as discussed in Chapter 19, finds that the money demand in the euro area is more stable relatively to the UK and the US, implying a more stable *LM* curve. ■

ISLM model in the long run

So far in our *ISLM* analysis, we have been assuming that the price level is fixed so that nominal values and real values are the same. This is a reasonable assumption for the short run, but in the long run the price level does change. To see what happens in the *ISLM* model in the long run, we make use of the concept of the **natural rate level of output** (denoted by Y_n), which is the rate of output at which the price level has no tendency to rise or fall. When output is above the natural rate level, the booming economy will cause prices to rise; when output is below the natural rate level, the slack in the economy will cause prices to fall.

Because we now want to examine what happens when the price level changes, we can no longer assume that real and nominal values are the same. The spending variables that affect the *IS* curve (consumer expenditure, investment spending, government spending and net exports) describe the demand for goods and services and are *in real terms*; they describe the physical quantities of goods that people want to buy. Because these quantities do not change when the price level changes, a change in the price level has no effect on the *IS* curve, which describes the combinations of the interest rate and aggregate output *in real terms* that satisfy goods market equilibrium.

Figure 21.10 shows what happens in the *ISLM* model when output rises above the natural rate level, which is marked by a vertical line at Y_n. Suppose that initially the *IS* and *LM* curves intersect at point 1, where output $Y = Y_n$. Panel (a) examines what happens to output and interest rates when there is a rise in the money supply. As we saw in Figure 21.2, the rise in the money supply causes the *LM* curve to shift to LM_2, and the equilibrium moves to point 2 (the intersection of IS_1 and LM_2), where the interest rate falls to i_2 and output rises to Y_2. However, as we can see in panel (a), the level of output at Y_2 is greater than the natural rate level Y_n, and so the price level begins to rise.

In contrast to the *IS* curve, which is unaffected by a rise in the price level, the *LM* curve is affected by the price level rise because the liquidity preference theory states that the demand for money *in real terms* depends on real income and interest rates. This makes sense because money is valued in terms of what it can buy. However, the money supply the media reports in euros is not the money supply in real terms; it is a nominal quantity. As the price level rises, the quantity of money *in real terms* falls, and the effect on the *LM* curve is identical to a fall in the nominal money supply with the price level fixed. The lower value of the real money supply creates an excess demand for money, causing the interest rate to rise at any given level of aggregate output, and the *LM* curve shifts back to the left. As long as the level of output exceeds the natural rate level, the price level will continue to rise, shifting the *LM* curve to the left, until finally output is back at the natural rate level Y_n. This occurs

FIGURE 21.10

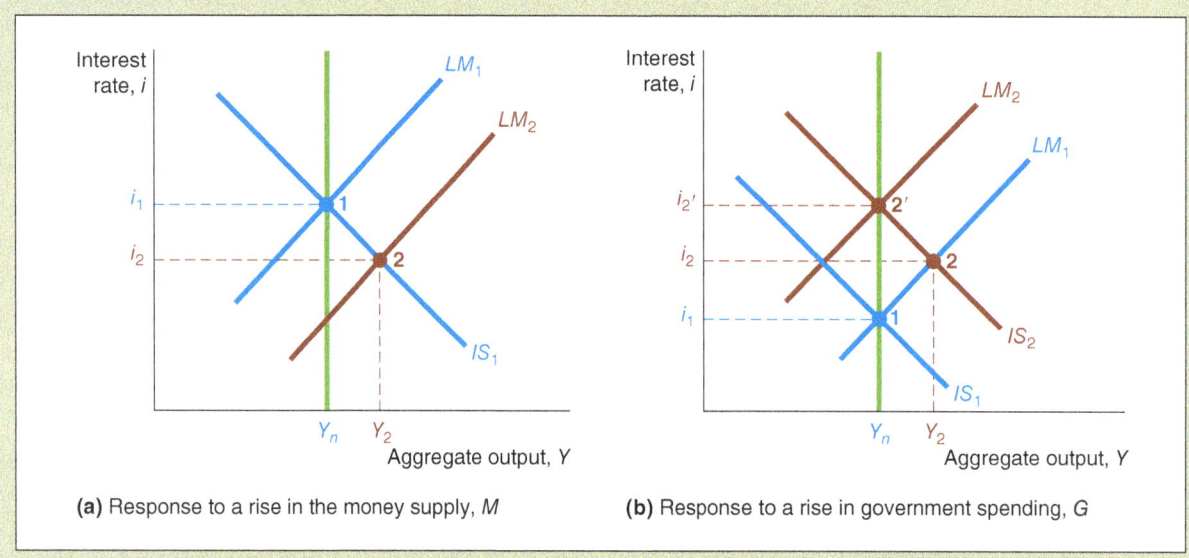

(a) Response to a rise in the money supply, *M*

(b) Response to a rise in government spending, *G*

ISLM model in the long run

In panel (a), a rise in the money supply causes the *LM* curve to shift rightward to LM_2, and the equilibrium moves to point 2, where the interest rate falls to i_2 and output rises to Y_2. Because output at Y_2 is above the natural rate level Y_n, the price level rises, the real money supply falls, and the *LM* curve shifts back to LM_1; the economy has returned to the original equilibrium at point 1. In panel (b), an increase in government spending shifts the *IS* curve to the right to IS_2, and the economy moves to point 2, at which the interest rate has risen to i_2 and output has risen to Y_2. Because output at Y_2 is above the natural rate level Y_n, the price level begins to rise, real money balances *M/P* begin to fall, and the *LM* curve shifts to the left to LM_2. The long-run equilibrium at point 2 has an even higher interest rate at i_2, and output has returned to Y_n.

when the *LM* curve has returned to LM_1, where real money balances *M/P* have returned to the original level and the economy has returned to the original equilibrium at point 1. The result of the expansion in the money supply in the long run is that the economy has the same level of output and interest rates.

The fact that the increase in the money supply has left output and interest rates unchanged in the long run is referred to as **long-run monetary neutrality**. The only result of the increase in the money supply is a higher price level, which has increased proportionally to the increase in the money supply so that real money balances *M/P* are unchanged.

Panel (b) looks at what happens to output and interest rates when there is expansionary fiscal policy such as an increase in government spending. As we saw earlier, the increase in government spending shifts the *IS* curve to the right to IS_2, and in the short run the economy moves to point 2 (the intersection of IS_2 and LM_1), where the interest rate has risen to i_2 and output has risen to Y_2. Because output at Y_2 is above the natural rate level Y_n, the price level begins to rise, real money balances *M/P* begin to fall, and the *LM* curve shifts to the left. Only when the *LM* curve has shifted to LM_2 and the equilibrium is at point 2, where output is again at the natural rate level Y_n, does the price level stop rising and the *LM* curve come to rest. The resulting long-run equilibrium at point 2' has an even higher interest rate at i_2 and output has not risen from Y_n. Indeed, what has occurred in the long run is complete crowding out: the rise in the price level, which has shifted the *LM* curve to LM_2, has caused the interest rate to rise to i_2, causing investment and net exports to fall enough to offset the increased government spending completely. What we have discovered is that even though complete crowding out does not occur in the short run in the *ISLM* model (unless the *LM* curve is vertical), it does occur in the long run.

Our conclusion from examining what happens in the *ISLM* model from an expansionary monetary or fiscal policy is that *although monetary and fiscal policy can affect output in the short run, neither affects output in the long run*. Clearly, an important issue in deciding on the effectiveness of monetary and fiscal policy to raise output is how soon the long run occurs. This is a topic that we explore in the next chapter.

ISLM model and the aggregate demand curve

We now examine further what happens in the *ISLM* model when the price level changes. When we conduct the *ISLM* analysis with a changing price level, we find that as the price level falls, the level of aggregate output rises. Thus we obtain a relationship between the price level and quantity of aggregate output for which the goods market and the market for money are in equilibrium, called the **aggregate demand curve**. This aggregate demand curve is a central element in the aggregate supply and demand analysis of Chapter 22, which allows us to explain changes not only in aggregate output but also in the price level.

Deriving the aggregate demand curve

Now that you understand how a change in the price level affects the *LM* curve, we can analyse what happens in the *ISLM* diagram when the price level changes. This exercise is carried out in Figure 21.11. Panel (a) contains an *ISLM* diagram for a given value of the nominal money supply. Let us first consider a price level of P_1. The *LM* curve at this price level is *LM* (P_1), and its intersection with the *IS* curve is at point 1, where output is Y_1. The equilibrium output level Y_1 that occurs when the price level is P_1 is also plotted in panel (b) as point 1. If the price level rises to P_2, then *in real terms* the money supply has fallen. The effect on the *LM* curve is identical to a decline in the nominal money supply when the price level is fixed: The *LM* curve will shift leftward to *LM* (P_2). The new equilibrium level of output has fallen to Y_2, because planned investment and net exports fall when the interest rate rises. Point 2 in panel (b) plots this level of output for price level P_2. A further increase in the price level to P_3 causes a further

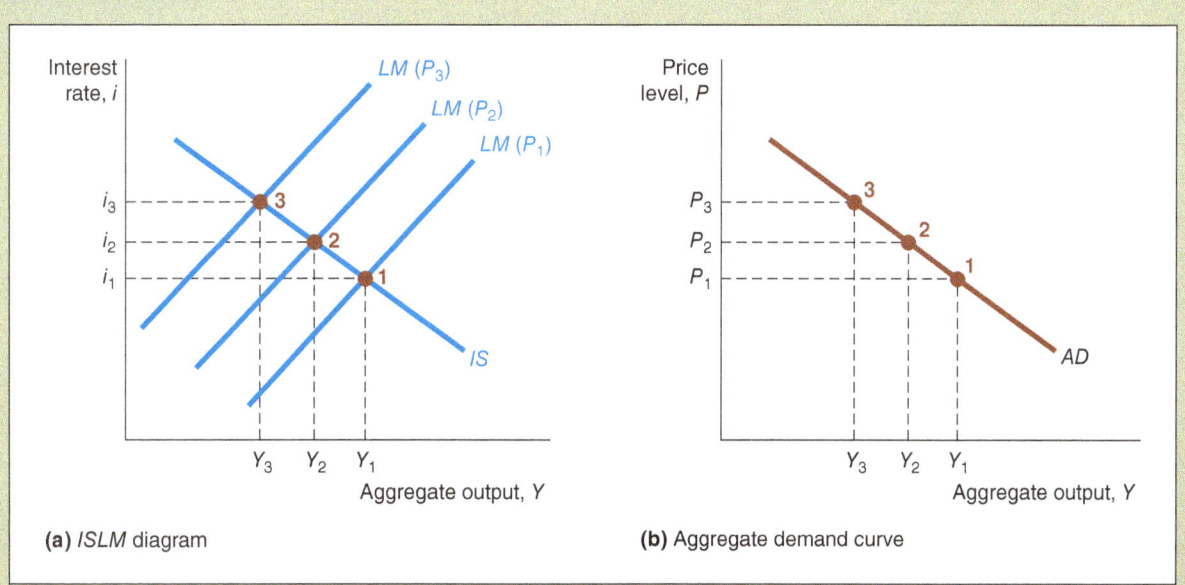

FIGURE 21.11

(a) *ISLM* diagram

(b) Aggregate demand curve

Deriving the aggregate demand curve

The *ISLM* diagram in panel (a) shows that with a given nominal money supply as the price level rises from P_1 to P_2 to P_3, the *LM* curve shifts to the left, and equilibrium output falls. The combinations of the price level and equilibrium output from panel (a) are then plotted in panel (b), and the line connecting them is the aggregate demand curve *AD*.

decline in the real money supply, leading to a further increase in the interest rate and a further decline in planned investment and net exports, and output declines to Y_3. Point 3 in panel (b) plots this level of output for price level P_3.

The line that connects the three points in panel (b) is the aggregate demand curve AD, and it indicates the level of aggregate output consistent with equilibrium in the goods market and the market for money at any given price level. This aggregate demand curve has the usual downward slope, because a higher price level reduces the money supply in real terms, raises interest rates and lowers the equilibrium level of aggregate output.

Factors that cause the aggregate demand curve to shift

$ISLM$ analysis demonstrates how the equilibrium level of aggregate output changes for a given price level. A change in any factor (except a change in the price level) that causes the IS or LM curve to shift causes the aggregate demand curve to shift. To see how this works, let's first look at what happens to the aggregate demand curve when the IS curve shifts.

Shifts in the IS curve

Five factors cause the IS curve to shift: changes in autonomous consumer spending, changes in investment spending related to business confidence, changes in government spending, changes in taxes and autonomous changes in net exports. How changes in these factors lead to a shift in the aggregate demand curve is examined in Figure 21.12.

Suppose that initially the aggregate demand curve is at AD_1 and there is a rise in, for example, government spending. The $ISLM$ diagram in panel (b) shows what then happens to equilibrium output, holding the price level constant at P_A. Initially, equilibrium output is at Y_A at the intersection of IS_1 and LM_1. The rise in government spending (holding the price level constant at P_A) shifts the IS curve to the right and raises equilibrium output to $Y_{A'}$. In

FIGURE 21.12

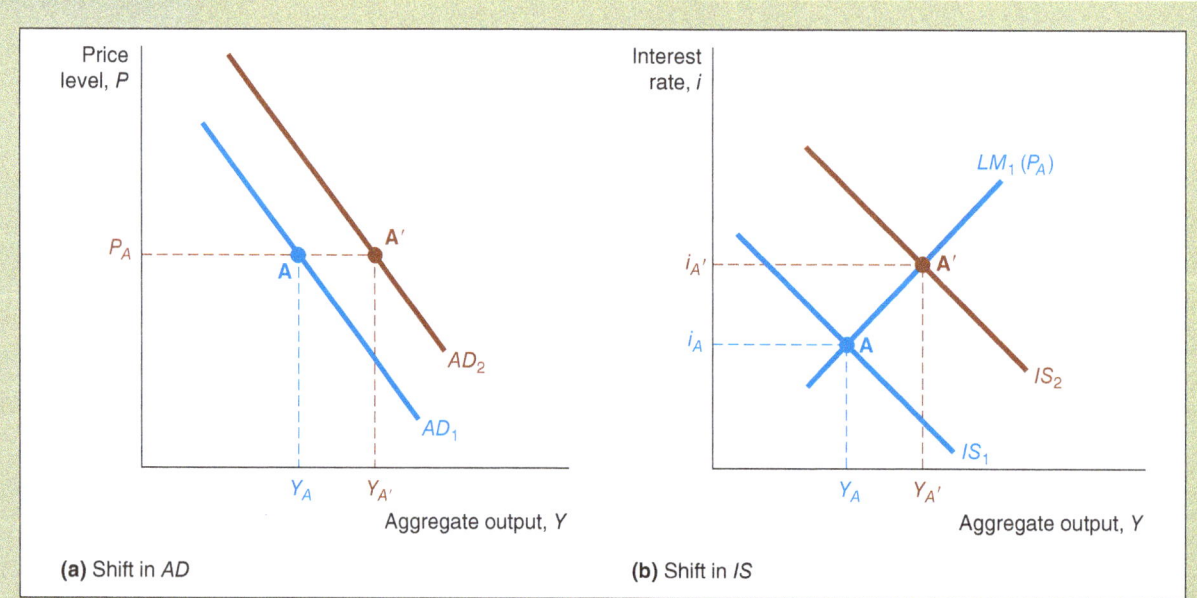

(a) Shift in AD **(b)** Shift in IS

Shift in the aggregate demand curve caused by a shift in the IS curve

Expansionary fiscal policy, a rise in net exports, or more optimistic consumers and firms shift the IS curve to the right in panel (b), and at a price level of P_A, equilibrium output rises from Y_A to $Y_{A'}$. This change in equilibrium output is shown as a movement from point A to point A in panel (a); hence the aggregate demand curve shifts to the right, from AD_1 to AD_2.

panel (a), this rise in equilibrium output is shown as a movement from point A to point A',
and the aggregate demand curve shifts to the right (to AD_2).

The conclusion from Figure 21.12 is that ***any factor that shifts the IS curve shifts the
aggregate demand curve in the same direction***. Therefore, 'animal spirits' that encourage
a rise in autonomous consumer spending or planned investment spending, a rise in
government spending, a fall in taxes or an autonomous rise in net exports – all of which
shift the *IS* curve to the right – will also shift the aggregate demand curve to the right.
Conversely, a fall in autonomous consumer spending, a fall in planned investment spending,
a fall in government spending, a rise in taxes or a fall in net exports will cause the aggregate
demand curve to shift to the left.

Shifts in the *LM* curve

Shifts in the *LM* curve are caused by either an autonomous change in money demand
(not caused by a change in *P*, *Y* or *i*) or a change in the money supply. Figure 21.13 shows
how either of these changes leads to a shift in the aggregate demand curve. Again, we are
initially at the AD_1 aggregate demand curve, and we look at what happens to the level of
equilibrium output when the price level is held constant at P_A. A rise in the money supply
shifts the *LM* curve to the right and raises equilibrium output to Y_A'. This rise in equilibrium
output is shown as a movement from point A to point A' in panel (a), and the aggregate
demand curve shifts to the right.

Our conclusion from Figure 21.13 is similar to that of Figure 21.12: ***holding the price
level constant, any factor that shifts the LM curve shifts the aggregate demand curve in
the same direction***. Therefore, a decline in money demand as well as an increase in the
money supply, both of which shift the *LM* curve to the right, also shift the aggregate demand
curve to the right. The aggregate demand curve will shift to the left, however, if the money
supply declines or money demand rises.

FIGURE 21.13

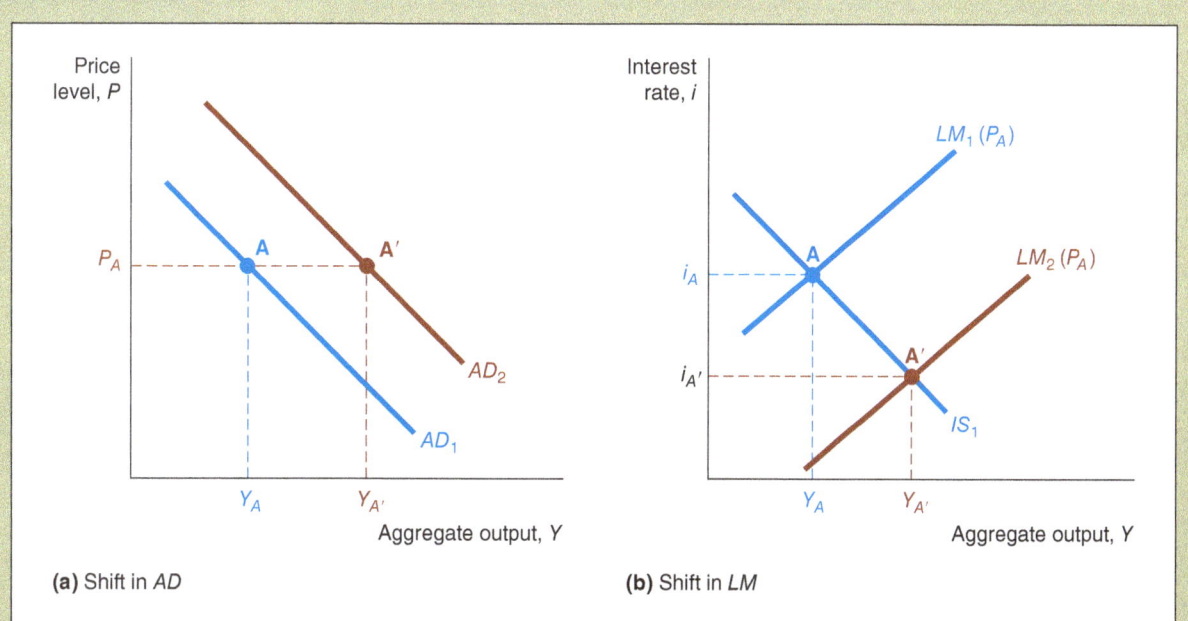

(a) Shift in *AD*   **(b)** Shift in *LM*

Shift in the aggregate demand curve caused by a shift in the *LM* curve

A rise in the money supply or a fall in money demand shifts the *LM* curve to the right in panel (b), and at a price level of
P_A, equilibrium output rises from Y_A to Y_A'. This change in equilibrium output is shown as a movement from point A to
point A in panel (a); hence the aggregate demand curve shifts to the right, from AD_1 to AD_2.

You have now derived and analysed the aggregate demand curve – an essential element in the aggregate demand and supply framework that we examine in Chapter 22. The aggregate demand and supply framework is particularly useful, because it demonstrates how the price level is determined and enables us to examine factors that affect aggregate output when the price level varies.

Summary

1 The *IS* curve is shifted to the right by a rise in autonomous consumer spending, a rise in planned investment spending related to business confidence, a rise in government spending, a fall in taxes or an autonomous rise in net exports. A movement in the opposite direction of these five factors will shift the *IS* curve to the left.

2 The *LM* curve is shifted to the right by a rise in the money supply or an autonomous fall in money demand; it is shifted to the left by a fall in the money supply or an autonomous rise in money demand.

3 A rise in the money supply raises equilibrium output, but lowers the equilibrium interest rate. Expansionary fiscal policy (a rise in government spending or a fall in taxes) raises equilibrium output, but, in contrast to expansionary monetary policy, also raises the interest rate.

4 The less interest-sensitive money demand is, the more effective monetary policy is relative to fiscal policy.

5 The *ISLM* model provides the following conclusion about the conduct of monetary policy: when the *IS* curve is more unstable than the *LM* curve, pursuing a money supply target provides smaller

output fluctuations than pursuing an interest-rate target and is preferred; when the *LM* curve is more unstable than the *IS* curve, pursuing an interest-rate target leads to smaller output fluctuations and is preferred.

6 The conclusion from examining what happens in the *ISLM* model from an expansionary monetary or fiscal policy is that although monetary and fiscal policy can affect output in the short run, neither affects output in the long run.

7 The aggregate demand curve tells us the level of aggregate output consistent with equilibrium in the goods market and the market for money for any given price level. It slopes downward because a lower price level creates a higher level of the real money supply, lowers the interest rate, and raises equilibrium output. The aggregate demand curve shifts in the same direction as a shift in the *IS* or *LM* curve; hence it shifts to the right when government spending increases, taxes decrease, 'animal spirits' encourage consumer and business spending, autonomous net exports increase, the money supply increases, or money demand decreases.

Key terms

aggregate demand curve p. 501

complete crowding out p. 495

long-run monetary neutrality p. 500

natural rate level of output, p. 499

policy mix p. 495

QUESTIONS AND PROBLEMS

All questions and problems are available in MyEconLab at **www.myeconlab.com/mishkin**.

1 If taxes and government spending rise by equal amounts, what will happen to the position of the *IS* curve? Explain this outcome with a Keynesian cross diagram.

2 What happened to the *IS* curve during the Great Depression when investment spending collapsed? Why?

3 What happens to the position of the *LM* curve if the central bank decides that it will decrease the money supply

to fight inflation and if, at the same time, the demand for money falls?

4 'An excess demand for money resulting from a rise in the demand for money can be eliminated only by a rise in the interest rate.' Is this statement true, false, or uncertain? Explain your answer.

*In Problems 5–15, demonstrate your answers with an **ISLM** diagram.*

5 Suppose the central bank reduces the money supply while the government raises taxes. What do you think will happen to interest rates and aggregate output?

6 'German re-unification can be understood as a combination of expansionary fiscal and restrictive monetary policy and may lead to no effect on aggregate output and an increase of the interest rate.' Do you agree with this statement? Why or why not?

7 Suppose that the central bank wants to keep interest rates from rising when the government sharply increases healthcare spending. How can the central bank do this?

8 Evidence indicates that lately the demand for money has become quite unstable. Why is this finding important to central bankers?

9 'As the price level rises, the equilibrium level of output determined in the *ISLM* model also rises.' Is this statement true, false, or uncertain? Explain your answer.

10 What will happen to the position of the aggregate demand curve if the money supply is reduced when government spending increases?

11 How will an equal rise in government spending and taxes affect the position of the aggregate demand curve?

12 If money demand is unaffected by changes in the interest rate, what effect will a rise in government spending have on the position of the aggregate demand curve?

Using economic analysis to predict the future

13 Predict what will happen to interest rates and aggregate output if a stock market crash causes autonomous consumer expenditure to fall.

14 Predict what will happen to interest rates and aggregate output when there is an autonomous export boom.

15 If a series of defaults in the bond market make bonds riskier and as a result the demand for money rises, predict what will happen to interest rates and aggregate output.

16 In the *ISLM* model of this chapter, we treat the exchange rate as an exogenous factor affecting the competiveness level and the net exports of a country. However, both fiscal and monetary policies can affect the exchange rate of those countries that are open to trade and where financial assets are free to circulate. Suppose that a country is open and its exchange rate is flexible. Using the *ISLM* model predict what will happen to aggregate output in response to an expansionary monetary policy. Will the effect be different from an expansionary fiscal policy?

17 Monetary policy in the euro area is controlled by the European Central Bank (ECB), but implemented in a decentralized manner by the individual national central banks. Consider a stylized monetary union made up of two countries, the Netherlands and Belgium. Suppose that the ECB instructs the Dutch central bank to increase the supply of money. Using the *ISLM* model predict what will happen to the interest rate and aggregate output of the Netherlands and Belgium?

18 Consider a stylized monetary union made up of two countries, Italy and Germany. Suppose that Italy unilaterally decides to boost income by raising government spending. Using the *ISLM* model predict what will happen to the interest rate and the aggregate output of Italy and Germany.

WEB EXERCISES

1 An excellent way to learn about how changes in various factors affect the *IS* and *LM* curves is to visit **www.fgn .unisg.ch/eurmacro/tutor/islm.html**. This site, sponsored by the World Bank, allows you to make changes and to observe immediately their impact on the *ISLM* model.

a Increase *G* from 200 to 500. What happens to the interest rate?
b Reduce *t* to 0.1. What happens to aggregate output *Y*?
c Increase *M* to 450. What happens to the interest rate and aggregate output?

2 Looking at the same site as you used in Question 1, **www .fgn.unisg.ch/eurmacro/Tutor/islm.html**, the exogenous parameters in this simulation are the MPC *(c)*, the sensitivity of money demand to income *(k)*, the sensitivity of money demand to the interest rate *(h)* and the sensitivity of investment to the interest rate *(b)*. For each of these parameters, explain what happens in the *ISLM* graph when they are *increased*. What happens to equilibrium output and the equilibrium level of the interest rate?

Notes

1 When the demand for money is affected by the interest rate, the usual case in which the *LM* curve slopes upward but is not vertical, some crowding out occurs. The rightward shift of the *IS* curve also raises the interest rate, which causes investment spending and net exports to fall somewhat. However, as Figure 21.5 indicates, the rise in the interest rate is not sufficient to reduce investment spending and net exports to the point where aggregate output does not increase. Thus expansionary fiscal policy increases aggregate output, and only partial crowding out occurs.

2 This result and many others in this and the previous chapter can be obtained more directly by using algebra. An algebraic treatment of the *ISLM* model can be found in an appendix to this chapter, which is on this book's website at **www .myeconlab.com/mishkin**.

3 The classic paper on this topic is William Poole, 'The optimal choice of monetary policy instruments in a simple macro model', *Quarterly Journal of Economics* 84 (1970): 192–216. A less mathematical version of his analysis, far more accessible to students, is contained in William Poole, 'Rules of thumb for guiding monetary policy', in *Open Market Policies and Operating Procedures: Staff Studies* (Washington, DC: Board of Governors of the Federal Reserve System, 1971).

4 It is important to recognize, however, that the crucial factor in deciding which target is preferred is the *relative* instability of the *IS* and *LM* curves. Although the *LM* curve has been unstable recently, the evidence supporting a stable *IS* curve is also weak. Instability in the money demand function does not automatically mean that money supply targets should be abandoned for an interest-rate target. Furthermore, the analysis so far has been conducted assuming that the price level is fixed. More realistically, when the price level can change, so that there is uncertainty about expected inflation, the case for an interest-rate target is less strong. As we learned in Chapter 4 and 5, the interest rate that is more relevant to investment decisions is not the nominal interest rate but the real interest rate (the nominal interest rate minus expected inflation). Hence when expected inflation rises, at each given nominal interest rate, the real interest rate falls and investment and net exports rise, shifting the *IS* curve to the right. Similarly, a fall in expected inflation raises the real interest rate at each given nominal interest rate, lowers investment and net exports, and shifts the *IS* curve to the left. In the real world, expected inflation undergoes large fluctuations, so the *IS* curve in Figure 21.9 will also have substantial fluctuations, making it less likely that the interest-rate target is preferable to the money supply target.

Useful websites

http://ingrimayne.com/econ/optional/ISLM/Limitations.html A paper discussing limitations of *ISLM* analysis.

http://macrotutor.weebly.com/4-is-lm-shifts-and-reactions.html Online macroeconomics tutorial focused on ISLM.

http://faculty.washington.edu/danby/islm/islmindx.htm An animated explanation of *ISLM*.

http://www.eurmacro.unisg.ch/macroeconomics.html Macroeconomics resources for students.

www.eurmacro.unisg.ch/tutor/mundellfleming_index.html An explanation of the open economy versions of the *ISLM* model.

MyEconLab Can help you get a better grade

MyEconLab®

If your exam were tomorrow, would you be ready? For each chapter, MyEconLab Practice Test and Study Plans pinpoint which sections you have mastered and which ones you need to study. That way, you are more efficient with your study time, and you are better prepared for your exams.

To see how it works, turn to page 19 and then go to: **www.myeconlab.com/mishkin**

CHAPTER 22

Aggregate demand and supply analysis

PREVIEW

In earlier chapters, we focused considerable attention on monetary policy, because it touches our everyday lives by affecting the prices of the goods we buy and the quantity of available jobs. In this chapter, we develop a basic tool, aggregate demand and supply analysis, that will enable us to study the effects of monetary policy on output and prices. **Aggregate demand** is the total quantity of an economy's final goods and services demanded at different price levels. **Aggregate supply** is the total quantity of final goods and services that firms in the economy want to sell at different price levels. As with other supply and demand analyses, the actual quantity of output and the price level are determined by equating aggregate demand and aggregate supply.

Aggregate demand and supply analysis will enable us to explore how aggregate output and the price level are determined. (The 'Following the financial news' box indicates where and how often data on aggregate output and the price level are published.) Not only will the analysis help us interpret recent episodes in the business cycle, but it will also enable us to understand the debates on how economic policy should be conducted.

Aggregate demand

The first building block of aggregate supply and demand analysis is the **aggregate demand curve**, which describes the relationship between the quantity of aggregate output demanded and the price level when all other variables are held constant.

Aggregate demand is made up of four component parts: **consumer expenditure**, the total demand for consumer goods and services; **planned investment spending**,[1] the total planned spending by business firms on new machines, factories and other capital goods, plus planned spending on new homes; **government spending**, spending by all levels of government (central and local) on goods and services (paper clips, computers, computer programming, missiles, government workers and so on); and **net exports**, the net foreign spending on domestic goods and services, equal to exports minus imports. Using the symbols C for consumer expenditure, I for planned investment spending, G for government spending and NX for net exports, we can write the following expression for aggregate demand Y^{ad}:

$$Y^{ad} = C + I + G + NX \tag{22.1}$$

Deriving the aggregate demand curve

Examining the effects of changes in the price level on individual components of aggregate demand is one way to derive the aggregate demand curve. The aggregate demand curve is downward-sloping because a lower price level ($P\downarrow$), holding the nominal quantity of money

Aggregate output, unemployment and the price level

Newspapers and Internet sites periodically report data that provide information on the level of aggregate output, unemployment and the price level in the main industrialized countries. Here is a list of the relevant data series, their frequency and when they are published.

Aggregate output and unemployment

- *Real GDP*: Quarterly (January–March, April–June, July–September, October–December); published three to four weeks after the end of a quarter.
- *Industrial production*: Monthly. Industrial production is not as comprehensive a measure of aggregate output as real GDP, because it measures only manufacturing output; the estimate for the previous month is reported in the middle of the following month.
- *Unemployment rate*: Monthly; previous month's figure is usually published on the Friday of the first week of the following month.

Price level

- *GDP deflator*: Quarterly. This comprehensive measure of the price level (described in the appendix to Chapter 1) is published at the same time as the real GDP data.
- *Consumer price index (CPI)*: Monthly. The CPI is a measure of the price level for consumers (also described in the appendix to Chapter 1); the value for the previous month is published in the third or fourth week of the following month. In order to have comparable measures of the price level, European countries compile the *Harmonized Index Consumer Price (HICP)*, which is based on the same typical 'basket' of goods and services bought by households in Europe.
- *Producer price index (PPI)*: Monthly. The PPI is a measure of the average level of wholesale prices charged by producers and is published at the same time as industrial production data.

(M) constant, leads to a larger quantity of money in real terms (in terms of the goods and services that it can buy, $M/P\uparrow$). The larger quantity of money in real terms ($M/P\uparrow$) that results from the lower price level causes interest rates to fall ($i\downarrow$), as suggested in Chapter 5. The resulting lower cost of financing purchases of new physical capital makes investment more profitable and stimulates planned investment spending ($I\uparrow$). Because, as shown in Equation 22.1, the increase in planned investment spending adds directly to aggregate demand ($Y^{ad}\uparrow$), the lower price level leads to a higher level of the quantity of aggregate output demanded ($P\downarrow \Rightarrow Y^{ad}\uparrow$) and so the aggregate demand curve slopes down as in Figure 22.1. Schematically, we can write the mechanism just described as follows:

$$P\downarrow \Rightarrow M/P\uparrow \Rightarrow i\downarrow \Rightarrow I\uparrow \Rightarrow Y^{ad}\uparrow$$

Another mechanism that generates a downward-sloping aggregate demand curve operates through international trade. Because a lower price level ($P\downarrow$) leads to a larger quantity of money in real terms ($M/P\uparrow$) and lower interest rates ($i\downarrow$), domestic assets become less attractive relative to assets denominated in foreign currencies, thereby causing a decline in the demand for domestic assets and a decline in the exchange rate for the domestic currency, denoted by $E\downarrow$ (as in Chapter 17). A reduction of the exchange rate, which makes domestic goods cheaper relative to foreign goods, then causes net exports to rise, which in turn increases aggregate demand:

$$P\downarrow \Rightarrow M/P\uparrow \Rightarrow i\downarrow \Rightarrow E\downarrow \Rightarrow NX\uparrow \Rightarrow Y^{ad}\uparrow$$

The fact that the aggregate demand curve is downward-sloping can also be derived from the quantity theory of money analysis in Chapter 19. The equation of exchange, $MV = PY$, indicates that if velocity stays constant, a constant money supply (M) implies that nominal

FIGURE 22.1

Shifts in the aggregate demand curve

A decrease in taxes ($T\downarrow$) or an increase in the money supply ($M\uparrow$), government expenditure ($G\uparrow$), net exports ($NX\uparrow$) or business or consumer optimism ($C\uparrow$, $I\uparrow$) increases aggregate demand at each aggregate price level and shifts the aggregate demand curve from AD_1 to AD_2.

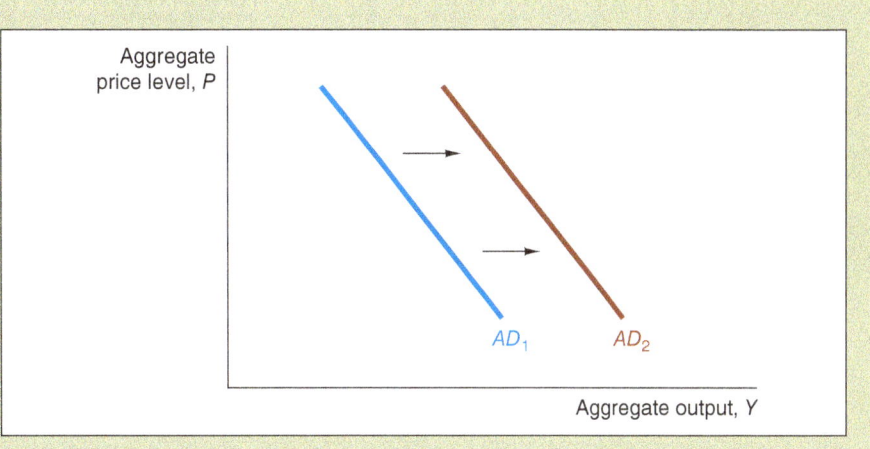

aggregate spending (PY) is also constant. When the price level falls ($P\downarrow$), aggregate demand must necessarily rise ($Y^{ad}\uparrow$) to keep aggregate spending at the same level.

Factors that shift the aggregate demand curve

The quantity theory analysis directly shows that an increase in the money supply ($M\uparrow$) shifts the aggregate demand curve to the right, because with velocity constant the higher money supply raises nominal aggregate spending ($PY\uparrow$) and hence at a given price level, the quantity of aggregate demand increases ($Y^{ad}\uparrow$). Hence an increase in the quantity of money increases the quantity of aggregate demand at each price level and shifts the aggregate demand curve to the right from AD_1 to AD_2 in Figure 22.1. The components approach to aggregate demand also indicates that changes in the money supply cause the aggregate demand curve to shift via the two mechanisms shown in the schematics above. For a given price level, a rise in the money supply causes the real money supply to increase ($M/P\uparrow$), which leads to a decline in interest rates ($i\downarrow$), an increase in investment and net exports (I, $NX\uparrow$) and an increase in the quantity of aggregate demand ($Y^{ad}\uparrow$), shifting the aggregate demand curve to the right from AD_1 to AD_2.[2]

In contrast to the quantity theory, the components approach suggests that other factors (manipulation of government spending and taxes, changes in net exports and changes in consumer and business spending) are also important causes of shifts in the aggregate demand curve. For instance, if the government spends more ($G\uparrow$) or net exports increase ($NX\uparrow$), the quantity of aggregate output demanded at each price level rises, and the aggregate demand curve shifts to the right. A decrease in government taxes ($T\downarrow$) leaves consumers with more income to spend, so consumer expenditure rises ($C\uparrow$). The quantity of aggregate output demanded at each price level also rises, and the aggregate demand curve shifts to the right. Finally, if consumer and business optimism increases, consumer expenditure and planned investment spending rise ($C\uparrow$, $I\uparrow$), again shifting the aggregate demand curve to the right. John Maynard Keynes described waves of optimism and pessimism as **'animal spirits'** and considered them a major factor affecting the aggregate demand curve and an important source of business cycle fluctuations.

Summary

The quantity theory and the components approaches to aggregate demand agree that the aggregate demand curve slopes downward and shifts in response to changes in the money supply. However, in the quantity theory approach, there is only one important source of movements in the aggregate demand curve – changes in the money supply. The components approach suggests that other factors – fiscal policy, net exports and 'animal spirits' – are equally important sources of shifts in the aggregate demand curve. Our discussion of the quantity theory and the components approach indicates that six factors can shift the aggregate demand curve: the money supply, government spending, taxes, net exports, consumer optimism and business optimism. The last two ('animal spirits') affect willingness to spend. The possible effect on the aggregate demand curve of these six factors (often referred to as **demand shocks**) is summarized in Table 22.1.

SUMMARY TABLE 22.1

Factors that shift the aggregate demand curve

Factor	Change	Shift in the aggregate demand curve
Money supply, M	⬆	
Government spending, G	⬆	
Taxes, T	⬆	
Net exports, NX	⬆	
Consumer optimism, C	⬆	
Business optimism, I	⬆	

Note: Only increases (↑) in the factors are shown. The effect of decreases in the factors would be the opposite of those indicated in the 'Shift' column. Note that the quantity theory approach views the money supply as the only important cause of shifts in the aggregate demand curve.

Aggregate supply

To complete our analysis we need to derive an **aggregate supply curve**, the relationship between the quantity of output supplied and the price level. In the typical supply and demand analysis, we have only one supply curve, but because prices and wages take time to adjust to their long-run level, the aggregate supply curve differs in the short and the long runs. First, we examine the long-run aggregate supply curve. We then derive the short-run aggregate supply curve and see how it shifts over time as the economy moves from the short run to the long run.

Long-run aggregate supply curve

The amount of output that can be produced in the economy in the long run is determined by the amount of capital in the economy, the amount of labour supplied at full employment, and the available technology. As discussed in Chapter 16, some unemployment cannot be helped because it is either frictional or structural. Thus at full employment, unemployment is not at zero, but is rather at a level above zero at which the demand for labour equals the supply of labour. This **natural rate of unemployment** is where the economy gravitates to in the long run.[3]

The level of aggregate output produced at the natural rate of unemployment is called the **natural rate of output**; it is where the economy settles in the long run for any price level. Hence the long-run aggregate supply curve (*LRAS*) is vertical at the natural rate of output, denoted by Y_n, as drawn in Figure 22.2.

Short-run aggregate supply curve

Because wages and prices take time to adjust to economic conditions, a process described by saying that wages and prices are *sticky*, the aggregate supply curve (AS_1) in the short run is upward-sloping, as depicted in Figure 22.3. To understand why the short-run aggregate supply curve is upward-sloping, we have to look at the factors that cause the quantity of output supplied to change. Because the goal of business firms is to maximize profits, the quantity of output supplied is determined by the profit made on each unit of output. If profit rises, more aggregate output will be produced, and the quantity of output supplied will increase; if it falls, less output will be produced, and the quantity of aggregate output supplied will fall.

FIGURE 22.2

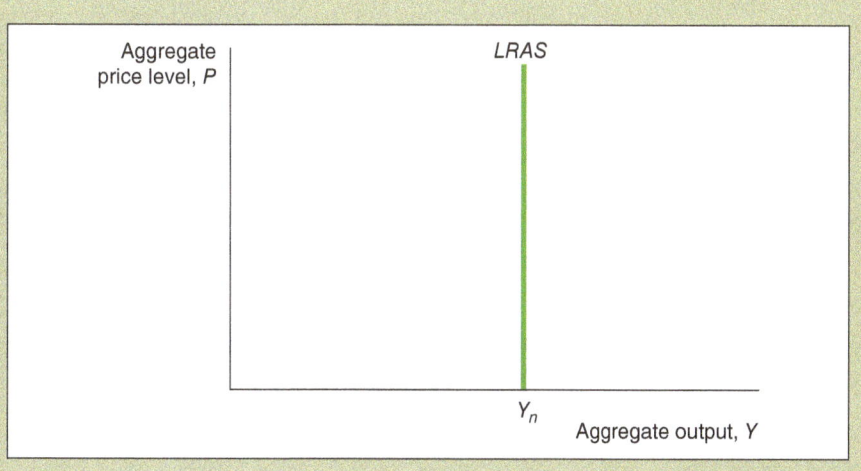

Long-run aggregate supply curve

The amount of aggregate output supplied at any given price level goes to the natural rate level of output in the long run, so that the long-run aggregate supply curve *LRAS* is a vertical line at Y_n.

FIGURE 22.3

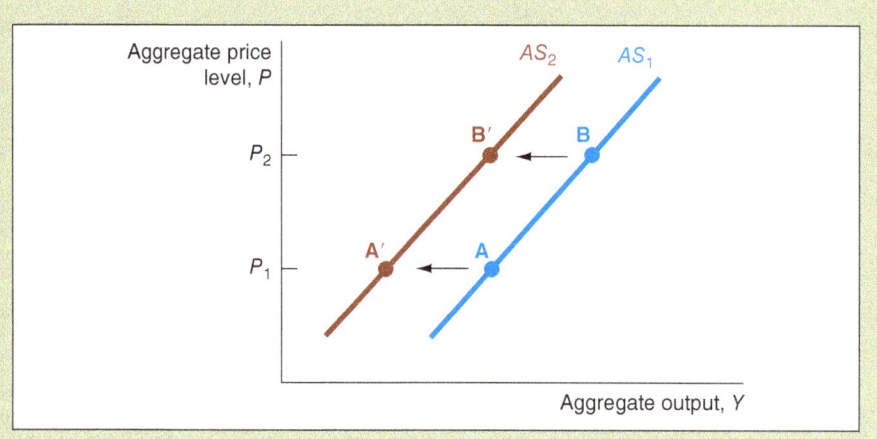

Aggregate supply curve in the short run

A rise in the costs of production shifts the short-run supply curve leftward from AS_1 to AS_2.

Profit on a unit of output equals the price for the unit minus the costs of producing it. In the short run, costs of many factors that go into producing goods and services are fixed; wages, for example, are often fixed for periods of time by labour contracts, and raw materials are often bought by firms under long-term contracts that fix the price. Because these costs of production are fixed in the short run, when the overall price level rises, the price for a unit of output will rise relative to the costs of producing it, and the profit per unit will rise. Because the higher price level results in higher profits in the short run, firms increase production, and the quantity of aggregate output supplied rises, resulting in an upward-sloping short-run aggregate supply curve.

Frequent mention of the *short run* in the preceding paragraph hints that the relationship between the price level and aggregate output embodied in the upward-sloping, short-run aggregate supply curve (AS_1 in Figure 22.3) may not remain fixed as time passes. To see what happens over time, we need to understand what makes the aggregate supply curve shift.[4]

Shifts in the short-run aggregate supply curve

We have seen that the profit on a unit of output determines the quantity of output supplied. If the cost of producing a unit of output rises, profit on a unit of output falls, and the quantity of output supplied at each price level falls. To learn what this implies for the position of the aggregate supply curve, let's consider what happens at a price level of P_1 when the costs of production increase. Now that firms are earning a lower profit per unit of output, they reduce production at that price level, and the quantity of aggregate output supplied falls from point A to point A'. Applying the same reasoning at price level P_2 indicates that the quantity of aggregate output supplied falls from point B to point B'. *What we see is that the short-run aggregate supply curve shifts to the left when costs of production increase and to the right when costs decrease*.

Factors that shift the short-run aggregate supply curve

The factors that cause the short-run aggregate supply curve to shift are ones that affect the costs of production: (1) tightness of the labour market, (2) expectations of inflation, (3) workers' attempts to push up their real wages and (4) changes in the production costs that are unrelated to wages (such as energy costs). The first three factors shift the short-run aggregate supply curve by affecting wage costs; the fourth affects other costs of production.

Tightness of the labour market

If the economy is booming and the labour market is tight ($Y > Y_n$), employers may have difficulty hiring qualified workers and may even have a hard time keeping their present employees. Because the demand for labour now exceeds supply in this tight labour market, employers will raise wages to attract needed workers, and the costs of production will rise. The higher costs of production lower the profit per unit of output at each price level, and the short-run aggregate supply curve shifts to the left (see Figure 22.3).

By contrast, if the economy enters a recession and the labour market is slack ($Y < Y_n$), because the demand for labour is less than the supply, workers who cannot find jobs will be willing to work for lower wages. In addition, employed workers may be willing to make wage concessions to keep their jobs. Therefore, in a slack labour market in which the quantity of labour demanded is less than the quantity supplied, wages and hence costs of production will fall, the profit per unit of output will rise, and the short-run aggregate supply curve will shift to the right.

The effects of tightness of the labour market on the short-run aggregate supply curve can be summarized as follows: *when aggregate output is above the natural rate, the short-run aggregate supply curve shifts to the left; when aggregate output is below the natural rate, the short-run aggregate supply curve shifts to the right*.

Expected price level

Workers and firms care about wages in real terms – that is, in terms of the goods and services that wages can buy. When the price level increases, a worker earning the same nominal wage will be able to buy fewer goods and services. A worker who expects the price level to rise will thus demand a higher nominal wage to keep the real wage from falling. For example, if Bob the Construction Worker expects prices to increase by 5%, he will want a wage increase of at least 5% (more, if he thinks he deserves an increase in real wages). Similarly, if Bob's employer knows that the houses he is building will rise in value at the same rate as inflation (5%), he will be willing to pay Bob 5% more. An increase in the expected price level leads to higher wages, which in turn raise the costs of production, lower the profit per unit of output at each price level and shift the aggregate supply curve to the left (see Figure 22.3). Therefore, *a rise in the expected price level causes the aggregate supply curve to shift to the left; the greater the expected increase in price level (that is, the higher the expected inflation), the larger the shift*.

Wage push

Suppose that Bob and his fellow construction workers decide to strike and succeed in obtaining higher real wages. This wage push will then raise the costs of production, and the aggregate supply curve will shift leftward. *A successful wage push by workers will cause the aggregate supply curve to shift to the left*.

Changes in production costs unrelated to wages

Changes in technology and in the supply of raw materials (called **supply shocks**) can also shift the aggregate supply curve. A negative supply shock, such as a reduction in the availability of raw materials (like oil), which raises their price, increases production costs and shifts the aggregate supply curve leftward. A positive supply shock, such as unusually good weather that leads to a bountiful harvest and lowers the cost of food, will reduce production costs and shift the aggregate supply curve rightward. Similarly, the development of a new technology that lowers production costs, perhaps by raising worker productivity, can be considered a positive supply shock that shifts the aggregate supply curve to the right.

The effect on the aggregate supply curve of changes in production costs unrelated to wages (supply shocks) can be summarized as follows: *a negative supply shock that raises production costs shifts the aggregate supply curve to the left; a positive supply shock that lowers production costs shifts the aggregate supply curve to the right.*[5] As a study aid, factors that shift the short-run aggregate supply curve are listed in Summary Table 22.2.

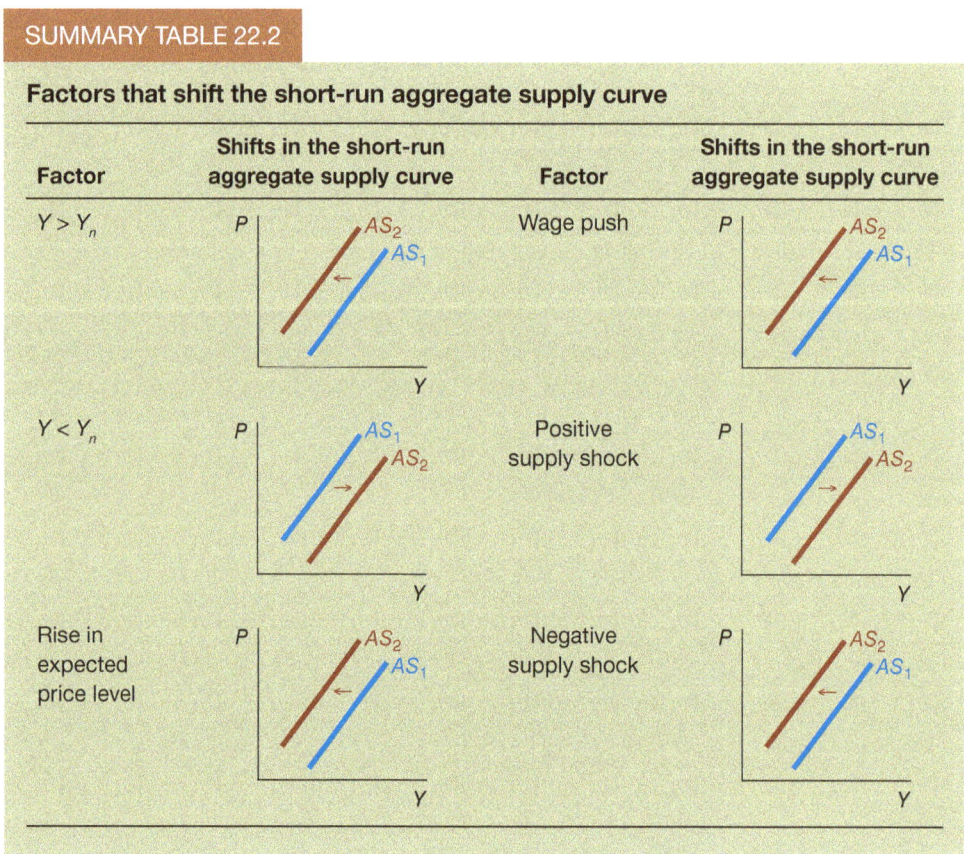

SUMMARY TABLE 22.2

Factors that shift the short-run aggregate supply curve

Equilibrium in aggregate supply and demand analysis

The equilibrium level of aggregate output and the price level will occur at the point where the quantity of aggregate output demanded equals the quantity of aggregate output supplied. However, in the context of aggregate supply and demand analysis, there are two types of equilibrium: short-run and long-run.

Equilibrium in the short run

Figure 22.4 illustrates a short-run equilibrium in which the quantity of aggregate output demanded equals the quantity of output supplied – that is, where the short-run aggregate demand curve *AD* and the aggregate supply curve *AS* intersect at point E. The equilibrium level of aggregate output equals Y^* and the equilibrium price level equals P^*.

As in our earlier supply and demand analyses, equilibrium is a useful concept only if there is a tendency for the economy to head toward it. We can see that the economy heads toward the equilibrium at point E by first looking at what happens when we are at a price level above the equilibrium price level P^*. If the price level is at P', the quantity of aggregate output supplied at point D is greater than the quantity of aggregate output demanded at point A. Because people want to sell more goods and services than others want to buy (a condition of *excess supply*), the prices of goods and services will fall, and the aggregate

FIGURE 22.4

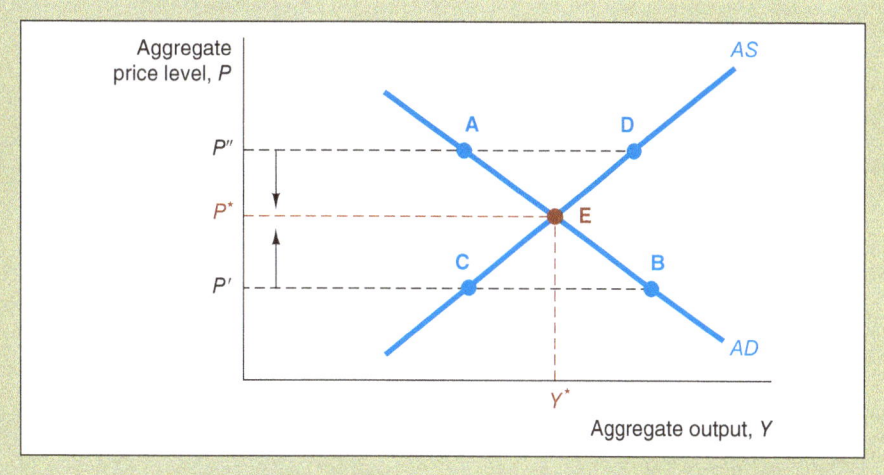

Equilibrium in the short run

Equilibrium occurs at point E at the intersection of the aggregate demand curve AD and the short-run aggregate supply curve AS.

price level will drop, as shown by the downward arrow. This decline in the price level will continue until it has reached its equilibrium level of P^* at point E.

When the price level is below the equilibrium price level, say at P', the quantity of output demanded is greater than the quantity of output supplied. Now the price level will rise, as shown by the upward arrow, because people want to buy more goods than others want to sell (a condition of *excess demand*). This rise in the price level will continue until it has again reached its equilibrium level of P^* at point E.

Equilibrium in the long run

Usually in supply and demand analysis, once we find the equilibrium at which the quantity demanded equals the quantity supplied, there is no need for additional discussion. In *aggregate* supply and demand analysis, however, that is not the case. Even when the quantity of aggregate output demanded equals the quantity supplied, forces operate that can cause the equilibrium to move over time if $Y^* \neq Y_n$. To understand why, we must remember that if costs of production change, the aggregate supply curve will shift.

As we saw earlier, the short-run aggregate supply curve will not remain stationary when aggregate output and unemployment differ from their natural rate: when $Y > Y_n$, labour markets are tight, production costs rise at any given price level and the short-run aggregate supply curve shifts to the left; when $Y < Y_n$, labour markets are slack, production costs fall at any given price level and the aggregate supply curve shifts to the right. Only when aggregate output and unemployment are at their natural rates is there no pressure from the labour market for wages to rise or fall. Under these conditions, there is no reason for the short-run aggregate supply to shift.

We look at how the short-run equilibrium changes over time in response to two situations: when short-run equilibrium is initially above the natural rate level and when it is initially below the natural rate level.

In panel (a) of Figure 22.5, the initial equilibrium occurs at point 1, the intersection of the aggregate demand curve AD and the initial short-run aggregate supply curve AS_1. Because the level of equilibrium output Y_1 is greater than the natural rate level Y_n, unemployment is less than its natural rate and excessive tightness exists in the labour market. This tightness drives wages up, raises production costs and shifts the aggregate supply curve to AS_2. The equilibrium is now at point 2, and output falls to Y_2. Because aggregate output Y_2 is still above the natural rate level, Y_n, wages continue to be driven up, eventually shifting the aggregate supply curve to AS_3. The equilibrium reached at point 3 is on the vertical long-run

FIGURE 22.5

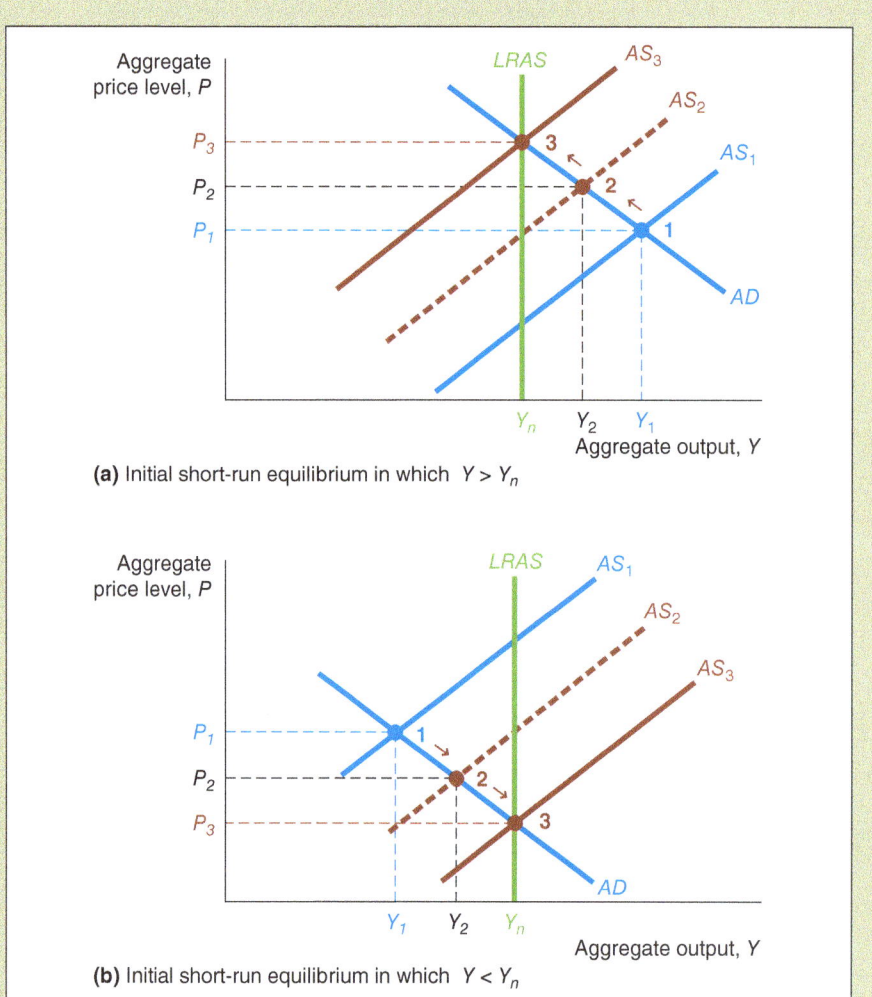

(a) Initial short-run equilibrium in which $Y > Y_n$

(b) Initial short-run equilibrium in which $Y < Y_n$

Adjustment to long-run equilibrium in aggregate supply and demand analysis

In both panels, the initial short-run equilibrium is at point 1 at the intersection of *AD* and *AS*$_1$. In panel (a), $Y_1 > Y_n$ so the short-run aggregate supply curve keeps shifting to the left until it reaches *AS*$_3$, where output has returned to Y_n. In panel (b), $Y_1 < Y_n$ so the short-run aggregate supply curve keeps shifting to the right until output is again returned to Y_n. Hence in both cases, the economy displays a self-correcting mechanism that returns it to the natural rate level of output.

aggregate supply curve (*LRAS*) at Y_n and is a long-run equilibrium. Because output is at the natural rate level, there is no further pressure on wages to rise and thus no further tendency for the aggregate supply curve to shift.

The movements in panel (a) indicate that the economy will not remain at a level of output higher than the natural rate level because the short-run aggregate supply curve will shift to the left, raise the price level and cause the economy (equilibrium) to slide upward along the aggregate demand curve until it comes to rest at a point on the long-run aggregate supply curve at the natural rate level of output Y_n.

In panel (b), the initial equilibrium at point 1 is one at which output Y_1 is below the natural rate level. Because unemployment is higher than its natural rate, wages begin to fall, shifting the short-run aggregate supply curve rightward until it comes to rest at *AS*$_3$. The economy (equilibrium) slides downward along the aggregate demand curve until it reaches the long-run equilibrium point 3, the intersection of the aggregate demand curve (*AD*) and the long-run aggregate supply curve (*LRAS*) at Y_n. Here, as in panel (a), the economy comes to rest when output has again returned to the natural rate level.

A striking feature of both panels of Figure 22.5 is that regardless of where output is initially, it returns eventually to the natural rate level. This feature is described by saying that the economy has a **self-correcting mechanism**.

An important issue for policymakers is how rapidly this self-correcting mechanism works. Many economists believe that the self-correcting mechanism takes a long time, so the approach to long-run equilibrium is slow. This view is reflected in Keynes's often quoted remark, 'In the long run, we are all dead'. These economists view the self-correcting mechanism as slow, because wages are inflexible, particularly in the downward direction when unemployment is high. The resulting slow wage and price adjustments mean that the aggregate supply curve does not move quickly to restore the economy to the natural rate of unemployment. Hence when unemployment is high, these economists, many of whom are followers of Keynes and are thus also known as **Keynesians**, are more likely to see the need for active government policy to restore the economy to full employment.

Other economists believe that wages are sufficiently flexible that the wage and price adjustment process is reasonably rapid. As a result of this flexibility, adjustment of the aggregate supply curve to its long-run position and the economy's return to the natural rate levels of output and unemployment will occur quickly. Thus these economists see much less need for active government policy to restore the economy to the natural rate levels of output and unemployment when unemployment is high. Indeed, Milton Friedman and his followers, known as **monetarists**, advocate the use of a rule whereby the money supply or the monetary base grows at a constant rate so as to minimize fluctuations in aggregate demand that might lead to output fluctuations. We will return in Chapter 24 to the debate about whether government policy should react in a discretionary fashion to keep the economy near full employment.

Changes in equilibrium caused by aggregate demand shocks

With an understanding of the distinction between the short-run and long-run equilibria, you are now ready to analyse what happens when an economy's aggregate demand curve shifts. Figure 22.6 depicts the effect of a rightward shift in the aggregate demand curve due to positive demand shocks: an increase in the money supply ($M\uparrow$), an increase in government spending($G\uparrow$), an increase in net exports ($NX\uparrow$), a decrease in taxes ($T\downarrow$), or an increase in the willingness of consumers and businesses to spend because they become more optimistic ($C\uparrow, I\uparrow$). The figure has been drawn so that the economy initially is in long-run equilibrium at point 1, where the initial aggregate demand curve AD_1 intersects the short-run aggregate supply AS_1 curve at Y_n. When the aggregate demand curve shifts rightward to AD_2, the economy moves to point 1', and both output and the price level rise.

FIGURE 22.6

Response of output and the price level to a shift in the aggregate demand curve

A shift in the aggregate demand curve from AD_1 to AD_2 moves the economy from point 1 to point 1'. Because $Y_1 > Y_n$, the short-run aggregate supply curve begins to shift leftward, eventually reaching AS_2, where output returns to Y_n and the price level has risen to P_2.

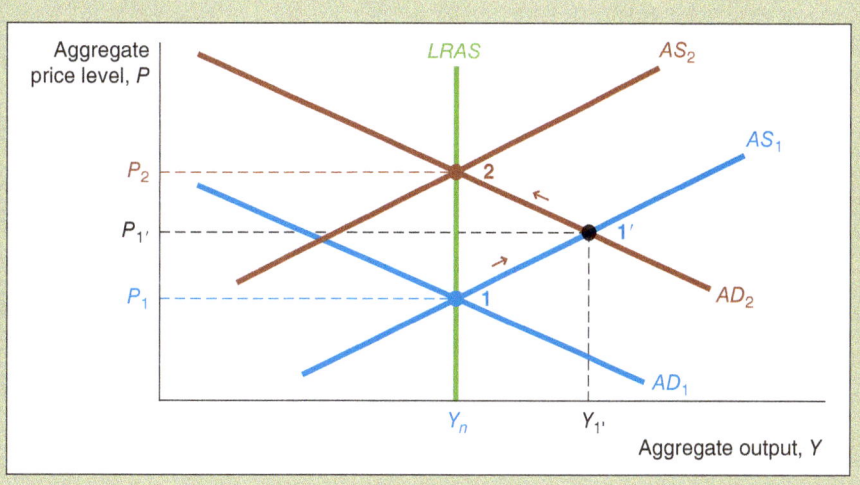

However, the economy will not remain at point 1′ in the long run, because output at $Y_{1′}$ is above the natural rate level. Wages will rise, increasing the cost of production at all price levels, and the short-run aggregate supply curve will eventually shift leftward to AS_2, where it finally comes to rest. The economy (equilibrium) thus slides up the aggregate demand curve from point 1′ to point 2, which is the point of long-run equilibrium at the intersection of AD_2 and the long-run aggregate supply curve (LRAS) at Y_n. *Although the initial short-run effect of the rightward shift in the aggregate demand curve is a rise in both the price level and output, the ultimate long-run effect is only a rise in the price level*.

Changes in equilibrium caused by aggregate supply shocks

Our understanding of the distinction between short-run and long-run equilibria allows us to analyse what happens when aggregate supply shocks shift the short-run aggregate supply curve. Suppose that the economy is initially at the natural rate level of output at point 1 when the short-run aggregate supply curve shifts from AS_1 to AS_2 in Figure 22.7 because of a negative supply shock (a sharp rise in energy prices, for example). The economy will move from point 1 to point 2, where the price level rises but aggregate output *falls*. A situation of a rising price level but a falling level of aggregate output, as pictured in Figure 22.7, has been labelled *stagflation* (a combination of the words *stagnation* and *inflation*). At point 2, output is below the natural rate level, so wages fall and shift the short-run aggregate supply curve back to where it was initially at AS_1. The result is that the economy (equilibrium) slides down the aggregate demand curve AD_1 (assuming that the aggregate demand curve remains in the same position) and returns to the long-run equilibrium at point 1. *Although a leftward shift in the short-run aggregate supply curve initially raises the price level and lowers output, the ultimate effect is that output and price level are unchanged (holding the aggregate demand curve constant)*.

Shifts in the long-run aggregate supply curve: real business cycle theory and hysteresis

To this point, we have assumed that the natural rate level of output Y_n and hence the long-run aggregate supply curve are given. However, over time, the natural rate level of output increases as a result of economic growth. If the productive capacity of the economy is

---

FIGURE 22.7

Response of output and the price level to a shift in short-run aggregate supply

A shift in the short-run aggregate supply curve from AS_1 to AS_2 moves the economy from point 1 to point 2. Because $Y_2 < Y_n$, the short-run aggregate supply curve begins to shift back to the right, eventually returning to AS_1, where the economy is again at point 1.

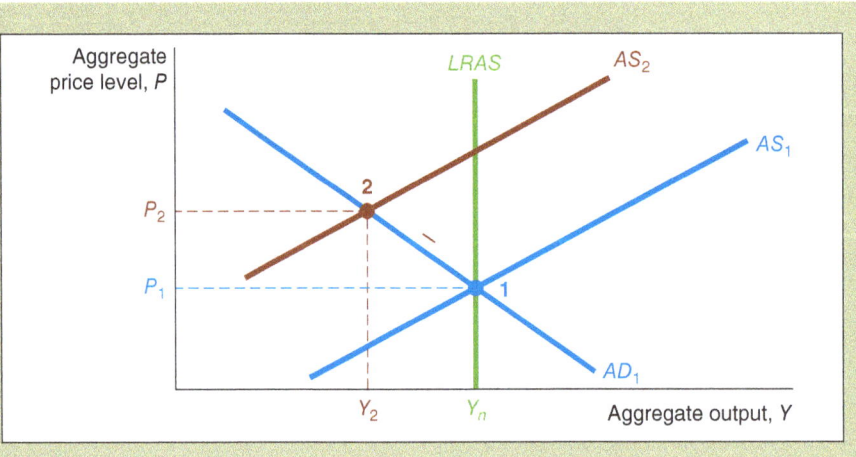

growing at a steady rate of 3% per year, for example, every year Y_n will grow by 3% and the long-run aggregate supply curve at Y_n will shift to the right by 3%. To simplify the analysis, when Y_n grows at a steady rate, Y_n and the long-run aggregate supply curve are drawn as fixed in the aggregate demand and supply diagrams. Keep in mind, however, that the level of aggregate output pictured in these diagrams is actually best thought of as the level of aggregate output relative to its normal rate of growth (trend).

The usual assumption when conducting aggregate demand and supply analysis is that shifts in either the aggregate demand curve or the aggregate supply curve have no effect on the natural rate level of output (which grows at a steady rate). Movements of aggregate output around the Y_n level in the diagram then describe short-run (business cycle) fluctuations in aggregate output. However, some economists take issue with the assumption that Y_n is unaffected by aggregate demand and supply shocks.

One group, led by Edward Prescott of the University of Minnesota, has developed a theory of aggregate economic fluctuations called **real business cycle theory**, in which aggregate supply (real) shocks do affect the natural rate level of output Y_n. This theory views shocks to tastes (workers' willingness to work, for example) and technology (productivity) as the major driving forces behind short-run fluctuations in the business cycle, because these shocks lead to substantial short-run fluctuations in Y_n. Shifts in the aggregate demand curve, perhaps as a result of changes in monetary policy, by contrast are not viewed as being particularly important to aggregate output fluctuations. Because real business cycle theory views most business cycle fluctuations as resulting from fluctuations in the natural rate level of output, it does not see much need for activist policy to eliminate high unemployment. Real business cycle theory is highly controversial and is the subject of intensive research.[6]

Another group of economists disagrees with the assumption that the natural rate level of output Y_n is always at the full employment level and is unaffected by aggregate demand shocks. These economists contend that the natural rate level of unemployment and output are subject to **hysteresis**, a departure from full employment levels as a result of past high unemployment.[7] When unemployment rises because of a reduction of aggregate demand that shifts the *AD* curve inward, the natural rate of unemployment is viewed as rising above the full employment level. This could occur because the unemployed become discouraged and fail to look hard for work or because employers may be reluctant to hire workers who have been unemployed for a long time, seeing it as a signal that the worker is undesirable. The outcome is that the natural rate of unemployment shifts upward after unemployment has become high, and Y_n falls below the full employment level. In this situation, the self-correcting mechanism will be able to return the economy only to the natural rate levels of output and unemployment, not to the full employment level. Only with expansionary policy to shift the aggregate demand curve to the right and raise aggregate output can the natural rate of unemployment be lowered (Y_n raised) to the full employment level. Proponents of hysteresis are thus more likely to promote activist, expansionary policies to restore the economy to full employment.

Conclusions

Aggregate demand and supply analysis yields the following conclusions (under the usual assumption that the natural rate level of output is unaffected by aggregate demand and supply shocks):

1 A shift in the aggregate demand curve – which can be caused by changes in monetary policy (the money supply), fiscal policy (government spending or taxes), international trade (net exports) or 'animal spirits' (business and consumer optimism) – affects output only in the short run and has no effect in the long run. Furthermore, the initial change in the price level is less than is achieved in the long run, when the aggregate supply curve has fully adjusted.

2 A shift in the aggregate supply curve – which can be caused by changes in expected inflation, workers' attempts to push up real wages, or a supply shock – affects output and prices only in the short run and has no effect in the long run (holding the aggregate demand curve constant).

3 The economy has a self-correcting mechanism, which will return it to the natural rate levels of unemployment and aggregate output over time.

Explaining past business cycle episodes

Aggregate supply and demand analysis is an extremely useful tool for analysing aggregate economic activity; we will apply it to several business cycle episodes. To simplify our analysis, we always assume in all three examples that aggregate output is initially at the natural rate level.

Negative supply shocks: the oil price shocks of 1973–75 and 1978–80

In 1973, industrialized countries were hit by a series of negative supply shocks. As a result of the oil embargo stemming from the Arab–Israeli war of 1973, the Organization of Petroleum Exporting Countries (OPEC) was able to engineer a quadrupling of oil prices by restricting oil production. In addition, a series of crop failures throughout the world led to a sharp increase in food prices. On top of these worldwide events, many countries were hit by domestic shocks which further affected their economies. For example, in the UK during the winter of 1973–74 the energy crisis was worsened by a series of strikes by coal miners and railway workers. In the US the termination of wage and price controls in 1973 and 1974 led to a push by workers to obtain wage increases that had been prevented by the controls. The thrust of these events caused the aggregate supply curve to shift sharply leftward, and as the aggregate demand and supply diagram in Figure 22.7 predicts, both the price level and unemployment began to rise dramatically (see Table 22.3).

TABLE 22.3

Unemployment and inflation during the negative supply shocks periods, 1973–75 and 1978–80

Year	Unemployment rate (%)	Inflation (year to year) (%)	Year	Unemployment rate (%)	Inflation (year to year) (%)
UK					
1973	3.7	9.3	1978	5.5	8.2
1974	3.7	16.6	1979	5.4	13.8
1975	4.5	24.7	1980	6.8	17.8
US					
1973	4.9	6.3	1978	6.0	7.6
1974	5.6	11.0	1979	5.8	11.3
1975	8.5	9.1	1980	7.2	13.5
Euro area					
1973	2.1	9.7	1978	4.7	7.6
1974	2.4	12.4	1979	5.0	8.6
1975	3.6	9.8	1980	5.3	11.3

Source: Office for National Statistics(ONS), OECD Economic Outlook, and Area Wide Model (AWM) Dataset.

The 1978–80 period was almost an exact replay of the 1973–75 period. By 1978, the economies had just about fully recovered from the 1973–75 supply shocks, when poor harvests and a doubling of oil prices (as a result of the overthrow of the Shah of Iran) again led to another sharp leftward shift of the aggregate supply curve. The pattern predicted by Figure 22.7 played itself out again – inflation and unemployment both shot upward (see Table 22.3).

Negative demand shocks: the anti-inflation policies of 1980-82

During the oil price shocks of the 1970s inflation soared to double-digit levels while the unemployment rate remained high in most countries around the world. To wring inflation out the system, the Federal Reserve under Chairman Paul Volcker put the US economy through two back-to-back recessions in 1980 and 1981–82 by increasing the federal funds rate from about 11% in 1979 to 20% by June 1981. Following a peak in inflation of nearly 18% in 1980, the British government run by Margaret Thatcher instructed the Bank of England to change policy in order to bring inflation down to normal levels. This policy was characterized by a sharp rise in interest rates and a gradual reduction in the growth of broad money.

Can our aggregate demand and supply analysis predict what happened? The answer is yes. These policy-driven negative demand shocks decreased household and business spending, causing a drop in aggregate demand and a shift of the aggregate demand curve to the left. The situation was exactly the opposite to that shown in Figure 22.6, and our aggregate demand and supply analysis predicts that unemployment would rise and inflation would fall. As we can see in Table 22.4, this prediction is what came to pass. Unemployment, which had been at around 7% in 1980, in 1982 rose to 10.7% in the UK and 9.7% in the US, while the annual rate of inflation fell from double-digit levels in 1980 to figures well below 5% in 1983. The American and the British administrations succeeded in bringing down inflation, but at high costs in terms of unemployment.

The perfect storm of 2007–9: negative supply shocks and the subprime financial crisis

Higher demand for oil from rapidly growing developing countries like China and India and slowing of production in places like Mexico, Russia and Nigeria drove up oil prices sharply from around the $60 per barrel level at the beginning of 2007. By the end of the year, oil prices had risen to $100 per barrel and reached a peak of over $140 in July 2008. The rise of oil prices along with other commodity prices caused the aggregate supply curve to shift sharply leftward. As the aggregate demand and supply diagram in Figure 22.7 indicates, the result was rises in both unemployment and inflation.

TABLE 22.4

Unemployment and inflation during the negative demand shocks period, 1980–3

Year	Unemployment rate (%)	Inflation (year to year) (%) UK	Unemployment rate (%)	Inflation (year to year) (%) US
1980	6.8	17.8	7.2	13.5
1981	9.6	11.8	7.6	10.4
1982	10.7	8.0	9.7	6.2
1983	11.5	4.7	9.6	3.2

Source: Office for National Statistics (ONS) and OECD Economic Outlook.

TABLE 22.5				
Unemployment and inflation during the perfect storm of 2007–9				
Year	Unemployment rate (%)	Inflation (year to year) (%)	Unemployment rate (%)	Inflation (year to year) (%)
	Euro area		UK	
2006	8.2	2.2	5.5	3.4
2007	7.4	2.1	5.4	4.3
2008	7.5	3.3	5.7	4.1
2009	9.4	0.3	7.6	−0.5
	US		Japan	
2006	4.6	3.2	4.1	0.2
2007	4.6	2.9	3.8	0.1
2008	5.8	3.8	4.0	1.4
2009	9.3	−0.3	5.1	−1.3

Source: Office for National Statistics(ONS) and OECD Economic Outlook, December 2001.

If this supply shock were not bad enough, the subprime financial crisis hit the US economy starting in August 2007, reaching a more virulent phase in the autumn of 2008 and affecting the euro area, the UK and Japan. As discussed in Chapter 9, the subprime financial crisis caused a contraction in both household and business spending, leading to a drop in aggregate demand and a shift of the aggregate demand curve to the left, the exact opposite of the situation depicted in Figure 22.6. Aggregate demand and supply analysis indicates that this would lead to a rise in unemployment, with some weakening of inflationary pressure. As our aggregate demand and supply analysis predicts, and as Table 22.5 shows, the result of this perfect storm of negative shocks was a recession starting in 2007–8, with unemployment rising in the euro area, the UK, the US and Japan. Also, as the aggregate demand and supply analysis predicts, inflation accelerated between 2006 and 2008. With the increase in the unemployment rate and the sharp decline of oil and other commodity prices after mid-2008, inflation fell rapidly in 2009 in all the countries in our sample. ■

Summary

1 The aggregate demand curve indicates the quantity of aggregate output demanded at each price level, and it is downward-sloping. The primary sources of shifts in the aggregate demand curve are changes in the money supply, fiscal policy (government spending and taxes), net exports, and the willingness of consumers and businesses to spend ('animal spirits').

2 The long-run aggregate supply curve is vertical at the natural rate level of output. The short-run aggregate supply curve slopes upward, because a rise in the price level raises the profit earned on each unit of production, and the quantity of output supplied rises. Four factors can cause the aggregate supply curve to shift: tightness of the labour market as represented by unemployment relative to the natural rate, expectations of inflation, workers' attempts to push up their real wages and supply shocks unrelated to wages that affect production costs.

3 Equilibrium in the short run occurs at the point where the aggregate demand curve intersects the short-run aggregate supply curve. Although this is where the economy heads temporarily, it has a self-correcting mechanism, which leads it to settle permanently at the long-run equilibrium where aggregate output is at its natural rate level. Shifts in either the aggregate demand or the short-run aggregate supply curve can produce changes in aggregate output and the price level in the short run.

Key terms

QUESTIONS AND PROBLEMS

All questions and problems are available in at **www.myeconlab.com/mishkin.**

1 If exports fall while imports rise, what happens to the aggregate demand curve?

2 If government expenditure goes down while taxes are raised to balance the budget, what happens to the aggregate demand curve?

3 Suppose that government spending is raised at the same time that the money supply is lowered. What will happen to the position of the aggregate demand curve?

4 Why does the aggregate demand curve shift when 'animal spirits' change?

5 If the euro increases in value relative to foreign currencies so that foreign goods become cheaper in the euro area, what will happen to the position of the short-run aggregate supply curve? The aggregate demand curve?

6 'Profit-maximizing behaviour on the part of firms explains why the short-run aggregate supply curve is upward-sloping.' Is this statement true, false, or uncertain? Explain your answer.

7 If huge budget deficits cause the public to think that there will be higher inflation in the future, what is likely to happen to the short-run aggregate supply curve when budget deficits rise?

8 If a pill were invented that made workers twice as productive but their wages did not change, what would happen to the position of the short-run aggregate supply curve?

9 When aggregate output is below the natural rate level, what will happen to the price level over time if the aggregate demand curve remains unchanged? Why?

10 Show how aggregate demand and supply analysis can explain why both aggregate output and the price level fell sharply when investment spending collapsed during the Great Depression.

11 'An important difference between Keynesians and monetarists rests on how long they think the long run actually is.' Is this statement true, false, or uncertain? Explain your answer.

Using economic analysis to predict the future

12 Predict what will happen to aggregate output and the price level if the Bank of England increases the money supply at the same time that UK government implements an income tax cut.

13 Suppose that the public believes that a newly announced anti-inflation programme will work and so lowers its expectations of future inflation. What will happen to aggregate output and the price level in the short run?

14 Predict the effect of a national sales tax on both the aggregate supply and demand curves and on aggregate output and the price level.

15 When there is a decline in the value of the euro, some experts expect it to lead to a dramatic improvement in the ability of euro area firms to compete abroad. Predict what would happen to output and the price level in the euro area as a result.

WEB EXERCISES

1 Go to **http://sdw.ecb.europa.eu** and download the average annual percentage changes in real GDP growth, the Harmonised Index of Consumer Prices (HICP) inflation rate and the unemployment rate of the euro area. After plotting these series in a diagram, try to explain the their main patterns since 2005? Do you see any relation between output growth and the unemployment rate?

2 Go to **http://www.ons.gov.uk/ons/index.html** and then click on 'Data'. Find the historical time series for real GDP and the unemployment rate of the United Kingdom and plot them since 2005. Can you identify any significant changes that can be related to the quantitative easing (QE) monetary policy implemented by the Bank of England since March 2009?

3 Go to **http://www.ons.gov.uk/ons/index.html** and then click on 'Data'. Find the historical time series for real GDP, the unemployment rate and the budget balance over GDP ratio of the United Kingdom and plot them since 2005. How large was the size of the fiscal austerity programme of the current coalition government? Do you see any clear relationship between these fiscal policy measures and the dynamics of output growth and unemployment?

4 Go to **http://research.stlouisfed.org/fred2/categories/12** and click on the Series ID link 'UNRATE' (Civilian Unemployment Rate). What has happened to the unemployment rate since the last reported figure in Table 22.5?

5 In the beginning of 2009, the Federal Open Market Committee warned in their statement dated 28 January 2009 that 'the Committee sees some risk that inflation could persist for a time below rates that best foster economic growth and price stability in the longer term'. Go to **http://research.stlouisfed.org/fred2/categories/9** and click on the Series ID link 'CPIAUCSL' (Consumer Price Index for All Urban Consumers: All Items-SA). Then click on the link '% Chg. From Yr. Ago'. What has happened to the inflation rate since the last reported figure in Table 22.5?

Notes

1 Recall that economists restrict use of the word *investment* to the purchase of new physical capital, such as a new machine or a new house, that adds to expenditure.

2 A complete demonstration of the components approach to the aggregate demand curve is given in Chapters 20 and 21.

3 A related concept is the *non-accelerating inflation rate of unemployment* (NAIRU), the rate of unemployment at which there is no tendency for the inflation rate to change.

4 The aggregate supply curve is closely linked to the Phillips curve discussed in Chapter 16. More information on the Phillips and aggregate supply curves can be found in an appendix to this chapter, which is on this book's website at **www.myeconlab.com/mishkin**.

5 Developments in the foreign exchange market can also shift the aggregate supply curve by changing domestic production costs. As discussed in more detail in Chapter 17, an increase in the value of the domestic currency makes

foreign goods cheaper at home. The decline in prices of foreign goods and hence foreign factors of production lowers home production costs and thus raises the profit per unit of output at each price level in the home country. An increase in the value of the domestic currency therefore shifts the aggregate supply curve to the right. Conversely, a decline in the value of the domestic currency, which makes foreign factors of production more expensive, shifts the aggregate supply curve to the left.

6 See Charles Plosser, 'Understanding real business cycles', *Journal of Economic Perspectives* (1989): 51–77, for a non-technical discussion of real business cycle theory.

7 For a further discussion of hysteresis, see Olivier Blanchard and Lawrence Summers, 'Hysteresis in the European unemployment problem', *NBER Macroeconomics Annual*, 1986, 1, ed. Stanley Fischer (Cambridge, MA: MIT Press, 1986), pp. 15–78.

Useful websites

http://sdw.ecb.europa.eu The Statistical Data Warehouse (SDW) of the ECB providing statistics for the euro area.

http://epp.eurostat.ec.europa.eu/portal/page/portal/eurostat/home/ The homepage of Eurostat, the EU's official statistical agency. It includes lots of economic data.

http://www.ons.gov.uk/ons/index.html Office for National Statistics (ONS) dataset for the United Kingdom.

www.bankofengland.co.uk/mfsd/iadb/NewIntermed.asp Bank of England's statistical interactive dataset.

www.bls.gov The home page of the Bureau of Labour Statistics lists information on unemployment and price levels.

www.census.gov/compendia/statab Statistics on the US economy in an easy-to-understand format.

www.research.stlouisfed.org/fred2/ A database of US economic data hosted by the Federal Reserve Bank of St. Louis.

CHAPTER 23

Transmission mechanisms of monetary policy: the evidence

PREVIEW

Since 1980, the European countries have been on a roller coaster, with output, unemployment and inflation undergoing drastic fluctuations. At the start of the 1980s, UK inflation was running at double-digit levels, and the economy plunged into the 1980–2 recession, the most severe economic contraction in the post-war era – the unemployment rate climbed to over 11.8% in 1984, and only then did the inflation rate came down to below the 5% level. The 1980–2 recession was then followed by a long economic expansion that reduced the unemployment rate to around 7% in the 1989–90 period. As a result of the US savings and loan crisis and the panic that followed, in 1990–2 the UK economy again plunged into recession. Subsequent growth in the economy was sluggish at first but eventually sped up, lowering the unemployment rate to around 5% in the late 1990s and the beginning of the 2000s. This almost 18-year-long period of growth was finally put to an end by the subprime financial crisis and the subsequent deep slowdown of the US economy. The United Kingdom officially slipped into recession in January of 2009 and the unemployment rate rose quickly to levels close to 8%. The other European countries were not immune to these developments and during this period they witnessed large output-growth slowdowns and increases in unemployment rates. In light of large fluctuations in aggregate output (reflected in the unemployment rate) and inflation, and the economic instability that accompanies them, policymakers face the following dilemma: what policy or policies, if any, should be implemented to reduce fluctuations in output and inflation in the future?

To answer this question, monetary policymakers must have an accurate assessment of the timing and effect of their policies on the economy. To make this assessment, they need to understand the mechanisms through which monetary policy affects the economy. In this chapter, we examine empirical evidence on the effect of monetary policy on economic activity. We first look at a framework for evaluating empirical evidence and then use this framework to understand why there are still deep disagreements on the importance of monetary policy to the economy. We then go on to examine the transmission mechanisms of monetary policy and evaluate the empirical evidence on them to better understand the role that monetary policy plays in the economy. We will see that these monetary transmission mechanisms emphasize the link between the financial system (which we studied in the first three parts of this book) and monetary theory, the subject of this part.

Framework for evaluating empirical evidence

To develop a framework for understanding how to evaluate empirical evidence, we need to recognize that there are two basic types of empirical evidence in economics and other scientific disciplines: **structural model evidence** examines whether one variable affects another by using data to build a model that explains the channels through which this variable affects the other; **reduced-form evidence** examines whether one variable has an effect on another simply by looking directly at the relationship between the two variables.

Suppose that you were interested in whether drinking coffee leads to heart disease. Structural model evidence would involve developing a model that analysed data on how coffee is metabolized by the human body, how it affects the operation of the heart and how its effects on the heart lead to heart attacks. Reduced-form evidence would involve looking directly at whether coffee drinkers tend to experience heart attacks more frequently than non-coffee-drinkers.

How you look at evidence – whether you focus on structural model evidence or reduced-form evidence – can lead to different conclusions. This is particularly true for the debate on the importance of monetary policy to economic fluctuations.

Structural model evidence

The components analysis of aggregate demand discussed in Chapter 22 is specific about the channels through which the money supply affects economic activity (called the **transmission mechanisms of monetary policy**). This approach examines the effect of changes in the money supply on economic activity by building a **structural model**, a description of how the economy operates using a collection of equations that describe the behaviour of firms and consumers in many sectors of the economy. These equations then show the channels through which monetary and fiscal policy affect aggregate output and spending. A structural model might have behavioural equations that describe the workings of monetary policy with the following schematic diagram:

$$M \Rightarrow i \Rightarrow I \Rightarrow Y$$

The model describes the transmission mechanism of monetary policy as follows: the change in the money supply M affects interest rates i, which in turn affect investment spending I, which in turn affects aggregate output or aggregate spending Y. Structural model evidence on the relationship between M and Y looks at empirical evidence on the specific channels of monetary influence, such as the link between interest rates and investment spending.

Reduced-form evidence

The quantity theory approach to aggregate demand does not describe specific ways in which the money supply affects aggregate spending. Instead, it suggests that the effect of money on economic activity should be examined by looking at whether movements in Y are tightly linked to (have a high correlation with) movements in M. Reduced-form evidence analyses the effect of changes in M on Y as if the economy were a black box whose workings cannot be seen. The reduced-form way of looking at the evidence can be represented by the following schematic diagram, in which the economy is drawn as a black box with a question mark:

$$M \Rightarrow ? \Rightarrow Y$$

Advantages and disadvantages of structural model evidence

The structural model approach has the advantage of giving us an understanding of how the economy works. If the structure is correct – if it contains all the transmission mechanisms and channels through which monetary policy can affect economic activity – the structural model approach has three major advantages over the reduced-form approach.

1 Because we can evaluate each transmission mechanism separately to see whether it is plausible, we can gather more evidence on whether monetary policy has an important effect

on economic activity. If we find that monetary policy significantly affects economic activity, for example, we will have more confidence that changes in monetary policy actually cause the changes in economic activity; that is, we will have more confidence on the direction of causation between M and Y.

2 Knowing how changes in monetary policy affect economic activity may help us predict the effect of changes in M on Y more accurately. For example, expansions in the money supply might be found to be less effective when interest rates are low. Then, when interest rates are higher, we would be able to predict that an expansion in the money supply would have a larger impact on Y than would otherwise be the case.

3 By knowing how the economy operates, we may be able to predict how institutional changes in the economy might affect the link between changes in M and Y. For instance, in the United Kingdom, during the 1970s the Bank of England instituted a policy of trying to control the money supply by creating constraints on the commercial banks' ability to create deposits. This policy was called the 'corset'. Commercial banks were not allowed to grow their deposits beyond certain limits. The results were that the commercial banks encouraged large-volume depositors to deal directly with large-credit obligors or to deposit offshore, creating 'disintermediation'. Disintermediation means that financial intermediation is going on but is not part of the official statistics. When the corset was abolished, all the deposits that were not recorded because of disintermediation came back into the system and M3 began to rise rapidly coinciding with the time the UK government was trying to control the money supply and meet medium-term monetary targets (see Chapter 16). It has been argued that the sharp rise in interest rates in 1980 in the UK was a response to a rise in the growth of M3 which was not the effect of loose money but measures of the money supply that were formerly hidden coming back to the surface. Consequently interest rates were higher than they need have been and the 1980–1 recession could have been less severe than it actually was.[1] Because of the rapid pace of financial innovation, the advantage of being able to predict how institutional changes affect the link between changes in M and Y may be more important now than in the past.

These three advantages of the structural model approach suggest that it is better than the reduced-form approach *if we know the correct structure of the model*. Put another way, structural model evidence is only as good as the structural model it is based on; it is best only if all the transmission mechanisms are fully understood. This is a big *if*, as failing to include one or two relevant transmission mechanisms for monetary policy in the structural model might result in a serious misjudgement about the impact of changes in M on Y.

However, structural models may ignore the transmission mechanisms for monetary policy that are most important. For example, if the most important monetary transmission mechanisms involve consumer spending rather than investment spending, the structural model (such as the $M\uparrow \Rightarrow i\downarrow \Rightarrow I\uparrow \Rightarrow Y\uparrow$ model we used earlier), which focuses on investment spending for its monetary transmission mechanism, may underestimate the importance of an increase in the money supply to economic activity.

Advantages and disadvantages of reduced-form evidence

The main advantage of reduced-form evidence over structural model evidence is that no restrictions are imposed on the way monetary policy affects the economy. If we are not sure that we know what all the monetary transmission mechanisms are, we may be more likely to spot the full effect of changes in M on Y by looking at whether movements in Y correlate highly with movements in M.

The most notable objection to reduced-form evidence is that it may misleadingly suggest that changes in M cause changes in Y when that is not the case. A basic principle applicable to all scientific disciplines, including economics, states that *correlation does not*

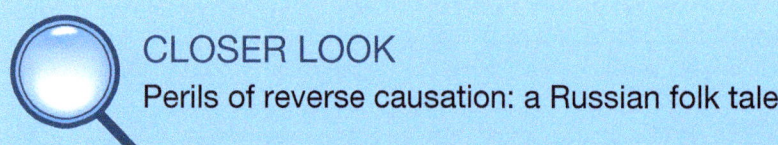

CLOSER LOOK
Perils of reverse causation: a Russian folk tale

A Russian folk tale illustrates the problems that can arise from reverse causation. As the story goes, there once was a severe epidemic in the Russian countryside and many doctors were sent to the towns where the epidemic was at its worst. The peasants in the towns noticed that wherever doctors went, many people were dying. So to reduce the death rate, they killed all the doctors.

Were the peasants better off? Clearly not.

necessarily imply causation. That movement of one variable is linked to another doesn't necessarily mean that one variable *causes* the other.

Suppose, for example, you notice that wherever criminal activity abounds, more police patrol the street. Should you conclude from this evidence that police patrols cause criminal activity and recommend pulling police off the street to lower the crime rate? The answer is clearly no, because police patrols do not cause criminal activity; criminal activity causes police patrols. This situation is called **reverse causation** and can produce misleading conclusions when interpreting correlations (see the 'Closer look' box, 'Perils of reverse causation: a Russian folk tale').

The reverse causation problem may be present when examining the link between changes in money and aggregate output or spending. Our discussion of the conduct of monetary policy in Chapter 16 suggested that when the central bank has an interest-rate target, higher output may lead to a higher money supply. If most of the correlation between M and Y occurs because of the central bank's interest-rate target, controlling the money supply will not help control aggregate output, because it is actually changes in Y that are causing changes in M, rather than the other way around.

Another facet of the correlation–causation question is that an outside factor, yet unknown, could be the driving force behind two variables that move together. Coffee drinking might be associated with heart disease not because coffee drinking causes heart attacks but because coffee-drinkers tend to be people who are under a lot of stress and the stress causes heart attacks. Getting people to stop drinking coffee, then, would not lower the incidence of heart disease. Similarly, if there is an unknown outside factor that causes M and Y to move together, controlling M will not improve control of Y.

Conclusions

No clear-cut case can be made that reduced-form evidence is preferable to structural model evidence, or vice versa. The structural model approach offers an understanding of how the economy works. If the structure is correct, it predicts the effect of monetary policy more accurately, allows predictions of the effect of monetary policy when institutions change, and provides more confidence in the direction of causation between M and Y. If the structure of the model is not correctly specified because it leaves out important transmission mechanisms of monetary policy, it could be very misleading.

The reduced-form approach does not restrict the way monetary policy affects the economy and may be more likely to spot the full effect of changes in M on Y. However, reduced-form evidence cannot rule out reverse causation, whereby changes in output cause changes in money, or the possibility that an outside factor drives changes in both output and money. A high correlation of money and output might then be misleading, because controlling the money supply would not help control the level of output.

Armed with the framework to evaluate empirical evidence we have outlined here, we can now use it to evaluate the empirical debate on the importance of monetary policy to economic fluctuations.

APPLICATION

The debate on the importance of monetary policy to economic fluctuations

We can apply our understanding of the advantages and disadvantages of structural model versus reduced-form evidence to a debate that has been going on for more than 70 years: how important is monetary policy to economic fluctuations? The followers of Milton Friedman, known as *monetarists*, tended to focus on reduced-form evidence and found that changes in the money supply are very important to economic fluctuations. Early followers of John Maynard Keynes, known as *Keynesians*, focused on structural model evidence based on the components approach to determination of aggregate demand, which was less likely to find that monetary policy is important. We evaluate the evidence that monetarists and Keynesians brought to bear on the importance of monetary policy using the analysis we developed in the previous section.

Early Keynesian evidence on the importance of money

Although Keynes proposed his theory for analysing aggregate economic activity in 1936, his views reached their peak of popularity among economists in the 1950s and early 1960s, when the majority of economists had accepted his framework. Although most Keynesians currently believe that monetary policy has important effects on economic activity, the early Keynesians of the 1950s and early 1960s characteristically held the view that *monetary policy does not matter at all* to movements in aggregate output and hence to the business cycle.

Their belief in the ineffectiveness of monetary policy stemmed from three pieces of structural model evidence:

1 During the Great Depression, interest rates on US Treasury securities fell to extremely low levels; the three-month Treasury bill rate, for example, declined to below 1%. Early Keynesians believed monetary policy affected aggregate demand solely through its effect on nominal interest rates, which in turn affected investment spending; they believed that low interest rates during the Great Depression indicated that monetary policy was easy (expansionary) because it encouraged investment spending and so could not have played a contractionary role during this period. Because monetary policy was not capable of explaining why the worst economic contraction in US history had taken place, early Keynesians concluded that changes in the money supply have no effect on aggregate output – in other words, money doesn't matter.

2 Early empirical studies found no linkage between movements in nominal interest rates and investment spending. Because early Keynesians saw this link as the channel through which changes in the money supply affect aggregate demand, finding that the link was weak also led them to the conclusion that changes in the money supply have no effect on aggregate output.

3 Surveys of business people revealed that their decisions on how much to invest in new physical capital were not influenced by market interest rates. This evidence further confirmed that the link between interest rates and investment spending was weak, strengthening the conclusion that money doesn't matter. The result of this interpretation of the evidence was that most economists paid only scant attention to monetary policy before the mid-1960s.

Objections to early Keynesian evidence

While Keynesian economics was reaching its ascendancy in the 1950s and 1960s, a small group of economists at the University of Chicago, led by Milton Friedman, adopted what was then the unfashionable view that money *does* matter to aggregate demand. Friedman and his disciples, who later became known as monetarists, objected to the early Keynesian interpretation of the evidence on the grounds that the structural model used by the early Keynesians was severely flawed. Because structural model evidence is only as good as the model it is based on, the monetarist critique of this evidence needs to be taken seriously.

In 1963, Friedman and Anna Schwartz, a researcher at the National Bureau of Economic Research, published their classic monetary history of the United States, which showed that, contrary to the early Keynesian beliefs, monetary policy during the Great Depression was not easy; indeed, it had never been more contractionary.[2] Friedman and Schwartz documented the massive bank failures of this period and the resulting decline in the money supply. Hence monetary policy could explain the worst economic contraction in US history, and the Great Depression could not be singled out as a period that demonstrates the ineffectiveness of monetary policy.

A Keynesian could still counter Friedman and Schwartz's argument that monetary policy was contractionary during the Great Depression by citing the low level of interest rates. But were these interest rates really so low? Although interest rates on US Treasury securities and high-grade corporate bonds were low during the Great Depression, interest rates on lower-grade bonds, such as Baa corporate bonds, rose to unprecedented high levels during the sharpest part of the contraction phase (1930–3). By the standard of these lower-grade bonds, then, interest rates were high and monetary policy was tight.

There is a moral to this story. Although much aggregate economic analysis proceeds as though there is only *one* interest rate, we must always be aware that there are *many* interest rates, which may tell different stories. During normal times, most interest rates move in tandem, so lumping them all together and looking at one representative interest rate may not be too misleading. But that is not always so. Unusual periods (like the Great Depression), when interest rates on different securities begin to diverge, do occur. This is exactly the kind of situation in which a structural model (like the early Keynesians') that looks at only the interest rates on a low-risk security such as a Treasury bill or bond can be very misleading.

There is a second, potentially more important, reason why the early Keynesian structural model's focus on nominal interest rates provides a misleading picture of the tightness of monetary policy during the Great Depression. In a period of deflation, when there is a declining price level, low *nominal* interest rates do not necessarily indicate that the cost of borrowing is low and that monetary policy is easy – in fact, the cost of borrowing could be quite high. If, for example, the public expects the price level to decline at a 10% rate, then even though nominal interest rates are at zero, the real cost of borrowing would be as high as 10%. (Recall from Chapter 4 that the real interest rate equals the nominal interest rate, 0, in this case, minus the expected rate of inflation, −10%, so the real interest rate equals $0 - (-10\%) = 10\%$.)

You can see in Figure 23.1 that this is exactly what happened during the Great Depression: real interest rates on US Treasury bills were far higher during the 1931–3 contraction phase of the depression than was the case throughout the next 40 years.[3] As a result, movements of *real* interest rates indicate that, contrary to the early Keynesians' beliefs, monetary policy was extremely tight during the Great Depression. Because an important role for monetary policy during this depressed period could no longer be ruled out, most economists were forced to rethink their position regarding whether money matters.

Monetarists also objected to the early Keynesian structural model's view that a weak link between nominal interest rates and investment spending indicates that investment spending is unaffected by monetary policy. A weak link between *nominal* interest rates and investment spending does not rule out a strong link between *real* interest rates and investment spending. As depicted in Figure 23.1, nominal interest rates are often a very misleading indicator of real interest rates – not only during the Great Depression, but in later periods as well. Large deviations between nominal and real interest rates are not a unique feature of the United States. For instance, Figure 23.2 shows that from the early 1920s till the mid-1930s, the UK real interest rate was persistently higher than the nominal rate, whereas the following 30 years were characterized by systematic negative real interest rates. Because real interest

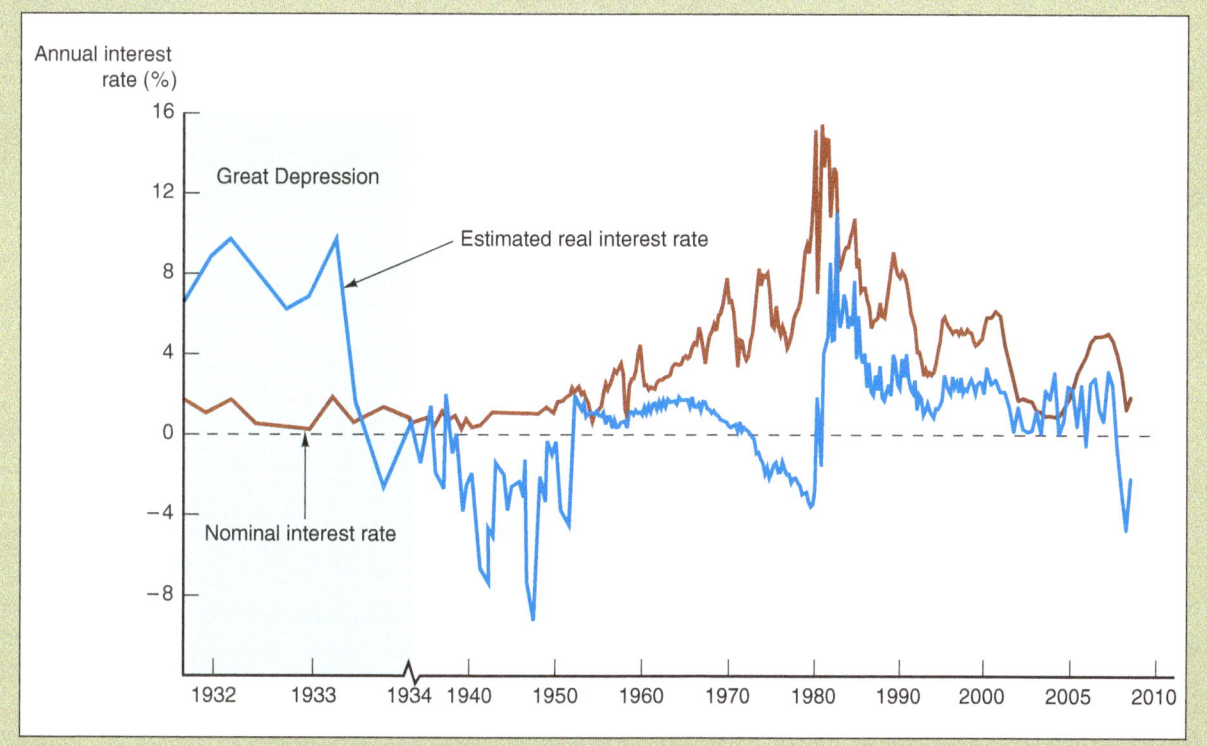

Real and nominal interest rates on US three-month treasury bills, 1931–2008

Sources: Nominal rates from *www.federalreserve.gov/releases/h15/update/*. The real rate is constructed using the procedure outlined in Frederic S. Mishkin, 'The real interest rate: an empirical investigation', *Carnegie-Rochester Conference Series on Public Policy* 15 (1981): 151–200. This involves estimating expected inflation as a function of past interest rates, inflation and time trends, and then subtracting the expected inflation measure from the nominal interest rate.

rates more accurately reflect the true cost of borrowing, they should be more relevant to investment decisions than nominal interest rates. Accordingly, the two pieces of early Keynesian evidence indicating that nominal interest rates have little effect on investment spending do not rule out a strong effect of changes in the money supply on investment spending and hence on aggregate demand.

Monetarists also asserted that interest-rate effects on investment spending might be only one of many channels through which monetary policy affects aggregate demand. Monetary policy could then have a major impact on aggregate demand even if interest-rate effects on investment spending are small, as was suggested by the early Keynesians.

Early monetarist evidence on the importance of money

In the early 1960s, Milton Friedman and his followers published a series of studies based on reduced-form evidence that promoted the case for a strong effect of money on economic activity. In general, reduced-form evidence can be broken down into three categories: (i) *timing evidence*, which looks at whether the movements in one variable typically occur before those in another; (ii) *statistical evidence*, which performs formal statistical tests on the correlation of the movements of one variable with another; and (iii) *historical evidence*, which examines specific past episodes to see whether movements in one variable appear to cause those in another. Let's look at the monetarist evidence on the importance of money that falls into each of these three categories.

FIGURE 23.2

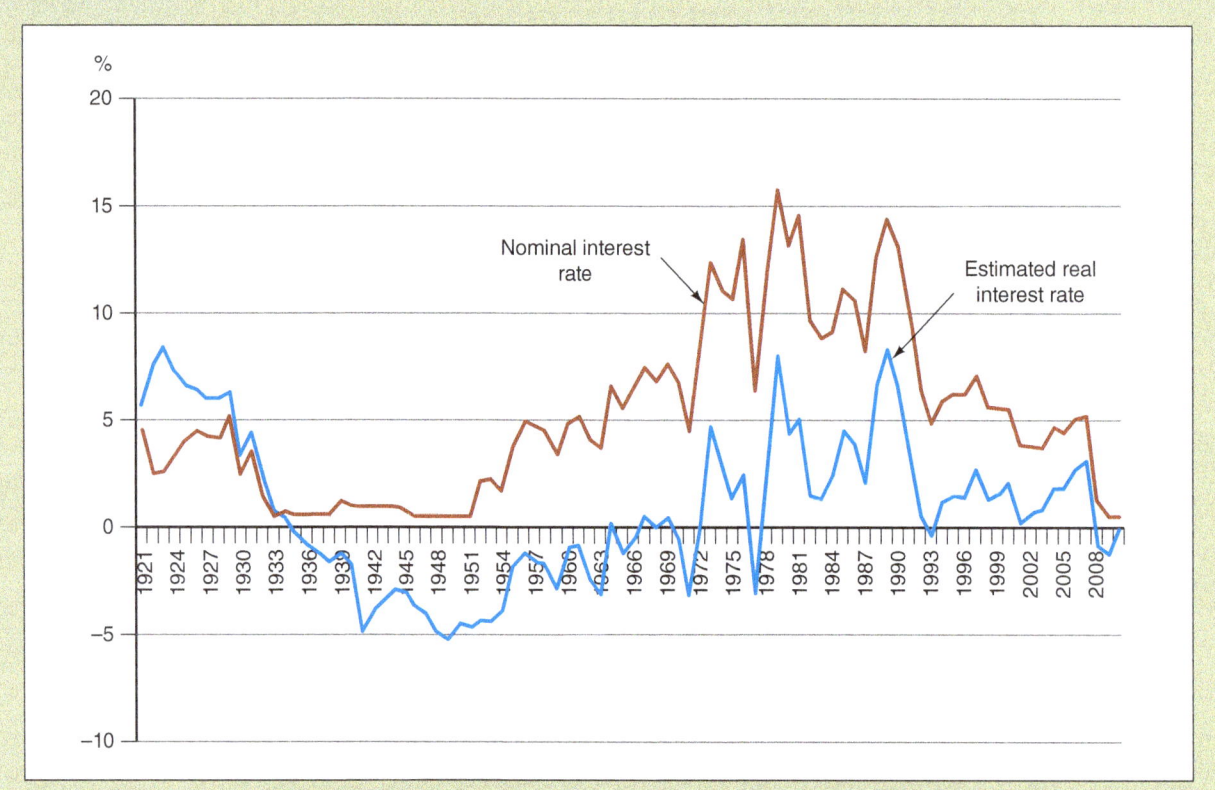

Real and nominal interest rates on UK three-month treasury bills, 1921–2010

Sources: Nominal rates from Office for National Statistics (ONS). The real rate is constructed using the procedure outlined in Frederic S. Mishkin, 'The real interest rate: an empirical investigation', *Carnegie-Rochester Conference Series on Public Policy* 15 (1981): 151–200. This involves estimating expected inflation as a function of past interest rates, inflation and time trends, and then subtracting the expected inflation measure from the nominal interest rate.

Timing evidence

Monetarist timing evidence reveals how the rate of money supply growth moves relative to the business cycle. The evidence on this relationship was first presented by Friedman and Schwartz in a famous paper published in 1963.[4] Friedman and Schwartz found that in every business cycle over nearly a century that they studied, the money growth rate always declined before output did. On average, the peak in the rate of money growth occurred 16 months before the peak in the level of output. However, this lead time could vary, ranging from a few months to more than two years. The conclusion that these authors reached on the basis of this evidence is that money growth causes business cycle fluctuations, but its effect on the business cycle operates with 'long and variable lags'.

Timing evidence is based on the philosophical principle first stated in Latin as *post hoc, ergo propter hoc*, which means that if one event occurs after another, the second event must have been caused by the first. This principle is valid only if we know that the first event is an *exogenous* event, an event occurring as a result of an independent action that could not possibly be caused by the event following it or by some outside factor that might affect both events. If the first event is exogenous, when the second event follows the first we can be more confident that the first event is causing the second.

An example of an exogenous event is a controlled experiment. A chemist mixes two chemicals; suddenly his lab blows up and he with it. We can be absolutely sure that the cause of his demise was the act of mixing the two chemicals together. The principle of *post hoc*, *ergo propter hoc* is extremely useful in scientific experimentation.

Unfortunately, economics does not enjoy the precision of hard sciences like physics or chemistry. Often we cannot be sure that an economic event, such as a decline in the rate of money growth, is an exogenous event – it could have been caused by an outside factor or by the event it is supposedly causing. When another event (such as a decline in output) typically follows the first event (a decline in money growth), we cannot conclude with certainty that one caused the other. Timing evidence is clearly of a reduced-form nature because it looks directly at the relationship of the movements of two variables. Money growth could lead output, or both could be driven by an outside factor.

Because timing evidence is of a reduced-form nature, there is also the possibility of reverse causation, in which output growth causes money growth. How can this reverse causation occur while money growth still leads output? There are several ways in which this can happen, but we will deal with just one example.[5]

Suppose that you are in a hypothetical economy with a very regular business cycle movement, plotted in panel (a) of Figure 23.3, that is four years long (four years from peak to peak). Let's assume that in our hypothetical economy, there is reverse causation from output to the money supply and movements in the money supply and output are perfectly correlated; that is, the money supply M and output Y move upward and downward at the same time. The result is that the peaks and troughs of the M and Y series in panels (a) and (b) occur at exactly the same time. Therefore, no lead or lag relationship exists between them.

Now let's construct the rate of money supply growth from the money supply series in panel (b). This is done in panel (c). What is the rate of growth of the money supply at its peaks in years 1 and 5? At these points, it is not growing at all; the rate of growth is zero. Similarly, at the trough in year 3, the growth rate is zero. When the money supply is declining from its peak in year 1 to its trough in year 3, it has a negative growth rate, and its decline is fastest sometime between years 1 and 3 (year 2). Translating to panel (c), the rate of money growth is below zero from years 1 to 3, with its most negative value reached at year 2. By similar reasoning, you can see that the growth rate of money is positive in years 0 to 1 and 3 to 5, with the highest values reached in years 0 and 4. When we connect all these points together, we get the money growth series in panel (c), in which the peaks are at years 0 and 4, with a trough in year 2.

Now let's look at the relationship of the money growth series of panel (c) with the level of output in panel (a). As you can see, the money growth series consistently has its peaks and troughs exactly one year before the peaks and troughs of the output series. We conclude that in our hypothetical economy, the rate of money growth always decreases one year before output does. This evidence does not, however, imply that money growth *drives* output. In fact, by assumption, we know that this economy is one in which causation actually runs from output to the level of money supply, and there is no lead or lag relationship between the two. Only by our judicious choice of using the *growth rate* of the money supply rather than its *level* have we found a leading relationship.

This example shows how easy it is to misinterpret timing relationships. Furthermore, by searching for what we hope to find, we might focus on a variable, such as a growth rate, rather than a level, which suggests a misleading relationship. Timing evidence can be a dangerous tool for deciding on causation.

Stated even more forcefully, 'one person's lead is another person's lag'. For example, you could just as easily interpret the relationship of money growth and output in Figure 23.3 to say that the money growth rate lags output by three years – after all, the peaks in the money growth series occur three years after the peaks in the output series. In short, you could say that output leads money growth.

We have seen that timing evidence is extremely hard to interpret. Unless we can be sure that changes in the leading variable are exogenous events, we cannot be sure that the leading variable is actually causing the following variable. And it is all too easy to find what

FIGURE 23.3

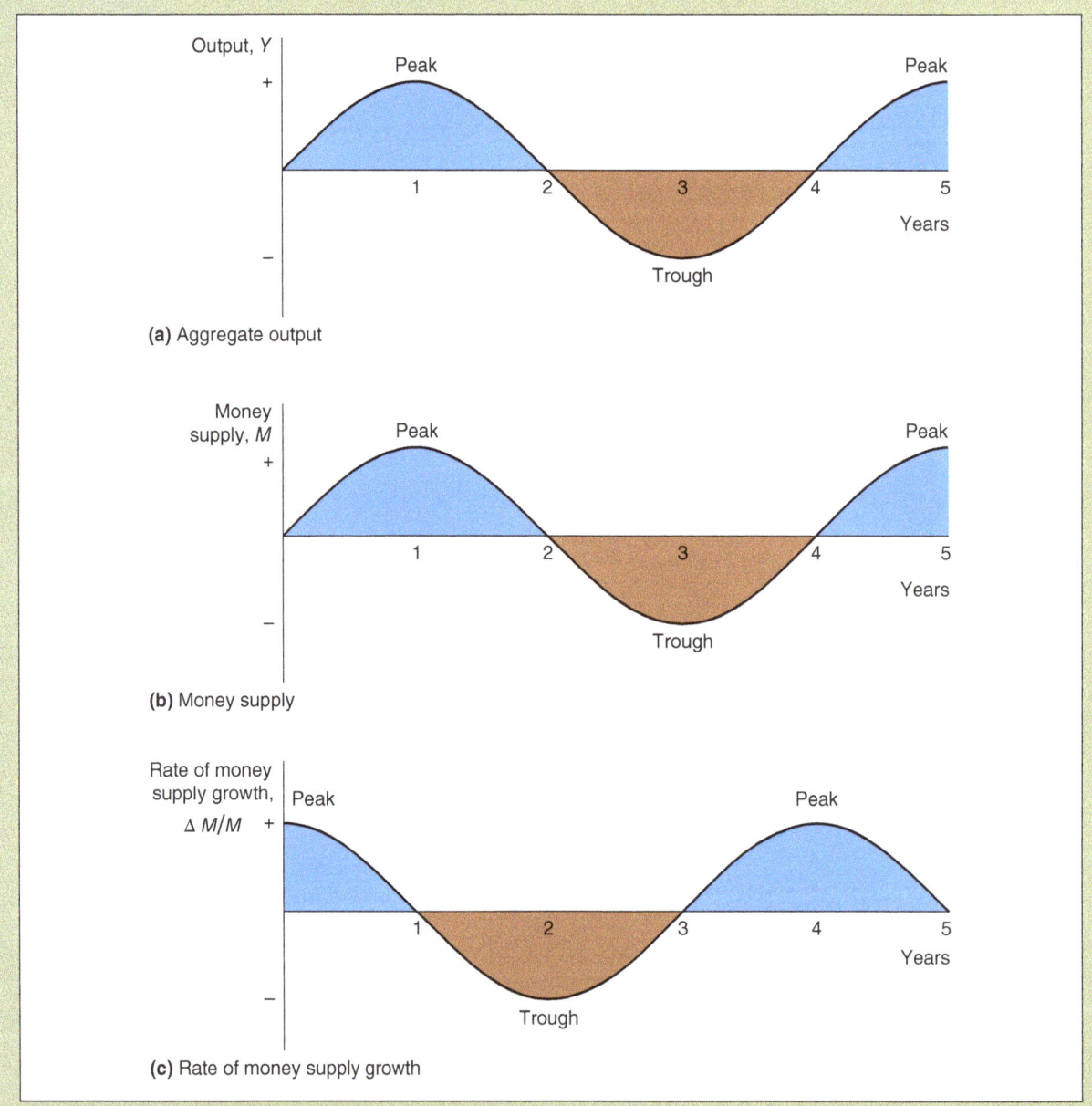

(a) Aggregate output

(b) Money supply

(c) Rate of money supply growth

Hypothetical example in which money growth leads output

Although neither M nor Y in panels (a) and (b) leads the other (that is, their peaks and troughs coincide), $\Delta M/M$ has its peaks and troughs one year ahead of M and Y, thus leading both series. (Note that M and Y in panels (a) and (b) are drawn as movements around a positive average value; a plus sign indicates a value above the average, and a minus sign indicates a value below the average, not a negative value.)

we seek when looking for timing evidence. Perhaps the best way of describing this danger is to say that 'timing evidence may be in the eyes of the beholder'.

Statistical evidence

Monetarist statistical evidence examined the correlations between money and aggregate output or aggregate spending by performing formal statistical tests. Again in 1963 (obviously a vintage year for the monetarists), Milton Friedman and David Meiselman published a paper that proposed the following test of a monetarist model against a model used by early Keynesians.[6] In the Keynesian components framework, investment and government spending were sources of fluctuations in aggregate demand, so Friedman and Meiselman constructed a 'Keynesian' autonomous expenditure variable A equal to investment spending plus government spending. They characterized the Keynesian components model as saying that A should be highly correlated with aggregate spending Y, while the money supply M should not. In the monetarist model, the money supply is the source of fluctuations in aggregate spending, and M should be highly correlated with Y, while A should not.

A logical way to find out which model is better would be to see which is more highly correlated with Y: M or A. When Friedman and Meiselman conducted this test for many different periods of US data, they discovered that *the monetarist model wins!*[7] They concluded that monetarist analysis gives a better description than Keynesian analysis of how aggregate spending is determined.

Several objections were raised against the Friedman–Meiselman evidence:

1 The standard criticisms of this reduced-form evidence are the ones we have already discussed: reverse causation could occur, or an outside factor might drive both series.
2 The test may not be fair because the Keynesian components model is characterized too simplistically. Keynesian structural models commonly include hundreds of equations. The one-equation 'Keynesian' model that Friedman and Meiselman tested may not adequately capture the effects of autonomous expenditure. Furthermore, Keynesian models usually include the effects of other variables. By ignoring them, the effect of monetary policy might be overestimated and the effect of autonomous expenditure underestimated.
3 The Friedman–Meiselman measure of autonomous expenditure A might be constructed poorly, preventing the 'Keynesian' model from performing well. For example, orders for military hardware affect aggregate demand before they appear as spending in the autonomous expenditure variable that Friedman and Meiselman used. A more careful construction of the autonomous expenditure variable should take account of the placing of orders for military hardware. When the autonomous expenditure variable was constructed more carefully by critics of the Friedman–Meiselman study, they found that the results were reversed: the 'Keynesian' model won.[8] A later study on the appropriateness of various ways of determining autonomous expenditure does not give a clear-cut victory to either the 'Keynesian' or the monetarist model.[9]

Historical evidence

The monetarist historical evidence found in Friedman and Schwartz's *A Monetary History* has been very influential in gaining support for the monetarist position. We have already seen that the book was extremely important as a criticism of early Keynesian thinking, showing as it did that the Great Depression was not a period of easy monetary policy and that the depression could be attributed to the sharp decline in the money supply from 1930 to 1933 resulting from bank panics. In addition, the book documented in great detail that the growth rate of money leads business cycles, because it declines before every recession. This timing evidence is, of course, subject to all the criticisms raised earlier.

The historical evidence contains one feature, however, that makes it different from other monetarist evidence we have discussed so far. Several episodes occur in which changes in the money supply appear to be *exogenous* events. These episodes are almost like controlled experiments, so the *post hoc, ergo propter hoc* principle is far more likely to be valid: if the decline in the growth rate of the money supply is soon followed by a decline in output in these episodes, much stronger evidence is presented that money growth is the driving force behind the business cycle.

One of the best examples of such an episode is the increase in reserve requirements in 1936–7 by the Federal Reserve, which led to a sharp decline in the money supply and in its rate of growth. The increase in reserve requirements was implemented because the

Federal Reserve wanted to improve its control of monetary policy; it was not implemented in response to economic conditions. We can thus rule out reverse causation from output to the money supply. Also, it is hard to think of an outside factor that could have driven the Fed to increase reserve requirements and that could also have directly affected output. Therefore, the decline in the money supply in this episode can probably be classified as an exogenous event with the characteristics of a controlled experiment. Soon after this experiment, the very severe recession of 1937–8 occurred. We can conclude with confidence that in this episode, the change in the money supply due to the Fed's increase in reserve requirements was indeed the source of the business cycle contraction that followed.

A Monetary History also documented other historical episodes, such as the bank panics of 1907 and other years in which the decline in money growth again appears to have been an exogenous event. The fact that recessions have frequently followed apparently exogenous declines in money growth is very strong evidence that changes in the growth rate of the money supply do have an impact on aggregate output. Recent work by Christina and David Romer, both of the University of California, Berkeley, applies the historical approach to more recent data using more sophisticated statistical techniques and also finds that monetary policy shifts have had an important impact on the aggregate economy.[10]

Overview of the monetarist evidence

Where does this discussion of the monetarist evidence leave us? We have seen that because of reverse causation and outside-factor possibilities, there are some serious doubts about the conclusions that can be drawn from timing and statistical evidence alone. However, some of the historical evidence in which exogenous declines in money growth are followed by business cycle contractions does provide stronger support for the monetarist position. When historical evidence is combined with timing and statistical evidence, the conclusion that monetary policy does matter seems warranted.

As you can imagine, the economics profession was shaken by the appearance of the monetarist evidence, because up to that time most economists believed that money does not matter at all. Monetarists had demonstrated that this early Keynesian position was probably wrong, and it won them a lot of converts. Recognizing the fallacy of the position that money does not matter does not necessarily mean that we must accept the position that money is *all* that matters. Many Keynesian economists shifted their views toward the monetarist position, but not all the way. Instead, they adopted an intermediate position: they allowed that money, fiscal policy, net exports and 'animal spirits' all contributed to fluctuations in aggregate demand. The result has been a convergence of the views on the importance of monetary policy to economic activity. However, proponents of a new theory of aggregate fluctuations called *real business cycle theory* are more critical of the monetarist reduced-form evidence that money is important to business cycle fluctuations because they believe there is reverse causation from the business cycle to money (see the 'Closer look' box 'Real business cycle theory and the debate on money and economic activity'). ∎

Transmission mechanisms of monetary policy

After the successful monetarist attack on the early Keynesian position, economic research went in two directions. One direction was to use more sophisticated monetarist reduced-form models to test for the importance of money to economic activity.[11] The second direction was to pursue a structural model approach and to develop a better understanding of channels (other than interest-rate effects on investment) through which monetary

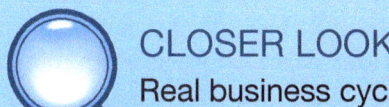

CLOSER LOOK
Real business cycle theory and the debate on money and economic activity

New entrants to the debate on money and economic activity are advocates of *real business cycle theory*, which states that real shocks to tastes and technology (rather than monetary shocks) are the driving forces behind business cycles. Proponents of this theory are critical of the monetarist view that money matters to business cycles because they believe that the correlation of output with money reflects reverse causation; that is, the business cycle drives money, rather than the other way around. An important piece of evidence they offer to support the reverse causation argument is that almost none of the correlation

between money and output comes from the monetary base, which is controlled by the monetary authorities.[*] Instead, the money–output correlation stems from other sources of money supply movements that, as we saw in Chapter 14, are affected by the actions of banks and depositors, and are more likely to be influenced by the business cycle.

[*]Robert King and Charles Plosser, 'Money, credit and prices in a real business cycle', *American Economic Review* 74 (1984): 363–80; and Charles Plosser, 'Understanding real business cycles', *Journal of Economic Perspectives* 3 (Summer 1989): 51–78.

policy affects aggregate demand. In this section we examine some of these channels, or *transmission mechanisms*, beginning with interest-rate channels, because they are the key monetary transmission mechanism in the *ISLM* and *AD/AS* models you have seen in Chapters 20, 21 and 22.

Traditional interest-rate channels

The traditional components view of the monetary transmission mechanism can be characterized by the following schematic, which shows the effect of an expansionary monetary policy:

$$\text{expansionary monetary policy} \Rightarrow i_r\downarrow \Rightarrow I\uparrow \Rightarrow Y\uparrow \qquad (23.1)$$

where an expansionary monetary policy leads to a fall in real interest rates ($i_r,\downarrow$), which in turn lowers the cost of capital, causing a rise in investment spending ($I\uparrow$) thereby leading to an increase in aggregate demand and a rise in output ($Y\uparrow$).

Although Keynes originally emphasized this channel as operating through businesses' decisions about investment spending, the search for new monetary transmission mechanisms recognized that consumers' decisions about housing and **consumer durable expenditure** (spending by consumers on durable items such as automobiles and refrigerators) also are investment decisions. Thus the interest-rate channel of monetary transmission outlined in Equation 23.1 applies equally to consumer spending, in which *I* also represents residential housing and consumer durable expenditure.

An important feature of the interest-rate transmission mechanism is its emphasis on the *real* (rather than the nominal) interest rate as the rate that affects consumer and business decisions. In addition, it is often the real *long*-term interest rate (not the real short-term interest rate) that is viewed as having the major impact on spending. How is it that changes in the short-term nominal interest rate induced by a central bank result in a corresponding change in the real interest rate on both short- and long-term bonds? The key is the phenomenon known as *sticky prices*, the fact that the aggregate price level adjusts slowly over time, meaning that expansionary monetary policy, which lowers the short-term nominal interest rate, also lowers the short-term *real* interest rate. The expectations hypothesis of the term structure described in Chapter 6, which states that the long-term interest rate is an average of expected future short-term interest rates, suggests that a lower real short-term interest rate, as long as it persists, leads to a fall in the real long-term interest rate. These lower real interest rates then lead to rises in business fixed investment, residential housing investment, inventory investment and consumer durable expenditure, all of which produce the rise in aggregate output.

That the real interest rate rather than the nominal rate affects spending provides an important mechanism for how monetary policy can stimulate the economy, even if nominal interest rates hit a floor of zero during a deflationary episode. With nominal interest rates at a floor of zero, a commitment to future expansionary monetary policy can raise the expected price level ($P^e \uparrow$) and hence expected inflation($\pi^e \uparrow$), thereby lowering the real

CLOSER LOOK
The pass-through of retail bank rates in the euro area

The adjustment of retail bank rates in response to changes in policy rates plays a key role in the monetary transmission mechanism, above all in those countries which have predominantly bank-based financial systems. A quick and complete **pass-through** will have a larger impact on borrowing and saving behaviour of firms and households, whereas a slow and incomplete one will make monetary policy less effective. Therefore the timing and size of the pass-through may considerably affect the strength of the monetary transmission mechanism. For policymakers this raises the crucial question about the factors likely to affect banks' interest-rate-setting behaviour when monetary policy conditions change. As the list of factors is quite extensive only a few major aspects will be discussed here.

First, the degree of competition among banks plays a key role. In a fully competitive banking sector for example a decrease in the policy interest rate may feed into lower retail loan rates relatively quickly since most banks may prefer to avoid a loss in market share likely to be accompanied by a lack of adjustment in credit yields. In contrast a low level of competition may induce a bank to postpone a reduction in loan rates in order to increase its profit margin. Hence less competition from other banks (and alternative non-bank financing sources) may be associated with a more sluggish pass-through of interest rates.

Second, uncertainty about the future course of monetary policy may prevent a smooth transmission process. If, for instance, a change in monetary policy is perceived to be temporary and likely to be reversed in the near future banks may decide not to react at all or to adjust only deposit and loan contracts with short maturities.

Third, administrative costs that originate from the implementation of new loan and deposit rates may exceed the costs of keeping rates at a non-equilibrium level. The financial resources devoted to, for instance, labour, computing and customer notification may simply outweigh the expected loss in revenues when retail rates are held stable. Administrative costs, also known as 'menu costs', may therefore counteract a quick and complete pass-through of interest rates.

Finally, the existence of adverse selection and moral hazard problems may prevent a bank from an upward adjustment in yields offered on loans. Given that a rise in lending rates may attract less solvent borrowers being more likely to fail on their debt, the expected return on a bank's loan portfolio may fall as a result of higher loan retail rates. Thus in order to maximize the expected return on loans a bank may not fully adapt loan rates to a rise in the official interest rate. Accordingly adverse selection and moral hazard problems are potential constraints to the pass-through process when monetary policy becomes more restrictive.

Given the above discussion, it is interesting to ask what the empirical evidence on the pass-through is. As observed in Figure 15.5, money market rates (for instance the EONIA in the euro area) closely mirror changes in the key official interest rates set by the ECB. But how do bank rates respond to market rates with a similar maturity? Figure 23.4 shows the dynamics of selected short-term retail bank lending and deposit rates of the euro area against changes in the EONIA and the three-month Euribor (the interest rate at which euro banks lend to each other unsecured funds at three month maturity) since the beginning of 2003. We can observe that bank rates have broadly followed the two market rates, but in a rather sluggish manner and not fully.

Recent empirical research based on econometric models for the euro area confirms that the pass-through is not only slow but also incomplete.* These studies find that on average less than 50% of a given change in the correspondent market rate is passed on to borrowers and

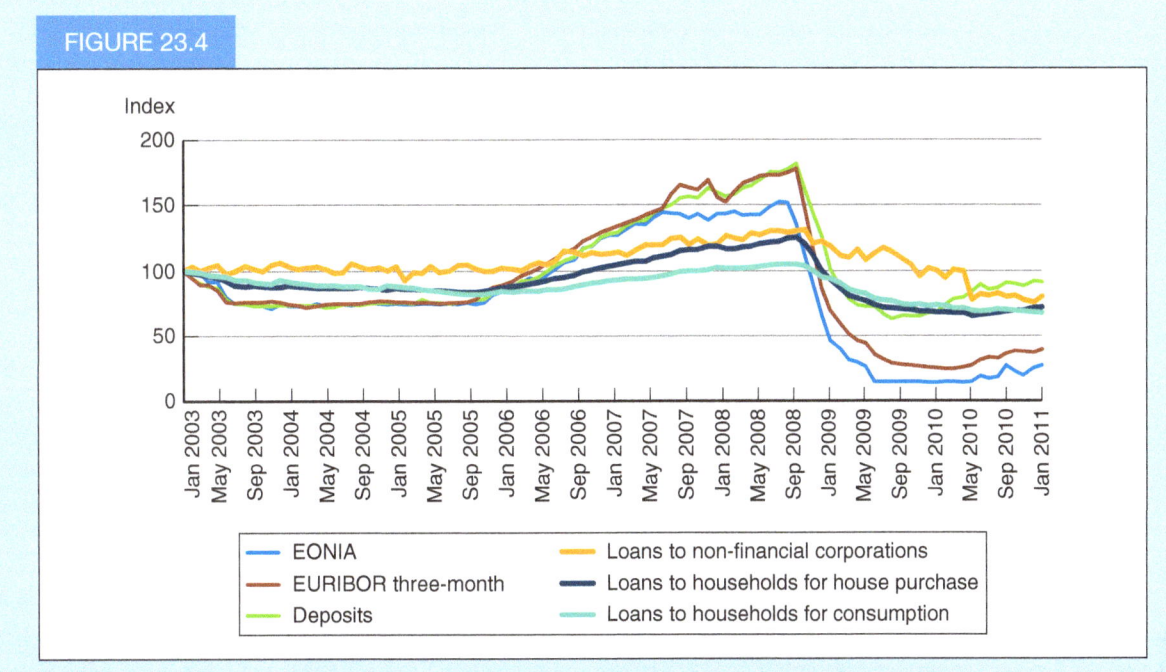

FIGURE 23.4

Selected short-term retail bank lending and deposit rates, the EONIA and Euribor (January 2003 = 100)

Sources: Own calculations from MFI interest rates on euro-denominated deposits and loans by euro area residents available from the ECB Statistical Data Warehouse, *http://sdw.ecb.europa.eu/home.do.*

the responsiveness of deposit rates is documented to be even lower. Moreover, it usually takes several months for retail rates to adjust. A different picture emerges from the UK literature where the empirical evidence points towards a quicker and more complete pass-through. This is consistent with a more competitive banking system.

* See Claudia Kwapil and Johann Scharler, 'Interest rate pass-through, monetary policy rules and macroeconomic stability', *Journal of International Money and Finance* 29 (March 2010): 236–51, and Gabe de Bondt, 'Retail bank interest rate pass-through: new evidence at the euro area level', *ECB Working Paper* (April 2002), No. 136.

interest rate ($i_r = [i - \pi^e]\downarrow$) even when the nominal interest rate is fixed at zero and stimulating spending through the interest-rate channel:

$$\text{expansionary monetary policy} \Rightarrow P^e\uparrow \Rightarrow \pi^e\uparrow \Rightarrow i_r\downarrow \Rightarrow I\uparrow \Rightarrow Y\uparrow \qquad (23.2)$$

This mechanism thus indicates that monetary policy can still be effective even when nominal interest rates have already been driven down to zero by the monetary authorities. Indeed, this mechanism is a key element in monetarist discussions of why the US economy was not stuck in a liquidity trap (in which increases in the money supply might be unable to lower interest rates, discussed in Chapter 19) during the Great Depression and why expansionary monetary policy could have prevented the sharp decline in output during that period. This is also a key mechanism underlying the recent unconventional policies implemented by the major central banks during the recent global financial crisis (see Chapter 15 and the Application 'The subprime recession and quantitative easing' later in this chapter).

Some economists, such as John Taylor of Stanford University, take the position that there is strong empirical evidence for substantial interest-rate effects on consumer and investment spending through the cost of capital, making the interest-rate monetary transmission mechanism a strong one. His position is highly controversial, and many researchers, including Ben Bernanke, now the chairman of the Fed, and Mark Gertler of New York University, believe that the empirical evidence does not support strong interest-rate effects operating through the cost of capital.[12] Indeed, these researchers see the empirical failure of traditional interest-rate monetary transmission mechanisms as having provided the stimulus for the search for other transmission mechanisms of monetary policy.

These other transmission mechanisms fall into two basic categories: those operating through asset prices other than interest rates and those operating through asymmetric information effects on credit markets (the **credit view**). (These mechanisms are summarized in the schematic diagram in Figure 23.5.)

Other asset price channels

As we saw earlier in the chapter, a key monetarist objection to the Keynesian analysis of monetary policy effects on the economy is that it focuses on only one asset price, the interest rate, rather than on many asset prices. Monetarists envision a transmission mechanism in which other relative asset prices and real wealth transmit monetary effects onto the economy. In addition to bond prices, two other asset prices receive substantial attention as channels for monetary policy effects: foreign exchange rates and the prices of equities (stocks).

Exchange rate effects on net exports

With the growing internationalization of economies throughout the world and the advent of flexible exchange rates, more attention has been paid to how monetary policy affects exchange rates, which in turn affect net exports and aggregate output.

This channel also involves interest-rate effects, because, as we saw in Chapter 17, when domestic real interest rates fall, domestic assets become less attractive relative to assets denominated in foreign currencies. As a result, the value of domestic assets relative to other currency assets falls and the domestic currency depreciates (denoted by $E\downarrow$). The lower value of the domestic currency makes domestic goods cheaper than foreign goods, thereby causing a rise in net exports ($NX\uparrow$) and hence in aggregate output ($Y\uparrow$). The schematic for the monetary transmission mechanism that operates through the exchange rate is

$$\text{expansionary monetary policy} \Rightarrow i_r\downarrow \Rightarrow E\downarrow \Rightarrow NX\uparrow \Rightarrow Y\uparrow \qquad (23.3)$$

Recent research has found that this exchange rate channel plays an important role in how monetary policy affects the domestic economy.[13]

Tobin's q theory

James Tobin developed a theory, referred to as *Tobin's q theory*, that explains how monetary policy can affect the economy through its effects on the valuation of equities (stock). Tobin defines q as the market value of firms divided by the replacement cost of capital. If q is high, the market price of firms is high relative to the replacement cost of capital, and new plant and equipment capital is cheap relative to the market value of firms. Companies can then issue stock and get a high price for it relative to the cost of the facilities and equipment they are buying. Investment spending will rise, because firms can buy a lot of new investment goods with only a small issue of stock.

Conversely, when q is low, firms will not purchase *new* investment goods because the market value of firms is low relative to the cost of capital. If companies want to acquire capital when q is low, they can buy another firm cheaply and acquire old capital instead. Investment spending, the purchase of new investment goods, will then be very low. Tobin's q theory gives a good explanation for the extremely low rate of investment spending during the Great Depression. In that period, stock prices collapsed, and by 1933 stocks were worth only one-tenth of their value in late 1929; q fell to unprecedented low levels.

The crux of this discussion is that a link exists between Tobin's q and investment spending. But how might monetary policy affect stock prices? Quite simply, when monetary

FIGURE 23.5

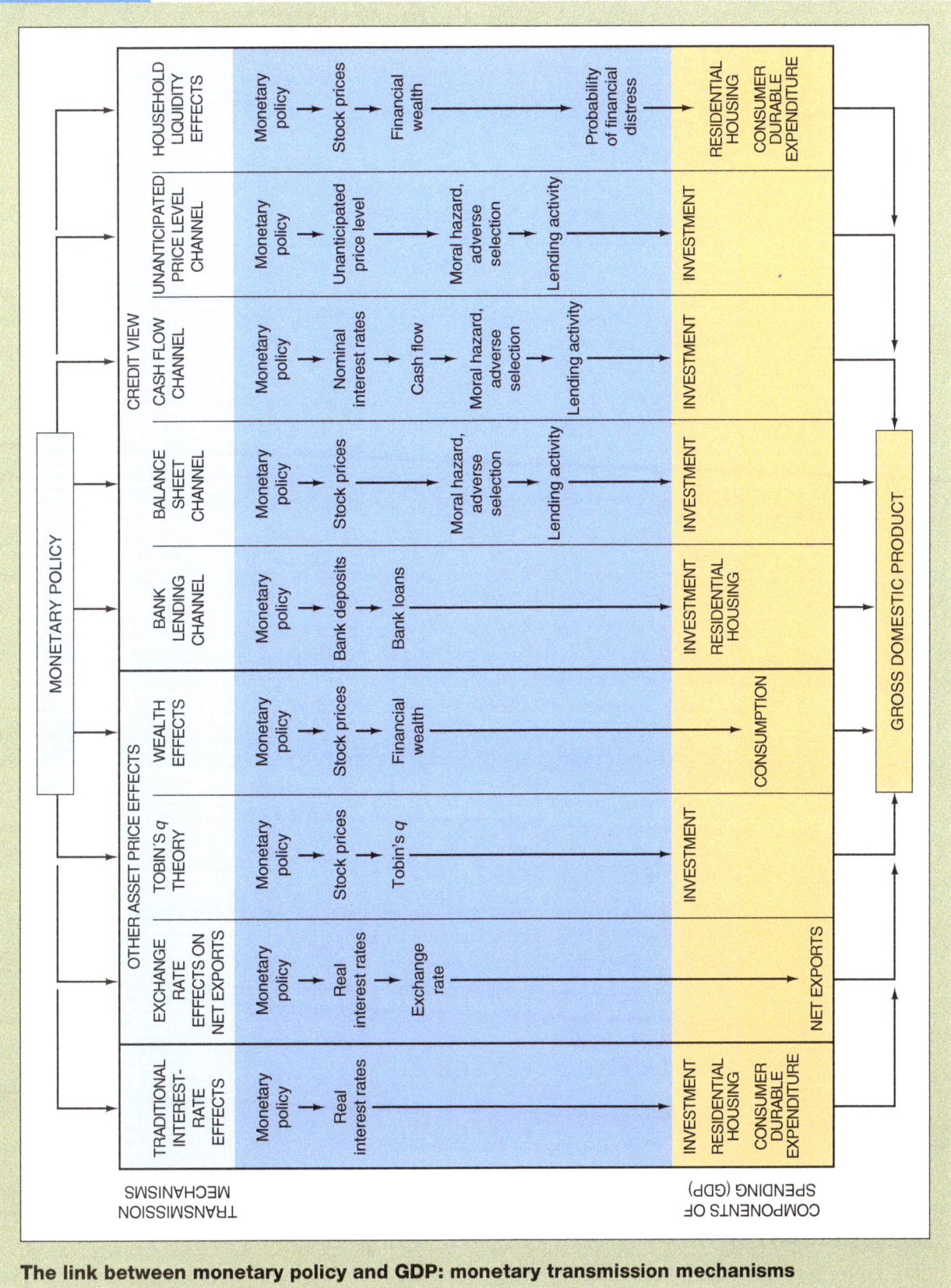

The link between monetary policy and GDP: monetary transmission mechanisms

policy is expansionary, the public finds that it has more money than it wants and so gets rid of it through spending. One place the public spends is in the stock market, increasing the demand for stocks and consequently raising their prices.[14] Combining this with the fact that higher stock prices (P_s) will lead to a higher q and thus higher investment spending I leads to the following transmission mechanism of monetary policy:[15]

$$\text{expansionary monetary policy} \Rightarrow P_s\uparrow \Rightarrow q\uparrow \Rightarrow I\uparrow \Rightarrow Y\uparrow \qquad (23.4)$$

Wealth effects

In their search for new monetary transmission mechanisms, researchers also looked at how consumers' balance sheets might affect their spending decisions. Franco Modigliani was the first to take this tack, using his famous life cycle hypothesis of consumption. **Consumption** is spending by consumers on non-durable goods and services.[16] It differs from *consumer expenditure* in that it does not include spending on consumer durables. The basic premise of Modigliani's theory is that consumers smooth out their consumption over time. Therefore, what determines consumption spending is the lifetime resources of consumers, not just today's income.

An important component of consumers' lifetime resources is their financial wealth, a major component of which is common stocks. When stock prices rise, the value of financial wealth increases, thereby increasing the lifetime resources of consumers, and consumption should rise. Considering that, as we have seen, expansionary monetary policy can lead to a rise in stock prices, we now have another monetary transmission mechanism:

$$\text{expansionary monetary policy} \Rightarrow P_s\uparrow \Rightarrow \text{wealth}\uparrow \Rightarrow \text{consumption}\uparrow \Rightarrow Y\uparrow \quad (23.5)$$

Modigliani's research found this relationship to be an extremely powerful mechanism that adds substantially to the potency of monetary policy.[17]

The wealth and Tobin's q channels allow for a general definition of equity, so they can also be applied to the housing market, where housing is equity. An increase in house prices, which raises their prices relative to replacement cost, leads to a rise in Tobin's q for housing, thereby stimulating its production. Similarly, housing and land prices are extremely important components of wealth, so rises in these prices increase wealth, thereby raising consumption. Monetary expansion, which raises land and housing prices through the Tobin's q and wealth mechanisms described here, thus leads to a rise in aggregate demand.

Credit view

Dissatisfaction with the conventional stories that interest-rate effects explain the impact of monetary policy on expenditures on durable assets has led to a new explanation based on the problem of asymmetric information in financial markets (see Chapter 8). This explanation, referred to as the *credit view*, proposes that two types of monetary transmission channels arise as a result of information problems in credit markets: those that operate through effects on bank lending and those that operate through effects on firms' and households' balance sheets.[18]

Bank lending channel

The bank lending channel is based on the analysis in Chapter 8, which demonstrated that banks play a special role in the financial system because they are especially well suited to solve asymmetric information problems in credit markets. Because of banks' special role, certain borrowers will not have access to the credit markets unless they borrow from banks. As long as there is no perfect substitutability of retail bank deposits with other sources of funds, the bank lending channel of monetary transmission operates as follows: expansionary monetary policy, which increases bank reserves and bank deposits, increases the quantity of bank loans available. Because many borrowers are dependent on bank loans to finance their activities, this increase in loans will cause investment (and possibly consumer) spending to rise. Schematically, the monetary policy effect is

$$\text{expansionary monetary policy} \Rightarrow \text{bank deposits} \uparrow$$
$$\Rightarrow \text{bank loans} \uparrow \Rightarrow I \uparrow \Rightarrow Y \uparrow \qquad (23.6)$$

An important implication of the credit view is that monetary policy will have a greater effect on expenditure by smaller firms, which are more dependent on bank loans, than it will on large firms, which can get funds directly through stock and bond markets (and not only through banks).

Though this result has been confirmed by researchers, doubts about the bank lending channel have been raised in the literature, and there are reasons to suspect that this channel may not be as powerful as it once was.[19] The first reason is that current regulations no longer impose restrictions on banks that hinder their ability to raise funds.[20] Nowadays banks have easy access to wholesale money markets to meet their funding needs, and large banks can issue bonds and CDs. Second, the worldwide decline of the traditional bank business of making loans funded by deposits has rendered the bank lending channel less potent. As discussed in Chapter 12, some of this business has been replaced by a shadow banking system in which bank lending has been replaced by lending via the securities markets.

Despite these trends, many economists still believe that this channel plays an important role in the monetary transmission mechanism, above all in those countries with a bank-based financial system. Table 23.1 shows that at the end of 2009 bank loans in the euro area and the UK were respectively 142% and 195% of GDP, while for the US this ratio was 56%. Moreover, bank loans to non-financial corporations in the euro area and the UK were around 50% and 35%, respectively, whereas in the US they were only 22%. The fact that European firms rely much more on bank sources of financing is not only consistent with what we observed in Chapter 8, but also with the fact that the amount of outstanding debt securities issued by the non-financial corporations in the euro area was 8% of GDP, less than half of the same ratio in the US. With these figures in mind, it is not surprising that economists have found the bank lending channel is operative in euro countries.[21]

A lesson from the above discussion is that the structure of the financial system has crucial implications for the relative importance of the individual transmission channels and the overall effectiveness of monetary policy across countries. Unfortunately for policymakers and in particular central banks, financial systems evolve over time and this leads to changes in the impact of monetary policy that are difficult to quantify. In this respect, assessing how the financial structure is altering the monetary transmission mechanism is of fundamental importance.

TABLE 23.1

Bank loans and debt securities in the euro area, the UK and the US (% of GDP)

	Total bank loans (1)	Bank loans to non-financial corporations (2)	Debt securities issued by non-financial corporations (3)
Euro area	141.5	52.4	7.8
United Kingdom	194.6	34.7	1.0
United States	55.6	22.0	19.5

Sources: For the euro area and the US, the figures refer to the information provided in Table 2.8 and 2.13 of ECB (2011), *The Monetary Policy of the ECB*. UK bank loans are collected from the Bank of England and UK debt securities from the Bank for International Settlements (BIS). Data refer to the end of 2009.

Balance sheet channel

Like the bank lending channel, the balance sheet channel arises from the presence of asymmetric information problems in credit markets. In Chapter 8, we saw that the lower the net worth of business firms, the more severe the adverse selection and moral hazard problems in lending to these firms. Lower net worth means that lenders in effect have less collateral for their loans, so their potential losses from adverse selection are higher. A decline in net worth, which raises the adverse selection problem, thus leads to decreased lending to finance investment spending. The lower net worth of businesses also increases the moral hazard problem because it means that owners have a lower equity stake in their firms, giving them more incentive to engage in risky investment projects. Because taking on riskier investment projects makes it more likely that lenders will not be paid back, a decrease in businesses' net worth leads to a decrease in lending and hence in investment spending.

Monetary policy can affect firms' balance sheets in several ways. Expansionary monetary policy, which causes a rise in stock prices ($P_s\uparrow$) along the lines described earlier, raises the net worth of firms and so leads to higher investment spending ($I\uparrow$) and aggregate demand ($Y\uparrow$) because of the decrease in adverse selection and moral hazard problems. This leads to the following schematic for one balance sheet channel of monetary transmission:

$$\text{expansionary monetary policy} \Rightarrow P_s\uparrow \Rightarrow \text{firm's net worth}\uparrow \Rightarrow \text{adverse selection}\downarrow,$$
$$\text{moral hazard}\downarrow \Rightarrow \text{lending}\uparrow \Rightarrow I\uparrow \Rightarrow Y\uparrow \qquad (23.7)$$

Cash flow channel

Another balance sheet channel operates by affecting *cash flow*, the difference between cash receipts and cash expenditures. Expansionary monetary policy, which lowers nominal interest rates, also causes an improvement in firms' balance sheets because it raises cash flow. The rise in cash flow increases the liquidity of the firm (or household) and thus makes it easier for lenders to know whether the firm (or household) will be able to pay its bills. The result is that adverse selection and moral hazard problems become less severe, leading to an increase in lending and economic activity. The following schematic describes this additional balance sheet channel:

$$\text{expansionary monetary policy} \Rightarrow i\downarrow \Rightarrow \text{firms' cash flow}\uparrow \Rightarrow \text{adverse selection}\downarrow,$$
$$\text{moral hazard}\downarrow \Rightarrow \text{lending}\uparrow \Rightarrow I\uparrow \Rightarrow Y\uparrow \qquad (23.8)$$

An important feature of this transmission mechanism is that *nominal* interest rates affect firms' cash flow. Thus this interest-rate mechanism differs from the traditional interest-rate mechanism discussed earlier, in which the real interest rate affects investment. Furthermore, the short-term interest rate plays a special role in this transmission mechanism, because interest payments on short-term (rather than long-term) debt typically have the greatest impact on households' and firms' cash flow.

A related mechanism involving adverse selection through which expansionary monetary policy that lowers interest rates can stimulate aggregate output involves the credit-rationing phenomenon. As discussed in Chapter 10, credit rationing occurs in cases where borrowers are denied loans even when they are willing to pay a higher interest rate. This is because individuals and firms with the riskiest investment projects are exactly the ones that are willing to pay the highest interest rates, for if the high-risk investment succeeds, they will be the primary beneficiaries. Thus higher interest rates increase the adverse selection problem and lower interest rates reduce it. When expansionary monetary policy lowers interest rates, less risk-prone borrowers make up a higher fraction of those demanding loans, so lenders are more willing to lend, raising both investment and output, along the lines of parts of the schematic in Equation 23.8.

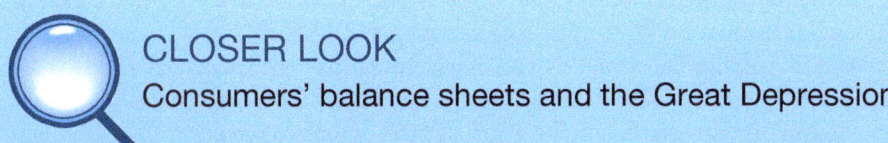

CLOSER LOOK
Consumers' balance sheets and the Great Depression

The years between 1929 and 1933 witnessed the worst deterioration in consumers' balance sheets ever seen in the United States. The stock market crash in 1929, which caused a slump that lasted until 1933, reduced the value of consumers' wealth by $737 billion (in 2000 dollars), and, as expected, consumption dropped sharply (by over $100 billion). Because of the decline in the price level in that period, the level of real debt consumers owed also increased sharply (by over 20%). Consequently, the value of financial assets relative to the amount of debt declined sharply, increasing the likelihood of financial distress. Not surprisingly, spending on consumer durables and housing fell precipitously: from 1929 to 1933, consumer durable expenditure declined by over 50%, while expenditure on housing declined by 80%.*

*For further discussion of the effect of consumers' balance sheets on spending during the Great Depression, see Frederic S. Mishkin, 'The household balance sheet and the Great Depression', *Journal of Economic History* 38 (1978): 918–37.

Unanticipated price level channel

A third balance sheet channel operates through monetary policy effects on the general price level. Because in industrialized countries debt payments are contractually fixed in nominal terms, an unanticipated rise in the price level lowers the value of firms' liabilities in real terms (decreases the burden of the debt) but should not lower the real value of the firms' assets. Monetary expansion that leads to an unanticipated rise in the price level ($P\uparrow$) therefore raises real net worth, which lowers adverse selection and moral hazard problems, thereby leading to a rise in investment spending and aggregate output as in the following schematic:

$$\text{expansionary monetary policy} \Rightarrow \text{unanticipated } P\uparrow \Rightarrow \text{firms' real net worth}\uparrow$$
$$\Rightarrow \text{adverse selection}\downarrow, \text{ moral hazard}\downarrow \Rightarrow \text{lending}\uparrow \Rightarrow I\uparrow \Rightarrow Y\uparrow \qquad (23.9)$$

The view that unanticipated movements in the price level affect aggregate output has a long tradition in economics: it is the key feature in the debt-deflation view of the Great Depression outlined in Chapter 9.

Household liquidity effects

Although most of the literature on the credit channel focuses on spending by businesses, the credit view should apply equally well to consumer spending, particularly on consumer durables and housing. Declines in bank lending induced by a monetary contraction should cause a decline in durables and housing purchases by consumers who do not have access to other sources of credit. Similarly, increases in interest rates cause a deterioration in household balance sheets, because consumers' cash flow is adversely affected.

Another way of looking at how the balance sheet channel may operate through consumers is to consider liquidity effects on consumer-durable and housing expenditures, which were found to be important factors during the Great Depression (see the 'Closer look' box, 'Consumers' balance sheets and the Great Depression'). In the liquidity effects view, balance sheet effects work through their impact on consumers' desire to spend rather than on lenders' desire to lend. Because of asymmetric information about their quality, consumer durables and housing are very illiquid assets. If, as a result of a bad income shock, consumers needed to sell their consumer durables or housing to raise money, they would expect a big loss because they could not get the full value of these assets in a distress sale. (This is just a manifestation of the lemons problem described in Chapter 8.) In contrast, if consumers held financial assets (such as money in the bank, stocks or bonds), they could easily sell them quickly for their full market value and raise the cash. Hence, if consumers expect a higher likelihood of finding themselves in financial distress, they would rather hold fewer illiquid consumer-durable or housing assets and more liquid financial assets.

A consumer's balance sheet should be an important influence on his or her estimate of the likelihood of suffering financial distress. Specifically, when consumers have a large amount of financial assets relative to their debts, their estimate of the probability of financial distress is low, and they will be more willing to purchase consumer durables or housing. When stock prices rise, the value of financial assets rises as well; consumer-durable expenditure will also rise because consumers have a more secure financial position and a lower estimate of the likelihood of suffering financial distress. This leads to another transmission mechanism for monetary policy, operating through the link between money and stock prices:[22]

$$\text{expansionary monetary policy} \Rightarrow P_s\uparrow \Rightarrow \text{value of households' financial assets}\uparrow$$
$$\Rightarrow \text{likelihood of financial distress}\downarrow$$
$$\Rightarrow \text{consumer–durable and housing expenditure}\uparrow \Rightarrow Y\uparrow \quad (23.10)$$

The illiquidity of consumer-durable and housing assets provides another reason why a monetary expansion, which lowers interest rates and thereby raises cash flow to consumers, leads to a rise in spending on consumer durables and housing. A rise in consumer cash flow decreases the likelihood of financial distress, which increases the desire of consumers to hold durable goods or housing, thus increasing spending on them and hence aggregate output. The only difference between this view of cash flow effects and that outlined in Equation 23.8 is that it is not the willingness of lenders to lend to consumers that causes expenditure to rise but the willingness of consumers to spend.

Why are credit channels likely to be important?

There are three reasons to believe that credit channels are important monetary transmission mechanisms. First, a large body of evidence on the behaviour of individual firms supports the view that credit market imperfections of the type crucial to the operation of credit channels do affect firms' employment and spending decisions.[23] Second, there is evidence that small firms (which are more likely to be credit-constrained) are hurt more by tight monetary policy than large firms, which are unlikely to be credit-constrained.[24] Third, and maybe most compelling, the asymmetric information view of credit market imperfections at the core of the credit channel analysis is a theoretical construct that has proved useful in explaining many other important phenomena, such as why many of our financial institutions exist, why our financial system has the structure that it has and why financial crises are so damaging to the economy (topics discussed in Chapters 8 and 9). The best support for a theory is its demonstrated usefulness in a wide range of applications. By this standard, the asymmetric information theory supporting the existence of credit channels as an important monetary transmission mechanism has much to recommend it.[25]

APPLICATION   The subprime recession and quantitative easing

With the advent of the subprime financial crisis in the summer of 2007, central banks around the world began a very aggressive easing of monetary policy. The Fed dropped the target federal funds rate from 5.25% to 0% over a fifteen-month period from September 2007 to December 2008. In a similar vein, the Bank of England (BoE) reduced the official bank rate from 5.75% to 0.5% from December 2007 to March 2009. The ECB reacted slightly later than the Fed and the BoE, but quite aggressively as well. Its main refinancing rate was dropped from 4.25% in July 2008 to 1% in May 2009. At first, it appeared that the central banks' actions would keep the growth slowdown mild and prevent a recession.

However, the economy proved to be weaker than expected, with a recession first hitting the US in December 2007, soon followed by an economic decline in the UK and the euro area countries. Why did the economy become so weak despite this unusually rapid reduction in the central banks' policy instrument?

The subprime meltdown led to negative effects on the economy from many of the channels we have outlined above. The rising level of subprime mortgage defaults, which led to a decline in the value of mortgage-backed securities and CDOs, led to large losses on the balance sheets of financial institutions. With weaker balance sheets, these financial institutions began to deleverage and cut back on their lending. With no one else to collect information and make loans, adverse selection and moral hazard problems increased in credit markets, leading to a slowdown of the economy. Credit spreads also went through the roof with the increase in uncertainty from failures of so many financial markets. The decline in the stock market and housing prices also weakened the economy, because it lowered household wealth. The decrease in household wealth led to restrained consumer spending and weaker investment, because of the resulting drop in Tobin's q.

With official interest rates almost at zero, and concerns about the risk of deflation associated with the severe recession, central banks started implementing unconventional policies (see Chapter 15 for a discussion). The Bank of England, for instance, directly injected money into the economy, primarily by purchasing government and corporate bonds from private sector institutions like insurance companies, pension funds, banks and non-financial firms (see the box 'Quantitative easing' in Chapter 15). But how can quantitative easing stimulate aggregate demand?

The underlying transmission channels are closely linked to what we have learned in this chapter.[26] First, by buying assets from banks, the central bank increases the holding of excess reserves of the banking sector, which, via the bank lending channel, leads to higher supply of lending to firms and households. Secondly, by buying gilts from non-banks (for example pension and insurance funds), a central bank increases the amount of cash in the portfolios of these institutions and incentivizes asset managers to invest in riskier instruments like corporate bonds and equities. This will push up the prices of these assets, stimulating consumption and investment through wealth, Tobin-q and balance-sheet effects. Moreover higher asset prices lead also to lower yields which make it cheaper for companies to raise finance from the capital market. The effectiveness of this 'portfolio balance' effect is thought to have been important in the UK.

Quantitative easing can also reinforce the traditional interest rate channel. Asset purchase programmes may signal future intentions about the likely path of policy rates. For instance, with its asset purchase programme the Bank of England, although not committing to maintain policy rates low in the future as the Fed did (see Chapter 15), gave a clear signal that it would have maintained a loose monetary policy. On the one side, these signals can have immediate effects on lowering long-term rates due to market participants' expectations of low future short-term rates. On the other side, by signalling its determination to avoid the risk of inflation falling below the medium-term target, the Bank of England managed to increase inflation expectations, that with nominal interest rates at very low levels contributed to lower real interest rates (see Figure 23.2).

The overall effects of QE are difficult to quantify as uncertainty remains of what would have happened in the absence of these actions. Nevertheless, the predominant view is that these unconventional measures helped to prevent further disruptions in the financial system, and contributed to preventing the risk of deflation. ■

Lessons for monetary policy

What useful implications for central banks' conduct of monetary policy can we draw from the analysis in this chapter? There are four basic lessons to be learned.

1 It is dangerous always to associate the easing or the tightening of monetary policy with a fall or a rise in short-term nominal interest rates. Because most central banks use short-term nominal interest rates – typically, the interbank rate – as the key operating instrument for monetary policy, there is a danger that central banks and the public will focus too much on short-term nominal interest rates as an indicator of the stance of monetary policy. Indeed, it is quite common to see statements that always associate monetary tightenings with a rise in the interbank rate and monetary easings with a decline in the rate. This view is highly problematic, because – as we have seen in our discussion of the Great Depression period – movements in nominal interest rates do not always correspond to movements in real interest rates, yet it is typically the real and not the nominal interest rate that is an element in the channel of monetary policy transmission. For example, we have seen that during the contraction phase of the Great Depression, short-term interest rates fell to near zero, yet real interest rates were extremely high. Short-term interest rates that are near zero therefore do not indicate that monetary policy is easy if the economy is undergoing deflation, as was true during the contraction phase of the Great Depression. As Milton Friedman and Anna Schwartz have emphasized, the period of near-zero short-term interest rates during the contraction phase of the Great Depression was one of highly contractionary monetary policy, rather than the reverse.

2 Other asset prices besides those on short-term debt instruments contain important information about the stance of monetary policy because they are important elements in various monetary policy transmission mechanisms. As we have seen in this chapter, economists have come a long way in understanding that other asset prices besides interest rates have major effects on aggregate demand. As we saw in Figure 23.3, other asset prices, such as stock prices, foreign exchange rates, and housing and land prices, play an important role in monetary transmission mechanisms. Furthermore, the discussion of such additional channels as those operating through the exchange rate, Tobin's q and wealth effects provides additional reasons why other asset prices play such an important role in the monetary transmission mechanisms. Although there are strong disagreements among economists about which channels of monetary transmission are the most important – not surprising, given that economists, particularly those in academia, always like to disagree – they do agree that other asset prices play an important role in the way monetary policy affects the economy.

The view that other asset prices besides short-term interest rates matter has important implications for monetary policy. When we try to assess the stance of policy, it is critical that we look at other asset prices in addition to short-term interest rates. For example, if short-term interest rates are low or even zero and yet stock prices are low, land prices are low, and the value of the domestic currency is high, monetary policy is clearly tight, not easy.

3 Monetary policy can be highly effective in reviving a weak economy even if short-term interest rates are already near zero. We have recently entered a world where inflation is not always the norm. Japan, for example, recently experienced a period of deflation when the price level was actually falling. One common view is that when a central bank has driven down short-term nominal interest rates to near zero, there is nothing more that monetary policy can do to stimulate the economy. The transmission mechanisms of monetary policy described here indicate that this view is false. As our discussion of the factors that affect the monetary base in Chapter 14 indicated, expansionary monetary policy to increase liquidity in the economy can be conducted with open market purchases, which do not have to be solely in short-term government securities. For example, purchases of foreign currencies, like purchases of government bonds, lead to an increase in the monetary base and in the money supply. Moreover, as experienced in the recent quantitative easing policies following the financial crisis, central banks can also focus their asset purchases on long-term bonds, reducing yields and making it cheaper for companies to raise finance. This increased liquidity and a commitment to future expansionary monetary policy helps revive the economy by raising general price-level expectations and by deflating other asset prices, which then stimulate aggregate demand through the channels outlined

here. Therefore, monetary policy can be a potent force for reviving economies that are undergoing deflation and have short-term interest rates near zero. Indeed, because of the lags inherent in fiscal policy and the political constraints on its use, expansionary monetary policy is the key policy action required to revive an economy experiencing deflation.

4 Avoiding unanticipated fluctuations in the price level is an important objective of monetary policy, thus providing a rationale for price stability as the primary long-run goal for monetary policy. As we saw in Chapter 16, central banks in recent years have been putting greater emphasis on price stability as the primary long-run goal for monetary policy. Several rationales have been proposed for this goal, including the undesirable effects of uncertainty about the future price level on business decisions and hence on productivity, distortions associated with the interaction of nominal contracts and the tax system with inflation, and increased social conflict stemming from inflation. The discussion here of monetary transmission mechanisms provides an additional reason why price stability is so important. As we have seen, unanticipated movements in the price level can cause unanticipated fluctuations in output, an undesirable outcome. Particularly important in this regard is the knowledge that, as we saw in Chapter 9, price deflation can be an important factor leading to a prolonged financial crisis, as occurred during the Great Depression. An understanding of the monetary transmission mechanisms thus makes it clear that the goal of price stability is desirable, because it reduces uncertainty about the future price level. Thus the price stability goal implies that a negative inflation rate is at least as undesirable as too high an inflation rate. Indeed, because of the threat of financial crises, central banks must work very hard to prevent price deflation.

APPLICATION Applying the monetary policy lessons to Japan

Until 1990, it looked as if Japan might overtake the United States in per capita income. Since then, the Japanese economy has been stagnating, with deflation and low growth. As a result, Japanese living standards have been falling further and further behind those in the United States. Many economists take the view that Japanese monetary policy is in part to blame for the poor performance of the Japanese economy. Could applying the four lessons outlined in the previous section have helped Japanese monetary policy perform better?

The first lesson suggests that it is dangerous to think that declines in interest rates always mean that monetary policy has been easing. In the mid-1990s, when short-term interest rates began to decline, falling to near zero in the late 1990s and early 2000s, the monetary authorities in Japan took the view that monetary policy was sufficiently expansionary. Now it is widely recognized that this view was incorrect, because the falling and eventually negative inflation rates in Japan meant that real interest rates were actually quite high and that monetary policy was tight, not easy. If the monetary authorities in Japan had followed the advice of the first lesson, they might have pursued a more expansionary monetary policy, which would have helped boost the economy.

The second lesson suggests that monetary policymakers should pay attention to other asset prices in assessing the stance of monetary policy. At the same time interest rates were falling in Japan, stock and real estate prices were collapsing, thus providing another indication that Japanese monetary policy was not easy. Recognizing the second lesson might have led Japanese monetary policymakers to recognize sooner that they needed a more expansionary monetary policy.

The third lesson indicates that monetary policy can still be effective even if short-term interest rates are near zero. Officials at the Bank of Japan have frequently claimed that they have been helpless in stimulating the economy, because short-term interest rates had fallen to near zero. Recognizing that monetary policy can still be effective even when interest rates are near zero, as the third lesson suggests, would have helped them to take monetary policy actions that would have stimulated aggregate demand by raising other asset prices and inflationary expectations.

The fourth lesson indicates that unanticipated fluctuations in the price level should be avoided. If the Japanese monetary authorities had adhered to this lesson, they might have recognized that allowing deflation to occur could be very damaging to the economy and would be inconsistent with the goal of price stability. Indeed, critics of the Bank of Japan have suggested that the bank should announce an inflation target to promote the price stability objective, but the bank has resisted this suggestion.

Heeding the advice from the four lessons in the previous section might have led to a far more successful conduct of monetary policy in Japan in recent years.[27] ■

Summary

1 There are two basic types of empirical evidence: structural model evidence and reduced-form evidence. Both have advantages and disadvantages. The main advantage of structural model evidence is that it provides us with an understanding of how the economy works and gives us more confidence in the direction of causation between money and output. However, if the structure is not correctly specified, because it ignores important monetary transmission mechanisms, it could seriously underestimate the effectiveness of monetary policy. Reduced-form evidence has the advantage of not restricting the way monetary policy affects economic activity and so may be more likely to capture the full effects of monetary policy. However, reduced-form evidence cannot rule out the possibility of reverse causation or an outside driving factor, which could lead to misleading conclusions about the importance of money.

2 The early Keynesians believed that money does not matter, because they found weak links between interest rates and investment and because low interest rates on Treasury securities convinced them that monetary policy was easy during the worst economic contraction in US history, the Great Depression. Monetarists objected to this interpretation of the evidence on the grounds that (a) the focus on nominal rather than real interest rates may have obscured any link between interest rates and investment; (b) interest-rate effects on investment might be only one of many channels through which monetary policy affects aggregate demand; and (c) by the standards of real interest rates and interest rates on lower-grade bonds, monetary policy was extremely contractionary during the Great Depression.

3 Early monetarist evidence falls into three categories: timing, statistical and historical. Because of reverse causation and outside-factor possibilities, some serious doubts exist regarding conclusions that can be drawn from timing and statistical evidence alone. However, some of the historical evidence in which exogenous declines in money growth are followed by recessions provides stronger support for the monetarist position that money matters. As a result of empirical research, Keynesian and monetarist opinion has converged to the view that money does matter to aggregate economic activity and the price level. However, Keynesians do not agree with the monetarist position that money is *all* that matters.

4 The transmission mechanisms of monetary policy include traditional interest-rate channels that operate through the cost of capital and affect investment; other asset price channels such as exchange rate effects, Tobin's q theory and wealth effects; and the credit view channels – the bank lending channel, the balance sheet channel, the cash flow channel, the unanticipated price level channel and household liquidity effects.

5 Four lessons for monetary policy can be drawn from this chapter: (a) it is dangerous always to associate monetary policy easing or tightening with a fall or a rise in short-term nominal interest rates; (b) other asset prices besides those on short-term debt instruments contain important information about the stance of monetary policy because they are important elements in the monetary policy transmission mechanisms; (c) monetary policy can be highly effective in reviving a weak economy even if short-term interest rates are already near zero; and (d) avoiding unanticipated fluctuations in the price level is an important objective of monetary policy, thus providing a rationale for price stability as the primary long-run goal for monetary policy.

Key terms

consumer durable expenditure p. 537

consumption p. 542

credit view p. 540

pass-through p. 538

reduced-form evidence p. 526

reverse causation p. 528

structural model p. 526

structural model evidence p. 525

transmission mechanisms of monetary policy p. 526

QUESTIONS AND PROBLEMS

All questions and problems are available in MyEconLab at **www.myeconlab.com/mishkin.**

1 Suppose that a researcher is trying to determine whether jogging is good for a person's health. She examines this question in two ways. In method A, she examines whether joggers live longer than non-joggers. In method B, she examines whether jogging reduces cholesterol in the bloodstream and lowers blood pressure; then she asks whether lower cholesterol and blood pressure prolong life. Which of these two methods will produce reduced-form evidence and which will produce structural model evidence?

2 If research indicates that joggers do not have lower cholesterol and blood pressure than non-joggers, is it still possible that jogging is good for your health? Give a concrete example.

3 If research indicates that joggers live longer than non-joggers, is it possible that jogging is not good for your health? Give a concrete example.

4 Suppose that you plan to buy a car and want to know whether a BMW car is more reliable than a Volkswagen. One way to find out is to ask owners of both cars how often their cars go in for repairs. Another way is to visit the factories producing the cars and see which one is built better. Which procedure will provide reduced-form evidence and which structural model evidence?

5 If the BMW car you plan to buy has a better repair record than a Volkswagen, does this mean that the BMW car is necessarily more reliable? (BMW car owners might, for example, change their oil more frequently than Volkswagen owners.)

6 Suppose that when you visit the BMW and Volkswagen car factories to examine how the cars are built, you have time only to see how well the engine is put together. If Volkswagen engines are better built than BMW engines, does that mean that the Volkswagen will be more reliable than the BMW car?

7 How might bank behaviour (described in Chapter 14) lead to causation running from output to the money

supply? What does this say about evidence that finds a strong correlation between money and output?

8 What operating procedures of the central banks (described in Chapter 16) might explain how movements in output could cause movements in the money supply?

9 'In every business cycle in the past 100 years, the rate at which the money supply is growing always decreases before output does. Therefore, the money supply causes business cycle movements.' Do you agree? What objections can you raise against this argument?

10 How did the research strategies of Keynesian and monetarist economists differ after they were exposed to the earliest monetarist evidence?

11 In the recent subprime recession, the value of ordinary shares in real terms fell dramatically. How might this decline in the stock market have affected aggregate demand and thus contributed to the severity of this recession? Be specific about the mechanisms through which the stock market decline affected the economy.

12 'The cost of financing investment is related only to interest rates; therefore, the only way that monetary policy can affect investment spending is through its effects on interest rates.' Is this statement true, false, or uncertain? Explain your answer.

13 Predict what will happen to stock prices if the money supply rises. Explain why you are making this prediction.

14 Franco Modigliani found that the most important transmission mechanisms of monetary policy involve consumer expenditure. Describe how at least two of these mechanisms work.

15 'The monetarists have demonstrated that the early Keynesians were wrong in saying that money doesn't matter at all to economic activity. Therefore, we should accept the monetarist position that money is all that matters.' Do you agree? Why or why not?

WEB EXERCISES

1 The introduction of the euro required the ECB to work out its own monetary transmission mechanism. Using both the official monetary transmission mechanism page

(**www.ecb.europa.eu/mopo/intro/transmission/html/ index.en.html**) and selected ECB articles (for example, 'Monetary policy transmission in the euro area, a decade after the introduction of the euro', *ECB Monthly Bulletin* article, May 2010 (**http://www.ecb.europa.eu/pub/pdf/ other/mb201005en_pp85-98en.pdf**), summarise the key features of the transmission channels of monetary policy decisions within the euro area.

2 Figure 23.1 shows the relationship between estimated real interest rates and nominal interest rates. Go to **www .martincapital.com** and click on 'US financial data', then on 'US financial charts' and finally to 'Charts on nominal versus real interest rates' to find data showing the spread between real interest rates and nominal interest rates. Discuss how the current spread differs from that shown most recently in Figure 23.1. What are the implications of this change?

3 Figure 23.3 discusses business cycles. Go to the CEPR's Euro Area Business Cycle Dating Committee **www.cepr. org/data/dating/** and review the material reported on recessions.

(a) What is the formal definition of a recession?

(b) What are the problems with the definition?

(c) How does the CEPR's methods compare to three Ds used by the National Bureau of Economic Research (NBER) to define a recession in the United States (**http://www. econlib.org/library/Enc1/Recessions.html**)?

(d) Review Chart 1. What trend is apparent about the length of recessions in the euro area and the United States?

4 Go to **http://sdw.ecb.europa.eu** and click on 'Money Banking and Financial Markets' and then on 'MFI interest rate' to find data showing the loans and deposits interest rates in the Euro area countries. Download some key retail interest rates of two eurozone countries of your choice and plot them against the EONIA and the three-month Euribor interest rates. Discuss whether the two countries differ from each other in terms of the bank pass-through. Can you name country-specific factors justifying these differences?

5 Go to **www.bankofengland.co.uk/publications/other/ monetary/montrans.pdf** and read this document which provides a discussion of the monetary transmission mechanism in the United Kingdom. Try to answer the following questions:

(a) What would be the effect of an increase in official interest rates if all mortgages were fixed-interest-rate loans?

(b) How does an interest rate rise alter the disposable income (and as a result the consumption) of borrowers and savers?

(c) What is the order of magnitude of the impact of a policy change on GDP?

Notes

1 Another example is provided in the US. Before 1980, the so-called Regulation Q was still in effect. This regulation imposed restrictions on interest payments on savings deposits, meaning that the average consumer would not earn more on savings when interest rates rose. Since the termination of Regulation Q, the average consumer now earns more on savings when interest rates rise. If we understand how changes in the interest rates paid on savings affect consumer spending, we might be able to say that a change in monetary policy, which affects interest rates, will have a different effect today than it would have had before 1980.

2 Milton Friedman and Anna Jacobson Schwartz, *A Monetary History of the United States, 1867–1960* (Princeton, NJ: Princeton University Press, 1963).

3 In the 1980s, real interest rates rose to exceedingly high levels, approaching those of the Great Depression period. Research has tried to explain this phenomenon, some of which points to monetary policy as the source of high real rates in the 1980s. For example, see Oliver J. Blanchard and Lawrence H. Summers, 'Perspectives on high world interest rates', *Brookings Papers on Economic Activity* 2 (1984): 273–324; and John Huizinga and Frederic S. Mishkin, 'Monetary policy regime shifts and the unusual behavior of real interest rates', *Carnegie-Rochester Conference Series on Public Policy* 24 (1986): 231–74.

4 Milton Friedman and Anna Jacobson Schwartz, 'Money and business cycles', *Review of Economics and Statistics* 45, Suppl. (1963): 32–64.

5 A famous article by James Tobin, 'Money and income: *post hoc, ergo propter hoc*', *Quarterly Journal of Economics* 84

(1970): 301–17, describes an economic system in which changes in aggregate output cause changes in the growth rate of money but changes in the growth rate of money have no effect on output. Tobin shows that such a system with reverse causation could yield timing evidence similar to that found by Friedman and Schwartz.

6 Milton Friedman and David Meiselman, 'The relative stability of monetary velocity and the investment multiplier', in *Stabilization Policies*, ed. Commission on Money and Credit (Upper Saddle River, NJ: Prentice-Hall, 1963), pp. 165–268

7 Friedman and Meiselman did not actually run their tests using the *Y* variable because they felt that this gave an unfair advantage to the Keynesian model in that A is included in *Y*. Instead, they subtracted A from *Y* and tested for the correlation of *Y* – A with M or A.

8 See, for example, Albert Ando and Franco Modigliani, 'The relative stability of monetary velocity and the investment multiplier', *American Economic Review* 55 (1965): 693–728.

9 See William Poole and Edith Kornblith, 'The Friedman–Meiselman CMC paper: new evidence on an old controversy', *American Economic Review* 63 (1973): 908–17.

10 Christina Romer and David Romer, 'Does monetary policy matter? A new test in the spirit of Friedman and Schwartz', *NBER Macroeconomics Annual, 1989*, 4, ed. Stanley Fischer (Cambridge, MA.: MIT Press, 1989), pp. 121–70.

11 The most prominent example of more sophisticated reduced-form research is the St. Louis model, which was developed at the Federal Reserve Bank of St. Louis in the

late 1960s and early 1970s. It provided support for the monetarist position, but is subject to the same criticisms of reduced-form evidence outlined in the text. The St. Louis model was first outlined in Leonall Andersen and Jerry Jordan, 'Monetary and fiscal actions: a test of their relative importance in economic stabilization', *Federal Reserve Bank of St. Louis Review* 50 (November 1968): 11–23.

12 See John Taylor, 'The monetary transmission mechanism: an empirical framework', *Journal of Economic Perspectives* 9 (Fall 1995): 11–26, and Ben Bernanke and Mark Gertler, 'Inside the black box: the credit channel of monetary policy transmission', *Journal of Economic Perspectives* 9 (Fall 1995): 27–48.

13 For example, see Ralph Bryant, Peter Hooper and Catherine Mann, *Evaluating Policy Regimes: New Empirical Research in Empirical Macroeconomics* (Washington, DC: Brookings Institution, 1993); and John B. Taylor, *Macro-economic Policy in a World Economy: From Econometric Design to Practical Operation* (New York: Norton, 1993).

14 See James Tobin, 'A general equilibrium approach to monetary theory', *Journal of Money, Credit, and Banking* 1 (1969): 15–29. A somewhat more Keynesian story with the same outcome is that the increase in the money supply lowers interest rates on bonds so that the yields on alternatives to stocks fall. This makes stocks more attractive relative to bonds, so demand for them increases, raises their price, and thereby lowers their yield.

15 An alternative way of looking at the link between stock prices and investment spending is that higher stock prices lower the yield on stocks and reduce the cost of financing investment spending through issuing equity. This way of looking at the link between stock prices and investment spending is formally equivalent to Tobin's q theory; see Barry Bosworth, 'The stock market and the economy', *Brookings Papers on Economic Activity* 2 (1975): 257–90.

16 Consumption also includes another small component, the services that a consumer receives from the ownership of housing and consumer durables.

17 See Franco Modigliani, 'Monetary policy and consumption', in *Consumer Spending and Money Policy: The Linkages* (Boston: Federal Reserve Bank, 1971), pp. 9–84.

18 Surveys of the credit view can be found in Ben Bernanke, 'Credit in the macroeconomy', *Federal Reserve Bank of New York Quarterly Review* (Spring 1993): 50–70; Ben Bernanke and Mark Gertler, 'Inside the black box: the credit channel of monetary policy transmission', *Journal of Economic Perspectives* 9 (Fall 1995): 27–48; Stephen G. Cecchetti, 'Distinguishing theories of the monetary transmission mechanism', *Federal Reserve Bank of St. Louis Review* 77 (May – June 1995): 83–97; and R. Glenn Hubbard, 'Is there a 'credit channel' for monetary policy?', *Federal Reserve Bank of St. Louis Review* 77 (May–June 1995): 63–74.

19 For example, see Valerie Ramey, 'How important is the credit channel in the transmission of monetary policy?', *Carnegie-Rochester Conference Series on Public Policy* 39 (1993): 1–45; and Allan H. Meltzer, 'Monetary, credit (and other) transmission processes: a monetarist perspective', *Journal of Economic Perspectives* 9 (Fall 1995): 49–72.

20 The US provides a good example in this respect. Prior to the mid-1980s, certificates of deposit (CDs) were subjected to reserve requirements and Regulation Q deposit rate ceilings, which made it hard for US banks to replace deposits that flowed out of the banking system during a monetary contraction. With these regulatory restrictions abolished, banks can more easily respond to a decline in bank reserves and a loss of retail deposits by issuing CDs at market interest rates that do not have to be backed up by required reserves.

21 See Michael Ehrmann, Leonardo Gambacorta, Jorge Martinez-Pages, Patrick Sevestre and Andreas Worms, 'Financial systems and the role of banks in monetary policy transmission in the euro area', in Ignazio Angeloni, Anil K Kashyap and Benoit Mojon, eds, *Monetary Policy Transmission in the Euro Area* (Cambridge: Cambridge University Press, 2003).

22 See Frederic S. Mishkin, 'What depressed the consumer? The household balance sheet and the 1973–1975 recession', *Brookings Papers on Economic Activity* 1 (1977): 123–64.

23 For a survey of this evidence, see R. Glenn Hubbard, 'Is there a "credit channel" for monetary policy?', and Ignazio Angeloni, Anil K. Kashyap and Benoit Mojon, eds, *Monetary Policy Transmission in the Euro Area* (Cambridge: Cambridge University Press, 2003).

24 See Mark Gertler and Simon Gilchrist, 'Monetary policy, business cycles, and the behavior of small manufacturing firms', *Quarterly Journal of Economics* 109 (May 1994): 309–40. There is also some empirical evidence that small banks are less capable to issue bonds and CDs and the bank lending channel operating through these banks might be stronger. See Anil Kashyap and Jeremy Stein, 'What do a million observations on banks say about the transmission of monetary policy', *American Economic Review* 90 (June 2000): 407–28.

25 Recently a new channel of monetary transmission has been proposed by the literature, the so-called 'risk-taking channel'. The latter stresses the fact that changes in the policy rate may affect economic activity by changing the risk-taking capacity of financial intermediaries, thus shifting market risk premiums and the supply of credit. For instance, with low nominal interest rates (and as a result reduced interest rate margins) bank-asset managers may 'search for yields' and be incentivized to switch to riskier assets with higher expected returns. Additionally, low interest rates may boost asset and collateral values as well as incomes and profits, which in turn can reduce risk perceptions and/or increase risk tolerance, which encourages risk taking. These mechanisms are extensively discussed in Raghuram Rajan, 'Has financial development made the world riskier?', *NBER Working Paper*, no. 11728 (2005), Claudio Borio and Haibin Zhu, 'Capital regulation, risk-taking and monetary policy: a missing link in the transmission mechanism?', *Bank for International Settlements Working Paper*, no. 268 (2008), and Tobias Adrian and H. Song Shin, 'Financial intermediaries and monetary economics', in B.M. Friedman and M. Woodford, eds, *Handbook of Monetary Economics*, Vol. 3 (Amsterdam: Elsevier, 2010).

26 A detailed description of the quantitative easing policy of the Bank of England is contained in Michael Joyce, Matthew Tong and Robert Woods, 'The United Kingdom's quantitative easing policy: design, operation and impact', *Bank of England Quarterly Bulletin* (2011): 200–12.

27 For a more detailed critique of recent monetary policy in Japan, see Takatoshi Ito and Frederic S. Mishkin, 'Two decades of Japanese monetary policy and the deflation problem', *National Bureau of Economic Research Working Paper No. 10878* (November 2004).

Useful websites

www.ecb.europa.eu/mopo/intro/transmission/html/index.en.html The ECB outlines its transmission mechanism of monetary policy.

http://sdw.ecb.europa.eu The Statistical Data Warehouse (SDW) of the ECB providing retail banks' interest rates for the euro area countries.

www.ecb.europa.eu/stats/keyind/html/sdds.en.html Provides euro area economic and financial data collected by Eurostat and the ECB.

www.cepr.org/data/dating/ Website documenting the official recessions of the euro area.

http://www.ons.gov.uk/ons/datasets-and-tables/index.html Provides all data collected by the UK national statistics office.

http://www.nber.org/cycles.html NBER's official designation of US Business Cycle Expansions and Contractions.

CHAPTER 24

Money and inflation

PREVIEW

Since the early 1960s, when the inflation rate hovered between 1% and 4%, the UK has suffered from higher and more variable rates of inflation. By the late 1960s, the inflation rate had climbed beyond 5%, and by 1974, it reached the double-digit level. Following a peak of nearly 25% in 1975 inflation rates remained at very high levels until the early 1980s. After strong anti-inflationary policies the remainder of the decade saw a slowdown of inflation to around 6%. In the 1990s the UK experienced a further decline of inflation to around 4%. This downward trend extended into the new century, however with a slight reversal in 2008 and 2011 when inflation climbed above the 4% level. Inflation, the condition of a continually rising price level, has become a major concern of politicians and the public, and how to control it frequently dominates the discussion of economic policy.

How do we prevent the inflationary fire from igniting and end the roller-coaster ride in the inflation rate of the past 40 years? Milton Friedman provided an answer in his famous proposition that 'inflation is always and everywhere a monetary phenomenon'. He postulated that the source of all inflation episodes is a high growth rate of the money supply: simply by reducing the growth rate of the money supply to low levels, inflation can be prevented.

In this chapter, we use aggregate demand and supply analysis from Chapter 22 to reveal the role of monetary policy in creating inflation. You will find that as long as inflation is defined as the condition of a continually and rapidly rising price level, almost all economists agree with Friedman's proposition that inflation is a monetary phenomenon.

But what *causes* inflation? How does inflationary monetary policy come about? You will see that inflationary monetary policy is an offshoot of other government policies: the attempt to hit high employment targets or the running of large budget deficits. Examining how these policies lead to inflation will point us toward ways of preventing it at minimum cost in terms of unemployment and output loss.

Money and inflation: evidence

The evidence for Friedman's statement is straightforward. *Whenever a country's inflation rate is extremely high for a sustained period of time, its rate of money supply growth is also extremely high*. Indeed, this is exactly what we saw in Figure 1.6, which shows that countries with the highest inflation rates have also had the highest rates of money growth. The long-run relationship between the average inflation rate and the average rate of money growth is even clearer when looking at a large sample of 110 countries, as shown in Figure 24.1. The graph indicates a positive, essentially one-to-one, correlation between money growth and inflation, which shows that the countries with the highest inflation rates have also the highest rates of money growth. This link is apparent not only on a

FIGURE 24.1

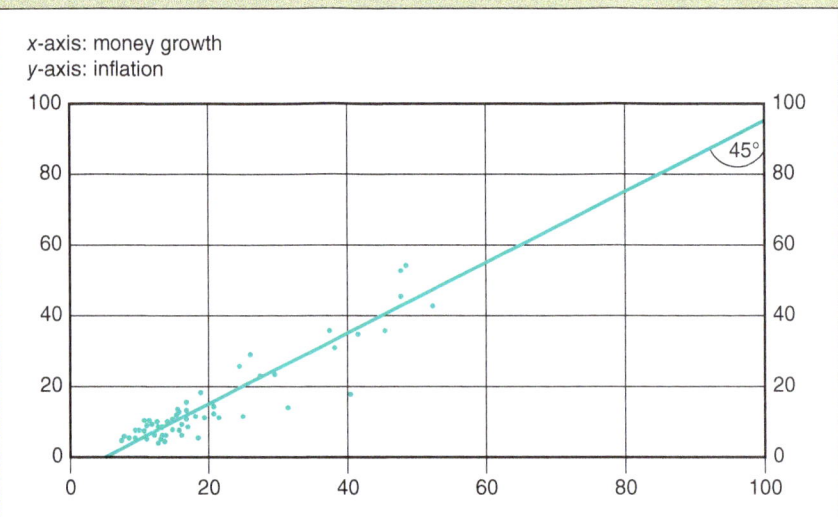

Average inflation rate versus average rate of money growth for 110 countries, 1960–90

Source: George McCandless and Warren Weber, *Some monetary facts*, Federal Reserve Bank of Minneapolis Quarterly Review, 19, 3 (1995): 1–11. Money growth is based on the monetary aggregate M2. Data from IMF.

cross-section of countries but also over time. For instance, Figure 24.2 shows that money growth and inflation in the United Kingdom moved closely together for most of the period going from 1875 to 2009. However, it seems that the relationship between inflation and money growth has weakened over the low-inflation period prevailing since the mid-1980s.[1] Figure 24.3 shows the money growth and inflation in the euro area from 1975 till 2010. We can clearly see that there is a robust long-run relationship between monetary growth and inflation, which is consistent with the prominent role of money in the ECB monetary policy strategy (see Chapter 16 for a full discussion).

FIGURE 24.2

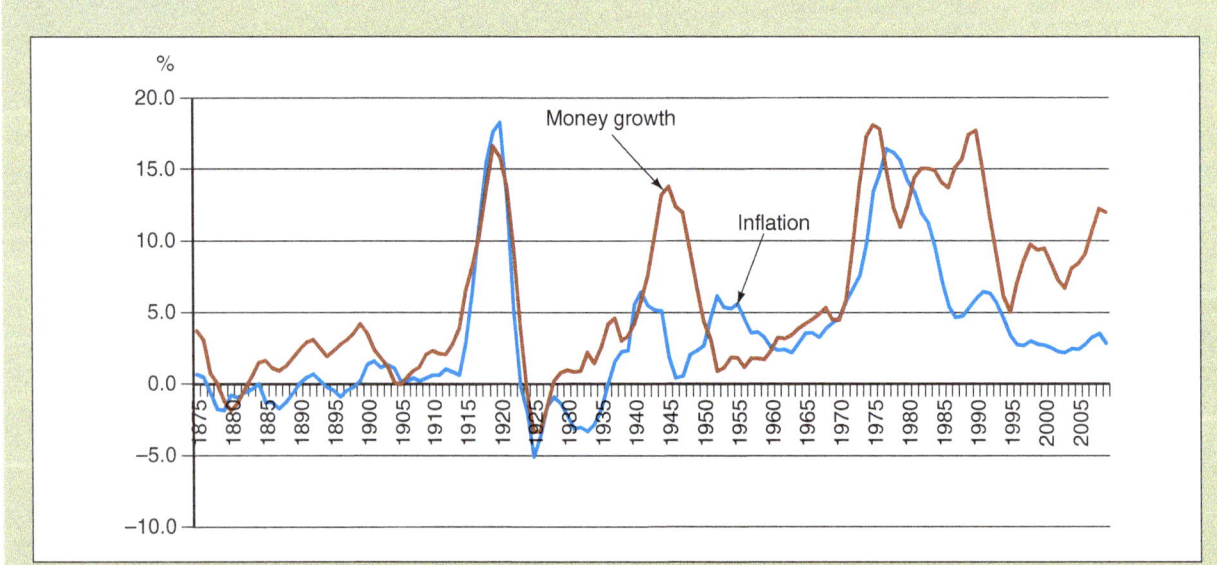

Inflation and money growth in the UK, 1875–2009

Source: Luca Benati, Long run evidence on money growth and inflation, ECB Working Paper Series No. 1027 (2009). Five-year moving averages of annual percentage changes. Information may be obtained free of charges through the ECB's website.

FIGURE 24.3

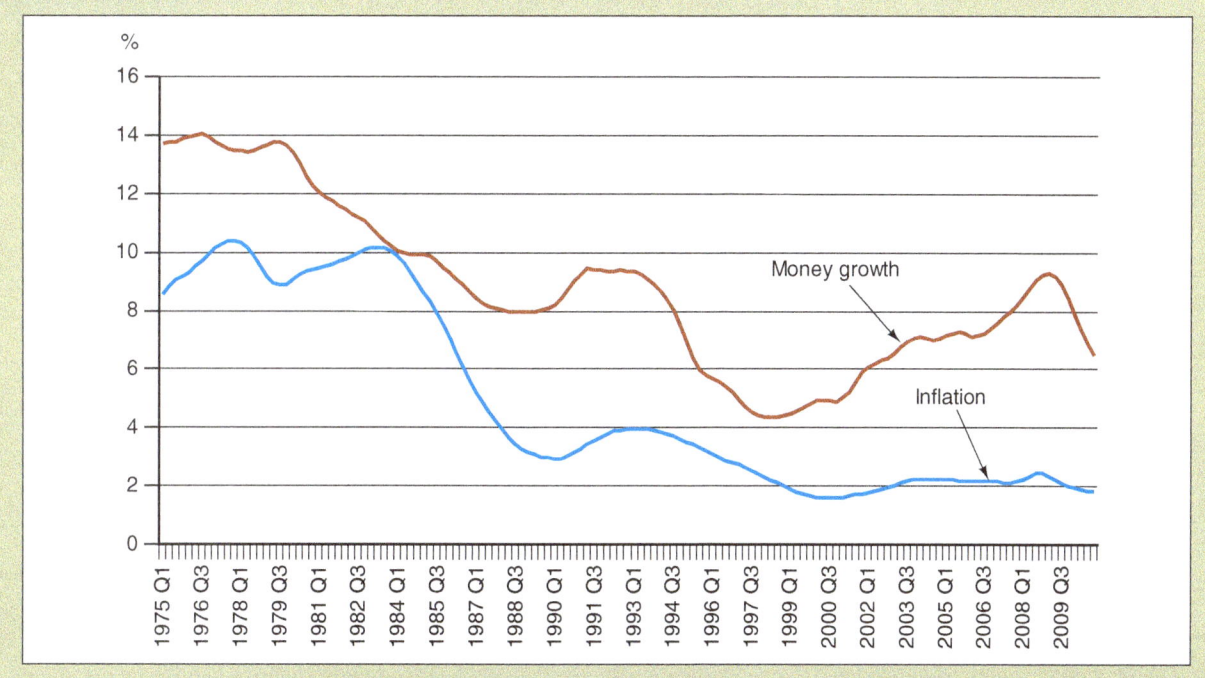

Inflation and money growth in the euro area, 1975–2010

Source: Money growth is based on the monetary aggregate M3 and inflation on the HICP index. Both series are taken from the Area Wide Model (AWM). Five-year moving averages of annual percentage changes.

Evidence of this type seems to support the proposition that extremely high inflation is the result of a high rate of money growth. Keep in mind, however, that you are looking at reduced-form evidence, which focuses solely on the correlation of two variables: money growth and the inflation rate. As with all reduced-form evidence, reverse causation (inflation causing money supply growth) or an outside factor that drives both money growth and inflation could be involved.

How might you rule out these possibilities? First, you might look for historical episodes in which an increase in money growth appears to be an exogenous event; a high inflation rate for a sustained period following the increase in money growth would provide strong evidence that high money growth is the driving force behind the inflation. Luckily for our analysis, such clear-cut episodes – hyperinflations (extremely rapid inflations with inflation rates exceeding 50% per month) – have occurred, the most notorious being the German hyperinflation of 1921–3.

German hyperinflation, 1921–3

In 1921, the need to make reparations and reconstruct the economy after World War I caused the German government's expenditures to greatly exceed revenues. The government could have obtained revenues to cover these increased expenditures by raising taxes, but that solution was, as always, politically unpopular and would have taken much time to implement. The government could also have financed the expenditure by borrowing from the public, but the amount needed was far in excess of its capacity to borrow. There was only one route left: the printing press. The government could pay for its expenditures simply by printing more currency (increasing the money supply) and using it to make payments to the individuals and companies that were providing it with goods and services. As shown

FIGURE 24.4

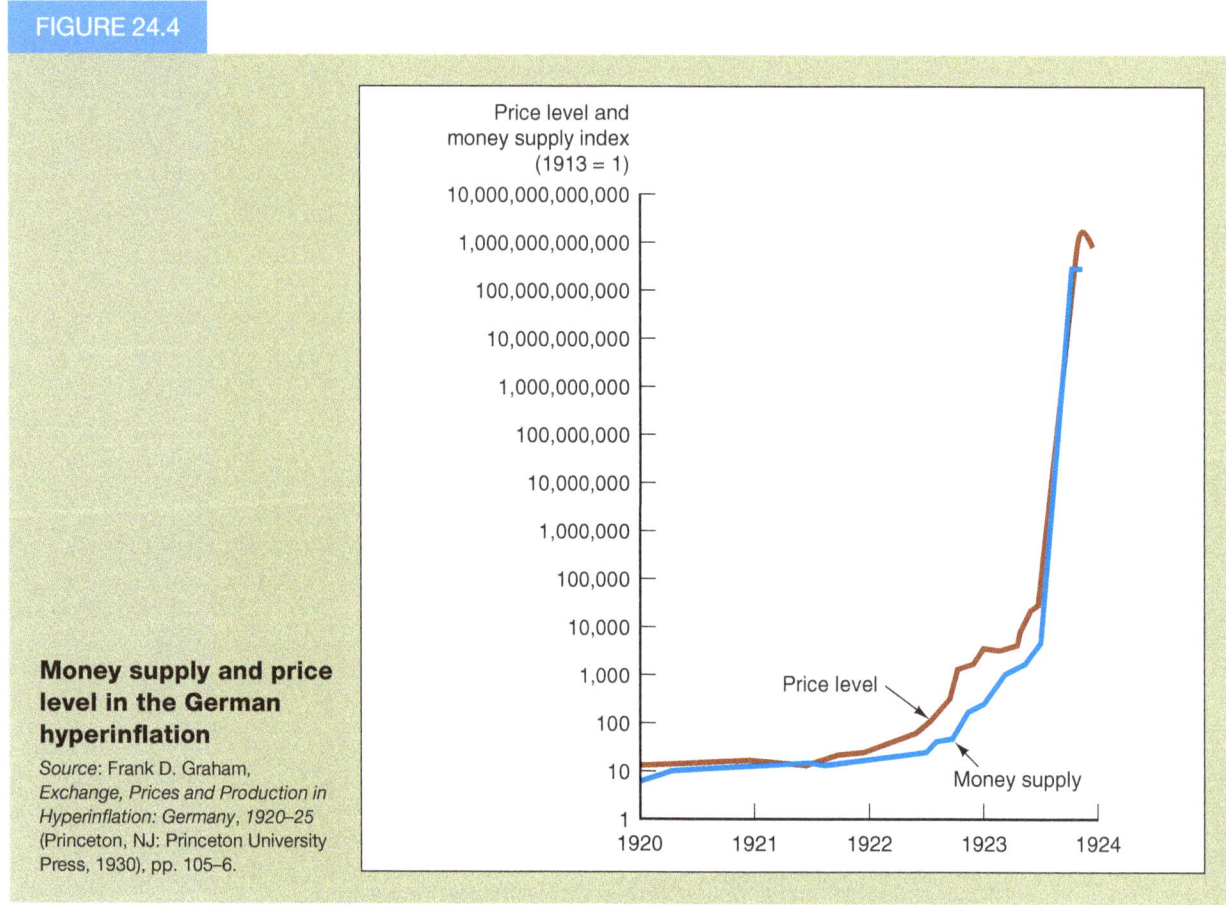

Money supply and price level in the German hyperinflation

Source: Frank D. Graham, *Exchange, Prices and Production in Hyperinflation: Germany, 1920–25* (Princeton, NJ: Princeton University Press, 1930), pp. 105–6.

in Figure 24.4, this is exactly what the German government did; in late 1921, the money supply began to increase rapidly, and so did the price level.

In 1923, the budgetary situation of the German government deteriorated even further. Early that year, the French invaded the Ruhr, because Germany had failed to make its scheduled reparations payments. A general strike in the region then ensued to protest the French action, and the German government actively supported this 'passive resistance' by making payments to striking workers. As a result, government expenditures climbed dramatically, and the government printed currency at an even faster rate to finance this spending. As displayed in Figure 24.4, the result of the explosion in the money supply was that the price level blasted off, leading to an inflation rate for 1923 that exceeded 1 million per cent!

The invasion of the Ruhr and the printing of currency to pay striking workers fitted the characteristics of an exogenous event. Reverse causation (that the rise in the price level caused the French to invade the Ruhr) is highly implausible, and it is hard to imagine a third factor that could have been a driving force behind both inflation and the explosion in the money supply. Therefore, the German hyperinflation qualifies as a 'controlled experiment' that supports Friedman's proposition that inflation is a monetary phenomenon.

Recent episodes of rapid inflation

Only one country has recently topped Germany in the high inflation league. In December 2008, Zimbabwe's annual inflation rate was estimated at $6\frac{1}{2} \times 100^{108}$%. Yes, that's a lot of zeros. In April 2009, the Zimbabwe authorities abandoned printing of the Zimbabwean dollar and since then all trade has been made in foreign currencies like the euro, the British pound and the American dollar.

The explanation for Zimbabwe's hyperinflation is the same as Germany's during its hyperinflation: extremely high money growth because the weak government of Robert Mugabe was unwilling to finance government expenditures by raising taxes, which led to a very high budget deficit financed by money creation.

Note that the inflation rate is high in all cases in which the high rate of money growth can be classified as an exogenous event. This is strong evidence that high money growth causes high inflation.

Meaning of inflation

You may have noticed that all the empirical evidence on the relationship of money growth and inflation discussed so far looks only at cases in which the price level is continually rising at a rapid rate and so inflation is persistent. It is this definition of inflation that Friedman and other economists use when they make statements such as 'inflation is always and everywhere a monetary phenomenon'. This is not what your friendly newscaster means when reporting the monthly inflation rate on the nightly news. The newscaster is only telling you how much, in percentage terms, the price level has changed from the previous month. For example, when you hear that the monthly inflation rate is 1% (12% annual rate), this indicates only that the price level has risen by 1% in that month. This could be a one-shot change, in which the high inflation rate is merely temporary, not sustained. Only if the inflation rate remains high persistently for, say, several years will economists say that inflation has been high.

Accordingly, Milton Friedman's proposition actually says that upward movements in the price level are a monetary phenomenon *only* if this is a sustained process. When *inflation* is defined as a persistent and rapid rise in the price level, almost all economists agree with Friedman's proposition that money alone is to blame.

Views of inflation

Now that we understand what Friedman's proposition means, we can use the aggregate demand and supply analysis learned in Chapter 22 to show that large and persistent upward movements in the price level (high inflation) can occur only if there is a continually growing money supply.

How money growth produces inflation

First, let's look at the outcome of a continually growing money supply (see Figure 24.5). Initially, the economy is at point 1, with output at the natural rate level and the price level at P_1 (the intersection of the aggregate demand curve AD_1 and the short-run aggregate supply curve AS_1). If the money supply increases steadily over the course of the year, the aggregate demand curve shifts rightward to AD_2. At first, for a very brief time, the economy may move to point 1' and output may increase above the natural rate level to Y', but the resulting decline in unemployment below the natural rate level will cause wages to rise, and the short-run aggregate supply curve will quickly begin to shift leftward. It will stop shifting only when it reaches AS_2, at which time the economy has returned to the natural rate level of output on the long-run aggregate supply curve.[2] At the new equilibrium, point 2, the price level has increased from P_1 to P_2.

If the money supply increases the next year, the aggregate demand curve will shift to the right again to AD_3, and the short-run aggregate supply curve will shift from AS_2 to AS_3; the economy will move to point 2' and then to point 3, where the price level has risen to P_3. If the money supply continues to grow in subsequent years, the economy will continue to

FIGURE 24.5

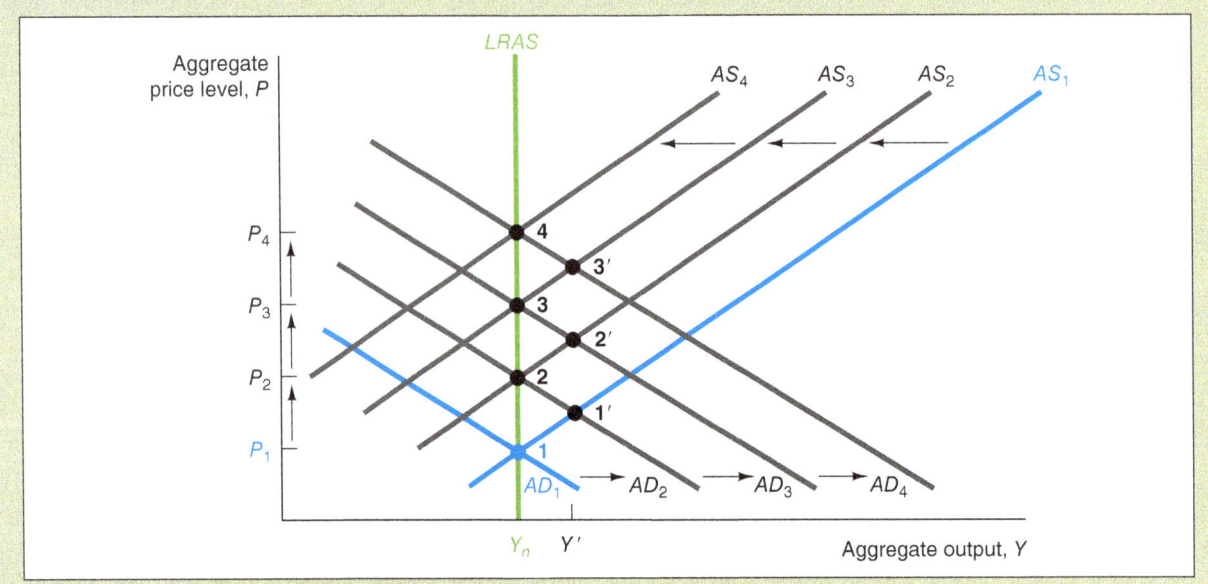

Response to a continually growing money supply

A continually growing money supply shifts the aggregate demand curve to the right from AD_1 to AD_2 to AD_3 to AD_4, while the short-run aggregate supply curve shifts to the left from AS_1 to AS_2 to AS_3 to AS_4. The result is that the price level rises continually from P_1 to P_2 to P_3 to P_4.

move to higher and higher price levels. As long as the money supply grows, this process will continue, and inflation will occur. *High money growth produces high inflation*.

Can other factors besides money growth produce a sustained inflation?

In the aggregate demand and supply analysis in Chapter 22, you learned that other factors besides changes in the money supply (such as fiscal policy and supply shocks) can affect the aggregate demand and supply curves. Doesn't this suggest that these other factors can generate persistent high inflation? The answer, surprisingly, is no. To see why high inflation is always a monetary phenomenon, let's dig a little deeper into aggregate demand and supply analysis to see whether other factors can generate high inflation in the absence of a high rate of money growth.

Can fiscal policy by itself produce inflation?

To examine this question, let's look at Figure 24.6, which demonstrates the effect of a one-shot permanent increase in government expenditure (say, from €500 billion to €600 billion) on aggregate output and the price level. Initially, we are at point 1, where output is at the natural rate level and the price level is P_1. The increase in government expenditure shifts the aggregate demand curve to AD_2, and we move to point 1', where output is above the natural rate level at Y_1. Because of this, the short-run aggregate supply curve will begin to shift leftward, eventually reaching AS_2, where it intersects the aggregate demand curve AD_2 at point 2, at which output is again at the natural rate level and the price level has risen to P_2.

The net result of a one-shot permanent increase in government expenditure is a one-shot permanent increase in the price level. What happens to the inflation rate? When we move

FIGURE 24.6

Response to a one-shot permanent increase in government expenditure

A one-shot permanent increase in government expenditure shifts the aggregate demand curve rightward from AD_1 to AD_2, moving the economy from point 1 to point 1′. Because output now exceeds the natural rate level Y_n, the short-run aggregate supply curve eventually shifts leftward to AS_2, and the price level rises from P_1 to P_2, a one-shot permanent increase but not a continuing increase.

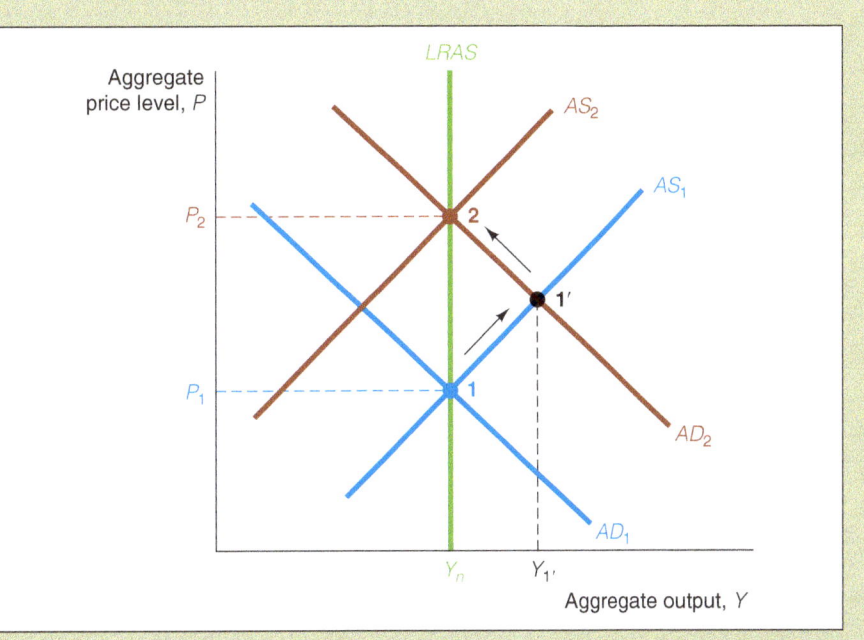

from point 1 to 1′ to 2, the price level rises, and we have a positive inflation rate. But when we finally get to point 2, the inflation rate returns to zero. We see that the one-shot increase in government expenditure leads to only a *temporary* increase in the inflation rate, not to persistent inflation in which the price level is continually rising.

If government spending increases continually, however, we *could* get a continuing rise in the price level. It appears, then, that aggregate demand and supply analysis could reject Friedman's proposition that inflation is always the result of money growth. The problem with this argument is that a continually increasing level of government expenditure is not a feasible policy. There is a limit on the total amount of possible government expenditure; the government cannot spend more than 100% of GDP. In fact, well before this limit is reached, the political process would stop the increases in government spending. As revealed in the continual debates in Europe and the US over balanced budgets and government spending, both the public and politicians have a particular target level of government spending they deem appropriate; although small deviations from this level might be tolerated, large deviations would not. Indeed, public and political perceptions impose tight limits on the degree to which government expenditures can increase.

What about the other side of fiscal policy – taxes? Could continual tax cuts generate an inflation? Again the answer is no. The analysis in Figure 24.6 also describes the price and output response to a one-shot decrease in taxes. There will be a one-shot increase in the price level, but the increase in the inflation rate will be only temporary. We can increase the price level by cutting taxes even more, but this process would have to stop – once taxes reach zero, they can't be reduced further. We must conclude, then, that ***persistent high inflation cannot be driven by fiscal policy alone***.[3]

Can supply-side phenomena by themselves produce inflation?

Because supply shocks and workers' attempts to increase their wages can shift the short-run aggregate supply curve leftward, you might suspect that these supply-side phenomena by themselves could stimulate inflation. Again, we can show that this suspicion is incorrect.

Suppose that a negative supply shock – for example, an oil embargo – raises oil prices (or workers could have successfully pushed up their wages). As displayed in Figure 24.7, the

FIGURE 24.7

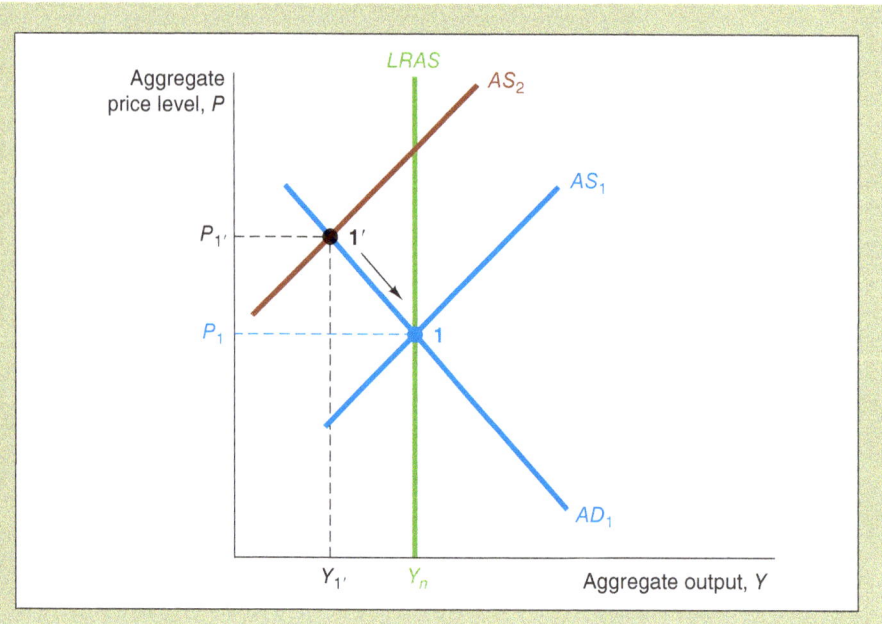

Response to a supply shock

A negative supply shock (or a wage push) shifts the short-run aggregate supply curve leftward to AS_2 and results in high unemployment at point 1'. As a result, the short-run aggregate supply curve shifts back to the right to AS_1, and the economy returns to point 1, where the price level has returned to P_1.

negative supply shock shifts the short-run aggregate supply curve from AS_1 to AS_2. If the money supply remains unchanged, leaving the aggregate demand curve at AD_1, we move to point 1', where output is below the natural rate level and the price level P_1 is higher. The short-run aggregate supply curve will now shift back to AS_1, because unemployment is above the natural rate, and the economy slides down AD_1 from point 1' to point 1. The net result of the supply shock is that we return to full employment at the initial price level and there is no continuing inflation. Additional negative supply shocks that again shift the short-run aggregate supply curve leftward will lead to the same outcome: the price level will rise temporarily, but persistent inflation will not result. The conclusion that we have reached is the following: *supply-side phenomena cannot be the source of persistent high inflation*.[4]

Summary

Our aggregate demand and supply analysis shows that persistent high inflation can occur only with a high rate of money growth. As long as we recognize that inflation refers to a continuing increase in the price level at a rapid rate, we now see why Milton Friedman was correct when he said that '*Inflation is always and everywhere a monetary phenomenon*'.

Origins of inflationary monetary policy

Although we now know *what* must occur to generate a persistent rapid inflation – a high rate of money growth – we still can't understand *why* persistent high inflation occurs until we have learned how and why inflationary monetary policies come about. If everyone agrees that inflation is not a good thing for an economy, why do we see so much of it? Why do governments pursue inflationary monetary policies? Because there is nothing intrinsically desirable about inflation and because we know that a high rate of money growth doesn't happen of its own accord, it must follow that in trying to achieve other goals, governments end up with a high money growth rate and high inflation. In this section, we will examine the government policies that are the most common sources of inflation.

High employment targets and inflation

The first goal most governments pursue that often results in inflation is high employment. In the euro area and the UK, a high level of employment constitutes a major policy objective as long as it is consistent with price stability. Before the strong commitment to price stability in the past European countries' governments often pursued a high employment target with little concern about the inflationary consequences of their policies. This was true especially in the 1970s, when the governments began to take a more active role in attempting to stabilize unemployment.

Two types of inflation can result from an activist stabilization policy to promote high employment: **cost-push inflation**, which occurs because of negative supply shocks or a push by workers to get higher wages, and **demand-pull inflation**, which results when policymakers pursue policies that shift the aggregate demand curve to the right. We will now use aggregate demand and supply analysis to examine how a high employment target can lead to both types of inflation.

Cost-push inflation

In Figure 24.8, the economy is initially at point 1, the intersection of the aggregate demand curve AD_1 and the short-run aggregate supply curve AS_1. Suppose that workers decide to seek higher wages, either because they want to increase their real wages (wages in terms of the goods and services they can buy) or because they expect inflation to be high and wish to keep up with inflation. The effect of such an increase (similar to a negative supply shock) is to shift the short-run aggregate supply curve leftward to AS_2.[5] If government fiscal and monetary policy remains unchanged, the economy would move to point 1' at the intersection of the new short-run aggregate supply curve AS_2 and the aggregate demand curve AD_1. Output would decline to Y', below its natural rate level Y_n, and the price level would rise to P_1.

FIGURE 24.8

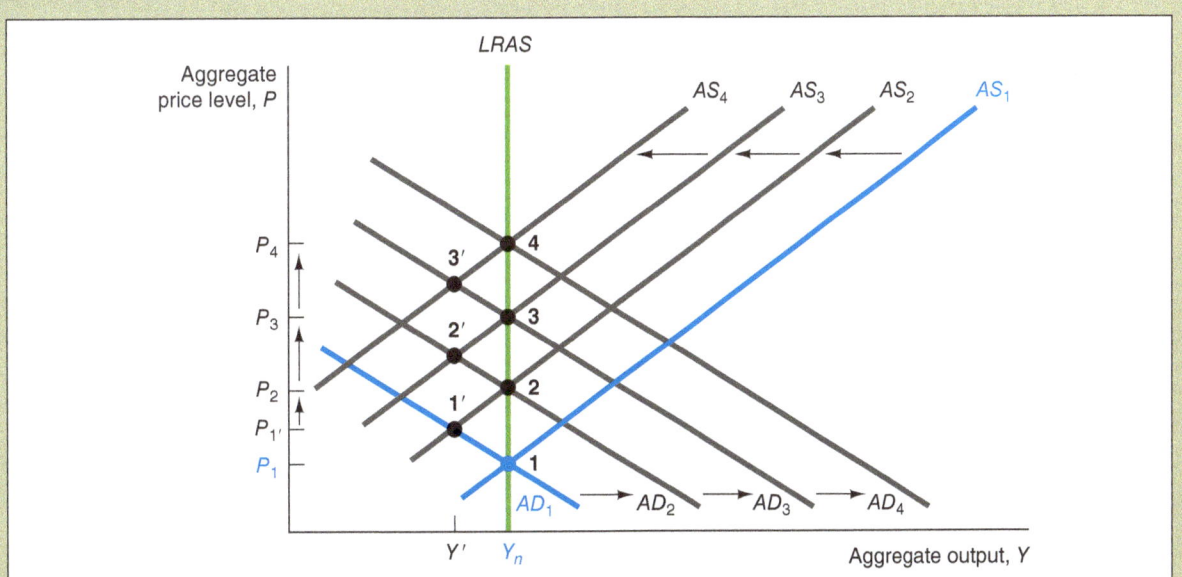

Cost-push inflation with an activist policy to promote high employment

In a cost-push inflation, the leftward shifts of the short-run aggregate supply curve from AS_1 to AS_2 to AS_3 and so on cause a government with a high employment target to shift the aggregate demand curve to the right continually to keep unemployment and output at their natural rate levels. The result is a continuing rise in the price level from P_1 to P_2 to P_3 and so on.

What would activist policymakers with a high employment target do if this situation developed? Because of the drop in output and resulting increase in unemployment, they would implement policies to raise the aggregate demand curve to AD_2, so that we would return to the natural rate level of output at point 2 and price level P_2. The workers who have increased their wages have not fared too badly. The government has stepped in to make sure that there is no excessive unemployment, and they have achieved their goal of higher wages. Because the government has, in effect, given in to the demands of workers for higher wages, an activist policy with a high employment target is often referred to as an **accommodating policy**.

The workers, having had their cake and eaten it, might be encouraged to seek even higher wages. In addition, other workers might now realize that their wages have fallen relative to their fellow workers', and because they don't want to be left behind, these workers will seek to increase their wages. The result is that the short-run aggregate supply curve shifts leftward again, to AS_3. Unemployment develops again when we move to point 2', and the activist policies will once more be used to shift the aggregate demand curve rightward to AD_3 and return the economy to full employment at a price level of P_3. If this process continues, the result will be a continuing increase in the price level – a persistent cost-push inflation.

What role does monetary policy play in a cost-push inflation? A cost-push inflation can occur only if the aggregate demand curve is shifted continually to the right. The first shift of the aggregate demand curve to AD_2 could be achieved by a one-shot increase in government expenditure or a one-shot decrease in taxes. But what about the next required rightward shift of the aggregate demand curve to AD_3, and the next, and the next? The limits on the maximum level of government expenditure and the minimum level of taxes would prevent the use of this expansionary fiscal policy for very long. Hence it cannot be used continually to shift the aggregate demand curve to the right. But the aggregate demand curve *can* be shifted continually rightward by continually increasing the money supply – that is, by going to a higher rate of money growth. Therefore, *a persistent cost-push inflation is a monetary phenomenon because it cannot occur without the monetary authorities pursuing an accommodating policy of a higher rate of money growth.*

Demand-pull inflation

The goal of high employment can lead to inflationary monetary policy in another way. Even at full employment, some unemployment is always present because of frictions in the labour market, which make it difficult to immediately match unemployed workers with employers. An unemployed carworker of Land Rover in Liverpool may not know about a job opening in the electronics industry in Southampton or, even if he or she did, may not want to move or be retrained. So the unemployment rate when there is full employment (the natural rate of unemployment) will be greater than zero. If policymakers set a target for unemployment that is too low because it is less than the natural rate of unemployment, this can set the stage for a higher rate of money growth and a resulting persistent inflation. Again we can show how this can happen using an aggregate supply and demand diagram (see Figure 24.9).

If policymakers have an unemployment target (say, 4%) that is below the natural rate (estimated to be between $4\frac{1}{2}\%$ and $5\frac{1}{2}\%$ currently), they will try to achieve an output target greater than the natural rate level of output. This target level of output is marked Y_T in Figure 24.9. Suppose that we are initially at point 1; the economy is at the natural rate level of output but below the target level of output Y_T. To hit the unemployment target of 4%, policymakers enact policies to increase aggregate demand, and the effects of these policies shift the aggregate demand curve until it reaches AD_2 and the economy moves to point 1'. Output is at Y_T, and the 4% unemployment rate goal has been reached.

If the targeted unemployment rate was at the natural rate level between $4\frac{1}{2}\%$ and $5\frac{1}{2}\%$ there would be no problem. However, because at Y_T the 4% unemployment rate is below the natural rate level, wages will rise and the short-run aggregate supply curve will shift in to AS_2, moving the economy from point 1' to point 2. The economy is back at the natural

FIGURE 24.9

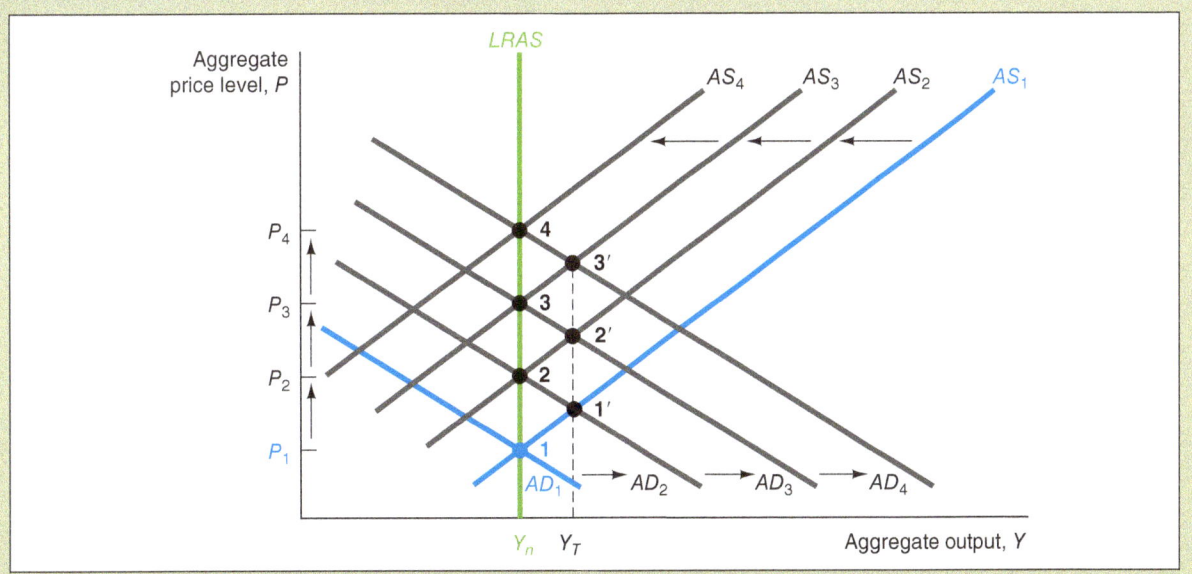

Demand-pull inflation: the consequence of setting too low an unemployment target

Too low an unemployment target (too high an output target of Y_T) causes the government to shift the aggregate demand curve rightward from AD_1 to AD_2 to AD_3 and so on, while the short-run aggregate supply curve shifts leftward from AS_1 to AS_2 to AS_3 and so on. The result is a continuing rise in the price level known as a demand-pull inflation.

rate of unemployment, but at a higher price level of P_2. We could stop there, but because unemployment is again higher than the target level, policymakers would again shift the aggregate demand curve rightward to AD_3 to hit the output target at point 2′, and the whole process would continue to drive the economy to point 3 and beyond. The overall result is a steadily rising price level – a persistent inflation.

How can policymakers continually shift the aggregate demand curve rightward? We have already seen that they cannot do it through fiscal policy, because of the limits on raising government expenditures and reducing taxes. Instead they will have to resort to expansionary monetary policy: a continuing increase in the money supply and hence a high money growth rate.

Pursuing too low an unemployment rate target or, equivalently, too high an output target is the source of inflationary monetary policy in this situation, but it seems senseless for policymakers to do this. They have not gained the benefit of a permanently higher level of output but have generated the burden of an inflation. If, however, they do not realize that the target rate of unemployment is below the natural rate, the process that we see in Figure 24.9 will be well under way before they realize their mistake.

Because the inflation described results from policymakers' pursuing policies that shift the aggregate demand curve to the right, it is called a *demand-pull inflation*. In contrast, a *cost-push inflation* occurs when workers push their wages up. Is it easy to distinguish between them in practice? The answer is no. We have seen that both types of inflation will be associated with higher money growth, so we cannot distinguish between them on this basis. Yet as Figures 24.8 and 24.9 demonstrate, demand-pull inflation will be associated with periods when unemployment is below the natural rate level, whereas cost-push inflation is associated with periods when unemployment is above the natural rate level. To decide which type of inflation has occurred, we can look at whether unemployment has been above or below its natural rate level. This would be easy if economists and policymakers actually knew how to measure the natural rate of unemployment; unfortunately, this difficult research question is still not fully resolved by the economics profession. In addition, the distinction between cost-push and demand-pull inflation is blurred, because a cost-push inflation can be initiated by a demand-pull inflation: when a demand-pull inflation produces higher inflation rates, expected inflation will eventually rise and cause workers to demand higher wages so that their real wages do not fall. In this way, demand-pull inflation can eventually trigger cost-push inflation.

Budget deficits and inflation

Our discussion of the evidence on money and inflation suggested that budget deficits are another possible source of inflationary monetary policy. To see if this could be the case, we need to look at how a government finances its budget deficits.

Government budget constraint

Because the government has to pay its bills just as we do, it has a budget constraint. There are two ways we can pay for our spending: raise revenue (by working) or borrow. The government also enjoys these two options: raise revenue by levying taxes or go into debt by issuing government bonds. Unlike us, however, it has a third option: the government can create money and use it to pay for the goods and services it buys.

Methods of financing government spending are described by an expression called the **government budget constraint**, which states the following: the government budget deficit *DEF*, which equals the excess of government spending *G* over tax revenue *T*, must equal the sum of the change in the monetary base ΔMB and the change in government bonds held by the public ΔB. Algebraically, this expression can be written as follows:

$$DEF = G - T = \Delta MB + \Delta B$$

To see what the government budget constraint means in practice, let's look at the case in which the only government purchase is a €100 million supercomputer. If the government convinces the electorate that such a computer is worth paying for, it will probably be able to raise the €100 million in taxes to pay for it, and the budget deficit will equal zero. The government budget constraint then tells us that no issue of money or bonds is needed to pay for the computer, because the budget is balanced. If taxpayers think that the supercomputer is too expensive and refuse to pay taxes for it, the budget constraint indicates that the government must pay for it by selling €100 million of new bonds to the public or by, in effect, printing €100 million of currency to pay for the computer. In either case, the budget constraint is satisfied; the €100 million deficit is balanced by the change in the stock of government bonds held by the public ($\Delta B = $ €100 million) or by the change in the monetary base ($\Delta MB = $ €100 million).

The government budget constraint thus reveals two important facts: *if the government deficit is financed by an increase in bond holdings by the public, there is no effect on the monetary base and hence on the money supply. But, if the deficit is not financed by increased bond holdings by the public, the monetary base and the money supply increase.*

There are several ways to understand why a deficit leads to an increase in the monetary base when the public's bond holdings do not increase. The simplest case is when the government's treasury has the legal right to issue currency to finance its deficit. Financing the deficit is then very straightforward: the government just pays for the spending that is in excess of its tax revenues with new currency. Because this increase in currency adds directly to the monetary base, the monetary base rises and the money supply with it, through the process of multiple deposit creation described in Chapter 14.

In many countries, however, the government does not have the right to issue currency to pay for its bills. In this case, the government must finance its deficit by first issuing bonds to the public to acquire the extra funds to pay its bills. Yet if these bonds do not end up in the hands of the public, the only alternative is that they are purchased by the central bank.

For the government bonds not to end up in the hands of the public, the central bank must conduct an open market purchase, which, as we saw in Chapter 14, leads to an increase in the monetary base and in the money supply. This method of financing government spending is called **monetizing the debt** because, as the two-step process described indicates, government debt issued to finance government spending has been removed from the hands of the public and has been replaced by high-powered money. This method of financing, or the more direct method when a government just issues the currency directly, is also, somewhat inaccurately, referred to as **printing money** because high-powered money (the monetary base) is created in the process. The use of the word *printing* is misleading because what is essential to this method of financing government spending is that the monetary base increases when the central bank conducts open market purchases, just as it would if more currency were put in circulation.

We thus see that a budget deficit can lead to an increase in the money supply if it is financed by the creation of high-powered money. However, earlier in this chapter you have seen that persistent inflation can develop only when the stock of money grows continually. Can a budget deficit financed by printing money do this? The answer is yes, if the budget deficit persists for a substantial period of time. In the first period, if the deficit is financed by money creation, the money supply will rise, shifting the aggregate demand curve to the right and leading to a rise in the price level (see Figure 24.5). If the budget deficit is still present in the next period, it has to be financed all over again. The money supply will rise again, and the aggregate demand curve will again shift to the right, causing the price level to rise further. As long as the deficit persists and the government resorts to printing money to pay for it, this process will continue. *Financing a persistent deficit by money creation will lead to a sustained inflation*.

A critical element in this process is that the deficit is persistent. If temporary, it would not produce an inflation because the situation would then be similar to that shown in Figure 24.6, in which there is a one-shot increase in government expenditure. In the period when the deficit occurs, there will be an increase in money to finance it, and the resulting rightward shift of the aggregate demand curve will raise the price level. If the deficit disappears in the next period, there is no longer a need to print money. The aggregate demand curve will not shift further, and the price level will not continue to rise. Hence the one-shot increase in the money supply from the temporary deficit generates only a one-shot increase in the price level, and a persistent inflation does not develop.

To summarize, *a deficit can be the source of a sustained inflation only if it is persistent rather than temporary and if the government finances it by creating money rather than by issuing bonds to the public.*

If inflation is the result, why do governments frequently finance persistent deficits by creating money? The answer is the key to understanding how budget deficits may lead to inflation.

Budget deficits and money creation

Although industrialized countries have well-developed money and capital markets in which huge quantities of their government bonds, both short- and long-term, can be sold, this is not the situation in many small and developing economies. If these countries run budget deficits, they cannot finance them by issuing bonds and must resort to their only other alternative, printing money. As a result, when they run large deficits relative to GDP, the money supply grows at substantial rates, and a persistent inflation results.

Earlier we cited Germany in the 1920s and Zimbabwe more recently which had high inflation rates and high money growth as evidence that inflation is a monetary phenomenon. The countries that had high money growth are precisely the ones that had persistent and extremely large budget deficits relative to GDP. The only way to finance the deficits was to print more money, so the ultimate source of their high inflation rates was their large budget deficits.

In all episodes of hyperinflation, huge government budget deficits are also the ultimate source of inflationary monetary policies. The budget deficits during hyperinflations are so large that even if a capital market exists to issue government bonds, it does not have sufficient capacity to handle the quantity of bonds that the government wishes to sell. In this situation, the government must also resort to the printing press to finance the deficits.

So far we have seen why budget deficits in some countries must lead to money creation and inflation. Either the deficit is huge or the country does not have sufficient access to capital markets in which it can sell government bonds. Ignoring the recent budgetary developments for a moment, neither of these scenarios seems to describe the situation in the British economic history. True, the British deficits were large in the mid-1970s and early 1990s but even so, the magnitude of these deficits relative to GDP was small compared to the deficits of countries that have experienced hyperinflations: the UK deficit as a percentage of GDP reached a peak of 8% in 1993, whereas Argentina's budget deficit sometimes exceeded 15% of GDP. Furthermore, because the UK has a very well-developed government bond market, it can issue large quantities of bonds when it needs to finance its deficit.

Whether the budget deficit can influence the monetary base and the money supply depends critically on how the central bank chooses to conduct monetary policy. If the central bank pursues a policy goal of preventing high interest rates (a possibility, as we have seen in Chapter 16), many economists contend that a budget deficit will lead to the printing of money. Their reasoning, using the supply and demand analysis of the bond market in Chapter 5, is as follows: when the Treasury issues bonds to the public, the supply of bonds rises (from B_1^s to B_2^s in Figure 24.10), causing bond prices to fall from P_1 to P_2 and hence interest rates to rise. If the central bank considers the rise in interest rates undesirable, it will buy bonds to prop up bond prices and reduce interest rates. The net result is that the government budget deficit can lead to open market purchases, which raise the monetary base (create high-powered money) and raise the money supply. If the budget deficit persists so that the quantity of bonds supplied keeps on growing, the upward pressure on interest rates will continue, the central bank will purchase bonds again and again, and the money supply will continually rise, resulting in a persistent inflation.

Economists such as Robert Barro of Harvard University, however, do not agree that budget deficits influence the monetary base in the manner just described. Their analysis (which Barro named **Ricardian equivalence** after the nineteenth-century British economist David Ricardo) contends that when the government runs deficits and issues bonds, the public

FIGURE 24.10

Interest rates and the government budget deficit

When the Treasury issues bonds to finance the budget deficit, the supply curve for bonds shifts rightward from B_1^s to B_2^s. Many economists take the position that the equilibrium moves to point 2 because the bond demand curve remains unchanged, with the result that the bond price falls from P_1 to P_2 and the interest rate rises. Adherents of Ricardian equivalence, however, suggest that the demand curve for bonds also increases to B_R^d, moving the equilibrium to point 2', where the bond price is unchanged at P_1, so that the interest rate does not rise and there is no need for the central bank to buy bonds and increase the money supply.

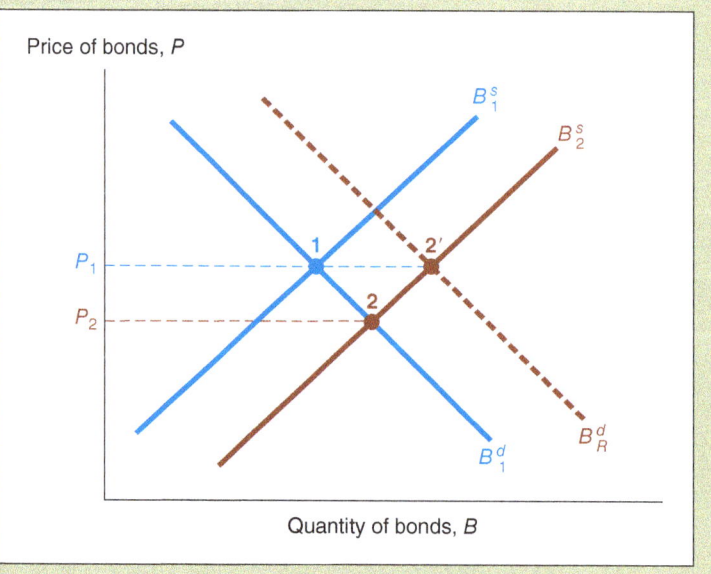

recognizes that it will be subject to higher taxes in the future to pay off these bonds. The public then saves more in anticipation of these future taxes, with the net result that the public demand for bonds increases to match the increased supply. The demand curve for bonds shifts rightward to B_R^d in Figure 24.10, leaving the bond price and interest rate unchanged. There is now no need for the central bank to purchase bonds to keep the interest rate from rising.

To sum up, although persistent high inflation is 'always and everywhere a monetary phenomenon' in the sense that it cannot occur without a high rate of money growth, there are reasons why this inflationary monetary policy might come about. The two underlying reasons are the adherence of policymakers to a high employment target and the presence of persistent government budget deficits.

APPLICATION ## Explaining the rise in UK inflation, 1960–80

Now that we have examined the underlying sources of inflation, let's apply this knowledge to understanding the causes of the rise in UK inflation from 1960 to 1980.

Figure 24.11 documents the rise in inflation in those years. In the 1960s inflation was relatively moderate, varying between 1% and 5%; from the early 1970s, inflation rates dramatically picked up, leading to an average annual inflation of around 13% during this decade. How does the analysis of this chapter explain this rise in inflation?

The conclusion that inflation is a monetary phenomenon is given a fair amount of support by the period from 1960 to 1980. As Figure 24.11 shows, in this period, there is a close correspondence between movements in the inflation rate and the monetary growth rate from two years earlier. (The money growth rates are from two years earlier, because research indicates that a change in money growth takes that long to affect the inflation rate.) The rise in inflation from 1960 to 1980 can be attributed to the rise in the money growth rate over this period. But you have probably noticed that in 1979–80, the inflation rate is well above the

FIGURE 24.11

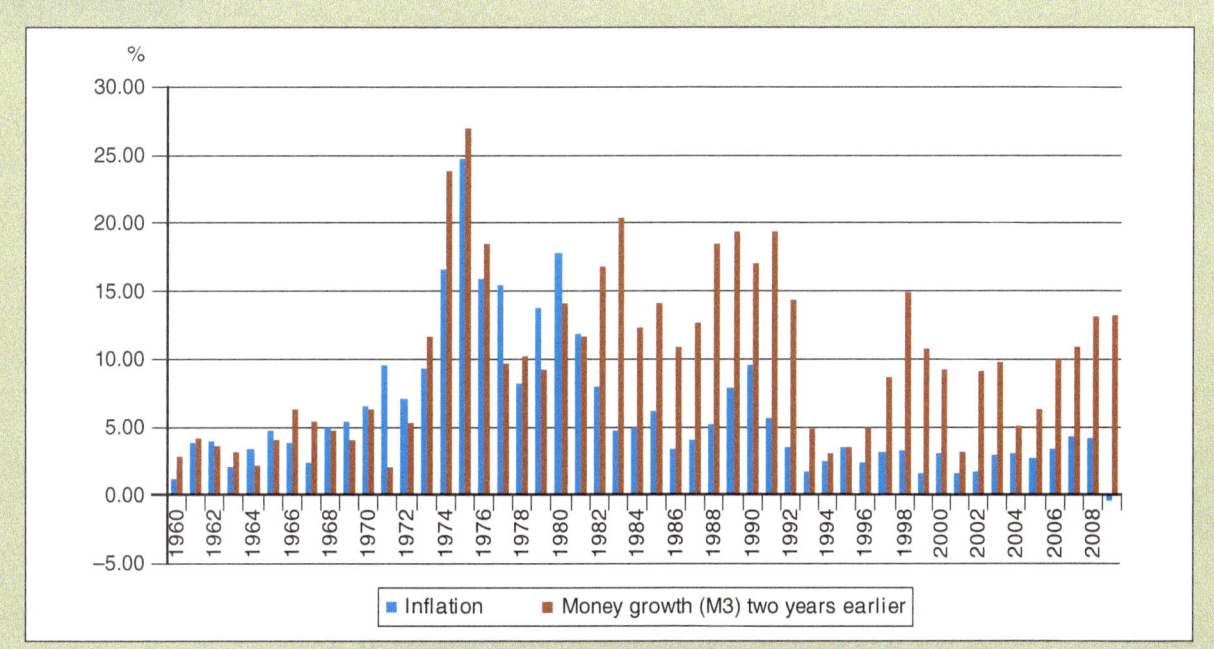

Inflation and money growth in the UK, 1960–2009

Source: Luca Benati, 'Long run evidence on money growth and inflation', ECB Working Paper Series No. 1027 (2009). Information may be obtained free of charges through the ECB's website.

money growth rate from two years earlier. You may recall from Chapter 22 that temporary upward bursts of the inflation rate in those years can be attributed to supply shocks from oil and food price increases that occurred in 1978–81.

However, the linkage between money growth and inflation after 1980 is not at all evident in Figure 24.11. The breakdown of the relationship between money growth and inflation is the result of substantial gyrations in velocity in the 1980s and 1990s (documented in Chapter 19). For example, the early 1980s was a period of rapid disinflation (a substantial fall in the inflation rate), yet the money growth rates in Figure 24.11 do not display a visible downward trend until after the disinflation was over. (The disinflationary process in the 1980s will be discussed in another application later in this chapter.) Although some economists see the 1980s and 1990s as evidence against the money–inflation link, others view this as an unusual period characterized by large fluctuations in interest rates and by rapid financial innovation that made the correct measurement of money far more difficult (see Chapter 3). In their view, this period was an aberration, and the close correspondence of money and inflation is sure to reassert itself. However, this has not yet occurred.

What is the underlying cause of the increased rate of money growth that we see occurring since the 1970s? We have identified two possible sources of inflationary monetary policy: government adherence to a high employment target and budget deficits. Let's see if budget deficits can explain the move to an inflationary monetary policy by plotting the ratio of government debt to GDP in Figure 24.12. This ratio provides a reasonable measure of whether government budget deficits put upward pressure on interest rates. Only if this ratio is rising might there be a tendency for budget deficits to raise interest rates, because the public

FIGURE 24.12

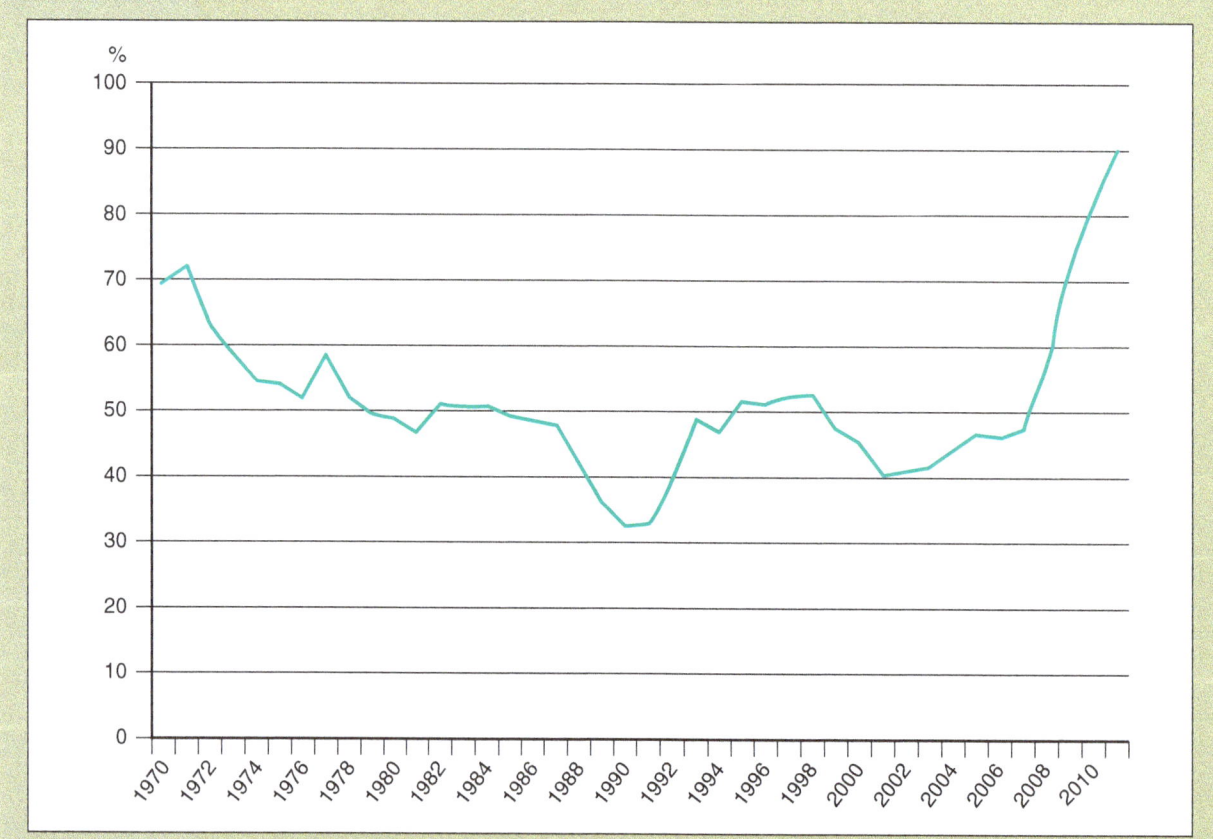

Government debt-to-GDP ratio, 1970–2011

Source: OECD Economic Outlook, December 2011. The government debt refers to the general government gross financial liabilities.

FIGURE 24.13

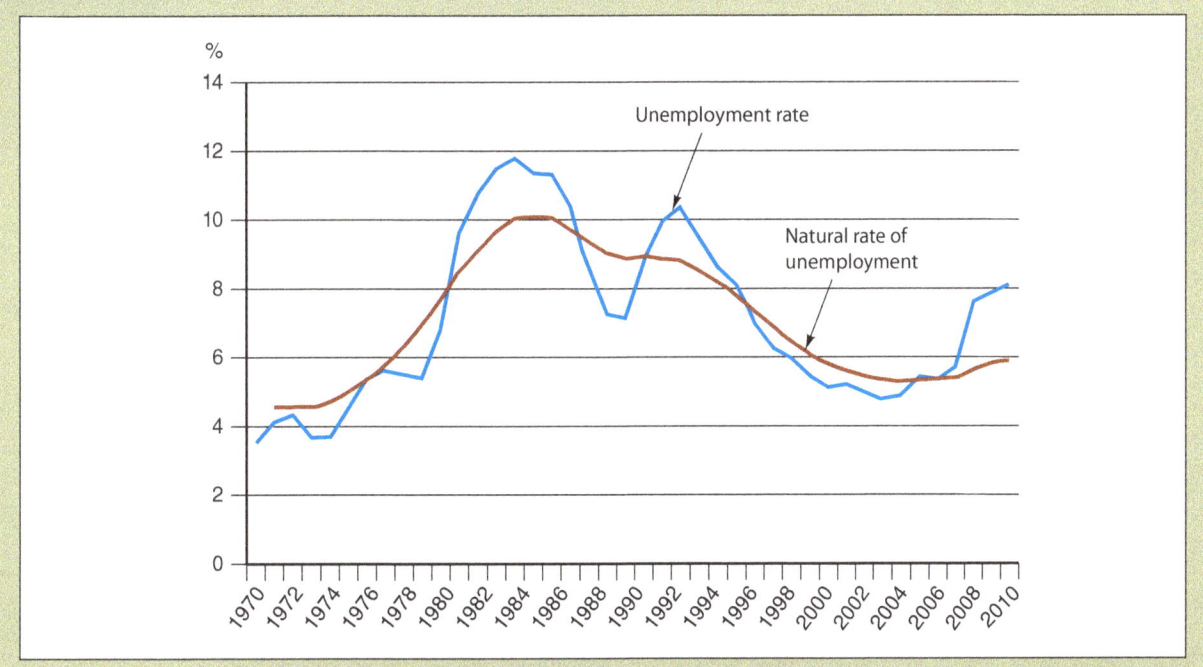

Unemployment and the natural rate of unemployment, 1970–2011

Sources: OECD Economic Outlook, December 2011. The natural rate of unemployment is proxied by the non-accelerating inflation rate of unemployment (NAIRU) estimated by the OECD.

is then being asked to hold more government bonds relative to their capacity to buy them. Surprisingly, over the course of the 20-year period from 1970 to 1990, this ratio was falling, not rising. Thus UK budget deficits in this period did not raise interest rates and so could not have encouraged the Bank of England to expand the money supply by buying bonds. Therefore, Figure 24.12 tells us that we can rule out budget deficits as a source of the rise in inflation in this period.

Because politicians were frequently bemoaning the budget deficits in this period, why did deficits not lead to an increase in the debt-to-GDP ratio? The reason is that in this period, UK budget deficits were sufficiently small that the increase in the stock of government debt was still slower than the growth in nominal GDP, and the ratio of debt to GDP declined. You can see that interpreting budget deficit numbers is a tricky business.[6]

We have ruled out budget deficits as the instigator; what else could be the underlying cause of the higher rate of money growth and more rapid inflation in the 1970s? Figure 24.11, which compares the actual unemployment rate to the natural rate of unemployment, shows that the economy was experiencing unemployment below the natural rate in all but one year between 1971 and 1980. This suggests that in the 1970s, the UK economy was experiencing the demand-pull inflation described in Figure 24.9.

Policymakers apparently pursued policies that continually shifted the aggregate demand curve to the right in trying to achieve an output target that was too high, thus causing the continual rise in the price level outlined in Figure 24.9. This occurred because there was a wide belief among policymakers, economists and politicians that the low unemployment levels of the 1950s and 1960s had become the norm in the UK. In hindsight, most economists today agree that policymakers substantially underestimated the natural rate of unemployment throughout the 1970s, as shown in Figure 24.13. The result of this inappropriate unemployment target was the beginning of the most sustained inflationary episode in UK history. ▪

The discretionary/non-discretionary policy debate

All economists have similar policy goals – they want to promote high employment and price stability – and yet they often have different views on how policy should be conducted. Advocates of discretionary policy, that is, policy to eliminate high unemployment whenever it appears, regard the self-correcting mechanism through wage and price adjustment (see Chapter 22) as very slow. Opponents of discretionary policy, by contrast, believe that the performance of the economy would be improved if the government avoided discretionary policy reactions to eliminate unemployment. We will explore this policy debate by first looking at what the policy responses might be when the economy experiences high unemployment.

Responses to high unemployment

Suppose that policymakers confront an economy that has moved to point 1′ in Figure 24.14. At this point, aggregate output Y_1 is lower than the natural rate level, and the economy is suffering from high unemployment. Policymakers have two viable choices: if they are proponents of non-discretionary policy and do nothing, the short-run aggregate supply curve will eventually shift rightward over time, driving the economy from point 1′ to point 1, where full employment is restored. The discretionary policy alternative is to try to eliminate the high unemployment by attempting to shift the aggregate demand curve rightward to AD_2 by pursuing expansionary policy (an increase in the money supply, increase in government spending, or lowering of taxes). If policymakers could shift the aggregate demand curve to AD_2 instantaneously, the economy would immediately move to point 2, where there is full employment. However, several types of lags prevent this immediate movement from occurring.

1 The *data lag* is the time it takes for policymakers to obtain the data that tell them what is happening in the economy. Accurate data on GDP, for example, are not available until several months after a given quarter is over.

FIGURE 24.14

The choice between discretionary and non-discretionary policy

When the economy has moved to point 1′, the policymaker has two choices of policy: the non-discretionary policy of doing nothing and letting the economy return to point 1 and the discretionary policy of shifting the aggregate demand curve to AD_2 to move the economy to point 2.

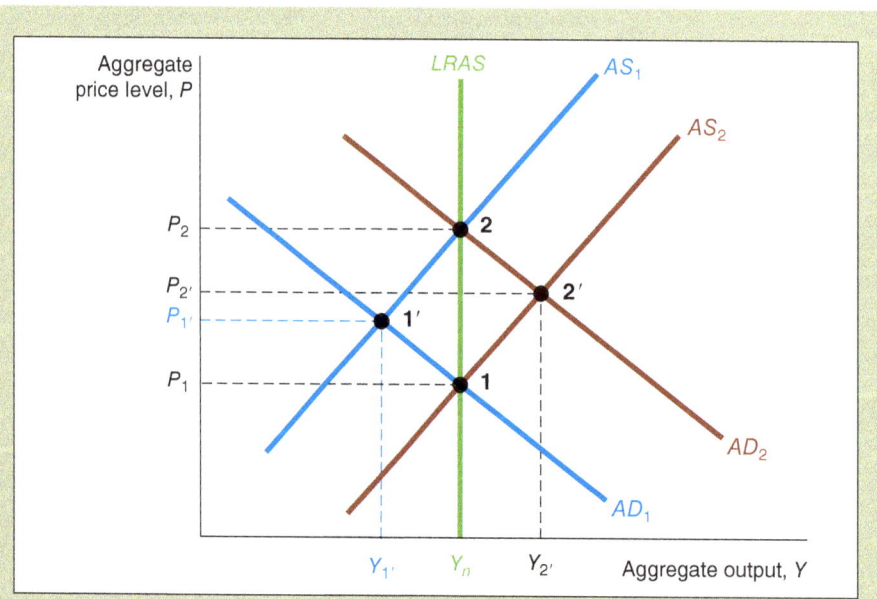

2 The *recognition lag* is the time it takes for policymakers to be sure of what the data are signalling about the future course of the economy. For example, to minimize errors, statistical offices will not declare the economy to be in recession until at least six months after it has determined that one has begun.

3 The *legislative lag* represents the time it takes to pass legislation to implement a particular policy. The legislative lag does not exist for most monetary policy actions such as open market operations. It is, however, important for the implementation of fiscal policy, when it can sometimes take six months to a year to get legislation passed to change taxes or government spending.

4 The *implementation lag* is the time it takes for policymakers to change policy instruments once they have decided on the new policy. Again, this lag is unimportant for the conduct of open market operations because central banks can purchase or sell bonds almost immediately. Actually implementing fiscal policy may take time, however; for example, getting government agencies to change their spending habits takes time, as does changing tax tables.

5 The *effectiveness lag* is the time it takes for the policy actually to have an impact on the economy. An important argument against discretionary policy is that the effectiveness lag is long (often a year or longer) and variable (i.e. there is substantial uncertainty about how long this lag is).

Discretionary and non-discretionary positions

Now that we understand the considerations that affect decisions by policymakers on whether to pursue discretionary versus non-discretionary policy, we can examine when each of these policies would be preferable.

Case for discretionary policy

Advocates of discretionary policies view the wage and price adjustment process as extremely slow. They believe that non-discretionary policy is costly, because the slow movement of the economy back to full employment results in a large loss of output. This means that, even though the five lags described may result in delay of a year or two before the aggregate demand curve shifts to AD_2, the short-run aggregate supply curve likewise moves very little during this time. The appropriate path for policymakers to pursue is thus a discretionary policy of moving the economy to point 2 in Figure 24.14.

Case for a non-discretionary policy

Opponents of discretionary policy view the wage and price adjustment process as more rapid than advocates of discretionary policies do and consider non-discretionary policy less costly because output is soon back at the natural rate level. They suggest that a discretionary policy of shifting the aggregate demand curve to AD_2 is costly, because it produces more volatility in both the price level and output. The reason for this volatility is that the time it takes to shift the aggregate demand curve to AD_2 is substantial, whereas the wage and price adjustment process is more rapid. Hence, before the aggregate demand curve shifts to the right, the short-run aggregate supply curve will have shifted rightward to AS_2, and the economy will have moved from point 1' to point 1, where it has returned to the natural rate level of output Y_n. After adjustment to the AS_2 curve is complete, the shift of the aggregate demand curve to AD_2 finally takes effect, leading the economy to point 2' at the intersection of AD_2 and AS_2. Aggregate output at $Y_{2'}$ is now greater than the natural rate level ($Y_2 > Y_n$) so the short-run aggregate supply curve will now shift leftward back to AS_1, moving the economy to point 2, where output is again at the natural rate level.

Although the discretionary policy eventually moves the economy to point 2 as policymakers intended, it leads to a sequence of equilibrium points – 1', 1, 2' and 2 – at which both output and the price level have been highly variable: output overshoots its target level of Y_n, and the price level falls from $P_{1'}$ to P_1 and then rises to P_2' and eventually to P_2. Because this variability is undesirable, policymakers would be better off pursuing non-discretionary policy which just lets the economy move to point 1.

Expectations and the discretionary/non-discretionary debate

Our analysis of inflation in the 1970s demonstrated that expectations about policy can be an important element in the inflation process. Allowing for expectations about policy to affect how wages are set (the wage-setting process) provides an additional reason for pursuing a non-discretionary policy.

Do expectations favour non-discretionary policy?

Does the possibility that expectations about policy matter to the wage-setting process strengthen the case for non-discretionary policy? The case for discretionary policy states that with slow wage and price adjustment, the discretionary policy returns the economy to full employment at point 2 far more quickly than it takes to get to full employment at point 1 if nothing is done. However, the argument for discretionary policy does not allow for the possibility (1) that expectations about policy matter to the wage-setting process and (2) that the economy might initially have moved from point 1 to point 1' because an attempt by workers to raise their wages or a negative supply shock shifted the short-run aggregate supply curve from AS_2 to AS_1. We must therefore ask the following question about discretionary policy: will the short-run aggregate supply curve continue to shift to the left after the economy has reached point 2, leading to cost-push inflation?

The answer to this question is yes *if* expectations about policy matter. Our discussion of cost-push inflation in Figure 24.8 suggested that if workers know that policy will be accommodating in the future, they will continue to push their wages up, and the short-run aggregate supply curve will keep shifting leftward. As a result, policymakers are forced to accommodate the cost push by continuing to shift the aggregate demand curve to the right to eliminate the unemployment that develops. The accommodating, discretionary policy with its high employment target has the hidden cost or disadvantage that it may well lead to inflation.[7]

The main advantage of a non-accommodating, non-discretionary policy, in which policymakers do not try to shift the aggregate demand curve in response to the cost push, is that it will prevent inflation. As depicted in Figure 24.7, the result of an upward push on wages in the face of a non-accommodating, non-discretionary policy will be a period of unemployment above the natural rate level, which will eventually shift the short-run aggregate supply curve and the price level back to their initial positions. The main criticism of this policy is that the economy will suffer protracted periods of unemployment when the short-run aggregate supply curve shifts leftward. Workers, however, would probably not push for higher wages to begin with if they knew that policy would be non-accommodating, because their wage gains will lead to a protracted period of unemployment. A non-accommodating, non-discretionary policy may have not only the advantage of preventing inflation but also the hidden benefit of discouraging leftward shifts in the short-run aggregate supply curve that lead to excessive unemployment.

In conclusion, *if workers' opinions about whether policy is accommodating or non-accommodating matter to the wage-setting process, the case for discretionary policy is much weaker*.

Do expectations about policy matter to the wage-setting process?

The answer to this question is crucial to deciding whether discretionary or non-discretionary policy is preferred and so has become a major topic of current research for economists, but the evidence is not yet conclusive. We can ask, however, whether expectations about policy do affect people's behaviour in other contexts. This information will help us know if expectations regarding whether policy is accommodating are important to the wage-setting process.

As any good negotiator knows, convincing your opponent that you will be non-accommodating is crucial to getting a good deal. If you are bargaining with a car dealer over price, for example, you must convince him that you can just as easily walk away from the deal and buy a car from a dealer on the other side of town. This principle also applies to conducting foreign policy – it is to your advantage to convince your opponent that you will go to war (be non-accommodating) if your demands are not met. Similarly, if your opponent thinks that you will be accommodating, he will almost certainly take advantage of you. Finally, anyone who has dealt with a two-year-old child knows that the more you give in (pursue an accommodating policy), the more demanding the child becomes. People's expectations about policy *do* affect their behaviour. Consequently, it is quite plausible that expectations about policy also affect the wage-setting process.[8]

Discretionary versus non-discretionary: conclusions

The following conclusions can be generated from our analysis: advocates of discretionary policy believe in the use of policy to eliminate excessive unemployment whenever it develops, because they view the wage and price adjustment process as sluggish and unresponsive to expectations about policy. Proponents of non-discretionary policy, by contrast, believe that a discretionary policy that reacts to excessive unemployment is counterproductive, because wage and price adjustment is rapid and because expectations about policy can matter to the wage-setting process. Proponents of non-discretionary policy thus advocate the use of a policy rule to keep the aggregate demand curve from fluctuating away from the trend rate of growth of the natural rate level of output. Monetarists, who oppose discretionary policy and who also see money as the sole source of fluctuations in the aggregate demand curve, in the past advocated a policy rule whereby the central bank keeps the money supply growing at a constant rate. This monetarist rule is referred to as a **constant-money-growth-rate rule**. Because of the unstable velocity of monetary aggregates (see Chapter 19), monetarists such as Bennett McCallum and Alan Meltzer of Carnegie-Mellon University have advocated a rule for the growth of the monetary base that is adjusted for past velocity changes.

As our analysis indicates, an important element for the success of a non-accommodating, non-discretionary policy rule is that it be *credible*: the public must believe that policymakers will be tough and not accede to a cost push by shifting the aggregate demand curve to the right to eliminate unemployment. In other words, government policymakers need credibility as inflation-fighters in the eyes of the public. Otherwise, workers will be more likely to push for higher wages, which will shift the aggregate supply curve leftward after the economy reaches full employment at a point such as point 2 in Figure 24.14 and will lead to unemployment or inflation (or both). Alternatively, a credible, non-accommodating, non-discretionary policy rule has the benefit that it makes a cost push less likely and thus helps prevent inflation and potential increases in unemployment. The following application suggests that recent historical experience is consistent with the importance of credibility to successful policymaking.

| APPLICATION | Importance of credibility to British victory over inflation |

In the 1970s, policymakers had little credibility as inflation-fighters – a well-deserved reputation, as they pursued a discretionary, accommodating policy to achieve high employment. As we have seen, the outcome was not a happy one. Inflation soared to double-digit levels, while the unemployment rate remained high. To wring inflation out of the system, the newly elected Conservative government under Margaret Thatcher embarked on a policy of monetarism aimed at lower money supply growth. The tightening of monetary policy was accompanied by the implementation of additional austerity measures. The deflationary policy stance characterized by higher interest rates, higher taxes and less government spending, put the British economy into a severe recession in the early 1980s. (The data on inflation, money growth and unemployment in this period are shown in Figures 24.11 and 24.13.) Only after the 1980–2 recession – with unemployment rising above the 10% level – did the government establish credibility for its anti-inflation policy. By the end of 1983, inflation was running at a rate of less than 5%.

One indication of the higher credibility came in 1983, when the money growth rate accelerated dramatically and yet inflation did not rise. Workers and firms were convinced that if inflation reared its head, the British authorities would pursue a non-accommodating policy of quashing it. They did not raise wages and prices, which would have shifted the aggregate supply curve leftward and would have led to both inflation and unemployment. Despite the success of anti-inflation policy, unemployment remained at high levels during the mid-1980s. Whereas some economists attribute the low employment during this period to structural changes in the UK economy, others blame the strong disinflationary fiscal and monetary policy of the Thatcher government. Undisputedly, however, British victory over inflation was achieved, but arguably the government obtained credibility the hard way, causing unprecedented high levels of unemployment.[9] ◼

Summary

1 Milton Friedman's famous proposition that 'inflation is always and everywhere a monetary phenomenon' is supported by the following evidence: every country that has experienced a sustained, high inflation has also experienced a high rate of money growth.

2 Aggregate demand and supply analysis shows that high inflation can occur only if there is a high rate of money growth. As long as we recognize that by inflation we mean a rapid and continuing increase in the price level, almost all economists agree with Friedman's proposition.

3 Although high inflation is 'always and everywhere a monetary phenomenon' in the sense that it cannot occur without a high rate of money growth, there are reasons why inflationary monetary policy comes about. The two underlying reasons are the adherence of policymakers to a high employment target and the presence of persistent government budget deficits.

4 Advocates of discretionary policy believe in the use of policy to eliminate excessive unemployment whenever it occurs because they view wage and price adjustment as sluggish and unresponsive to expectations about policy. Opponents of discretionary policy take the opposite view and believe that discretionary policy is counterproductive. In addition, they regard the credibility of a non-accommodating anti-inflation policy as crucial to its success.

Key terms

accommodating policy p. 564

constant-money-growth-rate
   rule p. 575

cost-push inflation p. 563

demand-pull inflation p. 563

discretionary policy p. 572

government budget constraint
   p. 566

monetizing the debt p. 567

printing money p. 567

Ricardian equivalence p. 568

QUESTIONS AND PROBLEMS

All questions and problems are available In My EconLab at **www.myeconlab.com/mishkin.**

1 'There are frequently years when the inflation rate is high and yet money growth is quite low. Therefore, the statement that inflation is a monetary phenomenon cannot be correct.' Comment.

2 Why do economists focus on historical episodes of hyperinflation to decide whether inflation is a monetary phenomenon?

3 'Because increases in government spending raise the aggregate demand curve, fiscal policy by itself can be the source of inflation.' Is this statement true, false, or uncertain? Explain your answer.

4 'A cost-push inflation occurs as a result of workers' attempts to push up their wages. Therefore, inflation does not have to be a monetary phenomenon.' Is this statement true, false, or uncertain? Explain your answer.

5 'Because government policymakers do not consider inflation desirable, their policies cannot be the source of inflation.' Is this statement true, false, or uncertain? Explain your answer.

6 'A budget deficit that is only temporary cannot be the source of inflation.' Is this statement true, false, or uncertain? Explain your answer.

7 How can the central bank's desire to prevent high interest rates lead to inflation?

8 'If the data and recognition lags could be reduced, discretionary policy would more likely be beneficial to the economy.' Is this statement true, false, or uncertain? Explain your answer.

9 'The more sluggish wage and price adjustment is, the more variable output and the price level are when a discretionary policy is pursued.' Is this statement true, false, or uncertain? Explain your answer.

10 'If the public believes that the monetary authorities will pursue a discretionary policy, a cost-push inflation is more likely to develop.' Is this statement true, false, or uncertain? Explain your answer.

11 Why are discretionary policies to eliminate unemployment more likely to lead to inflation than non-discretionary policies?

12 'The less important expectations about policy are to movements of the aggregate supply curve, the stronger the case is for discretionary policy to eliminate unemployment.' Is this statement true, false, or uncertain? Explain your answer.

13 If the economy's self-correcting mechanism works slowly, should the government necessarily pursue discretionary policy to eliminate unemployment?

14 'To prevent inflation, the central bank should follow Teddy Roosevelt's advice: "Speak softly and carry a big stick"'. What would the central bank's 'big stick' be? What is the statement trying to say?

WEB EXERCISES

1 Figure 24.11 reports the inflation rate from 1960 to 2009. As this chapter states, inflation continues to be a major factor in economic policy. Go to the ONS' Consumer Price Indices page **www.ons.gov.uk/ons/rel/ cpi/consumer-price-indices/index.html** and download the latest figures on CPI inflation in the UK. Move data into Excel using the method described at the end of Chapter 1. Graph this data and compare it to Figure 24.11.

(a) Has inflation increased or decreased since the end of 2009?

(b) When was inflation at its highest?

(c) When was inflation at its lowest?

(d) Have we ever had a period of deflation? If so, when?

2 It can be an interesting exercise to compare the purchasing power of the pound sterling over different periods in history. Go to **www.bankofengland.co.uk/ education/inflation/calculator/index1.htm** and use this calculator to compute the following:

(a) If a new home cost £1,000 in 1950, what would it have cost in 2010?

(b) The average household income in 2008 was about £40,000. How much would this have been in 1945?

(c) An average new car cost about £20,000 in 2008. What would this have cost in 1945?

(d) Using the results you found in Exercises (b) and (c), does a car consume more or less of average household income in 2008 than in 1945?

3 The official measure of inflation in the euro area is the Harmonised Index of Consumer Prices (HICP). Eurostat, the official EU statistical agency, has a dedicated page on the HICP (**http://epp.eurostat.ec.europa.eu/portal/page/ portal/hicp/introduction**). From this site:

(a) Find out the key differences between the HICP and the Consumer Price Indices (CPI).

(b) Using the inflation dashboard (**http://epp.eurostat. ec.europa.eu/inflation_dashboard/**) find out what country in the EU has the highest and lowest overall HICP rate in the most recent month.

(c) Using the same inflation dashboard, graph the overall HICP rate since 2006. What patterns do you observe?

Notes

1 For a discussion of the decline in the money growth–inflation correlation over recent decades see Luca Benati, 'Long run evidence on money growth and inflation', ECB Working Paper Series No. 1027 (March 2009), and Bennett T. McCallum and Edward Nelson, 'Money and inflation', in *Handbook of Monetary Economics*, ed. Benjamin M. Friedman, edn 1, vol. 3, ch. 3, pp. 97–153 (Elsevier, 2010).

2 There is a possibility that the short-run aggregate supply curve may immediately shift in toward AS_2, because workers and firms may expect the increase in the money supply, so expected inflation will be higher. In this case, the movement to point 2 will be very rapid, and output need not rise above the natural rate level. (Some support for this scenario from the theory of rational expectations is discussed in Chapter 25.)

3 The argument here demonstrates that 'animal spirits' also cannot be the source of inflation. Although consumer and business optimism, which stimulates these groups' spending, can produce a one-shot shift in the aggregate demand curve and a temporary inflation, it cannot produce continuing shifts in the aggregate demand curve and persistent inflation. The reasoning is the same as before: consumers and businesses cannot continue to raise their spending without limit because their spending cannot exceed 100% of GDP.

4 Supply-side phenomena that alter the natural rate level of output (and shift the long-run aggregate supply curve at Y_n) can produce a permanent one-shot change in the price level. However, this resulting one-shot change results in only a temporary inflation, not a continuing rise in the price level.

5 The cost-push inflation we describe here might also occur as a result either of firms' attempts to obtain higher prices or of negative supply shocks.

6 Another way of understanding the decline in the debt/GDP ratio is to recognize that a rise in the price level reduces the value of the outstanding government debt in real terms – that is, in terms of the goods and services it can buy. So even though budget deficits did lead to a somewhat higher nominal amount of debt in this period, the continually rising price level (inflation) produced a lower real value of the government debt. The decline in the real amount of debt at the same time that real GDP was rising in this period then resulted in the decline in the debt/GDP ratio. For a fascinating discussion of how tricky it is to interpret deficit numbers, see Robert Eisner and Paul J. Pieper, 'A new view of the federal debt and budget deficits', *American Economic Review* 74 (1984): 11–29.

7 The issue that is being described here is the time-inconsistency problem described in Chapter 16.

8 A recent development in monetary theory, new classical macroeconomics, strongly suggests that expectations about policy are crucial to the wage-setting process and the movements of the aggregate supply curve. We will explore why new classical macroeconomics comes to this conclusion in Chapter 25, when we discuss the implications of the rational expectations hypothesis, which states that expectations are formed using all available information, including expectations about policy.

9 Thomas Sargent, 'Stopping moderate inflations: the methods of Poincaré and Thatcher', in *Inflation, Debt, and Indexation*, ed. Rudiger Dornbusch and M. H. Simonsen (Cambridge, MA: MIT Press, 1983), pp. 54–96, discusses the problems that Thatcher's policies caused and contrasts them with more successful anti-inflation policies pursued by the Poincaré government in France during the 1920s.

Useful websites

http://sdw.ecb.europa.eu/The home page of the Statistical Data Warehouse, the ECB's interactive database, from which selected indicators of the euro area can be downloaded.

http://epp.eurostat.ec.europa.eu/portal/page/portal/hicp/introduction The inflation page of Eurostat, the official EU statistical agency.

http://www.ons.gov.uk/ons/rel/cpi/consumer-price-indices/index.html The Consumer Price Indices page of the Office for National Statistics.

http://www.bankofengland.co.uk/education/Pages/inflation/default.aspx The Bank of England's 'Inflation tools' page has some useful references and links.

ftp://ftp.bls.gov/pub/special.requests/cpi/cpiai.txt Download historical inflation statistics for the US going back to 1913. These data can easily be moved into Microsoft Excel using the procedure discussed at the end of Chapter 1.

CHAPTER 25

Rational expectations: implications for policy

PREVIEW

After World War II, economists, armed with models (such as the *ISLM* model) that described how government policies could be used to manipulate employment and output, felt that discretionary policies could reduce the severity of business cycle fluctuations without creating inflation. In the 1960s and 1970s, these economists got their chance to put their policies into practice (see Chapter 24), but the results were not what they had anticipated. The economic record for that period is not a happy one: inflation accelerated, the rate often climbing above 10%, while unemployment figures deteriorated from those of the 1950s.[1]

In the 1970s and 1980s, economists, including Robert Lucas of the University of Chicago and Thomas Sargent, now at New York University, used the rational expectations theory discussed in Chapter 7 to examine why discretionary policies appear to have performed so poorly. Their analysis cast doubt on whether macroeconomic models can be used to evaluate the potential effects of policy and on whether policy can be effective when the public *expects* that it will be implemented. Because the analysis of Lucas and Sargent has such strong implications for the way policy should be conducted, it has been labelled the *rational expectations revolution*.[2]

This chapter examines the analysis behind the rational expectations revolution. We start first with the Lucas critique, which indicates that because expectations are important in economic behaviour, it may be quite difficult to predict what the outcome of a discretionary policy will be. We then discuss the effect of rational expectations on the aggregate demand and supply analysis developed in Chapter 22 by exploring three models that incorporate expectations in different ways.

A comparison of all three models indicates that the existence of rational expectations makes discretionary policies less likely to be successful and raises the issue of credibility as an important element affecting policy outcomes. With rational expectations, an essential ingredient to a successful anti-inflation policy is the credibility of the policy in the eyes of the public. The rational expectations revolution is now at the centre of many of the current debates in monetary theory that have major implications for how monetary and fiscal policy should be conducted.

The Lucas critique of policy evaluation

In his famous paper 'Econometric policy evaluation: a critique', Robert Lucas presented an argument that had devastating implications for the usefulness of conventional **econometric models** (models whose equations are estimated with statistical procedures) for evaluating policy.[3] Economists developed these models for two purposes: to forecast economic activity and to evaluate the effects of different policies. Although Lucas's critique had nothing to say about the usefulness of these models as forecasting tools, he argued that they could not be relied on to evaluate the potential impact of particular policies on the economy.

Econometric policy evaluation

To understand Lucas's argument, we must first understand econometric policy evaluation: how econometric models are used to evaluate policy. For example, we can examine how the central bank uses its econometric model in making decisions about the future course of monetary policy. The model contains equations that describe the relationships among hundreds of variables. These relationships are assumed to remain constant and are estimated using past data. Let's say that the central bank wants to know the effect on unemployment and inflation of a decrease in the interest rate from 5% to 4%. It feeds the new, lower interest rate into a computer that contains the model, and the model then provides an answer about how much unemployment will fall as a result of the lower interest rate and how much the inflation rate will rise. Other possible policies, such as a rise in the interest rate by one percentage point, might also be fed into the model. After a series of these policies have been tried out, the policymakers at the central bank can see which policies produce the most desirable outcome for unemployment and inflation.

Lucas's challenge to this procedure for evaluating policies is based on a simple principle of rational expectations theory from Chapter 7: *the way in which expectations are formed (the relationship of expectations to past information) changes when the behaviour of forecasted variables changes.* So when policy changes, the relationship between expectations and past information will change, and because expectations affect economic behaviour, the relationships in the econometric model will change. The econometric model, which has been estimated with past data, is then no longer the correct model for evaluating the response to this policy change and may consequently prove highly misleading.

Example: The term structure of interest rates

The best way to understand Lucas's argument is to look at a concrete example involving only one equation typically found in econometric models: the term structure equation. The equation relates the long-term interest rate to current and past values of the short-term interest rate. It is one of the most important equations in macroeconometric models because the long-term interest rate, not the short-term rate, is the one believed to have an impact on aggregate demand.

In Chapter 6, we learned that the long-term interest rate is related to an average of expected future short-term interest rates. Suppose that in the past, when the short-term rate rose, it quickly fell back down again; that is, any increase was temporary. Because rational expectations theory suggests that any rise in the short-term interest rate is expected to be only temporary, a rise should have only a minimal effect on the average of expected future short-term rates. It will cause the long-term interest rate to rise by a negligible amount. The term structure relationship estimated using past data will then show only a weak effect on the long-term interest rate of changes in the short-term rate.

Suppose the central bank wants to evaluate what will happen to the economy if it pursues a policy that is likely to raise the short-term interest rate from a current level of 5% to a permanently higher level of 8%. The term structure equation that has been estimated using past data will indicate that there will be just a small change in the long-term interest rate. However, if the public recognizes that the short-term rate is rising to a permanently higher level, rational expectations theory indicates that people will no longer expect a rise in the short-term rate to be temporary. Instead, when they see the interest rate rise to 8%, they will expect the average of future short-term interest rates to rise substantially, and so the long-term interest rate will rise greatly, not minimally as the estimated term structure equation suggests. You can see that evaluating the likely outcome of the change in central bank policy with an econometric model can be highly misleading.

The term structure example also demonstrates another aspect of the Lucas critique. The effects of a particular policy depend critically on the public's expectations about the policy. If the public expects the rise in the short-term interest rate to be merely temporary, the response of long-term interest rates, as we have seen, will be negligible. If, however, the public expects the rise to be more permanent, the response of long-term rates will be far greater. *The Lucas critique points out not only that conventional econometric models cannot be used for policy evaluation, but also that the public's expectations about a policy will influence the response to that policy.*

The term structure equation discussed here is only one of many equations in econometric models to which the Lucas critique applies. In fact, Lucas uses the examples of consumption and investment equations in his paper. One attractive feature of the term structure example is that it deals with expectations in a financial market, a sector of the economy for which the theory and empirical evidence supporting rational expectations are very strong. The Lucas critique should also apply, however, to sectors of the economy for which rational expectations theory is more controversial, because the basic principle of the Lucas critique is not that expectations are always rational but rather that the formation of expectations changes when the behaviour of a forecasted variable changes. This less stringent principle is supported by the evidence in sectors of the economy other than financial markets.

New classical macroeconomic model

We now turn to the implications of rational expectations for the aggregate demand and supply analysis we studied in Chapter 22. The first model we examine that views expectations as rational is the *new classical macroeconomic model* developed by Robert Lucas and Thomas Sargent, among others. In the new classical model, all wages and prices are completely flexible with respect to expected changes in the price level; that is, a rise in the expected price level results in an immediate and equal rise in wages and prices because workers try to keep their *real* wages from falling when they expect the price level to rise.

This view of how wages and prices are set indicates that a rise in the expected price level causes an immediate leftward shift in the short-run aggregate supply curve, which leaves real wages unchanged and aggregate output at the natural rate (full-employment) level if expectations are realized. This model then suggests that anticipated policy has no effect on aggregate output and unemployment; only unanticipated policy has an effect.

Effects of unanticipated and anticipated policy

First, let us look at the short-run response to an unanticipated (unexpected) policy such as an unexpected increase in the money supply.

In Figure 25.1, the short-run aggregate supply curve AS_1 is drawn for an expected price level P_1. The initial aggregate demand curve AD_1 intersects AS_1 at point 1, where the realized price level is at the expected price level P_1 and aggregate output is at the natural rate level Y_n. Because point 1 is also on the long-run aggregate supply curve at Y_n, there is no tendency for the aggregate supply to shift. The economy remains in long-run equilibrium.

Suppose the central bank suddenly decides the unemployment rate is too high and so makes a large open market purchase that is unexpected by the public. The money supply increases, and the aggregate demand curve shifts rightward to AD_2. Because this shift is unexpected, the expected price level remains at P_1 and the short-run aggregate supply curve remains at AS_1. Equilibrium is now at point 2′, the intersection of AD_2 and AS_1. Aggregate output increases above the natural rate level to $Y_{2'}$ and the realized price level increases too.

FIGURE 25.1

Short-run response to unanticipated expansionary policy in the new classical model

Initially, the economy is at point 1 at the intersection of AD_1 and AS_1 (expected price level = P_1). An expansionary policy shifts the aggregate demand curve to AD_2, but because this is unexpected, the short-run aggregate supply curve remains fixed at AS_1. Equilibrium now occurs at point 2' – aggregate output has increased above the natural rate level to $Y_{2'}$, and the price level has increased to $P_{2'}$.

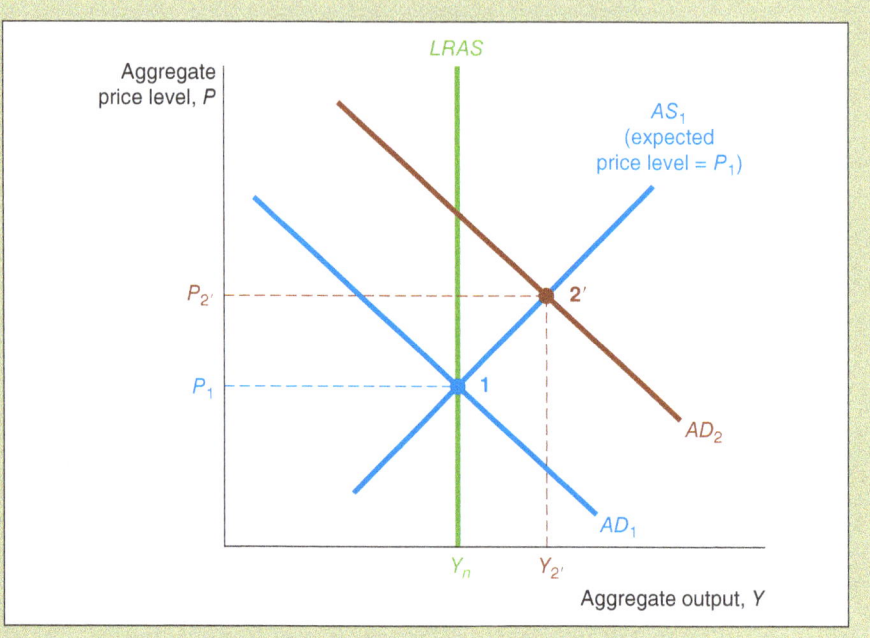

If, by contrast, the public expects that the central bank will make these open market purchases to lower unemployment because they have seen the central bank do this in the past, the expansionary policy will be anticipated. The outcome of such anticipated expansionary policy is illustrated in Figure 25.2. Because expectations are rational, workers and firms recognize that an expansionary policy will shift the aggregate demand curve to the right and will expect the aggregate price level to rise to P_2. Workers will demand higher wages so that their real earnings will remain the same when the price level rises. The short-

FIGURE 25.2

Short-run response to anticipated expansionary policy in the new classical model

The expansionary policy shifts the aggregate demand curve rightward to AD_2, but because this policy is expected, the short-run aggregate supply curve shifts leftward to AS_2. The economy moves to point 2, where aggregate output is still at the natural rate level but the price level has increased to P_2.

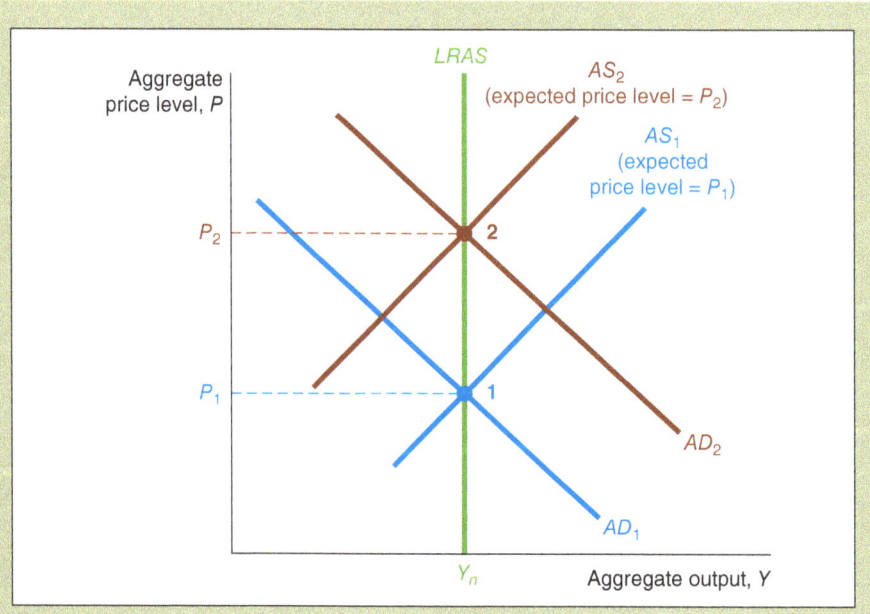

run aggregate supply curve then shifts leftward to AS_2 and intersects AD_2 at point 2, an equilibrium point where aggregate output is at the natural rate level Y_n and the price level has risen to P_2.

The new classical macroeconomic model demonstrates that aggregate output does not increase as a result of anticipated expansionary policy and that the economy immediately moves to a point of long-run equilibrium (point 2) where aggregate output is at the natural rate level. Although Figure 25.2 suggests why this occurs, we have not yet proved why an anticipated expansionary policy shifts the short-run aggregate supply curve to exactly AS_2 (corresponding to an expected price level of P_2) and hence why aggregate output *necessarily* remains at the natural rate level. The proof is somewhat difficult and is dealt with in the box 'Proof of the policy ineffectiveness proposition'.

The new classical model has the word *classical* associated with it because when policy is anticipated, the new classical model has a property that is associated with the classical economists of the nineteenth and early twentieth centuries: aggregate output remains at the natural rate level. Yet the new classical model allows aggregate output to fluctuate away from the natural rate level as a result of *unanticipated* movements in the aggregate demand curve. The conclusion from the new classical model is a striking one: ***anticipated policy has no effect on the business cycle; only unanticipated policy matters***.[4]

This conclusion has been called the **policy ineffectiveness proposition**, because it implies that one anticipated policy is just like any other; it has no effect on output fluctuations. You should recognize that this proposition does not rule out output effects from policy changes. If the policy is a surprise (unanticipated), it will have an effect on output.[5]

CLOSER LOOK
Proof of the policy ineffectiveness proposition

The proof that in the new classical macroeconomic model aggregate output *necessarily* remains at the natural rate level when there is anticipated expansionary policy is as follows. In the new classical model, the expected price level for the short-run aggregate supply curve occurs at its intersection with the long-run aggregate supply curve (see Figure 25.2). The optimal forecast of the price level is given by the intersection of the aggregate supply curve with the anticipated aggregate demand curve AD_2. If the short-run aggregate supply curve is to the right of AS_2 in Figure 25.2, it will intersect AD_2 at a price level lower than the expected level (which is the intersection of this aggregate supply curve and the long-run aggregate supply curve). The optimal forecast of the price level will then not equal the expected price level, thereby violating the rationality of expectations. A similar argument can be made to show that when the short-run aggregate supply curve is to the left of AS_2, the assumption of rational expectations also is violated. Only when the short-run aggregate supply curve is at AS_2 (corresponding to an expected price level of P_2) are expectations rational because the optimal forecast equals the expected price level. As we see in Figure 25.2, the AS_2 curve implies that aggregate output remains at the natural rate level as a result of the anticipated expansionary policy.

Can an expansionary policy lead to a decline in aggregate output?

Another important feature of the new classical model is that an expansionary policy, such as an increase in the rate of money growth, can lead to a *decline* in aggregate output if the public expects an even more expansionary policy than the one actually implemented. There will be a surprise in the policy, but it will be negative and drive output down. Policymakers cannot be sure if their policies will work in the intended direction.

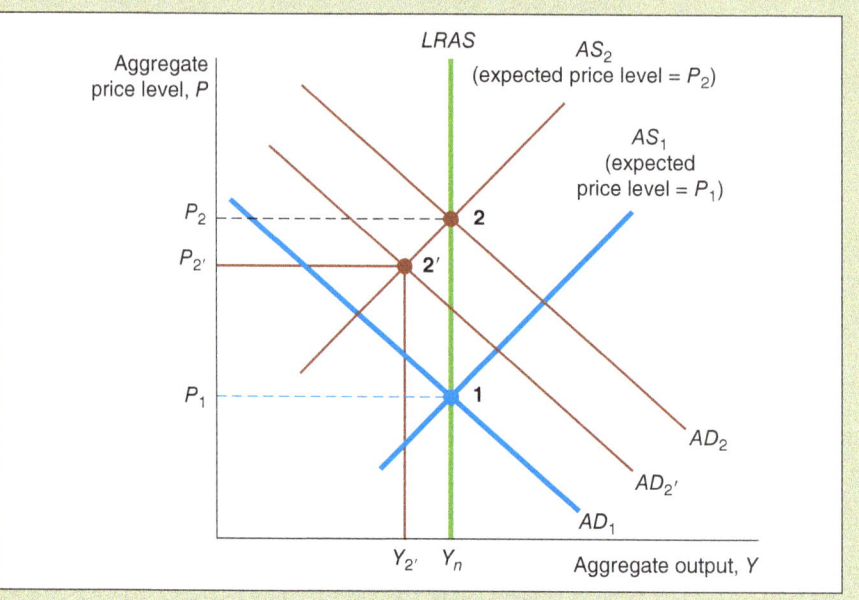

Short-run response to an expansionary policy that is less expansionary than expected in the new classical model

Because the public expects the aggregate demand curve to shift to AD_2, the short-run aggregate supply curve shifts to AS_2 (expected price level $= P_2$). When the actual expansionary policy falls short of the public's expectation (the aggregate demand curve merely shifts to $AD_{2'}$), the economy ends up at point 2', at the intersection of $AD_{2'}$ and AS_2. Despite the expansionary policy, aggregate output falls to $Y_{2'}$.

To see how an expansionary policy can lead to a decline in aggregate output, let us turn to the aggregate supply and demand diagram in Figure 25.3. Initially we are at point 1, the intersection of AD_1 and AS_1; output is Y_n, and the price level is P_1. Now suppose that the public expects the central bank to increase the money supply to shift the aggregate demand curve to AD_2. As we saw in Figure 25.2, the short-run aggregate supply curve shifts leftward to AS_2, because the price level is expected to rise to P_2. Suppose that the expansionary policy engineered by the central bank actually falls short of what was expected so that the aggregate demand curve shifts only to $AD_{2'}$. The economy will move to point 2', the intersection of the short-run aggregate supply curve AS_2 and the aggregate demand curve. The result of the mistaken expectation is that output falls to $Y_{2'}$, while the price level rises to $P_{2'}$, rather than P_2. An expansionary policy that is less expansionary than anticipated leads to an output movement directly opposite to that intended.

Implications for policymakers

The new classical model, with its policy ineffectiveness proposition, has two important lessons for policymakers: it illuminates the distinction between the effects of anticipated versus unanticipated policy actions, and it demonstrates that policymakers cannot know the outcome of their decisions without knowing the public's expectations regarding them.

At first you might think that policymakers can still use discretionary policy to stabilize the economy. Once they figure out the public's expectations, they can know what effect their policies will have. There are two catches to such a conclusion. First, it may be nearly impossible to find out what the public's expectations are, given that the public consists of several million citizens. Second, even if it were possible, policymakers would run into further difficulties, because the public has rational expectations and will try to guess what policymakers plan to do. Public expectations do not remain fixed while policymakers are plotting a surprise – the public will revise its expectations, and policies will have no predictable effect on output.[6]

Where does this lead us? Should the central bank and other policymaking agencies pack up, lock the doors and go home? In a sense, the answer is yes. The new classical model implies that discretionary stabilization policy cannot be effective and might have undesirable effects on the economy. Policymakers' attempts to use discretionary policy may create a fluctuating policy stance that leads to unpredictable policy surprises, which in turn cause undesirable fluctuations around the natural rate level of aggregate output. To eliminate these undesirable fluctuations, the central bank and other policymaking agencies should abandon discretionary policy and generate as few policy surprises as possible.

As we have seen in Figure 25.2, even though anticipated policy has no effect on aggregate output in the new classical model, it *does* have an effect on the price level. The new classical macroeconomists care about anticipated policy and suggest that policy rules be designed so that the price level will remain stable.

New Keynesian model

In the new classical model, all wages and prices are completely flexible with respect to expected changes in the price level; that is, a rise in the expected price level results in an immediate and equal rise in wages and prices. Many economists who accept rational expectations as a working hypothesis do not accept the characterization of wage and price flexibility in the new classical model. These critics of the new classical model, called *new Keynesians*, object to complete wage and price flexibility and identify factors in the economy that prevent some wages and prices from rising fully with a rise in the expected price level.

Long-term labour contracts are one source of rigidity that prevents wages and prices from responding fully to changes in the expected price level (called **wage–price stickiness**). For example, workers might find themselves at the end of the first year of a three-year wage contract that specifies the wage rate for the coming two years. Even if new information appeared that would make them raise their expectations of the inflation rate and the future price level, they could not do anything about it because they are locked into a wage agreement. Even with a high expectation about the price level, the wage rate will not adjust. In two years, when the contract is renegotiated, both workers and firms may build the expected inflation rate into their agreement, but they cannot do so immediately.

Another source of rigidity is that firms may be reluctant to change wages frequently even when there are no explicit wage contracts, because such changes may affect the work effort of the labour force. For example, a firm may not want to lower workers' wages when unemployment is high, because this might result in poorer worker performance. Price stickiness may also occur because firms engage in fixed-price contracts with their suppliers or because it is costly for firms to change prices frequently. All of these rigidities (which diminish wage and price flexibility), even if they are not present in all wage and price arrangements, suggest that an increase in the expected price level might not translate into an immediate and complete adjustment of wages and prices.

Although the new Keynesians do not agree with the complete wage and price flexibility of the new classical macroeconomics, they nevertheless recognize the importance of expectations to the determination of short-run aggregate supply and are willing to accept rational expectations theory as a reasonable characterization of how expectations are formed. The model they have developed, the *new Keynesian model*, assumes that expectations are rational but does not assume complete wage and price flexibility; instead, it assumes that wages and prices are sticky. Its basic conclusion is that unanticipated policy has a larger effect on aggregate output than anticipated policy (as in the new classical model). However, in contrast to the new classical model, the policy ineffectiveness proposition does not hold in the new Keynesian model: anticipated policy *does* affect aggregate output and the business cycle.[7]

Effects of unanticipated and anticipated policy

In panel (a) of Figure 25.4, we look at the short-run response to an unanticipated expansionary policy for the new Keynesian model. The analysis is identical to that of the new classical model. We again start at point 1, where the aggregate demand curve AD_1

FIGURE 25.4

Short-run response to expansionary policy in the new Keynesian model

The expansionary policy that shifts aggregate demand to AD_2 has a bigger effect on output when it is unanticipated than when it is anticipated. When the expansionary policy is unanticipated in panel (a), the short-run aggregate supply curve does not shift, and the economy moves to point U, so that aggregate output increases to Y_U and the price level rises to P_U. When the policy is anticipated in panel (b), the short-run aggregate supply curve shifts to AS_A (but not all the way to AS_2 because rigidities prevent complete wage and price adjustment), and the economy moves to point A so that aggregate output rises to Y_A (which is less than Y_U) and the price level rises to P_A (which is higher than P_U).

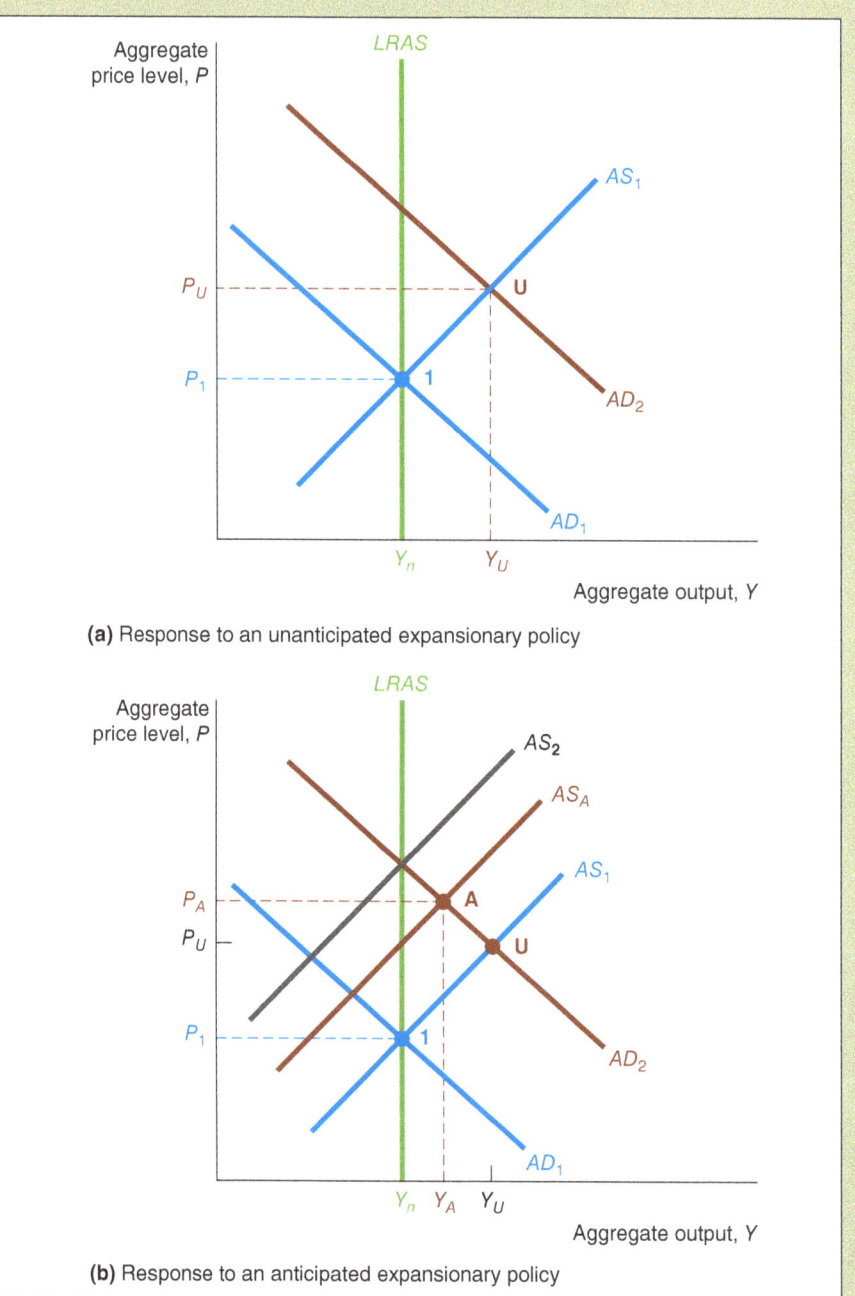

(a) Response to an unanticipated expansionary policy

(b) Response to an anticipated expansionary policy

intersects the short-run aggregate supply curve AS_1 at the natural rate level of output and price level P_1. When the central bank pursues its expansionary policy of purchasing bonds and raising the money supply, the aggregate demand curve shifts rightward to AD_2. Because the expansionary policy is unanticipated, the expected price level remains unchanged, leaving the short-run aggregate supply curve unchanged. Thus the economy moves to point U, where aggregate output has increased to Y_U and the price level has risen to P_U.

In panel (b), we see what happens when the central bank's expansionary policy that shifts the aggregate demand curve from AD_1 to AD_2 is anticipated. Because the expansionary policy is anticipated and expectations are rational, the expected price level increases, causing wages to increase and the short-run aggregate supply curve to shift to the left. Because of rigidities that do not allow *complete* wage and price adjustment, the short-run aggregate supply curve does not shift all the way to AS_2 as it does in the new classical model. Instead, it moves to AS_A, and the economy settles at point A, the intersection of AD_2 and AS_A. Aggregate output has risen above the natural rate level to Y_A, while the price level has increased to P_A. *Unlike the new classical model, in the new Keynesian model anticipated policy does have an effect on aggregate output.*

We can see in Figure 25.4 that Y_U is greater than Y_A, meaning that the output response to unanticipated policy is greater than to anticipated policy. It is greater because the short-run aggregate supply curve does not shift when policy is unanticipated, causing a lower price level and hence a higher level of output. We see that *like the new classical model, the new Keynesian model distinguishes between the effects of anticipated and unanticipated policy, with unanticipated policy having a greater effect.*

Implications for policymakers

Because the new Keynesian model indicates that anticipated policy has an effect on aggregate output, it does not rule out beneficial effects from discretionary stabilization policy, in contrast to the new classical model. It does warn policymakers that designing such a policy will not be an easy task, because the effects of anticipated and unanticipated policy can be quite different. As in the new classical model, to predict the outcome of their actions, policymakers must be aware of the public's expectations about those actions. Policymakers face similar difficulties in devising successful policies in both the new classical and new Keynesian models.

Comparison of the two new models with the traditional model

To obtain a clearer picture of the impact of the rational expectations revolution on our analysis of the aggregate economy, we can compare the two rational expectations models (the new classical macroeconomic model and the new Keynesian model) to a model that we call, for lack of a better name, the *traditional model*. In the traditional model, expectations are *not* rational. That model uses adaptive expectations (mentioned in Chapter 7), expectations based solely on past experience. The traditional model views expected inflation as an average of past inflation rates. This average is not affected by the public's predictions of future policy; hence predictions of future policy do not affect the aggregate supply curve.

First we will examine the short-run output and price responses in the three models. Then we will examine the implications of these models for both stabilization and anti-inflation policies. As a study aid, the comparison of the three models is summarized in Table 25.1. You may want to refer to the table as we proceed with the comparison.

Short-run output and price responses

Figure 25.5 compares the response of aggregate output and the price level to an expansionary policy in the three models. Initially, the economy is at point 1, the intersection of the aggregate demand curve AD_1 and the short-run aggregate supply curve AS_1. When the expansionary policy occurs, the aggregate demand curve shifts to AD_2. If the expansionary policy is *unanticipated*, all three models show the same short-run output response. The traditional model views the short-run aggregate supply curve as given in the short run, while the other two view it as remaining at AS_1 because there is no change in the expected price level when the policy is a surprise. Hence, when policy is *unanticipated*, all three models indicate a movement to point 1', where the AD_2 and AS_1 curves intersect and where aggregate output and the price level have risen to Y_1 and P_1 respectively.

The three models

Model	Response to unanticipated expansionary policy	Response to anticipated expansionary policy	Can discretionary policy be beneficial?	Response to unanticipated anti-inflation policy	Response to anticipated anti-inflation policy	Is credibility important to successful anti-inflation policy?
Traditional model	$Y\uparrow, P\uparrow$	$Y\uparrow, \pi\uparrow$ by same amount as when policy is unanticipated	Yes	$Y\downarrow, \pi\downarrow$	$Y\downarrow, \pi\downarrow$ by same amount as when policy is unanticipated	No
New classical macro-economic model	$Y\uparrow, P\uparrow$	Y unchanged, $P\uparrow$ by more than when policy is unanticipated	No	$Y\downarrow, \pi\downarrow$	Y unchanged, $\pi\downarrow$ by more than when policy is unanticipated	Yes
New Keynesian model	$Y\uparrow, P\uparrow$	$Y\uparrow$ by less than when policy is unanticipated, $P\uparrow$ by more than when policy is unanticipated	Yes, but designing a beneficial policy is difficult	$Y\downarrow, \pi\downarrow$	$Y\downarrow$ by less than when policy is unanticipated, $\pi\downarrow$ by more than when policy is unanticipated	Yes

Note: π represents the inflation rate.

The response to the *anticipated* expansionary policy is, however, quite different in the three models. In the traditional model in panel (a), the short-run aggregate supply curve remains at AS_1 even when the expansionary policy is anticipated, because adaptive expectations imply that anticipated policy has no effect on expectations and hence on aggregate supply. It indicates that the economy moves to point 1', which is where it moved when the policy was unanticipated. The traditional model does not distinguish between the effects of anticipated and unanticipated policy: both have the same effect on output and prices.

In the new classical model in panel (b), the short-run aggregate supply curve shifts leftward to AS_2 when policy is anticipated, because when expectations of the higher price level are realized, aggregate output will be at the natural rate level. Thus it indicates that the economy moves to point 2; aggregate output does not rise, but prices do, to P_2. This outcome is quite different from the move to point 1' when policy is unanticipated. The new classical model distinguishes between the short-run effects of anticipated and unanticipated policies: anticipated policy has no effect on output, but unanticipated policy does. However, anticipated policy has a bigger impact than unanticipated policy on price level movements.

The new Keynesian model in panel (c) is an intermediate position between the traditional and new classical models. It recognizes that anticipated policy affects the aggregate supply curve, but due to rigidities such as long-term contracts, wage and price adjustment is not as complete as in the new classical model. Hence the short-run aggregate supply curve shifts only to $AS_{2'}$, in response to anticipated policy, and the economy moves to point 2', where output at $Y_{2'}$ is lower than the Y_2 level reached when the expansionary policy is unanticipated. But the price level at P_2 is higher than the level P_1 that resulted from the unanticipated policy. Like the new classical model, the new Keynesian model distinguishes between the effects of anticipated and unanticipated policies: anticipated policy has a smaller effect on output than unanticipated policy does but a larger effect on the price level. However, in contrast to the new classical model, anticipated policy does affect output fluctuations.

FIGURE 25.5

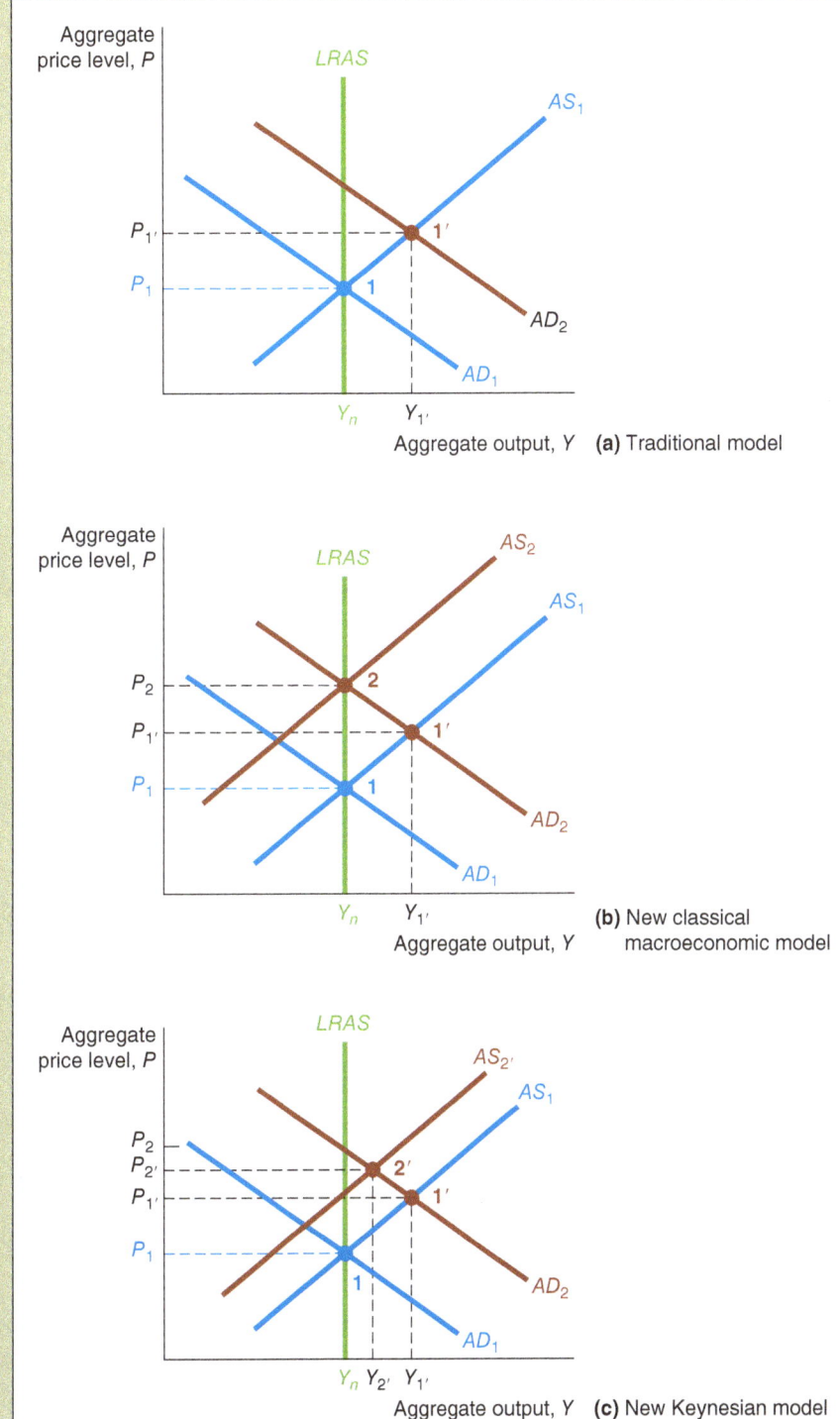

Comparison of the short-run response to expansionary policy in the three models

Initially, the economy is at point 1. The expansionary policy shifts the aggregate demand curve from AD_1 to AD_2. In the traditional model, the expansionary policy moves the economy to point 1' whether the policy is anticipated or not. In the new classical model, the expansionary policy moves the economy to point 1' if it is unanticipated and to point 2 if it is anticipated. In the new Keynesian model, the expansionary policy moves the economy to point 1' if it is unanticipated and to point 2' if it is anticipated.

Stabilization policy

The three models have different views of the effectiveness of *stabilization policy*, policy intended to reduce output fluctuations. Because the effects of anticipated and unanticipated policy are identical in the traditional model, policymakers do not have to concern themselves with the public's expectations. This makes it easier for them to predict the outcome of their policy, an essential matter if their actions are to have the intended effect. In the traditional model, it is possible for discretionary policy to stabilize output fluctuations.

The new classical model takes the extreme position that discretionary stabilization policy serves to aggravate output fluctuations. In this model, only unanticipated policy affects output; anticipated policy does not matter. Policymakers can affect output only by surprising the public. Because the public is assumed to have rational expectations, it will always try to guess what policymakers plan to do.

In the new classical model, the conduct of policy can be viewed as a game in which the public and the policymakers are always trying to outfox each other by guessing the other's intentions and expectations. The sole possible outcome of this process is that discretionary stabilization policy will have no predictable effect on output and cannot be relied on to stabilize economic activity. Instead, it may create a lot of uncertainty about policy that will increase random output fluctuations around the natural rate level of output. Such an undesirable effect is exactly the opposite of what the discretionary stabilization policy is trying to achieve. The outcome in the new classical view is that policymakers should be non-discretionary and promote as much certainty about their policy actions as possible.

The new Keynesian model again takes an intermediate position between the traditional and the new classical models. Contrary to the new classical model, it indicates that anticipated policy *does* matter to output fluctuations. Policymakers can count on some output response from their anticipated policies and can use them to stabilize the economy.

In contrast to the traditional model, however, the new Keynesian model recognizes that the effects of anticipated and unanticipated policy will not be the same. Policymakers will encounter more uncertainty about the outcome of their actions, because they cannot be sure to what extent the policy is anticipated. Hence a discretionary policy is less likely to operate always in the intended direction and is less likely to achieve its goals. The new Keynesian model raises the possibility that a discretionary policy could be beneficial, but uncertainty about the outcome of policies in this model may make the design of such a beneficial policy extremely difficult.

Anti-inflation policies

So far we have focused on the implications of these three models for policies whose intent is to eliminate fluctuations in output. By the end of the 1970s, the high inflation rate (then over 10%) helped shift the primary concern of policymakers to the reduction of inflation. What do these models have to say about anti-inflation policies designed to eliminate upward movements in the price level? The aggregate demand and supply diagrams in Figure 25.6 will help us answer the question.

Suppose that the economy has settled into a sustained 10% inflation rate caused by a high rate of money growth that shifts the aggregate demand curve so that it moves up by 10% every year. If this inflation rate has been built into wage and price contracts, the short-run aggregate supply curve shifts and rises at the same rate. We see this in Figure 25.6 as a shift in the aggregate demand curve from AD_1 in year 1 to AD_2 in year 2, while the short-run aggregate supply curve moves from AS_1 to AS_2. In year 1, the economy is at point 1 (intersection of AD_1 and AS_1); in the second year, the economy moves to point 2 (intersection of AD_2 and AS_2), and the price level has risen 10%, from P_1 to P_2. (Note that the figure is not drawn to scale.)

Now suppose that the central bank decides that inflation must be stopped and ends the high rate of money growth so that the aggregate demand curve will not rise from AD_1. The policy of halting money growth immediately could be costly if it leads to a fall in output. Let's use our three models to explore the degree to which aggregate output will fall as a result of an anti-inflation policy.

First, look at the outcome of this policy in the traditional model's view of the world in panel (a). The movement of the short-run aggregate supply curve to AS_2 is already set in

FIGURE 25.6

Anti-inflation policy in the three models

With an ongoing inflation in which the economy is moving from point 1 to point 2, the aggregate demand curve is shifting from AD_1 to AD_2 and the short-run aggregate supply curve from AS_1 to AS_2. The anti-inflation policy, when implemented, prevents the aggregate demand curve from rising, holding it at AD_1. (a) In the traditional model, the economy moves to point 2′ whether the anti-inflation policy is anticipated or not. (b) In the new classical model, the economy moves to point 2′ if the policy is unanticipated and stays at point 1 if it is anticipated. (c) In the new Keynesian model, the economy moves to point 2′ if the policy is unanticipated and to point 2″ if it is anticipated.

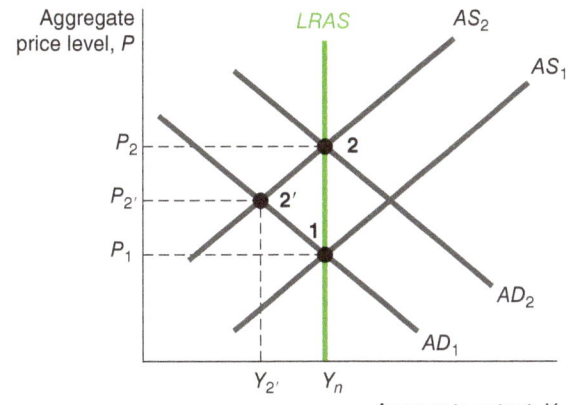

(a) Traditional model

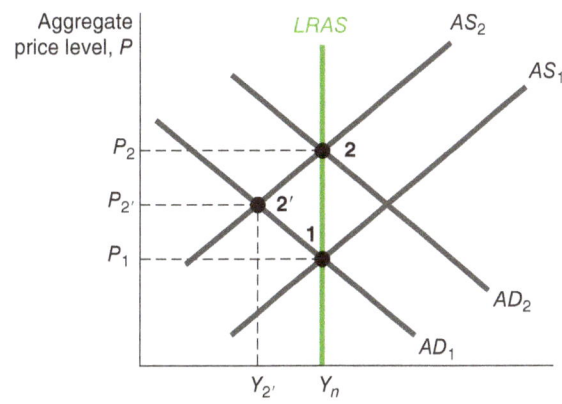

(b) New classical macroeconomic model

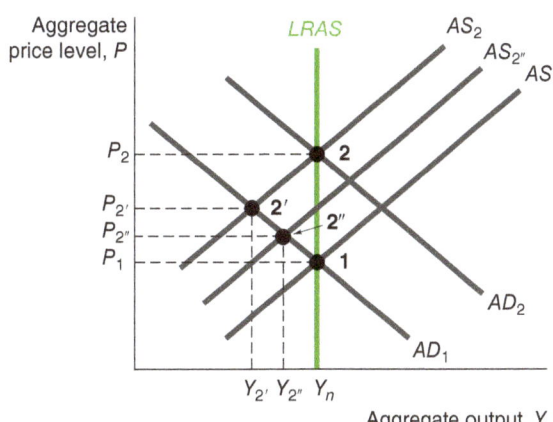

(c) New Keynesian model

place and is unaffected by the new policy of keeping the aggregate demand curve at AD_1 (whether the effort is anticipated or not). The economy moves to point 2 (the intersection of the AD_1 and AS_2 curves), and the inflation rate slows down because the price level increases only to $P_{2'}$ rather than P_2. The reduction in inflation has not been without cost: output has declined to Y_2, which is well below the natural rate level.

In the traditional model, estimates of the cost in terms of lost output for each 1% reduction in the inflation rate are around 4% of a year's real GDP. The high cost of reducing inflation in the traditional model is one reason why some economists are reluctant to advocate an anti-inflation policy of the sort tried here. They question whether the cost of high unemployment is worth the benefits of a reduced inflation rate.

If you adhere to the new classical philosophy, you would not be as pessimistic about the high cost of reducing the inflation rate. If the public *expects* the monetary authorities to stop the inflationary process by ending the high rate of money growth, it will occur without any output loss. In panel (b), the aggregate demand curve will remain at AD_1, but because this is expected, wages and prices can be adjusted so that they will not rise, and the short-run aggregate supply curve will remain at AS_1 instead of moving to AS_2. The economy will stay put at point 1 (the intersection of AD_1 and AS_1), and aggregate output will remain at the natural rate level while inflation is stopped because the price level is unchanged.

An important element in the story is that the anti-inflation policy be anticipated by the public. If the policy is *not* expected, the aggregate demand curve remains at AD_1, but the short-run aggregate supply curve continues its shift to AS_2. The outcome of the unanticipated anti-inflation policy is a movement of the economy to point 2'. Although the inflation rate slows in this case, it is not entirely eliminated as it was when the anti-inflation policy was anticipated. Even worse, aggregate output falls below the natural rate level to $Y_{2'}$. An anti-inflation policy that is unanticipated, then, is far less desirable than one that is anticipated.

The new Keynesian model in panel (c) also leads to the conclusion that an unanticipated anti-inflation policy is less desirable than an anticipated one. If the policy of keeping the aggregate demand curve at AD_1 is *not* expected, the short-run aggregate supply curve will continue its shift to AS_2, and the economy moves to point 2 at the intersection of AD_1 and AS_2. The inflation rate slows, but output declines to $Y_{2'}$, well below the natural rate level.

If, by contrast, the anti-inflation policy is *expected*, the short-run aggregate supply curve will not move all the way to AS_2. Instead it will shift only to $AS_{2'}$ because some wages and prices (but not all) can be adjusted, so wages and the price level will not rise at their previous rates. Instead of moving to point 2' (as occurred when the anti-inflation policy was not expected), the economy moves to point 2", the intersection of the AD_1 and $AS_{2'}$ curves. The outcome is more desirable than when the policy is unanticipated – the inflation rate is lower (the price level rises only to $P_{2''}$ and not P_2), and the output loss is smaller as well ($Y_{2''}$ is higher than Y_2).

Credibility in fighting inflation

Both the new classical and new Keynesian models indicate that for an anti-inflation policy to be successful in reducing inflation at the lowest output cost, the public must believe (expect) that it will be implemented. In the new classical view of the world, the best anti-inflation policy (when it is credible) is to go 'cold turkey'. The rise in the aggregate demand curve from AD_1 should be stopped immediately. Inflation would be eliminated at once with no loss of output *if the policy is credible*. In a new Keynesian world, the cold-turkey policy, *even if credible*, is not as desirable, because it will produce some output loss.

John Taylor, a proponent of the new Keynesian model, has demonstrated that a more gradual approach to reducing inflation may be able to eliminate inflation without producing a substantial output loss.[8] An important catch here is that this gradual policy must somehow be made credible, which may be harder to achieve than a cold-turkey anti-inflation policy, which demonstrates immediately that the policymakers are serious about fighting inflation. Taylor's contention that inflation can be reduced with little output loss may be overly optimistic.

Incorporating rational expectations into aggregate supply and demand analysis indicates that a successful anti-inflation policy must be credible. Evidence that credibility plays an important role in successful anti-inflation application policies is provided by the dramatic end of the Bolivian hyperinflation in 1985 (see the Global box: 'Ending of Bolivian hyperinflation: a successful anti-inflation programme'). The disinflationary policies implemented by the EU countries in the 1990s provide another clear example in this respect. Before joining the EMU, many southern European countries like Italy, Greece, Spain and Portugal suffered from chronic high inflation rates mostly due to their lack of internal discipline and institutions. In order to meet the inflation convergence criterion set by the Maastricht Treaty (see the Application 'Maastricht inflation criterion as entry condition to EMU'), during the 1990s these countries went through a credible disinflationary process which led to a substantial reduction in inflation, with only a moderate increase in unemployment. But establishing credibility is easier said than done. You might think that an announcement by policymakers that they plan to pursue an anti-inflation policy might do the trick. The public would expect this policy and would act accordingly. However, that conclusion implies that the public will believe the policymakers' announcement. Unfortunately, that is not how the real world works.

GLOBAL
Ending the Bolivian hyperinflation: a successful anti-inflation programme

The most remarkable anti-inflation programme in recent times was implemented in Bolivia. In the first half of 1985, Bolivia's inflation rate was running at 20,000% and rising. Indeed, the inflation rate was so high that the price of a movie ticket often rose while people waited in line to buy it. In August 1985, Bolivia's new president, Victor Paz Estenssoro, announced his anti-inflation programme, the New Economic Policy. To rein in money growth and establish credibility, the new government took drastic actions to slash the budget deficit by shutting down many state-owned enterprises, eliminating subsidies, freezing public-sector salaries and collecting a new wealth tax. The finance ministry was put on a new footing; the budget was balanced on a day-by-day basis. Without exceptions, the finance minister would not authorize spending in excess of the amount of tax revenue that had been collected the day before.

The rule of thumb that a reduction of 1% in the inflation rate requires a 4% loss of a year's aggregate output indicates that ending the Bolivian hyperinflation would have required halving Bolivian aggregate output for 1,600 years! Instead, the Bolivian inflation was stopped in its tracks within one month, and the output loss was minor (less than 5% of GDP).

Certain hyperinflations before World War II were also ended with small losses of output using policies similar to Bolivia's,[9] and a more recent anti-inflation programme in Israel that also involved substantial reductions in budget deficits sharply reduced inflation without any clear loss of output. There is no doubt that credible anti-inflation policies can be highly successful in eliminating inflation.

APPLICATION   Maastricht inflation criterion as entry condition to EMU

As discussed in Chapter 18, the Maastricht Treaty, which was signed in 1991, establishes that in order for an EU member country to join the Economic and Monetary Union (EMU) it has to fulfil four main convergence criteria, all of which stress macroeconomic convergence between countries before accession to the euro area. One of these criteria determines that the inflation rate in the acceding country should not exceed the average of the three lowest inflation rates in the EU plus 1.5%. As shown in Table 25.2, due to lack of national discipline and institutions, during the 1980s the southern European countries of Greece, Spain, Italy and

Portugal experienced high levels of inflation relative to countries like Germany, which had a central bank with a credible low-inflation reputation. Before the monetary union started, these candidate member countries had to show that they cared about low inflation, and in order to meet the inflation requirement during the 1990s they went through a disinflationary process characterized by restrictive monetary and fiscal policies. These anti-inflationary policies led to a substantial reduction in inflation which allowed them to join the EMU, with only a relatively small increase in the unemployment rate. Could the credibility of these anti-inflation policies, especially in their final phases, have contributed to reduce these negative effects?

Some economists answer yes, using diagrams like panels (b) and (c) of Figure 25.6. The main concern of an anti-inflation policy implemented by a country that lacks credibility, is that it makes it harder for the public to believe that this policy would actually be pursued when the government announced its intention to do so. Consequently, the short-run aggregate supply curve would continue to rise from AS_1 to AS_2 as in panels (b) and (c). Under these circumstances, when the government actually keeps the aggregate demand curve from rising to AD_2 by implementing anti-inflationary policies, the economy can move to a point like 2' in panels (b) and (c), and significant unemployment may result. As our analysis in panels (b) and (c) of Figure 25.6 predicts, with low credibility, the inflation rate can only be reduced with high costs in terms of unemployment.

But why did the southern European countries experience only moderate increases in their respective unemployment rates? The answer is simple. Instead of moving to point 2', thanks to the substantial fiscal adjustment which showed a credible commitment of the government towards the reduction of inflation, the economy moved to point 2" in panel (c). Reduction of budget deficits thus led to a rapid drop in inflation and a smaller loss of output. For instance, beside the tight monetary policy stance needed to disinflate, Greece implemented a substantial fiscal adjustment with the fiscal deficit falling from about 10% of GDP in 1995 to around 3% in 1999. At the same time, the Greek parliament approved central bank independence and provided the Bank of Greece with a mandate to achieve price stability. All these factors strengthened the credibility of the disinflationary process and contributed to limit the output loss. The conclusion is that when the government takes actions that will help the central bank adhere to anti-inflation policies, the policy will be more credible and more likely to succeed.

TABLE 25.2

Average inflation rates across selected euro area countries

	1980–89	1990–98	1999–2011
Germany	2.9	2.8	1.6
Greece	19.5	9.8	3.2
Spain	10.2	4.4	2.8
Italy	11.2	4.4	2.3
Portugal	17.6	6.4	2.5

Source: Figures are average annual percentage changes and refer to CPI inflation up to 1998 and to HICP inflation afterwards. Data are taken from the OECD Economic Outlook, December 2011.

Past experiences of policymaking suggest that central banks have not always done what they set out to do. For instance, during the 1970s, the chairman of the Federal Reserve Board, Arthur Burns, repeatedly announced that the Fed would pursue a vigorous anti-inflation policy. The actual policy pursued, however, had quite a different outcome: the rate of growth of the money supply increased rapidly during the period, and inflation soared. Such episodes reduced the credibility of the Federal Reserve in the eyes of the public and, as predicted by the new classical and new Keynesian models, had serious consequences. The reduction of inflation that occurred from 1981 to 1984 was bought at a very high cost;

the 1981–2 recession that helped bring the inflation rate down was one of the most severe recessions in the post-World War II period.

The government can play an important role in establishing the credibility of anti-inflation policy. We have seen that large budget deficits may help stimulate inflationary monetary policy, and when the government and the central bank announce that they will pursue a restrictive anti-inflation policy, it is less likely that they will be believed *unless* the government demonstrates fiscal responsibility. Another way to say this is to use the old adage, 'Actions speak louder than words'. When the government takes actions that will help the central bank adhere to anti-inflation policy, the policy will be more credible.

Impact of the rational expectations revolution

The theory of rational expectations has caused a revolution in the way most economists now think about the conduct of monetary and fiscal policies and their effects on economic activity. One result of this revolution is that economists are now far more aware of the importance of expectations to economic decision making and to the outcome of particular policy actions. Although the rationality of expectations in all markets is still controversial, most economists now accept the following principle suggested by rational expectations: expectations formation will change when the behaviour of forecasted variables changes. As a result, the Lucas critique of policy evaluation using conventional econometric models is now taken seriously by most economists. The Lucas critique also demonstrates that the effect of a particular policy depends critically on the public's expectations about that policy. This observation has made economists much less certain that policies will have their intended effect. An important result of the rational expectations revolution is that economists are no longer as confident in the success of discretionary stabilization policies as they once were.

Has the rational expectations revolution convinced economists that there is no role for discretionary stabilization policy? Those who adhere to the new classical macroeconomics think so. Because anticipated policy does not affect aggregate output, discretionary policy can lead only to unpredictable output fluctuations. Pursuing a non-discretionary policy in which there is no uncertainty about policy actions is then the best we can do. Such a position is not accepted by many economists, because the empirical evidence on the policy ineffectiveness proposition is mixed. Some studies find that only unanticipated policy matters to output fluctuations, while other studies find a significant impact of anticipated policy on output movements.[10] In addition, some economists question whether the degree of wage and price flexibility required in the new classical model actually exists.

The result is that many economists take an intermediate position that recognizes the distinction between the effects of anticipated and unanticipated policy but believe that anticipated policy can affect output. They are still open to the possibility that discretionary stabilization policy can be beneficial, but they recognize the difficulties of designing it.

The rational expectations revolution has also highlighted the importance of credibility to the success of anti-inflation policies. Economists now recognize that if an anti-inflation policy is not believed by the public, it may be less effective in reducing the inflation rate when it is actually implemented and may lead to a larger loss of output than is necessary. Achieving credibility (not an easy task in that policymakers often say one thing but do another) should then be an important goal for policymakers. To achieve credibility, policymakers must be consistent in their course of action.

The rational expectations revolution has caused major rethinking about the way economic policy should be conducted and has forced economists to recognize that we may have to accept a more limited role for what policy can do for us. Rather than attempting to fine-tune the economy so that all output fluctuations are eliminated, we may have to settle for policies that create less uncertainty and thereby promote a more stable economic environment.

Summary

1 The simple principle (derived from rational expectations theory) that expectation formation changes when the behaviour of forecasted variables changes led to the famous Lucas critique of econometric policy evaluation. Lucas argued that when policy changes, expectations formation changes; hence the relationships in an econometric model will change. An econometric model that has been estimated on the basis of past data will no longer be the correct model for evaluating the effects of this policy change and may prove to be highly misleading. The Lucas critique also points out that the effects of a particular policy depend critically on the public's expectations about the policy.

2 The new classical macroeconomic model assumes that expectations are rational and that wages and prices are completely flexible with respect to the expected price level. It leads to the policy ineffectiveness proposition that anticipated policy has no effect on output; only unanticipated policy matters.

3 The new Keynesian model also assumes that expectations are rational but views wages and prices as sticky. Like the new classical model, the new Keynesian model distinguishes between the effects from anticipated and unanticipated policy: anticipated policy has a smaller effect on aggregate output than unanticipated policy. However, anticipated policy does matter to output fluctuations.

4 The new classical model indicates that discretionary policy can be only counterproductive, while the new Keynesian model suggests that activist policy might be beneficial. However, because both models indicate that there is uncertainty about the outcome of a particular policy, the design of a beneficial discretionary policy may be very difficult. A traditional model in which expectations about policy have no effect on the short-run aggregate supply curve does not distinguish between the effects of anticipated and unanticipated policy. This model favours discretionary policy, because the outcome of a particular policy is less uncertain.

5 If expectations about policy affect the short-run aggregate supply curve, as they do in the new classical and new Keynesian models, an anti-inflation policy will be more successful (will produce a faster reduction in inflation with smaller output loss) if it is credible.

6 The rational expectations revolution has forced economists to be less optimistic about the effective use of discretionary stabilization policy and has made them more aware of the importance of credibility to successful policymaking.

Key terms

econometric models p. 579

inflation rate p. 593

policy ineffectiveness
proposition p. 583

wage–price stickiness p. 585

QUESTIONS AND PROBLEMS

All questions and problems are available in MyEeconLab at **www.myeconlab.com/mishkin**.

1 If the public expects the central bank to pursue a policy that is likely to raise short-term interest rates permanently to 5% but the central bank does not go through with this policy change, what will happen to long-term interest rates? Explain your answer.

2 If consumer expenditure is related to consumers' expectations of their average income in the future, will an income tax cut have a larger effect on consumer expenditure if the public expects the tax cut to last for one year or for ten years?

Use an aggregate demand and supply diagram to illustrate your answer in all the following questions.

3 Having studied the new classical model, the new head of the central bank has thought up a surefire plan for reducing inflation and lowering unemployment. He or she announces that the central bank will lower the rate of money growth from 10% to 5% and then persuades the other members of the council to keep the rate of money growth at 10%. If the new classical view of the world is correct, can his plan achieve the goals of lowering inflation and unemployment? How? Do you think this plan will work? If the traditional model's view of the world is correct, will the chairman's surefire plan work?

4 'The costs of fighting inflation in the new classical and new Keynesian models are lower than in the traditional model.' Is this statement true, false, or uncertain? Explain your answer.

5 The new classical model is an offshoot of the monetarist framework because it has a similar view of aggregate supply. What are the differences and similarities between the monetarist and new classical views of aggregate supply?

6 'The new classical model does not eliminate policymakers' ability to reduce unemployment because they can always pursue policies that are more expansionary than the public expects.' Is this statement true, false, or uncertain? Explain your answer.

7 Which principle of rational expectations theory is used to prove the proposition that stabilization policy can have no predictable effect on aggregate output in the new classical model?

8 'The Lucas critique by itself casts doubt on the ability of discretionary stabilization policy to be beneficial.' Is this statement true, false, or uncertain? Explain your answer.

9 'The more credible the policymakers who pursue an anti-inflation policy, the more successful that policy will be.' Is this statement true, false, or uncertain? Explain your answer.

10 Many economists are worried that a high level of budget deficits may lead to inflationary monetary policies in the future. Could these budget deficits have an effect on the current rate of inflation?

Using economic analysis to predict the future

11 Suppose that a treaty is signed limiting armies throughout the world. The result of the treaty is that the public expects military and hence government spending to be reduced. If the new classical view of the economy is correct and government spending does affect the aggregate demand curve, predict what will happen to aggregate output and the price level when government spending is reduced in line with the public's expectations.

12 How would your prediction differ in Problem 11 if the new Keynesian model provides a more realistic description of the economy? What if the traditional model provides the most realistic description of the economy?

13 The chairman of the central bank announces that over the next year, the rate of money growth will be reduced from its current rate of 8% to a rate of 2%. If the chairman is believed by the public but the central bank actually reduces the rate of money growth to 5%, predict what will happen to the inflation rate and aggregate output if the new classical view of the economy is correct.

14 How would your prediction differ in Problem 13 if the new Keynesian model provides a more accurate description of the economy? What if the traditional model provides the most realistic description of the economy?

15 If, in a surprise victory, a new administration is elected to office that the public believes will pursue an inflationary policy, predict what might happen to the level of output and inflation even before the new administration comes into power. Would your prediction differ depending on which of the three models – traditional, new classical and new Keynesian – you believed in?

WEB EXERCISES

1 In 1995 Robert Lucas won the Nobel Prize in economics. Go to **http://nobelprize.org/nobel_prizes/economics/** and locate the press release on Robert Lucas. What was his Nobel Prize awarded for?

2 In 2011 Thomas Sargent (together with Christopher Sims) won the Nobel Prize in economics. Go to **http://nobelprize .org/nobel_prizes/economics/** and locate the press release on Thomas Sargent. What was his Nobel Prize awarded for?

Notes

1 Some of the deterioration can be attributed to supply shocks in 1973–5 and 1978–80.

2 Other economists who have been active in promoting the rational expectations revolution are Robert Barro of Harvard University, Bennett McCallum of Carnegie-Mellon University, Edward Prescott of Arizona State and Neil Wallace of Pennsylvania State University.

3 *Carnegie-Rochester Conference Series on Public Policy 1* (1976): 19–46.

4 The new classical view, in which anticipated policy has no effect on the business cycle, does not imply that anticipated policy has no effect on the overall health of the economy. For example, the new classical analysis does not rule out possible effects of anticipated policy on the natural rate of output Y_n, which can benefit the public.

5 Thomas Sargent and Neil Wallace, '"Rational" expectations, the optimal monetary instrument, and the optimal money supply rule', *Journal of Political Economy* 83 (1975): 241–54,

first demonstrated the full implications of the policy ineffectiveness proposition.

6 This result follows from one of the implications of rational expectations: the forecast error of expectations about policy (the deviation of actual policy from expectations of policy) must be unpredictable. Because output is affected only by unpredictable (unanticipated) policy changes in the new classical model, policy effects on output must be unpredictable as well.

7 For a comprehensive and advanced treatment of the new Keynesian model see Jordi Galí, *Monetary Policy, Inflation and the Business Cycle: an Introduction to the New Keynesian Framework* (Princeton, NJ: Princeton University Press, 2008).

8 John Taylor, 'The role of expectations in the choice of monetary policy', in *Monetary Policy Issues in the 1980s* (Kansas City: Federal Reserve Bank, 1982), pp. 47–76.

9 For an excellent discussion of the end of four hyperinflations in the 1920s, see Thomas Sargent, 'The ends of four big inflations', in *Inflation: Causes and Consequences*, ed. Robert E. Hall (Chicago: University of Chicago Press, 1982), pp. 41–98.

10 Studies with findings that only unanticipated policy matters include Thomas Sargent, 'A classical macroeconometric model for the United States', *Journal of Political Economy* 84 (1976): 207–37; Robert J. Barro, 'Unanticipated money growth and unemployment in the United States', *American Economic Review* 67 (1977): 101–15; and Robert J. Barro and Mark Rush, 'Unanticipated money and economic activity', in *Rational Expectations and Economic Policy*, ed. Stanley Fischer (Chicago: University of Chicago Press, 1980), pp. 23–48. Studies that find a significant impact of anticipated policy are Frederic S. Mishkin, 'Does anticipated monetary policy matter? An econometric investigation', *Journal of Political Economy* 90 (1982): 22–51; and Robert J. Gordon, 'Price inertia and policy effectiveness in the United States, 1890–1980', *Journal of Political Economy* 90 (1982): 1087–117.

Useful websites

www.federalreserve.gov/pubs/feds/2001/200113/200113pap.pdf The Federal Reserve recently published a paper discussing the new Keynesian model and price stickiness.

http://www.econlib.org/library/Enc/RationalExpectations.html Thomas Sargent provides a brief definition of rational expectations.

www.imf.org/external/pubs/ft/spn/2010/spn1003.pdf An IMF paper by Oliver Blanchard, Giovanni Dell'Ariccia and Paolo Mauro critically reviewing the current macroeconomic policy framework.

GLOSSARY

accommodating policy An activist policy in pursuit of a high employment target. **564**

accountability The obligation of an independent institution (like a central bank) to justify and explain its decisions and actions to the public and democratically elected institutions and to respond to concerns about its policy. **295, 354**

adaptive expectations Expectations of a variable based on an average of past values of the variable. **135**

adjustment mechanism A mechanism that helps the economy's output to return to equilibrium. According to the theory of Optimal Currency Area (OCA), two adjustment mechanisms helping to restore equilibrium are through wage flexibility and labuor mobility. **435**

adverse selection The problem created by asymmetric information *before* a transaction occurs: the people who are the most undesirable from the other party's point of view are the ones who are most likely to want to engage in the financial transaction. **36**

agency theory The analysis of how asymmetric information problems affect economic behaviour. **154**

aggregate demand The total quantity of output demanded in the economy at different price levels. **464, 507**

aggregate demand curve A relationship between the price level and the quantity of aggregate output demanded when the goods and money markets are in equilibrium. **501, 507**

aggregate demand function The relationship between aggregate output and aggregate demand that shows the quantity of aggregate output demanded for each level of aggregate output. **468**

aggregate income The total income of factors of production (land, labour, capital) in the economy. **20**

aggregate output The total production of final goods and services in the economy. **9**

aggregate price level The average price of goods and services in an economy. **9**

aggregate supply The quantity of aggregate output supplied by the economy at different price levels. **507**

aggregate supply curve The relationship between the quantity of output supplied and the price level. **511**

alt-A mortages Mortgages for borrowers with higher expected default rates than prime borrowers, but with better credit records than subprime borrowers. **184**

anchor currency A currency to which other countries' currencies are pegged. **411**

'animal spirits' Waves of optimism and pessimism that affect consumers' and businesses' willingness to spend. **471, 509**

appreciation Increase in a currency's value. **384**

arbitrage Elimination of a riskless profit opportunity in a market. **138**

asset A financial claim or piece of property that is a store of value. **4**

asset management The acquisition of assets that have a low rate of default and diversification of asset holdings to increase profits. **213**

asset market approach An approach to determine asset prices using stocks of assets rather than flows. **85**

asset-price bubbles Increases in asset prices in the stock and real estate markets that are driven well above their fundamental economic values by investor psychology. **181, 373**

asset transformation The process of turning risky assets into safer assets for investors by creating and selling assets with risk characteristics that people are comfortable with and then using the funds acquired by selling these assets to purchase other assets that may have far more risk. **36**

asymmetric information The unequal knowledge that each party to a transaction has about the other party. **36**

asymmetric shocks An asymmetric shock is a demand or supply shock that hits only one of the countries in a monetary union. **435**

automated banking machine (ABM) One location that provides an automated teller machine (ATM), an Internet connection to the bank's website, and a telephone link to customer service. **261**

automated teller machine (ATM) An electronic machine that provides banking services 24 hours a day. **261**

automatic transfer The fiscal transfer that automatically takes place in a monetary union when different regions or countries are hit by asymmetric shocks. **437**

autonomous consumer expenditure The amount of consumer expenditure that is independent of disposable income. **465**

balance of payments A bookkeeping system for recording all payments that have a direct bearing on the movement of funds between a country and foreign countries. **410**

balance-of-payments crisis A foreign exchange crisis stemming from problems in a country's balance of payments. **419**

balance sheet A list of the assets and liabilities of a bank (or firm) that balances: total assets equal total liabilities plus capital. **205**

bank failure A situation in which a bank cannot satisfy its obligations to pay its depositors and other creditors and so goes out of business. **232**

Bank of England (BoE) The central bank of the United Kingdom. **281**

bank panic The simultaneous failure of many banks, as during a financial crisis. **178**

Bank Rate The official interest rate of the Bank of England. **333**

banks Financial institutions that accept money deposits and make loans (such as commercial banks, savings and loan associations, and credit unions). **8**

Basel Accord An agreement that required that banks to hold as capital at least 8% of their risk-weighted assets. **238**

Basel Committee on Banking Supervision An international committee of bank supervisors that meets under the auspices of the Bank for International Settlements in Basel, Switzerland. **238**

behavioural finance A subfield of finance that applies concepts from other social sciences such as anthropology, sociology, and, particularly, psychology to understand the behaviour of securities prices. **143**

Board of Governors of the Federal Reserve System A board with seven governors (including the chairman) that plays an essential role in decision making within the Federal Reserve System. **282**

bond A debt security that promises to make payments periodically for a specified period of time. **4**

borrowed reserves A bank's borrowings from the central bank. **307**

Bretton Woods system The international monetary system in use from 1945 to 1971 in which exchange rates were fixed and the US dollar was freely convertible into gold (by foreign governments and central banks only). **413**

brokers Agents for investors; they match buyers with sellers. **26**

bubble A situation in which the price of an asset differs from its fundamental market value. **142**

budget deficit The excess of government expenditure over tax revenues. **12**

budget surplus The excess of tax revenues over government expenditures. **12**

business cycles The upward and downward movement of aggregate output produced in the economy. **9**

capital Wealth, either financial or physical, that is employed to produce more wealth. **25**

capital account An account that describes the flow of capital between a country and other countries. **411**

capital adequacy management A bank's decision about the amount of capital it should maintain and then acquisition of the needed capital. **213**

capital market A financial market in which longer-term debt (generally with original maturity of greater than one year) and equity instruments are traded. **27**

capital market instruments Debt and equity instruments with maturities of greater than one year. **29**

capital mobility A situation in which foreigners can easily purchase a country's assets and the country's residents can easily purchase foreign assets. **405**

cash flows Cash payments to the holder of a security. **61, 131**

central bank The institution that oversees the banking system and is responsible for the amount of money and credit supplied in the economy; in the euro area, the European Central Bank; in the United Kingdom, the Bank of England; and in the United States, the Federal Reserve System. **12**

certificate of deposit It is a debt instrument sold by a bank to depositors that pays an annual interest of a given amount and at maturity pays back the original purchase price. **28**

cheque A cheque is an instruction from a customer of a bank to transfer money from his account to someone else's account when she deposits the cheque. **50**

collateral Property that is pledged to the lender to guarantee payment in the event that the borrower is unable to make debt payments. **151**

collateralized debt obligations (CDOs) Securities that paid out cash flows from subprime mortgaged-backed securities in different tranches, with the highest tranch paying out first, while lower ones paid out less if there were losses. **184**

commercial paper A short-term debt instrument issued by large banks and well-known corporations. **28**

commodity money Money made up of precious metals or another valuable commodity. **50**

common stock A security that is a claim on the earnings and assets of a company. **5**

compensating balance A required minimum amount of funds that a firm receiving a loan must keep in a cheque account at the lending bank. **223**

complete crowding out The situation in which expansionary fiscal policy, such as an increase in government spending, does not lead to a rise in output because there is an exactly offsetting movement in private spending. **495**

conflicts of interest A manifestation of the moral hazard problem, particularly when a financial institution provides multiple services and the potentially competing interests of those services may lead to a concealment of information or dissemination of misleading information. **167**

consol A perpetual bond with no maturity date and no repayment of principal that periodically makes fixed coupon payments. A consol is also called a perpetuity. **68**

constant-money-growth-rate rule A policy rule advocated by monetarists, whereby the central bank keeps the money supply growing at a constant rate. **575**

consumer durable expenditure Spending by consumers on durable items such as automobiles and household appliances. **537**

consumer expenditure The total demand for (spending on) consumer goods and services. **464, 507**

consumption Spending by consumers on non-durable goods and services (including services related to the ownership of homes and consumer durables). **542**

consumption function The relationship between disposable income and consumer expenditure. **465**

conventional monetary policy tools The usual tools of monetary policy that the central bank uses to control the money supply and interest rates: open market operations, lending and deposit facilities, and reserve requirements. **326**

convergence criteria The four criteria of the Maastricht Treaty that must be fulfilled by each country before it can adopt the euro, namely a stable price level, sound public finances, a stable exchange rate and low and stable long-term interest rates. The Convergence Criteria are also known as the Maastricht Criteria. **436**

convertible bonds A special form of corporate bonds that have the additional feature of allowing the holder to convert them into a specified number of shares of stock at any time up to the maturity date. **31**

corporate bonds These long-term bonds are issued by corporations with very strong credit ratings. The typical corporate bond sends the holder an interest payment twice a year and pays off the face value when the bond matures. **31**

costly state verification Monitoring a firm's activities, an expensive process in both time and money. **160**

cost-push inflation Inflation that occurs because of the push by workers to obtain higher wages. **563**

coupon bond A credit market instrument that pays the owner a fixed interest payment every year until the maturity date, when a specified final amount is repaid. **64**

coupon rate The monetary amount of the yearly coupon payment expressed as a percentage of the face value of a coupon bond. **64**

credit boom A lending spree when financial institutions expand their lending at a rapid pace. **181**

credit counterparts model A model of money supply determination which focuses on bank lending to the private sector as the main determinant of the quantity of money. **321**

credit easing Altering the composition of the central bank's balance sheet in order to improve the functioning of particular segments of the credit markets. **343**

credit-rating agencies Investment advisory firms that rate the quality of corporate and municipal bonds in terms of the probability of default. **111**

credit rationing A lender's refusal to make loans even though borrowers are willing to pay the stated interest rate or even a higher rate or restriction of the size of loans made to less than the full amount sought. **223**

credit risk The risk arising from the possibility that the borrower will default. **213**

credit view Monetary transmission mechanisms operating through asymmetric information effects on credit markets. **540**

currency Paper money and coins. **28, 46**

currency board A monetary regime in which the domestic currency is backed 100% by a foreign currency and in which the note-issuing authority, whether the central bank or the government, establishes a fixed exchange rate to this foreign currency and stands ready to exchange domestic currency at this rate whenever the public requests it. **431**

current account An account that shows international transactions involving currently produced goods and services. **410**

current yield An approximation of the yield to maturity that equals the yearly coupon payment divided by the price of a coupon bond. **69**

dealers People who link buyers with sellers by buying and selling securities at stated prices. **26**

debt deflation A situation in which a substantial decline in the price level sets in, leading to a further deterioration in firms' net worth because of the increased burden of indebtedness. **183**

default A situation in which the party issuing a debt instrument is unable to make interest payments or pay off the amount owed when the instrument matures. **28, 110**

default-free bonds Bonds with no default risk, such as German government bonds. **110**

deleveraging When financial institutions cut back on their lending because they have less capital. **181**

demand curve A curve depicting the relationship between quantity demanded and price when all other economic variables are held constant. **82**

demand-pull inflation Inflation that results when policymakers pursue policies that shift the aggregate demand curve. **563**

demand shocks Shocks that can shift the aggregate demand curve, including changes in the money supply, changes in government expenditure and taxes, changes in net exports and changes in consumer and business spending. **510**

deposit facility The standing facility in which banks can make overnight deposits at the central bank. Such deposits are remunerated at a pre-specified deposit rate. **341**

deposit outflows Losses of deposits when depositors make withdrawals or demand payment. **213**

deposit rate The interest rate at which banks can make overnight deposits at the central bank. The deposit rate is normally set 100 basis points below the official interest rate. **327**

depreciation Decrease in a currency's value. **384**

devaluation Resetting of the fixed value of a currency at a lower level. **414**

direct method In the direct method, the exchange rate is quoted as units of domestic currency per unit of foreign currency. **384**

dirty float An exchange rate regime in which countries attempt to influence their exchange rates by buying and selling currencies (also called a *managed float regime*). **413**

discount bond A credit market instrument that is bought at a price below its face value and whose face value is repaid at the maturity date; it does not make any interest payments. Also called a zero-coupon bond. **64**

discount rate The interest rate that the Federal Reserve charges banks on discount loans. **340**

discount window The Federal Reserve facility at which discount loans are made to banks. **340**

discretionary policy Policy to eliminate high unemployment whenever it appears on a discretionary basis. **572**

disposable income Total income available for spending, equal to aggregate income minus taxes. **465**

diversification Investing in a collection (**portfolio**) of assets whose returns do not always move together, with the result that overall risk is lower than for individual assets. **36**

dividends Periodic payments made by equities to shareholders. **26, 131**

dollarization The adoption of a sound currency, like the US dollar, as a country's money. **431**

dual mandate A central bank mandate that features two co-equal objectives: price stability and maximum employment. **280**

duration analysis A measurement of the sensitivity of the market value of a bank's assets and liabilities to changes in interest rates. **225**

e-cash Electronic money that is used on the Internet to purchase goods or services. **51**

econometric model A model whose equations are estimated using statistical procedures. **579**

Economic and Monetary Union (EMU) The process that led to the single currency, the euro, and the single monetary policy in the euro area. **286, 433**

economies of scale The reduction in transaction costs per euro of transaction as the size (scale) of transactions increases. **35**

economies of scope The ability to use one resource to provide many different products and services. **167, 263**

efficient market hypothesis The application of the theory of rational expectations to financial markets. **136**

e-finance A new means of delivering financial services electronically. **9**

electronic money (e-money) Money that exists only in electronic form and substitutes for cash as well. **51**

emerging market economics Economies in an earlier stage of market development that have recently opened up to the flow of goods, services and capital from the rest of the world. **189**

Enhanced Credit Support (ECS) The non-standard measures taken by the European Central Bank and the Eurosystem during the financial crisis. **337**

equation of exchange The equation $MV = PY$, which relates nominal income to the quantity of money. **445**

equities Claims to share in the net income and assets of a corporation (such as common stock). **25**

equity capital See *net worth*. **158**

equity multiplier (EM) The amount of assets per euro of equity capital. **218**

euro overnight index average (EONIA) A measure of the effective interest rate prevailing in the overnight interbank market of the euro area. It is calculated as a weighted average of the interest rates on unsecured overnight lending transactions denominated in euros, as reported by a panel of contributing banks. **327**

Eurobonds Bonds denominated in a currency other than that of the country in which they are sold. **33**

Eurocurrencies A variant of the Eurobond; foreign currencies deposited in banks outside the home country. **33**

eurodollars US dollars that are deposited in foreign banks outside the United States or in foreign branches of US banks. **33**

European Banking Authority (EBA) The European Banking Authority (EBA) was set up in January 2011 to oversee national bank regulators in the European Union (EU) and if necessary provide a common framework of regulation. **247**

European Central Bank (ECB) The central bank of the euro area. The ECB is located in Frankfurt, Germany. **53, 286**

European Monetary System (EMS) The European Monetary System (EMS) was an arrangement between European leaders established in March 1979 where most European countries linked their currencies to prevent large fluctuations relative to one another. **192**

European System of Central Banks (ESCB) It is composed of the European Central Bank and the national central banks of all the EU countries. The ESCB includes the Eurosystem and the national central banks of the EU countries whose currency is not the euro. **286**

European Union (EU) The EU is an economic and political union of 27 member states which are located primarily in Europe. **286**

Eurosystem The central bank system of the euro area. It comprises the European Central Bank and the national central banks of the EU countries whose currency is the euro. **286**

eurozone (or euro area) The area formed by the EU countries whose currency is the euro and in which the single monetary policy is conducted by the European Central Bank. **179**

excess demand A situation in which quantity demanded is greater than quantity supplied. **84**

excess reserves Reserves in excess of required reserves. **208, 302**

excess supply A situation in which quantity supplied is greater than quantity demanded. **84**

exchange rate The price of one currency stated in terms of another currency. **381**

Exchange Rate Mechanism (ERM) The ERM was one of the key elements of the European Monetary System (EMS) in which the exchange rate between every pair of currencies of the participating countries was not allowed to fluctuate outside narrow limits around a fixed exchange rate. **192**

exchange rate overshooting A phenomenon whereby the exchange rate changes by more in the short run than it does in the long run when the money supply changes. **398**

exchange-rate peg Fixing the value of the domestic currency to the value of another currency, so the exchange rate is fixed. **427**

exchange-rate targeting See *exchange-rate peg* **427**

exchanges Secondary markets in which buyers and sellers of securities (or their agents or brokers) meet in one central location to conduct trades. **27**

Executive Board One of the decision-making bodies of the European Central Bank. It consists of the president, vice-president and four other members who are appointed by common agreement of the heads of states of the euro area countries. **286**

expectations theory The proposition that the interest rate on a long-term bond will equal the average of the short-term interest rates that people expect to occur over the life of the long-term bond. **116**

expected return The return on an asset expected over the next period. **81**

expenditure multiplier The ratio of a change in aggregate output to a change in investment spending (or autonomous spending). **469**

face value A specified final amount paid to the owner of a coupon bond at the maturity date. Also called par value. **64**

fair-value accounting In which assets are valued in the balance sheet of what they could sell for in the market. **242**

federal funds rate The interest rate on overnight loans of deposits at the Federal Reserve. **327**

Federal Funds Rate Target The official interest rate of the Federal Reserve System. **334**

Federal Open Market Committee (FOMC) The committee that makes decisions regarding the conduct of open market operations; composed of the seven members of the Board of Governors of the Federal Reserve System, the president of the Federal Reserve Bank of New York, and the presidents of four other Federal Reserve banks on a rotating basis. **282**

Federal Reserve banks The 12 district banks in the Federal Reserve System. **282**

Federal Reserve System (the Fed) The central banking authority responsible for monetary policy in the United States. **000**

fiat money Paper currency decreed by a government as legal tender but not convertible into coins or precious metal. **50**

financial crisis A major disruption in financial markets that is characterized by sharp declines in asset prices and the failures of many financial and non-financial firms. **8, 176**

financial derivatives Instruments that have payoffs that are linked to previously issued securities, used as risk reduction tools. **260**

financial engineering The process of researching and developing new financial products and services that would meet customer needs and prove profitable. **184, 259**

financial globalization The process of economies opening up to flows of capital and financial firms from other nations. **190**

financial intermediaries Institutions (such as banks, insurance companies, mutual funds, pension funds and finance companies) that borrow funds from people who have saved and then make loans to others. **7**

financial intermediation The process of indirect finance whereby financial intermediaries link lender–savers and borrower–spenders. **35**

financial liberalization The elimination or restrictions on financial markets. **179**

financial markets Markets in which funds are transferred from people who have a surplus of available funds to people who have a shortage of available funds. **3**

financial panic The widespread collapse of financial markets and intermediaries in an economy. **41**

financial supervision (prudential supervision) Overseeing who operates financial institutions and how they are operated. **240**

fiscal policy Policy that involves decisions about government spending and taxation. **12, 437**

Fisher effect The outcome that when expected inflation occurs, interest rates will rise; named after economist Irving Fisher. **91**

fixed exchange rate regime A regime in which central banks buy and sell their own currencies to keep their exchange rates fixed at a certain level. **411**

fixed investment Spending by firms on equipment (computers, aeroplanes) and structures (factories, office buildings) and planned spending on residential housing. **467**

fixed-payment loan A credit market instrument that provides a borrower with an amount of money that is repaid by making a fixed payment periodically (usually monthly) for a set number of years. **64**

floating exchange rate regime An exchange rate regime in which the values of currencies are allowed to fluctuate against one another. **411**

foreign bonds Bonds sold in a foreign country and denominated in that country's currency. **33**

foreign exchange intervention An international financial transaction in which a central bank buys or sells currency to influence foreign exchange rates. **407**

foreign exchange market The market in which exchange rates are determined. **6**, **381**

foreign exchange rate See *exchange rate*. **6**

forward exchange rate The exchange rate for a forward transaction. **383**

forward transaction A transaction that involves the exchange of bank deposits denominated in different currencies at some specified future date. **383**

free-rider problem The problem that occurs when people who do not pay for information take advantage of the information that other people have paid for. **155**

fully amortized loan See *fixed-payment loan* **64**

futures contract A contract in which the seller agrees to provide a certain standardized commodity to the buyer on a specific future date at an agreed-on price. **259**

gap analysis A measurement of the sensitivity of bank profits to changes in interest rates, calculated by subtracting the amount of rate-sensitive liabilities from the amount of rate-sensitive assets. **225**

generalized dividend model Calculates that the price of stock is determined only by the present value of the dividends. **132**

GIIPS The group of the euro area countries mostly affected by the eurozone sovereign debt crisis. They are Greece, Ireland, Italy, Portugal and Spain. **196**

goal independence The ability of the central bank to set the goals of monetary policy. **281**

gold standard A fixed exchange rate regime under which a currency is directly convertible into gold. **411**

Gordon growth model A simplified model to compute the value of a stock by assuming constant dividend growth. **132**

Governing Council The supreme decision-making body of the European Central Bank. It comprises all the members of the Executive Board and the governors of the national central banks of the countries whose currency is the euro. **286**

government budget constraint The requirement that the government budget deficit equal the sum of the change in the monetary base and the change in government bonds held by the public. **566**

government spending Spending by the government on goods and services. **464**, **507**

gross domestic product (GDP) The value of all final goods and services produced in the economy during the course of a year. **12**, **20**

hedge To protect oneself against risk. **259**

hierarchical mandate A mandate for the central bank that puts the goal of price stability first, but as long as it is achieved other goals can be pursued. **280**

high-powered money The monetary base. **303**

hyperinflation An extreme inflation in which the inflation rate exceeds 50% per month. **49**

hysteresis A departure from full-employment levels as a result of past high unemployment. **519**

incentive-compatible Having the incentives of both parties to a contract in alignment. **162**

income The flow of earnings. **47**

index-linked bond A bond whose interest and principal payments are adjusted for changes in the price level, and whose interest rate thus provides a direct measure of a real interest rate. **76**

indirect method In the indirect method, the exchange rate is expressed as units of foreign currency per unit of domestic currency. **384**

inflation The condition of a continually rising price level. **10**

inflation rate The rate of change of the price level, usually measured as a percentage change per year. **593**

inflation targeting A monetary policy strategy that involves public announcement of a medium-term numerical target for inflation. **354**

initial public offering (IPO) Shares of newly issued stock. **168**

instrument independence The ability of the central bank to set monetary policy instruments. **281**

interest parity condition The observation that the domestic interest rate equals the foreign interest rate plus the expected appreciation in the foreign currency. **405**

interest rate The cost of borrowing or the price paid for the rental of funds (usually expressed as a percentage per year). **4**

interest-rate risk The possible reduction in returns associated with changes in interest rates. **73**, **213**

intermediate target Any of a number of variables, such as monetary aggregates or interest rates, that have a direct effect on employment and the price level and that the central bank seeks to influence. **366**

International Monetary Fund (IMF) The international organization created by the Bretton Woods agreement whose objective is to promote the growth of world trade by making loans to countries experiencing balance-of-payments difficulties. **413**

international reserves Central bank holdings of assets denominated in foreign currencies. **407**

inventory investment Spending by firms on additional holdings of raw materials, parts and finished goods. **467**

inverted yield curve A yield curve that is downward-sloping. **116**

investment banks Firms that assist in the initial sale of securities in the primary market. **26**

IS **curve** The relationship that describes the combinations of aggregate output and interest rates for which the total quantity of goods produced equals the total quantity demanded (goods market equilibrium). **476**

junk bonds Bonds with ratings below Baa (or BBB) that have a high default risk. **111**

Keynesian A follower of John Maynard Keynes who believes that movements in the price level and aggregate output are driven by changes not only in the money supply but also in government spending and fiscal policy and who does not regard the economy as inherently stable. **517**

labour mobility The degree of mobility of the labour force from one region or country to another. **437**

large, complex banking organizations (LCBOs) Large companies that provide banking as well as many other financial services. **264**

law of one price The principle that if two countries produce an identical good, the price of this good should be the same throughout the world no matter which country produces it. **385**

lender of last resort Provider of reserves to financial institutions when no one else would provide them to prevent a financial crisis. **341**

lending facility A standing facility in which banks can borrow (against eligible collateral) overnight reserves from a central bank at a lending rate. **327, 339**

lending rate The interest rate set by the central bank in its standard lending facilities. The lending rate is normally set 100 basis points above the official interest rate. **327**

liabilities IOUs or debts. **24**

liability management The acquisition of funds at low cost to increase profits. **213**

liquid Easily converted into cash. **26**

liquidity The relative ease and speed with which an asset can be converted into cash. **49, 81**

liquidity management The decisions made by a bank to maintain sufficient liquid assets to meet the bank's obligations to depositors. **213**

liquidity preference framework A model developed by John Maynard Keynes that predicts the equilibrium interest rate on the basis of the supply of and demand for money. **95**

liquidity preference theory John Maynard Keynes's theory of the demand for money. **449**

liquidity premium theory The theory that the interest rate on a long-term bond will equal an average of short-term interest rates expected to occur over the life of the long-term bond plus a positive term (liquidity) premium. **121**

liquidity services Services financial intermediaries provide to their customers to make it easier for them to conduct their transactions. **35**

LM **curve** The relationship that describes the combinations of interest rates and aggregate output for which the quantity of money demanded equals the quantity of money supplied (money market equilibrium). **476**

loan commitment A bank's commitment (for a specified future period of time) to provide a firm with loans up to a given amount at an interest rate that is tied to some market interest rate. **223**

loan sale The sale under a contract (also called a secondary loan participation) of all or part of the cash stream from a specific loan, thereby removing the loan from the bank's balance sheet. **226**

longer-term refinancing operations (LTROs) A category of open market operations by the European Central Bank that normally are carried out with a monthly frequency and a maturity of three months. **334**

long-run monetary neutrality See *monetary neutrality*. **500**

long-term With reference to a debt instrument, having a maturity of ten years or more. **25**

M1 The narrowest measure of money, which includes the most liquid means of payment available. M1 consists of currency in circulation as well as demand deposits and other chequable deposits held in depository institutions. **53**

M2 A measure of money that typically adds to M1 saving deposits and time deposits. The exact definition of M2 differs considerably from one country to another. **53**

M3 A broad measure of money that adds to M2 specific financial instruments. It is calculated by central banks such as the ECB and the Bank of England. The Federal Reserve System discontinued measuring M3 in March 2006. **53**

Maastricht Treaty The agreement signed on 7 February 1992 by the members of the European Community in Maastricht, Netherlands. The Treaty is the building stone of the process towards monetary unification in Europe. **280**

macro-prudential regulation Regulatory policy to affect what is happening in the credit markets in the aggregate. **375**

main refinancing operations (MROs) Weekly reverse transactions (purchase or sale of eligible assets under repurchase agreements or credit operations against eligible assets as collateral) that are reversed within two weeks and are the primary monetary policy tool of the European Central Bank. **334**

Main Refinancing Rate (MRR) The official interest rate of the European Central Bank which is applied in the main refinancing operations in the euro area. **334**

managed float regime An exchange rate regime in which countries attempt to influence their exchange rates by buying and selling currencies (also called a dirty float). **411**

management of expectations Term that refers to the commitment of the Fed to keeping the federal funds rate at zero for an extended period in order to cause the long-term interest rate to fall. **000**

marginal lending facility The European Central Bank's standard lending facility in which banks can borrow (against eligible collateral) overnight loans from the national central bank at the marginal lending rate. **339**

marginal lending rate The interest rate charged by the European Central Bank for borrowing at its marginal lending facility. The marginal lending rate is normally set 100 basis points above the main refinancing rate. **339**

marginal propensity to consume The slope of the consumption function line that measures the change in consumer expenditure resulting from an additional euro of disposable income. **465**

mark-to-market accounting An accounting method in which assets are valued in the balance sheets at what they would sell for in the market. **242**

market equilibrium A situation occurring when the quantity that people are willing to buy (demand) equals the quantity that people are willing to sell (supply). **84**

market fundamentals Items that have a direct impact on future income streams of a security. **139**

maturity Time to the expiration date (maturity date) of a debt instrument. **25**

maturity transformation Process by which banks accept short maturity deposits and convert them into long maturity loans. **210**

medium of exchange Anything that is used to pay for goods and services. **47**

monetarism The view that the money supply is the primary source of movements in the price level and aggregate output. **458**

monetarist A follower of Milton Friedman who sees changes in the money supply as the primary source of movements in the price level and aggregate output and who views the economy as inherently stable. **517**

monetary aggregates The measures of the money supply used by the Federal Reserve System (M1 and M2). **52**

monetary base The sum of the Fed's monetary liabilities (currency in circulation and reserves) and the US Treasury's monetary liabilities (Treasury currency in circulation, primarily coins). **302**

monetary neutrality A proposition that in the long run, a percentage rise in the money supply is matched by the same percentage rise in the price level, leaving unchanged the real money supply and all other economic variables such as interest rates. **397**

monetary policy The management of the money supply and interest rates. **11**

Monetary Policy Committee (MPC) The committee in the Bank of England that has the responsibility for formulating monetary policy. **281**

monetary targeting A monetary policy strategy in which the central bank announces that it will achieve a certain value (the target) of the annual growth rate of a monetary aggregate. **351**

monetary theory The theory that relates changes in the quantity of money to changes in economic activity. **9, 445**

monetary union A monetary union is formed when two or more countries abandon their own national currencies for a common currency managed by a common central bank. These countries fix their exchange rates irrevocably and irreversibly towards the common currency. **432**

monetizing the debt A method of financing government spending whereby the government debt issued to finance government spending is removed from the hands of the public and is replaced by high-powered money instead. Also called *printing money*. **567**

money (money supply) Anything that is generally accepted in payment for goods or services or in the repayment of debts. **9**

money market A financial market in which only short-term debt instruments (generally those with original maturity of less than one year) are traded. **27**

money multiplier A ratio that relates the change in the money supply to a given change in the monetary base. **312**

money supply The quantity of money. **9**

moral hazard The risk that one party to a transaction will engage in behaviour that is undesirable from the other party's point of view. **345, 37**

mortgage-backed securities Securities that cheaply bundle and quantify the default risk of the underlying high-risk mortgages. **184**

mortgages Loans to households or firms to purchase housing, land or other real structures, in which the structure or land itself serves as collateral for the loan. **29**

multiple deposit creation The process whereby, when the central bank supplies the banking system with 1 euro of additional reserves, deposits increase by a multiple of this amount. **307**

NAIRU (non-accelerating inflation rate of unemployment) The rate of unemployment when demand for labour equals supply, consequently eliminating the tendency for the inflation rate to change. **370**

National Central Bank (NCB) A central bank of a country of the European Union (EU). **53, 286**

natural rate level of output The level of aggregate output produced at the natural rate of unemployment at which there is no tendency for wages or prices to change. **499, 511**

natural rate of unemployment The rate of unemployment consistent with full employment at which the demand for labour equals the supply of labour. **278, 511**

net exports Net foreign spending on domestic goods and services, equal to exports minus imports. **464, 507**

net interest margin (NIM) The bank's interest income from assets minus interest expenses of funds divided by earning assets. **255**

net worth The difference between a firm's assets (what it owns or is owed) and its liabilities (what it owes). Also called *equity capital*. **158**

nominal anchor A nominal variable such as the inflation rate, an exchange rate or the money supply that monetary policymakers use to tie down the price level. **277**

nominal interest rate An interest rate that does not take inflation into account. **73**

non-accelerating inflation rate of unemployment See *NAIRU*. **370**

non-borrowed monetary base The monetary base minus borrowed reserves. **307**

off-balance-sheet activities Bank activities that involve trading financial instruments and the generation of income from fees and loan sales, all of which affect bank profits but are not visible on bank balance sheets. **226, 238**

official interest rate The policy interest rate set by the central bank. This is called the Main Refinancing Rate in the euro area, the Bank Rate in the United Kingdom and the Federal Funds Rate Target in the United States. **327**

official reserve transactions balance The current account balance plus items in the capital account. **411**

open market operations The central bank's buying or selling of bonds in the open market. **283, 303**

open market purchase A purchase of bonds by the central bank. **303**

open market sale A sale of bonds by the central bank. **303**

operating instrument A variable that is very responsive to the central bank's tools and indicates the stance of monetary policy (also called a policy instrument). **366**

opportunity cost The amount of interest (expected return) sacrificed by not holding an alternative asset. **96**

Optimal Currency Area (OCA) A geographical area that is better served by a single currency that by several currencies. **435**

optimal forecast The best guess of the future using all available information. **135**

originate-to-distribute model A business model in which the mortgage is originated by a separate party, typically a mortgage broker, and then distributed to an investor as an underlying asset in a security. **185**

overnight interbank interest rate The interest rate for overnight interbank loans such as the EONIA (euro overnight index average) in the euro area, the SONIA (sterling overnight index average) in the United Kingdom and the Federal Funds Rate in the United States. **326**

over-the-counter (OTC) market A secondary market in which dealers at different locations who have an inventory of securities stand ready to buy and sell securities 'over the counter' to anyone who comes to them and is willing to accept their prices. **27, 326**

par value See *face value*. **64**

pass-through The adjustment of retail bank interest rates in response to changes in the official interest rate set by the central bank. **538**

payments system The method of conducting transactions in the economy. **50**

perpetuity See *consol*. **68**

Phillips curve theory A theory suggesting that changes in inflation are influenced by the state of the economy relative to its production capacity as well as to other factors. **370**

planned investment spending Total planned spending by businesses on new physical capital (e.g. machines, computers, apartment buildings) plus planned spending on new homes. **464, 507**

policy ineffectiveness proposition The conclusion from the new classical model that anticipated policy has no effect on output fluctuations. **583**

policy instrument A variable that is very responsive to the central bank's tools and indicates the stance of monetary policy (also called an operating instrument). **366**

policy mix The contemporaneous implementation of monetary and fiscal policies. **495**

political business cycle A business cycle caused by expansionary policies before an election. **294**

portfolio A collection or group of assets. **36**

preferred habitat theory A theory that is closely related to liquidity premium theory, in which the interest rate on a long-term bond equals an average of short-term interest rates expected to occur over the life of the long-term bond plus a positive term premium. **122**

present discounted value See *present value*. **61**

present value Today's value of a payment to be received in the future when the interest rate is *i*. Also called *present discounted value*. **61**

price stability Low and stable inflation. **275**

price transparency The situation in which consumers of different countries sharing the same currency are able to compare prices of the same goods and services. **433**

primary market A financial market in which new issues of a security are sold to initial buyers. **26**

principal–agent problem A moral hazard problem that occurs when the managers in control (the agents) act in their own interest rather than in the interest of the owners (the principals) due to different sets of incentives. **159**

printing money See *monetizing the debt*. **567**

prudential supervision See *financial supervision*. **240**

quantitative easing (QE) An expansion of the central bank's balance sheet. This policy was implemented by the Bank of England and the Fed during the recent financial crisis. **335**

quantity theory of money The theory that nominal income is determined solely by movements in the quantity of money. **446**

quotas Restrictions on the quantity of foreign goods that can be imported. **388**

rate of capital gain The change in a security's price relative to the initial purchase price. **71**

rate of return See *return*. **71**

rational expectations Expectations that reflect optimal forecasts (the best guess of the future) using all available information. **135**

real business cycle theory A theory that views real shocks to tastes and technology as the major driving force behind short-run business cycle fluctuations. **519**

real exchange rate The rate at which domestic goods can be exchanged for foreign goods; i.e. the price of domestic relative to foreign goods denominated in domestic currency. **386**

real interest rate The interest rate adjusted for expected changes in the price level (inflation) so that it more accurately reflects the true cost of borrowing. **74**

real money balances The quantity of money in real terms. **450**

real terms Terms reflecting actual goods and services one can buy. **74**

recession A period when aggregate output is declining. **9**

reduced-form evidence Evidence that examines whether one variable has an effect on another by simply looking directly at the relationship between the two variables. **526**

regulatory arbitrage A process in which banks keep on their books assets that have the same risk-based capital requirement but are relatively risky, such as a loan to a company with a very low credit rating, while taking off their books low-risk assets, such as a loan to a company with a very high credit rating. **238**

repurchase agreement (repo) An arrangement whereby the central bank, or another party, purchases securities with the understanding that the seller will repurchase them in the near future. **29, 333**

required reserve ratio The fraction of deposits that the central bank requires be kept as reserves. **208, 302**

required reserves Reserves that are held to meet the central bank's requirement that for every euro of deposits at a bank, a certain fraction must be kept as reserves. **208, 302**

reserve currency A currency, such as the euro or the US dollar, that is used by other countries to denominate the assets they hold as international reserves. **413**

reserve requirements Regulation making it obligatory for depository institutions to keep a certain fraction of their deposits in accounts with the central bank. **208**

reserves Banks' holding of deposits in accounts with the central bank plus currency that is physically held by banks. **208, 302**

residual claimant The right as a stockholder to receive whatever remains after all other claims against the firm's assets have been satisfied. **131**

restrictive covenants Provisions that restrict and specify certain activities that a borrower can engage in. **152**

retail price index (RPI) An index that measures the average of the prices paid by consumers for a fixed basket of consumer goods and services. **76**

return The payments to the owner of a security plus the change in the security's value, expressed as a fraction of its purchase price. More precisely called the *rate of return*. **71**

return on assets (ROA) Net profit after taxes per euro of assets. **218**

return on equity (ROE) Net profit after taxes per euro of equity capital. **218**

revaluation Resetting of the fixed value of a currency at a higher level. **415**

reverse causation A situation in which one variable is said to cause another variable, when in reality the reverse is true. **528**

reverse repurchase agreement (reverse repo) An arrangement whereby the central bank, or another party, sells securities and the buyer agrees to sell them back in the near future. **333**

Ricardian equivalence Named after the nineteenth-century British economist David Ricardo, it contends that when the government runs deficits and issues bonds, the public recognizes that it will be subject to higher taxes in the future to pay off these bonds. **568**

risk The degree of uncertainty associated with the return on an asset. **35, 81**

risk premium The spread between the interest rate on bonds with default risk and the interest rate on default-free bonds. **110**

risk sharing The process of creating and selling assets with risk characteristics that people are comfortable with and then using the funds acquired by selling these assets to purchase other assets that may have far more risk. **35**

risk structure of interest rates The relationship among the interest rates on various bonds with the same term to maturity. **108**

secondary market A financial market in which securities that have previously been issued (and are thus second-hand) can be resold. **26**

secondary reserves Short-term US government and agency securities held by banks. **208**

secured debt Debt guaranteed by collateral. **152**

Securities Markets Programme (SMP) An ECB programme for conducting interventions in the euro area public and private debt securities markets to ensure depth and liquidity in dysfunctional market segments. **337**

securitization The process of transforming illiquid financial assets into marketable capital market instruments. **184**, **262**

security A claim on the borrower's future income that is sold by the borrower to the lender. Also called a financial instrument. **4**

segmented markets theory A theory of term structure that sees markets for different-maturity bonds as completely separated and segmented such that the interest rate for bonds of a given maturity is determined solely by supply of and demand for bonds of that maturity. **120**

seignorage The revenue a government receives by issuing money. **432**

self-correcting mechanism A characteristic of the economy that causes output to return eventually to the natural rate level regardless of where it is initially. **516**

shadow banking system A system in which bank lending is replaced by lending via the securities market. **258**

short sales Borrowing stock from brokers and then selling the stock in the market, with the hope that a profit will be earned by buying the stock back again ('covering the short') after it has fallen in price. **143**

short-term With reference to a debt instrument, having a maturity of one year or less. **25**

sight deposit Sight deposits are bank accounts that allow the owner of the account to write cheques to third parties or to draw cash out of ATMs without loss of interest. **207, 310**

simple deposit multiplier The multiple increase in deposits generated from an increase in the banking system's reserves in a simple model in which the behaviour of depositors and banks plays no role. **310**

simple loan A credit market instrument providing the borrower with an amount of funds that must be repaid to the lender at the maturity date along with an additional payment (interest). **62**

single banking market The single banking market of the EU allows consumers to purchase financial services from any part of the EU and for financial intermediaries to supply financial services to any part of the EU. The aim of the single banking market is to foster competition and greater efficiency in banking. **252**

smart card A stored-value card that contains a computer chip that lets it be loaded with digital cash from the owner's bank account whenever needed. **51**

special drawing rights (SDRs) An IMF-issued paper substitute for gold that functions as international reserves. **417**

speculative attack A situation in which speculators engage in massive sales of the currency. **192**

spinning When an investment bank allocates shares of hot, but underpriced initial public offerings to executives of other companies in return for their companies' future business with the investment bank. **168**

spot exchange rate The exchange rate for a spot transaction. **383**

spot transaction The predominant type of exchange rate transaction, involving the immediate exchange of bank deposits denominated in different currencies. **383**

Stability and Growth Pact (SGP) An agreement signed by EU leaders in 1997 to ensure fiscal discipline of EU member states. The Stability and Growth Pact imposes constraints on the national fiscal policies of EU countries. **435**

state-owned banks Banks that are owned by governments. **165**

sterilized foreign exchange intervention A foreign exchange intervention with an offsetting open market operation that leaves the monetary base unchanged. **409**

stock A security that is a claim on the earnings and assets of a company. **5, 29**

stockholders Those who hold stock in a corporation. **130**

store of value A repository of purchasing power over time. **49**

structural model A description of how the economy operates, using a collection of equations that describe the behaviour of firms and consumers in many sectors of the economy. **526**

structural model evidence Evidence that examines whether one variable affects another by using data to build a model illustrating the channels through which this variable affects the other. **525**

structured credit products Securities that are derived from cash flows of underlying assets and are tailored to have particular risk characteristics that appeal to investors with different preferences. **184**

structured investment vehicles (SIVs) Securities similar to CDOs in that they pay off cash flows from pools of assets such as mortgages; however, instead of being issued as long-term debt as in CDOs, they are issued as asset-backed commercial paper. **186**

subprime mortgages Mortgages for borrowers with poorer credit records. **184**

supply curve A curve depicting the relationship between quantity supplied and price when all other economic variables are held constant. **84**

supply shock Any change in technology or the supply of raw materials that can shift the aggregate supply curve. **513**

T-account A simplified balance sheet with lines in the form of a T that lists only the changes that occur in balance sheet items starting from some initial balance sheet position. **211**

tariffs Taxes on imported goods. **388**

Taylor principle The principle that the monetary authorities should raise nominal interest rates by more than the increase in the inflation rate. **370**

Taylor rule Economist John Taylor's monetary policy rule that explains how the official interest rate is set by the central bank. **369**

term structure of interest rates The relationship among interest rates on bonds with different terms to maturity. **108**

theory of asset demand The theory that the quantity demanded of an asset is (1) usually positively related to wealth, (2) positively related to its expected return relative to alternative assets, (3) negatively related to the risk of its return relative to alternative assets, and (4) positively related to its liquidity relative to alternative assets. **82**

theory of efficient capital markets See *efficient market hypothesis*. **136**

theory of purchasing power parity (PPP) The theory that exchange rates between any two currencies will adjust to reflect changes in the price levels of the two countries. **386**

time deposit Deposit that normally cannot be withdrawn before the maturity date but incurs a penalty if withdrawn before the maturity date. **207**

time-inconsistency problem The problem that occurs when monetary policymakers conduct monetary policy in a discretionary way and pursue expansionary policies that are attractive in the short run but lead to bad long-run outcomes. **277**

Tobin tax A tax on all foreign exchange transactions proposed by James Tobin in order to curb excessive exchange-rate fluctuations. Nowadays the term 'Tobin tax' is commonly applied to the idea of a broader financial transaction tax. **421**

trade balance The difference between merchandise exports and imports. **410**

transaction costs The time and money spent trying to exchange financial assets, goods or services. **35**

transmission mechanisms of monetary policy The channels through which the money supply affects economic activity. **526**

transparency Transparency means that the central bank provides the general public and the markets with all relevant information on its strategy, assessments and policy decisions in an open, clear and timely manner. **354**

Treasury bill A short-term debt instrument of the UK government, which is issued in one-, three- and six-month maturities to finance the government spending. **28**

unconventional monetary policy tools Non-interest-rate tools central banks use to stimulate the economy: liquidity provision, asset purchases, commitment to future monetary policy actions. **326**

underwrite Purchase securities from a corporation at a predetermined price and then resell them in the market. **41**

unemployment rate The percentage of the labour force not working. **9**

unexploited profit opportunity A situation in which an investor can earn a higher than normal return. **138**

unit of account Anything used to measure value in an economy. **48**

unsecured debt Debt not guaranteed by collateral. **152**

unsterilized foreign exchange intervention A foreign exchange intervention in which a central bank allows the purchase or sale of domestic currency to affect the monetary base. **408**

vault cash Currency that is physically held by banks and stored in vaults overnight. **208**

velocity of money The rate of turnover of money; the average number of times per year that a euro is spent in buying the total amount of final goods and services produced in the economy. **446**

venture capital firm A financial intermediary that pools the resources of its partners and uses the funds to help entrepreneurs start up new businesses. **161**

virtual bank A bank that has no building but rather exists only in cyberspace. **261**

wage flexibility When wages respond fully to changes in the expected price level. **437**

wage–price stickiness When a source of rigidity prevents wages from responding fully to changes in the expected price level. **585**

wealth All resources owned by an individual, including all assets. **47**

World Bank The International Bank for Reconstruction and Redevelopment, an international organization that provides long-term loans to assist developing countries in building dams, roads and other physical capital that would contribute to their economic development. **413**

World Trade Organization (WTO) An organization headquartered in Geneva, Switzerland, that monitors rules for the conduct of trade between countries (tariffs and quotas). **413**

yield curve A plot of the interest rates for particular types of bonds with different terms to maturity. **116**

yield to maturity The interest rate that equates the present value of payments received from a credit market instrument with its value today. **64**

zero-coupen bond See *discount bond*. **64**

INDEX